THE PAPERS OF
THOMAS JEFFERSON

THE PAPERS OF

Thomas Jefferson

Volume 20
1 April to 4 August 1791

JULIAN P. BOYD, EDITOR

RUTH W. LESTER, ASSISTANT EDITOR

PRINCETON, NEW JERSEY
PRINCETON UNIVERSITY PRESS

1982

DEDICATED TO THE MEMORY OF

ADOLPH S. OCHS

PUBLISHER OF THE NEW YORK TIMES

1896-1935

WHO BY THE EXAMPLE OF A RESPONSIBLE

PRESS ENLARGED AND FORTIFIED

THE JEFFERSONIAN CONCEPT

OF A FREE PRESS

ACKNOWLEDGMENTS

As INDICATED in the first volume, this edition was made possible by a grant of $200,000 from the New York Times Company to Princeton University. Since this initial subvention, its continuance has been assured by additional contributions from the New York Times Company; by the grant of the Ford Foundation to the National Archives Trust Fund Board as explained in Volume 17; by the Fellowship bestowed on the Editor by the John Simon Guggenheim Memorial Foundation; and by other benefactions from the Charlotte Palmer Phillips Foundation, Time Inc., and from such loyal supporters of the enterprise as James Russell Wiggins and David K. E. Bruce. In common with other editions of historical documents, *The Papers of Thomas Jefferson* is a beneficiary of the good offices of the National Historical Publications and Records Commission, tendered in many useful forms through its officers and dedicated staff. For these and other indispensable aids generously given by librarians, archivists, scholars, and collectors of manuscripts, the Editors record their sincere gratitude.

FOREWORD

Iₙ ₜₕₑ last months of his life, Julian Boyd concentrated on completing the Editorial Note that he titled "Fixing the Seat of Government," which he referred to as the L'Enfant note. Although this note appears first in the volume, he left it for last because he considered it the most difficult and time-consuming. He had begun drafting the conclusion for it and, in fact, had stopped in mid-sentence to take a telephone call or ponder his choice of words. He was never able to return to it.

The L'Enfant note, printed here essentially as drafted, never benefited from Mr. Boyd's scrupulous re-examination and possible corrections, but his conclusion about the roles of Jefferson and L'Enfant in preparing a plan for the new capital of the nation is clear. His final notes reveal a concern for what Fiske Kimball correctly described as the apotheosis of Pierre L'Enfant more than a century after his employment. Even as they praised his genius as a city planner, the architects, historians, and heads of government planning agencies who thought they had resurrected his reputation ironically denied him the one claim L'Enfant hoped would win him fame and fortune: that of originality, of envisioning some innovative departure from the Old Order exemplified in European cities. Instead, his advocates found, his plan for the seat of government reflected his European training in art and engineering. It is not surprising that the efforts to trace European influences in his plan were carried to historically inaccurate extremes, nor can it be denied that the apotheosis had its utilitarian objects. In his Editorial Note, Mr. Boyd attempted to restore balance to the evaluation of L'Enfant's contribution and to show that "Jefferson's impress upon the plan for the capital is far greater than has been realized."

At one point, while reflecting on the significance of the development of the capital rather than on the mythology surrounding L'Enfant and his role in it, Mr. Boyd wrote what perhaps best represents his final conclusion: "Like the nation itself, appropriately, the capital of this 'Grand Empire' of L'Enfant's vision was viewed in idealistic terms by those who founded it – as something triumphing over the Gothic decadence of corrupt Europe, becoming noble in simplicity and grandeur as in Rome and Athens and in Jefferson's view looking far beyond. But in actuality, as proved by a history of nearly two centuries, it, like the nation, exhibited its conflicts, its corruptions, its mistakes, its human errors of judgment and attempts at justification. It is perhaps in this sense a better reflection of the character of the people than any symbolic plan of beauty and republican utility that even Jefferson, much less L'Enfant, could have devised." This, we believe, is how he would have ended his essay had he been able to do so.

Several questions and notes written throughout the manuscript over the past few years required our attention and led to some small changes in the original annotation. While scanning this material, we found evidence to suggest that Mr. Boyd might have intended to bring together another group of related letters. An essay entitled "Sources of Foreign Intelligence" would have introduced six documents: Secretary of State to Gouverneur Morris, 26 July 1791; Secretary of State to the President, 27 July 1791; The President to the Secretary of State, 28 July 1791; Secretary of State to William Short, 28 July 1791; Secretary of State to the President, 30 July 1791; and The President to the Secretary of State, 30 July 1791. We have separated these letters and printed them in chronological order.

Julian Boyd left a scholarly legacy that will be long appreciated by the practitioners of the craft of historical editing. Most historians who began editing after 1950 started in Princeton, asking for advice on setting up a project and compiling materials for printing. The "Boyd method" of accessioning documents and transcribing them lives on in dozens of locations throughout the country. His new method of transcription was called to the attention of a wide audience when the editors of the *Encyclopedia of American History* included a section on it. Nevertheless, the editors of that book, and most historical editors, have failed to realize that the new methods and high standards that have made these volumes famous were established by Mr. Boyd *specifically* for Thomas Jefferson's papers. He did not believe that every collection of papers of every historical figure warranted the same treatment, although he believed that if one intended to transcribe papers for letterpress publication, the job should be done with accuracy and fidelity. It was his overriding concern that the papers of Thomas Jefferson – one of four or five collections of papers he considered fundamentally important in the history of our nation – be prepared and published in a comprehensive edition of such high standards that later editions would be unnecessary. He would want to be remembered for that, and Volumes 1-20 of *The Papers of Thomas Jefferson* are a proper monument to his achievement.

Our preparation for publication of this last number has required few corrections or revisions; in all cases of doubt we have attempted to present the material in accordance with Mr. Boyd's style and principles of editing. He believed that each scholar must do his own editing and expected that future volumes would necessarily reflect differences. This twentieth volume is vintage Boyd, however, and it is satisfying to have had a hand in presenting it as such.

CHARLES T. CULLEN

10 November 1980

GUIDE TO EDITORIAL APPARATUS

1. TEXTUAL DEVICES

The following devices are employed throughout the work to clarify the presentation of the text.

[. . .], [. . . .]	One or two words missing and not conjecturable.
[. . .]¹, [. . . .]¹	More than two words missing and not conjecturable; subjoined footnote estimates number of words missing.
[ ]	Number or part of a number missing or illegible.
[roman]	Conjectural reading for missing or illegible matter. A question mark follows when the reading is doubtful.
[*italic*]	Editorial comment inserted in the text.
⟨*italic*⟩	Matter deleted in the MS but restored in our text.
⟦ ⟧	Record entry for letters not found.

2. DESCRIPTIVE SYMBOLS

The following symbols are employed throughout the work to describe the various kinds of manuscript originals. When a series of versions is recorded, *the first to be recorded is the version used for the printed text.*

Dft	draft (usually a composition or rough draft; later drafts, when identifiable as such, are designated "2 Dft," &c.)
Dupl	duplicate
MS	manuscript (arbitrarily applied to most documents other than letters)
N	note, notes (memoranda, fragments, &c.)
PoC	polygraph copy
PrC	press copy
RC	recipient's copy
SC	stylograph copy
Tripl	triplicate

All manuscripts of the above types are assumed to be in the hand of the author of the document to which the descriptive symbol pertains. If not, that fact is stated. On the other hand, the following types of manuscripts are assumed *not* to be in the hand of the author, and exceptions will be noted:

FC   file copy (applied to all forms of retained copies, such as letter-book copies, clerk's copies, &c.)

Tr   transcript (applied to both contemporary and later copies; period of transcription, unless clear by implication, will be given when known)

3. LOCATION SYMBOLS

The locations of most documents printed in this edition from originals in private hands, from originals held by institutions outside the United States, and from printed sources are recorded in self-explanatory form in the descriptive note following each document. The location symbols BL and PRO are used for documents in the British Library and the Public Record Office in London, respectively. The locations of documents printed from originals held by public institutions in the United States are recorded by means of the symbols used in the National Union Catalog in the Library of Congress; (explanation of how these symbols are formed is given above, Vol. 1: xl). The symbols DLC and MHi by themselves will stand for the collections of Jefferson Papers proper in these repositories; when texts are drawn from other collections held by these two institutions, the names of the particular collections will be added. The list of symbols appearing in each volume is limited to the institutions represented by documents printed or referred to in that and previous volumes.

BL   British Library, London

CLSU   University of Southern California Library, Los Angeles

CLU   William Andrews Clark Memorial Library, University of California at Los Angeles

CSM   Colonial Society of Massachusetts, Boston

CSmH   Henry E. Huntington Library, San Marino, California

Ct   Connecticut State Library, Hartford

CtHi   Connecticut Historical Society, Hartford

CtY   Yale University Library

DeHi   Historical Society of Delaware, Wilmington

DLC   Library of Congress

DNA   The National Archives, with identifications

of series (preceded by record group number) as follows:

AL	American Letters
CD	Consular Dispatches
DCI	Diplomatic and Consular Instructions
DD	Diplomatic Dispatches
DL	Domestic Letters
FL	Foreign Letters
LAR	Letters of Application and Recommendation
MLR	Miscellaneous Letters Received
MTA	Miscellaneous Treasury Accounts
NL	Notes from Legations
NWT	Northwest Territory Papers
PC	Proceedings of Board of Commissioners for the District of Columbia
PCC	Papers of the Continental Congress
PDL	Printing and Distribution of the Laws
SDC	State Department Correspondence
SDR	A Record of the Reports of Thomas Jefferson, Secretary of State for the United States of America
SWT	Southwest Territory Papers

G-Ar	Georgia Department of Archives and History, Atlanta
ICHi	Chicago Historical Society, Chicago
IHi	Illinois State Historical Library, Springfield
IMunS	St. Mary of the Lake Seminary, Mundelein, Illinois
InHi	Indiana Historical Society, Indianapolis
MB	Boston Public Library, Boston
MBA	Archives, State House, Boston
MBAt	Boston Athenæum, Boston
MdAA	Maryland Hall of Records, Annapolis
MdAN	U.S. Naval Academy Library, Annapolis
MdHi	Maryland Historical Society, Baltimore
MeHi	Maine Historical Society, Portland

MH	Harvard University Library
MHi	Massachusetts Historical Society, Boston
MHi:AM	Adams Manuscripts, Massachusetts Historical Society
MiU-C	William L. Clements Library, University of Michigan
MoSHi	Missouri Historical Society, St. Louis
MWA	American Antiquarian Society, Worcester, Massachusetts
NA	New York State Library, Albany
NBu	Buffalo Public Library, Buffalo, New York
NcD	Duke University Library, Durham, North Carolina
NcU	University of North Carolina Library, Chapel Hill
NhD	Dartmouth College Library, Hanover, New Hampshire
NhHi	New Hampshire Historical Society, Concord
NHi	New-York Historical Society, New York City
NjHi	New Jersey Historical Society, Newark
NjMoW	Morristown National Historical Park, Morristown, N.J.
NjP	Princeton University Library
NK-Iselin	Letters to and from John Jay bearing this symbol are used by permission of the Estate of Eleanor Jay Iselin.
NN	New York Public Library, New York City
NNC	Columbia University Libraries, New York City
NNP	Pierpont Morgan Library, New York City
NNS	New York Society Library, New York City
O	Ohio State Library, Columbus
OCHP	Historical and Philosophical Society of Ohio, Cincinnati
OHi	Ohio State Archaeological and Historical Society, Columbus
PBL	Lehigh University Library
PHC	Haverford College Library
PHi	Historical Society of Pennsylvania, Philadelphia
PHMC	Pennsylvania Historical and Museum Commission, Harrisburg
PP	Free Library, Philadelphia

PPAP	American Philosophical Society, Philadelphia
PPL	Library Company of Philadelphia
PRO	Public Record Office, London
PU	University of Pennsylvania Library
PWW	Washington and Jefferson College, Washington, Pennsylvania
RPA	Rhode Island Department of State, Providence
RPAB	Annmary Brown Memorial Library, Providence
RPB	Brown University Library
Vi	Virginia State Library, Richmond
Vi:USCC	Ended Cases, United States Circuit Court, Virginia State Library
ViHi	Virginia Historical Society, Richmond
ViRVal	Valentine Museum Library, Richmond
ViU	University of Virginia Library
ViU:McG	McGregor Library, University of Virginia
ViU:TJMF	Manuscripts deposited by the Thomas Jefferson Memorial Foundation in the University of Virginia Library
ViW	College of William and Mary Library
ViWC	Colonial Williamsburg, Inc.
VtMC	Middlebury College Library, Middlebury, Vermont
VtMS	Secretary of State, Montpelier, Vermont
WHi	State Historical Society of Wisconsin, Madison

4. OTHER SYMBOLS AND ABBREVIATIONS

The following symbols and abbreviations are commonly employed in the annotation throughout the work.

Second Series   The topical series to be published as part of this edition, comprising those materials which are best suited to a topical rather than a chronological arrangement (see Vol. 1: xv-xvi)

TJ   Thomas Jefferson

TJ Editorial Files   Photoduplicates and other editorial materials in the office of *The Papers of Thomas Jefferson*, Princeton University Library

TJ Papers   Jefferson Papers (applied to a collection of manuscripts when the precise location of a given document must be furnished, and always preceded by the symbol for the institutional repository; thus "DLC: TJ Papers, 4:628-9" represents a document in the Library of Congress, Jefferson Papers, volume 4, pages 628 and 629)

RG   Record Group (used in designating the location of documents in the National Archives)

SJL   Jefferson's "Summary Journal of Letters" written and received (in DLC: TJ Papers)

SJPL   "Summary Journal of Public Letters," an incomplete list of letters written by TJ from 16 Apr. 1784 to 31 Dec. 1793, with brief summaries, in an amanuensis' hand except for six pages in TJ's hand listing and summarizing official reports and communications by him as Secretary of State, 11 Oct. 1789 to 31 Dec. 1793 (in DLC: TJ Papers, at end of SJL)

V   Ecu

f   Florin

£   Pound sterling or livre, depending upon context (in doubtful cases, a clarifying note will be given)

s   Shilling or sou. (Also expressed as /)

d   Penny or denier

ₜ   Livre Tournois

℔   Per (occasionally used for pro, pre)

5. SHORT TITLES

The following list includes only those short titles of works cited with great frequency, and therefore in very abbreviated form, throughout this edition. Their expanded forms are given here only in the degree of fullness needed for unmistakable identification. Since it is impossible to anticipate all the works to be cited in such very abbreviated form, the list is appropriately revised from volume to volume.

Adams, *Works*   Charles Francis Adams, ed., *The Works of John Adams*, Boston, 1850-56, 10 vols.

Adams, *Diary*   *Diary and Autobiography of John Adams*, ed. L. H. Butterfield and others, Cambridge, 1961, 4 vols.

AHA   American Historical Association

AHR   *American Historical Review*, 1895-

Ammon, *Monroe*   Harry Ammon, *James Monroe*, New York, 1971

Annals   *Annals of the Congress of the United States: The Debates and Proceedings in the Congress of the United States . . . Compiled from Authentic Materials by Joseph Gales, Senior*, Washington, Gales & Seaton, 1834-56, 42 vols. All editions are undependable and pagination varies from one printing to another. The edition cited here has this caption on both recto and verso pages: "History of Congress." Another printing, with the same title-page, has "Gales & Seatons History" on verso and "of Debates in Congress" on recto pages. Those using the latter printing will need to employ the date or, where it is lacking, to add approximately 52 to the page numbers of *Annals* as cited in this volume.

ASP   *American State Papers: Documents, Legislative and Executive, of the Congress of the United States*, Washington, Gales & Seaton, 1832-61, 38 vols.

Atlas of Amer. Hist.   James Truslow Adams and R. V. Coleman, eds., *Atlas of American History*, New York, Scribner, 1943

Bear, *Family Letters*   Edwin M. Betts and James A. Bear, Jr., eds., *Family Letters of Thomas Jefferson*, Columbia, Missouri, 1966

Bemis, *Jay's Treaty*   Samuel Flagg Bemis, *Jay's Treaty: A Study in Commerce and Diplomacy*, New Haven, 1962, rev. edn.

Bemis, *Pinckney's Treaty*   Samuel Flagg Bemis, *Pinckney's Treaty: America's Advantage from Europe's Distress, 1783-1800*, rev. edn., New Haven, 1960

Betts, *Farm Book*   Edwin M. Betts, ed., *Thomas Jefferson's Farm Book*, Princeton, 1953

Betts, *Garden Book*   Edwin M. Betts, ed., *Thomas Jefferson's Garden Book, 1766-1824*, Philadelphia, 1944

Beveridge, *Marshall*   Albert J. Beveridge, *The Life of John Marshall*, Boston, 1916

Biog. Dir. Cong.   *Biographical Directory of the American Congress, 1774-1949*, Washington, 1950

B.M. Cat.   British Museum, *General Catalogue of Printed Books*, London, 1931-; also *The British Museum Catalogue of Printed Books, 1881-1900*, Ann Arbor, 1946

B.N. Cat.   Bibliothèque Nationale, *Catalogue général des livres imprimés. . . . Auteurs*, Paris, 1897-1955

Brant, *Madison*   Irving Brant, *James Madison*, Indianapolis, 1941-61, 6 vols.

Bryan, *National Capital*   W. B. Bryan, *History of the National Capital*, New York, 1914-1916, 2 vols.

Burnett, *Letters of Members*   Edwin C. Burnett, ed., *Letters of Members of the Continental Congress*, Washington, 1921-1936, 8 vols.

Butterfield, *Rush*   *Letters of Benjamin Rush*, ed. L. H. Butterfield, Princeton, 1951, 2 vols.

Cal. Franklin Papers   I. Minis Hays, ed., *Calendar of the Papers of Benjamin Franklin in the Library of the American Philosophical Society*, Philadelphia, 1908, 6 vols.

Carter, *Terr. Papers*   *The Territorial Papers of the United States*, ed. Clarence E. Carter, Washington, 1934-62, 26 vols.

Cutler, *Cutler*   William Parker Cutler, *Life, Journals, and Correspondence of Rev. Manasseh Cutler*, Cincinnati, 1888, 2 vols.

CVSP   William P. Palmer and others, eds., *Calendar of Virginia State Papers ... Preserved in the Capitol at Richmond*, Richmond, 1875-1893

DAB   Allen Johnson and Dumas Malone, eds., *Dictionary of American Biography*, N.Y., 1928-1936

DAE   Sir William A. Craigie and James Hulbert, eds., *A Dictionary of American English*, Chicago, 1938-1944

DAH   James Truslow Adams, ed., *Dictionary of American History*, N.Y., 1940, 5 vols., and index

DeConde, *Entangling Alliance*   Alexander DeConde, *Entangling Alliance; Politics & Diplomacy under George Washington*, Durham, N.C., 1958

DNB   Leslie Stephen and Sidney Lee, eds., *Dictionary of National Biography*, 2d ed., N.Y., 1908-1909

Dumbauld, *Tourist*   Edward Dumbauld, *Thomas Jefferson American Tourist*, Norman, Oklahoma, 1946

Elliot's *Debates*   Jonathan Elliot, ed., *The Debates of the Several State Conventions on the Adoption of the Federal Constitution ... together with the Journal of the Federal Convention*, 2d ed., Philadelphia, 1901, 5 vols.

Evans   Charles Evans, comp., *American Bibliography*, Chicago, 1903-1955

Fitzpatrick, *Writings*   John C. Fitzpatrick, ed., *The Writings of George Washington*, Washington, 1931-44, 39 vols.

Ford   Paul Leicester Ford, ed., *The Writings of Thomas Jefferson*, Letterpress Edition, N.Y., 1892-1899, 10 vols.

Freeman, *Washington*   Douglas Southall Freeman, *George Washington*, N.Y., 1948-1957, 6 vols.; 7th volume by J. A. Carroll and M. W. Ashworth, New York, 1957

Fry-Jefferson Map   Dumas Malone, ed., *The Fry & Jefferson*

Map of Virginia and Maryland: a Facsimile of the First Edition, Princeton, 1950

Gottschalk, *Lafayette, 1783-89* Louis Gottschalk, *Lafayette between the American and the French Revolution (1783-1789),* Chicago, 1950

Greely, *Public Documents* Adolphus Washington Greely, ed., *Public Documents of the First Fourteen Congresses, 1789-1817: Papers Relating to Early Congressional Documents,* Washington, 1900

HAW Henry A. Washington, ed., *The Writings of Thomas Jefferson,* N.Y., 1853-1854, 9 vols.

Hening William Waller Hening, ed., *The Statutes at Large; Being a Collection of All the Laws of Virginia,* Richmond, 1809-1823, 13 vols.

Henry, *Henry* William Wirt Henry, *Patrick Henry, Life, Correspondence and Speeches,* N.Y., 1891, 3 vols.

Humphreys, *Humphreys* F. L. Humphreys, *Life and Times of David Humphreys,* New York, 1917, 2 vols.

Hunt, *Madison* Gaillard Hunt, ed., *The Writings of James Madison,* New York, 1900-1910, 9 vols.

JCC Worthington C. Ford and others, eds., *Journals of the Continental Congress,* 1774-1789, Washington, 1904-1937, 34 vols.

Jefferson Correspondence, Bixby Worthington C. Ford, ed., *Thomas Jefferson Correspondence Printed from the Originals in the Collections of William K. Bixby,* Boston, 1916

Jenkins, *Records* William Sumner Jenkins, ed., *Records of the States of the United States of America* (Library of Congress and University of North Carolina, 1950)

JEP *Journal of the Executive Proceedings of the Senate of the United States . . . to the Termination of the Nineteenth Congress,* Washington, 1828

JHD *Journal of the House of Delegates of the Commonwealth of Virginia* (cited by session and date of publication)

JHR *Journal of the House of Representatives of the United States,* Washington, Gales & Seaton, 1826-

JS *Journal of the Senate of the United States,* Washington, Gales, 1820-21, 5 vols.

JSH *Journal of Southern History,* 1935-

Ketcham, *Madison* Ralph Ketcham, *James Madison,* New York, 1971

Kimball, *Jefferson* Marie Kimball, *Jefferson,* New York, 1943-1950, 3 vols.

King, *King*   C. R. King, ed., *The Life and Correspondence of Rufus King, Comprising His Letters, Private and Official, His Public Documents, and His Speeches, 1755-1827*, New York, 1894-1900, 6 vols.

L & B   Andrew A. Lipscomb and Albert E. Bergh, eds., *The Writings of Thomas Jefferson*, Washington, 1903-1904, 20 vols.

L.C. *Cat.*   *A Catalogue of Books Represented by the Library of Congress Printed Cards*, Ann Arbor, 1942-1946; also *Supplement*, 1948-

Library Catalogue, 1783   Jefferson's MS list of books owned or wanted in 1783 (original in Massachusetts Historical Society)

Library Catalogue, 1815   *Catalogue of the Library of the United States*, Washington, 1815

Library Catalogue, 1829   *Catalogue: President Jefferson's Library*, Washington, 1829

Loubat, *Medallic history*   J. F. Loubat, *The Medallic History of the United States of America, 1776-1876*, New York, 1878, 2 vols.

Maclay, *Journal*   Edgar S. Maclay, ed., *Journal of William Maclay, United States Senator from Pennsylvania, 1789-1791*, New York, 1890

Madison, *Letters and Other Writings*   James Madison, *Letters and Other Writings of James Madison*, Philadelphia, 1865

Malone, *Jefferson*   Dumas Malone, *Jefferson and his Time*, Boston, 1948-1981, 6 vols.

Mason, *Papers*   Robert A. Rutland, ed., *Papers of George Mason, 1725-1792*, Chapel Hill, 1970, 3 vols.

Mathews, *Andrew Ellicott*   Catharine Van Cortlandt Mathews, *Andrew Ellicott, his life and letters*, New York, 1908

Mayo, *British Ministers*   Bernard Mayo, ed., "Instructions to the British Ministers to the United States 1791-1812," American Historical Association, *Annual Report*, 1936

Mays, *Pendleton*   David John Mays, ed., *Letters and Papers of Edmund Pendleton, 1734-1803*, Charlottesville, 1967, 2 vols.

Miller, *Hamilton*   John C. Miller, *Alexander Hamilton Portrait in Paradox*, New York 1959

Mitchell, *Hamilton*   Broadus Mitchell, *Alexander Hamilton*, New York 1957, 1962, 2 vols.

MVHR   *Mississippi Valley Historical Review*, 1914-

Notes, ed. Peden   William Peden, ed., *Notes on the State of Virginia*, Chapel Hill, 1955

NYHS, *Quar.*   New-York Historical Society *Quarterly*, 1917-

NYPL, *Bulletin*   New York Public Library *Bulletin*, 1897-

OED   Sir James Murray and others, eds., *A New English Dictionary on Historical Principles*, Oxford, 1888-1933

Padover, *National Capital*   Saul K. Padover, ed., *Thomas Jefferson and the National Capital*, Washington, 1946

Peterson, *Jefferson*   Merrill D. Peterson, *Thomas Jefferson and the New Nation*, New York, 1970

PMHB   *Pennsylvania Magazine of History and Biography*, 1877-

Randall, *Life*   Henry S. Randall, *The Life of Thomas Jefferson*, N.Y., 1858, 3 vols.

Randolph, *Domestic Life*   Sarah N. Randolph, *The Domestic Life of Thomas Jefferson, Compiled from Family Letters and Reminiscences by His Great-Granddaughter*, Cambridge, Mass., 1939

Rowland, *George Mason*   Kate Mason Rowland, *Life of George Mason, 1725-1792*, New York, 1892, 2 vols.

Sabin   Joseph Sabin and others, comps., *Bibliotheca Americana. A Dictionary of Books Relating to America*, N.Y., 1868-1936

St. Clair, *Narrative*   Arthur St. Clair, *A Narrative of the Manner in which the Campaign against the Indians . . . was Conducted . . .* , Philadelphia, 1812

St. Clair, *Papers*   William Henry Smith, ed., *The St. Clair Papers. The Life and Public Services of Arthur St. Clair*, Cincinnati, 1882, 2 vols.

Setser, *Reciprocity*   Vernon G. Setser, *The Commercial Reciprocity Policy of the United States*, Philadelphia, 1937

Shipton-Mooney Index   Clifford K. Shipton and James E. Mooney, comps., *National Index of American Imprints through 1800, The Short-Title Evans*, 1969, 2 vols.

Sowerby   E. Millicent Sowerby, comp., *Catalogue of the Library of Thomas Jefferson*, 1952-1959, 5 vols.

Sparks, *Morris*   Jared Sparks, *Life of Gouverneur Morris*, Boston, 1832, 3 vols.

Swem, *Index*   Earl G. Swem, comp., *Virginia Historical Index*, Roanoke, 1934-1936

Swem, "Va. Bibliog."   Earl G. Swem, comp., "A Bibliography of Virginia History," Virginia State Library, *Bulletin*, VIII (1915), X (1917), and XII (1919)

Syrett, *Hamilton*   *The Papers of Alexander Hamilton*, ed. Harold C. Syrett and others, New York, 1961-1979, 27 vols.

TJR   Thomas Jefferson Randolph, ed., *Memoir, Correspondence, and Miscellanies, from the Papers of Thomas Jefferson*, Charlottesville, 1829, 4 vols.

Tucker, *Life*   George Tucker, *The Life of Thomas Jefferson*, Philadelphia, 1837, 2 vols.

Turner, *CFM*   F. J. Turner, "Correspondence of French Ministers, 1791-1797," AHA, *Ann. Rept.*, 1903, II

U.S. Statutes at Large   Richard Peters, ed., *The Public Statutes at Large of the United States ... 1789 to March 3, 1845*, Boston, 1855-1856, 8 vols.

Van Doren, *Franklin*   Carl Van Doren, *Benjamin Franklin*, New York, 1938

Van Doren, *Secret History*   Carl Van Doren, *Secret History of the American Revolution*, New York, 1941

VMHB   *Virginia Magazine of History and Biography*, 1893-

WMQ   *William and Mary Quarterly*, 1892-

CONTENTS

CONTENTS

CONTENTS

CONTENTS

CONTENTS

CONTENTS

CONTENTS

CONTENTS

ILLUSTRATIONS

Following Page 384

WILLIAM SHORT (1759-1849)

A native of Surry County, Virginia, and a graduate in 1779 of the College of William and Mary, Short joined Jefferson in Paris in November 1784, becoming his private secretary and later secretary of legation. When Jefferson returned to the United States in 1789, Short became chargé d'affaires in Paris. Disappointed that Washington named Gouverneur Morris minister to France early in 1792, he accepted the post of minister at The Hague.

Portrait by Rembrandt Peale; original in the College of William and Mary. (*Courtesy of the Frick Art Reference Library*)

JOSHUA JOHNSON (1742-1802)

Washington appointed Johnson U.S. consul in London in 1790 after Johnson's business collapsed. In May 1791 he sent reports on the status of the brigantine *Rachel*. His daughter, Louisa Catherine, married John Quincy Adams in 1797. When President Adams appointed him superintendent of stamps in 1800, a tie vote at confirmation was broken by Jefferson in favor of Johnson.

Portrait by Edward Savage. (*Courtesy of the Massachusetts Historical Society*)

SKETCH OF THE FEDERAL CITY, 1791

A press copy of Jefferson's suggestions for laying out the federal district, drawn between 10 and 21 March 1791. The original disappeared after George Washington turned it over to Pierre L'Enfant. (*Courtesy of the Library of Congress*)

L'ENFANT'S PLAN OF THE SEAT OF GOVERNMENT, 1791

After this plan was engraved and laid before Congress, Washington described it as containing Jefferson's instructions to the engraver. The pencilled changes made by Jefferson were directed not to the engraver, however, but to Andrew Ellicott, who prepared the final copy for the engraver. (*Courtesy of the Library of Congress*)

TITLE-PAGE AND ENDORSEMENT OF PAINE'S "RIGHTS OF MAN"

Jefferson was "thunderstruck" when he saw his letter printed on the verso of the dedication page in Samuel Harrison Smith's Philadelphia edition of Paine's book. Without the inference of endorsement, the book might have received only passing interest. With it, a national controversy developed. (*Courtesy of the American Philosophical Society*)

"CONTRASTED OPINIONS OF PAINE'S PAMPHLET"

This popular cartoon reflects the reaction and alarm aroused in England — here caricatured by George III, Pitt, and Queen Charlotte — by the threat of subversion. (*Courtesy of the Lewis Walpole Library, Farmington, Connecticut*)

ILLUSTRATIONS

VOCABULARY OF THE UNQUACHOG INDIANS

Jefferson wrote this list on an address leaf while interviewing the Unquachog Indians on Long Island during his northern journey with James Madison in the spring of 1791. (*Courtesy of the American Philosophical Society*)

GEORGE BECKWITH (1753-1823)

When Lord Dorchester became Governor General of British North America, Beckwith joined him in Canada and made trips to New York to obtain information for the British. Jefferson refused to talk with Beckwith, who then established a continuing association with Alexander Hamilton. In 1791 Beckwith relayed information on Indian affairs between Hamilton and Dorchester.

The portrait by S. W. Reynolds is a mezzotint after J. Eckstein; original in the British Museum. (*Courtesy of Newsweek Book Division*)

Volume 20

1 April to 4 August 1791

JEFFERSON CHRONOLOGY

1743 · 1826

1743.	Born at Shadwell, 13 Apr. (New Style).
1760.	Entered the College of William and Mary.
1762.	"quitted college."
1762-1767.	Self-education and preparation for law.
1769-1774.	Albemarle delegate to House of Burgesses.
1772.	Married Martha Wayles Skelton, 1 Jan.
1775-1776.	In Continental Congress.
1776.	Drafted Declaration of Independence.
1776-1779.	In Virginia House of Delegates.
1779.	Submitted Bill for Establishing Religious Freedom.
1779-1781.	Governor of Virginia.
1782.	His wife died, 6 Sep.
1783-1784.	In Continental Congress.
1784-1789.	In France as commissioner to negotiate commercial treaties and as minister plenipotentiary at Versailles.
1790-1793.	U.S. Secretary of State.
1797-1801.	Vice President of the United States.
1801-1809.	President of the United States.
1814-1826.	Established the University of Virginia.
1826.	Died at Monticello, 4 July.

VOLUME 20

1 April 1791 to 4 August 1791

10 Apr.	Suggestions to L'Enfant on fixing the seat of government.
10 Apr.	Negotiates payment of U.S. debt to France.
17 Apr.	Advice on unofficial diplomacy on Indian Affairs.
26 Apr.	Forwards Paine's *Rights of Man* to printer.
17 May- 19 June	Northern journey with Madison.
31 May	Joshua Johnson reports on case of brigantine *Rachel*.
14 June	Visits Unquachog Indians and records their vocabulary.
4 Aug.	Freneau informs TJ of proposals for *National Gazette*.

THE PAPERS OF
THOMAS JEFFERSON

◄══════════►

Fixing the Seat of Government[1]

EDITORIAL NOTE

> We are about founding a City which will be one of the
> first in the World, and We are governed by local and
> partial Motives.
> — John Adams, *Diary*, 23 Sep. 1789

Adams' observation, apt at the time and prophetic of what was to come, was
made during the embittered debates of the First Session when, quite unex-
pectedly, the old and divisive issue of fixing the permanent seat of government
disturbed the councils of the new government. In that contest the North was
pitted against the South and the West against both in the struggle to determine
whether the national capital would be situated on the Delaware, the Susquehanna, the Patuxent, or the Potomac. When the last was chosen in the famous
compromise of 1790, there followed a second conflict exhibiting local and partial
motives among individuals and communities along the river from tidewater to

[1] The phrase is that of Washington himself, written after a decisive event in the history
of the capital (Washington to La Luzerne, 10 Aug. 1790, *Writings*, ed. Fitzpatrick, xxxi,
84).

the Conococheague. After Washington announced by proclamation the site of the Federal District – a choice he had made even before undertaking a tour for the ostensible purpose of deciding among rival locations[2] – a third opportunity for the display of interested motives presented itself. The competing claims of owners of land from Carrollsburg on the Eastern Branch to Georgetown up-river, together with those lying between in the area of Funkstown or Hamburg, were not of such magnitude as to disrupt the nation or to divide it along sectional lines.

But the problem of accommodating these local rivalries to the public interest involved more than the cost per acre of lands needed for the Capitol, the President's House, the departmental offices, and other public uses. Maryland citizens on whom Washington relied for aid in solving the problem – Daniel Carroll, William Deakins, Jr., and Benjamin Stoddert – had long since been warned by Jefferson that the opportunity to keep the Federal City on the Potomac might be lost forever if lands, funds, and buildings for government use were not speedily provided.[3] Washington soon added his own powerful promptings. As he was fully aware, many hoped and believed that Philadelphia – long the commercial, cultural, and political center and now designated as the temporary capital – would remain the permanent seat of government. Evidence of this became public soon after passage of the Residence Act when the City of Philadelphia made known its plans to erect public buildings for the accommodation of the President and Congress on a plan "equally superb and elegant with any . . . in America." This, declared a Philadelphia editor, would not only mean important additons to the city but would insure that at the end of the ten-year period fixed by law "the idea of moving the seat of government to the Westward (alias Connogochegue) will be rendered truly ridiculous."[4] Within two months the Mayor and Aldermen of Philadelphia had applied to the Pennsylvania legislature for funds to erect a Federal Hall rivalling that of New York and a President's House commensurate with the dignity of the office occupied by Washington. Again the Philadelphia editor exclaimed: "And shall we consider a residence of ten years, and very probably a century, as worth building a Federal Hall for? . . . Let us therefore join hand and heart and set about it."[5]

Pennsylvania leaders were more discreet than the journalist. While keeping their ultimate aims hidden, they provided immediate accommodations on the square where independence had been declared and postponed public discussion of the sensitive topic until the President had departed on his southern tour. When in the last days of the session a bill was introduced in response to the Philadelphia petition, an acrimonious debate took place. In this contest, revealing yet another example of contending local views, members from the western parts of the state were in the opposition while those from Philadelphia and the eastern counties pressed for immediate adoption. Albert Gallatin charged

[2] See Editorial Note and group of documents on locating the Federal District, at 24 Jan. 1791.

[3] TJ's report of meeting with Carroll, Stoddert, and Deakins at Georgetown, [14 Sep. 1790], Document II in group at 29 Aug. 1790.

[4] Quoted by the New York *Daily Advertiser* of 2 Aug. 1790 (with the allusion to Conococheague added), from Brown's *Federal Gazette* of 26 July 1790.

[5] New York *Daily Advertiser*, 7 Sep. 1790, quoting a Philadelphia paper of 4 Sep. 1790.

that the bill was founded on "wrong, dangerous, and dark principles." Its intent, he argued, was to have the temporary capital made permanent. Since Congress had already designated the Potomac and the President had chosen the permanent site for the seat of government, he thought such a step by one state seemed an improper attempt at bribery, contrary to the good of the nation as a whole. The voice of the back country, unequally represented though it was and divided between those who favored a location on the Potomac and those who preferred one on the Susquehanna, nevertheless prevailed over the formidable forces of the metropolis. The bill was postponed to the next session.[6]

Jefferson duly reported these proceedings to the President, who affected an indifference belied by his actions.[7] If Pennsylvania should actually go beyond the provisions already made for a temporary residence and provide lands and buildings for the indefinite future, then prompt and decisive action was clearly necessary to keep the capital on the Potomac. Washington quickly made use of the threat. Warning the Commissioners not to reveal his own sentiments on the subject, he quoted the brief paragraph in Jefferson's letter informing him of the Pennsylvania bill. This, he declared, "marks unequivocally in my mind, the designs of that state, and the Necessity of exertion to carry the Residence Law into effect."[8] A month later, after having read the debates and learned of the outcome, he repeated the warning and reminded the Commissioners that "the further consideration of a certain measure in another state stands postponed; for what reason is left to their own information or conjectures."[9] Such proddings had been typical of his words and actions ever since the Residence Act was enacted.

During these months, while urgently seeking to reconcile conflicting interests and bring the Federal City into being as quickly as possible, Washington generally turned to the Secretary of State for advice. But there could be no doubt, as Jefferson himself recognized, that the President was in command and that the ultimate decisions, whether authorized by law or arising from a profound fear of failure, were his to make. "If they have plac'd . . . the business

---

[6] Albert Gallatin and John Smilie, both from western Pennsylvania, were the chief protagonists for postponement, while William Bingham and Samuel Powel, both from Philadelphia, argued for immediate passage. The bill passed the House by a vote of 42 to 15, but the Senate voted for postponement 9 to 6. The text of the bill and an account of the debates appeared in Bache's *General Advertiser*, 6, 7, 9, 11, 12, and 13 Apr. 1791. Powel, pressed by those who believed that the bill had been deliberately held back to the final days of the session when attendance was thin and the schedule crowded, argued that it had not been possible to bring it forward earlier. But this was clearly disingenuous: the memorial of the City of Philadelphia had been presented three months earlier and the committee to which it was referred had unanimously recommended favorable action on the 14th of February. At the close of the debate Powel revealed the real intent when he declared it to be to the honor and advantage of Pennsylvania to keep the seat of government in Philadelphia "as long as possible." To have brought in the bill earlier, with Powel's close friend the President dominating the scene, would have created an awkward situation.

[7] TJ to Washington, 27 Mch. 1791; Washington to TJ, 1 Apr. 1791.

[8] Washington to the Commissioners, 3 Apr. 1791 (*Writings*, ed. Fitzpatrick, XXXI, 263-4). Two days earlier Washington had given Deakins and Stoddert the same information accompanied by a similar warning (Washington to Deakins and Stoddert, 1 Apr. 1791, same, XXXI, 262-3).

[9] Washington to the Commissioners, 7 May 1791 (same, XXXI, 286-8).

under the direction of the Executive," James Monroe observed in the summer of 1790, "it will most probably succeed."[10] Success was finally achieved. But the route to the ultimate goal was long and tortuous and many of the difficulties encountered along the way, as well as mistakes that were made, could be attributed in large part to the sense of urgency Washington felt and impressed upon all involved. Fixing the capital permanently upon the Potomac was indeed such a controlling factor in his thinking as to cause him to relegate the planning of this new seat of empire to secondary status, with unexpected and lasting consequences.

I

The first step to be taken after the Federal District had been defined, as Madison had pointed out, was to fix the site for the public buildings and to "provide for the establishment or enlargement of a town within the district" for the Federal City.[11] No authority had been conferred upon the President or the Commissioners to acquire lands for this purpose, hence the consent of landowners was necessary. Some might prove recalcitrant, others unknown or incompetent. At the crucial meeting Jefferson held in the autumn of 1790 with Carroll, Deakins, and Stoddert, he "supposed that the assembly of Maryland would interpose to force the consent of infant or obstinate proprietors for a reasonable compensation."[12] The mere hint was sufficient. Within a few weeks the Maryland legislature complied. But that body limited the delegated right of eminent domain to the exact number of acres owned by the numerous dispersed landowners of German descent in Maryland and Pennsylvania who held title to lots in the old projected town of Hamburg.[13] This dubious coincidence pointed inescapably to that area as the site already chosen for the location of the public buildings. So also did another suggestion made by Jefferson at this important meeting – that "proprietors of those spots of land most likely to be fixed on" for the Federal City make it possible under the Residence Act for the Commissioners to receive lands and to raise funds for erecting buildings. The signs indicating a choice of site near Georgetown had been so clear for so long that few if any at the meeting could have misread them. In consequence, as Jefferson must have anticipated, the principal owners of land in the vicinity promptly came forward, offering to deed their property on such terms as Washington considered reasonable and just, provided the Federal City should be located on their properties. They conceded that their own interests were involved, but, turning Jefferson's admonition around, warned that a site distant

[10] Monroe to TJ, 26 July 1790.

[11] Madison's advice on means of executing the Residence Act, [before 29 Aug. 1790], Document I in group at 24 Jan. 1791.

[12] TJ's Report to Washington, [14 Sep. 1790], Document II in group at 29 Aug. 1790.

[13] The Maryland legislature passed such an act on 28 Nov. 1790. Hamburg, or Funkstown, located a mile and a half below Georgetown, covered 130 acres – the amount of land stated in the Act – had been laid out in 1768 by Jacob Funk and consisted of 287 lots belonging to about 150 proprietors (Deakins and Stoddert to Washington, 9 Dec. 1790, DLC: Washington Papers; plat of Hamburg is reproduced in Library of Congress catalog of an exhibition, *District of Columbia Sesquicentennial* [Washington, 1950], Plate 19).

from Georgetown could raise "Doubts . . . whether after all, the Seat of government would be on Patowmack."[14]

Despite these maneuvers which pointed so obviously to a choice of site in the neighborhood of Georgetown, Jefferson had earlier drawn an outline locating the Federal City in the vicinity of Carrollsburg on the Eastern Branch. His idea of appealing to the self-interest of landowners in order to obtain lands and funds was advanced as a suggestion, one which such an experienced land speculator as Washington scarcely needed and which indeed he may have prompted. But in submitting the sketch Jefferson discussed details about the use of public lands as if the President had already decided against the Georgetown location. As set forth in his plan for using three hundred of the fifteen hundred acres he thought necessary for the new town, these details — the width of streets, the shape of lots, the height of buildings, the size of squares — were all offered as matters to be considered. He thought each square should consist of about eight acres, with two squares allocated for the President's House, offices, and gardens, one each for the Capitol and the Market, and *nine* — about a fourth of the whole number — to be set aside for "the Public walks," a term reflecting his hope of creating in the new capital such pleasant parks and gardens as he had enjoyed in the great cities of Europe.[15] The manner in which he discussed these points indicates clearly that he thought Washington had already chosen the area at the confluence of the Eastern Branch and the Potomac, contrary to all that he had indicated earlier. If so, was this a feint such as Washington later contrived to bring the Georgetown landowners to agree to more acceptable terms? It is difficult to believe that it was. During the whole of these negotiations extending over a period of almost a year before the choice of site for the Federal City was revealed to the public, all of the evidence suggests that Washington shared his views with Jefferson, at times with him alone. The circumstances indicate that — at least until the largely self-serving activities of Carroll, Deakins, and Stoddert began to promise beneficial results to the public — the down-river site had been chosen and that Washington had informed Jefferson of the fact.

This initial — and temporary — focus on the Eastern Branch is understandable. That location offered an excellent harbor and Jefferson's rough outline indicated that wharves and mercantile houses should be built along its right bank, with the public buildings and walks facing the Potomac. It must have occurred to him as well as to Washington that Philadelphia itself offered a striking confirmation of the generally accepted idea that the Federal City would be both the nation's capital and a commercial center. While George Mason, whose advice was sought by Jefferson at Washington's behest, had revealed his decided

[14] TJ's report to Washington on the meeting at Georgetown, [14 Sep. 1790]; TJ to Washington, 17 Sep. 1790, and form of conveyance given to Carroll; proposals of the Georgetown landowners, [13 Oct. 1790]; Documents II, IV, and VI in group at 29 Aug. 1790. To Carroll alone TJ had suggested the plan of having landowners in the whole of the Federal District give up half of their holdings. This brought forward a second proposal by the Georgetown proprietors: that they retain every third lot and give up the remainder for a Federal City of 3,000 acres instead of one of 1,500 suggested by TJ (Deakins to Washington, 18 Nov. 1790, DLC: Washington Papers).

[15] See TJ's suggestions to Washington, 29 Aug. and 14 Sep. 1790 (Documents I and II in group at 29 Aug. 1790).

preference for Georgetown, he had also thought "the Eastern Branch . . . an admirable position, superior in all respects to Alexandria."[16] These circumstances, added to the rivalry of the Carrollsburg and Georgetown interests, suggest that the idea of embracing both areas within the limits of the Federal City was developed not long afterwards. Such an extended plan also held forth the promise that more adequate funds would accrue through the sale of public lands in accordance with the suggestion Jefferson had advanced.

There can be no doubt, however, that by the 24th of January, when Washington announced his choice of site for the Federal District, he had decided to locate the public buildings for both executive and legislative branches near Georgetown between the Tiber and Rock Creek. One proof of this is found in the instructions given by him early in February to Deakins and Stoddert, engaging them under an injunction of "the most perfect secrecy" and all the dispatch compatible with success to buy lands in the vicinity of Georgetown. These instructions, drawn by Jefferson in accordance with Washington's views, outlined the comparative advantages of Carrollsburg and Georgetown as if the choice of site for the public buildings and offices were undecided. The agents, instructed to purchase lands as if for themselves but actually for the public, were thus entrusted with a state secret — but not with all of it. They were given a rough sketch of the three hundred or so acres desired, a tract equivalent to what Jefferson in his first proposals had deemed necessary for public use. They were told specifically that lands along the Tiber — particularly those belonging to David Burnes, though his name was not mentioned — were indispensable and should be sought before any other purchases were attempted. The success of their secret undertaking, Washington assured them, would help him decide between two locations about whose respective advantages his mind "had been so long on the balance."[17] The competition, so the instructions pretended, was for the location of the Federal City, not just for the site of the public buildings. But this screen, behind which Washington hoped to conceal both the extent already decided upon for the former and the choice already made for the latter, was scarcely impenetrable. The mere authorization to purchase a certain amount of land in a precisely defined area, even when limited to deeds in fee simple and conditioned upon a twelve-months' credit, could scarcely help conveying its real meaning to agents whose own interest would insure their best efforts: the choice lots naturally would lie in the vicinity of the public buildings. The flimsiness of the screen, together with the secrecy of the effort, was soon disclosed.

II

In the discussions following passage of the Residence Act, Madison had assumed that the Commissioners would have charge of the laying out of the Federal City and would develop their own plans for the public buildings or

[16] TJ to Washington, 17 Sep. 1790 (Document IV in group at 29 Aug. 1790).

[17] Washington to Deakins and Stoddert, 3 Feb. 1791 (Document I). Reasons for attributing the draft of this letter to TJ are discussed in the note to it. Another confirmation of Washington's choice of site is that he had received news that the Georgetown proprietors would make cessions of their lands and asked Edmund Randolph, through TJ, to prepare forms of conveyances as soon as possible (TJ to Randolph, [6?] Mch. 1791).

would submit to the President those "obtained from ingenious Architects."[18] This, in the view of Senator Maclay and others, would have been in accordance with the law and the intent of Congress. But Washington's desire for prompt action was too great to permit such important decisions to be left to others, even to those whom he had chosen and in whom he had confidence. Letters patent giving authority to the Commissioners had been issued at the time he announced his choice of location for the Federal District, but Thomas Johnson, Daniel Carroll, and David Stuart did not begin their deliberations for another two months. During this time Washington chose Andrew Ellicott to run the experimental lines of the Federal District. That competent and reliable engineer could also have defined the streets and boundaries of the Federal City in accordance with plans made by Jefferson or anyone else. Later, in fact, he was obliged to render essential services in this respect. But in his urgency to see the capital visible on the landscape as early as possible, Washington made a fateful choice early in 1791 which caused delay, created many obstacles, threatened to defeat his aims, and in the end left an ineradicable impression upon the capital of the nation.

This was his selection of Pierre Charles L'Enfant, the thirty-seven-year-old French engineer and architect who had served during the war, was a member of the Cincinnati, had designed its insigne and diploma, and was best known for his performance in converting New York's City Hall into Federal Hall to accommodate Congress at the beginning of the new government. Soon thereafter, following the 1789 debates over the location of the Federal District, L'Enfant had made known to the President his desire to be appointed surveyor general and to be assigned the task of planning the capital of "this vast Empire."[19] Others had also applied or had been recommended for this responsibility, including the more experienced British-born architect Joseph Clark who had demonstrated his talents in his work on the public buildings at Annapolis. A few months before the choice was made, Chancellor Hanson of Maryland, a man whom Washington respected and who was well acquainted with what Clark had done for the capital of Maryland, recommended him to the President in these words: "I consider the public works which in this city he has planned, superintended, and conducted, to be monuments of superior taste, judgment and skill. From his works, from his drawings . . . from his activity and attention to business . . . from the manner in which he exercised his authority, from the attachment and obedience of his workmen; in short, from every thing which I have either seen or heard, I do not scruple to declare, that I believe no man on the continent better qualified than Mr. Clark to act in that line, in which he is ambitious of serving the United States."[20] This was high praise concerning a man whose architectural achievements Washington was of course aware of because of his frequent visits to Annapolis. A few weeks later the Chancellor gave Clark a letter of introduction to the President, repeated his opinion that there was "no person in America better qualified for executing the trust, or

[18] Madison's advice on executing the Residence Act, [before 29 Aug. 1790], Document I in group at 24 Jan. 1791.

[19] L'Enfant to Washington, 11 Sep. 1789 (DLC: Washington Papers).

[20] Hanson to Washington, 2 Aug. 1790 (same). Alexander Contee Hanson (1749-1806) was held in such respect by Washington that he was about to be offered the post of District Judge for Maryland when he was appointed Chancellor, an office he held for the remainder of his life.

employment which he sollicits," and said that Clark would lay before him his plans and proposals.[21] Tench Coxe was another who came forward with his ideas concerning the capital, but did not seek employment in executing them.[22] The historian William Gordon also advanced interesting suggestions.[23] John Macpherson put forward his own claims. "I mean to draw a plan for the whole City!" he exclaimed. "I now form ideas what it will be a Hundred years hence. . . . If built as I hope it will be, its inhabitants will be warmer in the Winter and cooler in the summer, than any other people on Earth that live in the same latitude!"[24] Washington prudently ignored the well-known Philadelphia eccentric. But if he gave any consideration at all to Clark's proven merits as a professionally trained engineer and architect, no record of the fact has been found.

Instead, he placed his confidence in one who, whatever his talents, lacked those qualities of character and professional discipline which Clark so evidently possessed. It is not known whether Washington made the choice in response to L'Enfant's application or whether he did so at the prompting of friends and patrons of the engineer, among them Alexander Hamilton, Henry Knox, and Robert Morris. A few months later when he felt called upon to justify the appointment, he said that his knowledge of L'Enfant as a man of science and taste indicated that, "for projecting public works; *and carrying them into effect*, he was better qualified than any one who had come within my knowledge in this Country, or indeed in any other."[25] The defensive nature of the testimonial is understandable. There can be little doubt, however, that the appointment was dictated in large measure by Washington's sense of urgency. On this assignment, the most important in his life, L'Enfant proved to be eccentric, proud, indiscreet, opinionated, ambitious for fame and glory, and so incapable of grasping the real nature of his professional status that, within the year, he had to be dismissed because he refused to accept directions even from the President in whom the law had vested final authority. But, while he had had

[21] Hanson to Washington, 10 Nov. 1790 (same). Washington endorsed both this and the earlier letter, but apparently answered neither.

[22] Coxe thought the Federal City should have been built on the Virginia side of the Potomac, but recognized that the political difficulties facing any effort to make the change in the law were "very obvious." He sought to improve upon Philadelphia by providing for wide lots, placing markets in squares instead of in streets, and managing water courses for more effective sewers. Citing the Friends' and Christ Church burial grounds, he raised the question whether cemeteries should be permitted within its limits. He also suggested, as L'Enfant did later, that public lands be set aside and donated to religious organizations under proper precautions (Tench Coxe, "Remarks on the laying out of the federal city, and on the manner of building"; unsigned and undated, but in Coxe's hand and probably made for TJ's use in Feb. or Mch. 1791; MS in DLC: TJ Papers, 80: 13882-5).

[23] Gordon, writing from England, was under the impression that the Federal City would be located at Sheperdstown. He knew the locality and offered advanced ideas about means of supplying water and conveying sewage. He also thought it of "the utmost consequence" that all government records be isolated from other buildings and so constructed "as to be in no danger of suffering by fire, water, damps or other enemies" (Gordon to Washington, 31 Jan. 1791, DLC: Washington Papers). Even so ardent an advocate of the preservation of archives as TJ did not make such a suggestion as this (see TJ to Hazard, 17 Feb. 1791).

[24] Macpherson to Washington, 9 Mch. 1791 (DNA: RG 59, MLR).

[25] Washington to Stuart, 20 Nov. 1791 (*Writings*, ed. Fitzpatrick, xxxi , 420; emphasis supplied).

no experience in planning a city, he was available, he had some politically powerful friends, he was a war veteran who had been wounded in service, and, perhaps most important of all, time was pressing.[26] While Washington assigned to his Secretary of State some of the more vexatious problems relating to the Federal City, there is no evidence that he consulted him on the appointment of L'Enfant. Jefferson unquestionably had his own ideas about the planning of the capital, some of which he disclosed to the President from time to time. He also undoubtedly had serious reservations about the essential features of L'Enfant's plans. But on this he appears to have remained discreetly silent while giving generous assistance to L'Enfant even when Washington made decisions which, for good or ill, became irrevocable by virtue of his unquestioned cachet. Jefferson's unswerving loyalty in this instance, as with so many others who have served the Chief Executive through history, also brought him on occasion the uncongenial duty of trying to justify presidential actions in terms incompatible with the facts.

Later, when insurmountable difficulties developed, Jefferson explained that Washington had given L'Enfant his initial assignment because Daniel Carroll had not been able to act as a Commissioner while serving as a member of Congress. This "accidental circumstance," he added, "alone gave an appearance of an original interference by the President, which it neither was, nor is, his intention to practice." L'Enfant, in brief, had been sent forward to the two other Commissioners, "under whose employment and direction he was explicitly informed . . . he was to act."[27] But this was said after Washington had been forced against his will to declare L'Enfant's services at an end. There is nothing in the contemporary record or in Washington's actions at the time of the appointment or afterward to justify the explanation given. Both before Carroll became a Commissioner and for a long while after he and the others assumed their responsibilities, Washington gave instructions to L'Enfant either directly or through Jefferson acting for him and with his approval. The Commissioners themselves, often uninformed until after important decisions had been made, were understandably puzzled about the nature of their role under the law. They were also, up to a point, discreetly deferential. It was not until after L'Enfant had flatly defied their authority that they were driven to ask for a clear understanding of the terms on which he had been engaged to serve. "From several intimations," they declared some months later in revealing terms, "we considered the business as resting more on us than heretofore."[28] They were indeed

[26] An adequate biography of L'Enfant is much needed. The accounts by Fiske Kimball in DAB and by John W. Reps in *Monumental Washington* (Princeton, 1967) are excellent but brief. Both are judicious in their appraisal of the role of TJ during L'Enfant's short connection with the planning of the capital. Both, in varying degrees, also embrace the estimate of L'Enfant which has emerged at the beginning of the twentieth century, which Kimball correctly designated as the apotheosis of the designer, and which is reflected in works by Elizabeth S. Kite, *L'Enfant and Washington* (Baltimore, 1929), H. Paul Caemmerer, *The life of Pierre Charles L'Enfant* (Washington, 1950), Elbert Peets, *On the art of designing cities: Selected essays of Elbert Peets*, ed. Paul D. Spreregen (Cambridge, Mass., 1968), and J. L. Sibley Jennings, Jr., "Artistry as Design: L'Enfant's Extraordinary City," *Quar. Jour. of the Library of Congress*, XXXVI (1979), 225-78. See below.

[27] TJ to George Walker, 26 Mch. 1792.

[28] Commissioners to Washington, 21 Oct. 1791 (DNA: RG 42). In his "Observations" of 11 Dec. 1791 about L'Enfant's attempt to justify his conduct, TJ made this remarkably candid statement to Washington: "I do not know what have been the authorities given

by that time being given burdensome duties to perform. But the original interference which Jefferson so unconvincingly sought to justify was to continue, providing only another of many testimonials to the prevailing sense of urgency so keenly felt by Washington. No one could reasonably doubt that in all of the maneuvers to establish the Federal City as soon as possible, the President was in the saddle, guiding with a tight rein and also making frequent applications of the spur. L'Enfant seems to have been the only one who failed to recognize this inescapable reality.

If the Commissioners were kept in the dark about the terms under which L'Enfant was engaged or the degree of authority given him orally or in writing, history has also been denied this information. All that is known is that late in January, within a few days after Washington announced the location of the Federal District, L'Enfant received a letter which determined his future relationship to the permanent seat of government. This crucial communication has never been found. It was not written by Washington, though of course it was done at his prompting and with his sanction. Nor was Jefferson called upon to draft it, as he was in so many instances involving instructions, proclamations, conveyances, and agenda of proceedings for establishing the Federal District and the Federal City. Instead, the task was assigned to Daniel Carroll, who for professed reasons of delicacy would not serve as a Commissioner while a member of Congress but who nevertheless consented to act as agent in this matter so decisively affecting the future of the national capital. The only clue to the contents of Carroll's letter is to be found in Jefferson's communication to the Commissioners written about the same time. From this we learn that Washington "thought Major L'Enfant peculiarly qualified to make such a Draught of the ground as will enable himself to fix on the spot for the public Buildings."[29] From later developments we may safely conclude that no contract was offered and no terms of compensation discussed. We may be equally certain that Carroll urged upon L'Enfant the same need for a quick discharge of his assignment that had caused Andrew Ellicott to be sent off post-haste in the middle of winter to run the experimental lines of the Federal District. If L'Enfant replied in writing to the invitation extended on behalf of the President, his letter has not been found. Despite Washington's insistence upon dispatch and L'Enfant's own expressed eagerness to take part in planning the seat of empire, more than a month elapsed before the engineer appeared to receive his orders. The cause of the delay is not known. But his tardy responses to other calls for prompt action suggest that responsibility for the late beginning lay with him.

III

It was during the final hectic days before Congress adjourned that Jefferson gave L'Enfant his first official assignment. Assuming that the authoritative source of the orders would be taken for granted — or perhaps because this had been made clear in preceding discussions — he did not feel it necessary to say

him *expressly* or by *implication*." The choice of words and the emphasis given them reveal much about Washington's manner of dealing with one of his closest advisers.

[29] TJ to the Commissioners, 29 Jan. 1791 (Document IX in group at 24 Jan. 1791). Washington's letter to L'Enfant of 13 Dec. 1791 (*Writings*, ed. Fitzpatrick, XXXI, 443) confirms the fact that his "first official notice" came from Carroll. See TJ to Walker, 26 Mch. 1792.

that these came from the President and reflected his wishes. As Jefferson's brief summary of Carroll's letter had shown, the initial assignment given L'Enfant was quite limited. He was merely to make a topographical survey of the hills, valleys, morasses, and water courses within a specified area and to produce drawings of the "particular grounds most likely to be approved for the site of the federal town and buildings." He was not given explicit directions to act under the Commissioners as Jefferson later claimed: that agency, invested though it was with legal authority, was not even mentioned. He was instructed instead to report progress to the Secretary of State "about twice a week, by letter." This, as Washington must have directed and as Jefferson indicated, would enable him to draw L'Enfant's attention "to some other objects" which he had not at that moment sufficient information to define.[30] L'Enfant was to begin his survey on the Eastern Branch.

A precise topographical survey was of course essential to enable the President to designate the "particular grounds" for the public buildings. But at this stage it was not necessary to carry into effect the decision already arrived at that these would be in the vicinity of Hamburg on the Tiber — those other objects about which Jefferson pretended not to have sufficient information. The pretense was necessary, arising as it obviously did from the decision of the President not to permit L'Enfant to share the "inviolable secrecy" surrounding the operations of Deakins and Stoddert. L'Enfant was not even told what these surreptitious emissaries were doing on behalf of the public. On the same day that Jefferson gave him his limited assignment, he also drafted Washington's letter to the two agents — again at the president's direction and with his approval — warning them not to be misled because L'Enfant's survey was confined to "the Eastern branch, the Patowmac, the Tyber, and the road leading from George town to the ferry on the Eastern branch." Washington assured them that *"nothing further"* had been communicated to L'Enfant. He had already told them to suspend efforts to induce David Burnes to come to terms. This, his letter made clear, had been only a diversionary tactic and they were now authorized to resume negotiations with him.[31] The restriction imposed on L'Enfant's first assignment was another and related stratagem which Washington hoped would make it easier for Deakins and Stoddert to acquire the indispensable lands he had fixed upon for the federal buildings.

L'Enfant had been instructed to proceed with such dispatch as to have his survey ready for Washington on his arrival in Georgetown later in March. His limited assignment was far less arduous than that given to Ellicott, who was also expected to have his preliminary survey of the Federal District ready at the same time. Ellicott did accomplish his mission with remarkable promptness and efficiency, despite inclement weather, an attack of influenza, and a lack of competent assistants. But mists and rains which had not impeded him in his more formidable task presented to L'Enfant "an insuperable obstacle." Also,

[30] TJ to L'Enfant, [2] Mch. 1791. Ellicott had been given directions to proceed with all dispatch possible to plat the courses of the Eastern Branch and the Tiber, and to report progress (TJ to Ellicott, 2 Feb. 1791, Document XI in group at 24 Jan. 1791). He evidently accepted the assignment the same day and reported frequently thereafter. See Ellicott to TJ, 14 Feb. 1791 (Document XII in same group).

[31] Washington to Deakins and Stoddert, 2 Mch. 1791 (emphasis in original). Directions to suspend negotiations had been given on 28 Feb. 1791 (*Writings*, ed. Fitzpatrick, XXXI, 225).

instead of confining himself to a topographical survey of the precise area to which his instructions limited him, he explored on horseback the lands along the Potomac from the Eastern Branch to the Tiber and beyond to Rock Creek, including "the heights . . . as far up as thier Springs." He reported that the area between the Eastern Branch and the Tiber afforded a less desirable location for the city because the elevations "behind george town absolutly command the whole."[32] With his European background and his exuberant nature, it was natural enough for him to seek out those commanding positions which, in addition to providing grand vistas, would also afford the protection and security he deemed necessary. But this was not what he had been ordered to do.

Worse, L'Enfant's explorations on horseback beyond the area and outside the specific duty assigned him exposed the feint Washington had devised to induce Burnes and other landowners in the neighborhood of Georgetown to sell on reasonable terms. His indiscreet talk did even more to nullify the strategy. Immediately after his arrival in Georgetown, Deakins and Stoddert reported the disturbing news to Washington.[33] The press also informed the public. Only three days after L'Enfant came on the scene, the local gazette announced that he had been "employed by the President of the United States to survey the lands contiguous to Georgetown, where the Federal City is to be put. . . . He is earnest in the business and hopes to be able to lay a plan of that parcel of land before the President on his arrival in this town."[34] This could only have come from L'Enfant.

On learning of these indiscretions, Washington did L'Enfant the justice to suppose that his opinions were "promulgated . . . as much probably from complaisance as judgment." But if these impressions were allowed to stand uncontradicted, his own strategy could be defeated. Thus committed publicly by his own agent, he found himself in such an embarrassing situation that his initial impulse was to declare "at *once* the Site of the public buildings" as already determined. Faced with this dilemma, he sought the counsel of his Secretary of State.[35] Jefferson undoubtedly advised against an immediate announcement, urging instead that L'Enfant be instructed to enlarge the area of his survey to include the grounds between the Tiber and Rock Creek. This would at least have the appearance of confirming what L'Enfant had already said and done but would not be final. Washington approved, perhaps the more readily because he had just received another letter concerning L'Enfant's activities. Jefferson had already drafted additional instructions indicating that the site on the Eastern Branch had considerable advantages but that other strong reasons "independent of the face of the ground" pointed toward the second area to be surveyed. Then, after consulting with Washington, he put the essence of the message in a postscript. L'Enfant was to try to keep "the public mind . . . in equilibrio between these two places" until the President's arrival so as to poise the expectations of the Georgetown and Carrollsburg interests.[36] This

[32] L'Enfant to TJ, 11 Mch. 1791 (Document III).

[33] Deakins and Stoddert to Washington, 11 Mch. 1791, not found but acknowledged as of that date in Washington's response of the 17th (Document V).

[34] *Maryland Journal*, 18 Mch. 1791, under a Georgetown dateline of the 12th.

[35] Washington to TJ, 16 Mch. 1791 (Document IV).

[36] TJ to L'Enfant, 17 Mch. 1791 (Document VII). L'Enfant only began his first assignment on the day this letter was written. He had already decided to go on to the vicinity of Rock Creek before he received it (L'Enfant to TJ, 20 Mch. 1791, Document VIII).

was perhaps an even more difficult assignment than having L'Enfant conduct a topographical survey in rain and mist, but its success or failure mattered less than another decision made at the same time.

On learning from Deakins and Stoddert that the owners of lots in Hamburg had agreed to cede them to anyone authorized by the President to accept title, Washington gave them the required authority. He knew that in doing so this would expose them as agents of the public, but his willingness to make the disclosure provided one further proof of his conviction that the lands along the Tiber and in the vicinity of Hamburg were indeed indispensable. With the few days remaining, Washington's hope that conveyances of Hamburg lands might be available for use as bargaining weights in negotiations with the Georgetown and Carrollsburg proprietors was impossible of realization. In the fall of 1790 it had taken several weeks for the agents even to find out the number of lots in Hamburg and the names of the their widely scattered owners.[37] But Jefferson's prudent advice did enable the President to avoid a premature announcement of the site chosen for public uses. More important, it gave Washington the chance to bring his presence to bear in the negotiations.

IV

A week after L'Enfant received his assignment, Jefferson, already pressing Washington on the urgent demands from the West to confront Spain on the Mississippi question and trying to effect a possible concert of European powers against British navigation laws, began preparing essential papers for him to use in the Georgetown negotiations. The first was a proclamation drafted on the 10th of March but not to be issued until these negotiations had been concluded. Its chief object was to announce the decision to place the Capitol, the President's House, and the public offices in the vicinity of Hamburg.[38] The next day, just as he had done in the preparations for locating the Federal District, Jefferson drew up a list of matters requiring attention, headed by the suggestion that the Commissioners be called into action. This assignment of priority may have been prompted by regard for what the law required as well as by a concern for local and authoritative guidance of L'Enfant's activities. Jefferson's own role in acting as a channel transmitting the President's decisions could scarcely have been a congenial one, even when Washington found his advice acceptable. Also, with the Commissioners authorized to exercise their lawful responsibility, Jefferson must have known that his own suggestions for the Federal City could

[37] Washington to Deakins and Stoddert, 17 Mch. 1791 (Document v and its enclosure of same date). The form of conveyance sent with this letter was that drawn by Edmund Randolph in response to TJ's letter of [6?] Mch. 1791. When Washington passed through Georgetown in 1790 on his way to Philadelphia, Deakins and Stoddert at his request inquired at once of Jacob Funk in Washington County asking a particular state of the lots in Hamburg. Information about the 287 lots owned by about 150 proprietors in Maryland and Philadelphia did not come to them until the 8th of December (Deakins and Stoddert to Washington, 9 Dec. 1790, DLC: Washington Papers).

[38] Proclamation by the President, 30 Mch. 1791 (Document xiii in group at 24 Jan. 1791). An entry in SJPL proves that TJ drafted the proclamation on the 10th of March. It is important to note that in his draft TJ made a clear distinction between the general area already chosen for public uses and the precise sites still to be determined. The passage concerning the former he placed within brackets and then, for Washington's guidance, indicated that a decision as to the latter, "being conjectural, will be to be rendered conformable to the ground when more accurately examined."

be effectively conveyed to them through Daniel Carroll, either by himself or by Madison. Other objects that he listed for Washington's attention concerned deeds from landowners, determination of the precise sites for the Capitol and the President's House, the laying off of the town by the Commissioners in accordance with the terms of the proposed proclamation, and the designation of reserved areas for public buildings, a town house, a prison, a market, and "public walks."[39]

It was in this period of intense application to matters of foreign and domestic policy that Jefferson drew up his well-known but often misrepresented second sketch for the Federal City. That key document, together with the draft of the proclamation and other papers pertaining to the new capital, he handed over sometime before noon on the 21st of March when Washington departed from Philadelphia. It is important to note that the central feature of this plan was a precise reflection of Washington's decision concerning the location of the Capitol, the President's House, and lands for other public uses. This significant fact, often overlooked, is implicit in the employment of Deakins and Stoddert and in the instructions given them to acquire lands in the area designated. It is given explicit proof in the exact congruity of Jefferson's sketch with the terms of the draft proclamation announcing the choice of site. This area, which he envisioned as the heart of the capital, lay on the right bank of the Tiber, with public parks, gardens, and walks facing the river and providing long vistas downstream. Jefferson had had in contemplation such open spaces for public ornament and use when he drew his first sketch in the summer of 1790 placing the center of the capital on the Eastern Branch. But, whatever the accidental or other causes which led Washington to shift the focus to the Tiber, his decision was both fortunate and enduring. Jefferson's concept of extensive public parks and gardens along the waterfront, its possibilities thus enhanced by transference intact to a more appropriate terrain, may rightly be regarded as the origin of what would eventually become one of the chief glories of the national capital.[40]

[39] TJ's list of "Objects which may require the attention of the President at George T." (see Document II).

[40] The sketch (see illustration in this volume) is known to exist only in TJ's press copy (DLC: TJ Papers, 80:10805), the original having disappeared after Washington turned it over to L'Enfant. It is undated but usually and incorrectly assigned the date of 31 Mch. 1791. All that can be said with certainty is that it was drawn sometime between 10 and 21 Mch, 1791.

W. B. Bryan, *History of the National Capital* (New York, 1914), I, 130, was the first to note the relationship between TJ's plan for public walks and parks with the later development of the Mall. In this work Bryan reproduced TJ's sketch under the caption "Jefferson's Plan of the Mall." Fitzpatrick called this "misleading" (Washington, *Writings*, ed. Fitzpatrick, XXXI, 271), but Reps, a careful student of the origins of the Federal City, concludes that the spatial relationship between the Capitol and the President's House was similar in TJ's sketch to that in L'Enfant's plan and that TJ's conception of " 'public walks' may be regarded as the genesis of L'Enfant's great mall" (*Monumental Washington* [Princeton, 1967], p. 10). It is important to note, however, that TJ did not separate the key public buildings at the great distance later defined for them. Nor, so far as the evidence indicates, did L'Enfant, who at this precise moment was urging a location adjoining Georgetown to take advantage of the vistas provided by the heights in that vicinity (L'Enfant to TJ, 11 Mch. 1791, Document III). TJ, knowing, as L'Enfant did not, where Washington had decided to place the public buildings, sought to encompass distant views along the river front and thus first sketched in this location the open spaces later incorporated, with some modification, in L'Enfant's plan.

His sketch shows clearly that the area chosen for government buildings and other public uses overlapped the town of Hamburg, the outlines of which are shown with the President's House near its center. It is not known what particular survey he used to define the boundaries of that paper town, but it was one precise enough to inform him that its streets would pose "a considerable obstacle" because they were oriented differently from those in his own plan, in which all the avenues and streets ran with the cardinal points of the compass.[41] The plat that he used was probably one obtained by Deakins and Stoddert at the President's request, possibly even that which still exists.[42] More important, another feature of his sketch not found in any previous map or chart is the recording of soundings of the Potomac from the mouth of the Tiber to Rock Creek. In *Notes on Virginia* written a decade earlier, Jefferson had indicated at a few locations the depth of the river channel from its mouth to Alexandria and the head of tidewater. But this information he must have drawn from his incomparable collection of atlases, geographies, and voyages dating back to the middle of the 17th century.[43] The Fry and Jefferson map which he improved for the 1787 Stockdale edition of *Notes on Virginia* did not include such soundings, even for the Chesapeake estuary. While Joshua Fisher's chart of the Delaware of 1756 had given mariners full information of the sort, no atlas or map available to Jefferson at the time is known to have included such data for the Potomac. Both for the survey of the river in the vicinity chosen for the Federal City and for the recording of soundings, he was probably obliged to depend upon some manuscript map drawn especially for the purpose. If so, it was most likely provided by Andrew Ellicott, who, after surveying the experimental lines of the Federal District, had been directed by Jefferson to occupy himself in "running the meanderings of the Eastern branch, and of the river itself, and other waters which . . . merit an exact place in the map of the Territory."[44] The supposition is made all the more plausible by subsequent directions given or inspired by Jefferson. In September the Commissioners, instructing L'Enfant to begin preparation of "A Map of the City of Washington, in the Territory of Columbia," informed him that Ellicott would provide soundings of the Eastern Branch.[45] These orders emerged from a meeting attended by Jefferson. Given his insistence upon the importance of presenting such information in the map of the City, it is reasonable to suppose that the suggestion came from him. Later, finding that soundings were not inserted in the first engraved plan of the City, he sought to have them added to the plate. The omission, among other things, led to his demand for rectification in the second map published in 1792.[46]

[41] Washington to Deakins and Stoddert, 17 Mch. 1791 and enclosure (Document v).

[42] MS plat of Hamburg in DLC, showing boundaries, streets, and numbered lots of the town. This survey is described and reproduced in facsimile in Library of Congress exhibition catalogue, *District of Columbia Sesquicentennial* (Washington, 1950).

[43] For the best reflection of TJ's interest in geography, cartography, travel voyages, and related subjects – one of the largest groups in his library – see Sowerby, Nos. 3818-4172.

[44] TJ to Ellicott, 2 Feb. 1791 (Document xi in group at 24 Jan. 1791). Such a map may have been included in one of Ellicott's missing letters to TJ.

[45] Commissioners to L'Enfant, 9 Sep. 1791 (DNA: RG 42, PC).

[46] On receiving the first impressions of the *Plan of the City of Washington in the Territory of Columbia* (engraved by Samuel Hill, Boston, 1792), TJ thought them proofs, sent one to the Commissioners, suggested that Ellicott could inform them whether the sound-

But the source of Jefferson's information is less important than the fact of his insistence upon presenting the kind of information merchants and mariners would need if, as all desired, the capital would become a center of commerce like London or Philadelphia. As his sketch shows, Jefferson knew that the Potomac at the mouth of the Tiber contained no water for commerce. This he took to be an advantage, since the absence of wharves and mercantile houses would leave "a fine open prospect for those attached to government" while the river at the mouth of Rock Creek would suit merchants because of the depth of water there. In shifting his 1790 plan from the Eastern Branch to the Tiber, he was compelled by the nature of the terrain to reverse his means of achieving the two objects. But in both instances he kept firmly in view the concept of the useful and the ornamental which he had long since imbibed from his classical studies. L'Enfant also envisioned the two objects, but he never recorded river soundings in any map of the City attributable to him and is not known to have suggested the need for publishing such information.

The plan of the City which Jefferson submitted to Washington has often been criticized as limited in extent by comparison with the projections of L'Enfant. In fact its area comprehended about the fifteen hundred acres which the President hoped would emerge from negotiations with the Georgetown and Carrollsburg proprietors. Washington had been assured that those of Georgetown would permit the extension of the limits to double that size if the landowners should be allowed to retain every third lot. This was apparently unacceptable.[47] In fact Jefferson himself had suggested in the autumn of 1790 that the idea of letting the owners retain half of the lots be carried throughout the entire Federal District, embracing sixty-four thousand acres. But this, he thought, might have been pressing matters too much and so he confided the greatly expanded concept only to Daniel Carroll. Both the extent of his plan and the trebling of the area which came when Washington arrived in George-town derived from the effort to accommodate the contending interest of land-owners. It was this realistic factor, not L'Enfant's expansive views, which determined the outer boundaries of the City. What distinguished Jefferson's plan, as might have been expected, was its pragmatism coupled with a concern for the grand and beautiful. Half of the lots in squares adjacent to those reserved for public uses, being the most valuable, were to be "sold in the first instance." The remainder were to be "laid off in future" and were expected to increase in value as the City grew outward from its center.[48] This recognition of reality

---

ings had been in the original, and, if not, urged that they be inserted in the "proof" to be sent to Boston. But it was too late. TJ had received prints, not proofs, and by then the plate itself was already on the way to Philadelphia. The omission of soundings, the size, and other imperfections of the Boston engraving undoubtedly led him to insist on publishing the larger, more accurate, and more complete Philadelphia engraving of 1792. See Blodget to TJ, 5 July 1792; TJ to Commissioners, 11 July 1792; TJ to Blodget, 12 July 1792; Carroll to TJ, 13 and 25 Oct. 1792; Commissioners to TJ, 5 Nov. and 5 Dec. 1792; TJ to Commissioners, 13 Nov. 1792. TJ ordered his chief clerk not to distribute any of the "small plans" until there should be copies of the large ones to accompany them (George Taylor to Commissioners, 10 Jan. 1793). For reproductions of the 1792 engraving, see Reps, *Monumental Washington*, p. 23-4. The soundings there given were reproduced in the 1793 engraving of Ellicott's topographical map of the Federal District.

[47] Deakins to Washington, 18 Nov. 1790 (DLC: Washington Papers).

[48] See illustration of TJ's 1791 sketch in this volume. Reps, *Monumental Washington*,

stood in sharp contrast to L'Enfant's idea of a series of localities — paper towns, so to speak, comparable to those of Hamburg and Carrollsburg — whose development, he insisted, should be pressed simultaneously with all other objects.

The sketch which Jefferson handed to the President just before he departed for Georgetown, embracing Washington's decision as to both the extent and the site chosen for public use, was only a bare skeleton of the reality he envisioned. We know that a month earlier, after L'Enfant had been given his invitation, Washington intimated that he wished Jefferson to accompany him to Georgetown to assist in fixing the site of the public buildings and in laying out the plan of the town. We also know that, in addition to his sketch, Jefferson presented his "general ideas" on the subject, among which we may be assured was his preference for architectural models of antiquity for the Capitol and those of later ages — such as the Hôtel de Salm in Paris which he so greatly admired — for the President's House.[49] But pressing public affairs and the need for some respite after months of intensive labors kept him in Philadelphia.

Even so, Washington found himself caught between the two opposed personalities and their disparate views. On the one hand was his Secretary of State, a pragmatic idealist whose extensive study of European ideas of taste and grandeur, ancient and modern, was informed by a thorough understanding of the principles of the new republic and the practicalities it faced. On the other was L'Enfant, Washington's old comrade in arms whose ideas for the capital were steeped in the traditions of his homeland but untempered by the realities of the nation whose "President's Palace and Congress House" he dreamed of in such ecstatic terms, always aiming at something novel and original which would bring him fame. Faced with these opposed embodiments of taste and temperament, the choices that Washington made between them tells us much of himself. Anxious and urgent, perhaps assured also that he could withhold approval of any proposals which on mature consideration and under other circumstances might prove unacceptable, he concentrated on the business of reconciling the competing local interests whose recalcitrance might frustrate all his hopes. In pursuing this primary goal, he seems not to have been aware of the magic his presence on the scene would work, bringing to bear a force which none dared openly oppose.

V

Washington arrived in Georgetown early on the 28th of March, conferred with Ellicott and L'Enfant, was honored at a public dinner, and the next day, in a thick mist, was joined by the Commissioners in an unsatisfying inspection of the land. That evening, at his request, the proprietors of Georgetown and Carrollsburg met him at his lodgings in Suter's Tavern. There, speaking bluntly, he warned them that their contentions were not compatible with either the public interest or their own. They could injure the cause by procrastination, but neither could command funds adequate to the object in view. Indeed, he assured them, "both together did not comprehend more ground nor would afford greater means than was required for the federal City; and instead of

p. 10, 12, estimates the total area covered by TJ's sketch at about 2,000 acres and adds: "Jefferson has sometimes been described as the advocate of a mere village for the new capital city, but this drawing and its marginal notes clearly refute this charge."

[49] TJ to Randolph, 24 Feb. 1791; TJ to L'Enfant, 10 Apr. 1791 (Document XII).

contending which of the two should have it they had better, by combining more offers make a common cause of it." He drove the point home with an Aesopian metaphor all understood: while contending for the shadow they might lose the substance. Then, moving from stern warnings about the dangers of delay, he drew their attention to the future prospects and "the good effects that might proceed from a Union" – good effects for both public and private interests. It is scarcely surprising that the next day the competitive groups united in signing an agreement whose terms and unanimity must have exceeded Washington's most ardent expectations. On arriving at Mount Vernon on the evening of the 31st, he confided to his diary with unmistakable satisfaction the feelings induced by this signal accomplishment.[50] He immediately reported the result to Jefferson, outlining the essential terms of the agreement and expressing gratification that even "the obstinate Mr. Burns" had signed.[51]

The spirit of harmony and of enthusiastic support was such that Washington did not need to disclose his choice of site for public uses. He therefore deleted from the draft proclamation the paragraph which contained its chief reason for being issued.[52] Nor, of course, did he show to the proprietors Jefferson's proposed sketch of the capital. On the day he arrived at Mount Vernon, the *Virginia Gazette* of Alexandria announced that the President for two or three days had been "assiduously employed in examining the lands from the Eastern branch upwards, in order to ascertain the most eligible spot for the seat of the federal buildings."[53] He had indeed explored the area but not for the purpose stated. As in the case of his journey up the Potomac in 1790, the ostensible object had long since been determined. Someone who was fully cognizant of the negotiations with the proprietors informed the press flatly that "The spot for the public buildings is not yet fixed."[54] This was incorrect, but, in the prevailing aura of good will, it was the impression Washington felt it necessary and indeed proper to leave upon all. The informed gentleman who gave this unqualified assurance would have needed little prompting to do so.

While the proclamation had been stripped of its essential paragraph and was

[50] Washington, *Diaries*, ed. Fitzpatrick, IV, 152-5.

[51] Washington to TJ, 31 Mch. 1791 (Document IX). Daniel Carroll sent James Madison a copy of the agreement, referred him to the newspapers for intelligence on the subject, and added: "The union of the George Town and Carrollsburgh interests, has given a Cast to this business more favourable than was expected even by its friend. It was a union I have most ardently wished for and promoted on public and personal considerations" (Carroll to Madison, 6 Apr. 1791, DLC: Madison Papers).

[52] See proclamation of 30 Mch. 1791 (Document XIII in group at 24 Jan. 1791) for the deleted paragraph.

[53] *Virginia Gazette*, 6 Apr. 1791, under an Alexandria dateline of 31 Mch. 1791.

[54] *Maryland Journal*, 1 Apr. 1791, "Extract of a letter from a gentleman at Georgetown to his friend in this town dated yesterday." Because of this and other statements in the letter, particularly the exact definition of the boundaries of the City, Daniel Carroll seems the most likely one to have written it.

Deakins was another who was privy to the President's decision. Soon afterward, Francis Cabot and Mr. Green wrote to the Commissioners expressing their pleasure that the President had designated the area in the vicinity of Georgetown for the Federal City. They conceived that this meant "the buildings for the accommodation of the public will soon be commenced" in that area. In offering to undertake contracts for the supply of materials, they referred the Commissioners to Deakins for their "Character and connexions" (Cabot and Green to Commissioners, 16 May 1791, DNA: RG 42).

issued immediately at Washington's insistence, newspapers throughout the country announced another feature which had been also omitted — the precise boundaries of the Federal City as defined in the meeting with the proprietors. Jefferson had received from Washington a rough indication of its extent, but he probably first learned from Bache's *General Advertiser* that the President had "ordered the federal city to be laid off, extending from George-town with the river, to the mouth of the Eastern-branch, and up the Eastern-branch about two miles, from thence a line drawn to intersect the road leading from George-town to Bladensburg, about half a mile from the Ford on Rock-creek, and with the road to the creek, and down the creek to the river."[55] These boundaries embraced an area of about forty-five hundred acres, treble what Jefferson had included in the sketch reflecting Washington's views prior to the meeting. Further, the agreement of the proprietors authorized the President to retain any number of squares he deemed proper for public purposes. On learning of this Jefferson seized the favorable moment to urge that very liberal reserves should be made. In making the suggestion he clearly hoped that Washington would go beyond the expanded areas for public use as defined in his sketch. He thought the reconciling of the contending interests and the emergence of such a greatly expanded area for the Federal City a "really noble" accomplishment.[56]

The successful termination of the negotiations was itself enough to lift the spirits of Washington and other advocates of the Potomac site. But this unexpected trebling of the area for the Federal City — almost certainly a result of Washington's argument that the contending proprietors should not only unite but contrive other offers of land — also held out the promise that sales of public lots would be proportionately augmented. The well-informed correspondent who gave the essential facts to the press expressed confidence that such sales would "produce the sum of *Three Hundred Thousand Pounds*."[57] Others, equally susceptible to the fever, predicted that even larger sums would accrue to the public and private interest, all tending to insure the permanent existence of the capital on the Potomac. A few, expressing themselves privately in letters or anonymously in the press, voiced doubts. Suppose, Jonathan Williams asked Henry Knox, Congress should determine at some future date not to keep the capital on the Potomac? Who then would reimburse the purchasers as required by the agreement?[58] Another skeptic from Hartford looked with scorn upon the idea of building a town which would be overrun with Congress in session and then would lie empty and idle during its recesses. If it should be so situated as to attract the trade of an extensive country, the capital might in time arise there. "But otherwise," he declared, "neither grants of money, nor acts of Congress, will have the least effect. We may expend ten millions of money in erecting accommodations for people, but if the place is not naturally designed

[55] *General Advertiser*, 7 Apr. 1791, from a Baltimore dateline of 1 Apr. 1791.
[56] TJ to Washington, 10 Apr. 1791 (Document XIII).
[57] *Maryland Journal*, 1 Apr. 1791, "Extract of a letter from a gentleman at George-town to his friend in this town dated yesterday" (emphasis in original). See note 54.
[58] Williams to Knox, 18 Apr. 1791 (MHi: Knox Papers). Williams had been shown over the site of the Federal City by Ellicott. "The location for the City appears to me judicious," he wrote, "as it unites as much as possible the objects of health, convenience, and beauty; but whether these should be considered in the extent of a Virginian's ideas . . . I will not undertake to determine. The size is only about 5000 acres."

for business, people will not live there. . . . It is a proper scheme for men in concert, who deal much in visionary theories, but very little in experience. Such are too many of the southern gentlemen, who, with industrious abilities, and good hearts, want that knowledge, which is acquired only in the detail of business. I had rather be guided in my opinions by one experienced man of business, than by a hundred theorists . . . versed only in books."[59] But the achievement at Georgetown as reported so widely in the press turned ridicule and disdain into sober thoughts. These reports, together with those of Andrew Ellicott and others, so Lear informed Washington, "have created a serious and to many an alarming expectation, that the law for establishing the permanent seat of Government will be carried fully into effect."[60]

Washington was justifiably elated, but the prevailing spirit of harmony had no effect upon the sense of urgency which he pressed upon all. Even when he felt, somewhat prematurely, that the business was "thus happily finished," he gave on departing from Georgetown "some directions . . . to the Commissioners, the Surveyor, and Engineer with respect to the mode of laying out the district, surveying the grounds for the City and forming them into lots."[61] Beyond this the precise nature of the instructions is not known. But two days after the agreement was signed, he took care to obtain a copy of it with the signatures attached. He insisted that in order to achieve the great object of uniformity and beauty, regulations governing public buildings should also apply to the proprietors as a condition of their grants. Above all, he urged a speedy completion of the good work that had begun so auspiciously.[62] "It is of the greatest moment," he warned the Commissioners, "to close this business with the Proprietors . . . that consequent arrangements may be made without more delay than can be avoided." New conveyances would be needed and should be executed so that the sale of lots might proceed with expedition. To the Commissioners, as well as to Deakins and Stoddert, he exploited the warnings that he professed to see in the Pennsylvania debates.[63] Such precautions in the midst of victory were as characteristic as they were well-advised. By the time Washington reached Charleston early in May discontents had arisen among the proprietors to such an extent that he felt his own word challenged by misconceptions or misrepresentations of the terms he had set forth.[64] The result was

[59] *Hartford Courant*, 11 Apr. 1791, cited in various papers, including the *Virginia Gazette* of 27 Apr. 1791. The origin of the comment, the allusion to Virginians in concert, and above all, the reference to those theorists versed only in books—a remark which seems aimed at TJ—suggest that the author was Noah Webster, who had pronounced convictions on such subjects and who had only recently ridiculed TJ's Report on Weights and Measures (see TJ to Madison, 10 Jan. 1791, and its enclosure).

[60] Lear to Washington, 24 Apr. 1791 (DLC: Washington Papers).

[61] Washington, *Diaries*, ed. Fitzpatrick, IV, 154.

[62] Washington to Deakins and Stoddert, 1 Apr. 1791 (*Writings*, ed. Fitzpatrick, XXXI, 262-3; Dft in DLC: Washington Papers, entirely in Washington's hand).

[63] Washington to the Commissioners, 3 Apr. 1791 (*Writings*, ed. Fitzpatrick, XXXI, 263-4).

[64] Commissioners to Washington, 14 Apr. 1791 (DLC: District of Columbia Papers). Daniel Carroll reported these disagreements to Madison. The major objection, made by Notley Young, Robert Peter, and other proprietors, was that Washington had been given power to go beyond the limits of some 4,000 acres as first defined by him. Another—that respecting regulations for public buildings apply also to private ones—was omitted from the agreement because of haste, but was inserted in deeds (Carroll to Madison, 6 and

a long, angry, and explicit letter revealing clearly which public question was uppermost in his mind. These unfortunate and unexpected difficulties, he warned, "arise to darken, perhaps to destroy the fair prospect . . . presented when I left Georgetown."[65]

But while the Commissioners were left to wrestle with forms of conveyance, deeds, and other troublesome details, Washington assumed responsibility for making important decisions which, under the law, should have fallen to them. He was able to do this because the terms of the agreement with the proprietors gave him sole power to direct the City to be laid off in whatever manner he pleased and to reserve whatever number of squares for public use he might think proper. In consequence, at this moment of elated hopes before leaving Georgetown, he gave L'Enfant instructions about laying out the City within the greatly expanded limits he had achieved. This was a critical and even fateful assignment, but, unlike the admonitions and directions to the Commissioners, its controlling terms were apparently not reduced to writing. The authority conveyed to the architect, however, can be reasonably deduced from two sources – the expressions of a naturally exuberant L'Enfant and the laconic statement of Washington himself.

All that L'Enfant had been able to give Washington on his first limited assignment was a rough pencil outline which "Steel remained unfinished." But, he reported to Jefferson, the President had directed the "delination of a grand plan . . . conformable to the ideas which I took the liberty to hold before him." The development of this plan, he added, "the President has left to me without any restriction so Ever."[66] To Alexander Hamilton, to whom L'Enfant was not required to report but with whom he felt more congenial than with the Secretary of State, he gave a much longer and more revealing account. It is not surprising that he took to himself credit for having resolved the conflicting interests among the proprietors and having determined whether Carrollsburg or Hamburg offered the best site for the Federal City. He said he had only followed directions to survey both tracts, but he could not help "when contemplating the whole local Feeling some concerned at seeing the advantages which [the Eastern Branch] offered likely to be trample upon from a necessity of securing the Establishments by begoning it no matter were." Nevertheless, he added, "I vantured the chance and gave imagination its full Scope in invading all the propriety of all, on a supposed more extensive location in which I comprehended the tow situations in competition and carring on my scheme further . . . and progressive improvement, I vantured some remarks thereon . . . to the President on his arrival at this place and was fortunate enough to see meet with his approbation." This new plan, he added, determined the President to delay rather than to secure whatever extent of territory was needed. The result was

23 Apr. 1791, DLC: Madison Papers). As indicated by notes on the second of these letters, Madison carried it with him on the northern journey with TJ and of course shared both documents with him, just as he had done with others when authorized to do so by Carroll.

[65] Washington to the Commissioners, 7 May 1791 (*Writings*, ed. Fitzpatrick, XXXI, 286-8).

[66] L'Enfant to TJ, 4 Apr. 1791 (Document x). Washington's agreement with the proprietors, 31 Mch. 1791 (DNA: RG 42, PC) created the Deed of Trust which successive Attorneys General recognized as giving Washington sole authority to plan the Federal City.

an accommodation which not even the most optimistic speculator had expected — the allocation of some six thousand acres for the Federal City. L'Enfant praised the location: "No position in all america can be more susceptible of grand improvement, more capable of promoting the rapide Increases of a city or Better situated to secure an infinity of advantages to gouvernement." Echoing the talk of speculators, he spoke of the great competition for lots that had already begun in the most eligible spot for "the capital of this extensive empire." Nothing, he concluded, would more promote the general good than for the people of the East to become interested "in the advancement of this business, in becoming at this early periode proprietor in this federal district were an acquisition of lots or of ground undelinated as such must in the end prove of infinit advantage to the purchasser." The planner and the dreamer had by now become infected with the enthusiasm of the speculator. But the overriding consideration, as L'Enfant exultantly confided to both Jefferson and Hamilton, was his claim that the President had charged him with full and unrestricted responsibility for "delinating a plan for the City."[67]

Both the words and actions of Washington lend confirmation to L'Enfant's claim. He knew that he possessed ultimate authority to approve, alter, or reject any proposals that might be made, but his exalted confidence in L'Enfant's competence to discharge the assignment with zeal and distinction undoubtedly was the controlling factor in his bestowal of such extensive responsibility. Despite L'Enfant's indiscreet talk two weeks earlier which placed him in such an embarrassing situation, Washington now confided to him information that he withheld from both the Commissioners and the public. This he did by turning over to L'Enfant a number of papers pertaining to the Federal City. These, he thought, would not provide any material advantages, but, having been drawn by different persons under different circumstances, they might be usefully compared with L'Enfant's own ideas of a proper plan for the capital. The rather gratuitous disparagement of the materials offered may have arisen from mere politeness. But Washington's words take on another meaning in light of the fact that the first of these documents was what he described as a "rough sketch by Mr. Jefferson." That sketch, he added, "was done under an idea that *no* offer, worthy of consideration, would come from the Land holders in the vicinity of Carrollsburg . . . and therefore was accommodated to the grounds about George town."[68] This statement was both inaccurate and misleading. The sketch had been prepared by Jefferson to incorporate Washington's choice of location for the public buildings and to accord with the announcement of that decision which he had proposed to make in the proclamation. Moreover, the plan of the City thus outlined with Washington's approval had in fact been extended to the Eastern Branch to propitiate the Carrollsburg

[67] L'Enfant to Hamilton, 8 Apr. 1791 (Syrett, *Hamilton*, VIII, 253-6). Hamilton thanked L'Enfant for his full communication and asked for a continuation of his observations (Hamilton to L'Enfant, 24 May 1791, same, VIII, 354-5).

[68] Washington to L'Enfant, 4 Apr. 1791 (*Writings*, ed. Fitzpatrick, XXXI, 270-1). While Washington had not informed TJ of the general area covered by the agreement with the proprietors (Washington to TJ, 31 Mch. 1791), he of course had to give to the one whom he had directed to survey and lay off the City a fairly precise definition of its boundaries. But his withholding from L'Enfant the choice of location for the public buildings could only have strengthened the architect's conviction that he had been authorized to plan the capital without any restriction whatever.

interest. But to this concealment of what the sketch represented, then and later, Washington added another. This was in the form of a map on a larger scale, drawn without reference to any particular spot for public buildings and other uses. This document has never been identified and is not known to exist. It may have been a mere sketch outlined by Washington himself or one prepared by Ellicott at his request to accord with the extended boundaries of the City as agreed upon with the proprietors. All that is known with certainty is that, as Washington assured L'Enfant, it covered a more extended area than did Jefferson's sketch and, unlike that, did not indicate the location of the Capitol, the President's House, and other public areas. In brief, with this document and his comment on it, Washington conveyed the impression that Jefferson's plan had been rendered obsolete by the reconciliation of the contending interests and that the choice of site for public purposes was still undetermined. He may have done this, as he had tried vainly to do two weeks earlier, to induce L'Enfant to keep the expectations of the two interests poised. He may have done it to give L'Enfant full scope in developing his own ideas. Or, having recently experienced L'Enfant's indiscreet talk, he may have made the disparaging reference to Jefferson's sketch for the same reason that he had deleted the essential paragraph from the proclamation. Whatever his motive, the concealment of his own views from the Commissioners and from the public was greater than what he withheld from L'Enfant.

Jefferson's sketch and other papers were turned over to L'Enfant by Washington confidentially, to be used only for his "*private* inspection." Yet within little more than two weeks the confidence thus bestowed, which evidently had been shared up to that moment only with Jefferson, was violated. To William Loughton Smith, member of Congress from South Carolina, L'Enfant showed all of his plans and surveys, rode with him about the whole area of the City, defined its boundaries, and pointed out the eminences, sites for canals, quays, bridges, and public walks. L'Enfant was enraptured with the prospect, according to Smith's testimony: " 'nothing,' he says, 'can be more admirably adapted for the purpose; nature has done much for it, and with the aid of art it will become the wonder of the world.' "[69] Smith's account leaves no doubt that the papers shown by the enthusiastic engineer included Jefferson's sketch. Washington never reported to Jefferson what disposition he had made of it. In turning it over to L'Enfant and virtually dismissing it as useless while concealing its true nature and his own approval of it, he must also have refrained from passing on those "other ideas" about the planning of the capital which Jefferson had held out to him in Philadelphia. L'Enfant, though required by Washington to report to the Secretary of State, also said nothing to him of the sketch.

But Washington's disparagement of it, coupled with his statement that it had been drawn on the supposition that the Carrollsburg interests would bring forth no acceptable offer, led L'Enfant to misread the communication and to suppose that the President really desired the City to be located on the Eastern Branch. Perhaps his original assignment confining his survey to that area, together with the postscript to Jefferson's letter urging him to keep public expectations poised between the two locations, also served to mislead. Certainly if Washington had not withheld his own decision about the center of the capital

[69] *Journal of William Loughton Smith*, ed. Albert Mathews (Cambridge, 1917), p. 60-2. Smith shared L'Enfant's enthusiasm for the site and suggested that the City be called *Washingtonople*.

as reflected in Jefferson's sketch, L'Enfant could scarcely have made the error he did. In any case, his response was what he thought the President wanted. In a long memorandum he argued that the Eastern Branch was the most eligible spot "for the first settlement of a grand City, and one which if not the only within the limits of the Federal territory, is at least the more advantageous in that part lying between the Eastern Branch and Georgetown." As for the means of navigation, the advantages of that excellent stream far transcended those of the river at Georgetown. Manufacturing establishments, warehouses for naval and mercantile uses, arsenals, and other useful structures could be built for three miles up its meanderings. On the ridge leading to Jenkins' Hill, many desirable spots were available for public edifices. "From these hights," L'Enfant thought, "every grand building would rear with a majestic aspect over the Country all around and might be advantageously seen from twenty miles off." These for ages would be the central part of the City, "facing on the grandest prospect of both . . . branches of the Potomac." Three miles up the Eastern Branch, a bridge could be built linking the City to the North, with another over the Potomac at the head of navigation connecting it with the South. Growth at both extremities would undoubtedly be rapid, provided immediate attention should be given to open a direct and spacious avenue from one bridge to the other. Less than a month earlier, L'Enfant had found the site near Georgetown preferable because of its commanding heights. His shift to the Eastern Branch, though he did not know it, paralleled what Jefferson had proposed months earlier. Like Jefferson, he would later bring forth a plan embracing the location that Washington had already chosen.

But L'Enfant could not remain content merely to advocate the superior advantages of the area he mistakenly thought the President preferred. At the close of his memorandum, again perhaps influenced by Washington's disparaging comment, he launched an attack on what he conceived to be the kind of planning Jefferson's rough sketch represented. Without the advantage of its informative background or a knowledge of Jefferson's vision of the capital, he misinterpreted the sketch as much as he had misread Washington's intent. To achieve his grand plan, L'Enfant pointed out, regular assemblages of houses and a city laid out in squares, with streets parallel and uniform, were not only not necessary: these were appropriate only on a plain where there were no interesting eminences and where it became indifferent which way the streets were oriented. "But on any other ground," he declared, "a plan of this sort must be defective, and it never would answer for any of the spots proposed for the Federal City, and on that held here as the most eligible it would absolutely annihilate every of the advantages enumerated . . . and along injure the success of the undertaking. – Such regular plans indeed, however answerable they may appear upon paper or seducing as they may be on the first aspect to the eyes of some people must even when applyed upon the ground the best calculated to admit of it become at last tiresome and insipid and it never could be in its origin but a mean continuance of some cool imagination wanting a sense of the real grand and truly beautiful only to met with where nature contributes with art and diversifies the objects."[70] The obvious personal allusion revealed a gross

<hr>

[70] L'Enfant to Washington, undated (MS in DLC: District of Columbia Papers). Kite, *L'Enfant*, p. 43, accepting the date of 26 Mch. 1791 usually attributed to this memorandum, added that it was "undoubtedly . . . handed by L'Enfant to the President" while he was at Georgetown. At the same time she points out that the outburst against TJ's

misconception of the mind and character of the man from whom L'Enfant at this moment sought and received assistance nowhere else obtainable.

VI

At the meeting with the proprietors, Washington had taken care to observe "that before the city could be laid out, and the spot for the public buildings precisely fixed on, the water courses were to be levelled, the heights taken &ca. &ca."[71] The words "precisely fixed on" were carefully chosen, reflecting his wish to leave the impression of a suspended decision. Running the levels of the water courses and taking the altitude of heights was of course the task L'Enfant had not yet carried out. Despite that failed assignment, Washington encouraged him to face the much more formidable task of determining the style and character of the Capitol, the President's House, and other public buildings. It is not known whether he, Carroll, Stuart, or anyone else informed L'Enfant of Jefferson's collection of plans of European cities or urged him to borrow them. But in making his request that Jefferson procure for his use maps of cities, ports, docks, and arsenals, L'Enfant also asked an extraordinarily busy Secretary of State to provide a description of the number and nature of the public buildings required. All of this he wished to have "as speedily as possible." He made it clear that he scorned the idea of imitation, but would use such materials – even defective ones – to achieve something different "on a new and orriginal . . . plan."[72] Within two days of receiving the request, Jefferson forwarded a dozen large and accurate maps of European cities he had systematically gathered while travelling in Europe. He offered these freely as long as they were needed, but naturally asked that they be returned. There is no evidence that L'Enfant ever acknowledged this assistance or returned the maps. The request for a

sketch was made after L'Enfant had received Washington's letter of 4 Apr. 1791. The memorandum was of course written after that date and, as internal evidence proves, before the ceremonies held in Alexandria on 15 Apr. 1791, when the first marker in the boundaries of the Federal District was fixed.

Reps, *Monumental Washington*, p. 14, thinks it doubtful that "this almost violent denunciation of the gridiron plan" was provoked by L'Enfant's examination of TJ's sketch. This assumption, running counter to the generally accepted view, was perhaps prompted by the date usually attributed to the memorandum which would have made its composition prior to L'Enfant's receipt of the sketch from Washington. But the very violence of L'Enfant's denunciation, together with its overtones of personal feeling, undoubtedly arose from his recent acquisition of the sketch Washington had disparaged. Once again, L'Enfant seemed to echo what he perceived to be the President's own views.

[71] Washington to Commissioners, 7 May 1791 (*Writings*, ed. Fitzpatrick, XXXI, 287).

[72] L'Enfant to TJ, 4 Apr. 1791 (Document x). Jennings finds it significant that five of the eight cities which L'Enfant named – Madrid, Naples, Venice, Genoa, and Florence – were located in southern Europe and that what he did "clearly and pointedly request were the plans of compact, intimate eighteenth-century cities that had limited vistas, alamedas, avenues, and paseos" (Jennings, "L'Enfant's Extraordinary City," p. 231-2, 237). The fact is that L'Enfant asked TJ to procure for him "what Ever map may fall within your reach, of *any* of the different grand city now existing" and named several cities only as examples. Even with respect to these, he declared, he "would reprobate the Idea of Imitating" (L'Enfant to TJ, 4 Apr. 1791, Document x, emphasis added). The significance Jennings found in L'Enfant's naming five southern European cities lies primarily in the support he supposed it gave to his hypothesis about the sources of L'Enfant's design.

tabulation of the number and nature of the public buildings Jefferson answered with silence, knowing from experience how much time and thought would be required for that demanding task. He was aware at the time that L'Enfant had not completed his first and much simpler assignment, and assured him there was yet time enough to address these other important undertakings. The assurance may have been prompted also by his desire to persuade the President on his return about those "other ideas" he had advanced, among them — as he also indicated to L'Enfant — his preference of the models of antiquity for the Capitol and those of later times for the President's House.[73]

This well-known preference of the Secretary of State may also have resulted in the effort at this time to borrow from Richmond the plaster model of the Roman temple at Nîmes which Jefferson had procured in France for use in building the Capitol of Virginia, then under construction. It is possible that Washington himself advanced the suggestion since it was his close friend David Stuart who informed L'Enfant of the existence of the model. L'Enfant, according to Stuart, expressed a wish to see it and Stuart made the request of Governor Randolph. "If there is no impropriety in it," he wrote, "I would beg you to send it to him by the stage. . . . If not adopted it shall be returned immediately."[74] The governor was astonished. "I did not suppose," he responded, "that you expected the model of the Capitol in Plaister of Paris to be forwarded by the stage. I therefore called upon Mr. Hay [one of the Directors of Public Buildings] for such drafts of the House as had been sent from France by Mr. Jefferson. You will receive inclosed in a small Tin Case a Draft of the Ground Plat, together with a side and front View of the Building, which I beg may be returned as soon as Major L'Enfant can take copies of them, as I am told they are essentially necessary for the completion of some work here."[75]

There is no evidence to show what L'Enfant thought of the maps of cities sent by Jefferson or the drawings of the Maison Carrée transmitted from Richmond. What is certain is that Washington's direct and indirect prodding had produced no results. By October the Commissioners were prompted to request L'Enfant to "prepare a draft of the public buildings" for their inspection. He promised to do so as soon as he found himself disengaged from the still incomplete assignment of mapping the Federal City.[76] Before departing for the opening of the Second Congress, Washington conferred with L'Enfant at Mount Vernon and no doubt gave him his own conception of what was desired. The Capitol especially, he felt, "ought to be upon a scale far superior to any thing in *this* Country" and the President's House should be designed in commensurate

[73] TJ to L'Enfant, 10 Apr. 1791 (Document XII).

[74] David Stuart to Beverley Randolph, 11 July 1791 (CVSP, V, 342).

[75] Randolph to Stuart, 25 July 1791 (Vi: Executive Letter Book). Stuart himself promised to return the drawings as soon as L'Enfant had done with them (Stuart to Randolph, 5 Aug. 1791, CVSP, V, 356). No evidence has been found that the drawings were returned to Governor Randolph or to the Directors of Public Buildings and they are not now in the Virginia State Archives. TJ's retained copies of the "Ground Plat" and the front and side elevations of the Maison Carrée are in MHi (Fiske Kimball, *Thomas Jefferson Architect* [Boston, 1916], Nos. 110, 115, and 116). These of course were not the copies made available to L'Enfant.

[76] Commissioners to Washington, 21 Oct. 1791 (DNA: RG 42). Since this request was made immediately after Washington had conferred with the Commissioners, there can be little doubt that the prompting originated with him.

terms even though not executed all at once.[77] L'Enfant undoubtedly shared the opinion that the two principal edifices should be architecturally imposing. But no evidence has been found that such ideas or models as he may have had in mind ever reached the stage of usable drawings. Certainly he never submitted plans for these structures either to the President or to the Commissioners. Washington, in his final letter to the man whom he had so ardently supported, told L'Enfant candidly that five months had been lost by this additional failure in meeting an assignment. It was only at that critical juncture that Jefferson prepared his own "Idea of the public buildings to be erected at the Federal seat," but, since a competition had been set in motion, this was expressed in terms of needs and functions rather than style.[78] Also, once again, he drew up a list of matters for the Commissioners to consider. Among these was the employment of Ellicott to finish laying off the City—that other assignment L'Enfant had left unfinished even with Ellicott's indispensable assistance.[79]

When Washington arrived home from his southern tour in mid-June, L'Enfant was able to submit to him only an incomplete and hastily drawn plan of the City. In an apologetic letter, he again solicited Washington's indulgence. "My whole attention," he explained, "was given to the combination of the general distribution of the Grand Local as to an object of most immediate moment and of Importance. To this I yielded Every other Consideration . . . having first determined some principal points to which I wished making the rest subordinate. I next made the distribution regular with streets at right angle *north-south* and *East-west*." Though the plan was obviously incomplete, it included the essential elements of L'Enfant's concept of the capital, with radial avenues cutting across the rectangular pattern, connecting the focal points he hoped would aid rapid settlement, providing "reciprocity of sight" toward distant objects, and bringing outer roads into the center of the City. The area above the Tiber, L'Enfant explained, was "the elligible spot to lay the Foundation . . . not because this point being central is the most likely to diffuse an Equallity of advantages trough the whole territory and in return to derive a benefit proportional to the rise of the valu but because the nature of the local is such as will make Every thing concur to render a settlement there prosperous." In this center he located the President's House and the buildings to house the State, Treasury, and War departments. L'Enfant's explanation not only shows that he had come to a fresh understanding of what the President desired and had therefore altered his earlier views: it also proves that his diagonals had been superimposed on the gridiron plan with its streets aligned as Jefferson had suggested and that the open spaces for public walks and gardens beyond

[77] Note by Washington to TJ's list of agenda for the Commissioners, [5 Mch. 1792]. Washington described the assignment to L'Enfant as a "compliment intended to be paid you in depending *alone* upon your plans for the public buildings" (Washington to L'Enfant, 28 Feb. 1792, *Writings*, ed. Fitzpatrick, xxxi, 488-9). A few days later TJ also declared that five months had been lost by dependence on L'Enfant and that he had done nothing to prepare such plans (TJ to Walker, 1 Mch. 1792). On Washington's futile effort to obtain plans from L'Enfant at the last moment, see Washington to TJ, 22 Feb. 1792, and TJ to L'Enfant of the same date.

[78] Undated MS by TJ, later described by him as "copy of paper I gave to the President and to the Commissioners in 1791." His assignment of the date is obviously erroneous (see document at 6 Mch. 1792).

[79] TJ's list of agenda for the Commissioners [5 Mch. 1792].

the Tiber were now viewed by him as providing long vistas downstream as well as an appropriate spot "to Erect the Grand Equestrian" statue of Washington. In brief, the center of the capital and its principal features as set forth in Jefferson's sketch were here preserved, probably not because L'Enfant approved of the concept but perhaps because he had become convinced that the President did.[80]

But there was one notable exception. This concerned L'Enfant's suggestion that there was no spot so advantageous for the Capitol as the bluff "on the west end of Jenkins heights which stand as a pedestal waiting for a monument." On the basis of this statement and its expression in the map handed to Washington, the dramatic shift in the relationship of the two principal public buildings of the capital has been attributed to L'Enfant as his inspired choice. So far as the record shows, this suggestion in L'Enfant's letter is indeed the earliest known evidence of the proposal. But did the idea originate with L'Enfant, who earlier had made a very different choice? Or did he advance it because, as with other recommendations, he now knew this to be Washington's preference? The answer lies in the realm of conjecture, but it is very probable that the idea originated with the President. Washington scarcely needed to be told by L'Enfant or anyone else that distributing the public buildings, placing the Capitol in the vicinity of Carrollsburg, pressing for its erection simultaneously with the building of the President's House, and trying thus to promote settlement near the Eastern Branch would go far to keep the precariously united interests from disrupting his plans. But again, as in the compromises over the location of the Federal District, there was a price to pay. How could the separation of the executive and legislative branches by so great a distance be explained and justified? Washington's experience of government in Williamsburg, New York, and Philadelphia provided arguments enough for maintaining contiguity. Even L'Enfant felt obliged to try to justify the rejection of such lessons drawn from experience. But whether Washington originated the idea or not, he gave it his sanction, thus fixing for all time the site of the Capitol on what was then called Jenkins' Hill. The question at once arises: why did he find it necessary to make the decision at the time and in the manner he did? To all appearances there was no more pressing need for this than there had been three months earlier. He was about to leave for Philadelphia. There he could have conferred with Jefferson, Madison, and others to whom, earlier and later, he turned at critical moments for advice on matters pertaining to the capital. There he could have issued a proclamation setting forth what he had deleted from the earlier one and, at the same time, have explained his altered choice of site for the Capitol. But on this occasion there was no presidential proclamation, no request of Jefferson for advice, not even an advance warning from Mount Vernon. Perhaps, as in his decision on the location of the Federal District, Washington felt it prudent to let his choice go unexplained without even the benefit of an official announcement.

Jefferson must have learned of this important decision from the public press.

[80] L'Enfant to Washington, 22 June 1791 (DNA: RG 42). So far as is known, the plan annexed to this letter is no longer extant. That it was a preliminary version of the one L'Enfant submitted to Washington in August and that, after some modification, it incorporated the essential features of the later plan cannot be doubted (Richard W. Stephenson, LC *Qu. Jour.*, xxxvi [1979], 208; Reps, *Monumental Washington*, p. 15). See note 88 for further discussion.

Brown's *Federal Gazette*, citing a Georgetown dateline of the 2d of July, gave the particulars, as did other newspapers. The President had put the finishing hand to the location of the Federal City on the 30th of June. While misunderstandings had prevailed when Washington left Georgetown in the spring, the unknown author reported, "the moment he appeared, all difficulties vanished." All narrow considerations were abandoned and the landowners cheerfully made conveyances to gratify the utmost wishes of the President. Then – and then only, it appears – "he submitted to the inspection of the proprietors, and a large number of gentlemen attending, a plan of the city, which had for several weeks occupied the time and talents of Col. L'Enfant, assisted by the Baron de Graff, and which, with some small alterations, he determined to adopt." At the close of this news account which so clearly bears evidence of official prompting, came the only announcement of importance: "By this plan, and the President's explanations, it appears that the buildings for the Legislature are to be placed on Jenkins' Hill, on the land of Daniel Carroll, Esq. of Duddington . . . and that the houses of the President, and for the great Department of State, are to be situated on the rising ground adjoining Hamburg, within one mile of George-town, and about one and a quarter from the houses of legislation." This arrangement, newspapers reported, "afforded the most general approbation, satisfying each interested individual, that his particular interest was as much consulted as a due attention to the public convenience and the public interest, which was the primary object, would any way warrant."[81]

Individual interests, for the moment at least, may have appeared satisfied. But there were many who thought the public interest and convenience had not been consulted. As soon as the fact became known an indignant citizen, writing as *Amicus*, challenged the decision to place the legislative buildings a mile and a half from those of the President and other officers of government. Holding the Commissioners responsible for a choice with which they had had nothing to do, *Amicus* blamed them for failing to recognize the convenience and propriety of making the principal buildings of government contiguous to each other. But, proving that he knew where the responsibility lay, he pointed out that there were two parties among the proprietors, both anxious to have the value of their lands increased by their vicinity to the public buildings. If the buildings were to be erected on the lands adjacent to Georgetown, then the Carrollsburg party would be disgusted; if on the hill nearest Carrollsburg, then the citizens of Georgetown would take it in dudgeon. Thus a compromise had taken place "and something . . . given up to both parties merely to quiet them, without sufficient regard to the general good or to public opinion." *Amicus* was certain the Commissioners had acted without bias, but he said every person with whom he had discussed the matter had joined him in condemning the

---

[81] Brown's *Federal Gazette*, 5 July 1791, under a Georgetown dateline of 2 July. When Washington met the Commissioners on the 28th, he found that all of the proprietors save three had signed conveyances. He induced the Commissioners to send an express asking that these proprietors do so at once. Their anxiety, they explained, arose from the "expectation that the President will not declare the places for the public buildings till the Deeds are signed" (Commissioners to Oden and others, 28 June 1791, DNA: RG 42). Obviously, just as he had done in March, Washington held these proprietors in suspense about a decision already made, using this as a means of persuading them to reach an accommodation. The strategy, as before, brought immediate results (Oden to the Commissioners, 28 June 1791, same).

decision because of countless inconveniences that would result to the President, to members of Congress, to heads of department, and to every citizen having business to do with government. Even in the conduct of ordinary business, he insisted, committees would be hampered in their deliberations, the drafting of bills would be impeded, the transmission of those passed and the return of those signed would be delayed, and, among other baneful consequences, essential consultations with heads of departments would be frustrated. But in the frantic closing days before Congress adjourned, it would become "absolutely necessary to employ post-horses, and establish relays . . . [with] committee-men secretaries, and public officers, full gallop, whip and spur, jostling each other, and kicking up a dust to the great merriment of the honest citizens of Goose-creek." *Amicus* indicated that the Commissioners' unfortunate decision need not be final. He therefore appealed to the President to withhold his sanction and order all public buildings to be erected in the vicinity of each other. This, he thought, would "unquestionably give more satisfaction to the public, whose wishes ought to be attended to in preference to those of a few interested individuals in the environs of Georgetown."[82]

The conclusion seems inescapable that *Amicus* pointed unerringly to the real reason for the decision to locate the Capitol so far removed from the buildings of the executive branch. Just as local and partial views over the years had so often affected every question pertaining to the national capital, so must such factors have influenced this important decision. The silence of Washington and Jefferson on the subject lends eloquent support to the supposition. So also with respect to the time, the place, and the manner of announcing the fact. It is difficult to believe that such a pragmatist as Washington departed from his earlier decision to place the Capitol in the vicinity of Hamburg merely because L'Enfant, seeing Jenkins' Hill as a pedestal waiting for a monument, had made the suggestion. Having already shown how anxious he was to gain approval by advancing or altering proposals conformable to what he conceived the President's preferences to be, L'Enfant cannot plausibly be regarded as the originator of the idea, much less as the sole source of whatever persuasions were brought to bear upon Washington to induce him to accept it.

VII

Immediately after Washington made this surprising choice of site for the Capitol, the Commissioners urgently called upon the proprietors to provide exact surveys of their holdings so that these could be laid out "distinctly on the general Plat of the City." This, they pointed out, should be done speedily and was essential before any lots could be sold.[83] Three months earlier L'Enfant had written enthusiastically about the prospect of "infinit advantage to the purchaser" of lots which would be defined on his "grand and general plan for the local distribution of the city."[84] But by the first of August, with the sale announced for the 17th of October, there was still no such map available. At

---

[82] *Amicus*, in Bache's *General Advertiser*, 12 July 1791.

[83] Commissioners to Proprietors, 30 June 1791 (DNA: RG 42). Two months later, with L'Enfant in Philadelphia, the Commissioners urgently repeated their request and directed that all claims be turned over to Ellicott, "the sooner the better" (Commissioners to Proprietors, 9 Sep. 1791, same).

[84] L'Enfant to Hamilton, 8 Apr. 1791 (Syrett, *Hamilton*, VIII, 255).

that moment newspapers were reporting that Ellicott was "busily employed in the federal city in opening streets, laying off squares, lots, &c." and that three thousand workmen were expected to begin work on the public buildings the following spring.[85] Ellicott was indeed busily engaged but the optimistic announcement concealed much.

The Commissioners voiced their anxiety to the President: the plan of the City was not going forward as they wished. They hoped Ellicott could continue his useful work for another month, in which case the sale might still be held even if the map were incomplete. L'Enfant, they added, would soon leave for Philadelphia to lay his plans before the President "for . . . confirmation." The expression clearly indicates that their approval had not been sought, but they knew enough about the general plan to foresee some difficulties its adoption might produce. "We cannot help repeating our wish," they wrote, "that in the new laying out of Carrolsburgh and Hamburgh as little alteration and appropriation as may be, may take place, for we shall unavoidably have difficulties enough, to reconcile private interests with public views."[86] In making this appeal to Washington, the Commissioners revealed their awareness that only he, if anyone, could induce L'Enfant to alter his plan and spare them the threatened difficulty.

Two weeks later, having heard nothing further, Washington displayed his own concern. Writing at his request, Jefferson informed L'Enfant in a rather blunt letter that the President had been expecting him for some time, that he wished to know whether and when he would arrive, and that not even the laying out of the lots should cause further delay. Then, perhaps to encourage haste, he referred to suggestions made in Philadelphia for laying off the lots to add to the convenience of purchasers and the profit of sellers and for "engraving a Map of the Federal territory." He went further and laid the foundation for future difficulties by assuring L'Enfant that the right of issuing such a map lay with him or Ellicott.[87] This acknowledgment of a private right to issue the first map of the capital being prepared under authority of the government was surprisingly casual, especially coming at a time when the President, the Commissioners, and Jefferson himself were hoping for the completion of a plan of the City that could be displayed at the October sale.

L'Enfant did not respond, but on arriving in Philadelphia late in August he went directly to the President and laid before him a map of the Federal City. This map, he generously acknowledged, owed much to the labors of Andrew

---

[85] "A letter from Maryland, dated George Town, Aug. 1." This item was widely copied in the press (*New Hampshire Gazette*, 31 Aug. 1791).

[86] Commissioners to Washington, 2 Aug. 1791 (DNA: RG 42).

[87] TJ to L'Enfant, 18 Aug. 1791. L'Enfant later claimed that the Commissioners had deprived him of substantial sums that should have come to him from the sale of his map, which he described as "my property." He intimated that he had been prevented from obtaining copyright first by the Commissioners and then by Washington's assurances that all of his "drawing and prints plate &ca. were to have been protected." The amount due him over ten years he estimated as the equivalent of 25,000 copies sold at $2.00 each (L'Enfant to TJ, 12 Mch. 1802). In view of these extravagant claims and misrepresentations, it should be noted that in his letter of 18 Aug. 1791 TJ referred to an engraving of the Federal District, no doubt intending that this would include the plan of the Federal City. Ellicott's topographical map of the Federal District of 1793 encompassed both objects and also employed a format TJ recommended. Ellicott did not expect and of course did not receive compensation from the sale of these maps.

Ellicott, whose assistance he hoped could be continued for three months longer. In an accompanying letter he referred to it as "the anexed map of doted lines" and said that it had been altered in accordance with Washington's directions.[88] These directions presumably had been given when L'Enfant visited Mount Vernon and submitted a plan which the President exhibited to the Commissioners, proprietors, and others on the 29th of June.[89] On that occasion Washington told the assemblage that the map would only "convey . . . the general ideas of the City." Also, being justifiably apprehensive that objections might be raised, he gave assurance that "some deviation from it would take place — particularly in the diagonal streets or avenues, which would not be so numerous; and in the removal of the President's house more westerly for the advantage of higher ground." Following the presentation, he had recorded in his diary the pleasure he felt when "a general approbation of the measure seemed to pervade the whole."[90] What other alterations Washington may have sug-

[88] L'Enfant to Washington, 19 Aug. 1791 (DNA: RG 42). In 1930 Lawrence Martin, Chief of the Division of Maps of the Library of Congress, advanced the opinion that the "map of doted lines" was one which L'Enfant might have directed Benjamin Ellicott to prepare late in 1791 or early in 1792, but that it was more likely one made in the summer of 1791 by or under the direction of L'Enfant and presented to Washington with this letter (*Report of the Librarian of Congress* [Washington, 1930], p. 165-7). Caemmerer, *L'Enfant*, p. 162, rejects these suppositions and concludes instead that it was the map L'Enfant gave to Washington in June. Reps, *Monumental Washington*, p. 15 (where the map is illustrated as Fig. 8), accepts Martin's theory that it was transmitted with the letter of 19 Aug. Stephenson, LC *Qu. Jour.*, xxxvi (1979), 208-9, suggests that it may have been done by Benjamin Ellicott sometime in Dec. 1791, thus agreeing in substance with Martin's first supposition. So, in effect, does Ehrenberg, who suggests also that L'Enfant intended to use it, together with his "original plan" presented in August, in an updated version suitable for engraving (same, p. 285). Jennings, however, claims that it has no relationship to L'Enfant's 1791 plan and that it agrees in every instance with the 1792 engraving, which he identifies as the Ellicott plan (same, p. 245, 246). Since the map prepared by Ellicott for engraving was based on L'Enfant's plan, though departing from it in some respects, Jennings' suppositions of course are self-contradictory.

The manuscript generally referred to as the "map of doted lines" is without title, author, date, or scale. Its system of streets, squares, and circles is presented but no names are given. Its sole legend reads: "All the Lines coloured red are finished and those coloured yellow are intended to be compleated this Season." It is this statement which, as indicative of the purpose for which the sketch was prepared, makes plausible the suggestions advanced in variant terms by Martin, Stephenson, and Ehrenberg. The draftsmanship by which the watercourses and topographical features are set forth with such precision also indicate the hand of Benjamin or Andrew Ellicott. Some of the features reflect modifications made when Andrew Ellicott was preparing a map to be engraved. But was this done *before* or *after* the drafting of that map? The allusion to surveys to be completed "this season" could not have referred to the winter of 1791-1792, thus suggesting that the "map of doted lines," based on the L'Enfant plan and on materials in the possession of the Ellicotts, was drawn at or about the time Andrew Ellicott was preparing to resume surveying in the spring of 1792.

[89] L'Enfant to Washington, 22 June 1791, to which he "anexed . . . an Incompleat drawing" (DNA: RG 42). It has been generally assumed that L'Enfant presented this letter and plan on a visit to Mount Vernon sometime between 22 and 27 June, but the fact is not recorded in Washington's diary. The drawing has not been identified and is not known to exist. Reps, *Monumental Washington*, p. 15; and Stephenson, LC *Qu. Jour.*, xxxvi [1979], 208, state that it has been lost.

[90] Washington, *Diaries*, ed. Fitzpatrick, iv, 200-1.

gested is not known. But the significant fact is that the distinguishing element of the plan had been given presidential sanction. L'Enfant was elated. Washington's approval, he declared, had satisfied his highest ambition.

But even after two months, this modified version of his map was still incomplete. In the accompanying letter, which he had written before leaving Georgetown, L'Enfant, as before, sought to justify the unfinished assignment. This time he could not complain of the hazards of fog, mist, and snow. But the multiplicity of difficulties arising from the need to fix points at great distances and to determine with exactness the acute angles and intersecting lines, he pointed out, had made the task more tedious than had been expected. Felled trees which the owners wished to preserve but were unwilling to remove had added to the obstacles. Despite repeated requests the proprietors had not returned surveys of their holdings, hence it would be impossible to have the lots recorded on the map before the sale. Also, even with a map available, few could make proper judgments of the relative advantages of different localities. Lots that would command the highest prices at the sale were those along the grand avenue connecting the Capitol and the President's House, as well as those on "the grand walk from the water cascade under the federal House to the president park . . . and also the severals squar or area such as are Intended for the Judiciary courts the national bank – the grand church – the play House, Market &c. Exchange." This, together with the small initial deposit required, would attract a few speculators with neither the means nor the inclination to promote the success of the enterprise. The sale, therefore, was premature and would not produce a tenth of what could be expected after a "general plan . . . of the City" could be distributed to the public throughout the country. If held on the announced date, it would not only set an unfortunate precedent: it would also bring down disgrace upon the whole business. So far as the sale was concerned, his argument implied, the unfinished state of the map was a matter of little or no consequence.

The important consideration, L'Enfant insisted, was "not to confine the Idea to the Erecting of a congress House and a Presidial palace, other Exertions being necessary to prompt and encourage private undertakings – them alone can forme the Establishment Enswerable to its objects, and to rise the City a City in Fact it is Indispensable to Consider every of the Improvements proposed in the plan as being part most Essential to the framing of the principal." It was of the first importance to do everything possible to serve the mercantile community, with the canal from the Tiber to the Eastern Branch being "of absolut necessity."[91] The streets from the river to the grand avenue would soon be filled with shops, businesses of all sorts, houses, and accommodations for officials

[91] Late in July Robert Peter had addressed a proposal to Washington about the building of wharves between Rock Creek and the Tiber, saying that L'Enfant had expressed the wish that he join the public in doing so. Washington thought the idea commendable, but referred the letter to the Commissioners, who declined (Peter to Washington, 20 July 1791; Commissioners to Peter, 2 Aug. 1791; Commissioners to President, 2 Aug. 1791, DNA: RG 42; Washington to Peter, 24 July 1791; Washington to Commissioners, 24 July 1791, *Writings*, ed. Fitzpatrick, xxxi, 323). Shortly thereafter George French, certainly with L'Enfant's knowledge and perhaps at his prompting, made a proposal for the canal between the Tiber and the Eastern Branch which L'Enfant thought so essential. This, too, the Commissioners declined (Commissioners to French, 2 Aug. 1791, DNA: RG 42).

and members of Congress. Further, L'Enfant added, the President's earlier approval had inspired him to devise a plan for donating several squares among the different states. These would be the focal points of settlements "all along of those transveral and divergents avenues were none of them will be lost nor . . . to distant from the Federal House or the president palace." These communities would gradually become connected, forming from the outset a chain of improvements around the center of the City. This integrated plan, with each part contributing to the good of the whole, was the only way the grand enterprise could succeed. Success would result not from an unfortunate sale, but from the negotiation of a loan, with the public lots being pledged as security and held in reserve for the inevitable increase in value. "Of that success," L'Enfant concluded, "I wished to promot in the delination of a plan wholy new, and which combined on a grand scale will require Exertions above what is the idea of Many but the which not being beyond your power to procur make me promise the securing of them . . . the operation of a magnitude so worthy of the concern of a grand Empire."[92] Washington's earlier approval had obviously stimulated L'Enfant to greater efforts to achieve novelty and grandeur. It also led him once again to warn against what he conceived to be the limited vision of others, as exemplified for him in Jefferson's sketch. His concept of a surrounding chain of settlements, each with its square donated to one of the states, was the most conspicuous addition to his previous plan. This was a proposal whose potentially adverse political implications L'Enfant evidently did not perceive – and against which Washington had no need to be warned.

With his map unfinished, L'Enfant's argument that the sale should be deferred until it could be widely distributed in complete form seemed persuasive. So also with respect to his insistence upon the need to support mercantile interests, to build wharves, to dig a canal, to provide space for shops and businesses of all sorts, and to negotiate a loan by which both public and private interests would be served. Though expressed in his own distinctive orthography and interspersed with characteristic flights of imagination, the letter is so exceptional among L'Enfant's writings as to suggest the presence of a prompting – and interested – hand at his side.[93] Certainly this defense of his plan was prepared with unusual care and in full knowledge that there were those who

[92] L'Enfant to Washington, Georgetown 19 Aug. 1791 (DNA: RG 42). As indicated below, Washington did not reveal this document to TJ.

[93] If anyone helped guide L'Enfant in developing his argument, Francis Cabot would seem to have been the most likely one. Cabot had been highly recommended by his Massachusetts friends to the President, the Vice-President, and others as one greatly interested in promoting the Federal City. He had just settled in Georgetown, become acquainted with L'Enfant, shared – and may have stimulated – his suggestion to Alexander Hamilton that easterners would invest in lands in the capital, and at this time was planning to accompany L'Enfant to Philadelphia to discuss his various plans for the City with Washington and Jefferson (Carroll to TJ, 29 July 1791). The likelihood that Cabot did accompany L'Enfant to Philadelphia is indicated by TJ's receipt of Carroll's letter of introduction only on 29 Aug., shortly after L'Enfant arrived there. Carroll described Cabot as a "sensible, intelligent Gentleman" with respectable connections – one of them, of course, being George Cabot, Senator from Massachusetts. For Washington's later doubts about Cabot, see his letter to David Stuart, 8 Mch. 1792 (*Writings*, ed. Fitzpatrick, XXXI, 507). It was Cabot whom L'Enfant engaged to buy a lot for Tobias Lear at the October sale.

would oppose or wish to modify it. As events would prove, Washington was clearly impressed.

But he was also caught between the Commissioners' appeal for assistance in preparing for the sale he had insisted upon and L'Enfant's argument calling for its postponement. Worse, the Commissioners' plea for modifying a plan the President had publicly approved was challenged by L'Enfant's call for immediate and continued action on every aspect of his general concept. Confronted with this first serious conflict between the Commissioners and L'Enfant, Washington turned to his Secretary of State. The extent of his concern is indicated in the conferences he immediately called for discussion of the issues raised. These took place immediately after L'Enfant laid his altered plan before the President. It is not known with certainty who took part. Washington presided. Jefferson only said that "certain persons" were present, but this was probably a circumlocution. All of the circumstances indicate that L'Enfant, having taken his case directly to the President, was not a participant. Certainly Jefferson and Madison were the chief advisors. It was they who received Washington's views and, as his representatives, were authorized to present their conclusions at a meeting of the Commissioners to be called at once. The matters discussed, according to Jefferson's account, were those brought up in the Commissioners' appeal and in two separate letters from Daniel Carroll to the President, one of which enclosed a plat of Carrollsburg as reinforcement of their position.[94] These subjects could scarcely have been canvassed without an examination of both that plat and L'Enfant's map of the Federal City. Washington must of course have made these available. But there can be no doubt that he withheld from those engaged in the discussions L'Enfant's letter opposing the sale as premature and arguing against any change in his plan. To the distinctive elements of that plan Washington was already committed as publicly as if he had issued a proclamation to that effect. He recognized the Commissioners' problem, especially with respect to Carrollsburg, but he took his stand unequivocally in support of L'Enfant's general concept. "To settle something with respect to *that* place and Hambg. *which will not interfere with the general Plan* is difficult," he wrote Jefferson less as expressing an opinion than as giving a directive, "but essential."[95]

This unequivocal support of L'Enfant's plan is confirmed by a remarkable list of matters to be discussed at the conferences which Washington himself drafted. Based in large part upon L'Enfant's letter, the list was put in the form of questions which of course need not have been raised if that letter had been made available to Jefferson and Madison or if L'Enfant had taken part in the discussions. Nowhere in this unusual document — the only one Washington is known to have drawn up on matters relating to the capital instead of having Jefferson perform the task — did he indicate that some of its key questions were drawn directly from L'Enfant. His first query establishes the point: would circumstances make postponement of the sale advisable? If not, in what areas should the sale of lots take place? Should a bridge over the Eastern Branch be built? Would it be prudent to negotiate a loan for carrying out the different operations within the City? Should the initial cash payment for lots purchased

[94] TJ to the Commissioners, 28 Aug. 1791; TJ to Johnson, 29 Aug. 1791.
[95] Washington to TJ, 29 Aug. 1791 (second emphasis added).

be increased? Should the canal be begun and Robert Peter's proposal to construct wharves be undertaken? Would it not be advisable to have a map of the Federal District engraved in a single sheet so as to comprehend "the plan of the Town"? And, to confront the issue between the Commissioners and L'Enfant, what compromise could be made with the Carrollsburg and Hamburg interests by which the plan of the Federal City might be preserved? While these and other topics were clearly prompted by L'Enfant's letter, there were significant omissions. There were no allusions to the outlying settlements, to the allotment of squares to the states, to the donation of land for religious societies, or to the giant cascade at the western bluff of Jenkins' Hill. Nor of course was there any mention of the decision to place the Capitol on that eminence. The squares for that edifice, as well as those for the Executive branch, were merely to be "considered as appropriated." In brief, the President's unexplained choice of site for the Capitol was irrevocable. We may reasonably assume, therefore, that during the discussions Jefferson and Madison treated it with discreet silence.

But on questions prompted by L'Enfant's letter, on those raised by the Commissioners, and on points which Jefferson himself urged in the conferences, Washington was given the kind of considered advice he desired. The sale should go forward. On the choice of lots to be sold, the "leading interests" should be accommodated. As to the idea of a public loan, even the proposal would be dubious without legislative authority and probably unsuccessful until a sale established something like the value of lands sold. The bridge, the wharves, and the canal should be postponed until funds were available. Meanwhile, preparations for the public buildings should be pressed forward as indispensable. But L'Enfant's point about the insufficiency of the required cash deposit was recognized as valid, with the resultant recommendation that the initial payment be more than trebled. Washington's questions had also included some based on suggestions made by Jefferson the year before, especially those relating to building regulations within the City. The answers concerning materials and height of private structures were such as he had long advocated. To these questions Jefferson added others during the conferences which also reflected his particular interests — running the post road through the City, having the streets run North-South and East-West, seeing that soundings of the Eastern Branch were supplied to the engraver of the map, and providing names for the streets, City, and District. But his previous suggestion that the taste of the new town might be improved if engravings of some of the handsomest private structures in Europe should be distributed free to the inhabitants of Georgetown was one on which Washington appears to have made no comment. Jefferson's additions to the list of topics also treated that point with silence.[96]

It was presumably after these discussions that the President asked L'Enfant to see him for an hour on the afternoon of the 27th of August. What transpired at their meeting is not known. Washington may have touched on some of the

---

[96] Washington's list of questions — thirteen in Washington's hand, six in TJ's — was undated but obviously was drawn in its original form on 28 Aug. 1791, under which date it is printed below. The point L'Enfant made about the low cash deposit was not among the questions framed by Washington, but evidently came up in the discussion of L'Enfant's proposal of a loan. The recommendation was that it be increased from 8% of the purchase price to 25%. The Commissioners approved and announced the increase immediately after TJ and Madison met with them (Advertisement, 9 Sep. 1791, DNA: RG 42).

conclusions reached at the conferences, but, understandably, he seems to have delegated to Jefferson and Madison the task of informing L'Enfant of all of the details and of discussing with him any differences that might arise. On the 31st Jefferson did invite L'Enfant to dine with him and Madison the next day, alone, to discuss "several matters relative to George town."[97] No evidence has been found that L'Enfant accepted the invitation. If he did, nothing is known of what transpired. Jefferson and Madison set out the next day for Georgetown, where they met with the Commissioners in an all-day session on the 8th of September, presenting to them the result of the conferences in Philadelphia. The Commissioners were "preadmonished," Jefferson reported, that the President wished them to make their decisions freely and in accord with their own views. Since the manner in which Washington had phrased the question about a compromise with the landholders of Hamburg and Carrollsburg revealed his own commitment to L'Enfant's plan, the answer was an evasion — a liberal compromise would be better than discontents or disputed titles. Such a compromise, offered by Thomas Johnson, put the matter out of dispute and so, for the moment at least, L'Enfant's plan was left intact. On this and all other points the Commissioners gave their unanimous approval to what had been agreed upon in Philadelphia. The sale which L'Enfant so strongly opposed would take place as announced. The President himself expected to be present and had already obligated Jefferson to attend.[98] The Commissioners, well knowing the effect of Washington's presence on previous occasions, scheduled their next meeting for the afternoon preceding the sale.

VIII

At his first meeting with the Commissioners in April Washington had urged that a plan of the City be published in time for a sale of lots before the Second Congress assembled.[99] But it was not until four months later, faced with L'Enfant's still incomplete map and appealed to by the Commissioners, that he addressed the problem with urgency. At the conferences late in August his question as to whether it would be desirable to have an engraving of the District that would include the City was answered in the affirmative. But, perhaps as a reflection of Jefferson's incautious letter to L'Enfant about his or Ellicott's right to publish such a map, the final decision was left in suspense: should it be issued by authority of the Commissioners or by the "Artists"?[100] The Commissioners

[97] TJ to L'Enfant, 31 Aug. 1791. In referring to "George town" TJ of course meant the Federal City. He and Madison left Philadelphia on the 2d. Washington remained there until the 15th.

[98] TJ to Washington, 8 Sep. 1791; TJ to Madison, 18 Aug. 1791.

[99] Daniel Carroll to James Madison, 23 Apr. 1791 (DLC: Madison Papers). Carroll indicated that the timing of the sale was to give members of the Congress from the North as well as the South an opportunity to attend. The strategic value of having members of Congress personally interested in the Federal City could not have escaped the attention of so experienced an investor in lands as Washington. On principle, TJ stood opposed to the use of such influence (TJ to Eppes, 15 Feb. 1783; TJ to Nash, 11 Mch. 1783).

[100] MS of Washington's list of agenda, at 28 Aug. 1791. This was Washington's final query. Below it TJ noted the decision to suspend consideration. In referring to "Artists" he clearly employed the word in its now obsolete sense, meaning persons skilled in the useful arts — specifically, as his letter of 19 Aug. 1791 to L'Enfant shows, the architect and the engineer, not the engraver.

decided that this should be done under their own direction, with sales benefiting the public.[101] But in informing L'Enfant of this and other decisions in their first written direction to him, they tempered authority with discretion. The manner of naming streets was made explicit. So also with respect to soundings of the Eastern Branch and the proposed post road through the City, which Ellicott would define and which they ordered to be recorded on the map. Then, in a postscript, they directed 10,000 copies of the map to be "struck on the best terms and as soon as possible" — an astonishingly large order which would have required the preparation of several plates. Its title would bear the names they had chosen for the City and District and the designation Jefferson had consistently employed in referring to the latter as a Territory — *A Map of the City of Washington, in the Territory of Columbia*. But the Commissioners' orders concerning the engraving and distribution of the map were provisional, being based upon the assumption that L'Enfant might have received other and contrary directions.[102] The assumption was well-founded.

Despite the agreement during the conferences in Philadelphia that the Commissioners should decide whether and under whose auspices the map should be published, plans had already been set in motion to have this done in Philadelphia. With L'Enfant in the city for that purpose, Washington authorized him to proceed. He apparently did not inform the Commissioners of this and no evidence has been found that L'Enfant responded to their directions. With time growing short and Washington angered over the proposal to build an executive mansion in Philadelphia, he allowed almost a month to elapse before inquiring of Lear about the progress of the map, at the same time directing that some of the first copies struck off be sent to him and the remainder "disposed of as was agreed on."[103] Only a week before the sale was to take place he received news of the complete failure of the effort.

Primary responsibility for this would seem to rest upon L'Enfant, but the engraver to whom he entrusted the task was not faultless. L'Enfant's choice, made in the very center of American printing, fell upon one Pigalle, a native of France, about whom and whose work little is known and that not favorable.[104] Presumably Pigalle was given the pressing assignment late in August when L'Enfant arrived in the City. Early in October, in response to an inquiry from

[101] TJ to Washington, 8 Sep. 1791.

[102] Commissioners to L'Enfant, 9 Sep. 1791 (DNA: RG 42). Of the 10,000 copies ordered, L'Enfant was to let the President have as many as he desired, leave half of the remainder in Philadelphia subject to their orders, and send the other half to them. They assured him that this draft for the cost would be honored.

[103] Washington to Lear, 2 Oct. 1791 (*Writings*, ed. Fitzpatrick, XXXI, 381-2). It is not known what disposition of the engraving Washington had ordered. On his response to Samuel Powel, Miers Fisher, and others about the plan for an executive mansion, see Washington to Powel, 20 Sep. 1791; to Fisher, 20 Sep. 1791; and to Lear, 26 Sep. 1791 (same, XXXI, 372-4, 376-8). The mansion was built 1792-1797 on a lot occupying the entire western side of 9th street between Market and Chestnut. It was never occupied by Washington.

[104] Pigalle (or Pigal) was evidently a recent arrival in Philadelphia. He is not listed in the Census of 1790 or in the city directories of the period. He was at work in New York in 1795 and usually signed his engravings "Pigalle," which William Dunlap called "crudely executed copper-plates" (Dunlap, *History of the rise and progress of the arts of design in the United States* [Boston, 1918], III, 327; Groce and Wallace, *Dictionary of artists in America* [New Haven, 1957], p. 506).

L'Enfant, Tobias Lear discovered that the plate had only then been prepared for engraving. Pigalle later added another explanation for the delay. The map left with him was so incorrect as to be unusable. Only "the large draft" which L'Enfant had carried back to the Federal City would suffice. This, so Pigalle informed Lear, he had asked L'Enfant to make available.[105] Neither the request nor any response to it has been found. But, somewhat surprisingly in view of his later conduct, L'Enfant told Lear it was his "earnest wish that [the engravings] might be struck off, before the sale, if they should be done in almost any manner."[106] Quite understandably, Washington found it inexplicable that the deficiency of the map had not been discovered earlier, especially since L'Enfant had been "detained many days in Philadelphia to prepare and fit it for the purpose." But he held the engraver responsible, expressly exonerating L'Enfant.[107]

Actually two manuscript maps were involved, both incomplete. One was referred to by L'Enfant as the "small draft" he had left with Pigalle. The other was a reduction taken from L'Enfant's "great Map" which had been prepared by Etienne Sulpice Hallet, another recently arrived native of France who began it at L'Enfant's request. Long afterward L'Enfant claimed that these maps had been placed in Washington's hands and that the Commissioners, acting surreptitiously through an agent in Philadelphia, had procured copies and prevailed upon the President to have it published. The account is confused and inaccurate, but Lear did get from Pigalle the small draft — not Hallet's reduction — and showed it to a few persons. The engraver had said that it was of "no manner of use to him" but Lear thought it at least provided a good general idea of both the location and the design.[108] While L'Enfant was in Philadelphia, Washington asked for his map — presumably his large working plan — to show to some gentlemen.[109] Also, L'Enfant himself informed Lear that a "Mr.——" had pressed him for a copy and suggested that Hallet's "outlines," together with the small draft, might satisfy his needs.[110] In this manner, through the intercession of the President, his secretary, and L'Enfant, a few interested individuals were able to obtain information not available to those who attended

[105] Lear to L'Enfant, 6 Oct. 1791 (DLC: Digges-L'Enfant-Morgan Papers). Lear acknowledged L'Enfant's letter of the 3rd (which has not been found) and said that, immediately on receiving it, he called on Pigalle and was greatly surprised to be told that it would not be possible to have a single print struck off before the end of the month. The next day, accompanied by Edmund Randolph, he again pressed the engraver to have some prints "struck off, in any manner, by the 12th or 14th." But the effort was ineffectual even with the aid of the Attorney General (Lear to Washington, 9 Oct. 1791, DLC: Washington Papers).

[106] Lear to Washington, 6, 9, and 11 Oct. 1791 (same); L'Enfant's request appears in the first as quoted from L'Enfant's (missing) letter of the 3rd.

[107] Washington to Lear, 14 Oct. 1791 (*Writings*, ed. Fitzpatrick, xxxi, 388); Washington to Stuart, 20 Nov. 1791 (same, xxxi, 421).

[108] Lear to Washington, 11 Oct. 1791 (DLC: Washington Papers). Hallet described his reduction as drawn on "silk paper in order to save Time but Majr. L'Enfant being at a Hurry took back his original before the reduction could be finished." He also said that he turned it over to Lear at the request of the President (Hallet to James R. Dermott, 25 Jan. 1794, same). See L'Enfant to TJ, 12 Mch. 1802 and its accompanying memorandum.

[109] Lear to L'Enfant, 1 Sep. 1791 (DLC: Digges-L'Enfant-Morgan Papers).

[110] L'Enfant to Lear, 19 Oct. 1791 (same).

the sale. Pigalle was undoubtedly dilatory and not a master of his craft, but his appraisal of the draft as inaccurate conforms to what is known of L'Enfant's unfulfilled promises to produce a finished plan. More important is the testimony of Andrew Ellicott, who thought it fortunate that engravings of this "first plan" had not been available because the map was so incorrect as not to justify a sale based upon it.[111] Thus ended in failure the first episode in the confused history of the early mapping of the Federal City.[112]

But this failure, not in itself of material consequence, was only a prelude to more serious conflicts in which L'Enfant disregarded or defied the Commissioners' authority. It was only two weeks after he had expressed a desire to have almost any kind of engraving of his map available for use at the sale that he adamantly refused to permit the Commissioners or the purchasers of lots to inspect his large general plan. This defiance of legal authority was compounded by acts of personal interest and favoritism. Benefiting from information withheld from the public, L'Enfant purchased one lot for himself and another for Tobias Lear, thus improperly involving both himself as the officially designated planner of the City and the personal secretary of the President.[113] It is scarcely conceivable that L'Enfant would have refused to display his map if the President had attended the sale as planned, but an accidental circumstance forestalled such an improbable confrontation. Although Washington knew precisely when the sale would take place, he had been "thunderstruck" a few days earlier to discover he had miscalculated the date Congress would convene. Thus forced to alter his plans and hasten on to Philadelphia, he passed through Georgetown on the 17th, announced the terms and conditions of building within the City, and authorized the Commissioners to proceed with the sale. That night he stopped at Bladensburg and at dawn the next day asked for a report of the number of lots sold and the amount received for them.[114] The result was disappointing.[115] By the same post Washington received news of L'Enfant's refusal to permit use of his map.

[111] Washington to Stuart, 20 Nov. 1791 (*Writings*, ed. Fitzpatrick, xxxi, 421-2).

[112] The best account of the early mapping of the Federal City is that by Ehrenberg, covering the years 1791 to 1818 (LC *Qu. Jour.*, xxxvi [1979], 279-319).

[113] L'Enfant to Lear, 19 Oct. 1791 (DLC: Digges-L'Enfant-Morgan Papers).

[114] Washington to the Commissioners, 17 Oct. and to Stuart, 18 Oct. 1791 (*Writings*, ed. Fitzpatrick, xxxi, 394, 395). TJ and Madison had spent the night of the 16th with Washington at Mount Vernon and of course were with him when he met with the Commissioners early on the 17th. They joined Washington at Bladensburg the same day and thus could only have attended the first part of the sale, which continued through the 18th. TJ, who on principle refused to engage in land speculation or to permit it to intrude upon public duty, would no doubt have been pleased to avoid lending his official presence at all had not Washington previously imposed upon him the obligation to attend (TJ to Madison, 18 Aug. 1791).

[115] Stuart to Washington, 19 Oct. 1791, enclosing list of sales, number of lots, and prices paid. Only 30 lots were sold in six squares for a total of £3,292 Pennsylvania currency (also current in New Jersey, Maryland, and Delaware, at $2.666 for £1 sterling), all of the lots being at some distance from the President's House (DLC: Washington Papers). Despite the disappointing news, Washington reported to Congress the next week that sales justified every expectation of "ample funds for carrying on the necessary public buildings" (Annual Message, 25 Oct. 1791, *Writings*, ed. Fitzpatrick, xxxi, 400). Privately Daniel Carroll gave Madison the particulars of the sale and expressed the hope that they could proceed more effectually in the spring – information which Madison undoubtedly shared with TJ (Carroll to Madison, 21 Oct. 1791, DLC: Madison Papers).

The most unusual account of the sale came from L'Enfant himself, who not only boasted of his act of defiance but was indiscreet enough to do so in an indirect message to the President. Writing to Tobias Lear, he admitted the results had not been propitious but claimed that higher prices were due entirely to the care he took to "prevent the exhibition of the general plan." By this means, he declared, purchasers were unable to compare their acquisitions with lots better situated. He asked Lear to communicate this to the President, being confident that he would approve and thus regret the less that engravings of the map had not been available. Pigalle's plate was therefore useless. It could not be completed with accuracy unless sent abroad or executed under his own eyes. This, L'Enfant concluded, could not be done until he returned to Philadelphia at the beginning of winter.[116] As he had intended, Lear submitted the letter to Washington.

In their report to the President the Commissioners' comment on L'Enfant's insubordination was restrained. Though they had been publicly embarrassed, Stuart merely remarked that if they had been able to exhibit "a general plan . . . it would have aided the sale considerably."[117] But Washington, obviously shocked, voiced feelings the Commissioners and others undoubtedly shared. The deliberate withholding of the map, he declared, gave him "a degree of surprise and concern not easy to be expressed."[118] While L'Enfant's letter to Lear had been expressly intended for the President and set forth an opinion with which he wholly disagreed, he chose not to make a direct or official response to it. Nor did he ask Jefferson to speak for him. Instead, unable to overlook L'Enfant's confident assumption that his action would be given presidential sanction, he employed "a direct channel, though not an official one" to express his disapproval. The channel he chose was Tobias Lear, but to Lear's communication Washington himself "engrafted sentiments of admonition, and with a view also to feel [L'Enfant's] pulse under reprehension."[119] Unfortunately this letter seems to have been lost to history, but it may be safely assumed that Washington composed the unofficial reproof with his usual regard for L'Enfant's sensibilities. As he later explained to the Commissioners, he had given the engineer to understand he did not share his opinion that withholding the map was either proper or advantageous. He praised L'Enfant in extravagant terms, but lamented that men of genius almost invariably should be "under the influence of an untoward disposition, or . . . sottish idle, or possessed of some other disqualification by which they plague all those with whom they are concerned." He had not expected, however, "to have met with such perverseness in Major L'Enfant."[120]

Jefferson was also concerned, but he could scarcely have shared Washington's surprise. While he was not shown the L'Enfant-Lear letters until later when even more egregious conduct on the part of L'Enfant made it necessary, he clearly perceived that the occasion called for something more than an indirect and unofficial admonition tempered by respect for one thought to possess the attributes of genius.

---

[116] L'Enfant to Lear, 19 Oct. 1791, enclosed in Washington to TJ, 30 Nov. 1791.

[117] Stuart to Washington, 19 Oct. 1791 (DLC: Washington Papers).

[118] Washington to Stuart, 20 Nov. 1791 (*Writings*, ed. Fitzpatrick, xxxi, 419).

[119] Washington to TJ, 30 Nov. 1791, enclosing copies of the L'Enfant-Lear exchange and other papers.

[120] Washington to Stuart, 20 Nov. 1791 (*Writings*, ed. Fitzpatrick, xxxi, 419).

IX

With the legally constituted channels of authority being confused, the mapping of the City virtually stalled, the actual progress on the site impeded by conflicting views over essential goals, and the ultimate object threatened by the ever-present contentions of landed interests, it is not surprising that Jefferson should have seized the opportunity presented by L'Enfant's conduct to lay two proposals before the President. First, repeating an earlier recommendation, he suggested that the surveyors be directed to lay out lots along the Potomac from Rock Creek to the Eastern Branch and then proceed "a-breast . . . towards the back part of the town." By this means they would pass the main avenue between the Capitol and the President's House before spring. Thus the next sale would be expedited and could take place without injury to either the Georgetown or the Carrollsburg interests. Focussed on the center of the City and on the need to reach an accommodation, the proposal stood in sharp contrast to L'Enfant's insistence upon an integrated development of his plan as a whole, with its ornamental and essential elements going forward simultaneously. Jefferson's second proposition was put in the form of a question, but its implicit comment on L'Enfant's behavior at the October sale and on the danger of still further difficulties ahead was unmistakable. "Will not the present afford you a proper occasion," he asked the President, "of assuring the commissioners that you leave every thing respecting L'Enfant to them?"[121] This key question, the answer to which was suggested both by law and by principles of orderly administration, was put to the President on the very day his unofficial reproof was given to L'Enfant through Lear.

Two weeks later Washington recommended to the Commissioners Jefferson's proposal for laying out the City lots, offering it for their consideration as "the opinion of intelligent and well informed men, now in this City." At the same time he informed them that in his indirect communication to L'Enfant he had "given him to understand . . . that he must, in future, look to the Commissioners for directions." L'Enfant, he added, was soon expected in Philadelphia. He assured the Commissioners that he would then try to reach some understanding with him of the terms upon which he would serve the public. He did not wish to have the "goodly prospect clouded by impediments . . . or injured by disagreements which would only serve to keep alive the hopes of those who are enemies to the Plan."[122] But even as Washington sought to placate both sides, L'Enfant provided the most extreme example he had yet given of his contempt for the authority of the Commissioners. In so doing, though he could scarcely have intended or even realized it, he also treated with disdain the message Washington had sought to convey through Lear. This further evidence of his estrangement from reality came with the destruction by his orders of a house belonging to Daniel Carroll of Duddington.

Before leaving for Philadelphia in August to lay his general plan before the President, L'Enfant had given directions to the surveyors to remove all obstructions falling within the limits of streets and other public property. Carroll, whose house was begun even before the Federal District had been defined, was given the impression by L'Enfant that his plan would not be final until approved

---

[121] TJ to Washington, 6 Nov. 1791.

[122] Washington to Stuart, 20 Nov. 1791 (*Writings*, ed. Fitzpatrick, XXXI, 421). Washington asked Stuart to lay before the Commissioners the sentiments expressed in this lengthy letter but only "for their private information."

by the President. Having received no word from him that the house would intrude upon public property, he proceeded with its construction. His kinsman, Daniel Carroll the Commissioner, was rightly apprehensive. Ellicott, however, assured him in L'Enfant's absence that only about six feet of the structure fell upon a street which "coud *without the least possible injury* to the plan be altered so as to leave the House Clear." In giving this assurance Ellicott was injudicious enough to promise that he would inform L'Enfant and would hold himself accountable for this being done.[123] After the Commissioners' meeting on the 18th of November, L'Enfant told David Stuart he had written Carroll that his house would have to come down. Stuart directed him to place the matter before the Commissioners at their next meeting if Carroll did not choose to comply. But on the 20th, with L'Enfant absent in Virginia, workmen acting on his orders began demolition. In anticipation of this Carroll had gone to Annapolis and obtained from Chancellor Hanson a preventive injunction ordering L'Enfant to desist and summoning him to appear in December. But it was too late. On his return L'Enfant took charge and on the 25th – the very day of the Commissioners' meeting – he caused Carroll's house to be razed.[124] Not content with removing that small part deemed an intrusion upon a street, he had the whole demolished, claiming that he did so by authority of the President.[125]

The Commissioners, naturally resentful of such an extraordinary act of de-

[123] Undated statement by Daniel Carroll, enclosed in a confidential letter to Madison, 29 Nov. 1791 (DLC: Madison Papers). A note appended to the statement indicates that it was shown to Thomas Johnson at the time of the sale. This would assign it a date on or before 17 Oct. 1791, which seems likely. Washington himself was informed at that time of the dispute over the house (Washington to the Commissioners, 18 Dec. 1791, *Writings*, ed. Fitzpatrick, xxxi, 446). Kite, *L'Enfant and Washington*, p. 80, on the basis of an examination of L'Enfant's plan, contends that Carroll "had appropriated for his own purposes an eminence that had been selected from the beginning by L'Enfant, and later approved by the President as one of those focal points essential to the symmetry of the City. . . . It was not therefore a question of moving the house farther back but of its entire elimination from the selected site." This supposition, together with its hint that Carroll "appropriated" the site after L'Enfant had chosen it, is contradicted by the evidence. All contemporary records mention the intrusion as partial and as lying upon a street. The house was built on land belonging to Carroll and its foundations had been laid months before L'Enfant was appointed – before even the choice of site for the Federal District had been announced.

[124] Commissioners to the President, 8 Jan. 1792, enclosing papers concerning the destruction of Carroll's house (DNA: RG 42). During L'Enfant's absence the Commissioners had ordered the workmen to desist. In informing L'Enfant of this, they said that even if the demolition had been absolutely necessary, their "opinion ought to have been previously taken on a subject so delicate and interesting" (Commissioners to L'Enfant, 25 Nov. 1791, same). See also Daniel Carroll's letters to Madison on the subject, 25 and 29 Nov. and 13 and 21 Dec. 1791 (DLC: Madison Papers). Carroll wrote in confidence, but he undoubtedly expected Madison to share his communications with TJ.

[125] Washington indignantly denied this, assuring the Commissioners that Carroll's house had been destroyed "against his consent, and without authority from yourselves or any other person, for you have done me but justice in asserting that [L'Enfant] had no such authority from me" (Washington to the Commissioners, 1 Dec. 1791, *Writings*, ed. Fitzpatrick, xxxi, 432). The house was still incomplete when destroyed. Washington thought the brick walls were up but the structure not yet covered, as perhaps it had not been when he passed through in October (Washington to the Commissioners, 18 Dec. 1791, same, xxxi, 446). This may explain why Carroll was anxious to proceed toward completion before the onset of winter.

fiance, were nevertheless fearful that prosecution of the illegal act would only multiply those impediments and disagreements which, as Washington had warned, would give delight to the enemies of the great object. One consequence they had to face was the understandable but baseless rumor that the Commissioners themselves had given their sanction to L'Enfant's action. Another was the possibly adverse effect upon their recent Memorial to the Maryland General Assembly asking for legislation which, among other things, would encourage the great object by making it possible for aliens to own land in the Federal District.[126] Since they had been openly defied, they were of course powerless to bring L'Enfant to terms. It seems likely, therefore, that one of the Commissioners may have prompted Daniel Carroll of Duddington to lay his case before the President, even though such urging was scarcely necessary. L'Enfant, who claimed from the outset that he acted under the President, left Carroll no alternative but to state his case directly to the only authority his opponent recognized. This he did on the day after the workmen began to destroy his house. So, on the same day, did L'Enfant.

On receiving their communications, Washington bluntly told Carroll that he should have laid his grievance before the Commissioners, "to whom," he declared, "all matters respecting the Federal District are now committed." While Carroll had agreed to the removal of his house if it were proved a public nuisance, Washington thought a simple fact would decide the issue. Was the building in whole or in part in the street? This begged the question, but, relying on L'Enfant's assurances, he regarded the point as established. Dismissing Carroll's argument that other houses had been built in streets and allowed to remain, he made a distinction between those already existing and one under construction – even one begun before the Federal District had been defined. This in effect made Carroll's house a nuisance per se, an interpretation which could scarcely have been sustained at law. Washington did not consult his Attorney General on the point but offered Carroll the choice of one of two alternatives. The house could be pulled down and re-erected at public expense in the spring in accord with regulations governing private buildings or it could be completed by Carroll and occupied for six years, after which it would have to be removed "with no other allowance from the public than a valuation for the Walls in the present state of them."[127] The question whether the house actually was a public nuisance was not faced. The still unfinished map of the Federal City, a correct version of which Washington had so recently insisted upon as an urgent need, was accepted as determinative. He also complicated matters further by sending L'Enfant a copy of his letter to Carroll, though in

[126] Commissioners to Benjamin Stoddert, 25 Nov. 1791, disavowing any "share in the transaction" and urging him to do his best to counteract "unfavourable impressions . . . respecting the memorial" (DNA: RG 42). On the same day the Commissioners assured Washington they had taken every step within their power to prevent unfavorable action on the memorial (Commissioners to Washington, 25 Nov. 1791, same). See also Carroll to Madison, 25 Nov. 1791 (DLC: Madison Papers). Carroll had shown TJ and Madison a copy of the memorial when they were in Georgetown early in September. The desired legislation was passed and in submitting a copy of the Act, Carroll said that this had given great relief to his mind, "much oppressed by the disagreeable business we have lately had on hand" (Carroll to Madison, 12 Dec. 1791, same; *Laws of Maryland* [Annapolis, 1792], Ch. xlv).

[127] Washington to Carroll of Duddington, 28 Nov. 1791 (*Writings*, ed. Fitzpatrick, xxxi, 429-30).

doing so he did not reprove him for his failure to submit the issue to the Commissioners. Nor did he say to L'Enfant as he had to Carroll that all matters pertaining to the Federal District had been placed in their hands. He did, however, urge the need for harmony: "it will always be found sound policy to conciliate the good-will rather than provoke the enmity of any man, where it can be accomplished without much difficulty, inconvenience or loss."[128]

But the choice presented to Carroll had become irrelevant even before it was offered. Washington had just dispatched the letters when he "learned with real mortification the account of the demolition of Mr. Carrolls house by Major L'Enfant."[129] He was indeed more than mortified, and with good reason. There was a distinct possibility that Daniel Carroll of Duddington might prosecute L'Enfant. If this should happen, the enemies of the Potomac location would be provided with still another and more powerful weapon to use.

Three weeks had passed since Jefferson had urged that the Commissioners be given full authority over L'Enfant. Washington is not known to have made any response to the suggestion, but now, faced with a much graver situation, he informed him of his unofficial communication to L'Enfant through Lear, made their correspondence and other papers available to him, and sought his counsel. He recognized that the time had come to give L'Enfant decisive instructions — but not so decisive, he made clear, as to risk the serious misfortune of losing his services. "At the same time," he added, "*he must know*, there is a line beyond which he will not be suffered to go . . . or we shall have no Commissioners."[130] Jefferson's response was immediate and went to the heart of the issue: the definition of L'Enfant's status would have to be made explicit, not indirectly and unofficially but by the President himself. He therefore drafted two letters for Washington to sign, one to L'Enfant, the other to the Commissioners. The former was brief, pointed, and unequivocal. L'Enfant had violated the law, and the law would have to take its course. Though his services were valued and still desired, he would be employed in the arrangements of the Federal City in future only on condition that he conduct himself "in subordination to the Commissioners, to the laws of the land, and to the rights of it's citizens." Like the Commissioners, Jefferson was well aware of Washington's dread of losing L'Enfant, and in submitting the draft he acknowledged that it might be too severe. What he obviously feared was that Washington might think it so and issue the directive in less decisive terms. To obviate this possibility, he took care to emphasize two facts which he had reason to believe would carry weight. First, his draft had been prepared after a conference with Madison and thus had his approval. Second, the President's sentiments as conveyed through Lear should have been respected, but L'Enfant had wholly disregarded that message.[131] Washington approved Jefferson's draft and indeed strengthened it by emphasizing the authority of the Commissioners: in future L'Enfant was to act in subordination to them and to regard them as standing between himself and the President. But, always concerned for L'Enfant's feelings, he then added two conciliatory paragraphs.[132]

[128] Washington to L'Enfant, 28 Nov. 1791 (same, XXXI, 430-1).
[129] Washington to the Commissioners, 1 Dec. 1791 (same, XXXI, 432-3).
[130] Washington to TJ, 30 Nov. 1791.
[131] TJ to Washington, 1 Dec. 1791, enclosing draft of letter to L'Enfant of same date.
[132] Washington to L'Enfant, 2 Dec. 1791 (*Writings*, ed. Fitzpatrick, XXXI, 434-5; the text as printed is typographically defective, obscuring the meaning of an important

Despite the stern warning to L'Enfant that the law had been violated and would have to take its course, Jefferson managed in his draft of the President's letter to the Commissioners to convey a hint intended to avoid what all feared – prosecution of L'Enfant by Carroll. If the offender should be spared, he suggested, it should be made known to him that he owed such protection entirely to the Commissioners and that there would be no intercession by the President on his behalf. Washington not only allowed the hint to stand but reinforced it by composing a letter to Daniel Carroll of Duddington very different in tone from his recent one. It would be unfortunate, he wrote, "if disputes amongst the friends to the federal City should Arm the enemies of it with weapons to wound it." To this appeal on behalf of the public good he added another touching Carroll's private interest. Such disputes, he concluded in terms which seemed almost threatening, "may injure you more on the large scale in the general sale of the lots than you can possibly gain by going into a court of Chancery."[133] In transmitting this letter through the Commissioners, Washington gave them leave to destroy it or transmit it to Carroll as they thought best.[134] Thus powerfully fortified, Jefferson's hint had effect. The Commissioners, though incensed at L'Enfant's conduct, made good use of Washington's letter and Carroll agreed to drop all legal proceedings. On learning of this from Jefferson, Washington was understandably gratified.[135]

But once again the hope for harmonious relations proved illusory. L'Enfant, seeing himself as one unfairly accused, if not indeed as an object of malice and persecution, attempted to justify his destruction of Carroll's house in letters both to the Commissioners and to the President. Having arrived in Georgetown on the evening of the 6th of December after an absence of ten days in Virginia, he replied the same day to the Commissioners' claim that they should have been consulted even if demolition of the house had been absolutely necessary. L'Enfant not only rejected the claim but maintained that the measure he took could in no way be challenged. He had no doubt the Commissioners, on mature reflection, would agree, hence there had been no need for him to refer the question to them. In matters of such nature as to require their attention, he said that he would always be disposed to respect the authority vested in them by law. But he trusted that, in future, they would never interfere with his operations except in justifiable cases of appeal from individuals. Not surprisingly, the Commissioners treated the condescending letter with silence. It was not until the next day that L'Enfant addressed himself to the President. In a

passage). For Washington's additions, see notes to TJ's draft under 1 Dec. 1791. PrC in Washington's hand in DLC: Washington Papers.

[133] Washington to Carroll of Duddington, 2 Dec. 1791 (*Writings*, ed. Fitzpatrick, XXXI, 433). For TJ's similar proposal that proceedings against one of L'Enfant's subordinates, Isaac Roberdeau, be dropped, see his letter to Commissioners, 6 Mch. 1792.

[134] Washington to Commissioners, 1 Dec. 1791 (same, XXXI, 433-4). For Washington's alterations in TJ's text, see notes to his draft of same date.

[135] Commissioners to TJ, 10 Dec. 1791; Washington to TJ, 14 Dec. 1791. L'Enfant declared to one of the Commissioners that he wished Carroll had gone ahead and sought his remedy at law. He also told Washington that he had hastened his return from Virginia to meet his adversaries and – out of respect for the law and the justice of his cause – to submit to the sheriff, who had been waiting for him three days (L'Enfant to Washington, 7 Dec. 1791, DLC: Digges-L'Enfant-Morgan Papers). It is most unlikely that the sheriff had been waiting at all. Certainly no summons was served.

letter quite different in tone from that to the Commissioners, he wrote as if in response to Washington's of the 28th of November, in which of course there was no mention of the destruction of Carroll's house. L'Enfant did not refer to the blunt directive of the 2d of December, but it is clear that he had that letter before him as he wrote. Yet, knowing precisely what Washington's sentiments were, he sought to justify his action as expedient, proper, and based on principles which had guided his conduct from the beginning. He apologized for not having explained earlier why he had proceeded as rapidly as he did in demolishing the house. He placed the entire blame on Daniel Carroll of Duddington and denounced him as a worthless individual who sought to benefit from his own folly, being prompted by his kinsman the Commissioner. Neither in this letter nor in any other, so far as is known, did L'Enfant acknowledge Washington's directive making him wholly subordinate to the Commissioners.[136]

While the Commissioners could ignore L'Enfant's communication, Washington had no such choice. It was now obvious that his unequivocal instructions had had no more effect than the indirect message transmitted through Lear. This time, however, he did not delay. Immediately on receiving L'Enfant's letter, he turned it over to Jefferson and sought his advice. The response was a formal report entitled "Observations on Majr. L'Enfant's letter." This, like Jefferson's draft letter of a few days earlier, was written at a time when he was hard-pressed preparing bills, resolutions, and reports on such matters as the consular establishment, the patent system, the Barbary pirates, the worsening commercial relations with France, and the crucial negotiations with the newly arrived British minister. But while his recent answer to the same key question had been expressed with brevity and force, the document he now submitted was a critical analysis of a case whose inherent weakness required no such elaborate response. The contrast in the manner of presentation suggests that Jefferson was less concerned with L'Enfant's vain attempt to justify himself than with Washington's hesitant use of authority in handling an increasingly confused and intractable subordinate. If so, the nature of the response involved a question of delicacy requiring both tact and candor. He delayed submitting his "Observations" for two days, perhaps because he wished to consult Madison — as he almost certainly did — and perhaps because he felt the vigor and bluntness of his criticism might offend Washington and thus defeat his purpose.[137]

In precise and unmistakable terms he dismissed L'Enfant's arguments as legally and otherwise untenable. The attempt at justification, he indicated at the outset, was based on a self-serving contradiction: on the one hand L'Enfant

[136] L'Enfant to Commissioners, 6 Dec. 1791; L'Enfant to Washington, 7 Dec. 1791 (DLC: Digges-L'Enfant-Morgan Papers; texts partly printed in Kite, *L'Enfant and Washington*, p. 85-9 and 89-91). Kite's supposition that L'Enfant had not received Washington's directive of the 2d when he wrote on the 7th is rendered implausible not only by the tone and context of L'Enfant's communication of the 7th but also by the speed of the post, which normally required only three days from Philadelphia to Georgetown, sometimes less. L'Enfant's letter of the 7th was in TJ's hands by the 9th. On the 10th L'Enfant wrote Washington again, but that letter has not been found.

[137] TJ's "Observations" is recorded in SJPL under 9 Dec. 1791, but was not submitted to Washington until the 11th. No covering note of transmittal has been found and none is recorded in SJPL. Hence Jefferson probably handed it to Washington in person.

maintained that Carroll's house was an intrusion on public property while on the other he asserted that the President had not yet finally approved the plan, hence his judgment as to what constituted a street could not be anticipated. The former argument Jefferson rejected as unwarranted, the latter he accepted as solidly grounded. To qualify as public property, he pointed out, streets would have to be defined in recorded deeds, sales, or partitions, with a copy of the definitive plan annexed. That plan, he took care to emphasize, was still open to alteration. There was, then, no such thing as an established street. Possessing a right of soil as tenant in common with the public, Carroll therefore could not have created a nuisance as defined by law. As for L'Enfant's claim that he had as much right to pull down a house as to cut down a tree, he had no authority to do either. The destruction of a tree might be overlooked, but any man whose house had been illegally destroyed would bring suit, subjecting the accused to large damages in a civil suit and to a heavy fine and imprisonment in a criminal action. In any case, writing as one experienced surveyor to another, Jefferson pointed out that trees and small obstructions, if insuperable, might be removed, while anyone who could not designate streets and lots even when a line passed through such an obstacle as a house could know little of geometry — that is, of the method of surveying by offset lines. L'Enfant's act, therefore, was palpably unnecessary, illegal, and contrary to the known sentiments of the President. It was further proof of his continuing inability to acquiesce under lawful authority.

In his effort to defend himself, L'Enfant had requested that a line of demarcation be drawn between his powers and those of the Commissioners. This provided Jefferson with an opportunity to restate the issue with more care and precision than he had yet done. What should the line be and who should draw it? Under the law, he argued, the Commissioners possessed the whole executive authority over the Federal District, standing between their subordinates and the President, who could only approve or disapprove certain of their acts. But the deeds of trust from the proprietors gave him sole execution of everything pertaining to the laying out of the town. Hence, while Washington had authority to draw such a line, there was no need or reason for doing so. The Commissioners were disposed to follow implicitly the President's wishes, while L'Enfant had not shown comparable moderation or acquiescence. Any attempt to define their separate spheres would only enable him to meet them "foot to foot, and chicane and raise opposition to their orders whenever he thinks they pass his line." The only means of preventing him from giving constant trouble to the President, therefore, would be to subject him to the unlimited control of the Commissioners. "We know," he reminded Washington, "the discretion and forbearance with which they will exercise it."[138] Recognizing as Washington himself did that the Commissioners, acquiescent and forbearing though they had been, were becoming more and more disturbed by L'Enfant's continuing defiance, Jefferson added this remarkably candid statement touching the heart of the issue: "I do not know what have been the authorities given him *expressly* or by *implication*." Coming from one who had been called upon so often for advice concerning the Federal City, the choice of words and the emphasis given them reveal much about Washington's manner of dealing with one of his closest advisors. In brief, his "Observations" implied, both the Commissioners and the

[138] TJ to Washington, 11 Dec. 1791, enclosing "Observations on Majr. L'Enfant's letter of Dec. 7. 1791."

Secretary of State needed to have L'Enfant's status defined in explicit terms. Most important of all, one who continued so intransigently on a course of insubordination should be required to respect those terms.

Jefferson's rebuttal of an essentially indefensible case was persuasive. Washington himself drafted the response to L'Enfant's letter, basing its main point on the "Observations" and in some respects adding strength to its emphatic terms. "I have received your letter of the 7th. instant," he wrote L'Enfant, "and can only once more, and now for all, inform you that every matter and thing which has relation to the Federal district, and the City within it, is committed to the Commissioners . . . that it is from them you are to derive your powers, and the line of demarcation for your government is to be drawn by them." He reminded L'Enfant that his first official communication had come from one of the Commissioners – Daniel Carroll, upon whom L'Enfant's letter had cast aspersions – and that all directions received by him since then should have been from them. Washington also pointed out that they had shown every disposition to listen to his suggestions, to adopt his plans, and to support his authority for carrying them into effect so far as these seemed reasonable, prudent, and consistent with their own powers. "But having said this in more instances than one," he concluded, "it is rather painful to reiterate it."[139]

Words could scarcely have been less ambiguous. A few days later Washington sent a copy of the letter to the Commissioners, describing it accurately as one that would admit of no misconstruction. As before, however, he sought to mitigate the force of his unmistakable directive. This time he did not appeal to both sides to reconcile their differences, but urged instead that the Commissioners extend to L'Enfant some measure of the authority that had been so unqualifiedly vested in them. After a lengthy analysis of L'Enfant's motives, behavior, and talents – coupled with an astonishing opinion holding Daniel Carroll of Duddington equally blamable for what had happened – he asked the Commissioners to consider "whether it might not be politic to give [L'Enfant] pretty general, and ample powers for *defined* objects; until you shall discover in him a disposition to abuse them." Such a mark of confidence, he thought, would gratify his pride and excite his ambition.[140] In making this suggestion Washington could not have been unaware that L'Enfant's pride and ambition were such conspicuous traits of character as to call less for stimulation than for the kind of restraint he had just administered. He certainly knew, as the affair of Carroll's house proved beyond doubt, that L'Enfant did not hesitate to abuse even those powers delegated to him by the President. Why, then, did he advance a proposal which, aside from weakening his own explicit instructions, amounted in effect to a rejection of Jefferson's warning that any attempt to delineate the separate spheres of the Commissioners and their subordinate would only lead to constant trouble? The most plausible answer would seem to be that Washington accepted the risk because he feared the loss of a man he regarded as irreplaceable might jeopardize the great object of keeping the capital on the Potomac. This is also indicated by the manner in which he made the suggestion. He did this not in a formal presidential communication but in a private letter which the Commissioners were expressly enjoined not to mingle with their public papers. Though the categorical definition of L'Enfant's status had been

[139] Washington to L'Enfant, 13 Dec. 1791 (*Writings*, ed. Fitzpatrick, XXXI, 442-3). Washington enclosed a copy of this letter in his to TJ of 14 Dec. 1791.

[140] Washington to the Commissioners, 18 Dec. 1791 (same, XXXI, 445-8).

prompted by Jefferson, this unofficial letter modifying its terms was not shared with him. Thus the decisive official posture exhibited by the President to his Secretary of State became transmuted into the weaker stance manifested in a form known only to the Commissioners.

The result, as before, was greater confusion of the lines of authority. L'Enfant himself apparently never acknowledged Washington's instructions. Certainly the reiterated and explicit command that he subject himself in all things to the Commissioners fell on deaf ears. That hitherto acquiescent body, flaunted a few weeks later by L'Enfant's subordinates, felt compelled to warn Washington that their own honor and duty required more of them than a continued tolerance of such affronts. With not a spade of clay turned up for bricks and with L'Enfant's workmen excavating the foundations for a Capitol not yet designed and digging wide and deep ditches to accord with plans of the City still subject to alteration, they felt it necessary to know and approve all that was being done. They would lament the loss of L'Enfant, but, they added, "we owe something to ourselves and to others which cannot be given up."[141] The destruction of Carroll's house had also given alarm to the proprietors and added to their confusion about the sources of authority.[142] Thus did Washington, profoundly concerned as he was about everything affecting the Federal City and possessing as he did ultimate authority over its planning, contribute more than anyone else to the developing sense of uncertainty. As he had done in the past and would continue to do throughout his presidency, he honored more in the breach than in the observance his official pronouncement to L'Enfant that "every matter and thing which has relation to the Federal district, and the City within it, is committed to the Commissioners." Believing that the question of fixing the seat of government was one of the two great issues which might decide the fate of the new government, he made every aspect of its progress a matter of personal and official concern.[143] This is understandable. But such direct involvement in all matters great and small inevitably meant that Washington's towering influence would be brought to bear upon all decisions, producing ultimately both the success of the enterprise and a number of otherwise avoidable mistakes. The most immediate effect during L'Enfant's connection with the Federal City was a steady deepening of the already murky air of confused authority.

Meanwhile the Commissioners, anxious to avoid a repetition of complaints that information had been withheld at the October sale, were determined not

[141] Commissioners to Washington, 7 Jan. 1792 (DNA: RG 42).

[142] Commissioners to Washington, 21 Dec. 1791, enclosing memorial of the proprietors and expressing fear that the hopes they had expressed in theirs of the 10th to TJ about getting matters settled with Carroll of Duddington would be frustrated (DNA: RG 42). See Washington to TJ, 25 Dec. 1791, and its enclosures; to TJ of 14 and 15 Jan. 1792, and their enclosures; Washington to the Commissioners, 17 Jan. 1792 (*Writings*, ed. Fitzpatrick, xxxi, 461). It was only after the proprietors had expressed their alarm over the destruction of the house that Washington sought the advice of Attorney General Randolph. The result was that the public ultimately was obliged to pay for damages done illegally by L'Enfant (Washington to Randolph, 31 Jan. 1792, same, xxxi, 470-1).

[143] "The two great questions of funding the debt and fixing the seat of government," he wrote in 1790, ". . . were always considered by me as questions of the most delicate and interesting nature which could possibly be drawn into discussion. They were more in danger of having convulsed the government itself than any other points" (Washington to La Luzerne, 10 Aug. 1790, same, xxxi, 84).

to announce another until maps could be completed and "everybody . . . have a Chance for the object of their choice."[144] Washington concurred. He expected L'Enfant in Philadelphia late in November and assured the Commissioners he would impress upon him the need for dispatch in producing a "correct draught of the City."[145] Writing directly to L'Enfant, he expressed his earnest desire "that correct Engravings of the City be . . . properly disseminated (*at least*) throughout the United States" before the sale should take place.[146] As shown by his proposal to expedite the next sale and by his various suggestions for mapping the District and the City, Jefferson fully shared this concern. But when L'Enfant finally appeared in Philadelphia in the last days of December, his map was yet unfinished and his capacity for defying authority far from diminished. The ultimate confrontation with the President came within a few weeks.

X

Shortly before the October sale, a newspaper essayist, obviously more interested than his use of the pseudonym *A Spectator* implied, presented to the public a glowing account of the capital as conceived by L'Enfant. "The plan of the city, agreeably to the directions of the President of the United States," *Spectator* wrote, "was designed, and drawn, by the celebrated Major L'Enfant; and is an inconceivable improvement upon all other cities in the world, combining not only convenience, regularity, elegance of prospect, and a free circulation of air, but every thing grand and beautiful that can possibly be introduced into a city." Since the plan would be published early the following month, *Spectator* announced, there would be no need to describe its features – and then proceeded to do so. He indicated the locations of the Capitol and the President's House as well as the "houses for the great departments of state, the Supreme-Court House, and the Judiciary Offices, and National Bank, the General Exchange, and the several Market-Houses, with a variety of other public buildings . . . all arranged with equal propriety, judgment and taste." West of the Capitol and South of the President's House there were "two great Pleasure-Parks, or Malls . . . ornamented at the sides with a variety of public gardens and elegant buildings." There were also many open areas interspersed throughout the City, fifteen of the best of which might be named for the states of the union and used for statues, obelisks, or columns to the memory of their favorite military heroes or statesmen. The transverse avenues and diagonal streets would facilitate transportation and avoid the insipid sameness of such cities as Philadelphia and Charleston. The great avenues would have brick pavements ten feet wide and gravel walks of twice that width planted with trees on each side, with eighty feet of paved street for carriages in the center. The description of the City concluded with another tribute to L'Enfant:[147]

[144] Commissioners to the President, 21 Oct. 1791 (DNA: RG 42). The Commissioners said that they had consulted L'Enfant and Ellicott about the probable time when all would be in readiness for the next sale. Both thought this would be about the middle or end of June.

[145] Washington to Stuart, 20 Nov. 1791 (*Writings*, ed. Fitzpatrick, XXXI, 421, 423).

[146] Washington to L'Enfant, 28 Nov. 1791 (same, XXXI, 431).

[147] "Description of the city of Washington" by *A Spectator*, published in *Maryland Journal*, 30 Sep. 1791, and *Gazette of the United States*, 8 Oct. 1791.

Among the many fortunate circumstances which have attended this country, during the present administration in government, the residence of Major L'Enfant in America at this time, may be considered as one of the most material. . . . The public buildings, now planned by this great engineer and architect, and carrying on under his orders, will be superb and elegant, and such as will do honor to the capital of a great and prosperous empire.

The details presented in this article, the praise heaped upon L'Enfant, the claim that his concept of the capital would cause it to transcend in beauty and grandeur all other cities of the world, and the quite unfounded assertion that elegant public buildings had been planned by him and were being constructed under his direction make it clear that *Spectator* was a zealous promoter of the Federal City and also had access to special sources of information. So, too, does his fear that the capital might not remain on the Potomac. *Spectator* conceded that Congress had power to repeal the Residence Act, but declared that "so grossly to violate public and private faith would not be mentioned in a congress of fiends in Pandemonium." Nor, he warned, could Congress interfere with private grants by individuals and states, stop the construction of houses by the proprietors, or prevent them from proceeding to build the Federal City. By the controlling terms of the trust agreement with the President, he implied, they could not be thwarted even by the highest law-making authority in the land.

It is equally obvious that *Spectator* could not have presented so exact and detailed a description of the projected plan had L'Enfant not given his assistance. Only he could have supplied such precise information as that giving locations of the public buildings, the width and arrangement of walks along the avenues, and, among other features, the areas proposed to be set aside for use of the states. The claim that this capital of a great empire would be superior to all other cities of the world, together with other extravagancies, only echoed such words of L'Enfant as may be found in his letters to the President. He had already shown himself disposed to cooperate with the proprietors and they in turn found him useful in advancing their interests. It is thus not surprising that, just prior to the sale of lots, *Spectator* should have obtained access to L'Enfant's plan. This is proved by the detailed descriptions and the language employed – for example, the words taken from the title describing the plan as designed by L'Enfant "agreeably to the directions of the President" – which could only have come from that source. *Spectator*'s assurance that the plan was about to be published could only have referred to the one Pigalle was then supposed to be preparing. But the maps being used for that purpose were at that time in Philadelphia. It is virtually certain, therefore, that the only map L'Enfant could have made available to *Spectator* was his large or general working plan which, a few days later, he refused to permit the Commissioners to use at the sale.

But to whom did L'Enfant make available such privileged information, thus in effect collaborating with a private individual screened behind a pseudonym? The beneficiary of this act of favoritism who signed himself so inappropriately as A *Spectator* was undoubtedly Francis Cabot, a member of the prominent mercantile and shipping family of Massachusetts. Cabot had been recommended to the President, the Vice-President, and others as a person greatly interested in promoting the Federal City. He had recently settled in Georgetown and quickly became intimate with L'Enfant. He also gained the confidence of Daniel

Carroll and obtained from him a letter of introduction when, late in August, he planned to accompany L'Enfant to Philadelphia at the time the latter laid his plan of the City before the President. Carroll described Cabot as "a sensible, intelligent Gentleman" with respectable connections – prominent among whom was his brother George Cabot, who had just been elected Senator from Massachusetts.[148] At the request of Tobias Lear on behalf of himself and friends from New England, L'Enfant engaged Francis Cabot to purchase a lot at the sale. For this speculative venture in which L'Enfant himself was involved, he must have made his general map available to Cabot just as he had done in giving assistance to *Spectator*. In these early months Cabot also seems to have gained the confidence of the President as well as the Commissioners. When in December he delivered to Jefferson a letter from Andrew Ellicott, he was described as "a Gentleman . . . of information" and also as "a zealous friend to the City."[149] But within a few months these initial evidences of confidence in Cabot had begun to erode.[150]

However gratified Washington may have been by the encomiums heaped upon L'Enfant, he could scarcely have failed to be disturbed by *Spectator*'s unauthorized disclosures. He was obliged soon to address Congress, whose members may well have wondered why, if copious and precise details about a plan of the capital designed by direction of the President could be made available to an anonymous newspaper scribbler, such information could not be given to them. He was not prepared to act on the advice of John Jay that his Annual Message include a general though cautious comment on "the Proceedings in the Business of the fœderal District."[151] But with *Spectator*'s assurance that the map of the City would be published early in October, Washington in his message could scarcely avoid referring to the plan. What made his embarrassment all the more acute was his knowledge that, once again, L'Enfant had acted innocently and contrary to his wishes because an official secret had not been confided to him. The fact is that neither Washington nor Jefferson had informed L'Enfant of the crucial decision taken early in September at the conferences in Philadelphia and confirmed at the later meetings in Georgetown when Jefferson and Madison obtained the concurrence of the Commissioners in the President's views. That decision was to leave blank the squares appropriated for public use except those for the legislative and executive branches, all others to remain undesignated until wanted for defined purposes.[152] This of course meant eliminating from the map Pigalle was supposed to be engraving

[148] Carroll to TJ, 29 July 1791. The letter was delivered on the 29th of August. This was only a day or so after L'Enfant arrived in Philadelphia, which indicates that Cabot did accompany him as planned.

[149] Ellicott to TJ, 30 Nov. 1791.

[150] Early in 1792 Washington had begun to doubt Cabot's sincerity and by the end of the year he thought "an antidote is necessary to the poison which Mr. F——s C——t is spreading . . . that the accomplishment of the Plan [for the Federal City] is no more to be expected than the fabric of a vision, and will vanish in like manner" (Washington to David Stuart, 8 Mch. and 30 Nov. 1791, *Writings*, ed. Fitzpatrick, xxxi, 507; xxxii, 244). Washington always retained his confidence in Senator George Cabot.

[151] Jay to Washington, 23 Sep. 1791 (DLC: Washington Papers). Jay even suggested that, if necessary, details about the state of affairs in the Federal District might be conveyed in a special message.

[152] See TJ's notes of Commissioners' meeting with TJ and Madison, 8 Sep. 1791, enclosed in TJ to Washington of that date.

such explanatory references as those setting aside squares for the national bank, the non-sectarian church, and the symbolic uses of the fifteen states. The Commissioners, in their first written communication to L'Enfant defining other matters that had been decided upon, did not mention this important decision which so directly affected his plan.[153] Hints may have been thrown out to L'Enfant at the prior meetings in Philadelphia and the failure to inform him of the decision may have been prompted by Washington's usual care to avoid giving him offense, but this only deepened the embarrassment caused by *Spectator*'s article. It is understandable, therefore, that in his Annual Message Washington treated the subject with caution. He also joined *Spectator* in exaggeration: the October sale had been favorable, there was a prospect that ample funds would be provided for the necessary public buildings, the Federal City had been laid out according to a plan which would be laid before Congress.[154] But this promise to submit the plan only brought on further embarrassment.

Despite Washington's urgent appeal to L'Enfant to come forward with a more "correct draught of the City," several weeks passed with no news from Georgetown save the usual accounts of disturbing conflicts. Early in December Francis Cabot arrived in Philadelphia, perhaps bearing the discouraging but accurate news that there would be still further delay in L'Enfant's coming. Immediately thereafter, Washington sent to the Senate and House of Representatives "the plan of a City that has been laid out within the District . . . fixed upon for the permanent seat of the Government of the United States."[155] There was no further comment or explanation. Washington later claimed that the letter of transmittal indicated the plan was sent only "as a matter of information, to show what state the business was in."[156] But this was said years after the event and after a legal challenge had been raised on the plausible ground that submission of the plan indicated official approval. In fact, the language employed both in his Annual Message and in his brief note of transmittal conveyed the impression that the City had already been laid out. This was undoubtedly intended. In brief, at this time, Washington found it expedient to have Congress and the public regard the plan submitted as the one that had received presidential sanction. *Spectator*'s promotional essay, with its even more misleading and inaccurate statements, helped confirm the impression.

The plan of the Federal City thus hesitantly and ambiguously presented to Congress was one of the two then in Washington's possession — Hallet's reduction from L'Enfant's large plan and the one L'Enfant called his "small draft." The former was only an unfinished outline and scarcely appropriate for submission to Congress. The latter, according to Pigalle, was quite useless for engraving but Lear thought it provided "a good general idea of the spot and plan of the City."[157] Washington, embarrassed by the long delay in keeping his promise to Congress, must have concluded that it was acceptable enough

[153] Commissioners to L'Enfant, 9 Sep. 1791 (DNA: RG 42).

[154] Annual Message, 25 Oct. 1791 (*Writings*, ed. Fitzpatrick, XXXI, 400).

[155] Washington to the Senate and House of Representatives, 13 Dec. 1791 (same, XXXI, 444).

[156] Washington to the Commissioners, 20 Feb. 1797 (same, XXXV, 395).

[157] Lear to Washington, 11 Oct. 1791 (DLC: Washington Papers). Lear himself indicated that the small draft would be needed to explain Hallet's outline reduction. See notes 108 and 110.

for his purposes. He subsequently described it in terms which leave no doubt that it was the one usually designated as the L'Enfant plan of 1791.[158]

This remarkable document, the earliest map of the Federal City known to be extant, has long been accorded the esteem and subjected to the scrutiny its importance warrants.[159] But its evolution as a manuscript of changing character has remained hidden beneath the layers of erasures, additions, and cancellations which determined its ultimate form. Its developing characteristics during the first six months of its existence – at the time drawn, at the time submitted to Congress, and at the time altered for engraving – need therefore to be examined. This is necessary also because its generally accepted designation, which properly recognizes L'Enfant as author of its more conspicuous features, has obscured the number and importance of characteristics others added to it or removed from it. In its final form it became indeed a Jefferson document of considerable importance in the planning of the capital.

XI

There can be little doubt that this was the manuscript L'Enfant submitted to Washington late in August and described as the "anexed map of doted lines."[160] Ellicott later referred to it as "the original plan" and said that it was a mixture of conjecture and fact.[161] With most of the field work yet to be done, reliance upon conjecture was unavoidable and lines not then laid out on the ground were designated on the plan in its original state. These cannot now be distinguished. But it may be said with some assurance that when L'Enfant delivered the plan to Washington late in August it lacked two outstanding features later given it. The first was the attribution of authorship in the cartouche – "By Peter Charles L'Enfant." The second and more conspicuous was the extended text containing general observations on the plan, descriptions of streets and avenues, and keyed references to its outstanding elements. These

---

[158] Washington to the Commissioners, 1 Dec. 1796 (*Writings*, ed. Fitzpatrick, xxxv, 305).

[159] See latest studies by Stephenson, Jennings, and Ehrenberg in LC *Qu. Jour.*, xxxvi (1979), and works cited there by Kite, Caemmerer, and others. Stephenson and Jennings, prompted perhaps by the many alterations, describe this "small draft" as L'Enfant's working or master plan. This, in the Editor's opinion, is an unwarrantable conclusion. L'Enfant's master or working plan was in their opinion the large or general map which he guarded so closely and from which, according to his own testimony, the "small draft" was copied. The large or general plan was probably the one submitted to the proprietors and others on 29 June 1791. If so, it was the one which later came into the possession of Francis Cabot, who turned it over to Samuel Davidson, who in turn gave it back to L'Enfant around 1800 (Davidson to L'Enfant, 16 Jan. 1802, *Records of the Columbia Historical Society*, ii, 141-2).

[160] L'Enfant to Washington, 19 Aug. 1791 (DNA: RG 42). The absence of street designations and especially the title given in the cartouche – "Plan of the City, intended for the Permanent Seat of the Government of the United States" – prove that its basic features were set down before the Commissioners met with TJ and Madison early in September and decided upon the name of the City.

[161] TJ to Johnson, 8 Mch. 1792. The Commissioners' inquiry had referred to the "original plan" and TJ employed the same term, referring to the "small draft" then in hand.

textual details, first outlined in L'Enfant's letter presenting the plan to Washington, were probably elaborated in incomplete form while L'Enfant was in Philadelphia early in September. Then, or perhaps soon after he left, some of the results of Ellicott's surveys produced further additions. Among these, it may be reasonably supposed, was the statement that Ellicott by celestial observation had drawn a true meridian line passing at right angles through another line at the site of the Capitol and, after precise survey, had made these the basis on which the whole plan was to be executed.[162]

That these detailed descriptions went through a series of changes, were originally set down on a separate paper or papers, and were then copied fair to accompany the plan submitted to Congress seems beyond question. When first published in Freneau's *National Gazette*, these explanatory passages were described as "annexed to the plan . . . sent to Congress by the President."[163] Their text at that stage contained many variations from the form later given them in the manuscript, including one complete sentence which does not appear in the latter.[164] One such variant occurs in the passage describing Ellicott's method of running the basic lines by celestial observation. There the text as sent to Congress refers to "the *above* plan," while the expression ultimately employed in the manuscript reads "*this* plan"[165] — an alteration explainable only on the supposition that, as submitted to Congress, the descriptive passages were on a separate paper subjoined to the manuscript. Also, while the central features of the plan were subjected to numerous erasures and alterations, the entire text of the general observations, descriptions, and references as recorded on the manuscript contains not a single change. This part, then, must represent a fair copy of an earlier and separate form as submitted to Congress, at which time the manuscript was evidently blank in those considerable areas now containing the descriptive texts. It follows of course that these would have been placed there after their appearance in revised form in the *National Gazette*. No

[162] There seems little reason to doubt that Ellicott himself inserted this explanation of his method in the early stage of the description of the plan. He took an obvious and justifiable pride in the professional exactness of his work, explaining it at some length in communications to the American Philosophical Society, of which he was a member. In surveying both the Federal District and the Federal City, he employed a transit and equal altitude instrument which he made and used in running the western boundary of New York ("A Letter from Mr. Andrew Ellicott, to Robert Patterson," 2 Apr. 1795, *Trans.*, Am. Phil. Soc., IV [1799], 32-51).

Ultimately Ellicott, like L'Enfant but for very different reasons, fell into disfavor with the Commissioners and abandoned work on the Federal City, leaving the northern part unsurveyed. Ellicott wished the President to hear his case but Washington declined to give him the consideration he had given L'Enfant (TJ to Ellicott, 22 Mch. 1793; Ellicott to TJ, 26 Mch. 1793).

[163] *National Gazette*, 2 Jan. 1792 (emphasis added). It is pertinent to recall that when L'Enfant delivered the map to Washington he referred to it as "the plan . . . annexed" and "the anexed map" (L'Enfant to Washington, 19 Aug. 1791, DNA: RG 42). Since L'Enfant's accompanying letter was a detailed explanation of the principal elements of the plan, it seems obvious that, at that time, it did not have or need the kind of descriptive passages it had when submitted to Congress. The text as printed in the *National Gazette* was copied exactly by the *Gazette of the United States*, 4 Jan. 1792, except for the addition of a headline reading "New City of Washington."

[164] See notes for details of variants; see also Stephenson's article, LC *Qu. Jour.*, XXXVI (1979), 207-24.

[165] Emphasis added.

document containing these descriptive texts as they evolved prior to submission to Congress is known to exist.

The manuscript plan also shows one alteration in Jefferson's engrossing or calligraphic hand which was clearly made before it was submitted to Congress. The change does not represent that form of his hand at its best, being written over some erased wording. But the lettering, perhaps hastily inserted, is unmistakably his.[166] The alteration, which occurs at the heavily erased area in and about the presidential square, reads "President's house." This substitution must have replaced some form of L'Enfant's invariable reference to the residence of the Chief Executive as a palace – including such variants as "the palace," "a presidial palace," and "the President palace."[167] Such a designation, as Jefferson surely perceived, would have aroused the anger of those who were already beginning to complain of monarchical tendencies in the administration.

Other changes in the evolving manuscript plan took place soon after it was submitted to Congress. When L'Enfant arrived in Philadelphia in the last days of December, he immediately waited upon the President. Washington earnestly impressed upon him the need to produce a plan suitable for engraving. L'Enfant promised to do so. Before leaving Georgetown, he had directed Benjamin Ellicott to record all of the field work resulting in actual measurements. This, together with his original or general plan, L'Enfant explained, was intended as the basis for a map on a reduced scale proper for engraving. He later claimed that Ellicott's draft had not been made available to him. L'Enfant would not say it was intentionally withheld, but he offered this as the reason for his not being able to comply with his promise to the President. He also explained that after obtaining the "sketch" left with Pigalle – that is, the one recently submitted to Congress – he turned it over to Ellicott, urged him to finish as much as he could without his large map, and thereafter "daily attended the progress of the business in all its stages" so that together they could correct and complete the reduced plan for the engraver.[168] L'Enfant thus had the "small draft" in his possession for only a brief time. But during that time, two or three days after his arrival, he must have made available to Freneau the general observations about the plan which the *National Gazette* – no doubt to the consternation of Washington and Jefferson – published on the 2d of January. Before doing so, L'Enfant himself or someone at his prompting must have inserted in the cartouche of the manuscript the words "By Peter Charles L'Enfant" which accompanied the passages reprinted in the newspapers. The lettering is slanted

[166] TJ's astonishing retention of his early training in draftsmanship, such as any student taught to survey and draw plats was required to do, is best illustrated in the engrossing or calligraphic hand with which, as Secretary of State and for high secrecy, he personally wrote official documents in their entirety.

[167] Before the plan and the descriptive texts were submitted to Congress, L'Enfant in no discoverable instance employed the words "President's house." In his letter to Washington of 22 June 1791 submitting the first incomplete plan he employed the word "palace" six times in such variant forms as those quoted above. In the letter of 19 Aug. 1791 delivering the "annexed map," he referred to the Chief Executive's "palace" in different forms no less than five times. It can scarcely be doubted therefore that the map itself carried the designation to which he had become so habituated over the months he had been working on it.

[168] L'Enfant to Lear, 17 Feb. 1792 (*Records*, Col. Hist. Soc., II [1899], 144-5). For Washington's urgent directions about producing a correct map for engraving, see his letter to L'Enfant of 28 Feb. 1792 (*Writings*, ed. Fitzpatrick, XXXI, 488-9).

and crowded, differing both from the careful draftsmanship in other parts of the manuscript and from Jefferson's insertion of the words "President's house."

Once again, however, L'Enfant had failed to keep his promise to the President. Instead of pursuing that task with the sense of urgency Washington had impressed upon him, he spent much time drafting a grandiose proposal calling for the expenditure of some $300,000 and the employment of more than a thousand men during the coming season. To meet these and other anticipated needs for the next four years, he suggested that a loan of a million dollars be negotiated. This, he said, had already been "offered from Holland" and would insure the success of the enterprise — a suggestion indicating that, as before, he was in consultation with his friend the Secretary of the Treasury. He warned the President that "unless some shining progress is made in the grand work," no foreign or American companies would lend their support. Above all, he thought there should be at the head of the operation a Director General with full authority over all employed in it, including the power of appointment and removal. "I feel a diffidence from the actual state of things," he declared, "to venture further in the work, unless adequate provisions are made."[169]

L'Enfant said nothing in this extraordinary document about the pressing assignment Washington had given him three weeks earlier, but the implication of his message was clear. He wished to be made Director General, with full authority over the planning and execution of all operations, or — the warning was delicately phrased yet unmistakable — he would have no further connection with the planning of the capital. In brief, this was one further rejection of the President's repeated and unequivocal directions placing L'Enfant under direct control of the Commissioners. Ironically, even as he drafted these proposals, events in the Federal City of his own doing destroyed any hope there may have been that they would be favorably considered. His subordinates, Isaac Roberdeau and others, acting under his directions, had defied the Commissioners, had been discharged, and Roberdeau had been placed under arrest. On the very day that Washington received L'Enfant's proposals he assured the Commissioners of his full support of their actions. To Jefferson he expressed himself more emphatically. "The conduct of Majr. L'Enfant and those under him," he wrote, "astonishes me beyond measure — and something more even than appears, must be meant by them!"[170] Apparently Washington did not respond to L'Enfant's letter or comment on the elaborate proposals.

Early in 1792 Andrew Ellicott appeared in Philadelphia and was surprised to find that no preparations had been made for publishing L'Enfant's plan.[171]

[169] L'Enfant to Washington, 17 Jan. 1792, enclosing plan of "Operations Intended for the Ensuing Season in the Federal City" (DNA: RG 42). See TJ's letter of 6 Mch. 1792 to the Commissioners enclosing this and other estimates. The letter and the plan of operations are printed in Kite, *L'Enfant and Washington*, p. 110-16, 117-32. The reference to the availability of a loan in Holland, the suggestion that the proceeds be lodged in the hands of the Secretary of the Treasury, and the boldness of the proposal suggest that the guiding hand of Alexander Hamilton may have influenced its composition. So also with respect to L'Enfant's talks with foreign ministers suggesting that offers of lots be made available for their residences.

[170] Washington to TJ, 18 Jan. 1792; Washington to Commissioners, 17 Jan. 1792 (DNA: RG 42). On the Roberdeau episode, see Commissioners to Washington, 7 and 9 Jan. 1792 (same). See also Washington to TJ, 14 and 15 Jan.; 7, 9, and 11 Feb. 1792.

[171] Ellicott to Commissioners, 23 Feb. 1792 (DNA: RG 42).

Washington himself later declared that if it had not been for the materials Ellicott brought with him, no engraving from that plan would probably have been produced.[172] Ellicott, who enjoyed Jefferson's confidence and respect as well as the esteem of such leading men of science as Franklin and Rittenhouse, had long since demonstrated his competence in surveying state boundaries and in laying out the Federal District and a large part of the Federal City.[173] It is thus not surprising that when L'Enfant failed to keep his promise, Washington decided to turn the task over to the man who had proved himself prompt and dependable in meeting his assignments. But his decision rested only partly upon Ellicott's presence and L'Enfant's failed promise. The determining factor was apparently what Washington called the "untoward temper" L'Enfant had displayed since his arrival in late December.[174] It was this, not the transfer of responsibility for preparing the plan for engraving, which led to L'Enfant's ultimate separation. After pressing upon him the urgent need to have the map prepared for publication, Washington left to others responsibility for trying to reach an accommodation with the increasingly intractable engineer. First of all, early in January and clearly at the request of the President, Jefferson invited L'Enfant to dine with him privately to discuss affairs of the Federal City.[175] If the meeting took place, nothing is known to have come of it. By early February L'Enfant reiterated his ultimatum, making it all the more explicit by combining it with a defense of Roberdeau's defiance of the Commissioners. The "confidence which from the beginning . . . you have placed in me," he wrote Washington, "enjoins me to renounce the pursuit unless the power of effecting the work with advantage to the public, and credit to myself is left me."[176] At that moment George Walker, one of the interested landowners and a confidant of L'Enfant, arrived in Philadelphia and Washington urged Jefferson to contrive a meeting with him at his place. But Walker turned out to be an ineffective intermediary, being both partial and unreliable.[177] By the 11th of February Washington had concluded that it was time to bring the matter to issue. He consulted both Jefferson and Madison. Within four days thereafter, having procured L'Enfant's

[172] Washington to Commissioners, 20 Feb. 1797 (*Writings*, ed. Fitzpatrick, xxxv, 395).

[173] In 1789, in applying for the position of Geographer, Ellicott said correctly that he was encouraged to do so by "some of the first scientific characters" and claimed that he and Rittenhouse were the "only practical surveyors and astronomers in the United States" who made their own instruments (Ellicott to Washington, 16 May 1789, DLC: Washington Papers). Among those who supported his application and testified to his scientific talents as well as his integrity and industry were Benjamin Franklin, Robert Patterson, David Rittenhouse, John Ewing, Robert Andrews, and the Rev. James Madison; see their letters of various dates in Aug. 1789 in DLC: Washington Papers, except for the last dated 5 May 1789 and addressed to James Madison (DLC: Madison Papers) and that of Franklin, dated 10 Aug. 1789, which is in the form of a certificate (DLC). The best account of Ellicott's career, together with illustrations of instruments made by him and by Rittenhouse and others for his use, is Silvio Bedini's "Andrew Ellicott, Surveyor of the Wilderness," *Surveying and Mapping*, xxxvi (June 1976), 113-35. Ellicott was elected a member of the American Philosophical Society in 1785, though his certificate is dated 20 Jan. 1786 (same, p. 118).

[174] Washington to David Stuart, 8 Mch. 1792 (*Writings*, ed. Fitzpatrick, xxxi, 503).

[175] TJ to L'Enfant, 7 Jan. 1792.

[176] Caemmerer, *Life of L'Enfant*, p. 201.

[177] Washington to TJ, 9 Feb. 1792.

plan from the Ellicotts, Jefferson submitted his suggested alterations, together with the draft of a letter from himself to L'Enfant on behalf of the President.[178]

Washington's authorization to Jefferson to propose alterations in the plan seems not to have been given in writing. L'Enfant, being dealt with through an intermediary, perhaps learned through his friend Walker of the transfer of responsibility for the map to Ellicott. As L'Enfant himself explained, "Mr. Andrew Ellicott gave me to understand that he was ordered by Mr. Jefferson to attend himself to that business" and that an engraver had already been engaged. L'Enfant expressed confidence that this order could not mean the map would be published without his knowledge or concurrence. He therefore decided to give the matter no more concern, being convinced the plan could not be completed without recourse to the large map then in his possession.[179] This he withheld. "Major L'Enfant refused us the use of the Original!" Ellicott exclaimed to the Commissioners. "What his motives were, God knows."[180] Yet despite this and other handicaps, Ellicott was able within a few days to produce a map of the City and present it to the President. Both Washington and the Commissioners were concerned about its accuracy and, at the President's request, Jefferson queried Ellicott closely on the point. After comparing both versions, he felt assured that the defects of L'Enfant's "original plan" had been corrected by Ellicott's actual surveys and that his draft could be relied upon with the "utmost minuteness."[181]

Ellicott's achievement in so brief a period and in spite of L'Enfant's refusal to cooperate was indeed remarkable, resulting in the engraving by Samuel Hill of Boston issued some months later. But since that version is generally though imprecisely referred to as the Ellicott plan of 1792, it is important to note that his contribution lay primarily if not wholly in the corrections and verifications he was able to supply from his own field work, not in the alterations and departures from L'Enfant's design that were incorporated in his draft.[182] L'Enfant himself originated the idea that such changes were made by Ellicott. While Ellicott's rendition was in progress, he inspected it at his former colleague's home. "This draft to my great surprise," he explained in a message intended for the President, "I found . . . most unmercifully spoiled and altered from the original plan to a degree indeed evidently tending to disgrace me and ridicule the very undertaking." L'Enfant found it difficult to believe one whom he had

[178] Washington to TJ, 11 and 15 Feb. 1792.

[179] L'Enfant to Lear, 17 Feb. 1792 (*Records*, Col. Hist. Soc., II [1899], 145). Ellicott reported to the Commissioners that, on reporting to the President and Secretary of State that no preparation had been made for engraving the plan, he was ordered to prepare one (Ellicott to the Commissioners, 23 Feb. 1792, DNA: RG 42).

[180] Ellicott to the Commissioners, 23 Feb. 1792 (same). Ellicott said that he completed the map with the aid of his brother and had delivered it to the President on the preceding Monday (the 20th). Thus, even handicapped as he was by L'Enfant's refusal to cooperate, Ellicott completed his task in about three weeks. See also Washington to the Commissioners, 6 Mch. 1792 (*Writings*, ed. Fitzpatrick, XXXI, 497-9).

[181] TJ to Johnson, 8 Mch. 1792 (private). In referring to the "original plan," TJ of course meant the manuscript which had been submitted to Congress and which he then had in hand for comparison with Ellicott's revision.

[182] Ellicott's draft evidently has not survived and is known only through the Samuel Hill engraving of 1792 and through the larger engraving by Thackara and Vallance of Philadelphia which included further changes, notably the addition of soundings in the Potomac.

always treated with candor as a friend should "harbour a design so inconsistent, as to endeavour to destroy the reputation of one whose contempt for the little machinations of envy, has left him unguarded against the treachery of false friends." Warning against the consequences of offering the public an erroneous map, he added in a postscript that he had that day requested Ellicott to send him his plan together with other drafts so that he might correct its errors and thus expedite the engraving.[183]

But it was too late. Acting as he was under supervision of the Secretary of State by direction of the President, Ellicott naturally declined the request. Because of L'Enfant's own behavior, the opportunity to have anything further to do with the plan of the capital had been permanently removed from his hands.

XII

It was during this brief period in February when Ellicott labored to produce a reliable map that L'Enfant's evolving manuscript received most of the alterations given it by Jefferson with the President's concurrence. Washington, who later identified that document as the one laid before Congress, described it as containing "(tho' almost obliterated) the directions given to the Engraver, by Mr. Jefferson, with a pencil, what parts to omit."[184] The changes made by Jefferson were not directed to the engraver, but to Ellicott, whose resultant draft – presumably no longer extant – was employed by the engraver. These alterations were more numerous than is generally believed, though they did not and were not intended to destroy the basic concept or to bring its author into disrepute as L'Enfant charged. Jefferson undoubtedly had strong reservations about the design and even anticipated some of the problems that would be created by its radial avenues and streets – such, for example, as those posed for the designers of angular buildings. But he was also well aware that Washington desired a minimum of changes to be made in a plan which he wished to become fixed in the public mind and which, as he was led to believe, had met with "universal applause."[185] Yet, even after L'Enfant had removed himself from all connection with the planning of the capital and after Ellicott's draft had been submitted, Washington asked Jefferson whether it would be advisable to permit him to suggest alterations in his plan. This was a suggestion perhaps prompted by Washington's sensitiveness to L'Enfant's "having become a very discontented man," but it was hedged by two prudent conditions: any alterations by L'Enfant would have to be made within a certain time and means to prevent "any thing unfair" would have to be available.[186] Jefferson must have advised against such a reopening of the closed door.

[183] L'Enfant to Lear, 17 Feb. 1792 (*Records*, Col. Hist. Soc., II [1899], 145-7).

[184] Washington to the Commissioners, 1 Dec. 1796 (*Writings*, ed. Fitzpatrick, XXXV, 305).

[185] Washington to David Stuart, 8 Mch. 1792 (same, XXXI, 507). Washington added the qualification "so far as my information goes." Given the President's immense personal and official authority, few would have had the temerity to challenge a plan laid before Congress as having been "Projected agreeable to the direction of the President." But Washington surely knew that the Commissioners, some of the proprietors, and Jefferson himself were not enthusiastic about certain features of the plan.

[186] Washington to TJ, [27?] Feb. 1792. A few days earlier Washington had suggested

One of the most conspicuous of Jefferson's alterations was the replacement of L'Enfant's title: "Plan of the City, intended for the Permanent Seat of the Government of the United States. Projected agreeable to the direction of the President of the United States, in pursuance of an Act of Congress, passed the Sixteenth of July MDCCXC, establishing the Permanent Seat at the head of Patowmac." This was inexact, repetitive, and geographically incorrect, besides being chronologically outmoded. There was not space within the cartouche for Jefferson to indicate a more appropriate version. The one substituted must, therefore, have been given to Ellicott on a separate piece of paper. In brevity, in precision, and in emphasis, as well as in its reflection of Jefferson's insistence upon territorial status for the Federal District, his altered version was characteristic: "Plan of the City of Washington in the Territory of Columbia ceded, by the States of Virginia and Maryland to the United States of America, and by them established as the Seat of their Government, after the year MDCCC." This, then, was not just a plan of the City intended for the capital, but one for the permanent seat of government as established by authority of the United States. No mention of its site was needed because the map itself defined the location. The substitution also absolved the President of responsibility for having directed the planning. Then, in a change which aroused L'Enfant's indignation, came Jefferson's omission of L'Enfant's name as author of the plan. Ellicott has received blame for this deletion, the more so since it has been assumed that it was he who left intact the passage describing his own role in fixing the base point by celestial observation. But it is Jefferson who must be held responsible both for retaining this description of Ellicott's method and for omitting L'Enfant's name. As for the former, assurance to any prospective investors that the plan could be relied upon for accuracy was a primary consideration. Ellicott, a man of probity and competence, possessed a name and a reputation that would lend credibility to the assurance. Those principally concerned – the contending proprietors – had witnessed his indefatigable labors in running the lines of the Federal District and in surveying the streets and lots of the Federal City, to say nothing of his observations of the annular eclipse of 1791.[187] Retention of Ellicott's name may have been prompted by the need to assure the public that the map was reliable, but it also served as a well-deserved recognition of his services which at this moment, as Washington himself recognized, were essential.

But why should Jefferson have caused the name of L'Enfant to be withdrawn, especially since Freneau's *National Gazette*, Fenno's *Gazette of the United States*, and *Spectator*'s more widely printed essay had already given him public recognition as author of the plan? It might be argued that he did so because he knew others had contributed to L'Enfant's basic design. Washington, for example, had chosen the site of the President's House and almost certainly had made the radical departure which fixed the location of the Capitol – not, presumably, because of an inspiration of L'Enfant but because of the need to placate contending land interests. Jefferson himself, in offering a qualified gridiron

---

similar concessions to gratify L'Enfant, provided he accepted the conditions proposed for his continuance in office and could point out any radical defects or others causing unnecessary delay (Washington to TJ, 22 Feb. 1792).

[187] Ellicott's observations of the eclipse made at Georgetown 2 Apr. 1791 (Ellicott to TJ, 13 Apr. 1801); see Ellicott to Patterson, 2 Apr. 1795 (*Trans.*, Am. Phil. Soc., IV [1799], 48-9).

plan and in providing for parks, public walks, and what proved to be the germinal idea of the Mall, had left a distinct impress upon the plan. But this argument for his deletion of L'Enfant's name, implying as it does an uncharacteristic lack of generosity on his part, does not seem persuasive. Jefferson never attached his own name to any of his architectural drawings, even those of a public nature such as his plans for the City of Richmond and the Capitol of Virginia. Why, then, the suppression which he knew would be highly offensive to L'Enfant and perhaps equally so to his supporters in Georgetown?

The most plausible explanation seems to lie in events of recent weeks in which L'Enfant had been the central figure – his destruction of Carroll's house, his failure to produce a finished map, his conflict with the Commissioners over the Roberdeau incident, his refusal to cooperate with Ellicott by withholding his large working plan, his issuance of what amounted to an ultimatum along with his grandiose proposals, and his almost eager willingness to see both the Carroll and Roberdeau matters proceed to litigation so as to provide him with a public forum for exposing what he considered the malevolent and prejudiced behavior of the Commissioners. In these and other ways L'Enfant had greatly enlarged his already formidable reputation for contentious, erratic, and defiant behavior. He had never been the celebrated figure whom *Spectator* hailed as one whose timely presence in the land was the nation's good fortune, but he was now making it manifest in many ways that his name and reputation if not his unpredictable behavior might in future prove a handicap to the achievement of the main object. Thus, on receiving L'Enfant's elaborate proposals in mid-January, Washington became increasingly aware that the time had come when terms would have to be agreed upon by which L'Enfant could be continued in service. Yet, two days after Ellicott submitted his draft and just as the final crisis approached, he observed the absence of L'Enfant's name on the map. "The Plan I think," he wrote Jefferson, "ought to appear as the work of L'Enfant. – The one prepared for engraving not doing so, is, I presume, one cause of his dissatisfaction."[188] This, in effect, amounted to a presidential directive. Yet Jefferson, very likely with the support of Madison who had been called into the discussions about L'Enfant's future status, prevailed against it, perhaps by persuading Washington on grounds amply fortified by experience that such recognition of the unpredictable L'Enfant might prove politically and otherwise embarrassing. That such an argument must have been employed is suggested also by the next most conspicuous deletion that Jefferson made in the plan. This one affected L'Enfant's cherished ideas as well as his name.

This deletion reached the heart of the matter, for it struck out the entire body of observations by which L'Enfant sought to explain and extol his concept of an undertaking having "a degree of splendour and greatness unprecedented."[189] In these passages he had keyed his references by capital letters to pertinent spots on the map – letters which of course were eliminated along with the explanations. The first item defined the location of the equestrian statue of George Washington which had been authorized by Congress in 1783. Others specified a historic column from which all distances throughout the continent were to be measured; a column to celebrate the beginning of a navy and to "stand a ready Monument to consecrate its progress and Atchievements"; a

[188] Washington to TJ, [22 Feb. 1792].
[189] L'Enfant to Washington, 19 Aug. 1791 (DNA: RG 42).

number of grand fountains for which a constant and abundant supply of water was available from more than twenty-five springs; a grand cascade forty feet high and a hundred yards wide descending the western slope of the hill on which the Capitol would stand; the "Grand Avenue" four hundred feet wide connecting the "Congress Garden with the President's park," with houses on each side; an extensive area near the President's House with lots "best calculated for spacious houses and gardens, such as may acommodate foreign Ministers, &c."; and, eastward of the capital, an avenue a mile long whose pavement on each side would pass under an arched way where shops would be most conveniently and agreeably situated.

But these were chiefly symbolic and ornamental details. An essential element of L'Enfant's plan called for outlying focal points to be built up simultaneously with the whole. These might have become mere paper settlements, but L'Enfant proposed a bold expedient to promote their growth. Fifteen squares would be set aside for the states, with each expected to provide improvements – or to subscribe funds in addition to the value of the land – for symbolic statues, columns, or other ornaments perpetuating the memory of notable figures of the Revolution and of those sages and heroes in whose paths the youth of succeeding generations would be invited to tread. In addition, there would be a Church for national purposes, such as public prayer, thanksgivings, funeral orations, and other notable occasions. This edifice would be assigned to the use of no particular sect, but would be equally open to all. Other squares or areas not appropriated for public use would be made available for all religious sects, as well as for colleges, academies, and societies whose purposes were national in scope.[190]

These and other provisions contained unmistakable potential for controversy, something Washington was most anxious to avoid. Even the proposed equestrian statue of himself could have contributed its share to any public discussion, just as Francis Hopkinson had once satirically suggested putting it on wheels for a peripatetic Congress that would move between alternate capitals.[191] The column intended to celebrate the beginning of a navy and such ornamental

---

[190] Significantly, in his description of the plan when first presented to Washington in August, there were some elements that were later eliminated or modified. For example, L'Enfant had included a site for the Bank of the United States, an institution which had already figured in the controversy over the location of the capital. He had also included a national theater, a market, and an exchange. All of these elements were omitted from the explanatory passages before the plan was submitted to Congress, perhaps because – except for the market and the exchange – of their inherent capacity for generating controversy. See L'Enfant to Washington, 19 Aug. 1791 (DNA: RG 42).

[191] See G. E. Hastings, *Francis Hopkinson* (Chicago, 1926), p. 383. On the day after Washington submitted L'Enfant's plan to Congress, Théophile Cazenove, possibly inspired by the proposal to place it at the crossing of the two main axes west of the Capitol and south of the President's House, described Ceracchi's model of an equestrian statue of Washington surrounded by eight groups of emblematic figures. He praised the artistry of "Mr. Scheraki" and expressed the hope that the national sentiment for the President "parlera plus haut que l'oeconomie" (Cazenove to his Principals, 14 Dec. 1791, Holland Land Company Papers, Archives of the City of Amsterdam). See Ceracchi to Washington, 31 Oct. 1791, enclosing a copy of his memorial to Congress describing the equestrian statue. It would be of bronze and rise 60 feet high and be surrounded by four emblematic figures (DLC: Washington Papers). See also TJ to Commissioners, 9 Apr. 1791; Commissioners to TJ, 11 and 14 Apr. 1791.

features as the grand fountains and the impressive cascade near the Capitol could also have been expected to provoke ridicule as well as debate. In a land where dissident sects had supported and made possible Jefferson's statute erecting a wall of separation between church and state, the proposed national church — even one open to all sects, Christian and other — and the donation of public lands to various denominations would almost certainly have brought on a storm of controversy. But perhaps most politically explosive of all was L'Enfant's proposal for squares to be set aside for the fifteen states, with each defining the use of its own and appropriating public funds for the purpose. Publication of this proposal would have amounted to a virtual guarantee that continuing and divisive debate would take place in every part of the nation, characterized no doubt by the kind of satiric cartoons and newspaper squibs that had ridiculed the removal of Congress to Philadelphia. The specter of this threat to the fixing of the permanent capital on the Potomac, reviving as it doubtless would have the debates of the preceding decade, must surely have caused this part of L'Enfant's plan to fall in that category of omissions which Washington "deemed essential."[192]

While omission of these potentially disruptive passages must have been prompted by such pragmatic considerations, L'Enfant's well-meant effort to have all of the states physically represented at the capital probably inspired a less risky gesture toward national unity — one which had the additional merit of requiring no public funds and of avoiding protracted public discussions. This was the device of naming fifteen of the avenues for the states. It is not known by whom this proposal was advanced, but it would have been characteristic of Jefferson. With Washington convinced a current of opposition in Philadelphia had set "so strongly against every thing that relates to the Federal district that it is next to impossible to stem it," it seems scarcely accidental that L'Enfant's grand avenue between the Capitol and the President's House should have been named Pennsylvania or that the two major avenues northward and southward of it should have honored Massachusetts and New York.[193]

As for the distinctive element of L'Enfant's plan — what he called the divergent avenues — Washington, Jefferson, Ellicott, and the landowners felt in varying degrees that there were too many. Washington had assured the proprietors the preceding June that some of these would be eliminated, and L'Enfant, in presenting his revised plan in August, informed him that alterations had accordingly been made.[194] But now additional changes reflecting such objections took place. Instructions for these were also no doubt given to Ellicott by Jefferson in separate memoranda or in personal consultation, not by pencilled notes on L'Enfant's plan. Only two or three of the latter are discernible on the

[192] Washington to the Commissioners, 20 Feb. 1797 (*Writings*, ed. Fitzpatrick, xxxv, 395).

[193] Washington to David Stuart, 8 Mch. 1792 (same, xxxi, 506). The general distribution of names, of course, allocated those in the northern part of the City to northern states and those below to southern states — though Kentucky Avenue fell to the eastward.

[194] Washington, *Diaries*, ed. Fitzpatrick, iv, 200-1. Ellicott, perhaps knowing that his views were shared by Washington and Jefferson, informed the Commissioners after L'Enfant's departure that he had always thought there were too many diagonals and too many squares. But he apparently assumed that L'Enfant had decided upon the location of the Capitol, which he thought unfortunate (Ellicott to Commissioners, 11 Apr. 1792, DNA: RG 42). See Jennings' criticism of Ellicott for alterations in the plan which he assumed were his (LC *Qu. Jour.*, xxxvi [1979], 274-5).

manuscript – for example, Jefferson's deletion of L'Enfant's designation of the Capitol as "Congress house" and substitution of the proper term.[195] But while alterations in squares, circles, and diagonal avenues and streets were not designated on the manuscript, these may be observed by comparison of the manuscript with the engravings. The most obvious of these changes was the elimination of the boundary of the presidential park running southeastwardly. The entire area from the President's House southward to the Potomac, with the substitution of an eastern boundary running due North-South, was left open to take advantage of the down-river vistas Jefferson had projected in his sketch. In one instance a diagonal avenue was lengthened. In order to balance Virginia Avenue with those named for Pennsylvania and Massachusetts, it was considerably extended, causing it to cut across the Mall and what was then the mouth of the Tiber and to extend on to the western boundary of the City. A few of the shorter diagonals were eliminated, including those reaching into a circle in Georgetown – also eliminated – which L'Enfant, without consulting either Washington or the Commissioners, had persuaded the proprietors to cede to him in trust for the public use. In general, so far as possible, numbers of odd triangular parcels were eliminated and squares where several avenues converged were made less irregular. One circle designated for a fountain was eliminated and the arrangement of the space north of the President's House was altered.[196] But the distinguishing feature of L'Enfant's plan – its divergent avenues and radial streets connecting the proposed outer settlements with the center – was left virtually intact.

Thus altered by Jefferson with Washington's approval, the draft prepared by Ellicott was ready for the engravers. Ellicott himself thought it would serve that purpose better than L'Enfant's large map which had been withheld. The engravers he chose were James Thackara and John Vallance of Philadelphia – both Americans, he informed the Commissioners in an obvious allusion to L'Enfant's choice of Pigalle some months earlier.[197] But that firm could not promise delivery in less than eight weeks. Washington feared the delay might be as many months. Again, looking upon this as "misteriously strange," he suspected that the growing number of opponents in Philadelphia might resort to any kind of subterfuge to keep the capital in that city. Were there any good engravers in Boston, he asked Jefferson? If so, would it not be advisable to procure a copy of Ellicott's draft "(under some other pretext) and send it there, or even to London without any one (even Ellicot's) being appris'd of it?"[198] This astonishing proposal to keep Ellicott in the dark, reflecting as it did the depth of Washington's anxiety, was unnecessary. It so happened that Samuel Blodget, Jr., a wealthy Bostonian recently settled in Philadelphia and now embarking on a bold and speculative career as promoter of the Federal City, had just offered to raise a loan of half a million dollars to purchase lots and erect houses there. After Jefferson had compared Ellicott's draft with L'Enfant's small plan, he engaged Blodget to have it engraved in Boston. Samuel Hill was slow in producing the plate, which was also unsatisfactory in size, in

[195] See the L'Enfant plan of 1791 as illustrated in this volume.

[196] Washington to Commissioners, 20 Feb. 1797 (*Writings*, ed. Fitzpatrick, xxxv, 395); Alexander White to TJ, 8 Aug. 1801.

[197] Ellicott to the Commissioners, 23 Feb. 1792 (DNA: RG 42).

[198] Washington to TJ, 4 Mch. 1792; Washington to the Commissioners, 6 Mch. 1792 (*Writings*, ed. Fitzpatrick, xxxi, 498-9); TJ to Johnson, 8 Mch. 1792.

craftsmanship, and in omitting the soundings Jefferson had insisted upon. He received the plate, together with four proofs, only in mid-summer and at once showed his disappointment in the results. The task of preparing a larger and more professional engraving was then put in the hands of those Ellicott had first employed, Thackara and Vallance. Further difficulties ensued when the printer reported that his press had broken down twice and he was able to run off only one hundred copies at a time. In consequence the improved engraving was not available at the deferred sale in October, but in sending copies abroad through American ministers and consuls, Jefferson insisted that the Hill prints be withheld until they could be accompanied by copies of the larger and better one.[199] It was the superior engraving which by usage and presidential sanction came to be regarded as the first official version of L'Enfant's Plan.

XIII

The predictable end of L'Enfant's connection with the Federal City came late in February after Washington had exhausted every means through intermediaries to avoid such an outcome. When the first approach through Jefferson failed early in January, Washington then urged him to negotiate through L'Enfant's supporter, George Walker. This, too, had no effect. Apparently Washington himself next called in Walker who reported on the 11th and 12th of February that L'Enfant declined putting his ideas in writing, asserting as justification that he had already explained to the President his views concerning the Commissioners. Washington then summoned Jefferson and Madison to a conference on the 16th, when Jefferson's alterations in the plan and his draft letter to L'Enfant were considered. On the 20th Washington received and approved Ellicott's rendition of L'Enfant's Plan and at the same time authorized Jefferson to dispatch the letter to L'Enfant that had been under consideration for almost a week.

This carefully drawn statement of the views of the President made it clear at the outset that he desired L'Enfant's services to be continued. But the unavoidable condition by which Washington's desires could be met had to be stated with unmistakable precision: the law required that if L'Enfant chose to make his services available, he would have to act in subordination to the Commissioners. But, again reflecting Washington's persistent effort to conciliate, Jefferson assured L'Enfant that the Commissioners would receive his proposals, decide on plans to be pursued, and then submit them to the President. In the final analysis, therefore, the one in whom L'Enfant professed to have implicit trust and whose esteem he most desired, would be the final judge of any plans and proposals he might submit. Further, speaking for Washington, L'Enfant could depend upon the Commissioners' good sense, discretion, and zeal in conforming to the judgment and desires of the President. By the same token, the Commissioners could be depended upon to cast into oblivion any disagreeable differences that might have taken place in the past. In brief, Jefferson made clear, he was charged by the President to persuade L'Enfant to continue.

[199] The printer was presumably Robert Scot. See Blodget to TJ, 5 July 1792; TJ to the Commissioners, 11 July 1792; TJ to Blodget, 12 July 1792; Carroll to TJ, 13 and 25 Oct. 1792; Stuart and Carroll to TJ, 5 Nov. 1792; TJ to the Commissioners, 13 Nov. 1792; Commissioners to TJ, 5 Dec. 1792; George Taylor to the Commissioners, 10 Jan. 1793; TJ to Gouverneur Morris, 12 Mch. 1793.

The law, as had been made plain to L'Enfant, much earlier, posed the inescapable condition but, so the conciliatory effort at precision argued, this need not be regarded as an insuperable obstacle to plans that L'Enfant might bring forward. The letter embodying this conciliatory appeal made on behalf of the President was handed to George Walker for conveyance to L'Enfant.[200]

Despite various overtures made by Washington in this and previous communications in an effort to achieve an amicable solution, several days passed with no reply from L'Enfant. George Walker left for Georgetown without indicating how Jefferson's letter had been received. In the meantime, L'Enfant's latest communication, written on the 17th to Tobias Lear but intended expressly for the President, attacked the Ellicott brothers, charged them with destroying the character of his plan with intent to injure his reputation, and sought to place upon them responsibility for his own failure to prepare a map suitable for engraving. Then, repeating the threatening implications of his prior communications, L'Enfant added: ". . . it is the last letter I propose to write interfering in matters relating to the city until some sistem, or arrangement is formed by the President whereby with certainty I may know in what manner in future the business is to be conducted."[201]

Presumably, even in the face of this thinly veiled threat, L'Enfant's flat statement that this would be the last of his communications on the subject until the President met his conditions, Washington dispatched Lear to have a personal interview with L'Enfant and to try to remove some of his misconceptions.[202] But even this direct appeal through Washington's personal secretary was contemptuously rejected. With the President having done everything permitted by the law, by his immense official and personal prestige, and by the ordinary rules of civility, L'Enfant dismissed Lear with the remark that he wished to hear no more on the subject. Washington quite understandably regarded this as an insult to his high office and to himself.[203] It is to be doubted whether Washington had reached such heights of intense anger since Monmouth.

On the 26th of February L'Enfant finally condescended to respond to the conciliatory appeal made by Jefferson in behalf of the President. In a long, belligerent and confused response to that appeal, L'Enfant implied that the President had been mistaken or misled in his views.

Since the President and the Secretary of State were convinced that the Commissioners acted from unbiased zeal, he would be obliged to present evidence to the contrary. What L'Enfant called evidence was a series of unqualified and unsubstantiated charges that the Commissioners were jealous, misled by

[200] TJ to L'Enfant, 7 Jan. 1792; Washington to TJ, 15 and 22 Jan. 1792; TJ to L'Enfant, 22 Feb. 1792; TJ to Walker, 1 Mch. 1792; Walker to TJ, 9 Mch. 1792.

[201] L'Enfant to Lear, 17 Feb. 1792 (DLC: Digges-L'Enfant-Morgan Papers); printed in full in Kite, *L'Enfant and Washington*, p. 140-3.

[202] Washington to Commissioners, 16 Mch. 1792. Most writers on the subject have assumed that Washington sent Lear on the evening of February 26, after he had called an urgent conference with Jefferson, Madison, and Randolph to come to a final solution. This seems most implausible. With L'Enfant having declared he would write nothing and with the passage of several days during which no response was received to Jefferson's letter, it seems highly improbable that Washington, on reading L'Enfant's long, confused, and adamant rejection of that appeal, would have made such a last-minute desperate effort.

[203] Washington to TJ, 14 Mch. 1792.

partisan interests, little addicted to business, and remarkably deficient even in matters falling within their sphere, such as contracts, supplies, and finance. He would not go into the matter of the destruction of the house of Daniel Carroll of Duddington since he had already presented his justification to the President for that action. As for the Commissioners' highly injudicious procedure against Roberdeau, they would have to stand condemned by every dispassionate observer. To this presumption that Washington had not been dispassionate in his approval of the Commissioners' actions, L'Enfant, as on previous occasions, added an unmistakable threat. Since Roberdeau and others were acting under his orders, he, L'Enfant, would have to take his stand with them at their trial. "I shall be obliged," he declared, "publicly to expose these transactions in my own Justification, to [the Commissioners'] dishonour, and to the evident disadvantage of the General Cause." As for himself, he had always acted upon the purest principle, proceeding "steadfastly . . . and disregardless of Clamour, and Cavils." In view of the unfriendly attitude of the Commissioners toward every measure he proposed, he had concluded, despite the President's confidence in him, that he could no longer act subject to their will and caprice. "If therefore," he concluded, "the Law absolutely requires without any equivocation that my continuance shall depend upon an appointment from the Commissioners, I cannot, nor would I upon any Consideration submit myself to it."[204]

Upon receiving this latest and most emphatic rejection of Washington's long series of patient overtures – one that he would not "upon any consideration" withdraw – Jefferson sent it at once to Washington. Then, immediately on reading it in mid-afternoon of the 26th, Washington realized at once that the time for a final decision had arrived. He thereupon summoned Jefferson, Madison, and Randolph to meet him early the next morning, being determined to rest the decision on the best ground and with the best advice. He could not at the moment think of any other to invite to the conference.[205] Although no record of the fact has been found, Washington subsequently included Alexander Hamilton among those invited to the conference. He presumably did this because he knew that Hamilton was a friend and patron of L'Enfant and because he wanted to rest the decision on grounds that would be fair to L'Enfant.

The outcome was a foregone conclusion. The notification to L'Enfant was of course sent by Jefferson at the President's instruction, but, surprisingly, its text was drafted by Alexander Hamilton. The decision was clearly unanimous and one for which there was no alternative: if, as indicated in L'Enfant's response to Jefferson and in his conversation with Lear, L'Enfant absolutely declined acting under the authority of the existing Commissioners, then, despite the President's desire to have L'Enfant continue to serve, the condition stipulated was "inadmissible, and your services must be at an end."[206] On the following

[204] L'Enfant to TJ, 26 Feb. 1792.

[205] Washington to TJ enclosing TJ to L'Enfant, 22 Feb. 1792 and L'Enfant to TJ, 26 Feb. 1792. In suggesting that these documents be transmitted to Madison because he was "better acquainted with the *whole* of this business than any other," Washington obviously meant that, through Daniel Carroll, Madison was better informed of the dispute between the Commissioners and L'Enfant. Since Jefferson had been Washington's closest adviser on all matters pertaining to the Federal City over the past year and a half, this seems the most obvious explanation for what would otherwise have been a tactless and unnecessary remark. The gravamen of the issue was the relationship of the Commissioners and L'Enfant because L'Enfant himself had made it so.

[206] TJ to L'Enfant, 27 Feb. 1792.

day Washington gave L'Enfant his own explanation of the inevitability of the decision. The continuation of L'Enfant's services, he wrote, would have been pleasing if this could have been on terms compatible with law. Every effort had been made to accommodate L'Enfant's wishes to this ineluctable principle, except dismissing the Commissioners, which could not be done on grounds of propriety, justice, or policy.[207] Jefferson immediately informed George Walker that L'Enfant's response to Lear was the unequivocal declaration that he would act on no condition but the dismissal of the Commissioners or his being made independent of them. "The latter is impossible under the law, and the former too arrogant to be answered," L'Enfant had been notified, and "that his services were at an end." Walker's response to this was that the proprietors were much alarmed by "This dismission of Major L'Enfant." Criticizing L'Enfant himself, Walker warned that the affairs of the capital might come into public investigation if means could not be adopted by which L'Enfant could be continued. Walker enclosed a communication from the proprietors with the hope that it would be laid before the President. Jefferson did so and pointedly indicated that "The retirement of Majr. L'Enfant had been his own act."[208] Walker and the proprietors, identifying themselves as such in order to emphasize the depths of their concern, admitted the unreasonableness of L'Enfant's conditions but added that if he could be induced to accept such arrangements as might properly be made, they hoped his seeking to do so would not "deprive forever the City of the services of a man of acknowledged Capacity and Merit, who has already been found highly useful."[209] Jefferson also laid this brief communication before the President. His response was that anyone desiring employment in the Federal City, whether L'Enfant or anyone else, would have to apply directly to the Commissioners.

XIV

What had L'Enfant achieved in his eleven months of service? The record is clear. Both Washington and Jefferson accused him of losing five months because he had not come forward with plans for the public buildings. This was unfair to expect of a man also given responsibility for planning a new capital. The long history of the planning of the Capitol and the President's House would in future prove it so. But what of L'Enfant's first duty? After repeated promises, he had four times come forward with incomplete plans, none of which was suitable for publication. Ellicott was only stating the obvious when he called the "original plan" largely conjectural. Although designed for execution on the base lines established by Ellicott, L'Enfant's plan – an imaginative site plan projected for the future – had to be committed to paper if it were to have the influence he desired. Of the projected plan, finally laid out in 1793, the only part of its concept which can beyond question be attributed to L'Enfant involves what he called the "divergent avenues" cutting across the basic gridiron and resulting in squares, triangles, circles, and other irregularly shaped areas which have been praised beyond measure as if born of inspired genius.[210]

[207] Washington to L'Enfant, 28 Feb. 1792 (*Writings*, ed. Fitzpatrick, XXXI, 488-9).
[208] TJ to Walker, 1 Mch. 1792; Walker to TJ, 9 Mch. 1792; TJ to Walker, 14 Mch. 1792.
[209] Walker to TJ, with enclosures, 21 Mch. 1792.
[210] For a comment on this incomplete conclusion, see the foreword to this volume.

I. George Washington to William Deakins, Jr. and Benjamin Stoddert

GENTLEMEN   Philadelphia Feby. 3d. 1791

In asking your aid in the following case permit me at the same time to ask the most perfect secrecy.

The federal territory being located, the competition for the location of the town now rests between the mouth of the Eastern branch, and the lands on the river, below and adjacent to Georgetown. – In favour of the former, Nature has furnished powerful advantages. – In favour of the latter is it's vicinity to Georgetown, which puts it in the way of deriving aids from it in the beginning, and of communicating in return an increased value to the property of that town. – These advantages have been so poised in my mind as to give it different tendencies at different times. – There are lands which stand yet in the way of the latter location and which, if they could be obtained, for the purposes of the town, would remove a considerable obstacle to it, and go near indeed to decide what has been so long on the balance with me.

These are, first, the lands on the S West side of a line to be run from where the Road crosses Goose creek (in going from Georgetown to the Eastern branch) to the corner of Charles Beatty's lot, including by the plat of Beatty and Orme the house of William Pearce; or, if the whole of this parcel cannot be obtained, then secondly so much as would lie within a line to be run from the said ford, or thereabouts, to the middle of the line of cession which extends from the corner of Beatty's lot, as above mentioned to its termination on Goose Creek. Thirdly, the lands of Mr. Carrol between Goose Creek, the River and Mr. Young, to the same ford of the Creek.

The object of this letter is to ask you to endeavor to purchase these grounds of the owners for the public, particularly the 2d. parcel, but as if for yourselves, and to conduct your propositions so as to excite no suspicion that they are on behalf of the public.

The circumstances of the funds appropriated by the States of Virginia and Maryland, will require that a twelve month's credit be stipulated, in order that they may cover you from any inconvenience which might attend your personal undertakings. – As the price at which the lands can be obtained would have it's weight also with me, I would wish that in making your bargains you should reserve to yourselves a fortnight's time to consider, at the end of which you should be free to be off or on, but the seller not so. This will admit your writing to me and receiving my definitive answer.

A clear purchase is so preferable to every other arrangement, that I should scarcely think any other worthy attention.

I am obliged to add that all the dispatch is requisite which can consist with the success of your operation, and that I shall be glad to hear by post of your progress, and prospect of the accomplishment of this business, in whole or part. I am Gentn. Yr. Most Obed. Hble Ser.   Go: Washington

P.S. That my description of the lands required in the foregoing letter may be more clearly understood, and my wishes further explained, I enclose you a rough (and very rough indeed it is) copy of the ceded tracts, Roads &ca. of Messrs. Beatty and Orme's Survey; adding thereto lines of augmentation. – To obtain the lands included within the lines A B & C is my first wish, and next to that the lands within the lines D E & F; but those within the lines D E, and along the Creek to C, are indispensably necessary: and being not over 250 Acres might, I suppose, be easily obtained. – It ought to be the first essay and I wish to know as soon as possible the result of it, before any others are directly attempted.   GW

PrC (DLC: Washington Papers); entirely in Washington's hand. FC (same). Enclosure not found.

The substance, the style, and the secrecy surrounding the instructions here given to Deakins and Stoddert make it virtually certain that TJ drafted the letter, as he did in other cases involving location of the site of the Federal City. The designation "federal territory," reflecting TJ's preference at this time and later for the name and form of government he hoped would be adopted for the Federal District, and the repeated use of "it's" for the possessive pronoun seem to be conclusive evidence of TJ's hand in the composition. There can be no doubt that Washington and TJ discussed and shared the very secret move here taken and it is very likely that both men went over the composition draft, perhaps with Washington adding the postscript to TJ's text just as he did in other instances involving these hidden negotiations.

II. Thomas Jefferson to George Washington

Objects which may merit the attention of the President at George T.

The Commissioners to be called into action.

Deeds of cession to be taken from the landholders.

Site of the Capitol and President's house to be determined on.

Proclamation completing the location of the territory and fixing the site of the Capitol.

Town to be laid off.

Squares of reserve to be decided on for the Capitol, Presidents house, offices of government, town house, prison, market, public walks.

Other squares for present sale designated.

Terms of sale to be settled. As there is not as yet a town-legislature in existence, and things may be done before there is one to prevent them which yet it would be desireable to prevent, it would seem justifiable and expedient that the President should form a Capitulary of such regulations as he may think necessary, to be observed until there shall be a town-legislature to undertake this office; such capitulary to be indented, signed, sealed and recorded according to the laws of conveyance in Maryland, and to be referred to in every deed of reconveyance of the lots to purchasers, so as to make a part thereof. – The same thing might be effected by inserting special covenants for every regulation in every deed: but the former method is the shortest. I cannot help again suggesting here one regulation formerly suggested, to wit, to provide for facilitating the extinguishment of fires, and the openness and conveniency of the town by prohibiting houses of excessive height, and making it unlawful to build on any one's purchase any house with more than two floors between the common level of the earth and the eves, nor with any other floor in the roof than one at the eaves.

To consider in what way the contracts for the public buildings shall be made, and whether as many bricks should not be made this summer as may employ bricklayers in the beginning of the season of 1792. till more can be made in that season.

With respect to the amendment of the location so as to include Bladensburgh, I am of opinion it may be done with the consent of the legislature of Maryland, and that that consent may be so far counted on, as to render it expedient so to declare the location at once. The location **A.B.C.D.A.** having been once made, I consider as obligatory, and unalterable but by consent of parties, except so far as was necessary to render it practicable by a correction of the beginning. That correction might be lawfully made either by stopping at the river, or at the spring of Hunting creek, or by lengthening the course from the courthouse so as that the second course should strike the mouth of Hunting creek. I am of opinion therefore that the beginning at the mouth of Hunting creek is legally justifiable. But I would advise the location **E.F.G.H.E.** to be hazarded so as to include Bla-

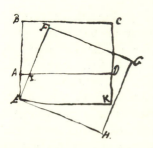

densburgh, because it is a better location, and I think will certainly be confirmed by Maryland. That state will necessarily have to pass another act confirming whatever location shall be made, because her former act authorized the delegates *then* in office to convey the lands. But as they were not located, no conveyance has been made, and those persons are now out of office and dispersed. Suppose the non-concurrence of Maryland should[1] defeat the location **E.F.G.H.E.** it can only be on this principle that the first location **A.B.C.D.A.** was valid and unalterable but by mutual consent. Then their non-concurrence will reestablish this first location **A.B.C.D.A.** and the 2d. location will be good for the part **E.I.D.K.E.** without their concurrence, and this will place us where we should be were we now to complete the location **E.B.C.K.E.** Consequently the experiment of amendment proposed can lose nothing, and may gain, and probably will gain, the better location.

When I say it can lose nothing, I count as nothing the triangle **A.I.E.** which would be in neither of the two locations. Perhaps this might be taken in afterwards either with or without the consent of Virginia.

TH: JEFFERSON
March 11. 1791.

PrC (DLC); faded and partly overwritten (see Vol. 10: 288, note 1). Entry in SJPL reads: "[1791. Mar.] 11. Note of Agenda at the 10 mi. sq."

TJ's suggested alteration in the lines of the Federal District was not approved by Washington (see Vol. 17: 463 and Editorial Note on locating the Federal District, at 24 Jan. 1791).

[1] TJ first wrote "suppose Maryland should insist on an adherence."

III. Pierre Charles L'Enfant to Thomas Jefferson

SIR [Georgetown] Friday March the 11 – 1791.

I have the Honor of Informing you of my arrival at this place where I could not possibly reach before wednesday last and very late in the Evening after having travelled part of the way on foot and part on horse back leaving the broken stage behind.

On arriving I made it my first care immediatly to wait on the mayor of the town in conforming with the direction which you gave me – he appeared to be much surprised and he assured me he had received no previous notice of my coming nor any instruction relating to the business I was sent upon – however nex day (yesterday morning) he made me a kind offer of his assistance in procuring for me three or Four men to attend me in the surveying and this being the only thing I was in need of Every matter as been soon arrenged. I am only at present to regret that an heavy rain and thick mist which has been incessant Ever since my arrival here dose put an insuperable obstacle to my wish of proceeding immediatly to the survey. Should the weather continu bad as there is Every apparence it will I shall be much at a loss how to make a plan of the ground you have pointed out to me and have it ready for the President at the time when he his Expected at this place. I see no other way if by Monday next the weather dose not change but that of making a rough draft as accurat as may be obtained by viewing the ground in riding over it on horsback as I have already done yesterday through the rain to obtain a knowlege of the whole. I rote from the easterne branch towards georgetown up the heights and down along side of the bank of the main river and along side of goose and Rock creeks as far up as thier Springs.

As far as I was able to juge through a thick Fog I passed on many spots which appeared to me realy beautiful and which seem to disput with each other who command In the most Extansive prospect on the wather. The gradual rising of the ground from carrollborough toward the ferry Road, the levell and Extensive ground from thence to the bank of the potowmack as far as Goos Creek present a situation most advantageous to run streets and prolong them on grand and far distant point of view. The wather runing from spring at some distance into the creeks appeared also to me possible to be conducted without much labour so as to forme pounds for watering Every part of that spot. The remainder part of the ground toward george town is more broken. It may affords pleasents seats but altho' the bank of the river betwen the tow creek can command as grand a prospect as any of the other spots its seem to be less commendable for the establessement of a city not only because the level surface it present is but small but because the heights from behind george town absolutly command the whole.

No part of the ground betwen the eastern branch and george town can be say to be of a commanding nature. On the contrary it appear at first sight as being closely surronded — however in advancing toward the easterne branch these heights seem to sink as the waves of a tempestuous sea and when considering the intended city on that grand Scale on which it ought to be planed it will appear that the only height which would unavoidably batter in it, a small town may easily be comprehended in the limit and be of such a one as rendered by a proper menagement in the appropriation of the building that may be there erected a mean of protection and of security.

Such are sir the few remark which I have been able to make in a[1] journey when the badness of the weather much impeded my progress. I therefore hope for your Indulgence in hazarding to comunicate them to you.[2] I have the Honor to be sir with very great respect

Dft (DLC: Digges-L'Enfant-Morgan Papers); with numerous interlineations and deletions, two of which are noted below. The missing RC indicated place of origin, for TJ recorded it in SJL as received on 16 Mch. 1791 from Georgetown.

[1] This word interlined in substitution for "my first," deleted.

[2] L'Enfant first wrote and then deleted: "and beg you will assure the president."

IV. George Washington to Thomas Jefferson

My dear Sir   [16 March 1791]

Enclosed is the last letter I have received from Messrs. Deakins and Stoddart. – What step had I best take to bring matters to a close with Burn's, and by declaring at *once* the site of the public buildings, prevent some inconvenience which I see may arise from the opinions promulgated by Mr. L'Enfont? as much probably from complaisance as judgment. – Yrs,   Go: Washington

RC (DLC); addressed: "Mr. Jefferson": endorsed by TJ as received 16 Mch. 1791. Entry in SJPL reads: "[Mch.] 16. G. W. to Th: J. on site of public buildings. Burns." Enclosure: Deakins and Stoddert to Washington, [11 Mch. 1791], not found but from Washington's response on the 17th (Document v) it is clear that, in addition to conveying information about the will-ingness of the inhabitants of Washington county to cede their lots in Hamburg, their letter indicated that L'Enfant had expressed opinions in Georgetown contrary to what they knew Washington's views to be (Washington to Deakins and Stoddert, 2 Mch. 1791; TJ to L'Enfant, 2 Mch. 1791; see Editorial Note above).

V. George Washington to William Deakins, Jr. and Benjamin Stoddert

Gentlemen   Philadelphia March 17th. 1791

In order to avail the public of the willingness expressed by the inhabitants of Washington county, as mentioned in your letter of the 11th. to sign a paper ceding their lots in Hamburg, on being requested by any person under my direction, I have written the inclosed letter, which if you think it will answer the desired end, you will be so good as to dispatch to them, with the necessary propositions in form. I am aware that by this means it will become known that you are acting for the public: but there will be no reason for keeping this longer secret after my arrival at George town.

With respect to Mr. Burns I will confer with you on my arrival as to what is best to be done in his case, should you not have obtained a cession from him in the mean time.

Dft (DLC: Washington Papers); in TJ's hand except for dateline and docketing in Washington's; at foot of text: "Messrs. Deakins & Stoddard." PrC (DLC); lacks dateline. Entry in SJPL reads: "[Mar. 16.] draught of letter from G. W. to Deakins & Stoddert." Their letter of the 11th has not been found (but see note, Washington to TJ, 16 Mch. 1791, preceding). Enclosure: printed below.

E N C L O S U R E

George Washington to William Deakins, Jr. and Benjamin Stoddert

GENTLEMEN   Phila. March 17th. 1791

On passing thro George town I propose to examine the ground between that town and the Eastern branch, and on that examination to fix on a site for the public buildings. Should there be any circumstances in favour of the ground next adjoining to George town, I foresee that the old town of Hamburg will be a considerable obstacle, as the streets of that will probably not coincide with those which might be proposed for the federal city. On behalf of the public I should be much pleased if the proprietors of lots in that town would voluntarily consent to cede them at such price as may be set on the adjacent lands which have been or shall be ceded. I will ask the favor of you to have application made to them in time for their decision to meet me at George town.

Dft (DLC: Washington Papers); in TJ's hand except for dateline, which is in Washington's; at foot of text: "Messieurs Deakins & Stoddert." PrC (DLC); lacks dateline.

VI. George Washington to Thomas Jefferson

Thursday Evening [17 Mch. 1791]

The P. has just received the enclosed.—He prays Mr. Jefferson to write by tomorrows Post to Majr. L'Enfont agreeably to what was mentioned this morning.

RC (DLC); addressed: "Mr. Jefferson"; endorsed by TJ as received 17 Mch. 1791. Entry in SJPL reads: "[1791. Mar.] 17. G. W. to Th: J. concerning Lenfant." Enclosure not identified.

VII. Thomas Jefferson to Pierre Charles L'Enfant

SIR   Philadelphia Mar. 17. 1791.

Your favor of the 11. inst. has been duly recieved. Between the date of that and your reciept of the present, it is probable that the most important parts of the ground towards the Eastern branch will have been delineated. However, whether they are or not, as the President will go on within two or three days, and would wish to have under his eye, when at Georgetown, a drawing also of the principal lineaments of the ground between Rock creek and the Tyber, you are desired, immediately on the reciept of this, to commence the survey of that part, beginning at the river, and proceeding towards the parts back of that till his arrival. If the meanders of these two creeks and of the river between them should not have been already laid down either by yourself or Mr. Ellicot, it is desired that Mr. Ellicot should immediately do this while you shall be employed on the interior ground, in order that the work may be as much advanced as possible on the arrival of the President, and that you will be so good as to notify this to Mr. Ellicot.[1] – I am with great esteem Sir Your most obedt. humble servt.

TH: JEFFERSON

P.S. There are certainly considerable advantages on the Eastern branch: but there are very strong reasons also in favor of the position between Rock creek and Tyber independant of the face of the ground. It is the desire that the public mind should be in equilibrio between these two places till the President arrives, and we shall be obliged to you to endeavor to poise their expectations.

RC (DLC: Digges-L'Enfant-Morgan Papers); at foot of text: "Majr. L'Enfant." PrC (DLC). FC (DNA: RG 59, DCI).

As originally drafted, this letter had no postscript. It was composed in response to the President's query of the 16th (see Document IV) and shown to Washington on the morning of the 17th. After that consultation, TJ added the postscript with its important reflection of the President's concern over L'Enfant's indiscretion. He then submitted the letter again and in response

the President wrote: "The Postscript to your letter of this morning is quite sufficient for the purpose intended. G.W." (Washington to TJ, [17 Mch. 1791]; RC in DLC; addressed: "[M]r. Jefferson"; endorsed by TJ as received 17 Mch. 1791; not recorded in SJL).

[1] This sentence originally ended with " . . . the President." TJ then crowded in the concluding clause, perhaps at the time he added the postscript.

VIII. Pierre Charles L'Enfant to Thomas Jefferson

SIR   Georgetown Mars the 20 – 1791

On the 17 ult. the change of the weather at last having permitted me to proceed to the Eastern Branch I deed on the afternoon of that day sat about the survey, but the variety of the weather has been such since as has much impeded my progress. I have only been able, to this day, to lay down of that part which lay betwen the eastern branch and the tiber so much as Includ Jenkins Hill and all the water course from round Carroll point up to the ferry landing leaving for a better time some swampy pats which were rendered absolutly impasable by the Eavy rain which overflowing all the low ground determined me to confine myself on the heigh land. – I Expected to have before this day attempted to lay down somme part of those laying betwen the tyber and Rock creek had not a fall of snow and stormy wind which succeeded for these three day past prevented me. I hope to morrow will prove more favorable for me to proceed laying down those part which you prescribe in the letter which I this moment receive From Mr. Ellicot who brought it himself to me and shall according to your direction join his Endeavour to mine in runing as much as possible of the wather course as may serve connect the whole of our differents surveys together. I have the Honor to be with great respect Sir your most humble and most obeident servant,   P. C. L'ENFANT

RC (DLC: District of Columbia Papers); endorsed by TJ as received 24 Mch. 1791.

IX. George Washington to Thomas Jefferson

DEAR SIR   Mount-Vernon March 31st. 1791.

Having been so fortunate as to reconcile the contending interests of Georgetown and Carrollsburg, and to unite them in such an agreement as permits the public purposes to be carried into effect on an extensive and proper scale, I have the pleasure to transmit to you the enclosed proclamation, which, after annexing your counter signature and the seal of the United States, you will cause to be published.

The terms agreed on between me, on the part of the United States, and the Landholders of Georgetown and Carrollsburg are – That all the land from Rock-creek along the river to the eastern-branch and so upwards to or above the ferry including a breadth of about a mile and a half, the whole containing from three to five thousand acres is ceded to the public, on condition that, when the whole shall be surveyed and laid off as a city, (which Major L'Enfant is now directed to do) the present Proprietors shall retain every other lot – and, for such part of the land as may be taken for public use, for squares, walks, &ca., they shall be allowed at the rate of Twenty five pounds per acre. – The Public having the right to reserve such parts of the wood on the land as may be thought necessary to be preserved for ornament &ca. The Landholders to have the use and profits of all their ground until the city is laid off into lots, and sale is made of those lots which, by the agreement, become public property. No compensation is to be made for the ground that may be occupied as streets or alleys.

To these conditions all the principal Landholders except the purchaser of Slater's property who did not attend have subscribed, and it is not doubted that the few who were not present, will readily assent thereto. Even the obstinate Mr. Burns has come into the measure. The enlarged plan of this agreement having done away the necessity, and indeed postponed the propriety, of designating the particular spot, on which the public buildings should be placed, until an accurate survey and subdivision of the whole ground is made, I have left out that paragraph of the proclamation.

It was found, on running the lines that the comprehension of Bladensburg within the district, must have occasioned the exclusion of more important objects – and of this I am convinced as well by my own observation as Mr. Ellicott's opinion. With great regard and esteem, I am dear Sir, Your most obedient Servant,

Go: Washington

RC (DLC); in the hand of William Jackson except for signature; endorsed by TJ as received 5 Apr. 1791 and so recorded in SJL. Dft (DNA: RG 59, MLR); also in Jackson's hand but having numerous deletions and interlineations in Washington's hand. FC (DNA: RG 59, SDC); agrees generally with Dft but varies in phraseology from both Dft and RC. Enclosure: The President's proclamation of 30 Mch. 1791 (see Editorial Note).

For an account of "the obstinate Mr. Burns," and a map showing his holdings see E.M.B. Morganston, "Davy Burnes, his Ancestors and their Descendants," Columbia Hist. Soc., *Records*, L (1948-1950), 103-35.

X. Pierre Charles L'Enfant to Thomas Jefferson

SIR   jeorge town April the 4th. 1791

I would have reproched myself for not having writen to you as regularly as you had desired I Should were it not for Circumstances to which you will I doubt not attribut this Seeming neglect in approving of the considerations which made me give the whole of my time to forwards as much as possibly could be the busines I had to performe. Great as were my Endeavour to that End it Steel remained unfinished at the moment of the President arrival at this place were I could present him no more but a rough drawing in pincel of the severals Surveys which I had been able to run. – Nevertheless the president Indulgent disposition making him account for the difficulties Encontered, I had the satisfaction to see the little I had done agreable to his wish, and the Confidence with which he has been pleased since to Honor me in ordering the survey to be continued and the deliniation of a grand plan for the local distribution of the City to be done on principle conformable to the ideas which I took the liberty to hold before him as the proper for the Establishement being to heigly flatering to my Embition to Fail Exerting the best of my hability. It shall be from this moment my Endeavour to Enswer the president Expectation in preparing those plans and having them ready for the time of his return from the Southern tour.

I Shall in the mean while, sir, beg for Every information respecting all what may in your jugement appear of most immediate importance to attend to as well as relating to Every desirable Establishement which it will be well to forsee although delaying or perhaps leaving the Execution thereof to a natural succession of time to Effect.

The number and nature of the publick building with the necessary appendix I Should be glad to have a Statement of as speedily as possible. And I would be very much obliged to you in the meantime if you Could procur for me what Ever map may fall within your reach, of any of the differents grand city now Existing such as for Example, as London, madry, paris, Amsterdam, naples, venice, genoa, florence together with particular maps of any such sea ports or dock yards and arsenals as you may know to be the most compleat in thier Improvement for notwithstanding I would reprobate the Idea of Imitating and that contrary of Having this Intention it is my wish and shall be my Endeavour to delinate on a new and orriginal way the plan the contrivance of which the President has left to me without any restriction so Ever. Yet the contemplation of what Exist of well improved Situation, iven the parrallel of these with deffective ones, may serve to suggest a variety of new Ideas and is necessary to refine and Strengthen the Jugement particularly in the present instance when having to unite the usfull with the Comodious and agreable viewing these will by offering means for comparing Enable me the better to determine with a certainty the propriety of a local which offer an Extensive field for combinations. I have the Honor to be with great respect Sir your most humble and most obeident servant,

P. C. L'Enfant

RC (DLC: District of Columbia Papers); endorsed by TJ as received 9 Apr. 1791 and so recorded in SJL.

XI. Daniel Carroll to Thomas Jefferson

Sir   George Town Apr. 6th. 1791
The inclosed for Mr. Madison is open for your perusal and information.

The prospect before us respecting the great object of the Seat of Govt. is pleasing at present here. I shall have occasion probably at times to communicate to you what may occur, and shall embrace every occasion of assuring you that, I am, sr. with very great regard & esteem, yr. respectful & obt Servt.   Danl Carroll

P.S. I expect we shall in a few days proceed to take proper deeds.

RC (DLC); endorsed by TJ as received 9 Apr. 1791 and so recorded in SJL. Enclosure printed below.

ENCLOSURE

Daniel Carroll to James Madison

My dear Sir   George Town Apr. 6th. 1791
I have flattered myself with hopes of receiving a line from you with information of the time you woud be at this place. On enquiry however I find it incertain whether you wou'd not turn your face to the East. Shou'd that not be the Case, I claim your promise of letting me know when I may expect to see you, and hope you will arrange matters so as not to be in a hurry to proceed when you get to this place. – I refer you to the George Town paper for some intelligence respecting the Federal City. The Union of the George Town and Carrollsburgh interests, has given a Cast to this business more favourable than

was expected even by its friends. It was a union I have most ardently wish'd for and promoted on public and personal considerations.

I inclose the articles of Agreement, sign'd by all the proprietors of Land within the propos'd limits of the City, so far as to compleat this important object with a Condemnation of a Small piece of land the right of a person insane, and by an accommodation respecting the Lotts in Hamburgh and Carrollsburgh to a Condemnation of some Lotts in each of those places, as the proprietors cannot be come at.

It is propos'd that both these places shall be Subject to be lay'd out again. – At the time the principal proprietors of the two interests agreed to a compromise, it was propos'd and agreed too that the private property shou'd be subject to the same regulations respecting the buildings &ca. as shou'd be thought proper for the public; this was in the hurry omitted to be inserted in the articles sign'd. We hope however to obtain it in the deeds. I wish much to see you & am My dear Sr, allways & Sincerely yr affe. friend & Servt.   DANL CARROLL

Present my compliments to Mrs. House and Mrs. Triste, and assure them of my esteem and regard. – Send the inclosd note to Fenno.

RC (DLC: Madison Papers); addressed: "Mr. Madison – for Mr. Jefferson's perusal." Enclosure: Agreement of the land-owners, "in consideration of the great benefits we expect to derive from having the Federal city laid off upon our lands," to convey in trust to the President or the commissioners or such persons as he should appoint, "by good and sufficient deeds in fee simple, the whole of our respective Lands which he may think proper to include within the lines of the Federal City," on these conditions: (1) the President to "have the Sole power of directing the Federal City to be laid off in what manner he pleases," and to retain any number of squares "he may think proper for public Improvements or other public uses," with only the lots laid off to be equally and fairly divided between the public and the individuals as soon after the city is laid off as may be; (2) the proprietors to receive no compensation for streets, but any land taken for public buildings or any kind of public use to be paid for at the rate of £25 per acre; (3) the woods on the lands to be the property of the owners and any

desired to be left standing by the President to be compensated for at a just valuation in addition to the £25 per acre for the land; (4) each proprietor to have the "Full possession and use of his land . . . untill sold and Occupied by the purchasers"; (5) where the public streets and lots permit, each proprietor to possess his buildings, improvements, and grave yards, paying to the public £12 10 per acre; but where the public streets, lots, and squares do not permit this and it becomes necessary to remove such buildings and improvements, the proprietors to be paid a reasonable value; and (6) none of the stipulations in the agreement to affect lots owned by the subscribers in Carrollsburg or Hamburg (unsigned MS in clerk's hand in DLC: Madison Papers, misdated 13 [for 30] Mch. 1791). The full text of agreement, dated 30 Mch. 1791 and signed by Robert Peter, David Burnes, Uriah Forrest, Benjamin Stoddert, and others, is in Columbia Hist. Soc., *Records*, XXXV-XXXVI (1935), 44-6. Enclosed note to Fenno has not been found.

XII. Thomas Jefferson to Pierre Charles L'Enfant

Sir   Philadelphia Apr. 10. 1791.

I am favored with your letter of the 4th. inst. and in compliance with your request I have examined my papers and found the plans of Frankfort on the Mayne, Carlsruhe, Amsterdam Strasburg, Paris, Orleans, Bordeaux, Lyons, Montpelier, Marseilles, Turin and Milan, which I send in a roll by this post. They are on large and accurate scales, having been procured by me while in those respective cities myself. As they are connected with the notes I made in my travels, and often necessary to explain them to myself, I will beg your care of them and to return them when no longer useful to you, leaving you absolutely free to keep them as long as useful. I am happy that the President has left the planning of the town in such good hands, and have no doubt it will be done to general satisfaction. Considering that the grounds to be reserved for the public are to be paid for by the acre, I think very liberal reservations should be made for them, and if this be about the Tyber and on the back of the town it will be of no injury to the commerce of the place, which will undoubtedly establish itself on the deep waters towards the Eastern branch and mouth of Rock creek; the water about the mouth of the Tyber not being of any depth. Those connected with the government will prefer fixing themselves near the public grounds in the center, which will also be convenient to be resorted to as walks from the lower and upper town. – Having communicated to the President, before he went away, such general ideas on the subject of the town, as occurred to me, I make no doubt that, in explaining himself to you on the subject, he has interwoven with his own ideas, such of mine as he approved: for fear of repeating therefore what he did not approve, and having more confidence in the unbiassed state of his mind, than in my own, I avoid interfering with what he may have expressed to you. Whenever it is proposed to prepare plans for the Capitol, I should prefer the adoption of some one of the models of antiquity which have had the approbation of thousands of years; and for the President's house I should prefer the celebrated fronts of Modern buildings which have already received the approbation of all good judges. Such are the Galerie du Louvre, the Gardes meubles, and two fronts of the Hotel de Salm. But of this it is yet time enough to consider. In the mean time I am with great esteem Sir Your most obedt. humble servt.,   Th: Jefferson

RC (DLC: Digges-L'Enfant-Morgan Papers); addressed: "Majr. L'Enfant at George-town Maryland"; franked; postmarked: "11 AP" and "FREE." PrC (DLC). FC (DNA: RG 59, PCC No. 120).

XIII. Thomas Jefferson to George Washington

SIR   Philadelphia Apr. 10. 1791.

I had the honor of addressing you on the 2d. inst. which I presume would overtake you at Richmond. The present I imagine will not overtake you till you get to Wilmington. Since my last I have been honoured with your two letters of March 31.[1] and two others of Apr. 4. one of which was circular. A copy of this I sent to the Vice-president, and as Colo. Hamilton has asked a consultation on a letter of Mr. Short's we shall have a meeting with the Vice-president tomorrow. I will then ask their advice also on the communication to Colo. Beckwith relative to the supplies to the Indians. – Finding, within a day or two after my letter to you of Mar. 27. that Putnam was gone to the Westward, I detained my letter to him, and applied to Genl. Knox from whom I obtained some information on the Eastern boundary. No official information of the affair of Moose island is received here. Perhaps it is on the road to you. Nor do we hear anything more of the disturbance said to have arisen on the borders of New York. – I have asked the favour of my friend Mr. Madison to think on the subject of the Consular commission to Mr. Barclay. So far as we have done so and conferred together as yet, we are both of opinion it may be used; but we shall think and confer further. I presume your only doubt arose on the constitutional pow-ers to 'supply vacancies' during the recess of Congress. – There was an omission also (which might strike your mind) of the limitation of the commission 'till the end of the next session of Congress.' As the constitution limits them, this clause is always useless; however as it does no harm, it has been usually inserted in the commissions. But in the case of Mr. Barclay such a clause would require a very awkward explanation to the Emperor of Marocco: and as Mr. Bar-clay is apprised of the constitutional determination of his commission it was thought better to omit the useless expression of it. – The acquisition of ground at George town is really noble. Considering that only £25. an acre is to be paid for any grounds taken for the public, and the streets not be to counted, which will in fact reduce it to about £19. an acre, I think very liberal reserves should be made for the public. Your proclamation came to hand the night of the 5th. Dunlap's and Bache's papers for the morning of the 6th. being already filled, I could only get it into Brown's evening paper of the 6th. On the 7th. the bill for the federal buildings passed the representatives here by 42. to 10. but it was rejected yesterday by 9. to 6. in the Senate, or, to speak more exactly, it was postponed till the next session. In the mean time spirited proceedings at George town will probably, under the continuance of your patronage, prevent the revival of the bill. I received last night from Majr. L'Enfant a request to furnish him any plans of towns I could, for his examination. I accordingly send him, by this post, plans of Frankfort on the Mayne, Carlsruhe, Amsterdam, Strasburg, Paris, Orleans, Bordeaux, Lyons, Montpelier, Marseilles, Turin and Milan, on large and accurate scales, which I procured while in those towns respectively. They are none of them however comparable to the old Babylon, revived in Philadelphia, and exemplified. While in Europe I selected about a dozen or two of the handsomest fronts of private buildings of which I have the plates. Perhaps it might decide the taste of the new town, were these to be engraved here, and distributed gratis among the inhabitants of George town. The expence would be trifling.

I inclose you extracts from a letter of Mr. Short's of Jan. 24. One of Jan. 28. has since come to hand, containing nothing but a translation of the letter said to have been written by the emperor to the king of France, but which he suspects to be a forgery, a forged bull of the pope having lately appeared in the same way. He says very serious differences have arisen between the minister of Prussia at Liege, and the Imperial commanding officer there.

I also inclose the debates of the Pennsylvania assembly on the bill for the federal buildings, and the bill itself; and have the honor of to be with sentiments of the most perfect respect & attachment Sir Your most obedient & most humble servt.,   TH: JEFFERSON

RC (DNA: RG 59, MLR); endorsed by Washington. PrC (DLC). For extracts of William Short to TJ, 24 Jan. 1791, see Vol. 18: 610.

[1] Thus in text: actually Washington's letter of 31 Mch. and 1 Apr. 1791.

To Richard Harison

SIR   Philadelphia Apr. 1. 1791.

The recess of Congress now permitting me to resume the subject of my letter of Aug. 12. which was circular, I have the honor of acknoleging the receipt of yours of Sep. 3. and Dec. 4. together with the papers which accompanied the latter. These, with the observations you have been so good as to make on the subject of British debts and property will enable us to give answers as to the proceedings of N. York whenever the British government shall think proper to come forward. – The other object, that of procuring a complete set of the laws of every state for the use of the federal government, is extremely important. I must therefore ask the favor of you to send forward the volumes you mention to have procured in your letter of Sep. 3. and still beg the continuation of your attention to the procuring any others which may be necessary to complete our collection, and of which you are the best judge. Whenever you will be so good as to notify me of the cost of those already procured, and so from time to time of those to be procured, you shall be immediately reimbursed by a bank-post-note. I am in hopes the apparent necessity of having such a collection made and deposited here will apologize to you for the trouble I have asked you to take herein, and pray you to accept my thanks for the same and assurances of the esteem with which I have the honor to be Sir Your most obedt. & most humble servt, TH: JEFFERSON

RC (NNS); addressed: "Richard Harrison esquire Attorney for the U.S. New York"; franked; postmarked: "1 AP"; endorsed. PrC (DLC). FC (DNA: RG 59, PCC No. 120).

TJ's circular of 12 Aug. 1790 to the various District Attorneys asking about possible infractions of the Treaty of Peace by the several states was to prepare himself for discussions of the major problems of American debts owed British merchants and the continued occupation of the western posts which would have to be confronted when diplomatic relations with Great Britain were established. Although TJ's report of 15 Dec. 1790 made it clear that the next step in this direction would have to come from Great Britain, he had every reason to believe at this time that the well-publicized threat of adoption of a navigation act at the next Congress would prompt such a move. Hence, as indicated by the above letter and others of the same date from Lewis and to Read and Sitgreaves, TJ took advantage of the first moment of leisure after the adjournment of Congress to address himself to the subject in a characteristic anticipation of need.

To Benjamin Hawkins

DEAR SIR   Philadelphia April 1. 1791.

At Mrs. Trist's desire I forward to you about a dozen beans of three different kinds, having first taken toll of them as she had done before. They are of the scarlet flowering kinds. This is all I know of them. The most beautiful bean in the world is the Caracalla bean, which though in England a green house plant, will grow in the open air in Virginia and Carolina. I never could get one of them in my life. They are worth your enquiry.

Some friendly Indians have been killed near Fort Pitt lately, on a trading visit, by a party of Virginians. This will not only defeat the measures set on foot for peace, but spread the war wider. There has been also a small fracas on our disputed territory to the Eastward, by our sheriff's levying taxes on the inhabitants of Moose island, who as to that article, wished to be neutrals. – A sale of 1,200,000 acres of land by Mr. R[obert] M[orris] in Europe and the purchase of 5. millions more is the report of the day. Things were going on well in France by the last authentic accounts. The English papers have since killed the D. of Orleans. It seems to be thought that the affairs of Europe are by no means settled, and that the late pacification has only covered a fire which will burst out again immediately. Adieu. Your's affectionately,   TH: JEFFERSON

PrC (DLC). The date is blurred and appears to be 1792, under which date the letter is printed in L & B, XIX, 93-4, but internal evidence and the entry in SJL establish the correct date as given above.

From William Lewis

Philadelphia, 1 Apr. 1791. Acknowledges his of yesterday. Getting laws required by that of 12 Aug. last borders on the impossible, otherwise TJ would have had no further trouble. He sent to TJ at New York by Timothy Hurst a folio volume of all laws enacted in Pennsylvania before Revolution, except those repealed or expired, together with 14 pamphlets containing all between 1 Oct. 1781 and 30 Nov. 1784. These, added to such as TJ had before, were all up to 22 Sep. 1785 and all he could procure. He has no note of what he later sent, but is glad to know they are brought up to 1790 "because I verily believe it to be utterly impossible for any person to collect a complete sett of the Laws in the whole city. I have several times applied to the Printer of our Laws; I have prevailed on the Speaker of the General Assembly to direct the Clerks to search among all the Laws and Minutes of the Legislature and I have applied to several of my Friends . . . most likely to have such as you wanted, and . . . there still remained a Deficiency. If therefore you will please to send me such as you have . . . not bound, I will compleat your sett from my own, have them bound, and my Index copied at the End of them by one of my Clerks. . . . I know of no other way by which you can be supplied, and the inconvenience to me will be but trifling till I can replace them in some way or other. – Although the Index to my sett may not be so good as you might make, it is perhaps better than your Clerks would be able to furnish."

RC (DNA: RG 59, MLR); at foot of text: "The Honble. Mr. Jefferson"; endorsed by TJ as received 1 Apr. 1791 and so recorded in SJL.

To George Read, Jr.

SIR   Philadelphia Apr. 1. 1791.

Having now leisure to resume the subject of my letter of Aug. 12. which was circular, I have the honor to acknolege the receipt of yours of Nov. 4. with the acts therewith forwarded. The making a complete collection, to be deposited at the seat of the general government, of all the laws in force in every state, or which have been in force, is so important, that I must ask a continuation of your attention to the procuring a copy of the collection of Delaware laws printed in 1752. and which some casualty may hereafter perhaps throw in your way. I shall thank you for a copy of those now under revisal whenever they shall appear. On notifying to me the cost of those already sent or hereafter to be sent, you shall be immediately re-imbursed by a bank-post-bill, with many thanks from him who has the honor to be with great respect Sir Your most obedt. & most humble servt,   TH: JEFFERSON

PrC (DLC); at foot of text: "George Read junr. esq. Delaware." FC (DNA: RG 59, PCC No. 120).

TJ had especially asked Read, District Attorney for Delaware and son of the senator from that state, to procure a copy of *Laws of the Government of New-Castle, Kent and Sussex* (Philadelphia, Franklin & Hall, 1752) – a work Read reported as difficult to obtain (Read to TJ, 4 Nov. 1790). But it seems that he was sent two other volumes instead. In response to the above letter, Read said that after diligent effort he had persuaded "a young Gentleman resident in the State" to let him have the first and second volumes of the laws and that he would send the third as soon as it came from the press. He had been obliged to pay three guineas to the owner, he reported, "that being the price which he supposed the new edition ... to be procured at, when published." He drew upon TJ for the sum involved (Read to TJ, 27 Oct. 1791; RC in DNA: RG 59, MLR; endorsed by TJ as received 26 Nov. 1791). The work sent was probably the two-volume edition of *Laws of the Government of New-Castle, Kent and Sussex upon Delaware* (Wilmington, 1763). TJ apparently did not acknowledge Read's acquisition.

To William Short

DEAR SIR   Philadelphia Apr. 1. 1791.

The bearer hereof, Mr. Daniel Ludlow, a merchant and citizen of New York, being about to go to Europe and probably to France, for the purpose of establishing mercantile connections, I take the liberty of introducing him to you. The assurances I recieve of his worth and respectability are such as to merit any services or kindnesses you can render him, and shall be considered as personal obligations on Dear Sir Your affectionate friend & servt,

                                        TH: JEFFERSON

PrC (DLC).

Ludlow, a prominent New York merchant, was obviously unknown to TJ. The assurances of his worth and respectability must have come from Alexander Hamilton, of whom Ludlow had requested letters of introduction to be used in Europe (Ludlow to Hamilton, 23 Apr. 1791, Syrett, *Hamilton*, VIII, 304).

To John Sitgreaves

SIR   Philadelphia Apr. 1. 1791.

Having now leisure, since the adjournment of Congress, to resume the subject of my circular letter of Aug. 12. I have the honour to acknowledge the reciept of your favor of Dec. 6. and to thank you for the papers forwarded with it on the subject of British debts and property. The other object of my letter, that of procuring a complete copy of all the laws in force or which have ever been in force, to be deposited here for the use of the general government is so important as to induce me to ask a continuance of your attention to it. Mr. Iredell's revisal when published will be desireable: and as far as a collection can be made of the *printed* laws omitted in that we shall be glad of it. It is not proposed to go to the expence of manuscript copies. Tho I had asked the favor of you to make this collection, while you were attorney for the district, and you are no longer in this office, yet as you have been so good as to begin it, and I hope it will not be a trouble of long duration, may I hope that you will be so obliging as to go through with it by picking up whatever may occur in print to fill up the omissions of Mr. Iredell's collection. Whenever at any time you will be pleased to notify to me the cost of these articles, you shall be immediately reimbursed by a bank post note. I have the honor to be with great respect & esteem Sir Your most obedt. & most humble servt.,   TH: JEFFERSON

PrC (DLC); at foot of text: "John Sitgreaves esq. N. Carola." FC (DNA: RG 59, PCC No. 120).

In 1787 James Iredell (1751-1799) was directed by the North Carolina legislature to collect and revise all of the acts then in force. The resultant *Laws of the State of North-Carolina*, a compilation rather than the sort of revisal that TJ sought to achieve for Virginia, was published in 1791. Sitgreaves did not comply with TJ's request until 1792, when he forwarded an unspecified number of volumes of North Car-olina laws that presumably included that of Iredell and at the same time promised to collect others subsequent to the period covered by Iredell — 1715 to 1790 (Sitgreaves to TJ, 21 June 1792, missing but recorded in SJL as received on 3 July 1792). In sending him the post bill for these volumes, TJ thanked Sitgreaves for his promise to send subsequent acts, "the completing this collection being extremely desirable" (TJ to Sitgreaves, 12 July 1792; PrC in DLC; FC: DNA, RG 59, PCC No. 120). Sitgreaves evidently did not fulfill his promise, for there is no further correspondence on the subject. TJ, who was more assiduous than any other American of his generation in collecting laws for private as well as official use, acquired a copy of Ire- dell's *Laws* for his own remarkable collec- tion of manuscript and printed statutes (Sowerby, No. 2165).

From George Washington

DEAR SIR   Mount Vernon April 1st. 1791

I have had the pleasure to receive your letter of the 27th. ult. with the papers which accompanied it.

Referring to your judgment whether a commission, similar to that intended for Mr. Barclay, may be given without the agency of the Senate, I return both papers to you signed, in order that the one you deem most proper may be used.

Your opinions respecting the acts of force which have already taken place, or may yet take place on our boundaries, meet my concurrence, as the safest mode of compelling propositions to an amicable settlement and it may answer a good purpose to have them suggested in the way you mention. – Should this matter assume a serious aspect during my absence I beg you to communicate particulars with all possible dispatch.

The most superb edifices may be erected, and I shall wish their inhabitants much happiness, and that too very disinterestedly, as I shall never be of the number myself.

It will be fortunate for the American public if private Speculations in the lands, still claimed by the Aborigines, do not aggrevate those differences, which policy, humanity, and justice concur to deprecate.

I am much indebted to your kind concern for my safety in travelling. No accident has yet happened either from the high-hanging of the carriage, or the mode of driving. The latter I must continue as my Postilion (Giles) is still too much indisposed to ride the journey.

It occurs to me that you may not have adverted to Judge Putnam's being in the Western Country at present. – Perhaps General Knox can furnish you with the maps you want, or they may be found among those that are in my study in Philadelphia.

I expect to leave Mount Vernon, in prosecution of my Southern tour, on tuesday or wednesday next. I shall halt one day at Fredericksburgh and two at Richmond. Thence I shall proceed to Charlestown by the way of Petersburg, Halifax, Tarborough, Newbern, Wilmington, and George Town, without making any halts between Richmond and Charleston but such as may be necessary to accomodate my journey. I am sincerely and affectionately Yours,

Go: WASHINGTON

RC (DLC); at foot of text: 'Thos. Jefferson Esqr. Secy of State"; endorsed by TJ as received 5 Apr. 1791 and so recorded in SJL. Dft (DNA: RG 59, MLR); in the hand of William Jackson, with complimentary close and signature added by Washington. FC (DNA: RG 59, SDC); in Jackson's hand, with complimentary close, signature, and docketing added by Washington.

Washington's response to TJ's information about the bill introduced in the Pennsylvania legislature "for building a federal hall, house for the President &c." (TJ to Washington, 27 Mch. 1791) was construed by TJ to mean that the President intended to retire at the end of his term in 1793. On the basis of this construction, he at once made a determination of his own. On receiving the above letter, as he stated some months later, "my mind was immediately made up to make that the epoch of my own retirement from those labors of which I was heartily tired" (Memorandum of conversations with Washington, 1 Mch. 1792).

TJ was also given another concern at this critical juncture of affairs when he and the President had such harmonious relations and when their views about policy toward Great Britain were so much in accord. This arose from his fear that a serious accident might happen to Washington in his travels southward. On 23 Mch. 1791 the *Gazette of the United States* stated that the President had departed "in a new chariot and six . . . a superior specimen of mechanical perfection." This was an opinion in which TJ certainly did not concur. His concern was indeed so great as to lead him to warn Washington that the coach was top-heavy because of the spring mountings, a condition aggravated by the fact that it was driven by a coachman rather than by a postillion mounted on the near horse of the leaders of the six-horse team (TJ to Washington, 27 Mch. 1791). Washington was not using the splendid coach of state that had been made for him in 1780 by George Bringhurst of Philadelphia. That coach, of which Washington was justifiably proud, had been thoroughly repaired, embellished, and accoutered in 1790 by the Philadelphia carriage makers, David and Francis Clark, but was thought both too heavy and too ornate for the gruelling journey southward over several hundred miles of rough roads. The Clarks were able to provide the President with one of two new coaches presumably brought from England, one of which belonged to the wife of Samuel Powel, mayor of Philadelphia. The latter came to rest at Mount Vernon in 1801 and, being referred to as "Washington's White Chariot," initiated a controversy which should never have arisen. The coach used on Washington's southern journey was sold by the executors of his estate in 1802 and was evidently broken up for souvenirs (Freeman, *Washington*, VI, 296n.; Washington to Lear, 5 Sep. and 14 Nov. 1790; Washington to David and Francis Clark, 17 Sep. 1790, *Writings*, ed., Fitzpatrick, XXXI, 111, 115-16, 154; David and Francis Clark to Washington, 13 Sep. 1790, DLC: Washington Papers; Lear to Washington, 24 Oct. 1790, Microfilm of Feinstone Collection, No. 774).

Washington not only survived the journey without serious accident but actually gained weight. TJ's concern about the safety of the coach, like that he had manifested during Washington's illness the previous year, testifies to his conviction that much depended on the President's life (TJ to Short, 27 May 1790).

From James Maxwell

Norfolk, 2 Apr. 1791. Acknowledging TJ's of 29th ult. On receiving former letter, he at once applied to Major Lindsay who had TJ's six boxes of furniture immediately sent to Richmond and who said Brown acknowledged their receipt and said he had been waiting for wagons to sent them up country. – On receiving TJ's former order for cider, he immediately applied to gentlemen he could rely on at Suffolk, Smithfield, Cabin Point, and Back River "(being the places of greatest reputation for Cyder) and their general answer was that they had made none they could recommend," due to a remarkably warm fall, the apples rotting too fast, and their having to distill them into brandy. But on receiving TJ's last he applied again and hopes soon to be able to send "3 or More Bbls: of Cyder and shall be happy I may get such as may meet with Your Approbation."

RC (MHi); endorsed by TJ as received 19 Apr. 1791 and so recorded in SJL.

To George Washington

SIR   Philadelphia Apr. 2. 1791.

I had the honor of addressing you on the 27th. Ult. since which letters are received of Jan. 24. from Mr. Carmichael, and of Jan. 3. and 15. Madrid, and Feb. 6. and 12. Lisbon, from Colo. Humphreys. As these are interesting and may tend to settle suspense of mind to a certain degree I shall trouble you with quotations from some parts and the substance of others.

Colo. H. says 'I learn from other good authority, as well as from Mr. Carmichael, that all representations of Gardoqui (when minister in America) tended to excite a belief that the most respectable and influential people throughout the U.S. did not wish to have the navigation of the Missisipi opened for years to come, from an apprehension such event would weaken the government and impoverish the Atlantic states by emigrations. It was even pretended that none but a handful of settlers on the Western waters and a few inhabitants of the Southern states would acquiesce in the measure.' – This is the state of mind to which they have reverted since the crisis with England is passed, for during that the Count de Florida Blanca threw out general assertions that we should have no reason to complain of their conduct with respect to the Missisipi; which gave rise to the report it's navigation was opened. The following passages will be astonishing to you who recollect that there was not a syllable in your letters to Mr. G. M. which looked in the most distant manner to Spain. Mr. Carmichael says 'something however might have been done in a moment of projects and apprehension had not a certain negociation carried on on our part at London, transpired, and which I think was known here rather from British policy than from the vigilance of the Marquis del Campo.

Entirely unacquainted with this manoeuvre, although in correspondence with the person employed I was suspected to be in the
secret. This suspicion banished confidence, which returns by slow
degrees. This circumstance induced me to drop entirely my correspondence with G.M. To continue it would have done harm, and
certainly could do no good. I have seen extracts of the President's
letter communicated to the Duke of Leeds, perhaps mutilated or
forged to serve here the views of the British cabinet. I do not yet
despair of obtaining copies of those letters through the same channel
that I procured the first account of the demands of G.B. and the
signature of the late convention.' Colo. Humphreys says 'the minister
had intimations from del Campo of the conferences between Mr.
Morris and the Duke of Leeds, which occasioned him to say with
warmth to Mr. Carmichael now is your time to make a treaty with
England. Fitzherbert availed himself of these conferences to create
apprehensions that the Americans would aid his nation in case of
war.' Your genuine letter could have made no impression. The
British court then must have forged one, to suit their purpose, and
I think it will not be amiss to send a genuine copy to Carmichael,
to place our faith in it's just ground. The principal hope of doing
any thing now, is founded, either on an expected removal of the
count de F.B. from the ministry, in which case persons will be
employed who are more friendly to America, or to the bursting out
of that fire which both gentlemen think but superficially covered.
Mr. Carmichael justifies himself by the interception of his letters.
He has shewn the originals to Colo. H. He concludes his present
letter with these words. 'Relying on the good opinion of me that
you have been pleased to express on many occasions, I intreat you
to engage the President to permit me to return to my native country.'
Colo. Humphreys on the subjects of his justification and return says
(after speaking of the persons likely to come into power) 'Mr. Carmichael being on terms of intimacy with the characters here, is
certainly capable of effecting more at this court than any other
American. He is heartily desirous of accomplishing the object in
view at all events, and fully determined to return to America in 12.
or 18. months at farthest. He has expressed that intention repeatedly.
To be invested with full powers, perhaps he would be able to do
something before his departure from the continent.' In his letter of
Jan. 15. he says 'Mr. Carmichael's ideas are just: his exertions will
be powerful and unremitting to obtain the accomplishment of our
desires before his departure from this country. The task will now
be difficult if not impracticable.' In that of Feb. 6. he says, 'Mr.

Carmichael is much mortified that so many of his dispatches have miscarried. By the original documents, which I have seen in his hands, I am convinced he has been extremely assiduous and succesful in procuring early and authentic intelligence. It is difficult for a person at a distance to form an adequate judgment of the embarrasments to which a public man, situated as he was, is subjected, in making written communications, from such an inland place, and under such a jealous government. He appears disgusted with the country and the mode of life he is compelled to lead. He desires ardently to return to his native land; but he wishes to distinguish himself first by rendering some essential service to it if possible.'

I propose to write to Mr. Carmichael that your absence prevents my asking the permission he desires, that as it is natural he should wish to do something which may make favorable impressions here before his return and an opportunity is now offered him, I will suspend asking his recall till I hear further from him.

Governour Quesada, by order of his court, is inviting foreigners to go and settle in Florida. This is meant for our people. Debtors take advantage of it and go off with their property. Our citizens have a right to go where they please. It is the business of the states to take measures to stop them till their debts are paid. This done, I wish a hundred thousand of our inhabitants would accept the invitation. It will be the means of delivering to us peaceably, what may otherwise cost us a war. In the mean time we may complain of this seduction of our inhabitants just enough to make them believe we think it very wise policy for them, and confirm them in it. This is my idea of it. I have the honour to be with sentiments of the most perfect respect & attachment, Sir, Your most obedt. & most humble servt,

Th: Jefferson

RC (DNA: RG 59, MLR); endorsed by Washington. PrC (DLC). FC (DNA: RG 59, SDC).

The complete texts of Humphreys' letters and that of Carmichael as here extracted are printed above under the dates given. Washington was "astonished . . . exceedingly" at the report of the British misuse of his letter to Morris of 13 Oct. 1789 (Washington to TJ, 13 Apr. 1791). For a comment on the Morris mission and on the new policy toward Spain which Washington had just approved, see Editorial Notes to grouped documents at 12 July 1790 and 10 Mch. 1791, in which the latter attempts an explanation of Gardoqui's misrepresentation of American attitudes and points out that Washington himself differed from his fellow Virginians on this issue. The "originals" of his dispatches which Carmichael showed to Humphreys, thus misleading him and causing TJ in turn to be misled, may have been drafts which were never dispatched (see note to TJ to Carmichael, 11 Apr. 1791; TJ to Humphreys, 11 Apr. 1791). Two such are in DNA: RG 233, House Records, 27A-G 7.4 (claim of the heirs of Carmichael). One of these, undated but ca. Dec. 1789, states that his dispatches to the Secretary for Foreign Affairs were not as detailed as he could wish for "want of a Cypher"; the other, written at some time after TJ took office, promised to write more fully to the Secretary of State. COLO. H and G.M. were David Humphreys and Gouverneur Morris.

TJ had learned of Governor Quesada's invitation only the day before, when Henry Knox in a letter of 1 Apr. 1791 (missing, but recorded in SJL as received the same day) sent him two documents. The first was Quesada's proclamation of 20 Nov. 1790 announcing that settlers to Louisiana and Florida would be obliged to pay their own passages and sustain themselves after arrival; that they must take an oath of allegiance to the King, with lands being granted free in proportion to the number of laborers in the family; that there would be no molestation on account of religion, but only Catholicism could be practised publicly; that every family could "bring their property of whatever kind free of all duties" and would be obliged to take up arms in defense of the province against all enemies; that all settlers should be of good character and be planters or tradesmen who would be beneficial to the province; that grants of land of 100 acres would be made to the head of the family, with 50 acres for "every other person white or coloured" in the family; that those who desired more land and could cultivate it would be given an additional 1,000 acres; that the land should be properly cultivated and the width of each tract should be one-third its length; and that, while the government would reward the industrious planters, it would punish those of a contrary character (Tr in DNA: RG 59, MLR; attested 1 Apr. 1791 by John Stagg, Jr., as a true copy from that on file in the War Office; endorsed by TJ). The second document (Tr also attested by Stagg on the same date and in the same series) was an extract of a letter from Captain Henry Burbeck to the Secretary of War, dated at Fort Tammany, 15 Mch. 1791, saying that he had been instructed to try to stop all Negroes from escaping into Florida; that since the Governor's proclamation saying that protection would not be given to such persons, none had deserted; that lately another proclamation, which he enclosed, had been issued inviting settlers into the province; that in consequence a number of citizens from Georgia and Carolina who were greatly in debt had deserted their creditors, fled to Florida, and put themselves under the protection of the Spaniards; and that a few days earlier he had been at the Spanish garrison on Amelia Island where he saw a number of such families who had "near five hundred Negroes with them."

To William Brown

SIR   Philadelphia Apr. 4. 1791.

Your favor of Mar. 21. came to hand on the 24th. and as it proposed a different statement from mine of the 17th. and I was too much engaged to open the papers on that subject, I have not been able to take it up till now. The interval of the war has been usually settled at 8. years. You state it at 3. months less. This trifle is not worth notice, and besides is lessened by an error of a month in the next article to your prejudice, and by the lapse of time between Mar. 21. and your recieving this. I therefore close with you, and inclose you a bank post bill for ninety seven dollars six cents equal to twenty one pounds sixteen and nine pence sterling @ 4/6 to the dollar, on reciept of which be pleased to give me a full discharge against all persons. Of this indeed I never suspected I had any need, believing firmly my tobacco had covered the whole account. To convince you that I have been grounded in this expectation, and in requiring a higher price for my tobacco I subjoin the weights of 13. hogsheads made on the same plantations which came here a few days ago. They average very near 1300. ℔. nett, and Mr. Lieper has given me 5. Dollars a hundred and the rise of the market till September, which is £14-6 sterl. a hogshead and the rise. He agrees that he never bought better tobacco and such has been it's reputation for 40. years. Add to this that tobacco is now lower here than it was in 1772. However the matter is now settled for better for worse: I am glad of it, and am with great esteem Sir your most obed. humble servt.,

TH: JEFFERSON

PrC (MHi); at foot of text TJ listed numbers and weights of thirteen hogsheads, ranging in net weight from 1,216 to 1,421 pounds and averaging 1,288 pounds.

Brown's letter of 21 Mch. 1791, recorded in SJL as received on the 24th, has not been found. Since Charles Carroll had been chosen by Brown to present his dubious claim, TJ sent the above letter to him unsealed (TJ to Carroll, 4 Apr. 1791). TJ clearly did not believe himself to be the debtor but settled for $97.06 to be free of the claimant, this sum "being agreed to be the balance of old dealings between T. Adams, Perkins, Buchanan & Brown and myself" (Account Book, this date). Brown did not acknowledge the above letter but forwarded the receipt to Carroll (Carroll to TJ, 10 Apr. 1791). Jefferson's calculation of the duration of the war at exactly eight years covered the period from the beginning of hostilities on 19 Apr. 1775 to their cessation on 19 Apr. 1783 (TJ to McCaul, 4 Jan. 1787; TJ to Jones, 5 Jan. 1787).

From Edward Carrington

Richmond, 4 Apr. 1791. Acknowledging TJ's of the 4th ult. enclosing commission as supervisor; he is duly sensible of "this additional evidence of the Confidence reposed in me by the President, and the Senate of the United States, and . . . particularly obliged by the very polite and friendly sentiments" of TJ accompanying the communication. He would have acknowledged this earlier but for several weeks he has been "out of the way of the post office."

The Secretary of the Treasury has forwarded Act with compensations allowed, but, it having just been received, "my opportunity of considering the subject upon the ground of personal advantage has been too slight to give me full satisfaction as to that Point." But his acceptance is decided on another ground – "the frequent suggestions of some amongst us, that the office cannot be safely undertaken. The act has been much misrepresented, and a refusal to accept in the first person appointed, would afford a sanction to these suggestions, which might greatly promote popular discontent." Far from apprehending danger, he is convinced the measure will become more and more satisfactory as it is explained.

RC (DNA: RG 59, MLR); endorsed by TJ as received 9 Apr. 1791 and so recorded in SJL.

In expressing gratitude for TJ's very polite and friendly sentiments, Carrington did not realize that the expressions were those of a form letter sent in identical phraseology to all supervisors in transmitting their commissions: "The President of the United States desiring to avail the public of your services as Supervisor for the District of Massachusetts, I have now the honor of enclosing you the Commission, and of expressing to you the sentiments of perfect esteem with which I am Sir Your most obedient & most humble Servant, Th: Jefferson" (TJ to Nathaniel Gorham, 4 Mch. 1791; FC in DNA: RG 59, PCC No. 120; form letter to all other supervisors and form of commission in same, all dated 4 Mch. 1791). This was the precise form that TJ also employed in sending other commissions, such as those for attorneys, judges, and other officials (e.g., TJ to Stephen Jacobs, 4 Mch. 1791; TJ to Daniel Carroll, 4 Mch. 1791, same). Carrington's opinion that the excise tax would meet with public approval was one shared by Washington, who said that the prediction "vehemently affirmed by many, that such a law could never be executed in the southern states, particularly in Virginia and North Carolina," had been disproved and that in his tour through the South it had been given general approbation (Washington to Humphreys, 20 July 1791, *Writings*, ed. Fitzpatrick, xxxi, 319). Henry Lee, however, entertained a contrary view, and events would in time sustain him (see TJ to Madison, 21 June 1791).

The above letter was evidently the last that passed between TJ and Carrington, whose political leanings brought to an end a relationship that had never been close.

To Charles Carroll

DEAR SIR   Philadelphia Apr. 4. 1791.

Mr. Brown having agreed to settle our balance at £21. 16s. 9d. sterling principal and interest, I have acceded in order to be done with it. Since you have been so good as to be privy to this whole matter, I take the liberty of sending my last letter on the subject, open, through your hands, that you may see that I have been grounded in my belief that I owed nothing, a belief that is still unshaken. Will you be so kind as to take from Mr. Brown a discharge in full for me against all persons, partners, assignees &c. on delivering to him the inclosed letter and bank bill for 97.06. dollars?

We hear that the British parliament is about to allow American grain carried there in *British bottoms* for re-exportation, to be stored rent-free. If so, we must make *British bottoms* lading, with wheat here, pay that rent before they sail in the form of an additional duty, so as to keep our vessels on a level with them. I am told the British merchants are already ordering all shipments of this article to be made in British bottoms. – By the latest authentic accounts, affairs in France were going on most perfectly well. Be pleased to accept assurances of the cordial esteem & respect of Dear Sir Your affectionate humble servt.,   TH: JEFFERSON

Tr (ViU). PrC (DLC); mutilated, so that the end of some lines in right margin are lost and have been supplied from Tr. Enclosure: TJ to Brown, 4 Apr. 1791.

From John Browne Cutting, Tench Coxe, and perhaps Benjamin Vaughan, TJ had received copies of Hawkesbury's report of 1790 which led to the introduction of the Corn Bill and its attempted revision of existing laws (see TJ to Coxe, ca. 28 Feb. 1791; Coxe to TJ, undated and printed in Vol. 18: 461, but prior to the foregoing and both probably written ca. 20 Mch. 1790). TJ's anxiety about the rent-free warehousing clause which he voiced in this and other letters arose from its threat to the American carrying trade and from the desire of farmers and shippers to have direct access to other than English markets. To a much greater extent than he knew at the time, his concern was shared by many both in England and in the United States. Even Lord Sheffield and Sir John Sinclair, whose political views differed widely from his own, pamphleteered against Hawkesbury's bill (for TJ's copies of Hawkesbury's report and various tracts for and against the bill, see Sowerby, Nos. 3591, 3592, 3593, and 3594). Private communications from both sides of the Atlantic warned Hawkesbury of the ill consequences of enactment. Thomas Eccleston, one of the largest grain farmers of Lancashire, strongly protested passage on behalf of the landed interest in that quarter (Eccleston to Hawkesbury, 2 Feb. 1791, BL, Add. MSS. 38226, f. 52). John Ross, merchant of Philadelphia, employed language in writing to a mercantile firm of Liverpool which the Secretary of State could not have used but would have approved: "I sincerely wish . . . that your Parlia[ment] may continue its Career to Curb our Trade from the firm persuasion this Country must re[ap the] fruits in a very short time. You are under Burthens too heavy for you to bear

. . . and we are not only hearty young and enterprizing, but free and independent . . . and amply provided to make its inhabitants the happiest and greatest of any hitherto known" (John Ross to Messrs. Corrie, Gladstone, and Bradshaw, 18 June 1791; MS mutilated and words supplied in brackets; BL, Add. MSS. 38226, f. 242-3; Edgar Corrie was one of Hawkesbury's advisers who railed at the blind and violent "prejudices . . . against warehousing Corn at the Public Expense" and who wrote a reply to Sinclair's pamphlet; Corrie to Hawkesbury, 1 Mch. 1791, BL, Add. MSS. 38226, f. 73-5; for TJ's copy of Corrie's reply to Sheffield, see Sowerby, No. 3593). In sending TJ a copy of his own pamphlet opposing the bill, Sinclair assumed they would be in disagreement. TJ assured him they were not on this particular point, but silently elaborated by sending in return a copy of Tench Coxe's reply to Sheffield's *Observations on the commerce of the American states*, describing it as "written by a very judicious hand" (Sinclair to TJ, 14 May 1791; TJ to Sinclair, 24 Aug. 1791).

Just a week after TJ wrote the above letter the warehousing clause which disturbed him so much was defeated in the House of Commons by a narrow vote. On another vote a month later Sheffield reported to Arthur Young: "We rejected the warehousing clause . . . by the Chairman's Vote only" (Sheffield to Young, 12 Mch. 1791, BL, Add. MSS. 38127). The contest continued for some time but the clause was finally eliminated.

From Joshua Johnson

London, 4 Apr. 1791. Encloses accounts of the Greenland fishery for 1789 and 1790, the former perfect but the latter not, due to incomplete "returns of *success*," though an exact copy of that given parliament; also list of ships fitted out for Southern fishery in 1789, though it is impossible to foretell their success since some may be out two or three years. These accounts procured after "considerable trouble and expence." His next object is to get account of success of outgoing ships for 1790 and incoming for 1789 and 1790. – He has not been unmindful of the cod fishery, but these accounts will be voluminous and as he fears TJ will think expense in getting them too great he will await further orders.

"The situation this Government has placed *herself in*, gives me full employment in watching their Movements, and protecting the citizens of the United States; from the Number of ships put into Commission, and the Scarcity of Seamen, they have been *obliged* to adopt, their usual *arbitrary* System in pressing, and of course some of our Seamen may be laid hold of; tho' *no longer than Saturday*, I received an assurance from the *Duke of Leeds' office*, that any one under that predicament, should be immediately liberated on demand." He has taken precaution to grant protections to crews of American ships that choose them. — He is awkwardly situated as to appointment of agents as he does not know the President's intentions concerning vice-consuls. Consuls for other countries depute agents accountable to them. Since these will be useful during armament of British fleet, he will do the same unless directed to the contrary.

RC (DNA: RG 59, CD); endorsed by TJ as received 21 June 1791 and so recorded in SJL. Dupl (same); in margin: "⅌Colo. Smith in Packett." Enclosures: (1) "A List of Ships on the Greenland and Davis's Straits Whale Fishery 1789," showing a total of 178 ships, 52 of which were from London, which accounted for a total of 553½ whales (the half being credited to *Norfolk* out of Yarmouth) and 5,101 tons of oil (Tabular list of vessels, captains, dates of arrival, and cargoes in DLC: TJ Papers, 53: 9025; another copy in DNA: RG 59, MLR). (2) Similar list for 1790, but incomplete (DLC: TJ Papers, 59: 10111). (3) "A List of Ships, cleared out for the Southern Whale Fishery," between 1 January and 31 December 1789, showing a total of 46 ships, 42 of which were from London, and giving the amount of tonnage and number of men but no cargoes (DLC: TJ Papers, 53: 9024; endorsed by TJ).

To Nicholas Lewis

DEAR SIR   Philadelphia Apr. 4. 1791.

A little intermission of public business on the separation of Congress and departure of the President permits me now to turn my attention for a moment to my own affairs. Finding that *good tobacco* sold tolerably well here, and being assured that the tobacco of the red lands in Albemarle and Bedford were perfectly known here, and commanded always the highest price, I wrote to Mr. Hylton at Richmond to send me 20. hhds. of mine to this place, with a view, if it should be liked, to order the whole crop here before it should be otherwise disposed of. There were at the warehouse but 13. hhds. weighing 16,744. ℔. nett, which was all of the Albemarle tobacco. It arrived here, and on view of it, I have sold that and the whole crop (except the fired part of the Bedford tobacco) for 5. dollars the hundred. Deducting from this the costs of removal it is equal to a sale at Richmond at 27/3 the hundred, and deducting 9d. for credit till Sep. it may be called 26/6 ready money at Richmond. I am now therefore to desire that you will be so good as to dispose of the fired part of the Bedford tobacco where and how you please, (I understood there would be about 14,000 ℔. of it) subjecting the money to my order, that I may divide it between Lyle and Hanson, according to the arrangements taken before I left home; and that you will have the residue hurried to Richmond by every possible exertion, and there be put under Mr. Hylton's orders, to whom I write this day to forward it. I believe that this place will hereafter be the best market for my tobacco especially when it shall be low in Virginia. – Wheat is at a dollar here. I am anxious to hear what money Wilson has furnished, and is likely to furnish. Of the £525 supposed in his hands £125. were destined for Dr. Currie, £160. for Dobson, and £240. to assist the other articles of reciept in paying the general list of debts. The sale of my tobacco here with the 14,000 ℔. to be sold by you will enable me to make the annual paiment of £700. sterl. to Lyle and Hanson punctually. Mr. Eppes has received £100. of Bannister's debt, and paid it to Dobson. He has also paid £110. more to Dobson from the funds of Mr. Wayles's estate: but as I do not wish to get rid of one debt by incurring another, I have begged of him to replace Mr. Wayles's £110. by calling on Wilson for so much out of the £160. in his hands as was destined for Dobson. – I am anxious to hear that the mortgages are taken from Ronald for his purchase, because I am proposing to Hanson and Lyle to assign them over to them, on condition they will consider it as an absolute payment of so much, and give me a discharge.

On enquiry from many farmers I find that Buckwheat unless critically managed, does injury to lands. They consider whiteclover, not too much fed, as the best improver of lands. You know how much I have at heart the preservation of my lands in general, and particularly the hill side where my orchard is, below the garden, and round the North side of the hill. I will therefore repeat my request to have as much white clover seed gathered and bought as can be, and sowed first in the orchards, and then in other places as formerly recommended. Be pleased to present me most affectionately to Mrs. Lewis, and accept assurances of the esteem with which I am Dear Sir Your sincere friend & servt.,   TH: JEFFERSON

P.S. I had forgotten to observe that the warehouse and shipping expences of the residue of the tobacco which is to come here, will be to be paid in Richmond, and will amount to 15. or 16.£. As I would not have Mr. Hylton advance this, I will be obliged to you to have it paid to him out of the fired tobacco to be sold in the country; or if that cannot be ready in time, let it be paid from any other fund, and replaced when that tobacco shall be sold. I write him word that you will place this sum in his hands before he ships the tobacco. If the overseer's shares can be bought so as to make a profit worth the trouble and advances, they might come on with the rest, and the money shall be remitted to any body they please in Richmond by the first post after the tobacco arrives here. In this you will be so good as to do what to you shall seem best.

Th: J.

PrC (CSmH); blurred and slightly mutilated, so that two or three words have been lost and are supplied from Tr (ViU).

Unofficial Diplomacy on Indian Affairs

I. THE PRESIDENT TO THE SECRETARIES OF STATE, TREASURY, AND WAR,
4 APR. 1791

II. THE PRESIDENT TO THE SECRETARY OF STATE,
4 APR. 1791

III. THE SECRETARY OF STATE TO THE PRESIDENT,
17 APR. 1791

IV. MEMORANDUM OF A CONVERSATION BETWEEN
JAMES MADISON AND GEORGE BECKWITH,
[18 APR. 1791]

EDITORIAL NOTE

I have from my arrival in this country endeavoured to preserve peace, and to extend it to friends and neighbours. . . . You may communicate these sentiments, as occasion may require, and your discretion direct.
— *Lord Dorchester to George Beckwith,*
27 June 1790

It will be fortunate for the American public if private Speculations in the lands, still claimed by the Aborigines, do not aggravate those differences, which policy, humanity, and justice concur to deprecate.
— *George Washington to Thomas Jefferson,*
1 Apr. 1791

In the spring of 1791 the governments of Great Britain and the United States became suddenly aware that mounting hostilities between American frontiersmen and western Indians threatened to jeopardize larger interests, thus complicating still further the relations between the two countries. On the initial stage of his journey southward, Washington received the "truly alarming" news of the killing of supposedly friendly Indians in western Pennsylvania by a party of Virginians. He feared, as did Jefferson, that this would defeat peaceful measures and expand the war.[1] Close on the heels of this disturbing incident came reports of clashes between Americans and Canadians at Passamaquoddy and in northern New York.[2] Washington was concerned enough to direct that any further developments of a serious nature be communicated to him with all possible dispatch.[3]

Across the Atlantic, at the same time but for different reasons, Lord Grenville was equally anxious for news. The hostilities between the Americans and the Indians were of "so alarming a nature," he wrote to Lord Dorchester, "as to make me very anxious for further Dispatches." He instructed the Governor General to take every measure possible to promote conciliation.[4] Such prodding was about the last thing that Dorchester needed. From the moment he returned to Canada as viceroy, the critical state of Indian affairs and the fear of an American assault on the British posts had been his paramount concern. The Indians, aggrieved because lands reserved to them by royal proclamation, by treaties, and by the Quebec Act of 1774 had been surrendered to the United States at the Treaty of Peace, were increasingly clamoring for protection against the westward-thronging Americans.[5] Their sense of betrayal and their distrust of British compacts could not be easily assuaged by annual gifts, pensions, and supplies. Because mounting hostilities brought distress to the lucrative commerce in fur, influential traders were equally insistent upon gaining protection for their interests. Far from being able to meet these urgent appeals, Dorchester found himself in a virtually defenseless position. The strongest of the forts depended upon Indian auxiliaries – a dubious reliance at best – and all of them were so weakly garrisoned as to invite the kind of humiliation the British had experienced at Ticonderoga in 1775.

For several years Dorchester had been warning his government of the dangers inherent in a policy of inaction. If the ministry insisted upon retaining the posts, this would require greatly augmented expenditures for additional troops, military stores, and Indian supplies – the last including the guns, knives, and powder that were so essential for hunting but were also useful in war. If adequate defensive measures could not be taken, Dorchester advised that it would be better to destroy the forts than permit them to be seized by American troops. "The most injudicious of all," he bluntly warned his government early in 1787, "is *no resolution*; remaining in an impotent state, and yet holding those places in defiance of powerful neighbors, who have set their hearts upon them; and who sooner or later will certainly assault them, if left in their present situation."[6] From the very beginning of hostilities Dorchester had done his best through orders to the commandants of the posts and to the Superintendent of Indian Affairs to avoid any active support of the Indians, and, if they were unable to

---

[1] Knox to Washington, 27 Mch. 1791 (DLC: Washington Papers); Washington to Knox, 1 Apr. 1791 (*Writings*, ed. Fitzpatrick, xxxi, 259-60); TJ to Hawkins, 1 Apr. 1791.

[2] TJ to Washington, 27 Mch. 1791.

[3] Washington to TJ, 1 Apr. 1791.

[4] Grenville to Dorchester, 7 Mch. 1791 (PRO: CO 42/73).

[5] See A. L. Burt, *United States, Great Britain and British North America* (New Haven, 1940); W. E. Stevens, *Northwest fur trade, 1763-1800* (Urbana, 1928).

[6] Dorchester to Sydney, 16 Jan. 1787 (PRO: CO 42/50; marked "secret"; emphasis in original); same to same, 14 Oct. 1788 (PRO: CO 42/61).

restrain them, to try to confine the hostilities to as narrow a scope as possible. In this prudent course he consistently received the approval of the British ministry.[7]

But fears of aggression, also mingled with professions of peaceable and conciliatory dispositions, were expressed by officials of the American government. When frontier settlers and troops were slain by Indians bearing British knives, tomahawks, and muskets, it was not difficult for those in government or the people at large to believe that this was done with the connivance if not at the prompting of British officials. Such convictions came all the more easily because, as both the President and the Secretary of State knew from official experience, British commanders had utilized Indian marauders during the late war. The two nations were now at peace, but Washington had long suspected that Indian depredations on the frontiers were aided and abetted by British traders and commandants.[8] Such suspicions seemed to be confirmed by the large amounts of arms and supplies delivered to the Indians from British posts just prior to Harmar's expedition. No doubt suspicion would have hardened into conviction had it been known that Grenville, on his own initiative and much to Dorchester's surprise, had almost doubled the requisitioned amount of Indian supplies because of the threat of war with Spain.[9] By the spring of 1791, with various newspaper accounts inflaming the public mind in America and giving concern to the ministry in England, Washington had indeed become convinced that "the notoriety of this assistance has already been such as renders enquiry into particulars unnecessary."[10] Jefferson shared this view. While he privately disapproved of the administration's military strategy, he and the President were fully in accord in believing that peace could be achieved only by the use of force.[11]

With fears of aggression entertained on both sides of the boundary and in the absence of diplomatic relations, both governments moved simultaneously to employ unofficial channels of communication. It is indicative of his awareness of the dangers posed by border clashes that Jefferson himself proposed that Beckwith be used to keep Dorchester from misconceiving American determination to use force if necessary.[12] In this instance as on previous occasions, however, unofficial diplomacy was capable of creating as well as preventing misunderstandings. One of the principal reasons for this lay in the fact that the American Cabinet was deeply divided. Another was that no one in the gov-

[7] Sydney to Dorchester, 5 Apr. 1787; Grenville to Dorchester, 16 Sep. 1791 (PRO: CO 42/50 and 42/21).

[8] In 1786 Washington said he had no doubt that Great Britain was "at this moment sowing the seeds of jealousy and discontent among the various tribes of Indians on our frontiers" (Washington to Knox, 26 Dec. 1786, *Writings*, ed. Fitzpatrick, XXIX, 124). Washington to Gouverneur Morris, 17 Dec. 1790; Washington to Humphreys, 20 July 1791 (same, XXXI, 174, 320).

[9] Dorchester thought "a considerable mistake" had been made, since Indian goods valued at more than £10,000 that were not requisitioned in 1789 had been dispatched (Dorchester to Grenville, 10 Nov. 1790; Grenville to Dorchester, 30 Apr. 1791, PRO: CO 42/72-3). The 1789 supplies arrived just before the Harmar expedition; those not requested came some time afterward.

[10] Washington to TJ, 4 Apr. 1791 (see Document II).

[11] For TJ's opinion of the administration's military operations against the Indians, see Editorial Note and Document II in group of documents at 10 Mch. 1791.

[12] TJ to Washington, 27 Mch. 1791.

ernment was more actively concerned about improving commercial and political relations with England than the Secretary of the Treasury. It is thus not surprising that Hamilton was the first to try to neutralize the threat to his policies arising from hostilities with the Indians.

I

In fact, Hamilton had foreseen the danger on the western frontier and had already taken steps to prevent misconceptions of American aims by the Canadian government. In 1790, unknown to the President and the Secretary of State, he had privately disclosed to George Beckwith the plans for the expedition against the Shawnee and Miami tribes even before Washington had authorized St. Clair to launch the attack. This of course nullified Jefferson's emphatic advice to Washington not to lose the calculated element of surprise by revealing its object to Lord Dorchester in advance.[13] Beckwith reported to Dorchester that Hamilton took this responsibility upon himself "to prevent any alarm at our posts." Hamilton of course knew that Washington had instructed St. Clair to give the commanders of the posts timely though not prior notice of the purpose of the expedition, and he therefore took care to caution Beckwith not to speak of this secret information at the seat of government.[14] Shortly afterwards, prompted by the same concerns, Hamilton assured Beckwith that "The Speeches or declarations of any person whatever in the Indian country . . . suggesting hostile ideas respecting the forts, are not authorized by this government." On the contrary, he declared, Dorchester's conduct toward the Indians was regarded by the administration as strong proof of his disposition to promote harmony and friendship.[15] Reports at this time about the purchase of Indian captives and plunder by traders at Detroit prompted Hamilton to approach Beckwith once more. "I have conferred with Mr. Sargent," he informed the agent, ". . . but on the whole there is no foundation for the idea that you support them in their hostility towards us; however, in the critical state of the two countries, if I may be permitted to say it, prudence would dictate the most pointed instructions to your officers at Detroit."[16] In giving these assurances Hamilton spoke as if for the administration, though nothing

[13] See Editorial Note and Document XI in group of documents on the war crisis of 1790, at 12 July 1790.

[14] Beckwith's undated report of the interview, which probably took place ca. 21-22 Aug. 1790, was received by Dorchester on the 11th of the following month and transmitted by him to Grenville on 25 Sep. 1790 (PRO: CO 42/69). Knox, with Washington's approval, had instructed St. Clair to let the British officers know "at a proper time" that the real object of the expedition was punitive, directed only at the Indians (Knox to St. Clair, 23 Aug. 1790, ASP, *Indian Affairs*, I, 98). When St. Clair did this as early as 12 Sep. 1790, Washington described the announcement as "certainly premature" (Washington to Knox, 4 Nov. 1790, *Writings*, ed. Fitzpatrick, XXXI, 144).

[15] Undated continuation of Hamilton's conversation with Beckwith, enclosed in Dorchester's dispatch to Grenville of 25 Sep. 1790, along with that cited in foregoing note (PRO: CO 42/69).

[16] Hamilton's conversation with Beckwith, [17 Oct. 1790], enclosed in the latter's dispatch to Grenville of 3 Nov. 1790 (PRO: FO 4/12). Beckwith sent a longer version to Dorchester, including the passage quoted above, which Dorchester forwarded to Grenville on 20 Nov. 1790 (PRO: CO 42/72). The text Beckwith sent to Grenville appears in Syrett, *Hamilton*, VII, 111-15.

in the words or actions of Washington and Jefferson suggests that they shared such sentiments or would have condoned their expression, least of all to an unaccredited British agent.

Early in 1791, with increasing evidence of Indian hostilities following Harmar's defeat, Beckwith himself brought to Philadelphia one William Macomb, a Detroit trader, to give Hamilton an account of affairs in the western country in order to explain "any misconceptions, or errors arising from misinformation." This interview was perhaps arranged as a result of the publication of the report by Harmar to the Secretary of War in which he stated that the "villanous traders would have been a principal object of attention" if the Miami village had not been abandoned before the attack — something the traders themselves had feared and complained about to Dorchester.[17] With Beckwith acting as interrogator, Macomb testified that it was impossible the traders could have persuaded the Indians to begin or continue the war since this would be ruinous to their trade. In fact, he asserted, bankruptcies at Detroit would take place as a result of hostilities already begun. He also declared unequivocally that the traders had not purchased Indian plunder and that the government had given out no supplies to them prior to Harmar's expedition, all of them agreeing that the Indians' defeat of Harmar would only cause them to "become infinitely more troublesome" than before. In this interview Hamilton was quoted by Beckwith as saying that the conversation "had given a new light to many things in the western country" and that the argument of the traders' self-interest in promoting peace was "a strong circumstance in opposition to the idea entertained by our military men."[18]

It is clear from this interrogation that Macomb was well-informed and that he shared the concern of leading fur traders about American military expeditions against the Indians. Hamilton asked some pointed questions, but Macomb responded with apparent candor and confidence. The interrogation was recorded verbatim and those present were precisely identified. In both respects this was so uncharacteristic of Beckwith's normal manner of reporting as to suggest that Hamilton may have called in one of the departmental clerks to make a literal transcript of the questions and answers. This would have been a natural and prudent procedure, especially in view of the widespread public suspicions that fur traders and British officers had given support to the Indians. It would also seem appropriate for him to have placed this important testimony before the President and the Secretary of State, especially if he was convinced that it contradicted popular suspicions and also threw much new light on the western situation. Macomb's intelligence was all the more significant because, being volunteered by Beckwith, it represented exactly the kind of conciliatory effort to avoid misunderstandings and miscalculations which Hamilton himself had been making.

Yet, so far as the record reveals, Hamilton did not report to Washington or Jefferson either the nature of Macomb's testimony or the fact that the interview had taken place. He may have deemed it imprudent to make such a report because his attempt of the preceding summer to persuade them that Beckwith had brought proposals of an alliance had failed to convince either Washington

[17] Harmar to Knox, 4 Nov. 1790 (ASP, *Indian Affairs*, I, 104).
[18] "A Conversation: Mr. Hamilton, Mr. Wm. Macomb of Detroit, and Lieutenant Colonel Beckwith," 31 Jan. 1791 (PRO: CO 42/73; text in Syrett, *Hamilton*, VII, 608-13).

or Jefferson, though apparently neither had suspected his deceptive role in that incident.[19] Also, being well aware that both the President and the Secretary of State shared the belief of military officers and the public at large that British officials and traders were actively supporting the Indians with arms and supplies, he was scarcely in a position to bring forward a witness whose testimony, however valid, could be immediately discounted as originating in self-interest — a point that he had himself made in questioning Macomb. But the conclusive reason for believing that Hamilton did not report the meeting is to be found in the consequences of an extraordinary move that he made then or at some other interview in January while Beckwith was in Philadelphia.

II

Early in 1791 Hamilton appealed to Lord Dorchester, through the British agent, to use his good offices in bringing the Indian hostilities to a close. This was a secret and unauthorized overture and it was of course unknown to the President and the Secretary of State. Because of its significance as coming from the Secretary of the Treasury and because it coincided so fully with the desires of both Dorchester and Grenville, Beckwith must have followed his usual practice of recording this conversation with the man who was his chief source of information within the administration. Since Hamilton's appeal was to Dorchester, Beckwith did not send a transcript of the interview to Grenville or even inform him of it. His letters to Dorchester transmitting this important news, together with the record of the interview with Macomb, evidently have not survived.

Yet there can be no doubt either as to the fact or the nature of Hamilton's appeal. The Governor General himself, obviously gratified, went so far as to describe it as a "request of interference with the Western Indians."[20] Dorchester's actions show that while he regarded it as an urgent appeal from an influential member of the Cabinet, he was aware that the request could in no sense be considered as a formal and official act by the American government. Hence, eager as he was to lend encouragement, Dorchester caused his carefully phrased response to be sent to Beckwith over the name of his aide, Henry Motz. There were in fact two responses, both written on 10 February 1791. It is significant that the first of these, more formal than the second, dealt exclusively with the appeal for intermediation, as if Dorchester intended it to be laid before the Secretary of the Treasury or the President himself.

As the first response made clear, Hamilton had told Beckwith that Dorchester's "exertion of his influence with the Western Indians to bring about a general tranquillity, would be considered in the United States as a friendly act, and that there was a disposition to give those Indians security in their lands, and to take every fair method of making them quiet and easy." In restating and replying to this appeal, Dorchester lamented the hostilities and wished "it to be fully understood, that the being instrumental in putting an end to these calamities would give him great satisfaction." He was obliged to point out that the means of effecting an accommodation did not depend upon himself. But, being anxious to make his good offices available, he left the door open by saying

[19] See Editorial Note and group of documents on the war crisis of 1790, at 12 July 1790.

[20] Dorchester to Grenville, 14 June 1791 (PRO: CO 42/73).

that Beckwith – that is, by implication, Hamilton and the administration for which he had presumed to speak – could easily perceive that he could take no step as intermediary "without being authorized by one or the other of the contending parties, nor without being specifically informed of their designs, claims, and pretentions."[21] Stripped of its circumlocution, what this meant was that if Dorchester were given official authorization and a statement of grievances by both parties, he was prepared to act. The next move would have to be made by Hamilton, who had initiated the unofficial communications.

Dorchester's hope that this would lead to more authoritative action is revealed in his second and simultaneous response to Beckwith, which obviously was not meant to be shown to Hamilton though some of its contents were intended for him. In this letter Beckwith was directed to communicate directly to Grenville any matters of interest, "particularly if [Dorchester's] answer to the application for his interference with the Indians should lead to any further steps of consequence in that business." In this response Dorchester also sought to alleviate Hamilton's concern about the ministry's reported coolness toward Gouverneur Morris. In addition he gave emphatic support to Macomb's testimony denying that presents and arms had been supplied to the Indians at the time of Harmar's expedition. He pointed out that the general spirit and language of the Americans had "operated ever since the peace against a connexion between the two countries," but he also recognized that many distinguished characters in the eastern states had "seen through the clouds that have been raised with so much industry to mislead the people."[22] Such a tribute to the policies pursued by Hamilton and others of his persuasion shows how clearly Dorchester grasped the implications of Hamilton's overture. Speaking to each other through a confidential intermediary, he and the Secretary of the Treasury were equally concerned lest the greater interests of the two countries be jeopardized by hostilities with a few tribes of Indians.

Although Dorchester had said in the indirect reply to Hamilton that he could not act until authorized by one or the other of the contending parties, he had no need to resort to circumlocution in seeking such authorization from the Indian tribes. Writing to Sir John Johnson on the same day, he revealed in explicit terms his desire to be fully prepared in case the United States should make an official request that he act as mediator:[23]

I have often expressed my concern at the hostilities between the United States and the Western Indians, and that I should feel great satisfaction in being instrumental in putting an end to these calamities. – I do not know how far this may be in my power; but, wishing to be fully prepared, in case the opportunity should offer, you will be pleased to take such means, as you may think effectual, to learn, with certainty and dispatch, the nature and extent of the specific terms, on which the confederated Indian nations may be disposed to establish a general tranquillity and friendship with the United States, together with the grounds of equity, justice, and policy, on which they may think it expedient, and incumbent on them to insist for their honor

[21] Henry Motz to Beckwith, 10 Feb. 1791 (PRO: CO 42/72). In the letter cited in preceding note Dorchester referred to Motz' two communications as "my answer to the request of interference with the Western Indians."

[22] Motz to Beckwith, 10 Feb. 1791 (same).

[23] Dorchester to Johnson, 10 Feb. 1791 (same).

and interest. – As the Indians themselves are the best judges of the extent of their own confidence, they should be made clearly to understand that there is not the smallest desire to obtain any knowledge of their views and designs, but what they themselves of their own free choice may think proper to communicate.

Both this direct instruction to the Superintendent of Indian Affairs and the veiled language of the message to Hamilton testified to Dorchester's eagerness to seek an accommodation. So, too, did his promptness in forwarding to Grenville copies of his two letters to Beckwith and his directive to Johnson. The extraordinary speed with which news of Hamilton's overture came to Dorchester and was acted upon by him is another indication of the importance that both he and Beckwith attached to it. Beckwith's three letters had taken less than ten days to get from Philadelphia to Quebec in deep winter, a feat that must have required an express riding under urgent orders. This remarkable accomplishment was perhaps equalled on the return of the messenger. If so, Beckwith must have received the responses to Hamilton's appeal about the time that Congress adjourned on the fourth of March.[24]

In view of this speedy exchange, especially since it resulted in such encouragement from Dorchester, it is not likely that Beckwith lost any time in revealing the good news to Hamilton. Precisely when he did so is not known, but the two men certainly met and discussed Dorchester's response some time before Washington departed on his journey southward in mid-March. The timing could scarcely have been less propitious for Hamilton. If there had ever been any possibility that the President and the Secretary of State would support Hamilton's appeal to Dorchester, that possibility had wholly disappeared with Washington's messages to Congress in mid-February disclosing, in very blunt language, the failure of the mission of Gouverneur Morris. This unexpected move, together with the real possibility that Madison's navigation bill retaliating against Great Britain would be adopted at the next session, threw Hamilton and his supporters upon the defensive and made it prudent for him to be very circumspect in his efforts to counteract policies he so consistently opposed.[25] A month earlier Dorchester's encouraging response to his appeal would have been welcome. Now it was an embarrassment for the Secretary of the Treasury who had invited it. Nevertheless, undaunted as always, Hamilton made a characteristic reply when Beckwith disclosed the first and more formal of Dorchester's two replies.

"If the United States were at war with a great or respectable nation," he declared, "a foreign mediation under certain circumstances might be desirable." Even so, while an application for this purpose would be official, it would be made "to the administration at home" and not to any of its officers abroad. But, Hamilton asserted, this was not a war between sovereign states. It was one being waged by the United States against "certain vagrant tribes who cannot

---

[24] In the second communication from Motz to Beckwith of 10 Feb. he acknowledged receipt of his "three letters of January marked K. L. M." The last was Beckwith's report of his conversation with Hamilton and Macomb of 31 Jan. 1791. Hamilton's appeal thus was conveyed over five hundred miles in ten days or less. Dorchester sent copies of Motz' two replies and of the Macomb interview to Grenville on 19 Feb. 1791 (PRO: CO 42/72).

[25] See Editorial Note and group of documents at 15 Dec. 1790.

be considered to be on the footing in which such a system as this would place them, however it may be our interest and policy to close hostilities, which are attended with trouble and expence, and which indeed may be excited by our frontier people, from interested Motives: as an Indian war leads to the spending money in their country as well as to the gratification of their individual resentments." Hamilton presumably did not mention the interest army contractors and land speculators also had in the continuance of the war, but the essential point could not be escaped by pointing elsewhere. Dorchester had believed, with reason, that he was responding to a specific "request for interference." To this Hamilton could only say to Beckwith that "the thing in its existing shape is inadmissible, and I could not submit such a paper to the President's consideration." The significant phrase "such a paper" could only mean that Dorchester had intended his carefully phrased response to be shown to Hamilton and by him to the President. But this presented an insuperable obstacle. For if Washington had seen Dorchester's communication, he would have known at once that his Secretary of the Treasury had initiated the unauthorized appeal for intermediation. Under the circumstances, it was not possible for Hamilton to transmit the information in a garbled and misleading version as he had done with another message from Dorchester the preceding summer.[26] In that case, the Governor General had initiated the exchange and his message could easily be manipulated. In this, not even the most adroit subterfuge could conceal the fact that Dorchester's communication was a response to an overture.

But Hamilton was not one to be intimidated by obstacles. "In suggesting the measure of an interference or rather of a pacific recommendation on the part of Lord Dorchester," he informed Beckwith, "I acted altogether as an individual, and my judgment led me to this from the sense of the thing, and from my conceiving the fomenting such a war could never be any object for such a government as yours. On the contrary I have concluded from those explanations which I have received by your means . . . that your trading interests would be advanced, by the re-establishment of peace." This conveyed nothing not already known, for Dorchester had never assumed that Hamilton's appeal was an act of the government. But despite his acknowledged inability to lay "such a paper" before the President, Hamilton boldly renewed his effort, again professing to speak as a private individual. "We shall take occasion in the course of the summer to mark a pacific disposition to the Indians in general and to those hostile tribes in particular," he assured Beckwith. "We shall suggest to them the idea of a meeting to discuss the objects of difference, and if Lord Dorchester would suggest that a friendly accomodation and settlement would be a pleasing circumstance to your Government, it might have a tendency to promote it: in all this, I do not speak ministerially to you, although I am sure the thing is so, and that it would not only advance this object but tend to forward the establishment of those greater national points which I have frequently touched upon in our different conversations."[27]

In plainer terms, Hamilton at once denied speaking officially and gave assurance that his renewed request for Dorchester to bring his influence to bear for peace represented the official views of the United States government. Even with his initial overture turning out to be embarrassingly effective, he could

[26] See Editorial Note and group of documents on the war crisis, at 12 July 1790.
[27] "Conversation relative to the request of interference with the Western Indians"; enclosed in Dorchester to Grenville, 14 June 1791 (PRO: CO 42/73).

not refrain from repeating it, asking only that Dorchester initiate the suggestion and thus remove the obstacle while screening his own actions from the President. Such was the measure of Hamilton's unremitting efforts to protect those greater national points which lay at the heart of his policy.

III

In London, almost at the moment Hamilton was renewing his appeal to Dorchester, Lord Grenville was also expressing alarm about the threats to larger national interests being posed by the American war against the Wabash and Miami tribes. In urging the Governor General to make every effort possible to promote conciliation, he declared that "no termination of this business could be so desireable as an adjustment of the points in dispute, between the United States and the Indians, under the good offices of this Country." This was not only desirable in itself, but such an intermediation "would probably at the same time afford an opening for settling in some manner satisfactory to both Parties the difficulties which have occurred to prevent the execution of that part of the Treaty of Peace . . . which relates to the cession of the Forts."[28] Even as Grenville considered this hopeful possibility, another instrument in the indirect channels of communication inspired by Hamilton and his supporters gave him an unexpected opportunity to communicate his concern directly to the friends of the British interest in America.

William Stephens Smith, chosen to communicate privately to the British ministry the anxieties aroused by the failure of Gouverneur Morris' mission and the hopes for some evidence of a friendly disposition in commercial matters, had arrived in London early in 1791. For weeks he had sought an interview with someone in the ministry to whom he could communicate the concern that Hamilton and others had long been expressing to Beckwith. Even though he had the backing of influential associates of Robert Morris, he had not succeeded in this effort until, early in April, he was granted a one-hour appointment with Grenville, who was about to become Secretary for Foreign Affairs. No record of this interview exists except that given by Smith himself in a long and unintentionally revealing report to the President – one that he had shown first of all to Hamilton and others.[29] While Grenville presumably granted the appointment primarily because of the importunations of Henry Dundas and others, he was also undoubtedly influenced by his desire to say something to the young American about the dangers arising from hostilities between the United States and the western Indians. He courteously received Smith's prepared statement – a remarkably blunt document warning that France was strengthening "her party in America by acts of kindness and attention to the United States," while England was threatening "much injury to the British interest in America" by her uniform though perhaps unintentional neglect[30] – and then raised some questions of his own about American policy toward the Indians.

According to Smith, Grenville spoke officially as minister when he declared that the question of the military posts would necessarily have to be faced, not only because of the importance of the fur trade and its connection with the

[28] Grenville to Dorchester, 7 Mch. 1791 (PRO: CO 42/73).

[29] See Editorial Note and group of documents at 15 Dec. 1790.

[30] Smith to Colquhoun, 4 Apr. 1791 (MiU-C: Melville Papers; quoted above Vol. 18: 257).

commercial and manufacturing interests of the nation, but also because of the government's obligation to secure the frontiers and protect the natives. Grenville spoke candidly about American policy toward the Indians and its effect on British interests. He stated that he was very sorry to see the United States

> . . . carrying on vigorous hostile measures against them, that in consequence of it the British trade had been very materially affected the two Last seasons and would be totally destroyed unless some measures were taken to accommodate the differences, and that he had noticed some observations in a late American Paper tending to impress the public mind with opinions that England countenanced the depredations of the savages on the frontier.

Grenville emphatically denied that the ministry had given such countenance. He then declared it to be his duty to convey the impression "that England could not with perfect indifference, see a tribe of Indians extirpated, from whom they received such advantages, without endeavouring in some degree to shelter them, but he flattered himself with the expectation that America would not proceed to too great extremities on this subject."

This could be taken as an expression of confidence or as a thinly veiled warning, but it caused Smith to bristle. However, he restrained himself sufficiently to convince the minister – so he reported to Washington – that, on unresolved questions arising from the Treaty of Peace, the United States would not be reluctant to enter into any investigation of matters "properly presented by a minister, always having in view the perfect fulfilment of the treaty, in such a manner, as not to bear hard upon either of the contracting parties, or to wound the feelings of either in the explanation" of its articles. Having voiced this noncommittal opinion, Smith then presumed to show Grenville where the true interests of England lay. He was certain that the minister sent to negotiate with the United States would soon be convinced that the fur trade of England would be benefited rather than otherwise if British troops were withdrawn within their own proper limits. Indeed, if this were done, the rapidly increasing settlements on the American side of the boundary would be an advantage to English commercial and manufacturing interests. As for the security of the frontiers, such a removal was "absolutely invited" because then "the troops and inhabitants of the United States together with the intermediate lakes would form an insurmountable barrier between the . . . belligerent Savages and the British inhabitants both of upper and lower Canada." This audacious suggestion conveniently overlooked the need expressed by Grenville for governmental protection to the Indians, but Smith was not daunted by the realities a responsible minister would have to take into consideration. He went so far as to suggest that such a withdrawal of the troops might possibly be a point on which "America would not object to enter into a defensive treaty with England so far as it would relate to mutual security against the savages on the frontiers of their respective territories." This conjecture, which perhaps had its origin in the hope entertained by Hamilton and others for treaty connections going beyond mere commercial arrangements, also overlooked existing political realities in Smith's native land.

So, too, did his expression of confidence that his countrymen would accept Grenville's assurance that the ministry "totally discountenanced the Idea of at present aiding and abetting those Savages in the depredations they had made and were still making on some defenceless parts of the American frontier." As for Grenville's concern over newspaper comments to the contrary, Smith thought it understandable that a printer might feel justified in making such observations "when in the packs and Haversacks of Indians slain in battle were found British provisions, it was impossible to ascertain, whether it was procured from the British Garrisons in way of Barter for furs or other articles of Indian traffic or whether it was supplyed for the purpose of enabling them to carry on the expedition." Smith nevertheless expressed the belief that "those at the head of the Government of America entertained too favourable an opinion of the Characters of the present administration of England to suspect them of being capable of countenancing such inhuman and barbarous incursions." Departing still further from reality, Smith was confident Grenville "would not suspect any gentlemen in the administration of the Government of America could for a moment believe that the ministers of England could be capable of such measures." The President and the Secretary of State must have read this inaccurate expression of their views less with surprise than with a better understanding of what the young diplomat had unwittingly revealed about himself and those whom he represented.

In reporting to Washington, Smith was careful to emphasize that he had spoken as an individual and that the views he had expressed to Grenville could in no sense be regarded as a commitment of the United States. This was assuredly true. But in justifying American policy toward the Indians, he employed language as if on behalf of the nation:[31]

> . . . I felt no diffidence in asserting that the Conduct of the United States towards the Savages on their frontiers was more strongly marked with Justice and benevolence than that of any power who had ever yet come in contact with them . . . that America was willing at any period to make peace with them upon those express principles, which had produced tranquility to every other nation and of which she might rather boast than be ashamed. And that she felt herself perfectly competent not only to chastise, but even if necessary to extirpate, still she would blush at exercising that power unless authorized by necessity and preceded by every conciliatory proposal that Justice could warrant or the Circumstances of the case admit of. That the war was by no means sought on our part, but being forced into it for the security of our settlements and protection of our frontiers, and in every stage of its progress continuing to hold in one hand mild and honourable terms of peace, while the other grasped the necessary weapons of war, it would be rather probable that we should pursue the war, with vigour, untill peace the only object of it, was obtained, rather than check those exertions under any apprehension that England would side with the Savages in such a cause. . . . but even if [the ministry] should take the side hinted at, America could only act one uniform part Viz. being satisfyed of the Justness of her Cause and the integrity of her intentions she doubtless would pursue her measures with firmness and leave the event.[32]

On its face, this expression of a determination to prosecute the war regardless of what Great Britain might do seemed closer to the views of Jefferson than to those of Hamilton. But coupled as it was with Smith's hope that the American position as the victim of aggression would be better understood if "Ministers

[31] Smith to Washington, 6 June 1791 (DLC: Washington Papers).
[32] Thus in MS.

would but give themselves the trouble of Examining the question," it accorded with the appeals that Hamilton and others had been making indirectly through Beckwith for more than a year. Presuming to express his conception of the views of the administration and indeed of the American people, Smith had actually spoken in behalf of those whom the ministry regarded as friends of "the British interest in America."

Thus when the unofficial envoy arrived in New York in June, he did not tarry but "went immediately to communicate the particulars to the Secretary of the Treasury" and then – in a long, inaccurate, and unintentionally revealing statement – to the President. George Beckwith did not see Smith as he passed through the city, but the general scope of the interview with Grenville was communicated to him "by a Member of the Senate, whose dispositions are in favor of an English interest."[33] Beckwith was gratified with this information because it accorded so well with assurances of the friendly disposition of the ministry that he had given some individuals on his recent trip to New England. On his return to Philadelphia on June 15, Beckwith found that Hamilton thought Grenville's comments generally "pleasing and promising," especially because of the ministry's reported determination to discuss the commercial concerns of the two countries and to establish formal diplomatic relations. To this Hamilton made a single exception. "One part only of this conversation was of a nature to excite some regret, or rather of doubt on our part," he declared. This fly in the ointment was Grenville's comment about American policy toward the Indians. Hamilton observed that this comment could be taken either as a mere expression of desire that the hostilities be brought to an end because of the injuries done to British trade, or as a warning that the British government might be forced by its obligations to intervene on the side of the Indians.

The latter interpretation Hamilton found ominous and disturbing. He declared to Beckwith that it was to the interest of the United States to make peace whenever this could be done on proper terms, but that, under existing circumstances, there was no alternative but to prosecute the war because the very safety of the nation required it. "I should feel extremely concerned," Hamilton told Beckwith, "if a fair prospect of a happy settlement of the affairs of the Two Countries, should be prevented by a consideration of this comparitively trivial nature."[34] This was what Smith reportedly had said to Grenville, but without the force born of Hamilton's deep and abiding concern lest his policies be jeopardized. That concern could scarcely have been alleviated when, a month later, the President – employing the words of the Secretary of State – informed Smith that his communication corresponded very exactly with what had been learned of British intentions as a result of the mission of Gouverneur Morris. Both the indirect appeal to Dorchester through Beckwith and that to Grenville through Smith had ended in failure.

[33] Beckwith to Grenville, 14 June 1791 (PRO: FO 4/12).

[34] "Conversations with a gentleman in Office, Philadelphia June 15th. [i.e., 16th] 1791"; enclosed in Beckwith to Grenville, 31 July 1791 (PRO: FO 4/12; text in Syrett, *Hamilton*, VIII, 475-7). Beckwith sent Dorchester an account of this conversation which contained both more and less than that sent to Grenville, though both are in agreement on that part of the interview discussed here (this version includes the code number for Hamilton and is dated 16 June 1791; enclosed in Dorchester to Grenville, 27 July 1791; PRO: CO 42/83).

While these surreptitious communications were in progress, Washington unintentionally complicated matters still further for Hamilton by authorizing the use of Beckwith to convey a very different kind of message. This quite unexpected move originated in a suggestion made by Jefferson, who, in informing the President of disturbing clashes between Canadians and Americans on the northeastern boundary, urged a policy of restraint but, if necessary, a resort to force. "If the idea meets your approbation," he wrote Washington, "it may prevent a misconstruction by the British, of what may happen, should I have this idea suggested in a proper manner to Colo. Beckwith."[35] He did not explain what he meant by a proper manner. But in view of his scruples against discussing public matters with Beckwith, he obviously intended any communication to be indirect, unofficial, and yet sufficiently authoritative to convince the British agent that it reflected the government's position. Washington agreed that this might be "the safest mode of compelling propositions to an amicable settlement."[36]

But as he reflected further upon the matter, border incidents in the East must have appeared far less exigent than those arising from the Indian war in the West. On that extended field the danger of miscalculation seemed to increase daily. Washington's suspicion that the British were aiding the hostile tribes had long since become conviction, providing further proof of the ease with which either government could misconstrue the intent of the other in the absence of diplomatic relations. Thus, three days after approving Jefferson's suggestion, Washington proposed that a far bolder, even peremptory, message be sent to Quebec. Assuming British aid to the western Indians to be so notorious as to make inquiry needless, he thought the national interest demanded that Dorchester be required to put a stop to such unwarranted interference in American affairs. Indeed, he went so far as to authorize Jefferson to convey this message directly — that is, officially as Secretary of State — or through Beckwith, whom he thought "peculiarly designated to be the channel of an indirect intimation." But, having begun his letter on the dubious assumption that Jefferson would concur in thinking the national interest compelled such a blunt approach, Washington concluded by authorizing him to act or not as he judged best.[37]

Since these instructions were directed solely to the Secretary of State and expressly authorized him to make the decision, Jefferson was not required to seek the advice of other members of the Cabinet. Nevertheless, he did so, perhaps because soon thereafter he received the President's circular directing the heads of departments to consult on any serious and important matters that might arise during his absence.[38] In accordance with Washington's directions, Jefferson immediately sent a copy of his letter to the Vice-President.[39] Hamilton

[35] TJ to Washington, 27 Mch. 1791.

[36] Washington to TJ, 1 Apr. 1791.

[37] Washington to TJ, 4 Apr. 1791 (Document II).

[38] The President to the Secretaries of State, Treasury, and War, 4 Apr. 1791 (Document I).

[39] TJ to John Adams, 8 Apr. 1791: "Th: Jefferson presents his respects to the Vice-president of the U.S. and has the honor to inclose him the copy of a letter from the President, just now received" (RC in MHi: AM; FC in DNA: RG 59, PCC No. 120;

assumed that he had done so and on Saturday the 9th of April informed Adams he had just received a letter from William Short which he wished to submit to the Vice-President and the heads of departments in accordance with the President's instructions. He asked Adams to name a time and place for the meeting as early as convenient.[40] This had the effect, perhaps unintended, of making the Vice-President the surrogate of the President in convening the Cabinet. But no one understood better than John Adams that the constitutional function of the Vice-President was confined to the legislative branch and that, in the American system, the Secretary of State was deemed to rank first among the heads of departments. His response to Hamilton that afternoon explained that he and Jefferson had "accidentally" met before he had had an opportunity to reply and that they had "agreed to propose a meeting at [Jefferson's] House at two o'clock on Monday the 11th," if this should be agreeable to Hamilton and Knox.[41] Protocol was thus accommodated, but in fact the meeting had been initiated by Hamilton. In informing Washington of Hamilton's desire for a consultation, Jefferson said that he would seek his colleagues' advice on the proposed communication to Beckwith about supplies to the Indians.[42]

What transpired in the Cabinet discussion on the 11th can only be deduced from incomplete and unsatisfactory evidence. Hamilton's official letters to Washington of the 10th and 14th announced only the question he proposed to lay before the Cabinet, the reasons for it, and the decision that had been reached.[43] Jefferson's account, set down a week after the event, left much unrecorded. This was in part because Hamilton and Knox had withheld essential information and in part because Jefferson himself deemed it best not to disclose to Washington all that he knew. His account of the discussion concerning the proposed message to Beckwith omitted a significant fact which, if revealed, would surely have called for an explanation involving his colleagues, thereby perhaps leading to further disharmony in the Cabinet. Full disclosure would also have limited his own choice of alternatives.[44]

---

enclosure: Washington to TJ, Hamilton, and Knox, 4 Apr. 1791; Tr in MHi: AM, in Remsen's hand; Document I).

[40] Hamilton to Adams, 9 Apr. 1791 (Syrett, *Hamilton*, VIII, 258).

[41] Adams to Hamilton, 9 Apr. 1791 (same, VIII, 258). TJ later recalled that he had invited them to dine with him to discuss the matter (including the Attorney General) and that this was the only time the Vice-President "was ever requested to take part in a cabinet question" (TJ's introduction to the *Anas*, written in 1818 but obviously with Washington's letter of 4 April 1791 before him). In this he erred: Adams' opinion was sought several times.

[42] TJ to Washington, 10 Apr. 1791.

[43] Hamilton wrote Washington on the 11th about another matter and said there was nothing else "worth communication" save that given in his official dispatch enclosed therewith. This has been taken to mean that Hamilton wrote a second and official dispatch on the 11th which has not been found (Syrett, *Hamilton*, VIII, 277). But the enclosure in the letter of the 11th was obviously the official one of the 10th announcing his intention to discuss Short's authority to negotiate loans and giving his reasons for removing the limitations upon it. Hamilton's letter of the 14th merely recorded the action of the Cabinet on the matter. Washington's response identifies the substance of both letters clearly but erred in saying that the first was written on the 11th, thereby creating the impression that Hamilton wrote two letters on that date (Syrett, *Hamilton*, VIII, 270-1, 277, 288, 330).

[44] TJ to Washington, 17 Apr. 1791 (Document III). The omission, discussed below,

The first topic discussed by the Cabinet concerned the letter which Hamilton had just received from William Short and which, in order to have "certain measures . . . taken upon it," had been his declared reason for initiating the meeting.[45] That letter announced the successful negotiation of a loan for 2.5 million guilders, the agreement of the Amsterdam bankers to accept a reduction in their commission, the very favorable position of American credit, and the possibility held forth by the financiers that, if war did not break out, the United States might be able in little more than a year to borrow from 9 to 12 million guilders, provided each loan should amount to 3 million guilders and be followed by the next whenever a favorable moment occurred.[46] On the day before the Cabinet met, Hamilton informed Washington that he intended to lay Short's letter before his colleagues and ask them to consider whether it would not be expedient to authorize a further loan of 3 million guilders. To the President, but not to the Cabinet, he urged that Short's instructions be changed so as to allow him to open successive loans for the same amount after the preceding one had been fully subscribed and without waiting for the President's sanction.[47] In brief, Hamilton was proposing that the precautionary limitations on Short's authority be removed. It was Jefferson himself who had suggested these restrictions the preceding year in order to enable the American agent to act more independently of the "wonderfully dexterous" bankers of Amsterdam. Washington had incorporated the limitations almost verbatim in his instructions to Hamilton.[48] But now, convinced by the Secretary of the Treasury that the favorable rating of American credit, the repayment of the debt to France, the need to avoid any delays in borrowing, and the prudence of taking advantage of favorable conditions in the money market of Amsterdam required that Short be given wider latitude, the President agreed to Hamilton's suggestion.[49]

There was in fact no reason why the Secretary of the Treasury should have asked his colleagues to discuss the question of altering or removing restrictions in instructions given by the President to himself. Nor indeed was there anything in Short's letter calling for immediate action or possessing the sort of urgency Washington had had in mind in directing the heads of departments to consult together. That letter did not expressly request confirmation of the loan Short had so successfully negotiated. Nor did it in any way suggest that the restrictions on the power to borrow funds be altered. Short was so little concerned on this point he did not deem it necessary to inform the Amsterdam bankers that his authority was limited to loans of a million dollars and that no new one could be made until the preceding one had been expressly confirmed by the President. Indeed, as he expressed it to Hamilton, "I do not think it probable that this latter condition will occasion any delay as a confirmation may generally be received in three months."[50] In fact, on the advice of both bankers and brokers, Short had agreed to postpone opening the loan for more than two months when conditions promised to be especially favorable for American credit.

---

pertains to the initial decision authorizing Knox to approach Beckwith on the proposal made by Washington.

[45] Hamilton to Adams, 9 Apr. 1791 (Syrett, *Hamilton*, VIII, 258).
[46] Short to Hamilton, 2 Dec. 1790 (same, VII, 175-87).
[47] Hamilton to Washington, 10 Apr. 1791 (same, VIII, 270).
[48] For TJ's suggested restrictions, see his opinion on fiscal policy, 26 Aug. 1790.
[49] Washington to Hamilton, 7 May 1791 (Syrett, *Hamilton*, VIII, 330).
[50] Short to Hamilton, 2 Dec. 1790 (same, VII, 175-87).

Under these circumstances, it is clear that the sense of urgency which led to the calling of the Cabinet meeting did not arise from the nature of Short's communication. Presumably by employing arguments he had set forth in his letter to the President, Hamilton was able to persuade his colleagues that immediate authorization should be given Short to negotiate a new loan for 3 million guilders even though this would violate Washington's instructions both as to the required sanction and as to the amount of the loan.[51] Jefferson's explanation to the President is explicit and revealing. The Secretary of the Treasury, he reported, placed before them Short's letter announcing the contract for the new loan and the reasons for postponing its execution until February 1791. Jefferson then quoted Short as saying there was every reason to hope the loan would be filled before it would be possible for him to receive the President's orders to open another, though these would be awaited according to his instructions. But this, Jefferson pointed out, would have caused a month's delay and those attending the meeting felt that if Washington himself had known the circumstances, he would have approved the decision. One of the reasons for their unanimous determination, he added, was that Short himself had "pressed the expediting the order that the stoppage of the current in our favor might be as short as possible."[52]

But the fact is that no such request and no such call for an urgent decision can be found in Short's letter. Far from pressing for the President's confirmation of the loan, Short had said that he anticipated no delay in the business because of the need to await it. Clearly, Jefferson could not have made such a categorical statement if he had actually read Short's letter or if he had heard it read. The most plausible explanation for the discrepancy between what Short had actually written and what Jefferson reported is that the Secretary of the Treasury had placed the letter before the group – a manuscript of about five thousand words in Short's minuscule, crabbed hand – and instead of reading it had summarized its contents, not as they were but as he wished them to be. Only in this manner, it seems, could he have created the sense of urgency that led to the unanimous decision on a point Short had not even raised. Only thus, it would appear, could that letter have been used as a justification for convening the Cabinet.

The supposition seems to be supported in the contrast between Hamilton's urgency in expediting the loans and his lack of it in making use of funds thus acquired. Thenceforth Short's complaints, both to the Secretary of the Treasury and to the Secretary of State, concerned the embarrassments he lay under and the needless interest costs incurred because of long-delayed instructions from the Secretary of the Treasury as to the disposition of funds already borrowed. While Hamilton had convinced the Cabinet that it was important and indeed urgent to authorize another loan, Short felt that it would have been advantageous if the one just negotiated had been delayed an additional two or three months in order to save the double interest charges on unused funds in the bankers' hands and on that paid on the debt to France.[53] But the most compelling reason for assuming that Short's letter was deliberately manipulated

[51] Hamilton to Short, 13 Apr. 1791; Hamilton to Washington, 14 Apr. 1791 (same, VIII, 280-2, 288).

[52] TJ to Washington, 17 Apr. 1791 (Document III).

[53] See, for example, Short's rather blunt comment to Hamilton, 3 June 1791 (Syrett, *Hamilton*, VIII, 412-25), and his even stronger expressions in his letter to TJ of 2 May 1791.

and misrepresented by Hamilton is that there was another object brought up for discussion by the Cabinet which had not been announced and which, for private concerns if not for the national interest, did possess an undeniable urgency. In brief, all of the evidence suggests that the letter from Short was only the excuse, not the real reason that prompted Hamilton to call for a meeting of the Cabinet.

V

The second subject discussed by the Cabinet was brought forward by the Secretary of War, undoubtedly by prearrangement with the Secretary of the Treasury and almost certainly at the instigation of others in and out of government. It, too, had an ostensible as well as a real but hidden object, with the Indian war in the West providing cover for schemes of land speculation in the East. While Indian affairs fell within the province of the Secretary of War, Henry Knox at this moment would not seem to have needed any new undertakings to divert him from his primary duty of prosecuting the war. He was already helping sow the seeds of St. Clair's defeat by the favoritism shown to William Duer as the concealed contractor for army supplies and by his and Duer's involvement in equally surreptitious negotiations for the purchase of two million acres of Maine lands.[54] In addition to this grandiose real estate venture, he was simultaneously pursuing his old and illusory dream of tapping the agricultural wealth of the upper Connecticut valley by means of a canal connecting it with the Charles river at Boston.[55] Knox was a man of energy and enterprise, but in the spring and early summer of 1791 his official duties suffered neglect because of the time and attention he gave to personal concerns. He also allowed private interests to affect public policy in the matter that he brought up for discussion on April 11th.

Jefferson's account of the Cabinet meeting merely states that the Secretary of War expressed his apprehension, based on "some suspicious circumstances," that the Six Nations might be induced to ally themselves with the hostile tribes in the West. Knox therefore proposed that Colonel Timothy Pickering be sent on a mission to the Iroquois to confirm them in their neutrality. This of course would require a tribal convocation and, as Knox optimistically calculated, would cost "about $2000."[56] If the Secretary of War explained what the suspicious circumstances were, Jefferson did not record the fact. To Washington, writing on the day before the Cabinet meeting, Knox indulged in speculation based on unconfirmed rumor. He knew that the President considered the recent

[54] See Editorial Note and group of documents at 10 Mch. 1791 for a discussion of these activities of Knox, Duer, and their associates.

[55] Less than a week before the Cabinet meeting Knox announced to William Smith, Isaiah Thomas, and William Hull his plan to undertake the experiment. He acknowledged that many people thought his scheme Utopian, but on 8 Apr. 1791 he engaged John Hills, a bibulous and imprudent man, to make the survey. By the end of summer David Cobb encouraged Knox to believe that the canal would yield a conservatively estimated $90,000 per annum in tolls or 10% net profit (Knox to Smith, Thomas, and Hull, 7 Apr. 1791; Articles of Agreement with Hills, 8 Apr. 1791; Hills to Knox, 30 June and 3 Aug. 1791; Henry Jackson to Knox, 21 Aug. 1791; David Cobb to Knox, 10 July and 4 Sep. 1791, all in MHi: Knox Papers).

[56] TJ to Washington, 17 Apr. 1791 (Document III).

murder of friendly Indians on Beaver Creek a truly alarming outrage that might widen the war.[57] Now, only a few days later, Knox reported that a party of Delaware Indians had killed nine men, women, and children on the Allegheny within twenty miles of Fort Pitt and had so blindly enraged the inhabitants as to endanger The Cornplanter and his party of Senecas. Had this happened, Knox concluded, the war unquestionably would have become general. "Affairs being so critical with the Six Nations," he informed the President, "I have judged it adviseable to assemble them as soon as possible, in order to brighten the Chain of Friendship and prevent all jealousies. . . . I shall lay this subject before the Vice-President and the other heads of departments tomorrow for their approbation."[58]

The Vice-President and heads of departments accepted Knox' recommendation and authorized the appointment of Pickering as agent to assemble the Six Nations. But in fact they had no alternative. For two days earlier Knox had dispatched an express to Pickering at Wilkes-Barré directing him "instantly" to send runners to assemble the chiefs "as early as possible . . . *to brighten the Chain, and to remove all Causes of jealousies and discontents.*" He accompanied this with an advance of $250 to pay for messengers; announced that he would at once procure blankets, strouds, and other gifts; and authorized contracts for the Indians' rations during the treaty. He directed Pickering to repair immediately to Philadelphia for instructions and declared that the holding of the treaty was "perfectly compatible with the orders and designs of the President of the United States."[59] The assertion served to cloak the business with executive authority but, as Knox well knew, this was not a precise or accurate statement. All members of the Cabinet were aware – as the President had reminded them only a few days since – that every expedient to achieve a peaceful settlement with the western tribes and to retain the friendship of those in treaty with the United States, the Six Nations included, had been adopted and was already in operation. Early in February The Cornplanter, head warrior of the Senecas, had pledged his nation's friendship and had gone on a mission of peace to the western tribes at the behest of the government. Just a month later Colonel Thomas Procter had been dispatched on an urgent and secret mission for the same purpose, with instructions to invite The Cornplanter and other leaders of the Six Nations to join him on the journey. It was immediately thereafter that Knox set in motion his unauthorized plan having the same ostensible purpose.

Even if a sudden emergency had required such action, the Secretary of War

[57] Washington to Knox, 1 Apr. 1791 (*Writings*, ed. Fitzpatrick, XXXI, 259).

[58] Knox to Washington, 10 Apr. 1791 (DLC: Washington Papers). Six weeks later Knox informed Washington that the Vice-President and heads of departments had concurred with him in the need to hold the treaty, not only to prevent the Six Nations from joining the western tribes, "but if necessary to induce them to join the troops of the United States" (Knox to Washington, 30 May 1791; same). But this was an afterthought. Pickering's instructions to this effect were not drawn up until two weeks after the Cabinet meeting. Knox told the agent to be particularly importunate in urging the Six Nations to send some of their young warriors to join St. Clair's army. He did this on his own authority but declared it to be the expectation of the President. Besides enlarging the object of the treaty beyond what the Cabinet had authorized, this directive, as it turned out, would have had a disastrous effect if Pickering had not prudently ignored the instruction.

[59] Knox to Pickering, 9 Apr. 1791 (MHi: Knox Papers; emphasis in original).

had just received positive instructions from the President as to the course to be followed in such cases. Washington's letter to the heads of departments, which arrived in Philadelphia just the day before Knox gave his urgent instructions to Pickering, was a positive delegation of authority to members of the Cabinet to consult on any serious and important matters arising during his absence. Washington had assured the Cabinet that he would approve all proper and legal actions taken in accordance with this directive. The meaning was unmistakable: his sanction would extend only to those measures decided upon by the heads of departments in consultation.[60] Yet Knox disregarded this directive and acted precipitately on his own authority. In placing the matter before his colleagues he was asking not that the question be decided by them but that the action already taken be approved. Whether he informed his colleagues of the fact or not, the first step leading ultimately to the lighting of the Iroquois council fire on the Tioga river in mid-summer, at an assemblage of more than a thousand sachems, chiefs, warriors, women, and children, had already been taken and was irreversible. The Secretary of War, on his own authority, had committed the government.

In doing so, Knox could not have been unaware that a delay of only two days for consultation with the heads of departments could scarcely have affected the declared purpose of the treaty one way or the other. Under the best of circumstances, the Six Nations could not be assembled for several weeks. The wagons carrying the bales of presents and supplies would not be dispatched for another month. Pickering was obliged to come to Philadelphia for instructions and these, instead of being delivered in three days as Knox had promised, were only handed to him three weeks after the Cabinet met. The actual circumstances ruled out the need for such haste as to cause Knox to disregard the President's instructions and to pre-empt his colleagues' right to decide whether a real emergency existed. All of the evidence suggests that he did so not because the situation was critical or even pressing, but because disapproval by the Cabinet would have thwarted the undisclosed purpose of the treaty. This presumably was a risk he dared not take.

One indication that something other than the public interest was involved is to be found in the manner in which Knox offered the agency to Pickering. The ostensible object had been set forth in explicit terms in Knox' official letter of the 9th of April directing him to convene the Six Nations. On the same day, Knox appealed to Pickering's friend and business associate, Samuel Hodgdon, to convey a private message which could not be put in the official communication. Hodgdon, a Philadelphia merchant and land speculator, complied in veiled but revealing terms. "On the business being explained to me," he wrote Pickering, "I hesitated not to declare you would undertake the business proposed. This will bring you to the City . . . *where every thing will be fully understood.* I know it will call you from your agricultural pursuits at an unfavorable season — but sir, in my opinion, the object in view will warrant you doing it. I consult your interest — you must determine finally."[61] With Knox' official communication in hand, Pickering could scarcely have mistaken his partner's hint about private interest and the need for an understanding concerning some object beyond the declared intent of keeping the Six Nations

---

[60] Washington to the heads of departments, 4 Apr. 1791 (Document I).
[61] Hodgdon to Pickering, 9-10 Apr. 1791 (MHi: Pickering Papers; emphasis added).

neutral. He accepted at once, dispatched runners to the Six Nations, and set out for Philadelphia. During the next two weeks he consulted Hodgdon, saw Knox almost daily, and conferred with the Massachusetts land speculator, Oliver Phelps.[62] The presence of the latter in Philadelphia provided another indication that the official reason for the treaty was not the real one. The fact is that Knox had given no supporting evidence, not even confirmed rumors, to show that the Iroquois were threatening to abandon their recent pledge of neutrality and friendship. As the official charged with oversight of Indian affairs, he could not have been unaware that the attitude of those tribes was just the opposite of what he had led the President and the Cabinet to believe it was.

It was as a league of peace that the Iroquois Confederacy, by astute diplomacy, the rule of law, and the use of force, had sustained its hegemony through three centuries over a vast region bounded by the Hudson, Illinois, and Ottawa rivers and the Chesapeake Bay. But the *pax iroquoia* was now at an end. Its nations were disunited and its people scattered. Under the multiplied pressures of the expanding frontier, the increasing interference of land speculators using political influence to achieve their ends, and the emergence of rivalries among such leaders as Joseph Brant and The Cornplanter, the Iroquois tribes not only did not pose a threat at this juncture but gave every indication of their desire to remain at peace and under the protection of the United States. Indeed, the situation was such that the Indians, while accepting the invitation to the treaty with some eagerness, were puzzled as to why the chain so recently brightened needed to be burnished again. They were not alone. Even Pickering, in extending the invitations, had anticipated that the Six Nations would wonder for what special purpose they were being assembled. He could only assure them that the pledges of peace recently given were pleasing to the government and that openness and frankness would characterize this further renewal of friendship.[63]

On the day after the Cabinet meeting, Knox informed Governor Clinton of the approaching treaty and appealed to him to use every influence upon Joseph Brant, the Mohawk leader, to induce him to make a journey of conciliation to the western Indians – the very task which the government had just persuaded Brant's arch-enemy, The Cornplanter, to undertake.[64] The appeal was unfor-

[62] Pickering's journal, 20 Apr.-20 July 1791 (MHi: Knox Papers). Six weeks earlier Pickering, anxious as he was for a federal appointment, had declined the more remunerative post of quartermaster general on the western expedition – an assignment for which he was far more experienced than in treating with Indians. In that case, too, Knox had offered special inducements through Hodgdon. The contrasting responses indicates that in the present instance Pickering clearly grasped his partner's meaning. On the offer and declination of the post of quartermaster general, see Knox to Lear, 25 Feb. 1791 (DLC: Washington Papers); Knox to Pickering, 25 Feb. 1791; Hodgdon to Pickering, 25 Feb. 1791; and Pickering to Hodgdon, 28 Feb. 1791 (all in MHi: Pickering Papers). Early in 1791 Knox had also offered Pickering the post of superintendent of the Six Nations, but this too he declined (Pickering to Washington, 15 Jan. 1791; Dft in MHi: Pickering Papers; RC in DLC: Washington Papers). For an excellent account of the decline of the Iroquois Confederacy and Robert Morris' ultimate success in purchasing the lands, see Anthony F. C. Wallace, *The death and rebirth of the Seneca* (New York, 1970), p. 149-83.

[63] Pickering to the Sachems, Chiefs, and Warriors of the Six Nations, 17 Apr. 1791 (MHi: Pickering Papers).

[64] Henry Knox to George Clinton, 12 Apr. 1791 (Tr enclosed in Knox to Pickering, 2 May 1791; both in MHi: Pickering Papers; ASP, *Indian Affairs*, I, 168).

tunate. Clinton, who had reasons of his own for supporting the kind of policy Brant had recently described as "the wicked mode of calling them out in separate nations or parties," had just advised the President to resist all attempts to reunite the Six Nations. Assuming correctly that Knox was aware of this, Clinton began his response with the icy supposition that Washington had given the Secretary of War discretionary power to pursue a contrary course. In words that revealed the warmth of his opposition to the action Knox had taken, he restated his own conception of what the government's Indian policy should be:[65]

> I observe, with some regret, that the measure of attempting a convention of the whole six nations, hath been resolved and acted upon. It cannot be unknown to you, that those nations are at present disunited by private animosities; that there subsists not among them, mutual intercourse and confidence, sufficient to lead to a general combination, or to effect (without the interposition of the agents of the United States) a general congress . . . even for the purpose of deliberation; that this disunion produces impotency and secures inaction, and that, if we should revive their importance, by renewing their union, we may give power and vigor, which we cannot with certainty direct, and over which we shall, with much trouble and expence, have an uncertain control.

Unable to refute the arguments, Knox could only respond that the decision to convene the Six Nations had appeared highly expedient at the time. But, offended by Clinton's vigorous opposition, he asserted that the authority for making the decision rested upon his statutory responsibility for Indian affairs and, he added incorrectly, on the President's instructions to him "upon the objects of the department during his absence." In an apparent effort at conciliation, he informed Clinton that the Senecas had been the principal object in view and that the tribes to the eastward had been invited only because it would have been impolitic to omit them.[66] This of course was not the explanation Knox had given to the President and to the Cabinet. But it is evident that his strategy was directed at the Senecas not merely because they were the main body of the Six Nations, but also because their influence was essential to the real purpose of the treaty. This is made clear by events which took place before and after the Cabinet meeting.

Late in 1790 The Cornplanter and other Seneca chieftains journeyed to Philadelphia and delivered a remarkably blunt speech to the President charging the government with failure to keep its promise to make the Indians secure on their lands.[67] Oliver Phelps was also in the capital at that time, engaged in negotiations with Robert Morris concerning the pre-emption rights to about four million acres of land stretching westward to Lake Erie from Morris' earlier purchase from Phelps and Gorham of more than a million acres. Shortly after Phelps' departure, The Cornplanter and his entourage made another speech to the President openly accusing Phelps of fraud and of defaulting on the terms

[65] Clinton to Knox, 27 Apr. 1791 (ASP, *Indian Affairs*, I, 167); Clinton to Washington, 1 Feb. 1791 (DLC: Washington Papers).

[66] Knox to Clinton, 11 May 1791 (ASP, *Indian Affairs*, I, 168).

[67] The Cornplanter, Half-Town, and Great Tree to the President, 1 Dec. 1790 (Tr enclosed in Knox to Pickering, 2 May 1791; MHi: Pickering Papers; text printed in ASP, *Indian Affairs*, I, 206-8).

of the purchase made of the Six Nations in 1788.[68] Having just dispatched William Temple Franklin to England to sell those lands, Robert Morris was understandably concerned over this public challenge to the validity of the title and the adverse effect it could be expected to have upon negotiations then under way for the much larger tract. "[T]he whole affair," Morris wrote to Phelps and Gorham,[69]

> has made disagreeable impressions. The Indians will be indisposed to sell the remainder of the Lands. The British are encouraging and will encourage them not to part with them, and probably the Government of the United States may refuse to authorize the holding of a Treaty for further purchase until the Indians shall be satisfied as to their Complaints respecting Mr. Livingston and Mr. Phelps. . . . I am now pretty well convinced that no body can surmount the obstacles which will occur in this business, so well as we can. This sentiment is the result of a full Consideration of the subject and I deem my own assistance as essentially necessary.

This indeed was the case. With Samuel Ogden as his agent and with Representative Jeremiah Wadsworth interested, Morris succeeded in acquiring the right of pre-emption from Massachusetts on the 5th of March.[70] Ogden's success was of course public information, but just before Washington departed for the South it also became known to some that Robert Morris was the actual purchaser. Théophile Cazenove reported the general judgment to be that he had made an excellent deal.[71]

Efforts to remove the disagreeable impressions made by The Cornplanter's accusations against Phelps were equally successful. Showered with gifts and attention, the Seneca leader now expressed gratitude to the President and pledged the friendship of his people.[72] In his instructions to Pickering, Knox expressed confidence in The Cornplanter's attachment and fidelity. Soon thereafter, more privately, he wrote: "The Cornplanter may be depended upon through all the changes of policy. . . . [He] is our friend from the solid ties of interest, and we must rivet it by all ways and means in our power."[73] The

[68] The Cornplanter, Half-Town, and Great Tree to the President, 10 Jan. 1791 (same, I, 208-9).

[69] Morris to Phelps and Gorham, 20 Jan. 1791 (NA: Phelps-Gorham Papers).

[70] The principal documents on the history of the tract — including Massachusetts' disposal of the right of pre-emption of 1 Apr. 1788; the Indian deed to Phelps and Gorham of 8 July 1788; the deed from the latter to Morris of 28 Nov. 1790 for that part on which the Indian title had been extinguished; the resolution of the Massachusetts legislature of 5 Mch. 1791 to sell the pre-emptive right to the residue of the lands to Samuel Ogden; the covenants between the Massachusetts commissioners for the sale to Ogden; and the assignment of those covenants from Ogden to Morris of 26 Apr. 1791 — are presented in Miers Fisher's *Brief of the Titles of Robert Morris* (Philadelphia, 1791). Henry Jackson reported to his friend Henry Knox on the day after the agreement that Ogden had closed the purchase of Massachusetts' right to the western tract at £100,000 lawful specie and that Ogden as agent had given the names of Robert Morris and Jeremiah Wadsworth as the real purchasers (Jackson to Knox, 6 Mch. 1791; MHi: Knox Papers).

[71] Cazenove to his Amsterdam principals, 19 Mch. 1791 (Cazenove Letter Book, Archives of the City of Amsterdam). TJ knew that Morris was the real purchaser (TJ to Washington, 27 Mch. 1791).

[72] The Cornplanter, Half-Town, and Big Tree to the President, 7 Feb. 1791 (ASP, *Indian Affairs*, I, 144).

[73] Knox to Pickering, 2 May and 13 June 1791 (MHi: Pickering Papers).

marked change in attitude that took place between The Cornplanter's arrival in Philadelphia and his departure a few weeks later suggests that influences other than the pledges of friendship and protection given by the President must have been brought to bear. Joseph Brant, the Mohawk sachem who had been most influential in arranging the sale of lands to Phelps and Gorham in 1788, denounced The Cornplanter and accused him of seeking bribes from those whom he had charged with fraud.[74] Whether the solid ties of interest included bribery or not, The Cornplanter had been appeased in a manner that could only have been satisfying to Robert Morris and those associated with him in the new purchase. This, as Morris had told Phelps and Gorham in January, was essential if the government were to be persuaded to hold a treaty.

News that arrived from London only a day or two after Washington departed on his southern journey was even more gratifying to Morris. On the 15th of February William Temple Franklin had signed preliminary articles with Patrick Colquhoun for the sale of one million acres of the tract Morris had acquired from Phelps and Gorham in 1790. When the final contract was completed on the 17th of March, with the wealthy William Pulteney, Earl of Bath, as the principal purchaser, the price agreed upon was £75,000 sterling, almost treble the amount Morris had agreed to pay for the tract.[75] The news that Morris had made an estimated profit of £50,000 sterling created a sensation in Philadelphia. Jefferson reported it to Washington, pointedly reminding him that the Indian title to these lands had been extinguished, but that this was not the case with the remaining four millions to which Morris had only acquired the right of pre-emption. "Perhaps," Jefferson added, "a sale may be made in Europe to purchasers ignorant of the Indian right."[76] He obviously feared another such imposition upon the Indians and potential investors as had been so recently exhibited in the activities of the Yazoo and Scioto companies. But those enterprises had raised warning signals. The contract for Morris' sale to the Pulteney Associates included a prudent clause making him responsible for extinguishing all claims of Indians and squatters. Morris was also well aware that under the Act of 1790 title to Indian lands could be validated only when publicly negotiated at a treaty held under the auspices of the federal government.

With The Cornplanter appeased and Massachusetts' right of pre-emption to four million acres acquired, Morris needed only to persuade the government to hold a treaty at which his speculation might be expected to yield far greater profit than that just realized. He had already told Phelps and Gorham that the government might refuse but that his assistance in overcoming this and other obstacles was essential. The assertion was less a boast than a well-grounded recognition of political realities. Knox was already engaged in land speculation

[74] Brant to the Secretary of War, 25 Feb. 1791, enclosed in Knox to Pickering, 18 May 1791 (same).

[75] By the agreement with Phelps and Gorham of 10 Aug. 1790, Morris had acquired a million acres for £30,000 Massachusetts currency in payments extending from 1 Jan. 1791 to 1 Dec. 1792. Thus at the time of the sale to the Pulteney Associates he had made only the first payment of £5,000. See Barbara Graymont, "New York State Indian Policy after the Revolution," New York History, LVII (Oct. 1976), 438-74; Barbara A. Charnow, "Robert Morris: Land Speculator," New York History, LVIII (Apr. 1977), 195-220; and Laurance M. Hauptman, "Senecas and Subdividers: Resistance to Allotment of Indian Rights in New York, 1785-1906," Prologue, IX (Summer 1977), 105-16.

[76] TJ to Washington, 27 Mch. 1791; see also TJ to Currie, 24 Mch. 1791, and to Hawkins, 1 Apr. 1791.

on a large scale. Hamilton himself was a shareholder in the Ohio Company. Rufus King, long an influential legislator in behalf of enterprises of land speculators and one of the commissioners who had settled the dispute between Massachusetts and New York over the lands involved, had just informed Hamilton of the activities of land speculators in New York and had expressed his confidence that the government would pursue "all prudent steps . . . to keep the Six Nations quiet."[77] With Jeremiah Wadsworth already interested and with other stalwart supporters of Hamiltonian policies not averse to participating in such a promising speculation, Morris had every reason to expect he could persuade the government to call for a treaty. It is not to be supposed that he, Hamilton, or Knox would have been so indiscreet as to let the public record disclose any private motives underlying the decision to convene the Six Nations. But that there was an understanding and that both Hamilton and Knox were aware of Morris' desire to extinguish the Indian title as quickly as possible is beyond question.

Immediately after the Cabinet authorized the treaty, Morris dispatched an agent to the Genesee country to find out whether the Indians were disposed to make another sale. Knox no doubt was already aware of this before Pickering informed him of the fact.[78] Soon thereafter, Morris made a hasty journey to Boston to confer with Nathaniel Gorham about a resurvey of the line between the old and new purchases and to conclude arrangements with Massachusetts officials. While there he told Gorham that he would certainly attend the treaty himself in order to effect a purchase. Gorham pressed his partner Phelps to attend also and to be certain of arriving at the place of rendezvous by the 15th of June when Morris, a punctual man, would unquestionably be present.[79] While Knox knew of Morris' plans, he did not warn Pickering in his official instructions or in private communications against possible interference by private interests in the conduct of the public negotiations. Aware as he was of Washington's strong feelings about the harmful effect of land speculators on the government's Indian policy, Knox thus offered further evidence of the real purpose of the treaty by this silence in the records, reinforced as it was by his knowledge of Morris' plans and expectations.

Those glowing expectations seemed on the point of realization when an insuperable obstacle presented itself. While Morris was absent in Boston, the Six Nations, in unmistakable terms, made known their unyielding opposition to any further sale of their lands. Early in May General Israel Chapin at Canandaigua reported that Morris' agent was at work among the Indians and that the result was ominous. "I hope Mr. Morris nor any other person," he wrote to Pickering, "will endeavor to purchase any lands of the Indians at

[77] Extract of a letter from King to Hamilton, 24 Mch. 1791, which Hamilton forwarded to Washington on 27 Mch. 1791 (Syrett, *Hamilton*, VIII, 212-13, 217-18).

[78] Pickering to Knox, 12 May 1791, in which he reminded Knox that, while in Philadelphia, he had given this information to him and had informed him that Morris had "employed one Ewing to endeavour to purchase lands of the Indians, or at least to feel their dispositions on that subject" (MHi: Pickering Papers).

[79] Gorham to Phelps, 15, 17, and 24 May 1791; Phelps to Gorham, 22 May 1791 (NA: Phelps-Gorham Papers). Morris left Philadelphia on 2 May and arrived home on the 29th (Lear to Washington, 8 May 1791, DLC: Washington Papers; Remsen to Currie, 2 June 1791, MHi).

present: for it is my opinion it will be attended with very ill consequences."[80] Pickering forwarded this warning to Knox and added strength to it: another trusted informant had reported that "the Indians would not endure the idea of parting with any more of their lands."[81] A preliminary gathering of about thirty chieftains at Canandaigua had assured Pickering's agent that "the Senecas and the Six Nations generally . . . would readily join the United States in the War against the Western Indians, provided they could be protected in return" – but that they were adamant in opposing any attempt to purchase more of their lands.[82]

Soon after Morris returned to Philadelphia, Hamilton and Knox called upon him and revealed the disappointing news. General Chapin's emphatic warning, together with similar admonitions from Clinton and Brant which arrived about the same time, made this unavoidable. There is no record of what took place at the conference, but Knox transmitted the result to Pickering in simple terms: "Mr. Morris will not attempt to purchase any lands at present."[83] Morris himself confirmed the understanding that had been reached. "Upon a consultation with Colo. Hamilton and General Knox," he wrote to Pickering, "I have agreed not to make any proposition to the Indians at this Treaty for the purchase of any part of their land, therefore nothing need to be said to them on that subject."[84] These revealing words convey the unmistakable implication that the private explanations given by Knox to Pickering through Hodgdon's cryptic message two days before the Cabinet meeting included a disclosure of Morris' reasons for desiring a treaty to be held. Had this not been so, there would have been no need for Morris to inform Pickering that his plan had been abandoned as a result of the consultation with Hamilton and Knox. The significant but unrecorded conference, the agreement to abandon the original object, the unexpressed assumption that Pickering was fully informed of the plan and hence needed to be given explicit directions to say nothing of it – all provided eloquent testimony concerning the real object for which the Secretary of War, with the support of the Secretary of the Treasury, had advocated the treaty in the first place.

When at last the Treaty of Newtown was formally begun on the 4th of July, Pickering soon found that the Six Nations wished nothing so much as to remain at peace with the United States and to be secure in their lands. He prudently disregarded that part of his instructions urging that some warriors be sent to join St. Clair's army. This, he discovered, would have been as strongly opposed as any effort to purchase the Indians' lands. Thus while the first of the two

[80] Chapin to Pickering, 5 May 1791 (MHi: Pickering Papers).
[81] Pickering to Knox, 12 May 1791 (same).
[82] Pickering's notes of Captain Samuel Bowman's report, "taken from his mouth" at Wilkes-Barré on 11 May 1791 (same).
[83] Knox to Pickering, 13 June 1791 (same).
[84] Morris to Pickering, 12 June 1791 (same). Morris explained that he thought it best not to attend the treaty in person after giving up the plan to attempt a purchase, but that his two sons would be present to witness the spectacle of an Indian treaty. He asked Pickering to present them to the Indians and to announce himself "as the owner of the preemptive right to that Tract of Country lying West of the Genesee River as far as Lake Erie." He had even prepared a speech to this effect, which he said one of his sons would deliver if Pickering approved. No evidence that the speech was delivered has been found.

ostensible objects of the treaty was achieved with predictable ease, the second was a complete failure. The latter was ignored in the appraisal of the results by Knox, who also made no allusion to the cost of the treaty that was so far beyond the estimate he had given the Cabinet. Instead, he reported to the President that Pickering had, "with great ability and judgement, carried into effect the objects of his mission, by cementing the friendships between the United States and the . . . Indians." He predicted that "the good effects flowing from this Council, will be manifestly conspicuous."[85] But when Washington received the voluminous papers from Pickering, he was upset and demanded an immediate conference with the Secretary of War.[86] Knox had no alternative but to face the grim reality. For the fact is that, two days before the treaty ended, Pickering had ratified a lease of about 64,000 acres lying on both shores of Lake Cayuga that had been granted by the Cayuga nation to one John Richardson. When he learned too late the significance of what he had done, Pickering sought to justify himself by saying that the Indians had demanded it, that if he had refused they would have been much angered, and that he had followed the advice given him by local magistrates and others. Unfortunately, so Knox represented him as saying, he had kept no copy of the instrument or of his ratification and had neither among his papers. This was not true. Pickering not only had retained copies of both documents: he had in fact drafted the lease himself.[87]

But one ineluctable fact could not be concealed. The right of pre-emption to these lands belonged not to any individual but to the state of New York. These were reservation lands assigned to the Cayugas, though only a handful of that tribe had remained there after the main body had moved elsewhere. Richardson and those whom he represented had for some time been squatters on this almost unoccupied tract. Also, as Pickering certainly knew and as Knox probably did when their reports were handed in, Abraham Hardenbergh and other New York speculators, who had long been casting covetous eyes upon these rolling hills and valleys of the lake region, had bitterly denounced the confirmation of the Richardson lease.[88] Governor Clinton, a not disinterested observer, was well aware of this fact. Timothy Pickering, generously disposed as he was toward the natives but no less so toward his fellow land speculators,

[85] Knox to Washington, 17 Aug. 1791 (DLC: Washington Papers).

[86] Tobias Lear to John VanderBrock, 25 July 1791, returning Pickering's papers to Knox and informing him that the President wished to see him "as soon as may be" concerning them (DLC: Washington Papers). Knox at this time was in New York consulting Duer about their land speculations.

[87] Pickering to Knox, 16 Aug. 1791; Pickering to Washington, 27 Aug. 1791; Dft of lease to Richardson in Pickering's hand, 16 July 1791; deed of Cayugas to Richardson, 16 July 1791 (all in MHi: Pickering Papers). Knox to the President, 17 Aug. 1791 (DLC: Washington Papers).

[88] Hardenbergh to Pickering, 22 July 1791, enclosing Clinton's letter of 17 May 1791 directing him to remove the squatters and bring them to condign punishment so as to prevent further complaint from the Indians (MHi: Pickering Papers). A few weeks after the treaty, Clinton's instruction was carried out in almost savage terms. A sheriff's posse of about fifty men evicted from fifteen to twenty families living on the land leased by Richardson and burned their homes. It was said that this "fiery Process" was carried out without regard to the age, sex, or state of health of the settlers (Obadiah Gore to Pickering, 22 Oct. 1791; Joseph Kinney to Pickering, 24 Oct. 1791, same).

had thrown the authority of government upon the wrong side of the conflict and in doing so had committed a capital error. His ratification of the lease to Richardson at a public treaty and as commissioner of the United States was, in plain terms, illegal. "This measure," the Secretary of War was obliged to report to the President, "was entirely unauthorized by his instructions, is contrary to the constitution and laws of New York, and to the Constitution and laws of the United States."[89]

It was embarrassing enough for Knox to have to report Pickering's illegal acts to the President but far more so to have to acknowledge this to Governor Clinton, who had disapproved the treaty in the first place. In doing so, Knox explained that the commissioner's desire to accomplish his mission had led him incautiously to yield to the earnest request of the Cayugas by confirming the Richardson lease and, on the insistence of the Senecas, to certify a grant of land to the two daughters of Ebenezer Allen by a Cayuga woman. Despite this, by command of the President, both actions were explicitly disavowed as being "considered . . . entirely null and void by the United States."[90]

Washington evidently did not realize how greatly private interests had influenced the Cabinet during his absence. Though he looked elsewhere for the springs of these actions, his response shows how clearly he perceived the ill effects produced by the treaty. Early in October he directed the Attorney General to examine the laws for securing Indians' lands, restraining states or individuals from purchasing them, and forbidding unauthorized intercourse with the natives. He asked Randolph to suggest such additional laws as would remedy defects and enable the President to enforce obedience. Such a measure would be indispensably necessary to establish peace and to avoid the expense and horrors of continual hostilities, Washington wrote, "for unless adequate penalties are provided that will check the spirit of speculation in lands and will enable the Executive to carry them into effect, this Country will be constantly embroiled with, and appear faithless in the eyes not only of the Indians but of the neighbouring powers also."[91] At the opening of Congress a few days later Washington laid before the Senate Pickering's instructions and other documents. He declared that the Six Nations had been convened "for the purpose of conciliation . . . at a critical period" and added that "it might not have been necessary to have requested your opinion on this business, had not the Commissioner, with good intentions, but incautiously, made certain ratifications of lands, unauthorized by his instructions, and unsupported by the Constitu-

---

[89] Knox to the President, 17 Aug. 1791 (DLC: Washington Papers). Pickering's confirmation of the grant of land from the Senecas to the two daughters of Ebenezer Allen, though insisted upon by the Cayugas, was also against the law (Allen to Pickering, 4 July 1791; Pickering's undated memorandum of the Cayuga chieftains' explanation of the Allen grant, to which he added a note that the daughters had been granted 18,640 acres, or more than their tribal share; draft by Pickering of his official certificate of the Allen grant, which he had explained in full Council and then signed, sealed, and delivered, all in MHi: Pickering Papers).

[90] Knox to Clinton, 17 Aug. 1791 (ASP, *Indian Affairs*, I, 169; Tr in DLC: Washington Papers). Washington approved the letter and directed that it be sent forward "without delay" (Lear to Knox, 17 Aug. 1791, same).

[91] Washington to the Attorney General, 10 Oct. 1791 (*Writings*, ed. Fitzpatrick, XXXI, 386-7; Dft in Washington's hand in DNA: RG 59, MLR).

[131]

tion."[92] The Senate, with Robert Morris and other leading purchasers of Indian lands present, saw fit not to take action.[93]

Such, in part, were the consequences of actions taken by the Secretary of War during the President's absence. The Indians who had not needed to be conciliated were left puzzled and somewhat embittered. The solid ties of interest that had been employed in the spring to bind The Cornplanter and to secure him and the powerful Seneca nation had begun to weaken in the autumn. The private land speculations of the Secretary of War had diverted him from his duty to prosecute the war in the West. Relations with the governor of an important state had been needlessly impaired. The law — the very law read by the Commissioner of the United States at the opening of the conference at which he promised to speak plain words of truth — had been so flagrantly and publicly violated that his acts were necessarily disavowed by the government he represented. Nothing of good had been achieved and the seeds of much ill had been planted.

VI

After the Cabinet had approved the convening of the Six Nations, Jefferson "then mentioned to the gentlemen the idea of suggesting thro' Colo. Beckwith, our knolege of the conduct of the British officers in furnishing the Indians with arms and ammunition, and our dissatisfaction." Although Washington had left the decision entirely up to him as to whether to make a formal or informal approach to Beckwith — or indeed to act at all — he nevertheless produced the President's letter and sought the advice of his colleagues. As might be expected, Jefferson preferred a communication less peremptory and more in accord with his own style of diplomacy than that suggested by Washington. He rested his argument on the law of nations and suggested a message to this effect: that "tho an annual present of arms and ammunition be an innocent act in time of peace, it is not so in time of war: that it is contrary to the laws of neutrality for a neutral power to furnish implements to either party at war, and that if their subjects should do it on private account, such furnitures might be seised as contraband."[94] This begged the question whether the laws of neutrality applied in a war carried on not between sovereign states but — as Hamilton had expressed it to Beckwith — with "certain vagrant tribes" who were not members of the society of nations. In using such an argument Jefferson at least sought to convey the government's views in terms more consonant with diplomatic propriety than those suggested by Washington.

Even as modified, however, a statement which accepted reports of British aid to the Indians as uncontroverted fact and which went no further than to express "dissatisfaction" would have been an emphatic contradiction of what Hamilton, for some time past, had been saying to Beckwith about the attitude

[92] Washington to the Senate, 26 Oct. 1791 (JEP, I, 85; Tr in DLC: Washington Papers). Washington directed that Knox himself present the letter and accompanying papers.

[93] These and other matters on Indian affairs, including The Cornplanter's speeches, were referred to committee. Its final report was submitted on 27 Jan. 1792, recommending that the papers be filed in the office of the Secretary and that it be discharged. The report was agreed to (JEP, I, 88, 91, 99, 100; ASP, *Indian Affairs*, I, 206-20).

[94] TJ to Washington, 17 Apr. 1791 (Document III).

of the administration. It was to be expected, therefore, that he would object to the idea of making such a communication to Dorchester and would seek to block it even in spite of Washington's emphatic urging. For if the President's suggestion should have been approved by the heads of departments, this would at once have placed Hamilton in a delicate and embarrassing position with respect to Beckwith. Worse, he might even have been exposed before his own government as one already engaged in confidential communications with the agent in which his views were represented as those of the administration — something Hamilton and his supporters in the Senate had repeatedly cautioned the British agent not to divulge. In this situation Hamilton had little if any choice but to inform his colleagues that, as Jefferson reported to Washington, Beckwith had consulted him on the subject and had assured him the British government had given the Indians nothing more than the annual present at the customary period. This could only have referred to the reply by Dorchester to Hamilton's appeal in January asking him to exercise his influence with the Indians. Dorchester's response clearly had been intended as an indirect message to the government, but Hamilton had already told Beckwith it was "inadmissible" to lay such a paper before the President.

Understandably, the Secretary of the Treasury did not wish to reveal to his colleagues what he had declined to lay before the President. He thus left them with the mistaken impression that it was Beckwith and not himself who had taken the initiative. But this only made him the more vulnerable. One of those present at the Cabinet meeting — almost certainly it was Jefferson — believed it necessary to inform Beckwith that even the giving of annual presents had attracted the attention of government. "I thought it the more material," Jefferson reported to Washington, "lest, having been himself the first to speak of it, he might suppose his excuses satisfactory, and that therefore they might repeat the annual present this year."[95] This suggestion, supported by Jefferson's argument about the duties of neutrals in time of war, was difficult for Hamilton to counter, particularly in view of Washington's pronounced feelings on the subject. He therefore acquiesced, but evidently sought to put himself in a position to guide the subsequent discussions with Beckwith. The decision finally reached by the Cabinet was one which "fully coincided with the judgement of the President . . . in making an *informal representation* through Lt. Colo. Beckwith . . . who it was sure would not fail to communicate to Lord Dorchester substantially what should be mentioned on the occasion."[96] But if there was unanimity on this point, there surely could not have been on the question which naturally followed: who should communicate the view of government to Beckwith?

Should it be the Secretary of the Treasury who, according to his own statement, had already been approached by the agent on the subject? Should it be the Secretary of War, who had oversight over Indian affairs? Should it be the Secretary of State? On every score the responsibility would seem to have rested most appropriately on Jefferson, not only because Washington had authorized him to act but also because the message, however informal, was intended for a foreign government. Nevertheless, it was the Secretary of War whom the Cabinet directed to communicate the government's concern to Beckwith. It is

[95] TJ to Washington, 17 Apr. 1791 (Document III).
[96] Knox' memorandum of his interview with Beckwith, 11 Apr. 1791 (MHi: Pickering Papers; emphasis in original).

plausible to suppose that it was Hamilton who made the suggestion. Jefferson acquiesced, though it is clear from his subsequent actions that he had little if any confidence that the views of the President would be adequately conveyed by the Secretary of War. It is significant that, in reporting the Cabinet's decision, he did not inform Washington that Knox had been chosen as its spokesman. Obviously, the omission was deliberate.[97]

Knox lost no time in carrying out his assignment. In his account of the conversation with Beckwith, which took place the same day, he began somewhat formally by stating that the Vice-President, the Secretary of State, the Secretary of the Treasury, and the Secretary of War had met in consequence of the President's desire that they "consult on certain points." Among other objects considered, he pointed out, the Secretary of State had produced a letter from the President "wherein was stated the reports . . . in circulation relatively to the Indians receiving supplies of ammunition from the british posts and intimating the propriety of making some representation either formal or informal in order to prevent in future the evil effects of such supplies." Following this prefatory comment, Knox explained that he had been asked to make the communication and that he had done so that very evening when Beckwith was at his house with other company.

"I mentioned to him at first with seeming indifference," Knox stated in his memorandum, "that I supposed he had remarked in the newspapers the paragraphs which spoke with some warmth of the supplies which the Indians had received from the british garrisons. He instantly replied he had and he supposed I alluded to some intimations of that nature taken from an Albany paper." To judge from the silence in the memorandum, Knox evidently did not confirm or deny the supposition. Knox reported that Beckwith then went into some detail to prove that the suspicions were unfounded, that no extraordinary supplies had been given the Indians, and that, because of the ill will generated by the "ungracious manner" in which the British government had behaved toward the natives by surrendering their lands to the United States at the Treaty of Paris, annual presents had been given with no other object than to make some retribution for injuries they had received. According to his account, Knox then explained that the United States had become involved in the war much against its inclinations:

> That it was its object to observe towards the indians a liberal system – That we wanted nothing of the Indians but peace – That the general government could not observe with indifference the depredations of the Indians, which seemed to grow out of indistinct circumstances – That we had offered them peace the last year – That we were still willing to make peace with them but that it was determined not to suffer any more of their depredations – That if peace could not be made the General Government were determined to convince the indians of its power – That in the process of this business it would have a pernicious effect [upon the relations of] Great Britain and the U. S.[98] if the Indians were supplied with Arms and ammunition from the

[97] TJ to Washington, 17 Apr. 1791 (Document III).

[98] Phrasing within brackets supplied. Knox first wrote: "it would have a pernicious effect if the Indians were supplied with Arms and ammunition" and then garbled the passage by inserting an ampersand before "effect" and by interlining "the Great Britain and the US" after that word. What he obviously intended to say was that the continuance of such supplies would have a pernicious effect upon relations between the two countries.

british posts — That it were to be hoped that Lord Dorchester would find it proper to discontinue any such until the contest was settled in order to kill all appearances of interference.

To this appeal for suspending the customary annual presents Beckwith "did not seem to answer explicitly," but pointed out circumstances to show that it was against both the dignity and the interest of Great Britain to support the Indians in a war with the United States. Knox did not indicate what these circumstances were, but his reported response was an enthusiastic concurrence. "I heartily assented," he wrote, "and observed that I was persuaded that the event would shew that there was not any just cause for such a suspicion." Upon Beckwith's remark that the disposition of Great Britain toward the United States had been made manifest by its intention to appoint a minister, "the conversation ended."[99]

While relations between Knox and Beckwith were cordial and at times convivial, the nature of the occasion at which their conversation took place is not known.[100] If, as the memorandum suggests, their discussion occurred in company, this could only have served to weaken the force of the government's message. Nor is it apparent for whom Knox intended his rather formal record. Since the first part contained nothing not already known to his colleagues, it is plausible to suppose that the report was intended for the President. If so, no copy of it has survived among Washington's carefully preserved papers. It is even more significant that Knox made no mention of the interview in his letters to Washington. Nor can any copy of his memorandum be found among the papers of Adams, Hamilton, or Jefferson. It apparently exists only in the composition draft which Knox retained in his own files. No allusion to it or indeed to the conversation between Knox and Beckwith on the evening of the 11th has been discovered. It is particularly noteworthy that neither Jefferson nor any other person present at the Cabinet meeting, so far as is known, reported the interview to the President. Even Beckwith failed to comment upon it in his reports to his superiors.

In view of these puzzling silences in the record, one can only fall back upon surmise. If the draft had been shown to Hamilton, as seems likely, it is plausible to assume that he gave Knox the prudent advice to abandon it and instead only to mention to Jefferson and perhaps to Adams that he had conveyed the message as directed. For what is known with certainty is that Knox' remarks to Beckwith about the pernicious effects of Indian hostilities upon larger interests of the two nations was only an echo of what Hamilton had already said in his recent appeals to Dorchester through Beckwith. Far from expressing the government's dissatisfaction as Washington had intended, Knox had placed the emphasis on newspaper accounts and then had sought to justify American policy toward the Indians. From this defensive posture he had launched not a protest but an

[99] Dft (MHi: Knox Papers; at head of text: "Memorandum of a conversation which passed between the subscriber and Lt. Colonel Beckwith who seems charged with some sort of informal political commission by Lord Dorchester. Evening of the 11th of April 1791").

[100] An example of this is found in a letter from Beckwith to Knox inviting him to dine at the City Tavern. "Anxious to promote the benign purposes of peace!" he wrote, "good humor! and intercourse! I am happy at all times in the being employed in whatever may have a tendency to promote such objects, which cannot conclude better than by a little eating and drinking" (Beckwith to Knox, 2 Oct. 1791, MHi: Knox Papers).

appeal. His expression of confidence that there were no just grounds for sus-
pecting the British would aid the Indians was exactly the opposite of the kind
of message the President's letter had suggested.

Jefferson obviously suspected that Knox would discharge his assignment in
this manner. Proof of this came soon after the Cabinet meeting when he turned
to Madison, showed him Washington's letter, and asked him to talk privately
with Beckwith. As he explained to the President, he had done this because
Beckwith and Madison resided at the same boardinghouse and he therefore
had requested the latter to "find some occasion . . . to reason with him on the
subject, as from himself, but so as to let him see that government thought as
himself did."[101] Clearly the choice of Madison to do what Knox had failed to
do was not based on mere convenience but on Jefferson's confidence that
through this channel the message would be conveyed to the British agent with
such clarity and force as to make its meaning unmistakable. His confidence
was fully justified. Madison did not approach Beckwith casually or hastily as
Knox had done but waited for a suitable opportunity. When it came on the
evening of the 17th, he came at once to the heart of the matter. He made it
clear that, aside from the widespread public belief that the Indians were being
supplied with implements of war from British posts, the President had received
information which he regarded as conclusive proof of the fact. This was indeed
made so explicit that Beckwith could not counter the statement without seeming
to contradict the President himself. Being confronted with a completely different expression of the government's views from that given him by Knox, he
could only declare that it was impossible such aids "could have proceeded
directly or indirectly from the British Government, or even have had the sanction or countenance of the authority on the spot." He stood on solid ground
in reiterating his assurances to Madison that the whole spirit and policy of his
government was opposed to Indian hostilities and that this was also in accord
with the sentiments and even the orders of Dorchester.

But there remained the intractable fact of Washington's conviction to the
contrary. Beckwith vainly sought to be informed of the particular proofs that
had led the President to such a conclusion. Perhaps prompted by the quite
different impressions he had received from the Secretary of War, he hinted with
equal lack of success at his desire to be put in direct communication with the
Secretary of State. He suggested that, if there were just grounds for complaint,
he might be given a regular statement for "communication of it in *any mode*
that might be thought not improper." It is understandable that Beckwith, long
in the habit of confidential exchanges with Hamilton, should have wanted to
communicate with a Secretary of State whose concept of official decorum had
led him to regard it as improper to hold discussions on public matters with an
unaccredited agent. Madison's response to Beckwith's obvious hint was polite
but conclusive: the President's views could probably not be conveyed in any
way "more authentic" than was being done in this private conversation. Moreover, Madison pointed out, the message to be communicated – that aid to the
Indians should be stopped – did not depend upon its form. Nor, in view of
Dorchester's reputation for humanity and prudence, would absolute proof be
required. Thus the question whether to use formal or informal channels of
communication between the governments was irrelevant. Whatever the source

[101] TJ to Washington, 17 Apr. 1791 (Document III).

of military aid, "it was in every case to be expected that the abuse would be corrected," the more so since the Indians were within the United States and their supplies for use in war came from a foreign source. Confronted with Madison's unyielding representation of the President's views, Beckwith made another unsuccessful effort to ascertain the grounds upon which they were based, professing to be uncertain how to report information "so vague . . . and communicated under such reserve." After insistent questioning which left him free to cite Madison by name, he asked that the intelligence received by the President be repeated, obviously in order that he might be able to identify the source of his information. When Madison complied, Beckwith assured him that he would report to Dorchester by the first opportunity and would transmit to him any answer that might be received.[102]

In submitting his careful report of the interview to Jefferson, Madison may have given him additional comments in a letter written the next day, but that letter has not been found.[103] Since the heads of departments had specifically authorized Knox to communicate the President's message to Beckwith, it is virtually certain that Jefferson did not inform his colleagues either of his choice of Madison or of the latter's report. It is significant that he kept no record of the conversation either in his personal or official files, perhaps because of his strict rule against having any public relations with the British agent. Nor, possibly for the same reason, did he send a copy of Madison's memorandum to Washington. Instead he gave him a succinct account of the interview in which he made it clear that Beckwith had responded "on very different ground from that on which he had placed it with Colo. Hamilton" and that he had been made aware that his former apologies to the Secretary of the Treasury had not been satisfactory to the government. On its face this would seem to place upon Beckwith an onus properly assignable to Hamilton, much as Jefferson had done during the war crisis of 1790. But these comments seem to take on a different meaning in light of Jefferson's report that Beckwith had tried "to induce a formal communication" from him as Secretary of State; that, on being made to realize this could not be done, he had complained of not being sufficiently noticed by government, however informal his character; and that, while he had been in New York before Jefferson came into office, "he had not been regularly turned over" to the Secretary of State. In this context Jefferson seemed to be calling attention to the contrast between his refusal to communicate officially with a person having no public character and Hamilton's very different posture. Far from fixing responsibility upon Beckwith for the discrepancy between the statement made by Hamilton and the report of Madison, Jefferson may thus have been hinting that it was the administration's end of the channel of communication that was unreliable. Further, and more important, his assurance that Beckwith would inform Dorchester of "the general information . . . received and our sense of it" may have been intended to suggest that the message would get through because a reliable channel had been chosen.[104]

But Beckwith did not keep his promise to Madison. Understandably, this may have been due to the confusing and contradictory representations he had received in recent weeks from those presuming to speak for the administration.

[102] All quotations in the foregoing account of the interview are taken from Madison's record of the conversation (see Document IV and its notes).

[103] Madison to TJ, 18 Apr. 1791, recorded in SJL as received on the 20th.

[104] Jefferson to Washington, 24 Apr. 1791.

While he had speedily transmitted Hamilton's earlier appeals and the responses made to them, there is no evidence that he reported either to Dorchester or to Grenville the conversations he had had with Knox and Madison. He was well aware of Dorchester's growing concern over American misrepresentations of British policy toward the Indians and of his hope that both sides, acting with moderation, would avoid all hasty resolves as being "highly injudicious, dangerous to the public tranquillity, and of no use whatever."[105]

In mid-summer Beckwith read in the *Gazette of the United States* an account of the narrative of Thomas Rhea, an American captive of the Indians, whose statements he declared to be so devoid of truth and so diametrically opposed to Dorchester's orders that he made a formal protest to the Secretary of the Treasury. Hamilton agreed that the man's account was extremely particular but improbable; denied that the United States had made an effort to have warriors of the Six Nations join them against the hostile tribes; and, having read one of the Indian speeches at the recent treaty with the Six Nations, declared it to be most convincing proofs that the Canadian government's influence was being used to promote peace.[106] Soon thereafter Knox informed Beckwith that he had given St. Clair specific orders to assure the western tribes that the United States desired nothing of them but peace and that they would be secured in the lands and other claims.[107] His and Hamilton's communications to the agent were both consistent and consonant with the pacific aims of Dorchester and the British ministry. But they did not reflect accurately the views of the President and the Secretary of State, who also desired peace but insisted upon a different kind of message to Dorchester.

Washington himself provided the strongest proof of this in a comment upon efforts at mediation which he did not realize had originated with Hamilton. As a result of the latter's appeal, Dorchester had sought to obtain from the western tribes a clear definition of their grievances. In consequence, late in the summer, Joseph Brant led a delegation of chieftains and warriors to Quebec where they presented complaints against both the United States and the British government. Dorchester met the latter as best he could by assuring them that when the King their Father made peace with the United States he had marked out a boundary which did not mean giving away their lands but implied no more than that he would not extend his interference beyond that line. In response to other charges he defended the United States, declaring that ill-informed individuals must have made false reports about the army in the West and its actions. He also repeated his assurances that he would be glad to be instrumental

---

[105] Henry Motz to George Beckwith, 6 May 1791 (Canadian Archives, Ser. Q, vol. 50-1, p. 106). Beckwith wrote Grenville on the day of his interview with Madison but made no mention of Indian affairs or of his conversations with Knox and Madison (Beckwith to Grenville, 17 Apr. 1791, PRO: FO 4/12).

[106] The narrative of Thomas Rhea, which appeared in the *Gazette of the United States*, 12 July 1791, was sent to Knox by General Richard Butler. Knox forwarded it to Washington (ASP, *Indian Affairs*, I, 196-7). Beckwith's "recent communications with a gentleman in office" was enclosed in his letter to Grenville of 31 July 1791 (PRO: FO 4/12; text printed in Syrett, *Hamilton*, VIII, 544-6). In the same letter Beckwith reported upon the Treaty of Newtown and said that the Six Nations had pledged strict neutrality and had returned home "perfectly satisfied."

[107] Beckwith to Grenville, 26 Aug. 1791, enclosing an account of his conversations with "gentlemen of distinction" in the government (PRO: FO 4/12). The interview with Knox took place on 5 Aug. 1791.

in restoring peace if it were in his power to do so. "It would give me great pleasure while I am in England," he concluded, "to hear that peace is established in your country, upon a true and solid foundation, and that you live in comfort and security with your families, sowing your fields and following your hunts to our mutual advantage. . . . I recommend it to you not to lose sight of this desirable object. Brothers, could I be instrumental in bringing this good work about, my pleasure would be still greater."[108]

This speech, as neutral in its attitude toward the two sides as Dorchester could afford to be, was as much a response to Hamilton's appeal for intermediation as it was an expression of Dorchester's own wishes. In forwarding a copy to Beckwith he was confident it would be so interpreted. Beckwith did grasp its intent and decided to make "a direct and formal communication of it to the executive government."[109] With both Washington and Jefferson absent in Virginia, he sent the speech to Hamilton, as perhaps he would have done in any case since he had had no direct communication with either the President or the Secretary of State. In doing so he expressed the hope that Dorchester's address to the Indians might "have a tendency to dispel the remaining prejudices of individuals, and to promote the peace of the frontiers."[110] Since Beckwith had formally submitted it "for the information of the Executive Government," Hamilton had no choice but to see that it came to the attention of the President. This presented for him an even more embarrassing choice than Dorchester's earlier response to his appeal which he had declined to submit to Washington, for any discussion of the address by the entire administration carried the danger that his role might be exposed. Confronted with this possibility, his response was threefold. First, he sent Dorchester's speech and Beckwith's letter to Knox because they dealt with Indian affairs, an action appropriate enough. Second, he sought to cast doubt upon the authenticity of the document by referring to it as "a paper purporting to be a speech of Lord Dorchester." Beckwith's signature on the document certifying it to be a true copy of the the original sufficiently testified to its authenticity. So also did the form, the substance, and the reiterated expression of Dorchester's desire to act as an intermediary, as Hamilton knew only too well. Finally, he informed Knox that Beckwith in conversation had made certain stipulations; that no use should be made of the speech that might be disagreeable to Dorchester; that it should not be published in the newspapers; and that no copy should be given to any officer on the western expedition. "I consider myself as having received the paper with these qualifications," Hamilton concluded, "and generally under the idea of a discreet and delicate use of it."[111] Hamilton had good reason to accept such stipulations and may indeed have advised Beckwith on the point as he had done on previous occasions. In reporting to Dorchester, Beckwith only stated that he had sub-

[108] Speech of Lord Dorchester "To the Chiefs and warriors deputed by the confederated Indian nations of the Ottawas, Chippaways, Potawatamies, Hurons, Shawanese, Delawares, Tusturs, and the six nations," delivered at Quebec, 15 Aug. 1791 (Tr in DLC: Washington Papers; authenticated as a true copy by Beckwith, 2 Oct. 1791; Tr in CtHi: Wolcott Papers).

[109] Beckwith to Dorchester, 5 Oct. 1791 (PRO: CO 42/85). Dorchester received this letter while in London and sent it to Grenville the same day (Dorchester to Grenville, 15 Nov. 1791, same).

[110] Beckwith to Hamilton, 2 Oct. 1791 (Syrett, *Hamilton*, IX, 265).

[111] Hamilton to Knox, 3 Oct. 1791 (same, IX, 270).

mitted the speech "to the executive government under certain limitations and restrictions." But at the same time he declared that he himself would make it available to "many individuals, upon the meeting of Congress." His object in doing so, he explained, was to counteract some erroneous reports about it that had already been received in the United States.[112] Thus by his own account Beckwith extended his direct and formal communication to the administration at least to those members of the legislative branch with whom he was in the habit of exchanging views.

Without comment Knox forwarded Dorchester's speech and the letters of Beckwith and Hamilton to the President. Washington merely acknowledged receipt of the communication.[113] Dorchester's good intentions thus came up against Washington's stony silence. Soon thereafter news of St. Clair's stunning defeat dashed all hopes of a peaceful settlement by intermediation or otherwise. The administration, supported by public sentiment and by the Congress, then determined to achieve peace through force. On the other side of the border, those engaged in Indian trade who had been most hurt by the hostilities saw possibilities that might not occur again. With the Indians demanding the Ohio River as their boundary, some hoped that the unfortunate terms of the Treaty of Peace might be altered. If, wrote one, the boundaries desired by the Indians were fixed, "we shou'd secure our Posts, the Trade, and the Tranquillity of the Country."[114] The instructions concerning Indian affairs which George Hammond brought with him as minister to the United States enunciated the policy of neutrality and pacification that Dorchester and the ministry had long supported. But these were outmoded by the disaster that had befallen the American army in the West.

Unofficial diplomacy had failed in every instance to achieve what both governments desired. But even if Washington had known that one of the initiatives had originated in his own Cabinet, he could scarcely have expressed his opposition to foreign intercession more forcefully than he did on learning from Gouverneur Morris of the report made to William Pitt by Henry Dundas that the United States had asked Great Britain to mediate. "You may be *fully* assured, Sir," he responded, "that such mediation *never* was asked; that the asking of it *never* was in contemplation, and . . . that it not only never *will* be asked but would be rejected if offered. The United States will never have occasion, I hope, to ask for the interposition of that power or any other, to establish peace within their own territory."[115] Washington never knew that he

[112] Beckwith to Dorchester, 5 Oct. 1791 (PRO: CO 42/85).

[113] Knox to Washington, 4 Oct. 1791 with enclosures (DLC: Washington Papers); Washington to Knox, 10 Oct. 1791 (*Writings*, ed. Fitzpatrick, XXXI, 385). The suspicion Hamilton cast upon the "purported" speech by Dorchester was sufficient to cause inquiries to be made. The matter became known somehow to Charles Williamson, agent of the Pulteney Associates, a friend of Hamilton, and another informal British agent. Williamson "accidentally" discovered that one of General Simcoe's officers was in Philadelphia, and reported to Knox, accompanied by Pickering. "I was determined to know," he wrote, "whether the speech handed to us as Lord Dorchester's was a Forgery or not." In conversation with the officer, Williamson became convinced that it was not only authentic but represented the views of the British government as well as those of Dorchester (Charles Williamson to Henry Knox, dated "Friday 1 o'clock"; RC in MHi: Knox Papers).

[114] "Extract of a Letter from Niagara," 24 Nov. 1791 (PRO: CO 42/88).

[115] Washington to Morris, 21 June 1792 (*Writings*, ed. Fitzpatrick, XXXI, 62-3; "Private"). Washington added that he had long suspected the British ministry of wishing to

was commenting upon an appeal made by the Secretary of the Treasury to Lord Dorchester.

Thus when the Vice-President and members of the Cabinet dined with the Secretary of State, much was revealed about the opposed modes and principles of administration, but nothing was accomplished in the public interest. The meeting, nevertheless, made an unforgettable impression on Jefferson. Long afterward, reflecting upon the occasion, he said that when the cloth had been removed and the business dispatched, conversation turned to other matters and by some circumstance was led to the British constitution. He quoted John Adams as saying: " 'purge that constitution of its corruption, and give to its popular branch equality of representation, and it would be the most perfect . . . ever devised by the wit of man.' " Hamilton, he reported, paused and then declared: " 'purge it of its corruption, and give to its popular branch equality of representation, and it would become an *impracticable* government: as it stands at present, with all its supposed defects, it is the most perfect government which ever existed.' "[116] Thus it was that, from the time of the Cabinet meeting onward, Jefferson became convinced that Hamilton believed corruption to be essential to the government of a nation. He did not realize then or ever that corruption in the form of favoritism extended to a powerful member of the Senate had been allowed to intrude upon public concerns on that April day.

---

intermeddle and had received many evidences of the fact but that the attempt had "retarded, if . . . not entirely done away the idea." He was more convinced than ever that these interferences and the underhanded support of the Indians had caused all of the difficulties with the Indians.

[116] "Explanations of the 3. volumes bound in Marbled paper," 4 Feb. 1818 (DLC: TJ Papers, 212: 37846).

I. The President to the Secretaries of State, Treasury, and War

GENTLEMEN   Mount Vernon, April 4. 1791.

As the public service may require that communications should be made to me, during my absence from the seat of government, by the most direct conveyances, and as, in the event of any very extraordinary occurrence, it will be necessary to know at what time I may be found in any particular place, I have to inform you that unless the progress of my journey to Savannah is retarded by unforeseen interruptions it will be regulated (including days of halt) in the following manner.

I shall be on the 8th. of April at Fredericksburg

11th.	Richmond
14th.	Petersburg
16th.	Halifax

18th.	Tarborough
20th.	Newbern
24th.	Wilmington
29th.	Georgetown, South-Carolina
2nd. of May	Charleston, halting five days.
11th.	Savannah, halting two days.

Thence, leaving the line of the mail, I shall proceed to Augusta, and, according to the information which I may receive there, my return, by an upper road will be regulated. – The route of my return is at present uncertain, but in all probability, it will be through Columbia, Camden, Charlotte, Salisbury, Salem, Guilford, Hillsborough, Harrisburg, Williamsburg to Taylor's ferry on the Roanoke, and thence to Fredericksburg by the nearest and best road.

After thus explaining to you, as far as I am able at present, the direction and probable progress of my journey, I have to express my wish, if any serious and important cases should arise during my absence, (of which the probability is but too strong) that the Secretaries for the Departments of State, Treasury, and War may hold consultations thereon, to determine whether they are of such a nature as to require my personal attendance at the seat of government – and, if they should be so considered, I will return immediately from any place at which the information may reach me. – Or should they determine that measures, relevant to the case, may be legally and properly pursued without the immediate agency of the President, I will approve and ratify the measures, which may be conformed to such determination.

Presuming that the Vice-President will have left the seat of government for Boston, I have not requested his opinion to be taken on the supposed emergency. Should it be otherwise I wish him also to be consulted. – I am, Gentlemen, Your most obedient Servant,

Go: Washington

RC (DLC); in hand of William Jackson except for signature; at foot of text: "Thomas Jefferson, Alexander Hamilton, and Henry Knox Esquires Secretaries of the United States for the Departments of State, Treasury, and War"; endorsed by TJ as received 8 Apr. 1791 and so recorded in SJL. PrC (DLC: Washington Papers). Dft (DNA: RG 59, MLR); in Jackson's hand. Tr (DNA: RG 59, SDC). Another Tr (DNA: RG 59, PCC No. 120).

II. The President to the Secretary
of State

DEAR SIR   Mount-Vernon April 4. 1791.

You will readily agree with me that the best interests of the United States require such an intimation to be made to the Governor of Canada, either directly or indirectly, as may produce instructions to prevent the Indians receiving military aid or supplies from the british posts or garrisons. — The notoriety of this assistance has already been such as renders enquiry into particulars unnecessary.

Colonel Beckwith seems peculiarly designated to be the channel of an indirect intimation. Referring the mode and extent of communicating with him to your own discretion, I wish it may be suggested in such manner as to reach Lord Dorchester, or the officer commanding in Canada, that certain information has been received of large supplies of ammunition being delivered to the hostile Indians, from british posts, about the commencement of last campaign.[1] And, as the United States have no other view in prosecuting the present war against the Indians, than, in the failure of negociation, to procure, by arms, peace and safety to the inhabitants of their frontier, they are equally surprised and disappointed at such an interference[2] by the servants or subjects of a foreign State, as seems intended[3] to protract the attainment of so just and reasonable an object.

These are my sentiments on this subject at the present moment. Yet so unsettled do some circumstances appear that it is possible you may see a necessity either to treat it very delicately, or to decline acting on it altogether. — The option is therefore left to your judgment as events may make the one or the other the part of propriety.

The enclosed paper is transmitted and referred to you in the State I received it. — I am dear Sir, Your most obedient Servant,

                                          GO: WASHINGTON

RC (DLC); at foot of text: "The Secretary of State"; in the hand of William Jackson, except for signature; endorsed by TJ as received 7 Apr. but recorded in SJL and SJPL under 8 Apr. 1791. Dft (DNA: RG 59, MLR); in Jackson's hand; with a number of deletions and interlineations, three of which are noted below. FC (DNA: RG 59, SDC); with one or two slight variations in phraseology from text of RC. Enclosure not identified, but it is very likely that this was a copy of the subscription paper drawn up as a "union of interest" between the contending landowners of Georgetown and Carrollsburg; Washington had requested a copy of that instrument a few days earlier (Washington to Deakins and Stoddert, 1 Apr. 1791, *Writings*, ed. Fitzpatrick, XXXI, 262-3).

[1] Dft originally read: "...that the United States cannot any longer regard with in-

difference the aid which is afforded to the hostile tribes of indians by the british garrisons" and then the passage was altered to read as above.

² Dft originally read: "they ⟨cannot but⟩ ⟨necessarily⟩ ⟨regard with astonishment such⟩ must find the happiness of their citizens

and the dignity of their government deeply interested in preventing such interference" and the passage was then altered to read as above.

³ Dft originally read "may have a tendency" and was then altered to read as above.

III. The Secretary of State to the President

SIR   Philadelphia Apr. 17. 1791

I had the honor of addressing you on the 2d. which I supposed would find you at Richmond, and again on the 10th. which I thought would overtake you at Wilmington. The present will probably find you at Charleston.

According to what I mentioned in my letter of the 10th. the Vicepresident, Secretaries of the Treasury and war and myself met on the 11th. Colo. Hamilton presented a letter from Mr. Short in which he mentioned that the month of February being one of the periodical months in Amsterdam, when from the receipt of interest and refunding of capitals, there is much money coming in there, and free to be disposed of, he had put off the opening his loan till then, that it might fill the more rapidly, a circumstance which would excite the presumption of our credit; that he had every reason to hope it would be filled before it would be possible for him, after his then communication of the conditions to recieve your approbation of them, and orders to open a second; which however should be awaited, according to his instructions; but he pressed the expediting the order, that the stoppage of the current in our favor might be as short as possible. We saw that if, under present circumstances, your orders should be awaited, it would add a month to the delay, and we were satisfied, were you present, you would approve the conditions and order a second loan to be opened. We unanimously therefore advised an immediate order, on condition the terms of the 2d. loan should not be worse than those of the 1st. – Genl. Knox expressed an apprehension that the 6. nations might be induced to join our enemies; there being some suspicious circumstances; and he wished to send Colo. Pickering to confirm them in their neutrality. This he observed would occasion an expence of about 2000 dollars, as the Indians were never to be met empty-handed. We thought the mission adviseable. As to myself, I hope we shall give the Indians a thorough drubbing this summer, and I should think it better afterwards to take up the plan of liberal and repeated presents to them. This would be much the cheapest in the end, and would save all the blood which is now spilt: in time too it would produce a spirit of peace and friendship between us. The expence of a single expedition would last very long for presents. – I mentioned to the gentlemen the idea of suggesting thro' Colo. Beckwith, our knowlege of the conduct of the British officers in furnishing the Indians with arms and ammunition, and our dissatisfaction. Colo. Hamilton said that Beckwith had been with him on the subject, and had assured him they had given the Indians nothing more than the annual present, and at the annual period. It was thought proper however that he should be made sensible that this had attracted the notice of government. I thought it the more material, lest, having been himself the first to speak of it, he might suppose his excuses satisfactory, and that therefore they might repeat the annual present this year. As Beckwith lodges in the same house with Mr. Madison, I have desired the latter to find some occasion of representing to Beckwith that tho an annual present of arms and ammunition be an innocent act in time of peace, it is not so in time of war: that it is contrary to the laws of neutrality for a neutral power to furnish military implements to either party at war, and that if their subjects should do it on private account, such furnitures might be seised as contraband: to reason with him on the subject, as from himself, but so as to let him see that government thought as himself did.

You knew, I think, before you left us, that the British parliament had a bill before them, for allowing wheat, imported in *British* bottoms, to be warehoused rent-free. In order further to circumscribe the carrying business of the U.S. they now refuse to consider as an American bottom, any vessel not built here. By this construction they take from us the right of defining by our own laws what vessels shall be deemed ours and naturalized here; and in the event of a war, in which we should be neutral, they put it out of our power to benefit ourselves of our neutrality, by increasing suddenly by purchase and naturalization our means of carriage. If we are permitted to do this by building only, the war will be over before we can be prepared to take advantage of it. This has been decided by the Lords Commissioners of the treasury in the case of one Green, a merchant of New York, from whom I have recieved a regular complaint on the subject. – I inclose you the copy of a note from

Mr. King to Colo. Hamilton, on the subject of the appointment of a British minister to come here. I suspect it however to be without foundation.

Colo. Eveleigh died yesterday. Supposing it possible you might desire to appoint his successor as soon as you could decide on one, I inclose you a blank commission, which when you shall be pleased to fill up and sign, can be returned for the seal and countersignature. I inclose you a letter from Mr. Coxe to yourself on the subject of this appointment, and so much of one to me as related to the same, having torn off a leaf of compliment to lighten and lessen my inclosures to you. Should distributive justice give preference to a successor of the same state with the deceased, I take the liberty of suggesting to you Mr. Hayward, of S.C. whom I think you told me you did not know, and of whom you are now on the spot of enquiry. – I inclose you also a continuation of the Pennsylvania debates on the bill for federal buildings. After the postponement by the Senate, it was intended to bring on the reconsideration of that vote. But the hurry at winding up their session prevented it. They have not chosen a federal Senator. I have the honour to be with the most profound respect & sincere attachment, Sir, Your most obedient & most humble servt.,   TH: JEFFERSON

RC (DNA: RG 59, MLR); endorsed. PrC (DLC); consisting of first three pages only, the fourth page being in MHi. FC (DNA: RG 59, SDC). Enclosures: (1) Extract from Rufus King to Alexander Hamilton, 11 Apr. 1791, printed below; (2) Tench Coxe to the President, 16 Apr. 1791; (3) partial text of Coxe to TJ, 16 Apr. 1791 (the two last printed in group of documents at 16 Apr. 1791).

ENCLOSURE

Extract from Rufus King to Alexander Hamilton

New York 11th Apr. [i.e., ca. 9 Apr. 1791]

Mr. Elliot, who, it has been said, was appointed, will not come to America; owing, say his friends here, to a disinclination on his part, that has arisen from the death of his eldest, or only son. Mr. Seaton yesterday read me an extract of a letter from London, dated Feb. 2. and written as he observed by a man of information, which says 'Mr. Fraser is appointed Plenipotentiary to the U. S. of America, and will go out as soon as it is ascertained here that a correspondent character is appointed in America.' Although Mr. Elliot might not have been altogether adequate to the appointment, yet he would not have been a bad choice: it is questionable whether we can say even as much as that for Mr. Fraser, who is probably the gentleman lately resident with the Hanse towns, and formerly Consul at Algiers, and who is said to be a wrong-headed impetuous man. Should the information be correct, the appointment is not only unpromising, but it is also a pretty strong proof of the misguided opinions of the British administration concerning this country. Yours most sincerely,

R. KING

Tr (DNA: RG 59, MLR); entirely in TJ's hand. The recipient is not identified except in TJ's covering letter to Washington. The letter from which this passage was extracted has not been found, but it is clear that TJ erred in dating it the 11th. It was on that day that Hamilton himself sent the same extract to Washington and made it available to TJ (Hamilton to Washington, 11 Apr. 1791, Syrett, *Hamilton*, VIII, 277). Hence King's letter presumably was dated about two days earlier. TJ's transcript of the extract varies in a few minor details from that sent by Hamilton to Washington.

It seems clear that when the Cabinet met at TJ's house on the 11th Hamilton laid before the group the extract from a letter he had just received from Rufus King. It is not so clear why he should have disclosed information which proved to be incorrect and which contained King's allusion to the misguided opinions of the British ministry. A plausible explanation for this would seem to be that Hamilton was keenly aware of the view held by Washington which he made manifest in transmitting to the Senate at the close of the session the report on Gouverneur Morris' mission (see Editorial Note and group of documents at 15 Dec. 1790). TJ's concurring attitude had long

since been made evident to Hamilton and others. The revelation of King's assessment may therefore have been made as a gesture of agreement that did not exist. While TJ told Washington he thought the news of the appointment of a minister was without foundation, Hamilton gave no opinion when he transmitted the extract to Washington. He did say, however, that nothing else had happened other than what his official dispatch contained (the dispatch dealt with the call of the Cabinet meeting to discuss the revision of Short's instructions; Hamilton to Washington, 10 Apr. 1791, Syrett, *Hamilton*, VIII, 269). But much was happening during the week of the 11th of April in which the hand of the Secretary of the Treasury was felt – the meeting of the Cabinet with the hidden object of assisting Robert Morris to make a purchase of Indian lands, the projection of plans for a nationally supported manufacturing establishment, and the sanctioning if not the prompting of Tench Coxe's candidacy for the office of Comptroller.

For comment on Andrew Elliot and others who were being reported as chosen or under consideration for appointment as minister to the United States, see Editorial Note and group of documents at 15 Dec. 1790.

IV. Memorandum of a Conversation between James Madison and George Beckwith

[17 April] Philada.

Last evening offered the first opportunity of breaking to Col. B. the subject for which he has been thought a proper channel to the Governour of Canada. It was explicitly made known to him, that besides its being generally understood that the N. W. Indians were supplied with the means of war from their intercourse[1] with Detroit &c. the President had received information, which he considered as certain, that ample supplies of that sort had about the commencement of last campaign, been received by the hostile tribes from places at present in British hands. It was observed to him at the same time, that as the U. S. had no other object in the present war, but to effect and establish peace on their frontier, it was obvious in what light such a circumstance must be viewed by them. And as a further consideration heightening the colour of the fact, he was reminded that the Indians in question were without an exception, inhabitants of the acknowledged territory of the U. S. and consequently stood in a certain relation to them, well understood by the nations possessing territories on this continent.

The sum of his answer was that as a fact so stated, however unaccountable it might be, was not to be contradicted, he could only undertake to affirm that it was impossible it could have proceeded directly or indirectly from the British Government, or even have had the sanction or countenance of the authority on the spot. He multiplied assurances that the whole spirit and policy of their Government was opposed to Indian hostilities; and that the sentiments views and orders of Lord Dorchester discouraged them as much as possible. This he knew to be the case. He asked whether there were any particulars of time place or persons contained in the information to the President; whether there was any evidence that the articles[2] supplied were in greater quantities than were usual for other purposes than war, intimating that if there were just ground of complaint a regular statement and communication of it in *any mode* that might be thought not improper, would be most correspondent with the customary proceedings in such cases. For himself he should be very ready on receiving any such statements or communications to transmit them. He was here however not in any formal character, on the contrary in an informal one, a very informal one to be sure; and he entered into this conversation as between one private gentleman and another. He had indeed been a good while at N. York before, as well as here since the removal of the Government. He hoped his further stay would be rendered short by the arrival of some more authentic character. He was at N. York before Mr. Jefferson came into the office he now holds, and he believed it was known on what footing he was. Yet he had not in any respect been turned over to Mr. Jefferson, nor had any thing passed that could give him any pretensions to be in any communication with the Secretary of State. Such a communication was no doubt thought improper by the Secretary of State with so informal a character, though in a way ever so informal. He did not undertake to suppose it was not right, especially as different forms of Governments have different modes of proceedings &c.

The turn given to the conversation shewing pretty clearly a desire to make the occasion subservient to some further and direct intercourse with the Government it was thought proper, for that reason, as well as for avoiding the necessity of another conversation to reply at once that it was not probable the information received by the President would be made known to him in any way more authentic than the present; which it was true, as he had observed, was merely a conversation between two private gentlemen; but if the fact, that the President had received the information as stated, was made sufficiently credible, the proper effect of the communication need not depend on the mode of it. If the dispositions of Lord Dorchester were such as were described, and of which his reputation for humanity and prudence left no room to doubt, any evidence amounting to probability only would insure all the interference that might depend on him. The conduct of Governments toward formal and informal characters was certainly not within the compass[3] of this conversation. It was probable however that no distinction was made by the Government here, which was not made by all Governments, the difference between those characters seeming to lie not in the circumstance of the former being possessed of written and the latter of verbal authority; but in the greater publicity and formality of the written credentials from the proper source produced by the former. – The evident impropriety of the military supplies afforded to the Indians required no doubt that the countenance of the British Government or even the sanction of the officer on the spot ought not to be presumed as long as the fact could be otherwise explained; but as the effect of such aids was the same whether furnished by public authority or by vindictive or avaritious individuals, it was in every case to be expected that the abuse would be corrected. And the circumstance of the Indians in question being within the acknowledged limits of the U. S. and receiving the means of war against them from a foreign source was again brought into view as heightening the color of the affair. – With respect to the particulars of the fact, they did not seem to be material. In what degree the President was possessed of them could not be said. It might be difficult to ascertain the particulars and yet the general fact be sufficiently established. As the Indians at war traded with British subjects only, their being able to carry on hostilities[4] was[5] of itself sufficient evidence in the case. It might be difficult also to mark precisely the line between supplies for war and for hunting, but it was probable that not only the difference of quantity demanded, but other indications must leave little doubt of the purpose for which they were intended.[6]

Col. B. professed the strongest disposition to do any thing in his power having been actuated by this disposition in all his communications to Canada, but repeated his wish for more exact information on the subject. The intelligence was itself so vague, and was communicated to him under such reserve, that he was really at a loss how to represent it. "May I sir mention your name in the case"? He was answered, that from the nature of the conversation he would be under no restraint from mentioning any circumstance[7] relating to it he pleased. "May I Sir say that I have your permission to use your name?" Ansr. The permission being a part of the conversation he must be equally free to mention it if he thought fit; tho' it was not perceived to be a circumstance very material. "Will you be so good Sir as to repeat the information you mentioned to have been received by the President?" This request being complied with, he said he should certainly look out for the first opportunity of making the matter known to Lord D.[8] and if Mr. M. should be here on the receipt of an answer he should be made acquainted with it, repeating his declaration that it was impossible the British Government could in any respect have countenanced or approved any supplies to the Indians as an aid or encouragement to their hostilities.[9]   J. M.

Dft (DLC: Madison Papers); at head of text: "Substance of a Conversation held by Js. Madison Jr with Col. Beckwith, at the desire of Mr. Jefferson. (Copy) with Mr. Jefferson's file"; at foot of text: "(Copy)"; bottom of second leaf torn so that approximately six lines of the text are lost; there are numerous interlineations and deletions, of which some are indicated in textual notes below. Although Madison twice described this as a copy, it is obviously a rough draft. The allusion to "Mr. Jefferson's file" presumably means that the memorandum was to be filed among the TJ papers in Madison's own records. The document is undated but the interview undoubtedly took place on the evening of the 17th. The memorandum may have been drafted on the 18th, for in Madison's list of his letters to TJ compiled many years later he entered under that date: "1791. Apl. 18. conversation with Beckwith" (MS in DLC: Rives Papers).

[1] Madison first wrote "communication" and then deleted it.

[2] Madison first wrote "arms and ammunition" and then altered the text to read as above.

[3] Madison first wrote "purpose" and then deleted it.

[4] Madison first wrote "war" and then deleted it.

[5] Madison first wrote and then deleted "the most authentic proof."

[6] The bottom part of the second leaf of Dft is missing, so that about six lines of text are missing, of which only a few ascenders of letters in the first line remain and are indecipherable. The succeeding paragraph begins at the top of the fourth page. In consequence the missing text at the bottom of the third page consisted of an intervening paragraph.

[7] As first written, this passage read: ". . . that as the conversation was meant for his use he was certainly free to mention any

circumstance." Madison then altered this to read as above.

[8] As first written, this passage first read: ". . . and of making known to Ld. D. what had been *related* communicated to him respecting his"; Madison then altered the text to read as above.

[9] As first written, this passage read: ". . . repeating his observations with assurances with respect to the disposition and interest of the British Govt. with regard to Indian affairs &c. &c." Madison then altered the text to read as above.

To Robert and Peter Bruce

GENTLEMEN   Philadelphia Apr. 5. 1791.

I now inclose you a bank post-note for sixty six dollars and a half, which makes up the rent of the whole year for the house I rented of you in New York, according to the statement below, for which I will ask the favor of a reciept in full. I am Gentlemen Your most obedt. humble servt.,   TH: JEFFERSON

Messrs. Robert and Peter Bruce to Th: Jefferson Dr.

		£	s	d
1790. Aug. 4. To cash. (New York currency)		27	7	3
Dec. 2. To do.		28	0	0
To assumpsit of new tenant		27	10	0
1791. Apr. 5. To 66½ doll. now inclosed		26	12	

£ s d
109 9 3

Cr.

By rent of house from May 1. 1790. to May 1. 1791.   109 0 0

PrC (MHi).

TJ delivered the post note to Remsen and made the following entry in his Account Book on this date: "Note: it was put into an open letter from me to them." The new tenants to whom TJ had sublet the house were Nova Scotia merchants, who at first had demurred but finally accepted TJ's offer at half of the rental price. This would have amounted to £31-18-5½ but, owing to a miscalculation, TJ received only £27-10-0 (TJ to Remsen, 1 Oct. 1790). Even so, he characteristically overlooked the discrepancy and in the settlement paid a few shillings more than required.

From Francis Eppes

DR SIR   Eppington April 5th. 1791

Your favour of 4th[1] of March was deliverd me on sunday last. I am much oblig'd by the pleasure you express at my fortunate sale. If you are determin'd to sell I wou'd recommend it to you not to sell until about XMas or a little after as Colo. Skipwith intends to dispose of one hundred on the first of October.

My wishes with respect to Jack are that he shoud be brought up to some profession. The Law is what him and myself have thought of. However, shou'd you find his foundations too slender to be respectable in that line I wish you to direct his Studies to any thing else which you think most to his advantage. Indeed coud he study Law and write in your office also that wou'd be my choice. I have provided funds for his maintanace, tho' am really at a loss what allowance is necessary. This you will be so obliging as to inform me. He brings with him £60, forty five of which is in two bank notes. Those I have directed him to lodge with you. I must also request that you will make him account with you for all his expenditures as I well know Boys of his age in such a place as Philadelphia are as little capabel of following a proper line of conduct as a Ship a[t] Sea without Helm or Pilot. I hope you will find him well dispos'd to do every thing you require. I have ever found him very manageable and trust when he is put into the right track, he will pursue it with ardor and I hope profit. Jack is fully appris'd of my circumstances and he will be unpardonable if he exceeds the bounds of moderation in his expenditures. Any addition which you think necessary shall with pleasure be furnish'd. I only request to have timely notice, and the remittance shall be made. He has some books which will be sent him by water. Any others that you think necessary shall be furnish'd or the money to purchase them. I suppose every thing in that way can be more easily procur'd in Philidelphia than here. I he[ar]d by Martin a few days ago that they all were well at the mountain and were shortly to come down the country. I am with every wish for your health & Happiness Dr. Sir Your affect. Friend, FRANS. EPPES

P.S. When ever you come to Virginia and your time will not admit of your coming here we shall make a point of Visiting you provided we can have notice in time. F E

RC (DLC: Miscellaneous Manuscripts). Recorded in SJL as received 19 Apr. 1791.

This letter was delivered by John Wayles Eppes and thus the time of his arrival in Philadelphia is fixed by the date of its receipt. Within a month TJ had set him on a rigorous course of study at the College of Philadelphia and, more important, in his own office and under his supervision. TJ not only directed the young man's reading in history, government, and law, but also provided him with a unique opportunity for observing at first hand the conduct of public affairs (see Editorial Note at 13 Mch. 1791; also, note to TJ to Eppes, 15 May 1791). MARTIN was a slave at Monticello, at this time about 52 years of age.

¹ I.e., 14th.

To Richard Hanson

SIR   Philadelphia April 5. 1791.

In my letter of Nov. 7. I informed you that on settling the affairs of the year there were expected to be 69,000 ℔. of tobacco to be appropriated to the making my annual payment of £500. sterl. to you and £200. sterl. to Kippen & co. Finding that tobacco of that quality would sell better here than in Virginia and probably better than in England I ordered so much as was at the warehouse to be brought here, and by that sample have sold the whole crop at 5. dollars, except the 14,000 ℔. which was fired and is to be sold in Virginia. 55,000 ℔. here @ 5. dollars and 14,000 ℔. there at the country price, will I presume, after paying the charges of bringing the former here, nearly about cover the 700£ sterl. I have been obliged to credit till September, as the tobacco will then be considered as old tobacco which entitled me to 5/ the hundred more than I should have got, had I sold it as it is at present. But I have hopes that if the tobacco can all be got here in time I can discount the purchaser's bills at the bank in time for your payment.

I have sold to Mr. Ronald my Cumberland lands for £1076 sterling, half payable Jan. 1. 1796. the other half Jan. 1. 1797. both bearing interest from Oct. 5. 1790. He has given two separate bonds, and as a security for one of them he mortgages the whole lands purchased, and for the other bond he mortgages half his Beaverdam lands, which half I suppose of double the value of the bond for which it is a security. I had previously examined the records of Goochland and found these lands were under no incumbrance there. These two bonds would pay the whole of my instalment to you of the year 1797. and nearly half that of 1796. The dispositions which Mr. Jones and yourself have expressed of giving every indulgence in this business consistent with his security, induce me to hope, that as these bonds and mortgages would be a greater security to him than my simple bonds, you will give me my bonds for 1796. and 1797. in exchange for these, and for a bond to be executed for the balance of 1796. which Ronald's bonds will not cover. The bonds in that case shall be assigned to you, and the mortgages regularly transferred. By this means you will be safer than as you now stand, and I shall be absolutely discharged of my instalment of 1797. and part of that of 1796. and the payment of this year being made there will remain only 4. more instalments of 500£ each and a fifth of nearly that sum, for which I shall provide by further sales without counting on crops except for the first of them which will be due in 1792. before any money can probably be recieved on sales. My desire to get myself placed on sure ground as fast as possible induces me to make you the offer of these bonds and mortgages first. I will beg your immediate answer; as if you do not accept them, *as payment*, I must endeavor to avail myself of them otherwise. I am with much esteem Sir Your most obedt. humble servt,   TH: JEFFERSON

RC (NN). PrC (MHi).

On the terms agreed upon by TJ to discharge his share of the debt to Farell & Jones, see Editorial Note and Documents on the subject, Vol. 15: 642-77. Although Hanson himself had disposed of TJ's first bond to a person to whom his principals were indebted, he declined to accept a similar proposal by TJ. His curt refusal was no doubt disappointing to TJ, but it was also a tribute to the respect in which his bond was held and to the long and persistent effort he made to discharge the indebtedness (see Hanson to TJ, 30 Apr. 1791).

To Daniel L. Hylton

DEAR SIR   Philadelphia Apr. 5. 1791.

Your favor of Mar. 12. came to hand a fortnight ago and having given me reason to expect that the bill of lading for the vis-a-vis would come within a post or two, I have delayed answering in order to make one job of it. But not recieving the bill of lading, I trouble you again to send it forward. In the mean time I had enquiry made at New York whether any such captain as Towles had arrived there and am answered in the negative. I now inclose you a bank-post-note for 22. Doll. 75. cents equal to £6-16-6 the expences you were so kind as to disburse for the 13 hogsheads of tobacco. Their quality has been found of the very best according to the taste of this market, and I have consequently sold my whole crop, except about 14,000 ℔. of the Bedford tobacco which having been injured by the wet would not answer here. I have written to Mr. Lewis to sell that part in the country, and to hurry down all the rest from Bedford and Albemarle, which I expect will be about 39 or 40 thousand. I must trouble you to have this sent to me here, making the freight payable here. I am told the proper price is 20/ this money or 2 Dol. 66 cents pr. hhd. On this you will be pleased to do for the best. The inclosed letter to Mr. Lewis desires him to place 15. or 16.£ in your hand to pay the warehouse and shipping expences; to prevent adding that advance to the other trouble I am giving you, be so good as to send it by the Charlottesville post which calls at the printing office (Davies's I believe) the day of the week on which the paper comes out. If you can now and then drop me a line informing me how the tobacco comes in, I shall thank you. My cordial esteem to Mrs. Hylton and am Dear Sir Your affectionate humble servt., TH: JEFFERSON

PrC (MHi). Enclosure: "Philadelphia Apr. 5. 1791. The Inspectors of either warehouse at Richmond are hereby desired to deliver to Mr. Danl. L. Hylton or order, all my tobo. of the last crop which shall come from Albemarle, or Bedford. Out of the last they are desired however to except such hogsheads as shall appear to have been fired (as I am informed there was some) should that come to their warehouse, also to except out of both parcels any orders which may be given on them by Colo. N. Lewis or Mr. B. Clarke for overseer's shares. Th: Jefferson" (PrC in MHi).

To William Lewis

DEAR SIR   Philadelphia Apr. 5. 1791.

It is with some degree of shame that I accept the kind offer in your letter of the 1st. inst. However one may sometimes do for the public what they would not do for themselves. I therefore send you our whole collection of loose laws, to be filled up as you propose. I would beg that the copying of your index or any other writing in the business may be sent to be done at my office so as to take as much trouble off your hands as we can. For the same reason I will ask you to give the bookbinder &c. orders on me for the amount of their accounts. I am with great esteem & respect Dr. Sir Your most obedt. & most humble servt,   TH: JEFFERSON

PrC (DLC). FC (DNA: RG 59, PCC No. 120).

To Matthew McAllister

SIR   Philadelphia Apr. 5. 1791.

I have received your two favors of Oct. 24. and Dec. 24. as also the laws and proceedings you have been so kind as to collect. Those relative to British property and subjects will enable us, I presume to decide on any objections which may be derived on their part from proceedings of the state of Georgia. – With respect to the collection of the laws of Georgia, however desireable that a complete collection of all the laws of every state should be made at the seat of government, yet I do not think myself authorised to go to the expence of Manuscript copies. I will therefore only ask your further attention to collect any *printed* acts which may serve to complete our collection and may fall in your way, or to send the new revisal when it shall be published. With respect to the blanks in your account for the journey to Augusta, it was certainly never my intention to give you the trouble of such a journey for this business. I expected the whole would be done by written orders, or by personal ones where the gentlemen should happen to be on the spot. As an uniformity must be observed in the settlement of these accounts, I must await those which shall be rendered by the attorneys for the other states, and if they make similar charges, the whole shall be put into the Auditor's hands as the law requires to be settled by him as shall appear just. In the mean time as no question can arise about replacing the cost of what you have sent, and it is improper you should lay out of that, I inclose you a bank-post-note for 17. Dol. 14. cents, the amount, which will be paid by the collector of the customs at Savannah, and have the honor to be Sir Your most obedt. humble servt,

TH: JEFFERSON

PrC (DLC). FC (DNA: RG 59, PCC No. 120).

To Richard Potts

SIR   Philadelphia Apr. 5. 1791.

Your favor of Mar. 9. came to hand on the 23d. I was prevented by other pressing business from attending to it's contents, till two or three days ago, and then perceiving that you had sent the laws to me, and that they were not come to hand, I sent to Mr. Warder, who immediately delivered them. I now inclose you a bank-post-note for twenty five dollars and a quarter, the amount of the account you inclosed. I beg you to accept my thanks for your attention to this business one part of which was interesting to the state of Maryland and the other to the general Government, and have the honor to be with great esteem & respect Sir Your most obedt. & most humble servt,   TH: JEFFERSON

PrC (DLC); at foot of text: "Mr. Richard Potts Maryland." FC (DNA: RG 59, PCC No. 120).

From Mary Jefferson Bolling

DEAR BROTHER   Chesnut Grove april 6 1791

I receiv'd the favour of yours dateed october wherin I found a total disappointment of the happiness I had long flattered my self with of seeing you, it being at a time that our distress cannot be describ'd. It is too much for my pen so that I will not trouble you with it. You must now permit me to hail you grandfather and I do Sincearly congratulate you on the happy occation of pat'cyes safe recovry. Wee anticipate the pleashure of seeing you this spring as your anxiety must be very great to see the little Stranger.

I am sorry to tell you our sister Carrs ill health becomes seriously alarming. She has an obstanate languid fever that does not intermit for two or three days. When they leave her she is considerable weakened and they return very frequently. I very much fear these are dropsical simtoms. I have long wisht an oppertunity of answering yours. Had it not have been for Mr. Epps's politeness to me it was uncertain when I should have been gratified. Mr. Bolling Joins in love to you and apologyes for his negligence. The rest of my family Join in love. Adieu my dear brother may every blessing this life affords attend you are the most ardent wishes of your affectionate Sister   MARY BOLLING

RC (ViU: Moyer-Jefferson Papers); endorsed by TJ as received 19 Apr. 1791 and so recorded in SJL. Punctuation has been supplied. TJ's letter was that of 31 Oct. 1790.

THE LITTLE STRANGER: TJ's first grandchild was Anne Cary Randolph, to whom Martha gave birth on 23 Jan. 1791 (see TJ to Martha Jefferson Randolph, 9 Feb.

1791, in which he acknowledged her letter announcing the event; that letter has not been found). TJ's sister, Mary Jefferson (1741-1817), was married to Col. John Bolling of Chesterfield county on 24 June 1760. SISTER CARR: Martha Jefferson Carr, widow of TJ's friend Dabney Carr, suffered poor health but lived for another twenty years. She was three years younger than TJ.

From Elizabeth Wayles Eppes

DEAR SIR   Eppington, April 6. 1791.

I sincerely congratulate you on the birth of your fine Granddaughter. I am told she is a nun such. I wish'd much to have been with my dear Patsy, but it was impossible. I now please myself with the happiness of seeing them all soon. The number of advantages you would have for my dear Polly in Philadelphia I have no doubt must be very great, added to the happiness of your having her with you, tho' be assured my dear Sir it will always add to our happiness to have her with us. I never met a more governable temper.

Your kind intentions with regard to Wayles have delight'd me not a little, as I am sure if he follows your directions (which I hope there is no doubt of) I shall be completely happy. We all join in wishing you every blessing this life affords, Your affectionate friend,

E EPPES

RC (ViU); endorsed by TJ as received 19 Apr. 1791 and so recorded in SJL.

From William Temple Franklin

DEAR SIR   London 6 April 1791.

I received duly your obliging Favor of the 27 Novr. last, together with the M. S. of Negotiations; for which I beg you will receive my thanks, as well as, for the obliging Expressions of your Friendship; in promising to make my special Preferences known, relative to a foreign-Appointment – should Circumstances give place to it. – These I think may probably soon occur, as I understand a Minister to Congress, is appointed, and soon going out from France; – and another from this Court is much talked of, and will in all probability be sent out 'ere long. – A very considerable Report is gone in to the Privy Council, on the Connection between this Country and the United States: I have been promised a sight of it, but have not yet been able to procure it: – As soon as I do, I will take the liberty of informing you particularly of its Contents: – For the present, I have only been able to learn, that the Dispositions towards us are more favorable than formerly. That they entertain a greater Respect for us as a Nation; and that a Commercial Treaty with us is a desireable Object. – For these Dispositions we have nobody to thank but Ourselves. The Establishment of our new System of Government, and thereby our public Credit, has work'd this Change in our Favor, not only here, but throughout Europe.

Finding my Mitchels Map, would not be compleat, even with the addition of the Sheet you have – and as you appear to be desirous of having the whole, – I have sent you a Compleat one, by Col. Smith, who sails in the Packet.

Having had much other Business at hand, I have not been able to give as yet much attention to the Publication of my Grandfathers Works. But being now more at Liberty, I shall soon put them into the Press: – and you may rely on my following your Advice of printing them in 8° as also of my attending to the Hint you have been pleased to give me, on another Point.

I sent to Mr. Adams by a former Opportunity, several late Publications here, relative to the French Revolution; – and I requested him to let you have the Perusal of them, which I suppose he has done. – [Paynes *"Rights of Man"* was among them: – It has had a great Effect here: – and did the lower order of People read, and think for themselves, it would have a greater: The Cause of Liberty is every where gaining Ground – and Monarchy getting out of Fashion: – I am told the King here says he does not think it will last above his Time in this Country.

The late Alarmes of War with Russia, are by no means so pleasing to the Nation, as those occasioned by the recent Dispute with Spain. – But War is as yet very uncertain; and I hardly think it will take Place. – The Ministry are much abused by Opposition on the present State of Affairs.]¹ – The inclosed will shew on what Grounds, tho' otherwise a trifling Performance.

The Cause of Freedom and good Government is loosing some of its ablest Supporters. Mirabeau, it is said, is dead! – and Dr. Price lies dangerously Ill!!

I meet here with many who ask kindly after you; – among them, the Duke of Dorset, who is very particular in his Enquiries. He has mentioned to me that his Neice had wrote once or twice to your Daughter, since her return to America; but not receiving an Answer had suppos'd she meant to drop her Acquaintance; which his Neice much regretted. I ventur'd to assure his Grace, that that was not likely, and that possibly the letters might have mis-carried. You will take what Notice of this you may think proper.

I shall probably leave this for Paris in about 3 Weeks; where I shall be very proud of hearing from you, and being honor'd with Your Commands – Being with great Esteem Dr. Sir, Yr obliged humble Servt,   W. T. FRANKLIN.

RC (DLC); endorsed by TJ as received 21 June 1791 and so recorded in SJL.

Believing as he did in the essential need for confidentiality in diplomatic discourse, TJ had admonished Franklin – in THE HINT here referred to – against publishing such of his grandfather's letters or papers as might "not yet be proper to put into the possession of every body." At the same time he had returned to him the M.S. OF NEGOTIATIONS which, as a fragment of Benjamin Franklin's autobiography, gave an account of his fruitless efforts at reconciliation between Great Britain and the colonies (see TJ to Franklin, 27 Nov. 1790). For a discussion of Franklin's important action in transmitting an abstract of Hawkesbury's REPORT . . . TO THE PRIVY COUNCIL, see Editorial Note and group of documents at 15 Dec. 1790.

Franklin's gesture in sending a copy of Paine's *Rights of Man* to John Adams with the request that he let TJ read it was well-intended, but it could not have come at a more inopportune moment. Adams of course ignored the request, knowing well – as did

the general public also – that TJ had already seen the pamphlet and had commended it in terms that brought about an open break between himself and Adams (see Editorial Note and group of documents at 26 Apr. 1791). But one of the pamphlets sent by Franklin to Adams was transmitted to TJ: Calonne's *De l'état de la France* (London, 1790). It bore this inscription by Franklin: "Mr. Adams is desired after perusing this Work to lend it to Mr. Jefferson and Mr. Secy. Hamilton. W.T.F." (Sowerby, No. 2543). The fact that TJ retained the volume in his library – it still exists in the Library of Congress – suggests that Adams sent it first to Hamilton. For other pamphlets sent directly to TJ by Franklin, presumably without covering letters since none is recorded in SJL after that of 3 July 1793, see Sowerby, Nos. 2596, 2597, and 2598.

¹ Brackets in MS. TJ may have marked this passage for publication during the controversy over *Rights of Man*, but the text has not been found in any newspaper.

To Thomas Mann Randolph, Jr.

DEAR SIR   Philadelphia Apr. 6. 1791.

Your favor of Mar. 5. came to hand on the 24th. and that of Mar. 14. on the 1st. inst. With respect to Mr. Thompson it has been understood that his circumstances are desperate and that he is fond of the bottle. At the time the first appointments of consuls were made, their circumstances were not attended to, and an appointment or two took place of persons under embarrasments of that kind. We have since become sensible of the inexpediency of this, and it has latterly been a decisive objection. The second is not less so. The Consulship of Lisbon has been for some time sollicited by a citizen of this state, supported by the intercessions of the first characters in the state. The candidate is of the purest character possible, and his circumstances, not desperate, but embarrassed. If this last objection can be departed from, he will have it. But it lies for consideration till the next session of Congress. If what has been understood of Mr. Thompson is not founded, the consulship of Cadiz is open, and will be so till next Congress: and I think he might expect it. If you can inform yourself on these two points, I will bear him in mind, and as I shall see you at Monticello in the fall, you will then be so good as to communicate the result of your enquiries. There is a desire to comply with his wish and that of his friends, if he be proper for the office. A consul is the judge in all disputes between two citizens within his consulship, of whatever magnitude; he is the administrator too of all citizens dying therein, and as such may have great sums of money lodged in his hands. – I am glad you are about to undertake the examination of the Opossum. It is a great reflection on us that this phaenomenon in natural history is still so much unknown. The disappearance of the false pouch, supposed by Mr. Rittenhouse, will of course claim your attention. I suspect it to be an error. – With respect to the purchase of Edgehill you alone can judge of it's expediency. If you can pay for it, you will never repent of it. It is a valuable tract and a cheap one: but I think with you that to take the negroes with it, is taking it sadly burthened. Money laid out in negroes is thrown away. Perhaps Colo. Randolph would agree to let you have the land, and to sell the negroes either publicly or privately. He would get more for them in this way. Still if the land alone should be too much for you to pay for, it may be better not to risk your quiet of mind on it. I wish I could help you in it, but my own embarrasments bind me hand and foot. Were it not for this I would gladly take any part of the tract that might not suit you. Does Mr. Carter intend to sell or not? If he does, so that a large body of good mountain land could be bought at once, the following calculation might be worth making, to wit. For how much would the lands of Varina sell? How much mountain land would that sum purchase? How much can be cleared at Varina at present? How much would be cleared on the mountain land so to be bought, in the farming way? Which is most likely to increase in value? Which would best admit of partition in the case of several children? Which most convenient at present? &c. &c. Were this idea admissible at all, it would require mature consideration. I beg that you will take all the time you please to accomodate yourself with lands, remaining in your present situation as long as you can make it agreeable to yourself to do so. It is a comfort to me to contribute in any thing to your accomodation and happiness. I have received my daughter's letter, and will execute her wish for the calash for herself, and seeds for her friend. Present my warm love to them both. I have a great deal for the little Anne also, and am with sincere attachment Dear Sir Yours affectionately, Th: JEFFERSON

RC (DLC)

The Pennsylvania candidate for the consulate at Lisbon, supported by Robert Morris and other influential merchants, was John Telles. TJ might also have added that members of Congress from Massachusetts and merchants of that state had urged the appointment of John Bulkeley. Another candidate for the post was Thomas Appleton, who wrote from Paris on 10 July 1791 reminding TJ of his previous request and adding: "The extensive Commerce which exists between that port, and the United States has determined my establishment there if I should obtain the nomination. You will readily perceive the advantages which that place has over most others in Europe, and from this Circumstance I imagine there may be many applicants." Samuel Pleasants of Philadelphia had also recommended Thomas Thompson, but TJ reported to Washington that the latter was "a bankrupt and addicted to the bottle" (see Editorial Note on consular problems and TJ's report, 21 Feb. 1791; Humphreys to TJ, 3 May 1791; and Appleton to TJ, 10 July 1791, RC in DLC: Washington Papers, endorsed by TJ as received 22 Oct. 1791 and so recorded in SJL). Appleton, Bulkeley, Telles, and Thompson all failed to get the Lisbon appointment. It went instead to Edward Church, who had been appointed consul at Bilbao but not received there (Washington to the Senate, 3 May 1792, JEP, I, 121).

From James Currie

Richmond, 7 Apr. 1791. He had the honor and the pain of receiving TJ's friendly letter by Mr. Hamilton, and while sorry to learn the situation he could never make acknowledgments enough for TJ's "uncommonly friendly and very pointed attention to the business." After deliberating with anxiety, he ventured to impart the contents of TJ's letter to [Griffin], which he received with some emotion and wrote the enclosed. He says there are reasons which forbid Potter's admitting possession and knowledge of the property mentioned. He will explain when he meets you and until then he desires secrecy and will "make all appear clearly to your satisfaction as my friend." Currie will leave to TJ to decide whether to reveal contents of his letter to Potter privately. If property is sacrificed to do him justice, he will let TJ decide whether to make the purchase. Once secured, it will be in his power to be generous to him. He will write again by him "and leave the whole to your talents for real business and experienced friendship to myself. Pray secure me if possible." – P.S. Mrs. Eppes' family all well. Mrs. Skipwith has been here a month "to try the Effects of Electricity &ca. for some very serious nervous Complaints of some standing. I am sorry to say not with all the advantage I could wish. It has much mended Miss Skipwith's hearing."

RC (DLC); addressed: "The Honble. Thomas Jefferson Esqr. Secretary of State"; postmarked: "free" and "richmond April 8"; endorsed by TJ as received 14 Apr. 1791 and so recorded in SJL. Enclosure: John Tayloe Griffin to TJ, 7 Apr. 1791, informing him that he had read TJ's letter to Currie; that when he drew the bills he had in Philadelphia, as Potter knew, over $21,000 in public securities, of which two-thirds were in final settlement certificates and one-third in indents and state certificates; that he pledged his faith and honor as a gentleman to apply these to the settlement of the bills and to no other purpose; that he asks TJ to postpone further application to Potter until he arrives in Philadelphia, which will certainly be between the 15th and 20th of April; and that thereafter, again pledging these effects to the discharge of the bills, he desires no further indulgence (RC in DLC; endorsed by TJ as received 14 Apr. 1791 and so recorded in SJL). Griffin failed to depart as promised. His journey, he wrote from Richmond on the 15th, was postponed by important and unforeseen business. Again he promised to set out the following week and asked TJ to hold the bills, promising to discharge them on arrival. But it was not until May that he arrived with Currie's letter of 13 Apr. 1791 (Griffin to TJ, 15 Apr. 1791; RC in DLC; endorsed by TJ as received 21 Apr. 1791 and so recorded in SJL). Two years later he was still importuning TJ for favors and afraid to enter Philadelphia for fear of a debtor's prison (see Griffin to TJ, 16 June 1793; TJ to Griffin, 18 June 1793). See note to TJ's instructions for Remsen, 16 May 1791.

To John Harvie, Jr.

Dear Sir   Philadelphia Apr. 7. 1791.

The recess of Congress, and a relaxation in the business which immediately ensues their separation, permits me now to turn my attention a little to my own affairs. I resume therefore the subject of my letters to you of Jan. 11. and Nov. 2. 1790. and yours to me of Jan. 25. 1791. respecting my right to the 490. acres of land included in my order of council of Mar. 11. 1773. for 1000. acres, and also in my two entries of Oct. 21. 1774. for 400. acres each, surveyed for James Marks on a junior entry, and purchased from him and Colo. Randolph and patented by you.

With respect to the moiety of the 490. acres sold to you by Colo. Randolph, as I never had an idea of using my orders or entries to injure any right he had, so I will not now avail myself of them to injure any right he thought he had, and in consequence conveyed to you. And if I mention some circumstances on this subject, it is only to bring facts to rights, and to place myself in that point of view which a thousand such tracts of land would not induce me to relinquish. The transaction is a very antient one: no wonder therefore if Colo. Randolph's memory and my own confound some circumstances. Colo. Randolph says to you 'that about 18. or 20. years past I told him I had made an entry for him with the surveyor of Albemarle (Staples) for vacant lands adjoining Edgehill which I would have surveyed for him.'

Ans. Exactly 18. years ago, to wit in 1773. I obtained my order of council for 1000 acres adjoining Edgehill. I had understood that Colo. Randolph had an entry or survey there for either one or two hundred acres, which I apprehended was liable to a caveat, and I told him my order of council should cover it for him. I repeated the same thing to Bryan the surveyor from time to time, and it was the delay occasioned by seeking after the supposed lines of Colo. Randolph's survey, which prevented Bryan from making mine. Colo. Randolph therefore only mis-remembers my *covering* his entry for him, instead of my *making* an entry for him with Staples. This could not be, as Staples had been then dead 6. or 8 years, for I think he died in 1763. or 1764. before I came of age, and 3. or 4. years before I removed from Williamsburg to live in Albemarle. This is mentioned only to shew that there was foundation for the substance of what Colo. Randolph thinks he recollects, so far as that I was to *cover* an entry for him. The entry he was supposed by me to have was either of one or two hundred acres of land, which I am now satisfied had been surveyed before and patented to him, and is no part of either the 490. in question or my 485. However, I mention these things only to rectify ideas as to the fact. I never did, from my cradle to this moment, consider Colo. Randolph's interests as alien to me; I am much less disposed to do it after circumstances have in some degree identified our interests. I therefore relinquish all claim to the moiety of the 490. acres sold by him to you, and I hereby confirm the same so as to place him clear of any demand or responsibility on that account. And I reduce my claim to the moiety held under James Marks.

As to this moiety, my right rests on the general statement contained in my letters of Jan. 11. and Nov. 2. I shall now therefore only subjoin short sketches of answers to some objections contained in yours of Jan. 25.

You observe that you had never heard of my claim till I wrote to you on the subject. I never had an idea, my dear Sir, of your being in the least conusant of the transactions which I complain to have been smuggled into a semblance of right, during my absence from the country, to take my property from me. I know you to be as incapable of it as any man on earth, and from the bottom of my soul acquit you of it. But I expressly charge Mr. Marks with having made his entry, surveyed and sold it, knowing of my prior right, because he and I had one, if not more, pointed conversations on it, beforehand, and because he was expressly warned of my right by Bryan, who I agree with you was very reprehensible for surveying for Mr. Marks. Towards no man would he be so reprehensible as towards myself. But this does not lessen the mala fides of Mr. Marks, nor could he make his title the better by conveying it to an innocent purchaser.[1]

Obj. Your survey was returned in 1784. and open to a caveat till 1786. Ans. The survey was made after I left the country on public business, under public privilege and protection, and the term for a remedy by caveat run out before my return. I arrived at my own house the 23d. of December, 1789. and wrote to you on the subject the 11th. of the ensuing month.

Obj. When a grant has been fraudulently or surreptitiously obtained it will not stand in equity, but throughout this whole business your title wears a very different aspect.'

Ans. I again confirm, my dear Sir, the innocence of your conduct. But Mr. Marks knew of my right, and Mr. Bryan knew of it. It was fraud and surprise in the former and collusion in the latter to enter and survey what both knew to be mine. Bryan indeed says that he did it on 'Mr. Marks assuring him the land would be given up on my making it appear that my claim was prior.' This is a poor palliative for him. Your title, tho' innocently acquired by you, is still built on original wrong, and must stand or fall with that wrong. Let me add too that equity does not confine itself to the vacation of *fraudulent* or *surreptitious* grants; it reforms those also obtained by *error*. If Mr. Marks had obtained a grant of my lands, not knowing they were mine, Equity would vacate his grant.

I close with you in submitting this decision to indifferent persons. I repeat that the subject now claimed is only the moiety of the 490. acres which you hold under Mr. Marks. Whatever award shall be rendered, I make it obligatory on myself and my heirs. I would chuse that the arbitrators should be taken from among the judges, federal, or of the state, and would as live they should be the three eldest (Mr. Wythe excepted, whose peculiar friendship to me, I would not wish to embarrass with such a reference). I believe Mr. Pendleton, Mr. Blair and Mr. Lyons are of the oldest commissions. These or any others you please may decide it. I do not wish to lay any thing before them but this and my two former letters, in which the matter is stated as far as my time will permit. The letter from Bryan of Jan. 10. 1790. as also my original order of council and copies of my two entries are in possession of Colo. N. Lewis who can himself give perhaps some information on the subject. I recollect nothing else which can be material. If there is any important fact to be supported, other than these will support, I should wish to be apprised of it. Otherwise let the matter be settled whenever and wherever these gentlemen shall happen to be assembled. The sooner the better, and you in possessing my three letters, and at hand to procure from Mr. Lewis the documents before mentioned, can have it settled when you please. – I wish, my dear friend, I could have abandoned to you the whole instead of the half of these lands. But they adjoin on the back of my lands also, as on yours; they are most excellently timbered, and lying on the mountain which leads down into all my lands on that side of the river, are a valuable resource for that article. I am told too there is as much land in the tract, of the very first quality as would employ 8. or 10. hands for a tobacco plantation. Knowing my right to be the most antient, believing it the most just, having for 18. years been doing every thing in my power to have it completed, I hope I shall be viewed by you as only endeavoring to hold what is my own, not as attacking the property of another. It is not pleasant to have even differences of opinion about property with a friend, and especially with one whom I esteem as sincerely and highly as I do you: but it is comfortable at least, if one is to support a right, that it is against a reasonable competitor, and one as capable of a chearful acquiescence, as I am myself, under whatever award shall take place. In fine, be it yours, or be it mine, I shall for ever cherish the sentiments of cordial esteem & attachment with which I am, my dear Sir, Your sincere & affectionate friend,

TH: JEFFERSON

P.S. Your favor of Mar. 19. and the letter it inclosed are recieved. This shall be forwarded by a vessel which sails in a few days for Havre.[2]

PrC (MHi); first page only; second page in ViU: Edgehill-Randolph Papers; final four pages in CSmH, being attached to PrC of TJ to Ross, 6 May 1791. Tr (MHi); entirely in TJ's hand and probably made by him in 1795; at head of text in TJ's hand: "Copy."

The present letter, together with those of 11 Jan. and 2 Nov. 1790, states TJ's claim with precision. For a note on the other documents in the case and for a survey showing the location of the 490 acres in dispute, see TJ to Harvie, 11 Jan. 1790. CONUSANT: a legal term meaning cognizant or having an actual knowledge of a matter. As TJ had learned from Sir Edward Coke's *Institutes*, a conusant was one who, knowing of an agreement in which he had an interest, made no objection to it. In using this term, as in stating his case with such precision in the letters referred to, TJ seemed to be addressing himself less to Harvie than to the arbitrators to whom he urged that the matter be submitted.

[1] At this point in Tr, TJ added the following: "[add to all this that my prior right was on record, and a record is notice to all the world]."

[2] P.S. omitted from Tr.

From Adam Lindsay

Norfolk, 7 Apr. 1791. He has TJ's of the 17th ult. and is happy his papers arrived safe. – The myrtle candles desired are plentiful in fall but not to be got at this season, the weather being too warm to make them mold. With some difficulty he has got 54 ℔s. at an advanced price of 20 ₰lb. more than they would bring in the fall. He can procure any quantity TJ desires in that season. "Our spring ships arrives fast, the last Account from England is Febry. 28. England, Prussia and Holland . . . determin'd to force the Empress to a peace. A small detachment beloning to the English in India is cut off by Tippo Saib. France alarm'd at the Empire's troops being on her frontiers is fitting out a fleet to oblige their Colonies to desist from cutting on anothers throts. A small part of the town of Whitehaven sunk down owing to the pillars of the coal pitts giving way. You will please to excuse this small degression." – P.S. The candles shipped on *Netty*, Capt. Cunningham, the same vessel that carried TJ's papers.

RC (DLC); endorsed as received 14 Apr. 1791 and so recorded in SJL.

From Henry Skipwith

DEAR SIR   Richmond 7th. April 1791.

Since my confinement in this place, in consequence of Mrs. Skipwith's becoming a patient of Dr: Curries, I have left no stone unturned to become thoroughly acquainted with the ground upon which we stand respecting the Guineaman consigned to Randolph and Wayles. – My inquiries my dear Sir! have rather encreased than diminished my fears on this score. – It seems generally agreed, among the gentlemen of the law here, whose opinions I have taken, that Mr. Wayles's early death, after the Sale, clearly exonerated his representatives from any claims which might be made on them in consequence of this consignment, had it not been for an unfortunate paragraph in a letter written by him to Farell & Jones, dated Wil-

liamsburg May the 14th. 1772, which follows "This is to acknowledge your favor of the 3d. of February and to return thanks for your
good office in regard to the Guineaman intended here to Colol.
Randolph and myself and to give you every assurance, that whatever
engagements you may be kind enough to enter into on our behalf
shall be complyed with, without inconvenience or prejudice to yourselves and if you desire it, to share in the profits." This Hanson
considers as the rock of his salvation, and I fear it is but too obligatory
on us. – Marshall and Ronald and Innes are of opinion (and to me
it seems right) that if the engagement abroad, entered into by Farell
& Jones (on the part of Randolph and Wayles) with the African
house, was dated prior to this letter as mentioned above, that then
this paragraph as to us becomes a nullity. – How far this is the case
I know not, but on comparing the date of Mr. Wayles letter and
that of the one alluded to of the 3d. of Feby. from Farell & Jones
with the time of the arrival of the Guineaman, I cannot but hope
we may yet be saved. – On the 10th. of the month I shall remove
my family to Eppington, and in conjunction with Mr. Eppes, shall
endeavour to ascertain the certain date of the contract. Perhaps you
may know where a copy of it may be met with. The result of our
search you shall be made acquainted with. – Pray Sir! let me hear
from you on this disagreeable score. Anything you recommend shall
immediately be done. Nothing on my part will be considered as
fatiguing. We have but little hope of redress from Richard Randolph's estate, as independent of the many incumbrances which are
laid on his land, it is a matter of much doubt here whether real
property can be subjected to the payment even of British debts. – After
making a tender of Mrs. Skipwith's warmest affection towards you,
and offering our prayers for a long continuance of your good health
and spirits, I beg leave to remain Dear Sir! Your affectionate friend,

HENRY SKIPWITH

Mrs. Skipwith has some thoughts of going to the Sweet springs
this Summer and taking Monticello in her way.

RC (DLC); endorsed by TJ as received
19 Apr. 1791 and so recorded in SJL.

The legal question involved here concerned the obligation of the estate of John
Wayles respecting the cargo of slaves
brought by *The Prince of Wales* and consigned by Farell & Jones to Wayles and
Randolph as joint partners in the venture.
Texts of the pertinent correspondence on
the subject, including Wayles' letter to Farell & Jones of 14 May 1772 partially quoted
and that of Farell & Jones to Wayles and
Randolph of 3 Feb. 1772 referred to above,
can be found in Vol. 15: 649-77. The
opinion of Andrew Ronald and John Marshall reads: "We are decidedly of opinion
that if any engagement relative to the consignment of a Guineaman to Randolph &
Wayles was entered into subsequent to the

receipt of Mr. Wayles' Letter of the 14th May 1772, that Messrs. Farrel & Jones have a good claim on the Writer of that Letter for indemnity. 1st. April 1791. Andrew Ronald J. Marshall." (RC in DLC); endorsed in Skipwith's hand: "Ronald & Marshall, Opinion."

This opinion was clearly given by the lawyers to Skipwith, not to TJ, who had always held that the Wayles estate was not liable in law or equity. For TJ's opposed and more considered opinion – with which Marshall ultimately came to agree – see his reply to Skipwith, 6 May 1791. The opinion of Innes has not been found.

From C. W. F. Dumas

The Hague, 8 Apr. 1791. The conferences at Reichenbach, The Hague, and Svishtov have placed the English and Prussians in a dilemma. He does not see how England can avoid bankruptcy or sustain Pitt, who is dominated by Grenville. He has just learned that the proposals by Denmark have been rejected. The Amsterdam regency is in bad humor. Some support it; others, their numbers growing, hope that the Phoenix will rise from the ashes. "Quoi-qu'il en soit, le nerf manque: l'argent." – He has drawn on the Amsterdam bankers for his account. P.S. He encloses a letter from a gentleman of The Hague to his kinsman, "*Store Keeper au March-Street*," which he hopes TJ's servant will deliver. Mirabeau died on the 4th. "Grande perte pour l'Assemblée nationale de France."

FC (Dumas Letter Book, Rijksarchief, The Hague; photostats in DLC). Recorded in SJL as received 29 June 1791. Enclosure: Dumas to Messrs. Willink, Van Staphorst, & Hubbard, 11 Apr. 1791, asking them to forward his dispatches "pour le Congrès" and advising them that he has drawn on them for his expenses for the last six months of 1790 (same).

From David Humphreys

Mafra, 8 Apr. 1791. In France uncommon agitation produced by journey of king's aunts to Rome. Great tumults in Paris. Repairing of Chateau de Vincennes, effort of mob to destroy it, and resultant confrontation with the national guard. Another dangerous affair at the Tuileries, involving misunderstanding between Lafayette and the mayor. "The Marquis is said to have acquired additional popularity by his promptness, decision and moderation in quelling these tumults. He is still not without his Enemies. . . . What, or whether any farther, calamities are in reserve, for that Kingdom, before its Revolution shall be completed, I pretend not to predict." Disorders in provinces and opposition of nobility and higher clergy lead malcontents to hope for counter-revolution. Threatened invasion under Prince de Condé, but the current of events authorizes expectation it will fail if attempted. – King much indisposed but recovered. Some new bishops consecrated in place of those refusing oath. Public property sells much higher than estimated; nearly 30 million in assignats burned. – Troubles in Geneva in mid-February now subsided. Bishop of Liège returned to his principality, but no cordial reconciliation. No perfect calm in Austrian Netherlands, where people have not lost sight of their objects. "As mankind have become more enlightened, the situation of Sovereigns and Subjects is wonderfully changed. A People, having once unsuccessfully attempted a Revolution and having found . . . they were not subjected to those rigorous punishments which used to be inflicted on Rebels" will be encouraged in efforts to redress their grievances and confirm their rights.

Conference at Svishtov, according to most recent advices, will not achieve peace between Russians and Turks. Letter of 16 Feb. from Vienna indicates that Convention of Reichenbach may before now have resulted in conclusive peace. Latest advices from North show Empress of Russia determined not to have peace imposed by mediating powers. Her affairs do not seem to be in that exhausted condition the English have long foretold. Nor, after amazing success, will she consent to have England and her allies dictate that everything "remain in the *original state*." But all Turks, save the Sultan, deprecate the war and wish peace, trembling for Constantinople. Ottoman government makes languid efforts and tries in vain to conceal its armies' disasters: "several men and women have been thrown alive into the Sea for speaking of them." If mediating powers do not extricate Turks by negociation, it remains to be seen whether they will succour them by the sword. "Opinions are various." It is understood they have unsuccessfuly sought further alliances with Denmark and Sweden. Russia seeks Danzig, England negociates with Poland. He encloses two papers of the British minister at Warsaw. Meantime, in England, naval preparations under way.

"Since the date of my last letter it has rained here every day, and at times with such abundance that the ground, which was before exceedingly parched with drought, does not require any more moisture at present. I do not know how extensively these seasonable showers have prevailed."

RC (DNA: RG 59, DD); at head of text: "(No.16)"; endorsed by TJ as received 21 June 1791 and so recorded in SJL. Tr (same). Enclosures: (1) Note of the English minister at Warsaw, 28 Jan. 1791, to the Deputies for Foreign Affairs informing them that he had just received a Declaration of his government on Polish affairs and expressing, "in the most distinct and unequivocal manner, the ardent desire of the King his Master to enter anew into political and commercial connections with his Majesty and the illustrious Republic of Poland." (2) Articles "circulated as [those] of the proposed Treaty between Great Britain and Poland," the first of which guaranteed treatment of the subjects of each state "as those of the most favored nation" and the second of which declared: "It shall be lawful to the subjects of each Nation to make their residences in either of the respective States, and to establish mercantile Houses where they please." The document outlined 16 articles in all (Tr of both enclosures, in Humphreys' hand, in DNA:

RG 59, DD; Tr in same).

Humphreys' lengthy account of affairs in France and northern Europe, based largely on newspapers such as the *Courier de l'Europe*, private letters, and pamphlets, reported events which William Short, being less isolated and having better sources of information both of a private and a public nature, had usually reported about a month earlier (see, for example, Short to TJ, 24 Jan., 22 and 25 Feb., and 4 and 11 Mch. 1791). Short, a close student of history and government and less impressed by the diplomatic corps and court affairs than Humphreys, was a more acute observer. But his dispatches were often delayed longer than those of Humphreys, as was the case with the one he sent on the same date as the above. What TJ probably would have valued most in this dispatch was a point Humphreys neglected to mention – the possible effect of the rains on Portuguese wheat production (see Humphreys to TJ, 31 Mch. 1791).

From William Short

DEAR SIR   Paris April 8. 1791.

My last was sent by the English packet a conveyance which I have constantly made use of since you have expressed the desire. I have no other opportunity of writing to you than by merchant vessels which have hitherto so illy served me as would prevent my making further use of them if I did not think it an indispensable duty on my part to give you the most regular information in my power. – This information would be more satisfactory perhaps if by communications from America I was better enabled to judge of the progression of affairs there and of course to examine those here in their relations with respect to them. Having yourself been perfectly in the way of appreciating the want of information from America it is useless for me to say any thing respecting it and of the effect which it necessarily produces on American affairs here. I know little of the wishes and less of the intentions of the United States under a variety of cases supposable. Still I have kept myself perfectly up to the events which take place on this side of the Atlantic in order to obtain and execute, as far as depended on me, such of their wishes and intentions as were capable of being reasoned into certainty.

The National Assembly continue as usual moving on slowly in the line of the constitution, and allowing themselves easily to be diverted from it by the circumstances which grow out of the moment. A decree has been lately passed however which has more the appearance of their intending to dissolve themselves than any thing which has been hitherto done. It is to beg the King to have executed immediately certain articles of a former decree which determined that lists should be made out of all the *citoyens actifs* of the several departments. This was grounded on the work of the present assembly drawing near to a conclusion and the propriety of soon issuing letters of convocation for a new legislature. The proposition was adopted unanimously and the motive of it much applauded. Still I do not think the present assembly will end soon or of themselves, first because I am persuaded that a large majority wish to remain as long as possible, and secondly because I think that movements abroad or disorders at home, the one arising from the imprudence and folly of the Refugees and the other from an habitual state of anarchy, will furnish the pretext for their remaining. By this means they will have the appearance of being continued by the force of circumstances and not of themselves, and thus secure their popularity.

An event which has produced a very uncommon and unexpected effect here is the death of M. de Mirabeau, after a short and violent illness of a few days. If you except a few of the aristocratical party who really desire the prolongation of disorder and a civil war, and of the demagogues of the assembly who saw in him their most formidable rival, he is universally regretted, and what is most extraordinary more at court than any where else. After having changed his party several times without changing his principles he had at length obtained an ascendency in the assembly of which there was no example. All parties believed him venal and faithless and yet all parties courted him and placed their confidence in him by a kind of impulse which it was almost impossible to resist. The general opinion was that he had made a large fortune and that of course he had now an interest in the re-establishment of order to secure it. Many also grounded their opinion of his interest in the forming and finishing of the government on a consideration that his talents put him above all in a well organised representative government whereas in disorder and confusion he was equalled and surpassed by many. It is certain that for some time past he had most strenuously supported the principles of efficient government, and had so perfectly impressed every one with the idea that he alone was capable of establishing one in this country that his death has produced a kind of dismay among them. Its influence has been equally powerful on the people of Paris for other reasons. – The enthusiasm of all has been exhibited in various ways. The different sections of Paris sent deputies to be present at the opening of the corpse in order to ascertain whether he had not been poisoned, which there was a strong disposition to believe. The municipality, department and patriotic clubs of Paris wear mourning for him. The national assembly have decreed that the new church of Ste. Genevieve should become the Mausolée des grands hommes, and that the ashes of Mirabeau should be deposed there. Future legislatures are to decree this honor to such as they judge worthy of it. The assembly, department, municipality, ministers, and thousands of citizens followed his corpse to this honorable place of interment. In fine the death of this extraordinary man is the greatest triumph of genius of which history furnishes an example, as well on account of those who rejoice it as of those who weep it.

Nothing further has been done by the assembly respecting the objects which interest American commerce. The diplomatick committees as well as M. de Montmorin have hopes of the assembly's reducing the difference of the duty paid on tobacco brought in

American or French vessels. The latter particularly wishes it because he has given instructions as he tells me to reclaim against the foreign tonnage imposed on their vessels in our ports. I shall leave nothing in my power undone to obtain such alterations to their several decrees as are desirable. I mentioned to you in my last letters that the duty on American oils was reduced to six livres the quintal and that under the *arrêt du conseil* the foreign and internal duties were 5ᵗ 18s.6d. the quintal. I imagine you will have this made known particularly in the eastern states.

There seems as far as I can learn much disposition to go into the cultivation of tobacco, in the southern provinces as well on account of its former prohibition as the fondness for novelty. Some of the deputies with whom I have conversed however say it will be only a small number of the richer cultivators who will make the experiment, that the peasantry in general are ignorant and so much attached to routine that they will not adopt a new system until the example of their neighbours shall have proved it advantageous. On the whole I suppose it very uncertain what will be done, and think that time and a short experience will change the decree so as to discourage the home cultivation.

You will have been informed by the English papers of the King's message to both houses of Parliament. We know nothing further officially. I find a general opinion here that war will ensue, and it is certain that every day which passes without clearing up the cloud renders the storm still more probable. Yet there is so much to be gained by peace and lost by war for the principal parties that I cannot help thinking they will find out some means of trafficking a pacification. In that case the Porte and Poland will make the sacrifices. Should war however take place, it seems to me that England and Holland will be in a disagreeable position, the first because Russia presents so few vulnerable parts to English force, and the second because the strong Imperial army in the low countries will have an opportunity of immediately insulting their territory. This would unquestionably endanger the present government as the patriotic party would be roused, and once roused would go as far as their forces would allow them towards a total overthrow if they found themselves supported by the Emperor.

I beg the favor of you to give the inclosed to the Secretary of the Treasury. This letter will be sent to Havre where I learn there is a vessel which will sail for Philadelphia in five or six days without fail. I hope and yet I know not why that it will be more fortunate than those hitherto sent by that conveyance. I am with sentiments of the most perfect attachment Dear Sir, your obedient humble servant

W: SHORT

PrC (DLC: Short Papers); at head of text: "No. 63." Tr (DNA: RG 59, DD); recorded in SJL as received 8 July 1791. Enclosure: Short to Hamilton, 9 Apr. 1791, discussing the possibility of transferring the American debt from France to capitalists of Genoa; warning of the danger that interested French officials might be able to obtain passage of a decree by the National Assembly concerning the debt; and urging as he had done before that the ignorance of European financiers be offset by regular publication of authentic documents such as Hamilton's report on the establishment of a national bank, the proceedings of Congress, the amount of duties collected, and so on. Short concluded by showing how the bankers for the United States at Amsterdam even had access to information in his own dispatches to Hamilton: "The houses at Amsterdam are regularly furnished with such information and papers, but my former letters will have shewn you how far it is from their interest to render them public. The following extract of a letter which I recieved the day before yesterday from one of them will shew you to what length this information goes – 'Mr Hamilton had received your letter to him of the day previous to our consenting to negotiate the future loans of Congress at 4. p. cent charges advising him you did not doubt of a loan being opened at 4½ p. cent charges or perhaps at 4. p. cent. We therefore expect soon his eventual orders for disposal of the monies of the March loan which being now more than half disposed of we shall be able to make a fine remittance immediately on the arrival of his directions, and we trust be able to conclude for a new loan on your first application to effect it, as well as to raise in a much shorter time than we formerly imagined the needful monies to pay off the arrears of interest and instalments of principal due to France by the U. S. so good is the credit actually enjoyed here by America'" (PrC in DLC: Short Papers; printed in Syrett, *Hamilton*, VIII, 260-4).

On the question of the debt to France and the disposition of funds borrowed by Short, Washington had directed that the Secretary of the Treasury and the Secretary of State act in concert. Short naturally assumed that his letters to Hamilton on the subject, such as the one enclosed with the above, would be shared with TJ. This was not the case (see Editorial Note and documents on the debt, at 10 Apr. 1791). But what Hamilton did not disclose to his colleague he confidentially revealed to Théophile Cazenove, who promptly reported such information to his principals – among them Van Staphorst, who of course made this available to Willink and Hubbard. Only a week after Short warned Hamilton in the enclosure to the above that the American agents in Amsterdam should not be thus favored, Cazenove informed one of the houses he represented that he had been shown Short's letter of 2 Dec. 1790, that Hamilton would make others available in future, and that Short had reported future loans might be negotiated at 5% interest and only 4% commission (Cazenove to Pieter Stadnitski, 14 Apr. 1791, Cazenove Letter Book, Holland Land Company Papers, Archives of the City of Amsterdam). In his response to Short Hamilton enclosed an authenticated statement of duties collected on imports from 1 Oct. 1789 to 30 Sep. 1790, but he failed to comment on Short's warning that information in his official dispatches to the Secretary of the Treasury had been made available to the American bankers. On Short's urging that loans might be obtained to better advantage in Genoa or elsewhere, Hamilton submitted his dispatches to Washington and recommended that restrictions be removed so as to permit Short to borrow when, where, and in what amounts he deemed advisable, subject to limits imposed by laws. Washington readily agreed. A year earlier he had sought TJ's advice on such questions and had accepted one limitation proposed by TJ. This time he did not (Hamilton to Washington, 29 July 1791; Washington to Hamilton, 29 July 1791, Syrett, *Hamilton*, VIII, 587, 588; see TJ's recommendation, 26 Aug. 1790). In informing Short that he had been given full latitude in making loans, Hamilton added:

"You will now find yourself in condition to embrace any favorable opportunities which may present in either of the Countries which have been mentioned by you or in any other whatsoever. I hinted to you on a former occasion that the market of London would not be an undesirable one. And I have some reason of late to suppose that it might not be found an impracticable one" (Hamilton to Short, 1-2 Aug. 1791, same, IX, 1-3).

From Charles Carroll

Annapolis, 10 Apr. 1791. TJ's of the 4th received. Yesterday morning he gave Brown TJ's letter, paid him the bank note, and took a receipt which he hopes will be satisfactory. He has kept a copy of latter, encloses original, and is "glad on both your accounts that this affair is thus finally adjusted and settled."

"I flatter myself Congress will during the next Session adopt decisive and adequate measures for the encouragement and support of our navigation. Great Britain, as it strikes me, is the only power, which can rival us in the carrying trade, and the only one disposed to extend her own navigation on the depression of ours. In a matter however of so much consequence, by which the temporary interests of some of the States, and the interests of leading individuals in all, may be affected, we can not proceed with too much caution; for we ought not to hazard any measure, we are not determined to go thro' with." He is happy to hear affairs in France go so well: "on the success of the Revolution in that country not only the happiness of France, but the rest of Europe, and perhaps our own depends. I wish sincerely freedom to all the nations of the earth; to France from education, and gratitude I feel a particular attachment: with such feelings, it is not surprising that I should view with anxious care the proceedings of the national Assembly; I own my doubts of a happy issue to their new system do not arise so much from the opposition of the dignified Clergy, and noblesse, as from the fear of disunion, the side views and factions combinations and cabals amongst the popular party. God send my apprehensions may be entirely groundless."

RC (DLC); endorsed by TJ as received 14 Apr. 1791 and so recorded in SJL. Enclosure not found.

On Carroll's role as intermediary in the collection of a doubtful claim by William Brown, see note to TJ to Brown, 4 Apr. 1791, which was the letter Carroll gave to the claimant. — Carroll's statement that Great Britain was the only power "disposed to extend her own navigation on the depression of ours" was perhaps an intended echo of TJ's own blunt language in the Report on Fisheries, in which he arraigned Great Britain for "exparte regulations . . . for mounting their navigation on the ruins of ours." His calling for the utmost caution and his advising against "any measure, we are not determined to go thro' with" was unquestionably inspired, as were similar expressions by others in the Senate, by the fear that TJ's Report on Commerce would call for a navigation act because, as his Report on Fisheries had warned, British regulations detrimental to American commerce could "only be opposed by counter-regulations on our part." For a comment on the sensation caused by the publication of TJ's blunt language in the Report, see Editorial Note to Report on Fisheries, 1 Feb. 1791.

From Mercy Otis Warren

Plymouth, Massachusetts, 10 Apr. 1791. Transmitting a volume of her poems to be registered for copyright.

RC (DNA: RG 59, MLR); at foot of text: "Honble. Mr. Jefferson"; endorsed by Remsen as received 31 Dec. 1791 but not recorded in SJL.

The volume sent for copyright was Mrs.

Warren's *Poems, Dramatic and Miscellaneous* (Boston, 1790), of which she had already presented a personal copy to TJ (see TJ to Mrs. Warren, 25 Nov. 1790; Sowerby, No. 4439).

The Debt to France
The Proposals of Schweitzer, Jeanneret & Cie.

I. LOUIS GUILLAUME OTTO TO THOMAS JEFFERSON, 10 APR. 1791

II. THOMAS JEFFERSON TO ALEXANDER HAMILTON, 10 APR. 1791

III. ALEXANDER HAMILTON TO THOMAS JEFFERSON, 12 APR. 1791

IV. ALEXANDER HAMILTON TO THOMAS JEFFERSON, 15 APR. 1791

V. THOMAS JEFFERSON TO LOUIS GUILLAUME OTTO, 7 MAY 1791

EDITORIAL NOTE

> If any negotiation with any prince or State to whom any part of the said Debt may be due, should be requisite, the same shall be carried on thro' the person, who . . . now is, or hereafter shall be charged with transacting the affairs of the United States with such Prince or State, for which purpose I shall direct the secretary of State, with whom you are in this behalf to consult and concert, to cooperate with you.
> — *George Washington to Alexander Hamilton, 28 Aug. 1790*

The question of liquidating the loans made by France to the United States not only affected the relations of the two countries: it also added another element to the domestic partisan conflicts which increasingly made the alliance an uneasy one. Throughout his years as minister to France, Jefferson had been deeply concerned about the accumulating arrearages of interest and the delinquent payments on the principal of the debt. Even before the adoption of the Constitution, he urgently pressed Washington, Madison, and Jay to have the new government emulate the British in levying taxes to amortize any loan negotiated and in never failing to be punctual in payment of interest. This, he assured Washington, would not only establish American credit but also remove "those causes of bickering and irritation which should not be permitted to subsist with

[175]

a nation with which it is so much our interest to be on cordial terms as with France."[1]

A year earlier Lambert, Comptroller General of Finances, was shocked to find the United States so far behind in its obligations. He urged Montmorin to press the matter and instructions were given to Moustier, who had just been appointed minister to the United States.[2] Moustier, regarding the debt much as he did the weakness of the United States under the Confederation, made the representation as required, but urged his government to be patient. In his view the loans constituted a powerful leverage to be retained for use in some unforeseen contingency, such as a rapprochement between England and the new republic. "We are linked to the United States," he argued, "neither by commerce, nor by habits, nor by feelings, nor even by those sentiments of gratitude which they should feel; the loan of His Majesty is the sole link which still binds the two powers."[3] Such an argument, in face of the worsening financial plight of France, was not convincing to Lambert, Necker, or other financial officers of the King. Montmorin was obliged to transmit their views to Moustier, though then and always he held that the United States should not be urged to the point of distress or inconvenience.[4] The debt was by no means the only bond between the two nations, as Moustier professed to believe, but it was a persistent source of irritation.

The political consequences of the French loans to the United States were magnified because they presented a glowing promise of profit to speculators. The adoption of the Constitution and the rapid recovery of the United States helped give stability to its credit, while the revolutionary movement in France brought on increasing depreciation of the livre in relation to the florin. In these circumstances, as the loans were payable in livres, it is not surprising that speculators on both sides of the Atlantic brought forth various schemes for purchase of the American debt. Since their success depended upon approval by both governments, it followed of course that there had to be dealings with elective and appointed officials in France and in the United States, some of whom were not averse to speculation on their own account.

Nor is it surprising that on this, as on all other major questions of policy, the councils of the American government were divided. The President might direct the Secretary of the Treasury to consult and concert his plans with the Secretary of State, who was required to cooperate. But even his explicit command did not always produce compliance.

I

Two days after Alexander Hamilton was appointed Secretary of the Treasury, he called upon the French minister to the United States and informed him of

[1] TJ to Washington, 2 May 1788; TJ to Madison, 3 May 1788; TJ to Jay, 4 May 1788. For other letters by TJ on the subject and for his plan to sustain American credit by making provisions for the French and other foreign debts, see citations in Editorial Note and group of documents at 18 Nov. 1788.

[2] Lambert to Montmorin, 6 Oct. 1787; Montmorin to Lambert, 4 Nov. 1787 (Arch. Aff. Etr., Corr. Pol., E.-U., XXXII; photocopies in DLC).

[3] Moustier to Montmorin, 28 Aug. 1788 (translated from the French; same).

[4] Montmorin to Necker, 30 Nov. 1788; Montmorin to Otto, 24 Jan. 1791 (same, XXXIII and XXXV).

his plans to ask Congress to authorize loans in Holland to liquidate all American debts, foreign and domestic. He was confident that this would be done, that customs and other revenues would sustain the expenses of government, and that the Dutch loans would enable the United States to discharge the French debt according to the terms of the contracts. Then, almost as an afterthought, Hamilton asked Moustier whether he knew of a company formed in France to buy the debt. The minister cautiously replied that he had heard rumors to this effect both in Europe and in America but that his instructions contained nothing about such a plan.

In reporting the conversation to Montmorin, Moustier revealed more than he had disclosed to Hamilton. He said that he knew several French capitalists had already raised a fund of a million piastres to buy the debt; that this was the principal object of Brissot de Warville's journey to America in the latter part of 1788; and that, in promoting the scheme, he had become closely linked with the Assistant Secretary of the Treasury, William Duer, whom Moustier regarded as the greatest *agioteur* in the United States. From this and other circumstances he believed that the Secretary of the Treasury himself, because of his relations with well-known speculators, would not be sorry to see such a speculation succeed.[5] The suspicion, so far as the record reveals, is without foundation. But the connections were indisputable. Aside from William Duer, there were other friends or supporters of Hamilton's policies who aspired to profit from the debt to France — among them, Gouverneur Morris, Robert Morris, William Constable, Andrew Craigie, and Daniel Parker. One of the most persistent promoters of such schemes was the Boston merchant James Swan, who had made a fortune during the war, had lost it, and had gone to France in an ultimately successful effort to get rid of his own accumulated debts by various speculations. Swan was unacquainted with Hamilton, but he was a friend of Henry Knox and tried to persuade him to use his influence with the President and the Secretary of the Treasury to gain their approval of one plan to buy the American debt to France.[6]

There is no evidence that Knox, who was then deeply immersed in his own speculations in Maine lands, responded to these overtures. In fact, no member of the administration ever gave official sanction to the speculators' schemes, however much the aims of friends and supporters may have been privately condoned. After Moustier's recall some Senators did speak privately and urgently to the French chargé because, so Otto thought, they considered the debt as a bond attaching America to France while others wished to fund it

[5] Moustier to Montmorin, 17 Sep. 1789 (same, XXXIV; an extract of this dispatch, so far as it relates to the conversation with Hamilton, is in Syrett, *Hamilton*, v, 366-8). Just before Gouverneur Morris departed for France, William Duer called on Rufus King, informed him of the plans of Brissot de Warville and the capitalists he represented to speculate in the debt to France, and said that Morris hoped to unite with them for the same object. He also conferred with Samuel Osgood (member of the Board of Treasury), Henry Knox, and Jeremiah Wadsworth, all of whom agreed that it would be useful in promoting the plan if King should accept appointment as minister to Holland. King was not indisposed to the idea, and replied that, consistent with the duties of the office, it would be a great satisfaction to "promote the interest of my friends" (MS in King's hand, dated 21 Dec. 1788, NHi; printed in Charles R. King, *Rufus King* [New York, 1894], I, 623-4). Nothing resulted from Duer's efforts save to illustrate the manner in which speculators sought to use government to promote their private interests.

[6] This was the proposal of Schweitzer, Jeanneret & Cie.

through Holland loans and thus indirectly strengthen the ties with England.[7] In France, official sponsorship and even connection with plans of various groups to speculate in the American debt appeared more open, resulting in one instance in the bestowal of ministerial approval. Moustier himself, inadvertently or not, may have contributed to this result.

Late in 1788, perhaps because of his hostility to plans of European and American capitalists whom Brissot represented, Moustier had urged his government to make no arrangements with any group or company which sought to acquire the debt. Instead, in a memoir based on his assumption that this was a bond to be preserved, he proposed that the ministry should acquire masts, ship timber, naval supplies, and other American produce to meet the needs of its marine. These products would be purchased by bills of exchange drawn on the Treasury of the United States in the amount of the annual interest due. This, Moustier argued, would achieve the double object of preserving the debt for political manipulation in some future contingency and of increasing commercial relations between the two countries.[8] Hamilton's private talk with the departing minister, followed by a confidential communication, encouraged Moustier to hope that his proposal would be adopted. His confidential letter has not been found, but its purpose is clear, both because Moustier commented upon it and because Hamilton gave similar promptings to the Marquis de Lafayette and to William Short. One of his first objects, he declared to the former, would be the debt due to France. He was not in a position to communicate officially since Congress had taken no action on the subject, but he contemplated a speedy payment of arrearages of interest and adequate provision for that to become due in future. He therefore ventured to say to Lafayette as a friend that it would be a valuable accommodation to the United States if installments on the principal could be suspended for a few years. He thought it best on every account that the offer of such an arrangement "should come unsolicited as a fresh mark of good will" on the part of the French government.[9] Postponement of installments on the principal not only accorded with the views of Moustier: it also happened to coincide with those of Gouverneur Morris, Daniel Parker, and others of Hamilton's supporters who sought to buy the whole American debt if France would give them title to the arrearages of

[7] Otto to Montmorin, 30 Oct. 1789 (Arch. Aff. Etr., Corr. Pol., E.-U., xxxiii; photocopies in DLC); Montmorin to Necker, 3 July 1790, referring Otto's dispatch to him (same, xxxv). In acknowledging the dispatch, Montmorin said only that the question had been raised of transferring the debt to Holland and that the ministry had been assured this would be agreeable to the American government (Montmorin to Otto, 10 July 1790, same, xxxv).

[8] Moustier's memoir was enclosed in his dispatch of 25 Dec. 1788 (same, xxxiv; see also Moustier to Montmorin, 17 Sep. 1789, same). This proposal antedated and possibly inspired a similar plan developed by James Swan, though the Boston merchant hoped to profit both from the sale of naval stores and from the acquisition of the debt.

[9] Hamilton to Lafayette, 6 Oct. 1789 (Syrett, *Hamilton*, v, 425-6). Hamilton enclosed this letter in one to Short in which he made it plain that he did not intend to make an official request of this nature but would be gratified if "the thing might come about in the form of a voluntary and unsolicited offer." He hoped that some indirect hint might be given to insure this (Hamilton to Short, 7 Oct. 1789, same, v, 429-30). Moustier's comment on Hamilton's missing letter to him, which was dated about the same time, is to be found in the memoir accompanying his dispatch to Montmorin of 14 Oct. 1789 (Arch. Aff. Etr., Corr. Pol., E.-U., xxxiv; see also Syrett, *Hamilton*, v, 428-9).

interest. If this were done, so Short reported to Hamilton, they would agree to the condition of postponing payment on the principal for five or six years, which he thought would "square perfectly" with Hamilton's wishes.[10]

Moustier, bearing Hamilton's letters to Lafayette and Short, arrived in Paris shortly after Necker, Director General of Finances, had recommended to the National Assembly that the American debt be used as security for a loan to be negotiated in Holland. Necker had also listened to proposals from a group of Amsterdam bankers to buy the entire debt. Their plan was so persuasive to him that even the American agents in Holland – Wilhem & Jan Willink, Nicholas & Jacob Van Staphorst, and Nicholas Hubbard – had joined the group for fear their plan would succeed without them. Upon Moustier's arrival, however, they withdrew. The recalled minister, so it was reported, had been " 'instructed by Congress to oppose any negotiation of that kind.' "[11] The claim, which must have originated with Moustier in an exaggerated interpretation of Hamilton's confidential communication, was of course without foundation. But it had the effect of causing Willink, Van Staphorst, & Hubbard to indicate that they might support the proposals of Morris, Parker, and their French and American associates.

In the complicated intrigues and negotiations which followed in the next two months, Gouverneur Morris seemed to be the commanding figure. Equally at home in the salons as in the official and financial circles of Paris, he pressed forward with characteristic boldness and self-confidence. He thought Necker honest and disinterested but a poor financier, and in the very home of the minister did not hesitate to ridicule his insistence upon obtaining security for the performance of a contract involving so large a sum as 40 million livres. When the Amsterdam bankers of the United States demanded three-fourths of the shares, Morris told them that this was not at all admissible, that half should be reserved for the American houses he represented, and that he could carry the proposition through without their assistance. To such threats and intimidations he added native gifts of charm wholly devoid of obsequiousness. Both Short and Lafayette, so he claimed, thought his plan an excellent means of protecting American interests and providing timely assistance to France in a moment of need. Morris also won over Montmorin, who approved the proposal and promised to urge its adoption by Necker. Ternant, soon to be named minister to the United States, did not wholly approve but thought the distressed state of French finances required some relief of the sort. Moustier, perhaps because of the proposal he himself had made long since, did what he could to defeat Morris' hopes.

The American bankers in Amsterdam were so apprehensive that they dispatched their partner Hubbard to Paris to advance their own proposal for the purchase of 6 million livres of the debt. By mid-January Short was able to report that this plan had been rejected by Necker as being too small to bring before the National Assembly. Morris, believing that he had convinced Hubbard, hoped that he would persuade his houses of the wisdom of uniting with himself, Parker, and their associates. Jacob Van Staphorst, who represented them in Paris, had already been persuaded. But as January wore on he received

[10] Short to Hamilton, 30 Nov. 1789 (Syrett, *Hamilton*, v, 570-4).

[11] The fact that Short, in reporting to Hamilton, placed the statement within quotation marks indicates that he considered Moustier to be the source of the reports (Short to Hamilton, 30 Nov. 1790, same).

only excuses from his partners in Amsterdam for their delayed decision. On Saturday the 30th of January, with his plan still being looked upon favorably by Necker and Montmorin, Morris' confidence waned and he confided to his diary: "I have for some Days past had disagreeable forebodings about the Affair negotiating in Holland."[12]

The devastating blow fell the very next day. Jacob Van Staphorst brought the news that his partners had not only refused to be connected with Morris' plan either as associates or on commission, but had opened a loan for 3 million florins on behalf of the United States. They had also informed Hamilton and Necker of this and urged them not to accede to Morris' proposal. Morris regarded this as betrayal of a solemn promise. Necker, so he reported, was vexed and disappointed. Short, who had just concluded a letter to Hamilton stating that it was certain Necker had decided to accept the proposal, added a postscript expressing his astonishment at the action of the Amsterdam bankers, at the reasons given in justification for it, and at their misrepresentation of his own position. Morris, about to depart on his mission to London, informed Necker that he might be employed by the United States and in that case motives of delicacy would prevent him from negotiating further about the debt, but that he would do all in his power to see that the minister's wishes were met.

On the day the blow fell, Morris gave Hamilton a succinct account of the affair, ridiculing the justifying reasons given by the bankers in their letter to the Secretary of the Treasury. Proving that he knew of Hamilton's plans – perhaps from Moustier, Lafayette, or Short – he declared that the proposal advanced by him in behalf of a "Society of Friends to America" would have obtained for the United States "the needful Time required for their Accomodation without a farthing of Expence and without the Pain of Soliciting it from this Court."[13] His report to Robert Morris also showed that he still entertained hopes for the proposal. But William Short accurately predicted that the unauthorized loan – made by the bankers, as Morris realized, out of self-interest and in order to defeat his plan – would prevent anything further being done by the ministry until the wishes of the United States became known. In fact, the bankers' action had been anticipated even before Moustier's arrival when, in order to defeat other speculations in the debt to France, they urged Jefferson with the least possible delay to obtain power to negotiate loans at Amsterdam in order to

[12] Gouverneur Morris, *Diary*, ed. Davenport, I, 392; the complicated story can be followed in the *Diary*, I, 317-20, 323-8, 332, 334, 351, 356, 366, 377; see also Short to Jay, 15 Dec. 1789, and 2 and 12 Jan. 1790 (DLC: Short Papers). Morris' opinion of Necker is given in his long letter to Washington, 24 Jan. 1790, in which he avoids all mention of the proposed purchase of the American debt (DLC: Washington Papers). William Short paid high tribute to Morris' powers of persuasion, his eloquence, his authority, and his ability to anticipate the course of events (Short to Morris, 12 Sep. 1790, quoted in Morris, *Diary*, ed. Davenport, I, 590-3).

[13] Morris to Hamilton, 31 Jan. 1791 (Syrett, *Hamilton*, VI, 234-9); Short to Hamilton, 28-31 Jan. 1791 (same, VI, 227-32); Willink, Van Staphorst, & Hubbard to Hamilton, 25 Jan. 1790 (same, 210-18); Gouverneur Morris to Robert Morris, 1 Feb. 1790 (Morris, *Diary*, I, 401). Within two days of receiving the disappointing news from Amsterdam, Morris had conceived another plan "grounded on the Misconduct of Messrs. Willinks and Staphorsts"; he also spent several days in Amsterdam trying to offset what those houses had done. But Morris' hopes proved less well-founded than Short's prediction (same, I, 402, 403, 406, 420, 453).

provide for a considerable part of the debt due France – an object which they correctly believed he had very much at heart.[14]

II

One consequence of the unauthorized loan was to make Necker even more impatient to receive payments on the American debt. To William Short he complained at length that the bankers had taken this precipitate step "to prevent his completing the negotiation . . . begun for the transfer of the American debt in a manner which would have been honorable and advantageous" for the United States and France as well as for the promoters. He thought the American government could not refuse to discharge a part of its debt now that it was in possession of 3 million livres and he asked Short to give him an order on Willink, Van Staphorst & Hubbard in that amount. Short of course declined, having no power to do so and not knowing whether the loan would be approved. He duly reported this to Hamilton and asked for instructions. Four months later, during which time the financial situation of France deteriorated and Necker's impatience increased, he repeated his appeal.[15]

Hamilton, who evidently did not respond to Gouverneur Morris' letter, assured the bankers that he was pleased with their action because it had put a stop to negotiations whose success would have been "an unwelcome circumstance."[16] He did not think the loan would create an unfortunate precedent, was confident it would be approved, and, despite Short's support of the proposal of Morris and others, commended him for his "very prudent and judicious" conduct.[17] To Washington he characterized the loan as "without previous authority, and in that view exceptionable." He thought sanctioning it would create a precedent inconsistent with the national dignity and interest, but that acceptance might be accompanied by prohibition against anything of the sort in future.[18] Washington approved and Hamilton, attributing to the bankers a sense of the delicacy of their action, felt he need not press upon them "the inadmissibility of any thing of a like nature in future; however cogent the motives to it."[19]

Another result of the loan was to create embarrassment for Washington. With the passage of the Acts of 4 and 12 August 1790 authorizing the President to borrow up to $14 million to provide for the foreign and domestic debt of the United States – legislation which gave the stamp of approval to policies Hamilton had disclosed to Moustier a year earlier – the President was faced with the problem of announcing to Congress a loan made prior to these enactments. Hamilton had prudently refrained from informing Washington of the unauthorized transaction until after Congress had acted. But as the time approached for the second Congress, he included in his notes for the President's

[14] Willink, Van Staphorst, & Hubbard to TJ, 13 Aug. 1789; TJ to Jay, 27 Aug. 1789. Washington transmitted both of these letters to Hamilton for his opinion (Lear to Hamilton, 18 Jan. 1790, Syrett, *Hamilton*, VI, 185).

[15] Short to Hamilton, 4 Apr. and 3 Aug. 1790 (same, VI, 349, 516-18).

[16] Hamilton to Willink, Van Staphorst & Hubbard, 7 May 1790 (same, VI, 409).

[17] Hamilton to Short, 29 May 1790 (same, VI, 446-7).

[18] Hamilton to Washington, 26 Aug. 1790 (same, VI, 569-70).

[19] Hamilton to Willink, Van Staphorst & Hubbard, 28 Aug. 1790 (same, VI, 580-2).

address an item announcing the loan. Washington struggled with his own draft, which opened with the statement that the loan had been made in accordance with authority granted at the previous session. Then, recognizing that this was not justified by the facts and that everyone would realize the patent impossibility of negotiating a loan in Amsterdam in the short interval between sessions, he sent a private note to Hamilton confessing that he was at a loss how to frame the announcement properly and asking that he be supplied with a new draft – by that afternoon if convenient.[20] Hamilton must have complied, but his version has not been found. The result as embodied in the message to Congress was a compromise which, while retaining the assurance that the loan was made under authority of Congress, covered this inaccuracy with the statement that "some provisional measures had previously taken place" respecting it.[21] This ambiguity concealed the fact that the initiative had been taken by the bankers, not by the administration.

Robert Morris and any other members of Congress interested in the "Society of Friends to America" whose plans had been frustrated by the bankers would of course have known the facts. But another significant change in Washington's draft seemed designed to obviate, at least for the time being, closer scrutiny by Congress. As originally phrased by Washington, the concluding sentence of his draft read: "The terms of it, with the disposition as far as made, the Secretary of the Treasury is directed to communicate." This was a variant of the wording Hamilton himself had suggested.[22] But as revised and incorporated in the message, the passage read: "The Secretary of the Treasury has my directions to communicate such further particulars as may be requisite for more precise information."[23] The Acts of Congress of course required an accounting of the disposition of funds borrowed, but neither the President nor the Secretary of the Treasury could at that time have provided such information. The less specific language, which eliminated all reference to disposition of the funds borrowed, points directly to the influence of the Secretary of State on this part of the message.

Late in August, in accordance with his instructions, Hamilton had conferred with Jefferson, had informed him of Washington's preference of William Short as the agent to negotiate the loans, and Jefferson had agreed to the appointment.[24] That the two heads of department thus acted in concert, at least in the beginning, is also shown in the fact that Hamilton referred Short to the Secretary of State for instructions as to the timing of payment on the debt to France.[25] It was probably Hamilton's decision to limit the amount of the payment to half of the 3 million florins the Amsterdam bankers had made

[20] Washington to Hamilton, [3? Dec. 1790], enclosing his own draft (both in same, VII, 189). See note 28 for reasons in support of the conjectured date.

[21] Second annual message, 8 Dec. 1790 (Washington, *Writings*, ed. Fitzpatrick, XXXI, 165). Acting under Washington's authorization, Hamilton in his letter and commission to the Amsterdam bankers had already accepted their "provisional" loan by virtue of the powers granted by Congress to the President (Hamilton to Willink, Van Staphorst & Hubbard, 28 Aug, 1790, with commission bearing same date, Syrett, *Hamilton*, VI, 581-5).

[22] Hamilton's suggestions for the message, 1 Dec. 1790 (same, VII, 173).

[23] Annual message, 8 Dec. 1790 (Washington, *Writings*, ed. Fitzpatrick, XXXI, 165).

[24] Hamilton to Washington, 3 Sep. 1790 (Syrett, *Hamilton*, VII, 22-3).

[25] Hamilton to Short, 29 Aug. and 1 Sep. 1790 (same, VI, 585-6; VII, 6-13).

available. Jefferson knew of the limitation and evidently did not object to it, even though it had long been his desire to liquidate the debt as speedily as possible. Nevertheless, his own instructions to Short called for at least a temporary delay. He hoped that a judicious timing of the payment might help procure concessions favorable to American commerce with the French West Indies. Jefferson left the timing of the payment up to Short, being confident he could forward this "great object" by assuring Montmorin measures had been taken by the United States to pay very shortly all arrearages of principal and interest. He assumed as a matter of course that Short could find excuses for delay until the propitious moment arrived.[26]

Under these circumstances, it is understandable that Jefferson would not have wished the President to give Congress any reason, at that time, to request information about the disposition of the funds. The evasive language employed in the revised passage of the annual message, departing as it did from the specific terms of the drafts of both Hamilton and Washington, suggests that Jefferson had persuaded the President to concur in his strategy of delayed payment, even though Washington had directed Hamilton to make payments of arrearages of interest and instalments on principal of the debt "with all convenient dispatch."[27] If so, the revised paragraph must have come from the pen of the Secretary of State.[28]

On other points, however, it seems clear that the Secretary of the Treasury did not concert matters with the Secretary of State as Washington had directed. One such involved advantages to be gained in making payments on the debt. While France had borrowed florins in Holland in order to make the loans to the United States, payments on the debt in depreciated livres held out inducements as obvious to the Secretary of the Treasury as to private speculators. "You will no doubt avail the United States of all proper advantages," Hamilton instructed Short, "in making the negotiation . . . which the course of Exchange between Paris and Amsterdam will admit. It is probable, that your bills will command a premium that will more than indemnify our Treasury for the charges of the Loan, so far as the amount of this payment to France" of 1.5 million livres.[29] The assumption was well-founded. Later Hamilton was able to report to Washington that the exchange between France and Holland afforded

[26] TJ to Short, 26 Aug. 1790. Hamilton had instructed the bankers not to reveal that half of the 3 million florins would be paid to France. They in turn had asked their partner, Jacob Van Staphorst, to respect the confidence. The latter, however, divulged the information to James Swan and Le Couteulx. The fact could not have been kept secret because the letter from the bankers to Van Staphorst had gone through the post and Hamilton's letters on the subject went through the hands of Montmorin. In this situation, Short said he had no alternative but to tell the minister the payment would be made as soon as he could command the funds (Short to TJ, 6 and 25 Nov. 1790).

[27] Washington to Hamilton, 28 Aug. 1790 (Syrett, *Hamilton*, VI, 579).

[28] In further support of this assumption, it should be noted that Washington wrote TJ on 3 Dec. 1790 and that, in response, TJ composed paragraphs for the annual message in addition to those he had already submitted (see note to TJ's draft of other items, 29 Nov. 1790). Both Washington's letter and TJ's response are missing. But it is plausible to suppose that Washington, after revealing to Hamilton his difficulty in phrasing the passage, also consulted TJ on the point, especially since it involved both the Treasury and State departments. If so, one of the additional paragraphs composed by TJ in response to Washington's letter was probably this one.

[29] Hamilton to Short, 29 Aug. 1790 (same, VI, 585-6).

a benefit of more than 10% on the payment of this sum – that is, more than the interest and commission charges for that part of the loan.[30] This was a policy on which Short needed no instructions. On the eve of his departure for Amsterdam, he was called into consultation by Montmorin and Dufresne, Director of the Royal Treasury, to have the payments made by bills of exchange drawn on the American bankers in florins. Short agreed, but on arriving in Holland he discovered that upwards of 2 million livres had already been remitted, this being so highly advantageous that 1.25 million florins purchased about 3.6 million livres. Even a letter from Dufresne asking that payment be made in Amsterdam so as to avoid enormous losses because of depreciation did not prevent him from making arrangements which gave the benefit to the United States. Recognizing that "what was loss for France was gain for us," Short even took gratification in reporting these transactions to the Secretary of State.[31] Jefferson obviously had not been consulted about the policy on which Hamilton and Short had such united views.

It is equally certain Hamilton did not inform Jefferson that, while opposing certain private speculations in the debt to France, he had left the door open for others which might be considered more solidly grounded. In his instructions to Short, he had referred to the "late negotiations" by Gouverneur Morris and others to purchase the debt to France and added: "Whether any arrangement of this nature will be a desireable accommodation to France; whether persons of real capital, who would not in the execution be obliged to use means prejudicial to the Credit of the United States, would be willing to embark in such a plan; whether it would not prove an obstacle to other loans which we may have occasion to make for other purposes are circumstances essential in determining its elegibility which cannot be known to me, and can only be accurately judged of by one, on the spot." He warned Short, however, that propositions of such a nature should not come from the United States; that the government should only be put in the position of sanctioning what other parties desired of it; and that in no event should such an arrangement injure the national reputation "or place us in the light of a people desirous of making hard bargains at the expence of friends."[32]

Hard bargains might be inadmissible when speculators sought to gain the same benefit for themselves that Hamilton and Short were pleased to take advantage of on behalf of the government. But Jefferson, making no comment to Short either on his failure to delay payments to achieve commercial conces-

[30] Hamilton to Washington, 14 Apr. 1791 (same, VIII, 288).

[31] Short to TJ, 25 Nov. 1790. Ironically, the payment which Dufresne wished to have paid in Amsterdam to avoid loss was the sum of 570,000 florins due to bankers there on account of loans made by France to the United States (Short to Hamilton, 18 Dec. 1790, Syrett, *Hamilton*, VII, 348-57). The arrangements for this payment made by Short, which he admitted in the letter to TJ might not square with Dufresne's ideas, included an Amsterdam banker whom he mistakenly considered to be associated with Ferdinand Grand, banker to the United States in Paris. This brought on a sharp reprimand from Grand, who pointed out that this was contrary to the terms of the treaty negotiated by Franklin. Short was forced to say that he had acted at the request of Montmorin and Dufresne; in doing so, he expressed the fear that Grand might carry his complaint to the President and Congress (Grand to Short, 25 Feb. 1791; Short to Grand, 3 Mch. 1791, copies of both of which were enclosed in Short to Hamilton, 11 Mch. 1791, Syrett, *Hamilton*, VIII, 170, 178, 179).

[32] Hamilton to Short, 1 Sep. 1790 (same, VII, 12).

sions or on his gratification at being able to have the United States profit from the depreciated livre, felt otherwise. Proof of this – and of the failure of the Secretary of the Treasury to act in concert with the Secretary of State on this matter as Washington had required – is to be found in their attitudes toward the only speculative proposal to gain the approval and recommendation of the French ministry, that of Schweitzer, Jeanneret & Cie.

III

News of passage of legislation authorizing the President to borrow $14 million to liquidate foreign and domestic debts had an immediate impact in Europe. When Short succeeded in negotiating the 2.5 million florin loan on extremely favorable terms and had it taken up within two hours – an unprecedented tribute to the rising credit of the United States – he was embarrassed more than ever by bankers, speculators, and French officials. For months he had been without instructions as to the disposition of the funds and pled with Hamilton for guidance, both to avoid double interest on money borrowed but idle and to enable him to "meet questions . . . which certainly will be asked."[33] The prediction was accurate. When Short learned in late May that Hamilton intended 1.5 million florins to be paid to France, he bluntly told the Secretary of the Treasury that the delay in employing money borrowed had not only added to the cost, but had created suspicions among French officials who could not understand why, with funds available, payments on the American debt could not be made. He found it impossible to convince them that the delay was not deliberately calculated in order to profit from the rapid depreciation of *assignats*. He was embarrassed by the ministry's probing on this point but regretted more that the American debt had attracted the attention of speculators – among them six new members of the Treasury – who had sought the intercession of Lafayette and Condorcet. His embarrassment was made worse by Hamilton's unexplained instructions to withhold half a million of the funds to be paid to France. He could not understand the reasons for this, did not know when he would be given directions, and said that he would avoid questions as much as possible. "It is tautology to add," he reminded Hamilton, "that as this sum is already in the hands of the bankers the U. S. will be paying an unnecessary interest until it is employed."[34]

Speculators in and out of office made Short's predicament worse, especially when Jean Gaspard Schweitzer and François Jeanneret sought ministerial support for their proposals to buy the American debt. These Paris bankers, claiming they represented Genoese capitalists who had more than 54 million livres available for the purpose, were unknown in Amsterdam and Short suspected they were mere adventurers without character or reputation who were put forward as a screen to conceal the real promoters in and out of office. He was convinced that their proposals would never have received the attention of

[33] Short to Hamilton, 17 Feb., 4 and 11 Mch., 9 Apr., 4 May 1791 (same, VIII, 51-7, 158-60, 170-1, 260-1, 324-5).

[34] Short to Hamilton, 3 June 1791, acknowledging receipt of Hamilton's letter of 13 Apr. 1791 (same, VIII, 280-2, 412-25). At the time Hamilton gave these instructions, he informed TJ that 1.5 million florins of the loan were destined for France, but he did not tell him that half a million had been withheld for further instructions (Hamilton to TJ, 15 Apr. 1791, Document IV following).

Montmorin if Lambert and some members of the Treasury and Committee of Finance had not interested themselves in the matter.[35] The suspicions seem justified, the more so because Schweitzer, Jeanneret & Cie. – or their hidden supporters – saw fit to make use of James Swan to influence American officials.

Swan was an obvious choice for the purpose. He had already negotiated a contract with the Minister of Marine to furnish naval supplies and was advancing proposals to supply American salt provisions, to be paid for in orders on the Treasury of the United States in settlement of the debt to France at the rate of 6 million livres annually. This plan had been blocked by the American bankers in Amsterdam on the ground that the government was greatly averse to the transfer of any part of the debt to individuals – an attitude which they knew to be that of the Secretary of State. Swan thereupon appealed to Jefferson because of his known interest in promoting commercial ties with France and urged him to persuade the President and Secretary of the Treasury to support the plan. He added that those concerned in the venture were Le Couteulx and "two bankers" whom they might choose, besides Daniel Parker, Gouverneur Morris, Robert Morris, and himself.[36] He did not bother to inform Jefferson that on the same day he had offered an interest in the operation to the Secretary of War. In the letter to Knox – in which Swan enclosed the letter to Jefferson to be read and then sealed before delivery – he gave the same names of the

[35] Short to Hamilton, 18 Dec. 1790, 11 Mch. and 3 June 1791 (same, VII, 348-57; VIII, 170, 412-25).

Jean Gaspard Schweitzer (1754-1811) was the son of a prosperous Zurich merchant. An enthusiast and idealist, student of philosophy and science, and ardent supporter of the French Revolution, he came into his inheritance and settled in Paris in 1786 as head of the banking firm of Schweitzer, Jeanneret & Cie. For purposes of speculation he left considerable sums in the hands of his friend and junior partner, also a native of Switzerland, while he devoted himself to political and social movements. Jeanneret's speculations were at first profitable and Schweitzer, installed in a magnificent hôtel in rue Taitbout, kept *table ouverte* and received Lafayette, Barnave, Saint-Pierre, Mirabeau, and others. Mirabeau, whom he idolized, took advantage of his generosity, and by 1788 Jeanneret had to confess that all of the funds entrusted with him had been lost. Schweitzer was obliged to dispose of his estate in Switzerland, sacrifice three-fourths of his interest in his father's old firm, sell his collection of books, prints, and objets d'art, lease half of his hôtel, and reduce the number of servants. There is thus no doubt that, as Short suspected, he was acting for a hidden group of capitalists and French officials in the effort to purchase the debt to France. In 1795 he joined with James Swan to supply grain and salt provisions to the French armed forces. He followed Swan to Boston by some months, only to discover that his partner had engaged in far-reaching speculations, the result of which left Swan with his fortune re-established and Schweitzer impoverished. Swan even sold him claims to an immense tract of land in the Southwest, where the visionary banker hoped to establish "un État modèle où seraint pratiques la religion de la nature, la communauté des biens, une tolérance universelle" (F. Barbey, *Suisses hors Suisse* [Paris, 1914], p. 299). Returning to France in 1801 ill and ruined, he died there ten years later. Although his bank was established in rue Taitbout in 1786, near where TJ had lived the year before, there is no evidence that the two men ever met. (For other biographical details, see Jean Bouchary, *Les Manieurs d'Argent à Paris du XVIIIe Siècle* [Paris, 1939], I, 103-17.)

[36] Swan to TJ, 3 Oct. 1790. Swan stated that he had kept Short informed of all steps taken and that "he entered from the first moment fully into the views of the Contract"; this scarcely accords with Short's own report of the matter (Short to TJ, 3 Oct. and 6 Nov. 1790).

interested persons that he had given to Jefferson and informed him that there was a blank share for those in America who might take part. "If you for yourself and friends would take that share, should the business go on," he added, "name the persons in whose names it should be entered and it shall be done without your being known in the matter."[37] So far as the record shows, neither Knox nor Jefferson responded to this or any other appeals made by Swan concerning the contract, though the discrepancy between his letters to the two heads of department silently testifies to his knowledge of the man.

The plan of Swan and Le Couteulx soon gave way to that of Schweitzer, Jeanneret & Cie., who were probably the unnamed "two bankers" to whom Swan referred in his letters to Jefferson and Knox. One reason for the successor scheme, which eliminated Swan's proposal for payment in produce, was that Jacob Van Staphorst had disclosed to Swan that arrangements had been made to pay 1.5 million florins on the American debt. Le Couteulx had immediately revealed this to the Committee of Finance with whom they had been negotiating. Within two weeks after the disclosure, Schweitzer, Jeanneret & Cie. laid their proposal before Lambert, Comptroller General of Finances, in a covering letter which revealed their knowledge that the United States could only pay the amount that had been authorized by Hamilton. Claiming to represent several rich capitalists, they proposed as a benefit both to France and the United States to purchase the entire sum of the debt, which they estimated at 36,710,000 livres. So urgent were they that they pressed Lambert immediately to recommend to Montmorin that he send copies of their proposal in duplicate to Short in Amsterdam. They stressed the importance of completing the transaction at once: all could be done if Short would simply sign his acceptance on one of the duplicates. But if, contrary to their understanding, Short should claim he had no power to do this, they and their friends would do all they could to remove any obstacles. In that case, they would ask Montmorin to state what sort of plan would be acceptable to him.[38] Lambert, already prepared, transmitted the duplicate copies of the plan to Montmorin, strongly urging its adoption and requesting that if Short felt it did not meet the intentions of the United States, he should be asked to submit a plan which he would accept.[39] Montmorin promptly complied by sending the two duplicates to Short and asking for his decision at the earliest moment possible. For further infor-

---

[37] Swan to Knox, 3 Oct. 1790 (MHi: Knox Papers; the concluding part of this letter is separated from the beginning and is to be found as an undated item in Reel 47 of the microfilm edition of the Knox Papers, published by the Massachusetts Historical Society).

[38] Schweitzer, Jeanneret & Cie. to the Comptroller General, 22 Nov. 1790, enclosed in Lambert to Montmorin, 26 Nov. 1790 (Arch. Aff. Etr., Corr. Pol., E.-U., xxxv; Tr in DLC: Short Papers, printed as enclosed in Short to Hamilton, 18 Dec. 1790, in Syrett, *Hamilton*, vii, 360-1; Trs in English and French in MHi: Knox Papers, as enclosed in Swan to Knox, 27 Dec. 1790; Tr in DNA: RG 59, MLR, as enclosed in Gouverneur Morris to Washington, 27 May 1791). Trs of the enclosed proposals, 22 Nov. 1790, in Arch. Aff. Etr., Corr. Pol., E.-U., xxxv, and in all of the sources named, except that Short did not enclose the actual proposal in his to Hamilton of 18 Dec. 1790, hence it is not in Syrett. These and other pertinent documents as enclosed in letters of Short, Swan, or others will be cited below only in one manuscript or printed form.

[39] Lambert to Montmorin, 26 Nov. 1790 (Arch. Aff. Etr., Corr. Pol., E.-U., xxxv; text printed in Syrett, *Hamilton*, vii, 358-9, from Tr in DLC: Short Papers).

mation he referred Short to Antoine Bernard Caillard, French chargé at The Hague.[40]

Before leaving Paris for Amsterdam, Short had informed Montmorin of the legislation authorizing funds to be borrowed for payment on the debt. This, he thought, had determined the French government not to listen to any speculators' schemes for buying the American debt. Thus he was ill prepared for Montmorin's letter and its enclosures: the scheme, as he saw at once, was to receive florins from the United States and to pay in depreciated livres. This hope of immense gain was one he and the American bankers shared in order to secure the profit for the government. His response to Montmorin was emphatic. Returning both copies of the proposals with the comment that he had no power to make such an engagement, Short could not refrain from saying how distressing it would be for the United States if France thought her interest lay in arrangements which could compromise the credit of her ally. He also thought it essential to point out that the purpose of the authorizing legislation concerning the debt seemed to be entirely unknown to the French government and that it would augur ill for the United States if the fate of its credit should be placed in hands which entered into engagements so lightly.[41] This was an indirect if blunt commentary on Lambert, but Short was determined if possible to persuade Montmorin to keep the matter from being debated in the National Assembly.

Schweitzer, Jeanneret & Cie. and their associates in and out of office were not so easily blocked. They brought forth a new proposal to lend the United States 10 million livres on terms as favorable as those offered by the Amsterdam bankers. They also had James Swan appeal to Short to try to gain his acceptance. Again Short said that he had no power to enter into such an engagement and urged Swan to use any influence he might have with the company to put a stop to the negotiations.[42] Swan claimed that he had tried but in the same breath urged Short to accept the new proposal because of its "neatness and honesty."[43] Swan transmitted the letter to the company. Schweitzer, accompanied by Swan, called on Montmorin and informed him of Short's declination and of their new proposal. Then by special courier to Amsterdam, they informed Short of what they had done and asked him to state what difficulties if any remained so that they might bring the matter to a conclusion. Short reiterated that he had no power to act and that the only motive he could have for examining their proposal at all was that it seemed to be acceptable to Montmorin. He added that he would immediately transmit this or any other

[40] Montmorin to Short, 30 Nov. 1790 (Dft in Arch. Aff. Etr., Corr. Pol., E.-U., xxxv, which differs slightly from RC in DLC: Short Papers as printed in Syrett, *Hamilton*, vii, 357-8). Lambert enclosed a copy of this letter in his response to Schweitzer, Jeanneret & Cie. on 30 Nov. 1790 (Tr in MHi: Knox Papers). See also Montmorin to Lambert, 29 Nov. 1790, promising to forward Short's response immediately on receiving it; Montmorin to Caillard, 30 Nov. 1790, enclosing his letter to be delivered to Short (Dfts of both in Arch. Aff. Etr., Corr. Pol., E.-U., xxxv).

[41] Short to Montmorin, 8 Dec. 1790 (RC in Arch. Aff. Etr., Corr. Pol., E.-U., xxxv). Short sent a copy of this to Hamilton as enclosure No. 3 in his letter of 18 Dec. 1790 (incorrectly identified in Syrett, *Hamilton*, vii, 355, as Short to Swan, 9 Dec. 1790).

[42] Short to Swan, 9 Dec. 1790 (PrC in DLC: Short Papers).

[43] Swan to Short, 12 Dec. 1790 and another of the same date, copies of both of which were enclosed in Short to Hamilton, 18 Dec. 1790 (Syrett, *Hamilton*, vii, 361-4).

plan meeting with the minister's approval to the President, who alone had the power to accept. This he duly reported to Montmorin, but warned that, if he should think the interest of France required the sale of the American debt, the persons designated should be known and of irreproachable repute and that the negotiation should be made public only after having been communicated to the President. These conditions were necessary, he reminded Montmorin, in order not to block the operations already begun for the discharge of the debt. "I have every reason to believe," he added, "that the loan will be perfectly fulfilled and that the United States will be able presently to liquidate all of their debts. I am persuaded that I have no need of repeating to you, Monsieur, that they regard their debt to France as the most sacred and whose complete discharge they hold most at heart."[44] In reporting these developments to Hamilton, Short suggested that if the Genoese capitalists interested in the plan could be induced to accept the conditions stated in his letter to Montmorin and would pay France in livres while accepting American obligations in florins so as to give the United States the benefit, it might be arranged to have them initiate the proposal. In any event, he thought his letter to Montmorin would probably put an end to the negotiations of Schweitzer, Jeanneret & Cie.[45]

What that letter did instead was to cause the company to turn its attention to the United States. This took the form of an assignment to James Swan to try to gain acceptance in America not of the revised proposal that had failed to win Short's approval but of the original offer to lend the United States about 40 million livres to discharge the debt to France. In making the assignment, the company pointed out what Swan already knew—that that plan had been given the approval of Lambert and Montmorin but had not been accepted by Short because of his lack of authority. "In this situation," they wrote, "we have need of a friend of the President who would be able to expedite acceptance of our proposal and to remove any obstacles that might arise. The advantageous reports we have had of your talents and rectitude, have induced us to have full confidence in you and to beg you to have the goodness to take charge of our interests and to pursue them yourself or through your friends."[46] Swan, who very probably suggested this step, accepted the company's offer of 7,000 livres sterling for the agency. On the same day and in a private communication to Henry Knox, Swan urged him to use his influence with the President, the Secretary of the Treasury, and any others to have it approved. To aid in accomplishing this, he made a sacred promise to turn over to Knox the fee—and a greater sum if necessary. "It is a great point gained having it accepted already by the Ministry here," he added, "and I do not see how it can be refused on your side of the water. . . . Would Duer be of some service in this? You know who will do best. He might work H[amilton]." In a postscript added three

[44] Short to Montmorin, 19 Dec. 1790 (translation from RC in Arch. Aff. Etr., Corr. Pol., E.-U., xxxv; text printed from PrC in DLC: Short Papers in Syrett, *Hamilton*, vii, 365-7). See also Swan to Short, 14 Dec. 1790; Schweitzer, Jeanneret & Cie. to Short, 14 Dec. 1790; and Short's reply of 17 Dec. 1790, all enclosed in Short to Hamilton, 18 Dec. 1790, and printed in same, vii, 364-5, 434-5, where the last is presented as an enclosure in Short to Hamilton, 15 Jan. 1791, though in fact the enclosure in that letter was one from Schweitzer, Jeanneret & Cie. to Short of 27 Dec. 1790 (missing).

[45] Short to Hamilton, 18 and 30 Dec. 1790 (Syrett, *Hamilton*, vii, 348-57, 392-6).

[46] Schweitzer, Jeanneret & Cie. to Swan, 27 Dec. 1790 (translation from Tr in MHi: Knox Papers).

days later, Swan added: "Pray sound Mr. Jefferson on this, or get someone to do it. I am afraid of him, merely because Mr. Short may have misled him. For God's sake, get it effected. It is all America can wish, and all that France desires: and is what is necessary to make the concern'd here perfectly satisfied."[47] He evidently felt so certain of obtaining support that he endorsed the bankers' letter to him giving Knox full right to the fee. There is no evidence that Knox responded to the crass effort to purchase his influence. The company, however, were more successful in their efforts to gain the support of French officials.

IV

On the same day that Swan made his urgent appeal to Knox, Schweitzer, Jeanneret & Cie. informed Short that they would accept the offer made in his letter of the 14th. Transmitting to him all of the documents pertaining to the subject which Short already possessed and had made available to Hamilton, they asked that he present their proposal to the President.[48] Early in January they reported this action to Montmorin and urged that the documents be communicated to the French minister in America, together with the most pressing instructions to solicit a prompt decision.[49] Montmorin, under pressure from the Treasury and the Committee of Finance, complied, but couched his instructions to Otto in terms far from pressing:[50]

> You will have the goodness to meet with Mr. Jefferson on the proposition. . . . We naturally desire, considering the situation of our finances, that this may coincide with the views of General Washington and that he will decide to accept it: but you will observe that we subordinate our convenience to that of the United States and that if the proposed operation is contrary to it, our intention is not to insist upon it. Whenever efforts have been made to engage us to transfer our credit to foreigners, we have refused for fear that it would be disagreeable to Congress. The present case is not the same, since it is simply a question of filling up a loan which that body has itself authorized. I recommend this affair to your zeal and prudence.

In transmitting a copy of this dispatch to Short, Montmorin said that it gave him less difficulty to agree to the company's request because he had made

[47] Swan to Knox, 27-30 Dec. 1790 ("Private"; MHi: Knox Papers). With this Swan enclosed the bankers' letter of assignment, copies of their original proposals, and of the correspondence on the subject – their letter to Lambert of 22 Nov. 1790, Lambert's reply of 30 Nov. 1790, their letter to Short of 14 Dec. and Short's reply of 17 Dec. 1790, together with copies of Lambert to Montmorin of 26 Nov. 1790 and Montmorin's reply of 29 Nov. 1790 (Tr in French, 12 pages, with translation; MHi: Knox Papers).

[48] Schweitzer, Jeanneret & Cie. to Short, 27 Dec. 1790. Short enclosed this in his letter to Hamilton of 15 Jan. 1791 but said that it added nothing to what he had already sent. While the letter has not been found, its purport is clear from Short's comment and from the company's letter to Montmorin (see following note and Short to Hamilton, 15 Jan. 1791, Syrett, *Hamilton*, VII, 427-34).

[49] Schweitzer, Jeanneret & Cie. to Montmorin, 10 Jan. 1791 (RC in Arch. Aff. Etr., Corr. Pol., E.-U., XXXV). Montmorin replied on 20 Jan. 1791 (Dft in same).

[50] Montmorin to Otto, 24 Jan. 1791 (translation of Dft in same, with notation that the communication was placed in the hands of Schweitzer, who took responsibility for sending it to its destination; Tr in DLC: Short Papers, without date, enclosed in Short to Hamilton, 7 Feb. 1791, and printed in Syrett, *Hamilton*, VIII, 12; Tr in MHi: Knox Papers, also without date, enclosed in Swan to Knox, 27 Jan. 1791).

acceptance entirely dependent upon the convenience of the United States. At the same time, he left it up to Short to decide whether he had sufficient authority to make a conditional arrangement with Schweitzer, Jeanneret & Cie. Short did not mention this when he transmitted a copy of the dispatch to Hamilton, but he felt certain that the Secretary of the Treasury would be perfectly satisfied because all had been left to the President to decide. He thought Montmorin himself did not expect the proposal to be accepted.[51] Short did not send Montmorin's letter or his dispatch to Hamilton, assuming that these would have been made available by Otto before his letter arrived. He may also have been content merely to describe their contents because of the hint Montmorin had given him about the possibility of concluding a provisional arrangement. But a few weeks later he sent copies of both, perhaps because in the meantime he said he had learned what he formerly suspected – that Schweitzer and Jeanneret were "entirely without credit or capital and . . . of a character which shews it would be unsafe to treat with them. Their offers being supported by the minister is the only circumstance which entitles them to any kind of attention."[52]

James Swan, with the optimism of an inveterate speculator, thought otherwise. He forwarded Montmorin's dispatch to London to go by the February packet and at the same time informed Henry Knox of its contents. He also told him that Short's refusal to act in the matter had been freely criticized in the Committee of Finance, whose members felt that the United States could not rightfully or honestly refuse the offer. "This step," he said of Montmorin's action, "can't but make the Affair go now, as America can form no reasonable objections to borrow money of these men on the same terms as they can in Holland; nor to replace their debt to France by this occasion, especially when she stands so much in need of it. . . . I trust still for your exertions in this affair, and be assured of my truest gratitude."[53]

Short had assumed that his dispatches to the Secretary of the Treasury about the speculation and to the Secretary of State about general political and commercial affairs would be shared by each other. This was far from being the case. While his communications to Hamilton had been held up for weeks by wind-bound vessels at Texel, Swan's urgent appeals to Knox enclosing all of the documents on the case went by way of London and the English packets. That the essential facts were known first to Hamilton and that he did not reveal what he knew to Jefferson is clear.

[51] Montmorin to Short, 24 Jan. 1791 (Arch. Aff. Etr., Corr. Pol., E.-U., xxxv).

[52] Short to Hamilton, 11 Mch. 1791 (PrC in DLC: Short Papers, printed in Syrett, *Hamilton*, VIII, 170-4, with Montmorin to Short, 24 Jan. 1791, as enclosure, the dispatch to Otto having been assumed to be an enclosure in Short's dispatch of 7 Feb. 1791, same, VIII, 10-12). The letter itself makes it clear that both were enclosed, but why Short delayed sending them for a month after having assumed Otto would already have made his instructions known is puzzling.

Gouverneur Morris, a shrewd judge of bankers whether in Paris, Amsterdam, or London, at first opposed the proposal of Schweitzer, Jeanneret & Cie. and at this time was as doubtful as Short about their reliability. But when a member of the firm – probably Schweitzer – called on him and was queried about their financial support, the answer given convinced him that they could command ample capital for the venture (Morris to Washington, 27 May 1791, enclosed in Lear to Hamilton, 15 Aug. 1791, and printed in Syrett, *Hamilton*, IX, 63-7). See below.

[53] Swan to Knox, 27 Jan. 1791 (MHi: Knox Papers).

For late in March Théophile Cazenove, reporting on a conversation he had just had with the Secretary of the Treasury, informed the Amsterdam houses he represented for investments in America that a company of French and Genevans had offered to buy from the French government its claim on the United States and that he had been promised a copy of the proposals. He was erroneously led to believe that these had been sent by Short to Jefferson. Cazenove evidently pressed Hamilton for further information, for two weeks later he reported to his principals that the proposals had been sent to someone not in the Treasury department and that his informants had made a great mystery of it. In this second conversation Hamilton revealed to Cazenove that he had just received from Short a letter of the 2d of December referring him for further details to a previous letter not then received; that from the little he wrote, it appeared Short had not consented to the plan, although it had been agreed to by Montmorin; that it had originated with the house of De Lessart, Comptroller of Finance; and that its execution would not require raising funds in Holland. On the basis of statements made to him by Hamilton, Cazenove was able to assure his principals that Short had no authority to conclude such an arrangement and that the Secretary of the Treasury would not favor one which put it in the power of a single company to control such a mass of claims and to manipulate it in such a way as to interfere with his general financial plans.[54]

The information given by Hamilton to Cazenove could only have come from Henry Knox, who clearly was the unidentified person not in the Treasury department to whom Cazenove alluded. Short's dispatch of the 2d of December had not even mentioned the speculation. That of the 18th of December enclosing the pertinent documents was not received by Hamilton until four days after the last of these conversations with Cazenove.[55] Short did not and could not have reported Montmorin's acceptance of the scheme until after the 24th of January. Nor did he mention the involvement of De Lessart or convey the impression that he would report on the matter to the Secretary of State. But Swan's urgent appeals to Knox, particularly that of the 27th of December which enclosed copies of the proposal and of the relevant correspondence, provided all of the details Hamilton was able to give to Cazenove, including the erroneous statement that the ministry had approved the plan at that date. Thus Hamilton, through his colleague in the Cabinet, was able to inform Cazenove of the essential facts of the case and to state his own views of the speculation before he received the same information from the Secretary of State.

It is understandable that Hamilton should not have wanted Cazenove to know that this information had come privately and through an inappropriate

[54] Cazenove to his principals (Pieter Stadnitski, N. & J. Van Staphorst, P. & C. van Eeghen, and Ten Cate & Vollenhoven), 29 Mch., 6 and 11 Apr. 1791 (Cazenove Letter Book, Holland Land Company Papers, Archives of the City of Amsterdam).

[55] Short to Hamilton of 18 Dec. 1790 was enclosed in his to TJ of 30 Dec. 1790, which TJ received on 14 Apr. 1791. The letters from Short that Hamilton had received at this time were those of 2 Dec. 1790 and 25 Jan. 1791. Only the latter referred very briefly to the proposal of Schweitzer, Jeanneret & Cie. (Hamilton to Short, 13 Apr. 1791, Syrett, Hamilton, VIII, 280-2); in this acknowledgment Hamilton said that the nature of the company's offer had been made known to him in "a communication through the Chargé des affaires of France to the Secretary of State" (see Documents I and II following).

channel. It is also understandable that he should have thus made a confidant of a foreign individual instead of communicating what he knew to Jefferson, despite Washington's instruction that he consult with him on matters concerning foreign loans and the debt to France. For in these conversations with Cazenove Hamilton had other objects in mind. In the first one he revealed his intention to create the Society for Establishing Useful Manufactures (SUM), an enterprise for which he sought and procured investments from the houses Cazenove represented. Among these were the Van Staphorsts, one of the banking firms which represented the United States in Amsterdam. Hamilton at the same time revealed to Cazenove his plans for the deferred annuities – useful information for the Holland capitalists who were already profiting from investments in American securities. The agent naturally asked his principals to hold this in confidence. Knowing that the American bankers would learn of it through the Van Staphorsts, Hamilton also assured the agent that Short's letter of the 2d of December had gratified him in its tribute to their zeal, talents, and credit, thus bringing to bear all that the United States could desire in respect to the loans being negotiated. Cazenove duly transmitted to his superiors this flattering but obvious misrepresentation of what Short had actually said in his cogent analysis of various Amsterdam banking houses and their practices.[56]

V

On the 4th of April Otto received Montmorin's instructions and all pertinent documents concerning the proposal of Schweitzer, Jeanneret & Cie. He immediately called upon the Secretary of State, who confessed that he was entirely ignorant of the matter despite dispatches recently received from Short. Thus, without making a formal representation, Otto had given Jefferson the essential facts some days before he presented his written communication with the relevant documents. At this initial interview Jefferson gave Otto his views of what the attitude of the government would be. He assured the chargé that Short had no power to conclude so important a transaction, being authorized only to make a loan very inferior to the one proposed; that the Holland financiers knew he could not open a new loan until the first had been approved; that it was the intention of the President to have the entire debt to France liquidated by payments made to the Royal Treasury in specie; that he feared no ill would result from the proposal because of the solicitous interest Montmorin himself had taken to prevent it; but that it would be necessary to await Washington's decision on his return from his southern tour.[57] Thus, speaking provisionally for the government, Jefferson gave his own views and a message of compliment to Montmorin a week before he submitted Otto's formal note and its accompanying documents to Hamilton and asked what substantive answer should be given.[58] This conversation with Otto took place on the day that Jefferson received Short's communication of the 24th of January which did not mention

[56] Cazenove to his principals, 11 Apr. 1791 (Cazenove Letter Book, Holland Land Company Papers, Archives of the City of Amsterdam). See also Editorial Note, Vol. 19: 454-7, for more detailed comment on Hamilton's successful effort to get Cazenove to invest for his principals in SUM.
[57] Otto to Montmorin, 4 Apr. 1791 (Arch. Aff. Etr., Corr. Pol., E.-U., xxxv).
[58] Otto to the Secretary of State, 10 Apr. 1791; TJ to Hamilton, 10 Apr. 1791 (see Documents I and II following).

the company's proposal but which enclosed the one of the 18th of December to Hamilton in which its nature was fully documented. But one important difference between Hamilton's conversation with Cazenove and that of Jefferson with Otto is that the Secretary of the Treasury disclosed useful information to a private individual with other objects in mind, while the Secretary of State gave a tentative response to a communication from the accredited representative of a foreign power. Five days after his conversation with Otto, Jefferson happened to learn from John Adams that Hamilton, in accordance with authorization given by Washington before his departure, had called a meeting of the heads of department for the ostensible purpose of giving more latitude to Short in the negotiation of loans.[59] Having thus learned from the Vice President that the stated purpose of the meeting concerned the loans being negotiated by Short – a subject to which the proposals of Schweitzer, Jeanneret & Cie. were obviously related – it seems clear that on the next day, which happened to be a Sunday, Jefferson prompted Otto to transmit to him the relevant documents. These he immediately dispatched to Hamilton, undoubtedly for the purpose of having the related subjects discussed at the meeting called for the next day. It is not likely that, with Knox present and in full possession of the facts through letters received from Swan, Hamilton would have desired such a discussion by the full Cabinet. His written opinion was not given until the day after the meeting.[60]

Another and more important difference between what the Secretary of the Treasury said privately to Cazenove and what the Secretary of State said officially to Otto was the assurance given by Jefferson that the entire debt to France would be paid in specie. He had long since learned of Short's gratification that the first payment was one in which 1.5 million florins commanded 3.6 million livres. If he had not already known that the Secretary of the Treasury shared this view, he was made aware of it when he received Hamilton's first communication declaring the company's proposal was inadmissible because, among other reasons, it would entail the loss of the benefit of exchange. This factor was given even more emphasis when Hamilton sent him a carefully excised version of Short's letter of the 18th of December.[61] Being thus made aware of their differing views about the value and mode of payment, Jefferson may have hoped to bring the issue before the President by placing Hamilton on record. In his reply to Otto, however, he merely summarized the argument given by Hamilton, minimized the factor of exchange by referring only to "the change of the place of payment," avoided repeating his own assurance that the debt would be paid in specie, and said nothing about having to await a final decision from the President.[62] Otto found the reasons given by Jefferson "peu satisfaisantes." In the meantime the chargé had several conversations with the Secretary of the Treasury, who emphasized his apprehensions about entrusting

[59] See Editorial Note and group of documents on indirect diplomacy, at 4 Apr. 1791. Hamilton to Adams, 9 Apr. 1791; Adams to Hamilton, 9 Apr. 1791; Hamilton to Washington, 10 Apr. 1791 (Syrett, *Hamilton*, VIII, 258, 270-1). After receiving Hamilton's letter on Saturday the 9th, Adams said that he accidentally fell in with TJ and that the latter had suggested a meeting at his house on the 11th.

[60] See Documents I, II, and III following.

[61] Hamilton to TJ, 12 and 15 Apr. 1791 (Documents III and IV following).

[62] TJ to Otto, 7 May 1791 (Document V following).

such a large mass of American obligations in the hands of individuals. Hamilton also gave him the erroneous impression that, in negotiating the last loan, Short had promised to accord the American bankers the preference for those to be negotiated later. Otto, accepting Hamilton's objection to the proposal of Schweitzer, Jeanneret & Cie. as conclusive, considered the matter closed and reported to Montmorin that it would be useless to press it further.[63]

The absence of full communication on the subject between Hamilton and Jefferson is also reflected in the manner in which each reported to Short the result of the exchange with Otto. Hamilton thought the sole advantage of the company's proposal lay in its prolonging the period of reimbursement and one of the main reasons for rejecting it was that it would subject "the United States . . . to the loss arising from a less favourable course of exchange." He also held out the hope that other and better offers to buy the debt would be made on terms that Short would be able to accept.[64] Jefferson held quite different views and expressed them in the form of positive instructions. Reminding Short how strongly the United States desired to pay off the debt and what good prospects there were for borrowing the whole sum, he added: "Under these dispositions and prospects it would grieve us extremely to see our debt pass into the hands of speculators, and be subjected ourselves to the chicaneries and vexations of private avarice. We desire you therefore to dissuade the government as far as you can prudently from listening to any overtures of that kind, whether native or foreign, to inform them without reserve that our government condemns their projects, and reserves to itself the right of paying no where but into the Treasury of France, according to their contract."[65] Nothing could have been more explicit as a statement of the government's policy, nor more at odds with Hamilton's view of what the policy should be.

Even as these conflicting instructions were being dispatched, the continuing depreciation of the livre brought renewed activity on the part of French officials and speculators. Dufresne, Director of the Royal Treasury, concerted with Montmorin to prevail upon Short to prevent further loss by the declining rate of exchange.[66] Caught between the American bankers in Amsterdam and these official pressures, an embarrassed Short referred the problem to Hamilton.[67] The same circumstances produced a new appeal by Schweitzer, Jeanneret & Cie. and their official supporters. Short declined to treat with them and referred them to Ternant, who was about to depart as minister to the United States. He told him, however, that if the ministry approved, if Ternant could be fully satisfied about their capital resources, and if the terms were fair, he would recommend that Hamilton accept their offer. In reporting this to Hamilton, Short said that if Ternant undertook to act on the proposal he would be authorized to give more advantageous terms than those submitted by the com-

[63] Otto to Montmorin, 7 May 1791 (Arch. Aff. Etr., Corr. Pol., E.-U., xxxv). On 6 July 1791 Montmorin transmitted to Schweitzer, Jeanneret & Cie. TJ's letter of 7 May 1791 rejecting the company's offer (Dft in same).

[64] Hamilton to Short, 13 Apr. 1791 (RC in DLC: Short Papers; printed in Syrett, Hamilton, VII, 280-2).

[65] TJ to Short, 25 Apr. 1791.

[66] Dufresne to Montmorin, 12 Apr. and 17 May 1791 (Arch. Aff. Etr., Corr. Pol., E.-U., xxxv).

[67] Short to Hamilton, 19 June 1791 (Syrett, Hamilton, VIII, 488-93).

pany. But he added: "The exchange between Paris and Amsterdam is now more than 20. p. cent in favor of the latter. This is the real standard by which you should be guided."[68]

James Swan, transmitting to Henry Knox the new proposal of the company, argued otherwise. He pointed out that the Committee of Finance had requested Dufresne to write to Short that as the money derived from the recent loan "was to pay the very sum borrowed by Congress, it was expected that it would be paid Ecu, contre Ecu, without the benefit of exchange." Since this had fallen so low as 20%, he thought the United States could not honorably take advantage of the misfortunes of her ally. To do this, he told Knox, "would appear as an Agiotage which the Government would not suffer, since they would claim the hard Crowns, as advanced to Congress."[69] In brief, what the government could not itself do, it could authorize a company of speculators to do for their own private benefit.

Gouverneur Morris added his voice to the conflicting counsels. He addressed himself not to the Secretary of the Treasury as he had done early in 1790 or to the Secretary of State, but to the President. In giving Washington a brief history of the affair, he referred to his letter to Hamilton of 31 January 1790, in which he had "hinted at the means of turning to useful Account a very precipitate step of the public agents in Holland." In his lengthy communication Morris left Washington with the erroneous impression that he had withdrawn from any concern with the debt on being sent on the public mission to England. He argued that since the United States was not in a position to pay the debt, a bargain by which the period of payment could be prolonged without loss to either party would be desirable. Nor could the nation "take Advantage of those Necessities [of France] which the Succor afforded to America . . . occasioned." He added that in a conversation with one who was engaged in the affair, he had been given proof that "People of the first Fortune" were concerned in it. He did not mention Schweitzer, Jeanneret & Cie. and he did not in precise terms recommend approval of their proposals. But he pointed out that the bargain desired could only be made with the French government or with individuals. This begged the question as to the purpose of the Holland loans and the effect such bargaining would have upon them. But, warning that any requests by the United States for further delays in payment would have to be given the consent of the National Assembly and the debates there would not be pleasant, Morris left no doubt as to which course he would recommend: "A Bargain with Individuals has the Advantage of bringing in the Aid of private Interest to the Support of our Credit, and what is of very great Consequence

[68] Short to Hamilton, 3 June 1791 (same, VIII, 412-25). Ternant told Short that he was not satisfied about the resources of the company. Schweitzer, Jeanneret & Cie. to Montmorin, 7 Apr. 1791 (Arch. Aff. Etr., Corr. Pol., E.-U., XXXV; photocopies in DLC). Montmorin acknowledged their letter on 29 Apr. 1791 and said that, while their plan appeared useful, he could take no further step to procure its acceptance. He forwarded the letter to Short the same day, repeating his favorable opinion of the proposal but leaving the matter up to Short (same).

[69] Swan to Knox, 27 May 1791, with a postscript of the 10th of June enclosing a power of attorney given by Schweitzer, Jeanneret & Cie. in blank, authorizing the unnamed person to present to the President the new proposal and to accept any modifications that might be required, subject to their final approval (both in MHi: Knox Papers). Swan gave a very different account to TJ, but thought their interest "near the minister" and other official support promised success (Swan to TJ, 2 June 1791).

EDITORIAL NOTE

it would leave us at Liberty to make Use of that Credit for the Arrangement of our domestic Affairs."[70] The phrasing was more elegant, but in essence this was the same argument Swan had urged in his communication with Knox: the United States could not honorably profit from the necessities of France, but it could permit private speculators to do this.

Montmorin declined the company's request for instructions to Ternant to press their proposals officially, referring them instead to Short. Ternant arrived early in August to take up his duties. Far from recommending adoption of the proposal of Schweitzer, Jeanneret & Cie., he made a representation against the advantage that had been taken of France by way of payments in depreciated currency. Jefferson drafted a response which reflected his own consistent views of the subject but which he knew was not in accord with those of Hamilton and Short as reflected in their words and actions. In submitting the draft to Hamilton for his suggestions, he reminded him that the response to Ternant would have to meet the approval of the President. Hamilton, perhaps not knowing whether Jefferson had already consulted Washington, offered a re-phrasing of the final sentence which eliminated the assurance that payments would be made in their just value and also deferred settlement of the question of depreciation and the rate of exchange to the time of final liquidation of the debt. But what remained was unequivocal. Speaking for the President, Jefferson gave the pledge of the government that it would entertain "no idea of paying their debt in a depreciated medium."[71] Hamilton duly reported the decision to Short.[72]

This was by no means an insignificant victory for the Secretary of State in his defense of a settlement of the debt that would be just and honorable. But it was far from ending the irritations and partisan conflicts which clustered about the American obligation as long as it existed.

[70] Morris to Washington, 27 May 1791 (DNA: RG 59, MLR; printed in Syrett, *Hamilton*, IX, 63-7). Washington requested Hamilton to draft a reply to Morris (Lear to Hamilton, 15 Aug. 1791, same, IX, 61). Lear sent with this all of the documents that Morris had enclosed: copies of the proposals of the company as enclosed in their letter to Lambert, 22 Nov. 1790; Lambert to Montmorin, 26 Nov. 1790; Montmorin's reply, 29 Nov. 1790; Lambert to Schweitzer, Jeanneret & Cie., 30 Nov. 1790; the company to Short, 14 Dec. 1790; Short's reply, 17 Dec. 1790; the company to Short, 27 Dec. 1790, and to Montmorin, 10 Jan. 1791; Montmorin's reply to the company, 20 Jan. 1791; Montmorin to Otto, 24 Jan. 1791 (Trs of all, in French, in DNA: RG 59, MLR).

Hamilton's draft of Washington's response to Morris (not found) was far more carefully composed than those he gave to TJ for rejecting the company's proposal (see Washington to Morris, 12 Sep. 1791, *Writings*, ed. Fitzpatrick, XXXI, 366-8; Documents III and IV following).

[71] TJ to Hamilton, 31 Aug. 1791; Hamilton to TJ, 31 Aug. 1791; TJ to Ternant, 1 Sep. 1791.

[72] Hamilton to Short, 1 Sep. 1791 (Syrett, *Hamilton*, IX, 158-62).

I. Louis Guillaume Otto to Thomas Jefferson

Dimanche matin. 10. Avril. 1791.

Le Chargé des Affaires de France a l'honneur de presenter ses respects à Monsieur le Secretaire d'Etat et de lui envoyer la Correspondance qui a eu lieu concernant la proposition faite par Messrs. Schweizer et Jeanneret de rembourser la dette des Etats unis envers Sa Majesté. Il le supplie de vouloir bien lui renvoyer ces pieces et lui en donner son opinion avant le depart du batiment, qui doit faire voile pour le Havre vers la fin de cette Semaine.

RC (DNA: RG 59, NL); endorsed by TJ as received 10 Apr. 1791 and so recorded in SJL. TJ returned the enclosures to Otto, and these cannot be identified with certainty. They cannot have included all that Short sent to Hamilton, which included those written by Swan (for identification of these enclosures, see Editorial Note, notes 38, 40, 41, 44, 48, 50, and 52). But it is certain that Otto sent to TJ with this note the proposals of Schweitzer, Jeanneret & Cie. of 22 Nov. 1790 and the exchanges among the company, Lambert, Montmorin, and Short, copies of which Gouverneur Morris sent to Washington in his letter of 27 May 1791 (for identification of these, see note 70 to Editorial Note. These probably did not include Montmorin's instructions to Otto of 24 Jan. 1791, a copy of which Montmorin had sent to Short.

II. Thomas Jefferson to Alexander Hamilton

[Philadelphia] Apr. 10. 1791.

Th: Jefferson has the honor to send to the Secretary of the Treasury a note just received from Mr. Otto with copies of a correspondence between certain bankers desirous of lending 40. millions of livres to the U. S. the French ministers and Mr. Short. He will ask the Secretary of the Treasury's consideration of these papers, and that he will be so good as to return them to him with the substance of the answer he would wish to have given to Mr. Otto. It is probable indeed we shall soon receive the same correspondence from Mr. Short with his observations on the offer made.

RC (DLC: Hamilton Papers); endorsed. Not recorded in SJL or SJPL. For enclosures see note to Document I preceding.

III. Alexander Hamilton to Thomas Jefferson

Sir   Treasury Department April 12th. 1791

I have perused the papers communicated to you by the Chargé des Affaires of France. The propositions to which they relate, as far as they are understood, appear to me inadmissible. The only advantage they offer to the United States is a prolongation of the time of reimbursement. The rate of interest is to remain the same, and the place of payment, according to the probable course of exchange, is to be altered for the worse, from Paris to Amsterdam. A premium of five ℔ Cent is also required, while the charges on the loans we make in Holland do not exceed four.

There is however a proposition which is not understood. It is this, that the exchange on the sum to be paid at Paris and received at Amsterdam shall be regulated according to the *Tariff* announced in the law of Congress. Now there is nothing in the laws of the United States to which I can apply the term Tariff. It is possible however that Mr. Short's letters when received may throw light on this point and some others, which may give a different complexion to the business.

But there are various collateral considerations in relation to the transfer of the debt due from the United States to France, affecting the credit and financial operations of this country, which will make it in almost any form a delicate operation. It is desireable on every account to make expeditious payment to France; but this desire must be conciliated with that of invigorating and perfecting the system of public credit of the United States. And in adhering to this idea there is the additional inducement of a tolerable prospect of satisfying the claims of France in a manner perhaps as expeditious and probably more efficacious than would be incident to an acquiescence in the proposed plan. – I have the honor to be, with great respect and esteem Sir Your obedt. servant,

Alexander Hamilton
Secy of the Treasury

RC (DLC: Madison Papers); in clerk's hand, except for signature; at foot of text: "The honorable Thomas Jefferson Esqr. Secretary of State." Not recorded in SJL.

IV. Alexander Hamilton to Thomas Jefferson

SIR   Treasury Department, 15 April 1791

The letter you sent me from Mr. Short and others which I have received, since mine to you, confirm the view of the subject therein taken. This you will perceive from the following passages extracted from one of them. "Since then (speaking of former overtures) another Company has presented itself for the same object, with a scheme by which the United States are to make the *sacrifices* on which *they count* for their profits." "The object of this Company is, as you will see, to pay livres tournois in their present depreciated State and to receive from the United States florins at the usual exchange. By this means France would receive from them *as much as she is entitled to receive from us*, but we should be obliged to pay the Company *much more than we are obliged to pay France*." "Had I had powers competent to the purpose,[1] I should not have thought myself justified to have opened such a negotiation where there was *all loss* and *no prospect of advantage* to the United States." "I must also add that the house which makes these propositions is *entirely unknown* here and that I never heard even their names at Paris, which proves that *it must be an inconsiderable one*." Consequently the credit of the United States would be in imminent danger of suffering in their hands.

I have authorised Mr. Short to apply a million and a half of florins of the loan he has opened to the use of France, and shall press as large payments, as may be practicable, to her.

I take it for granted that the Court of France will not attempt any operation with the debt, without the consent of the United States. Any thing of this sort, considering the efforts which are making on our part, to discharge the debt, would certainly be very[2] exceptionable. Indeed[2] I do not see how any valid disposition of the debt of a sovereign power can be made without its consent; but it would be disagreeable to have to use this argument. I trust it will never be rendered necessary. – I have the honor to be, with great respect, Sir, Your obedt. Servant,   ALEXANDER HAMILTON

RC (DLC: Madison Papers); in clerk's hand except for signature and two interlineations in Hamilton's hand (see note 2 below); endorsed by TJ as received 15 Apr. 1791 and so recorded in SJL. The extracts made by Hamilton are from Short's letter to him of 18 Dec. 1790, enclosed in his to TJ of 30 Dec. 1790. Both were received by TJ on 14 Apr. 1791, and that to Hamilton was forwarded to him the same day. The italicized passages were not underscored in Short's letter, but whether emphasis was given by Hamilton or by some later hand cannot be determined. For one instance of a departure from Short's text, see note 1 below.

As indicated in the Editorial Note, Short assumed as a matter of course that his dispatches to the Secretary of the Treasury pertaining to the loans and to the debt to France would be shared with the Secretary of State. Thus he did not forward to TJ the various documents enclosed in his letters to Hamilton of 18 Dec. 1790, 15 Jan. 1791, 7 Feb. 1791, and 11 Mch. 1791. Neither did he keep TJ informed of the complicated maneuvers of Schweitzer, Jeanneret & Cie. and their supporters in and out of office. His assumption that a full and free exchange of information would take place between the two heads of department is understandable. The subject under discussion involved both finance and American foreign relations. Also, as Short knew, it was for this reason that Washington had required consultation and concerted action by the two members of the Cabinet having responsibility in these areas. But that Short's assumption was ill-founded is proved – among other things – by the above letter in which, instead of enclosing the full text as Short had supposed would be done, Hamilton excluded far more from the lengthy dispatch than he included. Also, while assuring TJ that he had authorized Short to apply 1.5 million florins to the debt to France and would "press as large payments, as may be practicable, to her," he failed to disclose that a third of this sum was being withheld for further instructions.

Thus, while Short's letter was intended for TJ's eyes as well as for Hamilton's, the Secretary of State never saw the perceptive account therein of the Dutch money lenders, undertakers, and brokers or Short's observations on the status of American credit in Europe. This would have added little to what TJ had learned from personal experience in 1788 when he persuaded John Adams to negotiate a loan in order to sustain American credit during the transition to a form of government which had power to tax. But among the parts of the letter that Hamilton excluded there was much else about the scheme of Schweitzer, Jeanneret & Cie. then formally under discussion

between the Secretary of State and the French chargé d'affaires. Short opened this topic with a statement about the attitude of the French ministry which TJ should have seen as Short intended: "I have informed you of the several attempts which have been made to speculate on the debt due by the U. S. They were averted by different means, but particularly by the governments acquiring full information of the value of that debt. At the time of my leaving Paris the ministry were fully determined as far as depended on them to listen to no negotiation of that sort. This put an end to the schemes of those who placed their profits in the sacrifices to be made by France." Short then gave a brief history of the negotiations of Schweitzer, Jeanneret & Cie. that was documented by his enclosures. The latter included the two letters from Swan of 12 Dec. 1790 and also that written two days later (Syrett, *Hamilton*, VII, 361-5). These of course were not included in the documents TJ received from Otto. Hamilton also excluded Short's remarks about Lambert and about his own response to Montmorin: "As this [the proposal of Schweitzer, Jeanneret & Cie.] was envelopped in such a manner as not to strike the Comptroller General, he espoused it with much warmth and recommended [it] to M. de Montmorin. That minister wrote me a letter on the subject. . . . You will see that the minister has misstated a little my conversation with him, though it is of no consequence. As I had no power to act I thought it best to rest my answer on that footing, but as I feared the company meant to submit their offers to the assembly where a discussion of them could not have failed to have been inconvenient at least, perhaps injurious, I wished to stop it if possible in the hands of the minister, and therefore added the observations contained in my answer. . . ." Hamilton also excluded Short's account of the subsequent pressures from Swan and from the company which induced him to write to Montmorin and "to shew that the U. S. did not refuse absolutely every kind of negotiation, and that there was a real insufficiency of power." To this Short added and Hamilton excluded the following: "I thought it probable this would put an end to the prosecution of this business without the U. S. being placed in an unfavorable light in the assembly in case of the matter being carried there. It is particularly important that we should be well regarded there at present as the discussion of the objects of our commerce in France is now open."

Perhaps most significant of all, Hamilton did not reveal Short's comment about the Genoese capitalists who were reputedly connected with the scheme. In these remarks he indicated his willingness to negotiate with them as potential purchasers of the debt: "You observe it is stated as if they [the Genoese capitalists] were wholly interested. Should they be induced to change their interests in the French funds to the American debt, and in order to effect this change submit to the loss of exchange, viz. pay France the number of livres, and receive the American new obligations here in florins of the value of those livres at the present rate of exchange, this which would be perfectly just would at the same time be advantageous to the U. S." Short admitted that this would involve risk by placing the obligations in private hands, but he added: "on the other hand the wants of America would cease as far as relate to the loans to be made for the liquidation of the debt due to France. Should it be thought proper to set on foot the conditional negotiation mentioned in my letter to M. Montmorin it will be then seen whether such a scheme would be acceptable to the Genoese and that without its coming from the U. S." (Short to Hamilton, 18 Dec. 1790; printed with enclosures in Syrett, *Hamilton*, VII, 348-68).

The extracts made by Hamilton from the letter of Short thus failed to reveal the latter's willingness to place the debt in the hands of presumably more reliable capitalists. But what he did disclose was sufficient to show that, on the matter of taking advantage of the depreciated value of the livre in order to benefit the United States — that is, to take advantage of the distressed situation of the ally — Short had proved himself to be more Hamiltonian than Jefferson in his views. TJ recognized the fact and treated it with silence. But in his instructions to Short he made it clear that the policy of the government was altogether different and that it condemned *all* speculators' plans to buy the debt, whether these originated at home or abroad (TJ to Short, 25 Apr. 1791).

The protégé and surrogate son of the Secretary of State, who was increasingly revealing his differing attitude toward the political situation in France, paid little if any attention to these unequivocal instructions. Within the year Short was suggesting to Hamilton that the first banking firm in Paris, Boyd & Ker, might be induced to pay off the entire remaining debt to France at one stroke. He argued that Boyd & Ker — an English house — were connected with the richest person in France, the Marquis de Laborde, banker to Louis XV; with Henry Hope & Co., the leading banking firm in Amsterdam; and, through that house, with their London correspondents. If such powerful auxiliaries invested in American funds, this would do much to support their credit (Short to Hamilton, 24 Mch. 1791, Syrett, *Hamilton*, XI, 178-85). Hamilton replied that he would be gratified to see the plan to settle the debt through Boyd & Ker carried into execution. Speaking as if for the Secretary of State, he informed Short that, if the assistance of the new minister to France, Gouverneur Morris, would help to carry the plan into effect, he would be "instructed to co-operate" (Hamilton to Short, 14 June 1792, printed in same, XI, 519-20). Hamilton did not need to point out that American funds in the hands of houses so closely connected with England might be expected to strengthen Anglo-American relations.

[1] What Short actually wrote in his letter of 18 Dec. 1790 was: "Had I power I should not have thought myself justified. . . ."

[2] This word interlined in RC by Hamilton.

V. Thomas Jefferson to Louis Guillaume Otto

S<small>IR</small>   Philadelphia May 7. 1791.

I have now the honour to return you the propositions of Messrs. Schweizer, Jeanneret & co. which have been submitted to the Secretary of the Treasury. He does not think they can be acceded to on the part of the United States. The greater premium demanded than what we now pay, the change of the place of payment, the change of the bankers whom we have always employed for others unknown to us, the danger of risking our credit by putting such a mass of our paper into new hands, will I dare say appear to you, Sir, substantial reasons for declining this measure; and the more so as the new instructions given to Mr. Short are to raise money as fast as our credit will admit; and we have no reason to suppose it cannot be as soon done by our antient bankers as by others. Our desire to pay our whole debt, principal and interest, to France is as strong as hers can be to recieve it, and we believe that, by the arrangements already taken, it will be as soon done for her, and more safely and advantageously for us, than by a change of them. We beg you to be assured that no exertions are sparing on our part to accomplish this desireable object, as it will be peculiarly gratifying to us that monies advanced to us in critical times should be reimbursed to France in times equally critical to her. I have the honour to be with sentiments of the most perfect esteem & respect, Sir, your most obedient & most humble servant,   T<small>H</small>: J<small>EFFERSON</small>

PrC (DLC). FC (DNA: RG 59, PCC No. 120). For enclosures see note to Document I preceding.

To William Carmichael

S<small>IR</small>   Philadelphia Apr. 11. 1791

I wrote you on the 12th. of March, and again on the 17th. of the same month, since which I have received your favor of January 24th. wherein you refer to copies of two letters, also to a paper No. 1. supposed to be enclosed in that letter: but there was nothing enclosed. You speak particularly of several other letters formerly forwarded, but not a single one was ever received of later date than May 6th. 1789. and this of January 24th. is all we possess from you since that date. I enclose you a list of letters addressed to you on various subjects and to which answers were, and are, naturally expected; and I send you again copies of the papers in the case of the Dover Cutter which has been the subject of so many of those letters, and is the subject of the constant solicitation of the parties here. A final decision on that application therefore is earnestly desired. When you consider the repeated references of matters to you from hence, and the total suppression of whatever you have written in answer, you will not be surprised if it had excited a great degree of uneasiness. We had enquired whether private conveyances did not occur from time to time from Madrid to Cadiz, where we have vessels almost constantly, and we were assured that such conveyances were frequent. On the whole, Sir, you will be sensible that, under the jealous Government with which you reside, the conveyance of intelligence requires as much management as the obtaining it: and I am in hopes that in future you will be on your guard against those infidelities in that line, under which you and we have so much suffered.

The President is absent on a journey through the Southern States from which he will not return till the end of June, consequently I could not sooner notify him of your desire to return: but even then I will take the liberty of saying nothing to him on the subject till I hear further from you. The suppression of your correspondence has in a considerable degree withdrawn you from the public sight. I sincerely wish that before your return you could do something to attract their attention and favor and render your return pleasing to yourself and profitable to them, by introducing you to new proofs of their confidence. My two last letters to you furnish occasions. *That of a co-operation against the British navigation act, and the arrangement of our affairs on the Missisipi. The former, if it can be effected, will form a remarkable and memorable epoch in the history and freedom of the ocean:*[1] *Mr. Short will press it at Paris and Colo. Humphreys at Lisbon: the latter will shew most at first: and as to the latter be so good as to observe always that the right of navigating the Missisipi is considered as so palpable, that the recovery of it will produce no other sensation than that of a gross injustice removed. The extent and freedom of the port for facilitating the use of it, is what will excite the attention and gratification of the public. Colo. Humphreys writes me that all Mr. Gardoqui's communications while here, tended to impress the court of Madrid with the idea that the navigation of the Missisipi was only demanded on our part to quiet our Western settlers, and that it was not sincerely desired by the Maritime states. This is a most fatal error and must be completely eradicated, and speedily, or Mr. Gardoqui will prove to have been a bad peacemaker. It is true there were² characters, whose stations entitled them to credit, and who, from geographical prejudices, did not themselves wish the navigation of the Missisipi to be restored to us, and who believed perhaps, as is common with mankind, that their opinion was the general opinion. But the sentiments of the great mass of the Union were decidedly otherwise then, and the very persons to whom Mr. Gardoqui alluded, are now come over to the opinion heartily that the navigation of the Missisipi, in full and unrestrained freedom, is indispensibly necessary, and must be obtained by any means it may call for. It will be most unfortunate indeed if we cannot convince Spain that we make this demand in earnest but by acts which will render that conviction too late to prevent evil.³*

Not knowing how better to convey to you the laws and Gazettes than by committing them to the patronage of Colo. Humphreys, I now send through that channel the laws of the 2d. and 3d. sessions of Congress, and the newspapers. – I have the honor to be with great esteem, Sir, Your most obedt. & most humble servt.

PrC (DLC); in a clerk's hand, unsigned; partly in code, accompanied by MS of text *en clair* in another clerk's hand. Dft (Lloyd W. Smith, Madison, N.J., 1946); entirely in TJ's hand; undated, unaddressed, and unsigned; endorsed by Remsen: "To Mr. Carmichael April 11th 1791"; in margin, opposite the bracketed passages to be encoded, TJ wrote on each of the two pages: "to be in cypher." FC (DNA: RG 59, DCI). Enclosures: (1) List of the 14 public letters to Carmichael, with summaries of their subjects, written by Jay as Secretary for Foreign Affairs from 19 Mch. 1785 to 7 Dec. 1789; in a separate column showing Carmichael's answers (three in number between 14 Aug. 1786 and 6 May 1789), there is the following note opposite the entry for Jay's letter of 14 Mch. 1786 "instructing him to terminate business respecting South Carolina Frigate and Dover Cutter and to send a cypher": "Receipt of this Letter acknowledged in one of 14 Aug. 1786"; also, opposite the entry for Jay's letter of 1 Dec. 1786 concerning "business and papers relative to So. Carolina Frigate" there is the following: "Receipt acknowledged 19 Augt. 1787 Conversation with the Minister on the subject 6 May 1789" (i.e., as reported in Carmichael's letter of that date). Following a note indicating the point at which Jay's letters ceased and TJ's began, there is a list of four of TJ's public letters between 11 Apr. and 29 Aug. 1790,

to which no responses had been received (FC in DNA: RG 59, DCI; PrC, in another clerk's hand, in DLC: TJ Papers, 63: 10830-2).

(2) John Mangnall to Congress, Teneriffe, 15 July 1780, referring to his earlier appeal of 27 Apr. 1780 and stating other particulars not mentioned therein: that the cutter *Dover*, chased into the port of Santa Cruz by an English vessel of superior force, had been condemned as a lawful Spanish prize and converted into a cruiser about the islands by decree of the "auditor or judge [Degurra] . . . a very old man, naturally ill-natured and cruel, entirely ignorant of the merits of this cause, and would if it was in his power do us [the officers and men of *Dover* who had been "enticed" on shore by deceit and not even permitted to recover their clothes, books, or papers] every injury"; that *Dover*, manned by Spaniards, had fallen in with an English vessel, *Resolution*, and "fired to bring her too and they not immediately lowering their sails, a few guns were fired at them which immediately sunk her," 21 men being killed and 22 taken prisoner; and that he had that morning petitioned for permission to embark for Virginia on the brig *Jenny* of Edenton and proceed to Philadelphia, but has received no answer.

(3) John Mangnall to Congress, Teneriffe, 16 July 1780, stating that the evening before he had received the General's an-

swer: "he must have time to consider of it"; that he thought none who had acted as officers on *Dover* would be permitted to leave until orders were received from Madrid; and that they therefore hoped Congress would "demand us, and the Cutter, as soon as possible."

(4) John Mangnall's account of *Dover*, Philadelphia, 22 Sep. 1780, stating that she was originally French, built at Le Havre, and, after being taken as an English prize, was bought by some "Gentlemen in London," lengthened 18 feet at Dover, and copper-sheathed at London; that she sailed from Foy, Cornwall, 13 Jan. 1780, and "on the 13th April she was cut out of Madeira Road by part of the people on board, and carried into St. a Cruse Teneriffe on the 17th of the same month, with an Intent to disembark thirty Prisoners, and then to have proceeded" to Philadelphia; that the captain, second lieutenant, surgeon, purser, and about 12 men were on shore when *Dover* was taken (i.e., by those who carried her to Santa Cruz); and that she was a fine cutter, mounting 20 guns, and had "small Arms, Cutlasses, Pole Axes, and boarding Spikes for seventy Men."

(5) Extract of letter from James Lovell to John Jay, Philadelphia, 4 June 1781, enclosing resolution of Congress of 27 Sep. 1780 and a copy of his letter to "a Gentleman in Teneriffe [McCarrick of Santa Cruz] to serve as a Memorandum in Case you have not already procured Justice for Mr. Mangnall and his associates who took the Dover Cutter. . . . Mangnall has been unfortunate from the time he left this Place, last October. He is now here. I do not know whether this is the Matter referred to in the Letter of Mr. Carmichael Decr. 24th: when he says 'The Minister also engaged to do Justice to certain Americans who carried a British Privateer to the Canaries' "; the enclosed letter to McCarrick, Philadelphia, 4 Oct. 1780, acknowledged his of 22 July 1780 to James Smith (a former member of Congress) introducing Mangnall and asked him to forward to John Jay in Madrid a packet on Mangnall's business communicated to him by order of Congress.

(6) Resolution of Congress, 14 Oct. 1777: "Whereas the British nation have received into their Ports, and condemned in their Courts of Admiralty as Lawful Prize several Vessels and their Cargoes belonging to these States which the masters and mariners, in breach of the Trust and Confidence reposed in them, have betrayed and delivered to the Officers of the British Crown, Resolved, therefore, that any vessel or cargo, the Property of any British Subject, not an Inhabitant of Bermuda or any of the Bahama Islands, brought into any of the Ports or Harbors of any of these United States by the master or mariners, shall be adjudged lawful Prize and divided among their Captors, in the same Proportion as if taken by any continental Vessel of War."

(7) Resolution of Congress, 27 Sep. 1780, that Mangnall's letters be referred to John Jay and that he be instructed to try to obtain for the captors of *Dover* the benefits intended by their resolution of 14 Oct. 1777, their intent being that "the whole Profit of the Capture be divided among the Captors."

(8) Extract of letter from Silvester Gray to the Secretary for Foreign Affairs, 13 Dec. 1785, stating that he and Shuker had been induced to capture *Dover* because of their "barbarous usage" while prisoners on board an English man-of-war, for which they "swore to retaliate the first opportunity"; that he and Shuker had been commissioned officers in the service of the United States since the beginning of the war, while he had "sailed out of . . . Philadelphia these 25 years mate and master of a ship"; that "There was an English Privateer laying in the Road of twenty Guns, the same time and thirty of our men and officers on shore . . . and dare not come out after us. There was not one officer on deck till we were out of Gun shot of the Garrison but myself. Mr. Shuker employed securing the Arms and officers and Sailors that might oppose us, to prevent murder"; that he anchored at Santa Cruz on 15 Apr. 1780, and the next day "the General and his attendants came on board, and much admired the vessel and her weight of metal, as she had burned several of their fishing craft a few days before"; that, as Jay had been informed several times while in Madrid, the General of Teneriffe had no right "to take the vessel in the manner he did"; that he has heard nothing about the matter since he and Shuker left Cadiz in 1782; and that

he hopes Jay will use his influence with the Court of Madrid since they had "run such a risk in this attempt" and he would always regard *Dover* as his property until she was paid for, concluding: "The value is £8000 pounds sterling to the owners in London, and I think she has been worth sixteen thousand pounds sterling to the King of Spain since she has been in his service these four years past."

(9) Extract of letter from Jay to Gray, 29 Dec. 1785, acknowledging the foregoing and saying that he had heard nothing about the *Dover* matter since he left Madrid, when it was being considered by the minister, who said that he had ordered the necessary inquiries to be made; and that he would forward a copy of Gray's letter to Carmichael and press him to attend to the business, adding: "His answer will doubtless enable me to give you particular and I hope satisfactory information on the subject."

(10) Extract of a letter from Samuel Cook to the Secretary for Foreign Affairs, 27 Feb. 1786, reading: "I am the mournful aged parent of Rutherford Cook, who after a lingering illness died in the month of October last, who often made mention of your goodness and kindness to him, for which I return you my thankful acknowledgment. – Captain Throop, a kinsman of mine and bearer of this, waits on you to know what information you may give him relative to the prize money in which my son was concerned, due from the Court of Spain on account of the british Cutter by him and others captured."

(11) Extract of a letter from Silvester Gray to the Secretary for Foreign Affairs, "dated 29th. (suppose) September 1786," acknowledging Jay's of 29 Dec. 1785 and desiring to know what response the American minister in Spain had made to his inquiry.

(12) Secretary for Foreign Affairs to Gray, 3 Oct. 1786, saying that he had that moment received the foregoing; that, after receiving no account from the chargé d'affaires in Madrid, he had written him on the *Dover* matter on 14 Mch. 1786 but had "not yet received his answer, nor any further intelligence respecting it." PrC, in clerk's hand, of all of the foregoing enclosures in DLC: TJ Papers, 63: 10883-99; FC in another clerk's hand in DNA: RG 59, DCI, where enclosures numbers 5 through 12 are given by title only because full texts of all were of course available in the files of the Secretary for Foreign Affairs.

The story of the cutter *Dover* is sufficiently outlined in the enclosures to the above letter, but two points require comment. First, the resolution of Congress of 14 Oct. 1777, like the prize decrees of British admiralty courts against which it retaliated, was an overt invitation to masters and mariners on British vessels to "breach . . . the Trust and Confidence reposed in them" – that is, in a word, to commit the serious crime of barratry or worse under promise of both immunity and material gain. American seamen, whose language and habits made it so easy for them to find berths on British vessels, were not slow to take advantage of this war-time measure which in effect legalized acts of piracy. Within a few weeks after adoption of the resolution, the mate and crew of a vessel bound from Grenada to British-occupied New York with a cargo of rum and sugar seized command of her, carried her into Charleston, and had her condemned as their prize. This, wrote the president of Congress, "is the first retort upon that species of British policy calculated for encouraging infidelity and treachery among seamen in the service of these States. I have no doubt but that in a few Months they will experience an hundred fold retaliation of their infamous example, which nothing but dire necessity would have induced virtuous Americans to Copy" (Henry Laurens to James Duane, 24 Dec. 1777, Burnett, *Letters of Members*, II, 597). The results scarcely fulfilled the prophecy and necessity cloaked other motives, but *Dover*, taken over by Silvester Gray, John Mangnall, and other members of her crew while her officers were ashore, was one of a number of vessels lost to their British owners by virtue of Congress' retaliatory measure. In her case, however, as the enclosures indicate, the promised benefits were reaped by the Spanish government rather than by the captors – and under claim of legality even more dubious than that under which they had acted in making the seizure. After more than a decade of fruitless effort on the part of Mangnall and others, he petitioned Congress, and an embarrassed Secretary of State was obliged to report that, though the matter had been pressed in the strongest terms by Jay and himself, no information had been received about what had been or was likely to be done (TJ's report on Mangnall's petition, 14 Nov. 1791; TJ to Carmichael, 6 Nov. 1791).

Second, as prior and subsequent developments proved beyond doubt, a good share of the responsibility for this outcome rested upon the negligent American chargé d'affaires in Madrid, William Carmichael. Five years before the above letter was written, John Jay as Secretary for Foreign Affairs had urged Carmichael to press the matter and had followed this up with subsequent inquiries. After taking office as Secretary of State, TJ had addressed no less than eight communications to Carmichael before sending the above, concerning such important issues as slaves escaping into Florida, navigation of the Mississippi, and TJ's hope for a concert of European powers against Great Britain's navigation act. To these Carmichael had made only one response, which was largely self-pitying, exculpatory, and even boastful about his own performance but which referred TJ to Humphreys for information about Spanish affairs and alarmed him by alleging forgery or misuse of Washington's letter to Gouverneur Morris (Carmichael to TJ, 24 Jan. 1791; TJ to Washington, 2 Apr. 1791). Humphreys' report of conversations with Carmichael, his claim to have seen the "originals" of his many dispatches that had miscarried, and his portrayal of the chargé as desirous of performing some essential service before returning home undoubtedly influenced the tone and substance of the above letter, wherein some of Humphreys' own phrases are used or paraphrased (Humphreys to TJ, 15 Jan. and 6 Feb. 1791).

But, while TJ expressed himself with restraint and gave Carmichael the benefit of the doubt by alluding to the "total suppression" of whatever he might have written, it seems clear that his own opinion as to the real cause had already been formed. Less than a month earlier, he had pointedly indicated to Carmichael that Humphreys' letter from Madrid, written within twenty-four hours after his arrival there, had been received promptly. He had also demanded "a full explanation of this suspension of all information from you" and had warned that final judgment would be suspended only "for . . . a reasonable time" (TJ to Carmichael, 17 Mch. 1791; see also TJ to Short, 24 Jan. 1791). TJ's well-grounded suspicion that the cause of the silence lay more with the chargé than with the Spanish government was soon confirmed. During the remainder of the year he wrote Carmichael five letters, the last two of which pressed him to report on the *Dover* case, but received no answer (TJ to Carmichael, 16 May, 23 June, 24 Aug., and 6 and 29 Nov. 1791). Exactly a year after writing the above TJ informed Carmichael: "I am still without letters from you: only one having been received since I came into office, as has often before been mentioned in my letters to you" (TJ to Carmichael, 9 Apr. 1792). Thus, while the above letter was influenced by Humphreys' mistaken appraisals, its appeal to Carmichael to distinguish himself by some essential service to his country was also evidence of TJ's hope that a concert of European powers against British mercantilist policies might be realized (see Editorial Note to group of documents at 15 Mch. 1791). This was as illusory as the expectation that Carmichael would take advantage of the opportunity to redeem himself. A year later the suspended judgment became final when, on TJ's recommendation, William Short was appointed to negotiate a treaty with Spain on crucial issues so long neglected. The measure of his reliance on Carmichael is shown in the fact that his detailed instructions were sent only to Short, that no duplicate was made, and that he was given explicit directions about gaining diplomatic immunity for the protection of his papers (TJ's Report to Washington; TJ to Short [private]; and TJ to Carmichael and Short, all dated 18 Mch. 1792). Short had no need of the admonition given above that "the conveyance of intelligence requires as much management as the obtaining it": he took the obvious precaution of sending important dispatches to Humphreys by courier under the protection of the Portuguese ambassador to Spain (see, for example, Carmichael and Short to TJ, 18 Apr. and 5 May 1793). Thereafter, the dispatches from the commissioners were frequent, were replete with information and cogent observations, and were models of disciplined diplomatic communication. They were of course written by Short.

¹ In Dft TJ first wrote "in naval history and freedom" and then altered the passage

to read as above.

² In Dft TJ first wrote and then deleted "certain."

³ The passage in italics is in code and is taken from Dft, the text being verified by the Editors employing Code No. 11.

To David Humphreys

DEAR SIR   Philadephia Apr. 11. 1791.

I wrote you Mar. 15. with postscripts of the 18th. and 19th. Since that yours of Jan. 3. No. 10. Jan. 15. No. 11. from Madrid, and Feb. 6. No. 12. and Feb. 12. No. 13. from Lisbon are received. They covered a letter from Mr. Carmichael, the only one we have from him of a later date than May 1789. You know that my letter to him, of which you were the bearer, took notice of the intermission of his correspondence, and the one inclosed to him in my letter to you of Mar. 15. being written when this intermission was felt still stronger, as having continued so much longer, conveyed stronger marks of dissatisfaction. Tho' his letter now received convinces us he has been active in procuring intelligence, yet it does not appear that he has been equally assiduous in procuring means of conveyance, which was the more incumbent on him in proportion as the government was more jealous and watchful. Still however I wish him to receive the letter now inclosed for him herein, as it softens what had been harder said, and shews a disposition rather to look forward than backward. I hope you will recieve it in time to forward with the other. It contains important matter, pressing on him, as I wish to do on you, and have done on Mr. Short, to engage your respective courts in a *co-operation in our navigation act.* – *Procure us all the information possible as to the strength, riches, resources, lights and dispositions, of Brazil. The jealousy of the Court of Lisbon on this subject will of course inspire you with due caution in making and communicating these enquiries.*¹ – The acts of the three sessions of Congress, and Fenno's papers from Apr. 1790. were sent you with my last. You will now receive the continuation of Fenno's paper. I send for Mr. Carmichael also laws and newspapers, in hopes you may find some means of conveying them to him. I must sometimes avail myself of your channel to write to him till we shall have a Consul at Cadiz. – I have the honour to be with great & sincere esteem Dear Sir your most obedt. humble servt.,

TH: JEFFERSON

RC (NjP); partly in code, with interlinear decoding in Humphreys' hand; endorsed. PrC (DLC); accompanied by MS of text *en clair* on a separate leaf. FC (DNA: RG 59, DCI).

[1] The passage in italics is in code, and Humphreys' decoding has been verified by the Editors, employing Code No. 8.

To David Humphreys

DEAR SIR   Philadelphia Apr. 11. 1791.

There has been published at Madrid, by some bishop who had been to Mexico, and found there an original collection of the letters of Cortez, a book containing those letters. I do not know how it happened that I did not ask the favor of you to procure this book for me. I now supply the omission, and add a request to procure also la historia del Amirante D. Christoval Colomb by Fernando Colomb, his son, in Spanish, or Ulloa's translation of it into Italian, or Cotolendi's translation into French, or all three of them. I am in hopes there are such communications between Madrid and Lisbon as to enable you to get them for me. I have received Mr. Bulkeley's letter and samples of wine. The Termo, and Torres are exactly what I had in view. As it will not be time to order wines over till the hot months are past, I shall in July inclose them an order and a bill of exchange for a pipe of the oldest Termo they can procure, this being the most approved of the six qualities they sent me. This will be in time for the wine to be shipped in September. As I shall probably send to them annually, I will add to my bills of exchange for them, any little disbursements for the books or other thing I may trouble you for. I am with great esteem Dear Sir Your friend & servt,

TH: JEFFERSON

RC (NjP); at head of text: "Private." PrC (DLC).

TJ had learned about the publication of Cortez' letters before leaving Paris, when he acquired a copy of J. F. Bourgoing's three-volume *Nouveau voyage en Espagne* (Paris, 1789), in which the collection published by the Archbishop of Mexico was mentioned (Sowerby, No. 3899). It is significant that, in remedying the omission, TJ appealed to Humphreys in Lisbon rather than to Carmichael in Madrid, to whom he had written on the same day in a letter to be forwarded by Humphreys. This was only another indication of TJ's growing conviction that the chargé could not be depended upon (see note, TJ to Carmichael, 11 Apr. 1791). Ironically, TJ's long quest for Lorezana y Butron's *Historia de Nueva-España, escrita por su Esclarecido Conquistador Hernan Cortes, aumentada con otros documentos, notas* (Mexico, 1770) came to a successful conclusion through the efforts of Carmichael, who appealed to Lorezana y Butron himself, then Archbishop of Toledo. The copy that TJ ultimately received was procured by him after "a great deal of trouble." TJ's copy still survives in the Library of Congress (Sowerby, No. 4120; James Blake to TJ, 6 June 1795). It came to TJ only after Carmichael's death.

So, too, did the memorial of the French and Spanish capitalists concerning the possibility of a canal through the Isthmus of Panama. The latter was an item TJ had long urged Carmichael to procure for him as "a vast desideratum for reasons political and philosophical" (TJ to Carmichael, 3 June 1788). In the period when he was alert and unafflicted, Carmichael had labored to meet this request and had reported frequently concerning it (Carmichael to TJ, 14 Apr., 24 July, 9 Sep. 1788, and 26 Jan. 1789). When and how he succeeded is not known. But late in life, when TJ presented the manuscript to the American Philosophical Society, his failing memory led him to give the credit to the Chevalier Bourgoing (TJ to DuPonceau, 6 Dec. 1817, quoted above in note to TJ to Carmichael, 3 June 1788, in which the Editors mistakenly accepted TJ's statement as correct). TJ had forgotten that both the *Historia de Nueva-España* and the manuscript on the proposed canal were gifts from Carmichael, transmitted to him by his widow and acknowledged by him twenty years earlier (TJ to James Blake, 29 Feb. 1796; TJ to Mrs. Carmichael, 8 May 1797).

MR. BULKELEY'S LETTER: An entry in SJL shows that TJ received a letter of 18 Jan. 1791 from John Bulkeley & Son, Lisbon, on 28 Feb. 1791. Another entry records the receipt on 30 Mch. 1791 of a letter from the same merchants, probably a duplicate of the first. Neither has been found, but see TJ to Bulkeley & Son, 13 July 1791. On Humphreys' relation with Bulkeley, see note to Humphreys to TJ, 3 May 1791.

From William Lindsay

Norfolk, *12 Apr. 1791*. Maxwell has informed him of TJ's inquiry about his furniture. Two days after getting TJ's of 10 Jan., he forwarded the goods to James Brown in Richmond, who says they arrived safely, and he had written "your Manager to send Waggons to convey them to your House." – He has been informed lately of a package for TJ addressed to him but sent by mistake to Lindsay's hotel, subsequently forwarded by Lindsay to TJ. He wishes to eradicate any impression TJ may have gained from these incidents that he was wanting in attention.

RC (MHi); endorsed by TJ as received 20 Apr. 1791 and so recorded in SJL.

From James Currie

Richmond, *13 Apr. 1791*. This will be delivered to TJ by Dr. John Griffin, whose letter to TJ about his bills on Potter was enclosed in one from Currie and has no doubt been received. Currie will be under greater obligation to TJ when the bills are paid; he hopes Potter will not have to make sacrifices, but if so he thinks himself entitled to that advantage more than any other creditor. Once the debt is secured, he does not wish to take "any ungenerous advantage of his situation." Griffin has promised to explain to TJ the cause of Potter's failure to confess assets because of fear of attachment in Griffin's hand to secure some other debt. He will inform TJ of this on settling his business with [Robert] Morris and he will be much satisfied if TJ will give him his friendly advice in the matter. "All your friends at Monticello were well some days ago. The President . . . arrived here on Monday afternoon, on which Evening he viewd the Capitol (now entirely coverd with Lead) and yesterday visited the Canal and went quite up from Harris the manager's house thro the Locks accompanied by the Directors of the Canal and several other Gentlemen here in 2 fine new Batteau's of David Ross's who had his Watermen, dressd in red Coaties on the Occasion, and lookd well. He dined yesterday with the Governor, and this Day dines at the Eagle by invitation of the Citizens and leaves this to Morrow on his way South Ward." He will be happy to hear from TJ about the bills as soon as he has seen Griffin, who promises to wait on him as soon as he gets to Philadelphia. "P.S. The . . . time the Batteaux took in passing the 2 locks was 7 Minutes and 4 seconds by a stop watch."

RC (DLC); addressed: "The Honble. Thomas Jefferson Esqr. Secretary of State Favord. by Jno. T. Griffin Esqr."; endorsed by TJ as received 7 May 1791 and so recorded in SJL.

From George Washington

Dear Sir   Richmond April 13th. 1791

Your letter of the 2d. came to my hands at this place. – Part of it did as you supposed, and might well suppose, astonished me exceedingly.

I think it not only right that Mr. Carmichael should be furnished with a copy of the genuine letters to Mr. G. Morris, but that Mr. Morris[1] should also know the result of his conferences with the Duke of Leeds at the Court of Madrid. – The contents of my official letters to him you are acquainted with. My private ones were few, and nothing in either of them relative to England or Spain; how it comes to pass therefore that such interpretations as the extracts recite, should be given, he best can account for.

Being hurried, I shall only add that I shall proceed on my Journey to morrow, and from good information have a dreary one before me in some parts thereof. – Yrs. sincerely,   Go: Washington

P.S. The footing upon which you have placed Mr. Carmichael[2] is good.   GW.

RC (DLC); endorsed by TJ as received 19 Apr. 1791 and so recorded in SJL. Tr (DNA: RG 59, SDC); with two variations, as noted below.

Although TJ had suggested that it might be well to send to Carmichael the full text of Washington's letter to Gouverneur Morris of 13 Oct. 1789, he apparently thought better of it and did not do so. Nor did he adopt Washington's suggestion that Morris be acquainted with the result of his conference with Leeds (TJ to Morris, 26 July 1791, the text of which TJ submitted to Washington for approval). Perhaps this was due to TJ's natural "disposition rather to look forward than backward" (TJ to Humphreys, 11 April 1791), but more likely Carmichael's silence led him to question the reliability of the allegation.

[212]

[1] Washington inadvertently omitted Morris' name in RC; it has been supplied from Tr.

[2] Tr reads: "Mr. Carmichael's application" — that is, his requesting leave to return to America.

From Alexander Hamilton

SIR   Treasury Department 14th April 1791.

It was the intention of the President that you and myself should take such measures as appeared to us eligible towards carrying into execution the Resolution empowering him to procure artists from Europe towards the establishment of a mint.

It appears to me of great importance, if still practicable, to acquire Mr. Droz and the terms mentioned in the enclosed note when applied to so pre-eminent an Artist do not seem extravagant. Mr. Droz however ought to be bound to give his service for not less than a year after his arrival in the United States. I should think it advisable too that some *determinate* allowance should be concerted with him as an equivalent for the expenses of himself and servant. It may be per day.

With regard to *instruments*, such as are indispensable and *difficult* of execution ought to be procured in Paris.

The having a person who is *practically* and accurately skilled in the assaying of Metals is of course an essential part of the establishment meditated. None such has hitherto been found in the United States. If one can be procured from France on terms not immoderate, I am of opinion that it will be expedient to procure him; unless it should appear upon enquiry that Mr. Droz is himself perfectly equal to this part of the business also. The requisite apparatus for making the assays ought in the first instance to be brought from Europe.

In the engagement of such a person it is highly important that no mistake should be made. He ought to be a man not only well skilled in the business, but altogether *trust worthy*.

If the payment of compensations could be deferred 'till after the services have been performed it would give security to the United States.

The requisite dispositions will be made to enable Mr. Short to possess himself of the funds which the execution of this trust may require. I have the honor to be, with great respect and esteem, Sir Your Obedient humble Servant,   ALEXANDER HAMILTON

Tr (DLC: Short Papers); at foot of text: "The Honble. Thomas Jefferson"; in the hand of George Taylor; on verso in an unidentified hand is the following: "Droz gra-

veur, rue des maçons Maison du Me-
nuisier derriere St. André des arts. Mr. De
La Corbure á Laffinage rue Guenegaud"
(enclosed in TJ to Short, 25 Apr. 1791).
PrC of another Tr (DLC); also in Taylor's
hand, as is another Tr in DNA: RG 59,
PCC No. 120. Recorded in SJL as received 15 Apr. 1791. Enclosure: Extract
from Grand to TJ, undated (printed below
as enclosure TJ to Short, 25 Apr. 1791).

From Daniel L. Hylton

Richmond, 14 Apr. 1791. TJ's of 5th received on 12th, enclosing bank note
for $22.75 and letter for Colo. Lewis which was sent by private hand the same
day, there being no post established from Richmond to Charlottesville. Encloses
bill of lading for the vis-à-vis. He was mistaken in name of vessel: that on
which it was shipped was lost at sea between New York and Philadelphia and
all the crew except one perished. The bill of lading also shows a small box
shipped at the same time: it contained lamps for the vis-à-vis. – He will ship
TJ's tobacco as directed and advise him as it comes in. He encloses bill of
lading for the 4 hhds. now at the warehouse being shipped by [the *Thomas*],
Capt. Stratton, at the customary freight. The 13 hhds. last shipped when at
higher freight because vessels previously engaged to carry wheat before getting
to Richmond. Tobacco remains very low there, frequently selling from 17 to
20/ per cwt., "a price by no means adequate for the labour of the planter." Any
further orders will be attended to: it will "ever give me pleasure to have it in
my power to render you every service of a freind. Mrs. H. joins with me in
every wish for your happiness." [P.S.] Capt Stratton will leave on Monday
next. He "also takes charge of Mr. Eppes trunk directed to your care and to
whom remember me affectionately."

RC (MHi); at foot of text Hylton listed "Invoice of 4 Hhds. tobacco shipt on board
the Ths. Henry Stratton Master," averaging 1,216 pounds; endorsed by TJ as received
21 Apr. 1791 and so recorded in SJL.

To Charles Carroll

DEAR SIR   Philadelphia Apr. 15. 1791.

I recieved last night your favor of the 10th. with Mr. Brown's
reciept, and thank you for the trouble you have been so kind as to
take in this business.

Our news from the Westward is disagreeable. Constant murders
committing by the Indians, and their combination threatens to be
more and more extensive. I hope we shall give them a thorough
drubbing this summer, and then change our tomahawk into a golden
chain of friendship. The most economical as well as most humane
conduct towards them is to bribe them into peace, and to retain
them in peace by eternal bribes. The expedition of this year would
have served for presents on the most liberal scale for 100. years.

Nor shall we otherwise ever get rid of an army, or of our debt. The least rag of Indian depredation will be an excuse to raise troops, for those who love to have troops, and for those who think that a public debt is a good thing. Adieu my dear Sir. Yours affectionately,

TH: JEFFERSON

PrC (DLC); at foot of text: "Charles Carrol esq. of Carrolton."

TJ's brief exchange with Carroll, in which the Senator from Maryland acted as intermediary in the matter of a doubtful debt, brought on polite but sharp expressions of political differences. TJ hinted at retaliatory measures against Great Britain. Carroll responded with a warning about pursuing policies that the nation might not carry out. In the above, TJ's final sentence on Indian affairs and the national debt could not have concealed his hostility to modes of frontier warfare involving large expenditures for army contracts and his aversion to Hamilton's fiscal policies (TJ to Carroll, 4 Apr. 1791; Carroll to TJ, 10 Apr. 1791; see Editorial Note to group of documents on the Mississippi Question, at 10 Mch. 1791). On these and other matters the two men held irreconcilable views. The above letter ended their correspondence.

From John Chester

Wethersfield, 15 Apr. 1791. He would have acknowledged TJ's letter of 4 Mch. 1791 earlier, but he "wished a time to consider of the subject, and advise" with his friends. He has decided to accept appointment and will discharge duties of the office to the best of his ability. He requests TJ to inform President and "to assure him of my attachment to his person, and affection to the government over which he presides."

RC (DNA: RG 59, MLR). Not recorded in SJL. TJ's letter transmitted Chester's commission as supervisor of the excise for Connecticut. Such letters of acceptance have not been included except in this and other instances which reflect some hesitancy about taking on the duty of enforcing an unpopular act.

From Tench Coxe

[Philadelphia], 15 Apr. 1791. Encloses return of tonnage for one year, including several customhouse returns not received when Register made up former statement. It is in the form shown TJ in Feb., "except the interesting additions . . . exhibiting the European – African – Asiatic – West Indian and other Subdivisions of the American commerce, which have been since added. As far as my mind has been able to bring it up to view, the inward trade of the United States is exhibited in this paper." Collectors have been directed to add a column to their returns which, after June, will give similar data for the export trade. The Controller, who is responsible for forms, has given Coxe leave to make any alterations to procure needed information. He has Register's clerks making up current imports in same form and he proposes to do this for prior years to show quantities and kinds of imports from several foreign na-

tions. – "Should you desire to reserve a copy of the document now sent, I beg leave to remark that it may be expedient to confine it afterwards to your private office as you will perceive there are several delicate points . . . too visible to admit of an exposure to any, but very confidential members of the government."

He encloses plan of a manufacturing establishment which "may apply happily in the federal district." He is not certain any but fine arts desirable in actual seat, but in a tract of 64,000 acres there may be a location with great water power in which this plan might be put in execution. "It is a favorite idea of mine . . . that this country should endeavour to employ in [manufactures], as much as possible, the great labor saving machines. Agriculture being the most natural employment, and manufacturers being often an intemperate and disorderly class of people, modes of manufacture which do not require them, and which indeed in a certain degree supercede the occasion for them, appear to be very desirable. This sketch is meant to be disposed of as you may think proper," Coxe having retained a copy. He will only observe that "the mode of raising *the fund* was obtained from the Secretary of the Treasury, who has every reason to believe that an establishment embracing the principal ideas in the plan will be very soon attempted in New Jersey upon subscriptions from New York, New Jersey and Pennsylvania. It may be worth considering whether the Potomack Navigation company might not find it their interest to admit of sales of Shares for 6 ₱ Cent stock estimated at par, and when they shall have sold the whole a loan at 5¼ ₱ Cent might be effected. The public paper would yield an interest more than equal to what they would have to pay and when our funds rise to par the paper might be sold, and the debt in Specie discharged." [P.S.] "It appears that our fishing vessels exceed the number in the Registers return about 20 ₱ Cent. The discovery of this error is very Material, and pleasing."

RC (DLC); endorsed by TJ as received 15 Apr. 1791 and so recorded in SJL. Enclosures: (1) Tabulation of tonnage of vessels entering the United States from foreign ports between 1 Oct. 1789 and 30 Sep. 1790, together with coasting and fishing vessels, showing that vessels of American registry amounted to 492,100.1 tons; those of Great Britain 226,953.1; and those of France 13,801.4, with lesser amounts from Spain, Holland, Ireland, Portugal, and Denmark (dated 15 Apr. 1791, signed by Coxe and submitted in final form by Hamilton to the Senate on 25 Nov. 1791, ASP, *Commerce and Navigation*, I, 44-7). (2) "A Plan for a manufacturing establishment in the United States," which proposed that a corporation be chartered in one or more states capitalized at $500,000 payable by subscribers in stock of the Bank of the United States and in public securities; that these securities be used to borrow an additional half million in specie in Holland or elsewhere; that, after the total capital was subscribed, the stockholders should elect a board of directors to conduct the affairs of the corporation; that one person, residing at the site of the factories, be chosen to superintend the operations of the business at an annual compensation suitable to his character and qualifications, though not to engage otherwise in its affairs or be employed in any other trade or business; that the directors be authorized to purchase land on some navigable river with streams and water power sufficient to operate "water machinery and works, bleaching and tan yards, breweries, distilleries, or such other factories" as might be undertaken; that this tract of land be laid out as a town or in lots with convenient streets, these lots to be sold or leased to manufacturers and tradesmen; that the legislature be petitioned for the purpose of opening roads, turnpikes, canals, and improvements of inland navigation to the interior and also for authorization to hold lotteries to pay initial expenses and to dispose of lots "in order to interest a large number as well of the citizens of the United

States as of foreign countries in the proposed city"; and that application be made to Congress to have the post road go through the city and "to increase the duties upon such articles as shall be seriously and systematically undertaken, and otherwise to foster and encourage the institution."

Coxe added: "The objects to which the stock can be applied with the greatest advantage appear to be such articles as are of considerable bulk, of general consumption, consequently almost or absolutely of necessity, and which are either made by such labour saving machines, as the cotton mills, flax mills, rolling and slitting mills, the tilt hammer, forges, powder mills, paper mills &c. or by labour saving processes, such as glass works, tanning, steel making, brewing, distilling, glue making, starchmaking &c. or by labour-saving slight, as in the manufactory of wire; wool and cotton cards; printed cottons, linens and paper; shovels; hinges, nails &c. The two first classes promise the greatest profit, though the latter well deserves consideration. Glass works are of great importance to this country, and with an adequate capital would probably yield good returns, but they might not at present be conducted with the greatest advantage in the proposed city. But in those instances wherein there is coal at hand, they may be introduced there at once. The city of Bristol in Britain has fifteen capital Glasshouses in which coal alone is used, as it is supposed."

In conclusion, Coxe argued that the benefits of the plan would be (1) "That a capital in specie applied to labour saving machines &c. working in raw materials as cheap or cheaper than in Europe must yield a very handsome advance upon the six, seven, or eight percent produce of public funds or Bank Stock"; (2) "That the operation must favour the holders of the public debt and Bank Stock by creating a new object for them, and taking large sums out of the market"; (3) "That the purchase of lands at or near their value as farms which is a perfectly safe operation, promises, by the addition of[1] an extensive, well placed, healthy manufacturing establishment, to yield a very handsome profit to the concerned, by the mere advance upon the lots"; and (4) "That the freight, insurance, commissions in Europe or the United States, damage, costs of packages, customhouse charges, compensation for credit, storeage, carting, and importer's profit being 15 per cent upon every importation of the finest kinds of the goods we should manufacture in the first seven years, afford an advantage, more than double the medium dividends on Bank or public Stock: and that profits such as the European Manufacturers enjoy are moreover to be expected in all cases wherein labour-saving machines and processes are employed. These will enable the Society to avoid the means of manual labour, which, from the high rate of wages, is urged against such factories as are conducted, in that way, in the United States" (Tr in clerk's hand, undated, in DLC: TJ Papers, 80:13913-16; with one alteration in text noted below).

The plan for a manufacturing establishment enclosed in the above letter embodies in specific form the "favorite idea" of which Coxe had long been the foremost and best-informed advocate. It has been assumed that this plan was an elaboration of that outlined in the third number of Coxe's *Brief examination of Lord Sheffield's observations on the commerce of the United States*. Actually, what Coxe had written in that publication was only three or four sentences giving the essence of his scheme. This general description followed rather than preceded the plan outlined above (the third number appeared in Brown's *Federal Gazette* only on 13 May 1791 and in Carey's *American Museum* for April). Whether the particularized plan or the brief comment preceded the other is unimportant. The essential fact is that Coxe's proposal anticipated in precise terms the manufacturing complex which Hamilton, Duer, and others brought into existence with the Society for Establishing Useful Manufactures (J. S. Davis, *Essays in the Earlier History of American Corporations*, I, 349-53; Jacob E. Cooke, "Tench Coxe, Alexander Hamilton, and the Encouragement of American Manufactures," WMQ, XXXII [July 1975], 382-3). Coxe had been assisting the Secretary of the Treasury for some weeks in the preparation of his Report on Manufactures and it is certain that Hamilton, who lent his powerful influence to bring SUM into existence, discussed the nature of the plan with Coxe before it was drafted and sent to TJ. He may very well have prompted

Coxe to give concrete expression to this favorite idea of the Assistant Secretary, for late in March he informed Théophile Cazenove of his project and promised to give him a copy of the plan within eight or ten days (Cazenove to the Amsterdam houses he represented, 29 Mch. 1791, Cazenove Letter Book, Holland Land Company, Archives of the City of Amsterdam).

Coxe's explanation that he sent the plan to TJ because it might "apply happily in the federal district" has been construed to be disingenuous, if not a ruse, in an effort to please and disarm the Secretary of State (Cooke, WMQ, XXXII [July 1975], 384). The more plausible reason would seem to lie elsewhere. Coxe knew, as did everyone, how deeply Washington was interested in the Federal District and the Potomac Company as well. He could scarcely have expected TJ to embrace the plan for a manufacturing city with the enthusiasm that Hamilton displayed. In urging TJ to make such disposition of the plan as he thought proper, he may only have hoped that it would be brought to Washington's attention. This supposition is supported by one alteration that Coxe made in his draft of the plan. As copied by his clerk, it first called for locating the establishment at the seat of some state government – this obviously because most state capitals were located at the head of tidewater with water power usually accessible. This provision Coxe struck out, as if to emphasize his interest in an operation in the Federal District distinct from the one he said Hamilton expected would be established in New Jersey (see note 1 below). In his own thinking Coxe envisioned manufacturing establishments located throughout the states, but this plan obviously called for a grand national enterprise such as Hamilton had in view.

The question immediately arises, then, as to whether the hand of the Secretary of the Treasury may have influenced Coxe to transmit such a plan to the Secretary of State. Within the space of a single week Hamilton, taking advantage of the President's absence, had manipulated a meeting of the Cabinet in the hope of enabling Robert Morris to make another purchase of a vast tract of land from the Indians and, for perhaps ulterior motives, had had a hand in Tench Coxe's vain application for the Comptrollership of the Treasury. He had also disclosed to Théophile Cazenove, but not to Washington, his hope to create a great manufacturing enterprise under the aegis of the government. Under these circumstances, fearing as he and his supporters did that TJ's influence with the President was rising and that his proposed navigation bill might be adopted at the next session, Hamilton may well have influenced Coxe to send the plan to TJ in the hope that it would be forwarded to the President.

When Washington supported the efforts of Henry Lee and James Madison to establish a manufacturing metropolis at the Falls of the Potomac, TJ gave no encouragement to their hope of obtaining funds for the venture in Europe (see Editorial Note to group of documents on the location of the Federal District, at 24 Jan. 1791). If Coxe, or Hamilton, hoped to gain his influence with the President for a similar enterprise near the Federal District, or in New Jersey, he was doomed to disappointment. TJ treated Coxe's proposal with silence. His real opinion of it was expressed two days later in a letter to James Monroe (TJ to Monroe, 17 Apr. 1791).

[1] These two words interlined in Coxe's hand in substitution for "combination of the Seat of a State Government with," deleted.

To Adam Lindsay

SIR   Philadelphia Apr. 15. 1791.

I recieved last night your favour of the 7th. instant inclosing the note for 54. ℔. myrtle wax candles. I thank you for your kind attention to this little commission, and now inclose you a bank post note for eleven dollars sixty cents the amount of the candles and box. This post note will be paid by any collector of the customs. The parcel you now send me will serve as a trial, as I never used this kind of candle. If it answers I will avail myself of your friendly offer by writing to you in the fall for more. The vessel is not yet arrived here. I am with great esteem Sir Your most obedt. humble servt,   TH: JEFFERSON

PrC (DLC).

Tench Coxe

Seeks Office as Comptroller of the Treasury

I. TENCH COXE TO THOMAS JEFFERSON, 16 APRIL 1791

II. TENCH COXE TO THE PRESIDENT, 16 APRIL 1791

III. THOMAS JEFFERSON TO TENCH COXE, 17 APRIL 1791

EDITORIAL NOTE

Mr. Jefferson . . . came here probably with a too partial idea of his own powers, and with the expectation of a greater share in the direction of our councils than he has in reality enjoyed. I am not sure that he had not peculiarly marked out for himself the department of the Finances.
 — *Alexander Hamilton to Edward Carrington,*
26 May 1792

So that if the question be By whose fault is it that Colo. Hamilton and myself have not drawn together? the answer will depend on that to two other questions; Whose principles of administration best justify, by their purity, conscientious adherence? and Which of us has, notwithstanding, stepped farthest into the controul of the department of the other?
 — *Thomas Jefferson to George Washington,*
9 September 1792

In his pioneering work *The Federalists*, Leonard D. White, an able scholar in the field of administrative history, agreed with both friendly and hostile critics of Hamilton that the Secretary of the Treasury went far beyond the limits of his own department in seeking to give effect to his policies. "Hamilton's active intervention in the field of foreign affairs," he wrote, "set off an administrative feud that was to dominate the scene from 1791 to 1793." The breach between the two Cabinet officers arose from profound differences over principles of administration, but White saw its origins in a mutual disregard of lines of departmental jurisdiction. He charged the Secretary of State with taking the initiative in the spring of 1791 and continuing in a series of assaults by which Jefferson sought to place Tench Coxe in the Treasury or even to break up the Department itself. "So far as has been ascertained," White wrote, "Jefferson's first move against Hamilton occurred on April 17, 1791. . . . [He] took a bold step in undertaking, without consultation with Hamilton, to forward the appointment of Coxe to the second position of the Treasury Department. He apparently was assured of Coxe's personal loyalty at this early date, although the tie was not generally known until later. Jefferson, however, exposed himself to an almost certain rebuff from the President, whose decision would naturally be governed primarily by the advice of the head of the department concerned. Jefferson also laid bare to Hamilton his intrigue to place his own man in the center of Hamilton's department – a challenge which the Secretary of the Treasury was not likely to overlook."[1]

This interpretation of Coxe's desire to be appointed Comptroller of the Treasury has been advanced in one form or another from 1791 to the present. Since White gave the legend his formidable sanction in 1948, it has not been challenged and the facts concerning the episode have not been sufficiently ascertained. Not surprisingly, it was the Secretary of the Treasury himself who first pointed the finger of suspicion at Jefferson as seeking to infiltrate his department. All of the evidence indicates that the traditional view is unwarranted and that the role played by Hamilton calls for further scrutiny.

I

On Saturday, the 16th day of April 1791, Andrew Brown's *Federal Gazette* carried the following brief announcement: "Died, this morning, Nicholas Eveleigh, Esq. Comptroller of the Treasury of the United States." Eveleigh, born in Charleston about 1748, spent almost half of his life in England, where he was educated. Returning to America in 1774, he became an officer of the 2d South Carolina regiment and in 1781 and 1782 served as a delegate to Congress. In 1789 he was appointed Comptroller of the Treasury, but when he arrived in New York in November to take office, he was so indisposed as to be of no assistance to the Secretary of the Treasury.[2] For some months before his death he had been unable to perform the duties of his office, and in the last few weeks "every prospect of his recovery . . . vanished."[3]

This not unexpected event created the first vacancy in a key office in the executive branch since the inception of the new government. The Comptroller, as watchdog of the Treasury, had responsibility for reviewing the Auditor's settlement of accounts and claims, for supervising loan officers and collectors of customs, for prosecuting delinquent collectors and debtors, for making certain that funds were expended in accordance with law, and, as Tench Coxe expressed it, for undertaking "preparatory political investigations."[4] Important as the office was, Eveleigh's death produced only a vacancy, not a crisis. More than a month earlier the Secretary of the Treasury had given notice that some of the functions of the office were being performed by Eveleigh's chief clerk

[1] Leonard D. White, *The Federalists* (New York, 1948), p. 224-5.
[2] Eveleigh was nominated and confirmed on 11 Sep. 1789 (JEP, I, 25); Alexander Hamilton to Elizabeth Hamilton, [Nov. 1789] (Syrett, *Hamilton*, V, 579).
[3] Tobias Lear to Washington, 17 Apr. 1791 (DLC: Washington Papers).
[4] Coxe to TJ, 16 Apr. 1791 (Document I).

under his own supervision.[5] As in Eveleigh's previous illness, Hamilton himself no doubt took on other duties of the Comptroller's office, probably with the aid of the Assistant Secretary and the Auditor. With the President absent on his southern tour, there could have been no discussions with him about potential candidates for the vacancy. In fact, no appointment was made until Congress met more than six months later.[6] Yet the scramble over the appointment of a successor began even before the death of the incumbent.

Hamilton was the first to act. This is understandable, since as Secretary of the Treasury he was naturally concerned to see the second office in his department occupied by a competent, trustworthy, and compatible colleague. But beyond this there were practical political considerations of long standing which limited his choice. When the Treasury was being organized in 1789, Jeremiah Wadsworth, representative from Connecticut and a loyal supporter of Hamilton's policies, urged Oliver Wolcott, Jr. to offer himself as a candidate for some office in that department, assuring him of the unanimous support of himself and others of the Connecticut delegation in Congress. With such impressive sponsorship, Wolcott drafted a formal application to the President and transmitted it to Wadsworth. In so doing, he made it clear that he did not wish an office of a routine and burdensome nature which could only win him "the reputation of an honest, plodding fellow of little genius or ability." Since he had applied to the President, he recognized the impropriety of refusing any appointment, but he hoped Wadsworth would arrange matters so that no offer would be tendered unless it could be accepted "with some prospect of reputation."[7] Though he was only twenty-nine, Wolcott already had a reputation to sustain. He had served with Oliver Ellsworth as a commissioner to settle Connecticut's accounts with the United States, had been appointed Comptroller of state accounts, and had reorganized the finances of Connecticut so effectively

[5] Hamilton's circular to Commissioners of Loans, 9 Mch. 1791 (Syrett, *Hamilton*, VIII, 169).

[6] On his return from the South to Mount Vernon, Washington wrote Hamilton a private letter authorizing him to tell Wolcott that it was his intention to appoint him to the vacancy (Washington to Hamilton, 13 June 1791, same, VIII, 470). He also informed Lear at the same time (Washington to Lear, 15 June 1791, *Writings*, ed. Fitzpatrick, XXXI, 296). Earlier TJ had sent a blank commission to Washington to be filled with the name of his appointee and to be returned for countersignature, seal, and delivery (TJ to Washington, 17 Apr. 1791, with group of documents at 4 Apr. 1791). Instead, Washington returned the commission to Lear with directions to have it filled out and, when countersigned and sealed, delivered to Wolcott (William Jackson to Lear, 17 June 1791, FC in DLC: Washington Papers). TJ himself expected that the commission might be returned to him during his absence on the northern tour (see TJ's instructions to Remsen, 16 May 1791). This unusual procedure was not followed. Wolcott was nominated on 31 Oct. and confirmed 7 Nov. 1791, the date when the commission was issued (JEP, I, 86, 88; FC of Commission in DNA: RG 59, Permanent Commissions). TJ forwarded it to Wolcott three days later (TJ to Wolcott, 10 Nov. 1791, DNA: RG 59, PCC No. 120).

[7] Wadsworth to Wolcott, 12 Aug. 1789; Wolcott to Wadsworth, 15 Aug. 1789, enclosing Wolcott to the President of the same date (George Gibbs, *Memoirs of the Administrations of Washington and John Adams*, I [New York, 1846], 19-20). Because he doubted that Wolcott would accept appointment as Auditor, Wadsworth probably never transmitted the application to Washington and instead relied on his and Ellsworth's consultations with Hamilton. Wolcott's letter is not found among other letters of application in Washington's papers.

as to win the approval of the legislature. His financial experience and other qualifications gave him undeniably stronger claims than those of Eveleigh. Wadsworth, Ellsworth, and others in the Connecticut delegation strongly supported his desire to be Comptroller. But, despite their considerable influence with the administration, Eveleigh was nominated as Comptroller and Wolcott as Auditor.

When Senator Ellsworth informed Wolcott of this, he expressed an opinion that others of the Connecticut delegation shared: "your merit would have justified your standing higher in the list, but you are young enough to rise, and I believe you ought to accept the appointment."[8] Wadsworth, equally disappointed, also urged acceptance. "I did not like this," he informed Wolcott, "as it was my wish and hope you would have been comptroller."[9] Wolcott's response was polite but firm: "The office of Auditor will not answer the appointment which I had contemplated as proper for me. I must therefore decline it, though my objections do not arise from the salary, but from its dependence on another office, and from the nature of the service to be performed."[10] In responding to Wolcott, Wadsworth said that he would keep the refusal to himself and let the appointment go forward. "Mr. Trumbull and myself both gave our opinions before, that you would not accept," he added, "wishing you, as Col. Hamilton wished, to be comptroller."[11]

Whether he learned of Wolcott's refusal from Wadsworth or some other, Alexander Hamilton himself urged Wolcott's acceptance. "Your friends having expressed a doubt of your acceptance," Hamilton wrote Wolcott on the day after his appointment was confirmed, "I cannot forbear saying, that I shall be happy to find the doubt has been ill founded; as from the character I have received of you, I am persuaded you will be an acquisition to the department."[12] Even this powerful appeal did not bring forth an immediate acceptance. Wolcott replied that he was on his way to New York and would immediately wait on Hamilton "for the purpose of acquiring such information relative to the duties of the office as will enable me to come to a decision whether I shall accept or decline the appointment."[13] What took place at their interview is unknown. But Wolcott found Hamilton "a very amiable, plain man" whose character indicated that his fiscal measures would be prudent, sensible, and firm. He supposed the prospect of promotion might be remote, but on the advice of his friends in Congress he decided to accept the post he had first refused.[14] From that time forward he became a close friend, loyal supporter, and able subordinate of the Secretary of the Treasury. Having Eveleigh as his superior did not make more bearable the office that he had never wanted. But by accepting it and by

[8] Ellsworth to Wolcott, 12 Sep. 1789 (Gibbs, *Washington and Adams*, I, 21).

[9] Wadsworth to Wolcott, 13 Sep. 1789 (same, I, 21). Wadsworth added that Hamilton was "very anxious you should accept." Earlier, he had written Wolcott to ask if he would accept the lesser office. "You must move with the national government," he advised. "It will not be what I wish, but it will be in the way of something" (same, I, 21).

[10] Wolcott to Wadsworth, 10 Sep. 1789 (same, I, 21). This was written on the day before Washington nominated Wolcott as Auditor and two days before his appointment was confirmed (JEP, I, 25, 26).

[11] Wadsworth to Wolcott, 13 Sep. 1789 (Gibbs, *Washington and Adams*, I, 21).

[12] Hamilton to Wolcott, 13 Sep. 1789 (Syrett, *Hamilton*, V, 372).

[13] Wolcott to Hamilton, 17 Sep. 1789 (same, V, 377).

[14] Wolcott to his wife, 24 Sep. 1789; Wolcott to his father, 3 Nov. 1789 (Gibbs, *Washington and Adams*, I, 22, 23).

performing its arduous duties with distinction, Wolcott had no need in 1791 to apply for the post he had coveted since 1789. Nor, when it became vacant, could Wadsworth, Ellsworth, and Hamilton forget the arguments they had used to persuade him to accept the lesser office. The most persuasive of these was undoubtedly the promise of future advancement when the opportunity presented itself. The opportunity came with Eveleigh's death, and both Hamilton and Wadsworth recognized their commitment to Wolcott.[15]

II

Four days before Eveleigh's death, when everyone knew the office of Comptroller would soon be vacant, Hamilton wrote the following cryptic note to Wadsworth: "I am sorry to learn that a certain heresy makes a progress. But there must be a portion of nonsense in human affairs – I bear in mind my promise to you."[16] The allusion to heresy may or may not refer to Tench Coxe's ambition to be Comptroller and Hamilton's promise may or may not have referred to his commitment to Wolcott. Under the circumstances, the supposition has plausibility. But the fact is that in a conversation with Washington about a month before Eveleigh died, Hamilton urged that Wolcott be appointed to the anticipated vacancy. What Washington said in response is not known, but Wolcott's performance in office had confirmed his opinion of the man as an able official, respected alike for his ability, industry, and integrity.[17] Given Hamilton's recommendation and Wolcott's record, the choice appeared both logical and certain. James McHenry, a friend of Hamilton who concerned himself with matters of patronage, was not the only one who assumed that Wolcott would be made Comptroller.[18] Yet for some reason the Secretary of the Treasury, not content to let the matter rest on his original recommendation, immediately took steps to reinforce it. He did this in a manner so unusual as to indicate a feeling of genuine anxiety lest the office be given to someone else.

On the day following Eveleigh's death, Hamilton dispatched two letters to the President, the first being only a brief official communication announcing the "loss . . . of a good officer and an honorable and able man."[19] The second was a long private letter reminding Washington of their prior conversation on the subject, extolling Wolcott as an official whose distinguished record as Auditor proved that he had "all the requisites which could be desired; moderation

---

[15] In an undated letter to his father soon after Eveleigh's death, Wolcott wrote: "No appointment has, or can be made until intelligence is received from the President, who is now in the southern States. There will be much competition for the office; who will be successful I cannot say. I have full reason to believe, that the Secretary of the Treasury wishes that it may fall to me; which is some satisfaction, as he is a man of distinguished talents, and has had the best opportunity to judge of my qualifications" (Wolcott to his father, undated, Gibbs, *Washington and Adams*, I, 64). Hamilton's recognition of his prior commitment to Wolcott was explicitly revealed when he informed Coxe that circumstances "which originated at the time of Mr. Wolcotts appointment" as Auditor restrained him from supporting any other candidate (Coxe to TJ, 16 Apr. 1791; Document I).

[16] Hamilton to Wadsworth, 12 Apr. 1791 (Syrett, *Hamilton*, VIII, 279).

[17] Washington to Robert Morris, 16 June 1791 (*Writings*, ed. Fitzpatrick, XXXI, 298).

[18] McHenry to Hamilton, 3 May 1791 (Syrett, *Hamilton*, VIII, 321); Jonathan Williams to Henry Knox, 27 May 1791 (MHi: Knox Papers).

[19] Hamilton to Washington, 17 Apr. 1791 (Syrett, *Hamilton*, VIII, 290).

with firmness, liberality with exactness, indefatigable industry with an accurate and sound discernment a thorough knowlege of business and a remarkable spirit of order and arrangement." Indeed, Hamilton declared, the Auditor possessed to such an eminent degree "all the qualifications desireable in a Comptroller of the Treasury that it is scarcely possible to find a man in the United States more competent to the duties of that station than himself, *few* who would be equally so. It may be truly said of him that he is a man of *rare* merit." To one who respected the judgment of the Secretary of the Treasury as much as Washington did and who shared these views of Wolcott's qualifications, this might have seemed a fully adequate testimonial. Hamilton knew as well as other members of the Cabinet that the President preferred testimonials about candidates for office to be brief and to the point. Yet this was only the beginning. To his own encomiums he added the opinion that Wolcott was known to be regarded in the same light by members of Congress from different parts of the country. He argued, with reason, that promotion to a higher office within the department was consonant with justice while unrewarded talents would breed discouragement. Then, possibly as an afterthought, he added in the margin of the draft of his letter that Wolcott, as a man of nice sensibility who was conscious of his own merits, might resign if another were appointed Comptroller. In that case, he declared, "the Derangement of the department would truly be distressing to the public service." The blunt admonition suggests that Hamilton and Wolcott had discussed the vacancy and that, as in 1789, the latter had made his intentions known.

Nor was this all. Hamilton, like others in the administration, was well aware that a fundamental principle governing Washington's distribution of patronage was that it should be done with due regard to the claims of the various sections of the nation. Eveleigh was a Carolinian; Wolcott from Connecticut. Anticipating the difficulty, Hamilton pointed out that if Wolcott were promoted, the President might direct his inquiries in the South "on the principle of distribution" for the resultant vacancy in the office of Auditor. The principle thus accommodated, he addressed himself to what must have seemed an even more formidable obstacle. "In suggesting thus particularly the reasons which in my mind operate in favor of Mr. Woolcott," he wrote, "I am influenced by information that other characters will be brought to your view by weighty advocates, and as I think it more than possible that Mr. Woolcott may not be mentioned to you by any other person than myself, I feel it a duty arising out of my situation in the department to bear my full and explicit testimony to his worth; confident that he will justify by every kind of *substantial* merit any mark of your approbation, which he may receive."[20]

The first observation to be made about this remarkable statement concerns Hamilton's supposition that no one save himself would advocate Wolcott's appointment. Two others who did were close friends and supporters of the Secretary of the Treasury, Henry Knox in the Cabinet and Robert Morris in the Senate. On the same day that Hamilton dispatched his lengthy testimonial to the President, Henry Knox also addressed a private letter to Washington

[20] Hamilton to Washington, 17 Apr. 1791 (Dft in CtHi: Wolcott Papers; clerk's copy, with some inaccuracies, in same; Tr in DLC: Washington Papers; full text from Dft in Syrett, *Hamilton*, VIII, 291-4). The presence of the draft in Wolcott's papers does not necessarily indicate that Wolcott saw it at this time, since a number of file copies of other Hamilton letters later came into his possession.

for the same purpose, employing the same arguments and indeed similar phraseology. "Mr. Eveleigh the Comptroller of the Treasury died yesterday," Knox began. "There will be a number of candidates for his office, who will urge their several pretensions with some specious, and perhaps some weighty arguments. – Having been taught by your goodness to address myself to you unreservedly, and knowing your desire to learn through different mediums, existing opinions relative to candidates, I take the liberty of transmitting you mine on this occasion. – From the view I have taken of the subject, it seems to me, that more personal political and official considerations unite in favour of Mr. Wolcott . . . than in any other person within my knowledge. – He is in the exercise of habits necessary to the investigations of public accounts, and eminently possesses the talents to form proper judgements of the cases which may be in his department." Knox then restated and elaborated Hamilton's point about the geographical distribution of offices. "Should he not be appointed," he warned, "the State of Connecticut may think itself neglected, as some of its citizens are of opinion that it has not its proportion of the great offices of Government. . . . The general principle which you have been pleased justly to adopt of distributing offices according to the divisions of eastern middle and southern states may have its operation in this case, as a character from a southern state may be found for the Auditor's Office." Knox not only echoed Hamilton's argument about promotion within the department; he also revealed that he knew what his colleague's preference was: ". . . there appears to be a propriety and fitness, in advancing persons of integrity and highly approved conduct from a lower to a higher grade. And I beg leave to observe that this appointment would be most acceptable to the Secretary of the Treasury, a circumstance of great importance in the harmonious conducting of the business of the treasury."[21] Three days later Robert Morris added his influential testimony. His letter has not been found, but there can be no doubt that he stood with Hamilton and Knox in urging Wolcott's appointment.[22] It is scarcely to be credited that such close associates of Hamilton as Knox and Morris would have urged Wolcott's appointment if they had not known that this would meet with the approval of the Secretary of the Treasury. Indeed Knox had declared this to be the case. In consequence, Hamilton's statement to Washington that he thought he might be the only one to recommend Wolcott must be regarded with some doubt. Under the circumstances it seems plausible to assume that the effort was concerted and that it arose from a more than ordinary concern.

All were aware that there would be various applicants for the post of Comptroller. Along with common gossip, Hamilton's circular announcing Eveleigh's inability to discharge his duties had signalled the approaching vacancy and aroused the expectations of potential candidates. One such was Christopher Richmond, Auditor General of Maryland, who journeyed to Philadelphia armed with testimonials from such a friend of the President as Governor Thomas Johnson soliciting appointment "when any Office becomes vacant."[23] Peter V.

[21] Knox to Washington, 17 Apr. 1791 (RC, marked "Private," in DLC: Washington Papers).
[22] In acknowledging Morris' letter of 20 Apr., Washington gave no indication of its substance but said that he considered Wolcott's appointment "as due to the public service, and to his own merit" (Washington to Morris, 16 June 1791, *Writings*, ed. Fitzpatrick, xxxi, 298).
[23] Richmond to Washington, 7 Mch. 1791. Richmond's candidacy was supported by

B. Livingston recommended his friend John Kean for the post.[24] James McHenry advanced the name of John H. Purviance.[25] Washington's neighbor, Uriah Forrest, told the President that he thought Eveleigh's death opened up a vacancy for which he deemed himself best fitted.[26] Timothy Pickering, arriving in Philadelphia to receive instructions for the forthcoming treaty with the Six Nations, also told the President that if there were any place in the Treasury he felt competent to fill it was that of the Comptroller. He knew that there were other applicants, perhaps having learned this from Hamilton or Knox, with whom he was then in close consultation. Pickering was so urgent as to send his application in triplicate, but he asked no testimonials. "To you alone . . . I make my suit," he wrote the President, "without asking the patronage or recommendation of any man. Such aid cannot be necessary, nor proper, nor decent: for no patronage, no recommendation could make you *better acquainted with my character*: and that is the only ground on which a recommendation could pertinently be offered."[27]

Pickering was the most formidable of these candidates, but, asking no testimonials, he could not have been the one Hamilton had in mind when he wrote to Washington about applicants who would be supported by "weighty advocates." The one applicant he obviously had in mind was, like Wolcott, a member of his own department – Assistant Secretary of the Treasury Tench Coxe, who at this moment was proving himself a most useful coadjutor in the preparation of Hamilton's Report on Manufactures and in promoting the Society for Establishing Useful Manufactures, which Hamilton had so much at heart. The Secretary of the Treasury was thus confronted by two of his able subordinates who desired to fill the vacancy, both well qualified but with quite different pretensions. Already committed to Wolcott, he may have regarded their rivalry as less of a dilemma than as an opportunity to be exploited against his own rival in the Cabinet, as ultimately he did.

III

It was on the very day of Eveleigh's death that Hamilton discussed with Coxe the vacancy that had just occurred and the latter made known his desire to fill it. Each left an account of the conversation which contradicts the other in essential points. That of Hamilton seems the more contrived, first because the context of his account was his long letter to Washington recommending Wolcott, and second because, on its face, his report of the interview reveals obvious incongruities. To this may be added a peculiarity in the drafting of the letter itself which indicates that, contrary to the impression he sought to convey to the President, Hamilton wrote in consultation with someone else.

---

the following testimonials, among others: A. C. Hanson to Washington, 26 Mch. 1791; John Eager Howard to Washington, 15 Mch. 1791; William Paca to Washington, 25 May 1791; Daniel Carroll to Washington, 7 Mch. 1791 (RCs in DLC: Washington Papers).

[24] Livingston to Washington, 1 June 1791 (same).

[25] McHenry to Washington, 20 Apr. 1791 (same). Purviance had applied in 1789 for the office of Auditor or Register (Purviance to Washington, 14 Sep. 1789, same).

[26] Forrest to Washington, 27 Apr. 1791 (same).

[27] Pickering to Washington, 2 May 1791 (Dft in MHi: Pickering Papers; duplicate and triplicate in DLC: Washington Papers).

"There is another circumstance which I ought not to conclude without mentioning to you," Hamilton remarked near the end of his letter. "Mr. Coxe has signified to me his wish to be considered for the Office of Comptroller. On this point I have answered him and very sincerely to this effect 'I am well convinced that the office under your direction would be in perfectly good hands. On the score of qualification my preference would not incline to any other man and you have every reason to believe that on personal accounts none would be more agreeable to me. But I am equally well satisfied on the other hand that no man ought to be preferred to Mr. Woolcott on the score of qualification for the office, and this being the case, I am of opinion that the relation which his present station bears to that in question gives him pretensions superior to any other person.' He then asked me whether it would be disagreeable to me to make his wish known to you. To this my answer was in substance that I could have no possible objection to his doing it and that I would even do it myself" – at which point the draft ended in mid-page, Hamilton drew a looping line to the bottom, and the sentence was concluded on a new page and in another hand – "but that I apprised him it should be done in such a manner as would make it clearly understood to you that all circumstances considered I thought that Mr. Woolcott had a decidedly preferable claim." Hamilton's unidentified collaborator – the handwriting is not that of Morris, Knox, Wadsworth, Ellsworth, Huntington, or others who could have had an interest in promoting Wolcott's candidacy – then concluded the letter with assurances that the recommendation was grounded in an honest zeal for the public good and a firm conviction that the department and the government would be best served by making Wolcott Comptroller.[28]

Hamilton was as good as his word. But in making Coxe's desire known to the President as promised, he did so in a letter whose urgent advocacy of Wolcott's claims nullified the assurances he said he had given Coxe. Nor was this all. In the concluding part of his draft he quoted himself as saying to Coxe that on the score of qualification no one stood higher in his estimation than he. Then, in the next sentence, in precisely the same terminology and according to the same criterion, he ranked Wolcott first. Perhaps haste caused Hamilton to overlook the inconsistency. More likely the lapse resulted from a revision in the draft. As Hamilton phrased the passage originally, he accorded Coxe superiority "on the score of ability and integrity" and then altered the phrase to read "on the score of qualification," the identical terms on which he based the superior claim of Wolcott. This inconsistency may have prompted Hamilton's unidentified collaborator to complete the account of the conversation by saying that Coxe's wishes would be made known to the President in such a way as to indicate Hamilton's decided preference for Wolcott. The addition was scarcely necessary, for the whole thrust of Hamilton's letter to Washington was to make it abundantly clear what his preference was. But, as words attributed to Hamilton by another, the real effect of the unnecessary elucidation was to cast doubt on the reliability of Hamilton's report of the conversation. Coxe's account of what took place between him and his superior on the day Eveleigh died raises still further questions about Hamilton's version. But on one point both were agreed – that Coxe had revealed his desire for the appointment and that Hamilton had interposed no objection to his informing the President of the fact.

[28] Hamilton to Washington, 17 Apr. 1791 (Dft in CtHi: Wolcott Papers).

Coxe immediately drafted his letter of application.[29] But instead of sending it directly to the President as Pickering and others had done, he enclosed it in a letter to Jefferson, placing upon him the responsibility of deciding whether to forward it. In doing so he explained that it had been his intention to make his desire known to one "of the best and wisest members of the Administration" at as early a moment as decorum permitted. Within a few hours of Eveleigh's death that moment assuredly had not arrived. But Coxe justified his haste by saying that the Secretary of the Treasury had that afternoon led him into a free conversation on the subject. According to Coxe, Hamilton not only initiated the subject but also volunteered the information that he was restrained from recommending any other than Wolcott because of circumstances connected with his appointment as Auditor. Hamilton was also quoted as saying that he considered Coxe as well qualified for the vacancy as any other and that he would by no means advise him not to apply for the office.[30] This version of the conversation, which places responsibility upon the Secretary of the Treasury for opening the discussion, justified Coxe in drawing the inference that if Hamilton had not been restrained by his prior commitment, he would have been gratified by Coxe's appointment. It also suggests that Coxe, grasping at the opening, inquired whether his application for the office would be disagreeable to his superior. The fact that the inquiry was made is confirmed by Hamilton's own version of the interview. What is conspicuously lacking in Coxe's account is the assurance Hamilton said he gave that he himself would make Coxe's wishes known to the President. If Hamilton had actually given such assurances, it seems highly unlikely that Coxe would have refrained from mentioning the fact in his letter to Jefferson.

The principal question raised by these two divergent accounts is not whether Hamilton initiated the subject, though there seems no reason to doubt Coxe's assertion that he did. It is rather a question of the motives that prompted him to adopt an equivocal role in the matter. Having already anticipated the vacancy a month earlier by recommending Wolcott, Hamilton by a simple statement to this effect could surely have deterred Coxe from becoming a rival for the post against the declared preference of his superior. Why, instead, did Hamilton present his own situation as limited by circumstances and make complimentary allusions which, even by his own account, could not have failed to encourage Coxe to apply for the vacancy? Knowing this, did he intimate or even suggest that Coxe might be sponsored by those "weighty advocates" to whom he referred in his letter to Washington? Knowing also that Coxe had been friendly with the Secretary of State and useful to him in supplying information, did he mention Jefferson as one whose support might be obtained? The answers to such questions must remain in the realm of conjecture. But Hamilton's equivocation in the coversation with Coxe, his subsequent accusations, and Jefferson's carefully considered method of dealing with the problem suggest a plausible explanation.

IV

Hamilton unquestionably knew that Coxe's application had been forwarded to the Secretary of State and by him to the President. The fact is proved by

---

[29] Coxe to Washington, 16 Apr. 1791 (Document II below).
[30] Coxe to TJ, 16 Apr. 1791 (Document I below).

his subsequent accusation. In view of this, together with Jefferson's immediate response containing a characteristic but perhaps imprudent expression of politeness wishing him success, it seems very likely that Coxe promptly informed Hamilton of the fact, perhaps even by showing him Jefferson's brief note.[31] If so, such news coming on the 17th could have prompted Hamilton, Knox, and Morris to undertake what can most plausibly be described as an urgent and concerted effort to offset the effect of the supposed testimonial of the Secretary of State. Jefferson's mere allusion to the fact that he did not think it necessary to consult Madison as Coxe had suggested would have been enough to prompt fears of those "weighty advocates" of the claims of the Assistant Secretary of the Treasury.

What Hamilton and his supporters did not know, first of all, was that Jefferson did in fact inform Madison of Coxe's application, despite his assurance to Coxe that he felt no need to consult him on the question. His manner of doing this could scarcely have been a casual passing of information or discussion of the distribution of patronage in another department. As later developments indicate, Jefferson's disclosure to his most intimate collaborator must have arisen from growing suspicions concerning actions originating with the Secretary of the Treasury. For the important fact that he did not reveal to Coxe, and one that certainly could not have been known to Hamilton, was the manner in which he communicated Coxe's letter to the President. Coxe had asked not to be informed whether Jefferson had chosen to submit it to Washington *with his opinion* or to commit it to the flames. Jefferson disregarded the request and declined to accept its implication that transmission of the letter meant support of the applicant: he merely reported that he had sent it forward. More important, he kept silent about the significant use he made of Coxe's letter to himself. What he did was to tear off the first leaf of that letter and enclose it with Coxe's application in his own letter to the President. That communication was concerned with important matters of policy, and at its close Jefferson almost casually remarked: "Colo. Eveleigh died yesterday. Supposing it possible you might desire to appoint his successor as soon as you could decide on one, I inclose you a blank commission, which when you shall be pleased to fill up and sign, can be returned for the seal and countersignature. I inclose you a letter from Mr. Coxe to yourself on the subject of this appointment, and so much of one to me as related to the same, having torn off a leaf of compliment to lighten and lessen my enclosures to you. Should distributive justice give preference to a successor of the same state with the deceased, I take the liberty of suggesting to you Mr. Hayward of S. C. whom I think you told me you did not know, and of whom you are now on the spot of inquiry."[32] That was all.

Jefferson not only had not become an advocate of Coxe's appointment: he had instead suggested another candidate on the basis of Washington's well-known principle of geographical distribution of patronage. In fact, he deliberately refrained from making even an indirect comment on the merit of Coxe's application by transmitting along with it the first part of the letter from Coxe

[31] TJ to Coxe, 17 Apr. 1791 (Document III below).

[32] TJ to Washington, 17 Apr. 1791, with enclosures (Document II in group of documents on unofficial diplomacy, at 4 Apr. 1791). See note 1, Coxe to TJ, 16 Apr. 1791 (Document I below). The person to whom TJ referred was Thomas Heyward (1746-1809) of South Carolina, whom TJ had known in Congress in 1776. TJ had respect for Heyward, but the two men never corresponded.

to himself. In doing so he gave the President the erroneous impression that he had only "torn off a leaf of compliment to lighten and lessen" the enclosures. The part he retained – actually two leaves – did contain adulatory remarks, but it also embraced much else. In particular it included Coxe's request that Jefferson consult Madison and then decide whether he should transmit the application "with your opinion on the subject; or . . . commit it to the fire." For Jefferson to have included this portion of the letter would have justified the inference that, by the mere act of transmittal, he lent his support to the applicant. It is understandable that he should have wished to avoid giving Washington such an impression. But why indeed should he have disclosed any part of that letter to the President? This Coxe surely would not have expected or desired. Jefferson must have taken this unusual liberty with a private communication because, first of all, it clearly exculpated himself from any involvement with the rival candidacies of two officers in another department. Also, this leaf torn from Coxe's letter to himself clearly revealed the equivocal role played by Hamilton. Whether or not Jefferson accepted at face value Coxe's account of Hamilton's being restrained by circumstances from supporting any other than Wolcott, he surely understood that the mere transmittal of Coxe's application without such information would have placed him in the ambiguous position of opposing the declared candidate of the Secretary of the Treasury. Thus this leaf transmitted from Coxe's letter accomplished the double purpose of placing responsibility for Coxe's candidacy upon the Secretary of the Treasury and of keeping himself scrupulously clear of involvement. This unusual action placed before the President two contradictory accounts of the episode. Characteristically, Washington passed over both in silence when he accepted the recommendation of the Secretary of the Treasury.[33]

[33] In his response to TJ, as indicated above, Washington made no allusion to Coxe's letter or to the comptrollership (Washington to TJ, 17 June 1791). His letters to Hamilton and Morris declared his high opinion of Wolcott but referred to no other candidates (Washington to Hamilton, 13 June 1791, Syrett, *Hamilton*, VIII, 470-1; Washington to Morris, 16 June 1791, *Writings*, ed. Fitzpatrick, XXXI, 292, 298). Washington did instruct Lear to "use every *indirect* means" in his power to ascertain the public opinion of the fittest character to "fill the present Auditors Office (as *he* will be appointed Comptroler) with the greatest ability and integrity. Several have been brought to my view for the Comptrolers place (who I suppose would accept of the Auditors) as able and meritorious characters; among these are Mr. Richmond . . . Colonel Pickering, Mr. Kean, Colo. Drayton (a Gentn. of South Carolina) Colo. Forrest and others" (Washington to Lear, 15 June 1791, *Writings*, ed. Fitzpatrick, XXXI, 296-7). Coxe's name was not mentioned.

Other applicants for the office of Auditor were John Clark, Matthew Clarkson, William Davies, John Dawson (recommended by James Monroe), James Ewing, Thomas Irwin, Eleazar McComb, William Moultrie, and William Simmons – all from the middle or southern states (their letters and testimonials between 4 July and 6 Nov. 1791 are in DLC: Washington Papers, Series 7). Washington nominated Richard Harrison. The Senate held up confirmation until it could learn which of several Richard Harrisons was intended. When Washington informed the Senate that "Richard Harrison . . . is a merchant of Alexandria, in Virginia," the nominee was confirmed (JEP, I, 90, 91).

Before learning of Washington's intentions, Hamilton sought through McHenry's influence to persuade Otho H. Williams of Baltimore to become a candidate, but he declined. McHenry, representing Hamilton, then called on William Smith of the same place and finally persuaded him to let his name be put forward for the post. "I was obliged to intimate," McHenry reported, "that from the opinion you had of him, I could

Thus, far from engaging in "intrigue to place his own man in the center of Hamilton's department," Jefferson remained as aloof as possible from the contest. He had no need to do otherwise. Even if he had wished to engage in an intrigue of the sort, such an effort would have been wholly unnecessary. Coxe was already in the Treasury, he had for some time been supplying Jefferson with useful statistics, and at this moment he was engaged in writing his criticism of Lord Sheffield's *Observations* in which Jefferson's influence was apparent. Theirs was not the close collaboration it has been represented to be, but Coxe could not have been more useful to Jefferson whether as Comptroller or Assistant Secretary.[34] Yet, possibly because of this relationship and because of his anxiety about Jefferson's proposed navigation bill, Hamilton himself, even after learning that Wolcott would be appointed, initiated the baseless charge that Jefferson had attempted to infiltrate his department. Late in July Henry Lee heard gossip to this effect in New York and reported it to Madison. "Would you believe," Madison wrote Jefferson, "that this . . . has got into circulation in the shape of an attempt in you and myself to intermeddle with the Treasury department, to frustrate the known wishes of the head of it, and to keep back the lineal successor, from a Southern antipathy to his Eastern descent!"

Madison touched upon the rumor in conversation with Hamilton and thought he had convinced him that Jefferson's agency, with which he associated himself, "was the effect of complaisance rather than of solicitude for or against the candidates — and particularly that it was impossible from the very nature of the case, it would have involved the idea of thwarting his purposes in his own department." He added that this was not the only instance of "the most uncandid and unfounded things of a like tendency having been thrown into circulation."[35] A week later Madison declared to Jefferson that he thought it "a little singular . . . that so serious a face should have been put on it by ———— [Hamilton] who ought to have known the circumstances which explained the nature of the interference complained of." Madison seemed willing to accept Hamilton's assertion that another candidate whom he could not properly name had been "the channel thro' which he had received his wrong impressions."[36] Jefferson, less credulous, placed the origin of the unfounded rumor where it belonged. "Nobody could know of T. C.'s application but himself, H[amilton] you and myself. Which of the four was most likely to give it out at all, and especially in such a form? Which of the four would feel an inclination to excite an opinion that you and myself were hostile to every thing not Southern?"[37]

---

entertain no doubt but his appointment would be certain unless the President got entangled to the Southward" (McHenry to Hamilton, 3 May 1791, Syrett, *Hamilton*, VIII, 322). Only a day after Washington had instructed Lear to investigate the list of applicants, the *Federal Gazette* of 16 July 1791 carried this announcement: "We hear that the President has appointed William Smith of Baltimore as Auditor in the Treasury Department." Hamilton's candidate thus failed to get the appointment.

[34] For comment on TJ's relationship with Coxe, see Editorial Notes to group of documents on American commerce, at 31 Jan. 1791, and to that concerning TJ's hope for a European concert on navigation laws aimed at Great Britain, at 15 Mch. 1791; for a differing interpretation and more comprehensive treatment of the relations between TJ and Coxe, see Jacob E. Cooke, "The Collaboration of Tench Coxe and Thomas Jefferson," PMHB, C (Oct. 1976), 468-90.

[35] Madison to TJ, 24 July 1791.

[36] Madison to TJ, 31 July 1791.

[37] TJ to Madison, 27 July 1791.

The rhetorical questions answered themselves. The inescapable conclusion is that Hamilton not only played an equivocal role by permitting if not prompting Coxe to become the rival of his own candidate: he also exploited the incident in a deliberate distortion of the facts in a manner calculated to discredit Jefferson. That he should have resorted to such tactics in the spring of 1791 may be taken as a measure of the concern he felt over the growing influence of the Secretary of State. Ironically, within less than a fortnight, Jefferson's unintended public allusion to political heresies in his commendation of Paine's *Rights of Man* did more to diminish his influence with the President than anything Hamilton could have contrived.[38] Within another three months, when Tench Coxe sought the office of Postmaster General and asked Hamilton's counsel, the candidate appealed for support not to the Secretary of State but to the Secretary of War. "I am authorized by [the Secretary of the Treasury] to say in confidence *to you*," Coxe wrote to Henry Knox, "that tho he feels a wish that he may not bring forward the name of a person so nearly connected with him, he will give me his *entire support*."[39] This time there was no charge that the head of one department sought by intrigue to invade that of another.

[38] See Editorial Note to group of documents on the Paine incident, at 26 Apr. 1791.
[39] Coxe to Knox, 11 July 1791 ("Private," MHi: Knox Papers).

I. Tench Coxe to Thomas Jefferson

SIR   Saturday Evening April 16th. 1791.

The vacancy produced in the Treasury department by the death of the Comptroller has occasioned me to take the liberty of making this communication to you. It will not appear unnatural, that a person in my situation should be led, by the relation the offices of the Treasury bear to each other, to entertain a wish for the appointment, and I should, at as early a moment as decorum permitted, have done myself the honor to make that desire known to you. But Mr. Hamilton having led me this afternoon into a free conversation on the subject I find it proper to be more early in this communication than it was my intention to have been. There appear to be circumstances, which originated at the time of Mr. Wolcotts appointment to his present office, that operate to restrain the Secretary of the Treasury from moving in favor of any other person, and this information he gave me unasked. He entertains an opinion, also, that the relation between the offices of the Comptroller and Auditor creates a kind of pretension in the latter to succeed the former. He however added in a very kind and flattering way his opinion, that he should see as many public advantages resulting from the appointment of myself as any other person, and that he would by no means advise my declining to apply to the President.

The Station you fill in the Government together with the impressions I feel concerning[1] your character have long since determined me never to present myself as a candidate for the favor of the President without making my Intention known to you. I do not desire to obtain any appointment, if good reasons against it can be adduced to the President by the best and wisest members of the Administration.

You will indulge me, Sir, in passing by everything, that has relation to my Ability to execute the office either in regard to the modifications, which it may be requisite to give to the public accounts, or the preparatory political investigations, which I have always thought should regularly engage the Comptroller of the Treasury.

It is my wish, Sir, that you will do me the honor to transmit the enclosed letter to the President of the United States; but if on a conference between yourself and the honorable Mr. Madison, in whose Judgment I have an entire confidence, that it will be for any reason best to omit the Application I have a sincere wish that it may be suppressed. I feel exceedingly averse to any addition on my account to the unpleasing circumstances, which must too often be obtruded on the President's mind in the delicate and important duty of appointments to office.

It will relieve me from a great part of the pain I feel in making this application to you, if you will be pleased to reserve from me any communication of the disposition you make of the letter, which I have ventured to enclose, whether you may deem it best to transmit it with your opinion on the subject; or may think it most fit on the whole to commit it to the fire. — With the highest respect, I have the honor to be Sir your most obedient & humble Servant,

TENCH COXE

It is my intention to confine my views to yourself, and Mr. Hamilton, leaving it to your own ideas of propriety to converse with Mr. Madison. If a perfectly convenient opportunity presents it would be very much my wish.

RC (DNA: RG 59, MLR; consisting only of the first leaf of the letter as enclosed in TJ to Washington, 17 Apr. 1791, the remaining two leaves in DLC); the blank verso of the part retained by TJ endorsed by him as received 16 Apr. 1791 and so recorded in SJL. For comment on TJ's reasons for sending only the first part of the letter to Washington, see Editorial Note above. Note 1 below indicates the only part of the letter that Washington saw.

[1] The first leaf of the letter ends at this point and marks the conclusion of that part of the letter TJ sent to Washington.

II. Tench Coxe to the President

SIR   Philadelphia April 16th 1791

It is with the greatest hesitation that I contribute to the unpleasing circumstances that are obtruded on your mind by too numerous applications for public office. The decease of the Comptroller of the Treasury having created the necessity of an appointment, I most humbly beg leave to present myself to your consideration. The relation which exists between the offices of the Treasury and the respectful solicitude for the honor of your countenance which is felt by every good citizen and which is anxiously desired by every faithful Servant of the public will be received, I hope, Sir, in apology for this step. Honor and Emolument may be generally deemed the inducements to these applications, but I trust I do not deceive myself in the belief that these considerations do not influence me more decidedly than a sincere desire to evince the highest respect for the government of the United States and for the peculiar character of their Chief Magistrate. – I have the honor to be with the most profound respect Sir your most humble & most obedient servant,

TENCH COXE

RC (DLC: Washington Papers); endorsed by Lear. TJ enclosed the above letter in his to Washington of 17 Apr. 1791.

III. Thomas Jefferson to Tench Coxe

Apr. 17. 1791.

Th: Jefferson presents his compliments to Mr. Coxe and being to write to the President this morning, he has no hesitation to inclose to him Mr. Coxe's letter, and to assure Mr. Coxe of his wishes for success to the application. He has not waited to consult with Mr. M. because he should have lost a post in the conveyance of the letter, and that as to himself he had no doubts to consult about.

RC (CtY); addressed: "Mr. Coxe"; endorsed. Not recorded in SJL.

To James Monroe

DEAR SIR   Philadelphia Apr. 17. 1791.

Your favor of Mar. 29. 1791. came to hand last night. I sincerely sympathize with you on the step which your brother has taken without consulting you, and wonder indeed how it could be done, with any attention in the agents, to the laws of the land. I fear he will hardly persevere in the second plan of life adopted for him, as matrimony illy agrees with study, especially in the first stages of both. However you will readily perceive that, the thing being done, there is now but one question, that is What is to be done to make the best of it, in respect both to his and your happiness? A step of this kind indicates no vice, nor other foible than of following too hastily the movements of a warm heart. It admits therefore of the continuance of cordial affection, and calls perhaps more indispensably for your care and protection. To conciliate the affection of all parties, and to banish all suspicion of discontent, will conduce most to your own happiness also. – I am sorry to hear that your daughter has been unwell, and hope she is recovered ere this, and that Mrs. Munroe enjoys good health. – Affairs in France are still going on well. The late pacification between Spain and England has not been a reconciliation. It is thought the fire is but slightly covered, and may burst out should the Northern war spread as is expected. Great Britain is still endeavoring to plunder us of our carrying business. The parliament have a bill before them to admit wheat brought in *British* bottoms to be warehoused rent free, so that the merchants are already giving a preference to British bottoms for that commodity. Should we lose the transportation of our own wheat, it will put down a great proportion of our shipping, already pushed by British vessels out of some of the best branches of business. In order further to circumscribe our carrying, the Commissioners of the Treasury have lately determined to admit no vessel as American, unless built here. This takes from us the right of prescribing by our own laws the conditions of naturalizing vessels in our own country, and in the event of a war in which we should be neutral, prevents our increasing, by purchase, the quantity of our shipping, so as to avail ourselves of the full benefit of the neutrality of our flag. If we are to add to our stock of shipping only as much as we can build, a war will be over before we shall be the better of it. – We hear of continual murders in the Westward. I hope we shall drub the Indians well this summer and then change our plan from war to bribery. We must do as the Spaniards and English do, keep them in peace by liberal and constant presents. They find it the cheapest plan, and so shall we. The expence of this summers expedition would have served for presents for half a century. In this way hostilities being suspended for some length of time, a real affection may succeed on our frontiers to that hatred now existing there. Another powerful motive is that in this way we may leave no pretext for raising or continuing an army. Every rag of an Indian depredation will otherwise serve as a ground to raise troops with those who think a standing army and a public debt necessary for the happiness of the U.S. and we shall never be permitted to get rid of either. – Our treasury still thinks that these new encroachments of Gr. Brit. on our carrying trade must be met by passive obedience and non-resistance, lest any misunderstanding with them should *affect our credit, or the prices of our public paper.* New schemes are on foot for bringing more paper to market by encouraging great manufacturing companies to form, and their actions, or paper-shares, to be transferrable as bank-stock. We are ruined, Sir, if we do not over-rule the principles that 'the more we owe, the more prosperous we shall be,' 'that a public debt furnishes the means of enterprize,' 'that if ours should be once paid off, we should incur another by any means however extravagant' &c. &c. – Colo. Eveleigh died yesterday morning.[1] – Present me affectionately and most affectionately to Mrs. Monroe. I cannot be with you till September. Adieu, my dear Sir Your sincere friend & servt, TH: JEFFERSON

RC (NN). PrC (DLC).

[1] TJ first wrote "last night" and then altered this to read as above.

To Martha Jefferson Randolph

MY DEAR DAUGHTER   Philadelphia April. 17. 1791.

Since I wrote last to you, which was on the 24th. of March, I have received yours of March 22. I am indeed sorry to hear of the situation of Walker Gilmer and shall hope the letters from Monticello will continue to inform me how he does.[1] I know how much his parents will suffer, and how much he merited all their affection. – Mrs. Trist has been so kind as to have your calash made, but either by mistake of the maker, or of myself, it is not lined with green. I have therefore desired a green lining to be got, which you can put in yourself if you prefer it. Mrs. Trist has observed that there is a kind of veil lately introduced here, and much approved. It fastens over the brim of the hat and then draws round the neck as close or open as you please. I desire a couple to be made to go with the calash and other things. – Mr. Lewis not liking to write letters I do not hear from him: but I hope you are readily furnished with all the supplies and conveniences the estate affords. I shall not be able to see you till September, by which time the young-grandaughter will begin to look bold, and knowing. I inclose you a letter to a woman, who lives, I believe, on Buckisland. It is from her sister in Paris, which I would wish you to send express. I hope your garden is flourishing. Present me affectionately to Mr. Randolph & Polly. Your's sincerely my dear,　　　Th: JEFFERSON

RC (NNP). PrC (MHi).　　　　　　　soon after returning.

Thomas Walker Gilmer, eldest son of TJ's friend Dr. George Gilmer, had been studying medicine at Edinburgh and died

[1] TJ first wrote ". . . whether it be really hopeless" and then altered the passage to read as above.

From Joshua Johnson

London, 18 Apr. 1791. His of 27 Mch. and 4 Apr. sent by New York packet in care of Colo. Smith. Since then the press for seamen has become general, but he is pleased to report "not . . . one Complaint from our Countrymen," proving the Ministers have kept their promise not to molest American citizens. He thinks the government do not dare enter the Russian war because of opposition to it in both houses of Parliament and a universal dislike among the people. – "I find Lord Hawkesbury has drawn up a long Report, on the advantages and disadvantages, of the Trade between the United States and this Country, for the King, and Privy Council, fifty copies of which are now printing for their examination; I am endeavoring to procure a sight of one, and should I succeed I will transmit you, the most interesting outlines. It is said here, that Colo. Smith had previous to his departure several interviews with Lord Grenville, on the Subject of the United States, and that the Packet was detained to carry him out, that he might communicate them to Congress; it is probable it may be the Case, but if so I know nothing of it, as I was not consulted, or informed of their objects. – It is now said that Mr. Elliott has resigned, and don't go to America. It is whispered Mr. Peale of Manchester is to be the Man; I have reason to believe that the Ministers are very much divided on the Business; some thinking a Commercial regulation highly necessary, and others that it is of no consequence; as for my own part I begin to think it is of much less consequence to the United States, than it is to Great Britain, and that a judicious Navigation Act will soon prove, that I am right, and convince this proud People, that they are wrong."

He encloses account of all American vessels entering and leaving London from 1 Jan. to 31 Mch., in which are many unavoidable imperfections owing to inattention of captains. Also sends register of sloop *Nancy*, which was owned by Messrs. Constable & Co. of New York but on arrival took out British register. This led him to take from Capt. Seton the one enclosed to prevent improper use of it. TJ will please order its cancellation. – "The interruption to the British trade with Russia has given advantage to the American Shipping, and our Vessells are sought for with avidity, and on advantageous Terms to go to St. Petersburgh; I grant to[1] all passes, one of which you will find inclosed for your satisfaction. – The Fleet at Spithead is not half manned, and more difficulty is met with, in procuring Men, than could be expected, so that it is uncertain when they can Sail."

RC (DNA: RG 59, CD). Recorded in SJL as received 23 July 1791. Dupl (same); with minor textual variations. Enclosure: Certificate of registry of sloop *Nancy*, Peter Seton, master, showing that her owners were William Constable, Gouverneur Morris, and Robert Morris; that she was built in Bermuda and rebuilt in New York in 1786; that she was 61'8" long, 21'8" wide; and that she was a square-sterned vessel of 170 tons with a female figurehead (printed form, dated New York, 1 May 1790, and signed by Alexander Hamilton and others, same).

For comment on Hawkesbury's Report to the Privy Council and William S. Smith's single interview with Grenville, see Editorial Note to group of documents on commercial and diplomatic relations with Great Britain, at 15 Dec. 1791.

¹ This word omitted in RC and supplied from Dupl.

From Mary Jefferson

DEAR PAPA   Monticello, April 18th, 1791.

I received your letter of March 31st the 14th of this month; as for that of March 9, I received it some time last month, but I do not remember the day. I have finished Don Quixote, and as I have not Desoles yet, I shall read Lazarillo de Tormes. The garden is backward, the inclosure having but lately been finished. I wish you would be so kind as to send me seven yards of cloth like the piece I send you. Adieu, my dear papa. I am your affectionate daughter,

MARIA JEFFERSON

MS not found. Text taken from Randolph, *Domestic Life*, p. 199. Recorded in SJL as received 30 Apr. 1791.

Under TJ's prodding and now with Martha's supervision, Mary had been struggling with Spanish for three years, being given ten pages to master in a day (see TJ to Elizabeth Wayles Eppes, 12 July 1788 and 7 Mch. 1790; Mary Jefferson to TJ, 25 Apr. 1790, 23 May 1790, and 22 Jan. 1791; Martha Jefferson Randolph to TJ, 16 Jan. 1791). The work that she had not yet tackled was *Historia de la Conquista de Mejico* by Antonio de Solis (1610-1686), Spanish dramatist and historian. In 1787 TJ owned the two-volume edition published in Madrid in 1783-1784 (Sowerby, No. 4119). It is not known which edition of Cervantes' *Don Quixote* Mary was reading. Of the several editions owned by TJ, one (published in Paris in 1754) was read by him as a youth and still survives, bearing on its title-page in his hand "Ex libris Thomæ Jefferson" (Sowerby, No. 4347). The work which Mary was about to read was presumably *The life and adventures of Lazarillo de Tormes*.

To Richard Soderstrom

SIR   Philadelphia Apr. 18. 1791.

The bearer hereof Mr. Samuel Pleasants, being desirous of being made known to you on account of some matter of business, I take the liberty of presenting him to you as a person with whom I have had considerable acquaintance during the occasional stays I have made in Philadelphia, and that I have ever esteemed him to be a person of integrity, and in whom confidence might be fully placed for whatever he undertakes. But he is too well known in Philadelphia generally, and his character there too well established to need further testimony from me. I am happy to embrace this and every other opportunity of assuring you of the respectful consideration with which I have the honor to be Sir Your most obedt humble servt,

Th: Jefferson

RC (Mrs. John Jay Pierrepont, Ridgefield, Conn., 1961); endorsed. PrC (MHi).

From Thomas Barclay

[*Philadelphia*], *19 Apr. 1791*. He called at TJ's house on Thursday, but TJ "had just moved from the door on horseback." He is "distressed beyond measure" to inform him of circumstances which he fears will postpone or prevent his embarking for Morocco as agreed. Messrs. Willing, Morris & Swanwick some time back began two actions against him for balances due to French & Co. of Bordeaux and to Cathalan of Marseilles by a mercantile house of L'Orient in which he unhappily was a partner while attending public business in Paris. He is bound to appear, but as proofs of the accounts — both of which are disputable — have never arrived from Europe, the trial has been postponed. He has offered Swanwick, the active prosecutor, an assignment of all his effects for general benefit of creditors but he says he is not at liberty to accept it. It appears to him and to friends he has consulted that his wisest course is to submit to bankruptcy to prevent disputable accounts from taking precedence over "others . . . founded in justice and equity. — This is a shocking expedient but if I go to Morocco I must adopt it." This will take about 40 days. No vessel for Lisbon for three or four weeks, so this would only postpone voyage three weeks longer. When arrangements are made, he will depart at once if services still thought of value. — Had he known of extent of difficulties before Thursday, he would have informed TJ sooner. — The day after he last talked with TJ, he wrote Col. Humphreys to inform Chiappe of his expected arrival, so that his advice about procedure and presents could meet him on arrival in Lisbon. — He thinks the unforeseen delay and extremity to which he is driven, may make it proper[1] to resume the commission. On this he desires TJ's opinion and may be addressed "at Mr. Barclays No. 216 near Pine street."

RC (DNA: RG 59, CD); endorsed by TJ as received 20 Apr. 1791 and so recorded in SJL.

[1] Thus in MS. Barclay may have intended to write "improper."

From Nathaniel Cutting

Le Havre, 19 Apr. 1791. TJ's of 26 Nov. did not arrive in time to be acknowledged by *Henrietta*. The information he sent from St. Domingo would lead one to expect magnanimity of its legislature would be cordially received by National Assembly. On contrary, French commercial interests, aided by intrigues of La Luzerne, engaged Barnave and other leaders to oppose the colony's legal representatives. The legislature's most commendable actions were severely censured and most illiberal aspersions cast on characters of its members. Since their arrival in Paris they have been held as prisoners on parole. Vice-President of legislature when it left St. Marc published a pamphlet about political situation which confirms Cutting's information. He encloses a copy for TJ. As TJ may not have had opportunity to acquaint himself with state of culture and finance in the French part of St. Domingue, he transmits tables which he wrote for his amusement last year, being well authenticated and published by De Marbois in 1789. De Marbois states total export duty at £6,924,167-19-11, but equally respectable authority says this is "the amount *actually collected*; but to know what *it ought* to have been, one must add at least 25 ℔ Ct. on account of the quantity of Produce illicitly convey'd from the Colony." Thus the whole revenue of the colony may be estimated at £9,329,934-17-11. Late estimate of population gives 30,000 whites, 32,000 free persons of color, and 400,000 Negro slaves, but he believes latter number too low because many planters, to avoid capitation tax, do not report "more than ⅔ or ¾ of their Stock," so that there are actually supposed to be from 450 to 500,000 slaves. — A gentleman who has been comptroller of the customs informs him that trade of colony is carried on by 580 ships directly from France averaging 373⅓ tons, 110 Guineamen, 259 Spanish ships, and 763 American and other vessels, these figures being provided from accurate information for the year 1789. "The illicit Commerce takes off Produce sufficient to load 44 Ships of 300 Tons burthen each, per annum."

"I cannot help feeling interested in behalf of the persecuted Colonists. Indeed I think that every Free American who indulges Political Reflections must feel himself peculiarly interested in the Fate of the valuable and flourishing Colony of St. Domingue, which at some future period may possibly fall within the Jurisdiction of the Thirteen United States! At least one may venture to predict that such an intimate intercourse will one day be established between them as will mutually invigorate those principles of Constitutional Freedom which have apparently taken such deep root in both Countries, and will be productive of that Reciprocal advantage which is the most durable cement of Political Union."

He says nothing of the political state of Europe, particularly France, because TJ has infinitely better information and he has little opportunity for gaining political intelligence. But as to himself, he is most grateful for TJ's kind intentions to have him appointed consul at Le Havre. He acknowledges that he "cannot *afford* to accept that Office" but with equal candor declares that he has always been ambitious to render all possible service to his countrymen and that he would be much gratified by the appointment "as it would shew the World that I was honor'd with the Confidence of the Fathers of my Country." He has long desired to fix himself there in the mercantile line, as the city "is now very flourishing and its Port bids fair to become one of the most secure and commodious in Europe. – If the American trade to this place revives, and I could form an advantageous connexion here I should be happy in the proposed appointment."

But as the etiquette of the European world makes it necessary to preserve certain appearances, as one holding that office "should be able uniformly to support a decent, not to say an elegant style of living," as there is no salary attached, and as his limited finances will not permit him to bear these extra expenses, he cannot accept. Further, the office of vice-consul "is a Feather in the Cap of M. De la Motte, and I am convinced his abilities are every way adequate to the discharge of all Consular Duties at this Port."

He does not believe it necessary to appoint a consul in every commercial city. He has been told that Congress contemplates forming three great consular departments in France, in each of which a native American would be consul and where necessary a vice-consul appointed. He thinks this a judicious arrangement. The vice-consuls might be instructed to keep registers of all American vessels arriving – their names, tonnage, cargoes, officers, sailors, and passengers – from which abstracts could be sent to the consul every month, to be transmitted from the three departments to the secretary of the American embassy in Paris, who could select such parts as thought necessary to inform Congress. Such a record would reveal "the extent and importance of the Commercial Intercourse between America and France . . . and it might furnish Government with hints that might prove exceedingly beneficial with respect to forming Commercial Treaties, or partial Regulations of Trade." If published, it would help individuals in their trading ventures. Publication of names of passengers might lead to discovery of persons supposed dead, thus preventing much litigation over property. TJ's superior sagacity will suggest other advantages or perhaps discover obstacles making it impracticable.

"Allow me to congratulate you on the auspicious nuptials of your eldest Daughter, and to thank you for the Intelligence that both she and Maria are in health; may that invaluable Blessing ever give a zest to all their other Enjoyments!" He has again become a resident of Le Havre, and it will always make him happy to be able to render TJ any service. If he is honored with any letters, they may be addressed to himself or in care of his friends Messrs. Le Mesurier & Cie.

RC (DNA: RG 59, MLR); mutilated, so that parts of quotations are supplied from FC (MHi: Cutting Papers). Recorded in SJL as received 8 July 1791.

From William Knox

Dublin, 19 Apr. 1791. As stated in his of 26 Nov. last, he intended writing only half-yearly, but recent circumstances cause him to make earlier communication.

Impressment of seamen from American ships generally practised in England during late preparations against Spain: "commonly all the men were taken, and it was left to be proved afterwards that they were Americans born. If the proofs were such as a regulating captain approved of they were discharged, provided by sufferings . . . and want of provisions they had not been forced to enter for his Brittanick Majestys service. . . . no other circumstance than birth was admitted as constituting an American subject in England." He learned on 11th from Belfast that all sailors on five American vessels were taken by Captain Mackay of *Inspector*, sloop of war. He applied at once to Mr. Hobart, secretary to Lord Lieutenant who acts as principal secretary of state and who informed him that only the Lords of the Admiralty could afford relief. On his advice he applied to Mr. Stephens, secretary, and also wrote to Belfast urging every means to prevent sailors from being sent to Plymouth or Portsmouth. Yesterday in reply from thence he learned all save five had been returned, and these had been sent to Plymouth as British subjects, although some of them had been married and settled at Philadelphia 22 years. – He immediately warned American vessels at Limerick, Londonderry, Cork, and Newry but knew of no impressments at those ports. Three American vessels were in Dublin when news came from Belfast, but their departure was hastened, and before the press on the evening of the 14th they had cleared. – It is an object of great consequence to American commerce for regulation between U.S. and England determining American citizenship exclusive of birth. It is also important that all American sailors coming to British dominions should have their names in manifests as part of ship's attested papers, giving birth, size, age, and particular proofs. Under existing circumstances a captain may be induced to swear they are American born when they are not. A consul requesting release of impressed men on oath of a captain may thereby make himself liable to very unfavorable imputations to himself and his country.

He recommends a Mr. Pearce of Manchester, "an artist of extraordinary merit" about to sail for Boston who had been induced to visit Ireland "by a Mr. McCabe an eminent watchmaker of Belfast a man of considerable property, and of great mechanical genius. They have lately been associated in an application to the Parliament of this Country for encouragement to a loom of Mr. Pearce's construction, which is simple, cheap, and calculated to turn out more work with the labor of one person than . . . by two in some articles and three in others. This man will be a great acquisition to our Country where the high price of labor operates as a bar to the establishing of manufactories." He encloses a paper showing capabilities of the invention and also the report of a committee of the House of Commons on their petition. McCabe and Pearce are not satisfied with terms offered and latter goes to America. Knox did not think proper to give him a letter but promised to inform TJ of his plan: he "will . . . wait on you in Philadelphia, when I do not Doubt, he will give such proofs of his being an highly valuable acquisition to the United States, as to insure your protection and support." – Heavy storms during winter have very much injured American trade with Ireland, six vessels, chiefly from Philadelphia, have been lost, but no lives. The *Clara*, a large ship from New York, was wrecked on 23d. Feb. 2 or 3 miles from Dublin. "In disasters of this kind it too frequently happens both on the Irish and English coasts, that the people endeavor to plunder all they can." In this case when the captain asked him for protection, he applied to the Lord Mayor, who provided a civil officer and army guard, so that enough was recovered to pay expenses and wages of the men, who have all had passages provided for them to their own country.

RC (DNA: RG 59, CD); at head of text: "(No.2)"; endorsed by TJ as received 16 July 1791 and so recorded in SJL. Dupl (same); with the following postscript not in RC: "The only two printed papers I had were enclosed in the original letter via Liverpool. – I take the liberty of enclosing the copy of a Letter to Mr. Stephens Secretary to the British Admiralty, and his answer, by which it seems pretty clearly Demonstrated that the English Government is Determined for the present not to relinquish the Idea, that no seaman born in his Brittanick Majestys Dominions can transfer his allegiance. Dublin May 7th. 1791"; endorsed by TJ as received 15 Aug. 1791 and so recorded in SJL.

Enclosures with RC: (1) Copy of approval of Knox' appointment as consul, signed by Grenville for the King, 8 Nov. 1790, and registered by R. Hobart at Dublin Castle, 4 Dec. 1790. (2) Receipt for £1-12-6 from William Taylor, Dublin Castle, 17 Dec. 1790, for entering Knox' commission. (3) Receipt for £2-5-0 from William Mossop, Dublin, 17 Dec. 1790, for engraving consular seal. (4) Printed sheet issued by Thomas McCabe and William Pearce announcing that "Two Artists from Belfast" had invented a superior loom for weaving linen and cotton by which a very good workman, who in 64 hours would weave 30 yards of "900 Callico on a loom of the present Construction," would weave 59¼ yards of the same quality on the new one in 52 hours and 45 minutes; affidavits of "three intelligent Weavers" substantiating the facts with regard to the present mode of working, together with those of "the Rev. Dr. Bruce, and Mr. David Manson, Mathematician, of Belfast" with regard to the new loom; two pieces of "Callico woven on the new Construction" were stated to be in Dublin in the hands of one of the artists. The inventors further stated that in weaving linen their loom could produce more than double the quantity in the same time and of superior quality, as shown by the even and straight selvage consistently reproducible because done by machinery and not dependent on "the manual Dexterity of the Artist." They claimed that their loom was "extremely simple in its Construction, not liable to go out of Order, and easily repaired," and at six to six and a half guineas would cost little more than the present ones. (5) Printed "Report on the Petition of Thomas Macabe and William Pearsce," dated 14 Feb. 1791, by a committee of the House of Commons, giving an appraisal of their loom by several

dealers in linen and a professor of natural philosophy of Trinity College. The Committee reported that the loom could weave cotton and linen "with more expedition, ease and perfection" than the common loom; that it was "simple in its construction, easily kept in order," and would not cost "double the price of a common loom"; and that it would be highly advantageous to the linen and cotton manufactures of the kingdom. Enclosures with Dupl: (1) Copy of Knox to Philip Stephens, 12 Apr. 1791, asking that instructions be given as soon as possible to prevent impressment of American seamen and to restore those already taken. (2) Copy of Stephens to Knox, 21 Apr. 1791, stating that directions had been sent by that post to Captain Drury of the *Squirrel* to discharge the impressed seamen provided he should have good reason to believe that they were "actually Natives of any of the provinces belonging to the United States"; and that the Lords of the Admiralty did not deem it necessary to give particular instructions to officers of the navy not to impress such persons as they were "already restrained from impressing *Foreigners*, and the natives of those provinces must be considered in that light." All enclosures are in DNA: RG 59, CD.

Knox did not see fit to inform TJ that a letter of recommendation to the Secretary of State on behalf of William Pearce had been solicited by Thomas Digges. But, like many others, he had some reservations about the self-appointed sponsor of Pearce and other English artisans whom he encouraged to emigrate to America – an activity which the laws of England and Ireland forbade. Knox had inquired of Joshua Johnson about the man and Johnson, who had known Digges and his family in Maryland, responded: "I am always unwilling to say any thing of a man, unless I could that which is pleasing: be cautious of *T. D.*" (Johnson to Knox, 18 Apr. 1791, DNA: RG 59, CD; MNP 167/1). For other comments about Digges and his letters of introduction to TJ and the President recommending Pearce, see note to Digges to TJ, 28 Apr. 1791.

Knox' assumption that American seamen would continue to be impressed if they were native-born Britons, no matter how long they had resided in the United States as citizens, was well-founded. The doctrine of an indefeasible allegiance which could be severed only by consent of the sovereign had been imbedded in the common law for centuries (see note on impressment of Hugh Purdie and others, 17 Dec. 1790). TJ was one of the first to challenge this doctrine and to endeavor to replace it with the right of voluntary expatriation "which nature has given to all men, of departing from the country in which chance, not choice, has placed them" (*Summary View*, 1774; see Vol. 1:121). This was a position which he never surrendered (see TJ to Gallatin, 26 June 1806).

To Tench Coxe

Apr. 20. 1791.

Th: Jefferson presents his compliments to Mr. Coxe and returns him the table of shipping with thanks for the opportunity of examining it. He sends for Mr. Coxe's examination one of the returns, which Th: J. has required half-yearly from our Consuls in foreign ports, and will thank Mr. Coxe for any hints for it's improvement either by insertions or omissions.

RC (CtY); addressed: "Mr. Coxe"; endorsed. Not recorded in SJL.

From Tench Coxe

[*Philadelphia*], *20 Apr. 1791.* He received TJ's note while at breakfast. He will take up consular returns this evening and note such ideas as worthy TJ's consideration. – He encloses abstract of licensed fishing vessels, including all returns on which reliance may be placed. Greater part of difference between present and last return apparently due to deficient customhouse returns. But it may be safely calculated total tonnage of fishing vessels is 32,000 and probably [3]2,500 as Rhode Island was not then in union and some small returns yet to be received.

He cannot refrain from expressing his "sensibility at the receipt of Mr. Jefferson's note of Sunday last, and wherever considerations of fitness and the public good may occasion the President . . . to deposit the trust, he will duly feel the weight of his obligations to Mr. Jefferson." – He has not lost sight of question of storage of grain in English ports, "but from the infrequency of speculations to that Island and the shyness of the English part of the Trade in Philadelphia he has not yet grounded himself in the facts."

RC (DLC); MS slightly torn and one figure that is missing has been supplied conjecturally; endorsed by TJ as received 20 Apr. 1791 and so recorded in SJL.

To Charles Thomson

DEAR SIR   Philadelphia Apr. 20. 1791.

Mr. Madison and myself have been in the constant purpose, as soon as the roads should get a little smooth, to ride out some morning and pay our respects to you: the late rains have disappointed us in that respect.

The Philosophical society have appointed a committee, of which you are named, to collect materials for forming the natural history of the Hessian fly, the best means of preventing or destroying it &c. This committee meets tomorrow. I therefore send the bearer express, in hopes you will find it convenient to come. The meeting shall be fixed to any hour that may suit your convenience, if you will be so good as to notify it to me by a line by return of the bearer. I shall hope also that you will do me the favor to take your dinner with me, to which I shall endeavor to join the other three members of the committee. The object of the meeting is to plan and distribute our operations. I hope Mrs. Thompson and yourself enjoy good health. It is fortunate for you that you are scarcely within striking distance, or, in my habit of daily riding I should be troublesome to you. You will always make me happy by calling on me when you come to town, and if it be at the hour of three or a little after, I can always offer you soup, and you will generally be solus cum solo. I am with great sincerity Dear Sir Your affectionate humble servt,

TH: JEFFERSON

RC (DLC: Charles Thomson Papers); addressed: "Charles Thomson esquire"; endorsed. PrC (DLC).

It was TJ himself who had proposed that the American Philosophical Society appoint a committee to study the Hessian fly. He was its chairman, and the other members were Dr. Benjamin S. Barton, Dr. James Hutchinson, Charles Thomson, and Dr. Caspar Wistar (APS, *Procs.*, XXII, pt. 3 [July 1885], 14, 15, 19). For a comment on the committee's study, see Editorial Note and group of documents concerning the northern journey of TJ and Madison, at 20 May 1791.

From Jeremiah Wadsworth

Hartford, 20 Apr. 1791. Enclosed paper is sent by desire of several merchants of Connecticut trading to Hispaniola. Capt. Johnson is a man of good character and his information may be relied on.

RC (DNA: RG 59, MLR); at foot of text: "Thomas Jefferson Esqr. Secretary of State"; addressed: "The Secretary of the United States Philadelphia"; endorsed by TJ as received 30 Apr. 1791 and so recorded in SJL. Enclosure: Affidavit by Samuel Johnston of Middletown, Conn., stating that on 1 Dec. 1790 in Port-au-Prince he placed in "the hands of Major Porter an American by birth, then an Established Merchant there, a Cargo, to sell on Commission"; that on evening of 24 Dec. 1790 Porter died and the next day "all the Books, papers, and Merchandize belonging to him were taken Possession of by the Droit d'aubain Officer, and after a few days . . . all the property found in his possession, as well his own as . . . other peoples, was indiscriminately sold at Vendue, excepting some horses which remained unsold belonging to Capt. Freeman of New London" and Johnston; that a considerable "quantity of Cotten belonging to a Gentleman of Curraçoa" in Porter's hands on commission was also sold; that some time after this gentleman appeared, sued for his cotton, "and the same Court which had denied the Americans their property, that remained unsold, altho apply'd for in the same way gave the whole Amount of the Cotten to its owner independent of an Average"; that his own cargo "sold, and unsold the greatest part of which was passed into Major Porters Books, amounted to Twenty seven thousand Livres west India Currancy"; that, though he detained his vessels for almost two months after Porter's death, he "was not able to get one Single Dollar from the Administrator"; and that Many other persons from different parts of the Continent suffered more or less by the Death of Major Porter in the same way" (MS in DNA: RG 59, MLR; not dated and not attested).

To Benjamin Franklin Bache

Apr. 22 1791.

Th. Jefferson presents his compliments to Mr. Bache and sends him three gazettes of Leyden. He will send him five others (coming to Feb. 22) as soon as he has read them. He congratulates Mr. Bache on an observation he has heard very generally made of the improvement of his paper within some time past. He still wishes some means could be found of making it a paper of general distribution, thro' the states. The advertisements, perfectly useless there, occupying one half of the paper, renders the transportation too embarrassing. Th: J. is not printer enough to know if they could be thrown into the last half sheet (say pages 3 and 4.) which might be torn off or omitted for distant customers. Mr. Bache will be so good as to excuse these officious hints, which proceed from a wish to serve him, and from a desire of seeing a purely republican vehicle of news established between the seat of government and all it's parts.

RC (Franklin Bache, West Chester, Pa., 1942); endorsed. Not recorded in SJL.

The issues of the *Gazette de Leide* which TJ enclosed were probably transmitted with Short's dispatch of 25 Feb. 1791, written from Amsterdam, which TJ had received only the day before the above was written. If so, this would explain why he had not finished reading five of the numbers.

From Tench Coxe

[*Philadelphia*], *23 Apr. 1791*. He encloses some remarks on the consular return, made with the greater freedom because TJ will consider before adopting them. He also sends an example of the variations in the form of a return. No aspect to the check in favor of the revenue, which might be introduced, appears in it. He has retained one of Maury's returns to consider the application of these documents to that purpose.

RC (DLC); endorsed by TJ as received 23 Apr. 1791 and so recorded in SJL.

The consular form on which Coxe based his remarks was evidently one submitted by Maury, but it has not been found. Although TJ was as ardent a statistician as Coxe and far more devoted to system, he did not adopt the suggestions here advanced for a uniform and systematic mode of consular reporting. None of his several circular letters to American consuls required such a form — or indeed any other in addition to the general instructions given in his consular circular of 26 Aug. 1790 (see TJ's circulars of 13 May 1791, 31 May 1792, 14 Nov. 1792, and 21 Mch. 1793). That no specific form was adopted during TJ's tenure as Secretary of State is indicated by the action of his successor, Edmund Randolph, who in his circular letter of instructions to consuls of 31 Dec. 1794 enclosed TJ's letter of 26 Aug. 1790 as evidence of what information was required, whatever the form.

ENCLOSURE

Remarks on the Consular return.

1.

The "denomination of Vessel" would be an useful, and not a difficult column. It ought of course to be filled with the word *Ship* or *Snow* or *Brig* or *Schooner* or *Sloop* as the fact may be.

2.

If the column mentioned under head 1 be introduced, that which is now entitled "*Ship's* Name" should be varied to *Vessels* name.

3.

Between the column for the "*Master's name*" and that headed "*whence*" another column might be introduced to shew "of what place" the vessel is. Captain Cutts's ship Betsey, for example, though from North Carolina and for Pennsylvania, is known to be of Biddeford in the District of Maine. Besides the advantage of minute information for occasional use (an object which merits unremitted attention) this column would shew where the private shipping of the United States is owned, and of course what ports and what states carry for the rest of the Union, and what ports or what States give employment to the carriers.

4.

The column "*whence*" though properly *headed*, might be more instructively filled, it is conceived, by the name of the *Port* from whence the vessel may have arrived than the name of the State. The commerce of particular parts of the same state is much more in the hands of foreigners, than that of others. Norfolk and Alexandria and Washington and Wilmington in North Carolina are mentioned as exemplifications.

5.

The column "whither bound" might also, it is conceived, be more instructively filled with the name of the port, than of the State of destination.

6.

The number of boys employed in navigation exhibits an interesting fact in the state of the Nursery for Seamen and in regard to the modes in which we obtain them: It is useful also constantly to occasion in the minds of Masters and owners of vessels the contemplation of boys or apprentices. For these reasons the propriety of another column for the "Number of boys" is suggested.

7.

A column for the number of guns might have it's use in the beginning of a war by shewing the state of preparation in which our vessels are which are caught abroad. It might possibly apprise us early of vessels fitting in foreign ports for privateers under our flag, or of our own vessels doing so. It would also shew us the precise condition, in the material particular of arms, of such of our ships as are long employed abroad. In peace or in all cases of unarmed vessels there will be no trouble in inserting a nought in the column, and very little in filling it with the number of guns in time of war.

8.

A column expressing "*of what Nation,*" if thought proper, might also be inserted after the column headed "*Exporters.*"
On these two columns (No. 7 and 8) it may be remarked, that it is not uninteresting or unimportant to know, who are our foreign factors and the shippers of our supplies, whether citizens of the United States sojourning abroad, or foreigners of the country from whence they are shipt, or foreigners not of that country, who are enabled to monopolize trade by dint of capital, and who may be the servants of privileged mercantile companies.

9.

It might be of use if the citizenship of the Consignee were mentioned in a column headed with the words "of what nation." This column, if thought safe and useful would come most properly before that for the "Cargo outward."

10.

The column for the "Cargo outward" admits of an easy and very useful variation. In the case of the Commerce, Capt. Dobel, for example, there are blended in the list of 6 trunks, 1 Chest, and 10 barrels, parcels of printed cottons, silks, wrought Iron, fustian, muslinets &c. To a country that desires to know accurately the nature and sources of it's supplies and wherein the laws have hitherto necessarily placed about two thirds of it's imports under non enumerated or ad valorem duties, it will be found very useful to mention the number and kinds of packages, that contain the several species of goods. If five trunks of printed cottons, one trunk of silks, one chest of muslinets and fustians, and ten barrels of wrought iron were really the true description of the goods, it would be well to have it so inserted in the account of them; and so far as it is practicable the propriety of doing it hereafter is submitted.

It might prevent mistakes in the Inspection of these returns if they should give their abbreviations in a way not to be mistaken. I think it would require mercantile knowledge to determine what Mr. Maury means by the mark over staves and boards. He certainly means hundreds and not thousands, because the vessels would not, in several instances, contain the goods enumerated, if they were thousands. The letters N. M. are intended it is supposed, for *naval measurement*, but it is uncertain, though very material.

A direction to include vessels in these returns, though not *from* or *destined* for American ports will be useful. It is probable however that this is already within the Consuls instructions.

A similar return of foreign vessels arriving from and departing for the United States would be useful, omitting such columns as are manifestly useless, or the contents of which might not be attainable.

The returns might be made, if thought proper, quarterly instead of half yearly. Frequent and recent information in the present situation of the Commercial affairs of the United States is desirable. A session of Congress may be lost, and certain conveyances free of expence are to be had from the North in October, which in January cannot be had on account of the ice.

MS (DLC); entirely in Coxe's hand; undated.

From Delamotte

Le Havre, 24 Apr. 1791. He is now grateful to captain of *Le Vendangeur* for asking such high freight for TJ's carriages that he did not let him have them. The papers today announce her loss at sea, though the crew were saved. He hopes *Henrietta* will be more fortunate. – The present goes by *Pennsylvania*, Captain Harding, departing tomorrow. Twelve days ago he informed Short of her departure, but he has neither received a packet of recent date for TJ nor heard of the arrival of the servant to be sent to TJ. Perhaps they will yet arrive in time. – England is arming to support the Turks against Russia, which may bring peace between them. But the nation is strongly indisposed toward Pitt for bringing on great expenditures twice in so brief a time. He has lost much of his popularity. – Delamotte has not yet concerned himself with establishment of agents in his vicinity but is now doing so. When done he will inform TJ, who may dispose the agents directly.

Consuls of the United States are more embarrassed than those of any other nation by distressed seamen. Wherever fate places them, they are farther from home and aid given them thus of more importance than for those of any other nation, being augmented also by infrequency of ships to convey them home. Their speech also confuses, and a rascal from Ireland will get the aid due an American, especially in France, where there are no English consuls and where they take the American consul for theirs: it costs them only a lie. Or indeed an American, being suspected and not able to make himself known, will not get relief. This confusion may become of such importance as to compromise the United States with other powers in cases such as crime or other serious matters when the consuls exercise their authority on individuals thought to be American who turn out to be English. The means to obviate this would be to let no seaman embark without a passport, to be signed by the one to whom issued, certifying him to be an American citizen.

[249]

29 [Apr.] Capt. Harding departs tomorrow. Short informs him that the servant will go by another vessel. — Mr. Cutting, while awaiting better employment, works with us. He has shown Delamotte TJ's letter, from which he learns of Miss Jefferson's marriage and he felicitates TJ. He has also read what TJ says about the consulate, followed by offers on Delamotte's part and refusal on his. He knows the conditions governing vice-consuls and he urges TJ to insist, if the consulate should be advantageous for him.

RC (DNA: RG 59, CD); in French; endorsed by TJ as received 8 July 1791 and so recorded in SJL.

To Mary Jefferson

Philadelphia Apr. 24. 1791.

I have received my dear Maria, your letter of Mar. 26. I find I have counted too much on you as a Botanical and zoological correspondent: for I undertook to affirm here that the fruit was not killed in Virginia, because I had a young daughter there who was in that kind of correspondence with me, and who I was sure would have mentioned it if it had been so. However I shall go on communicating to you whatever may contribute to a comparative estimate of the two climates, in hopes it will induce you to do the same to me. — Instead of waiting to send the two vails for your sister and yourself round with the other things, I inclose them with this letter. Observe that one of the strings is to be drawn tight round the root of the crown of the hat, and the vail then falling over the brim of the hat is drawn by the lower string as tight or loose as you please round the neck. When the vail is not chosen to be down, the lower string also is tied round the root of the crown so as to give it the appearance of a puffed bandage for the hat. I send also inclosed the green lining for the Calash. J. Eppes is arrived here. Present my affections to Mr. R. your sister & niece. Your's with tender love,

TH: JEFFERSON

April 5. Apricots in blossom.
         Cherry leafing.
       9: Peach in blossom.
         Apple leafing.
      11. Cherry in blossom.

PrC (ViU).

To George Washington

SIR   Philadelphia Apr. 24. 1791.

I had the honour of addressing you on the 17th. since which I have recieved yours of the 13th. I inclose you extracts from letters received from Mr. Short. In one of the 7th. of Feb. Mr. Short informs me that he has received a letter from Mr. de Montmorin, announcing to him that the King has named Ternant his minister here. – The questions on our tobacco and oil have taken unfavorable turns. The former will pay 50. livres the thousand weight less when carried in French than foreign bottoms. Oil is to pay twelve livres a kental, which amounts to a prohibition of the common oils, the only kind carried there. Tobacco will not feel the effect of these measures till time will be given to bring it to rights. They had only 20,000 hhds. in the kingdom in Novemb. last, and they consume 2000 hhds. a month; so that they must immediately come forward and make great purchases, and not having, as yet, vessels of their own to carry it, they must pay the extra duties on ours. I have been puzzled about the delays required by Mr. Barclay's affairs. He gives me reason to be tolerably assured, that he will go in the first vessel which shall sail after the last day of May. There is no vessel at present whose destination would suit. Believing that even with this, we shall get the business done sooner than thro' any other channel, I have thought it best not to change the plan. – The last Leyden gazettes give us what would have been the first object of the British arms had the rupture with Spain taken place. You know that Admiral Cornish had sailed on an unknown destination before the Convention was recieved in London. Immediately on it's reciept, they sent an express after him to Madeira, in hopes of finding him there. He was gone, and had so short a passage that in 23 days he had arrived in Barbadoes, the general rendezvous. All the troops of the islands were collecting there, and Genl. Matthews was on his way from Antigua to take command of the land operations, when he met with the packet-boat which carried the counter orders. Trinidad was the object of the expedition. Matthews returned to Antigua, and Cornish is arrived in England. This island, at the mouth of the Oronoko, is admirably situated for a lodgment from which all the country up that river, and all the Northern coast of South America, Spanish, French, Dutch, and Portuguese, may be suddenly assailed.

Colo. Pickering is now here, and will set out in two or three days to meet the Indians, as mentioned in my last. – The intimation to Colo. Beckwith has been given by Mr. Madison. He met it on very different ground from that on which he had placed it with Colo. Hamilton. He pretended ignorance and even disbelief of the fact: when told that it was out of doubt, he said he was positively sure the distribution of arms had been without the knowlege and against the orders of Ld. Dorchester, and of the government. He endeavored to induce a formal communication from me. When he found that could not be effected, he let Mr. Madison percieve that he thought however informal his character, he had not been sufficiently noticed: said he was in N. York before I came into office, and that tho' he had not been regularly[1] turned over to me, yet I knew his character. In fine he promised to write to Ld. Dorchester the general information we had recieved and our sense of it; and he saw that his former apologies to Colo. Hamilton had not been satisfactory to the government. – Nothing further from Moose island nor the posts on the Northern border of New-York, nor any thing of the last week from the Western country.

Arthur Campbell has been here. He is the enemy of P. Henry. He says the Yazoo bargain is like to drop with the consent of the purchasers. He explains it thus. They expected to pay for the lands in public paper at par, which they had bought at half a crown the pound. Since the rise in the value of the public paper, they have gained as much on that, as they would have done by investing it in the Yazoo lands: perhaps more, as it puts a large sum of specie at their command which they can turn to better account. They are therefore likely to acquiesce under the determination of the government of Georgia to consider the contract as forfeited by non-payment. – I direct this letter to be forwarded from Charleston to Cambden. The next will be from Petersburg to Taylor's ferry; and after that I shall direct to you at Mount Vernon. I have the honor to be with sentiments of the most affectionate respect and attachment Sir Your most obedient & most humble servt,   TH: JEFFERSON

RC (DNA: RG 59, MLR); endorsed by Lear. PrC (DLC). Enclosures: Although TJ had received eight letters from Short since Washington's departure (his public dispatches between 2 Dec. 1790 and 22 Feb. 1791), the three extracts enclosed in the above letter were all taken from that of 16 Jan. 1791 (see notes to that letter which identify the extracts). In his letter to Washington of 10 Apr. 1791 TJ enclosed one extract from Short's dispatch of 24 Jan. 1791 (see note 5 to that letter for identification of extract).

In a note to Tobias Lear dated "Sunday Apr. 24. 1791." TJ explained his plans for communicating with the President during his travels southward: "Th: Jefferson presents his compliments to Mr. Lear. On calculating the march of the President, (at 200 miles a week) he determines to direct this day's letter to Cambden, next Sunday's to Taylor's ferry, and this day fortnight's to Mount Vernon. They will all probably get a little ahead of him: but this is the best fault. Should he travel a little faster than is expected, so as to get before his letters, they will never overtake him, conveyances across the country are so rare" (RC in ViU; not recorded in SJL). Although TJ communicated more regularly and more fully with Washington than did any other member of the administration, having failed to send his regular weekly letter only three times while he himself was travelling, his carefully calculated plan for having his letters wait for Washington's arrival failed almost completely. Of the eleven letters TJ wrote during Washington's travels, only those of the 2d and 10th of April and the 15th of May were received by the President before he returned to Mount Vernon. This was partly due to the laxness of the postal service in the southern states and partly to Washington's departure from his scheduled route on his return. Immediately on arriving home Washington wrote Hamilton a long letter explaining the circumstances and informing him of his plans so that if any pressing public matters came up, his location at a given time would be known. The letter closed "with affectionate regard," and nothing in it implied that the failure of communication was attributable to anything other than the reasons given (Washington to Hamilton, 13 June 1791, Syrett, *Hamilton*, VIII, 470-1). By comparison, Washington's brief letter to TJ two days later was almost curt, closing with "Your most obedient Servant" (Washington to TJ, 15 June 1791). Before this time the President was well aware of the publication of TJ's letter to Jonathan B. Smith and its criticism of heretical doctrines that had sprung up, a fact which must have influenced the difference in tone of the two letters as it undoubtedly did the future relations between TJ and Washington (see Editorial Note and group of documents at 26 Apr. 1791).

[1] TJ first wrote "formally" and then changed it to read as above.

From J. P. P. Derieux

Charlottesville, 25 Apr. 1791. Has just received TJ's of 24 Mch. and is most grateful for what TJ has written to Fenwick. If his hopes are realized he will owe this to TJ alone. If not, he will have the certainty that nothing in the world henceforth could move this unrelenting kinsman from the proceedings of an unjust mother. Hence, whatever the outcome of TJ's kind effort in his behalf, he will always be grateful. He thanks TJ for the good news of France, the more so because it can be depended on as from him and not from the distorted news of the gazettes. The constitution, it seems, begins to have good effect and he rejoices with all the nation. – He sends TJ a letter for Mde. Bellanger which he hopes will be sent to Mr. Short as soon as possible, since it contains matters on which he awaits a reply with the greatest impatience. – The wheat harvest promises at present to be very fine. They have lately had some very favorable showers, and if it turns warm, the crop will be considerable. He has seen TJ's mountain some days ago and can assure him that "il m'a paru le le plus beau des Environs." He would have thought the great drought in the north would have augmented the price of wheat, but this was only gazette news. – Mde. de Rieux, very flattered by TJ's kind recollection, sends her respect and to this he joins his greatest gratitude.

RC (MHi); in French; endorsed by TJ as received 5 May 1791 and so recorded in SJL.

To William Short

My late letters to you have been of the 8th. 12th. 15th. and 19th. of March. Your's recieved and unacknoleged are as follow.

No.49. dated Dec.2. rec'd Apr.8.	No.55. dated Feb.7. rec'd Apr.23.
51. 30. 14	56. 18. 23.
52. Jan. 16. 20	57. 22. 23.
53. 24. 4.	58. 25. 21.
54. 28. 9.	

Those still missing are Nos. 31. 44.

I consider the Consular convention as securing clearly our right to appoint Consuls in the French colonies. The words 'etats du roi' unquestionably extend to all his dominions. If they had been merely synonimous with 'la France' why was the alteration made? When I proposed that alteration, I explained my reasons, and it cannot be supposed I would offer a change of language but for some matter of substance. Again in the translation it is 'dominions of France.' This translation was submitted to M. de Montmorin and M. de Reyneval, with a request that they would note any deviation in it from the original, or otherwise it would be considered as faithful. No part was objected to. M. de Reyneval says we must decide by the instrument itself, and not by the explanations which took place. It is a rule, where expressions are susceptible of two meanings, to recur to other explanations. Good faith is in favour of this recurrence. However, in the present case, the expression does not admit of two constructions; it is co-extensive with the dominions of the king. I insist on this only as a reservation of our right, and not with a view to exercise it if it shall be inconvenient or disagreeable to the government of France. Only two appointments have as yet been made (Mr. Skipwith at Martinique and Guadaloupe and Mr. Bourne in St. Domingue) and they shall be instructed not to ask a regular Exequatur. We certainly wish to press nothing on our friends which shall be inconvenient. I shall hope that M. de Montmorin will order such attentions to be shewn to those gentlemen as the patronage of commerce may call for, and may not be inconvenient to the government. These gentlemen are most pointedly instructed not to intermeddle, by word or deed, with political matters. – My letter of Aug. [2][1] 1790. to Mr. Carmichael was delivered to him by Colo. Humphreys. – The report you mention of the prospect of our captives at Algiers being liberated has not taken it's rise from any authoritative source. Unfortunately for us there have been so many persons, who (from friendly or charitable motives, or to recommend themselves) have busied themselves about this redemption, as to excite great expectations in the captors, and render our countrymen in fact irredeemable. We have not a single operation on foot for that purpose but what you know of. And the more all voluntary interpositions are discouraged, the better for our unhappy friends whom they are meant to serve.

You know how strongly we desire to pay off our whole debt to France, and that for this purpose we will use our credit as far as it will hold good. You know also what may be the probability of our being able to borrow the whole sum. Under these dispositions and prospects it would grieve us extremely to see our debt pass into the hands of speculators, and be subjected ourselves to the chicaneries and vexations of private avarice. We desire you therefore to dissuade the government as far as you can prudently from listening to any overtures of that kind, and as to the speculators themselves, whether native or foreign, to inform them without reserve that our government condemns their projects, and reserves to itself the right of paying no where but into the treasury of France, according to their contract.

I inclose you a copy of Mr. Grand's note to me, stating the conditions on which Drost would come, and also a letter from the Secretary of the treasury expressing his ideas as to those terms, with which I agree. We leave to your agency the engaging and sending Mr. Drost as soon as possible, and to your discretion to fix the terms, rendering the allowance for expences certain, which his first proposition leaves incertain. Subsistence here costs about one third of what it does in Paris, to a housekeeper. In a lodging house the highest price for a room and board is a dollar a day for the master and half that for the servant. These facts may enable you to settle the article of expences reasonably. If Mr. Drost understands assaying, I should much rather confide it to him, than to any other person who can be sent. It is the most confidential operation in the whole business of coining. We should expect him to instruct a native in it. I think too he should be obliged to continue longer than a year if it should be necessary for qualifying others to continue his operations. It is not important that he be here till November or December, but extremely desireable then. He may come as much sooner as he pleases.

We address to M. La Motte a small box for you containing a complete set of the journals of the antient Congress, the acts of the last session of the federal legislature, and a continuation of the newspapers. – I am with great & sincere esteem, Dear Sir your affectionate friend & humble servt, TH: JEFFERSON

RC (DLC: Short Papers); endorsed by Short as received 11 June 1791. PrC (DLC). FC (DNA: RG 59, DCI). Enclosures: (1) Hamilton to TJ, 14 Apr. 1791, returning the following. (2) Extract from Grand to TJ: "If Mr. Droz be called to America for the Purpose of establishing a Mint there, it will be proper to make him acquainted with the Matter of which it is expected the money is to be made, as well Gold and Silver as Copper, that he may if judged expedient, have all the necessary Instruments made in Paris. In this Case they must be paid for by the Minister of the United States, to whom he engages to establish in the City where he may be placed, a mint for the Coinage of such money as will be required, more economical in every respect, and more perfect than any hitherto known; those which he has made in England being superior even to the 6 pieces which Mr. Jefferson saw him coin. For this purpose he demands, to be paid to himself at Paris, or to his Heirs, the Sum of 1000 Louis, and to have all the Expenses of his Voyage, Support, &c. &c. with those of his Servant, defrayed, until his return to France. These are nearly the same Conditions on which he contracted with Mr. Bolton, which will determine in Sept. next, when he shall be at liberty again to engage. If the United States, to remove every ambiguity, should prefer the fixing a certain daily Sum for the Expenses of his Voyage, his remaining, and

Support in America, and those of his Servant also, it would be proper to fix it so as that he shall receive clear of every Expense the 1000 Louis which he demands, and this Sum must be augmented in proportion to the Time he may be detained beyond the year, which he presumes sufficient to complete the Establishment" (PrC in DLC; FC in DNA: RG 59, DCI).

The extract of the second enclosure is undated and it cannot be known with certainty from which of Grand's letters it was taken. It may indeed be a copy of the "projet de Convention" with Droz which Grand enclosed in his letter to TJ of 28 Aug. 1790 and which, for reasons there stated, he had drafted for Droz. If so, it must have been this enclosure (or some adaptation of it) which TJ forwarded to the Secretary of the Treasury the day after he received it, describing it as a "note from Mr. Droz" (TJ to Hamilton, 24 Nov. 1790). Grand wrote again on 2 Sep. 1790, but that letter, which TJ received on the 15th of December, has not been found. It does not seem likely that the extract was taken from it, since it was probably either a duplicate of that of the 28th or merely a confirmation of the terms of the "projet de Convention" with Droz.

[1] TJ left a blank in MS, and the date has been supplied.

From William Short

DEAR SIR   Paris April 25. 1791.

Our information from America is as when I last wrote to you, that is to say, no lower than your letter of the 23d. of January. I have been waiting with much impatience to receive further intelligence for the reasons which I have repeated in my several letters.

Since my last the national assembly have extended to their islands and all their foreign possessions the decree which abolished the *droit d'aubaine* in France, as you will see by the *No. 104.* of the Moniteur, which will be sent by the way of Havre. The decree is to have a retrospective effect as to the foreign possessions so as to take place from the time of its being passed for France, viz. Aug. 6. 1790.

No other alterations have been as yet made on the decrees concerning the commerce of the United States. With respect to the duty on oils there is a circumstance which it is proper to mention. You know the different stages through which this business has gone. I was in Holland when the reduction took place to 6. ₶ the quintal and this it was observed in the letters to me put them very nearly on the same footing as under the *arrêt du conseil*. On my observing that by it they were subjected only to the 7. ₶ 10 per barrel and 10 sous per livre and that the letter of M. de Calonne previous to the *arrêt*, abolished expressly the *droit de fabrication a l'egard des huiles de baleine et spermaceti*, it was answered that although the importer did not pay any other duties, the oils paid them internally, and that the registers of the farm which had been examined by the committee of commerce proved it: – and further that the letter of the minister was of no effect, the *arrêt du Conseil* having not confirmed expressly the abolition. – Since my arrival here I have brought together the *Rapporteur* of the committee, and Mr. Barrett. They were not able to satisfy each other by their arguments. They are both to produce their proofs at the next meeting. The *Rapporteur* says if he does not shew by extracts from the registers of the farm that the oils paid the duties agreeable to his note sent to M. Ramond (and which I forwarded to you in my *No. 62*.) he will propose to the assembly to reduce them to the former value, and that he is sure of succeeding. Of this however I have my doubts, as I think the assembly will be prevented by those interested in the national fisheries from consenting to a further reduction at present. Time will certainly effect it, and probably remove entirely the duties on the importation of this article. According to the price at which it sells at present the duty of 6. ₶ the quintal is about 20 per cent on its value.

Paris has been for eight days past and still is in a degree of fermentation of which there is no example, as well on account of the cause which gives rise to it as its duration. – You know that by a decree of the national assembly passed last year, such ecclesiastics as refused to take an oath there prescribed were to be displaced and successors immediately appointed. All the Bishops were of this class except three or four and a great number of inferior clergymen. Those who took the oath and supplanted the nonjurors are considered by the devout as schismatick. Of course those who are really devotees, though friendly to the revolution, and all those who are hostile to the revolution whether devotees or not, refuse making use of the churches occupied by the new priests. As the number of parishes in the capital was much reduced, and the supernumerary churches were about to be sold, a society was formed for purchasing one of them and installing in it priests *non jurors*. The administrators of the department considering that freedom in the exercise of religion was allowed rented a church to this society, until the formalities of the sale could be completed. – It was to have been opened eight days ago. The citizens of the section in which the church stands assembled the night before, and urged on by a curate who has taken the oath and a few factious people, decided that it was unconstitutional to open other *catholic* churches than those established by the law. They accordingly had the doors shut the next morning and refused admittance to those who had rented it. The Mayor accompanied by the garde nationale went to the church to obtain a free entry but were unable or unwilling to carry their object into execution. The mob remained assembled at the door during the whole day. No attempt was made to disperse them and no other violence used on their part.

The same day mass was said in the King's chapel by a priest nonjuror. Some of the guards had murmured and shewn dispositions to prevent his Majesty's passing to the chapel, but the Marquis de la Fayette being called, had one of the mutinous arrested and thus procured tranquillity for the moment. These circumstances being known in the different quarters and among the people of Paris excited much uneasiness. Their alarms were increased by the emissaries of those who wish for disorder. The King's refusing from conscientious motives to make use of priests who had subscribed to the laws which he himself had sanctioned, together with the marked predilections shewn in favor of the displaced Bishops, (all of whom are hostile to the revolution) were considered as in fact changing his principles with respect to the constitution and a determination to violate the oath he had taken to maintain it.

Those who reflected saw no contradiction in the King's conduct and had no doubt of the purity of his intentions. But the people of Paris do not reflect. It was known that he proposed going the next day to pass the holy week at St Cloud. Papers were printed and circulated declaring the King a traitor, saying that relays of horses were prepared on the road that he might make his escape &c. When he got into his carriage the people and garde nationale in ranks before the horses refused to let them go. The Marquis de la Fayette exerted himself in vain to procure a passage for the carriage – an universal defection had taken place among the garde nationale. The

Marquis was insulted and menaced by several who were in a state of phrenzy. They were convinced the King meant to make his escape and supposed him an accomplice. The King remained in this situation in his carriage for two hours, during which time he heard from the guards and people around his carriage the most abusive expressions as well against himself as the Queen. He at length determined to abandon the plan of his departure for that day.

The next morning he went to the assembly and addressed them – in the speech herewith inclosed. In it he persisted in his determination to go to St. Cloud, but as yet he has not renewed the attempt. The national assembly did not dare to censure the conduct of the people and the guards, the department of Paris and the municipality still less, but as it was impossible for the two last not to take some step they addressed the King to assure him that the present unhappy circumstances proceeded from the distrust occasioned by his being surrounded by persons known to be hostile to the constitution. No exertion was made to find out other causes. This conduct of the assembly and members of administration is considered cowardly and base and shews clearly that they are guided absolutely by the will of the Paris mob. – The persons most noted about the King's person have quitted their places either of their own accord or by his request.

The Marquis de la Fayette determined immediately on being disobeyed to resign. He employed two days in taking the proper arrangements for this purpose and then sent his commission to the municipality. Immediately on its being known a general consternation spread itself throughout Paris. Numbers were preparing to leave the city. Deputies from the several battalions went to his house to assure him of their attachment and confidence and their determination to obey no other chief. The municipality in a body went also to entreat his remaining at the head of the guard. In order to avoid these sollicitations he had left his house and did not return till midnight. He found there the municipality in their habits of ceremony and the battalions under arms who had determined not to leave his house without seeing him. He promised his answer for the next day, when he went to the hotel de ville and delivered the speech inclosed. From that time the alarms increased. The procession of battalions to his house was without interruption. The King's journey to St. Cloud and the opening of the churches rented to private societies, which were the first causes of these disturbances, seemed entirely forgotton. The great object was to induce the Marquis to re-assume the command. The battalions all assembled and subscribed a new oath of obedience to him and for the execution of the law. They resolved to expel such as had been refractory and particularly a grenadier who for his leading opposition to the King's departure had been crowned in several of the patriotic societies of Paris. After so much sollicitation, and so much apprehension of ill entertained by all in the case of his refusal, he determined two days ago to receive again his commission. This circumstance has excited general satisfaction, and so long as the zeal of the present moment lasts will enable him to command the guard without opposition. It is certain however that [it] cannot last always, and that he must submit in the end to the impulsions they receive.

During the crisis which was attributed by most people to the King's scruples of conscience and appearance of tergiversation, it was manifest that the general attachment to him was subsiding daily. The current of public opinion with respect to the King, and with respect to Royalty in general seemed to be taking a direction that threatened a new revolution, or at least indicated that the present would be carried still further. The obnoxious persons around the King being dismissed had not sufficed to check the progress. In the addresses to the King he had been asked also to notify to the foreign courts his adhesion to the new constitution. You will see them in the papers sent by the way of Havre. In this situation of things a circular letter written by M. de Montmorin to the King's ministers at foreign courts was communicated by him to the assembly. I send it herewith, and you will not be surprized that it should have excited there a degree of enthusiasm and joy of which there is no example. The most exaggerated demagogues were those who were most forward in the expression of their satisfaction and thanks. A deputation was immediately sent to the King to express these sentiments of the assembly, and it was with difficulty that the whole body could be prevented from going.

From that moment the public voice has taken a change, and the sentiments or expressions at least of loyalty and attachment to the King's person have succeeded to the most exaggerated ideas of democracy. The day after communicating the letter to the assembly the King accompanied by such of his courtiers as are known to be attached to the revolution went as usual to hear mass at his parish where it is celebrated by a curate who has taken the new oath; and thus every thing for the moment is restored to the position it was in fifteen days ago, except that experience has now proved that no opposition will be made either by the assembly, department, or municipality to any movement of the people or a part of the people of Paris.

I have thought it proper to give you these details thus minutely because they will certainly have much influence on the affairs of this country in future. One effect which is already visible is the desire it has given many of the members of the assembly to finish their session and quit a ground that they foresee now will not be always tenable. These do not yet make the majority as I believe, though many are of a different opinion. It is constantly repeated now by the popular members of the assembly that letters of convocation will be issued in the course of the next month and that the present assembly will cease on the 14th. of July.

Advices are just received from the French islands. They are as late as the 8th. of March and bring an account of the arrival of the fleet and troops sent there in February last. There still remained much disorder. The regiment which had been for some time at S. Domingo commanded by M. Mauduit Duplessis who served in America during the late war, had gone into a perfect state of revolt and massacred him whilst endeavouring to give them the explanations they exacted respecting his conduct last summer when he had made them act against some of the inhabitants. – This insubordination seems to have been produced by the troops lately sent there, who together with the sailors of the fleet, were in full insurrection. The commandant of the fleet and the officers desire to be recalled. Two members of the municipality have arrived in France, sent to give an account of the present disturbances prevailing in the island.

A few days before an account of these disorders was received here forty five of the members of the colonial assembly kept *à la suite de l'assemblée nationale*, had signed a retraction of their errors and their submission to the decrees of the assembly relative to S. Domingo. They sollicit leave to return there. Nothing has been yet decided on respecting them, but the manner in which their petition and retraction was received shews that the assembly is happy to have an opportunity of releasing them, and that it will be done without opposition.

Preparations for war and negotiations for peace in the north of Europe are going on with redoubled activity. Every day which passes without bringing peace renders war more probable. Denmark has thrown herself into a posture of mediation which I think the menacing powers will make use of. The principal basis is a modification of the status quo offered by Russia and rejected by the triple alliance.

The war is manifestly unpopular in England. Should the minister not be able to extricate himself from prosecuting it, he will probably present some object in the Mediterranean to the national cupidity so as to render it more to the taste of the people, that is to say the merchants of London.

The French Minister will leave this place for Philadelphia in the course of the next month. This letter goes by the English packet and will carry you assurances of the sentiments of attachment & respect with which I have the honor to be Dear Sir, your most obedient servant,   W: SHORT

PrC (DLC: Short Papers); at head of text: "*No. 64*"; badly faded, so that some words are illegible and have been supplied from Tr (DNA: RG 59, DD). Recorded in SJL as received 23 July 1791. Enclosure: Montmorin's circular to French diplomats, 29 Apr. 1791 (printed as enclosure in Otto to TJ, 22 July 1791; Document IV in group of documents at 26 Apr. 1791 on the Paine episode).

Appointments of Vice-Consuls for Portugal

Philadelphia, 26 Apr.-6 July 1791. Commissions by Ignatius Palyart, Consul General for Portugal, appointing the following Vice-Consuls: under date of 26 Apr. 1791, James Barry for Maryland and Virginia, John Abrams for New York State, Francis James Ver Cnocke for South Carolina; under date of 6 July 1791, Richard Codman for Massachusetts.

Trs (DNA: RG 59, CD); four commissions in clerk's hand, signed by Palyart; the date for that of Codman is inserted in the hand of Remsen. No letter transmitting these copies to TJ has been found. Palyart had been appointed consul general for Portugal (see Palyart to TJ, 5 Oct. 1790).

From Joseph Fenwick

Bordeaux, 26 Apr. 1791. Encloses list of vessels entered and cleared in last six months, together with copy of his last. Since then, duty on American fish oil reduced from 12 to 6 ₶ per quintal, its present rate, but expects this to be modified as experience and commercial interest require. Encloses list of duties prior to 1 Apr. and in force since the 15th.

RC (DNA: RG 59, CD); in clerk's hand, signed by Fenwick; endorsed as received 9 July 1791 and so recorded in SJL. Enclosures: (1) copy of Fenwick to TJ, 22 Mch. 1791; (2) lists of vessels and duties, not found.

From Moustier

MONSIEUR   à Berlin le 26. Avril 1791

Les moyens de correspondance sont si difficiles entre l'Europe et l'Amerique, que je commençois à desesperer d'obtenir même des preuves de l'arrivée de mes lettres dans votre continent, lorsque j'ai reçu la reponse dont vous m'avez honoré le 3. de Decembre dernier. Une lettre de M. le President du 1er. 9bre. m'est parvenue en même tems. Je suis bien aise d'apprendre que le derangement de santé qui vous avoit empeché de vous occuper est entierement passé. Je suis très touché des regrets que vous voulez bien m'exprimer sur une contrarieté que j'ai eprouvée bien vivement de mon coté, de ce que la fortune m'ait fait croiser avec vous, Monsieur, avec qui j'aurois eû tant de satisfaction à pouvoir passer beaucoup de momens que j'aurois trouvés à tous égards bien interessans. On a vû recemment tant de jeux de cette même fortune qu'il ne faut plus repondre de rien, ainsi je ne renonce pas pour toujours à l'espoir de vous revoir. Quoiqu'il arrive, je reponds au moins de la durée des sentimens d'estime et d'attachement que je vous ai voués. — Je suis bien convaincu de la sincerité des regrets que vous m'exprimés sur les delais de la conclusion de notre constitution. Mais ce qu'il y a de plus malheureux, c'est que de longtems nous n'aurons la constitution qui NOUS *convient*. Les difficultés qui se sont opposés à l'établissement d'une telle constitution n'étoient pas insurmontables, mais il falloit de la bonne foi, de la probité, des lumieres et de la vigueur reunies. Tout cela s'est trouvé epars; tandis que l'ambition, l'avarice, l'envie, l'orgueil, la haine, la fourberie, le fanatisme, la perseverance, la violence, la terreur, la fausse eloquence, l'audace se sont combinées. Votre opinion est la mienne depuis longtems. J'ai dit tout haut et à gens qui auroit pû en faire leur profit. Qu'on finisse et qu'on prenne une constitution quelconque *à l'essai*. Le plus mauvais gouvernement vaut toujours mieux que l'anarchie dans laquelle nous vivons depuis 18. mois. Il faut bien que notre nation se forme par sa propre experience, puisqu'elle ne veut pas profiter de celle des autres ni même de celles de nos pères. J'ai parlé à des Sourds lorsque j'ai voulu citer les Etats Unis. Nos energumenes regardent votre constitution avec dedain. Ils en sont encore à se parer de vos rebuts, ils se sont emparés des materiaux de votre premier édifice pour construire le leur. Quand chacun sera bien las de tous les tâtonnemens auxquels on s'abandonne avec une fureur aveugle, alors on commencera à douter, et le doute disposera à recevoir la verité à la place de l'erreur qui en a pris le masque.

—Nous n'avons jusqu'àpresent de la liberté que le mot, mais dans le fait c'est la licence et la tyrannie populaire qui regnent. En supposant la vraie liberté, c'est à dire celle qui garantit la sureté personelle, et les proprietés, placée dans un centre, je pense que, quoique nous en fussions eloignés autrefois, nous en sommes plus eloignés aujourdhui, parce que nous nous sommes portés davantage à l'extrême opposé. Au reste, je vous expose mon opinion, qui peut etre erronée, mais à coup sûr est de bonne foi, avec cette liberté qui appartient toujours à un homme de bien dans quelques circonstances qu'il se trouve. Je n'aimois pas le regime ancien, je n'aime pas l'actuel, j'en espere un meilleur à l'avenir. Mais, quoiqu'il en soit, dans quelque pays que ce soit, je ne troublerai pas les gouvernements.

Le peu de details que vous m'avez donnés sur votre pays m'interessent infiniment. J'avois toujours presumé que le Cens feroit reconnoître une population plus considerable dans les Etats Unis qu'on ne supposoit. Vos operations seront bonnes, ou du moins n'auront jamais de grands inconveniens, parcequ'elles seront murement reflechies et pesées d'avance. Vous n'avez pas une Assemblée unique, qui fait des loix comme on monte à l'assaut. Il faut d'autres moyens pour prendre une bastille que pour construire un vaste edifice bien ordonné. Je n'ai pas été heureux dans la seule tentative que j'aie faite pour influer sur la legislation Françoise. J'ai eû pour moi des Sages, sont-ils les plus forts? Non, lorsque la force consiste dans les bras. Nous avons sacrifié une belle branche de revenu et brisé un des liens qui nous attachoit aux Etats Unis. Il y a des maux qui ne se reparent pas. Votre nation est bien différente de la nôtre. Aussi faut-il cultiver le fruit de la liberté d'une autre maniere chez nous que chez vous; je crois même que pour en faire usage, il lui faut un apprêt sans lequel il seroit ainsi que beaucoup de plantes, nuisibles dans leur etat naturel, qui ne sont salutaires qu'après une certaine preparation. La pêche, qui est un poison dans un pays, est un fruit bienfaisant dans un autre. N'en seroit-il pas de même de la liberté? Est-elle la même chez un peuple nouveau et presque entierement agricole, ou chez un peuple ancien, commerçant, agioteur, et en grande partie *citadin*? On ne m'accusera pas de ne pas aimer ma patrie, ni de n'être pas un homme très humain. Cependant, je suis loin de penser et surtout de vouloir agir comme nos docteurs modernes. Le peuple François ne trouvera jamais en moi un flatteur, par la même raison que je ne l'ai jamais été de la puissance. Je pense enfin que le peuple doit etre bien gouverné, mais qu'il ne doit pas gouverner parcequ'il n'en est pas capable. Il doit donner son approbation aux loix, il doit même indiquer les objets sur lesquels il croit en avoir besoin, elles ne doivent pas avoir de force sans lui, mais il ne doit pas être legislateur. Quand la majorité pensera comme celà en France, je serai à ses ordres pour les postes perilleux et laborieux. Tant qu'Elle pensera autrement, je ne conniverai pas aux manoeuvres par lesquelles on la tourmente.

Je jouis ici de beaucoup de loisir et de tranquillité. On ne manque de matieres à meditations nulle part. – On est tout occupé de préparatifs de Guerre, depuis la Mediterrannée jusqu'à la mer Baltique, et les mers d'Allemagne et Britanniques. *Quidquid deliram reges pleatuntur achivi.*

J'ai été bien surpris que ma recompense au retour des Etats Unis, puisqu'on ne vouloit pas que j'y retournasse, ait été la mission de Berlin. Je ne l'ai assurement pas sollicitée. J'ai obei, j'y fais de mon mieux, je paye mon tribut de la maniere qu'on juge la plus convenable. Ma santé est assez bonne parcequ'heureusement l'hiver a été singulierement doux. Je n'ai pas été si heureux en Amerique et c'est la seule chose dont, tout compensé, j'aie lieu de me plaindre. Quand vous aurez des moments de loisir, pensez à moi et donnez m'en des preuves. Ce sera toujours avec un vif interêt que je recevrai de vos nouvelles et de celles de votre pays par vous, Monsieur, à qui j'ai voué un attachement et une estime inalterable.

F. DE MOUSTIER

Par notre nouveau protocole, nous avons suprimé le *J'ai l'honneur d'etre &c.* – Mes amitiés à Mr. Maddison.

RC (DLC); endorsed by TJ as received 16 July 1791 and so recorded in SJL.

From William Short

DEAR SIR   Paris April 26. 1791.

Petit is now here and intends going by the French packet which will sail from L'Orient the 15th. of next month. He insisted on 100. a month and seemed convinced from your letter that you would think it fully reasonable. Of course as far as the arrangement depends on me his wages are fixed at that rate. I had supposed from his letters written whilst I was in Holland that he would have been glad to have gone for less.

The commission with which you charged me in your letter of Jan 24. (the last which I have had the pleasure of recieving from you) is executed and I think will be fully to your satisfaction. I shall send you by Petit the part you desired as well as the details respecting it. I shall send you also your reveille. – Chanterot is making the clock. The price he asks is the same with that of the salle des ventes (15. guineas). Of course I thought it best to employ him. It will be done in three weeks and immediately sent to Havre. Houdon sent the dress some time ago.

I suppose you will have seen Paine's answer to Mr. Burke on the French revolution. It has made much noise in England and pleases a good deal here. What surprizes me most is that he was not prosecuted for it, as he remained in London some time after its publication and it was the opinion of able lawyers that it was libellous in many parts and treasonable in still more. It is much in Paine's style, that is to say incorrect – with strong expressions and bold ideas. Adieu. Yr. friend,   W: SHORT

RC (DLC); at head of text: *"Private"*; endorsed by TJ as received 23 July 1791 and so recorded in SJL. PrC (DLC: Short Papers).

There is irony in the fact that Short's critical comment on Paine's *Rights of Man* was written on the very day that TJ penned his famous note to Jonathan B. Smith commending it in terms which brought acute embarrassment to him (see note, TJ to Smith, following). Separated from TJ and looking upon the revolutionary scenes from a different geographical and philosophical perspective, Short at this time exhibited an increasing departure from the views of his mentor concerning the direction in which the revolutionists were moving. His comments on the revolution to his friend William Nelson were not only perceptive but also more frank than he had been in his letters to TJ: "As far as I may judge from some newspapers which I have seen printed at N. York, and from a few letters which I have recieved it is much less approved there than they suppose in France, for they really consider themselves as either treading in our footsteps or soaring beyond us. The truth seems to me to be that this revolution like all others has changed with time its original aim which was good, justifiable and praiseworthy, viz to limit the Royal prerogative, check the monstrous and insupportable privileges of the clergy, nobility, *gens de finance* and the Parliaments, and to take measures for preventing such abuses in future by establishing a perma-

nent form of government. The people were willing in the beginning to have purchased this by paying all the immense debt previously contracted: – The court was imprudent enough to leave some matters of form unsettled, and one which was essential, the mode of deliberation among the several orders. To settle this begot ill blood amongst them. These skirmishes gave the commons an opportunity of trying their own strength, of feeling the weakness of the two other orders arising from their being haled by the people, of seeing the wavering timidity of the court. Their pretensions rose every day and for a long time were just because it was only asking for the restoration of a greater number of those rights which nature gave them and which no government has a right to take away. The court seeing this progress and fearing it would have no bounds determined imprudently to put every thing on one stake. They placed guards at the door of the assembly to keep out the members. These assembled in another place and bound themselves by oath not to separate until they had given a constitution to their country. This was what was desired by 23/24 of the kingdom. Mr. Necker's disgrace and banishment was the signal which brought these unequal parties into conflict. You know the principal events which followed. As men and particularly large bodies of men become corrupted by power and love to domineer, the national assembly has by degrees lost sight of their original object and instead of considering themselves merely as the passive channels through which the organization of government was to pass, instead of a body intended merely to delegate the powers of government, they have found it more agreeable to exercise those powers themselves. And of course for eighteen months past they have concerted in their body all those of an executive, judiciary, administrative and legislative nature. Accustomed to be thus more powerful and more despotic than any individual could be because they suppose themselves immediately authorized by the national will, they can have no desire to descend from such an eminence, which ambition and avarice both conspire to render agreeable to them. No time is fixed for their duration no limits to their powers, and yet the French consider themselves as perfectly free under such a government. There is no act of injustice and tyranny that they have not committed, no contradiction of the first principles of free government into which they have not fallen, and still as they consult popularity, endeavour to please the *canaille* of Paris, and bear their rod of iron on the smaller number only, they are supported by the greater.

. . . This is a black but as it appears to me a true picture of the present situation of France. Still I entertain firm hopes that definitively a free government will be established there one way or another. It may cost much blood perhaps, but it seems to me the principles of liberty are so generally diffused at present, that whenever a whole nation can be consulted fairly and quietly on the kind of government they chuse to live under they will adopt one which though more or less perfect in the beginning, will still have freedom for its basis, and the means of perfectibility. It is true the immense population of France, the great number of poor who have nothing to fear from disorder, their large army and their geographical position, are all principles which may vary the combinations on this subject, yet I think there are others which counterbalance them and which enable me to predict without pretending to the gift of prophecy, that France will acquire by this revolution the freest government in Europe" (Short to William Nelson, 21 Feb. 1791; RC in NjP).

Rights of Man
The "Contest of Burke and Paine
. . . in America"

EDITORIAL NOTE

> The way to make friends quarrel is to pit them in
> disputation under the public eye.
> — *Thomas Jefferson to George Washington,*
> *16 Apr. 1784*

> [Jefferson's] talents and Information I know very well
> and have Ever believed in His honor, Integrity, his Love
> of his Country, and His friends. I may Say to you that
> his Patronage of Paine and Freneau and his Entangle-
> ments with Characters and Politiks which have been
> Pernicious are and have long been a Source of Inquietude
> and anxiety to me.   — *John Adams to Tristram Dalton,*
> *19 Jan. 1797*

What James Monroe called "the contest of Burke and Paine, as reviv'd in America," bore a distinctly different character from its European counterpart.[1] Burke's *Reflections on the Revolution in France* and Paine's *Rights of Man*, two of the most notable political tracts in the English language, set forth in memorable terms their authors' commitment to diametrically opposed views of man and society.[2] In England the heroic contest between these two eloquent spokes-

[1] Monroe to TJ, 25 July 1791 (Document IX).

[2] The most thorough discussion of the controversy in England over Burke's *Reflections* and Paine's *Rights of Man* is R. R. Fennessy's *Burke, Paine, and the Rights of Man* (The Hague, 1963). Fennessy concedes that *Rights of Man* did not bring about a revolt of the workers, but contends that it did play a part in the "political transformation of the modern world" (p. 246, 247, 250). No comparable study of the public response in America to

men was heralded when Burke announced his stand even before his *Reflections* provoked Paine's scathing reply. Consistent with his inborn distrust of the people and his belief in a hierarchical ordering of society, he declared early in 1790 that the French had proved themselves the ablest architects of ruin that ever existed and that "an irrational, unprincipled . . . ferocious bloody and tyrannical democracy" had carried all before them.[3] When his *Reflections* appeared a few months later and sold thousands of copies in England, France, Italy, and Germany, defenders of hereditary monarchy hailed its author as the champion of their cause. In the nature of things, with revolutionary flames sweeping through Europe and exciting the masses, Paine's audience vastly outnumbered Burke's, as shown by the numbers of editions and sales of copies.

But the effect of the European contest could not be gauged by the convictions, the enthusiasms, or the numbers of their respective audiences. In France, it was to be expected that such ardent supporters of the revolution as Jefferson's friends the abbés Arnoux and Chalut would embrace Paine's *Rights of Man* as a defense of the humane principles of 1776 and 1789, hoping it would do for the British people what *Common Sense* had done for America. So, too, with another friend, the Chevalier de Pio, who declared that he had burned all of his books save those by Locke, Sidney, Rousseau, and Paine – though he, like all diplomats, retained his Machiavelli.[4] In England, it was to be expected that George III and Pitt would look upon Burke with grateful eyes, that a flood of pamphlets attacking him or praising Paine would issue from the presses, and that the workingmen's clubs would welcome *Rights of Man* as their political testament. So also could it have been expected that Fox would approve and Liverpool deprecate Paine's echo of the Jeffersonian doctrine that the earth belongs in usufruct to the living: "Every age and generation must be as free to act for itself, *in all cases*, as the ages and generations which preceded it. . . . Man has no property in man; neither has any generation a property in the generations which are to follow."[5]

On the European scene there were indeed few discernible or lasting consequences of this battle of the titans. Products rather than provokers of an age of revolution, Burke's *Reflections* and Paine's *Rights of Man* epitomized its agony and its opposed philosophies but did little if anything to alter the course of events. Their contribution was to express in unforgettable terms what already stood fixed in the minds of their adherents, confirming them in their beliefs and providing them with powerful weapons of propaganda. In England, with

the two classic works of Burke and Paine has yet been made. David F. Hawke's *Paine* (New York, 1974) is a very useful and perceptive biography of a man who failed in almost everything except as one of the greatest of political propagandists.

[3] Speech in the House of Commons, 9 Feb. 1790, an extract of which TJ caused to be printed in Fenno's *Gazette of the United States*, 1 May 1790 (see Vol. 16: 260-2). Burke's *Reflections* was published in Nov. 1790. On TJ's report to Paine on events in France, the framing of the Declaration of the Rights of Man, and the possible effect of his letter in strengthening Burke's convictions about the revolution in France, see TJ to Paine, 11 July 1789.

[4] Arnoux and Chalut to TJ, 20 May 1791; De Pio to TJ, 22 July 1791.

[5] On TJ's doctrine that the earth belongs to the living, see TJ to Madison, 6 Sep. 1789. Fennessy, *Burke, Paine, and the Rights of Man*, p. 263-6, presents a convenient listing of the many contemporary tracts and pamphlets on Burke's *Reflections* and Paine's *Rights of Man*. For a graphic representation of the varying reactions of George III, Pitt, Fox, and others to *Rights of Man*, see illustration of a popular cartoon in this volume.

even the workingmen's clubs choosing the path of peaceful reformation, the most noticeable effect was the wave of prosecution of authors and publishers of writings thought to be subversive. When *Rights of Man* was first published in March 1791, with five other editions appearing in the next two months, the government seriously considered indicting Paine but refrained from doing so. When the second part appeared early in 1792, a royal proclamation was issued calling upon magistrates to search out and report upon authors and printers of seditious writings. The decree embraced all dissidents — Joseph Priestley, Horne Tooke, and others — but Pitt admitted it was aimed at Paine because his writings "struck at hereditary nobility . . . the destruction of monarchy and religion, and the total subversion of the established form of government."[6] Late in May Paine was indicted for seditious libel. When his trial was postponed, he fled to France and in December was tried *in absentia* as a "wicked, malicious, seditious, and ill-disposed person."[7] He was convicted of treasonable and seditious libel, declared to be an outlaw, and *Rights of Man* was suppressed. The persecutions against authors and publishers were severe, some being convicted and jailed. But the wave of hysteria aroused by the threat of subversive dangers soon began to subside. The contest of Burke and Paine in Europe was like another brilliant burst of flame added to the general conflagration already raging.

In America, where monarchy had been rejected, where the workingmen labored on farms rather than in factories, and where the press was free, Burke's *Reflections* and Paine's *Rights of Man* would certainly have aroused interest but would scarcely have provoked a national controversy in a time of peace and relative stability. Many of course would have taken their stand with Burke. But surely the majority of the American people, once so passionately aroused by *Common Sense* and still remembering its epochal effect, would have felt otherwise. Instead of becoming participants in an expanding European contest between an opponent of revolution and one who had contributed so dramatically to the winning of their own, Americans generally might have done no more than welcome Paine's *Rights of Man* as another confirmation of their belief that they had opened a new era in human annals.

But one of those trivial accidents of history, big with unexpected consequences, decreed otherwise. What followed on this side of the Atlantic was not an echo of the European debate but a quite different kind of contest which aroused political passions all the more because it raised fundamental questions about the fate of the new experiment in self-government. Here the issue reached what Jefferson called "the holy cause of freedom," a concept whose religious overtones suggest the dangers of those heresies and schisms against which he had warned even before entering office.[8] Now, within a few days after Paine's *Rights of Man* arrived in the capital, Jefferson became the unexpected and extremely embarrassed surrogate for Paine. John Adams found himself silently occupying the role of Burke, with John Quincy Adams as *Publicola* defending him and attacking Jefferson. The American version of the contest of Burke and Paine had personal and political consequences that were important and enduring.

[6] Pitt's reply to a question by Fox on 25 May 1792 (*Parliamentary History*, XXIX, 1513).

[7] T. B. and T. J. Howell, *State Trials*, XXII (London, 1817), 358; see also, Fennessy, *Burke, Paine, and the Rights of Man*, p. 242-4; David F. Hawke, *Paine*, p. 250, 253-4.

[8] See Editorial Note and TJ's response to the citizens of Albemarle, 12 Feb. 1790.

The first printing of *Rights of Man* appeared in London on 22 February 1791, a date which prompted Paine to tip the dedication to the President into the first bound copies. That issue was recalled by the publisher within a few hours, but not until more than a hundred copies had been sold. Another publisher took over the sheets and brought out the first edition on the 16th of March. About four weeks later the first copies arrived in Philadelphia. One of these — Jefferson erroneously assumed it was the only one in the city — came into the hands of John Beckley, who lent it to James Madison. Being on the point of departing for New York, Madison passed it on to Jefferson with the request that it be returned to Beckley "within the day." But Jefferson, having a mass of private and public business to attend to before he and Madison left on their northern journey, had not finished reading it when Beckley called for it. Beckley must already have initiated arrangements for publication, but he allowed Jefferson to retain the copy and, perhaps that day or the next, wrote a note instructing him to forward it to the printer when he had done with it.[9] Jefferson promptly complied by sending it to the person whom Beckley had named. Urgency seemed to have marked every step taken since Beckley came into possession of the pamphlet. Unhappily for Jefferson, his own hasty compliance with Beckley's request brought on one of the most embarrassing incidents of his life.

The note that Jefferson dashed off was addressed to Jonathan Bayard Smith, whom he mistakenly assumed to be the brother of the man destined to bring out the first American edition of *Rights of Man*, Samuel Harrison Smith.[10] Jefferson later explained to Washington that he was "an utter stranger to J. B. Smith, both by sight and character."[11] There is no reason to doubt the statement, but it is remarkable that he did not know the man to whom his note was addressed. Smith was a prominent Philadelphia merchant. He had been a zealous supporter of the Revolution from the beginning and was active in civic and political affairs. He was a man of varied cultural interests, being a trustee of the University of Pennsylvania and of the College of New Jersey, of which he was a graduate. Both he and Jefferson were active members of the American Philosophical Society. The minutes of the Society are not clear as to whether both were present at the smaller meetings where they could scarcely have avoided becoming acquainted. But certainly both had been present a few weeks earlier at the large gathering of members who assembled in the Hall and marched to the German Lutheran Church for the memorial tribute to Franklin.[12] Under these circumstances Jefferson's certainty that he was ad-

[9] Beckley's note has not been found and is not recorded in SJL. It was enclosed in TJ to Smith, 26 Apr. 1791 (Document I), along with the copy of *Rights of Man*.

[10] Samuel Harrison Smith (1772-1845) was the only son of Jonathan Bayard Smith (1742-1812) and Susannah Bayard of Maryland, whose husband adopted her patronymic as his own middle name, doubtless to avoid confusion with another Philadelphian, a Quaker, named Jonathan Smith. TJ's error in mistaking the son for the brother has been perpetuated by almost all who have written about the episode. On the correct relationship, see sketch of Jonathan Bayard Smith in DAB; *Index* to PMHB on the two Jonathan Smiths; and J.G.B. Bulloch, *A history and genealogy of the families of Bayard, Houstoun of Georgia, and the descent of the Bolton Family* (Washington, 1919).

[11] TJ to Washington, 8 May 1791 (Document II).

[12] See Editorial Note and group of documents at 26 Jan. 1791; Am. Phil. Soc., *Procs.*, XXII (July 1885), 191-2.

dressing a stranger is surprising, though perhaps his assurance arose from the nature of Beckley's directions or from his own undeniable haste. But that he wrote under the conviction that he was addressing a stranger is confirmed by his error in presuming Jonathan Bayard Smith to be the brother instead of the father of the printer.

Samuel Harrison Smith was then nineteen years of age, four years out of college, and just about to begin his distinguished career as a publisher. It is not known whether he had his own printery at this time, but it seems most likely that the first American edition of *Rights of Man* was printed in the shop of Benjamin Franklin Bache, John Beckley's close friend and political ally. On the 29th of April Bache's *General Advertiser* carried this announcement:[13]

> In the Press, and speedily will be published by *Samuel Harrison Smith*, and sold by all Booksellers in the City, *Rights of Man*, Being an answer to Mr. Burke's attack on the French Revolution: By Thomas Paine author of Common Sense.

The work was indeed speedily issued. Smith's advertisement had appeared on Friday. The following Tuesday, the 3rd of May, the *General Advertiser* announced that *Rights of Man* was that day published. Exactly one week had elapsed since Jefferson transmitted Beckley's copy of the pamphlet to the father of the publisher.

Thus by Wednesday or Thursday at the latest, we may assume, Jefferson had received the three or four copies he had ordered. On opening the pamphlet, he was "thunderstruck," as he later described his feelings to John Adams, to read the publisher's preface. This unauthorized statement preceded even Paine's dedication to Washington:

> The following Extract from a note accompanying a copy of this Pamphlet for republication, is so respectable a testimony of its value, that the Printer hopes the distinguished writer will excuse its present appearance. It proceeds from a character equally eminent in the councils of America, and conversant in the affairs of France, from a long and recent residence at the Court of Versailles in the Diplomatic department; and, at the same time that it does justice to the writings of Mr. Paine, it reflects honor on the source from which it flows, by directing the mind to a contemplation of that Republican firmness and Democratic simplicity which endear their possessor to every friend of the 'Rights of Man.'

Then, with the opening sentence of Jefferson's note to Jonathan B. Smith omitted, there followed a direct quotation from the Secretary of State expressing extreme pleasure that with the republication of *Rights of Man* something at

[13] Presumably on the basis of rumor, the announcement declared it to be a sufficient recommendation of the celebrated pamphlet that its strictures on the English constitution had caused its author to be persecuted and his work suppressed (*General Advertiser*, 29 Apr. 1791). The advertisement was repeated in the issues of 3, 6, 8, 10, 12, and 14 May. Simultaneously, Andrew Brown announced in his *Federal Gazette* that he had been favored with a copy of Paine's pamphlet and promised to print it in full. He added that "in an eminent degree it deserves the attention and applause of all friends of freedom." The first installment, preceded by the dedication to Washington, appeared in the *Federal Gazette* on 30 Apr. 1791. Subsequent numbers followed on 2, 3, 4, 5, 6, 7, 9, and 10 May. Brown probably obtained his copy of *Rights of Man* from someone other than Beckley.

last would be said publicly against the "political heresies" that had sprung up in the United States.[14]

In identifying the Secretary of State as the one who had transmitted "a copy of this Pamphlet for republication" and in omitting the explanation that this had been done at Beckley's desire, Smith permitted his readers the plausible inference that it was Jefferson who had sponsored publication of the pamphlet.[15] The inference, perhaps born of youthful enthusiasm and inexperience, was no doubt unintended and certainly unwarranted, but it is not likely that any of Jefferson's opponents in or out of government failed to embrace it. Also, Smith's expressed hope that the Secretary of State would excuse the printing of the extract amounted in fact to a public admission that he had not sought or received permission to quote it. On this point, too, it is unlikely that contemporary readers made any allowance for Smith's disregard of the proprieties. Indeed, subsequent commentators on the episode, in varying terms, have described Jefferson's note to Smith as an indiscretion of the first magnitude for so experienced a politician.[16] But under the circumstances it was quite natural for Jefferson to express pleasure at the republication of a work which he felt would counter principles and measures he deemed hostile to republican government. He had never made any effort to conceal his fears about the tendency of federal measures — even at times, so Hamilton declared, expressing himself without due regard for delicacy.[17] There can be no doubt that Jefferson was extremely mortified to be brought onto the public stage where, as he told Washington, "to remain, to advance or to retire, will be equally against my love of silence and quiet, and my abhorrence of dispute."[18]

But while he genuinely abhorred public controversy, Jefferson's expression of his political convictions even to a stranger was characteristic. The indiscretion — or, more precisely, the impropriety — was that of the publisher.[19] Upon

[14] TJ to Jonathan Bayard Smith, 26 Apr. 1791 (Document I). The full title of the first American printing, designated on the title-page as the "Second Edition," reads: *Rights of Man: being an answer to Mr. Burke's attack on the French Revolution, by Thomas Paine, Secretary for Foreign Affairs to Congress in the American War and author of the work intitled Common Sense. Philadelphia: Re-printed by Samuel Harrison Smith. M.DCC.XCI.* While TJ ordered three or four copies of this edition, none owned by him is known to exist. See Sowerby, No. 2826.

[15] In its issue of 14 May 1791 Fenno's *Gazette of the United States* drew the inference explicitly by announcing that "The Secretary of State furnished the copy of Mr. Paine's Pamphlet, from which the second edition was published in this city." The paper then quoted, without comment, the "note to the printer" from the Secretary of State. Presumably because he feared the inference would be generally accepted, TJ categorically denied its validity (TJ to Randolph, 3 July 1791; Document V).

[16] See, for example, [E. M. Sowerby], *Library of Congress Qu. Jour.*, VIII (Nov. 1950), 83, 84; Edmund and Dorothy S. Berkeley, *John Beckley* (Philadelphia, 1973), p. 58.

[17] Hamilton to Edward Carrington, 26 May 1792 (Syrett, *Hamilton*, XI, 429).

[18] TJ to Washington, 8 May 1791 (Document II).

[19] In his explanation to Washington, TJ himself properly placed responsibility upon Smith: he said that he had been brought into the public dispute by "the indiscretion of a printer" (TJ to Washington, 8 May 1791; Document II). There is no evidence that TJ ever reproved Smith, directly or indirectly, for his unauthorized use of the note to his father. Indeed, when the second Philadelphia edition appeared later in the year, based on the fourth London edition, Smith made no change at all in his prefatory statement or in the extract of TJ's note as published in the first edition. By the end of the decade, TJ had become a friend, admirer, and patron of the young publisher. It was on his

young Smith, who admired Jefferson and sought only to pay tribute to his "Republican firmness and Democratic simplicity," must be placed responsibility for bringing on the American contest of Burke and Paine with its dramatic intensification of existing political cleavages. The unintended effect was all the greater because the publisher nowhere referred to Jefferson by name. The note of which he printed an extract, Smith stated with obvious pride, was that of the Secretary of State. He thus gave to Jefferson's private communication almost the status of an official commendation of Paine's *Rights of Man*, transforming a personal opinion into a pronouncement *ex cathedra* – so it was interpreted by *Publicola* and many other of Jefferson's opponents – that those cherishing different principles of government were guilty of heresy. This was Smith's ultimate impropriety.

II

Thus introduced, Paine's *Rights of Man* fell like a thunderclap on the quiet capital. The expressions of the Secretary of State more than the pamphlet itself, we may be sure, took precedence in the political gossip of the boardinghouses, the taverns, and the Philadelphia dinner tables. The first to make their resentment manifest were those whom Jefferson described in his letter to Washington as "some Anglomen" who thought his sanction of Paine's anti-monarchical ideas would give offense to the British government.[20] The President, he had good reason to know, could not fail to identify the principals among those to whom he alluded – Adams, Jay, Hamilton, Knox, and many of the Cincinnati.[21] To the Secretary of the Treasury and his supporters in Congress, already concerned about Jefferson's apparently growing influence with Washington, his aspersions on heretics were compounded by another vexing question. Had the President himself sanctioned Paine's dedication and thus lent his official patronage to the work? Even if Washington had been in the capital, the question could scarcely have been put directly to him.

But the British agent, George Beckwith, whether acting on his own initiative or being prompted by his American advisers, sought the answer from the President's secretary, Tobias Lear. This occurred at Martha Washington's soiree on Friday the 6th of May, three days after *Rights of Man* appeared in the bookshops. The feelings that had been aroused are clearly reflected in the verbatim account Lear gave to the President of his conversation with the British agent. He said it might furnish Washington with a moment's amusement:[22]

> B[eckwith]. Have you seen Mr. Paine's pamphlet in answer to Mr. Burke?
> L[ear]. I have not yet been favored with a perusal of the work; but have read some extracts from it which have been published in the papers.

urging that Smith moved to Washington and founded the *National Intelligencer*, the only one of TJ's several efforts to found a truly national journal of information and discussion which met his hopes. On his side, Smith did not hesitate to pronounce TJ in print – not once but several times – as the greatest of Americans.

[20] TJ to Washington, 8 May 1791 (Document II).

[21] In his private letter to Short, 28 July 1791, TJ identified these as the sect who favored government by king, lords, and commons. The general meeting of members of the Cincinnati was being held in Philadelphia at the time Paine's pamphlet appeared.

[22] Lear to Washington, 8 May 1791 (DLC: Washington Papers). Lear said that he repeated the conversation in the same words as nearly as he could recollect. He enclosed a copy of Smith's edition of *Rights of Man* in this letter.

EDITORIAL NOTE

B. I observe Mr. Paine has dedicated it to the President.

L. So I understand.

B. I am very much surprized at it; for it is always thought that the person to whom a book is dedicated approves the sentiments therein contained, as well as their tendency, and I should hope that *everything* in that Book did not meet the President's approbation.

L. Why?

B. Because there are many things in it which reflect highly on the British Government and Administration, and as it is dedicated to the President, it may lead to a conclusion that he approves of those things, and that the Author has his sanction for publishing them. Had Mr. Paine dedicated this pamphlet to General Washington, it would then have been considered as addressed to him in his personal capacity, and would not have excited the same ideas that are produced by its being dedicated to *the President of the United States*; for I believe it will appear somewhat singular, that a Citizen of the United States should write and publish a book in a foreign Country, containing many things highly disrespectful to the Government and Administration of the Country where he writes, and dedicate that book to the Chief magistrate of his own Country. It will naturally appear to the world that, from the dedication, it meets the approbation of the Chief Magistrate of the Country whereof the writer is a citizen, and I therefore conceive that Mr. Paine has not, in this instance, treated the President with that delicacy which he ought.

L. As I have not read Mr. Paine's book I can say nothing with respect to the sentiments or tendency of it relative to the Government and Administration of Great Britain. But it is well known that the President could not have seen it, or have had any knowledge of its contents before it was published, it would therefore be absurd to suppose, *merely from the circumstance of its being dedicated to him*, that he approves of every sentiment contained in it. Upon this ground, a book containing the most wicked or absurd things might be published and dedicated to the President without his knowledge, and this dedication would be considered as his having given his sanction to them. Or, a book might be written under the circumstances which you have observed that Mr. Paine's is, and contain many unjust and unjustifiable strictures upon the government and governors of the Country where the writer resides, and a dedication of it to the Chief Magistrate of his own Country would, according to your idea, cause such chief Magistrate to be considered as the patron of its author and the abettor of its sentiments. – If Mr. Paine has, in this instance, not acted with that delicacy and propriety which he ought, he must answer for it himself to those who are authorized to call him to an Account.

B. True! But, I observe, in the American Edition, that the *Secretary of State* has given a most unequivocal sanction to the book, as Secretary of State. It is not said as Mr. Jefferson.

L. I have not seen the American, nor any other edition of this pamphlet. But I will venture to say that the Secretary of State has not done a thing which he would not justify.

B. On this subject you will consider that I have only spoken as an individual and as a private person.

L. I do not know you, Sir, in any other Character.

B. I was apprehensive that you might conceive that, on this occasion, I meant to enter the lists, in more than a private Character.

At that moment some members of the Cincinnati entered the room "in form" to pay their respects to Mrs. Washington and the conversation ended.

But this was only a prelude to what Lear was able to report about the events of the next day. On Saturday the 7th Edmund Randolph and his wife dined informally with Mrs. Washington. After dinner Lear repeated to the Attorney General the substance of his conversation with Beckwith. Just as he concluded, someone called at the door for Randolph, who accompanied the caller to Mrs. Trist's boardinghouse. Some members of the Virginia delegation, including Madison, resided at her establishment. So did Colonel Beckwith. The circumstances suggest that Randolph may have been called away from the small gathering at Mrs. Washington's because of concerns aroused by Jefferson's commendation of *Rights of Man*. At any rate, while Randolph was at Mrs. Trist's, Beckwith came in and raised with him the same questions he had put to Lear. He must have done so in more explicit terms, for Randolph went at once to inform Jefferson. From Randolph, perhaps from others as well, Jefferson must have learned how "open mouthed" Hamilton and Beckwith were in thinking his note "likely to give offense to the court of London."[23] He surely would have agreed with Madison in thinking this a ridiculous fear. Beckwith himself, perhaps on advice from Hamilton, soon backed away from the position he had taken. The following Friday, again at Mrs. Washington's soiree, he called Lear aside, expressed apprehension that he might have appeared too much concerned about Paine's pamphlet, and repeated that he had only given his opinion as a private individual.[24] He did not bother to report to Dorchester or Grenville his earlier concern about the presumed affront to the British court.

But a more important object of Randolph's visit to Jefferson that Saturday evening was to put to him the question that Beckwith was far from alone in asking. Had he, as Secretary of State, authorized publication of his note to Smith? On obtaining the answer, Randolph sought out the President's secretary that same evening. The next day Lear was able to report to the President that the Secretary of State had given the Attorney General this assurance:[25]

> Mr. Jefferson said that so far from having authorized ['publication of the extract from his note which appeared prefixed to . . . Paine's Pamphlet'], he was exceedingly sorry to see it there; not from a disavowal of the approbation which it gave the work; but because it had been sent to the Printer, with the pamphlet for re-publication, without the most distant idea that he would think of publishing any part of it. And Mr. Jefferson further added, that he wished it might be understood that he did not authorize the publication of any part of his note.

Jefferson of course could assume from Randolph's role as intermediary that Lear would report this much to Washington. But, acutely embarrassing though it was, he had no alternative except to explain himself to the President in his own words. The next day, Sunday the 8th, Jefferson gave a full and explicit account to Washington. The letter was one of his weekly official reports, but there was no public event to discuss except the mortifying situation in which he found himself. He frankly acknowledged that in writing the note he had had the author of *Discourses on Davila* in mind and thought it unquestionable

[23] TJ to Madison, 9 May 1791 (Document III).
[24] Lear to Washington, 22 May 1791 (DLC: Washington Papers).
[25] Lear to Washington, 8 May 1791 (DLC: Washington Papers).

that Adams would regard the charge of political heresy as meant to injure him in the public eye. But, he declared, Adams was his friend, one of the most honest and disinterested men alive, and even after his apostasy to hereditary monarchy and nobility, they differed, but differed as friends should.[26] Since this undoubtedly was the way Jefferson believed friends should treat their political differences, it is possible – as he asserted in his letter to Madison the next day – that in conversation he made free to tell Adams he was a heretic. But it was one thing to do this in private and quite something else to say it in print for the whole nation to read. Knowing Adams as he did, Jefferson correctly assumed that he would regard the charge of heresy as aimed at himself. "I have just reason, therefore," he wrote Madison, "to think he will be displeased."[27] The conclusion was well grounded.

III

The Vice-President and Mrs. Adams left Philadelphia for Braintree on Monday the 2nd of May, the day before Smith's edition of *Rights of Man* came from the press. But copies of the London edition had become available a few days earlier and so Adams had been able to read the pamphlet before departing. Since that edition carried no endorsement by the American Secretary of State, his response to it was directed at the author's performance alone – and was even more emphatic than the opinion he held of *Common Sense*.[28] Benjamin Rush had asked Adams what he thought of *Rights of Man* – knowing already the substance of the answer – and Tobias Lear, who happened to be present, gave the President a graphic account of the response. "After a little hesitation," he wrote, the Vice-President "laid his hand upon his breast, and said in a very solemn manner, I detest that book and its tendency from the bottom of my heart." Writing after the appearance of Smith's edition, Lear added: "This publication of Mr. Jefferson's sentiments respecting Mr. Paine's pamphlet will set him in direct opposition to Mr. Adams's political tenets."[29]

No one was more acutely aware of this than Jefferson himself. Sometime before his own departure from the capital on the 17th of May he endeavored to conciliate his old friend by sending an indirect message through the Secretary of War. Though its nature may be gauged only as relayed by Knox, it clearly agreed in substance with the explanation Jefferson had already given the President. Knox reported to Adams that Jefferson had assured him the note to Smith was never intended for publication but had been written as a kind of apology for the detention of the pamphlet "longer than the impatience of the

[26] TJ to Washington, 8 May 1791 (Document II).

[27] TJ to Madison, 9 May 1791 (Document III).

[28] Early in 1776, when it was reported that Adams himself was author of *Common Sense*, he thought it manly and striking in style but deficient in its ideas of government (Adams to Abigail Adams, 19 Mch. 1776; MHi: AM). Later, when he considered it "ridiculous to ask any questions about Tom Paines Veracity, Integrity or any other virtue," he approved only the arguments in *Common Sense* in favor of independence – arguments which he himself had been "repeating again and again in Congress for nine months" (Adams, *Diary and Autobiography*, ed. Butterfield, III, 330-5).

The copy of *Rights of Man* that Adams read was very likely the one sent him by William Temple Franklin (see Franklin to TJ, 6 Apr. 1791). That copy had been sent some time before Franklin wrote TJ.

[29] Lear to Washington, 8 May 1791 (DLC: Washington Papers).

[277]

printer would admit." In making it clear that this had been a borrowed copy yielded up at the printer's insistence, Knox reflected Jefferson's desire to emphasize his role as a mere channel of communication and to repudiate that of sponsor into which he had been cast by political opponents. So also with respect to the charge of heresy. "Perhaps," Knox added, "the *political heresies* mentioned in the preface to the American edition of Paynes pamphlett . . . may occasion some uneasiness. . . . But[30] if this idea was aimed at your doctrines it ought not to create a moments pain. Conscious as you are, of the invariable pursuit of the public happiness, regulated by the sober standard of reason, it is not the desultory ebulition of this, or that man's mind that can divert you from your object.[31] For while human nature shall continue its course according to its primary principles, there will be a difference of judgment upon the same objects even among good men."[32] Knox had not been prompt in passing the message along, but the assurance it contained and the appeal not to let differences of opinion be divisive reveal Jefferson's prompting hand and his conciliatory purpose.

Adams did not so interpret the message. The death of his good friend Dr. Richard Price, he replied to Knox, had hurt him "more than the little flickerings of Politicks." Then, revealing both his sensitiveness to the charge of heresy and his conviction that it had been inspired by Jefferson's political ambition, he added:[33]

> The Preface to Paine's Nonsense has occasioned much Speculation. It is thought rather early for Electioneering. My head I thank God is not easily diverted from its Views nor my heart from its Resolutions; and therefore neither Paine nor his Godfather will much affect me, and I believe they will affect the Public as little. It only grieves me that a Character who stood high is so much lowered in the public Esteem.

The character for whom Adams grieved was assuredly not the author of *Rights of Man*, but the one whom he designated as Paine's godfather. Abigail Adams, no less positive, echoed her husband's views. Everywhere, she wrote to Martha Washington in a glowing account of their homeward journey, they beheld the face of peace and contentment and found the people happy and satisfied with their government. But she noted the exceptions: "There are however two inhabitants (envy and jealousy) who are not perfectly content, but as they are characters for whom I have an utter aversion I can only pitty their folly and avoid them."[34] With her husband publicly accused of heresy, the politically

---

[30] In his draft of this letter Knox first wrote the following and then, realizing its inappropriateness, deleted the words: "But over this *small affair* . . ." (Knox to Adams, 10 June 1791; Dft in MHi: Knox Papers).

[31] At this point Dft reads: ". . . that ought to give pain."

[32] Knox to Adams, 10 June 1791 (RC in MHi: AM). The full text is given in Adams, *Works*, ed. C. F. Adams, VIII (Boston, 1853), 503-4.

[33] Adams to Knox, 19 June 1791 (MHi: AM).

[34] Abigail Adams to Martha Washington, 25 June 1791 (MHi: AM). After the election of 1796, Abigail Adams gave a more charitable but less accurate account of the feelings that had been aroused: "There never was any publick, or private, animosity between Mr. Adams and Mr. Jefferson, upon the subject of Pains Rights of Man. There was a disagreement of sentiment. Mr. Jefferson 'does not look quite thro the Deeds of Men.' Time has fully disclosed whose opinion was well founded" (Abigail Adams to Elbridge Gerry, 31 Dec. 1796; Collection of Nathaniel E. Stein, illustrated in Sotheby Parke Bernet Inc. catalogue of sale, 30 Jan. 1979, Lot 1).

astute wife of the Vice-President felt no need to name the two inhabitants or to identify the object of envy as the second highest office in the land.

The Adamses were far from alone in believing that the charge of heresy was born of political ambition. But Jefferson's concern over Adams' "apostacy to hereditary monarchy and nobility" had arisen even before the new government was formed or either of them held office under it. The seeds of their political differences were planted at least as early as the time of Shays' Rebellion and soon germinated with the appearance of Adams' *Defence of the Constitutions of Government of the United States* in 1787.[35] Jefferson regarded that formidable treatise as incontrovertible evidence of Adams' belief in monarchy.[36] This conviction was steadily reinforced by all he had observed of Adams' writings and conduct after his return from Europe. In 1790, while passing through Philadelphia on his way to assume office, he discussed with Benjamin Rush the change that both had observed in Adams' political principles. This was a month before *Discourses on Davila* began appearing in the *Gazette of the United States*. These essays, coming from the pen of the Vice-President and being published in newspapers over a period of a year, disturbed Jefferson even more than Adams' *Defence* had. Rush, always candid and a devoted friend of both men, did not hesitate to tell Adams of his and Jefferson's concern. "In my notebook I have recorded a conversation that passed between Mr. Jefferson and myself on the 17th of March, of which *you* were the principal subject," he wrote. "We both deplored your attachment to monarchy and both agreed that you had changed your principles since the year 1776."[37] In a lengthy reply in which he deplored the stupid and mulish systems of the Ancient Dominion, Adams made no allusion to Rush's conversation with Jefferson. But he denied then

[35] See TJ to Adams, 20 Dec. 1786, 6 and 23 Feb. and 1 Mch. 1787; TJ to Abigail Adams, 21 Dec. 1786 and 22 Feb. 1787; Abigail Adams to TJ, 29 Jan. 1787; Adams to TJ, 1 Mch. 1787.

[36] It has been argued that TJ at first read Adams' *Defence* hastily, initiated plans for a French translation, and then permitted or connived at its "suppression" (Joyce Appleby, "The Adams-Jefferson Rupture and the First French Translation of John Adams' *Defence*," AHR, LXXIII [Apr. 1968], 1084-91). The argument for the suppression – or, more precisely, the abandonment – of the proposed translation is based on the plausible inference that the work was not regarded with favor by those in France who looked to America rather than to England for its model of government. William Short provided another cogent argument against translation: it was not the kind of work that would be read in Paris, except perhaps among a few men of learning, who would prefer the original (Short to TJ, 26 Mch. 1787). It should be noted that TJ did not initiate plans for the translation, but when proposals came to him he sought to obtain a good translator (Froullé to TJ, 17 Feb. 1787; TJ to Adams, 23 Feb. 1787). There is no evidence that he did anything further in connection with the proposed translation, either to promote or discourage publication.

[37] Rush to Adams, 13 Apr. 1790 (Butterfield, *Rush*, I, 546). It is puzzling that Rush said they had found their proofs in Adams' letter to William Hooper on a form of government for North Carolina. No such letter has been found, and Adams denied knowledge of it (same, I, 548, note 10, which contains a brief but excellent account of TJ's relations with Rush). Possibly Rush referred to a later newspaper or other printing of the "Hooper version" of Adams' *Thoughts on Government*, which, while it was the first of several versions written in 1776, differed from all others and presumably is that which appeared in the *Southern Literary Messenger*, XIII (Jan. 1847), 42-7. See Butterfield, *Rush*, I, 331-2.

Discourses on Davila first appeared in *Gazette of the United States* on 28 Apr. 1790 and was concluded exactly a year later with the issue of 27 Apr. 1791.

and always that he had ever advocated monarchy as a form of government for the United States.[38] Jefferson, however, never surrendered his conviction. "Can any one read Mr. Adams's defence of the American Constitutions," he asked late in life, "without seeing that he was a monarchist?"[39]

With Congress in recess and most members returned home, with the President, the Vice-President, and all heads of department save the Secretary of War absent from the capital, and with such seekers of political intelligence as John Beckley and George Beckwith touring New England, the angry passions aroused by Jefferson's charge of heresy seem to have quieted down. Only a few squibs in the newspapers, aimed at Burke or Paine according to the editors' preferences, had appeared by the time Jefferson left on his month's journey to the northward.[40] Before departing, he wrote to his English friend Benjamin Vaughan, expressing confidence that even suppression of *Rights of Man* could not prevent the ultimate reform of the British system of government. "We have some names of note here who have apostatised from the true faith," he acknowledged, "but they are few indeed, and the body of our citizens are pure and insusceptible of taint in their republicanism."[41] This, however, was confidence based on hope and intended for English consumption. Proof of its validity had to await the next phase of the American contest of Burke and Paine. That, unlike the first, was not confined to the partisan gossip of the capital but was waged in the newspapers of the nation.

IV

It was on Wednesday the 8th of June, with the publication in Benjamin Russell's *Columbian Centinel* of the first of eleven essays signed *Publicola*, that the contest moved from the more or less hidden maneuvers in the capital to the wider field of national debate. In his opening number *Publicola* paid tribute to Burke and Paine as illustrious characters equally devoted to the cause of liberty, but he found the former's indiscriminate censure of the National Assembly as objectionable as the unqualified praise bestowed upon it by the latter. Thus assuming the role of an impartial seeker of truth, *Publicola* then turned his attention to the preface of *Rights of Man* containing the note of the Secretary of State, which he said had been published in most newspapers. "I am somewhat at a loss to determine," he wrote, "what this very respectable gentleman means by *political heresies*. Does he consider this pamphlet of Mr. Payne's as the canonical book of political scripture? As containing the true doctrine of popular infallibility, from which it would be heretical to depart in one single point. . . . I have always understood, Sir, that the citizens of these States were possessed of a full and entire freedom of opinion upon all subjects civil as well as religious; they have not yet established any infallible criterion of *orthodoxy*, either in church or state: . . . and the only political tenet which they would stigmatize with the name of heresy, would be that which should attempt to impose an opinion upon their understandings, upon the single principle of authority." The people, *Publicola* declared, were not disposed to rally around the standard of any man. But if Paine were to be adopted as the holy father of their political

[38] Adams to Rush, 18 Apr. 1791 (MHi: AM).
[39] TJ to Short, 8 Jan. 1825.
[40] TJ to Washington, 8 May 1791 (Document II).
[41] TJ to Vaughan, 11 May 1791. See also TJ to Littlepage, 29 July 1791.

faith and *Rights of Man* be taken as "his Papal Bull of infallible virtue," then this testament of orthodoxy should be examined and if found to contain many spurious texts, false in their principles and delusive in their inferences, the apocryphal doctrines should be expunged. *Publicola* closed his first essay on a note of civility. Both Paine and Jefferson were entitled to the gratitude of their country. As for the latter: "He is a friend to free inquiry upon every subject, and he will not be displeased to see the sentiments which he has made his own, by a publick adoption, canvassed with as much freedom as is consistent with the reverence due to his character."[42]

In the *Columbian Centinel* for the next two months *Publicola* canvassed the sentiments of *Rights of Man* on a high level of public discourse, but with little reverence either for its ideas, its author, or its presumed sponsor. His style was restrained, his analyses of Paine's arguments cogent, and his frequent allusions to the American system of government laudatory. Paine was not only flagrantly in error in denying the existence of a British constitution, but had been proved so when the glorious Congress of 1774 defended their rights "by the immutable laws of nature, *the principles of the English Constitution*, and the several charters or compacts." While Paine asserted that the National Assembly, exercising the whole power of the nation, could do anything, he had also declared that it could not alter the constitution or bind future generations. But, *Publicola* insisted, while the British people had "delegated their whole collective power to a legislature, consisting of a king, lords, and commons" and had included even the power of altering the constitution, neither a mere "mechanical horror against the name of a king, or of aristocracy, nor a physical antipathy to the sound of an extravagant title, or to the sight of an innocent riband" could justify a people in laying violent hands upon so excellent a constitution. Its most serious defects arose not from inherent dangers, except in the matter of representation, but from a universal venality and corruption pervading all classes of men. The constitution may have been violated by tyrants – monarchical, aristocratical, or democratical – but it was always necessary to return to the foundation of natural and unalienable right. The American people, the most enlightened and most virtuous on the globe, had demonstrated this. For sixteen years they had endured tyrannical abuse and, being driven at last to separation, had recited their sufferings to the world to show how the misuse of delegated power had violated their natural rights. Even "the venerable character who drew up this declaration, never could believe that the rights of a nation, have no other limits, than its powers." The American Constitution united all of the advantages of those of France and England while avoiding the evils of both. Yet its delegation of the amending power to Congress and the state legislatures was, "according to the ideas emanating from Mr. *Paine*, and coming to us at the same time by reflection from the Secretary of State, . . . a very dangerous political heresy." So also with the location of power to make war and peace – "not the first instance in which Mr. *Paine*'s principles attack those of the constitutions of his country." But, *Publicola* concluded, if the principles advocated by the author of *Rights of Man* should in any instance be founded upon eternal truth, they should be respected. As for himself, he remained unconvinced of Paine's infallibility. Let

[42] The *Publicola* essays are most conveniently accessible in W. C. Ford's edition of *Writings of John Quincy Adams*, I (New York, 1913), 65-110. They appeared in Benjamin Russell's *Columbian Centinel* on 8, 11, 15, 18, 22, 29 June; 2, 9, 13, 20, and 27 July 1791.

the people, he urged, therefore "remain immovably fixed at the banners of our constitutional freedom, and not desert the impregnable fortress of our liberties, for the unsubstantial fabrick of visionary politicians."[43]

Thus did *Publicola* hurl the charge of heresy back at Jefferson, characterizing him at the same time as a visionary politician. His essays were not intended as a defense of Burke's *Reflections* or even of the particular form of the British constitution. Nor was Paine himself the primary object of attack. It was the prefatory note to *Rights of Man* which provoked Adams' cogent analysis of the pamphlet, making the Secretary of State the real target. This is indicated in the opening essay and proved by all that followed. Had not Jefferson, a friend to free inquiry upon every subject, civil and religious, hailed Paine's reply to Burke as the canonical book of political scripture? But had the people not refused to establish any infallible criterion of orthodoxy, either in church or state? Was not the only political tenet they would stigmatize as heretical one which imposed opinions solely on the basis of authority?

The questions were rhetorical but their intent was clear. *Publicola* based his attack on propositions the American people had pronounced self-evident. He appealed to the concept of natural, inalienable rights by which the nation had justified its existence and on which, as an immutable foundation, all forms of government rested. In asserting that the legitimate object of all government was to promote the happiness of the people, *Publicola* only echoed the rhetoric of the revolutionary generation. In tracing principles of right and justice back many centuries to the customary law of the Anglo-Saxons, he reflected opinions Jefferson himself had expressed about the earlier and uncorrupted British constitution. And in declaring that the only security against tyrannical abuses of delegated power lay in the honesty and enlightened spirit of the people, he consciously or unconsciously paraphrased the view expressed in *Notes on Virginia* that it is "the manners and spirit of a people which preserve a republic in vigour."[44] In these and other respects *Publicola* astutely chose the common ground. His purpose, he declared, was to examine those ideas set forth in *Rights of Man* "which are supposed to be directly opposite to principles acknowledged by the constitutions of our country." In other words, it was the Secretary of State who, in the name of orthodoxy and by an authoritarian pronouncement, had given official sanction to political heresy.

Standing on this solid ground of generally accepted principles, *Publicola* put Jefferson's defenders at a disadvantage, thereby turning the contest of Burke and Paine into an intensely partisan newspaper war marked by angry personal abuse. The essays, Benjamin Russell declared, had been reprinted in all of the most respectable newspapers to the southward. "His *animadverters*, not answerers," he added, "swarm like *Bees*; and, like *Drone-Bees*, they only *buz*."[45] *Brutus* in the *Columbian Centinel* and *Agricola, A Republican, The Ploughman* and *The Watchman* in the Boston *Independent Chronicle* were among those who sought to answer *Publicola* by charging him with advocating monarchy and aristocracy. In Massachusetts, in Pennsylvania, in Virginia, and elsewhere the

[43] This was the tenth number of *Publicola* and, to judge from this concluding passage, was evidently intended to be the last. But the number and violence of attacks upon the essays — "a torrent of abuse," Adams called it — provoked him to add an eleventh number in rebuttal. See below.

[44] *Notes*, ed. Peden, p. 165. [45] *Columbian Centinel*, 2 July 1791.

numbers and the anger of those making the charge were all the greater because most people shared Jefferson's belief that John Adams was *Publicola*. When this was asserted in the newspapers, Benjamin Russell felt obliged to assure the public that the Vice-President had "no more concern in the publication, than the author of '*Rights of Man*' himself."[46] Jefferson believed this to be an equivocation. The denial was not generally credited, he asserted, because Adams himself had not made it and because the style and sentiments indicated that *Publicola* and the author of the *Defence* and of the *Discourses on Davila* were the same.[47]

The "host of writers" who had arisen to defend Paine and Jefferson caused *Publicola* to add a final essay to the ten already published. Since these had "called forth a torrent of abuse, not upon their real author nor upon the sentiments they express, but upon a supposed author, and supposed sentiments," *Publicola* felt obliged to deny that the Vice-President either wrote or corrected them or gave his sanction to any opinions he had advanced. Further, the essays did not, as one of his attackers had asserted, " 'go to the press under the assumed patronage of his son.' " With this emphatic denial, *Publicola* then challenged all who had written "in support of Mr. Paine's infallibility, to produce a single passage . . . which has the most distant tendency to recommend either a monarchy or an aristocracy to the citizens of these States." He had never intended, he asserted, to defend the corruptions of the British system, or even to support its principles in theory except insofar as these had been incorporated in the American Constitution.[48]

The challenge could not be successfully met on the ground chosen by *Publicola*, but this did not affect the outcome. John Adams stood fixed in the public mind as *Publicola*, and some thought Jefferson himself had written the attacks by *Brutus, Agricola, Philodemus*, and others.[49] Thus the lines were drawn, with the Vice-President and the Secretary of State placed in public confrontation over fundamental principles of government. The merits of *Publicola*'s arguments were virtually ignored by the press, while Adams in the general view could not escape the stigma of political heretic. "It is a circumstance highly honourable to the political character of our country," proclaimed an editorial in Brown's *Federal Gazette*, "that an *host* of enlightened writers have arisen, in every part of the United States, to oppose the abominable *heresies of Publicola*."[50] The opinion was quoted or echoed in many other newspapers throughout the country. Russell's *Columbian Centinel* and Fenno's *Gazette of the United States* were the principal journals to take a stand on the side of *Publicola*. The bitter partisan warfare continued throughout the summer and, as the opening of the Second Congress approached, it became clear that the American contest of Burke and Paine had produced some very significant results, personal and political.

[46] Same.

[47] TJ to Monroe, 10 July 1791 (Document VI). As late as 1793 a London edition of the essays of *Publicola* appeared in pamphlet form as *An answer to Paine's Rights of Man. By John Adams, Esq.* (London, 1793). Madison was quick to note that the style of *Publicola* was not that of John Adams.

[48] *Columbian Centinel*, 27 July 1791.

[49] TJ to Monroe, 10 July 1791 (Document VI); TJ to Adams, 17 July 1791 (Document VIII).

[50] *Federal Gazette*, 11 July 1791.

The first and most obvious consequence was that the long-standing political divergencies of Adams and Jefferson were confirmed and brought to the point of open rupture. Jefferson knew at the outset that his charge of heresy would be interpreted both by Adams and the public as aimed at the Vice-President, and he vainly hoped that publication of his note would be little noticed. But on his return from the northern journey, after reading several numbers of *Publicola* and finding himself charged with having sponsored *Rights of Man* and proclaimed Paine's infallibility, he finally brought himself after much agonizing to appeal to Adams not to misconstrue his motives merely because *Publicola* and a host of writers had placed them as antagonists on the public stage. His explanation of the origin of his note was essentially the same as that he had given to Washington. He frankly acknowledged that he and Adams differed about the best form of government, but they differed as friends should. Perhaps to spare Adams' feelings, he did not indicate that the charge of political heresy had been inspired largely by *Discourses on Davila* or that he, like most others, had assumed Adams to be *Publicola*. The main thrust of his letter was conciliatory, written from a conviction that truth, between candid minds, could never do harm.[51]

Adams graciously accepted this explanation of Jefferson's motives. He professed not to know what form of government Jefferson preferred and, like *Publicola*, challenged anyone to find anything in his writings advocating the establishment of a monarchical system for the United States. But, far from placing responsibility for the bitter contest where Jefferson had, he traced it back to the "Striking . . . recommendation" of *Rights of Man* which had been so industriously propagated throughout the country. This, he asserted, had led the public to regard it as a direct and personal attack upon himself. To be sure, Adams blamed the misconduct on the printer for having sown the seeds of more evils than he could ever atone for. But while this was a regrettable breach of confidence, he made it clear that the printer had only exposed to the public the true source of all of the bitter consequences. The question asked everywhere, he insisted, "was What Heresies are intended by the Secretary of State?" And everywhere the answer propagated by press and partisans was false. It was Jefferson's charge of heresy and his sponsorship of *Rights of Man*, Adams clearly believed, that had brought on a display of ambition, intrigue, and unbridled political rivalries which he regarded as the most alarming he had ever witnessed. In citing particular evidences of these partisan animosities, he was careful to confine his observations largely to the "Stone House Faction" of Boston, led by John Hancock and Samuel Adams, and to indicate that it was the former who was seeking election as Vice-President. It was in this state of things, after his enemies and rivals had set up a hue and cry against him, overwhelming him with "floods and Whirlwinds of tempestuous abuse, unexampled in the History of this Country," Adams declared, that *Publicola* had come forward. He supposed his defender had done so because he thought Paine's pam-

---

[51] TJ to John Adams, 17 July 1791 (Document VIII). The essays of *Publicola* appeared in the *Gazette of the United States* between 18 June and 6 Aug. 1791. When TJ wrote Adams he had only seen the first seven essays. He of course knew at this time that the *Columbian Centinel* of 2 July 1791 had denied that John Adams was *Publicola*, for the denial had been promptly published in Philadelphia papers.

phlet – and, by implication, Jefferson's recommendation of it – had been "made Use of as an Instrument to destroy a Man, for whom he had a regard, whom he thought innocent, and in the present moment of some importance to the Publick." The long letter revealed how deeply Adams had been hurt, but he closed with an affecting reaffirmation of his long-standing friendship and esteem for Jefferson. "It was high time," he declared, "that you and I should come to an explanation with each other."[52]

But the effort of the two men to achieve a friendly understanding failed. Adams' supposition that Hancock was his arch-rival may only have been intended to spare Jefferson's feelings, for it was the Vice-President and the Secretary of State – as Jefferson had pointed out and as the public at large knew full well – who had been brought on stage as political antagonists, not Adams and Hancock. Adams of course understood this. His letter to Henry Knox had named Jefferson godfather to Paine because of his commendation of *Rights of Man* and had held him, not Hancock, guilty of premature electioneering. His circumlocution may have been accepted for what it was had he not traced all of his sufferings to the charge of heresy which his enemies and rivals had employed as an instrument to destroy him politically. Thus, his argument implied, the weapon had been forged by Jefferson and the Janizaries who had wielded it and every other kind of falsehood had called forth *Publicola* as the valiant defender of his innocence. This, added to *Publicola*'s indictment of the Secretary of State as official sponsor of Paine's heresies, was more than Jefferson could accept in silence.

Aroused to the point of indignation, he replied by naming *Publicola* as "the real aggressor in this business," knowing as he did so that John Quincy Adams was the reputed author of the essays. It was *Publicola*, he declared, who had misconstrued "a figurative expression" in his note and had brought him before the public by name. This, not the publication of his note, had provoked a host of writers to attack the Vice-President on the presumption that he was *Publicola*. Jefferson was incorrect in saying that not a single word had been published on the subject until the appearance of *Publicola*, but his account of the first phase of the contest was nearer the truth than Adams' version. *Publicola*, selecting as his target the one who had made the charge of heresy, had indeed provoked the responses of *Brutus* and a host of others throughout the nation. But in his effort to exculpate himself and to place responsibility upon *Publicola*, Jefferson did so at the expense of truth when he declared to Adams: "Indeed it was impossible that my note should occasion your name to be brought into question; for so far from naming you, I had not even in view any writing which I might suppose to be yours."[53] This was in direct contradiction to what Jefferson had told the President only a few days after his note appeared at the head of *Rights of Man*. In writing that note, he frankly admitted, he not only had in mind Adams' *Discourses on Davila* but also, long before *Publicola* aroused a storm of controversy, he was certain Adams would interpret it as aimed at himself.

Adams, who was neither pleased nor persuaded by the argument that his son was the aggressor and that Jefferson was "as innocent *in effect* as . . . in intention," did not deign to reply. The personal and political rift between the two old friends grew wider and deeper, making impossible a resumption of

[52] Adams to TJ, 29 July 1791 (Document x).
[53] TJ to Adams, 30 Aug. 1791 (Document xii).

their friendship until Benjamin Rush brought them together twenty years later. Even then, although they closed their careers with the most elevated exchange of political and philosophical correspondence in American literature, they never truly succeeded in recapturing their earlier trust and confidence — or in explaining themselves to each other.[54]

The national debate between *Publicola* and his adversaries thus fixed John Adams in the public mind, however unjustly, as an advocate of a monarchical form of government for the United States. In consequence, as James Monroe saw immediately, Jefferson's stature as a champion of the republican cause had been vastly magnified. Looking ahead to the coming elections when public opinion would disclose itself, he pointed out that Jefferson had been given an opportunity to cast his aid and talents on the popular side of the scales. Jefferson's political sentiments had never been questioned, Monroe concluded, but they had been "made known as well by the short note prefixt to Paines pamphlet, as a volume could do it."[55] Alexander Hamilton was also quick to read the political portents, which to him were ominous. At the beginning of the newspaper controversy, Jefferson quoted him as saying that Adams had been imprudent in stirring up the question and as predicting that "his business is done."[56] Several weeks later Hamilton revealed the depth of his concern by making a personal call on Jefferson. After giving a frank and rather formal statement of his own political views, he took pains to dissociate himself from Adams and his writings, particularly his *Discourses on Davila*, which he thought tended to weaken the national government. He had no doubt Adams' intentions were pure, but, he added: "whoever by his writings disturbs the present order of things, is really blameable, however pure his intentions may be."[57] It was at this time, so Hamilton later informed Washington, that he had been instrumental in preventing two or three persons from making "a very severe and systematic attack upon Mr. Jefferson" because of the persecution of Adams resulting from the note in Paine's pamphlet.[58] Such an exercise of restraint was

---

[54] See *The Adams-Jefferson Letters The complete correspondence between Thomas Jefferson and Abigail and John Adams*, ed. Lester J. Cappon (Chapel Hill, 1959).

[55] Monroe to TJ, 25 July 1791 (Document IX).

[56] TJ to Monroe, 10 July 1791 (Document VI).

[57] TJ's notes of a conversation with Hamilton, 13 Aug. 1791.

[58] Hamilton to Washington, 9 Sep. 1792 (Syrett, *Hamilton*, XII, 348). Even as he wrote this, Hamilton also, as *Catullus*, accused Jefferson of having eagerly seized the opportune appearance of *Rights of Man* "to answer the double purpose of wounding a competitor and of laying in an additional stock of popularity; by associating and circulating the name of Thomas Jefferson, with a popular production of a favorite writer, on a favorite subject." He accused TJ of lending his auspices as Secretary of State because, being linked to the dedication to the President, it would appear that *Rights of Man* was being promoted or at least patronized by the government. He also insinuated that TJ had inspired Smith's encomium upon himself by expressing his approval of *Rights of Man* in such a manner as was "calculated not only to do justice to the writings of Mr. Paine, but to do honor to Mr. Jefferson; by *directing the mind* to a contemplation of that *republican firmness* and *democratic simplicity*, which ought to *endear him* to every friend to the 'Rights of Man.'" This, Hamilton added, was a signal so well understood by TJ's partisans that a general attack immediately began: "The newspapers in different States resounded with invective and scurrility against the patriot, who was marked out as the object of persecution, and if possible of degradation." Adams, in brief, had been designated

surely not to protect Jefferson, as Hamilton implied. It testified rather to his clear perception that such a concerted attack would only have added fuel to the flames and made the Secretary of State loom even larger in the public estimation.

Jefferson himself was highly gratified with the overwhelming response of the people as reflected in the press. "I thank god," he wrote Paine, "that they appear firm in their republicanism, notwithstanding the hopes and assertions of a sect here, high in names, but small in numbers."[59] He gave full credit for this to the timely appearance of *Rights of Man*. So did Otto, the French minister, who had long been annoyed by *Discourses on Davila* and what he called Adams' diatribes against the revolution in France and the proceedings of the National Assembly. He had responded to these with great moderation, he reported, but the public had asserted itself with less reserve. "The gazettes abound with political darts of verse and epigram against Mr. Adams," he wrote, "and it is generally believed that the Vice-President will lose his place at the first election. It is Mr. Paine in particular who has brought about this revolution in spirits." But the salutary effect of *Rights of Man*, he added, had been greatly increased by the arrival of Montmorin's instructions containing the King's circular to all French diplomats signifying his acceptance of the constitution. This unprecedented document he had transmitted to the Secretary of State and promised to draw the attention of the public to its importance in every way possible.[60] When George Hammond arrived as minister from England, he, too, reported that Paine's pamphlet had produced a very open "diversity" between Jefferson and Adams. "The latter Gentleman in conversation (and I understand also in writing)," he added, "is very warm in his animadversions upon that event, and in his defence of the British constitution."[61]

Paine's *Rights of Man* was indeed an essential factor in the sequence of events, but it was Samuel Harrison Smith's improper use of Jefferson's note to his father and *Publicola*'s response to it which triggered the national debate, bringing immense popular support to Jefferson and stamping upon John Adams the undeserved but enduring appellation of monarchist. For years to come, and especially as the pivotal election of 1800 approached, Adams' political opponents did their best to revive the polemics of 1791.[62] His honest anger and indiscreet expressions did little if anything to mitigate the effect of their efforts. "Of course," wrote Gouverneur Morris in 1800, "the democrats and their demagogues, have had just cause to complain of the manner in which money is raised, and our expenditure is far from economical, so that no applause is to be expected on that score. — But the thing, which, in my opinion, has done most mischief to the federal party, is the ground given by some of them to

---

as clearly as if he had been named: the javelin thrown by TJ "went directly to its destination" (*Catullus* No. III appeared in *Gazette of the United States*, 29 Sep. 1792; Syrett, *Hamilton*, XII, 501-4).

[59] TJ to Paine, 29 July 1791 (Document XI). See also TJ to Paine, 19 June 1792 (Document XIII).

[60] Otto to Montmorin, 23 July 1791 (DLC: Adams Transcripts). See also Otto to TJ, 22 July 1791.

[61] Hammond to Grenville, 1 Nov. 1791 (BL: Dropmore Add. MSS 58939).

[62] As late as 1823 Tench Coxe, writing as *Sherman* and *Greene*, sought to attach the label "monarchist" to John Quincy Adams because he had written the *Publicola* essays (Jacob E. Cooke, *Tench Coxe and the early Republic* [Chapel Hill, 1978], p. 517n.).

believe, that they wish to establish a monarchy."[63] Adams was by no means the only one who had provided such grounds for the opposition, but he was unquestionably less reserved in expressing his political sentiments than any other member of his party.

With the newspapers of the nation keeping Jefferson and Adams at the center of the stage, it is understandable that another and perhaps more important consequence has escaped notice. This concerned the relations of Washington and Jefferson. The controversy opened just at the time Hamilton and his supporters began to be increasingly apprehensive that Jefferson's influence with the President was in the ascendant. The return of Adams' son-in-law, William S. Smith, and the failure of his unofficial mission to England coincided with the appearance of the first essay by *Publicola* and thus tended to confirm these fears.[64] Hamilton's call on Jefferson and his express disapproval of Adams' writings was perhaps another indication of his anxiety about the growing influence of the Secretary of State. Washington was undoubtedly concerned from the outset over the divisive controversy. On his return to Mount Vernon from his southern tour and before he had received Lear's letter informing him of his conversations with Beckwith and Randolph, he asked particularly that a copy of Paine's *Rights of Man* be sent by post so as to reach him at Georgetown, obviously to enable him to read the pamphlet on his journey back to the capital.[65] To Jefferson's prompt and candid explanation of his note to Smith, Washington returned only an icy silence. It is not known when he received Jefferson's explanation, though it was probably some time after his arrival in Philadelphia at the height of what Monroe called "the fever." Surprisingly, but perhaps because of the widespread popular support being given to Paine and because of what he had done for the American people in the struggle for independence, Jefferson, with the concurrence of Madison and acting indirectly through Edmund Randolph, recommended the author of *Rights of Man* for appointment as postmaster general. It is not surprising, however, that the recommendation was ignored – the appointment went instead to one who became an implacable opponent of Jefferson and all that he stood for, Timothy Pickering.[66] When, even before the American contest of Burke and Paine quieted down, Jefferson added to his public commendation of *Rights of Man* the bestowal of political patronage on Philip Freneau to help found the *National Gazette*, he planted another fertile seed of doubt in the President's mind which germinated in the even more bitter and divisive controversies of 1792.[67] It was in the midst of those turmoils that Washington, deeply angered by Freneau's attacks, finally acknowledged Paine's letter of the preceding year and his gift of fifty copies of *Rights of Man*. The letter was an acknowledgment, not a response, and obviously the delay reflected Washington's concern over the controversy and was not attributable, as he explained, merely to the pressure of official duties. There

[63] Gouverneur Morris to Rufus King, 4 June 1800 (Jared Sparks, *Life of Gouverneur Morris*, III [Boston, 1832], 128).

[64] See Editorial Note and group of documents at 15 Dec. 1790.

[65] Washington to Lear, 19 June 1791 (*Writings*, ed. Fitzpatrick, xxxi, 302).

[66] When TJ learned that Samuel Osgood's resignation had created a vacancy in the office, he informed Madison that he would "press Paine for it." Madison approved, but it was Edmund Randolph who actually submitted the nomination to Washington, along with the names of other candidates (see note to TJ to Madison, 10 July 1791).

[67] See Editorial Note and group of documents at 4 Aug. 1791.

was no mention of the dedicatory letter in the pamphlet. But Washington closed with an affirmation of his own sentiments: "I rejoice in the information of your personal prosperity; and as no one can feel a greater interest in the happiness of mankind than I do . . . it is the first wish of my heart, that the enlightened policy of the present age may diffuse to all men those blessings, to which they are entitled, and lay the foundation of happiness for future generations."[68]

The evidence is largely hidden in Washington's silence, but, viewing the relationship of the two men during the remainder of Jefferson's tenure as Secretary of State and over the ensuing years – marked as they were by the publication of the letter to Mazzei and other incidents which led ultimately to the withdrawal of Washington's friendship – it is difficult to escape the conclusion that the deterioration of the bonds of friendship, trust, and affection that once existed between the central figure of the Revolution and the pre-eminent spokesman for its moral and philosophical propositions had its origin in the unauthorized publication of Jefferson's letter to Jonathan Bayard Smith.

The Paine episode had one other lasting effect. It made Jefferson extraordinarily sensitive to the possibility that his private letters might improperly get into print. The note to Jonathan Bayard Smith was the first and one of the most excruciatingly embarrassing of such incidents, but it was by no means the last. When his words were garbled and misused for partisan purposes, as in the case of the famous letter to Mazzei, Jefferson suffered intensely. It was to John Adams himself that, late in life, he expressed his feelings on the subject most emphatically. Reading, he declared, was his delight. Then he added: "I should wish never to put pen to paper; and the more because of the treacherous practice some people have of publishing one's letters without leave. Ld. Mansfield declared it a breach of trust, and punishable at law. I think it should be a penitentiary felony."[69] Once, writing to a trusted political confidant, Jefferson agreed that an earlier letter of his might be shown to "a few *well tried friends*" but then suggested that it be thrown into the fire because his confidence had been so often abused and because he had suffered so much in being exhibited before the public in terms not meant for them. "I recieve letters expressed in the most friendly and even affectionate terms," he added, "sometimes perhaps asking my opinion on some subject. I cannot refuse to answer such letters, nor can I do it dryly and suspiciously. Among a score or two of such correspondents, one perhaps betrays me. I feel it mortifyingly; but conclude I had better incur

[68] Washington to Paine, 6 May 1792 (*Writings*, ed. Fitzpatrick, xxxii, 38-9). Although there is a text of this letter in TJ's hand in DLC and an entry under its date in SJPL reading "G. W. to Thos. Paine" – two facts which would seem to justify the inference that Washington asked TJ to draft the response to Paine – the text is of such a character as to prove that it is not a composition draft but that TJ was only copying from Washington's missing RC. The most plausible assumption is that Washington showed the letter to TJ before dispatching it and that TJ made an unusual abbreviated copy of it.

Washington's letter was in response to Paine's of 21 July 1791, accompanied by fifty copies of *Rights of Man*, which Paine wished the President to distribute to TJ and others. When the second part was published early in 1792, Paine sent a dozen copies to Washington, half of which were intended for TJ (Paine to TJ, 13 Feb. 1792; Paine to Washington, 13 Feb. 1792 [DLC: Washington Papers]; TJ to Paine, 19 June 1792 [Document xiii]; see Sowerby, No. 2826).

[69] TJ to Adams, 1 June 1822. Ironically, both this letter and Adams' reply of 11 June 1822 were published in the *Daily National Intelligencer*, 23 Dec. 1822. Why or by whom this was done is not clear.

one treachery, than offend a score or two of good people. I sometimes expressly desire that my letter may not be published; but this is so like requesting a man not to steal or cheat, that I am ashamed of it after I have done it."[70] The characteristic comment is revealing. As a man of honor, torn between his desire to state his views on government with candor and his fear that his words might be exploited by political opponents, as in the Paine and Mazzei incidents, Jefferson nevertheless did not permit his inner distress to be stifling. Throughout life he continued to express his views vigorously and eloquently, though at times he thought it prudent not to reveal all of his feelings to a correspondent whom he did not know well or in whose discretion he did not have full confidence.[71]

[70] TJ to Nathaniel Macon, 23 Nov. 1821. In another remarkable letter written the same year, TJ expressed his feelings emphatically: "But let me beseech you, Sir, not to let this letter get into a newspaper. . . . The abuse of confidence by publishing my letters has cost me more than all other pains, and makes me afraid to put pen to paper in a letter of sentiment. If I have done it frankly, in answer to your letter, it is in full trust that I shall not be thrown by you into the Arena of a newspaper" (TJ to C. Hammond, 18 Aug. 1821). See also TJ to John Norvell, 11 June 1807.

[71] See, for example, TJ to Horatio Gates Spafford, 10 Jan. 1816, in which he first expressed at some length his views about the attacks made upon him by "pious whining, hypocritical canting, lying and slandering" clergy and then, prudently, excised the whole passage. Spafford, however, was one who had the courtesy to ask permission to quote an extract from one of TJ's letters.

I. Thomas Jefferson to Jonathan B. Smith

Apr. 26. 1791.

Th: Jefferson presents his compliments to Mr. Jonathan B. Smith, and in consequence of the inclosed note and of Mr. Beckley's desire he sends him Mr. Paine's pamphlet. He is extremely pleased to find it will be re-printed here, and that something is at length to be publicly said against the political heresies which have sprung up among us. He has no doubt our citizens will rally a second time round the standard of Common sense.[1]

He begs leave to engage three or four copies of the republication.

RC (DLC: Jonathan Bayard Smith Papers); endorsed, in part: "Communicating a copy of Paine's Rights of Man for publication." Not recorded in SJL. Enclosure: In addition to the copy of *Rights of Man*, TJ enclosed Beckley's note requesting that it be forwarded. The note has not been found and is not recorded in SJL, but it was probably written and received on the same day TJ wrote the above.

In his letter to Randolph, TJ said that he thought so little of this note that he "did not even retain a copy of it" (TJ to Randolph, 3 July 1791; Document v).

[1] Only the two preceding sentences were published by Smith in his edition of *Rights of Man*. These were quoted exactly except for the use of the first person instead of the third at the beginning of each sentence.

II. Thomas Jefferson to George Washington

SIR Philadelphia May 8. 1791.

The last week does not furnish one single public event worthy communicating to you: so that I have only to say 'all is well.' Paine's answer to Burke's pamphlet begins to produce some squibs in our public papers. In Fenno's paper they are Burkites, in the others Painites. One of Fenno's was evidently from the author of the discourses on Davila. I am afraid the indiscretion of a printer has committed me with my friend Mr. Adams, for whom, as one of the most honest and disinterested men alive, I have a cordial esteem, increased by long habits of concurrence in opinion in the days of his republicanism: and even since his apostacy to hereditary monarchy and nobility, tho' we differ, we differ as friends should do. – Beckley had the only copy of Paine's pamphlet, and lent it to me, desiring when I should have read it, that I would send it to a Mr. J. B. Smith, who had asked it for his brother to reprint it. Being an utter stranger to J. B. Smith, both by sight and character, I wrote a note to explain to him why I (a stranger to him) sent him a pamphlet, to wit, that Mr. Beckley had desired it; and to take off a little of the dryness of the note, I added that I was glad to find it was to be reprinted, that something would at length be publicly said against the political heresies which had lately sprung up among us, and that I did not doubt our citizens would rally again round the standard of Common sense. That I had in my view the Discourses on Davila, which have filled Fenno's papers for a twelvemonth, without contradiction, is certain. But nothing was ever further from my thoughts than to become myself the contradictor before the public. To my great astonishment however, when the pamphlet came out, the printer had prefixed my note to it, without having given me the most distant hint of it. Mr. Adams will unquestionably take to himself the charge of political heresy, as conscious of his own views of drawing the present government to the form of the English constitution, and I fear will consider me as meaning to injure him in the public eye. – I learn that some Anglomen have censured it in another point of view, as a sanction of Paine's principles tends to give offence to the British government. Their real fear however is that this popular and republican pamphlet, taking wonderfully, is likely at a single stroke to wipe out all the unconstitutional doctrines which their bell-weather Davila has been preaching for a twelvemonth. I certainly never made a secret of my being anti-monarchical, and anti-aristocratical: but I am sincerely mortified to be thus brought forward on the public stage, where to remain, to advance or to retire, will be equally against my love of silence and quiet, and my abhorrence of dispute. — I do not know whether you recollect that the records of Virginia were destroyed by the British in the year 1781. particularly the transactions of the revolution before that time. I am collecting here all the letters I wrote to Congress while I was in the administration there, and this being done I shall then extend my views to the transactions of my predecessors, in order to replace the whole in the public offices in Virginia. I think that during my administration, say between June 1. 1779. and June 1. 1781. I had the honour of writing frequent letters to you on public affairs, which perhaps may be among your papers at Mount Vernon. Would it be consistent with any general resolution you have formed as to your papers, to let my letters of the above period come here to be copied, in order to make them a part of the records I am endeavoring to restore for the state? Or would their selection be too troublesome? If not, I would beg the loan of them, under an assurance that they shall be taken the utmost care of, and safely returned to their present deposit.

The quiet and regular movement of our political affairs leaves nothing to add but constant prayers for your health & welfare and assurances of the sincere respect and attachment of Sir Your most obedient & most humble servt,   TH: JEFFERSON

RC (DNA: RG 59, MLR); addressed: "The President of the United States. To be put into the mail for Petersburg the post master at which place is desired to forward it by the first safe conveyance to Taylor's ferry on the Roanoke, there to await the arrival of the President"; postmarked "9 MA" and "FREE"; docketed by the post-master at Petersburg as received there 14 May and forwarded; endorsed by Washington. PrC (DLC). FC (DNA: RG 59, SDC).

The squib in Fenno's *Gazette of the United States*, which TJ erroneously supposed to have been written by John Adams, was a satiric piece on a sermon by Richard Price as mentioned in Burke's *Reflections*. It ap-peared in the issue of 7 May under a Boston dateline of 23 Apr. 1791 and bore the heading "The *beautiful* and *sublime* of Blackguardism." It concluded with this allusion to the events of the preceding Oc-tober: "The actual murder of the King and Queen and their child, was wanting to the other auspicious circumstances of this '*beautiful* day.' The actual murder of the Bishops, though called for by so many holy ejaculations, was also wanting. A groupe of regicide and sacrelegious slaughter, was indeed boldly sketched, but it was only sketched. It unhappily was left unfinished, in this great history-piece of the massacre of innocents. What hardy pencil of a great master, from the school of the rights of men, will finish it, is to be seen hereafter."

III. Thomas Jefferson to James Madison

DEAR SIR   Philadelphia May. 9. 1791.

Your favor of the 1st. came to hand on the 3d. Mr. Freneau has not followed it: I suppose therefore he has changed his mind back again, for which I am really sorry. I have now before me a huge bundle of letters, the only business between me and my departure. I think I can be through them by the end of the week, in which case I will be with you by Tuesday or Wednesday, if nothing new comes in to delay me. Rittenhouse will probably not go. He says he cannot find a good horse. I shall propose to you when we tack about from the extremity of our journey, instead of coming back the same way, to cross over through Vermont to Connecticut river and down that to New-haven, then through Long-island to N.Y. and so to Philada. Be this however as you will. Our news from Virginie is principally of deaths, to wit, Colo. B. Harrison of Barclay, Turner Southall, Dixon the printer, Colo. Overton of Hanover, Walker Gilmer son of the Doctor. A Peter Randolph of Chatsworth has had a fit of madness, which he has recovered from. Wheat has suffered by drought: yet it is tolerably good. The fruit not entirely killed. At this place little new. – F. Hopkinson lies at extremities with regular epileptic fits, from which they think he cannot recover. Colo. Hamilton set out to-day for Bethlehem. Have you seen the Philadelphia edition of Paine's pamphlet? You know you left Beckley's copy in my hands. He called on me for it, before I had quite finished it, and desired me when done to send it to J. B. Smith whose brother was to reprint it. When I was proceeding to send it, I found it necessary to write a note to Mr. Smith to explain why I, a perfect stranger to him, sent him the pamphlet. I mentioned it to be by the desire of Mr. Beckley, and to take off a little of the dryness of the note, added currento calamo, that I was pleased to find it was to be reprinted here, that something was at length to be publicly said against the political heresies which had of late sprung up among us, not doubting but that our citizens would rally again round the standard of Common sense. I thought no more of this and heard no more till the pamphlet appeared to my astonishment with my note at the head of it. I never saw J. B. Smith or the printer either before or since. I had in view certainly the doctrines of Davila. I tell the writer freely that he is a heretic, but certainly never meant to step into a public newspaper with that in my mouth. I have just reason therefore to think he will be displeased. Colo. Hamilton and Colo. Beckwith are open mouthed against me, taking it in another view, as likely to give offence to the court of London. H. adds further that it marks my opposition to the government. Thus endeavoring to turn on the government itself those censures I meant for the enemies of the government, to wit those who want to change it into a monarchy. I have reason to think he has been unreserved in uttering these sentiments. — I send you some letters recieved for you. Adieu. Yours affectionately, TH: JEFFERSON

P.S. F. Hopkinson is dead. — Rittenhouse has agreed this afternoon to go with me as far as New York.

RC (DLC: Madison Papers). PrC (DLC); lacks postscript.

IV. James Madison to Thomas Jefferson

DEAR SIR   N. York May 12. 1791.

Your favor of the 9th. was received last evening. To my thanks for the several inclosures I must add a request that the letter to Baynton which came in one of them may be handed to him by one of your servants. The directory will point out his habitation.

I had seen Payne's pamphlet with the preface of the Philada. Editor. It immediately occurred that you were brought into the Frontispiece in the manner you explain. But I had not foreseen the particular use made of it by the British partizans. Mr. Adams can least of all complain. Under a mock defence of the Republican Constitutions of this Country, he attacked them with all the force he possessed, and this in a book with his name to it whilst he was the Representative of his Country at a foreign Court. Since he has been the 2d. Magistrate in the new Republic, his pen has constantly been at work in the same cause; and tho' his name has not been prefixed to his antirepublican discourses, the author has been as well known as if that formality had been observed. Surely if it be innocent and decent in one servant of the public thus to write attacks against its Government, it can not be very criminal or indecent in another to patronize a written defence of the principles on which that Government is founded. The sensibility of H[amilton] and B[eckwith][1] for the indignity to the Brit: Court is truly ridiculous. If offence could be justly taken in that quarter, what would France have a right to say to Burke's pamphlet, and the Countenance given to it and its author, particularly by the King himself? What in fact might not the U.S. say, whose revolution and democratic governments come in for a large share of the scurrility lavished on those of France.

I do not foresee any objection to the route you propose. I had conversed with Beckley on a trip to Boston &c. and still have that in view, but the time in view for starting from this place, will leave room for the previous excursion. Health recreation and curiosity being my objects, I can never be out of my way.

Not a word of news here. My letters from Virginia say little more than those you had received. Carrington says the returns have come in pretty thickly of late and warrant the estimate founded on the Counties named to me some time ago. As well as I recollect, these averaged upwards of 8000 souls, and were consider'd by him as under the general average. – Yrs. affecly.,   Js. MADISON JR.

RC (DLC: Madison Papers); a number of interlineations and deletions, at least one of which was made by Madison late in life (see below). Recorded in SJL as received 14 May 1791.

[1] At this point Madison interlined "Hammond-Bond" late in life, thus mistaking the initials "H and B" for George Hammond and Phineas Bond.

V. Thomas Jefferson to Thomas Mann Randolph, Jr.

DEAR SIR   Philadelphia July 3. 1791.

I wrote to Maria this day sennight, and to Martha three days before, to wit June 23. In this letter I asked information to be obtained from Colo. Lewis relative to my tobo. of which I had heard nothing. But having received the day after a letter from him, giving me full information, I mentioned in mine to Maria, that no notice should be taken of my desire expressed in the letter to her sister. Lest any accident should have happened to the letter to Maria, I repeat here that no enquiry of Colo. Lewis is necessary.

The President is not yet arrived; but we expect him the day after tomorrow. He has probably protracted his journey so as to avoid the ceremonies of tomorrow. – We expect daily to hear the event of the expedition under Genl. Scott into the Indian country. Perhaps you will hear it sooner than we shall. – Having nothing to communicate in the line of public news, I will state something personal. You will observe by the inclosed and preceding papers, that I am mentioned on the subject of Paine's pamphlet on the rights of man: and you will have seen a note of mine prefixed to that pamphlet, whence it has been inferred that I furnished the pamphlet to the printer and procured it's publication. This is not true. The fact was this. Mr. Beckley had the only copy of that pamphlet in town. He lent it to Mr. Madison, who lent it to me under the injunction to return it to Beckley within the day. Beckley came for it before I had finished reading it, and desired, as soon as I had done, I would send it to a Mr. Jonathan B. Smith whose brother was to reprint it. Being an utter stranger to Mr. J. B. Smith, I explained to him in a note that I sent the pamphlet to him by order of Mr. Beckley and, to take off somewhat of the dryness of the note, I added 'that I was glad to find it was to be reprinted here &c. as you have seen in the printed note. I thought so little of this note, that I did not even retain a copy of it: and without the least information or suspicion that it would be published, out it comes the next week at the head of the pamphlet. I knew immediately that it would give displeasure to some gentlemen, fast by the chair of government, who were in sentiment with Burke, and as much opposed to the sentiments of Paine. I could not disavow my note, because I had written it: I could not disavow my approbation of the pamphlet, because I was fully in sentiment with it: and it would have been trifling to have disavowed merely the publication of the note, approving at the same time of the pamphlet. I determined therefore to be utterly silent, except so far as verbal explanations could be made. The Vice president, who is at Boston, took up the cudgels under the name of Publicola. He is in turn assailed by a host of republican champions. I think it probable he will be aided by some of his compeers, but, more cautious than him, they will mask themselves better. For my part I am determined to let them write and wrangle as they please, without intermeddling in word or deed.

I am unable as yet to fix a time for my trip to Virginia. It must depend on the movements of the President. I foresee nothing in the public affairs which threatens impediment. Present me affectionately to my daughters, and believe me to be Dear Sir Yours sincerely,

Th: Jefferson

RC (DLC).

VI. Thomas Jefferson to James Monroe

Dear Sir   Philadelphia July 10. 1791.

Your favor of June 17. has been duly recieved. I am endeavoring to get for you the lodgings Langdon had. But the landlord is doubtful whether he will let them at all. If he will not, I will endeavor to do the best I can. I can accomodate you myself with a stable and coach house without any expence, as I happen to have two on hand:

and indeed in my new one I have had stalls enough prepared for 6. horses, which are 2 more than I keep. Of my success in procuring rooms I shall bring you news myself, tho' as yet the time of my visit to Albemarle is unfixed. Mr. Madison will both go and come with me. He is at present at New York. His journey with me to the lakes placed him in better health than I have seen him: but the late heats have brought on some bilious dispositions.

The papers which I send Mr. Randolph weekly, and which I presume you see, will have shewn you what a dust Paine's pamphlet has kicked up here. My last to Mr. Randolph will have given an explanation as to myself which I had not time to give when I sent you the pamphlet. A writer under the name of Publicola, in attacking all Paine's principles, is very desirous of involving me in the same censure with the author. I certainly merit the same, for I profess the same principles; but it is equally certain I never meant to have entered as a volunteer into the cause. My occupations do not permit it. Some persons here are insinuating that I am Brutus, that I am Agricola, that I am Philodemos &ca. &ca. I am none of them, being decided not to write a word on the subject, unless any printed imputation should call for a printed disavowal, to which I should put my name. A Boston paper has declared that Mr. Adams 'has no more concern in the publication of the writings of Publicola than the author of the Rights of man himself.' If the equivoque here were not intended, the disavowal is not entirely credited, because not from Mr. Adams himself, and because the stile and sentiments raise so strong a presumption. Besides to produce any effect, he must disavow Davila, and the Defence of the American constitutions. A host of writers have risen in favor of Paine, and prove that in this quarter at least the spirit of republicanism is sound. The contrary spirit of the high officers of government is more understood than I expected. Colo. Hamilton, avowing that he never made a secret of his principles, yet taxes the imprudence of Mr. Adams in having stirred the question and agrees that 'his business is done.' Jay, covering the same principles under the vail of silence, is rising steadily on the ruins of his friend. – The bank filled and overflowed in the moment it was opened. Instead of 20 thousand shares, 24 thousand were offered, and a great many unpresented who had not suspected that so much haste was necessary. Thus it is that we shall be paying 13. per cent per ann. for 8. millions of paper money instead of having that circulation of gold and silver for nothing. Experience has proved to us that a dollar of silver disappears for every dollar of paper emitted: and for the paper emitted from the bank 7. per cent profits will be received by the subscribers for it as bank paper (according to the last division of profits by the Philadelphia bank) and 6. per cent on the public paper of which it is the representative. Nor is there any reason to believe, that either the 6 millions of public paper or the 2. millions of specie deposited will not be suffered to be withdrawn, and the paper thrown into circulation. The cash deposited by strangers for safe keeping will probably suffice for cash demands. Very few subscribers have offered from Virginia or N. Carolina, which gives uneasiness to H. It is impossible to say where the appetite for gambling will stop. The land-office, the federal town, certain schemes of manufacture, are all likely to be converted into aliment for that rage. – But this subject is too copious for a letter and must be reserved for conversation. – The respite from occupation which my journey procured, has entirely removed my head-aches. Kiss and bless Mrs. Monroe and Eliza for Dear Sir Yours affectionately,   TH: JEFFERSON

RC (NN). PrC (DLC).

VII. James Madison to Thomas Jefferson

DEAR SIR   N. York July 13. 1791

I received last evening your kind enquiries after my health. My last will have informed you of the state of it then. I continue to be incommoded by several different shapes taken by the bile; but not in a degree that can now be called serious. If the present excessive heat should not augment the energy of the cause, I consider myself as in a good way to get rid soon of its effects.

Beckley has just got back from his Eastern trip. He says that the partizans of Mr. Adam's heresies in that quarter are perfectly insignificant in point of number – that particularly in Boston he is become distinguished for his unpopularity – that Publicola is probably the manufacture of his son out of materials furnished by himself – and that the publication is generally as obnoxious in New England as it appears to be in Pennsylvania. If Young Adams be capable of giving the dress in which publicola presents himself, it is very probable he may have been made the Editor of his Father's doctrines. I hardly think the Printer would so directly disavow the fact if Mr. Adams was himself the writer. There is more of method also in the arguments, and much less of clumsiness and heaviness in the stile, than characterize his writings. I mentioned to you some time ago an extract from a piece in the Poughkepsie paper, as a sensible comment on Mr. Adams' doctrines. The whole has since been re-published here, and is evidently from a better pen than any of the anti-publicolas I have seen. In Greenleafs paper of today is a second letter from the same quarter, which confirms the character of I have given of the author.

We understand here that 800 shares in the Bank committed by this City to Mr. Constable, have been excluded by the manner in which the business was conducted – that a considerable number from Boston met with the same fate – and that Baltimore has been kept out in toto. It is all charged on the manœuvers of Philada. which is said to have secured a majority of the whole to herself. The disappointed individuals are clamorous of course, and the language of the place marks a general indignation on the subject. If it should turn out that the cards were packed, for the purpose of securing the game to Philada. – or even that more than half the Institution and of course the whole direction of it have fallen into the hands of that City, some who have been loudest in their plaudits whilst they expected to share in the plunder, will be equally so in sounding the injustice of the monopoly, and the danger of undue influence on the Government.

The packet is not yet arrived. By a vessel arived yesterday news-papers are received from London which are said to be later than any yet come to hand. I do not find that any particular facts of moment are handed out. The miscellaneous articles come to me thro' Child's paper, which you get sooner than I could rehearse to you. It has been said here by the Anglicans that the President's Message to Congress on the subject of the commercial disposition of G.B. has been asserted openly by Mr. Pitt to be misrepresenta-tion – and as it would naturally be traced to Govr. Morris it has been suggested that he fell into the hands of the Chevr. Luzerne who had the dexterity to play off his negociations for French pur-poses. I have reason to believe that B-ck-th has had a hand in throwing these things into circulation. – I wish you success with all my heart in your efforts for Payne. Besides the advantage to him which he deserves, an appointment for him, at this moment would do public good in various ways. Always & truly yours,

Js. Madison Jr.

RC (DLC: Madison Papers); addressed; franked "Free" and postmarked: "N YORK july 14"; endorsed by TJ as received 16 July 1791 and so recorded in SJL. The address sheet contains a column of brief pencilled notes by TJ, as follows:

"√harvest   √Prussia's
√price of tobo.   media[tio]n.
√Freneau   √Denm[ark]
√T. P. [Thomas Paine]   √Empress.
   St. Domingo Congress   France
                √Scott.
                √Mazzei."

This was a list of topics TJ made for his response. All, whether checked or not, are alluded to in TJ to Madison, 21 July 1791.

As indicated in the Editorial Note to the group of documents on the war crisis of 1790, at 12 July 1790, it was Hamilton who suggested to Beckwith that Gouverneur Morris had fallen under the influence of La Luzerne and thus contributed to the coolness of the British ministry. Washington's message to Congress about the failure of Morris' mission not only alarmed Hamilton and his supporters but also made it easier for Beckwith, almost a year after the event, to accept and repeat the account which placed the blame upon Morris rather than upon the real author (see Editorial Note and group of documents on commercial and diplomatic relations with Great Britain, at 15 Dec. 1790). By the time Madison heard the rumor, responsibility for its origin would seem to have been firmly fixed upon Beckwith.

The two letters from the *Poughkeepsie Journal* which impressed Madison so much were published in the issues of 21 May and 20 June. Although he and TJ passed through Poughkeepsie only two days after the first letter appeared, Madison – and of course TJ – only saw it and the later one when they were reprinted in the *New-York Journal* of 2 and 13 July 1791. The author concealed his identity under the fiction that the letters were written by a correspondent abroad who was supposed to be instructing an American youth in a course of political studies. The contributor, who affected to be merely the channel of communication but was the actual author, signed himself *A Customer*. He advised the student – that is, the public – to imbibe deeply the writings on the American constitutions and to form an abiding attachment to them. He recommended first *The Federalist*, which, though written in haste and on the spur of the occasion, he considered "full of correct method, sound sense, and luminous prin-

ciples of liberty from beginning to end." Then *A Customer* turned to his real object, the writings of John Adams, particularly his *Defence* and his *Discourses on Davila*.

Adams' writings, he advised, "must be read with *some grains of allowance*. There is a great deal of learning, and a great number of useful and wise principles of government brought into view; but . . . he is attached to aristocratical and monarchical principles. My belief is founded on an attentive examination of his writings. This great master of politics is frequently, and pretty directly, inculcating a skepticism as to the goodness of republican governments, and a belief of the utility of hereditary monarchy, in terms which cannot but excite in the breast of those who are attached to the one, and who despise the other, a painful regret, and lively indignation. I wish to make a firm stand against such pernicious tenets. They are as directly in the face of our institutions and manners, as they are repugnant to our feelings and happiness." The *Discourses on Davila*, like all of Adams' other writing, revealed extensive learning and superior talents. They also pointed out one excellent truth that had long since been embodied in the American constitutions – the wisdom of dividing the executive, legislative, and judicial powers. But, *A Customer* added, "his writings have also inculcated, cherished, and propagated one abominable *heresy* that monarchy and aristocracy are compatible with permanent freedom, and probably essential to a wise, happy, and perfectly balanced constitution." TJ, Rush, and others then and later would have agreed with the author's observation that Adams had undergone, "since his residence in Europe, a very great change in his political principles." *A Customer* also anticipated TJ's later argument with Adams over the essential components of a natural aristocracy. Adams, in his *Defence*, had pointed out that the sources of inequality in every society – wealth, birth, and merit – constituted a natural aristocracy, a body of men containing the greatest collection of virtues and talents in a free government. "Fame and Fortune may be, and frequently are hereditary," *A Customer* observed, "but this is the first time I have ever heard a grave philosopher pronounce virtue and abilities to be so."

The first letter concluded by thanking

Adams for his years of labor and warning against the evils to which free government was exposed. "But," *A Customer* added, "I wish he would also warn us against the dangers of the opposite coast, to which he is steering our political vessel. . . . His writings have certainly the tendency (whatever may be his intention) to make people weary of republican government, and to sigh for the monarchy of England. To inculcate the doctrine, that men are not fit to choose their own rulers – that frequent elections are dangerous – that distinctions, not of virtue and talents, but of birth and fortune, are essential to the order of government – that riches and family should be the titles to preferment, and poverty the object of contempt. Such doctrines are deemed heresies in American politics."

A Customer's two letters, published before *Publicola*'s first number appeared, provided a carefully reasoned close to the first and less acrimonious phase of the contest of Burke and Paine in America. The second letter put the fictitious youth to whom it was supposedly addressed on guard, warning him that, while Adams as a patriot and philosopher stood high and illustrious because of his signal share in effecting the revolution and in concluding the Treaty of Peace, his opinions, like those of all others, were the proper object of criticism and inquiry. *A Customer* then proceeded to examine Adams' writings, to challenge his doctrines by citing historical evidence – including citations of Clarendon, Blackstone, *Notes on Virginia*, and other works – and contradicted Adams' assertion (later repeated in his address as President to the young workingmen of Philadelphia, greatly to TJ's indignation) that "The science of government has received very little improvement since the Greeks and Romans." On the contrary, declared *A Customer*, this was an age of political experimentation. Out of their own experience – the record of Connecticut, for example, in choosing their governors for a century and a half "with perfect harmony and . . . with the most undeviating discretion" – Americans had a right to conclude that self-government was possible. "But," he concluded, "admitting that it is still a matter of experiment, the cause of liberty, and of human happiness, requires that we should make the experiment with every possible advantage. It is not fair dealing for our most respectable writers to anticipate the decision, and give a wrong bias to the trial. . . . It would be deemed an odd way of encouraging a merchant to adventure his stock in foreign trade by recounting to him nothing but bankruptcies and shipwrecks; or to animate the soldier to war, by detailing only defeats, imprisonment and death."

The identity of *A Customer* has not been discovered. He was obviously a man of learning, well versed in classical writings on government, and – as the internal evidence proves – in law and jurisprudence as well. His letters were judicious, cogent, and restrained but forceful. His argument that Adams' writings tended to weaken the public confidence in government was one that Hamilton himself employed a few weeks later (see Editorial Note), but clearly the Secretary of the Treasury would not have penned many of *A Customer*'s passages. Since these two carefully reasoned, judicious critiques of Adams' writings were first published in Poughkeepsie, and considering their substance and style, it is plausible to suppose that Chancellor Robert R. Livingston may have written them. This supposition is given some confirmation by the fact that, after the *Publicola* essays began to appear, Livingston did compose a lengthy manuscript condemning the "new order of advocates of monarchy." The piece bears the title "Reflections on Monarchy" and was a direct outcome of the second phase of the controversy triggered by *Publicola* (MS in NHi: Robert R. Livingston Papers; cited by Alfred F. Young, *The Democratic Republicans of New York* [Chapel Hill, 1967], p. 208). The identity of *A Customer*, however, unfortunately remains in the realm of conjecture. His essays were deservedly reprinted in various newspapers, including the *Virginia Gazette*.

VIII. Thomas Jefferson to John Adams

Dear Sir   Philadelphia July 17. 1791.

I have a dozen times taken up my pen to write to you and as often laid it down again, suspended between opposing considerations. I determine however to write from a conviction that truth, between candid minds, can never do harm. The first of Paine's pamphlets on the Rights of man, which came to hand here, belonged to Mr. Beckley. He lent it to Mr. Madison who lent it to me; and while I was reading it Mr. Beckley called on me for it, and, as I had not finished it, he desired me as soon as I should have done so, to send it to Mr. Jonathan B. Smith, whose brother meant to reprint it. I finished reading it, and, as I had no acquaintance with Mr. Jonathan B. Smith, propriety required that I should explain to him why I, a stranger to him, sent him the pamphlet. I accordingly wrote a note of compliment informing him that I did it at the desire of Mr. Beckley, and, to take off a little of the dryness of the note, I added that I was glad it was to be reprinted here and that something was to be publicly said against the political heresies which had sprung up among us &ca. I thought so little of this note that I did not even keep a copy of it: nor ever heard a tittle more of it till, the week following, I was thunderstruck with seeing it come out at the head of the pamphlet. I hoped however it would not attract notice. But I found on my return from a journey of a month that a writer came forward under the signature of Publicola, attacking not only the author and principles of the pamphlet, but myself as it's sponsor, by name. Soon after came hosts of other writers defending the pamphlet and attacking you by name as the writer of Publicola. Thus were our names thrown on the public stage as public antagonists. That you and I differ in our ideas of the best form of government is well known to us both: but we have differed as friends should do, respecting the purity of each other's motives, and confining our difference of opinion to private conversation. And I can declare with truth in the presence of the almighty that nothing was further from my intention or expectation than to have had either my own or your name brought before the public on this occasion. The friendship and confidence which has so long existed between us required this explanation from me, and I know you too well to fear any misconstruction of the motives of it. Some people here who would wish me to be, or to be thought, guilty of improprieties, have suggested that I was Agricola, that I was Brutus &c. &c. I never did in my life, either by myself or by any other, have a sentence of mine inserted in a newspaper without putting my name to it; and I believe I never shall.

While the empress is refusing peace under a mediation unless Oczakow and it's territory be ceded to her, she is offering peace on the perfect statu quo to the Porte, if they will conclude it without a mediation. France has struck a severe blow at our navigation by a difference of duty on tobacco carried in our and their ships, and by taking from foreign built ships the capability of naturalization. She has placed our whale oil on rather a better footing than ever by consolidating the duties into a single one of 6. livres. They amounted before to some sous over that sum. I am told (I know not how truly) that England has prohibited our spermaceti oil altogether, and will prohibit our wheat till the price there is 52/ the quarter, which it almost never is. We expect hourly to hear the true event of Genl. Scott's expedition. Reports give favorable hopes of it. Be so good as to present my respectful compliments to Mrs. Adams and to accept assurances of the sentiments of sincere esteem & respect with which I am Dear Sir Your friend & servant,

Th: Jefferson

RC (MHi: AM); at foot of text in Adams' hand: "recd. at Boston July 28, 1791 ansd. July 29." PrC (DLC).

IX. James Monroe to Thomas Jefferson

Dear Sir   Wmsburg July 25. 1791.

Your favor of the 10th. found me here upon the business mention'd in my last. I left Mrs. M. at Monticello to remain till my return. I have been here near three weeks and shall leave it tomorrow on my way back. We have gone thro' the business, allotted to each his duty and are to meet again in Fredbg. on the 5th. of Octr. next. A part of our duty was to consolidate (when many were drawn) all the acts on one subject. The object, to make the law more perspicuous, by drawing its scatter'd parts into one view and repealing all preceding laws on such subject. A question arose in the Committee whether they were bound by this to prepare a bill conformable to the law as it stands, or provided they confin'd themselves to the subject, might propose on it any new project they thought fit. Of the latter opinion were Tazewell Tucker and Lee, Prentis Nelson and myself of the former. We were willing however that any member who conceiv'd the policy defective might prepare a bill for the purpose of amending it, which (having the approbation of the Committee) might accompany the other with the preference of the board, thus giving the legislature a fair alternative between them. In point of importance and labor the business is pretty equally divided between the members, but how these gentlemen above referr'd to, particularly Tucker and Lee, will execute their part in this respect is doubtful; we shall observe the principle contended for on our part strictly. – An attempt was made to protract our meeting untill that of the Assembly, to have it likewise at Richmond, with a view by managment of procuring admission into the house for the purpose of supporting the report. This has been urg'd by most of them and altho the time of meeting has been yeilded, yet the other object is not abandon'd. It is sought no doubt with other views by several than merely that of explaining the bills that will be submitted. Some of them certainly wish to avail themselves of such an opportunity of gaining the good wishes of that body for other purposes. – The contest of Burke and Paine, as reviv'd in America with the different publications on either side is much the subject of discussion in all parts of this state. Adams is universally believ'd to be the author of Publicola and the principles he avows, as well as those of Mr. B. as universally reprobated. The character of the publick officers is likewise pretty well known. At first it was doubted whether you would not be compell'd to give your sentiments fully to the publick, whether a respect for yourself and the publick opinion would not require it of you. Whilst the fever was at the height the opinion preponderated in favor of it. At present it appears unsettled, especially as Adams is not the avow'd author of Publicola, and so many writers have taken up the subject in your favor. Your other engagements which employ so much of your time necessarily, are certainly to be taken into the calculation and must have great weight. The publick opinion however will before long fully disclose itself on the subject of government, and as an opportunity has and is in some measure offer'd you to give the aid of your talents and character to the republican scale, I am aware you must have experienc'd some pain in repressing your inclinations on the subject. Your sentiments indeed, if they had been previously question'd, are made known as well by the short note prefixt to Paines pamphlet, as a volume could do it. – Dr. Lee is almost the only man I have heard answer that pamphlet or support that of his antagonist. Tis said however that his whole family are in harmony with him.

I am particularly thankful for your attention to our accomodation. We shall be happy in whatever you do in that respect and the more so the nearer you place us to yourself. Remember me to Mr. Madison. We are on our plantation surrounded by trees &ca. Very affecy. I am dear Sir sincerely yr. friend & servant,

JAS. MONROE

RC (DLC); endorsed by TJ as received 4 Aug. 1791 and so recorded in SJL.

X. John Adams to Thomas Jefferson

DEAR SIR   Braintree July 29. 1791

Yesterday, at Boston, I received your friendly Letter of July 17th. with great pleasure. I give full credit to your relation of the manner, in which your note was written and prefixed to the Philadelphia edition of Mr. Paines pamphlet on the rights of Man: but the misconduct of the person, who committed this breach of your confidence, by making it publick, whatever were his intentions, has Sown the Seeds of more evils, than he can ever attone for. The Pamphlet, with your name, to So Striking a recommendation of it, was not only industriously propagated in New York and Boston; but, that the recommendation might be known to every one, was reprinted with great care in the Newspapers, and was generally considered as a direct and open personal attack upon me, by countenancing the false interpretation of my Writings as favouring the Introduction of hereditary Monarchy and Aristocracy into this Country. The Question every where was What Heresies are intended by the Secretary of State? The Answer in the Newspapers was, The Vice Presidents notions of a limited Monarchy, an hereditary Government of King and Lords, with only elective commons. Emboldened by these murmurs soon after appeared the Paragraphs of an unprincipled Libeller in the New Haven Gazette, carefully reprinted in the papers of New York, Boston and Philadelphia, holding up the Vice President to the ridicule of the World, for his meanness, and to their detestation for wishing to Subjugate the People to a few Nobles. These were soon followed by a formal Speech of the Lieutenant Governor of Massachusetts very Solemnly holding up the Idea of hereditary Powers and cautioning the Publick against them, as if they were at that moment in the most imminent danger of them. These Things were all accompanied with the most marked neglect, both of the Governor and Lieutenant Governor of this State towards me; and alltogether opperated as an Hue and Cry to all my Ennemies and Rivals, to the old constitutional faction of Pensilvania in concert with the late Insurgents of Massachusetts, both of whom consider my Writings as the Cause of their overthrow, to hunt me down like a hare, if they could. – In this State of Things, Publicola, who, I Suppose thought that Mr. Paines Pamphlet was made Use of as an Instrument to destroy a Man, for whom he had a regard, [whom] he thought innocent and in the present moment [of] Some importance to the Publick, came forward.

You declare very explicitly that you never did, by yourself or by any other, have a Sentence of yours inserted in a Newspaper, without your name to it. And I, with equal frankness declare that I never did, either by myself or by any other, have a Sentence of mine inserted in any Newspaper Since I left Philadelphia. I neither wrote nor corrected Publicola. The Writer in the Composition of his Pieces followed his own Judgment, Information and discretion, without any Assistance from me.

You observe "That you and I differ in our Ideas of the best form of Government is well known to Us both." But, my dear Sir, you will give me leave to Say, that I do not know this. I know not what your Idea is of the best form of Government. You and I have never had a Serious conversation together that I can recollect concerning the nature of Government. The very transient hints that have ever passed between Us, have been jocular and Superficial, without ever coming to any explanation. If You Suppose that I have or ever had a design or desire, of attempting to introduce a Government of King, Lords and Commons [or] in other Words an hereditary Executive or an [h]ereditary Senate, either into the Government of the United States, or that of any Individual State, in this Co[ountry,][1] You are wholly mistaken. There is not Such a Thought expressed or intimated in any public writing or private Letter of mine, and I may Safely challenge all Mankind to produce Such a passage and quote the Chapter and Verse. If you have ever put Such a Construction on any Thing of mine, I beg you would mention it to me, and I will undertake to convince you, that it has no such meaning. Upon this occasion I will venture to Say that my unpolished Writings, although they have been read by a sufficient Number of Persons to have assisted in crushing the Insurrection of the Massachusetts, the formation of the new Constitutions of Pensilvania, Georgia and South Carolina and in procuring the Assent of all the States to the new national Constitution, Yet they have not been read by great Numbers. Of the few who have taken the pains to read them, Some have misunderstood them and others have willfully misrepresented them, and these misunderstandings and misrepresentations have been made the pretence for overwhelming me with floods and Whirlwinds of tempestuous abuse, unexampled in the History of this Country.

It is thought by Some, that Mr. Hancocks friends are preparing the way, by my destruction, for his Election to the Place of Vice President, and that of Mr. Samuel Adams to be Governor of this Commonwealth, and then the Stone House Faction will be sure of all the Loaves and Fishes, in the national Government and the State Government as they hope. The opposers of the present Constitution of Pensilvania, the Promoters of Shases Rebellion and County Resolves, and many of the Detesters of the present national Government, will undoubtedly aid them. Many People think too that no small Share of a foreign Influence, in revenge for certain untractable conduct at the Treaty of Peace, is and will be intermingled. The Janizaries of this goodly Combination, among whom are three or four who hesitate at no falshood, have written all the Impudence and Impertinence, which have appeared in the Boston Papers upon this memorable Occasion.

I must own to you that the daring Traits of Ambition and Intrigue, and those unbridled Rivalries which have already appeared, are the most melancholly, and alarming Symptoms that I have ever Seen in this Country: and if they are to be encouraged to proceed in their Course, the Sooner I am relieved from the Competition the happier I Shall be.

I thank you, Sir very Sincerely for writing to me upon this occasion. It was high time that you and I should come to an explanation with each other. The friendship which has Subsisted for fifteen years between Us, without the Smallest Interruption, and untill this occasion without the Slightest Suspicion, ever has been and Still is, very dear to my heart. There is no office which I would not resign, rather than give a just occasion for one friend to forsake me. Your motives for writing to me, I have not a doubt were the most pure and the most friendly and I have no suspicion that you will not receive this explanation from me in the same candid Light.[2]

I thank You Sir for the foreign Intelligence and beg leave to present You with the friendly compliments of Mrs. Adams, as well as the repeated Assurances of the friendship, Esteem and respect of Dear Sir Your most obedient and most humble servant,

JOHN ADAMS

RC (DLC); slightly mutilated, so that some words and parts of words have been lost; these have been supplied from FC and placed within brackets; at foot of text: "The Secretary of State of the United States of America"; endorsed by TJ as received 11 Aug. 1791 and so recorded in SJL. FC (MHi: AM); in the hand of Adams' young-est son, Thomas B. Adams. For slight variation in the texts, see notes below.

The UNPRINCIPLED LIBELLER IN THE NEW HAVEN GAZETTE, whose satiric squib appeared in its issue of 18 May 1791, charged Adams with being parsimonious. "The liberality of that gentleman," the anonymous author declared, "is worthy of notice. On his tour between Philadelphia and Boston his progress was impeded by means of a dangerous bridge being taken up to repair. The alacrity of the laborers . . . soon furnished the Sage with a temporary passage for himself, family, and retinue; which demonstrated their esteem for so illustrious a character. – And in token of respect for the attention shewn him, he *generously* conferred on the laborers *one quarter* of a *dollar*!! which must be considered a very liberal compensation to six or eight men for an hour's service, especially when we consider how *parsimonious* Congress have

been in stipulating his Salary." The piece was copied by newspapers throughout the country, especially in the middle and southern states (see Donald H. Stewart, *The opposition press of the Federalist period* [Albany, 1969], p. 831n.). See TJ's response to Adams' allusion to the New Haven piece (TJ to Adams, 30 Aug. 1791; Document XII).

[1] MS mutilated and part of this word editorially supplied; FC omits the phrase "in this Country."

[2] FC ends at this point.

XI. Thomas Jefferson to Thomas Paine

DEAR SIR   Philadelphia July 29. 1791.

Your favor of Sep. 28. 1790. did not come to my hands till Feb. 11. and I have not answered it sooner because it said you would be here in the Spring. That expectation being past, I now acknolege the reciept. Indeed I am glad you did not come away till you had written your 'Rights of man.' That has been much read here, with avidity and pleasure. A writer under the signature of Publicola attacked it. A host of champions entered the arena immediately in your defence. The discussion excited the public attention, recalled it to the 'Defence of the American constitutions' and the 'Discourses on Davila,' which it had kindly passed over without censure in the moment, and very general expressions of their sense have been now drawn forth; and I thank god that they appear firm in their republicanism, notwithstanding the contrary hopes and assertions of a sect here, high in names, but small in numbers. These had flattered themselves that the silence of the people under the 'Defence' and 'Davila' was a symptom of their conversion to the doctrine of king, lords, and commons. They are checked at least by your pamphlet, and the people confirmed in their good old faith.

Your observations on the subject of a copper coinage have satisfied my mind on that subject, which I confess had wavered before between difficulties. As a different plan is under consideration of Congress, and will be taken up at their meeting, I think to watch the proper moment, and publish your observations (except the Notes which contain facts relative to particular persons which I presume you would dislike to see published, and which are not necessary to establish the main object,) adding your name, because it will attract attention and give weight to the publication. As this cannot take place under four months, there is time for you to forbid me, if it should be disagreeable to you to have the observations published, which however I hope it will not be.

Genl. Scott has just returned from a succesful expedition against the Indians, having killed 32 warriors and taken 58. women and children, and burnt several towns. I hope they will now consent to peace, which is all we ask. – Our funds are near par; the crops of wheat remarkeably fine; and a great degree of general prosperity arising from 4. years successive of plentiful crops, a great diffusion of domestic manufacture, a return to economy, and a reasonable[1] faith in the new government. – I shall be happy to hear from you, and still more so to see you, being with great & sincere esteem Dr. Sir Your friend & servt,   TH: JEFFERSON

PrC (DLC).

Late in November, after receiving the above letter, Paine wrote to his friend John Hall: "I have received a letter from Mr. Jefferson who mentioned the great run [*Rights of Man*] has had there. It has been attacked by John Adams, who has brought an host about his ears from all parts of the Continent. Mr. Jefferson has sent me twenty-five different answers to Adams who wrote under the name of Publicola" (Paine to Hall, 25 Nov. 1791, Philip S. Foner, *The complete writings of Thomas Paine*, II [New York, 1945], 1322). Paine's misrepresentation of TJ's letter led David F. Hawke, *Paine*, p. 234, to the conclusion that TJ, in spreading rumor for fact about the authorship of the *Publicola* essays, had done his friend Adams a great disservice. This gossip, he added, "sealed Paine's hatred of Adams and Paine ever after pursued Adams with the ferocity he usually reserved for kings." Paine, however, needed no prompting on this score. He had long since joined TJ, Rush, and others in thinking that Adams had changed his political principles since 1776. Indeed, at this time, Paine boasted: "I had John Adams in my mind when I wrote [*Rights of Man*] and it has hit as I expected" (Paine to William Short, 2 Nov. 1791, Foner, *Writings of Paine*, II, 1320, from RC in PHi). Far from identifying Adams as *Publicola* in the above letter, TJ carefully concealed his opinion on the subject, thereby silently defining the

limits of his confidence in Paine's discretion.

Surprisingly, it was William Short's breach of TJ's confidence which enabled Paine to give Hall the erroneous impression that John Adams was *Publicola*. On the day before TJ wrote the above letter, he gave Short a brief account of the enthusiastic reception of Paine's pamphlet, the attack on it by "a writer under the name of Publicola," and the response "by a host of republican volunteers." He also expressed his fear that "the honestest man of the party will fall a victim to his imprudence on this occasion" – an expression which pointed unmistakably to Adams. But even with a correspondent in whom he had implicit confidence, TJ took pains to encode the passage of his letter naming Adams as first among those hoping "to make way for a king, lords and commons" in the United States (TJ to Short, 28 July 1791). Short sent to Paine a copy of this private letter and also forwarded to him the collection of anti-*Publicola* clippings from Bache's *General Advertiser* (Paine to Short, 2 Nov. 1791, Foner, *Writings of Paine*, II, 1320). From TJ's letter to Short and from these clippings, Paine drew the inference that John Adams was *Publicola* and passed the unfounded supposition on to his friend Hall. He also gave him the false impression that it was TJ himself who had sent him the anti-*Publicola* pieces.

Paine's "Thoughts on the Establishment of a Mint" was enclosed in his letter to TJ of 28 Sep. 1790 and is printed there. When Paine next wrote, he did not mention receipt of the above letter or comment on TJ's suggestion, perhaps because he was so disturbed over the appointment of Gouverneur Morris as minister to France (Paine to TJ, 13 Feb. 1792). In the meantime, TJ made the essay on the mint available to Freneau, who published it in the *National Gazette*, 17 Nov. 1791. The original manuscript has not been found, and so the names that TJ deleted cannot be known with certainty, but these must have included that of Robert Morris, whose plan for coinage had been criticized by TJ. The name of Gouverneur Morris, who had written on the subject, may also have appeared in the text (see Editorial Note and group of documents on coinage, at end of Apr. 1784).

¹ This word interlined in substitution for "great degree of," deleted.

XII. Thomas Jefferson to John Adams

MY DEAR SIR   Philadelphia Aug. 30. 1791.

I recieved some time ago your favor of July 29. and was happy to find that you saw in it's true point of view the way in which I had been drawn into the scene which must have been so disagreeable to you. The importance which you still seem to allow to my note, and the effect you suppose it to have had tho unintentional in me, induce me to shew you that it really had no effect. Paine's pamphlet, with my note, was published here about the 2d. week in May. Not a word ever appeared in the public papers here on the subject for more than a month; and I am certain not a word on the subject would ever have been said had not a writer, under the name of Publicola, at length undertaken to attack Mr. Paine's principles, which were the principles of the citizens of the U. S. Instantly a host of writers attacked Publicola in support of those principles. He had thought proper to misconstrue a figurative expression in my note; and these writers so far noticed me as to place the expression in it's true light. But this was only an incidental skirmish preliminary to the general engagement, and they would not have thought me worth naming, had not he thought proper to bring me on the scene. His antagonists, very criminally in my opinion presumed you to be Publicola, and on that presumption hazarded a personal attack on you. No person saw with more uneasiness than I did, this unjustifiable assault, and the more so, when I saw it continued after the printer had declared you were not the author. But you will perceive from all this, my dear Sir, that my note contributed nothing to the production of these disagreeable peices. As long as Paine's pamphlet stood on it's own feet, and on my note, it was unnoticed. As soon as Publicola attacked Paine, swarms appeared in his defence. To Publicola then and not in the least degree to my note, this whole contest is to be ascribed and all it's consequences.

You speak of the execrable paragraph in the Connecticut paper. This it is true appeared before Publicola. But it had no more relation to Paine's pamphlet and my note, than to the Alcoran. I am satisfied the writer of it had never seen either; for when I past through Connecticut about the middle of June, not a copy had ever been seen by anybody either in Harford or New Haven, nor probably in that whole state: and that paragraph was so notoriously the reverse of the disinterestedness of character which you are known to possess by every body who knows your name, that I never heard a person speak of the paragraph but with an indignation in your behalf, which did you entire justice. This paragraph then certainly did not flow from my note, any more than the publications which Publicola produced. Indeed it was impossible that my note should occasion your name to be brought into question; for so far from naming you, I had not even in view any writing which I might suppose to be yours, and the opinions I alluded to were principally[1] those I had heard in common conversation from a sect aiming at the subversion of the present government to bring in their favorite form of a King, lords, and commons.

Thus I hope, my dear Sir, that you will see me to have been as innocent *in effect* as I was in intention. I was brought before the public without my own consent, and from the first moment of seeing the effort of the real aggressor in this business to keep me before the public, I determined that nothing should induce me to put pen to paper in the controversy. The business is now over, and I hope it's effects are over, and that our friendship will never be suffered to be committed, whatever use others may think proper to make of our names.

The event of the King's flight from Paris and his recapture will have struck you with it's importance. It appears I think that the nation is firm within, and it only remains to see whether there will be any movement from without. I confess I have not changed my confidence in the favourable issue of that revolution, because it has always rested on my own ocular evidence of the unanimity of the nation, and wisdom of the Patriotic party in the national assembly. The last advices render it probable that the emperor will recommence hostilities against the Porte. It remains to see whether England and Prussia will take a part. Present me to Mrs. Adams with all the affections I feel for her and be assured of those devoted to yourself by, my dear Sir your sincere friend & servt,

TH: JEFFERSON

RC (MHi: AM); endorsed. PrC (DLC).

The EXECRABLE PARAGRAPH IN THE CONNECTICUT PAPER is identified and quoted in the note to Adams' letter to TJ of 29 July 1791 (Document x).

XIII. Thomas Jefferson to Thomas Paine

DEAR SIR   Philadelphia June 19. 1792.

I received with great pleasure the present of your pamphlets, as well for the thing itself as that it was a testimony of your recollection. Would you believe it possible that in this country there should be high and important characters who need your lessons in republicanism, and who do not heed them? It is but too true that we have a sect preaching up and panting after an English constitution of king, lords, and commons, and whose heads are itching for crowns, coronets and mitres. But our people, my good friend, are firm and unanimous in their principles of republicanism, and there is no better proof of it than that they love what you write and read it with delight. The printers season every newspaper with extracts from your last, as they did before from your first part of the Rights of man. They have both served here to separate the wheat from the chaff, and to prove that tho the latter appears on the surface, it is on the surface only. The bulk below is sound and pure. Go on then in doing with your pen what in other times was done with the sword; shew that reformation is more practicable by operating on the mind than on the body of man, and be assured that it has not a more sincere votary, nor you a more ardent well-wisher than, Dear Sir, Your friend & servt,   TH: JEFFERSON

PrC (DLC); at foot of text: "Thos. Paine esq." The pamphlets that TJ acknowledged were six copies of the second part of *Rights of Man*. Paine had sent Washington a dozen copies, designating half of them for TJ (Paine to TJ, 13 Feb. 1792; Paine to Washinton, 13 Feb. 1792, DLC: Washington Papers; see Sowerby, No. 2826).

It is significant that TJ allowed another decade to pass before he again wrote to Paine. During this critical period he allowed all of Paine's various letters to go unanswered (Paine to TJ, 20 Apr. 1792; 10 Oct. 1793; 1 Apr. and 10 May 1797; and 1, 4, 6, and 16 Oct. 1800). The reason seems obvious. A failure at almost everything save his great achievements as a political propagandist, Paine succeeded ultimately in alienating himself not only from such former friends as Washington, Adams, and TJ, but from the mainstream of events in England, France, and the United States as well. More and more he became obsessed with the idea that the American national character had deteriorated. "The neutral powers despise her for her meanness and her desertion of a common interest," he wrote TJ in 1797, "England laughs at her for her imbecility, and France is enraged at her ingratitude and sly treachery" (Paine to TJ, 1 Apr. 1797). His hatred of the Federalists was so violent as to suggest mental derangement, leading him into the seditious act of planning the conquest of the United States by France. His letters of 1800 were such that TJ felt obliged, shortly after becoming President, to restate his inaugural pledge and to warn Paine that the United States would not become involved in European contests – even, he added, "in support of principles which we mean to pursue" (TJ to Paine, 18 Mch. 1801).

From Francis Eppes

Bermuda Hundred, 27 Apr. 1791. Has consulted all our lawyers on *The Prince of Wales* and, on the basis of Wayles' letter of 14 May 1772, they "appear all very clear in their opinions that the Executors . . . will be answerable for the amount of the . . . cargo." The trial will be brought on in October if possible. "I hope you will be in Virginia at that time as I shall stand much in need of your advice and assistance. . . . You will be pleas'd to consider [Wayles' letter] and inform me what you think of it. Jack ear this must be with you. For gods sake indeavour to impress on his mind the necessity of his qualifying himself for some profession which will inable him to git his bread for shou'd this business go against us it will not be in my power to do much for him. We are all well and unite in wishing you every blessing this world affords."

RC (ViU); endorsed by TJ as received 10 May 1791 and so recorded in SJL.

For the lawyers' opinions on the liability of the estate of John Wayles in the matter of *The Prince of Wales*, see note to Skipwith's letter to TJ, 7 Apr. 1791, and TJ's reply to Skipwith, 6 May 1791.

From Thomas Digges

SIR   Belfast 28 April 1791.

I wrote you on the 24th. Ins. and am sorry to put you to the trouble of reading a second long Letter nearly upon the same Subject. It is of such importance to the Manufactures of our Country as to insure me your forgiveness. The Artist Mr. Wm. Pearce, mentiond in my former Letter and whose works you will have described at the end of this Letter, has finally determind to go for America with his Invention, and to fix there; And I have so little time before the Vessel sails to address The President and yourself on the subject of Pearce and McCabe getting a Patent or premium for their work, that I hope you will escuse haste and inaccuracys.

I before wrote You that a Box was forwarded to Mr. Geo. Woolsey Merchant of New York and a relation of McCabes, containing the materials and specifications for a new Invented double Loom, and so sent For the Inspection of the President and yourself as to obtain for the Inventors Pearce and McCabe a Patent, or such exclusive Benefit as the Laws of America provide for Artists who furnish new and usefull Inventions.

At that time I had my Eye upon Pearce and a strong hope of his going, but as His doing so much crashd with the present Interest of his Partner McCabe, I was necessiated to write to Yourself and the President in the stile I then did *as if Pearce was not to go*. He is now, very much to my satisfaction and pleasure, so engaged as not to be able to recede, without a forcible stop from the Government, who are making Laws and trying all possible means to stop the Emigration of Artists and their Tools. – I need not tell You that it is not only difficult to get such away, but highly dangerous to those concerned; Therefore the more secret it is kept the better. Pearce will bear this Letter to Yourself and a similar one to the President; together with the box before mentioned. For fear of a miscarriage of my former Letter I will annex to this a duplicate of my description of his sundry Looms &ca., as also to inform You that the Box contains a pair of double Temples near 7 ft. in length for spreading at the same time two pieces of Linin or Callico on one Loom, also a set of Headles, Elbow and Shuttle for Linen &ca. I have one satisfaction that should they miscarry, Pearce if He lives can make every atom of them (which I believe no other man can do) and with Him goes two ingenious workmen, Jameson and Hall, who can make most kinds of machinery such as spining Jennys, Billys, mules, Carding machines &ca. and they will be excellent *seconds* to Pearce who has been twice or thrice beset here by Emissarys from Manchester to inveigle Him back to England, and I doubt not but they will follow him for like purposes to America.

He puts his trust in the President and in You to whom it is with alacrity I have given every testimonial in my power of his industry, sobriety, worth and extraordinary [talents though he is low-bred and an ?] illiterate man. He is not rich tho an Independant man having [a sum ?] of money left in the hands of a friend in Manchester on whom he can draw, (which He has done to me for the advance of getting him and the other two out and for passage money &ca.). He has a wife and Family in England who will soon follow him, and I trust his invitations will lead a number of mechanic Artists to follow his fortunes. – I have given Him introductory Letters to Mr. Seton of N York, Conyngham & Nesbet, Governor Dickinson, my Brother at my home near Mt. Vernon, Colo. Fitzgerald &ca.

but with Express orders that no one shall have access to the Box but the President and yourself, for the disclosure of it to an ingenious artist or good drawer might pirate from McCabe and Pearce their Invention. – He wants nothing but health, waterfall, wood and Iron to carry him thro' any Manufactory and being delighted with my description of our Rivers and Falls &ca. it is with my advice He will wait upon Mr. Dickinson and look at the Brandywine mills &ca. &ca.

I hope by tomorrow He will be at Sea and in safety. It gives me great pleasure to have been the means of getting so valuable an Artist to our Country and I cannot too strongly recommend Him to Your patronage and every other aid He may want. I am with great respect & Esteem Yr. Obedt. & very Hle. Serv.,

THOS. DIGGES

If I can in *any way* assist or help You, I hope You wont spare Your commands. I shall be in England till Sepr. next and any direction will be to care of Mr. Josa. Johnson American Consul London, tho my stay will be chiefly in Yorkshire and the manufacturing towns of England. – I have wrote till I am nearly blind.

RC (DLC); top of first leaf worn so that some words are lost and have been given conjecturally in brackets (supplied), being based on similar expressions in other letters by Digges. Recorded in SJL as received 12 July 1791. Enclosure: Digges' description of Pearce's inventions, together with some information about the man and his claims, in part as follows: "Pearce came last from Doncaster in Yorkshire, and is the artist who erected the famous mills of Messrs. Cartwrights of that place, which dress the wool, spins and weaves it into Broad Cloth by force of water, steam, or horse (when I saw the works, they were forc'd by an Ox or Bull) and the Proprietors were making a fortune by it. – He also was the inventor of Arkwrights Spining and weaving Machinery . . . but was robbd of his invention by Arkwright (then a hairdresser and since made a Baronet from his Wealth) But Pearce and a Mr. Thos. Hayes, then a joint Artist in the work broke Arkwrights patent 'tho not till after he acquired a large fortune by it." There followed a description of Pearce's improvements on his four types of looms, the last of which was "for weaving three pieces of Thickset or Corduroys at once, with an additional invention of a flat piece of Iron with Cutters to cut the Thickset as he wove on (the Expence of cutting Thickset is 1½d. or 2d. pr yard). I did not see the cutting [work, but the] Pieces were all of Cotton of about 900 fine and nine yards pr. day was easy work. This was his neatest and best looking Loom, but the Linin one is far more valuable to this Country, and His Check one the more ingenious. . . . The intention of Messrs. Pearce and McCabe was to get a premium from the Irish Parliament for these vast improvements in manufacture, but after a long attendance and producing every possible and convincing proofs of their Utility, They were foild by a *party* ⟨. . .⟩; and by a trick in *Jobbing*, (for there is no publick works done in this Country without its becoming a *Job*). Ireland is likely to loose not only the invention but so ingenious an Artist as Pearce. He will I trust be a blessing to Our Country, where from the dearness and high price of Mechanic wages, all Manufacture must at first receive a Check; But by the aid of such Machinery and mill work as Pearce's, He will make *wood* and *water*, a vast substitute for manual Labour" (MS in Digges' hand, undated, in DLC: TJ Papers, 63: f. 10951;

a word or two heavily scored out and indecipherable, as indicated by the angle brackets; MS worn at top of leaf and some words are lost, being given in brackets [supplied] from a similar document of which a description follows). There is another description of Pearce's looms and of his relation with McCabe which is almost identical with the enclosure just described except for the final paragraph, which reads: "On Mr. Pearce's disappointment here, and becoming vexd with the Rulers of this Country, I got Him with some difficulty, and no little danger to Embark for America. An Express was sent from Dublin to stop Him, and the vessell was twice boarded and stopd in which He went by the Cutters. I saw him safe away in the Brig Endeavour Capn. Seward belonging to Portsmouth N H and who saild from hence the 3d. of May for New York. His wish is to Establish himself where a water fall in the vicinity of any great town can be easily obtained. He took out with Him the working artist who made his Looms (*Mr. Jameson*, who is Brother to Messrs. Jamesons Merchts Iron monger in London), also Jno. Hall another artist; and He went recommended (his purpose being first to obtain a Patent in America) to The President, to Mr. Wm. Seton N. York, Mr. Thos. Jefferson, Govr. Dickinson, Conyngham & Nesbit Phia, to Colo. Fitzgerald Alexa; Geo Diggs &ca. & ca. and also to Mr. Thos Russell Boston. His wish is to be near the Fœdral Town and He is bent upon looking at the Falls of Potowmack for His mill station before he fixes. T.D." (MS in DNA: RG 59, MLR; undated but after 3 May 1791 and obviously addressed neither to Washington nor to TJ. Its presence in the departmental files suggests that the recipient forwarded it either to the President or to the Secretary of State. The reference to Pearce's desire to locate near Federal City and at the Falls of the Potomac indicates that the most likely recipient was Henry Lee, who hoped to establish manufacturing and commercial enterprises at that site; see Lee to TJ, 6 Mch. 1789 and note to TJ's opinion on Virginia's textile proposal, at 3 Dec. 1790; Digges enclosed a similar document in his letter to Washington of 12 July 1791, DNA: RG 59, MLR.)

Thomas Attwood Digges (1742-1821), scion of a prominent Catholic family of Maryland whose seat lay across the Potomac from Mount Vernon, was trusted least by those who knew him best. The known testimony of contemporaries – with one very notable exception – was unanimously adverse. Benjamin Franklin's famous appraisal was so damning and so current at the time that Horace Walpole recorded it in his journals. On learning that Digges had embezzled charitable funds placed in his hands for the relief of suffering American prisoners, Franklin declared in outrage: "We have no name in our Language for such atrocious Wickedness. If such a Fellow is not damn'd it is not worth while to keep a Devil" (Franklin to William Hodgson, 1 Apr. 1781, DLC: Franklin Papers, printed in Francis Wharton, *Dipl. Corr. Am. Rev.*, IV, 345-6; Walpole's paraphrase – "that if Digges was not damned the devil would be useless" – appears in his Journal for Mch. 1782, Francis Steuart, ed., *The Last Journals of Horace Walpole* [London, 1910], p. 422). Joshua Johnson, who had known Digges well in London before the war, advised William Knox to "be cautious of T. D." (Johnson to William Knox, 18 Apr. 1791, DNA: RG 59, CD, MNP 167/1; see note to Knox to TJ, 19 Apr. 1791). Even Bishop Carroll of Baltimore, who did not know Digges at all but was well aware of his general reputation in Maryland, felt called upon to warn the Archbishop of Dublin against his intrigues in "coaliting Catholics with Presbyterians" in northern Ireland. Acknowledging that his family and connections were of the first respectability and that Digges himself was a person of "amazing address," Carroll declared that in his early youth he had been guilty of misdemeanors "indicating rooted depravity . . . and his friends, to rescue him from the hands of justice, and themselves from dishonour, sent him out of the country" (Carroll to the Archbishop of Dublin, 16 Apr. 1792, quoted in Lynn H. Parsons' "The Mysterious Mr. Digges," WMQ, XXII [July, 1965], 490-1, from Moran's *Spicilegium Ossoriense* [Dublin, 1884], 511-12).

The one exception among Digges' distrusting contemporaries was the President of the United States. Long a neighbor and friend of the family, George Washington said he had "no hesitation in declaring that the conduct of Mr. Thomas Digges towards the United States during the war

. . . and since so far as the same has come to my knowledge has not been only friendly, but I might add zealous." Washington believed, but did not assert as a fact, that during the war he had received useful communications directly from Digges and also through captives he had helped to escape, sent at "extreme hazard of discovery." But this distinguished testimonial, prudently qualified as it was, only revealed Washington's lack of personal knowledge of Digges' true character. "Until you mentioned the doubts . . . entertained of Mr. Digges' attachment to his country," Washington wrote to his friend John Fitzgerald, "I had no idea of its being questioned." In another important respect Washington's testimonial was an unintended confirmation of the general estimate of Digges' role during the war. For the fact is that legal proceedings had been instituted to have Digges' Maryland estate confiscated on the ground that he had remained loyal to England and had served the enemy. Washington spoke therefore as a character witness and at the request of counsel for the defense. Fitzgerald was confident that the President would not only do justice to Digges' character as a patriot, "but perhaps save an Estate to the descendants of an old friend and Neighbour, and to a family which . . . I have every reason to believe you honor with your friendship." Washington readily complied, but with an opinion which raised more questions than it answered. Whatever its value as legal evidence, the powerful influence of its author undoubtedly helped Digges retain possession of his ancestral patrimony (Fitzgerald to Washington, 14 Apr. 1794, RC in DLC: Washington Papers; Washington to Fitzgerald, 27 Apr. 1794, *Writings*, ed. Fitzpatrick, XXXIII, 340-2; in a postscript Washington added that he had talked with John Trumbull, who said that he was well acquainted with Digges in London and that he "always appeared well attached to . . . the United States"). Washington's testimony may have enabled Digges to live out his final days as a Maryland planter. But it could not sway the verdict of history.

Digges absented himself from his native land for more than thirty years, during most of which time his known activities served only to raise suspicions about what remained hidden from the record. Like the famous double-agent, Edward Bancroft,

another American expatriate whom he knew in London, Digges claimed to be a doctor, possessed affable manners, was admitted to respectable circles, and even wrote a mediocre novel whose chief title to remembrance is the doubtful claim that it was the first by an American. But there the parallel ends. Bancroft, a man of many talents, was so supremely skilled at deception that his treasonable activities remained hidden for a century, while Digges, an adventurer without any distinguishing competence, earned almost at once the well-merited distrust of those who knew him. With good reason he was accused at the time of being a liar, a speculator, a trader with the enemy, and a secret agent of the British government. The judgment of historians – again with a single exception – has overwhelmingly sustained that of his contemporaries. Every new accession of evidence has also confirmed the verdict. Even Digges' sole scholarly defender, William Bell Clark, conceded that he embezzled funds intended for the relief of prisoners and sought to excuse this on the ground that failure of remittances from home "forced Digges to substitute ingenuity for integrity" (Clark, "In Defense of Thomas Digges," PMHB, LXXVII [Oct. 1953], 381-438; for the attribution to Digges of *Adventures of Alonso* [London, 1774], see Robert H. Elias, "The First American Novel," *Amer. Lit.*, XII [Jan. 1941], 419-34, reprinted as an introduction to a facsimile edition of the novel [New York, 1943], and Robert H. Elias and Michael N. Stanton, "Thomas Atwood Digges and *Adventures of Alonso*," *Amer. Lit.*, XLIV [March 1972], 118-22; fresh information about Digges' intrigues in Ireland, raising new suspicions, is presented in Lynn Hudson Parsons' "The Mysterious Mr. Digges," WMQ, XXII [July 1965], 486-92).

There is abundant evidence, as Washington correctly testified, that Digges did much to encourage artisans to emigrate to America and to take with them models and drawings of various kinds of machinery. What Washington overlooked, however, was that this was a felonious endeavor against which Great Britain for a century had enacted laws with increasingly severe penalties (i.e., £500 sterling fine and twelve months in prison, under the then prevailing laws of both Great Britain and Ireland; see David J. Jeremy, "British Textile

Technology Transmission to the United States," *Business Hist. Rev.*, XLVII [Spring 1973], 24-6). This undeniable activity may have been inspired by patriotic feelings, as Washington believed, but the abundant evidence set forth in Digges' letters, flawed as it was by prevarication, unfounded claims, and poor judgment, suggests that he had other and less elevated objects in view. Among these, as Digges candidly admitted, was the desire to "get over some Tenantry, and among them Artists, to fix on lands I possess both in Virginia and Maryland not far from the new Federal Town" (Digges to Hamilton, 6 Apr. 1792, Syrett, *Hamilton*, XI, 242). Perhaps also Digges thought to rehabilitate his reputation at home by an activity which might be regarded by some as disinterested public service. But, however worthy his public or private motives, Digges was nevertheless engaged in industrial espionage of a criminal nature. This he compounded by seeking to enlist as accomplices the highest officers of his own government.

When Digges made a similar appeal to TJ in 1788, he received not only the blunt response that other than cotton manufacturing was impracticable in the United States, but also the unequivocal declaration that it was "not the policy of the government . . . to give any aid to works of that kind" (TJ to Digges, 19 June 1788; Digges to TJ, 12 May 1788; Henry Wyld to TJ, 20 May 1788). This was not enough to discourage such an enthusiast as Digges. Early in 1791, after a committee of the Irish House of Commons had reported favorably on Pearce's invention of a simple loom capable of weaving a double web simultaneously, Digges made himself sponsor, promoter, and, as the evidence suggests, exploiter of the inventor. Pearce was an ingenious artisan, unlettered, impracticable, and intemperate. But Digges, who made the highly implausible claim that Arkwright and Cartwright had got their machines by robbing Pearce of his inventions, came to look upon the mechanic as "somewhat like a second Archimedes" (Digges to Hamilton, 6 Apr. 1792, Syrett, *Hamilton*, XI, 244-5). The suggestion that Digges may have exploited Pearce and other artisans whom he urged to emigrate is found in the above letter, in which he asserted that Pearce was so engaged as not able to refrain from emigrating. This could only have meant that Pearce had made a binding agreement with Digges. The suggestion is also supported by Digges' claim that he had advanced passage money for Pearce and his two companions. But when Pearce arrived in the United States, it was William Seton who personally gave Pearce $120 for passage and other expenses because Digges had asked him to extend his patronage and protection to the mechanic (Seton to Hamilton, 11 June 1792, same, XI, 506-7).

Pearce, bearing Digges' several letters of introduction which sought to make the President, the Secretary of State, and others his secret accomplices, arrived at a propitious moment. At that time, unknown to all but a few, a small group of capitalists, speculators, and public officials, centered chiefly in New York and favored with the powerful influence of the Secretary of the Treasury, was trying to give reality to a dream of American manufactures long entertained by Tench Coxe. The result was the creation of the Society for Establishing Useful Manufactures (SUM) at the Falls of the Passaic. Some of those involved looked upon Alexander Hamilton as the true founder and he undoubtedly was the towering figure in the enterprise (see, for example, Archibald Mercer to Hamilton, 6 Apr. 1792, and Elias Boudinot to Hamilton, 26 Mch. 1793, Syrett, *Hamilton*, XI, 247-8; XIV, 245-6; for a careful appraisal of Coxe's role as the pioneering advocate, see Jacob E. Cooke, "Tench Coxe, Alexander Hamilton and the Encouragement of American Manufactures," WMQ, XXXII [July 1975], 369-92). This conjunction of events was fortunate for the Secretary of State as well as for the ingenious emigrant.

It was on the 12th of July that Pearce presented himself with his two most important letters of introduction at the homes of the President and the Secretary of State. If he bore Digges' letter of 24 Apr. 1791 as well as the above, no copy of it has been found and none of that date is recorded in SJL. TJ never answered Digges and had no need to do so. For on that same afternoon he received a note on the same subject from the President. "If Mr. Pearce merits the character given him by T: D.," wrote Washington, "he will unquestionably merit encouragement, and you can put him in the way to obtain it" (Washington to TJ,

12 July 1791, enclosing Digges' letter to him). This may have been predicated upon a condition, but it was unquestionably a command, phrased in a manner Washington had never before employed with his Secretary of State.

One can only imagine TJ's feelings on receiving this unequivocal directive. Just a few months had elapsed since the Secretary of State and the Attorney General had formally counselled the President against holding communication with an artisan exporting machines and models because such exports were against the law. On that occasion, the appeal had come from the State of Virginia and required an official response (see TJ's opinion at 3 Dec. 1790, initially approving the President's cooperation but later replacing this with his and Randolph's opinion against involvement; see Vol. 18: 124n.). Pearce's appeal, particularly in enjoining secrecy, was of a different character altogether. Before the week was over, TJ would learn that the American consul in Dublin had deemed it improper to give Pearce a letter of introduction (Knox to TJ, 19 Apr. 1791). Now, however, the President of the United States had required the Secretary of State to patronize a man who, however worthy, had violated British laws inculpating those who would give such encouragement. What TJ was directed to do went beyond the official duty of the Secretary of State and the other Commissioners of Patents to examine models and grant patents. That was an unavoidable obligation requiring adherence to the specific terms of a law applicable to all, citizens and aliens alike. A patent had in fact recently been granted to George Parkinson, another British emigrant who claimed to possess a "Knowledge of all the Secret Movements used in Sir Richard Arkwright's Patent Machine" (Cooke, WMQ, XXXII [July 1975], 381, citing an advertisement in *Federal Gazette*, 24 Mch. 1791, and claiming Parkinson had thus "announced that the American government had officially endorsed his evasion of those English laws to prevent emigration of artisans and purveyance of industrial secrets"; this is incorrect even as inference: no such statement appears in the advertisement and, if it had, would not have been allowed by the Commissioners of Patents to whom it had been submitted prior to publication). But Washington's terse command required the Secretary of State to go beyond his legal duty as patent officer and to give official encouragement to a person undeniably guilty of a felony. This presented a hard dilemma for one as scrupulously careful as TJ in separating public office from private interest. A significant indication of his attitude in facing this ethical problem is that he retained no single copy or record of his letters concerning the matter. The answer he gave to Washington – very likely an oral report – can only be conjectured. But of the nature of the solution which, fortunately, he found close at hand, there can be no doubt.

TJ had long been aware that Washington believed "the introduction of the late-improved Machines to abridge labour, must be of almost infinite consequence to America" (Washington to TJ, 13 Feb. 1789). He also knew that a year later, in addressing the second session of the First Congress, the President had declared the safety and interest of a free people required the promotion of "such manufactories, as tend to render them independent on others for essential, particularly for military supplies" (First Annual Address, 8 Jan. 1790, *Writings*, ed. Fitzpatrick, XXX, 491-2). In consequence of Washington's recommendation, the House of Representatives had called upon the Secretary of the Treasury to prepare a plan for the encouragement and promotion of manufactures. Why, then, had Washington not called upon Hamilton, whose thinking on the subject so closely paralleled his own, instead of referring Pearce to TJ whose opinions on the subject were quite different? The President's action, if limited to the mere matter of granting a patent, would have been understandable. But since it commanded the extension of official patronage and encouragement to the British artisan, TJ could scarcely relieve himself of the problem by asking the Secretary of the Treasury to do what he himself had been directed to do. Fortunately, Tench Coxe had recently sent him a copy of his plan for a manufacturing establishment (Coxe to TJ, 15 Apr. 1791). This presented the opportunity TJ needed and he immediately turned Pearce over to Coxe, thus approaching his Cabinet colleague in a characteristically indirect manner. Under a covering note to Coxe, written the same day, he received Washington's command (but not found and not recorded in SJL), TJ transmitted the letter Digges had written to the President recommending Pearce. Coxe responded with enthusiasm the next day, promising "to fix a man who appears of so much importance to the United States" (Coxe to TJ, 13 July 1791, and note). He was as good as his word and saw to it that Pearce came to the attention of the Secretary of the Treasury. This assured the future of the artisan for the next two years, under official patronage privately bestowed. Coxe himself drew up the petition to the Commissioners of Patents of "William Pearce, late of . . . Great Britain, but now of the city of Philadelphia, manufacturing machine maker." The application described the various machines Pearce had invented or improved and promised to prepare "models, descriptions and drawings . . . in so intelligible and complete a manner as fully to comply with the requisitions of the act of Congress to promote the useful Arts." The claimed inventions were minor except for one Pearce said had been contrived during a short stay in Ireland, called a "mulitplier" – a term here used for the first time and which Coxe may have suggested – "capable of weaving two, three and perhaps more pieces of goods at one time" (undated draft, but before 7 Dec. 1791, in Coxe's hand, addressed "To the honorable Thomas Jefferson, Henry Knox, and Edmund Randolph," PHi: Coxe Papers; a document listing Pearce's machines in much the same terms is in DLC: Hamilton Papers and is printed in Syrett, *Hamilton*, IX, 86n.).

Thus it was that the Secretary of the Treasury, through TJ's referral of Pearce to Coxe, became the artisan's sponsor. Hamilton was in Philadelphia at the time of the exchange between TJ and Coxe, but immediately thereafter he went to New York and received from the directors of SUM full authority to negotiate a charter, secure artisans, and make public the plans of the new enterprise through a prospectus which he drafted (Davis, *Essays in the earlier history of American corporations*, I, 370, 373-4; Hamilton's Prospectus, which appeared in various newspapers, is in Syrett, *Hamilton*, IX, 144-53). Within a month Hamilton had advanced $100 to Pearce in behalf of SUM for the construction of "certain

machines and models of Machines to be delivered to . . . Alexander Hamilton" (same, XI, 85-6). Early in September Pearce began constructing his looms and other machinery in two "stores" rented by Hamilton from John Nixon. The next month Hamilton rented two additional places of Nixon for the same purpose. Altogether, within the year he had advanced to Pearce the not inconsiderable sum of $2,340.90.

Pearce had not brought with him the drawings and models which Digges sought to make accessible only to the President and the Secretary of State, but had left these in New York in the custody of William Seton, cashier of the Bank of New York. On the basis of a letter written a year later by Seton, who had advanced funds to Pearce for passage and other expenses, Davis and other authorities have accepted at face value his statement that TJ had given him written assurance "all charges would be thankfully repaid" (Seton to Hamilton, 11 June 1792, Syrett, *Hamilton*, XI, 506-7). In this Seton was mistaken, confusing instructions from Tench Coxe with supposed assurances given directly by TJ. In his letter to TJ of 13 July 1791 Coxe enclosed a letter from Pearce to Seton authorizing him to deliver the two boxes of drawings and models to such person as the Secretary of State should direct. At the bottom of Pearce's letter TJ appended a note to Seton containing nothing more than an authorization to him to turn the boxes over to Coxe. This is the only communication of any sort TJ is known to have written at any time to Seton. Coxe had no alternative but to take responsibility for Pearce's models. But in transmitting Pearce's letter, he accompanied it with another in which he made this quite unauthorized statement: "The charge I will procure from the Secretary of State and remit to you" (Coxe to Seton, 15 July 1791, PHi: Coxe Papers; see note to Coxe to TJ, 13 July 1791). TJ of course had no authority – and certainly no inclination – to pledge funds for Pearce on behalf of either the government or SUM. Seton's statement to Hamilton, unsupported by any corroborative testimony and contradicted by all of the known evidence, cannot warrant the assertion that TJ "backed Coxe's request to reimburse Pearce for his expenses by assuring William Seton . . . that 'all charges,' including the Englishman's passage to America, 'would be thankfully repaid' " (Cooke, WMQ, XXXII [July 1975], 388n.; see also Cooke, *Tench Coxe*, p. 195-6n.). It was Coxe, not TJ, who asked Seton to pay Pearce's expenses, knowing full well that Hamilton would back the request – as, ultimately, he did (on the record of Hamilton's sponsorship of Pearce in this and other matters, see Syrett, *Hamilton*, IX, 85-6, 184, 214, 490, 509; X, 345-6; XI, 241-6, 247-8, 445, 566; XII, 22, 45, 83, 141-2, 217-8; XIV, 189, 245-6, 253-4, 302-3, 318-9, 419-21; XV, 107-8, 328-9, 391; see also Carroll W. Pursell, Jr., "Thomas Digges and William Pearce: An Example of the Transit of Technology," WMQ, XXI [Oct. 1964], 551-60).

Hamilton's patronage of Pearce and other immigrant artisans whom he engaged for SUM and his zeal in promoting that enterprise were inseparably connected with his remarkable Report on Manufactures, which had been under preparation for over a year and which would be presented at the approaching session of Congress. Just as the creation of SUM was expected by its principal founder to demonstrate the advantage to the national economy of measures advocated in the Report, so Hamilton hoped to gain further support for his policies by displaying, in the heart of the capital, the effectiveness of Pearce's labor-saving machinery. Being well acquainted with the President's interest in the development of essential American manufactures, he could not have been unaware of the value of such a practical demonstration. Thus, under his guidance and support, Pearce's "Cotton Manufactory" was in operation at No. 13 Penn Street just at the time when the Report on Manufactures was before Congress and under attack by Madison and others. Shortly after the session ended, a group of thirteen Philadelphia weavers inspected the establishment and gave public testimony of their findings. Pearce himself was not by trade a weaver, but the inspecting group agreed unanimously that "his abilities in mechanism are superior to any we ever saw, especially in his double loom." They expressed the hope that this and other of his improvements would "soon come into general use, and be found of great utility in the United States." They also hoped that, since their testimony was addressed to the public good, it would be inserted in "newspapers

... throughout the United States" (*Gazette of the United States*, 6 June 1792; also in the *National Gazette*, 4 June). All that is known of Pearce indicates that he was not endowed with entrepreneurial qualities but was instead a rather ingenious artisan who needed guidance. This, added to the fact that the newspaper in which this promotional appeal appeared was under the special patronage of the Secretary of the Treasury, suggests the likelihood that the guiding hand behind the glowing testimonial was that of Hamilton himself. Certainly his concern for SUM, the success of which he had so much at heart that he had declared his own reputation was committed, was deep enough to prompt such a national effort (Hamilton to Seton, 25 May 1792, Syrett, *Hamilton*, XI, 425).

It seems even more likely that it was the Secretary of the Treasury who, two weeks later, inspired an inspection of Pearce's establishment by a much more distinguished group. "On Tuesday last," the *Gazette of the United States* reported on 9 June 1792, "the President of the United States, and his Lady, attended by the Secretary of State, and the Secretary of the Treasury and his Lady, visited Mr. Pearce's Cotton Manufactory. The President attentively viewed the Machinery, &c. and saw the business performed in its different branches – which received his warmest approbation." But this early instance of the power of the presidency in the bestowal of approval was unavailing. The great national enterprise at Passaic to which Hamilton had so wholly committed himself was a generation ahead of its time. As TJ had warned Digges four years earlier, land was too cheap and labor too dear in America to promise success for such undertakings. To these underlying factors was added the visionary planning of L'Enfant, the haphazard management of Duer, and the ineffectiveness of some of the artisans. Within a few months Hamilton soon came to regard Pearce as "unsteady . . . and incapable of being kept within any bounds of order or œconomy" (Hamilton to Nicholas Low, 15 Apr. 1793, Syrett, *Hamilton*, XIV, 318-19). In the following year Pearce proved the point by meriting dismissal and absconding with some of the machines for which Hamilton had advanced money. These were recovered, but Pearce, hoping to establish a manufacturing plant at the Falls of Brandywine, met with misfortune and disappeared from historical record.

TJ was silent about the inspection of Pearce's manufactory in the summer of 1792. He must, however, have been interested in the improved machinery, whatever he may have thought of the political implications of an establishment so zealously promoted by the Secretary of the Treasury. Earlier, in responding to William Knox' recommendation of the artisan, TJ had remarked: "We consider Mr. Pearce as a valuable acquisition, and shall cherish him accordingly" (TJ to Knox, 31 May 1792). But this carried the tone of politeness rather than conviction. So far as the record shows, TJ extended no encouragement save to express an interest later in a cotton gin of Pearce's design. But this soon gave way to his greater interest in the invention of Eli Whitney (TJ to Pearce, 15 Dec. 1792; TJ to Whitney, 16 Nov. 1793). Even the specific directive from the President to extend encouragement to the artisan he avoided by diverting the responsibility to his colleague in the Cabinet, who he must have known would eagerly embrace it.

Within a month after he had done so, TJ received a long and learned essay from a French émigré urging that the rising American empire insure its future greatness by lending its support to infant industries; that it encourage European artisans to emigrate to the United States by paying their passage and offering them premiums; and that it endeavor to make itself independent of foreign nations for the manufactured articles its expanding population required. In some respects this argument of the new citizen went even beyond the position of Washington and Hamilton to which TJ had been so consistently opposed. Yet the Secretary of State, to whom the essay was addressed, caused it to be translated and silently released to Freneau's *National Gazette* shortly before Hamilton submitted his Report on Manufactures to Congress. The Secretary of the Treasury could have had little difficulty in guessing by whose hands this argument so corroborative of his own policies was made public. For a possible explanation of the motives that led TJ to take such an anomalous action, see Editorial Note and group of documents at 4 Aug. 1791.

From Pierre Guide

Baltimore, 28 Apr. 1791. His first concern on arriving there was to inform TJ and to forward dispatches given to him at Marseilles by Mr. Cathalan at the end of Jan. They would have come sooner, but he was blown off course by a northwest wind on 8 Mch. from the latitude of the Bermudas to Cap Français. The damage was so great that he was obliged to abandon his ship, under the Savoy flag, and to place a part of his cargo on a French ship. – He encloses letters of recommendation from Etienne Cathalan and from his brother Jean Baptiste Guide, who had the honor of meeting TJ at Turin in 1788, as he himself did. These call upon TJ to bestow his esteem and protection.

His brother informed TJ of the purpose of his voyage: to gain local knowledge for beginning a happy and extensive trade between the United States and the realm of Sardinia. Leaf tobacco is America's object of export, but to encourage merchants in it, articles imported under the American flag must be admitted as those of the most favored nation, since TJ will know that the American flag has been and is so favored in all Sardinian ports: for several ships consigned to his brother at Nice have been successfully exempted from all duties whatever through his care. Guide will see with great satisfaction that his observations "à V[otre] E[xcellence] ne lui deplussent pas et que Son amour pour l'accroissement et la prosperité du commerce la portat à faire accorder, s'il sera possible, aux liaisons naissantes que nouse allons entreprendre avec le

Pavillon Savoyard, les facilités et La protection dont elle daigna nous flatter à Nice lors de Son passage pour Turin." When he arrives in Philadelphia next month, he will ask a few moments of TJ's precious time, for his brother and he are convinced of the success of their enterprise if they can begin under auspices as happy and as efficacious as those of TJ. – Cathalan has delivered to him six barrels of olive plants and a box which he thinks is for TJ or the Agricultural Society of Philadelphia, consigned to Robert Gilmor & Co. from whom he hopes they may be received in good state: he took the best care of them possible. He encloses a summary of the first Savoyard cargo dispatched to the United States in the hope that, if he finds something that could please TJ's taste, he would so inform him, being convinced that TJ would not be offended by an offer "aussi sincere que naïve."

RC (DLC); at foot of text: "S. E. Monsr. De Jefferson ministre des affaires etrangeres a Philadelphie"; endorsed by TJ as received 30 Apr. 1791 and so recorded in SJL. Enclosures ("les plys"): (1) Stephen Cathalan, Jr., to TJ, 22 (two) and 26 Jan. 1791, one of the former being a letter of recommendation of Pierre Guide; (2) Jean Baptiste Guide to TJ, 17 Jan. 1791.

To William Smith

DEAR SIR   Philadelphia Apr. 28. 1791.

As the time allotted for Mr. Eppes's stay here is short in proportion to the objects of it, I am desirous of husbanding every hour of it possible. Lest I should not have explained myself sufficiently as to his objects at the college, I take the liberty of doing it now. In Mathematics he possesses already the first 6. and the 11th. and 12th. books of Euclid (having been four times over them in different schools) plain trigonometry, and as far as Quadratic equations in algebra. The latter may be usefully carried to Cubic equations (for the higher parts of Algebra, and fluxions, tho' charming to possess, would take more time than he now has to spare) there remains also to be acquired the Conic sections, spherical trigonometry, Astronomy, and to attend a course of natural philosophy chiefly for the experimental part. Whenever Dr. Smith's class is engaged on these objects, Mr. Eppes will attend him, laying aside every thing else for that purpose. Whenever the class is engaged about subjects which Mr. Eppes possesses already, I should be glad to have him at home that he may be pursuing those branches of reading in which I shall occupy him. I have taken the liberty of stating my views, relying on your goodness to forward them as far as can be done, and have the honour to be with great esteem, Sir, your most obedt. humble servt,   TH: JEFFERSON

RC (PHi). PrC (DLC); mutilated, the right half of leaf being lost.

From Sylvanus Bourne

Cape François, 29 Apr. 1791. Arrived and presented credentials on 16 Mch. Still awaits recognition "but cannot obtain any decision of the business: being constantly put off by the most equivocal and evasive Conduct on their part. One Day am informed that the Convention does not extend to the Colonies – the next that as my Commission is unaccompanied by a letter from the Secy. of State, they cannot acknowledge its authenticity, and again that as the Convention has never been transmitted to them from France they are not bound to notice it. I am sent from the assembly to the Govr. the Govr. to the assembly without obtaining satisfactory answer from either." He conceives such conduct to be in direct violation of Art. 29 of the commercial treaty and of the Consular Convention. Requests instructions and a letter to the Governor General specifically obviating their objections. Without this he doubts he can be established in face of determined opposition from admiralty officers who will "lose fees which they are ever ready to extort from our Countrymen. . . . I have ever made my official establishment the ground work of my mercantile one and without the former I shall lose many expected advantages." This and exaction of *droit d'aubaine* show the colonists' opposition to operation of any treaty. Only a few weeks ago the property of an American consignee who died at Port-au-Prince was seized as an escheat.

He is chagrined that Congress has again lost the Consular bill, thus placing public officers in a disagreeable predicament: "principles of liberal policy ought not to be thus neglected."

Politics in this island excites in turn pity and indignation. The northern and southern parts are bitterly opposed, while principles and motives "are clouded in mystic darkness." Both with equal fervor profess attachment to the National Assembly but differ much in evidence of it. Deputies are daily expected.

Questions whether the philanthropist can view the French conduct as leading these people from despotism to freedom. Hopes to hear from TJ by the "first conveyance."

RC (DNA: RG 59, CD); endorsed by TJ as received at Bennington, Vermont, 4 June 1791 and so recorded in SJL.

Only four days before Bourne made this first report of his difficulty in obtaining recognition, TJ expressed the view that the United States had a clear right to appoint consuls in the French West Indies (TJ to Short, 25 Apr. 1791). He had in fact held this position during the negotiations leading to the Consular Convention of 1788. But, anticipating that there would be objections, he cautioned both Short and Bourne not to press the claim if the French government should find it inconvenient or disagreeable to grant it (see TJ's circular to consuls, 13 May 1791, and note on the one sent to Bourne; see also TJ to Bourne, 14 Aug. 1791). This was characteristic of his style of diplomacy, as it was of Montmorin's. On learning of the problem presented by Bourne's appointment and on being given the mistaken information that an exequatur had been granted, Montmorin declared that this action placed the government in "un grand embarras" and gave instructions that the governor general be directed to consider it as *non-avenu*. At the same time, in pointing out that this was an exercise of sovereignty which could only belong to the monarch, he urged that any discussions that would be disagreeable to the United States be avoided (Montmorin to Thevenard, 30 July 1791; Thevenard to Montmorin, 21 July and 18 Aug. 1791, Arch. Aff. Etr., Corr.-Pol., E.-U., xxxv; photocopies in DLC). Earlier, on learning that Bourne and Skipwith had been appointed consuls in the islands, he had given emphatic instructions to Otto to make it clear to TJ that their nominations should remain without effect and that the Consular Convention did not include the French West Indies except with respect to the *droit d'aubaine* (Montmorin to Otto, 13 Nov. 1790, same).

From Charles François d'Anmours

Baltimore, 29 Apr. 1791. Introducing and recommending to TJ's "special protection" M. Pierre Zacharie of Lyons, an "ingenious mechanician of a family that has produced many men of merit in the mechanical branch of mathematicks, and who have received . . . several rewards and privileges." He is the inventor of a machine to clean harbors, found on examination there to be superior to a number of others. He goes to Philadelphia to solicit "an Exclusive patent for Establishing it in all the harbours of the U. States," conveying with him a model which he will submit to TJ.

"As I know, Sir, how familiar every Branch of Knowledge is to you and with what Zeal you Protect and Promote every object of public utility, I have on these two Principles, taken upon me to recommend both the machine and its inventor to your Patronage; Knowing not a better Judge of the merit of the one, and a more judicious and Benevolent Protector of the latter."

RC (DNA: RG 59, MLR); endorsed by TJ as received 4 May 1791 and so recorded in SJL.

On 24 Nov. 1791 a patent was granted to "Peter Zacharie" for his machine for cleaning docks or harbors (*List of patents granted . . . from April 10, 1790, to December 31, 1836* [Washington, 1872]).

From Louis Guillaume Otto

SIR,   Philadelphia, 29th April, 1791.

In consequence of orders which I have received from his Majesty, I have the honor herewith to transmit to you the law which fixes the disposition of the colours in the different kinds of flags, or other customary marks of distinction among ships of war and commercial vessels of the French nation. I request the favor of you to make this law known in the ports of the United States. And have the honour to be, With respectful attachment, Sir, Your most humble and Obedient servant,   OTTO

Text of letter and enclosures from Brown's *Federal Gazette*, 4 May 1791, no manuscript of either having been found in DNA: RG 59, NL or elsewhere. Enclosures: (1) Full text of the law of 31 Oct. 1790 as approved by Louis XVI in accordance with the decree of the National Assembly of 24 Oct. 1790 "Fixing the Disposition of the Colours in the different kinds of Flags, or other customary marks of distinction among ships of war, and commercial vessels," consisting of six Articles and a command to all tribunals, administrative bodies, and municipalities to have the law "transcribed in their registers, read, published, and posted up in their respective districts and Departments, and to execute it as a law of the Kingdom." The first Article, which displaced the Bourbon white flag with its fleurs-de-lis and substituted for it the national tricolor, read: "The Jack shall be composed of three equal stripes and placed vertically: The one nearest the staff shall be red, the center one white, and the third blue." (2) Proclamation of the King, 31 Oct. 1790, announcing the law of that date which determined the form of the French national flag, commanding all ships of war and commercial vessels to conform to its stipulations, and, after notification to foreign nations, forbidding all French vessels after 1 Apr. 1791 to use "any other than the National Flag." In SJL, TJ recorded receipt of Otto's letter and enclosures on 30 Apr. 1791.

From Pierpont Edwards

New Haven, 30 Apr. 1791. Encloses first code of laws enacted in Connecticut, published 1672. There are no laws extant of earlier date, perhaps because the charter obtained by Gov. Winthrop from Charles II in 1662, incorporating and uniting colonies of Hartford and New Haven which until then had been distinct and totally independent of each other, was procured without permission of New Haven, which for several years refused to act under the charter. The dispute was settled about 1672, and it is said this code was enacted immediately thereafter. – He also encloses revised code of 1702 and all laws from then to 1744. The laws from 1672 to 1702 not reenacted in revision of that year, and those between 1744 and 1750 are needed to complete TJ's collection. He does not despair of being able to procure them. He encloses, as requested, his bill of expenditures.

RC (DNA: RG 59, MLR); endorsed by TJ as received 5 May 1791 and so recorded in SJL.

From Richard Hanson

Petersburg, Virginia. 30 Apr. 1791. He has received TJ's of 5th inst. and that of 7 Nov., which would have been "answered in course had you not mentioned writing me again soon." He notes TJ's making such an advantageous sale of his tobacco. Farell & Jones, owing a debt to Colo. Edward Carter, gave power to Dobson to receive it and Hanson paid latter TJ's first bond "as it could make no difference to you, with whom you will please to settle it." – As for giving up TJ's bonds and taking Ronald's plus mortgage on lands as security, this "is what I cannot think of doing, for I can assure you that your Bonds without security is preferable with me to any others with Security. Besides, he might pay you sooner than me." If indulgence is needed, TJ may be assured of having a reasonable time as bonds fall due. He hopes his declining to exchange bonds will not be to TJ's disadvantage, but it would not be to Jones' interest to do so.

RC (MHi); endorsed by TJ as received 10 May 1791 and so recorded in SJL.

From David Humphreys

Mafra, Portugal. 30 Apr. 1791. On 13th Samuel Harrison, at instance of Jacob Dohrman, sent messenger from Lisbon to inform Humphreys that Dominick Joyce, merchant of Philadelphia, had written his brother Edward Joyce on 25 Feb.: "A Minister is appointed to your Court; Colo. Humphreys is the person." This and three others from Philadelphia received in extraordinary manner. An American brigantine, *Peggy*, Capt. Jacob De Hart, of Philadelphia was seen off the Tagus on 6th. Two or three days later the letters were found on beach at Cascaies, and on 12th they appeared at the Exchange, broken open.

He has received letter from Carmichael of 15 Apr. saying nothing material had yet taken place. A violent bilious and nervous disorder has kept him in bed last ten days, but he is recovering. He says: " 'I write now with a trembling hand, and am obliged to pause at every line. The Bile destroys my Spirits, and the Cholic, and the Emetics . . . shatter my Nerves. Great Changes have taken place here' " – Campomanes removed from Council and given sinecure – many other removals and promotions, about which he says: " 'were we *tete à tete* I might be able to develope the cause.' " He then proceeds: " 'You see that there are strong appearances of the war spreading in the North. I can never believe that G. Britain is really in earnest. All depends on Potemkin: the Empress has been firm hitherto, and I scarce think that money will buy him. – This Country is lulled into perfect Security; and the Disarmament is complete. – I have no official letters since those you brought me.' "

Bulkeley writes on 25th that British consul at Elsinore says general peace soon expected. Vague reports say Empress aims to go only to Constantinople to show England her prowess, and the Porte that it has been deceived. More certain that English fleet is vigorously preparing, and King's bounty to seamen extended to 30 May. – "Here all is peace and quietness, without innovation. A few Pasquinades against Administration have . . . lately been pasted up in Lisbon. The only Trait in the Queen's character which the Authors could find susceptible of being Caricatured was her great veneration for the Lady Abbess of the New Convent. I believe the Queen really merits the esteem of the Portuguese Nation." Rains have been plentiful, promise of harvest good, and price of wheat fallen. He sends this under cover to George C. Fox in Falmouth, through Bulkeley.

RC (DNA: RG 59, DD); at head of text "(No. 17)." Tr (same). Recorded in SJL as received 22 June 1791.

From Thomas Mann Randolph, Jr.

DEAR SIR,   Monticello April 30th 1791.

We are unhappy at not being able to transmit you as regular accounts from Monticello as you are desirous of having. The discontinuance of the post throws us entirely on the Waggons for the conveyance of our letters, a method not only irregular but extremely uncertain. It is particularly painful to us to be frequently in doubt from the same cause about the state of your health as there is nothing in which we are so much interested. Your letter of the 17th. March reached Monticello on the 19th of April and we often receive 2 or 3 packets at once. A sure opportunity by means of Bob who goes to Fredericksburg on a visit to his wife, induces us all to write at the same time.

I am sorry to let you know that I have little hopes of arriving at any thing absolutely conclusive this year, on the question concerning the Opossum. Being unluckily misinformed with respect to the time of the appearance of the young in the false pouch I was not extremely anxious to procure subjects till the first weeks of March had elapsed. Of four which I have examined one was in no way pregnant, the young of the other 3 were hanging at the teats in the false pouch, but were much larger, even those of the smallest brood, than a pea or a bean of which size it is said they have been seen in the same situation. The first had been taken in the middle of Winter before it had intercourse with the male and was kept alive till the beginning of April: the teats had the usual appearance of those of barren animals but the false pouch was as complete in every respect as in the other subjects. From this it appears that Mr. Rittenhouse was misinformed. – The young opossums kept themselves at the teat by pressing the extremity of it between the tongue and the end of the upper jaw: an attempt to separate them from it by drawing them forcibly away would have occasioned a considerable laceration, it was evident; but by opening the mouth gently with the end of a pin they were removed without the smallest marks of violence, altho the most particular attention was bestowed. From the most accurate observation of 10, which was the number of the youngest brood, no connecting membrane could be discovered. The little animals of that brood even when removed in this manner from the false pouch, if placed near it, easily found their way in again; yet they appear to be as imperfect as the fetus in the larger Quadrupedes a considerable time before its birth. Several of them are preserved in Spirits to be submited to your inspection. – The internal organs of generation in the Opossum are perfect in every respect. The Uterus Tyson I think, has remarked to have two cavities: these cavities however communicate with each other at some distance from the neck. Since my dissection it has occurred to me that there might be a passage from some part of the Vagina to the false belly and this shall be one of the chief objects of my next enquiry. I recollected Mr. Madisons idea of a communication between the Uterus directly and the false

[328]

belly but am convinced that there is no such passage. A way leading from some part of the Vagina is much more probable. The end at which my dissections immediately aimed was the discovery of a gravid Uterus, as that would have afforded decisive proof in favor of the Opinion of several European Naturalists (vid. Bonnet Contemplation de la Nature V.3. p.45. note) viz. that the time of gestation is extremely short with the Opossum and that parturition is with it a kind of natural Abortion.

I shall have it in my power soon to give you a more minute and particular account of my observations with any thing new which may occur.

I am sorry not to be able to give you a good account of the Diary you desired me to keep. I could only find one Thermometer in Richmond for Sale which was short, badly graduated and at an exorbitant price. I send you observations during the present month made with the old Spirit of Wine Thermometer in the Study.

Within 1st h. after Sunrise   last h. bef. Sunset

April 1. 29.3 44.f

    2. 29.1. 48.f.   Leontodon taraxacum fl.
                 Violae.1,2,3.

    3. 29.2. 34.f. 29.2. 43.f.

    4. 29.2. 40.f. 29.2 48.f. Silene – .Fragaria Vesca.

    5. 29.3. 43.f.

    6. 29.4. 44.f. 29.3. 48.c. Caprimulgus Europ. ap.

    7. 29.3. 44.f.

    8. 29.4. 44.f. 29.4. 48.f.

    9. 29.4. 43.f.

   10.

   11. 29.3. 48.f.

   12. 29.2. 54.c. 29.1. 66.f.

   13. 29.   64.c.

   14. 28.8. 55.f. 28.9. 56.f.a.r.& th. Hirundo
                  purpurea.

   15. 28.9. 49.f.

   16.   r.   28.9. 45.r.

   17. 28.9. 47.c.a.r. 28.9. 47.c.

   18. 29.   45.f. 29. 50.f.

   29.   29.3. 64.c. Turdus Rufus. Hirundo
                  Pelasgia.

   30. 29.3. 61.c. 29.3. 62.c.a.r. Lanius Tyrannus.
                  Trochilus

Colub. Parus — . Pl. Chionanthus Virg. Cypripedium Calc. Crataegus Crus ga Morus Rubra. Hyacin. comosus. Aquilegia Canad. Prunus Virg. Magnolia 3 pet. &c. between 18 and 30. The Chasm is occasioned by a trip to Varina. I have only noted the birds and a few plants, such of either only as appeared on the top of the Mountain. Dear Sir your most aff. & obed. Servt.

TH: M. RANDOLPH

RC (MHi); endorsed by TJ as received 7 May 1791 and so recorded in SJL.

Rittenhouse's opinion about the false pouch of the opossum is given in TJ's letter to Randolph of 24 Feb. 1791 and in that of 6 Apr. 1791 TJ felt that this was an erroneous conclusion. Immediately on receiving the above letter, he made it available to Rittenhouse (TJ to Rittenhouse, 8 May 1791). In DLC: TJ Papers, 96: 16488 there is an undated memorandum in Randolph's hand which may have been a part of the above letter or may have been included later in one of the many letters from TJ's son-in-law of which copies have not been found. The note reads as follows: "The teat is compressed at its extremity between the end of the tongue and the extremity of the upper jaw. 9 or 10 young ones were separated without any appearance of laceration. The orifices of the ears were not open in the young. The nostrils were, the jaws grown together except a small hole just sufficient to admit the teat, the eyes covered with a membrane as in puppies. When they were taken from the teat they crawled about very well and attempted to get into the false belly again or to conceal themselves in the hair. Their fæces were plain to be seen in the false belly. The uterus is double in this shape, communicating together."

The meteorological readings given above were made to accord with the pattern and abbreviations employed by TJ in his letter to Randolph of 24 Feb. 1791. BOB was Robert Hemings (b. 1762), a Monticello slave and one of the twelve children born to Betty Hemings, whose family formed a part of Martha Wayles Jefferson's patrimony (see Betts, *Farm Book*, p. 15, 451; Betts and Bear, *Family Letters*, p. 63-4, n.3). Bob, who was eventually freed by TJ, was given such freedom of travel that at times his master did not know where he was (TJ to Fitzhugh, 24 Aug. 1790).

From Peter Carr

MY DEAR SIR   Monticello. May. 1. 1791

My silence hitherto has proceeded from a supposition that you had little leisure to attend to any thing but the duties of your office and I learn from Colo. Monroe that this supposition has been well founded. My time since your departure has been employed principally in the study of the law following the course you marked out. The evenings have been divided between History, Philosophy, and Poetry. I am at present reading the 2d. vol of Ld. Raymond's Reports and am of opinion that most of the adjudications of Holt will stand their ground as long as English jurisprudence shall depend on the maxims and doctrines of the common law, or shall be supported by justice and equity. Vaughan is a most excellent Reporter, and remarkable I think for the soundness and perspicuity of his decisions. His deductions are strictly logical and one may easily see he has been very conversant with Euclid.

During the session of the district court in Charlottesville I attended in order to gain some knowledge of the practical part of the law; but found the proceedings conducted in so different a manner from what I had been taught by books on the subject, that I fear I gained but little. I know not what method a young man should pursue to become acquainted with this part of the law. It would be a very awkward thing to have it to learn after he comes to the bar, and yet I see no other more eligible means. Any thing which you shall say on this subject will be acceptable and shall be duly attended to. I saw Mr. Maury a few days ago and enquired of Dabney's progress &c., &c. His accounts are extremely flattering, both with Respect to his genius, application, and judgment. His dispositions are without a fault.

You were so good when you first returned from Europe as to direct that some debts which were left unpaid by me in Wmsburg. should be discharged. It is painful to me to inform you that this has not been done, and that I see very little probability of its being accomplished soon. After your unbounded beneficence it may appear to argue a want of delicacy in me to trouble you on this subject, but I am sure you will excuse it when you consider that a regard for my own reputation has been the inducement. My mother drew an order some time ago on Colo. Lewis for 60£, which he says shall be paid when your creditors pay him.

Garland Jefferson is a close student and goes on hopefully. I trust we shall see you in Virginia this autumn. Adieu my Dr Sir and believe me to be yr. unalterable & affectionate friend,

PETER CARR

RC (ViU); endorsed by TJ as received 7 May 1791 and so recorded in SJL.

To James Currie

DEAR SIR   Philadelphia May 1. 1791.

This will be delivered you by Mr. Cassinove a gentleman from Holland of distinction, wealth and merit. An acquaintance of a year's standing enables me to bear particular testimony to his worth as a man, and his talents as a man of business. Desirous that strangers of note should have opportunities of knowing the real character of my countrymen which I know will not suffer *on the whole* when compared with any others, I take the liberty of asking your attentions to him, and that you will be so good as to make him known to others whose acquaintance may be agreeable to him. I am with great & sincere esteem Dear Sir Your friend & servt,

TH: JEFFERSON

PrC (DLC).

MR. CASSINOVE: Théophile Cazenove (1740-1811), an investment agent for several Amsterdam banking houses, who was about to take a "petit trot" into Virginia and Maryland. He reported to a friend that their little club had scattered, that Count Andriani had given up the project of getting himself scalped and was off for Quebec and Newfoundland, and that all was tranquil in Philadelphia except that the beautiful and amiable Mrs. Bingham was ill, thus afflicting all (Cazenove to Edward Campbell, 25 Apr. 1791, Cazenove Letter Book, City Archives of Amsterdam). The circle in which Cazenove moved included Alexander Hamilton as its most important figure, but it did not include TJ, who for a brief period had also been an admirer of Anne Willing Bingham while in Paris.

On this date TJ wrote letters of introduction to Cazenove addressed to Currie, McClurg, Governor Randolph, Thomas Mann Randolph, and Bushrod Washington. The text of the last exists only in a fragment (PrC in DLC: TJ Papers, 69, f. 11948).

To William Drayton

SIR   Philadelphia May 1. 1791.

My mortification has been extreme at the delays which have attended the procuring the olive plants so long ago recommended by myself, so long ago agreed to by the agricultural society, and for which their money has been so long lying in the hands of a banker at Paris. I assure you Sir that my endeavors have been unremitting. In addition to the first small parcel which were sent soon after the reciept of your orders, I have now the pleasure to inform you that a second cargo is arrived at Baltimore consisting of 6. barrels which contains 40. young olive trees of the best species, to afford grafts, and a box of olives to sow for stocks. This I order on immediately to Charleston to the care of Messrs. Brailsford & Morris for you, and I inclose herewith a copy of the directions given for the manner of treating them. A third cargo is on it's way from Bordeaux, but for what port I have not learned. This consists of 2. barrels containing 44. olive trees of which 24 are very young. – I shall immediately write to my correspondent at Marseilles to send another cargo the ensuing winter. – I delivered to Mr. Izard a barrel of Mountain rice of last year's growth, which I recieved from the island of Bananas on the coast of Africa and which I desired him to share with you for the use of the society. The attention now paying to the sugar-Maple tree promises us an abundant supply of sugar at home:

and I confess I look with infinite gratification to the addition to the products of the U. S. of three such articles as oil, sugar, and upland rice. The last I value, in the hope it may be a complete substitute for the pestiferous culture of the wet rice. — I have the honour to be with great respect Sir Your most obedient & most humble servt,

TH: JEFFERSON

PrC (DLC). Enclosure: "Memorandum for the Olive Tries" transmitted in Cathalan's first letter of 22 Jan. 1791 and summarized there.

To Robert Gilmor & Company

GENTLEMEN   Philadelphia May 1. 1791.

I am just informed that there is arrived at Baltimore addressed to you by Mr. Cathalan of Marseilles 6. barrrels containing Olive trees, and a chest containing olives to sow, for me. I must beg the favor of you to send them by the first vessel to Charleston (S. C.) addressed 'to Messieurs Brailsford & Morris for Mr. Drayton.' As the success of this endeavour to introduce the culture of the olive tree into the U. S. depends on the plants arriving at their destination in due season, and that is now passing fast away, I must beg your attention to send them by the very first vessel bound from your port to that. Any expences which may not be payable at the port of delivery according to usage, I will answer on your notifying them to me. I have the honour to be Gentlemen Your most obedt. humble servt,   TH: JEFFERSON

PrC (DLC); at foot of text: "Messrs. Robert Gilmor & co."

Enclosure: TJ to Guide, 1 May 1791.

Robert Gilmor & Co. responded to the above on 3 May 1791, saying that the letter enclosed for Guide would be given him the next day; that, as directed by Cathalan, they immediately shipped the olives and olive trees to Brailsford & Morris by the *Fanny*, Capt. Vickery, with instructions to deliver them to Drayton; that she would sail with the first wind; that they had given particular directions to Capt. Vickery "to take care of them and to give them the air" when weather permitted; and that no expenses had been incurred there (RC in MHi; endorsed by TJ as received 6 May 1791 and so recorded in SJL).

To Pierre Guide

SIR   Philadelphia May. 1. 1791.

I received last night your favor of Apr. 28. as well as those of your brother and Mr. Cathalan, and experience at the same time regret from the accident to your vessel, and the pleasure of seeing a commencement of commerce between the dominions of his Sardinian majesty and the United states. How far the assortment you have brought may answer here, I am not merchant enough to say; but the prudent resolution of establishing yourself in America will soon enable you to assort your cargoes to the demand. No distinction being made here between the vessels of different nations, yours are of course received on an equal footing. You will soon also see Sir, that the laws of this country operate so equally on every man, as to place every one independant of the protection of another, and do for all what in other countries is done partially by the protection of the great. Hence, Sir, that protection which you are pleased to ask from me, and which should certainly be exercised, could there be occasion for it, will be limited to my good wishes for the success of your undertakings, and recommendations of you to others whenever occasions shall occur. This I shall chearfully do from motives of regard to yourself and brother, as well as wishes to see our countries connected usefully to both. – I thank you for the communication of your invoice. My wants in that way are confined to the consumption of a small family. I looked over the invoice with some eagerness in hopes of finding in it some of the kind of wine which I drank at Turin under the name of Nebiule. Should you be able, with convenience, to order, in any of your future invoices, five or six dozen bottles of that, *du meilleur cru*, I will take them thankfully. – I shall be glad to see you when you come to Philadelphia. In the mean time if any vessel were coming round from Baltimore to Philadelphia I should be glad to recieve the articles mentioned below, the amount of which shall be remitted to you as soon as you shall make it known to me. My object with respect to the wine being merely to distribute it here in the best houses, in order to recommend it from it's quality, which I know to be good, and from it's price, I will beg the favor of you to let me know at what price I may say to them that it can be procured in future. – I thank you for your particular attention to the olive trees, and I write to Messrs. Robert Gilmor & co. to ship them off immediately for Charleston. – I shall be absent from Philadelphia from the middle of this month to the middle of the next. If you could send me by the first stage (if the package will bear land-carriage) a single dozen of the Vin vieux de Nice, and the price, perhaps I may procure further orders from hence before I go. I am with great regard, Sir, your most obedt. humble servt.,

TH: JEFFERSON

3. douzaines de bouteilles de Vin vieux rouge de Nice. Douze livres de figues Marseillaises en boites (ou environ). Douze livres (ou environ) de Raisins sec de Smyrne.

PrC (DLC). NEBIULE: For TJ's description of this wine, see Vol. 11: 435.

From Mary Jefferson

DEAR PAPA   Monticello May 1

As Bob is going down the country to morrow we shall all write to you by this opportunity. We expect jenny and nancy Randolph here in july. Mr. Randolph has bought a horse called my heart and a saddle for me to ride out on also a pretty whip. My niece is prettier and prettier everyday. This place is beautiful now. The peaches cherrys and strawberries are very big allready and there are a great number. Adieu my dear Papa I am your affectionate daughter

MARY JEFFERSON

RC (MHi); endorsed by TJ as received 7 May 1791 and so recorded in SJL. Some punctuation has been supplied.

For identification of the slave BOB (Robert Hemings), see note to Randolph to TJ, 30 Apr. 1791. JENNY and NANCY were Virginia and Anne Cary Randolph, daughters of Col. Thomas Mann Randolph and sisters of Mary's brother-in-law. Two years after the above letter was written, Nancy

became involved in the notorious affair at Bizarre, about which much has been written without dispelling all of the misconceptions that have arisen. The most reliable account is to be found in the editorial note by Charles T. Cullen and Herbert A. Johnson, eds., *The Papers of John Marshall* (Chapel Hill, N.C., 1977), II, 161-78, which contributes new information and proves that Commonwealth *v.* Randolph was not in fact a trial but a hearing.

From James Madison

DEAR SIR   N York May 1. 1791.

Finding on my arrival at Princeton that both Docr. Witherspoon and Smith had made excursions in the Vacation, I had no motive to detain me there, and accordingly pursuing my journey I arrived here the day after I left Philada. My first object was to see Dorhman. He continues to wear the face of honesty, and to profess much anxiety to discharge the claims of Mazzei, but acknowledges that all his moveable property has been brought under such fetters by late misfortunes that no part of it can be applied to that use. His chief resource consisted of money in London which has been attached, improperly as he says, by his brother. This calamity brought on him a protest of his bills, and this a necessity of making a compromise founded on a hypothecation of his effects. His present reliance is on an arrangement which appeals to the friendship of his brother and which he supposes his brother will not decline when recovered from the misapprehensions which led him to lay his hands on the property in London. A favorable turn of fortune may perhaps open a prospect of immediate aid to Mazzei, but as far as I can penetrate he ought to count but little on any other resource than the ultimate security of the Western township. I expect to have further explanations however from Dorhman, and may then be better able to judge. I have seen Freneau also and given him a line to you. He sets out for Philada. today or tomorrow, though it is not improbable that he may halt in N. Jersey. He is in the habit I find of translating the Leyden Gazette and consequently must be fully equal to the task you have allotted for him. He had supposed that besides this degree of skill, it might be expected that he should be able to translate with equal propriety into French, and under this idea, his delicacy had taken an insuperable objection to the undertaking. Being now set right as to this particular, and being made sensible of the advantages of Philada. over N. Jersey for his private undertaking, his mind is taking another turn; and if the scantiness of his capital, should not be a bar, I think he will establish himself in the former. At all events he will give his friends there an opportunity of aiding his decision by their information and counsel. The more I learn of his character talents and principles, the more I should regret his burying himself in the obscurity he had chosen in N. Jersey. It is certain that there is not to be found in the whole catalogue of American Printers, a single name that can approach towards a rivalship.

I send you herewith a Copy of Priestley's answer to Burke which has been reprinted here. You will see by a note page 56 how your idea of limiting the right to bind posterity is germinating under the extravagant doctrines of Burke on that subject. Paines answer has not yet been received here. The moment it can be got Freneau tells me it will be published in Childs' paper. It is said that the pamphlet has been suppressed in England, and that the author withdrew to France before or immediately after its appearance. This may account for his not sending copies to his friends in this Country.

From conversations which I have casually heard, it appears that among the enormities produced by the spirit of speculation and fraud, a practice is spreading, of taking out administration on the effects of deceased soldiers and other claimants leaving no representatives. By this thievery if not prevented, a prodigious sum will be unsaved by the public, and reward the worst of its Citizens. A number of adventurers are already engaged in the pursuit, and as they easily get security as administrators and as easily get a Commission on the usual suggestion of being creditors, they desire nothing more than to ascertain the name of the party deceased or missing, trusting to the improbability of their being detected or prosecuted by the public. It cannot but have happened and is indeed a fact well understood that the unclaimed dues from the U. S. are of very great amount. What a door is here open, for collusion also if any of the Clerks in the Account offices are not proof against the temptation!

We understood in Philada. that during the suspension of the Bank Bill in the hands of the President, its partizans here indulged themselves in reflections not very decent. I have reason to believe that the licentiousness of the tongues of speculators and Tories far exceeded any thing that was conceived. The meanest motives were charged on him, and the most insolent menaces held over him, if not in the open streets, under circumstances not less marking the character of the party.

In returning a visit to Mr. King yesterday, our conversation fell on the Conduct of G. B. towards the U. S. which he evidently laments as much as he disapproves. He took occasion to let me understand, that altho' he had been averse to the appearance of precipitancy in our measures, he should readily concur in them after all probability should be over, of voluntary relaxations in the measures of the other party; and that the next session of Congress would present such a crisis if nothing to prevent it should intervene: He mentioned also that a young gentleman here (a son of W. Smith now Ch: Justice of Canada) gives out, as information from his friends in England that no Minister will be sent to this Country, until one shall have previously arrived there. What credit may be due to this person or his informers I do not know. It shews at least that the conversation and expectations which lately prevailed are dying away.

A thought has occurred on the subject of your mechanism for the table, which in my idle situation will supply me with another paragraph, if of no other use. The great difficulty incident to your contrivance seemed to be that of supporting the weight of the Castor without embarrassing the shortening and lengthening of the moveable radius. Might not this be avoided by suspending the Castor by a chain or chord on a radius above, and requiring nothing more of

yours than to move the swinging
apparatus: thus. A.B. moveable on
a shoulder at A. would be a necessary brace, and must allow C.D.
to pass thro' it and play from a to
b as the tongs are shortned or
lengthened. The use of C.D. would
be to connect F.G. and the tongs,
so as to make them move together
on the common perpendicular axis.
As the distance from C to D must
vary with the protraction of the
tongs, the connecting bar ought to
be long accordingly, and pass
through without being fixed to the
tongs. Its office would in that state

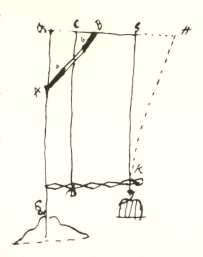

be sufficiently performed. The objections to this plan are 1. The
height of the perpendicular axis necessary to render the motion of
the Castor easy, and to diminish the degree in which it would mount
up at the end of the table. Perhaps this objection may be fatal. 2.
The necessity of adjusting the friction of the tongs so as not to be
inconvenient to the hand, and be sufficient to stop and hold the
castor at any part of the table. In this point of view perhaps a slide
on a spring would be better than the tongs. In that case C.D. might
be fixed, and not moveable in the brace. – By projecting F.G. to H.
the castor might be made to swing perpendicularly not at the part
of the table least distant, but at the mean distance from the Center,
and the difference between its greatest and least elevation and pressure diminished. But inconveniences of another sort might be increased by this expedient. If the tongs or slide were to be placed
not horizontally, but inclining so as to lessen the effect
of the pressure of the Castor without being less moveable
by the hand, the 2d objection might be lessened. It would
in that case be of less consequence to project the upper
radius as proposed. I am afraid you will hardly understand
what I have attempted to describe, and I have not time
if the thing deserved it, to write the letter over again for
the present mail.

RC (DLC: Madison Papers); unsigned;
endorsed by TJ as received 3 May 1791
and so recorded in SJL; verso of last page
also contains TJ's pencilled notes of subjects to be treated in his reply of 9 May

1791. Enclosure: Joseph Priestley's *Letters
to the Right Honourable Edmund Burke,
occasioned by his Reflections on the Revolution in France, &c.* (Birmingham, 1791).
The copy that TJ later acquired was the

reprint of the third edition by Hugh Gaines (New York, 1791). See Sowerby, No. 2544. For TJ's "idea of limiting the right to bind posterity," see Editorial Note and group of documents at 6 Sep. 1789.

To James McClurg

MY DEAR DOCTOR   Philadelphia May 1. 1791.

The bearer hereof, Mr. Cassinove, a gentleman from Holland of distinction, wealth and merit, being to pay a visit to Richmond and Norfolk, I am desirous of making him known to the men of worth of my own country, and them also to him. On this principle permit me to bring you and him together, persuaded you will find a mutual gratification in each other's society. He is particularly connected with the Van Staphorsts, bankers of the United States at Amsterdam, and very peculiarly skilled in that line of business. I am glad to avail myself of every occasion of bringing myself to your recollection, of assuring you that time has continued to fortify those sentiments of esteem & attachment which were inspired in earlier life, and which will continue to it's latest hours with dear Sir Your sincere friend & servt,   TH: JEFFERSON

PrC (DLC). See note to TJ to Currie, this date.

To James Maury

DEAR SIR   Philadelphia May 1. 1791.

Mr. Coxe, Assistant secretary of our treasury, interests himself in behalf of a Mr. Parkinson here, whose family is in your neighborhood, and who is desirous of having them brought here. I will thank you for your attention to any thing Mr. Coxe may desire on this subject, and as he is not known to you, I take a pleasure in assuring you that his faith and his ability to comply with whatever he may engage on behalf of Mr. Parkinson may be counted on with the utmost certainty and punctuality. – I am, Dear Sir, with great esteem & attachment Your sincere friend & humble servt,

TH: JEFFERSON

PrC (MHi).

Early in 1790 Tench Coxe had entered into partnership with the English artisan George Parkinson, who claimed to possess "the Knowledge of all the secret Movements used in Sir Richard Arkwright's Patent Machine" and who agreed to construct a model with his improvements upon it by which hemp, flax, wool, and silk could be woven into fabrics as well as cotton. The articles of agreement provided that the partners would share in all patent rights and profits and that Coxe would arrange for the passage of Parkinson's family from Liverpool to Philadelphia (Articles of agreement, 11 Jan. 1790, PHi: Coxe Papers; see Jacob E. Cooke, "Tench Coxe, Alexander Hamilton, and the Encouragement of American Manufactures," WMQ, XXXII [July 1975], 381, n. 45, where it is stated that Coxe arranged for the family's passage through James Maury). While TJ took no part in aiding the immigration of British artisans because it was forbidden by law, Coxe had recently saved him from the embarrassment of having to do so be-cause the President had directed it (see note to Digges to TJ, 28 Apr. 1791). Because of this and other instances in which Coxe had been useful to him — especially his assistance in the preparation of TJ's Report on Fisheries — TJ was no doubt pleased to reciprocate by lending his good offices in a matter which did not contravene British law. Coxe also applied directly to Maury, who made the necessary arrangements (Coxe to Maury, 4 May 1791; Maury to Coxe, 29 July 1791, PHi: Coxe Papers).

To Beverley Randolph

DEAR SIR   Philadelphia May 1.

The bearer hereof, Mr. Cassinove being on a visit to Richmond and perhaps Norfolk, I take the liberty of presenting him to your notice. He is a gentleman of distinction and merit from Holland, and under particular connections with the Van Staphorsts, bankers of the United States at Amsterdam. Satisfied that you will find a gratification in his society, and that any attentions you shall be pleased to shew him will be entirely merited and justified on his part, I shall only add that they will be considered as an obligation on him who has the honor to be with sentiments of great & sincere esteem & attachment Your Excellency's Most obedt. & Most humble servt.,   TH: JEFFERSON

PrC (DLC); at foot of text: "Governr. Randolph." See note to TJ to Currie, this date.

To Thomas Mann Randolph

MY DEAR FRIEND   Philadelphia May 1. 1791.

Permit me to introduce to you the bearer hereof Mr. Cassinove, a gentleman from Holland of distinction and worth, who is paying a short visit to Richmond and the lower parts of Virginia. You will find in him the polished manners of a traveller with the plainness of retirement. Desirous that he should see our country advantageously, and particularly the charms of our country-situations, I will ask of you to take him a day to Tuckahoe, when you shall be happening to visit it yourself, where he may see that hospitality and comfort which is so peculiarly ours. Present my affectionate respects to Mrs. Randolph & the family and accept assurances of the sincere esteem & attachment of Dear Sir Your affectionate friend & servt,

TH: JEFFERSON

PrC (MHi). See note to TJ to Currie, this date.

To Thomas Mann Randolph, Jr.

DEAR SIR   Philadelphia May. 1. 1791.

I have to acknowlege the reciept of your favour of Apr. 7. which came to hand on the 20th. I hope my letters on the subject of my tobacco have got to hand in time to prevent any contract there interfering with the sale I made here. I learn that 4. hhds. more are coming on. Being entitled to the highest price given before payment, I believe I shall be sure of 5⅓ dollars which will neat me 29/3 Virginia money. Your shipment to London and Mr. Madison's to Liverpool will give us a fair trial of the markets – We are still setting before fires here. The fruit in this country is untouched. I thank you for having replaced my dead trees. It is exactly what I would have wished. I shall be glad to hear how the white wheat, mountain-rice, Paccan and Sugar maples have succeeded. Evidence grows upon us that the U.S. may not only supply themselves the sugar for their own consumption but be great exporters. I have recieved a cargo of olive trees from Marseilles, which I am ordering on to Charleston, so that the U.S. have a certain prospect that sugar and oil will be added to their productions. No mean addition. I shall be glad to have a pair of puppies of the Shepherd's dog selected for the President. – A committee of the Philosophical society is charged with collecting materials for the natural history of the Hessian fly. – I do not think that of the weavil of Virginia has been yet sufficiently detailed. What do you think of beginning to turn your attention to this insect, in order to give it's history to the Phil. society? It would require some summers observations – Bartram here tells me that it is one and the same insect which by depositing it's egg in the young plumbs, apricots, nectarines and peaches renders them gummy and good for nothing. He promises to shew me the insect this summer. – I long to be free for pursuits of this kind instead of the detestable ones in which I am now labouring without pleasure to myself, or profit to others. In short I long to be with you at Monticello. Greet all the family tenderly for me. Yours, dear Sir, affectionately,

TH: JEFFERSON

PrC (DLC). Not recorded in SJL, unless the entry there on this date for a (missing) letter to Martha Jefferson Randolph was made in error, as is probable in view of TJ's practice of rotating his letters to his two daughters and son-in-law.

Randolph's "favour of Apr. 7." has not been found but is recorded in SJL as received 20 Apr. and as dated 4 Apr. 1791.

From Fulwar Skipwith

St. Pierre, 1 May 1791. The lack of an exequatur and tardiness of Congress in framing instructions or providing for consuls, the troubles of this island and consequent losses in commerce, added to the exhausted state of his finances, have driven him to the mortifying resolution to return to America until the obstacles can be removed and Congress "think proper to regulate the Consular Powers and Privileges." – Before the government here will recognize either his commission or the Convention [of 1788], official notification or an exequatur must be received from France. He has written Mr. Short but has had no reply. – The reasons for Congress' neglect of consuls best known to that honorable body, but he thinks appointments to French colonies prematurely made. Those holding such commissions suffer hardship, occupying as they do "the bare shadows of empty and expensive places, without profit or Privileges." – The arrival of a formidable land and sea force has provided an unnatural calm. "Under the winning masks of the *words* liberty and Patriotism, the ambitious and designing are still in movement, and in their train have gained a herd of fanatics, who feel no bounds to their rancour." The soldiery cannot be trusted and security in enforcing order by no means certain. – [P.S.:] By decree of the National Assembly, the port of Trinity is open to Americans without limitation as to time; that of Fort-Royal [Fort-de-France], the governor with consent of the council has declared free until after the hurricane months. It is his opinion and that of most men here that "the Planting interest will obtain a decree of the Nations for its remaining open."

RC (DNA: RG 59, CD, T/431); endorsed by TJ as received 21 June 1791 and so recorded in SJL. The postscript appeared in Brown's *Federal Gazette* of 7 July 1791 under the heading "Extract of a letter from St. Pierre (Martinique) of May 1, 1791" (Tr in DLC: TJ Papers, 59:10208). PrC of Tr (DLC: TJ Papers, 63:10976); endorsed by TJ: "French W. Indies."

To George Washington

Sɪʀ   Philadelphia May. 1. 1791.

I had the honour of addressing you on the 24th. Ult. which I presume you will have recieved at Cambden. The present is ordered to go from Petersburg to Taylor's ferry. I think it better my letters should be even some days ahead of you, knowing that if they ever get into your rear they will never overtake you. – I write to day indeed merely as the watchman cries, to prove himself awake, and that all is well, for the last week has scarcely furnished any thing foreign or domestic worthy your notice. Truxton is arrived from the E. Indies and confirms the check by Tippoo-Saib on the detachment of Colo. Floyd, which consisted of between 3. and 4000 men. The latter lost most of his baggage and artillery, and retreated under the pursuit of the enemy. The loss of men is pretended by their own papers to have been 2, or 300 only. But the loss and character of the officers killed, makes one suspect that the situation has been such as to force the best officers to expose themselves the most, and consequently that more men must have fallen. The main body with General Meadows at their head are pretended to be going on boldly. Yet Ld. Cornwallis is going to take the field in person. This shews that affairs are in such a situation as to give anxiety. Upon the whole the account recieved thro' Paris proves true notwithstanding the minister had declared to the house of Commons, in his place, that the public accounts were without foundation, and that nothing amiss had happened.

Our loan in Amsterdam for 2½ million of florins filled in two hours and a half after it was opened.

The Vice-president leaves us tomorrow. We are told that Mr. Morris gets £70,000. sterl. for the lands he has sold.

A Mr. Noble has been here, from the country where they are busied with the Sugar-maple tree. He thinks Mr. Cooper will bring 3000£'s worth to market this season, and gives the most flattering calculations of what may be done in that way. He informs me of another very satisfactory fact, that less profit is made by converting the juice into spirit than into sugar. He gave me specimens of the spirit, which is exactly whiskey.

I have arrived at Baltimore from Marseilles 40. olive trees of the best kind from Marseilles, and a box of the seed. The latter to raise stocks, and the former cuttings to engraft on the stocks. I am ordering them on instantly to Charleston, where if they arrive in the course of this month they will be in time. Another cargo is on it's way from Bordeaux, so that I hope to secure the commencement of this culture and from the best species. Sugar and oil will be no mean addition to the articles of our culture. – I have the honour to be with the greatest respect and esteem, Sir, your most obedt. & most humble servt.,   TH: JEFFERSON

RC (DNA: RG 59, MLR); addressed: "The President of the United States. To be lodged at Taylor's ferry on the Roanoke. To which place the post-master at Petersburg is desired to forward it by the first private conveyance. – For the Petersburg mail"; postmarked: "FREE" and "2 MA"; endorsed by Washington. PrC (DLC). FC (DNA: RG 59, SDC).

MR. NOBLE and MR. COOPER: Arthur Noble was an associate of William Cooper, founder of Cooperstown and ardent promoter of what has aptly been called the "Maple Sugar Bubble" of the late 18th century (Butterfield, *Rush*, I, 597n.; see also Butterfield, "Judge William Cooper (1754-1809): A Sketch of his Character and Accomplishment," *New York History*, XXX [Oct. 1949], 385-408; and Alfred Young, *The Democratic Republicans of New York* [1967], p. 262-7). As his letters of this date to Drayton, Randolph, and Washington make clear, TJ was one of the most optimistic advocates of the manufacture and use of maple sugar, not even excluding Tench Coxe and Benjamin Rush. TJ was familiar with Coxe's estimate in 1790, based on the unrealistic figures of Cooper, that the sugar consumption of the United States could be met by families engaged in home manufacture on only 263,000 acres – an estimate which Coxe conceded had "a wild and visionary appearance" (reprinted in Coxe's *View of the United States* [Philadelphia, 1794], p. 78-82). In the same year "a society of gentlemen" in Philadelphia published *Remarks on the manufacture of maple sugar: with directions for its further improvement* (Philadelphia, 1790). TJ obtained a copy and would surely have agreed with the authors' opening sentence: "He who enables another to obtain any necessary of life, either cheaper or more independently than heretofore, adds a new source of happiness to man; and becomes more or less useful, in proportion to the number of those who participate in the benefits of his discovery" (for description of TJ's copy, see Sowerby, No. 1224).

But, while joining in the sanguine belief that a new and extensive field had been opened in what the authors declared to be the cause of humanity, TJ went further and saw in this favored product a useful instrument of policy. Hence his indirect allusion to it in a private letter to Benjamin Vaughan which was clearly intended as a warning that the maple tree might enable the United States to be no longer dependent on the British West Indies for sugar (TJ to Vaughan, 27 June 1790). The British consul in Philadelphia, less optimistic than TJ about the possibility that enough sugar could be produced to meet the American demand and also to provide an article of export, nevertheless was as concerned about the potential threat as

Vaughan had been. He sent a copy of *Remarks on the manufacture of maple sugar* to the British ministry, with the result that the subject was discussed in Hawkesbury's Report to the Privy Council early in 1791 (Bond to Leeds, PRO, FO 4/8, f. 263-71).

Benjamin Rush sought to bolster TJ's hopes with the hope of still further benefits to be derived from maple sugar. In what purported to be a letter to TJ written at his request, Rush claimed that liquors he had prepared in tests for its strength in tea – samples of which were consumed by Alexander Hamilton, Henry Drinker, and several ladies – would even prevent worm diseases in children. He also pointed to the relief from pain Franklin had experienced after ingesting large quantities of blackberry jam. He suggested that maple trees should be protected by law and that the manufacture of sugar should be encouraged by government bounties. Looking upon this new spectacle in light of "the present opening prospects in human affairs," Rush thought it would be the means of making the slave trade unnecessary. He closed his eloquent plea by declaring that TJ used "no other sugar in his family than that which is obtained from the sugar Maple tree." He added, with some exaggeration, that TJ had already "planted an orchard of maple trees on his farm in Virginia" (Rush to TJ, 19 Aug. 1791; Am. Phil. Soc., *Trans.*, III [1793], 64-79). This production was in fact an essay, addressed less to TJ than to members of the American Philosophical Society. It cannot therefore be regarded as being a part of the Jefferson canon except in the form of address. No manuscript copy of it has been found, it was never acknowledged by TJ, and there is no record of it in SJL.

Three months after the above letter was written, Cooper and Noble sent Washington samples of maple sugar and expressed the belief that "a sufficient quantity of this sugar may be made in a few years to supply the United States" (Cooper and Noble to Washington, 7 Aug. 1791, DLC: Washington Papers). Washington planted maples at Mount Vernon in 1792 but he evidently did not share the optimistic belief of TJ, Coxe, Rush, Cooper, and others that sugar from the maple would displace that from cane.

To David Humphreys

Dear Sir   Philadelphia May 2d. 1791.

The bearer hereof Mr. John Wilcocks junr. having in contemplation to visit different Countries of Europe, and perhaps that of your Residence, with a view to commercial arrangements, I take the liberty of informing you that he is a citizen of the United States, son of Mr. Wilcocks the Recorder of Pennsylvania, and of a respectable character. As such I beg leave to make him known to you, and to recommend him, should he have occasion, to that patronage which the Citizens of the United States will naturally look for from the Representative of their Country in foreign parts. – I have the honor to be with sentiments of great respect and attachment, Dear Sir Your Most Obedient and Most humble Servant,

TH: JEFFERSON

RC (NjP); in hand of George Taylor, except for signature; addressed by TJ: "Col. Humphreys Lisbon"; endorsed. PrC (DLC); in Taylor's hand, not signed; at foot of text: "Mr. Short. Mr. Carmichael. Col. Humphreys." Entry in SJL also shows that identical letters were sent to Short and Carmichael.

From William Short

Dear Sir   Paris May 2. 1791.

I wrote to you on the 26th. of last month by the English packet and mentioned to you that Petit had been here some time and would go by the French which sails the 15th. from L'Orient. By the arrangement of the stages he finds that he shall be obliged to leave this place the 5th. Of course my letters to you by him will not be of so late a date as I had hoped.

I intended if he would not accept 3½ louis a month to have left the matter to have been arranged betwixt you and him on his arrival. I found him however startled at the idea of this sum, and so determined on the 100.^{tt} and so sure you would think it fully reasonable, after your letter to him, that I agreed with him as far as depended on me that the wages should be fixed at that rate. He understands it exclusive of his food. I was sure that on arriving at Philadelphia he would have insisted on the same and I knew you would not have disputed it with him after he had crossed the Atlantic. I hope you will both be satisfied and am only sorry that your separation has been prolonged till now, the more so as from your letter to Petit it would seem as if you had expected I should have removed any difficulties he might have had.

[345]

I send you by Petit the remains of what I recieved for you, agreeably to your desire. The secrecy you requested is fully observed. I put the object into M. de Gautier's hands. He separated with his own hands and in my presence, the picture[1] herewith sent. It is not mended because I did not chuse to let it go out of my hands here, where it would be well known; and because it will be easily put together in America. Gautier had the diamonds[1] disposed of for 9405. ₶ as you will see by the account which I shall get from him and inclose to you in this letter. Sequeville recieved immediately on his putting the picture into my hands (he would not take it sooner) 800.₶ with which he was perfectly satisfied. – Tolozan is at Lyons and expected here daily, which has prevented my writing to him. Immediately on his return I shall see him and present him the 1200.₶ that is to say ask his permission to put this sum into the hands of his Jeweller in order that he may furnish such a box as may please him. This I am told is the manner which is used with him.

The wines &c. have been paid for by M. Grand on my order. These sums will be deducted from the 9405.₶ and the bill of exchange of 500 and odd livres you sent me last winter. The rest will be remitted to V. Staphorst & Hubbard to be kept for you. You may therefore settle this matter with the P[resident] as to the wines: when his bills of exchange shall arrive they shall be deposed also with Staphorst & Hubbard, at your disposition or that of the P——— according as you may direct.

I am much mortified to learn from M. de la Motte that he was obliged to keep your carriages during the whole winter and that they have been forwarded, with the other articles sent you only this spring.

You will recieve by Petit your reveille watch mended by Chanterot who assures me it is now in perfect order. He is making the clock for 15. louis. He assures me also with respect to it that he does not gain a sol and that it is altogether for the honor and pleasure of serving you. It will be sent as soon as finished, by water to Havre. – Petit carries also a packet of books put into my hands for you by M. de la Lande of the academy of Sciences. He recieved them from Turin. M. de Condorcet has promised me also a copy of the memorial which induced the Bishop of Autun to change his plan of establishing the standard of weights and measures, and on which the decree of the assembly is founded. If I recieve it in time it shall be forwarded to you with this letter. – The supplement to your report has been delivered to the several persons to whom you sent it. – The newspapers as usual will be sent by Petit and also a

few numbers of a new journal called *logo graphique*. It is written on
a new invented plan approved by the assembly on a report of the
academy of sciences. A number of people sit round a table and each
writes one or a few words and by a stroke of the knee communicates
to his neighbour where he is to begin, so that in thus running the
words round the table a number of writers together keep pace with
the speaker. The journal is in much vogue on account of its exact-
itude and I therefore send it to you. – I think it would be proper
also that you should have the *proces verbaux* of the assembly. The
work is immensely voluminous and as delay will be attended with
no inconvenience I shall await your orders on the subject, or rather
hope you will give them to my successor, as the idea of remaining
in the present[2] situation months longer would be insupportable.

I do not mean by this that my wishes have entirely and suddenly
changed. But taking it for granted from your letters that I shall not
be appointed here I wish much to quit a posture which cannot be
agreeable in itself, and which becomes less so every day, by the idea
that when withdrawn in order to give place to another, the opinion
which is unavoidable, that it is want of merit in me will be increased
in proportion to the length of time I have remained here. Those
instances are common where this kind of residence and experience
give such a preference to the chargé par interim that he is preferred
in opposition to the birth fortune &c. of his concurrent and that in
countries where birth and fortune are powerful arguments. – In cases
where such arguments have no weight or do not exist, and in a
country where the experience and knowlege of foreign countries are
more rare than in any other, the chances in favor of the chargé par
interim are such that no person can be brought to entertain a doubt
of his succeeding and will be sure when the proof comes of their
error that it could only have arisen from his demerit. I do not mention
these as reasons which should have any influence on the appointment
but only as having much weight in making me wish that it should
be decided as soon as possible, and even that it should have been
decided immediately on your return to America and determination
to remain there. – I still however suppose with you that delay will
be favorable to me. And I imagine that after having acted here for
some time without a superior, I should be more likely than another
who had not done this to obtain an appointment of an inferior grade.
That at the Hague I suppose will be of that sort. Still what you
mention in your letter of Jan. 24. I should accept rather than nothing, not from a desire to be in Europe, but from a wish not to return
to America before my family and affairs should be in a different

position for it is impossible for me to persuade myself that I could succeed as you imagine 18 months hence in Virginia. Diplomatick appointments in small towns being much more in evidence than in such places as Paris or London, those of an inferior grade are still more disagreeable there. My first desire was to have remained here as I expressed it formerly much too fully. This has been much diminished since, first by the position of the country in general which renders it impossible for me or any body else to be essentially useful for the present, and secondly by the position of my friends, all of whom are rendered unhappy by the menacing aspect of affairs and many absolutely ruined by the effects of the revolution. — Further disorders which seem to me inevitable and which are looked forward to with horror, throw a gloom and anxiety on the society of Paris that renders its residence painful in the extreme. All those who have not taken too active a part in the revolution to be able to leave it, and who have means of subsisting abroad are preparing to go out of the country. The people often use violence to prevent their departure. This increases the apprehensions and consequent emigrations. The evil augmenting daily, it is feared the people will soon insist on the assembly's passing a decree for prohibiting further emigrations and recalling those who are absent, under penalty of double taxes, or some other more violent means. — This situation of things as you will easily concieve renders the residence of Paris very different from what it was formerly and increases every day with me a wish that I had left it last year, and been enabled by the situation of my family and affairs to have gone and settled myself at home agreeably to my wishes.

Another disagreeable circumstance arising from the present uncertainty of my position and the expectation of recieving every day information respecting it, is the impossibility of taking any fixed arrangement. Since my return from Holland I have lodged in an hotel garni as I mentioned to you. My appartment costs me 12½ louis a month. I did not think it proper to take an house or furnished lodgings by the quarter, because it was probable every day that the next would bring some decisive intelligence, and because I did not know whether the rent was to be allowed me in the present situation. I know that under the present system it is not to be allowed in the cases where there is an outfit. But in the case of a temporary appointment I suppose of course no outfit will be allowed. — With respect to my journey to Holland also I forgot to ask you what you had done in a similar case. I have charged only for the expences absolutely occasioned by the journey, viz. The purchase of a carriage and post horses. The carriage was my own which I have charged the same price for that I had refused for it ten days before I was ordered to take this journey. The tavern expences on the road and at Amsterdam for myself and servant I have considered as my own.

I mentioned to you in my last how the affair of oils stood and the difference of opinion between the *Rapporteur du comité* and Mr. Barrett, and the assurance of the Rapporteur of getting a reduction made if it was found that the American oils paid no internal duties. I have an extract at length from the registers of the farm which expresses their exemption from such duties. I have this moment recieved it so that I do not know what the Rapporteur will say to it. I have little hopes of his succeeding however being persuaded that the same causes which first induced the committee to prohibit American oils altogether and then to impose a duty of 12.ᵗᵗ and finally to fix it at 6.ᵗᵗ will prevent the assembly at present from lowering it. Still it is proper that it should not be left unessayed, and I shall accordingly shew the registers to the Rapporteur, who on his side was also to have them examined. I mentioned to you that the duty of 6.ᵗᵗ at the present price was about 20. per cent. Tobacco of the first quality is from 40.ᵗᵗ to 45.ᵗᵗ the quintal exclusive of the duty, so that as yet the decree has been favorable to the sale of that article. Time only can shew how far the home cultivation will be prejudicial to it.

Next to your own silence, which I had supposed would have been prevented by your own experience and sufferings here, and which I had fondly allowed myself to hope would have been obviated by your friendship for me, what surprizes me most is the being so long without hearing a single word from the Secretary of the treasury. He cannot but know how dear this costs the U.S. The first loan of 3. millions paid near a years interest before it was employed. That was under particular circumstances. The loan which I have made has now paid from one to three months interest. It was known such a loan was to be made and interest is still going on on a debt it is probably intended to re-imburse a part of. Whether this payment of double interest is intended or not I know not. In any event and to whatever use it may be intended to be appropriated it seems to me a most extraordinary circumstance that no orders should have been given, either to pay it here or to remit it to America. It is impossible to concieve that the object of the loan could have been to have remained in the hands of the bankers at Amsterdam. Had it been made as soon as I went to Amsterdam, there would have been now five months interest paid on it uselessly. – Unless more celerity is used in future the loans to be made by the U.S. will become an increased burthen instead of a relief. In my last letter to the Secretary of the Treasury I stated the present situation of American credit in Europe and the means of deriving the greatest advantage from it when the diplomatick appointments to this place, London and the Hague shall have been made. Should none be made to the latter place then the same powers or such powers as are thought necessary might be confided to those at the two other courts. I suppose no individual would consent to act alone in such a case.

In my letters which have gone through the post I have been averse to speaking to you concerning the present situation of the Marquis de la Fayette. He has committed several errors in the command which he has had and which fortune seemed to have placed in his hands for the preservation of his country. But these errors have all proceeded from his extreme honesty and delicacy. Unwilling to act on the court by terror, he had no other means of preventing them from doing many things disagreeable to the people. Unwilling also not to appear to have the court at his orders he was obliged to submit to responsability for actions not under his control. Desirous of pleasing all parties he has alternately displeased all. In order to lead his followers by persuasion he was often obliged to make promises that he could not perform or encourage hopes that he could not realize. Under these circumstances his popularity and of course his force has been declining for some time. In the late instance of opening churches for the non jurors and the departure of the King for St. Cloud, he was obliged to come to an issue with his guards who almost unanimously took the opposite side of the question, not from a want of confidence in him, but because the confidence was not sufficient to counteract their own feelings and sentiments. His resignation shewed they were more attached to him than any other. In order to induce him to re-assume the command they have all taken a new oath of obedience. At the same time the national assembly, the department and municipality all sided with the people, or at least did nothing to oppose their conduct. Under these circumstances nothing but the Marquis's known patriotism and disinterestedness could have supported him. Any other would have been considered as a traitor and condemned as such. Not withstanding the new oath it cannot be doubted that on any similar occasion and as soon as the present zeal shall be passed he would be disobeyed again. The demagogues of the assembly, viz Lameth, Barnave and Duport are his most violent enemies. They are taking much pains as they have done for some time to throw suspicions on his patriotism. The new oath is much censured by them as unconstitutional, and the Marquis blamed for admitting it. Time and their continued efforts will probably succeed. He sees it whenever he has time to look forward. By a false delicacy he refused from the beginning to recieve a salary or any part of his expences. They have been immense, and it is not doubted that his fortune will be entirely lost and dissipated. Mde. de la fayette feels this most sensibly and is exceedingly distressed at it. Her devotion and her attachment to her husband are in a constant conflict and render her, notwithstanding her really uncommon fortitude and courage, the most unhappy of women. On the whole I fear the Marquis will lose his popularity (though he will certainly always retain the love and esteem of all who know him well). I am sure he will lose his fortune and perhaps not live to see his country enjoying a government that will secure its peace and happiness. – He was induced to separate from the Lameths Duport &c. to whom as you know he was much attached, by designing men who wished to form a party that they might govern and by it govern the assembly. They knew the influence of the Marquis and his pliancy also. The party did not succeed. It on the contrary rivetted the popularity of the Jacobins, and now those men who made the Marquis de la Fayette quit them, and prevented his rejoining them as he often wished, finding that the Jacobins will throughout the kingdom influence the ensuing elections, have abandoned him to return to that class. The principal of these are the Abbé Sieyes, Bishop of Autun, Roederer. Condorcet also has joined them. The Marquis de la Fayette and Duke de la Rochefoucault refuse as yet to follow them. – The Marquis feels now as he has long done that he was wrong in quitting that club, but he thinks it would be indelicate at present to return there as his most bitter enemies are the chiefs of it. Unfortunately most of the garde nationale (and all the people) consider it as the receptacle of the purest patriotism, and are disposed to see with an evil eye their commandant witholding himself from it.

I mentioned to you in a former letter that Parker had become bankrupt. I fear much that I shall suffer in his downfall. The money which I had for some time had idle in Mr. Grands hands and which I had also lent to you for Congress during the time that M. Grand refused to make further advances, I committed to Parker in June 89. in order to vest it for me in the American funds. – I had no anxiety about it until all of a sudden I learned the embarassment into which his affairs had gone. I know not yet how it will be settled. If he can prevent my losing I have no doubt he will do it. His agents in America it is said are the principal cause of his failure. I shall suffer also much I fear by Colo. Skipwiths having kept my money in his hands instead of laying it out in certificates, agreeable to his solemn promise and my positive instructions after he had sollicited from me such instructions. Had he done as I wished I might now be settled in America and even on the eastern side of the mountains with some degree of comfort and satisfaction. – At present I must confine myself to regret so good an opportunity lost, and which will certainly never return, and endeavour to conform myself to circumstances. Whatever they may be I beg you to be assured that my sentiments for you will never change, that my gratitude for former proofs of your friendship & attachment is unalterable, and that nothing can prevent my remaining my dear Sir, most sincerely your friend & servant,

W: SHORT

RC (DLC); at head of text: *"Private"*; endorsed by TJ as received 19 July 1791 and so recorded in SJL. PrC (PHi). Enclosures: Gautier's account of the sale of some "objects" (identified below) has not been found, but on 22 Apr. Grand & Cie. informed Short that 9,405 livres had been received for their sale and credited to TJ's account (RC in DLC: Short Papers).

The "object" about which Short was required to exercise such secrecy was a miniature of Louis XVI, surrounded by diamonds, which was presented to TJ when it became known that he would not return to France as minister. Such traditional gifts to departing envoys were given by the king and, in the case of Adams and Franklin,

were accepted. TJ's instructions about what to do with the diamonds were given in his letter to Short of 24 Jan. 1791 (see Vol. 16: xliii and 362-3). After receiving the above letter, TJ carefully obliterated some words that would have revealed the nature of the object and what had been done with it (see note 1 below). The person who removed the stones from the picture and had them sold in Amsterdam was Jean Antoine Gautier, a member of the banking firm of Grand & Cie. TJ had known him while in France and had respect for him.

[1] TJ obliterated the two preceding words, which have been supplied from PrC.

[2] Short added the word "precarious" and then deleted it in RC but not in PrC.

From Causin

Paris, "rue neuve Ste. Martin. No.18." 3 May 1791. It is the tender and sad cry of a father and mother for a son that moves them to appeal to TJ on account of one of their children, who departed from Le Havre 12 May 1790 under care of the Scioto Company. They have received no news of him save one letter from Mr. De Boine, who says he saw him in Philadelphia. Because of this they beg TJ to aid him in returning to France. If he is not found or is in danger, their intent to make him free and happy will be seen by the enclosed extract of an act, duly attested by a notary, as well as a letter of their son, who bears the deed and a letter from Mr. Playfair. "Nous adresserons nos Voeux à l'être Supreme qui veille à la conservation des Jours prétieux de Monsieur."

RC (DNA: RG 59, MLR); endorsed by TJ as received 19 July 1791 and so recorded in SJL.

From Condorcet

[*Paris, ca. 3 May 1791.*] He encloses a copy of a report made to the Academy of Sciences on the determination of a unit of measure. TJ will perceive therein their reasons for rejecting the more simple idea of taking the length of the pendulum for the unit and availing themselves instead of the fortunate circumstance which placed within their reach the only meridian line of neither too great nor too small an extent, terminated by the sea at its two extremes and intersected by the 45° of latitude at about one-third of its length.

As a result of the decree of the National Assembly adopting the principles of the report, the Academy has created five committees. The first, consisting of Messrs. Cassini, Méchain, and Le Gendre, is to make the astronomical observations and measure the triangles. The second, Messrs. Monge and Meusnier, is to measure the angles. (Particular circumstances have induced him to associate himself with these two committees.) A third, Messrs. Borda and Coulomb, is to make observations on the pendulum. A fourth, Messrs. Lavoisier and Abbé Hauy, is to determine the weight of a given quantity of distilled water. And the fifth, Messrs. Tillet, Brisson, and Vandermonde, is to determine the relation of the ancient weights and measures to the toise and the pound. These committees are to begin their operations immediately. Condorcet will keep TJ informed of the results.

He offers thanks for the two works TJ was kind enough to send him. "They will instruct us in all that is needed for the success of our common aims. You have provided good proofs of the results. Permit me to count myself among those who will share them and accept the assurance of my respect."[1]

RC (NNP); undated but written on either 2 or 3 May 1791 (Short's letters of these dates refer to it first as promised and then as enclosed); endorsed by TJ as received on 19 July 1791 and so recorded in SJL. Tr (DLC); in George Taylor's hand; at head of text: "Letter from M. de Condorcet perpetual Secretary of the academy of Sciences at Paris to Mr. Jefferson, received 19 July 1791." The English translation in Tr omits the final paragraph. RC translated by the Editors.

Philip Freneau had not yet become translator for the Department of State when TJ received the above letter and its enclosed *Rapport* (printed below). But it is clear beyond doubt that the translation of both documents employed by the clerk of the Department of State in making the copies presented here was prepared by TJ himself and was very likely in the form of a rough draft. This is proved beyond question by the use of "it's" for the possessive, by the beginning of some sentences with a lower case letter, by clerical errors made in the texts prepared by the copyist, by interpolations of clarifying phrases not in the original, and above all by the scrupulous accuracy, conciseness of expression, and translation so smooth and unmistakable in style that it does not appear to be such. Freneau, as shown by documents translated by him, could not conceal the hand of the translator even in subjects less scientific and technical than the principles of metrology. But TJ, in the act of converting French into English from the execrable handwriting of Condorcet as well as from the philosophical expressions of the *Rapport*, revealed his own profound knowledge of the subject – and, in so doing, exposed himself as one who executed the (missing) translation employed by the copyist. He also did so in the exclusion from the final paragraph of Condorcet's letter of the complimentary allusion to his own classic Report on Weights and Measures.

This omission, together with the nature of the captions given to Condorcet's letter and the *Rapport* as translated, suggest that TJ caused a departmental clerk to transcribe both documents because he contemplated releasing the texts to the press. He may also have thought thereby to make them available to Rittenhouse or to members of the American Philosophical Society. The originals were not presented to the Society and no copy of the translations has been found in contemporary newspapers. If TJ did not in fact communicate to the public the translations he had so laboriously prepared, the reason for withholding them could not have arisen from any lack of interest in the subject. His own hope for a universal and decimalized system of weights, measures, and coinage based on a unit of measure accessible to all nations was one he pursued all his life (see Editorial Note and group of documents on his Report on Weights and Measures, 4 July 1790). The reason is rather to be sought in the nature of the Academy of Sciences' *Rapport*.

That document was submitted to the National Assembly on 26 Mch. 1791 as one consonant with the stipulations in the decree of the previous year on the report prepared by the Bishop of Autun: that, to achieve uniformity of weights and measures, a natural and invariable unit of measure should be fixed; that the only means of extending this system to other nations would be to get them to agree to the same unit; and that, in choosing it, nothing of an arbitrary nature should be permitted nor the particular situation of any people on the globe considered. The unit proposed by Talleyrand was the pendulum vibrating seconds at 45° latitude. TJ received news of Talleyrand's proposal and of the National Assembly's decree just as he was completing his own Report to Congress. He welcomed the choice of latitude 45° as the standard and immediately accepted it in substitution for his own choice of latitude 38°. He did so in the hope that this would result in a common measure on which

the systems of both nations would be based (TJ to Short, 26 July 1790). In his letter submitting the *Rapport* of the Academy of Sciences to the National Assembly, Condorcet not only asserted that it met the stipulations of the previous year; he also claimed that the spirit of enlightenment and the progress of fraternity among all peoples was its object: "The operation which the Academy proposes is the greatest ever undertaken, and it can only bring honor to the nation which will execute it. The Academy . . . desires, in a word, that if the principles and details of this operation could pass alone to posterity, it would be impossible to tell by what nation it had been ordered or executed. The establishment of uniformity of measures is of such great utility and importance that it should be acceptable to all peoples. . . . The Academy feels that it must embrace the views of all men and all centuries" (Condorcet to the President of the National Assembly, undated; translation by the Editors from *Procès-Verbal*, 26 Mch. 1791, p. 12-14).

Despite the grand sentiments, the recommendations of the Academy of Sciences represented a retreat from those advanced by Talleyrand a year earlier. TJ thoroughly disapproved the plan, found it "uncatholic," and, with blunt candor, gave his opinion to Condorcet: "I would rather have seen you depart from your Catholicism in religion than in your Philosophy" (TJ to Condorcet, 30 Aug. 1791). His obvious disappointment at this turn of events would seem to have provided sufficient reason for withholding Condorcet's letter and the report of the Academy of Sciences from the public.

[1] This paragraph is omitted in TJ's translation.

ENCLOSURE

Report to the Academy of Sciences on a Unit of Measure

[Paris, 19 March 1791]

The idea of founding the whole Science of measure upon an unit of length taken from nature, presented itself to mathematicians from the moment that they knew the existence of such an unit, and the possibility of determining it:

they saw that this was the only means of excluding every thing arbitrary from the system of measures, and of being sure of preserving it at all times the same, without it's being subjected to uncertainty from any event short of a revolution in the present system of nature. They judged also that such a system not belonging exclusively to any particular nation, might eventually be adopted by all. Indeed were we to adopt for an unit the measure of any particular country, it would be difficult to assign to the others reasons of preference sufficient to over-weigh that degree of repugnance not philosophical, perhaps, but at least very natural, which all nations have against an imitation which implies an acknowledgment of a certain inferiority. There would then be as many measures as there are great nations. Besides, were nearly the whole of them to adopt any one of these arbitrary standards, numberless accidents easy to be foreseen would produce doubts of the true admeasurement of the standard. And as there would be no exact means of testing it, there would, in time, be a disagreement in these measures. The diversity which exists at this day among those in use in different Countries is not so much owing to an original diversity existing at the period of their first establishment, as to changes occasioned in process of time. In short, little would be gained even in a single nation, by preserving any one of the units of length therein used, since it would be still necessary to correct the other imperfections of the system of measures, an operation which would be nearly as inconvenient for the greater part of them.

The units which appear most proper for serving as the basis of measure, may be reduced to three, the length of the pendulum; a quadrant of the Equatorial circle; and lastly a quadrant of a terrestrial meridian.

The length of the pendulum has appeared in general to merit preference, as it possesses the advantage of being more easily determined, and consequently more easily tested or verified, whenever accidents to the Standard should render it necessary. Add to this, that those who should adopt this measure already in use with another nation, or, who after having adopted it should have occasion to verify it, would not be obliged to send observers to the place where the operation would have been first made.

In fact the law of the lengths of the pendulum is sufficiently certain and sufficiently confirmed by experience to be employed in operations without danger of sensible error; and even if we were to disregard this law, still a comparison of the difference in the lengths of pendulums, once executed could always be verified, and thus the unit of measure become invariable for all the places where the comparison should have been made; and thus we might immediately rectify any accidental change in the Standards, or find the same unit of measure at any moment when we should resolve to adopt it. But we shall see hereafter that this last mentioned advantage can be made common to all natural measures, and that we may employ the observations on the pendulum to verify them, although such observations have not served as the basis for their determination.

In employing the length of the Pendulum it seems natural to prefer that of the simple pendulum, which vibrates seconds at the forty fifth degree of Latitude. The law of the lengths of simple pendulums from the Equator to the Pole, performing equal vibrations, is such that that of the pendulum at the forty fifth degree is precisely the mean of all these lengths, that is to say, it is equal to their sum divided by their number: it is equally a mean between the two extremes taken the one at the pole, the other at the equator, and between any two lengths whatever corresponding at equal distances, the one to the north, the other to the south of the same parallel. It would not then be the length of the pendulum under any determinate parallel which would in this case be the Unit of measure, but the mean length of the pendulums, unequal among themselves, which vibrate seconds in the different Latitudes.

We must observe, however, than an unit of measure thus determined has something arbitrary in it: the second of time is the eighty six thousand four hundredth part of a day, and consequently an arbitrary division of this natural unit; so that to fix the unit of length we not only employ a heterogeneous element (time) but an arbitrary portion of it.

We might, indeed, avoid this latter inconvenience by taking for unit the hypothetical pendulum which should make but a single vibration in a day, a length which divided into ten thousand millions of parts would give an unit for common measure, of about twenty seven inches; and this unit would correspond with a pendulum which should make one hundred thousand vibrations in a day: but still the inconvenience would remain of admitting a heterogeneous element, and of employing time to determine an unit of length, or which is the same in this case, the intensity of the force of gravity at the surface of the earth.

Now if it be possible to have an unit of length, which depends on no other quantity, it would seem natural to give it the preference. Besides, an unit of measure taken from the earth itself has the advantage of being perfectly analogous to all the actual measures which for the common uses of life we take on the earth, such as the distances between certain points of it's surface, or the extent of portions of that surface. It is much more natural in fact to refer the distance of one place from another to a quarter of a circle of the earth, than to refer it to the length of the pendulum.

We have thought it our duty then to decide in favour of this species of unit, and then again to prefer a quarter of a meridian to a quarter of the equator. The operations necessary to determine this last element cannot be executed but in countries so distant from us that they occasion expenses and difficulties far above the advantages which could be hoped from them; the verifications of them, whenever they should be deemed necessary would be more difficult for all nations, at least till the time when the progress of civilization shall reach the inhabitants under the equator, a time unfortunately very distant from us. The regularity of this circle is not more certain than the similitude, or the regularity of the meridians.

The length of the celestial arc corresponding with the space measured, is less susceptible of being determined with precision: in short we may say that every nation belongs to one of the meridians of the earth, but that only part of them are situated under the equator.

The quarter of a meridian of the earth then would be a real unit of measure, and the ten millionth part of it would be the unit for common use. It will be seen here that we renounce the ordinary division of the quarter of the meridian into ninety degrees, of the degree into minutes, of the minute into seconds; because we could not retain this ancient division without breaking in on the unity of the system of measures, since the decimal division answering to the arithmetical scale ought to be preferred for the measures in common use, and thus we should have, for those of length only, two systems of division, the one of which would be adapted to the great measures, and the other to the small ones. For example, the league could not be at the same time a simple division of a degree, and a multiple of the toise in round numbers. The inconveniencies of this double system would be perpetual, whereas those of changing it would be temporary, and they would fall principally on a small number of persons accustomed to calculation; and we have imagined that the perfection of the operation ought not to be sacrificed to an interest which in many respects we may consider as personal.

In adopting these principles we introduce nothing arbitrary into the system of measures, except the arithmetical scale by which their divisions must necessarily be regulated. Also in that of weights, there will be nothing arbitrary but the choice of a substance homogeneous and easy to be always obtained in the same degree of purity and density to which we must refer the weight of all other substances; as for instance, if we should for a basis chuse distilled water weighed *in vacuo*, or reduced to the weight it would be of in vacuo, and taken at the degree of temperature at which it passes from a solid to a fluid form. To this same degree of temperature all the real measures employed in the operations should have relation; so that in the whole system there would be nothing arbitrary but that which is so of necessity and from the nature of things. And even the choice of this substance and of this degree of temperature is founded on physical reason, and the retaining the arithmetical scale, is prescribed by a fear of the danger to which this change in addition to all the others, would expose the success of the whole operation.

The immediate mensuration of a quarter of a meridian of the earth would be impracticable, but we may obtain a determination of it's length by measuring an arc of a certain length, and inferring from thence the length of the whole, either directly, or by deducing from this mensuration the length of an arc of the meridian corresponding to the hundredth part of the celestial arc of ninety degrees, and so taken as that one half of this arc should be to the south and the other to the north of the forty fifth parallel. In fact, as this arc is the mean of those which from the equator to the pole answer to equal parts of the celestial arc, or which is the same thing, to equal distances of latitude, by multiplying this measure by a hundred, we shall find the length of the quarter of the meridian.

The increase of length in these terrestrial arcs follow the same law as those of the pendulum, and the arc which answers to this parallel is a mean of all the others, in like manner as the pendulum of the forty fifth degree is the mean of all the other pendulums.

It may be objected here that the law of the increments of length of the degrees from the equator towards the pole is not so well ascertained as that of the increments of the pendulum; although both are founded on the same hypothesis of the ellipticity of the meridians. It might be said that it has not been equally confirmed by observations; but 1st. there exists no other method of finding the length of a quarter of a circle of the earth. Secondly, there results from it no real inexactitude, since we have the immediate length of the arc measured with which that deduced from it will always have a known relation. Thirdly, the error which might be committed in determining the hundredth part of a quadrant of the meridian, would not be sensible. The hypothesis of the ellipticity cannot be far from reality in the arc whose length should be actually measured: it will represent necessarily, with sufficient exactness, the small portion of the curve almost circular and a little flatened, which forms this arc. And fourthly, if this error could be sensible, it might of necessary consequence be corrected by the same observations. There could be no error but such as could not be appreciated by observations.

The larger the measured arc is, the more exact would be the determinations

[357]

resulting therefrom. In fact the errors committed in the determination of the celestial arc, or even in the terrestrial measurements and that of the hypothesis will have the less sensible influence on the results in proportion as this arc is of greater extent. In fine there is an advantage in the circumstance that the two extremities happen to be, the one to the South, the other to the North of the parallel of forty five degrees, at distances, which without being equal, are not too disproportionate.

We will propose then an actual mensuration of an arc of the meridian from Dunkirk to Barcelona, comprising alike[1] more than nine degrees and an half: this arc will be of quite sufficient extent, and there will be about six degrees of it to the north, and three and a half to the south of the mean parallel. To those advantages is added that of having it's two extreme points equally in the same level of the sea: it is to satisfy this last condition which gives points in the same level, invariable and determined by nature, to increase the extent of the arc to be measured in order that it may be divided in a manner more equal; in fine to extend it beyond the Pyrenees, and free it from any inaccuracies which their effect on the instruments might produce, that we propose to prolong the measure to Barcelona. Neither in Europe nor in any other part of the world (without measuring an arc of much greater extent) can a portion of meridian be found which will satisfy the condition of having it's two extreme points in the level of the sea, and at the same time that of traversing the forty fifth parallel, unless it be the one now proposed, or another westward of this and extending from the coast of France to that of Spain. This last arc would be more equally divided by the parallel of forty five degrees;[2] but we have preferred that which extends from Barcelona to Dunkirk, because it is in the track of the meridian already traced in France, that there exists already an admeasurement of this arc from Dunkirk to Perpignan, and that it is some advantage to find in the work already done a verification of that now to be executed. In fact, if in the new operations we find in the distance from Perpignan to Dunkirk the same result in all it's parts, we shall have a reason the more for counting on the certainty of these operations. Should there be found any variations, by examining what are the causes, and where the error is, we shall be sure of discovering those causes and of correcting the error. Besides in following this direction we cross the Pyrennees where they are more passable.

The operations necessary for this work will be first, to determine the difference of Latitude between Dunkirk and Barcelona, and in general to make on that line all the astronomical observations which shall be deemed useful. 2d. to measure the old bases which were used for the measure of a degree made at Paris, and for the purpose of the map of France. 3d. to verify by new observations the suite of the triangles which were used for measuring the meridian, and to extend them to Barcelona. 4th. to make at the forty fifth degree observations for determining the number of vibrations which a simple pendulum equal to the ten millionth part of the arc of the meridian will make in a day in vacuo at the sea-side, and in the temperature of ice beginning to melt, in order that, this number being once known, the measure may be found again at any time by observations on the pendulum. By these means we unite the advantages of the system which we have preferred, and of that which takes for it's unit the length of the pendulum. These observations may be made before this ten millionth part is known: having in fact the number of vibrations of a pendulum of a given length, it will suffice to know afterwards the proportion of this length to this ten millionth part in order to deduce from thence with certainty the number required. 5th. to verify by new experiments, carefully made, the weight in vacuo of a given quantity of distilled water taken at the freezing point. And lastly, to reduce to the present measures of length the different longitudinal, superficial and solid measures used in commerce, and the different weights in use, to the end that we may be able afterwards, by the simple rule of three, to estimate the new measures when they shall be determined.

We see that these different operations require six separate commissions, each charged with one of these portions of the work. Those to whom the academy shall trust the work should be required at the same time, to explain to them the method which they propose to follow.

In this first Report we have confined ourselves to what relates to the unit of measure. We propose in another to present the plan of the general System to be established upon this unit. In fact, this first determination requires preliminary operations which will take time, and which should be previously ordered by the National Assembly. We have nevertheless sufficiently meditated on this plan and the results of the operations, as well for the measure of the arc of the meridian, as for the weight of a given quantity of water, are known so nearly, that we may assert at present, that in adopting the unit of measure which we have proposed, a general system may be formed, in which all the divisions may follow the arithmetical Scale, and no part of it embarras our habitual usages: we shall only say at present that this ten millionth part of a quadrant of the meridian which will constitute our common unit of measure will not differ from the simple pendulum but about a hundred and forty fifth part; and that thus the one and the other unit leads to systems of measure absolutely similar in their consequences.

We have not thought it necessary to wait for the concurrence of other nations either in deciding upon the choice of the unit of measure or in beginning the operations. In fact we have excluded from this choice every arbitrary determination: we have admitted no elements but those which belong equally to all nations. The choice of the forty fifth degree of Latitude was not determined by the position of France, it is not here considered as a fixed point of the meridian, but only as that to which the mean length of the pendulum, and the mean length of a given division of that circle correspond: in fine we have chosen the only meridian wherein an arc can be found terminating at both it's extremities at the level of the ocean, and cut by the mean parallel without being of too great extent, which would render it's actual mensuration too difficult. There is nothing here then which may give the smallest pretence for reproaching us with an affectation of pre-eminence.

We conclude therefore to present this Report to the National Assembly, praying it to order the proposed operations and the measures necessary for the execution of those which must be made on the territories of Spain.

Done at the Academy the 19th. of March 1791.

BORDA
LA GRANGE
LA PLACE
MONGÉ
CONDORCET

I certify the above copy to be conformable to the Original, and to the decision of the Academy. Paris March 21st. 1791.

CONDORCET, PERPETUAL SECRETARY

PrC (DLC); in hand of George Taylor; at head of text: "A Report made before the Academy of Sciences the 19th of March 1791, on the choice of a unit of measure." Translated by TJ from *Rapport sur le choix d'une unité de mesure lu à l'Academie des Sciences le 19 mars 1791* (Paris, 1791), printed by order of the National Assembly and appended to its *Procès-Verbal* for 26 Mch. 1791.

[1] A clerical error. The passage in the *Rapport* reads: ". . . un peu plus de neuf degrés et demi." The error must have been that of the transcribing clerk in view of the meticulous accuracy of TJ's translation.

[2] The *Rapport* does not include the equivalent of the phrase "of forty five degrees." TJ obviously made this interpolation for the sake of clarity.

From Benjamin Hawkins

DEAR SIR   Warren in NC 3rd. of May 1791

I had the pleasure to receive the letter you did me the honor to write to me of the 1st. of april enclosing some of the scarlet blosom beans; And the acts of the last Session of Congress under an envelope franked by you, for which I request you to accept my thanks. I wish you and Mrs. Trist may have been as fortunate with your beans as I am with mine, the largest and middle sized are up and promising; I imagine the largest to be the carnealla.

The unfortunate mistake of the Virginians will have disagreeable consequences. The Indians have no Idea of expiation other than blood for blood, and they risk every thing to obtain it.

Having been unwell since my return from Philadelphia I have not been from home or had an opportunity of hearing the sentiments of many of the people of this State on the acts of the federal Legislature. Some people of Virginia and of this State are of Opinion that the minority are ever in the right. They speak of Jackson as being left out by the people of Georgia with astonishment, he being the most virtuous, the most eloquent and best informed man in the house of representatives.

That spirit of rudeness which blazed out at the last session of our Legislature seems Perfectly stifled, the actors therein being ashamed of their conduct and desirous it should be forgotten. – With the most affectionate regard I have the honor Dear Sir Yr. most obedient Servant,   BENJAMIN HAWKINS

RC (MHi); addressed: "The Honble Thomas Jefferson Esqr. Secretary of State Philadelphia. Fav'd by Mr. De Corbean to Petersburg"; postmarked: "Petersburg May 6"; endorsed by TJ as received 12 May 1791 and so recorded in SJL.

James Jackson (1757-1806), native of England and representative from Georgia in the first Congress, was not re-elected to the second. He contested the election of Anthony Wayne and the seat was thereupon declared vacant. He twice served as Senator from Georgia. Jackson was a strong opponent of the Yazoo fraud, a lawyer known for his impassioned eloquence, and a man of not inflexible political principles. Hawkins' encomiums to his virtue, his eloquence, and his learning were obviously tinged with derision.

From David Humphreys

Mafra, Portugal, 3 May 1791. Acknowledging receipt by express from Bulkeley of TJ's of 15 Mch. – As minister, "I can only rely on my own zeal and the candour of those . . . concerned in administring the Government of my Country: and . . . it is a peculiar felicity that my communications are to be made through an Office entrusted to a Person from whose Instruction and Indulgence, I know, I have every thing to hope." He will present letter of credence without lost time. The articles in TJ's letter "will meet with due attention." He forwards English papers, brought by messenger who left Lisbon at one o'clock this morning. By him he received Dohrman's letter, this moment answered: copies of both enclosed, as well as list of arrivals sent by Harrison. He encloses duplicate of his last. "I am extremely obliged by your attention in sending me a complete set of the Laws, together with the entire series of the Gazette of the United States. Scarcely any thing could have been more useful – nothing more acceptable." P.S. He will write in a few days to TJ and Lear. Moderation of demands of Empress of Russia shown in rescript in one of the papers.

RC (DNA: RG 59, DD); at head of text: "(No. 18)"; endorsed by TJ as received 22 June 1791 and so recorded in SJL. Tr (same). Enclosures: (1) Jacob Dohrman to Humphreys, congratulating him on his appointment as minister and recommending vice-consuls who had served the United States, particularly Samuel Harrison (Dohrman to Humphreys, Lisbon, 2 May 1791; Tr in French). (2) Humphreys to Dohrman, acknowledging the foregoing, requesting that consulate business be conducted by same persons until he receives further instructions from the Secretary of State, and adding: "it is incompatible with the System adopted by the Supreme Executive to name any Foreigners as Consuls General. . . . The Secretary of State has only informed me, 'we shall name a Consul for the Port of Lisbon as soon as a proper Native shall occur.' – The distinguished services of your brother have been acknowledged by the American Government: those of yourself (since his departure for America) are not, I trust, unknown there. – I am returning to Lisbon; and desire you will do me the favor of dining with me on Sunday next at Williams's Hotel. I have also to desire you will invite Mr. Harrison and all the Captains of the Vessels from America" (Humphreys to Dohrman, Mafra, 3 May 1791). (3) Harrison's undated list of American vessels and cargoes in Lisbon: *Laurel*, James Wharton (wheat); *Betsey*, James Eagleston (flour for Bilboa); *Two Brothers*, John Hall (wheat), all from Philadelphia; *Venus*, Caleb Green, and *Good Hope*, John Burke, both from Alexandria and both laden with corn. One vessel had arrived the night before for which Harrison had no information (Trs of all three enclosures in Humphreys' hand in DNA: RG 59, DD; FCs of all in same).

Neither Humphreys' letter nor its enclosures conveyed his real views on consular appointments. As many another diplomat who enjoyed close personal relations with an incumbent President has done since, Humphreys in this and other instances expressed himself more freely to the Chief Executive than to the Secretary of State. A few days later, in a letter marked secret, he wrote Washington about consular appointments in Spain lest his letters to the Secretary of State "should have been so inexplicit as to leave your mind in doubt respecting the merits or pretensions of those persons." He professed to be disinterested in the decision and only desirous of removing "embarrassments" from Washington's mind. The Dohrmans, he thought, might be considered because of their services during and after the war. Though Jacob Dohrman did not seem to expect an appointment, he earnestly wished Harrison to be made vice-consul until a native American could be named, being anxious himself to have a share in the consignment business. Humphreys pointed out that Harrison had done all of the consulate business in Lisbon for some years and, on the basis of personal knowledge, he believed him "active, faithful, and intelligent in business and worthy of a vice-consular appointment until an American could be named consul" – which, he added pointedly, "will now, of course, be the case unless orders may be received to the contrary." Then he revealed his real preference: "Mr. John Bulkeley is my very good friend. He has taken uncommon pains to shew civilities to me, and continues to do the same. On every occasion evincing his politeness, hospitality and disposition to serve me. He is one of the wealthiest Merchants of the Factory, and a man well versed in business. I understand he has applied for the American Consulship. Indeed, he has intimated the same to me, and produced to my view a letter from Mr. Thomas Russel of Boston in answer to one from himself on the subject. Mr. Bulkeley has made a principal part of his fortune in the American Trade; and from a desire of extending his connections in it, has doubtless been useful to other Americans as well as to me: I conceive him to be a good Englishman and a true Merchant, in heart. – In time of the war, he conducted in general prudently: not, however (as I have understood) without being concerned in an English Privateer." In conclusion, Humphreys protested his disinterestedness perhaps a bit too much: "Truth, and the interest of the Republic are my only objects. I write at the desire of no Person, nor with the knowledge of any one. – For I can have no possible interest in the matter, nor the remotest byas to an option, distinct from what may comport with the public weal" (Humphreys to Washington, "*Secret*," 12 May 1791; RC in DLC: Washington Papers).

John Bulkeley was indeed a good friend of Humphreys and some years later became his father-in-law. He was a member of a prominent New England family who had remained loyal during the Revolution, but Humphreys clearly thought that as a native-born American there was no legal bar to his being made consul and that, as with many others, his disaffection to the patriot cause did not disqualify him for office. Bulkeley had in fact applied for the post, and his candidacy had been supported by influential Congressmen and merchants. TJ thought him a man of good character and later placed orders for wine with his firm. But, knowing that he had sided with the British in the Revolution, he had already advised Washington that "his birth and sentiments seem to set him aside." In acknowledging Humphreys' letters on the subject, neither TJ nor Washington commented upon his observations and recommendations concerning consular appointments. After all, matters of patronage lay beyond the province of a diplomat. The post at Lisbon was first offered to Stephen Moylan of New Jersey and finally, in 1792, given to Edward Church of Georgia, who in 1790 had been appointed consul at Bilbao but had not been received. Robert Morris and the mercantile communities of Philadelphia and New York had also failed to get their candidate appointed (see Editorial Note on consular problems, Vol. 19: 308-13 and Documents I and III; TJ's undated memorandum on consular commissions, DLC: TJ Papers, f. 11903; Church's Commission, 5 May 1792, DNA: RG 59, CC; JEP, I, 121; TJ to Humphreys, 13 July 1791; Washington to Humphreys, 20 July 1791, *Writings*, ed. Fitzpatrick, XXXI, 317-21).

From William Short

DEAR SIR   Paris May 3. 1791.

The fermentation of Paris which I mentioned to you in my last has continued subsiding since that time. But the regulation of the department for renting and selling churches to the catholics who adhere to the priests non-jurors, and the departure of the King for St. Cloud remain suspended. The regulation or *arreté* of the department when sent to the national assembly was referred to the committee of the constitution. It was the means of avoiding to pronounce on it until it could be seen whether it could be carried into execution, that is to say, whether the people of Paris would consent to it. The report is to be made now in a day or two and is in favor of the department. Should that pass quietly the King will probably attempt again to go to St. Cloud, and unless there should arise some new cause of popular disquietude no opposition will be made. The Marquis de la Fayette will use his influence in favor of it. As yet the zeal excited among the garde nationale of Paris by his resignation, and his resumption of the command at their sollicitation, still continues. In the nature of things this cannot last always; but it will last longer with him than any other person whatever. I fear that the government will not be organised in time to secure and inforce peace and good order as soon as the influence and popularity of the Marquis, by which the people have hitherto been persuaded into it in some degree, shall have ceased – or if organised, will not be found adequate to those purposes. The parties (which are already pronounced) will be violent and strong, the government feeble – of course disorder and confusion until experience shall have pointed out to the majority the only true and permanent remedy, a well established constitution and a government sufficiently energetic to control the factious and turbulent. This will certainly happen sooner or later. The liberty of the press, and the general information of the present age will probably accelerate that term, and give reasonable hopes, I think, that anarchy and faction formerly the road to despotism, may now lead to a free government.

The inhabitants of the capital are in a state of much joy and contentment occasioned by the abolition of the barriers of Paris. By the decree of the assembly you know all duties ceased the 1st. of this month. A procession of the municipality and garde nationale made the round accompanied by music and numberless crowds of people and had the iron grates taken down. I inclose you a tariff of the principal duties paid. The committee of imposition think it will be easy to supply the place of the various articles of revenue suppressed, by a direct tax of 300 millions, and indirect ones of nearly as much more, formed and collected on different principles more easy and more agreeable to the people. – It is a great and hazardous experiment of which the success in the first instance is at least questionable.

I informed you that on the report of the academy of Sciences the Bishop of Autun had changed his plan respecting weights and measures. The assembly have adopted it as it stands at present. I inclose it to you with a letter from M. Condorcet for you which he sent to me open as you will receive it. I think it highly probable the plan will be defeated by Spain's not admitting the French commissioners into that Kingdom. The jealousy of the court against every thing or person coming from France, and particularly connected with the national assembly, is beyond all conceptions. You will see by an office of the Spanish Ambassador communicated to the assembly, (in the Moniteur) that a line of troops is formed by Spain on the frontiers of France. It is said also that the court have such an horror of every thing that has the appellation of assembly, that they have forbidden that of the bank of St. Charles, lest something appertaining to revolution principles should grow out of it.

There is no doubt that the finances of that country are in a declining state. The present ministry are prodigal and will not ameliorate them. Thus foreign broils or internal disorders will probably present ere long favorable opportunities for those who have difficulties to settle with that country. I have had only distant conversations with the Spanish Ambassador relative to the Mississipi since my return from Holland and that without the appearance of seeking them, and in presence of indifferent persons. I observed that he extolled much the importance of the Floridas, and seemed to consider them as most valuable acquisitions. This was in answer to a question of an enemy to the present revolution here, who in considering the late war as a most distressing one for France, asked the Ambassador what Spain had gained by it. You will recollect what I mentioned formerly concerning his idea of territory. No. 44. It is impossible to form an opinion with certainty on such desultory conversations but as far as one may be formed I think, if war had taken place with England the Ambassador would have been for purchasing the friendship of the U.S. at any price but that as it is he would not be for acquiring it by a cession of territory nor even a cession of the navigation of the Mississipi. – Not knowing what would be the sentiments of the U.S. under present circumstances, I have thought it best not to shew too much anxiety in sounding the Ambassador. The extract of your letter to Carmichael, as you will suppose, has not been communicated to the person you mentioned.

The Ambassador is very anxious that a good understanding should be preserved with the U.S. and particularly that his court should know precisely what are their intentions with respect to the Missisipi. He told me that he had recommended one of his friends to be sent as minister to the U.S. But that on further information he had withdrawn this recommendation in favor of the Spanish governor on our Western frontier, and that he hoped he would be appointed, although he did not know him. He observed that he thought himself bound to make this sacrifice of his friendship in a case where it was so necessary to have a person well acquainted with the U.S. and particularly the western country. – This convinced me that he was for making full inquiry into our dispositions and particularly the dispositions of the western inhabitants before any thing decisive being done. He has probably hopes that they may be induced to become Spanish subjects in order to obtain the navigation of the Mississipi, and then contribute to preclude from it the citizens of the U.S. that their advantages may be the greater. His anxiety to have the Governor of that Country appointed minister is a strong indication that he is for the plan being pursued. – I have no intelligence from Mr. Carmichael since he has recieved your instructions. One or two short letters which he has written to me say nothing that has any relation to that subject, although one of them was by a private hand. I suppose therefore that nothing new has occurred, or which is more probable, that he might not think it proper or necessary to communicate it to me. I learn accidentally by a person from Madrid that Colo. Humphries passed about three weeks there on his way to Lisbon. The last intelligence I recieved from him was on his arrival in London. He then mentioned he was about to embark for Lisbon.

I mentioned to you in my last the extension of the decree abolishing the *droit d'aubaine*, as you will see by the journals of the assembly herewith sent. Since then nothing further has been done in any thing which concerns our commerce. With respect to the difference of duty paid by French and American vessels importing tobacco I have written to M. de Montmorin by his desire reclaiming against it on the principle of its being so great as to exclude American vessels from participating in the transportation of their own productions, the freight of an hogshead of tobacco being not more than 40.₶ whilst the excess of duty paid by an American vessel is 50.₶

He has answered me that he has sent my letter to the minister of finance and the diplomatick committee. This committee together with those of imposition and commerce are to consult on it the next week as I learn from the Duke de la Rochefoucauld. M. de Montmorin desires much to have the American and French vessels put on the same footing, having already given instructions to reclaim against the excedent tonnage to which French vessels are subjected in the ports of the U.S. Ternant also is exerting himself much with the committees in order to induce them to treat the productions and shipping of the U.S. more favorably.

I observe that he is much disposed to see a treaty of commerce entered into with America and thinks that government are fully authorized to do it. I do not suppose it proper to trouble you with my ideas of treaties of commerce in general, for several reasons, but with respect to one with this country in particular in its present situation, I cannot help observing that much caution should be used. Until government shall have acquired a degree of influence which it is far from having at present it will be doubtful whether their engagements would be confirmed, and probably would not be confirmed if such articles were entered into respecting their Islands particularly as the U.S. should certainly insist on. On the contrary when the government shall become sufficiently vigorous to lead the assembly, the moment will be more favorable and should not be lost. Even then perhaps a treaty should be confined to a few leading points. Time cannot but strengthen the demands of the U.S. Their increasing numbers and commerce and general prosperity will render their connexions more valuable, and what will have still more influence will render their friendship more necessary to those nations who have possessions in the West-Indies. It will be seen that the U.S. without desiring to have possessions there themselves will have it in their power to keep them in the hands of those nations to whom they are attached, and they will be attached to those who offer them the greatest commercial advantages there. France of course will be for inlisting us by our interest in the guarantee of her possessions in the islands instead of having it on paper only.

Time also will take the inhabitants of the colonies more out of the hands of the merchants of Bordeaux and Nantes, and render these also less influential in the assembly, by rendering them less necessary to the establishment of the constitution. – The French citizens of influence who are owners in the islands and of course desirous to extend the liberty of commerce as much as possible submit to the merchants of this country because they think their influence essential to the revolution. The inhabitants of the islands themselves who are here wish much for freedom of commerce, but they are obliged to unite with the merchants and submit to their terms, though their natural enemies, in order to secure two other points which they have much more at heart – 1. The subjecting the *gens de couleur*, free and landholders, to the white citizens, that is to say allowing them to fix in their colonial assemblies the privileges which those are to enjoy. 2. The continuation of the slave trade. – Until these two points are finally settled the islanders will unite with the merchants of France. – By their joint influence they will succeed. The committees to whom the first of these questions was referred agreed last night in a report which leaves to the colonial assemblies the decision of every thing relative to the state of *persons*. This is provisional and pronounces formally what the former decree had left to be interpreted as each should chuse, and thus gave rise to the disturbances which have since taken place.

No intelligence has been recieved from the West-Indies since that I mentioned in my last. It appears that the troops and fleet sent were in such a state of insubordination that they could not be counted on. I think they were sent from hence with an intention to make them inforce severely the wishes of the mother country and that the regulations with respect to commerce particularly would have been strictly carried into execution. The longer the inhabitants are accustomed to the present state of things the more difficult it will be to shut their ports altogether.

I am sorry to have heard nothing further from you since I mentioned the minister's idea with respect to the appointment of Consuls in the islands. Nothing more has passed between him and me respecting this. I know not how far you would wish to insist on it under present circumstances. If the minister is pushed at present he would certainly refuse it. Perhaps it might enter into your views to obtain the refusal explicitly. I hope I shall soon hear from you on this subject. Mr. Skipwith has written to me that neither the Governor or any person at Martinique has any cognizance of the consular convention, and desires I will take measures for procuring him an exequatur. This will be suspended of course for your orders.

I send you several publications which have appeared here on colonial subjects. Unfortunately for the present, the personal interests of those who are to decide on them are too much concerned to admit of lights from discussion. You will see that some of them are in favor of a free commerce, and you will easily judge of the weight that will be given to these arguments by the merchants of Bordeaux or Nantes.

I enclose you a paper given me by the Imperial Chargé des affaires to which he begs your attention. It will explain itself.

I have heard nothing of the affair of Schweighauser & Co. since you left this place until the inclosed paper was put into my hands some time ago by one of the party concerned with a request I would forward it to you. He urged me much to give him an order to sell the arms, and seemed to think it extraordinary that I declined doing any thing in it.

As yet it has been impossible for me to get from Dupré the medal he is making for M. de la Luzerne, although one side was finished many months ago. This delay is occasioned by his employing himself in opposition to several other artists to obtain the engraving of the dyes for the new coinage decreed by the national assembly. He has given me his word however that I shall have it in the course of this month and I count on it.

May 4. I have informed you of the causes of difference between this country and the Pope in spiritual matters. After much delay he has sent the Bref which I inclose you, and which is considered as the harbinger of excommunication against the bishops and priests who supplant the non-jurors. If we may judge of the people in general from those in Paris it will have little effect. They yesterday dressed up a figure in straw representing the Pope with his bref in one hand and they say a crucifix in the other, an inscription on his back of *guerre civile*. After parading him in the garden of the Palais Royal he was burnt to the great satisfaction of the immense crowds present. Intelligence had been recieved the day before that the Pope refused to recieve M. de Segur who was about to leave Paris in order to go and reside at Rome as successor to the Cardinal de Bernis. – During these circumstances the assembly was employed in discussing the question whether Avignon and the Comtat should be recieved as part of the Kingdom of France. The two parties in that country that is to say those for and those against the reunion to France are now in a state of war and have been for some time. Deserters from the French army, the French partisans at Avignon and citizens of the neighbouring departments, have run over the Comtat, carried devastation with them wherever they met opposition and forced the inhabitants to declare in favor of France. Carpentras is now besieged by this army of plunderers for the same purpose. The question of the reunion has been long before the assembly and referred to two of the committees. This state of things rendered a decision indispensable. The report of the committees made on Saturday last was for the re-union and there seemed no doubt it would be adopted. You will see the debates in the papers inclosed, as far as last night. The question was decided a few hours ago by yeas and nays, by a considerable majority against the reunion. The assembly rose after determining this point. They have not yet decided what measures they will take for stopping the disorders, which prevail in the Comtat occasioned by French citizens, and which threaten also the French territory. If I recieve the papers before Petit leaves this to-morrow I will forward them to you.

I learn in the instant that the house of Clermont-Tonnere one of the members of the assembly who was most violent in his opposition to the reunion has been surrounded by a mob for some harsh expressions used in his speech, and with difficulty prevented from being plundered by the arrival of the garde nationale who persuaded the people not to proceed to extremities.

Letters received to day from Vienna by some of the members of the Corps diplomatique mention that the Russian ambassador there had just recieved intelligence of a considerable victory gained over the Turks near Brailow, in which there were 3 or 4000 prisoners. I observed that the persons present when one of these letters was received, and particularly the new envoy of Poland, supposed the affair had been much exaggerated by the Russian ambassador at Vienna. I suppose it certain however that an engagement has taken place, and that the Russians were victorious. This may be considered as the opening of the campaign, and would seem to render peace less probable. Still as the Turks will probably not be consulted I think yet it will be concluded by the mediation of Denmark. It is believed that England and Prussia have already moderated their pretensions. The Empress certainly wishes much for peace, and finding now that the Turks are disposed to prefer another campaign to a separate negotiation, I think she will negotiate through Denmark in modifying the statu quo.

I am informed that the plan which the committees of the colonies &c. intend proposing to the assembly as agreed on the night before last is to have a congress assembled in the West Indies of deputies from the several islands who are to propose a constitution for the colonies to be submitted to the national assembly, that this congress shall particularly have the initiative in deciding *L'Etat des personnes* in the islands viz. the rights of the *gens de couleur libres*, and the condition of slaves and the slave trade. The footing on which their commerce is to be placed is also to be proposed by the Congress to the consideration of the national assembly. This is all that has transpired from the committee and is vague. They desire much to keep their decision unknown until they propose it to the assembly and they will then endeavour to run it through that body without discussion as they have done in two similar instances. I suppose it best not to appear too sollicitous about collecting the result of the committees, as the U. S. are considered with much jealousy by several of the members. They are sure that we have projects of conquest and a thousand other wild ideas. It is expected that this report will be made to the assembly immediately and of course published. You shall be informed of its result in due time. I have found the deputies of the colonies disposed of themselves to go as far as possible in their demands respecting their commerce, but ready to give them all up to secure the slave trade and the dependence of the *gens de couleur*.

The Minister of marine resigned some days ago. The reason he gave was that the colonies were not separated from his department. He considered himself inadequate to the place in its present situation. No successor is yet named. M. Le Hoc and M. Le Brasseur, both formerly employed under former ministers, are generally spoken of, and even De Moustier is mentioned by some.

I send you a memoire of M. Du Crest against the Duke of Orleans. I have been obliged to take a copy which has been used, not being able to find a new one. I have never read it but understand it gives a particular account of Arkwright's spinning machines and suppose it may be therefore useful. It is on that account that it is sent.

I take the liberty of inclosing you a letter for the Secretary of the Treasury which I ask the favor of you to give him. My last from him was Sep. 1. 90 and from you Jan. 23 and 24. 91. – I have the honor to be with sentiments of the most perfect respect & attachment, Dear Sir Your most obedient & most humble servant,

W: Short

PrC (DLC: Short Papers); at head of text: "No. 65"; extremely faded and blurred, so that some words have been supplied from Tr (DNA: RG 59, DD). Recorded in SJL as received 19 July 1791. Enclosures: (1) Condorcet to TJ, ca. 3 May 1791, with the report of the committee of the Academy of Sciences on a unit of measure which is printed as an enclosure to that letter; (2) The Marquis de Ducrest, *Mémoire . . . contre M. D'Orléans* (Paris, 1791); see Sowerby, No. 2287 for a description of TJ's copy; (3) Pope Pius VI (Giovanni Angelo Braschi [1717-1799]), *Bref du Pape Pie VI . . . au sujet de la constitution civile du clergé, décrétée par l'Assemblée Nationale* (Paris, 1791); see Sowerby, No. 2589; (4) Short to Alexander Hamilton, 4 May 1791 (printed in Syrett, *Hamilton*, VIII, 324-5).

Short's dispatch No. 44 was that of 21 Oct. 1790. The extract of TJ's LETTER TO CARMICHAEL was taken from that of 2 Aug.

1790. TJ directed Short to submit it, together with other papers, to Montmorin (TJ to Short, 10 Aug. 1790; See Documents II and VI in group on the war crisis, at 12 July 1790). COMTAT (or Comtat Venaissin) is the region in southeastern France bounded by Dauphiné, Provence, and Languedoc; it was under papal rule from 1274 to 1791. On the Diplomatic Medal to be executed by DUPRÉ, see TJ to Short, 30 Apr. 1790 (also Vol. 16: xli-xlii).

It is scarcely surprising that Short failed to send TJ a copy of his protest against the decree of the National Assembly subjecting tobacco imported in American vessels to prohibitive duties. Montmorin had requested Short to make such a representation, and, as he had already instructed Otto to protest against discriminatory tonnage duties laid on French vessels in ports of the United States, it is clear that he desired it to be expressed in equally vigorous terms so as to achieve authorization for a new treaty of commerce. Short complied by employing expressions TJ would not likely have used. After protesting that the tobacco decree amounted to a perfect prohibition against American vessels carrying this article of commerce, Short conveyed what could only be regarded as a threat of retaliation: "I cannot allow myself . . . to believe that it was the intention of the national assembly to have pronounced this prohibition, because it would not have been just, because it would be extending the principle of the navigation-act much beyond what has been done by other nations, even that whose principles on this subject have been so often and so justly condemned by the National Assembly – and because it would invite to, and even necessitate, counter-restrictions on the part of the United States; or in other words, would again lay the foundation for those fiscal shackles and embarassments which the National Assembly have so wisely and victoriously attacked on all other occasions. – Taking it for granted therefore . . . that if the multiplicity of important and pressing concerns which occupy the National Assembly should allow them to examine the effect of this part of the decree in its various consequences, that they would modify it in their wisdom so as to prevent its weakening the commercial ties of the two countries, I take the liberty of asking you to submit to them the considerations above stated. – I know that the duties to which French merchandises and vessels are subjected in the United States were mentioned by some at the time of passing this decree; but I cannot suppose that moderate duties imposed on foreign manufactures agreeably to the common usage of countries, and a tonnage duty on foreign vessels appropriated to purposes necessary for their accomodation in the American ports, could have been the cause of duties such as are imposed by this decree on the productions of the American soil (and which amount to much more than 100. p. cent) and of the real prohibition of American vessels" (Short to Montmorin, 6 Apr. 1791; RC in Arch. Aff. Etr., Corr. Pol., E.-U., XXXV; photocopies in DLC). Montmorin acknowledged Short's protest on 29 Apr. 1791 and said that he had sent copies to De Lessart and to the Diplomatic Committee. The result of the consultations of this and other committees was the decree of the National Assembly calling for a new treaty of commerce (Farbé to Montmorin, 18 June 1791, same). See Editorial Note and group of documents on the French protest against the Tonnage Acts, at 18 Jan. 1791.

From François André Danican (Philidor)

Paris, "Rue macon St. André No. 1[5?]." 4 May 1791. He encloses an important mémoire on the manufacture of arms about which TJ knows, and the report of a commission named by the Academy of Sciences at the invitation of the Minister of War to examine locks and the new means of manufacture employed to achieve identity of form and precision in the parts of locks, "ce qui fait le précieux de cette decouverte pour le Service des Troupes dans tous les cas le moin à porté de trouver des ressources pour les reparer, et qu'il seroit possible de faire Jouir le pays de paix que vous habitez."

RC (DNA: RG 59, MLR); slightly mutilated; endorsed by TJ as received 19 July 1791 and so recorded in SJL.

Philidor was the name of a family of French musicians whose proper surname was Danican, the former bestowed reputedly by Louis XIII in the 17th century. The person who signed the above letter as Philidor was François André Danican (1726-1795), the leading chess player of his time, whose *L'Analyze des echecs* marked an epoch in the history of the game. TJ owned a copy of the work (Sowerby, No. 1173). Since Philidor was a composer and shared TJ's interest in the manufacture of arms on the principle of interchangeable parts, the two may have met in Paris. For TJ's effort to promote use by the Army of the United States of guns manufactured on this principle, see his letters to Knox and Jay of 12 and 17 Sep. 1789.

From Pierre Guide

Baltimore, 5 May 1791. Acknowledging with deep gratitude TJ's flattering letter of 1 May. He is no less grateful for TJ's wishes for the success of his venture in extending trade with Sardinia. What he says about equality of admission of all foreigners is not very consoling since high duties fall heavily on some of their articles, but it is necessary to be patient as it is the law of the land. – He is most grateful for TJ's order for wine, figs, and raisins. He is sending by the stage a dozen bottles of the Vin Vieux Rouge de Nice and a box of dry Smyrna raisins. The Marseillaise figs were all spoiled by the length of the voyage, and he does not think it will do to send those of Provence, which are common and not well preserved. By the first occasion he will send the other two dozen bottles of wine, which he sells at four gourdes per dozen. The raisins, being "un objet de ma pacotille," he asks TJ to accept and hopes he will find them to his taste. He did not bring any Vin de Nebiule, but he will have some by the first ship his brother dispatches.

He sees that TJ is going to spend a couple of months in the country and will not return to Philadelphia until mid-July. His affairs will detain him longer than expected, and when he goes there he hopes he will be able to present his respects to TJ. – P.S. He will have to buy a ship here to send to Nice and thus will have to return home under an American flag. He asks TJ to inform him if it will be possible to obtain this flag and to have it under the command of Captain Barrett, who accompanies him and about whom his brother has spoken to TJ. Barrett intends to establish himself on the Continent. Guide will be grateful if TJ will have the kindness to aid him in this and to inform him of the course to take.

RC (DLC); addressed: "Sir Th. Jefferson Secretary of State Philadelphia"; endorsed by TJ as received 8 May 1791 and so recorded in SJL.

To David Ross

Sir   Philadelphia May. 6. 1791.

It has not been till now that I have been able to turn my attention again to the accounts in dispute between us, to your remarks on them, the letters therewith sent, and Mr. Nicolson's explanation of the article of tobacco delivered Mr. Elder. This last satisfies my mind, that the two heavy hogsheads supposed to be omitted in the credits, not having been delivered to Mr. Nicolson ought to be omitted. This makes a difference in the settlement of my money bond. The letters sent with your remarks, satisfy me that the article of cash £15. Dec. 15. 1781. was to be paid for in tobacco and render it probable that the article of salt £28-19 Dec. 2. 1782. was so to be paid for, and nothing else. A closer examination of the accounts have shewn me that the following four articles, viz. 1783. Aug. 30. 25/ Nov. 7. £3-0-5 1784. Mar. 26. £1-16. July 1. £5. making £11-1-5 should have been entered in the *Open account* I sent you. As the correction of these articles would have been troublesome to the Arbitrators, and I thought it my duty to save them all the trouble I could, I have undertaken to copy anew the statements I sent you, making the above alterations in them. I have also accomodated the Observations to the corrected statements and recopied them. To the whole I have added a Reply to your Remarks. Copies of these papers are now making out, and shall be sent you as soon as ready. The accounts will not differ from those sent you formerly in a single article except those above pointed out, and in the omission of the erroneous charge of 1783. Dec. 13. £4-10. corrected by a credit 1784. May 4. £4-10.

PrC (CSmH).

To Henry Skipwith

Dear Sir   Philadelphia May 6. 1791.

I have duly recieved your favor of April 7. on the subject of Mr. Wayles's responsibility for his joint-consignee in the case of the Guineaman. I have never considered this subject methodically, and therefore have not absolute confidence in the opinion I have formed on a superficial view of it. My ideas however I will hazard to you, however informal.

It is a principle in law that joint-interests and joint-powers pass over to the Survivor on the death of one of the persons joined. Such is the case of joint-tenancy, joint-obligors (if there be no words of severalty) joint executors, joint-commissioners, joint-trustees, joint-attornies, joint-consignees &c. To this rule I believe there is not a single exception. When survivorship takes place, the interest and authority passes over completely to the survivor; none remains in the representatives of the deceased, and consequently no responsibility. Except indeed as to the doings of their testator. If he was guilty of any thing wrong, personally, his representatives must answer it. Thus we are answerable for monies actually received by Mr. Wayles. – Had an action been brought during Colo. Randolph's life, it is known they could not have joined us in the action, because one obligor cannot be sued jointly with the executors of the other, the parties standing, as the law terms it, in different degrees. The action then, as to us, was certainly suspended during the survivorship of Colo. R. and it is a principle in law that a personal action, once suspended, is gone forever.

This being the decision of the Common law, is it a case in which Equity will interfere? 1. If it did interfere, it would clearly be to relieve us. But 2. it is not a case in which it can interfere, because it would be to controul a principle of the common law in the very case where it was intended to operate, which would amount to a repeal of it. This is beyond the powers of a court of equity. – So far then as this question stands on general principles, we are clear. The question then occurs whether there have been any covenants, written or verbal, to controul the general rules of the law, and to produce a covenanted responsibility where there was no legal one. I suppose the case to have been thus. A company of Guinea merchants send a ship to the coast of Africa [in 1771. I take for granted][1] Farrell and Jones, desirous of obliging two customers, Mr. Wayles and Colo. Randolph, obtain the consignment of this cargo to them in Feb. 1772. and then inform the consignees of it. Mr. Wayles May 14. writes the letter you mention in answer to theirs. They might recieve this the middle of June. At this time the vessel must have been on her way here, for she arrived in 10. or 11. weeks after. This renders it nearly certain that the consignment was previous to the reciept of Mr. Wayles's letter, and of course was not in consequence of it. That letter can only be considered therefore as a confirmation of what F. & J. had stipulated for the consignees for whom they became securities. They could well make themselves responsible to the consignors for the doings of both consignees and this they did; but it was impossible they could covenant that one consignee should be responsible for the other. This would have been void as a res inter alios acta. Accordingly it has never been pretended that there was any such special covenant. Then the letter, considered as a confirmation of the covenants of F. & J. cannot have produced a joint-responsibility which is not in these covenants. Was the letter intended as an original obligation of securityship by Mr. Wayles for Colo. R.? 1. F. & J. had not desired any such securityship from Mr. Wayles, and it is not probable he would have undertaken it so very wantonly. 2. The letter purports no such intention in him: it is only expressive of a general assurance that they will do their best. 3. The law, to establish an obligation, requires that there shall have been a clear and unequivocal intention in the mind of the party, to enter into the obligation, that there should have been an animus se obligandi. 4. Had Mr. Wayles solemnly said (the contract having been previously entered into by F. & J. and the consignment actually made) 'I oblige myself, in consideration of *what you have done*, to be responsible for Colo. R.' it would have been void, as being merely voluntary. The consideration for the pact, to wit. that F. & J. *had done so and so*, being past and executed, could not found an obligation. So if a man in consideration of a marriage *already taken place*, covenants or conveys; it is merely voluntary, a nudum pactum which will not raise a right. Cuningham's L. dict. being at my hand I find there under the head of 'Consideration' the case of Tutthill v. Roberts cited from Freeman 344. a decision by Hale that 'in consideration that one was bound for him for money owing, he did bargain and sell: this is no good consideration.' Then if Mr. Wayles 'in consideration that F. & J. were bound for him for money &c. had undertaken to do so and so, this is no good consideration.' I do think therefore that there is no general principles either of law or equity which produce a cross-responsibility, that there has been no special undertaking which has done it; not by F. & J. because they could not do it, and I am satisfied they have not pretended to covenant any such thing; nor by Mr. Wayles, because his letter had no such thing in view, and would have been voluntary and void if it had intended it. I have no fear but that the acts of consignment and securityship, passed between the owners and F. & J., were previous to the reciept of Mr. Wayles's letter, probably previous to their own letter of Feb. 3. I had in the year of Mr. Wayles's death the best law-authority to say there was no responsibility on our part on the general principles of law. — Still it is my opinion we should take every possible step to subject Colo. R's property, only taking care to do nothing new which may render us liable if we are not so already. – The marshalling of his assets will be an important circumstance to attend to because if F. & J. cannot as British creditors come on his land, let all the creditors who can come on them, be forced on them, that the personal estate may be left for the simple contracts.

I shall be happy to hear that Mrs. Skipwith's stay at Richmond has bettered her health, and that the trip to the Sweet springs shall do it still more. I am sure her friends at Monticello will be made happy by seeing her there. Would to god I could be of the party. It shall be so one of these days, without yet saying when. I would not give one hour of domestic and friendly society for an age of my present state. Present me affectionately to Mrs. Skipwith and the young people, and accept assurances of the sincere esteem & attachment with which I am Dear Sir Your sincere friend & servant,

TH: JEFFERSON

PrC (CSmH).

¹ Brackets in text.

From James Sullivan

Boston, 6 May 1791. Recommends for consular appointment Samuel Cooper Johonnot, grandson and only male descendant of "the late American Patriot Doctor Cooper." Johonnot "has had his education in France . . . has read Law under my direction, and has been about three years at the bar. His conduct has added much to the partiallity I general[ly] feel for my pupils." He has had a call to Demarara, and if the President intends to appoint a consul there or in the ports of Essequibo, Berbice, or Surinam, Sullivan will hold himself responsible for his conduct, "having the most unreserved confidence in his honor and integrity."

RC (DLC: Washington Papers); endorsed by TJ as received 12 May 1791 and so recorded in SJL.

Johonnot's grandfather, Samuel Cooper ("Silver-Tongued Sam"), was the famous clergyman and patriot of Boston who has been described in a none too sympathetic but very illuminating biographical sketch as having made a contribution to the Revolution "far greater than that of Paul Revere, perhaps as great as that of Sam Ad-ams" (Clifford K. Shipton, *Sibley's Harvard Graduates*, XI [Boston, 1960], 189-213, at p. 211). Cooper sent Johonnot to France, but whether the primary object was the young man's education or Cooper's own ardent support of the French alliance is a question. Johonnot was graduated from Harvard in the class of 1783, the year of his grandfather's death. He was appointed consul to Demarara on 2 Mch. 1793 (JEP, I, 135, 136).

From Barbier Demarais

Boston, 7 May 1791. He encloses a letter sent to him by Mlle. de Bruny from Guadeloupe for Mlle. Jefferson. He would have been pleased to present it to her in accordance with his promise, but public and private affairs cause him to return to Guadeloupe immediately. He plans to return soon to "votre bonne et agréable patrie" and to bring fresh news to Mlle. Jefferson from her friend.

RC (ViW); endorsed by TJ as received 17 May 1791 and so recorded in SJL. The enclosed letter from Mlle. de Bruny, a friend and schoolmate of Martha Jefferson at the Abbaye Royale de Pentemont, has not been found.

From Alexander Hamilton

Treasury Department May the 7th. 1791

The Secretary of the Treasury has the honor to inform the Secretary of State that there are in the bank of North America Bills at ten days sight for the sum of 32,175 Guilders, which the Cashier is directed to hold for him. A warrant is enclosed for the sum of 13000 dolls. in his favor, the money for which is intended to procure those bills for the Purpose of obtaining a recognition of the treaty with the new Emperor of Morocco.

RC (DLC); in a clerk's hand; endorsed by TJ as received 7 May 1791 and so recorded in SJL.

TJ had requested funds for the mission to Morocco in his letter to Hamilton of 12 Mch. 1791. The delay of almost two months in meeting the request was caused by Thomas Barclay's financial difficulties, which postponed his departure (Barclay to TJ, 19 Apr. 1791).

To Tobias Lear

May 7. 1791.

Th: Jefferson presents his compliments to Mr. Lear: he has been calculating the march of the President at 200. miles a week and he makes it as follows.

May 20. he will be at Augusta
   24. at Cambden
   26. Charlotte
   27. Salisbury
   28. Salem
   30. Guilford
   31. Hillsboro'

June 1. Harrisbg.

  2. Taylor's ferry

  7. Fredsbg

  8. Mt. Vernon.

On this view he is of opinion that tomorrow's letter, put into the Petersburg mail, may be tolerably certain of getting to Taylor's ferry before the 2d. of June, as he believes there cannot be a fortnight without a private conveyance occurring from Petersburg to Taylor's ferry. He intends so to direct his own letter of tomorrow.

RC (ViHi). Not recorded in SJL.

To Peter Carr

DEAR SIR   Philadelphia May 8. 1791.

I recieved last night your favor of the 1st. instant, your judgment of Ld. Holt is certainly right. He is the greatest lawyer England ever had, except Coke. Vaughan is a most learned and clear headed reporter. You will find what you have to read henceforward much lighter, than what you have passed; much less matter in more words. A volume every fortnight or three weeks may be read of the remaining reporters, common law and chancery. Ld. Kaim's principles of equity, Blackstone and Hawkins's P.C. will take time. For the practical part, it will be necessary to read some practical books. There are some published since my time which I am told are better than the older. However attendance at the Albemarle courts will still be of some service, however slovenly the practice there. Were you to undertake to draw the declarations, pleas &c. of some one of the lawyers for that court, and to attend at the clerk's table to answer to the cases as called, it would be beneficial. Mr. J. Walker of Orange would be instructive to you in this way, as he is a skilful pleader. – I am much pleased to hear of Dabney's progress, and dispositions. – When I left Monticello I was obliged to marshall the monies which were to be paid on particular monies which were to be recieved. I see in a copy of my memorandums that £72. due for you in Williamsburg, and the balance due from your father's estate to Dr. Walker, whatever it might be, were allotted to be paid out of monies to be raised by the sale of wheat, corn, and pork, and from some debts to be collected which however were thought to be in hands which would pay them pretty readily. Perhaps they have been less so than was expected. Some failure of this kind may have produced the delay of payment on the part of Mr. Lewis, or perhaps some persons to whom money was to be paid from the same funds, have swept off the first collections. The fund was abundantly sufficient when collected. I shall hope that further progress in this collection will have relieved or will soon relieve your anxiety. You may be assured that in every event the money destined for that payment shall be sacredly applied to it's destination: and I am assured the delay cannot be long. My unfortunate losses of property and particularly by the paper-money for which my lands were sold with a view to pay off Mr. Wayles's debt, leave this work to be done over again, and all my tobaccos mortgaged as it were for that object. It consequently cripples all my wishes and endeavors to be useful to others, and obliges me to carry on every thing starvingly. I am with great & sincere esteem Dear Sir Your affectionate friend & servt.

Th: Jefferson

RC (ViU). PrC (MHi).

To J. P. P. Derieux

Dear Sir   Philadelphia May. 8. 1791.

Your favor of Apr. 25. came to hand three days ago. The letter to Madame Bellanger will go by the French packet which sails from N. York this week. By advices from France of the last of February matters were going on perfectly well; here and there (particularly in Alsace, and at Strasburg) some commotion, but quiet very generally established elsewhere; the revenues beginning to become productive, the reciept greater than the expence, the church lands selling generally 50. percent above their estimated value, assignats a little above par. The clergy had not yet come in any considerable degree into the new ecclesiastical establishment, and I rather think the greater part of them were not likely to do so, before the last day allowed them. In this case they were to stand absolutely deprived, and successors to be appointed. However in all the cities the people were against them, so that nothing is apprehended beyond some little commotions in country places where the people are ignorant and happen to have an affection for their curate. Be pleased to present my respects to Madame de Rieux and to accept assurances of the esteem & attachment with which I am Dear Sir Your most obedt humble servt,   Th: Jefferson

PrC (DLC).

To Maxcey Ewell

Sir   Philadelphia May 8. 1791.

Your letters to Mr. Madison and myself have been duly recieved. We went together to the Auditor's office, and enquired into the state of your claim. The Auditor turned to your certificate which had come on from Mr. Hopkins, and was properly certified: but the whole of the certificates which stand in Majr. Claiborne's accounts as yours does, are obliged to wait till his accounts come on from Richmond. These we were told waited only for a safe conveyance, so that your claim will not be delayed longer than the forms render necessary. Still it is my opinion you cannot count on it for an immediate relief. I should hope that in the course of the present year it might be obtained. I shall be always ready to do any thing for you in it that I can. I am Sir Your very humble servt.,

Th: Jefferson

PrC (MHi).

To Mary Jefferson

My dear Maria   Philadelphia May 8. 1791.

Your letter of Apr. 18. came to hand on the 30th. That of May 1. I recieved last night. By the stage which carries this letter I send you 12. yards of striped nankeen of the pattern inclosed. It is addressed to the care of Mr. Brown merchant in Richmond, and will arrive there with this letter. There are no stuffs here of the kind you sent.

April 30. the lilac blossomed.

May 4. the gelder rose, Dogwood, Red bud, and Azalea were in blossom. We have still pretty constant fires here. I shall answer Mr. Randolph's letter a week hence. It will be the last I shall write to Monticello for some weeks, because about this day sennight I set out to join Mr. Madison at New York, from whence we shall go up to Albany and Lake-George, then cross over to Bennington and so through Vermont to the Connecticut river, down Connecticut river by Hartford to New-haven, then to New York and Philadelphia. Take a map and trace this rout. I expect to be back in Philadelphia about the middle of June. – I am glad you are to learn to ride, but hope your horse is very gentle, and that you will never be venturesome. A lady should never ride a horse which she might not safely ride without a bridle. I long to be with you all. Kiss the little one every morning for me, and learn her to run about before I come. Adieu my dear. Your's affectionately,   TH: JEFFERSON

PrC (ViU); at foot of text: "M. Jefferson."

To Martha Jefferson Randolph

MY DEAR DAUGHTER   Philadelphia May 8. 1791.

Your letter of April 13.[1] tho' it came to hand on the 30th. is yet to be acknowleged. That of May 1. I received last night, within seven days of it's date. The post from Richmond comes I believe in 4. days at this season of the year, so that our correspondence might be very prompt if you had a regular post from Charlottesville to Richmond. I thank you for all the small news of your letters, which it is very grateful to me to recieve. I am happy to find you are on good terms with your neighbors. It is almost the most important circumstance in life, since nothing is so corroding as frequently to meet persons with whom one has any difference. The ill-will of a single neighbor is an immense drawback on the happiness of life, and therefore their good will cannot be bought too dear. – The loss of my vis-a-vis, coming round by water from Richmond to this place taught me that it was best to trust nothing that way during the boisterous months of the winter and spring. I am afraid I have a second lesson of the same kind, as I had 4. hhds. of tobacco on board a Capt. Stratton, who was to sail from Richmond 3. weeks ago, but is not arrived here. On board him were J. Eppes's books and baggage. I fear he must be lost. I had been particularly waiting for him, as being a very careful man and going directly to Richmond, to send the Mattrasses &c. Tomorrow however I will have the packages finished, and send them by any other conveyance which occurs. They will contain as follows.

6. mattrasses.

A package of James's bedding from Paris. To be kept for him.

do.   Sally's do.

The Encyclopedie.
Buffon.
Tacitus.   } for Mr. Randolph.
Journaux de physique

Magazin des modes.
Sacontalá.   } for yourself.
Calash

Anacharsis for Maria.

Herrera. 4. vols. ⎫

History of Florida. 2. vols. ⎬ to be deposited in my library.

Acosta ⎭

A box containing 2. panes of glass for Mrs. Lewis.

Some Windsor chairs if the vessel can take them.

I am made happy by Petit's determination to come to me. I had not been able to assume the name of a housekeeper for want of a real housekeeper. I did not look out for another, because I still hoped he would come. In fact he retired to Champaigne to live with his mother, and after a short time wrote to Mr. Short 'qu'il mouroit d'ennui.' and was willing to come. I shall acknowlege the receipt of Mr. Randolph's letter next week. Adieu, my dear, with affectionate esteem to you both. Your's, TH: JEFFERSON

RC (NNP). PrC (MHi). Martha's letter of 18 Apr. 1791 is recorded in SJL as received on the 30th, but it has not been found. Her letter of 1 May 1791 is recorded in SJL as received on the 7th of May, but it is also missing.

[1] Thus in MS. Whether this is the correct date or whether TJ erred in the SJL entry cannot be determined. The former seems more likely, since that is the date of Mary's letter, also received on the 30th.

To David Rittenhouse

DEAR SIR   May 8. 1791.

You mentioned to me once, information which you had recieved and which satisfied you that the pouch of the Opossum disappeared after weaning the young. As I knew that Mr. Randolph intended this spring to make observations on that animal I communicated to him your information that he might pay particular attention to it. You will see what he says. Tho a single observation is not conclusive, yet the memory remains strong with me that, when a boy, we used to amuse ourselves with forcing open the pouch of the Opossum, when having no young, and the Sphincter was so strongly contracted as to render it difficult to find where we were to enter our fingers, and extremely difficult to introduce them. – The diary of the flowering of plants and appearance of birds may amuse you a minute. I observe the martin appeared there the 14th. of April. Here it was the 21st. this year, and exactly on the same day at New York the last year. The object of this diary is to shew what birds disappear in winter and when, and also to enable us to form a comparative view of the climates of that and this place, for I was to have kept a

similar diary here; but a town situation does not admit of it. – I am
Dear Sir Your's affectionately,   Th: Jefferson

RC (J. M. Fox, Philadelphia, 1946); addressed: "Mr. David Rittenhouse." PrC (DLC).
Enclosure: Randolph to TJ, 30 Apr. 1791.

From David Rittenhouse

Dr Sir   May 8th 1791

I thank you for a Sight of Mr. Randolph's Letter. I must Confess
I was pleased with Mr. Neville's account of the Opossum, because
it seemed to remove every difficulty on the Subject and at the same
time more nearly to connect the Vegitable and animal economy.
But I well know with what caution we ought to recive the testimony
of any individual. Mr. Randolph's observations however does not
shew that the young had been actualy excluded by its parent and
exposesed to the open air before they entered the false belly, which
is the thing that appears to me so very improbable, tho' indeed their
finding their way back again into it, when removed, takes away
much of that improbability. Neither does Mr. Randolph's account
absolutely contradict the disappearing of the pouch after its having
Nourished a sett of Young, because his Oppossum might have been
a Young female that never had brought forth. I hope he will continue
his attention to this curious subject. I sometime ago wrote to Isaac
Zane of Winchester, on this matter, but not received any answer. I
shall set down below the Corresponding observations on Barometer
and Thermometer with those of Mr. Randolph, tho' some allowance
ought to made for the time of day, as mine were I suppose generally
made one hour earlier. Yours sincerely,   D. Rittenhouse

		B.	T.		B.	T.	
April	1.	30.0	−40	11.	30.1	−42	
	2.		−48	12.	29.8	−40	at 3 oClock − 76°
	3.	30.1	−33	13.	29.5	−60	
	4.	30.1	−31	14.	29.55	−42	
	5.	30.05	−40	15.	29.5	−45	
	6.	30.3	−34	17.	29.5	−50	
	7.	30.25	−38	18.	29.75	−49	
	8.		−41	30.	29.8	−52	
	9.	30.27	−36				

RC (DLC); endorsed by TJ as received 8 May 1791 and so recorded in SJL.

From William Short

This letter goes by post in order to overtake Petit, who is the bearer of my No. 65., at L'Orient. You will learn with pleasure that the committee of constitution made their report yesterday on the subject of freedom, of religion, (in consequence of the proceedings of the department of Paris denounced to the assembly as mentioned already) and that it obtained the most complete triumph. The Bishop of Autun whose excommunication is commenced by the holy see was the reporter of the committee: and after execrating the term of toleration as tyrannical, since it supposed the right of prohibition, established as a natural right this most unbounded liberty in the expression of religious opinions whether by worship or otherwise. – His report as well as a speech of the Abbé Seyes on the subject are ordered to be printed by the assembly and shall be forwarded to you. It is not surprizing that such sentiments should be expressed by two philosophers. But it is really so that they should be received in such a manner as well by the *coté droit* of the assembly, as the people in the galleries, that neither the ecclesiastics or the Jansenists ventured to open their mouths against them, except indeed two, who were hissed from the beginning to the end of their speeches. It remains still to be seen what the people out of doors will do when the churches rented to those who follow the priests *non jurors* shall be opened. It is highly probable they will follow the impulsion of the assembly, but if they do not neither the assembly, nor department, nor municipality will enter into competition with them for carrying into execution the decree for the free exercise of the catholic religion, by what they now call *non conformists* or *non-jurors*.

The enemies of the Marquis de la fayette and of good order have already begun an attack on him. They are unwilling to await the natural decline of his popularity which must necessarily come with time. One of the 48 sections has assembled, and instigated by a demagogue of the party of the Lameths who is also a member of the department of Paris, resolved that having resigned his commission he could no longer be considered as commandant of the garde nationale until re-elected by the sections, and that all the acts which he should do in that quality, until they should have expressed their wish in their assemblies, were usurpation and tyranny. This resolution was printed yesterday and sent to the other sections. They have not yet assembled but they will all at present be against the

Joshua Johnson

William Short

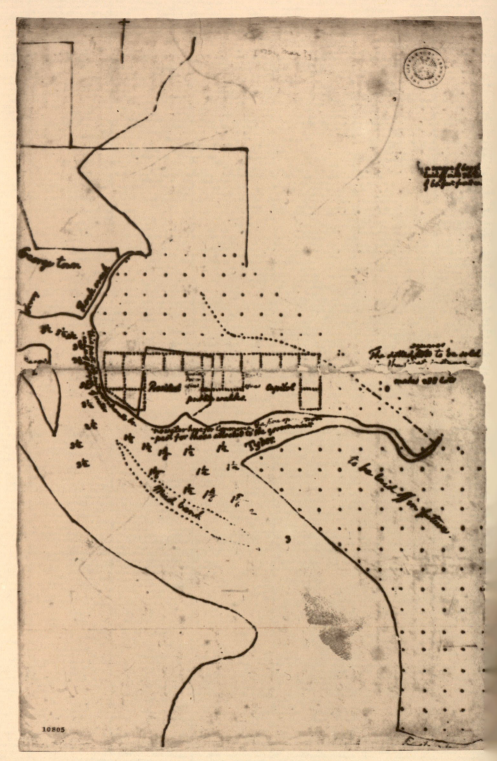

Sketch of the Federal City, 1791

L'Enfant's Plan of the Seat of Government, 1791

RIGHTS OF MAN:

BEING AN

ANSWER TO MR. BURKE's ATTACK

ON THE

FRENCH REVOLUTION.

BY

THOMAS PAINE,

SECRETARY FOR FOREIGN AFFAIRS TO CONGRESS IN THE AMERICAN WAR,

AND

AUTHOR OF THE WORK INTITLED *COMMON SENSE.*

Second Edition.

―――――――

PHILADELPHIA:

RE-PRINTED BY *SAMUEL HARRISON SMITH.*

M.DCC.XCI.

Title-page of Paine's *Rights of Man*

THE following Extract from a note accompanying a copy of this Pamphlet for republication, is so respectable a testimony of its value, that the Printer hopes the distinguished writer will excuse its present appearance. It proceeds from a character, equally eminent in the councils of America, and conversant in the affairs of France, from a long and recent residence at the Court of Versailles in the Diplomatic department; and, at the same time that it does justice to the writings of Mr. Paine, it reflects honor on the source from which it flows, by directing the mind to a contemplation of that Republican firmness and Democratic simplicity which endear their possessor to every friend of the " RIGHTS OF MAN."

After some prefatory remarks, the Secretary of State observes:

" I am extremely pleased to find it will be re-
" printed here, and that something is at length to
" be publicly said against the political heresies which
" have sprung up among us.

" I have no doubt our citizens will *rally* a second
" time round the *standard* of COMMON SENSE."

Endorsement of Paine's *Rights of Man*

C̶ONTRASTED OPINIONS OF PAINE'S PAMPHLET:

"Contrasted Opinions of Paine's Pamphlet" (*above*)

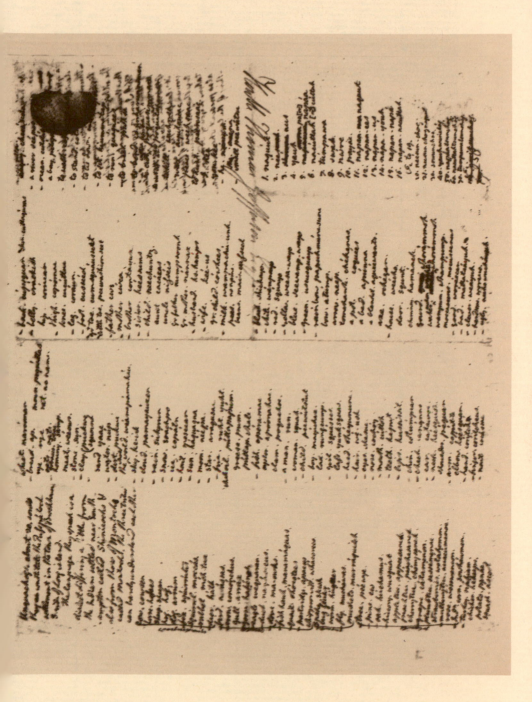

George Beckwith

one which has taken this resolution. This opposition will of course rather prolong the popularity of the Marquis than otherwise.

The report of the colonial and other committees mentioned in my last was made yesterday. The reporter insisted much on the necessity of adopting it without adjournment, as they had hitherto done on subjects of the kind. It appeared however that the dispositions of the assembly had changed. The proposition to decree without discussion was recieved with indignation, although founded in two precedents. It was decided by a great majority that the report of the committees should be first printed and then discussed in the assembly. The proposition of the committees was to confirm the decree of the 12th. of October last and to assemble a *comité-generale* of deputies from all the islands in the French part of the island of St. Martin, to decide on an uniform plan as to the *etat de personnes* viz. *gens de couleur* to be submitted to the national assembly. This adjournment for discussion is considered as a kind of victory, by those who are for the free of all colours having the same privileges. Still the point is doubtful. – Permanent regulations of commerce will not be entered into until this question is settled, and it was probably the intention of the committees that the Islanders should recieve one as the price of the other.

I mentioned to you in my last that the Pope refused to recieve M. de Segur as ambassador. The reason given as appears by a letter from M. de Montmorin to the Nuncio, communicated to the assembly is that the Pope will recieve no ambassador who has taken the oath prescribed, without restriction. M. de Montmorin observes in this letter that the King hopes there has been some error in the business, as it would be a means of breaking off all communication between the holy see and the French monarchy, and that not sending an Ambassador to Rome "*La dignité de la nation et celle de S. M. ne lui permettraient plus de conserver un nonce du Pape a Paris.*" The letter ends with this sentence. "*S. M. cependant par égard pour S. S. a par une attention particuliere pour V. E. suspendu le depart de M. de Segur en attendent[1] votre reponse, pour prendre le parti que le soin de sa dignité rendrait indispensable.*"

The diet of Poland have come to a determination to give the right of citizenship to the *Bourgeois* of the Republick. They have adopted the inverse system of France. Instead of taking the nobility from those who possessed it they have given it to those who had it not. The bourgeois have now the privileges of nobility, this being granted by an assembly of nobles almost unanimously and of their own accord is a strong proof of the progress of philosophy even in that region.

It is reported and generally believed that on the British Chargé des affaires at Copenhagen announcing to that court that a fleet of thirty ships of the line or more would be sent into the Baltic, and that his court flattered itself they would be recieved into the Danish ports and find there the supplies which should be necessary, orders were immediately given to arm in these ports. The activity with which it is said to be doing also would seem as if Denmark meant to be ready to act independently. Still it is certain that exposed as that country is by land and by water to Prussia and England, all that can be hoped for by Russia is a perfect neutrality. There is no doubt that the dispositions of the court if they could be followed would be warmly in favor of the Empress. The Baron Blome told me yesterday that the English fleet would be admitted into the Danish ports if they insisted on it, but that it would probably be with much precaution, such as recieving a few ships at a time &c.

The Russian minister here seems to use affectation in saying to every body that war will certainly take place in the North. The English Ambassador on the contrary is moderate, expresses his doubts, says it is possible they may be forced into the war, and other things of the kind. He does not pretend to deny that it is exceedingly unpopular in England, and it is evident that he considers it an impolitic step. The English cabinet are probably of the same opinion since the ultimatum last sent to Berlin to be concerted and accepted there and then forwarded to Petersburg contains modifications. The English Ambassador took so much pains to convince every body that they were not the cause of the resignation of the Duke of Leeds, that he persuaded fully most people that they were.

The prospect of this war occasions a strong preference in favor of American shipping. Still I observe from the late list of those which have passed the sound that much the greatest number is as usual, English, I mean in proportion to those of other nations. I have the honor to be with sentiments of the most perfect respect & attachment, Dear Sir your most obedient humble servant,

W: SHORT

PrC (DLC: Short Papers); at head of text: "*No. 66*"; badly faded, and some illegible words and phrases have been supplied from Tr (DNA: RG 59, DD). Recorded in SJL as received 19 July 1791.

[1] Thus in PrC and Tr. Montmorin's letter as recorded in *Archives Parlementaires*, xxv, 587-8 for the session of 5 May 1791 has "*et attendra.*"

From George Washington

Charleston, May 8th. 1791.

The round of business and of ceremony, which now engages my attention, only allows me leisure to acknowledge the receipt of your letter of the 10th. of last month, which will receive a more particular consideration. – I am, with great esteem, Sir, Your most obedient Servant,   Go: Washington

RC (DLC); in hand of William Jackson except for signature; endorsed by TJ as received at Albany 25 May 1791 and so recorded in SJL. In this TJ erred: he arrived at Albany only on the morning of the 26th, having lodged the previous night at Kinderhook, 20 miles below the city.

To Thomas Leiper

Sir   Philadelphia May 10. 1791.

Capt. Stratton arrived last night with the 4. hhds. of tobo. for which I gave you the bill of lading some time ago. He will call on you to-day. I should like that it were examined, because I believe, from the marks, that it is of the Bedford tobo. – I mentioned to you sometime ago that I believed I should have occasion for about 400. Dollars of this money, to be obtained by discount at the bank. As I leave town about the last of the week on a journey Northwardly, during which I shall need this money, I will beg the favor of a note for that sum in a form negociable at the bank. – I must beg that the painters may be ready to go to work on Monday, that the smell may be vanished before my return. I am Sir Your very humble servt,

Th: Jefferson

PrC (MHi).

To William Short

Dear Sir   Philadelphia. May 10. 1791.

I wrote you on the 25th. of April. Since that date nothing has occurred worth communication. On this day, in consequence of orders given, we expect a sudden incursion will be made from Kentuckey into the Indian country by a corps which will return immediately, and others repeat the same thing successively, till a force shall be collected sufficient to meet any numbers the enemy can bring into the field. So that by a greater, if not by the smaller, movements we may hope to bring them to peace.

You will see by the papers sent herewith that the public stocks here maintain their ground pretty equally. I am in hopes they may be considered as now stationary, a circumstance much to be desired in order to put an end to the spirit of gambling which their vibrations had produced.

I set out in a few days on an excursion Northwardly, from which I shall not return till the middle of next month: consequently I shall not till then write to you again. – I am with great & sincere esteem, Dear Sir your affectionate friend & humble servt,

Th: Jefferson

PrC (DLC). FC (DNA: RG 59, DCI). Recorded in SJL as a public letter.

To Pierpont Edwards

Sir   Philadelphia May 11. 1791.

I have duly recieved your favor of April 30. together with the volume of laws accompanying it: and have now the honour to remit you a post bill for 15. dollars 25. cents for your reimbursement, according to the account sent. Anxious to carry this collection of the laws of all the states to as perfect completion as possible, as well for the use of the general government, as for placing in a safe deposit one copy of the laws of all the states to which they may themselves be glad to recur hereafter, I take the liberty of solliciting a continuance of your attention to the subject, and of adding assurances of the esteem & respect with which I am Sir Your most obedt. & most humble servt,   Th: Jefferson

PrC (DLC); at foot of text: "Mr. Pierpont Edwards, New haven." FC (DNA: RG 59, PCC No. 120).

To James Lyle

Dear Sir   Philadelphia May 11. 1791.

In order to make provision for the payment of my debts to yourself and Farrell & Jones, I sold a tract of land to Mr. Ronald for £1076. pounds sterling, one half payable Jan. 1. 1796. the other half Jan. 1. 1797. with interest on the whole from Oct. 5. 1790. For the one half, I retain a mortgage on the lands sold; for the other half he mortgaged a moiety of his Beaverdam lands valued at the double of the bond; so that I have mortgages of the value of double the sum due. To propose your taking these bonds and mortgages as payment of my debt to Kippen & co. is indeed a proposition to postpone the times of payment as settled between us, but it offers in consideration of those delays a better security, to wit bonds backed by mortgages in exchange for my simple bonds, and whatever personal confidence you might have in me, I am not immortal, and the discharge of my bonds may fall into other hands. It would be an infinite relief to my mind, and the greatest favour in the world if you would take these two bonds and mortgages *in discharge of my* bonds. There would be a small matter overpaid to be refunded when recieved. If this cannot be done as to both let me beseech you to take the one payable Jan. 1. 1796. in lieu of your two last payments. It will delay the last, which is the greatest but five months, and will be infinite relief to me. I think I am sure that Mr. McCaul would do it were he here, and will approve it if done by you: because it serves me, and betters the security for the debt. Your answer will oblige Dear Sir your most obedt. humble servt, TH: JEFFERSON

PrC (MHi).

On the day before the above letter was written, TJ had received Richard Hanson's flat refusal of the same proposal, a disappointment that could hardly have been lessened by the statement of Hanson that he would rather have TJ's bond unsecured than that of anyone else with security (TJ to Hanson, 5 Apr. 1791; Hanson to TJ, 30 Apr. 1791). An entry in SJL shows that TJ received on 21 June a reply from Lyle dated 20 May 1791, but the letter has not been found. TJ's agreement with William Ronald, purchaser of the Elk Hill lands, is printed at 5 Oct. 1790.

To James Maxwell

SIR   Philadelphia May 11. 1791.

Being about to leave town, and not likely to return till the middle of next month, I am to acknowlege the reciept of your favor of Apr. 2. and to ask of you, if you should forward the cyder within that period, that you will be so good as to address it with your letter to 'Mr. Henry Remsen, chief clerk of the Secretary of state at Philadelphia,' who will remit the amount: otherwise if addressed to me the letter would remain unopened till my return. I am afraid the weather is getting full warm for it's removal: however of this you are the best judge, and what ever you do herein will be thankfully acknowleged by Sir Your most obedt. humble servt,

TH: JEFFERSON

PrC (MHi).

[389]

To Daniel Smith

SIR   Philadelphia May 11. 1791.

In acknowleging the reciept of your favor of Mar. 1. I take occasion at the same time to answer the query it proposed by observing that the reports from your office should contain periods of six months each. It would be well that they should end on the last days of June and December. Having nothing interesting to communicate I shall only add assurances of the esteem with which I am Dear Sir Your most obedt. humble servt,   TH: JEFFERSON

PrC (DLC). FC (DNA: RG 59, PCC No. 120).

To James Strange

SIR   Philadelphia May 11. 1791.

Your favor of Apr. 30. has been duly recieved. My separation from my books and papers of account, which are in Virginia renders it impossible to give any definitive answer here. I go home once a year with a view to attend to my private affairs, and shall be at home in the month of September next when I will attend to the subject of your letter and write to you. In the mean time I would observe to you that I am not the person to be applied to in the account against my father's estate. It probably is for articles furnished after my interests were separated from that estate which was about the year 1764. Mr. John Nicholas of Buckingham is the only acting executor, and can point out the persons responsible for the account. – With respect to those against myself and my mother, I shall be glad to recieve copies of the accounts, under what factors and at what places they arose, because it was the name of the factor generally and not of the firm which was known to the dealer. These may be sent to me here by post more safely than elsewhere. – I am Sir Your very humble servt,   TH: JEFFERSON

PrC (MHi). Recorded in SJL as "for Donald Scott & Co." Strange's letter of 30 Apr. is recorded in SJL as being from Richmond and as received 7 May 1791, but has not been found.

To Benjamin Vaughan

DEAR SIR   Philadelphia May 11. 1791.

It is rare that my public occupations will permit me to take up the pen for my private correspondencies however desireable to me. This must be my apology for being so late in acknowleging the reciept of your favors of Sep. 21 Oct. 21. Dec. 2. and 16. and Jan. 6. The parcels of Mountain rice from Timor came to hand too late in the last season to produce seed. I have sowed this spring some of the same, but it has not yet come up. I was fortunate in recieving from the coast of Africa last fall a cask of Mountain rice of the last year's growth. This I have dispersed into many hands, having sent the mass of it to S. Carolina. The information which accompanied this cask was that they have there (on the coast of Africa) 3. kinds of Mountain rice, which sowed at the same time, comes to harvest a month distant from each other. They did not say of which kind that is which was sent to me. The kind which ripens quickest will surely find sun enough to ripen it in our middle states.

I thank you, my dear Sir, for the Sacontalá, and for Smeaton's book: but the latter is of a value which obliges me to request you to put more reasonable bounds to your liberalities, neither the state of the sciences nor of the arts here putting it in my power to fulfill that reciprocity which my wishes would lead me to. – The Revolution of France does not astonish me so much as the Revolution of Mr. Burke. I wish I could believe the latter proceeded from as pure motives as the former. But what demonstration could scarcely have established before, less than the hints of Dr. Priestly and Mr. Paine establish firmly now. How mortifying that this evidence of the rotteness of his mind must oblige us now to ascribe to wicked motives those actions of his life which wore the mask of virtue and patriotism. To judge from what we see published, we must believe that the spirit of toryism has gained nearly the whole of the nation: that the whig principles are utterly extinguished except in the breasts of certain descriptions of dissenters. This sudden change in the principles of a nation would be a curious morsel in the history of man. – We have some names of note here who have apostatised from the true faith: but they are few indeed, and the body of our citizens are pure and insusceptible of taint in their republicanism. Mr. Paine's answer to Burke will be a refreshing shower to their minds. It would bring England itself to reason and revolution if it was permitted to be read there. However the same things will be said in milder forms, will make their way among the people, and you must reform at last.

We have great reason to be satisfied with the train of our affairs. Our government is going on with a firm and steady pace, our taxes, increasing with our population, are always ahead of our calculations, favorable seasons for several years past have given great crops of produce, and the increase of industry, economy, and domestic manufacture are very sensible. Our credit both at home and abroad is equal to our wishes. So that on the whole we are in as prosperous a way as a nation can well be. This shews the advantage of the changeableness of a constitution. Had our former one been unalterable (pardon the absurdity of the hypothesis) we must have gone to ruin with our eyes open. – We are in hopes the operations of this summer will bring our savage neighbors to accept our peace, friendship and good offices, which is all we desire of them. If you see Ld. Wycombe sometimes present my esteem to him; so also and ever to Dr. Price. I am Dear Sir with sincere attachment Your most obedt. & most humble servt, TH: JEFFERSON

RC (Mrs. Langdon Marvin, Hallowell, Maine, 1944); addressed: "Benjamin Vaughan esq. Jefferies square London"; endorsed. PrC (DLC).

TJ's letter to the printer of Paine's *Rights of Man*, with its indirect allusion to John Adams' political heresies, had been an indiscretion, but the more veiled reference here was calculated. So also was the glowing account of the firm and steady pace of the government, about whose divisions and conflicting policies no one was more troubled at this moment than TJ. Both comments, like his earlier intimation to Vaughan that maple sugar would make the nation independent of the British sugar islands for that commodity, were intended for English consumption.

The copy of the greatest Sanskrit drama, *Sakuntala*, by Kalidasa, the great Hindu poet of the fifth century A.D., which Vaughan sent to TJ was the translation by Sir William Jones (1746-1794), published in London in 1790 (Sowerby, No. 4435). TJ probably was less enthusiastic about this work than Vaughan was (see Vaughan to TJ, 21 Sep. 1790). But, as his allusion to it indicates, he fully appreciated the copy of the work by John Smeaton (1724-1792), the English engineer: *A narrative of the building and a description of the construction of the Edystone Lighthouse* (London, 1791; Sowerby, No. 4213).

The Rev. Richard Price, whom TJ greatly admired, never received TJ's felicitation. He died less than a month before the above letter was written.

To Jeremiah Wadsworth

SIR   Philadelphia May 11. 1791.

I have duly recieved your favour of April 20. The exemption from the Droit d'Aubaine in the French West Indies, has been for some time past a subject of attention. As the National assembly were abolishing it *in France* for all nations, I desired our Chargé des affaires there to see that the decree should be extended to all the *dominions* of France. His letters assure me that it will be done, so as to remove this grievance hereafter. With respect to the past, I believe it has been *judicially* determined in France that the exemption given by our treaty did not extend to their foreign possessions. Should Mr. Johnston however be disposed to try this matter, it will be requisite for him to obtain from Port au prince an authenticated record of the proceedings in his case. It would seem also that those in the case of the gentleman of Curracoa might be useful. These should be transmitted to some person in Paris to sollicit the government for him. Tho' it is not permitted that our Chargé des affaires there, or any where, should act as the private agent or sollicitor for any individual, yet he will lend his aid and influence whenever it may be just and useful, by official application. I have the honour to be with great esteem, Sir, your most obedt. and most humble servt, TH: JEFFERSON

PrC (DLC); at foot of text: "Honble. Jeremiah Wadsworth." FC (DNA: RG 59, PCC No. 120).

To Willink, Van Staphorst & Hubbard

GENTLEMEN   Philadelphia May 11. 1791.

I have now before me your favours of Sep. 3. and 30th. and approve of your compliance with Mr. Short's draughts therein mentioned. The error to your prejudice of one hundred florins in my draught of May 3. 1789. I was not able to correct till my papers arrived from France, and could be opened, so as to rectify the same error at the same time in my public accounts. This being done I have paid the hundred florins with interest to this day to Mr. Leroy, to wit forty five dollars, exchange @ 40. cents the florin, interest 6. per cent. per annum. Always mindful of your civilities and kindnesses, I shall be happy in every occasion of rendering you service, & of proving to you the esteem with which I have the honour to be Gentlemen Your most obedt. humble servt,

TH: JEFFERSON

PrC (DLC); recorded in SJL as "private." On this date Leroy & Bayard acknowledged TJ's payment of $45 and credited the amount to the Amsterdam firm (MS in DLC).

To Willink, Van Staphorst & Hubbard

GENTLEMEN   Philadelphia May. 11. 1791.

In my letter of Mar. 19. I inclosed you the Treasurer's bill on you for ninety nine thousand current gilders, erroneously calling them ninety thousand, and after specifying what calls were to be answered from them in the first instance, I mentioned that I would at a future day send further and final instructions for the application of the whole sum. This is destined to pay the salaries of Colo. Humphreys, Mr. Short, Mr. Carmichael and Mr. Dumas, the three former being allowed four thousand five hundred dollars a year, and Mr. Dumas the sum you have heretofore paid him; as also certain contingent expences for postage, couriers &c. defined to them either in general or occasional instructions. You will therefore be pleased to answer their draughts for their salaries and contingent expences, taking on ourselves the trust in their discretion as to the amount of their draughts for contingent expences. As they may at times be charged with special commissions from other departments for disbursements not to be made out of this fund, be pleased, in arranging the epochs and forms of their draughts, to desire that the draught when chargeable on this fund must express that it is to be paid 'for the department of state.' My separate responsibility for this fund forbids my permitting any disbursements to enter into the account which do not belong to it. I must beg the favor of you also to make up your account to the close of the last day of June this present year, into which no expences are to enter which preceded the 1st. day of July 1790. these being the dates of the appropriation of the law. I inclose you a duplicate of the treasurer's bill for 99,000 gilders, and am with great esteem Gentlemen Your most obedient & most humble servt.

Tʜ: Jᴇꜰꜰᴇʀsᴏɴ

PrC (DLC). FC (DNA: RG 59, DCI). Enclosure: Dupl of Treasurer's bill, triplicates of which Coxe had transmitted to TJ along with copies of the letter of advice, suggesting that these might be "connected by wafers to the Bills for 99000 Guilders on Amsterdam" (Coxe to TJ, 19 Mch. 1791; PHi: Coxe Papers).

Letters of advice were usually, though not always, sent separately, and properly, in advance of bills of exchange, but whether TJ followed Coxe's advice to attach them to the bills is not known. The bankers called TJ's attention not to the error he had made in the amount but to the fact that he had failed to endorse the bill. They therefore requested that "a second properly transferred" be sent (Willink, Van Staphorst & Hubbard to TJ, 20 May 1791; RC in DNA: RG 59, AR; recorded in SJL as received

4 Aug. 1791). Immediately on receiving this request, TJ forwarded the bill for 99,000 guilders and added: "I hope you will have recieved my letter of May 11.... and that your account of this fund from July 1. 1790. to June 30. 1791. inclusive is on it's way to me that I may recieve it in time to lay before Congress at their meeting. – Lest I should have omitted also to endorse the 1st. and 2d. of the bills for 32,175 currt. gilders, I enclose you a triplicate of that duly endorsed" (TJ to Willink, Van Staphorst & Hubbard, 5 Aug. 1791; PrC in DLC; FC in DNA: RG 59, DCI). In this hope TJ was disappointed. The bankers sent the account on receiving the above letter, but it reached TJ only after the adjournment of Congress and after he had written a stern admonition (Willink, Van Staphorst & Hubbard to TJ, 24 Oct. 1791; see TJ's letter of 23 Jan. 1792).

To Benjamin S. Barton and Others

Thursday May 12. 1791.

Th: Jefferson presents his respects to the gentlemen of the committee on the Hessian fly, and prays their attendance at the Hall of the Philosophical society tomorrow (Friday) at half after seven P.M. He has conjectured that that hour will be most convenient to them, and that not a moment of their time may be lost unnecessarily, he will attend himself at the very moment precisely, and for their own convenience asks the same of them. He leaves town on Sunday for a month, to set out on a journey which will carry him through N. York and the whole of Long island, where this animal has raged much. He is therefore anxious to take with him the decision of the committee and particularly prays of Dr. Barton to have his queries prepared to present to them.

RC (MB); addressed: "Doctor Barton 55. North 2d street." Not recorded in SJL.

From William Murray

SIR   Lexington May 12th. 1791.

I was honored with your letter of the 22d. of March and its inclosures by Governor St. Clair. – I have made every enquiry in my power into the business of O Fallon and believe the following to be a true state of it. He came into this Country about the Month of April last as the agent of what he called the South Carolina Yaszou company. He gave out that this Company had made a large purchase of Land from the State of Georgia and that they would give great encouragment to such as would remove there from this Country. Finding that he could not obtain a sufficient number of settlers in this way, about the Month of September he changed his plan and determined to raise a Body of Troops but on what terms I have not[1] been informed. In consequence of this resolution he named a number of Officers to whom he gave Commissions similar to the one you transmitted to me; contracted for a large quantity of Military Stores and for considerable supplies of provisions and drew bills for the amount of the whole on the Company in Charlestown. His bills were protested and the persons who were to have furnished the supplies then refused to deliver them. It is said that the Officers had engaged the number of men they had stipulated to raise and that nothing was wanting but the supplies to set them in motion, but they having been before disgusted with O Fallon deserted him to a man as soon as they heard that his bills had been protested. At the time these people engaged with him it was not known that he intended to make this settlement in opposition to the general Government: On the contrary it was supposed by the adventurers that the Company had a legal right to the lands under their purchase from Georgia and that by removing to that land they would offend none but the Spaniards and Indians.

The whole of this business was conducted quietly and without any public meeting that I have yet heard of. Under these circumstances I am of opinion that O'Fallon's conduct can only be considered as a conspiracy or an intention to levy War and that, as the War was never actually levied, it cannot amount to treason: that it cannot be treason because the War was not intended against the United States but only against their allies, and that it cannot be treason if the Country which it was to be carried on is out of the limit of the United States. – No such Assembly or meeting has even been held by these people as far as my information goes, as could legally be denominated an unlawfull assembly a rout or a riot.

From this view of the subject and in consequence of Mr. Randolph's Opinion I consulted with the Attorney Genl. for the State within this District. He viewed the matter in same light that I did and said that as a State officer he had nothing to do with it, as the only fact which appeared to him was the giving a Commission to raise men for a purpose to be executed out of the limits and jurisdiction of the State. Upon the whole I have Judged it most proper not to set on foot any prosecution against O Fallon untill I receive your further directions. – The situation in which he is at this time has served to confirm me in this resolution. He is totally without friends partizans or Money and must sink into obscurity unless he should be made an object of importance by a prosecution which could not be supported. – I will keep an attentive eye on his conduct and if he takes any new steps or if any alteration in the business shall take place which will make it proper to do so, I will instantly institute a prosecution against him.

If it shall be thought by Government necessary to institute one against him for what he has already done, I shall be ready to do it, but must request that the Attorney Genl. for the United States may be directed to point out the kind of prosecution which ought to be carried on. As this is a new and untrodden path under the present Government I flatter myself I shall stand excused in waiting for further directions; and in requesting that the business may be commenced under the opinion of a Gentleman of superior abilities and experience to what I pretend to possess. – I have the honor to be with the greatest respect & Esteem sir yr. mst. Obedient and Very Humble sert.,   WILLIAM MURRAY

N.B. I have published the President's proclamation and have no doubt it will effectually prevent any attempt to renew the scheme.

W. M.

RC (DNA: RG 76, Tennessee Claims); endorsed by TJ as received 9 Aug. 1791 and so recorded in SJL.

The opinion of the Attorney General in the O'Fallon matter, which TJ helped prepare, specifically stated that the prosecution be for a riot unless available testimony would "clearly subject him to the charge of treason" (see opinion, 14 Feb. 1791). TJ sent a copy of this opinion to Murray in his letter of 22 Mch. 1791, together with a copy of the President's proclamation of

19 Mch. 1791. TJ did not reply to the above letter, but undoubtedly he approved the decision to let O'Fallon sink into oblivion without being prosecuted. He must have made this recommendation to the President, for Lear returned Murray's letter with the comment that "the President . . . knows of nothing more to be done in the business" (Lear to TJ, 15 Aug. 1791; PrC in DNA: RG 59, MLR).

[1] This word omitted in RC though clearly intended.

Official Instructions for Thomas Barclay

SIR   Philadelphia May 13th. 1791

You are appointed by the President of the United States to go to the Court of Morocco for the purpose of obtaining from the new Emperor a recognition of our Treaty with his father. As it is thought best that you should go in some definite character, that of Consul has been adopted, and you consequently receive a Commission as Consul for the United States in the dominions of the Emperor of Morocco, which having been issued during the recess of the Senate will of course expire at the end of their next session. It has been thought best however not to insert this limitation in the Commission as being unnecessary, and it might perhaps embarrass. – Before the end of the next session of the Senate it is expected the objects of your mission will be accomplished.

Lisbon being the most convenient port of correspondence between us and Morocco, sufficient authority will be given to Col: Humphreys, Resident for the United States at that place, over funds in Amsterdam for the objects of your mission. On him therefore you will draw for the sums herein allowed, or such parts of them as shall be necessary. To that port too you had better proceed in the first vessel which shall be going there, as it is expected you will get a ready passage from thence to Morocco.

On your arrival in Morocco sound your ground, and know how things stand at present. Your former voyage there having put you in possession of the characters through whom this may be done, who may best be used for approaching the Emperor and effecting your purpose, you are left to use your own knowledge to the best advantage.

The object being merely to obtain an acknowledgment of the Treaty, we rely that you will be able to do this, giving very moderate presents. As the amount of these will be drawn into precedent on future similar repetitions of them, it becomes important. Our distance, our seclusion from the ancient world, it's politics and usages, our agricultural occupations and habits, our poverty, and lastly our determination to prefer war in all cases to tribute under any form and to any people whatever, will furnish you with topics for opposing and refusing high or dishonoring pretensions, to which may be added the advantages their people will derive from our commerce, and their Sovereign from the duties laid on whatever we extract from that country.

Keep us regularly informed of your proceedings and progress, by writing by every possible occasion, detailing to us particularly your conferences either private or public, and the persons with whom they are held.

We think that Francisco Chiappe has merited well of the United States by his care of their peace and interests. He has sent an account of disbursements for us amounting to 394 dollars. Do not recognise the account, because we are unwilling, by doing that, to give him a colour for presenting larger ones hereafter, for expences which it is impossible for us to scrutinize or controul. Let him understand that our laws oppose the application of public money so informally; but in your presents, treat *him* handsomely, so as not only to cover this demand, but go beyond it with a liberality which may fix him deeply in our interests. The place he holds near the Emperor renders his friendship peculiarly important. Let us have nothing further to do with his brothers or any other person. The money which would make one good friend, divided among several will produce no attachment.

The Emperor has intimated that he expects an Ambassador from us. Let him understand that this may be a custom of the old world, but it is not ours: that we never sent an Ambassador to any Nation.

You are to be allowed from the day of your departure till your return 166⅔ dollars a month for your time and expences, adding thereto your passage money and sea stores going and coming.

Remain in your post till the 1st. of April next, and as much longer as shall be necessary to accomplish the objects of your mission, unless you should receive instructions from hence to the contrary.

With your commission you will receive a Letter to the Emperor of Morocco, a cypher and a Letter to Col: Humphreys. — I have the honor to be with great esteem Sir Your most obedient & most humble servant

PrC of missing RC (DLC); in Remsen's hand, unsigned. Tr (NjP); entirely in clerk's hand; docketed in part: "for Colo Humphreys." FC (DNA: RG 59, DCI). Enclosures: (1) Commission to Barclay as consul for Morocco, 31 Mch. 1791 (FC in DNA: RG 59, CC). (2) Washington's letter to the Emperor of Morocco, 31 Mch. 1791: "Great and magnanimous Friend. — Separated by an immense Ocean from the the more ancient Nations of the Earth, and little connected with their Politics or Proceedings, we are late in learning the Events which take place among them, and later in conveying to them our Sentiments thereon. — The Death of the late Emperor, your Father and our Friend, of glorious Memory, is one of those Events which, tho' distant, attracts our Notice and Concern. Receive, great and good Friend, my sincere Sympathy with you on that Loss; and permit me at the same time to express the Satisfaction with which I learn the Accession of so worthy a Successor to the Imperial Throne of Morocco, and to offer you the Homage of my sincere Congratulations. May the Days of your Majesty's Life be many and glorious, and may they ever mark the Æra during which a great People shall have been most prosperous and happy under the best and happiest of Sovereigns. — The late Emperor, very soon after the Establishment of our Infant Nation, manifested his royal Regard and Amity to us by many friendly and generous Acts, and particularly by the Protection of our Citizens in their Commerce with his Subjects. And as a further Instance of his Desire to promote our Prosperity and Intercourse with his Realms, he entered into a Treaty of Amity and Commerce with us, for himself and his Successors, to continue Fifty years. The Justice and Magnanimity

of your Majesty leave us full of Confidence, that this Treaty will meet your royal Patronage also; and it will give me great Satisfaction to be assured, that the Citizens of the United States of America may expect from your Imperial Majesty, the same Protection and Kindness, which the Example of your Illustrious Father has taught them to expect from those who occupy the Throne of Morocco, and to have your royal Word that they may count on a due observance of the Treaty which connects the two Nations in friendship. — This will be delivered to your Majesty by our faithful citizen Thomas Barclay, whom I name Consul for these United States in the Dominions of your Majesty, and who to the integrity and knowledge qualifying him for that Office, unites the peculiar advantage of having been the Agent through whom our Treaty with the late Emperor was received. I pray your Majesty to protect him in the exercise of his functions for the patronage of the commerce between our two countries, and of those who carry it on. — May that God, whom we both adore, bless your Imperial Majesty with long life, health and success, and have you always, Great and magnanimous Friend, under his holy keeping. — Written at Philadelphia the thirty first day of March in the fifteenth year of our sovereignty and independence, from Your good and faithful friend George Washington by the President Thomas Jefferson" (FC in DLC; entirely in Remsen's hand; RC, also in his hand but signed by Washington and attested by TJ, was in possession of a private individual in Australia in 1973; Tr in DNA: RG 59, GRSD; all texts of the enclosure are those of the second version described below). TJ drafted Barclay's instructions as well as the letter to the Emperor. He submitted these to Washington, who, as an entry in SJPL shows, returned them in a covering note of 10 March 1791 (Washington's note is missing). Subsequently, when Barclay pointed out that if he were given no rank he would be received as an ambassador and commensurate gifts would be expected, TJ thereupon advised that he be sent as consul and submitted a blank commission for that purpose. He also drafted another letter to the Emperor not otherwise different from that signed by Washington "but as having a clause of credence in it" (TJ to Washington, 27 Mch. 1791). Washington signed both and left it to TJ to decide whether the commission could be issued without the approval of the Senate (Washington to TJ, 1 Apr. 1791). The text of the discarded letter to the Emperor which Washington signed early in March has not been found.

In voicing the policy of the government giving preference to "war in all cases to tribute under any form and to any people whatever," TJ expressed his own settled conviction, though even at the moment of making the declaration the position he had consistently held was being eroded (see Editorial Note to group of documents on trade with the Mediterranean, at 28 Dec. 1790). The instructions here given, while issued in pursuance of law, also conflicted with his equally consistent view that a treaty represented the compact of two sovereign powers and could not be affected by a change in the form of the government of either or by a succession to the throne. But the secret instruction authorizing the expenditure of $10,000 in gifts for the purpose of confirming a treaty already negotiated was in effect only the payment of tribute under another guise.

Confidential Instructions for Thomas Barclay

May 13th. 1791.

A private instruction which Mr. Barclay is to carry in his memory, and not on paper, lest it should come into improper hands.

We rely that you will obtain the friendship of the new Emperor, and his assurances that the Treaty shall be faithfully observed, with as little expence as possible. But the sum of ten thousand dollars is fixed as the limit which all your donations together are not to exceed.

PrC of missing RC (DLC); in Remsen's hand, unsigned. Tr (NjP); in clerk's hand, on verso of last page of copy of letter docketed in part: "for Colo. Humphreys." FC (DNA: RG 59, DCI). The text in PrC (and of course in that of the missing RC) is given on a separate sheet for obvious reasons.

To Francisco Chiappe

SIR   Phila. May 13. 1791.

Since my entrance into the office of Secretary of state I have been honoured with several of your letters, and should sooner have acknoleged the reciept of them but that I have from time to time expected the present occasion would occur sooner than it has done.

I am authorised to express to you the satisfaction of the President at the zeal and attention you have shewn to our interests and to hope a continuance of them.

Mr. Barclay is sent in the character of Consul of the U.S. to present our respects to his imperial Majesty for whom he has a letter from the President. We have no doubt he will receive your aid as usual to impress the mind of the emperor with a sense of our high respect and friendship for his person and character, and to dispose him to a cordial continuance of that good understanding so happily established with his father.

Our manner of thinking on all these subjects is so perfectly known to Mr. Barclay, that nothing better can be done than to refer you to him for information on every subject which you might wish to enquire into.[1] I am with great esteem Sir Your mo. ob. & mo. hble servt.

Dft (Lloyd W. Smith, Madison, N.J., 1946); at foot of text: "Mr. Francisco Chiappe"; docketed by Remsen. PrC of RC in Remsen's hand (DLC). FC (DNA: RG 59, DCI).

TJ in fact had not received any letters addressed to him by Francisco Chiappe since becoming Secretary of State: all during that period had been written to Jay as Secretary for Foreign Affairs or to Washington as "President of Congress." These were six in number and covered the period from 3 Aug. 1790 to 8 Nov. 1791. All are in DNA:

RG 360, PCC No. 98 (M-247/125) and are noted where transmitted to TJ (see, for example, Lear to TJ, 9 July 1791; also Editorial Note on commerce in the Mediterranean, at 28 Dec. 1790). Although both Francisco and Giuseppe Chiappe sent several letters to the President subsequent to this date which are to be found in the same series, the above communication closed the official relationship with the brothers (see TJ's instructions to Barclay, 13 May 1791).

[1] In Dft at this point TJ deleted the following: "He will particularly explain to you."

Circular to Consuls and Vice-Consuls

SIR   Philadelphia May 13th. 1791.

You will readily conceive that the union of Domestic with the Foreign affairs under the Department of State, brings on the head of this Department such incessant calls, not admitting delay, as oblige him to postpone whatever will bear postponing; hence, though it is important that I should continue to receive from time to time regular information from you of whatever occurs within your notice interesting to the United States, yet it is not in my power to acknowledge the receipt of your letters regularly as they come. I mention this circumstance that you may ascribe the delay of acknowledgment to the real cause, and that it may not produce any relaxation on your part in making all those communications which it is important should be received, and which govern our proceedings, though it is not in my power to note it to you specially.

I had hoped that Congress at their last Session would have passed a bill for regulating the functions of Consuls. Such an one was before them; but there being a considerable difference of opinion as to some of it's parts, it was finally lost by the shortness of the Session, which the Constitution had limited to the 3d. of March. It will be taken up again at the ensuing Session of October next; in the mean time you will be pleased to govern yourself by the instructions already given.

In general our affairs are proceeding in a train of unparalleled prosperity. This arises from the real improvements of our Government, from the unbounded confidence reposed in it by the people, their zeal to support it, and their conviction that a solid union is the best rock of their safety, from the favorable seasons which for some years past have co-operated with a fertile soil and genial climate to increase the productions of agriculture, and from the growth of industry, economy and domestic manufactures. So that I believe I may say with truth that there is not a Nation under the sun enjoying more present prosperity, nor with more in prospect.

The Indians on our frontier indeed, still continue to cut off straggling individuals or families falling in their way. An expedition against them the last summer was less successful than there was reason to expect: we lost in it about 100 men. The operations of the present summer will more probably bring them to peace, which is all we desire of them, it having been a leading object of our present Government to guaranty them in their present possessions, and to protect their persons with the same fidelity which is extended to it's own Citizens: we ask nothing of them but that they will accept our peace, friendship and services; and we hope soon to make them sensible of this, in spite of the incitements against us which they have been so much the dupes of. This is the general state of our affairs at present, as faithfully as I am able to to give it. — I am with great esteem Sir Your most obedient and Most Humble Servant,

Th: Jefferson

RC (Mrs. Laussat R. Rogers, New Castle, Del., 1962); in Taylor's hand; at foot of text: "James Yard Esqr." PrC (DLC); in clerk's hand, unsigned; at foot of text: "Nathaniel Barrett, Edward Church, Ebenezer Brush, John Street, James Yard" (the five to whom the circular was sent in the form given above). FC (DNA: RG 59, DCI); at head of text: "(Circular) To the Consuls and Vice Consuls of the United States"; at the foot of text are listed the foregoing five persons, together with the names and locations of ten consuls and vice-consuls to whom the circular was sent as above with additions as given below (additions described as postscripts in FC but, as indicated by some surviving recipients' copies, incorporated in the body of the letter immediately following the text of the circular):

(1) *To Sylvanus Bourne, consul at Hispaniola:* "Having received no letter from you since Novr. 30. I presume you are at the place of your residence. Particular reasons render it improper to press a formal acknowledgement of our Consuls in the French Colonies; for this purpose we must wait till circumstances shall render it less inconvenient to their government: in the mean time as to everything essential the same attention will be paid to yourself, your representations, and applications as if you were formally acknowledged. I am to recommend to you in the strongest terms not to intermeddle in the least by word or deed in the internal disputes of the Colony, or those with the Mother Country. Consider this as a family affair with which we have neither the right nor the wish to intermeddle. We shall expect however narratives of them from time to time" (in addition to FC, from which this and following addenda are taken, these texts of the circular to Bourne exist: RC in CtY, in Remsen's hand except for signature; Dupl in NjP, in Taylor's hand except for signature; PrC in Remsen's hand in DLC).

(2) *To Fulwar Skipwith, consul at Martinique:* this addendum is the same as that to Bourne, preceding, except for this initial sentence: "Your favors of August 30, September 18. October 10. and February 10. have been duly received" (RC in CtY, in Taylor's hand except for signature; PrC in DLC, unsigned).

(3) *To Joseph Fenwick, consul at Bordeaux:* "Your favors of November 4. 6. December 8. and January 15. have been received and their contents duly noted" (PrC in Taylor's hand in DLC).

(4) *To James Maury, consul at Liverpool:* "Your favors of November 1. 6. 20. and March 2. are received and their contents duly noted. I shall not be able to communicate to you the ultimate form for your returns, till I receive the observations of the other Consuls. In the mean time, if the owners of the cargo in and out cannot be known readily, we must be contented with the names of the Consignee and exporter, though the former would be preferable" (PrC in Taylor's hand in DLC).

(5) *To William Knox, consul at Dublin:* "After acknowledging the receipt of your favor of November 26. I have only to add assurances of the esteem with which I am &c." (PrC in clerk's hand in DLC).

(6) *To John M. Pintard, consul at Madeira:* "Your favors of November 26. January 23. February 10. and 11. are received and their contents duly noted. The matter suggested in the first of these and also in the last will depend on the Consular bill to be past. I am happy to learn the manifestations of the friendship of the Portuguese Government towards us which you mention: they may certainly count on corresponding dispositions on our part" (PrC in Remsen's hand in DLC).

(7) *To Joshua Johnson, consul at London:* "Your favors of November 2. 3. 5. 15. 30. February 25. and 26. have been received, and their contents duly noted. The want of coercive powers over American masters and mariners therein truly stated must await the passage of the bill before mentioned, and your jurisdiction over them till then, be considered as merely voluntary. For the same bill also must wait that part of your account which relates to the expenses attending the recognition of your Commission, its publication &c. being £10. 8, no law as yet passed having provided for the reimbursement of these charges; and as the reimbursement in your case would form a precedent for all others, and that too, in countries where their extent is unknown, it must be suspended till determined by the Consular bill. Having found it impracticable to obtain a bill of exchange for so small a sum as £3.6.7 sterling, the amount of the residue of the account, I have given the money to Mr. Russell, the bearer hereof for you" (RC in DNA: RG 59, CD, in Remsen's hand, except for signature; endorsed as received 29 June and as answered 10 Aug. 1791; PrC in DLC, unsigned).

(8) *To Stephen Cathalan, vice-consul at Marseilles:* "Your favors of September 1. 25. and January 22. 26. are received and their contents duly noted. – The olive plants by Mr. Guide have arrived at Baltimore. I pray you to send as early as you can the ensuing fall as many more as will make the cost of the whole amount to what I at first desired, observing the directions already given for your reimbursement and their

destination and address" (PrC in Remsen's hand in DLC).

(9) *To Delamotte, vice-consul at Le Havre*: "Your favors of July 15. August 22. 27. September 13. 22. October 28. November 20. 21. have been received and their contents noted. With respect to your disbursements for Benjamin Huls, an American sailor, be so good as to lay the account before Mr. Short who is authorized to reimburse them" (PrC in Taylor's hand in DLC).

(10) *To Thomas Auldjo, vice-consul for Poole*: "Your favors of October 5. 28. November 4. 7. and 23. have been received and their contents duly noted" (PrC in Taylor's hand in DLC).

In addition to the foregoing, the circular was sent to C.W.F. Dumas, agent at The Hague, with the following addendum: "I am to acknowledge the receipt of your favors of April 2. May 8. 17. 26. July 10. 14. September 7. 30. October 19. November 23. December 6. and 11. I now receive the Leyden gazette with great regularity by the British packet, and thank you for your attention to this with a request that it may be continued. – There is no doubt it would be desireable for us to receive our intelligence from Europe through a channel of our own, but the expence of an establishment of packet-boats would be beyond the value of the object for us, considering that our connection with Europe is less political than commercial, and that information of the latter kind may come safely through any channel. In fact if we attend to the whole amount of our civil list, we shall find that the expence of packet-boats would make a very sensible addition to it. The idea therefore, though good, must be suspended yet awhile. – Accept my thanks on the part of Government for the copy of Rymer you have been so good as to send us, and which is duly received, and be assured of the sincere esteem and attachment with which I have the honor to be, Sir Your most obedient & most humble Servant" (RC in DLC, in Remsen's hand except for signature; FC in Taylor's hand in DNA: RG 59, DCI).

TJ's report of the unbounded confidence of the people in the government, like the similar expressions in his letter to Vaughan written two days earlier, concealed his own concerns and the deep sectional and political divisions which posed genuine dangers to national cohesiveness. Here, on a wider scale, he was using the consular establishment to portray conditions which revealed his hopes rather than reality and to spread these optimistic hopes abroad. At least one member of the consular body acted in accord with the unexpressed intent and caused this part of the instructions to be published (see Delamotte to TJ, 25 July 1791).

To Alexander Donald

DEAR SIR   Philadelphia May 13. 1791.

My public occupations rarely permit me to take up the pen of private correspondence. I have still therefore to acknoledge the reciept of your favors of Oct. 5. 25. and Jan. 6. I find that at the date of the last you had not yet received mine of Nov. 25. covering a letter to Mr. Short. This I hope has fulfilled your wish as far as the unsettled state of things in France permitted. The farms being put down, and nothing else put up as far as I yet know, I think the general letter to Mr. Short was the best measure I could adopt. When a Regie shall be established, if there be among them any acquaintance of mine I shall give you a letter to him with that pleasure it ever gives me to be useful to you. I find as I advance in life I become less capable of acquiring new affections and therefore I love to hang by my old ones. In general I shall endeavor to impress on the French government the policy of recieving no tobacco from this country, but *directly*, and in *French* or *American* bottoms; therefore my efforts to serve you must be consistent with that idea. – Tobacco is low in Virginia, but I have sold mine here for 5. dollars, from which deduct half a dollar the expence of bringing it here. Wheat has been generally at a dollar and from that to a French crown, at this place, through the winter. The spring has been rather dry; however the new crops of grain have not suffered, materially. We have no public news worth detailing. Deaths in Virginia are Colo. Harrison of Barclay, Turner Southall, J. Dixon the printer, Colo. Overton of Hanover. The marriage of Mr. Tucker with Mrs. Carter of Corotoman, taken place or about to take place, is perhaps new to you. To this I will add what is not new, that I am with great & sincere esteem Dear Sir Your friend & servt,

Th: Jefferson

Bordeaux wines.

1. Red. There are 4. crops which are best and dearest, to wit Chateau-Margaux, all engaged to Jernon a merchant. Tour de Segur belonging to Monsieur Miromenil, 125. tons. Hautbrion, two thirds of which are engaged; the other third belongs to the Count de Toulouse at Toulouse, and De la Fite belonging to the President Pichard at Bordeaux. The last are in perfection at 3. years old, the three first not till 4. years. They cost about 1500.₶ the tun when new, and from 2000.₶ to 2400.₶ when ready for drinking. – The best red wines after the 4. crops are Rozan belonging to Madame de Rozan (who supplies me), Dabbadie ou Lionville, la Rose, Quirouen, Durfort. These cost 1000.₶ new, and I believe 1500.₶ to 1750.₶ fit for use. These wines are so nearly equal to the 4. crops that I do not believe any man can distinguish them when drank separately.

2. White wines. The wines made in the Canton of Grave are most esteemed at Bordeaux. The best crops are 1. Pontac belonging to M. de Lamont, 400.₶ the ton, new. 2. St. Brise belonging to M. de Pontac, 350.₶ the ton new. 3. de Carbonius belonging to the Benedictine monks. They never sell new, and when old they get 800.₶ the ton. – But the white wines made in the three parishes above Grave are more esteemed at Paris than the vins de Grave. These are 1. Sauterne, the best of all, belonging to M. de Luz-Saluce (who supplies me) 300.₶ the ton new and 600.₶ old. 2. Prignac. The

best is the President du Roy['s]. Same price. 3. Barsac. Best is the President Pichard's. Same price.

Add to all these prices 5. sous for bottles and bottling. You have no occasion for a letter. The only introduction and the sufficient one is the cash. If you should apply to Madame de Rosan or Monsieur de Luz-Saluce, if their stock of good wine should be low, it may add an inducement to them to name me. In all cases the owner is the person to be applied to. He will either send you none, or good. He never adulterates, because he would be a felo de se to do it. All the persons live at Bordeaux where not otherwise mentioned.

PrC (DLC).

To David Humphreys

DEAR SIR   Philadelphia, May 13th. 1791.

Mr. Thomas Barclay is appointed by the President of the United States to go to Morocco in the Character of Consul for the Purpose of obtaining from the new Emperor a Recognition of our Treaty with his Father.

Ten thousand dollars are appropriated for Presents in such Form and to such Persons as Mr. Barclay in his Discretion shall think best; and he is to receive for himself at the rate of Two thousand Dollars a year and his Sea expenses.

It is thought best that the money for these Purposes should be placed under your Controul, and that Mr. Barclay should draw on you for it. Thirty two thousand, one hundred and seventy five Gilders current are accordingly lodged in the Hands of our Bankers in Amsterdam, and they are instructed to answer your Draughts to that amount, you notifying them that they are to be paid out of the Fund of *March 3rd. 1791*, that this account may be kept clear of all others. You will arrange with Mr. Barclay the manner of making his Draughts so as to give yourself Time for raising the money by the Sale of your Bills.

A Confidence in your Discretion has induced me to avail the Public of that, in the Transaction of this Business, and to recommend Mr. Barclay to your Counsel and Assistance through the whole of it. I inclose you one Set of the Bills for 13,000 Dollars beforementioned, and a Copy of my Letter to the Bankers. Duplicates will be sent to them directly. I have the Honor to be, with great and sincere Esteem Dear Sir, Your most obedient and Most humble servant,

TH: JEFFERSON

RC (NjP); in clerk's hand except for signature; endorsed. Dft (Lloyd W. Smith, Madison, N.J., 1946); on recto of Dft of letter to Willink, Van Staphorst & Hubbard of this date; docketed in Remsen's hand. PrC of RC (DLC); unsigned. FC (DNA: RG 59, DCI). Although no enclosure other than the bills of exchange is referred to, TJ did enclose copies of his official and confidential instructions to Barclay of this date (both in NjP).

To William Short

DEAR SIR   Philadelphia May 13. 1791.

The bearer hereof Mr. James Jones proposing to visit Paris in a tour of travel, I take the liberty of recommending him to your acquaintance and friendly offices. The general worth of his character will sufficiently recommend him to you, and you will probably derive particular satisfaction from conversing with him on the subject of New Orleans, where having resided 20. years, he will be able to satisfy your curiosity on the subject of that country so interesting and so little known to us. I am with great & sincere esteem Dear Sir Your affectionate friend & servt,   TH: JEFFERSON

PrC (DLC).

To Willink, Van Staphorst, & Hubbard

GENTLEMEN   Philadelphia, May 13th. 1791.

Congress having thought proper, by their Act of March 3rd. 1791 to establish a Fund for a particular Purpose, which is under my Direction, I now enclose you Bills for Thirty two thousand, one hundred and seventy five current Gilders, to be credited to me in a special Account separate from all others, and which may be distinguished as that of the Fund of *March 3rd: 1791.* Whenever I either remit or draw on you for this Fund, I will specially name it. Colonel Humphreys, our Resident at the Court of Portugal is duly authorized to draw on this Fund, and you are desired to answer his Draughts to any amount within the Sum which shall be in your Hands for this particular Fund. He will always advise you when his Draughts are on this account. I have the Honor to be, Gentlemen, Your most obedient humble Servant,

Tr (NjP); in a clerk's hand, unsigned. PrC (DLC); in clerk's hand; "(Duplicate)" at top of page. FC (DNA: RG 59, DCI).

To James Lackington

Sir   Philadelphia May 14. 1791.

My removal from Paris to this place has probably been the cause of the intermission in my recieving your half yearly catalogues as usual. I will beg the favor of you to resume the practice of sending them to me, changing the former address to that of 'Thomas Jefferson Secretary of state Philadelphia, to the care of Messrs. Donald and Burton merchts. London.' On sending them to Messrs. Donald and Burton whose residence the London Directory states to be Angell court Throgmorton street, they will be regularly forwarded to me, and it will generally be in my power to lodge my order with you within 3. or 4. months after. I am Sir Your humble servt,

TH: JEFFERSON

PrC (MHi); at foot of text: "Mr. J. Lackington, bookseller, No. 46-47. Chiswell street, Moorfeilds."

From James Lyons

Sir   Hanover town. May 14th. 1791.

I received, a few weeks past, a letter from Dr. Currie of Philadelphia, informing me of his preparing for the press, a history of the diseases which occur in the different parts of America and which will be printed next month. As the design is laudable, and the work may be useful, tho' he is quite unknown to me, I have endeavoured to comply with his request for my assistance, by giving him such information on the subject, as I could from the short notice and the interruption of Medical practice. The pleasure, which you have always appeared to enjoy, in communicating information yourself, and in assisting those, who endeavoured the same, has induced me to address the inclosed to you, as it will be conveyed easily, I hope, and save the considerable expence of postage, without being any to you. That it may not be thought an unwarrantable liberty will give considerable satisfaction; and at the same time it affords a pleasing opportunity of assuring you, that I am, Sir, With the most respectful regard, Your very humbl. Servt.,   JAS. LYONS

RC (ViW); addressed: "The Honble Thomas Jefferson Esqr. Secretary of State Philadelphia"; endorsed by TJ as received at Bennington, Vt., 4 June 1791 and so recorded in SJL.

The work in preparation was *An historical account of the climates and diseases of the United States* (Philadelphia, 1792) by William Currie (1754-1828), a privately trained surgeon who engaged in contro-

versy with Benjamin Rush (L. H. Butterfield, ed., *Letters of Benjamin Rush*, II,
674n.). Currie was a founding member of
the College of Physicians and was elected
to the American Philosophical Society the

year his work was published. So far as the
record indicates, TJ did not respond to
Lyons' letter or engage in correspondence
with Currie.

To Thomas Mann Randolph

DEAR SIR   Philadelphia May 14. 1791.

I received your favor by Capt. Heath, and notice what is said
therein on the subject of the Marquee. Capt. Singleton has been
certainly misinformed as to the delivery of it at Monticello. You
know it was in the summer of 1782. I was at home the whole of
that summer. My situation at that time enables me to say with
certainty that I was not from home one day from the time the
Marquee was borrowed till late in the fall when I went to Ampthill
to have my children inoculated. It's delivery at Monticello therefore
is impossible. On my return from Ampthill I set out for this place
under an appointment to go to Europe. I left it among my written
instructions to have application made to you for the Marquee lest
some accident should happen to it. I have a strong idea too of having
either spoken or written to you on the subject, either then or the
ensuing year when I passed about 4. months in Virginia before my
final departure from it. If Capt. Singleton will be so good as to state
the proofs of the delivery, it may put us into a train of investigation,
to find where the loss ought to fall. On you it cannot be: on me I
know it to be impossible. Perhaps it may be traced to some person
responsible to P.R.'s estate. I am just setting out on a Month's
journey to the Northward. My affectionate respects to Mrs. Randolph and am with great esteem Dear Sir Your sincere friend &
servt,   TH: JEFFERSON

PrC (DLC); at foot of text: "Colo. TM Randolph."

To William Short

DEAR SIR   Philadelphia May 14. 1791.

The bearer hereof Mr. Russell proposing to visit Paris, I take the
liberty of introducing him to your notice. His father is the most
eminent merchant in Boston, I might perhaps have said in the
United states: his brother I believe you knew in France. Tho less

acquainted with himself I am authorised to assure you he will do justice to any marks of attention you will be so good as to shew him, which will also be considered as an obligation on Dear Sir Your friend & servt,   TH: JEFFERSON

PrC (MHi).

From Sir John Sinclair

Whitehall, 14 May 1791. He sends his best compliments, encloses some papers, and asks their acceptance by TJ. As to the Corn Laws, "they will not probably agree," but he sincerely wishes for some commercial arrangement between the two countries.

RC (DLC); endorsed by TJ as received 16 July 1791 and so recorded in SJL.

TJ shared the papers enclosed in this and a previous letter (25 Dec. 1790) with

Tench Coxe. See Coxe to TJ, 19 July 1791, and Vol. 18: 367n. Contrary to Sinclair's expectations, TJ was in close agreement with him on the Corn Laws. See TJ to Sinclair, 24 Aug. 1791.

To Thomas Sumter

DEAR SIR   Philadelphia May 14. 1791.

I am really mortified at the account I am obliged to give you of the fate of the ores you confided to my care. I gave them you know to Count Andriani whose regular chemical education, and his fondness for that study, together with his leisure, induced me to expect an attentive and scientific analysis of them. I enquired of him continually from time to time, and he always told me he was trying them with solvents, and that the solution was going on. Being about to take a journey myself, I sent two days ago to his lodgings to ask the result of his experiments, or at least the prospect of the result. To my surprise my messenger brought me word that he had left town on a long journey. I will certainly know on his return something definitive: but I confess to you I expect he has failed of success in his trial of them.

We have nothing very interesting or late from Europe. The revolution in France was still going on steadily, and securely. England and Prussia endeavoring to domineer Russia into a peace with the Porte on their own terms: and Russia shewing no symptoms of attention to them. Burke's pamphlet and the answers to him occupy much attention there and here. Payne's and Priestly's are excellent. The former is the best thing it's author ever wrote. – You mentioned to me two instances of Volcanic eruption in Carolina. I must beg of you to take the trouble of collecting all the facts you can relative to these, and to be so good as to communicate them to me. This phaenomenon is so absolutely unprecedented in our part of America as to excite much attention. — I have the honor to be with great & sincere esteem Dear Sir Your most obedient & most humble servt,

TH: JEFFERSON

PrC (DLC); at foot of text: "General Sumpter."

To James Currie

DEAR SIR   Philadelphia May 15. 1791.

I deferred making another application to Potter till Doctr. Griffin had so long overrun the time of his arrival that I thought it desperate and then went to Potter and shewed him Dr. G.'s letters. He expressed his astonishment and assured me in the most pointed terms that he had no property of his in his hands but the wine mentioned before, and that he did not know in whose hands his certificates were. His language was pointed, but there was something in his looks, which cannot be described and which left me in some doubt. On returning from him I learned that Dr. G. had been two days in town. Next day I called at his lodgings. Not at home. Again, he was at dinner. I then wrote a note and asked a meeting. He called on me and assured me that he was taking measures, and in a few days would arrange your bills. I waited till the day before yesterday, and as I was to leave town to-day on a journey of a Month Northward, I then wrote to desire he would take some final arrangement. No answer. I called there twice yesterday. Not within. Twice to-day one answer was he was gone into the country, and the second that he had not been in the house for 2. or 3. days. This alarmed me, and on enquiry I found he was become invisible; and I am now satisfied he means to do nothing. This is Sunday. I will go tomorrow and have his bills regularly protested, and as I set out in the afternoon I will leave them in the hands of Mr. Henry Remsen to call and call again to see if any thing can be done, till you shall have time to answer this and say what you would have done. Were it my case, and were I disposed to push the matter legally and knew of no other property, I would, on the hesitation I thought I discovered in Potter's countenance, levy an attachment in his hands, and risk the expence of guessing wrong against the chance of his really holding the property. It is kept secret merely to avoid it's being attached. — I write so far now, because I have more time at this moment than I shall have tomorrow. But I will not close my letter till the moment of my departure, that I may give you the last intelligence. Direct your answer to 'Mr. Henry Remsen chief clerk of the Secretary of State's office. Market Street 274.'

May 16. I have called again on Potter. He assures me he has never seen Dr. Griffin yet, and I feel myself better satisfied that he has nothing in his hands but the wine. Still that furnishes a sufficient ground for an attachment while you take the chance of their being something more. He points out two other brokers and a Vendue-master, whom he thinks likely to have property in their hands. Not having time now to search into this I have had the bills protested for non-acceptance (and paid 1 D.27 cents) so that you may bring an action if you please tho' they are not due. I leave them with Mr. Remsen who will search for the property, but do nothing more unless you order it. If you could find property in Virginia it would be better to proceed there. I am with great esteem Dr. Sir Your friend & servt, Th: Jefferson

PrC (MHi); at foot of text: "Dr. Currie."

To Francis Eppes

Dear Sir   Philadelphia May 15. 1791.

Jack's letters will have informed you of his arrival here safe and in good health. Capt. Stratton is also arrived, whom we considered as lost. Your favors of April 5. and 27. are recieved. I had just answered a letter of Mr. Skipwith's on the subject of the guineaman, and therefore send you a copy of that by way of answer to your last. I shall be in Virginia in October, but cannot yet say whether I shall be able to go to Richmond.

Jack is now set in to work regularly. He passes from 2. to 4. hours a day at the College, completing his courses of sciences, and 4 hours at the law, besides this he will write an hour or two to learn the stile of business and acquire a habit of writing, and will read something in history and government. The course I propose for him will employ him a couple of years. I shall not fail to impress on him a due sense of the advantage of qualifying himself to get a living independently of other resources. As yet I discover nothing but a disposition to apply closely. I set out tomorrow on a journey of a month to Lakes George, Champlain &c. and having yet a thousand things to do I can only add assurances of the sincere esteem with which I am Dr. Sir Your affectionate friend & servt,

TH: JEFFERSON

PrC (MHi). Enclosure: Copy of TJ to Skipwith, 6 May 1791.

To Elizabeth Wayles Eppes

MY DEAR MADAM   Philadelphia May 15. 1791.

I received your favor of Apr. 6. by Jack, and my letter of this date to Mr. Eppes will inform you that he is well under way. If we can keep him out of love, he will be able to go strait forward, and to make good way. I receive with real pleasure your congratulations on my advancement to the venerable corps of grandfathers, and can assure you with truth that I expect from it more felicity than any other advancement ever gave me. I only wish for the hour when I may go, and enjoy it entire. – It was my intention to have troubled you with Maria when I left Virginia in November, satisfied it would be better *for her* to be with you. But the solitude of her sister, and the desire of keeping them united in that affection for each other which is to be the best future food of their lives induced me to leave her at Monticello; and the rather as I proposed to bring her here as soon as I can find a good situation for her. In answer to a paragraph of Mr. Eppes's letter of Apr. 5. that it had been said I did not leave her with you for fear it should be too troublesome, I assure you that reason had no operation with me. I know that with such minds as his and yours, trouble is a pleasure when it is to serve our friends living or dead. I know you both too well to have a hesitation on that account, and the freedoms I have taken in that way have proved it. Adieu my dear dear madam. Yours affectionately,

TH: JEFFERSON

Tr (ViU); 19th-century transcript.

Ironically, TJ's desire to keep Jack from falling in love so that he would not be diverted from his studies – something he had himself experienced at about the same age – was defeated by his plan to bring Polly to Philadelphia. The two had known each other as children at Eppington, where Elizabeth Wayles Eppes had been such a a devoted surrogate mother that Polly "may be said to have been an Eppes in spirit before she became one in name" (Malone, *Jefferson*, III, 239). On his return to Philadelphia in the autumn of 1791, TJ brought Polly with him, and the affection of the two cousins for each other was given fresh stimulus. Jack was then eighteen and Polly thirteen. They were married during TJ's first year as Vice-President, with his unqualified approval.

To Daniel L. Hylton

DEAR SIR   Philadelphia May 15. 1791.

By Capt. Stratton I have recieved the 4. hhds. of tobo. Among these is one of those which had been injured by fire, and serves sufficiently to shew that tobacco of that quality cannot be sold here at any price. I must therefore ask your particular attention that there be no more of the fired tobacco sent here. I understood there were about 14,000 ℔., say 12 hhds. fired. Should there be no other means of distinguishing them from the good, I must be at the expence of having them opened and examined at Richmond. I suppose they will have been inspected at Lynchberg. Just setting out on a journey and a thousand things crowding on me I have only time to present my affections to Mrs. Hylton and assure you of the sincere esteem of Dr. Sir Your friend & servt.,   TH: JEFFERSON

PrC (MHi).

To the Mayor of Philadelphia

May 15. 1791.

Th: Jefferson presents his compliments to the Mayor of the city. He had understood there was a subscription paper for the relief of the sufferers by the late fire, which was handing about town, and expected he should have met it in turn. Not having as yet seen it and being about to leave town he asks permission to put into the hands of the Mayor the inclosed note for 25. dollars to be disposed of with the other donations for the same purpose.

RC (Dr. John A. Munroe, Santa Monica, Calif., 1951). Not recorded in SJL. The address cover is missing, but the note was sent to John Barclay, who was mayor of Philadelphia at the time.

On the evening of May 11th fire broke out in a livery stable on Dock Street near Third and spread rapidly. By midnight a score of wooden houses in the vicinity were in flames, and many people had been rendered homeless. Committees were appointed to collect subscriptions for the distressed, and a benefit performance was given in the South Street Theater (Scharf and Westcott, *History of Philadelphia*, I, 467).

To Thomas Mann Randolph, Jr.

DEAR SIR   Philadelphia May. 15. 1791.

Your favor of April 30. came to hand on the 7th. inst. and I thank you for your information relative to the Opossum, which I hope the next season will enable you to complete. You may count it as fortunate that so interesting an investigation remains still to be made, and that, being made with care and science, it cannot fail to attract general notice. – In my letter of last week I mentioned my fear that Capt. Stratton was lost, with J. Eppes's baggage and 4. hhds. of my tobacco. He is since arrived, and will sail tomorrow for Richmd. He has received on board the following parcels addressed to the care of Mr. James Brown merchant at Richmond.

TI. No. 1. A box of books. to wit. Encyclopedie. Buffon. Tacitus, and Journaux de Physique for yourself.

Sacontalá and the Magazins des modes for Patsy Anacharsis for Maria.

Herrera. The history of Florida, and Acosta to be put into the library.

No. 2. A box with 7. Venetian blinds for the windows at Monticello.

3. A box, containing your harness.

4. A box of linen and stockings of mine. The latter article will furnish a good deal of employment for Bet if opened and given out to her.

5. A bale, containing 4. mattrasses for the house, a calash for Patsy and 12. yds. striped Nankeen for Maria. I thought it safest to send this last by Stratton, and not by the stages as I had proposed in my letter to her.

6. A bale, containing 2. mattrasses for the house, and a box with two panes of glass for Mrs. Lewis.

7. A bale, containing Sally's bedding from France.

N.B. James's bedding is in one of the bales; I don't know which.

A dozen and a half Windsor chairs. They are loose and will probably be rubbed.

I hope my tobo. will all come on now as soon as possible, except that which was fired. One of those hhds. Stratton brought was of this kind, and cannot be sold here at all. I will thank you to desire Mr. Lewis to take effectual measures to retain there the fired tobo. as, should it come here, I shall be obliged to send it back again to Richmond, which will cost a dollar a hundred, the coming and going. I am afraid my letter of Feb. 9. to Mr. Lewis never got to hand. The objects of it were to inform him of the sale of my tobo. here, to press a final settlement of my bargain with Ronald, and to advertize the Elkhill lands for sale. Not having seen the advertisement in Davies's paper, has excited my fear that the letter miscarried.

Perhaps it may have been put into some other paper. For fear it should have miscarried I will add the same form for the advertisement at the end of this letter. That of Feb. 9. was important for the other two objects also. It certainly ought to have got to hand before the date of your letter of Apr. 4. wherein you say he was still waiting my directions relative to the tobacco. I set out tomorrow on a journey to lakes George and Champlain, down Connecticut river, and through Long island back to N. York and this place, so that you will not hear from me for a month to come. I inclose you Bache's as well as Fenno's papers. You will have percieved that the latter is a paper of pure Toryism, disseminating the doctrines of monarchy, aristocracy, and the exclusion of the influence of the people. We have been trying to get another *weekly* or *halfweekly* paper set up excluding advertisements, so that it might go through the states, and furnish a whig-vehicle of intelligence. We hoped at one time to have persuaded Freneau to set up here, but failed. In the mean time Bache's paper, the principles of which were always republican, improves in it's matter. If we can persuade him to throw all his advertisements on one leaf, by tearing that off, the leaf containing intelligence may be sent without over-charging the post, and be generally taken instead of Fenno's. I will continue to send it to you, as it may not only amuse yourself, but enable you to oblige your neighbors with the perusal. My love to Martha and Maria, and be assured yourself of the sincere attachment of Dear Sir Your's affectionately,

TH: JEFFERSON

FOR SALE.[1]. . . Note. I would leave Mr. Lewis to decide whether it is best to mention the price of the lands in the advertisement. If he thinks not, that may be struck out, and insert instead of it 'the purchase money to be paid by instalments in 1793. 4. 5. 6.' with interest from the delivery, &c.

RC (DLC).

[1] For the text of the advertisement, see note to TJ to Nicholas Lewis, 9 Feb. 1791, Vol. 19: 264.

To George Washington

SIR   Philadelphia May 15. 1791.
We are still without any occurrence foreign or domestic worth mentioning to you. It is sometime since any news has been recieved from Europe of the political kind, and I have been longer than common without any letters from Mr. Short.

Colo. Hamilton has taken a trip to Bethlehem. I think to avail myself also of the present interval of quiet to get rid of a headach which is very troublesome, by giving more exercise to the body and less to the mind. I shall set out tomorrow for New York, where Mr. Madison is waiting for me, to go up the North river, and return down Connecticut river and through Long-island. My progress of the North river will be limited by the time I allot for my whole journey, which is a month. So that I shall turn about whenever that renders it necessary. I leave orders, in case a letter should come from you covering the commission for Colo. Eveleigh's successor, that it should be opened, the great seal put to it, and then given out. My countersign may be added on my return. I presume I shall be back here about the time of your arrival at Mount-Vernon, where you will recieve this letter. The death of Judge Hopkinson has made a vacancy for you to fill. Should I pick up any thing in my journey, I will write it to you from time to time. I have the honor to be with sincere respect & attachment, Sir, your most obedient and most humble servt., Th: Jefferson

RC (DNA: RG 59, MLR); at foot of text: "The President of the U.S."; addressed: "The President of the United States. To be sent to Mount Vernon"; postmarked "15 ma" and "free"; endorsed by Washington. PrC (DLC). FC (DNA: RG 59, SDC).

To William Carmichael

Sir   Philadelphia May 16. 1791.

Mr. Swanwick informs me that the house of Morris, Willing & Swanwick have suffered a very considerable loss in the port of St. Andero, by an abuse of office, in having a cargo of corn thrown overboard as being bad, when it was in fact perfectly good. I know that in some countries of Europe it is often difficult to obtain justice against persons protected by court favor. In this, as in all other instances where our citizens shall have occasion to seek justice in the country of your residence, I would wish you to interfere just so far as by the influence of your character to counterbalance the undue protection of their opponents, so as that equal and impartial justice may be done them.

The regulation by which they suffer in the present instance, is, in it's nature extremely susceptible of abuse, and prevails, as I am told only in the ports of the bay of Biscay. The patronage of our commerce being the chief object of our diplomatic establishments abroad, you would render that an essential service could you obtain a repeal of this regulation, or an impartial exercise of it, if the repeal cannot be obtained; and in any event, a permission to re-export a cargo of grain condemned. I have the honour to be with great esteem & respect Sir Your most obedt. & most humble servt,

TH: JEFFERSON

PrC (DLC). FC (DNA: RG 59, DCI).

If Swanwick's information was given by letter, no copy of it has been found, and it is not recorded in SJL. For a comparable complaint of abuse at the hands of those "protected by court favor," see Swanwick to TJ, 14 Dec. 1790.

To Pierre Guide

SIR   Philadelphia May 16. 1791.

Being in the moment of setting out on my journey, I have just time to acknolege the receipt of your favor of the 5th. inst. and to note your information that you had sent off by the stage of that day a case of wine and some raisins for me. On repeated enquiries at the different stage-offices, I find it has never arrived here which I thought necessary to mention to you in order to excite your enquiries after it, as it may have been left somewhere on the road. I am in hopes before my return that which comes by water will be also come to hand. I am with great esteem Sir Your most obedt. humble servt,

TH: JEFFERSON

PrC (MHi).

To William Hay

DEAR SIR   Philadelphia May 16. 1791.

I have this morning had a conversation with Mr. Dobson a bookseller on the subject of your Encyclopedie; I told him if he could dispose of it at such an advance as he sells his own books at, so that you might get something like first cost for first cost you would take it in books. He thinks it possible, and will endeavor to dispose of it. He thinks the chance would be better if the books were here. Yet I doubt whether it is certain enough to go to the expence of sending them before a purchaser offers. – I cannot help supposing you might find a purchaser in Virginia, on your assuring them that I will have the remainder imported for them (they advancing the money) which I will chearfully do. I will also be still on the look-out for a purchaser myself. I am this moment setting out on a long journey, and can therefore only add assurances of the sincere esteem with which I am Dear Sir Your most obedt. humble servt,

TH: JEFFERSON

PrC (MHi).

To Nicholas Lewis

DEAR SIR   Philadelphia May 16. 1791.

When I wrote to Mr. Randolph yesterday I did not think I should have time to write to you, and therefore put into his letter some articles for you to which I must refer you. The present is merely to cover a letter of John Jefferson's which will explain to you his request to be still assisted in the recovery of his rights. I will thank you to have him furnished with what may be necessary to enable him to recover his own. The method you took before appears to me the best, that of undertaking to pay his lawyers &c. rather than to deliver the money to him, as I understand that he is not always in a condition to take care of it. I am anxious to learn what success Wilson has had in the collection of the monies we depended on him for. My affectionate respects to Mrs. Lewis, and am Dr. Sir Your sincere friend & servt,   TH: JEFFERSON

PrC (MHi). The enclosed letter from John Jefferson of Cumberland has not been found, but it was dated 28 Feb. 1791 and is recorded in SJL as received 21 Apr. 1791. For other aspects of his financial em-barrassments and TJ's instructions to Lewis for assistance in relieving them, see John Jefferson to TJ, 7 Jan. 1790, and TJ's reply, 14 Feb. 1790. See also TJ to Lewis, 7 Mch. 1790.

Jefferson's Instructions for Henry Remsen, Jr.

May 16. 1791.

Letters which come in time to reach Albany before the 25th. instant[1] may be sent to Albany. No newspapers to be forwarded, except Fenno's.

If a letter comes from the President, which seems to cover the commission for Mr. Eveleigh's successor, Mr. Remsen will be so good as to open it, put the great seal to it, and send it to the person, with an assurance that I shall countersign it on my return. In the mean time he can act.

Mr. Remsen will be so good as to recieve a check on the bank for 35. Dollars, of which on the close of the month 10. Doll. are to be paid to Francis, 10. D. to Philip and 5. D. to Brown. The residue is meant to cover any little demands arriving during my absence.

I expect some parcels of wine from Bordeaux for the President and myself. Mr Lear will recieve the President's as also a parcel for him from Havre. I do not know the quantity of mine, which with the incertainty of it's coming at all prevents my leaving the duties. If it should arrive as there would be danger of it's spoiling in a warehouse, perhaps Mr. Delany will let it come to my own cellars, on assurance that I will settle the duties on my return.

I expect 3 doz. of wine (as a sample) from Baltimore. Perhaps part of it may come by the stage. Also some cyder from Norfolk. The freight will be to be paid.

My tobo. as it comes, to be received by Mr. Lieper who will be so good as to pay the freight in my absence.

I leave with Mr. Remsen Mr. Griffin's bill on Potter, protested. I have taken the liberty to desire Dr. Currie to inform Mr. Remsen what he would have done with them, and I will pray him to execute what he shall desire. Also to enquire if Griffin has any property in the hands of the persons whose names I give to Mr. Remsen. – Griffin has promised most solemnly that he will, during the present week put into Mr. Remsen's hands paper to the whole amount of the bills. He will need pushing. Perhaps it may be prudent not to push so hard as to indispose him absolutely. It is very desireable to find out where his property is, yet so secretly as that he shall not know it.

RC (Lloyd W. Smith, Madison, N.J., 1946); at head of text: "Memoranda"; endorsed by Remsen: "Mr. Jefferson's directions May 16th. 1791." Not recorded in SJL.

[1] TJ first wrote "Letters which come before the 18th. instant may be sent to me at New York. Those which come before the 22d. may be sent to Albany" and then altered it to read as above.

To John Vaughan

May 16. 1791.

Th: Jefferson presents his compliments to Mr. Vaughan. He has sent one of Argand's double lamps to Mr. Bringhurst to have wick-racks fixed to it, and has directed him to deliver it to Mr. Vaughan, when done, for the use of the Philosophical society whose acceptance of it he asks. He presumes that if suspended over the middle of the table it will sufficiently light it.

RC (PPAP); addressed: "Mr. Vaughan." Not recorded in SJL.

From David Humphreys

Lisbon, 17 May 1791. He was presented to the Queen on the 13th, delivered his letter of credence, and, with the approval of the Minister of Foreign Affairs, expressed his discourse in English, a copy of which he encloses. The Queen, surrounded at the public audience by her ministers, the diplomatic corps, the nobility, the chief officers of the departments, and many ladies of the court, replied "on the spot . . . vivâ você, 'Her wish that the United States of America might in return enjoy all manner of prosperity.' " He also encloses a letter on the subject from the Minister for Foreign Affairs. This was the birthday of the Prince of Brazil, who assisted in the ceremony, and also the anniversary of the Queen's coronation, circumstances which caused "the numerous Company and splendid Gala of the Court. Great promotions took place; and undissembled satisfaction with Her Majesty, and the mild and happy administration of Her Government seemed universally to prevail. . . . P.S. I flatter myself with having opportunities, hereafter, of demonstrating in the most unequivocal manner every thing I have asserted respecting the mild Government and prosperous state of Portugal."

RC (DNA: RG 59, DD); at head of text: "(No.19)"; endorsed by TJ as received 24 Aug. 1791 and so recorded in SJL. Tr (same). Enclosures: (1) Copy of Humphreys' speech on being presented to the Queen, 13 May 1791: "May it please your Majesty! Although it has been my first care to become sufficiently acquainted with the Portuguese language, to understand the glorious exploits of Your Majesty's Ancestors recorded in it: yet I feel myself peculiarly distressed, at this instant, in not being able to explain, in that language, my sensibility of the honor conferred on me, by being placed near their AUGUST DESCENDANT and the Inheritor of all their VIRTUES, as the first Representative to this Court, from the American Nation. – With equal pain, I find myself unable to express, in the same tongue, the distinguished friendship of the United States of America for your Majesty: and particularly the grateful sense they entertain of the Orders, your Majesty has so repeatedly given, for your fleets to protect American ships from the hostile attacks of the piratical Powers of Bar-

bary. – For myself, it will constitute the greatest felicity of my life, and the most pleasing reflection to the latest period of it; if, in being the faithful Organ of expressing the sense of my Country, I may, in any degree, be the humble Instrument of promoting an extensive, happy and durable intercourse between the Subjects of your Majesty, and the Citizens of the United States of America. – And as I have a sincere pleasure in believing, that there do not exist, at this moment, on the face of the globe, any two Nations in more prosperous circumstances; so I am equally happy in a conviction, between no two nations better calculated to promote the mutual Interest and essential Prosperity of each Other" (DNA: RG 59, DD). (2) English and Portuguese texts (both in Humphreys' hand, as is the foregoing speech to the Queen) of Luis Pinto de Souza to Humphreys, 17 May 1791, acknowledging his of the 11th with the copy of the speech which he "had the honor of bringing by a translation to Her Royal Understanding" (same).

From George C. Morgan

Hackney, [England], 17 May 1791. He would not have presumed on an acquaintance of two or three hours had he not known TJ's respect for his uncle, Dr. Price, and his readiness to cooperate with him in serving two worthy gentlemen. Had he lived a few weeks longer, he would have applied to TJ himself. The bearers are men of property and great integrity. They leave beneficial connections in England to enter on flattering prospects of trade between the southern states and different parts of Europe. They conceive an introduction to "Mr. Washington may be of much Service to their Interest," and if TJ could procure this honor for them, his object is achieved. – He does not know whether his uncle ever acknowledged TJ's "little Treatise on Weights and Measures. He was much delighted with the Work, and still more with the evidence it conveyd that Dr. Franklin's retirement did not remove Philosophy from the Government of America." – He perceives from *Notes on Virginia* TJ's fondness for the arts as well as for scientific works. The former "are low, very low indeed in this country at present," but he would be proud to gratify TJ with any productions arousing his curiosity.

"How rapidly is the prospect of things brightening in France! When I had the pleasure of calling upon you in Paris, a most fiery storm seem'd to be gathering. But you saw further thro' the reigning Darkness and confusion than myself, and the friends of Mankind have to rejoice that Liberty is likely to be establish'd with the blood of those Millions which you estimated as Trifling Means in the purchase of so great an Object."

"In this Country the spirit of reformation is spreading very impetuously, nor has Mr. Payne the renowned Author of common Sense contributed a small portion of Fuel to the flame that is kindling. His answer to Mr. Burke is in all Hands. It is read in all Circles. It makes converts amongst all Parties. Thousands of it have been sold in England, and I am assured that in Ireland and Scotland, the printing Press is too slow in its Operations for the Avidity of the people. – Mr. Burke raves in the House of Commons and He finds that both his friends and the World desert him. Nor do the King's Ministers give any ear to his very open Advances of Good Will and Friendship.[1] But while he is indulging his Rage, His Pride will not allow him to mention the Object of it by his Name. In short, his unpitied and disregarded Fury is perhaps one of the most sure testimonies of that general Revolution which is now taking Place in the political partialities and Opinions of the Publick."[2]

"The General silence with which your government have regarded the struggles of the National Assembly, is what the Friends of America here would wish to account for honorably to their Character as *Citizens of the World*. My Uncle was amongst the rest who wish'd to have some reason assign'd for this singularity, besides such as are derived from partial Interests and local Considerations. Those Americans who plead your cause, urge the gratitude You owe to the *Court* of Versailles, and the *prudence* of not committing Yourselves in a dubious Cause. I hope your zeal for the Happiness of the World will have better advocates in the Ears of future generations. . . . with the most unfeigned Respect for Your Character and distinguished Talents, Yr. Hble Servt."

RC (ViW); addressed: "Mr. Jefferson, Minister of State in the United States of North America Philadelphia"; endorsed by TJ as received 19 Nov. 1791 and so recorded in SJL. TJ bracketed one paragraph (see note 2) and dispatched it to Freneau with the following pencilled note on address leaf: "Perhaps Mr. Freneau may think the paragraph marked within to be worth a place in his paper. The names of the persons from and to whom the letter was written not to be mentioned." With several grammatical emendations and the addition of one sentence not in the original, Freneau published the passage in the *National Gazette* of 21 Nov. 1791, giving it a fictitious date and describing it as "Extract of a letter from Hackney, England, September 2." See Editorial Note and group of documents at 4 Aug. 1791.

TJ had known and befriended Morgan in Paris (Morgan to TJ, 11 July 1789; TJ to Price, 12 July 1789; Price to TJ, 3 Aug. 1789).

[1] At this point Freneau inserted in the published version a sentence not in the original: "It is remarkable that in his debates he frequently refers to Paine's book, and thereby shews how much it galls him."

[2] TJ bracketed this paragraph at beginning and end as the one to be printed by Freneau.

To Thomas Leiper

Sir · New York May 19. 1791.

The day I left Philadelphia, I went for the first time up into the book-room which Mr. Carstairs is building, and then for the first time also observed he had left no place for the chimney. On asking an explanation I found that some how or other he had taken a notion from the beginning that there was to be none. I am sure he had it not from me. It is possible that I may not have particularly spoken of the chimney, looking on it as a thing of course, but I certainly never gave him the idea of having none. I meant to have spoke to you about it, but saw you only for a moment, and did not then think of it. Mr. Carstairs says there will be no difficulty in fixing the chimney, and promised to speak to you about it. I have thought it better to write to you that it may be done while you have the bricklayers and materials on the spot. I am in hopes they are already painting the inside of the house, and that I shall find every thing finished on my return. I am Sir Your very humble servt.

Th: Jefferson

PrC (MHi).

From the Abbés Arnoux and Chalut

Paris 20. mai 1791.

Notre legislature tant attendue, tant desirée et à la fin obtenue, tend à sa fin, notre cher Monsieur, et notre Constitution est presque achevée. Le mois de juillet prochain verra la fin et l'achevement de l'une et de l'autre, et dans ce meme tems la nouvelle legislature succedera à l'ancienne. Si notre constitution n'est pas parfaite, le tems, l'experience, la reflexion et de nouvelles lumieres la rendront moins imparfaite. La perfection absolue n'est pas le partage de L'homme, mais avec cette Constitution nous serons heureux. Comment ne le serions nous pas? Nous sommes maintenant tous egaux en droits par la loi; nous l'etions par la nature. Le despotisme nous en avoit privés. Les privileges des provinces et des hommes sont abolis. Ces distinctions impolitiques, immorales et odieuses de nobles, de roturiers et de serfs, ont disparu de la surface de la France. Le Clergé est devenu Citoyen et ses richesses, que la Cupidité avoit arrachées de l'ignorance et de la Superstition des peuples, servent à payer nos detes et nous sauvent d'une banqueroute. La magistrature n'est plus hereditaire. La peuple par ses electeurs nomme ses magistrats payés par la nation, et leurs jugements ne sont plus infectés d'une Criminelle Cupidité. Nos évechés sont reduits presque à moitié, et fixés au nombre de quatre-vingt deux. Les anciens eveques ont été remplacés à l'exception de deux, il y en a soixante et dix nouveaux en pleine activité que le peuple a nommé par ses electeurs, et ces nouveaux eveques remplissent leur place à la satisfaction et à l'édification du peuple. Les anciens n'oseroient pas paroitre dans leur ville episcopale. Leur luxe, leur oisiveté, leurs moeurs Les avoit rendus meprisables. Le Roi, dans l'ancien regime, les nommoit, c'est à dire Les ministres, les favoris et les Catins de la Cour. Les eveques n'étoient que les fruits de l'intrigue, de la Cabale et de la faveur; ce qu'on cherchoit le moins dans Leur choix étoit les talents et Les vertus.

Nous sommes libres comme vous, nos Loix nouvelles nous assurent notre Liberté, et notre obeissance à ces memes loix nous la conservera. Nos regards, depuis votre revolution, étoient amoureusement tournés vers vous, nous admirions vos loix, votre liberté, et nous nous plaignions de ne pas jouir ici des memes avantages. Notre revolution a fait cesser nos plaintes, nous sommes devenus Citoyens, et la porte du bonheur nous est ouverte. Nous Sommes heureux, nous le serons davantage à l'avenir. Les secousses de la revolution ont agité les esprits, le Calme commence à s'établir, il ne restera bientôt plus que l'inquietude Salutaire de l'amour de la Liberté qui Contient tous les pouvoirs delegués.

Avec les Sentiments de la philosophie que vous nous Connoissez, il nous est impossible de ne pas desirer que la revolution qui a Abattu le despotisme en France Le fasse disparoître chez tous nos voisins et sur la Surface du monde entier.

Croirez-vous que des membres de la chambre des pairs et de celle des Communes d'angleterre condamnent notre revolution? Cela est Cependant vrai. Les anglois membres du parlement sont presque tous Aristocrates et la majorité est vendue au gouvernement qui paye Cette prostitution par tous les emplois Corrupteurs que la nation a laissés à la disposition du Roi. Les anglois ennemis de notre revolution n'ont prosperé qu'avec les avantages d'un gouvernement moins vicieux que le nôtre. Ils voyent avec douleur que notre Constitution nous met au-dessus d'eux, et que nous sommes affranchis des vices politiques qui tôt ou tard leur feront perdre le peu de liberté qui leur reste. M. Payne, votre Concitoyen, dans un ouvrage plein de la logique, de la raison, et de la Connoissance des droits des hommes et des Societés, vient de prouver que M. Burke n'est qu'un sot et qu'un ignorant, ou bien qu'un homme d'une insigne mauvaise foi. Cet ouvrage vous est sans doute parvenu, il a fait fortune ici, et il pourroit être Contre le gouvernement anglois ce qu'a eté son Livre du Sens Commun.[1]

Les papiers anglois et françois vous parviennent. Il y a dans les premiers une partialité qui revolte, il semble que les journalistes soient payés pour Calomnier La france, sa revolution, sa Constitution. Vous Connoissez L'esprit et les principes de L'assemblée nationale. Les mensonges des journalistes ne font qu'exciter votre pitié, mais les ignorants adoptent les mensonges imprimés. Les journaux françois se sont multipliés à un point étonnant, il y en a chaque jour une Centaine qui sont Criés à tue-tete dans toutes les rues et sur toutes les places. Les trois quarts ne Contiennent que des choses fausses, des Calomnies, des erreurs, des personnalités Contre des gens de tous les états, contre l'assemblée nationale, contre le Roi, Contre les Ministres, Contre la Religion et Contre Dieu meme. Les Passions se nuancent selon Les differents interests. En general, tout ce qui étoit privilegié, tout ce qui étoit noble ou eglisier riche, tout ce que étoit magistrat, tout ce qui tenoit à la Cour et à ses abus est ennemi de la revolution. Les amis de la revolution écrivent pour, Ses ennemis ecrivent contre; c'est à la raison, c'est à la reflexion à discerner le vrai du faux. Quant aux decrets de l'assemblée nationale, il faut les juger selon Leur contenu et Les avoir tels qu'ils ont été rendus. Avec La Liberté de la presse, avec des amis et des ennemis, le vrai et le faux circulent également. Malgré les mal intentionnés, malgré les anticitoyens, la france restera libre. Le peuple sent tout le prix de la liberté et aucune puissance humaine ne pourroit étouffer ce Sentiment. Il a secoué le joug de la Superstition; il brave, il se moque des foudres de rome, les menaces de cette cour jadis si redoutable n'exitent que son mepris, il a vu le renouvellement des anciens eveques avec la Satisfaction qu'inspire la retraite d'un homme qu'on Craint et qu'on n'estime pas. Il a reçu les nouveaux Eveques avec des demonstrations de joye qu'on n'avoit jamais temoignée aux anciens: jugez par Là si la nouvelle Constitution civile du clergé Lui deplait.

Vous nous avez Souvent dit que si vous aviez à choisir entre un bon gouvernement et le jugement par les Jurés, vous prefereriez ce dernier au premier. Nous avons l'un et l'autre. Tout ce qui regarde le jugement par les jurés est decreté, et avant la fin de juin prochain Les procès criminels ne seront pas jugés autrement.

Il ne reste de l'ancien regime et de l'ancien gouvernement que le Souvenir des maux qu'ils nous ont Causés pour nous garantir de Leur retour. Les Ministres Si fiers Si despotes sont aujourdhui honnetes et obeissants à la loi. Il est vrai que leur administration par la raison et par la loi est plus penible que par l'arbitraire.

M. le Prince de Condé et M. D'Artois, frere du Roi, sont fugitifs depuis le premier jour de la revolution. Le premier est en Allemagne et l'autre à Turin. Ils sont desesperés de tout ce qui se passe en france. Ils étoient sous l'ancien regime des hommes puissants, ils faisoient ouvrir le tresor public où ils prennoient de quoi satisfaire à leur extravagante prodigalité. Leur profusion étoit fort avantageuse à leur alentour. Livrés à leurs flateurs, ayant tous les vices à leur service, ils n'etoient occupés que des objets de leur imagination et de leurs sens. Rien ne les contenoit, leur volonté étoit leur seule Loi. Par la nouvelle Constitution, ils ne sont plus que des Citoyens soumis aux memes Loix, ils ne disposeront plus des revenus publics. Ils auront les leurs, assez grands s'ils sont sages et économes; enfin, ils étoient des despotes, et ils ne peuvent plus être que des hommes libres, dependants comme les autres de la loi. S'ils pouvoient susciter des ennemis à la france pour y retablir l'ancien regime, ils se mettroient à la tete d'une armée pour assouvir leur rage. Ils ont beaucoup de mecontents avec eux, mais les mecontents ne peuvent faire que des efforts impuissants pour l'execution de leurs ridicules projets. Nous avons, independemment des troupes reglées, plus de deux millions de Citoyens sous les armes qui preferent la mort à l'esclavage. Avec cette force redoutable, qui peut nous attaquer? Nous sentons très bien que les rois voyent avec douleur notre revolution et les principes de notre Constitution. Ils Craignent que les grandes verités qui Circulent dans toute l'europe ne fassent ouvrir les yeux des peuples asservis. Ils auront beau faire, la lumiere percera partout. Les Societés doivent rentrer dans L'usage de tous les droits qu'on leur a volés.

La Liberté de Conscience et de religion est établie parmi nous, la diversité des opinions religieuses ne sera plus un motif de persecution. Convenez que notre raison a fait de grands progrès depuis peu d'années. De quelque religion que soit un homme, il aura le droit de pretendre à toutes les places. Les absurdités alloient si loin chez nous qu'il falloit un Certificat de Catholicité pour avoir la permission de vendre du Sel à petites mesures. Nous avons banni de notre Langue le mot tolerence, parce qu'il est absurde de l'employer pour l'exercice d'un droit. Chacun sera religieux à sa maniere. La seule chose qui vous deplaira peut être et qui est legalement établie, c'est que la nation Salarie exclusivement les fonctionnaires publics du Culte Commun. Il est quelque fois utile de transiger avec Les prejugés. Nous Sçavons que chez vous les choses à Cet egard ne sont pas sur le meme pied. Cependant vous avez des ministres de la religion qui ont des terres qui leur Servent de Salaires et que Ces terres ont été Concedées, ou par les parroisses ou par l'état. Les lumieres avec Le tems Corrigeront des abus qu'il seroit dangereux d'abolir dans le moment present.

Nous pensons que M. Short vous fait parvenir tous les decrets de L'assemblée nationale. C'est pas ses decrets que vous La jugerez, et votre jugement sera d'autant plus sûr que vous Connoissez la france, que vous L'avez vue dans le tems des plus grands abus et sous le regime le plus despotique. Vous avez connu nos moeurs, vous avez vu les premiers tems de la revolution. Toutes ces connoissances sont bien necessaires pour juger avec Connoissance de Cause notre revolution et notre Constitution.

Il est heureux pour nous d'avoir empeché une guerre Civile que les Aristocrates auroient bien voulu exciter, mais l'esprit du peuple étoit trop decidé pour La Liberté. Il n'étoit pas possible de le tromper et de l'égarer. Il faut que nos ennemis intérieurs contiennent leur rage et se bornent à Leurs vains desirs. Un jour ils beniront avec le peuple une revolution qui a assuré leurs personnes et leurs proprietés, avantage dont ils ne jouissoient pas sous L'ancien regime.

Nous ignorons si, dans vos etats unis, les gens de Couleur nés des pères et meres Libres jouissent chez vous de tous les droits de Citoyens actifs. Nous Sçavons que chez les anglois ces droits ne leur sont pas assurés. L'assemblée vient de decréter que les hommes de Couleur nés des peres et meres libres, en payant les taxes prescrites par la loi, sont declarés Citoyens actifs et eligibles. Ce decret n'a pas été rendu sans des grandes oppositions de la part des députés de nos isles, mais la justice et la verité ont triomphé. Comme les gens de Couleur sont plus nombreux que les blancs, ce decret les attachera davantage à notre Constitution et ils seront par là plus interessés à la deffense de nos isles et à leur prosperité.

Il est tems que nous finissions une lettre qui n'est deja que trop Longue. Les affaires de votre place auroient dû nous porter à abreger. Il n'est pas facile d'arreter une plume sur une matiere si interessante pour nous et pour l'espece humaine. Les gens heureux aiment à parler de leur bonheur, comme les malheureux aiment à entretenir de leurs maux. Ceux-ci les radoucissent et les premiers l'augmentent. Que ne nous est-il permis d'esperer qu'un jour toutes les Societés politiques ne seront plus livrées aux brigandages de la tirannie? Il faudroit pour cela éteindre dans l'homme la Soif des richesses et de la domination, et l'eclairer sur la justice, seule base du bonheur. Il faudroit lui faire envisager l'agriculture comme la Source de toute prosperité morale, politique et civile, et les arts comme des principes Corrupteurs S'ils ne sont pas Contenus dans des justes limites. Nous ne voulons pas Condamner les hommes à ne faire usage que de la hache et de la Scie. Cette austerité n'a jamais convenu qu'aux Spartiates, mais nous voudrions qu'un Luxe moins immoderé contentat nos desirs. La modestie et la Sobrieté qui Conviennent tant aux particuliers conviennent aussi à toutes les Societés. Nous voudrions que le travail fut par la necessité des choses le Saint devoir des hommes de toutes les Classes, pour bannir la Criminelle oisiveté, mère de tous les vices.

L'histoire de tous les tems semble ne pas nous permettre d'esperer ce nouvel ordre de choses. Les Societés se Corrompent en vieillissant et il faut rependre des torrents de Sang pour les regenerer. Nous esperons Cependant. Le desespoir nous rendroit plus malheureux, et l'esperance est notre Soulagement et notre bonheur. C'est ainsi que nous terminons notre Lettre.

Nous voudrions ecrire en meme tems à M. Adams et à M. Jay. Voudriez-vous permettre que Cette Lettre Leur fut Commune et leur faire parvenir L'assurance de notre estime et de notre amitié, avec nos hommages respectueux pour Mde. Adams et pour Mde. Jay.

Nous Comptions de vous envoyer encore deux volumes des ouvrages posthumes de notre ami L'abbé de Mably, mais l'impression n'en est pas achevée. Dès qu'ils seront imprimés nous aurons L'honneur de vous en envoyer trois exemplaires, un pour vous, et les deux autres pour M. Adams et pour M. Jay.

Quand vos affaires vous permettront de nous donner de vos nouvelles et de celles de votre païs, vous nous ferez un veritable plaisir. Quand nous pourrons faire quelque chose qui vous soit agreable, nous sommes à vos ordres et à votre Service. Vous nous trouverez toujours disposés à vous temoigner les Sentiments d'estime et d'amitié que vous nous avez inspirés et avec lesquels nous avons

L'honneur d'être Monsieur vos très humbles et très obeissants Serviteurs,

CHALUT ARNOUX

M. L'ambassadeur de france auprès de votre Congrès a bien voulu Se Charger de cette Lettre. Vous serez bien Content de son Esprit et de son Coeur. Vous trouverez en Lui un homme Sage qui remplira sa mission à la Satisfaction de la france et des etats unis. Son desir est de Concourir efficacement à la prosperité des deux nations. Toute sa politique Consistera dans la verité et dans les avantages respectifs. Vous le Connoissez et vous avez Surement sur son Compte les memes Sentiments que nous.

RC (DLC); in the hand of Arnoux; consisting of four leaves (f. 11129-32), with "No.1" written at the head of the first and "No. 2" at the beginning of the third (see note 1); endorsed by TJ on verso of fourth leaf as received 9 Aug. 1791 and so recorded in SJL. Following this is a misplaced leaf, undated and in the hands of Arnoux, TJ, and an unidentified person (f. 11133, endorsed by TJ: "Arnoux and Chalut"). On the recto of this leaf is a memorandum by Arnoux describing "Balsamum Canadense . . . une resine plus ou moins liquide, presque sans couleur et sans odeur, mais d'un gout de therebentine le plus agreable," believed to have come from a species of spruce found in Canada and Virginia. This note was written on behalf of TJ's friends the Devilles, who desired him to procure four to six pounds of the balm. The memorandum must have been given to him on the eve of his departure from France. Below Arnoux' memorandum TJ wrote various notes in which he tried to identify the species of tree. His notes were taken from St. Germain's Manuel des Végétaux, Miller's Dictionnaire des Jardiniers, Clayton's Flora Virginica, and Linnaeus' Systema Naturae, and from his investigation he concluded that if the tree were not one of two species described by Linnaeus and Clayton, "it does not grow in Virginia." Since the works he consulted were acquired by him in Paris and since his books did not arrive in America until the autumn of 1790, it follows that this attempt at identification was written down before he left Paris in 1789. Beneath this

notation by TJ on f. 11133, there appears the following in an unidentified hand: "No. 26 Hanover Square 8/ per ℔." This note was written by someone in New York directing TJ to the place where the balm could be procured, which happened to be the establishment of Oliver Hull & Son, druggists, next door to the book store and printery of Hugh Gaine. Within two weeks after his arrival in New York in the spring of 1790, TJ was able to report to Arnoux and Chalut that he had found in the city "the genuine Balsamum Canadense brought from Canada" and that it would be sent by the first vessel going directly to Le Havre (TJ to Arnoux and Chalut, 5 Apr. 1790). Three weeks later he purchased three quarts of the balm for 24 shillings, and late in May he informed Short that he had sent about "½ doz ℔. of Balsamum Canadense for Mr. Deville" by Crèvecoeur (TJ to Short, 27 May 1790; Account Book, 25 and 26 Apr. 1790). The shipment arrived and was presented to Deville by Short on TJ's behalf (Short to TJ, 9 Sep. 1790). The misplaced leaf therefore belongs in the period 1789-1790 and should have been noted there.

This letter closes TJ's correspondence with Arnoux and Chalut, the two abbés whose engaging manners, hospitality, and learning had won his respect and friendship soon after his arrival in Paris. TJ probably met them through John and Abigail Adams, who also had warm and friendly relations with them. They taught Adams French, and he had wondered with some amusement whether they were spies, since they had high connections and associated with members of the court (Adams, *Diary*, ed., L. H. Butterfield, II, 306; IV, 59-60). The abbés quite innocently suggested that TJ share this letter with Adams and Jay, another American friend of theirs, but it is virtually certain that he did not show it to either. Their glowing optimism about the course of the revolution, their extravagant praise of Paine and denunciation of Burke, and their tribute to American achievements in law and liberty arrived at a time when TJ was agonizing over his relationship with Adams because of his praise of Paine's *Rights of Man* and the ensuing public furor. The first letter he wrote Adams after receiving the above was one in which he exculpated himself and blamed *Publicola* without realizing that he was placing the blame upon John Quincy Adams (TJ to Adams, 30 Aug. 1791). In that letter he reaffirmed his confidence in the outcome of the revolution, but based this upon his own observations and did not refer at all to the letter from their mutual friends Arnoux and Chalut. The good abbés' enthusiasm for the revolutionary cause must indeed have seemed too far removed from reality for TJ to have made it available to the public through Bache's *General Advertiser* or Freneau's *National Gazette*, as he occasionally did with other communications. After Ternant, who bore the letter, gave him the information promised by Short about various interests in the National As-sembly that had prevented any modification of the tobacco and other decrees, TJ must have confined the abbés' optimism to his files (Short to TJ, 6 June 1791).

TJ undoubtedly retained his feeling for affection and respect for the two abbés for their "kindnesses beyond number," their patriotism, and their "love of mankind in general" which he said he would always remember (TJ to Arnoux and Chalut, 5 Apr. 1790). But he did not respond to this letter. Nor, evidently, did he receive the two final volumes of Abbé de Mably's *Œuvres posthumes* which they promised to send and which appeared later in the year (Sowerby, No. 2404; TJ had the first two volumes, published in 1790).

It is not surprising that the abbés should have recalled TJ's oft-expressed views about the fundamental importance of juries. He had guided their reading on the subject and was perhaps the more insistent in expressing views he held then and always because he had feared that the constitution being framed by the National Assembly would not include a guarantee of trial by jury. He thought the French were "not sensible of it's value" (TJ to Arnoux, 19 July 1789; TJ to Price, 8 Jan. 1789).

[1] The two leaves headed "No. 1" end at this point and are followed by those marked "No. 2." From this it appears that the letter originally consisted of two sheets of four pages each.

From Samuel Blackden

Dear Sir   Paris May 20th. 1791

I would not trespass upon your time which is so usefully employ'd in the service of the public, and so much to your own honor, if I did not believe that you would think me guilty of a want of confidence in your goodness and that I am insensible to the pleasure and alacrity with which you undertake and serve your country and your friends. If I take too much liberty you will pardon me, when you reflect that it proceeds from your own behavior towards me, that I am embolden'd to address you upon a subject which is of importance to our country, to posterity, and to the world at large.

Our inestimable friend Mr. Barlow, came to Europe upon a speculation which has not altogether succeeded, whatever it may do in future, and in consequence of new arrangements, made by his own desire and concurrence, he is at liberty to pursue any other object that presents.

To a judge like you, I need not speak of the Talents of our friend, they need no eulogium, but from the most intimate acquaintance with him, for three years under the same roof, I may be bold to say, that a more worthy man does not exist, nor a firmer son of universal liberty. He is no trimmer in France for the smiles and favors of the great, nor has he to please the Aristocrats ever been heard to say a single word against the constitution, of our happy country. That has been left to a speculating member of a former Congress, and a Governor who never had a Government. If our country loses Mr. Barlow through the embarassments of his fortune, she loses a diamond of the brightest water.

Mr. Barlow is inclined to write, but to write well a man should be at his ease. The inconveniences attendant upon a want of fortune, call of[f] the attention of the mind from the project upon which it ought to dwell. Poems and plays it is true have been wrote in garrets, and historys have been wrote in prisons but it is easy to perceive that the genius was cramped and that employment more than Fame was the object of the writing.

If merit of every sort could claim the attention of our country Mr. Barlow could not be overlook'd but as that is not always the case to whom shall we apply but to the Wise and the good, and happy is our lot that we may address our persuasions in a Government, in a plain and simple stile (freedom knows no intrigue) and thrice happy are we in this distant corner of the Earth, to know that we have still existing Our Washington our Jefferson and our Knox, whose Patriotism is too ardent to suffer the history of the revolution to expire in the Vapid pages of a Soulés or a Gordon. The doings of our Congress are worthy of an inspired pen (if any such ever existed). But to make it Sure that posterity may not be in Want of *a recital which will be read*, and which will fix these events on their minds, it is to be wished that those transactions may be Assigned to the pen of a Barlow.

To do then my dear Sir what our country wants, what posterity have a right to expect and look for, and what our friend is qualified to perform, will you use your endeavours to put him in such a situation as will in the intervals of his duty, afford him an Opportunity of writing Upon the most important event that occurs in the history of Mankind, an event which has put Europe in Motion, and which will probably be felt throughout the world. The ideas of freedom begin already to be felt even in Poland.

Many things must offer in your department that would accord with this National object, and I feel a confidence that you will not be offended at my writing in favor of a man, who is an honour to his country, and who may prove in his writings how useful he can be to Mankind when favord by such patronage. – Mrs. B. desires me to present her respectful compliments to you and your dear Children with which I am Dear Sir Most respectfully your Obliged hble servant,

S. BLACKDEN

RC (DLC: Washington Papers); at head of text in Remsen's hand: "S. Blackden. On Joel Barlow's situation"; endorsed by TJ as received 9 Aug. 1791 and so recorded in SJL.

It is not known if this appeal prompted TJ to recommend Barlow for appointment, but he did give the letter to Washington and a year later mentioned that Barlow was one of those whom he had rec-

ommended to the President (TJ to Washington, 9 Sep. 1792).

The GOVERNOR WHO NEVER HAD A GOVERNMENT was obviously Gouverneur Morris. The SPECULATING MEMBER OF A FORMER CONGRESS has not been identified, though it is clear that Blackden supposed TJ would guess his identity from the two clues provided.

To Joseph Willard

SIR   New York May 20. 1791.

I have the honor to inclose you a packet which came from France under cover to me.

I recieved several times, while in France, two copies, in sheets, of certain books printed in the king's press, and which had been procured from him as a present to two of our colleges by the Marquis de Chastellux. I knew from this gentleman himself that the college of Virginia was one to which such a present was ordered, but had no information as to the 2d. copy. I therefore forwarded it from time to time to Doctr. Franklin who had recieved and forwarded it while in France, taking for granted he knew it's destination and would send it on from Philadelphia. At the time of his death however there remained one of these parcels in his hands, which was sent to me in Philadelphia by his family. I have some idea that yours was the college to which this 2nd. copy was given. However of this you Sir can give me information, as in that case you must have been in the course of recieving them, and I will thank you for that information. If it be to your's that the present goes, it shall be forwarded as soon as I return to Philadelphia. I have the honor to be with great respect & esteem, Sir, Your most obedt. and most humble servt,

TH: JEFFERSON

PrC (DLC).

TJ was mistaken in thinking that the parcel of books in Franklin's custody at the time of his death was intended for Harvard College. It was destined instead for the College of Philadelphia. While in America the Marquis de Chastellux had been awarded honorary degrees by the latter institution and by the College of William and Mary. On his return to France, he was instrumental in persuading Louis XVI, through Vergennes, to present to these two colleges a number of works on history, science, geography, and exploration, among them many that were issued by L'Imprimerie Royale. Most of the 100 volumes given to the College of Philadelphia have survived and all of the works are listed in C. Seymour Thompson, "The Gift of Louis XVI," *University of Pennsylvania Library Chronicle*, ii (1934), 37-48, 60-7. Only two of those given to the College of William and Mary remain (see *Travels in North America . . . by the Marquis de Chastellux*, ed. Howard C. Rice, Jr. [Chapel Hill, 1963], i, 310-311; ii, 606).

An entry in SJL shows that Willard answered the above letter on 15 Oct. 1791 (recorded as received 1 Nov. 1791), but his reply has not been found. Since none of the volumes given to the College of Philadelphia by Louis XVI was issued later than 1783 and since there is no record of any addition to the gift after the original shipment was received in 1784, it seems that the institution for which the parcel was intended was not the recipient.

The Northern Journey of Jefferson and Madison

EDITORIAL NOTE

> There was every appearance of a passionate courtship
> between the Chancellor – Burr – Jefferson and Madison
> when the two latter were in Town. Delenda est Carthago
> I suppose is the Maxim adopted with respect to you.
> They had better be quiet, for if they succeed they will
> tumble the fabric of the government in ruins to the ground.
> Upon this subject however, I cannot say that I have the
> smallest uneasiness. You are too well seated in the hearts
> of the citizens of the northern and middle states to be
> hunted down by them.
> — *Robert Troup to Alexander Hamilton*,
> *15 June 1791*

Long before Hamilton's friend Robert Troup made this observation he had become convinced that the enemies of the Secretary of the Treasury were resolved to defeat his policies by destroying him politically. He saw this danger most ominously manifested in the southern states, particularly in Virginia. Now, as Jefferson and Madison paused in New York City at the beginning of their northward journey and were seen in company with Chancellor Livingston and Aaron Burr, Troup once again attributed to Hamilton's opponents the motto of destruction – *Delenda est Carthago.*[1] A coalition of the Livingstons and the Clintonians had just enabled Burr to defeat Hamilton's father-in-law, Senator Philip Schuyler, and had given a new aspect to the politics of New York. In these circumstances the cordiality exhibited between the Virginians and the victorious New Yorkers seemed to Hamilton's friends evidence of a plot to extend the opposition by creating a sectional alliance.

[1] Troup had used the phrase in his letter to Hamilton of 19 Jan. 1791 in which he warned that "We are going headlong into the bitterest opposition to the General Government" (Syrett, *Hamilton*, VII, 445; VIII, 478-9). His comment quoted above was written on the day Madison and Jefferson arrived back in New York, but the allusion was to their earlier stay in the city. See also Duer to Hamilton, 19 Jan. 1791 and Tillary to Hamilton, [Jan. 1791] (same, VII, 442-3, 614-16).

The "passionate courtship" which gave rise to the suspicion, if it existed at all, was certainly brief. Jefferson arrived in New York late on May 19th, two days behind schedule, and stopped at Elsworth's boardinghouse in Beekman Street. There he joined Madison, who had been in the city since late April. Early on the morning of the 21st, after dispatching his servant James Hemings to Poughkeepsie with the phaeton and his and Madison's horses, he boarded Captain John Cooper's sloop with Madison and started up the Hudson. Jefferson had spent only a single day in the city, during which time he bought a book and attended to several errands. He and Madison must have seen Livingston and Burr, and they unquestionably met Philip Freneau at dinner, possibly when all of those suspected of engaging in political intrigue were present.

Robert Troup was not the only one, or indeed the first, to entertain such suspicions. Two days after the travellers left the city the British Consul General, Sir John Temple, warned the Duke of Leeds that the "party and Politicks" of the Secretary of State were gaining ground and that he and Madison had "gone to the Eastern States, there to proselyte as far as they are able to a commercial war with Great Britain."[2] Lord Dorchester's agent and Hamilton's confidant, George Beckwith, shared these suspicions. Only a few weeks earlier he had received through Madison a stern message from the President and had been rebuffed when he sought to obtain from Jefferson the same kind of recognition Hamilton had accorded him.[3] Convinced that hidden political motives prompted Jefferson's travels, Beckwith decided to make a countervailing move. "[B]eing no stranger to the plans of this gentleman," he reported to Lord Grenville, "I esteemed it my duty in the present critical condition of the interests of the Empire and in this country, to precede Mr. Jefferson in New England, and it gives me much satisfaction to find, that my declarations to different individuals with whom I thought it necessary to converse freely have accorded perfectly with the assurances recently given to Colonel Smith in London."[4]

It is scarcely surprising that Beckwith found such perfect accord among those with whom he was in the habit of conversing freely, such as William Samuel Johnson, Philip Schuyler, John Jay, Jeremiah Wadsworth, and others who opposed Jefferson's principles. This seemed all the more obvious to Hamilton's supporters since the Secretary of State was then the embarrassed center of controversy because he had publicly praised Paine's *Rights of Man* and had denounced political heresies that had sprung up.[5] The opinions expressed to

[2] Temple to Leeds, 23 May 1791 (PRO: FO 4/12).

[3] See Editorial Note and Document IV in group of documents at 4 Apr. 1791.

[4] Beckwith to Grenville, 14 June 1791 (PRO: FO 4/12). On the assurances given Smith by Grenville, see Editorial Note and group of documents at 15 Dec. 1790.

[5] See Editorial Note and group of documents at 26 Apr. 1791. Beckwith was so concerned about the dedication of *Rights of Man* to the President and TJ's public endorsement of the work that he called on Tobias Lear and Edmund Randolph to voice his objections (Lear to Washington, 8 May 1791, DLC: Washington Papers). Jeremiah Wadsworth was one of those Beckwith visited in Connecticut, taking satisfaction in being able to assure him, as he doubtless did others, that "the best disposition exists in our government to establish an amicable connexion, between the two countries, upon fair and liberal principles" (Beckwith to Wadsworth, 31 May and 14 June 1791, CtHi: Wadsworth Papers). On the ineffectiveness of Beckwith's effort in the face of rising popular feelings about British policies, see Charles R. Ritcheson, *Aftermath of Revolution* (Dallas, 1969), p. 122.

Beckwith were perhaps similar to those voiced by Pierpont Edwards at a dinner in Connecticut, which included among those present the governor, members of the Council, and some of the Hartford Wits. "At this Table," Nathaniel Hazard reported to Hamilton, "Mr. Edwards ridiculed J—n and M—n's Tour, in which they scouted silently thro' the Country, shunning the Gentry, communing with and pitying the Shayites, and quarreling with the Eatables; nothing good enough for them." He added that if southern smoke provoked a northeast gale, the poet John Trumbull, who was among those present, would give their journey "A Canto . . . of stinging satire."[6]

Although several newspapers along the route announced the presence of Jefferson and Madison, satirical comment and attribution of political motives have not been found in their notices. What appears at first glance to be an exception to this was the comment of an Albany paper:[7]

On Thursday last this city was honored with the presence of Mr. Jefferson, Secretary of State, accompanied by the *Charles Fox* of America, the celebrated Madison. We are informed they are going north, as far as Lake Champlain, and then across the *fifteenth Constellation*, east to Connecticut river.

This announcement, which by its allusion to Fox correctly cast Madison in the role of leader of the opposition, was widely copied by other newspapers. Given the political bias of the editors, readers of Fenno's *Gazette of the United States* perhaps interpreted this as satire, while those of Childs and Swaine's *Daily Advertiser* might have read it as praise. It was in fact offered in high tribute by Barber's *Albany Register*, a journal ardently opposed to Federalist policies. There was indeed additional editorial comment in the same issue which sympathetic newspapers such as Neale and Lawrence's *Burlington Advertiser* and Bache's *General Advertiser* copied but which Fenno's *Gazette of the United States* and other papers of Federalist persuasion understandably omitted:[8]

It is to be regretted that their short stay in this city deprived our principal characters from paying that respectful attention due to their distinguished merit. While the President is exploring one extremity of the empire, these enlightened patriots are doing the same in the other. – How different this

---

[6] Hazard to Hamilton, 25 Nov. 1791 (Syrett, *Hamilton*, IX, 534).

[7] Quoted in the New York *Daily Advertiser*, 6 June 1791, in the *Federal Gazette* of 8 June 1791, and in the *Gazette of the United States*, 8 June 1791, all under an Albany dateline of 30 May. The only newspapers published in Albany at the time were the *Albany Gazette* and the *Albany Register*. No issue of the latter for Monday 30 May 1791 has been found. But both of the passages quoted above may safely be attributed to it because the *Albany Gazette* of that date contains no mention of the presence of TJ and Madison; because of the known political sympathies of the *Albany Register*; and because all newspapers quoting part or all of the passages assign the same Albany dateline. On 21 May 1791 the *Daily Advertiser* announced TJ's arrival in New York on the preceding day and his plan to make a tour northward accompanied by Madison. The *Federal Gazette* of 25 May 1791 and the *Poughkeepsie Journal* of 26 May 1791 made a similar announcement. So did the *Hudson Weekly Gazette* of 26 May 1791 and the Lansingburgh *American Spy* of 27 May 1791. For Richard Peters' comment on the comparison of Madison with Fox, see his letter to TJ, 26 June 1791.

[8] Bache's *General Advertiser*, 29 June 1791, taken from the *Burlington Advertiser* of 21 June, which in turn published the passage under an Albany dateline for 30 May. For reasons given in the preceding note both passages have been attributed to the opposition newspaper, the *Albany Register*.

from the leaders of the old corrupted empires of the east, (Pitt excepted) who are wallowing in every species of dissipation, regardless of the happiness or prosperity of their country, while ours are industriously prying into an accurate knowledge of the situation of every part of the union from personal observation. With such men at the helm we passengers can promise ourselves nothing less than a prosperous and pleasant voyage.

There were even more expressions of gratification that the ship of state was fortunate enough to be commanded by such statesmen as Washington, Jefferson, and Madison, but the maritime metaphor needed no elaboration. The Federalist *Albany Gazette* did not even notice the presence of the Virginians in the city.

After his return to New York, Madison learned of the accusation by Hamilton and others that Jefferson had tried to have Tench Coxe appointed as Comptroller of the Treasury. He cited this as not the only instance of "the most uncandid and unfounded things of a like tendency having been thrown into circulation."[9] The allusion must have been to such suspicions as those voiced by Troup, Trumbull, and others. No evidence has been found to indicate that Hamilton himself shared or expressed these suspicions. But it was left to his son to give them permanent form. In John C. Hamilton's view, there was no doubt that the travellers, after frequent interviews with Livingston and Burr, visited Governor Clinton "under the pretext of a botanical excursion to Albany, thence extended their journey to Vermont, and, having sown a few tares in Connecticut, returned to the seat of government."[10]

This interpretation, based upon the letters of Troup and Hazard which Hamilton found in his father's papers, not only fixed Federalist suspicions in American history but also provoked an unending debate over their validity. Some, accepting this version without question, have built upon it. Their view of the "botanizing excursion" is that Jefferson and Madison, in studying "*Clintonia borealis* and other hardy perennials in Ulster county and the neighborhood of Albany," took the first and most important step in forming a nation-wide opposition party through the creation of an alliance of New York and Virginia republicans.[11] Others, basing their conclusions on the total absence of any comment on political affairs by Madison or Jefferson during their journey or any subsequent written evidence to sustain the view that a partisan alliance had been established, have concluded that the trip "had no other object than a temporary relaxation from public cares."[12] Still others, recognizing that the

[9] Madison to TJ, 24 July 1791; see also Editorial Note and group of documents at 16 Apr. 1791.

[10] John C. Hamilton's documentary biography of his father, *History of the Republic of the United States, as traced in the writings of Alexander Hamilton*, IV (New York, 1859), 506.

[11] Morison and Commager, *The growth of the American Republic*, I (New York, 1937), 230; this interpretation remains unmodified in the 1977 edition. See also Morison, *The Oxford history of the American people* (New York, 1965), p. 331. Wilfred E. Binkley thought the intersectional entente set the permanent pattern of the party and that the "two statesmen-politicians extended their journey into New England, conferred with state leaders, and knit the local followings into the Republican coalition" (*American political parties: Their natural history* [New York, 1962], p. 78).

[12] William C. Rives, *Life and times of James Madison*, III (Boston, 1868), 191. This apparently was the first rebuttal of the view set forth by John C. Hamilton. Henry S.

two statesmen could scarcely have failed to inquire about politics or even to promote their own ideas of government, have held that they had no clearly defined political objective in view, least of all any intention of cementing alliances or creating a national opposition party. "Hamilton and his friends," writes one of Jefferson's biographers, "imagined political intrigue where there was none. . . . If any alliance or bargains were struck, with Livingston, Burr, Clinton, or anyone, they were very secret indeed, for they left no traces."[13]

This conclusion seems entirely warranted. Yet, while the interpretation of those who reject the idea of political plotting seems to accord best with the known facts, even the admission that political concerns were not wholly absent from the minds of the travellers has not been sufficiently comprehensive. In accepting Jefferson's suggested outline of the itinerary — which the travellers adhered to both as to route and timing — Madison wrote: "Health recreation and curiosity being my objects, I can never be out of my way."[14] This in all respects coincided with the aims of Jefferson, who after a winter and spring of drudgery had suffered attacks of his periodic headaches. But "curiosity" for both of the philosopher-statesmen included politics in its broadest sense as well as partisanship in its narrower meaning. Political inquiry for both was an integral part of their being and therefore, in the nature of things, could not be suspended during the northern journey. To suppose two men so constituted and so opposed to the tendency of national measures could have set aside their primary concerns even on a tour of recreation is to embrace a contradiction in terms. One of the clearest indications that the tour of relaxation did not mean the exclusion of political interests is to be found in Jefferson's directions about forwarding his official mail. The only newspaper that he asked to be included with his letters was Fenno's *Gazette of the United States*. This obviously was not because he admired its position but because he wished to be kept informed of any moves of his political opponents, particularly any comments that might be published concerning his praise of Paine's *Rights of Man*.

I

Ironically, it was the British agent George Beckwith who came closer to describing one of the primary objects Jefferson had in mind than any contem-

Randall, in a comment published the year before Hamilton's work appeared, dismissed the journey with the remark that TJ's "private memoranda of the journey are hardly worth transcribing" (*Life of Thomas Jefferson*, II [New York, 1858], 10).

[13] Merrill Peterson, *Thomas Jefferson and the new nation* (New York, 1970), p. 439-40. Others who share this view, with varying degrees of emphasis, are: Philip M. Marsh, "The Jefferson-Madison Vacation," PMHB, LXXI (Jan. 1947), 20-2; Dumas Malone, *Jefferson*, II, 359-63; Adrienne Koch, *Jefferson and Madison: The great collaboration* (New York, 1950), p. 115-16; Brant, *Madison*, III, 336-40; Dumbauld, *Tourist*, p. 172-7, 237-8; Noble E. Cunningham, *The Jeffersonian Republicans: The formation of party organization, 1789-1801* (Chapel Hill, 1957), p. 11-12; Alfred F. Young, *The Democratic Republicans of New York: The origins, 1763-1797* (Chapel Hill, 1967), p. 194-201. The last presents the most careful analysis of the political aspects of the journey and concludes: "The first leg of the . . . trip [in New York City] unquestionably was political. The rest very likely was not."

[14] Madison to TJ, 12 May 1791. For years Madison had wished to make a tour of the upper Hudson and the eastern states and had so expressed himself to TJ after an earlier period of sedentary occupations (Madison to TJ, 7 and 15 Sep. 1784).

porary and most subsequent commentators. "Mr. Jefferson's views," he wrote to Grenville, "have been to feel the pulse of the country and to advocate his favorite objects in behalf of France."[15] On both counts this was characteristic of Jefferson. Such had been his purpose in 1784 when he travelled through the eastern states and conversed with leading public figures in preparing himself to promote trade with France in behalf of the fisheries and the grain and salt provisions of New England as well as the tobacco and timber of the southern states. On that preparatory excursion he had been cordially received in New York and in the commercial centers of New England.[16] So also when he returned to the United States in 1789, one of his purposes was to possess himself anew of the spirit and ideas of his countrymen. "I know only the Americans of the year 1784," he wrote to David Humphreys. "They tell me this is to be much a stranger to those of 1789."[17] The shock he had experienced early in 1790 at the dinner tables of the capital, where he heard political views so different from those six years earlier, could only have magnified his desire to know whether the spirit of the people had also changed. The measures adopted by the First Congress — the impost, the assumption of state debts, the adoption of the excise tax, the creation of the national bank — undoubtedly deepened his concern. Hamilton's refusal to accommodate France on the relatively trivial question of the tonnage dues; the views on government which he had expressed at the Cabinet meeting on April 11th; those advanced by Adams at the same time and in his *Discourses on Davila*; even Noah Webster's ridicule of his proposed standard of measure — all served to make Jefferson more anxious to ascertain the temper of the general public.[18]

"Are the people in your quarter," he asked Chancellor Livingston early in 1791, "as well contented with the proceedings of our government, as their representatives say they are?"[19] He knew well enough what was being said in the South and West and was apprehensive of the consequences. Livingston's answer brought some encouragement as to what he might find in the North: "Our delegates deceive themselves if they believe that their constituents are satisfied with all the measures of government."[20] But Livingston also pointed to the danger of a sectional cleavage on all important measures, thus by implication pointing to the desirability of such a coalition of dissidents between North and South as had brought a measure of success to the efforts of the New York opposition. Before Congress adjourned Jefferson had talked of the heresies of some, but professed to believe that the great mass of the people were untainted.[21] On so vital a question, however, reassurance could scarcely be obtained at the seat of government. In 1789, after Congress had adjourned, Washington himself had undertaken a tour through the eastern states "to acquire knowledge of the face of the Country, the growth and agriculture

---

[15] Beckwith to Grenville, 14 June 1791 (PRO: FO 4/12).

[16] See Editorial Note and group of documents on northern commerce at May-July 1784.

[17] TJ to Humphreys, 18 Mch. 1789.

[18] See Editorial Notes and grouped documents on the French protest over tonnage views and on unofficial diplomacy, at 18 Jan. and 4 Apr. 1791. See also TJ to Madison, 10 Jan. 1791.

[19] TJ to Livingston, 4 Feb. 1791.

[20] Livingston to TJ, 20 Feb. 1791.

[21] TJ to Mason, 4 Feb. 1791.

thereof — and the temper and disposition of the inhabitants towards the new government."[22] This taking of the pulse of the people, as Beckwith expressed it, was also one of the principal objects of the journey of Jefferson and Madison. But where Washington had found this difficult because of the public attentions showered upon him everywhere he went, they could gauge the disposition of the people best by avoiding ceremony and conversing as much as possible with farmers, ferrymen, blacksmiths, tavern keepers, and, occasionally, newspaper editors and political leaders.

This is precisely what Jefferson and Madison did, neither seeking out nor avoiding the political leaders of either party, except perhaps in Connecticut. There is no evidence that they saw Governor Clinton at all. While in Albany they were cordially received by Philip Schuyler, who went beyond the call of civility in extending courtesies, but neither Jefferson nor Madison referred to this visit with the most distinguished political figure they are known to have met on their travels.[23] In Vermont they were guests of Governor Moses Robinson, an ardent republican who had just been elected to the Senate. The only reference Jefferson made to the visit concerned a balsam tree at the governor's home which he later identified as "the balsam poplar, Populous balsamifers of Linnaeus."[24] The stunning beauty of Lake George; the fragrance of the wild azalea; the forests of white pine, hemlock, balsam, and birch; the mosquitoes, gnats, fleas, rattlesnakes, and squirrels; the cherries, gooseberries, and strawberries in abundance; the historical sites of the Revolution such as Saratoga, Ticonderoga, Crown Point, and Bennington; the quality of the taverns along the way; the farm products of the Connecticut valley — these and other aspects of the country they were seeing for the first time were what the travellers noted in their sparse records of the journey.

II

But the silence in the documents does not mean that politics did not enter into the discussions along the way. Beckwith's observation about Jefferson's

[22] Washington, *Diaries*, ed. Fitzpatrick, IV, 14. Washington sought and received the approval of his proposal from Hamilton, Knox, Jay, and Madison (same, IV, 16, 17).

[23] Alfred F. Young, *The Democratic Republicans of New York* (Chapel Hill, 1967), p. 199, quoting in part Schuyler's letter to his son: "I have intreated Mr. Jefferson and Mr. Madison to take beds with you on their way to Lake Champlain. They are intitled to and will receive your best attentions. — Be so good as to accompany them over the grounds occupied . . . by the American and British Armies previous to the surrender of the latter and point out the ground on which the british piled their arms. — On their return the Gentlemen will proceed from your house to Bennington. Pray give them the road" (Philip Schuyler to John B. Schuyler, 26 May 1791, NN: Schuyler Papers). They did not stay overnight with either Schuyler or his son, despite the offer of hospitality.

[24] TJ to Madison, 21 June 1791. Madison and TJ breakfasted at Dewey's tavern in Bennington on the morning of June 4th. Their coming had been anticipated because of announcement of their plans in newspapers along the Hudson, one of which Anthony Haswell published in the *Vermont Gazette* of 6 June 1791 under a Lansingburgh dateline of May 27th. This advance knowledge perhaps led to Robinson's invitation. — The presence of the governor and his guests at the Congregational Church later brought forth a number of newspaper squibs. One, undoubtedly founded in nothing more substantial than political bias, quoted both TJ and Madison as saying they had not attended church in years (Sketch of Moses Robinson in A. M. Hemenway, *The Vermont Historical Gazetteer*, I [Burlington, 1868], 168-9). Both men had in fact attended the memorial services in Christ Church on 1 Mch. 1791 for Benjamin Franklin.

desire to promote his favorite objects in behalf of France finds support in what the travellers saw in the recently established whaling port of Hudson, with its textile mill for the manufacture of sailcloth and its thriving distillery capable of producing for export a thousand hogshead of rum annually. While at Hudson, Jefferson sought to persuade Captain Seth Jenkins, principal founder of the port, that better spirits could be made from wine than from molasses. In his view this would have had the double advantage for the United States of increasing trade with France and of lessening dependence upon the British West Indies for sugar. Jenkins remained unconvinced because of the higher cost of imported wines. But the very fact that Jefferson advanced the suggestion shows, as did his treatise on the whale fishery and many of his state papers, that he was thinking of trade as an instrument of politics.[25] Doubtless the idea was inspired by what he saw at Hudson rather than being a planned objective, but the incident illustrates well the fact that along the route he was alert to any opportunity to advance his policies. At Waterford on the same day he paid particular attention to the operation of a nail manufactory – something he later introduced at Monticello – and perhaps took some satisfaction in observing an infant industry which promised to decrease still further American reliance upon British manufactures.

The politics of commerce also became apparent when Jefferson and Madison arrived in Bennington. Anthony Haswell, editor of the *Vermont Gazette*, was a zealous republican who welcomed the travellers in phrases echoing those of the *Albany Register* published a week earlier:[26]

> How enlightened is the policy of American legislators and statesmen, in thus acquainting themselves with the state of population, situation, and extent of the empire to which their abilities are devoted; by these means they obtain a personal knowledge of the abilities and prejudices of the citizens of different parts, and find the surest mode of reconciling differences, from investigation of the causes whence they orginate.

As an editorial in Haswell's paper of June 13th noted, the Virginians candidly discussed public questions during their pause in the Vermont capital:

> Monday morning last the secretary of state to the american union, and mr. Maddison, member of congress from Virginia, left this town on their way to Connecticut. They expressed great satisfaction with the country through which they had passed on their tour; and from the affability and polite attention they paid the citizens of Bennington, and doubtless those of the different places they visited on their rout, it is reasonably to be presumed, they not only ingratiated themselves deeply with the discerning, but obtained, unreservedly, the sentiments of the people, and secured to themselves a fund of political knowledge, which cannot fail to render them more essentially serviceable to their country. They attended public worship on the Sabbath, and left the town before sunrise the next morning. Examples, like these, speak the gentleman of good breeding, and the man of business, and are worthy of imitation by all ranks and descriptions of men in our republic.

[25] In his discussions with Jenkins, TJ also brought up the subject of the fisheries trade. On his return he sent him a copy of his report, which Jenkins found commendable (TJ to Jenkins, 21 June 1791; Jenkins to TJ, 5 July and 7 Nov. 1791).

[26] *Vermont Gazette*, 6 June 1791; also printed in *New-York Journal*, 15 June 1791, under Bennington dateline.

Having paid them this tribute, Haswell then touched upon a subject which almost certainly had been inspired by Jefferson:

> It is reported from good authority, that accurate calculations have been made, by which it is ascertained beyond a doubt, that there are maple trees in the inhabited parts of the united states, more than sufficient, with careful attention, to produce sugar adequate to the consumption of its inhabitants. It is likewise said, that refineries are about being established, by some wealthy foreigners, resident in the union: by whom agents will be established in different parts, who will loan out kettles, &c. on reasonable terms, to persons unable to purchase. With these agents cash will likewise be lodged to purchase all the raw sugar in their power. This scheme, prosecuted to effect, cannot fail to be extensively beneficial to the community, but in the meantime, attention to our sugar orchards is essentially necessary to secure the independence of our country.

The concluding sentence echoed what Jefferson had written to a British friend exactly a year earlier about the sugar maple industry, expressing confidence that the nation could produce enough not only to meet its own needs but also to provide a surplus for export. That overly optimistic estimate was in the nature of a warning to Great Britain that the United States would no longer be dependent upon the cane sugar of the British West Indies. This happy prospect, Jefferson had pointed out, resulted from "late difficulties in the sugar trade" – a circumlocution for the exclusionary provisions of the British Navigation Act which he did not need to explain to his friend in England.[27] But now, more realistically, he shifted the emphasis by warning the Vermonters that careful attention to the planting and cultivation of maple orchards would be necessary to produce even enough to meet the domestic demand. While at Bennington he set the example by ordering sugar maple seed and declaring his intention to create an orchard at Monticello. This was an act of official encouragement as well as personal interest, born of the "Maple Sugar Bubble" created by such promoters as William Cooper and Benjamin Rush. But it did for the time being arouse the interest of other Vermonters besides the editor of the *Vermont Gazette*. Joseph Fay, from whom Jefferson ordered his seed, promised to plant a regular orchard the next spring and to encourage others to do so.[28]

Knowing Vermont's close relationship with Canada and having recently informed Washington about clashes between Americans and Canadians on the northeastern boundary, Jefferson in his political inquiries also touched on that subject. This is made clear not only in his report to Washington written during the pause in Bennington, but also in what the editor of the *Vermont Gazette* had to say in the same editorial in which he remarked about the fund of political knowledge the travellers had acquired:[29]

[27] TJ to Vaughan, 27 June 1790. TJ emphasized the same point in his letter to Joseph Fay, 30 Aug. 1791.

[28] *Vermont Gazette*, 13 June 1791; Joseph Fay to TJ, 9 Aug. 1791. On the "Maple Sugar Bubble," see *Letters of Benjamin Rush*, ed. L. H. Butterfield, i (Princeton, 1951), 587-99. See also Rush to TJ, 10 July 1791, an essay TJ had probably suggested on the eve of the northern tour.

[29] See TJ to Washington, 5 June 1791; *Vermont Gazette*, 13 June 1791.

It is found to be a question among the southern politicians of the union, whether, if Canada, Nova Scotia &c. should throw off their foreign dependence, it would be policy to annex these provinces to the already wide extended empire of the United States, or let them form an independent republic: Among northern politicians the annexing of Mexico and Peru to the union, should they assume independence of European domination, is a question equally important.

Haswell went on to point out that the late generous acts of Great Britain relating to Canada proved

that they are convinced their former conduct was wrong, in assuming a right to tax in all cases whatsoever; they now relinquish the right to tax in any case whatever. The reason . . . is obvious – the flame of liberty burns bright in France, the great body of Canadians retain their partialities therefore, for the mother country, when they see the shackels of despotism shaken off there, and reflect on the advantage of republican governments, enjoyed by their neighbors.

The words were Haswell's, but they must have been inspired by Jefferson's inquiries concerning Canadian affairs.

As the visitors enjoyed the hospitality of Governor Robinson in the hillside mansion overlooking the Walloomsac river, Anthony Haswell and others of congenial political sentiments must have been among the company. Another leading citizen with whom the visitors discussed politics freely was Joseph Fay, who as Secretary of State from 1778 to 1781 had taken a leading part in negotiating the entente between Vermont and Canada during the war. Alexander Hamilton, with good reason, considered him to be one of the two most important individuals in the state.[30] Perhaps at Governor Robinson's table, certainly in a conversation with Fay present, a far more immediate political topic than relations with Canada or promotion of the sugar industry came up – the controversy on both sides of the Atlantic over Paine's reply to Burke. The fact that such a subject could have been broached, however casually, is confirmation of Haswell's public statement that political conversations with the distinguished travellers had been carried on without reserve. As had happened during the Cabinet meeting on April 11, the merits of the British constitution came under discussion. Fay, who carried on an extensive correspondence with Canadians, defended the English system of government, though whether he did so in terms such as Adams and Hamilton had used at Jefferson's dinner table is not known. Jefferson or Madison or both must have made a response turning the discussion to Paine's *Rights of Man*. In any case, soon after they departed, Fay acquired a copy of the controversial work and was so impressed by its republican arguments and its criticism of the British government that he wrote Jefferson and formally retracted the contrary sentiments he had expressed in their discussions at Bennington. Now a thorough convert, he hailed the revolutionary movements in France, Poland, and elsewhere in Europe, considered the United States with its republican system to be the most favored power on earth, and concluded by asking that he be given "early information of the Politicks of the day." Jefferson had already subscribed to Haswell's

[30] Hamilton's remarks on a New York Act acknowledging the independence of Vermont, 28 Mch. 1787 (Syrett, *Hamilton*, IV, 134).

Vermont Gazette and he had asked Fay to have the Quebec paper also sent to him on a regular basis. Fay promised that these would come free of charge.[31]

During their week-end stay in Bennington the Virginians joined Governor Robinson in attending services at the Congregational church, whose pastor was the Rev. Job Swift, graduate of Yale, disciple of Timothy Dwight, and, like him, so convinced of the infidelity of Jefferson that during his presidency he omitted the customary prayer for the chief executive. With Vermont having just been admitted to the union, its capital was the center of intense partisan contests and, with such controversial political visitors in the congregation, the pastor, a prudent man, probably confined himself to his usual doctrinal sermon.[32] Having lately been obliged to differ with Nathaniel Chipman and Lewis R. Morris, the Vermont commissioners who had assumed that admission of the state to the union was a matter to be negotiated as between sovereign states, Jefferson very likely had sought no communication with the two Federalists.[33] Given the state of partisan feelings in Vermont at the time, this is understandable. But all the evidence indicates that nowhere else on the entire journey did the travellers find themselves in such a congenial political climate or discuss public affairs so unreservedly as when they stopped at Bennington and conversed with such republicans as Moses Robinson, Anthony Haswell, and Joseph Fay. In old age Jefferson remembered that the road from Saratoga to Northampton was mostly desert, but it was that part of the route which had produced the most extended evidence of their political discussions along the way.[34]

As they crossed over into the rich Connecticut valley, whose abundant produce Jefferson had tried so hard to promote in France, the political climate changed and so did the record left by the travellers. On entering the prosperous, well-settled Connecticut valley, Jefferson brought his journal to an abrupt end. No record survives of what he may have thought of the region of the Shaysites, of the new college at Williamstown, of the embryonic manufactures at Springfield and Hartford, or of the progress of commerce at New Haven. Next to the last of his travel notes had been written just two days before reaching Bennington. From there on the only note he added was at Middletown where he observed an "Axis in peritrochio" such as he had seen in Holland.[35] Although the travellers spent two nights in Hartford, possibly because Madison's horse was disabled, there can be little doubt that Pierpont Edwards was right in saying that they shunned the gentry, meaning of course such leading political figures as Oliver Wolcott, Senators Ellsworth and Johnson, and Representatives Sherman, Trumbull, and Wadsworth. There had been little communion among them even at the seat of government and the total absence of any record of discussions with them as Jefferson and Madison travelled quickly and unobtrusively through the state was to be expected. Representative William Loughton Smith of South Carolina, one of Hamilton's supporters, was at this time also making a tour of Connecticut. He, like Beckwith, was welcomed at the home of Jeremiah Wadsworth. But such hospitality as Philip Schuyler had

[31] Fay to TJ, 9 Aug. and 20 Sep. 1791; TJ to Fay, 30 Aug. 1791.

[32] Isaac Jennings, *Memorials of a century. . . . The early history of Bennington, Vt. and its First Church* (Boston, 1869), p. 92-9. See note 24.

[33] See Editorial Note and documents on the admission of Vermont and Kentucky, at 4 Mch. 1791. Chipman resided at Tinmouth and Morris at Springfield.

[34] TJ to Ellen Wayles Coolidge, 27 Aug. 1825.

[35] See TJ's Notes of his tour through Holland in 1788 (Vol. 13: 9).

extended at Albany was evidently not offered to the Virginians or sought by them.

A few months earlier John Trumbull made a comment which helps to explain why this was so. "Maddison in his constant opposition to every plan of the Secretary of the Treasury," he had written to John Adams, "seems dwindled from the Great Politician we once supposed him, to the insignificant leader of an impotent Minority. No man ever more mistook his real Interest, or the line of policy he ought to have pursued. He has lost all his popularity in this quarter."[36] It did not diminish the Connecticut politicians' hostility to Madison when they saw him travelling in the company of the Secretary of State, whose republican principles and opinions on American foreign policy, on education, on religion, and on the separation of church and state had long been known to the public through his *Notes on Virginia*, thus making him perhaps even more an object of partisan animus than Madison. Some observers, then and later, attributed Madison's supposed defection from his principles to the influence exerted by Jefferson on this journey.[37] But Madison had been leading the opposition to Hamiltonian measures long before Jefferson left France, and what made the Connecticut Federalists increasingly hostile toward the two collaborators was the mounting evidence that they did not speak for an impotent minority.

III

One of the primary objects Jefferson had in mind in planning the trip was to undertake a systematic study of the Hessian fly and the means of preventing its ravages. This inquiry produced one of the longest records of the journey and resulted in frequent stops and many interviews with farmers and others along the way. Jefferson's investigation of the insect was prompted by his scientific curiosity and his concern for the country's agriculture. But it was also touched with political concerns, both in respect to the national economy and to his desire to offset the effect of actions taken by Great Britain.

His interest in the subject was of long standing. In 1788 American wheat production had been severely reduced by the insect which in the United States came to be called the Hessian fly. To prevent infection of British crops, the government issued an Order in Council on 25 June 1788 temporarily prohibiting importation of American wheat. At the same time it requested Sir Joseph Banks, President of the Royal Society, to study the problem. This action has been regarded as one born of hard necessity because of Britain's dependence on American grain, but which Jefferson "rather typically" viewed as the result of a deep-laid plot.[38] Actually, being less concerned about the British embargo than about the public spreading of "a groundless alarm in those Countries in Europe where [American grain was] constantly and kindly received," Jefferson believed it to be a hostile act grounded in ignorance.[39]

As he had pointed out in 1789, the Hessian fly never existed in the grain

---

[36] John Trumbull (1750-1831) to John Adams, 5 Feb. 1791 (MHi: AM).

[37] Albert J. Beveridge, *Life of John Marshall*, II (Boston, 1916), 79; Beveridge based his conclusion on what he called an excellent account of the journey and of Madison's "defection" in Sydney H. Gay's *James Madison* (Boston, 1895), p. 184-5.

[38] Charles R. Ritcheson, *Aftermath of Revolution* (Dallas, 1969), p. 200.

[39] TJ to Vaughan, 17 May 1789.

and could not therefore be imported in shipments of wheat. At that time he had never seen the insect and his assertion was based on what he had just learned from the report of a conversation between Sir Joseph Banks and Thomas Paine in which the latter had made the same point. When Banks replied that the action was taken against the weevil, not the Hessian fly, Paine challenged the government's action on the ground that the former insect had existed for decades in America wherever wheat was grown and yet no prohibition against importing it had resulted.[40] It was shortly thereafter that Banks made his report to the Privy Council, basing his observations in large part on information received from George Morgan, Jeremiah Wadsworth, Samuel L. Mitchill, and other Americans, including Paine.[41] During the British embargo the price of wheat in London rose to above 40 shillings a bushel, while American exporters were selling it in other parts of Europe at roughly a tenth of that amount.[42] Jefferson was joined by many American farmers and shippers in expressing hostility to an act of the British government which denied them access to the more profitable market. Just before leaving France, he added to his library a work on the subject by the distinguished French agriculturalist, Duhamel du Monceau: *Histoire d'un insect qui devore les grains de L'Angoumois; avec les moyens que l'on peut employer pour le detruire*. At the same time he bought Arthur Young's *Proceedings of His Majesty's most honourable Privy Council, and information received, respecting an insect supposed to infest wheat of the territories of the United States of America*.[43] The latter work embodied the results of Sir Joseph Banks' investigation. Both served to strengthen Jefferson's conviction that the British embargo, even though temporary, was not a friendly act.

Against this background, despite the bountiful wheat crop of 1790 – that of Pennsylvania was virtually undamaged – Jefferson proposed that the American Philosophical Society undertake a systematic study of the Hessian fly. As early as 1768 the Society had urged its Committee on Husbandry to "consider whether any Method can be fallen on for preventing the damage done to Wheat, by what is called the Fly," but nothing had resulted.[44] At a meeting of the Society shortly before embarking on the northern tour, Jefferson proposed that a select committee be appointed to collect materials on the natural history of the insect and the best means of combatting it. The committee, whose charge was considerably enlarged by the addition of the clause "and whatever else may be interesting to agriculture," consisted of Jefferson as chairman, Dr. Benjamin S. Barton, Dr. James Hutchinson, Charles Thomson, and Dr. Caspar Wistar.[45] Jefferson summoned a meeting of the committee on the 21st of April. No record of its proceedings has been found. But for discussion at the next meeting,

[40] Paine to TJ, 16 Feb. 1789.

[41] Banks to the Privy Council, 2 Mch. 1789 (BL: Jenkinson Papers, Add. MSS. 38,224; much of the material Banks gathered is to be found in a microfilm of his papers in PPAP).

[42] Ritcheson, *Aftermath of Revolution*, p. 201.

[43] TJ's copy of Duhamel du Monceau's work was the Paris edition of 1762 (Sowerby, No. 738). Young's *Proceedings* was issued at Bury St. Edmonds in 1789 (Sowerby, No. 739).

[44] MS Minutes, PPAP, incorrectly quoted in Society's *Proceedings*, XXII, pt. 3 (July, 1885), 14, 15, as referring to "the Hessian fly."

[45] Same, p. 14, 15, 19.

scheduled for the 13th of May, he particularly requested that Barton bring "his queries" – presumably such as had been proposed at the first meeting.[46] This request must have been prompted by his desire to make use of the questionnaire on the northern tour, on which he expected to embark two days later.

Jefferson's notes on the Hessian fly taken down during the journey suggest the nature of Barton's queries. What were its characteristics from egg to insect? When did it first appear? What damage had been suffered? Did it attack other grains than wheat? What means of prevention had been tried and with what success? And, reflecting Jefferson's political concerns, was it ever known to attack the grain or be transported with it? The first stage of the journey was by water from New York to Poughkeepsie, but Jefferson began his inquiries on the 21st of May, perhaps as they moored for the night at Conklin's tavern. Above Poughkeepsie he obtained from one Conrad Lasher some of his most reliable information. From then on throughout the journey, even after he had parted from Madison in New York, his inquiries about the Hessian fly were pressed upon farmers, blacksmiths, tavern keepers, and such dignitaries as Philip Schuyler, Moses Robinson, Joseph Fay, William Floyd, and Sylvester Dering, whom Jefferson valued as one who had been "particularly serious in his observations."[47] Whatever suspicions the Federalists might have entertained about the narrow partisan aims of the journey, there can be no question that this systematic investigation of the Hessian fly was one of the principal objects Jefferson had in view.

Nor can there be any doubt that his persistent questioning brought responses far beyond the answers that he recorded in his notes along the way. After returning home he received a number of communications from those with whom he had talked on the journey and from some who had only heard of his investigation. Among the authors of these volunteered comments were some who had furnished information to Sir Joseph Banks, such as George Morgan.[48] On this subject of general concern there was no trace of a partisan animus among those who tried to give assistance. Even such a stout Federalist as Jeremiah

[46] TJ to Thomson, 20 Apr. 1790; TJ to Barton and others, 12 May 1791.

[47] See TJ's notes on the Hessian fly (Document II).

[48] George Morgan (1743-1810) was a member of the American Philosophical Society who carried on an experimental farm at "Prospect" in Princeton. He was the author of several articles on the Hessian fly which appeared in the *American Museum* in 1787 and other periodicals. The first of his communications to come to TJ was a copy of his "Letter to a Gentleman Farmer of Virginia," dated 31 July 1788. The second was his letter of 26 Aug. 1788 to Sir John Temple, written at Temple's request in consequence of the Order in Council prohibiting importation of American wheat. While agreeing with the opinion of Lasher and others that well-manured soil and the bearded wheat were sound preventive measures, Morgan believed that the insect was brought in by the Hessians and claimed credit for himself and a friend for having named it the Hessian fly as expressive of their sentiments of the "two Animals" – a designation they had industriously spread in the hope of passing it down "with all possible Infamy as a useful National Prejudice." He added: "It is now become the most opprobrious Term our Language affords and the greatest affront our Chimney Sweepers and even our Slaves can give or receive, is to call or be called Hessian" (Tr of both documents in Morgan's hand, endorsed by John Vaughan as "For the Committee of the American Philosophical Society"; DLC: TJ Papers, 41: 7075-8, 42: 9197-9202). Vaughan presumably transmitted Morgan's two communications to TJ in person, for no covering letter has been found and none is recorded in SJL.

Wadsworth evidently lent his hand to the business, although probably indirectly. Shortly after Jefferson returned to Philadelphia he received a letter from Wadsworth which has not been found but which must have covered one on the subject from William Robinson. In 1776 Robinson had examined the insect in its various stages with "an excellent microscope" and was convinced it had always been present but some unknown natural phenomenon had caused it to multiply and spread, as was "the Case with the canker Worm, and thousands of other insects, which no body conceives to have been imported."[49] Another firm Federalist, Senator John Laurance of New York, asked Samuel L. Mitchill for his opinion. The resultant "Short Memoir on the Wheat-Insect," dated Long Island 23 June 1791, attributed the name to the country people, who were "ever fond of ascribing every thing disagreeable to the Germans." Mitchill thought it understandable that the British government had been apprehensive about the possibility of importing the insect with American grain. But when Lord Dorchester had raised the question concerning imports from New York and Vermont, he had assured him "that most certainly there was *no Danger*." Mitchill also asserted that no effective preventive measures had been discovered, attributed their recent decline to "their Spontaneous disappearance," and thought only two facts had been clearly established: that the soil should be well manured and the seed sowed as late in the autumn as possible.[50]

Jefferson did not acknowledge these letters, perhaps because – with the possible exception of that from Wadsworth – they had come to him indirectly. Although he devoted a great deal of time to the subject during the journey, he was aware that such an investigation would require much more time and effort than he had been able to give to it in his hurried travels. To assist the American Philosophical Society's effort – and no doubt to try to arouse the interest of his son-in-law – he urged that young Randolph devote himself to similar inquiries.[51] The contributions that Jefferson valued most and did acknowledge were those of Ezra L'Hommedieu, Jonathan Havens, and Sylvester Dering. In thanking them for their communications, he said he thought it probable the committee would continue its inquiries through another year.[52] Some months later the committee met at his request and adopted a resolution calling upon all persons having any information about the natural history of the insect "to communicate the same by letter addressed to Thomas Jefferson, Esq. Secretary of State to the United States." In order to make the appeal as broad as possible, the committee compiled a series of queries to elicit the kind of information desired. The resolution and questionnaire were released to the press with the suggestion that "The republication of these Queries throughout the United States may essentially promote the interest of agriculture."[53] The response was minimal, with one Pennsylvanian addressing his answers to Cas-

[49] Robinson to Wadsworth, 29 June 1791 (RC in DLC: TJ Papers, 65: 11213; endorsed by TJ: "Hessian fly").

[50] MS in Mitchill's hand, DLC: TJ Papers, 65: 11198-9. Mitchill's Memoir was enclosed in his letter to John Vaughan, 23 June 1792 (DLC: endorsed by Vaughan and by TJ).

[51] TJ to Randolph, 1 May 1791.

[52] L'Hommedieu to TJ, 10 Sep. 1791; Havens and Sylvester to TJ, 1 Nov. 1791. See TJ's responses of 22 Dec. 1791.

[53] See the committee's announcement and questionnaire under 7 June 1792, printed in Freneau's *National Gazette* for 14 June 1792 and other papers.

par Wistar and evidently asking that his name be withheld.[54] Evidences of the reappearance of partisan feelings in this hard-fought election year may be found even in journals which published the committee's appeal and in the responses addressed not to the Secretary of State but to the Secretary of the American Philosophical Society – an institution already earning for itself the reputation of being unduly republican in spirit.

Perhaps because of the approaching "evanishment" of the Hessian fly and because of the chairman's increasingly arduous official duties, the committee never submitted a report. The archives of the Society do not contain even a copy of the questionnaire or any record of the committee's proceedings. All of the materials gathered under its auspices remained in the files of the chairman who had negotiated the investigation. But the episode, marked by Jefferson's insistent inquiries on a long and arduous journey, stands as another of many examples illustrating his conviction of the fundamentally important relationship between scientific inquiry and the principal objects of government.

IV

Jefferson's chief object on the last stage of the journey, so he informed the members of the Society's committee, was to continue his inquiries about the Hessian fly. He therefore proposed to travel from Connecticut through "the whole of Long Island, where this animal [had] raged much."[55] He did in fact pursue his investigations there.

But then another and more compelling attraction appeared which had nothing at all to do with politics or the natural history of an insect. On the 12th of June, after an all-night crossing of the sound, Jefferson and Madison landed at Oysterpond Point on Gardiner's Bay. That day and the next they proceeded across the island to the south shore and on the 13th lodged at Downs' tavern seven miles from the seat of General William Floyd. On the 14th they departed early, arriving at Mastic in time to breakfast with their old friend. Doubtless they would have pushed on after a brief visit with Floyd, for Jefferson was pressed to return to Philadelphia. But while there he learned that nearby, at the small settlement of Pusspátuck, there was a remnant of an Algonkian tribe, the Unquachog Indians. The result was that Jefferson and Madison spent most of the day with Floyd, who conducted his guests to the settlement. There, perhaps before they returned to dine with him in the afternoon, Jefferson recorded what two aged women of the tribe and a young girl gave him as the Unquachog equivalent of some two hundred English words.

That this was an unplanned, impromptu performance is proved by the character of the document on which Jefferson set down the vocabulary. If he had anticipated such an opportunity before leaving Philadelphia, he doubtless would have prepared in advance a list of English words of common usage similar to those containing a somewhat larger number he employed on other occasions for use by friends and government officials in recording other dialects. Without one of these more systematic forms at hand, he was obliged to record the Unquachog vocabulary on the blank space of the cover of a letter addressed to

[54] Undated letter from Chester county, Pennsylvania, to "Dear Caspar" (RC in DLC: TJ Papers, 80: 13,926; endorsed by TJ as "Anon"; given in summary in note to the committee's questionnaire, 7 June 1792).

[55] TJ to Barton and others of the committee, 12 May 1791.

himself, perhaps that of an invitation he had received along the route of his travels. The arrangement of the words followed in general his accustomed categories, but with variations which suggest a compilation drawn from memory rather than one executed in advance.[56] Affairs of state awaited him in Philadelphia, but these could be postponed at least for a few hours in the face of such an exigent appeal to deep-rooted intellectual interests.

For the fact is that the history and languages of the American aborigines had engaged Jefferson's interest from early youth and would remain with him throughout life. Even as a youngster he had excavated an Indian burial mound, employing the stratigraphic method which he conceived far in advance of its time. He had also formed an opinion early in life which he never surrendered – that knowledge of the aboriginal languages would be the most certain evidence of the Indians' origins which could be produced. He thought it lamentable that so many tribes had become extinct "without our having previously collected and deposited in the records of literature, the general rudiments at least of the languages they spoke." The most ardent collector and advocate of the preservation of historical records of his time, Jefferson suggested that if vocabularies of all the languages spoken by the native Americans were "deposited in all the public libraries, it would furnish opportunities to those skilled in the languages of the old world to compare them . . . and hence to construct the best evidence of the derivation of this part of the human race." He had already convinced himself that the radical differences in language among the Indians was in the order of twenty to one as compared with those of Asia. On the basis of this supposition, which he accepted as fact, he concluded that their origin was of greater antiquity than that of the Asiatics.[57]

Because he so deeply regretted the disappearance of many tribes and with them their languages, Jefferson had long since urged such informed persons as Benjamin Hawkins and Thomas Hutchins to record Indian vocabularies.[58] "This," he had assured Hawkins, "is an object I mean to pursue, as I am persuaded that the only method of investigating the filiation of the Indian nations is by that of their languages."[59] The presence of the dwindling tribe at the Pusspátuck settlement along the route of their travels gave Jefferson the chance to do what he had so long been asking others to help him accomplish. It is almost certain that this was not only the first Indian dialect that he personally recorded but also the only one.[60] The Unquachog vocabulary has

[56] See Document VII.

[57] *Notes*, ed. Peden, p. 97-102. See TJ to Ezra Stiles, 1 Sep. 1786, in which he repeats the argument that Asiatics were descended from American Indians, basing this on "the single Fact" of the greater diversity of radical languages among the latter.

[58] TJ to Hawkins, 28 Dec. 1783; TJ to Hutchins, 29 Dec. 1783. Both letters are missing, but entries in SJL reveal their subject. So, too, does Hawkins' response in which he promised that the vocabularies would be confined to "the most common objects in nature" (Hawkins to TJ, 14 June 1786).

[59] TJ to Hawkins, 4 Aug. 1787. TJ reiterated this conviction many times; see, for example, TJ to John S. Vater, 11 May 1811.

[60] A second Algonkian vocabulary has been erroneously attributed to him; see Franklin Edgerton, "Note on Early American Work in Linguistics" (APS, *Procs.*, LXXXVII [1944], 25-34). The error resulted from a notation made by Du Ponceau, who in transcribing a collection of Indian vocabularies in 1820 included one which he designated as "Vocabulary of the Delawares of New Jersey" and described as recorded "Decemb. 1792. Mr. Thos. Jefferson" (Du Ponceau's MS "Indian Vocabularies," p. 42-5; PPAP).

not been published heretofore, although Albert Gallatin made use of some of its words in his remarkable compilation and comparative study of aboriginal languages, *A synopsis of the Indian tribes . . . in North America.*[61]

From the time he first discussed Indian linguistics in *Notes on Virginia* Jefferson pursued his quest at every opportunity. He also became more and more anxious to insure preservation of the materials he had gathered. By 1800 his concern was such as to prompt him to take action for their safety. "I have now made up a large collection," he wrote Benjamin Hawkins in 1800, "and afraid to risk it any longer, lest by some accident it might be lost, I am about to print it. . . . I propose this summer to arrange my vocabularies for the press, and I wish to place every tongue in the column adjacent to it's kindred tongues."[62] He made some progress on the task despite the turbulent political activities of that election year, but the responsibilities of the presidency interrupted his effort. By 1806, however, he thought he had made such progress that within a year or two he would be able to publish the result.[63] But in the last year of his presidency the crises in public affairs were so pressing as to prevent his completion of what would have been the first American compilation for a comparative study of Indian languages. His collection, then numbering about fifty vocabularies, had been augmented by those brought back by Lewis and Clark. These he had not been able to add to his parallel-column digest and so he decided to put off the task until after he had returned to Monticello.

Under the circumstances this was no doubt unavoidable, but his long labors were chiefly in vain because of what he correctly termed an irreparable misfortune. As he left the presidency he caused the entire collection, including both his digest and the original vocabularies, to be packed in a box of stationery and shipped by water with about thirty other parcels of his personal belongings. This single package, containing irreplaceable manuscripts he had gathered over the past thirty years, attracted the attention of the boatmen, perhaps because of its weight and presumed valuable contents. These were indeed precious but not to those who may have been looking for liquor or silver. Out of ignorance and disappointment, as vandals had done with irreplaceable records over the centuries, the culprits threw the contents into the river. Some leaves and fragments of the vocabularies floated ashore and were later found in the mud. In his initial reaction to the tragic loss, Jefferson thought these were so few and so defaced that no general use could be made of them.[64] But some years later he presented all that had survived to the American Philosophical Society, where

[61] AAS, *Trans. and Colls.*, II (Cambridge, 1836), 35-6, 42.

[62] TJ to Hawkins, 14 Mch. 1800. Fourteen years earlier he had told Hawkins he would take care to dispose of his collection so that "it shall not be lost" (same to same, 13 Aug. 1786).

[63] TJ to Harris, 18 Apr. 1806.

[64] TJ to Barton, 21 Sep. 1809. Barton had asked TJ to assist him in preparing a revised edition of his *New views of the origin of the tribes and nations of America* (Philadelphia, 1797), which he had dedicated to TJ and in which he took issue with TJ's theory that the American aborigines were of greater antiquity than the peoples of Asia. Barton asked not for TJ's complete vocabularies but only for a "good selection of about ten or twelve words from each of them" (Barton to TJ, 14 Sep. 1809). The part of the collection saved was greater than TJ indicated. He lent a fragment of the Pawnee vocabulary compiled by Meriwether Lewis because Barton had said that he had not a word of that language. TJ asked that this be returned. Obviously, as this and his subsequent action proved, he properly valued the remnant that had been salvaged.

over the years Du Ponceau, Gallatin, and other scholars were able to make use of them.[65] Among the surviving documents was Jefferson's sixty-page digest, mutilated and mud-stained, which he had been unable to complete during the political turmoils of his final year in the presidency.[66]

The vocabulary of the Unquachogs also survived, but it showed no evidence of having been stained by water or mud. Perhaps this was because it had been kept among the notes of the Hessian fly and other records of the northern tour. Appropriately enough, it owed its existence to the earlier accident which had brought Jefferson and the three Unquachog women together. Even at that time their failure to produce equivalents for *cow, horse, sheep,* and other words of common usage indicated that their grasp of the native tongue had weakened. Jefferson was told that the dialects of the Shinicocks and Montauks on the eastern part of Long Island were said to be so different from that of the Unquachogs that the people of these Algonkian tribes could scarcely understand one another.[67] He perhaps regretted that he was unable to compile vocabularies for all three, but he did set down the sole surviving record of the dialect of the Unquachogs, doing so almost at the moment of its extinction. This was the one enduring achievement of the famous excursion.

And it does after all have one slight tinge of those political connections which have been seen by contemporary and subsequent commentators as evidence of hidden motives on the part of Jefferson and Madison. The detached cover on which the Unquachog vocabulary is recorded bears this address: "The Honble. Thomas Jefferson Esqr." The handwriting is that of Chancellor Livingston. The letter it covered has evidently not been preserved, but one may surmise that it was an invitation perhaps to dine with Burr on May 20th when the two travellers were preparing to depart northward. Jefferson's hiring a coach on that day would seem to support such a conjecture. If so, this would indicate that the initiative, whether for purposes of political discussion or merely for hospitality, was taken by the Chancellor, not by the Virginians. In either case the incident was of little moment.

But health, recreation, and curiosity about all aspects of the country through which Madison and Jefferson travelled, including especially the state of politics and partisan attitudes, were objects that had been successfully achieved in a journey which has been inaccurately described as a leisurely one.[68] The severe

[65] TJ to Du Ponceau, 17 Nov. and 30 Dec. 1817. For some treatments of TJ's study of Indian languages, see Clark Wissler, "The American Indian and the American Philosophical Society," APS, *Procs.*, LXXXV (1942), 189-204; Albert C. Baugh, "Thomas Jefferson, linguistic liberal," in *Studies for William A. Read*, N. M. Caffee and T. A. Kirby, eds. (Louisiana, 1940), p. 88-108; Mabel Morris, "Jefferson and the languages of the American Indians," *Modern Language Quarterly*, VI (1945), 31-4. See also, H. C. Montgomery, "Thomas Jefferson as a philologist," *Am. Jour. Philology*, LXV (Oct. 1944), 367-71.

[66] See illustration of one of the relatively undamaged pages showing TJ's method of compiling the parallel-column digest.

[67] Gallatin referred to TJ's comment about the linguistic differences of the Unquachogs, Shinicocks, and Montauks, but expressed the opinion that their languages seemed to differ more from those of New England than from each other (AAS, *Trans. and Colls.*, II [Cambridge, 1836], 42).

[68] TJ travelled in all 920 miles in 33 days. Considering the fact that he and Madison tarried two days in New York going and coming, one day each at Albany, Bennington,

headache which Jefferson had experienced during the winter and spring vanished with the escape from official drudgery. The political leaders with whom the travellers had had frank and extended conversations in Vermont gave them reason for more optimism than anything they encountered elsewhere. The chilly political climate of Connecticut they no doubt expected, and while Madison was disappointed for reasons of health in not being able to carry out his plan to visit Massachusetts, John Beckley had been feeling the political pulse of the people there and was able to give encouraging reports.[69] No partisan alliances had been effected in New York, but the most important political effort of the trip was one which Troup, Trumbull, and other Hamilton supporters failed to mention. This was the hope Jefferson and Madison entertained that they would succeed in persuading Philip Freneau to establish an opposition newspaper at the seat of government that would be national in scope. The breakfast at which Jefferson met Madison's Princeton classmate for the first time was perhaps decisive in giving reality to this hope.[70] With the opening of the Second Congress Freneau's *National Gazette* was inaugurated, giving the Federalists more to be concerned about than any alliance they supposed had been arranged between the Virginians and the New York republicans.

---

and Hartford, and spent a day and a half making little progress on Lake Champlain, this meant that the average day's travel was well over 30 miles, some of it over very rough terrain. The time consumed along the way in making inquiries about the Hessian fly, in inspecting the thriving port of Hudson, in touring the battlefields, in making the Unquachog vocabulary, and in purchasing shrubs at Prince's nursery in Flushing make the distance travelled all the more impressive.

[69] Beckley reported that John Adams' popularity in Boston had declined and that the articles of *Publicola* appeared to be "as generally obnoxious in New England as . . . in Pennsylvania" (Madison to TJ, 13 July 1791).

[70] See Freneau to TJ, 4 Aug. 1791, in which he refers to his discussion in New York with TJ and Madison about establishing the paper.

I. Jefferson's Journal of the Tour

1791.[1]   [21 May-10 June 1791]

May 22. Conklin's in the highlands. Found here the Thuya Occidentalis, called White cedar and Silverfir, called hemlock. [The former with an imbricated leaf, the latter with single pinnated leaves. Also the Candleberry myrtle.

23. Poughkeepsie. The White pine [5. leaved] Pitch-pine [3. leaved] Juniper [a shrub with decumbent stems about 8 f. long, with single leaves all round the stem, and berries used for infusing gin.]

24. Claverac. Azalea. [wild honeysuckle rose-coloured, on stems 4. f. high loaded richly with large flowers of a strong, pink fragrance. They say it bears an apple eateable]

27. Hudson. A manufacture of Duck beginning. 1000. barrels of salted herring exported annually. A distillery from which 1000 hhds of rum are annually exported.

Waterford. Saw nails made by cutting them with a pair of shears from the end of a bar of iron, the thickness of which corresponded with the thickness of the nail, and it's breadth with the length. We saw 120. cut off in a minute, and 24. headed in a minute, which would amount to 20. a minute cut off and headed. But they make habitually about 4000. a day. The iron formed into bars costs about 50 per cent more than nail rod. The sheers cost 9. dollars. The bit is sometimes welded to the sheers, sometimes fixed on with screws so as to be taken off to be ground. They are made at Lebanon in N. York. The lever vice for heading is very simple.

Cohoes. Sugar maple.

28. Still water. Polypod.

Saratoga. Ground oak.

Fort Edward. The small red squirrel.

29. Lake George. Honeysuckle [Lonicera] wild cherry with single fruit, the black gooseberry, Velvet Aspen, cotton Willow, paper birch or white birch, bass-wood wild rose, Spruce pine with single leaves all round the stem 1/3 I. long, with abundance of sugar maple pitch pine, white pine, silver fir, thuya, red cedar. The Thuya is much covered with a species of long moss of a foot long generally, but sometimes 4.f. Strawberries now in blossom and young fruit.

This lake is formed by a contour of mountains into a bason 36. miles long and from 1. to 4. miles wide, the hill sides shelving down to the water edge and only here and there leaving small intervals of low land, tolerably good.[2] Now and then are precipices of rock forming the bank of the lake, as well as hanging over it in immence heights. One of these is famous &c.[3] [famed by the name of Rogers's rock, the celebrated partisan officer of that name having escaped the pursuit of Indns. by sliding down it when covered with snow, and escaping across the lake then frozen over. The neighborhood of this lake is healthy but there are few inhabitants on it.] It's waters very clear, except just at the North end, abounding with salmon-trout of 7.lb.

weight, speckled or red trout, Oswego bass of 6. or 7.lb. weight, rock bass, yellow perch. There are sea-gulls in abundance, loons and some wild-ducks. Rattle snakes abound on it's borders. Two which we killed were of a sutty dark colour, obscurely checkered. It is infested[4] with swarms of musketoes and gnats, and 2 kinds of biting fleas. It is pretty much interspersed with small islands. It closes with ice about the last of December and opens from the 15th. to the 20th. of April. The difference between the height of it's water in spring and fall is about 2. feet. There is no lime stone immediately on the lake but abundance in the neighborhood on the East side.

31. Lake Champlain is a much larger but less pleasant water than L. George. It is about 110 miles long and from one to 15. miles broad. It is narrow and turbid from Ticonderoga to beyond the Split rock about 30. miles, where it is said to widen and grow more clear. It yields cat fish of 20 lb. weight, sturgeon, and salmon, also the fish found in L. George except the trout but in smaller quantities, and it is less infested with muske-toes and insects. The Eastern bank is of limestone laminated like slate, on the Western side is none, and it is remarkeable that to the Westward of this and L. George, the people are obliged to come to them from great distances for their limestone. The Western end is closed by high mountains of very indifferent lands, on the East side the lands are champaign, the Green mountains rising out of them at the distance of 20 or 25. miles and running parallel with the lake as far as the sight extends. These lands may be called good, and begin to be thickly seated. The growth on both sides the lake much the same as on lake George, to which add the yellow or 2. leaved pine, and the thistle in much abundance as to embarrass agriculture in a high degree. This lake is conjectured to be about 100 f. lower than L. George; the difference of it's level in spring and fall is about 3. f. It closes with ice about the last of November, and opens a few days before lake George. It is to be noted that we have seen no poplar, dogwood, nor redbud since we have passed the high-lands, nor any fruit trees but apples and here and there

a cherry tree. We have seen no persimmons in any place since crossing the Hudson.

June 2. From L. George to Sandy hill[5] the first three or 4. miles are over high hills which would seem avoidable by following a valley on the Eastern side. The hills are sandy and poor. The residue of the road is along a high plain of sand, limestone and round pebble crossed by 2 or 3. creeks which seem sufficiently copious and elevated to admit a canal of navigation to L. George on the North and the Hudson on the South, 8 miles distant in that part. The plains are pine barrens. We pass Wing's falls and Sandy hill falls of about 35 or 40. f. each on a bed of limestone in horizontal strata.

3. From Sandy hill to Fort Edward and McNeal's ferry 14. miles along the river side: some good lowlands, the highlands indifferent.

Middletown. Axis in peritrochio for drawing water. The wheel 6. f. diameter has the rope wound round it with the bucket, the axis 8. I. diameter has a weight appended sufficient to balance the bucket on the wheel when full of water. This weight descends to the ground outside of the well when the bucket is drawn up, and when you send down the bucket you wind up the weight.

MS (DLC: TJ Papers, 69: 11910); written in TJ's minuscule hand on a single leaf, with all but final six lines on recto; brackets in MS, the first not closed. Later, on the almost blank verso, TJ made additions to his notes on the Hessian fly, this part being confined to his observations in New Jersey on his return (see Document II, note 3).

[1] The initial entry, which TJ deleted, read: "May 21. Toppan sea. Upper end."

[2] At this point TJ wrote and then deleted: "Very few inhabitants around the lake."

[3] The passage enclosed was entered several lines below following the phrase ". . . interspersed with small islands." It has been placed here as a continuation of the incomplete allusion, as TJ obviously intended.

[4] TJ first wrote and then deleted the words "in the highest degree."

[5] These two words interlined in substitution for "Fort Edward," deleted.

II. Jefferson's Notes on the Hessian Fly

[24 May-18 June 1791]

Conrad Lasher. 16. miles above Poughkeepsie. The Hessian fly remains on the ground among the stubble of the old wheat. At ploughing time for sowing the new crop they rise in swarms before the plough horses. Soon after the wheat comes up they lay the egg in it, of the size of a nit, and will crack like it. He supposes the old fly dies in the winter. In the spring they begin to grow. [I saw them just below the highlands on the 21st. of May in the worm state, about as long as a grain of rye, and one third it's volume.[1] White, smooth and transparent.] In June the Chrysalis bursts and the insect comes out, brown like a flax seed, a little longer, and with wings. The egg is found from the joint nearest the ground. He has counted 120. on one stalk, always under cover of the blade. The stem decays in that part, turns yellow, the blades become erect,[2] and the plant dies. The farmers have found a remedy in what they call the new sort of wheat which is a white bearded wheat equal in quantity and quality to any kind they ever tended. It has a more vigorous stalk. He tried by highly dunging a piece of ground to give the old kind of wheat vigour enough to resist. For a while it promised fair, but the insect got the better at length and he made no more from that than any other. They are never in the grain or chaff. He thinks the fly does not generally remain in the straw when carried to the stack. Yet in one instance on threshing a stack in the spring, there were some found in the straw. He thinks they had no wings and consequently thinks they were dead. They have two wings naturally. The fly harms nothing.

The crop of the growth of 1785 was the first attacked. However that year they made a good deal. In 86. they destroyed all. So also in 87. and 88. These were the three years of it's principal rage. In 1789. his crop was of the new wheat. In 90. he had no insect, nor is there any this year 91. His neighbor who continues the old wheat had some flies in 89. but not so as to injure his crop. He never saw an instance of it in the new wheat but it has attacked rye a little. But never any thing else that he knows of.

Pulvar. 23. miles above Lashar's. The fly came first in 1787. into this neighborhood and destroyed the crops of 87. 88. 89. The people got the new sort of wheat which had a stronger stalk. Some tended that and the old kind at the same time. The old would be all destroyed and the new a little touched. Generally from 5. to 20 worms to a stem. The spring wheat more totally destroyed than the fall wheat. It attacked rye a little, oats a very little. There were a very few flies in 90. None this year 91. There would seem to be the best prospect possible of a good crop and then the moment it was getting into the ear it would all fall. The old kind of wheat is now rid of them. The worm is at first white, then becomes brown and a little bigger than a flea, then it bursts it's case and comes out a fly with two wings about the beginning of June.

Kenderhook. Shethar. A field of rye which he sowed in the spring for pasture was totally destroyed. In 1788 was the first mischief he had done. Not certain if any fly appeared the year before. They prevailed little here when at the worst. He thinks that they never destroyed above one tenth taking the neighborhood in general. All gone now.

Moore. 8 miles from Albany. The fly was first seen in 1787. A few only. 1788 they did the most mischeif. In 1789 less. In 1790 they were only in two or three places and very few. None this year. Some persons insist on having found the fly in their stacks in the spring when they went to threshing. Others suppose them mistaken, and that it was some other fly. [This proves that but a few at any rate survived winter.]

Albany. Genl. Schuyler. There might perhaps be some few in this neighborhood in 87. but in 88. about 1/10 of the wheat of the neighborhood was destroyed. In 89 much less. Perhaps none in 90. This year certainly none.

Waterford. Gregory. First appeared in 88. Then the most mischief. In 89. very few. None since

Benjamin. 11. miles above Waterford. Same exactly as Waterford.

Still-water. Dr. Willard. 15. miles above Waterford. The principal mischief was done in 1788. He has heard that a few were seen in 1787. There was very little injury in 89. None since.

Saratoga. Mr. Schuyler. He understood a few were seen in 87. In 88. they injured the Spring barley and nothing else. In 89. they did the same as to Spring barley but in a still less degree. None since.

F[ort] Edward. The fly was known here in 88. and 89. but not enough to do perceptible damage.

Sandy hill. 2 miles above. do.

F[ort] George. Never here at all.

Cambridge. Had a few in 1789. 90. Have heard of some this year, but never did any sensible injury. They showed themselves rather more in Spring grain. Colvin.

Bennington. Had a few in 89. 90. Have not heard if there are any this year. Never did any injury. Dewey. Fay. Robertson.

Pitsfeild and Dalton. In 88 first known but not to do mischief. In 89. about one third of the wheat in the neighborhood destroyed. In 90. a few but no harm. This year have not heard of any.

Northampton. In 88. first known but did no harm. In 89 rather more, but not sensibly injurious. In 90 still a few. This year none.

W. Springfeild. Some were seen in 87 but did no injury, yet it spread such an alarm that few people sowed wheat. They substituted rye in their grounds. The few who sowed wheat however had as good as ever in 88. Then in 89 every body sowed again and no harm done. Some say there are a few this year.

[Ju]ne 10. Sidon hill near Middletown. They appeared here first in 84. and did extreme mischief that year and 85. and 86. that the informant left off sowing wheat in 87. 8. 9. In 90 he had a good crop of the sowing of 89 and no fly. This year he knows of no fly.

Stranton's 5 miles from Guildford. They appeared here first in 1786. but did not very much injury that year. But every year since they have destroyed 1/3 or 1/2 and are as many this year as ever. They got the new kind of bearded wheat last year and this year a small quantity. They have not injured that more than rye. They have sometimes touched the rye a little. Have not meddled with oats.

[G]uilford. They came here about 86. and have done much mischief in the old wheat.

Oyster pond point. They came here about 86. Have done much mischief ever since. The yellow bearded wheat has been introduced. That is strong and attacked about as much as rye is. If that wheat gets the start they cannot hurt it. Has heard of none this year. Rufus Tupple.

Southold. 15 miles from Oyster pond point. Mrs. L'hommedieu's. The fly came here in 85. and destroyed the crops of that year, 86. and 87. Then they got the yellow bearded wheat which resisted them in a great degree but not entirely. But they got a piebald wheat from Goshen which they never touched and it is a fine white wheat. Besides this the farmers finding that the fly destroyed all weakly wheat got into the practice of manuring highly which contributed very much to prevent the ravages of the fly by making the wheat too vigorous for them: so that by the improvement of manure the country really has been benefited. In 88. 89. 90. no mischief done worth speaking of but in the old lands and old kinds of wheat. In these there are some this year.

The fly lays a maggot (not an egg) in the young wheat near the root. This becomes in the winter and spring a cocoon. Resembles flax seed and eats itself out of it's coat in May or June and comes out a fly. This fly appeared first in Flatbush near where the Hessians landed and the year after they landed, and they have travelled about 20 miles a year, more or less according to the winds.

The yellow bearded wheat was foreign wheat taken by the British (not known from whom) a bushel of which was sowed by a miller accidentally.

The fly cannot go Westwardly because repelled by the Westwardly winds.

Colo. Dearing of Shelter Isld. has been particularly serious in his observations on this fly.

Riverhead. Griffin. Fly was never at this place, nor for 4 or 5 miles all around it. Beyond that distance in every direction a plenty. The reason unassignable. This is 18. miles from Southold.

Morichie's. Downs's. Came into this neighborhood in 85. He had a very few that year, but not to do sensible injury. Has had none since. This neighborhood for some miles never affected by it. Cannot account for it.

Genl. Floyd. He observed that the fly travelled from West to East about 20 miles a year, but he went a journey N.E. and found they travelled much more in that direction because it was going before the wind, for at the season of their being able to fly the S.W. winds prevail. This is the reason they go slowly to the Westward.

Terry's. 22 miles from Genl. Floyd's. The fly came here in 85. and destroyed some fields of wheat entirely. However they have never prevailed on the S. side of the island near as much as on the N. side. They have for many years sowed the bearded wheat. No fly this year.

Hamstead. A few here this year.

Flushing. Prince. This insect first appeared at this place. The Hessians were stationed here in 76. and in 77: the insect appeared. It was very slow indeed in it's first extensions, not getting beyond the limits of this neighborhood for some years. He confirms the account of the origin of the yellow bearded wheat given by L'hommedieu. It was first sown by a miller in this neighborhood.[3]

Richmond. They came here a year or two after the war. They destroyed 3 crops. He (Turner) thought that their general period every where was of 3 years. The bearded wheat not hurt by them.

South Amboy. They came here about 2 years after the war. Have made general destruction ever since among the old wheat, but not the bearded. This is a sandy country and but little wheat raised.

A smith's shop 6 miles from S. Amboy. They came here in 83. or 84. and have destroyed 7 crops of the old kind of wheat. There have been fewer for 3 years past tho there are still some. He saw this year a feild sown part with the old wheat, part the bearded.

You might trace the very furrow where they changed. The old destroyed, the bearded not hurt.

Williamson. 14. miles from S. Amboy. The last good crop of wheat he has had was the summer after the peace. The year following all was destroyed, and so afterwards every year in a greater or less degree. They fluctuate, prevailing less some years, more the next. Last year for instance, they did little injury here. This year they will destroy two thirds. The bearded wheat is attacked, but less than the other. If wheat be sown early in the fall they will destroy it in the fall. It is better therefore sown late. About a month ago he saw some of the insects in the green chrysalis, others in the brown and the empty chrysalis of others, the fly having eaten itself out. It is when the chrysalis has turned brown that it resembles flax seed.

I found here some of the cocoons full and some empty. They were all of the size and color of flax seed.

Allentown. 14 miles from Burlington. This the 5th. harvest attacked here. 2/3 will be lost this year, to wit all the old kind of wheat and a little of the bearded. Last year the loss was still greater. The bearded wheat produces less, is more difficult to cut and thresh, and the chaff is useless.

MS (DLC: TJ Papers, 69: 11907-9); the first part of the notes was written by TJ in four columns on recto and verso of a folded address cover, postmarked and addressed "Hble Thos. Jeff[e]rson Philadelphia" in hand which appears to be that of Barbier Demarais, whose letter of 7 May 1791 was received by TJ on the day he departed from Philadelphia. The second part, from 17 to 19 June, was added to the verso of TJ's Journal of the Tour (see note 3 below and note to Document I). Brackets for first and second passages in MS.

One document on TJ's investigation of the Hessian fly is an undated anatomical description of the insect which has hitherto been assigned to 1791 but which was almost certainly written in June 1792. This consists of a single leaf and has the following at the top of its verso (DLC: TJ Papers, 69: 11909):

June 1. Mr. Williams brought several stalks with the Chrysalis of the Hessian fly in them, most were of the flax seed colour, one only was pale green.

    5. a fly found hatched in the morning. qu: how long[?] at 9. aclock laid eggs.
14. 3. do. hatched.
15. 1. do.

From this it is clear that TJ was conducting an experiment over a period of two weeks and that this could not have occurred while he and Madison were on their journey. On 1 June 1791 they were at the head of Lake George where the fly had not been seen in two years. The "Mr. Williams" who brought TJ the wheat stalks was probably Jonathan Williams, who in the spring of 1792 was in Philadelphia and who attended meetings of the American Philosophical Society when TJ was present. At that time the Committee of the Society of which he was chairman drew up and published its series of queries calling upon all persons having information about the natural history of the insect to communicate the same to TJ. TJ's anatomical description of the fly must therefore have been written at that time. It is given as a note to the Committee's questionnaire, which is dated 7 June 1792 (see note to that document; also TJ to Thomson, 20 Apr. 1791).

[1] TJ first wrote ". . . grain of wheat and half as thick" and then altered the passage to read as above.

[2] TJ first wrote ". . . the blades stand straight up" and then altered the passage to read as above.

[3] At this point TJ wrote "Contd." The continuation of his notes on the Hessian fly, consisting of all that follows, was written on the verso of his Journal (see note to Document I).

III. Thomas Jefferson to Henry Remsen, Jr.

DEAR SIR   Saratoga May 28. 1791.

I recieved at New York and Albany the letters and papers you were so kind as to forward thither. I am so far on my journey, and am now able to calculate with some probability my future course and progress. I shall go Northwardly still three days and then tack about, go to Bennington to Connecticut river, then down that and thro Long island to N. Y. and Philadelphia. I expect to be at Bennington the 5th. of June, at Hartford the 10th. and at N. York the 18th. and shall be glad to recieve at those places my letters, and Fenno's newspapers. Inconveniently situated for writing I can only add assurances of the esteem with which I am Dear Sir Your obedt. humble servt,

                                          TH: JEFFERSON

RC (MdHi); addressed: "Mr. Henry Remsen Philadelphia Market street No. 270"; franked; postmarked: "ALBANY" and "1 IV [JUNE]"; endorsed by Remsen as received 7 June 1791. Not recorded in SJL.

So far as the entries in SJL indicate, TJ did not receive any letters in New York

when he arrived on the 19th. The only letter recorded as received at Albany, which he reached on the morning of the 26th, is Washington's brief note of 8 May 1791. The papers that he mentions no doubt included Fenno's *Gazette of the United States* which he particularly asked to have forwarded.

IV. Thomas Jefferson to Mary Jefferson

MY DEAR MARIA   Lake George May 30. 91.

I did not expect to write to you again till my return to Philada., but as I think always of you, so I avail myself of every moment to tell you so which a life of business will permit. Such a moment is now offered while passing this lake[1] and it's border, on which we have just landed, has furnished the means which the want of paper would otherwise have denied me. I write to you on the bark of the

Paper birch, supposed to be the same used by the antients to write on before the art of making paper was invented, and which being called the Papyrus, gave the name of paper to the new invented substitute. I write to you merely to tell you that I am well, and to repeat what I have so often before repeated that I love you dearly, am always thinking of you and place much of the happiness of my life in seeing you improved in knowlege, learned in all the domestic arts, useful to your friends and good to all. To see you in short place your felicity in acquiring the love of those among whom you live, and without which no body can ever be happy. Go on then my dear Maria in your reading, in attention to your music, in learning to manage the kitchen, the dairy, the garden, and other appendages of the houshold, in suffering nothing to ruffle your temper or interrupt that good humor which it is so easy and so important to render habitual, and be assured that your progress in these things are objects of constant prayer with your's affectionately.

Dft (MHi); written on paper, with numerous interlineations and deletions. The RC, written on birch bark, has not been found.

TJ's remark that he would have been denied the opportunity to write Mary if birch bark had not been available needs qualification. That paper was scarce and that he carried little with him is proved by the scraps on which he recorded his travel notes, his comments on the Hessian fly, and his vocabulary of the Unquachogs. But while all three of his letters to Mary, Martha, and his son-in-law were written on bark, drafts of each of these were first written on paper, as were the letters to Washington and Remsen. He did not usually prepare drafts of his letters to his children, but in this case he evidently wished to have the texts in final form before copying them on bark.

[1] At this point TJ wrote the following and then deleted it: "which I desire you to take your map and look for." The deletion was obviously made because TJ remembered he had already made the suggestion (see TJ to Mary Jefferson, 8 May 1791).

V. Thomas Jefferson to Martha Jefferson Randolph

MY DEAR MARTHA   Lake Champlain May. 31

I wrote to Maria yesterday, while sailing on Lake George, and the same kind of leisure is afforded me today to write to you. Lake George is without comparison the most beautiful water I ever saw: formed by a contour of mountains into a bason 35 miles long, and from 2 to 4 miles broad, finely interspersed with islands, its waters limpid as chrystal and the mountain sides covered with rich groves of Thuya, silver fir, white pine, Aspen and paper birch down to the water edge, here and there precipices of rock to checquer the scene and save it from monotony. An abundance of speckled trout, salmon trout, bass and other fish with which it is stored, have added to our other amusements the sport of taking them. Lake Champlain, tho much larger, is a far less pleasant water. It is muddy, turbulent, and yields little game. After penetrating into it about 25 miles we have been obliged by a head wind and high sea to return, having spent a day and a half in sailing on it. We shall take our rout again thro Lake George, pass thro Vermont down Connecticut river, and through Long island to New York and Philadelphia. Our journey hitherto has been prosperous and pleasant except as to the weather which has been as sultry hot through the whole as could be found in Carolina or Georgia. I suspect indeed that the heats of Northern climates may be more powerful than those of Southern ones in proportion as they are shorter. Perhaps vegetation requires this. There is as much fever and ague too and other bilious complaints on Lake Champlain as on the swamps of Carolina. Strawberries here are in the blossom, or just formed. With you I suppose the season is over. On the whole I find nothing any where else in point of climate which Virginia need envy to any part of the world. Here they are locked up in ice and snow for six months. Spring and autumn, which make a paradise of our country, are rigorous winter with them, and a Tropical summer breaks on them all at once. When we consider how much climate contributes to the happiness of our condition, by the fine sensations it excites, and the productions it is the parent of, we have reason to value highly the accident of birth in such an one as that of Virginia.

From this distance I can have little domestic to write to you about. I must always repeat how much I love you. Kiss the little Anne for me. I hope she grows lustily, enjoys good health, and will make us all and long happy as the center of our common love. Adieu my dear. Your's affectionately, TH: JEFFERSON

RC (NNP); on birch bark, covered with silk crepeline because of its extreme brittleness. Dft (MHi); on paper, having a number of deletions, interlineations, and slight variations in phraseology.

VI. Thomas Jefferson to Thomas Mann Randolph, Jr.

DEAR SIR   Bennington in Vermont June 5. 1791.

Mr. Madison and myself are so far on the tour we had projected. We have visited in the course of it the principal scenes of Burgoyne's misfortunes, to wit the grounds at Still water where the action of that name was fought and particularly the breastworks which cost so much blood to both parties, the encampments at Saratoga and ground where the British piled their arms, and the field of the battle of Bennington, about 9 miles from this place. We have also visited Forts William Henry and George, Ticonderoga, Crown point &c. which have been scenes of blood from a very early part of our history. We were more pleased however with the botanical objects which continually presented themselves. Those either unknown or rare in Virginia were the Sugar maple in vast abundance, the Thuya, silver fir, White Pine, Pitch pine, Spruce pine, a shrub with decumbent stems which they call Junaper, an Azalea very different from the Nudiflora, with very large clusters of flowers, more thickly set on the branches, of a deeper red and high pink-fragrance. It is the richest shrub I have seen: the honey suckle of the gardens growing wild on the banks of Lake George, the paper birch, an Aspen with a velvet leaf, a shrub willow with downy catkins, a wild gooseberry, the wild cherry with the single fruit (not the bunch cherry), straw-berries in abundance.

From the Highlands to the lakes it is a limestone country. It is in vast quantities on the Eastern sides of the lakes, but none on the Western sides. The Sandy hill falls and Wing's falls two very re-markeable cataracts of the Hudson of about 35. or 40 feet each, between Fort Edward and Fort George, are of limestone, in hori-zontal strata. Those of the Cohoes on the West side of the Hudson and of 70. feet height we thought not of limestone. We have met with a small red squirrel, of the colour of our fox squirrel with a black stripe on each side, weighing about six ounces generally, and in such abundance, on Lake Champlain particularly, as that twenty odd were killed at the house we lodged in opposite Crown point the morning we arrived there, without going ten steps from the door. We killed three which were crossing the lakes, one of them just as he was getting ashore where it was three miles wide, and where, with the high winds then blowing, he must have made it 5. or 6 miles.

I think I asked the favor of you to send for Anthony in the season for inoculation, as well to do what is necessary in the orchard as to pursue the object of inoculating all the Spontaneous cherry trees in the fields with good fruit.

We have now got over about 400 miles of our tour, and have still about 450 more to go over. Arriving here on the Saturday evening, and the laws of the state not permitting us to travel on the Sunday has given me time to write to you from hence. I expect to be at Philadelphia by the 20th. or 21st. I am with great & sincere esteem, dear Sir yours affectionately, TH: JEFFERSON

RC (NNP); written on birch bark. Dft (DLC); on paper.

Vermont had only recently passed a law permitting any magistrate to authorize travel on Sunday for persons requesting a pass. Being the governor's guests, TJ and Madison obviously preferred to respect the law and customs of the state. Besides, on this week-end they were enjoying frank political discussions with Governor Robinson, the editor of the *Vermont Gazette*, and other figures (see Editorial Note).

ANTHONY was a slave at Monticello.

VII. Thomas Jefferson to George Washington

SIR   Bennington June 5. 1791.

In my last letter from Philadelphia, I mentioned that Mr. Madison and myself were about to take a trip up the North river as far as circumstances should permit. The levelness of the roads led us quite on to Lake George, where taking boat we went through that, and about 25 miles into Lake Champlain. Returning then to Saratoga, we concluded to cross over thro' Vermont to Connecticut river and go down that instead of the North river which we had already seen, and we are so far on that rout. In the course of our journey we have had opportunities of visiting Still water, Saratoga, Forts Wm. Henry and George Ticonderoga, Crown point, and the scene of Genl. Starke's victory.

I have availed myself of such opportunities as occurred to enquire into the grounds of the report that something disagreeable had taken place in the vicinities of the British posts. It seems to have been the following incident. They had held a small post at a blockhouse on the North Hero, an island on the Vermont side of Lake Champlain, and something further South than their principal post at the Point au fer. The Maria, hitherto stationed at the latter, for Custom-house purposes, was sent to the Block-house, and there exercised her usual visits on boats passing to and from Canada. This being an exercise of power further within our jurisdiction became the subject of notice and clamour with our citizens in that quarter. The vessel has been since recalled to the Point au fer, and being unfit for service, a new one is to be built to perform her functions. This she has usually done at the Point au fer with a good deal of rigour, bringing all vessels to at that place, and sometimes under such circumstances of wind and weather as to have occasioned the loss of two vessels and cargoes. These circumstances produce strong sensations in that quarter, and not friendly to the character of our government. The establishment of a custom-house at Alburg, nearly opposite to Point au fer, has given the British considerable alarm. A groundless story of 200 Americans seen in arms near Point au fer, has been the cause, or the pretext, of their reinforcing that place a few days ago with a company of men from St. John's. It is said here they have called in their guard from the Block-house, but the information is not direct enough to command entire belief.

On enquiring into the dispositions in Canada on the subject of the projected form of government there, we learn, that they are divided into two parties; the English who desire something like an English constitution but so modelled as to oblige the French to chuse a certain proportion of English representatives, and the French who wish a continuance of the French laws, moderated by some engraftments from the English code. The judge of their Common pleas heads the former party, and Smith the chief justice secretly guides the latter.

We encounter the Green mountains tomorrow, with cavalry in part disabled, so as to render our progress a little incertain. I presume however I shall be in Philadelphia in a fortnight. I have the honour to be with sentiments of the most perfect respect and attachment, Sir, Your most obedient & most humble servant,

Th: Jefferson

RC (DNA: RG 59, MLR); endorsed by Washington. PrC (DLC). Tr (DNA: RG 59, SDC). The existence of the press copy is the only – though conclusive – evidence that TJ carried his portable copying press on the journey, just as he did in travelling through southern France in 1787. Since he had promised Washington to inquire into the matters here reported, he no doubt carried the press specifically for the purpose of recording such official reports as this.

VIII. Jefferson's Vocabulary of the Unquachog Indians

[14 June 1791]

Unquachogs. About 20. souls. They constitute the Pusspátock settlement in the town of Brookhaven S. side of Long island.

The language they speak is a dialect differing a little from the

Indians settled near Southampton called Shinicocks and also from those of Montock called Montocks. The three tribes can barely understand each other.

quadrupeds

cow. čowsen
horse. hosses
sheep. sheeps.
hog. hog.
dog. arsúm
– fox. squírrútes
– squirrel. moccás.
– rabbet móh-tux
– deer. hátk

birds

– bird. aswássas.
– crow. concónchus.
gull. arráx
– goose. hakénah
– eagle wéquaran.
– duck. nanásecus.
– dove. má-owks.
– fish hawk. manamáquas.
– quail. ohócotees
– partridge. ápacus
whippoorwill. whácorees.

insects

– snake. skwk
– bug seukr
worm. húquer
– fly. mucháwas.
musketo. murráquitch

plants

– tree. péewye.
– pine. cw
– oak. húchemus.
– hiccory. wusquat
appletree. appeesanck.
peach tree. péachesanck
cherry tree. chérrysanck.
– grape. cátamenón.
plumb tree. sassémenac.
strawberries. wotáhomon.
– mulberry tree. accacúmenoc.
rose. wósowancon.
Indn. corn. sowháwmen.

– turkey nahiam.
chicken. kekeeps.
potato. panac.
squash. áscoot
wheat. maróomar
– bread. ap.
mouse. poquáttas
rat. no name.
rye. rye
– oats. oats.
tobacco. tobac.
hominy. samp.
meat. wéeows.
– stone. sun.
– clay. púckwe
–   ʃsquoint
sand yaac
– water. núp
– dirt. puckwé
the whole world. wáame-
    pámakíu.
– sky. ke-isk
– cloud. pamayaúxen
– rain. súkerun
– snow. soáchpo
– ice. copátn
– hail. mosécan
– sun. háquaqua
– moon. neépa.
– star. aráqusac
– fire. ruht. yuht.
whale oil. púttapapúm.
greese. pum.
whale. púttap.
– fish. opéramac.
oyster. apóonahac.
clam. poquahoc.
– a man. run.

— woman. squah.
— child. peewútstut
— boy. macúchax.
  lad. rungcump.
— girl. squásses.
  lass. yúnksquas.
— head. okéyununc.
— hair. wé-usk
— eyes. skésuc.
— nose. cochóy
— mouth. cúttoh
— teeth. képut
— lips. kussissit.
— chin. cotumpcan
— cheek. canánno
— ear. catáwoc.
— neck. keésquish.
  shoulder. péquan
— arm. copút-te
  elbow. keésquan.
— hand. coritché
— finger. coritcheus.
— nail. cocássac
— back. cúpsquan
  skin. cuttaqúras
— belly. cráckish
  hip. corúcan
— thigh. copómac
  knee. cucúttuc
— leg. coráun.
— foot. cusseéd
— grt. toe. cumsquáusseet
— little toe. peewasticonseet
— father cws
— mother cwca
— brother contàyux
— sister. keéssums
— child. neechuntz.
  aunt cacácas
  uncle nisséis
  Gr father numpsoonk
  Gr. mother. nánnax

— husband. ks-hamps
— wife. keé-us
  gr. child. cówhees
— milk. wampachú-unk
  peas. no name.
  beans. mais-cusseet
— black. shickayo.
— white. wámpayo
— red. squáyo
— yellow. weesa-wayo
— blue. seewamp-wayo
— green. uscusquáyo
— rainbow papuhmúncsunc
  bow. atúmp.
  arrow. neep.
  tomahawk. chékenas.
  a pot. coquées
  a bed. apúnna
  a blanket. aquéewants.
  axe. ochégan.
— house. weécho.
  door. squnt.
  chimney. hamánek
  gourd. ⟨quai⟩ whorámmok.
  watermelon. waghti-
    whorámmok
  wampum. whampump.
  mocassens. mocússenus
— good. woréecan
— bad. mattateáyuh.
— clever. weáyuh.
— handsome. woreeco.
— ugly. neeho wuchayuk
  a cross ⟨angry⟩ fellow.
    cheeáscota.
— a river seépus
— ocean. cutstúk
  a bay. petápagh
— to walk. copumusah
— to stand. cotofer
— to lie down. cutchéepur
— to sit. kiummatap.

−to run. quáquees

−to break. pẃksa

−to bend. co-unkarúnneman

to cut with a knife.
poquesímman.

to cut with an axe.
poquatáhaman

−to kill. wúhnsa.

war. ayutówac

−peace. weéhsaac

to hunt. peénsaac.

−I. née

−you. kee

−he. naácum.

⟨she. wéena⟩

−small peéwátsu

1. naqúut

2. nées

3. nus

4. yaut

5. pa [or] napáa

6. nacúttah [or] cúttah

7. túmpawa

8. swah.

9. nẃre

10. payac.

11. nápan-naquut

12. napan-ees

13. napan-us

14. nápan-yóut

15. napan-napá

16. napan-nacuttah.
&c. to 19.

20. neésun-chog

21. neesun chognaquut

30. sowunchog

40. yauhwunchóg

50. napáatsunchóg.

60. nacúttahtsunchog

70. tumpawatsunchog.
&c.

⟨100   norit sunchog⟩

−100. noquut pasit

−200. nees pasu

⟨300⟩

⟨god⟩ god. mánto.

a great god. masakéetmúnd.

devil. máttateáshet

−thunder. pataquáhamoc.

−lightening. wowosúmpsa.

The orthography is English. This Vocabulary was taken by Th: J. June 13. 1791.[1] in presence of James Madison and Genl. Floyd. There remain but three persons of this tribe now who can speak it's language. These are old women. From two of these, brought together, this vocabulary was taken. A young woman of the same tribe was also present who knew something of the language.

MS (PPAP); written on an address leaf entirely in TJ's hand except for the address: "Honble Thomas Jefferson Esq." which is in the hand of Robert R. Livingston (see Editorial Note). Tr (same); in hand of Peter S. Du Ponceau, transcribed in his volume of "Indian Vocabularies Collected September 1820," p. 46-8.

[1] Thus in MS. The travel notes in the Account Book show that TJ "visited the Unquachog Indians" on the 14th.

IX. Jefferson's Table of Distances and Rating of Inns

[17 May-19 June 1791]

			miles water	miles land
May	17.	Philadelphia to		
	19.	Eliz. town point		80.
		ferry to N. York	9	
	23.	Poughkeepsie. Hendrickson's*	83	
		Lasher's*		16
		Swartz's		12
		Katchum's		4
	24.	Pulvar's —		5
		Claverack*		8
		Hudson*		4
	25.	Kenderhook —		14
		Miller's		8
		Moore's		4
	26.	Albany*		8
		Troy		6
		Lansingboro'		2
		Waterford +		2
		Peeble's		4
	27.	Benjamin's —		7
		Dr. Willard's at Stillwater		4
		Ensign's*		4
		Saratoga		6
		McNeal's ferry +		3
	28.	Fort Edwd. — Baldwin's		11
		Sandy hill falls + Deane's		3
		Wing's falls		4
		Halfway brook		1
	29.	Ft. George + Hay's		7
		Lake George	36	
		Ticonderoga Hay's +	3	
	30.	Crown point	15	
		further into the lake	8	
	31.			

* good   + midling   − bad

		miles water	miles land
June. 1.	back to Fort George	62	
2.	Saratoga		29
3.	Cambridge. Colvin's		15
	Sickle's (battle of Bennington)		6
4.	Bennington. Dewy's*		9
	Bennington to Williamstown. Kiblock's		14
	Sloane's		4
	New Ashfeild		4
	Lanesboro' Wheeler's*		6
	Pittsfeild		6
June. 6.	Dalton. Mrs. Marsh's		4½
7.	Northampton Pomeroy's*		34
	West Springfeild Stebbins's +		18
	Suffeild. Hitchcock's*		9½
	Windsor		10
8.	Hartford. Fred. Bull's*		8
	Weathersfeild		4
	Middletown. Bigelow's +		11
	Durham		8
10.	Strandford's —		7
11.	Guilford Stone +		8
	Oysterpond point	35	
12.	Southold. Mrs. Peck's +		16
	Hubbard's		8
	Riverhead* Griffin's		10
13.	Moritchie's Downs's +		12
	Colo. Floyd's		7
	Hart's +		13
14.	Terry's +		9
	Strong's		6
	Udell's		6
	Bethpeg		10
	Hamstead		9
15.	Jamaica		10
	Brooklyn		12
16.	New York	1	
	Pauler's hook	1¼	
	Bergen point		9
	Staten island	3/4	

	miles water	miles land
Richmond		6
Billing's point		9
Perth Amboy	¼	
17. South Amboy	1	
Spotswood		10
Williamson's		4
Cranberry		6
18. Allentown		11
Crosswick's		4
Bordentown		4
Burlington		11
Duns's ferry		4
the ferry	3/4	
19. Philadelphia		16
	256 +	664 = 920

This calculation of distances with rating of inns where Madison and TJ lodged or dined is extracted from the Account Book (NN), where it was entered at 20 June 1791 after TJ arrived back in Philadelphia. It bears the caption "The stages and distances of my journey."

TJ did not begin to rate the inns and taverns along the way until he had joined Madison in New York and ceased to do so the day before they parted. The highest ratings, understandably, were given to those establishments in the well-settled parts of the Hudson and Connecticut valleys. Although Pierpont Edwards had said that the travellers grumbled at the "Eatables" and found nothing good enough for them (see Editorial Note), Connecticut inns with one exception were given TJ's top rating. Some indication of his criteria for the three cat-egories may perhaps be found in the inn where he and Madison stopped at Ticonderoga, located on the lake shore near Fort Ticonderoga in a stone building that had been known as "The King's Store." This inn was operated by the wife of Charles Hay (brother of Udney Hay, who had been deputy quartermaster at Ticonderoga during the Revolution). Mrs. Hay was a native of Quebec and she had operated an inn there. When Isaac Weld stopped at Mrs. Hay's Ticonderoga establishment only a few years after TJ and Madison were there, he was greatly surprised and pleased with both the service and the food, attributing this to her being a native of French Canada (Isaac Weld, *Travels*, I [New York, 1799], 293). TJ, perhaps judging Mrs. Hay's cuisine by his own French standards, rated her place only as "middling."

From Charles Carter

MY DR. FRIEND   Ludlow Town 21st May 91

Without any apology, for this intrusion, I beg leave to engage you in matter that deeply concerns me, and my Family. Your very kind letter to your relation Mrs. C when you were in Virginia has induced me to take this liberty. My second Son has compleated his Classical Education, under the Revd. Thomas Ryan; and is desirous of studying Physics. I wish to send him to Philadelphia, rather than a foreign Country, believing he can receive, as much instruction there, as at any other place. Some of my acquaintance have enquired the terms. Doctr. Rush demands a Fee of 100£ P.C. Bond and Shippen 80£. By some I am recommended to one, and by others to another. But by letters from Mr. Ths. Fitzhugh Knox a Relation, of our Friend of Chatham who now lives, in the Town of and studies under a Doctor Barton, I am induced to believe, this Fee is exorbitant. Doctr. Barton is professor of Botany and Natural History, stands high in the Physical line, and the Head of the Dispensary, and one of the Attendants, on the Hospital. Mr. Knox lives in his Family, has access, to his library and attends with him, his Patients. Tis supposed he will gain as much experience, as if he had paid, the exorbitant Fees. And for this he pays 50£ P.C. I wish to have advice on the matter. And that youl be so obliging, as to let me know in either case, the expence. The Boy is 17 years of age, is very fond of his Books, to which he has devoted his whole time. I have had him Enoculated. I some time since had presented me the Accounts of Wm. Ogle Esq. delivered to the House Commons. They are of no use to me, but I think may be so to you. I therefore sent you and beg your acceptance of the Book. Mrs. Carter begs to be affy. rembrd. to you. I am Dr. Sr. Yr. Aff. Friend & Hble. St.,

CHS. CARTER

RC (MHi); endorsed by TJ as received 21 June 1791 and so recorded in SJL.

TJ's letter to MRS. C. (Elizabeth Chiswell Carter) was that of 1 Oct. 1790. The work that Carter sent was *The accounts of*

William Ogle, Esq. Superintendent of the Newry Canals (Dublin, 1787). The original owner of TJ's copy, Samuel Martin, inscribed his name on the title-page and he may have been the one who presented it to Carter (see Sowerby, No. 2987).

From David Humphreys

Lisbon, 21 May 1791. Sends English papers. From talks with De Pinto and others, peace more expected to prevail than formerly. But newly arrived vessels from north bring nothing definite. By direct accounts from Paris at end of April, he finds tumults have subsided, Lafayette again in command of national guard, and his popularity and triumph complete despite English prophecies. The mischievous intrigues of the anti-constitutional faction react against them. "With unanimity and perseverance on the part of the Patriots, the French nation cannot fail of becoming more happy, powerful and glorious than any other on this Continent."

Meantime, he is pleased to belong to a nation "whose name is, at each succeeding time, pronounced with more and more respect, throughout the European World. Mankind begin to believe in the excellence and stability of our Government. Every day discovers fresh proofs, of enterprize and resources, flattering to the character of our Country." A few days ago, when captains of American ships showed satisfaction at appointment of minister, the largest merchantman fired a federal salute and displayed American flags. She belongs to a foreigner and trades with Baltic under American papers and captain "*because the premium of Insurance and expense of Navigation are cheaper than they would be under other Colours.*"

He attributes to rising reputation of America civilities he has everywhere received. Two or three days before being presented, he called on De Challon, French ambassador, with introduction from Marquis de la Luzerne, and on Walpole, British minister, with one from Lord St. Helens. Both were "extremely polite," and on 13th Walpole presented him to the diplomatic corps in the Queen's antechamber. Every person in that body returned his visit before the end of the second day.

He has had similar reception from "several Portuguese Characters of high distinction: particularly from D. John Carlos of Braganza, Duke of Alafoñes, Uncle to Her Majesty, Commander in Chief of Her Troops, and Governor of Estremadura." Without any hint whatever, he was introduced to him on the 12th, partook of a collation with him, the "Dutchess and many Ladies of the first families" at the palace where meets the Royal Academy of Sciences, of which he is president and over which he had just presided at an extraordinary session. "This Nobleman is perfectly elegant in his manners, and greatly beloved for the goodness of his heart. He has travelled through Europe, understands English and French, and is the Protector of Arts and Sciences in the Kingdom." He had previously read newspapers and other publications Humphreys had brought. On being presented to him "he told me in the most courteous possible manner, 'that he was already perfectly acquainted with me; that he admired the conduct and character of my country; and that he was disposed to render me every service in his power.'" After acknowledging his politeness in what he hoped was not an unbecoming manner, Humphreys said: "as we were a young Nation, but just emerging from . . . a long and distressing war, we must only hope to make gradual improvements, which I was happy in believing we were now doing." To which the Duke replied: " 'Young as your Nation is, it advances in improvements with the STEPS OF A GIANT (pas d'un Geant). It is not a compliment to tell you so. – I say what I mean – for it as ill becomes me of the House of Braganza to flatter, as it does a Citizen of the United States to be flattered.' " On the 13th the Duke received a new promotion.

For introduction to that illustrious personage, he was indebted to the Duke's most intimate friend, Abbé Corrêa, secretary of the Academy of Sciences, "one of the most liberal Philosophers of the age, an enthusiastic admirer of our Country, and certainly one of the best informed men on the subject of it (for a person who has not been there) I have ever met with in my life." TJ will perceive his manner of political thinking by what he said when Humphreys first saw saw him: " 'I look upon the U. S. of America to be the only hope and consolation of Mankind. Here in Europe we have ten thousand almost insurmountable obstacles to political happiness. — KINGS ARE BAD ENOUGH, BUT NOBILITY ARE THE DEVIL.' — A few days ago he remarked 'You and we have every circumstance in our favor to make us strictly and advantageously united. And England and Spain are (if I may use an expression that ought to be exploded) the natural enemies of both.' He declares that nothing but his age prevents him from going to the U. S. — He professes, however, that this Country is tranquil and prosperous, in a wonderful degree, under the present Reign: But that the public felicity is held by too precarious a tenure, it depending but too much on the Characters of the reigning Sovereign."

He is so much fatigued by paying and receiving visits, writing and copying letters, and making arrangements for a house that he must retire into the country for a few weeks lest his "health should suffer from some inconvenient plethorick symptoms, which the unusual life . . . has produced." The "public business can receive no detriment."

P.S. On further inquiry into character and conduct of Samuel Harrison as vice-consul, he finds his services not only indispensable but also highly approved by masters of vessels. — Humphreys thinks that "if the Philosophical Society of Philadelphia (of which I believe you are one of the principal officers) should think proper to admit the Duke of Alafões, the Chev. Luis Pinto de Souza Coutinho, and the Abbé Jose Corrêa de Serra, as Members," it would bring no discredit to the Society, be acceptable to them, prove useful to the cause of science in general, "and perhaps, not unprofitable to that of our Country in particular. If it would not encrease the number too much, I would also add the name of the Conde D. Diogo de Neronha, Ambassador . . . at Madrid. — His name is the first on the list of the members of the Royal Academy of Portugal."

RC (DNA: RG 59, DD); at head of text: "(No. 20)"; endorsed by TJ as received 7 July 1791 and so recorded in SJL. Tr (same).

Of those suggested by Humphreys for membership in the American Philosophical Society, only Corrêa da Serra was elected (1812). TJ was not an officer of the Society at this time, though he was an active member.

From Stephen Cathalan, Jr.

Marseilles, 23 May 1791. Hopes olive trees shipped on *Marie Antoinette*, Capt. Joseph Barret, will suffer "nothing else than a retardment"; if trees are damaged, he will replace them. Encloses O'Bryen and Stephens' letter of 25 March to the "Society of Philantropy." He has thanked Parret and de Kersey, who have spoken very warmly on the subject and have charged him to urge that a nation "who had so much sacrifice to conquer Liberty would not suffer a Longer time her fellow Citizens in Slavery." He thinks redemption and peace should be negotiated at same time, but Parret and de Kersey "say that with such People Politick can't obtain nothing" and that the prisoners should be redeemed first. He urges that they be given a regular monthly or weekly stipend, according to rank, to alleviate their suffering.

On 22 March he received his commission as vice-consul and his exequatur, but as the latter does not accord privileges of consul he has returned it with a petition to Montmorin to clarify his status. He has not yet heard from him or from Short.

The season is too far advanced to send TJ "Brugnols and Dried figs," but he will not fail to send some of their fruits next winter. A French vessel sails for New York from this harbor the first days of June. No American vessels since his last, only the French brig *La Virginie*, Capt. Dot, Français, which sailed from Philadelphia 29 March and arrived here on 11 May with "197 hogd. Tobacco, 17 Tierces Carolina Indigo, 29 Barls. Bees Wax, 173 Whale Bones, 140 Bels. Superfine flour." Lists prices current for tobacco and other commodities.

Affairs in France very critical; public credit much hurt. "God knows when Matters will take a fair Prospect." He presumes United States will retaliate against decrees of National Assembly.

RC (DNA: RG 59, CD); endorsed by TJ as received 20 Aug. 1791 and so recorded in SJL.

From Martha Jefferson Randolph

MY DEAR PAPA   Monticello May 23, 1791

As you have been so long without hearing from any of us Mr. Randolph begged me to write a few lines to you that you might not be uneasy. He had began to do it himself but was prevented by a very bad cut in his thumb. It is almost 5 weeks since *I* have recieved a letter from you which I attribute to the irregularity of the post: that of Charlottesville they say is reestablished. Anthony has been to innoculate your trees. We had strawberries here the 2d of this month and cherries I think the 9th tho they had had both some time before that at Richmond. As I did not expect to have written this week it was so late before I began that I am obliged to be very concise for fear of missing the post which is expected in town early this morning and by which I am in hopes of recieving a letter from you. Adieu My Dear Papa. We have all been in perfect health here and are extremly obliged to you for the veils you sent us. I am with the tenderest love your affectionate child,

M. RANDOLPH

The largest of the beans you sent me is come up and very flourishing but none of the others have as yet made their appearance.

RC (ViU); endorsed by TJ as received 21 June 1791 and so recorded in SJL.

From C. W. F. Dumas

The Hague, 24 May 1791. Cabinets of London and Berlin greatly embarrassed by the peace overtures of Empress of Russia and by the astonishing Polish revolution. Pitt is great in matters of internal finance and commerce, but below mediocrity in foreign affairs, having for more than three years been influenced by his kinsman, "le très-intriguant Grenville." He long ago predicted what events have proved: that the policy adopted is not his but that of his master. – Prince Edward has gone from Gibralter to Quebec with his regiment to extend its fortifications. Why? To hold the Canadians in check? Do they fear the Americans or the French? Neither will be aggressors. – In Holland people are diverted from their troubles by military maneuvers which will cost money and by the display of placards urging preachers to thank God for the continuation of civil and religious liberty procured by their Royal Highnesses, &c. &c. &c. – Apparently the concession of the Dutch East India Company will not be continued after its expiration. Government will take over its assets and debts and send out commissioners with power to change the governments of Batavia, Ceylon, &c. "En auront-ils la force? Je l'ignore." – He is greatly pleased with Paine's *The Rights of Man.* Shocked by the absurd and quixotic Burke, he prays God with all his heart that "our" illustrious President and august legislature will see the New World which they have made happy continue to regenerate the old by their example. "C'est dans ces sentiments que je vivrai et mourrai."

FC (Dumas Letter Book, Rijksarchief, The Hague; photostats in DLC); at head of text: "No.77"; with numerous deletions and interlineations. Recorded in SJL as received 18 Aug. 1791.

From Daniel L. Hylton

Dr Sir   Richmond Virginia May 29th. 1791

Your favour of 15th inst. have received some days past and shall pay attention to the contents, am concern'd to find one of the Hhds. tobacco shipt by Stratton was such, as you had describd in your former letter and exceptionable. This fault lays with the inspectors, as I had requested they would mark out those that had been fir'd. In future I shall attend to that circumstance and request them again to put a private mark on those that have been injur'd. Their is only two down and think they had better remain until a few more comes to be shipt together. So soon as a sufficiency is at the Warehouse I shall embrace the earliest opportunity in shiping them to you. – Our country is much alarm'd at the decission of the Northern judges respecting the payment of the british debts, without any provision for the payment of the negroes under the treaty or any part of their property taken from them during the War. If the same decission takes place in the Southern department in contraverting the laws of the state I know not where this business may end, as the determination of the people in this country, is not to Submit to the payment until the treaty is fully complyd with. The Southern and Northern states have been affected in different manners, one who unfortunately posses'd a species of property, which every liberal mind detests, have been borne off in great numbers after the treaty being sign'd, which infraction deprives this country of the very means in paying those debts from the depredation of those now claiming them. Surely congress can never suffer such injurys to their own citizens to pass over with impunity and commit so glaring injustice to them, by placing the british subjects on a better footing then their own, I wish this subject to be handled with a degree of caution by congress and the different judges, as the welfare of this great union will in some measure depend on that justice which the citizens of the united states demand of them. It will be well for the judges to weigh this subject with serious deliberations before they decide on a question in which their country is so deeply interested and by whose decissions materialy effect. Much may be said on this subject and would require a volume to enter in a full detail which is unnecessary, as I know you are a perfect master of it, having yourself (from my own knowledge) felt and experienc'd the loss of large sums from the great confidence plac'd in our laws before the common cement of the Union. I fear have trespass'd on your patience already too much, therefore drop this political subject and say with sincerity of heart wishing you every happiness Your Fd & St,

DANL. L. HYLTON

P.S. I have written Mr. E. Randolph for a paper he has either lost or mislaid in a Suit here he had to manage for me, which is a material one in the cause and on which I have now depending £100; if its lost, have requested the favour of him to send a certificate to you which be pleasd to forward to me.

RC (DLC); addressed: "Honble. Thomas Jefferson"; endorsed by TJ as received 21 June 1791 and so recorded in SJL.

From Mary Jefferson

MY DEAR PAPA   [Monticello] May 29

I am much obliged to you for the veil that you sent me and shall allways were it. I have began to learn botany and arithmetic with

Mr. Randolph. The mare that he bought for me is come. She is very pretty and is sister to brimmer. She can only trot and canter. The fruit was not killed as you thought. We have a great abundance of it here. Adieu Dear Papa I am your affectionate daughter,

MARY JEFFERSON

P.S. Little anna grows fast an is very pretty

RC (ViU); endorsed by TJ as received 21 June 1791 and so recorded in SJL.

Brimmer was a thoroughbred of distinguished lineage, purchased by TJ in 1790 (see note, TJ to Fitzhugh, 21 July 1790). Mary's statement that the mare sharing that lineage could only trot and canter—a dubious assertion as TJ surely knew—was no doubt intended to reassure him. He had already warned her never to be venturesome with the animal, asserting that "a lady should never ride a horse which she might not safely ride without a bridle" (TJ to Mary Jefferson, 8 May 1791).

From Harry Innes

DEAR SIR   Kentucky 30th. May 1791

I have the honor to acknowledge the reciept of your favor of the 7th. of March by my friend Mr. Brown and feel myself flattered by the polite terms in which you acknowledge the reciept of my Letter of July the 8th. and your readiness to enter into an Epistolary correspondence, which I shall with pleasure continue having your assent thereto.

If any circumstances in the line of Natural History shall occur in this Western Country it will be pleasing to me to communicate them to you, not only because it may afford you pleasure but thro' the same channel be handed to posterity if deserving to be recorded.

The Political Letter which I promised you hath not been written; I was unhappily obliged to leave the District last Fall to pay my last attentions to my ever dear and ever to be lamented Mrs. Innes, who took a trip to the Sweet Springs and left me on the 26th. of December last. This prevented my writing agreable to promise and in the interim the Arrangements of Government have in a great measure silenced our complaints, as their is at present a disposition to remedy our wants, by the active measures adopted against the Indians and to obtain the Navigation of the Mississippi, which were the subjects intended to have been written on. Should any thing hereafter occur in the Political line which may require the interference of Government I shall freely and candidly state it to you.

The late arrangements ordered by the President for carrying on Hostile operations against the Indians Northwest of the Ohio have been taken into consideration by the Commissioners and I hope the 1st. Detachment of Volunteers under the command of Genl. Scott are this day making their Stroke and crowning themselves with Laurels. Patriotism never shined with more lustre at any time during the late American Warr than on this occasion it hath in Kentucky. Many Field Officers and Subalterns of the Militia have stept into the ranks as common soldiers. Others have condescended to command in inferior Rank to that which they bare in their County and many private Gent. have become soldiers, among whom is our friend Brown.

The General must be highly flattered by his command; the Corps is equal to any that can be raised in the United States. Young, stout and healthy – well armed – well mounted and provided with 20 days provision from the No. Wt. bank of the Ohio, from whence they marched in high Spirits on the 23d. Inst. The Lieut. Colo. is Genl. Wilkinson – 1st. Major Colo. Robt. Todd formerly a Capt. in the Ilionois Regiment – 2d. Major Capt. Thos. Barbee of the Virginia Continental line.

Since the reception of your Letter I have seen Genl. Clarke and find he is writing the History of his Expeditions and will complete the work in the course of this summer. I entertain the same Ideas of his greatness that you do and consider him as a singular loss to the Western Country. I took the liberty of shewing him your Letter, from a hope, that it might cause him to reflect upon his present folly. He was perfectly sober, was greatly agitated by the Contents, observed it was friendly and shed Tears – a Sympathetic touch seised my Soul and I could not forbear accompanying him.

Some Tribe of Indians generally supposed to be Cherokees have been very troublesome this Spring on our Southern frontier. Some lives taken, several persons wounded, three or four taken prisoners and a number of Horses stolen. If the Treaty Governor Blount is about to hold does not produce a good effect the people of Kentucky will make a stroke on that nation this summer. It will not be difficult to produce proof enough against them since the Treaty of Hopewell. I fear and dread the consequences. – I am with great respect Dr Sir Your mo. ob. servt., HARRY INNES

RC (DLC); addressed: "The Honble. Thomas Jefferson Secretary of State Philadelphia"; endorsed by TJ as received 24 June 1791 and so recorded in SJL.

From James Yard

St. Croix, 31 May 1791. Has presented his commission to be reported to Copenhagen as required, but it has not been passed, and he has not "urged any Decision whatever." He believes he will be permitted to act without interruption. In the meantime he will collect information necessary to place "the Commerce of this Country in a clear Point of View."

RC (DNA: RG 59, CD); endorsed by TJ as received 25 June 1791 and so recorded in SJL.

The American Consul at London
Joshua Johnson and the Brigantine *Rachel*

I. WILLIAM GREEN TO THE SECRETARY OF STATE, 23 MAY 1791
II. JOSHUA JOHNSON TO THE SECRETARY OF STATE, 31 MAY 1791
III. WILLIAM GREEN TO THE SECRETARY OF STATE, 6 DEC. 1791

EDITORIAL NOTE

In your letter of instructions . . . you direct me to prevent any Vessell entering as an American *who is not such*, if in my power. I discover much abuse in this particular, but what can I say? The Register is granted to a Person in America, on his swearing that he is the sole owner, when it is notorious, that the Principal resides here, and that the Person, in whose name the Register is granted, is no more, or less, than an Agent, or Junior Partner. Whether it may be wise to abolish this kind of Property, or not, you can best Judge; but my own opinion is that we should not be too Scrupulous, as it gives employment to our Countrymen, and that of the Funds of Foreigners.   − *Joshua Johnson to Thomas Jefferson, 26 Feb. 1791*

You will be pleased . . . to give no countenance to the usurpation of our flag by foreign vessels, but rather indeed to aid in detecting it, as without bringing to us any advantage, the usurpation will tend to commit us with the belligerent powers, and to subject those vessels which are truly ours to harrassing scrutinies in order to distinguish them from the counterfeits.
− *Thomas Jefferson to American Consuls, 21 Mch. 1793*

When news arrived early in the summer of 1790 that England and Spain were on the verge of war, the administration firmly committed itself to a policy of neutrality, while at the same time seizing the opportunity to free the United States as much as possible from commercial restraints imposed by both powers. No one doubted that, if war came, there would be increasing resort to the usages of centuries by which belligerent nations had made a convenience of the flags of neutrals, thereby protecting their own trade while enriching the northern European commercial centers. Such had been the practice from the time of the Hanseatic League onwards. A state of war indeed only intensified strategies employed at all times when mercantile houses found their interest in concealing the true ownership and nationality of their trading vessels.

The mere threat of conflict in 1790 led at once to the appointment of an American consul at London and to Jefferson's instruction to him and other consuls to be on guard against granting entry or countenancing the sale of any vessel purporting to be American that was not truly such.[1] Simultaneously, the brigantine *Rachel* cleared New York for London under the command of Nicholas Duff, having on board William Green, a New York merchant who had suffered ruinous losses in the East India trade and who was en route to London to prosecute his case against those whom he held responsible. According to his own testimony, Green was the sole owner of *Rachel* and her cargo of potash, pig iron, and staves. He also testified that he had acquired her less than a month before from the well-known New York merchant, Nicholas Brevoort. On several occasions *Rachel* had been admitted to the ports of Great Britain and Ireland, the last time only three months before Green acquired her. But between that voyage and the one which carried her new owner to London, the possibility that England would soon be at war insured a closer scrutiny by customs and admiralty officials of both neutral ships' papers and seamen who claimed to be American citizens. Though her register was silent on the point, *Rachel* had been built in France some years earlier, a fact which, under the circumstances, was enough to guarantee that her papers would be examined with extreme care. She also had on board William Knox, brother of the Secretary of War, who had just been appointed consul at Dublin. Knox, unfortunately, happened to have in his baggage a fowling piece made by a famous London gunsmith which he was taking back for repairs as a favor to its owner, Henry Cruger.[2] Ironically, Knox also bore Jefferson's instructions to Joshua Johnson admonishing him to guard against vessels abusing the American flag.[3] Whether or not *Rachel* was such, the consequences were unfortunate for her, for her owner, and for the American consul at London who prosecuted her case so vigorously.

The case of *Rachel* leaves her true identity somewhat less certain than it

---

[1] TJ to Johnson, 7 Aug. 1790; TJ's instructions to American consuls, 26 Aug. 1790.

[2] Henry Cruger (1739-1829), like the previous owner of *Rachel*, belonged to a prominent mercantile family of New York, but his career was quite unusual. His father had placed him in a trading firm in Bristol, England, where he soon married the daughter of a banker, rose to prominence, and in 1774 stood with Edmund Burke for Parliament under the slogan "Burke, Cruger, and Liberty!" In Parliament he argued eloquently for reconciliation with the American colonies, but concurred in the general acceptance of the doctrine of parliamentary supremacy. He was defeated in 1780, elected mayor of Bristol in 1781, and returned to Parliament in 1784. In 1790 he declined to stand again and returned to the United States to spend the remainder of his life. Thus he had been in his native land only a few months before *Rachel* departed on her unhappy voyage (Henry C. Van Schaack, *Henry Cruger*, [New York, 1859]; DAB).

[3] Johnson to TJ, 2 Nov. 1790.

appeared to the Lords of the Treasury who, after deliberating two months, refused her entry because she had been built in France. Given the circumstances, this is understandable. But the incident, to which the American consul devoted such an unusual amount of time and effort and which he reported in more detail than he gave to any other, tells us a great deal about Joshua Johnson. Like the dispatch quoted above in which he innocently disclosed an intent not to be too scrupulous in preventing abuses of the American flag because these were beneficial to trade — a disclosure which must have shocked the Secretary of State, whose aim was precisely the opposite — Johnson's handling of the *Rachel* incident reveals much about himself, about his concept of his official role, and about his conduct as consul. The case is important not as an isolated example but as a reflection of the man and his setting at the capital where questions of crucial importance to American political and commercial relations were being decided.

I

So far as American interests were concerned, London was then, as Johnson himself declared, "the first City in the World."[4] There, and to a much lesser extent at Liverpool, Bristol, and other British ports, a large proportion of American commerce had resumed its accustomed channels, just as Lord Sheffield and others had predicted. But the old problems — American debts, difficulties with customs officials, impressment of seamen, and so on — had also continued and in many cases had been magnified by the lingering bitterness over the dismemberment of the empire and by the mercantilist policies of Lord Hawkesbury. This was a situation which called for all of the address and resourcefulness of a skilled diplomat. In the absence of formal diplomatic relations and as the only official representing the United States at the capital, Johnson was expected to go beyond the normal consular functions — to do "somewhat more," as Jefferson informed him, in providing political intelligence and acting in general as a quasi-diplomatic character.[5] Lacking ministerial rank made the unique assignment all the more difficult by depriving Johnson as consul of the opportunity to deal directly with the Secretary for Foreign Affairs, a handicap of which he was perhaps too sensitively aware. But there was a more serious impediment of which he seems not to have been sufficiently conscious.

This, a formidable obstacle which occasionally impeded his consular activities and even at times placed him at odds with his own government's policy, arose from the fact that Johnson had been absent from his native land since 1771. In that year, at the age of 29, he had gone to London as the resident partner of the recently formed Annapolis firm of Wallace, Johnson, and Davidson. This

---

[4] Johnson to Philip Stephens, Admiralty Office, 30 July 1791 (DNA: RG 59, CD; Johnson's letterbook as consul, hereafter referred to by its microfilm designation as MNP 167/1).

[5] TJ to Johnson, 7 Aug. 1790. A good example of TJ's expectation in this respect is the Purdie case, in which he gave Johnson specific instructions about the government's attitude and then, in a covering letter, directed him to reveal these to the Duke of Leeds as if on his own initiative (TJ to Johnson, 17 and 23 Dec. 1790). This characteristically indirect approach had the effect of making Johnson, in this instance, an unofficial diplomatic agent.

was the first group of colonial entrepreneurs to challenge with American capital the near monopoly enjoyed by British merchants in shipping goods to Maryland and Virginia and receiving consignments of tobacco in return – a system of trade and credit so disadvantageous to the colonists that, as Jefferson expressed it, their "debts had become hereditary from father to son for many generations, so that the planters were a species of property annexed to certain mercantile houses in London."[6] This rather overstated the case, but the hold of the British merchants was so firm that they naturally resented the effort of an American firm to break it. Johnson succeeded in part because of methods of duplicity such as he occasionally exhibited as consul. At the outset, facing a cold reception in London, he gained the support of the influential London merchant Osgood Hanbury only by assuring him that Wallace, Johnson, and Davidson had no intention of engaging in the tobacco trade. This sponsorship enabled him within a few weeks to dispatch a cargo of goods worth more than his firm's capital. Yet, almost immediately, he began urging his partners to do what he had assured Hanbury they would not do. Ultimately, they yielded to his arguments about the profits to be made in accepting tobacco shipments on consignment. By 1775 Johnson had shipped goods valued at £47,638 sterling and had sold 4,475 hogsheads of tobacco on consignment – some of it purchased by a London firm of which he was a silent member and about which he did not feel it necessary to inform his American partners. He was equally reticent with planters who sent tobacco on consignment, as on the occasion when he informed the shippers that he had sold their cargo at 7d sterling while, at the same time, he himself was disposing of tobacco at 12d. Within a short while Johnson had moved into a house near the Exchange, had adopted a mode of life he felt suited to a successful merchant, and had annoyed his partners with insistent demands that he be allowed additional compensation for living and business expenses.

When the firm was dissolved after the outbreak of hostilities, Johnson remained in London until 1778 seeking to carry on business by himself. This placed him in an ambiguous situation, with the result that at times he gave a double set of instructions to his ships, the one to show any inquiring English vessel that the cargo was intended for use by the royal forces in New York, the other indicating that the real destination was the Chesapeake. In that year Johnson removed to Nantes to engage in business and also to seek loans from France as agent for Maryland, an activity in which he claimed he was hampered by Benjamin Franklin. In 1779 Congress named him as agent to settle accounts with its commissioners and others in Europe, but failed to make provision for compensation. When Franklin asked him to come to Paris with a clerk so that, in Silas Deane's absence, they could go over unsettled accounts and adjust the business as best they could, Johnson flatly refused and asked that Congress appoint another in his place. He explained to William Carmichael that he was determined to resign both the Maryland agency and that of Congress because of the uncertainty of reimbursement for public services.[7]

[6] TJ's answers to Démeunier's queries, [Jan.-Feb. 1786], Vol. 10:27.

[7] Edward C. Papenfuse quotes Johnson as saying that he was resigning "his post as consul to Congress in Nantes" (*In pursuit of profit The Annapolis merchants in the era of the American Revolution, 1763-1805* [Johns Hopkins, 1975], p. 108). Johnson of course had not been appointed consul and actually did not serve as agent for the settlement of accounts. In his letter accepting the agency he quoted his response to Franklin in which he said he would handle any accounts except those of Jonathan Wil-

In 1781, with Johnson residing in Nantes, the firm of Wallace, Johnson and Muir was created to engage in the expanding tobacco trade with France and the marketing of French goods in the United States. The business of the house rapidly expanded in the post-war years, especially since it acted as an agent for Robert Morris under his contract guaranteeing the sale of 20,000 hogsheads of tobacco per annum for the three years ending in 1788. In 1783 Johnson returned to London, where the new firm far outstripped the success of the earlier one. But the collapse of Robert Morris' monopoly and the increasing competition of British merchants brought it into serious difficulties. Johnson himself contributed to the firm's problems. Charles Carroll, one of its most influential customers, complained that Johnson was not as punctual in correspondence or as attentive to business as formerly. Johnson's partners were so distressed over his mismanagement that the senior partner, Charles Wallace, went to London in 1785 to straighten matters out. In that year Wallace, Johnson, and Muir owed London creditors a staggering total of £240,000. By then Johnson and his partners had become so alienated in their personal relationships that dissolution of the firm was a foregone conclusion. In the spring of 1787 Johnson called together the major creditors and placed the firm's London affairs in their hands as trustees under an arrangement which assured him against arrest or suit for two years. On January 1, 1790, only a few months before Johnson was appointed consul, the firm was dissolved, but the acrimonious dispute over the division of its assets continued until Johnson's death in 1802. Just a few months before his appointment as consul Johnson announced that he would continue in the tobacco consignment business on his own, but with no intention of shipping cargoes. Soon thereafter, he described himself as the resident partner of a new house — Wallace, Johnson, and Morris — about which little is known.[8]

Johnson's long years of mercantile experience in London and Nantes reveal much about him and his manner of conducting business. He had experienced

---

liams — Franklin's grandnephew, with whom Johnson had fallen out. But only three months later he informed Congress that he had refused Franklin's request; declared that that body could not blame him since it could not expect him to leave his house and business "without an equivalent for it"; and suggested that another be appointed in his place (Johnson to Huntington, 12 Apr. and 20 July 1780, DNA: RG 360, No. 78, XIII, f. 139 and 146). Even so, Congress in 1781 authorized Johnson to settle the accounts of Schweighauser & Dobrée against the frigate *Alliance*. Again Johnson refused, and that tangled business fell to TJ after Congress took it up again in 1786 (JCC, XXI, 907; TJ to Schweighauser & Dobrée, 20 July 1788).

[8] Johnson described himself as resident partner of the firm in his letter to the Commissioners of the Customs, 4 Feb. 1791 (Tr in DNA: RG 59, CD; MNP 167/1). The firm is not mentioned in Papenfuse, *In pursuit of profit*, an excellent study on which the above account of Wallace, Johnson, and Davidson and Wallace, Johnson, and Muir is chiefly based. For other biographical details concerning Johnson and his family, see Edward S. Delaplaine, *Thomas Johnson* (New York, 1927); Samuel Flagg Bemis, *John Quincy Adams*, I (New York, 1949), 79-82; *Md. Hist. Mag.*, XLII (Sep. 1947), 214-15; Adams, *Diary*, ed. L. H. Butterfield, II, 300. In 1797, after his daughter Louisa was married to John Quincy Adams and his tobacco consignment business had failed, Johnson returned to the United States, settled in the city of Washington where he had invested in real estate, and was appointed by John Adams superintendent of stamps under the Federalist-inspired Stamp Act of 1800 which a Republican Congress soon repealed (*U. S. Statutes at Large*, I, 754-7; II, 845).

both successes and reverses, more than once fearing arrest as a debtor. He had not always been candid or even scrupulous in his relations with his partners and their customers. Under an appointment by Congress he had placed personal compensation above the performance of public duty. He was undeviating in his devotion to his country's cause and its interests as he conceived them. But his long absence abroad had put him more or less out of touch with the transforming events in America that had so greatly altered his countrymen's view of themselves, of their institutions, and of their relations with the rest of the world. In some ways his years in Europe had affected him much as Jefferson feared William Short, or any official representative, would be if he remained too long absent from his native land. A slight but revealing indication of this is to be found in Johnson's communications as consul to British officials, and even in those to Jefferson, in which he seemed to regard himself as being responsible to Congress rather than to the Executive, as if the structure of government had not been drastically altered since his appointment at Nantes. Another and more important manifestation was his emulation of the forms and practices of foreign consulates as he had observed them in France and England. This derivative influence affected his official conduct in various ways, some trivial and some serious, which neither the experience of European consuls in the United States nor the views of the Secretary of State would have sanctioned.[9] The first thing Johnson did on receiving his commission was to have two seals cut bearing the arms of the United States. He did not customarily wear the authorized uniform of a consul, but was prepared to do so on special occasions. On being granted his exequator, he expended a not insignificant sum in connection with that formality, a public charge quite customary with European consuls but unauthorized by American law, as Jefferson was obliged to inform him.[10]

But these were matters of slight significance as compared with the manner in which Johnson sought to maintain the dignity of his consulate and to protect that of his nation by emulating the practices of European consulates. Observing that other consuls were paid salaries and were given perquisites as well as authority denied him, Johnson was importunate in his plea for compensation and additional powers. There was merit in his argument, especially for a consul in London where so much American trade was centered. During his first year in office, Johnson spent an inordinate amount of time in appeals to officials in the Treasury, Customs, Admiralty, and Foreign Office concerning impressed seamen, deserters who claimed to be British subjects, crews charging their

[9] On the various conflicts between French consuls and local authorities in the United States concerning jurisdiction over deserting seamen, merchant vessels, maritime offenses as serious as barratry, and even ships of war in American territorial waters, see Editorial Note and documents on the Consular Convention of 1788 (Vol. 14: 66-180). TJ's views on consular establishments and their "inutility" for the United States are expressed in his letter to Montmorin, 20 June 1788.

[10] TJ to Johnson, 13 May 1791. Funds for secret intelligence were also authorized by law, but TJ told Johnson it would be worth 50 or 100 guineas to obtain the full text of Hawkesbury's report to the Privy Council. On a matter of such importance TJ was willing to take the risk of Congressional approval (TJ to Johnson, 29 Aug. 1791). Despite this authorization, Johnson was unable to obtain the report, but William Temple Franklin was fortunate enough to be able to send it to TJ at no cost (see Editorial Note, group of documents on commercial and diplomatic relations with Great Britain, at 15 Dec. 1790).

officers with cruelty, and vessels seized under the revival of an act of Charles II forbidding American vessels to trade with Guernsey and Jersey. The end of a war crisis brought effects worse than the cruelties of press gangs, when large numbers of sailors were thrown "loose on the World . . . in the most wretched starving situation," unable even to get a passage home.[11] There were also appeals from indigent Americans of all sorts, including women, who were stranded and needed aid. Not surprisingly, there were numerous impostors, sometimes as difficult to detect as a foreign vessel masquerading under the American flag.[12] There were also unusual cases, such as the Baltimore sea captain who became insane and whom Johnson, out of compassion, placed in suitable accommodations and finally paid for his burial expenses.[13] The burdens placed upon the London consulate were not only greater than those experienced by American consuls in France, Italy, Spain, and Portugal, but the advantages from trade were even less. "I am appointed to a place," Johnson wrote to the Secretary of State, "where every Merchant in America has his correspondent, and who will not remove his Business so long as he does well; but if the Captain of his Ship is arrested by a Seaman; or he gets into any Scrape, it falls on me to protect, and extricate him; whilst the Merchant is freed from any trouble, and he is reaping the Advantages of American favors."[14]

It is little wonder that, under these circumstances, Johnson became more importunate than any other person in the consular establishment — with the possible exception of Sylvanus Bourne — in urging that Congress provide compensation for services rendered the public. American consuls at Lisbon, Bordeaux, Marseilles, and other ports might be content with the prestige of the office, plus the undeniable trade advantages a consul in such places enjoyed. But Johnson was both blunt and insistent in urging that Congress establish regulations for the consular service, adopt European practices by levying tonnage and other duties on merchant vessels to provide for indigent seamen, and, especially, support their consulates in proper dignity by providing fees and salaries. Johnson animadverted at some length upon the subject even in his letter of acceptance, expressing the hope that Congress would be liberal enough to enable him to continue in office. Betraying his lack of familiarity with the divided sentiments of his countrymen on the need for a consular establishment, he soon followed this with information about consular regulations in France and elsewhere which he regarded as suitable models.[15] Even before Congress

[11] Johnson to TJ, 30 Sep. 1791. In addition, captains of American vessels also dumped ill and unfit seamen, leaving them as Johnson reported in "such poverty and distress as would rouse the feelings and compassion of the most hard-hearted." He suggested that the tactics of the Prussian consul in fixing responsibility upon owners of vessels for such cruelties might be emulated (Johnson to TJ, 26 Feb. 1791).

[12] "There are so many of them," Johnson wrote on one occasion, "that let us act as cautious as we can we shall by some be deceived" (Johnson to Thomas Auldjo, 23 May 1792, DNA: RG 59, CD; MNP 167/1).

[13] Johnson to TJ, 26 Feb. and 30 Sep. 1791; 6 Apr. 1792.

[14] Johnson to TJ, 30 Sep. 1791. In his letter of acceptance Johnson had pointed out that the consular business at London would give him more employment "than every other together" (Johnson to TJ, 2 Nov. 1790).

[15] Johnson to TJ, 2 and 30 Nov. 1790; 26 Feb. 1791. On the opposition in Congress to compensation for consuls, see TJ to Skipwith, 31 July 1791. William Maclay, arguing against any diplomatic establishment on the ground that the relations of the United States with other nations were commercial rather than political, declared that these could be handled "by consuls, who would cost us nothing" (Maclay, *Journal*, ed. Maclay, p. 257).

adjourned, he confided to James Maury that he had told the Secretary of State he would resign if adequate compensation were not provided by law.[16] In the spring of 1791, as he anxiously awaited news of the consular bill, he declared that he would not continue in office beyond the next Congress "unless something handsome is allowed me."[17] Late in May he was astonished that he had not received a line from Jefferson about the fate of the bill. When he learned from newspapers that Congress had adjourned without making any provisions for the consular system, he immediately proposed to William Knox and James Maury that they reach "a proper understanding and . . . have a memorial ready to present to Congress, pressing them to come to some decision." Johnson of course said nothing of this to the Secretary of State. Knox, who at first promised to draft such an appeal, advised instead that each should write individually to their "friends . . . and get them to interfere."[18] In his appeal to Jefferson, Johnson recited the burdens of his office and asked that his account of them be placed before the President so as to enable him to judge what compensation should be allowed and to "urge Congress to pass an act for that purpose." This suggestion, perhaps intended to bring Washington's friendship with the family to bear, was accompanied by Johnson's promise to persevere at least until he knew what was to be done at the next session.[19]

What happened at the next session was even more disappointing. One of the persons to whom Johnson had written—probably Robert Morris—had sent him a copy of the consular bill as soon as it passed the Senate. Johnson thought the result "miserably Parsimonious" on the part of Congress, though the House of Representatives had not yet acted.[20] The bill, he declared to Jefferson, "makes but a miserable compensation to me for the loss of time, vexation and trouble I have had."[21] This was disappointment enough, but when Johnson finally received the bill as passed and found he was obliged to give bond, he looked upon this as insult added to injury. He bluntly told Jefferson that he considered

[16] This referred to Johnson's letter of acceptance of 2 Nov. 1790, which could scarcely be regarded as containing a threat of resignation (Johnson to James Maury, 7 Feb. 1791, DNA: RG 59, CD; MNP 167/1).

[17] Johnson to Maury, 25 May 1791; Johnson to Knox, 18 Apr. 1791 (same).

[18] Johnson to Maury, 27 July and 9 Aug. 1791 (same). Knox, who at this time was in such straits that he had to borrow £100 to go to London in an effort to sell lands for his brother, had no expectation that Congress would provide compensation. But he wrote to Henry Knox of his conversations with Maury and Johnson, and added: "I imagine they will both resign. They are merchants and have families. They find the duties of their appointments very considerable and interfere so much with their other pursuits, exclusive of being attended with no small expence, that without some provision they cannot stand it" (William Knox to Henry Knox, 27 June 1791, MHi: Knox Papers).

[19] Johnson to TJ, 30 Sep. 1791. Johnson revealed to Maury that this letter was written in consequence of Knox' suggestion as the best mode of achieving their end. He added that he had written to the Secretary of State pressing for regulations of the consular office, "as well as provision for their Consul, or else I cannot give up my time" (Johnson to Maury, 17 Sep. 1791; Tr in DNA: RG 59, CD; MNP 167/1).

[20] Johnson to Maury, 6 Jan. 1792 (DNA: RG 59, CD; MNP 167/1). In a letter of the same date to Auldjo, a British subject who was vice-consul at Cowes, Johnson was more circumspect, merely stating that his "friend" had said the bill would pass the House of Representatives without alteration, but that he had not read it and could offer no opinion on its merits (Johnson to Auldjo, 6 Jan. 1792; for other comments by Johnson, see also Johnson to Maury, 16 Jan., 23 Feb., 9 Apr., and 20 May 1792; all in same).

[21] Johnson to TJ, 6 Apr. 1792.

the requirement a direct violation of the "promise" made when he was appointed and flatly declined to give bond. He of course understood what it would mean to defy the law and so gave assurance that he would "continue to execute the functions of the Office . . . for the benefit of my Country until the President shall be pleased to appoint some other person to take my Place."[22] Jefferson naturally rejected the idea of a promise violated or even made without lawful authority, praised Johnson for his faithful and useful services, and urged him to reconsider so that the President would not be obliged to appoint a successor who would meet the legal requirement. On the outbreak of war early in 1793 Johnson did reconsider and supplied the bond. Four months later he informed Jefferson of the fact.[23] Opposition in Congress to a salaried consular establishment may have worked a hardship in Johnson's case, but his long absence from home undoubtedly contributed to his failure to understand the reasons for it and to make him feel he had been ill-treated by the country he served, the more so since he thought Jefferson communicated with him too infrequently.[24]

For the same reasons, Johnson misjudged the feelings of his countrymen about the extent of consular powers. Having observed the customs of foreign consulates, he naturally sought to exercise the powers of his office in like manner and failed to realize that this would not have been tolerated in his native land. Perhaps unaware of the feelings aroused by clashes between state officials and British and French consulates in Norfolk, New York, and elsewhere during and after the war, Johnson sought coercive powers over merchant vessels and exclusive jurisdiction over disputes between masters and crews. Had he been closer in touch with sentiment in America, he might have known that there special privileges and immunities were extended to consuls by courtesy, that the law of nations did not apply to them, that it had been purposely excluded from the Consular Convention of 1788, and that, until Congress established regulations, state laws alone determined consular functions and jurisdiction.[25]

---

[22] Johnson to TJ, 9 Oct. 1792. Pinckney arrived in August and delivered TJ's instructions of 31 May 1792, enclosing copies of the consular act, which Johnson forwarded to Maury and Auldjo. After talking with Pinckney, Johnson told Maury that he had little expectation of being compensated for relieving destitute sailors and others: "I evade it where I can," he wrote, "but am often obliged to give assistance." He wrote Elias Vanderhorst that since Congress was not disposed to give compensation for "Loss of Time, Fatigue, or Expences," he had decided to quit the service and had so informed the Secretary of State (Johnson to Maury, 22 Aug. and 26 Dec. 1792; Johnson to Auldjo, 22 Aug. 1792; Johnson to Vanderhorst, 26 Dec. 1792; all in DNA: RG 59, CD; MNP 167/1).

[23] TJ to Johnson, 21 Mch. 1793. Johnson to Pinckney, 8 Apr. 1793 (DNA: RG 59, CD; MNP 167/1). Johnson did not settle his accounts with Pinckney as directed by TJ and explained that, since many of these were not allowed by law, he supposed they would have to be laid before Congress at the next session (Johnson to TJ, 24 Aug. 1793). Actually, most of his outlays were unauthorized, and Johnson later memorialized Congress for reimbursement.

[24] Johnson to TJ, 9 Oct. 1792. Johnson frequently complained to Maury of Jefferson's "neglect."

[25] See TJ to Newton, 8 Sep. 1791. TJ's views on an American consular establishment are well expressed in his letter to Jay of 14 Nov. 1788. His consistent policy was that consuls should not engage in commerce, that they should be paid at least in fees, and that they should not be subjects of the country in which they carried out their duties. See Eugene Schuyler, *American diplomacy and the furtherance of commerce* (London,

At the outset, Johnson sought detailed instructions even on such routine matters as the proper form for reporting entries and clearances of American vessels and their cargoes, sensibly suggesting the desirability of a uniform style of reporting for all consuls.[26] Surprisingly, systematic as he was, Jefferson failed to act upon the suggestion and issued only general instructions. Johnson wondered whether he had power even to administer oaths as other consuls did and urged that Congress adopt strict and explicit maritime regulations giving consuls coercive power over masters of vessels comparable to those in France. Lacking such authority, he thought his appointment would be of no avail and would "reduce our Country in the eyes of this Government."[27] He was particularly disturbed that American sailors were habitually running to petty attorneys on every frivolous pretext, but called this to the attention of the Secretary of State as a burden because he was obliged to intervene.[28] To his colleague James Maury, however, he put it in a quite different light. "In cases of Disputes between the Captains and their Men," he declared, "I do not suffer either the Courts of Justice, or the Commons to take cognizance of it, but order them before me. This is the custom of other Consuls, and I doubt not but you will pursue it and support the Dignity [and Honor of the office]."[29] Two weeks later he informed Maury that, until Congress prescribed their duties, he would follow the usages and customs of European consulates. "Wherever you can accommodate between Master and Men," he added, "it is best. But I do not hesitate interfering peremptorily, not only with them but with Proctors and Attorneys. I suffer them not by any means to interfere between Americans, as it is an invasion on the Honor and Dignity of our Office, as that takes Cognizance of all Disputes except the case of assault. Them the laws of the Country will punish."[30] The words, echoing those of the Comte de Moustier and Martin Oster protesting against the invasion of consular powers and immunities by local officials in the United States, provide a measure of the gulf separating Johnson's views and the role of the consular system as envisaged by his own government.

Indeed at times Johnson sought to support the honor and dignity of his office by going beyond the practices of European consulates. This was exemplified by his interference in the suit brought by two seamen against Captain Crozier of the American vessel *Greyhound*, threatened by the Admiralty with seizure unless the claims of the seamen were met. "I am at a loss to understand what

---

[1886]), p. 75; Burt E. Powell, "Jefferson and the Consular service," *Pol. Sci. Qu.*, XXI (1906), p. 626-38.

[26] Johnson to TJ, 2 Nov. 1790. To Maury, Johnson wrote: "It certainly would have been more pleasing had Congress enacted Marine Laws and forms for our government, but . . . we must form them ourselves, and the greater similarity we use I think the better, and for that purpose I enclose you copies of what I have adapted and delivered similar ones to Mr. Knox" (Johnson to Maury, 15 Nov. 1790, DNA: RG 59, CD; MNP 167/1).

[27] Johnson to TJ, 15 Nov. 1790. See also Johnson to TJ, 26 Feb. 1791 and 13 Apr. 1792.

[28] Johnson to TJ, 30 Nov. 1790.

[29] Johnson to Maury, 7 Feb. 1791 (DNA: RG 59, CD; MNP 167/1; the words in brackets are supplied, being such as Johnson usually employed in this context).

[30] Johnson to Maury, 24 Feb. 1791 (same).

the Lords of the Admiralty mean," Johnson wrote, "by interfering between Americans, the subjects of the United States. It is contrary to the Law of Nations and far from being friendly. . . . Should their Lordships persevere in their directions to you to arrest the Greyhound, I shall not appear in Court to contend the Matter, but you may pursue to Judgment, Condemnation, and Sale; then I will transmit to Congress those proceedings and be governed by their directions in future."[31] This was a fairly typical example of the harsh language which Johnson admitted he was often compelled to use. He thought the Admiralty would not dare "such a breach of the law of Nations."[32] The two seamen had left the *Greyhound*, joined the royal navy, and brought suit to recover their wages. Johnson thereupon informed Maury that he had a suit pending in the Court of Common Pleas "highly interesting to the Commercial Interest of all Europe."[33] He also invited all foreign consuls in London to attend the trial of this "Cause of the utmost consequence" so that they could transmit accounts of it to their respective courts.[34] Against the opinion of the Lord Advocate, Henry Erskine, and even contrary to the advice of his own attorney, Johnson refused to compromise, insisted upon a jury trial, and hoped to set a precedent which "would have ascertained the power of Consuls, and prevented those low R—— from teazing us any more." But in this he was disappointed, for at the last moment the suit was withdrawn. Johnson, feeling both frustrated and uneasy, then formed the quixotic scheme of drawing up a memorial to Parliament. He asked the other consuls in London to join him in signing it, hoping for the passage of a bill "to prevent . . . Attornies from entering Actions for Foreign Subjects against their Captains."[35] He freely and somewhat proudly reported all of this to James Maury, but revealed none of the circumstances to the Secretary of State. The only allusion that he made in his dispatches to this extraordinary effort to extend his authority and jurisdiction was to justify the expense of a suit which had accomplished nothing. He reported to Jefferson that he had been obliged to defend Captain Crozier because otherwise an ill precedent would have encouraged the crews of all vessels to sue for pay. Worse, veiling the truth in a self-serving equivocation, he asserted that he had succeeded and had protected American masters against all such "innovations."[36] Even the litigious Oster at Norfolk had not gone quite so far in asserting the authority and dignity of his office.

Jefferson, reflecting his own style of diplomacy, had been careful to warn Johnson and other consuls against fatiguing government officials with unimportant matters, but rather to husband their good dispositions for occasions of some moment, "never indulging in any case whatever a single expression which may irritate."[37] This prudent counsel was all the more applicable to Johnson as the only American official at the capital. The absence of formal diplomatic

---

[31] Johnson to George Gostling, Admiralty Office, 23 June 1791 (same).

[32] Johnson to Maury, 13 June 1791 (same). In a letter of the 30th, Johnson told Maury that he had appealed from the Commissioners of the Customs to the Lords of the Admiralty "and in many instances obliged to be harsh."

[33] Johnson to Maury, 24 Nov. 1791 (DNA: RG 59, CD; MNP 167/1).

[34] Johnson to the European consuls in London, [6] Dec. 1791 (same).

[35] Johnson to Maury, 6 Jan. 1792 (same).

[36] Johnson to TJ, 6 Apr. 1792. It is worth noting that all of this occurred after the *Rachel* incident had been closed.

[37] TJ's instructions to American consuls, 26 Aug. 1790.

relations, the sensitivity of many Englishmen to the humiliating defeat at the hands of colonials, the overbearing attitude of some American seamen – equalled and often exceeded by the insolence and even cruelty of British naval officials – the occasional smuggling and evasion of maritime regulations on the part of American mariners, the connivance of some American mercantile firms in the concealment of true ownership of vessels, all called for consular conduct of the utmost civility, restraint, and tact.[38] Johnson, however, seemed to regard himself as being in an adversary relationship with officials with whom he had to communicate. This was indeed at times the case, but the unusually burdensome and complicated problems he faced were not made less so by his rather free use of harsh, accusatory, and even threatening language. Further, under a system permitting consuls to engage in trade, disinterested reporting of commercial intelligence affecting the interests of the merchant-consul as well as others in trade presented inevitable conflict. It must be said that Johnson's dispatches did not adequately meet the duty placed upon him to report commercial intelligence of general concern to his countrymen.

This is strikingly illustrated in the contrast afforded by Jefferson's early schoolmate and life-long friend, James Maury, American consul at Liverpool. Maury also faced the problems of negligent captains, disputes between them and their crews, violations of customs regulations, and the harassments of Treasury and Admiralty officials, though in a less degree. But he never complained about lack of compensation, made no threats to resign because Congress did not provide it, did not reproach the Secretary of State for the infrequency of his communications and, when the consular bill was finally passed, did not hesitate to comply with the requirement for giving bond. On disputes between masters and crew his invariable approach was to seek an accommodation, feeling unauthorized to take further steps without instructions or statutory warrant.[39] Whereas Johnson made it clear that he thought one should not be too scrupulous about abuses of the American flag because this was good for trade, Maury made a particular effort to give effect to Jefferson's instructions on the point.[40] But what distinguished Maury's dispatches more than anything else from those of his colleague lay in the kind and importance of commercial information they conveyed. At the time when Johnson was defying the Admiralty and providing legal defense in the suit against the master of *Greyhound*, a matter of far greater importance – passage by Parliament of the Corn Law of 1791 – went entirely unnoticed in his dispatches. Jefferson, who was much concerned about the possible effect of this legislation on American farmers and on the relations between the two countries, received his first information of its passage as well as the first copy of its text not from Johnson at the capital, but from the American consul at Liverpool.[41] While Johnson omitted detailed commercial intelligence

[38] Jefferson himself had been nettled by the attitude of the British during his visit in 1786 (see TJ to R. H. Lee, 22 Apr. 1786; TJ to Jay, 22 and 23 Apr. 1786). As an example of the frictions created by American seamen, a Fourth of July episode at Liverpool had much disturbed both Maury and Johnson (Johnson to Maury, 27 July 1791, DNA: RG 59, CD; MNP 167/1). Despite Johnson's disclaimer, the facts of the case involving Purdie – and others that might be cited – sufficiently indicate the corresponding attitudes of British navy personnel (see documents on Purdie case, at Vol. 18: 310-42).

[39] Maury to TJ, 9 Sep. 1790; 2 Mch., 23 June, 12 and 29 July; and 13 Aug. 1791.

[40] Johnson to TJ, 26 Feb. 1791 (quoted above); Maury to TJ, 4 July 1793.

[41] TJ to Maury, 30 Aug. 1791; Maury to TJ, 23 June 1791. On TJ's concern about

from his dispatches, Maury caused to be printed a tabular form in which he could record and report fluctuations in price and demand of all of the principal articles of American produce. These he sent regularly to Jefferson with his own comments, such as the increase in the price of rice because of rainy weather, the steady market in tobacco despite news of a disastrous crop in America, the scarcity of potash and indigo, the current demand for cotton, the lack of demand for lumber, the advance in turpentine prices, and the stagnation of business due to "the Calamity of the times."[42] None of this kind of information appeared in Johnson's dispatches, nor did he bother to inform Jefferson of the proclamation prohibiting the export of wheat or give notice of the closing of British ports to the importation of foreign grain. Perhaps, as his dispatches occasionally indicated, Johnson thought the London newspapers he forwarded to the Secretary of State contained sufficient information of public interest. But these did not include the kind of detailed comment about commodity prices and their supply and demand that Maury provided. In brief, Maury's quite disinterested conduct of the consular office foreshadowed the professional service that was still a generation in the future: Johnson's revealed some of the disadvantages of having the office filled by a merchant whose private interests could scarcely avoid being at times in conflict with public duty. It is not surprising, therefore, that Jefferson expressed gratitude to the Liverpool consul for conveying intelligence "of considerable importance" or that, on receiving it, he sought to make it available to American farmers and merchants by releasing it on occasion both to Fenno's *Gazette of the United States* and to Freneau's *National Gazette*.[43]

When Jefferson notified Johnson of his appointment and told him that "somewhat more" would be expected of him as the only American official located at the capital, he may have implanted the hope that when diplomatic relations were established the consul would be made minister. This would have been a natural expectation and the enthusiasm with which Johnson entered upon his duties gives support to the inference that he entertained it. He began with a flurry of dispatches following one on the other, in the first of which he pointedly remarked that his duties would be heavier than those of all other consuls combined "until a superior appointment takes place"; that, while his rank did not entitle him to personal conferences with the Secretary for Foreign Affairs, discussions with his secretaries indicated "every wish, and inclination, on the part of Government, to support a friendly and good understanding with the United States"; and that George Aust, secretary to the Duke of Leeds, had expressed sanguine hopes of seeing a treaty of alliance or a treaty of commerce negotiated.[44] Five months later, despite all of the testimony in the Purdie case which had been so persuasive with Jefferson, Johnson said that he had heard of no American sailors being mistreated; that since his appointment he had met

---

the passage of the Corn Law, see TJ to McHenry, 28 Mch. 1791; TJ to Carroll, 4 Apr. 1791; TJ to Washington, 17 Apr. 1791.

[42] Maury to TJ, 14 Sep. 1791; 9 and 30 Apr., 8 and 27 May, 19 Sep., 7, 13, and 26 Nov., and 1 Dec. 1792; 16 Mch., 3 June, 4 July, and 7 Sep. 1793. While Johnson's dispatches virtually ceased after Pinckney's arrival in the autumn of 1792, Maury kept on sending his detailed commercial reports at frequent intervals.

[43] TJ to Maury, 12 Sep. 1793; see Maury to TJ, 7 Nov. 1792, which TJ sent to the two rival newspapers as an "Extract of a letter dated Liverpool Nov. 7. 92."

[44] Johnson to TJ, 2 Nov. 1790. In the first two months Johnson sent as many dispatches as he did during the last two years of TJ's tenure as Secretary of State.

with "every Assurance and Friendly disposition in this Government towards that of the United States"; and that he hoped the impending appointment of a British minister to the United States would "define the rights of the two Countrys, and produce an Amicable liberal and Just understanding."[45] While Johnson's communications with subordinate officials in the Customs, Admiralty, and Treasury offices at this time rather contradicted the assurances from the Foreign Office which he received with such confidence, his dispatches convey more than a hint that the task of representing the United States in any effort to reach a just understanding would be acceptable. With William S. Smith and William Temple Franklin both in London in the spring of 1791 and both ambitious to be charged with that responsibility, Johnson might justifiably have thought his own claim superior to theirs.[46] While conveying repeated indications of the cordial relations he enjoyed with the Foreign Office and the friendly dispositions expressed there, he may indeed have selected the *Rachel* incident to demonstrate his mode of conducting complicated negotiations. He thought it a "case . . . singularly hard" and he prosecuted it vigorously before all of the major departments of the British government.

III

Even the essential facts about the *Rachel* episode are not altogether free of doubt. Johnson referred to it as "a complicated affair," and so it was.[47] But it was not made less so by incomplete, conflicting, and imprecise testimony and especially by Johnson's failure to address himself, as his instructions required, to the central question as to whether the owner of the vessel had made a convenience of the American flag. When *Rachel* was detained late in October because she was French-built, William Green, her putative owner, first took the matter up with Treasury officials. Later he reported to Jefferson that the American consul had not intervened at the outset because he had only received news of his appointment and was without instructions at the time of *Rachel*'s arrival.[48] This is incorrect. Johnson's commission had reached him a week before *Rachel* arrived, but his instructions, specifically enjoining him to try to prevent all vessels entering as "American . . . which are not really of the United States," arrived on *Rachel* herself.[49] The fact that the brigantine was detained by customs officials precisely because she was suspected of being something other than her papers claimed should have alerted the consul to his duty. But during *Rachel*'s initial detention, Johnson stood silent, though not aloof. He and Green, both merchants, were in full accord in thinking it would be commercially advantageous and therefore justifiable for the United States to adopt European usages by which nations at war covered their navigation under the

[45] Johnson to TJ, 27 Mch. 1791; see also Johnson to TJ, 4 and 18 Apr. 1791.

[46] Johnson's communications with the Customs, Admiralty, and Treasury offices soon caused him to doubt the assurances he had at first accepted so confidently from the Foreign Office (see Johnson to TJ, 13 June, 10 July, and 12 Sep. 1791). On the aspirations of Smith and Temple, see Editorial Note and documents on commercial and diplomatic relations with Great Britain, at 15 Dec. 1790.

[47] Johnson to Maury, 13 June 1791 (DNA: RG 59, CD; MNP 167/1).

[48] Green to the Secretary of State, 23 May 1791 (Document I below).

[49] Johnson to TJ, 2 Nov. 1790, acknowledging TJ's letter to him of 7 Aug. and his instructions to American consuls of 26 Aug. 1790.

flags and papers of neutrals. In his first appeal to Jefferson, Green strongly argued for such a policy, urging abandonment of the British and American practice of inserting in a ship's papers the place where she was built. He may very well have been the sole owner of *Rachel* and her cargo as he claimed. But, if this were so, one wonders why, after her release, he felt it necessary to urge upon the Secretary of State a policy covering her even if she were owned by an alien, justifying this solely in terms of the wealth that would be derived from it and pointing particularly to Hamburg, "whose Flag is generally attended to as much upon the Ocean as if she had Twenty Sail of Line of Battle Ships to protect it from Injury and Insult."[50] It was just a month after this plea that Johnson, acknowledging the specific obligation imposed by his instructions and admitting the frequency of the abuse, dared to suggest that the policy of the government he represented should not be enforced too scrupulously.[51] The argument of the owner of *Rachel*, though based upon a narrow conception of the national interest, is understandable. But the same argument, coming from the consul, was in conflict with official instructions.

Rachel arrived at London while preparations for war were still in progress. Treasury officials, rarely prompt, gave no response to Green's appeal for two months and then, immediately after news of the Convention with Spain arrived, denied entry. Possibly they suspected that the real owner of the brigantine was a British subject, concealing the fact in order to avoid the disadvantage of the tonnage act of 1789, which favored American citizens. The ministry had long since warned against such discrimination and British consuls had reported the resultant concealments of ownership to avoid its effects.[52] Whatever the reason for denial of entry, *Rachel* remained in port for another month after her release. Green at first stated that this was due to the "oppressive circumstances" in which Captain Duff had been placed by the customs officials. Later he said that Duff's only offense had been to land the fowling piece brought by William Knox, thereby failing to point out that there had also been an altercation and the captain had ejected from his cabin the tidewaiter who initiated the prosecution.[53] Neither Green nor Johnson nor Duff explained why the captain should have been brought into court over an article found in the baggage of Knox or why that consul was not involved in the suit. But all stated that *Rachel* had been detained three months after her arrival, which is contrary to fact. *Rachel* had remained in port for a month after she was refused entry, according to their testimony, so that Duff could give bail, but she was not then under seizure. A more plausible explanation is that Jacob Wilkinson, the consignee, was awaiting word from Ostend before giving orders for her to proceed. Both Green and Duff, however, made liberal estimates of the loss to the owner because of the additional month's "detention."[54] Similar conflicts in the testimony occur

[50] Green to TJ, 21 Jan. 1791. *Rachel*'s register did not show where she was built (Johnson to TJ, 31 May 1791; Document III, enclosure C).

[51] Johnson to TJ, 26 Feb. 1791.

[52] On such abuses, see John Hamilton, British consul at Norfolk, to the Duke of Leeds, 25 May 1791 (PRO: FO 4/10, f. 63-5). See also Editorial Notes and documents on American commercial policy, at 18 June 1790.

[53] Green to TJ, 21 Jan. 1791 and 23 May 1791 (Document I). Duff himself volunteered the information that he had ejected the customs officer because he had tried to make his quarters "a Cooking place for his provision" (Affidavit of Duff, 4 Mch. 1791; Document II, enclosure B, note).

[54] *Rachel* was denied entry on 24 Dec. 1790. Her departure for Ostend was variously

in the more complicated circumstances of *Rachel's* return from Ostend in February, when Johnson promptly and vigorously took up her cause.

William Green informed Jefferson that Johnson did not intervene until the "pressing necessity of National Circumstance compelled him."[55] He did not explain the nature of the compulsion and, not surprisingly, there were conflicting accounts of the circumstances which produced his intervention. All of the testimony makes it clear that, on her outward voyage from Ostend, *Rachel* came to anchor off Spithead on the 21st of February. Captain Duff informed Johnson that her voyage to New York had been interrupted by permission of the consignee because it was "absolutely necessary" for him to discover the fate of the suit against himself. The customs officers at Portsmouth quoted Duff as saying he had come into port "*to await orders.*" Perhaps so, but there can be no doubt that the captain did submit to the Commissioners of the Customs a memorial which reached that body on the 24th. This appeal was certainly made with Johnson's knowledge and very likely with his assistance. Duff's request to compromise the matter was granted the very same day. Green must have advanced the amount of court costs and compensation to the tidewaiter who brought suit, since he later asked indemnification. The transaction had been concluded swiftly and Captain Duff learned of the result on the 25th.

But, unfortunately, he had not reported to the customs officials immediately on arrival. He explained that his delay was due to foul weather, though this had not prevented the revenue officers from coming on board on the 22d. Nor had it kept Duff from getting off his memorial to the Commissioners of Customs on the same day. He also gave conflicting testimony about the date he had reported to the Portsmouth customs officials. At first he stated that this was done on the 24th, a date corroborated by the officials. Later, under Johnson's directions to verify the date precisely, he altered this to the 23rd. This, unfortunately, confused the matter still further and made even more difficult Johnson's effort to prove that the report of the Commissioners of Customs had deviated from the truth in essential points. Johnson tried to reconcile the contradiction, but could only argue that the report had mistakenly given *Thursday* instead of *Tuesday* as the day when Duff announced *Rachel's* arrival. Tuesday fell on the 22d, a date that the captain had not mentioned in either of his contradictory statements. Worse, this would have weakened Johnson's argument still further by proving that the delay had not in fact occurred.

But the important point, which not even Duff denied, is that he had failed to report at once as required by law. Later, when he did submit *Rachel's* register and manifest, the customs officers at Portsmouth, perhaps already annoyed at his ignoring the maritime requirement, found that *Rachel* had on board brandy and gin in amounts not permitted by regulations. They seized her on the 2d

---

given in the testimony of Duff, Green, and Johnson as 17, 18, and 20 Jan. 1791. Duff even asserted that the vessel was detained by the Commissioners of the Customs until the 17th of January, yet, in calculating the loss caused by the detention – which he liberally estimated at £681 sterling – he correctly estimated the duration at 63 days (Affidavit of Duff, 17 Jan. 1791, enclosed in Green to TJ, 21 Jan. 1791). Green later claimed that *Rachel* had been detained 89 days from 22 Oct. 1790 to 18 Jan. 1791 (Green to TJ, 6 Dec. 1791; Document III). Johnson stretched the facts equally by estimating the detention at "upwards of twelve weeks" (Johnson to the Duke of Leeds, 25 Mch. 1791; Document II, enclosure c).

[55] Green to TJ, 23 May 1791 (Document I).

of March and Captain Duff set out for London that night. The next day he gave a written report to Johnson, who immediately intervened and demanded not only that the Commissioners of Customs release the brigantine, but that compensation be made for her detention. Three weeks later the Commissioners gave orders for *Rachel*'s release, subject to prosecution of the spirits in small quantities and satisfaction being made to the seizing officer. On receiving this information, Johnson appealed the next day not to the Lords of the Treasury but to the Secretary for Foreign Affairs, again requesting the vessel's release as well as full and ample compensation.[56] On the day of its receipt his memorial was referred by the Foreign Office to the Treasury and by that department to the Commissioners of Customs. Johnson viewed this as making the accused both judge and jury and again protested to the Duke of Leeds, more vigorously — and also inaccurately.[57] The reference to the Commissioners of the Customs was of course for report and recommendation. Not surprisingly, the Commissioners' report was at variance with the statements of Johnson and Duff. It recommended that, since *Rachel* and her captain had received all reasonable indulgence, they should be given no further relief.[58]

The issue might then have been closed. *Rachel* had been detained only three weeks in her second clash with authority and was free to proceed as soon as the necessary condition had been met. On another occasion Johnson himself stated that compensation to seizing officers was customary and, if it were deemed unreasonable, appeal could be made to the Treasury.[59] In the case of *Rachel*, however, his appeal directly to the Secretary for Foreign Affairs resulted in a delay of several weeks before he learned that it was fruitless. Meanwhile *Rachel* was losing money for her owner, had suffered damage at the hands of the officials, and the spirits in small packages had been "pillaged" in Johnson's view — prosecuted in that of the officials. But now Johnson turned upon the Commissioners of Customs, charged that their report did violence to the truth, professed not to understand what was meant by "*Satisfaction to the Seizing*

[56] Johnson to TJ, 31 May 1791 (Document II, enclosures B and C).

[57] Johnson to the Duke of Leeds, 19 Apr. 1791 (Document II, enclosure D). Johnson quite inaccurately stated that *Rachel* was then in the fifth month of her detention, a calculation that could not be justified whether he regarded both detentions as one or only referred to the second. Exactly a month later he stated that *Rachel* had been detained three months, which was still off the mark (Johnson to Commissioners of the Customs, 18 May 1791; Document II, enclosure H). Johnson also erred in referring to *Rachel*'s having been "stripped" of a part of her cargo — "pillaged" was the term he used in reporting the case to TJ. The customs officers were only enforcing regulations that had been established primarily to prevent mariners from smuggling spirits in small quantities. This was a practice with which Johnson himself was quite familiar, having engaged in it himself. When he first came to London in 1771 he wrote his partner John Davidson that he had found a way of slipping a few bottles of "good old speritt" past the customs officials and added: "Jonny you know we have studied the art of smuggling." The allusion suggests the kind of contribution which Davidson, as deputy naval officer at Annapolis, was able to make to the firm of Wallace, Johnson, and Davidson (Papenfuse, *In pursuit of profit*, p. 141, note 9).

[58] Commissioners of Customs to Lords of the Treasury, 29 Apr. 1791 (Document II, enclosure E).

[59] Johnson to Maury, 17 Sep. 1791 (DNA: RG 59, CD; MNP 167/1). See also Johnson to TJ on the similar condition for the release of the American vessels *Hope*, *Janet*, and *Thomas*.

Officers," and announced that he would report the transaction "to the Congress of the United States" and send copies of his view of the facts to the Duke of Leeds and to the Lords of the Treasury.[60] Without waiting for an answer from the Commissioners he sought to obtain one from the customs officers at Portsmouth, demanding that it be put in writing. When the officers reported that £60 would suffice, Johnson asked the Commissioners of Customs for a speedy answer as to whether *Rachel* could proceed on her voyage on payment of that amount. He did not submit the officers' letter to the Commissioners, presumably because it quoted Duff as saying he considered it a "very reasonable" sum. Nor did he send either to the Commissioners or to Jefferson the letter of Captain Duff concerning their reply which he sent by the same post.[61] Nothing had been gained by this rather circulatory mode of negotiation except delay and increased irritation on the part of all concerned. Far from husbanding the good disposition of government for important occasions as Jefferson had counselled, Johnson had made prodigal levies upon it in a case of questionable merit.

But this was by no means the end. On the 27th of April, just a month after the Commissioners of the Customs had ordered the release of *Rachel*, her boatswain and four members of the crew deserted and enlisted in the British navy, claiming to be subjects of the Crown despite the fact that they had signed on in New York as American citizens. This was not an unusual occurrence, considering the higher wages offered seamen by the Admiralty. Johnson himself had long since called Jefferson's attention to the problem.[62] But when the deserters sought to recover their wages and personal possessions that had been left on board, *Rachel* faced arrest and Johnson sprang to her defense. Already engaged in confrontation with the Foreign Office, Treasury, and Customs on her account, he now took on the Lords of the Admiralty. It was his policy, he confided to James Maury but not to the Secretary of State, to forbid captains of American vessels to pay the wages or deliver the clothes of seamen who deserted or entered the royal navy. "The *American Captain* in refusing to deliver the *American Sailors* cloaths, or pay his wages," he wrote to Maury about another case of the sort, "did perfectly right. In every instance I have forbid their doing either, and in many even not to pay the Wages of British Seamen, prest out of American ships. The first point I am clear in, and Government has given it up; on the second I took Sir William Scott's opinion and which is rather against me, tho in one instance the Admiralty has arrested a Ship at Portsmouth and that more than a month ago, threatening that they would sell her to pay the Mens wages in six days unless satisfied. I wrote the Admiralty to do as they pleased, that nothing should be paid, that I should protest and transmit the same to Congress, and take their instructions; they have done nothing, and if we were to act firmly, I dont believe they dare."[63] The vessel

[60] Johnson to the Commissioners of Customs, 18 May 1791 (Document II, enclosure H).

[61] Johnson to Duff, 18 May 1791; Duff to Johnson, 19 May 1791; Johnson to Commissioners of Customs, 24 May 1791; Officers of the Customs to Johnson, 20 May 1791 (Document II, enclosures I, K, L, M).

[62] Johnson to TJ, 2 Nov. 1790.

[63] Johnson to Maury, 13 and 30 June 1791 (DNA: RG 59, CD; MNP 167/1). Sir William Scott's opinion, solicited by Johnson, was based on the case of one James Cooper, a British subject, who on 28 Sep. 1790 signed articles at London as master of the American ship *Abigail* of Boston. After her voyage to Savannah and back, Cooper left

in question was *Rachel* and the Lords of the Admiralty had indeed dared to arrest her when the five seamen brought suit in the High Court of Admiralty. Johnson, in the most imperious language he had thus far employed, declared that the seamen were Americans, that they had violated their contract, and that by deserting they had forfeited their claim to wages. He demanded that the Admiralty give "instant, and effectual Orders to put an immediate stop to the perpetration of so insolent an Outrage."[64] The response was prompt, arriving just in time for Johnson to send it to the Secretary of State with other documents on the case of *Rachel*. It was also conclusive: all that was necessary for her release was for the owner or master of the vessel to settle the claims or let the High Court of Admiralty decide.[65]

Johnson, of course, had no more authority to forbid the master of *Rachel* – or any other vessel – to refuse payment than he had to compel American captains to report their entry and clearance. Presumably he was able to persuade Green that the Admiralty would not make good its warning that *Rachel* would be condemned and sold if the claims were not met. Certainly Johnson's confidence was not shaken. Simultaneously and in language as blunt as that he had used with the Admiralty, he repeated his earlier protests to the Treasury and to the Secretary for Foreign Affairs, now Lord Grenville. In the first of these communications he reiterated his demand that compensation be made for *Rachel*'s earlier detention and – again assuming authority which he did not possess – declared that he could not consent to the condition imposed for her release, characterizing it as "an arbitrary fine." In that to Grenville he asserted that his earlier memorial to Leeds complaining of a gross outrage had been referred for ultimate decision to those who had perpetrated it. This was not a very precise statement of what had occurred, but in both letters he announced his intention to transmit a report "to the Congress of the United States" by the June packet.[66] A month after *Rachel*'s arrest on the sailors' suit, Johnson still hoped for success. Late in June, repeating an earlier question, he asked George Aust "to inform him by the bearer whether Lord Grenville means to honor Mr. Johnson with any answer to his letter . . . or not." Grenville did not answer, but a week later Aust informed Johnson that the Commissioners of the Treasury had confirmed their former report and remained of the opinion that no further relief should be granted. On the 21st of July came the warning that, unless the seamen were paid, *Rachel* would be condemned and sold. Three days later Green prudently gave up the contest and agreed to the stipulations. He also compensated the customs officers who had seized her on the 2d of

---

her before the expiration of his articles and brought suit to recover wages withheld. Scott held that "If a Proclamation has issued for recalling British seamen from foreign service . . . it is the duty of British seamen so engaged to quit their service" and that British courts would sustain their claims to the proportion of wages earned (Opinion of Scott, 11 June 1791, in clerk's hand except for concluding opinion and signature; DNA: RG 59, CD, London; T-168/5).

[64] Johnson to Philip Stephens, Admiralty Office, 25 May 1791 (Document II, enclosures N and O).

[65] Philip Stephens to Johnson, 30 May 1791 (Document II, enclosure S).

[66] Johnson to Charles Long, Treasury Office, 27 May 1791; Johnson to Grenville, 27 May 1791 (enclosures Q and R). After sending off his dispatch of 31 May with its numerous enclosures, Johnson continued to press the Foreign Office for a decision on *Rachel* (Johnson to Aust, 6, 10, and 21 June 1791; DNA: RG 59, CD; MNP 167/1; Aust to Johnson, 6, 21, and 27 June 1791; same, CD, London; T-168/5).

March.[67] Had that condition been met at the time, the brigantine could have departed a month before the seamen deserted. Johnson's strategy of confrontation, with Green's acquiescence, had failed on every count.

The optimistic hopes of *Rachel*'s owner went even further beyond the bounds of reality. Before the year was out, Green submitted to Jefferson what he described as a sequel to Johnson's report, representing himself as having resisted "a Public Wrong and Indignity to the Independance of the United States." For this public service he hoped the federal government would have the humanity and wisdom to indemnify him for the losses he had sustained. His estimate of damages was liberal, amounting to $7,292 or almost two-thirds of the insured value of the vessel and her cargo. His treatment of the facts was equally loose. Jefferson would have had no difficulty in perceiving that, on the basis of Green's own reckoning, *Rachel* had not been detained by British authorities "for the Space of Nine Months."[68] Looking over the elaborate documentation of the case as reported by Johnson, he could have seen at once that the total period of detention amounted to no more than six months, and might have been reduced to half that period had the customary compensation been made when *Rachel* was ordered to be released late in March. Most of her time spent in idleness resulted from the vigorous insistence of the American consul who, in Green's words, intervened when "the pressing necessity of National Circumstance compelled him."

If Johnson had known the Secretary of State well or if he had read his instructions carefully, he might have guessed that the outcome was predictable. Jefferson acknowledged Johnson's dispatch, but made no direct comment then or ever on the merit of *Rachel*'s case. But his allusion in the same letter to the consul's abandonment of the case of Purdie may very well have been intended to apply equally to his espousal of *Rachel*: "We would chuse never to commit ourselves but when we are so clearly in the right as to admit no doubt."[69] Quite understandably, Jefferson did not even acknowledge Green's hopeless appeal for indemnification. Later, after Thomas Pinckney's appointment as minister to England, Green appealed in person to the Secretary of State for assistance in recovering the much larger losses he claimed he had sustained in trade with the East Indies. Before Pinckney departed, Jefferson had frequent discussions with him about Green's application and reached an understanding as to the position the government should take. "The magnitude of his losses," Jefferson

[67] George Gostling to Johnson, 14, 21, and 31 July (same). Even after Green had met the conditions for *Rachel*'s release, there was a final irritating exchange between Johnson and the Admiralty Office because of delay in transmitting the orders. Claiming that she was then in the 10th month of her detention, Green declared that if this had happened to a British vessel in the United States, they would have heard "a thousand infamous epithets, the least or most moderate of which would be that we were a race of Pirates as bad as the Algerines." When the orders still had not arrived four days later, Green asked Johnson to make one final effort. If this did not succeed, he declared that he would obey Johnson's orders as consul, "even to abandoning the vessel altogether to a set of Harpies, and to take my chance of redress from Congress" (Green to Johnson, 24 and 29 July; 2 Aug. 1791; DNA: RG 59, CD, London; T-168/5; Johnson to George Gostling, 28 and 30 July; Johnson to Green, 27 July, 1 and 3 Aug. 1791; DNA: RG 59, CD; MNP 167/1).
[68] Green to Secretary of State, 6 Dec. 1791 (Document III and enclosure).
[69] TJ to Johnson, 29 Aug. 1791.

later wrote to the minister, "will call for all the attentions and patronage we can give him consistently with those considerations of ultimate friendship and peace between the two nations which higher duties oblige us to cultivate." Jefferson left it up to Pinckney to decide when the case would justify official interposition.[70] All of this was set forth in a letter of introduction for Green to present to Pinckney, left unsealed for his inspection. Thus signalling the doubts that Jefferson entertained, it should have warned the merchant of the undisclosed grounds on which the Secretary of State and the minister to England had conditioned the possibility of official intervention.

These higher duties of ultimate peace and friendship, unfortunately, were such as Johnson lost sight of when striving most assiduously to meet them. That he should have chosen to document so fully such a dubious case as that of *Rachel* seems explicable only on the ground that he hoped to prove his qualifications for the rank of minister. At this juncture he knew that diplomatic relations between the two countries were about to be resumed. He was also aware that his situation required him to go somewhat beyond the normal consular functions. Indeed, in his later appeal to Congress to reimburse and compensate him for his services, he stressed the fact that in the absence of an American minister, he was obliged to act in a diplomatic capacity and to entertain "almost every American of respectability whose business or whose pleasure brought him to London."[71] He was conscious of the powerful political

[70] TJ to Pinckney, 12 Dec. 1792; Green to TJ, 8 and 11 June and 5 Dec. 1792. Green forwarded to Pinckney a copy of TJ's letter of 12 Dec. but was unable to proceed on his voyage to England to pursue his claim because of suits instituted against him there to recover from him much of his property, "which their own Judicature has annihilated" (Green to Pinckney, 6 Feb. 1793; DLC: Pinckney Papers).

Despite his precautionary instructions to Pinckney, TJ found Green's East Indian case useful in rebutting George Hammond's contention that English courts, without exception, gave American citizens and British subjects equal protection of the laws. After stating the facts in this and other cases, TJ declared: "These cases appear strong to us. If your Judges have done wrong in them, we expect redress. If right, we expect explanations" (TJ to Hammond, 29 May 1792). Even in this notable diplomatic argument TJ was careful to assume that the decision against Green might have been right and thus avoided a formal representation by the government. Soon after that exchange, Green sought the aid of the Secretary of the Treasury in avoiding a ruinous legal action in New York. In doing so he gave Hamilton the misleading impression that the government had interposed in his behalf. Because of Green's distress, Hamilton yielded and, through the agency of William Seton, succeeded for a brief while in postponing Green's difficulties (Hamilton to Seton, 17 July 1792; Seton to Hamilton, 23 July 1792; Green to Hamilton, 24 and 26 July 1792; Syrett, *Hamilton*, XII, 43-4, 79, 82, 110-11). After TJ left office, Green persisted in claiming the government's protection by again appealing to the Secretary of State. Randolph sought the opinion of the Attorney General, William Bradford, as well as that of Hamilton. Bradford found that the British judge was obliged to rule against Green according to the laws of the realm and the long-established doctrine of indefeasible allegiance; that Green had failed to appeal the decision and thus no complaint could be registered until the issue was decided by the court of last resort; and that the facts did not warrant any formal demand by the United States. Hamilton concurred in this opinion (Bradford and Hamilton to Randolph, 4 Nov.[-9 Dec.] 1794, same, XVII, 254-5).

Randolph forwarded their opinion to Green and informed him – in words similar to those used by TJ to Johnson on the Purdie case (TJ to Johnson, 29 Aug. 1791) – that the government could not commit itself in a doubtful case. But, feeling as others did that Green had justice on his side, he urged Jay and Pinckney to take the matter under

thrust of Jefferson's report on the fisheries and thought that the navigation act which had been referred to the Secretary of State would be enacted at the ensuing Congress.[72] It was therefore perhaps not accidental that, in submitting *Rachel's* case as proof of hostility on the part of the British government, he expressed the opinion that no response could be so effectual "as a retaliating Navigation Act."[73] As he must have realized, this placed him squarely in accord with the announced policy of the Secretary of State. But, if he were seeking ministerial appointment, the methods of conducting diplomatic discourse which he so elaborately revealed in the record of *Rachel* proved him to be his own worst advocate. It is not in this but in Jefferson's silence on the case that the importance of the episode lies, suggesting as it does the means by which he chose to attain great objects of policy. Jefferson was prepared to use the countervailing strategy of a navigation act because, as he pointed out to Sir John Sinclair, the failure to achieve amicable commercial relations between the United States and Great Britain could not be imputed to the former.[74] He was not prepared to jeopardize the ultimate goal of friendship and peace, most especially if this meant standing on so fragile a foundation as that revealed in the too amply documented case of *Rachel*. Civility, not harshness or belligerency, was his most characteristic trait in endeavoring to reach just and reasonable accommodations of interest among men and nations.

Within a year Jefferson's insistent warnings against abuses of the American flag became national policy upon passage by Congress of the Registry Act of 1792. This unprecedented legislation made ownership of vessels entirely by American citizens an indispensable requirement of registration. It prohibited sale to aliens of any interest in a vessel bearing the flag of the United States, under penalty of loss of registry and, in the event of proven fraudulence, for-

---

consideration discreetly and "in such a manner as may best promise success; but without committing our Government by a formal demand" (Randolph to Green, 11 Dec. 1794; DNA: RG 59, DL; Randolph to Jay, 11 Dec. 1794; same, CDI; pertinent extracts are in Syrett, *Hamilton*, XVII, 356-7). On Green's extravagant claims of losses in the East India case, see note to Green to TJ, 23 May 1791 (Document I).

[71] Johnson argued correctly that since the United States had no diplomatic representative in London for some time after he became consul he was "in some respects obliged to act in a diplomatic capacity, and a great part of his time was taken up in attending to such of the public Interests . . . as do not usually come within the extent of the consular functions." He also pointed out that this was during a war when his whole time was taken up in protecting American seamen, and that, having incurred expenses of some thousands of pounds, he had "not received the smallest compensation." He petitioned for reimbursement of £314.3.2 as well as for all expenses incurred in the service of the government (draft of petition to Congress, Georgetown, [28 Jan. 1800]; DNA: RG 59, CD, London T-168/5). Almost half a century later Louisa C. Adams and other heirs of Johnson petitioned Congress for a settlement of Johnson's account "upon principles of equity and justice," even to the extent of retroactive allowances or compensation as provided consuls by the acts of 19 Jan. 1836 and 3 Mch. 1837 (Petition to the Senate and House of Representatives, 22 July 1848, DNA: RG 233, Records of the House of Representatives).

[72] Johnson told Maury that he thought the navigation bill would pass "the next session with additional restrictions and severity" and that this would be "the means of compelling this Court to alter her system respecting the United States of America" (Johnson to Maury, 13 June and 24 Nov. 1791, same).

[73] Johnson to TJ, 31 May 1791 (Document II).

[74] TJ to Sir John Sinclair, 24 Aug. 1791.

feiture of both vessel and cargo. It provided that, upon sale or transfer of title of a vessel so registered, her certificate of registration should immediately be surrendered to the authorities. The Enrollment and Licensing Act of 1793 established even more stringent provisions to prevent abuse of the American flag.[75] Such legislation, designed to insure that vessels registered under authority of the United States should adhere strictly to its policy of neutrality, was difficult if not impossible to enforce. Much litigation resulted, and no doubt many more fraudulent practices went undiscovered. But the principle which Jefferson consistently upheld long before it became embodied in national law had been vindicated.

[75] *U.S. Statutes at Large*, I, 287-99, 305-18.

I. William Green to the Secretary of State

SIR   London the 23d. of May 1791.

I had the honour to address a letter to you on the 21st. of last January, concerning the conduct of the British Administration, with respect to the Brigantine Rachel, Nicholas Duff Master, belonging to the port of New York. I should not have sollicited the trouble of your attention to that detail from me, although both Vessel and Cargo were my own; if Mr. Johnson the Consul of the United States for this port had conceived his intervention warrantable, at the time of her arrival: but, as he had just then only received a notification of his own appointment, without any official Instructions for his line of conduct, he did not think it right without these to interest himself upon the business, until the pressing necessity of National Circumstance compelled him. From that moment I have been silent, unless with him; and he has had the goodness since to act with such energy of Public Spirit, as it is hoped will meet your approbation, although it has had no effect towards procuring redress.

This vessel is now in the seventh Month of her detaintion, since she left New York, three months on her first arrival, and four on her outward passage. She has been pillaged of a part of her Cargo, and the remainder is to be subject to an arbitrary fine. A very heavy Expence and Loss have been incurred, and yet no offence has been committed, except that of landing an English made fowling piece, part of the baggage of Mr. Knox, the Consul for Dublin, who came to England with me a passenger in the vessel.

Under the auspices of Mr. Johnson, I have nearly compleated the proofs of a damage, which I have sustained, as a Citizen and Subject of the United States, of somewhat more than Two hundred thousand Dollars, for which, notwithstanding the Treaty of Peace, I am not permitted to plead in a British Court of Justice; a lawful impediment being put in my way, as an American Creditor, to annul my claim against British Debtors. This business alone brought me to Europe last fall; but, as it is nearly accomplished, I shall embark shortly to return, when I shall be permitted to lay these proofs before you, for your inspection. I have the honour to be, with the greatest respect, Sir, Your most obedient, humble servant, WILLIAM GREEN

RC (DNA: RG 76, Great Britain, unsorted papers); at head of text: "(Duplicate)"; endorsed by TJ as received 20 Aug. 1791 and so recorded in SJL.

William Green, a merchant and native of England, became a naturalized citizen in Rhode Island in 1786. He later established himself in New York and engaged in the East India trade. In 1788 he dispatched a vessel and cargo from Philadelphia for Bengal. Under contract with John Buchanan and Robert Charnock, British merchants located at Ostend, Green shipped East India goods to his partners which, because of their bankruptcy and his own arrest and imprisonment at their suit, resulted in losses which he estimated at this time at £49,969.6.7¾ sterling. Among the proofs that he was gathering was an itemized statement of his losses, certified by a committee of Americans in London (Samuel Broome, John Browne Cutting, and Duncan Ingraham). In submitting his proofs to Johnson, Green declared that these "gentlemen of probity and experience and capacity . . . sat for several days as a Committee upon the investigation of the business under your auspices." Green claimed that he was denied recovery of his property

"by the extraordinary doctrine of Jurisprudence as delivered by that Oracle of Law, Lord Kenyon, whereby not only every British subject, but even every foreigner residing in England or in any Part of the British Dominions are declared to be absolved from every Debt which they owed to Mr. Green, and to be exempt from any responsibility to him for any property which he has placed in their hands." Claiming that he had embarked his fortune "as a Commercial Capitalist under the Flag and Protection of the United States of America," he submitted proofs to Johnson because of their magnitude, because his case affected the political interests of the United States, and because he hoped Johnson would "frame such a Report of the Circumstances and Truths of the Case as may accompany my application to Congress for redress and relief" (Green to Johnson, 25 June 1791, with enclosed notarial proofs and itemized account of losses; DNA: RG 59, London; T-168/5). Johnson made no report, but Green continued his efforts by appealing both to TJ and to his successor, Edmund Randolph. Both sympathized with him for his losses, but declined to commit the government to his case (see Editorial Note, note 70).

II. Joshua Johnson to the Secretary of State

SIR   London 31st. May 1791.

I have the honor to transmit you various Papers marked A B C D E F G H I K L M N O P Q R S respecting the seizure of the Brigantine, Rachel, Capt. Nicholas Duff, belonging to New York, at Portsmouth, by the Collector and Comptroller of his Britanick Majestys Customs. As this case is singularly hard, I have been the more anxious, to procure Justice to the injured, and support the Honor, and Interest of the United States, and which I hope will be approved by Congress; my different addresses to the Commissioners of the Customs may appear harsh; the evident inattention to the Body of Evidence, and state of facts laid before them, and their decision in direct opposition to Justice, will, I doubt not, fully justify me; at all events, I do not consider that I have gone beyond the bounds of my Duty, to Congress, or my Country.

I beg leave to remark to you, that the Rachel, Cap. Duff, took in her Cargo at Ostend, and on her outward bound passage touched at the Mother-Bank, for the purpose stated in paper A B. Should this Government be actuated, either by Jealousy, or any other cause, against the growing Commerce of the United States, they may pursue this system of conduct untill they have entirely interrupted our Navigation into the North Seas, unless checkt in Time; and I cannot point out any thing, that will so effectually do it, as a retaliating Navigation Act. As for seeking redress, by what is called Law here, the attempt by an American would be ridiculous, as is plainly proved by the decisions of the Commissioners, and Lords of the Treasury. – It would appear that Government, were not content with the unexampled cruelty exercised on the Property of Mr. Green, in the refusal, of suffering his Vessell to an Entry, in the first instance, and then seizing her on her returning passage, in the second; pillaging him of part of the Cargo, detaining the Vessell at a heavy expence for Seven Months, but also in addition, have imposed a fine to their officers; they carry their Revenge still farther, by having induced the Seamen to enter into the King's Service, see papers marked O and S, and in opposition to the proofs marked N, they send an Admiralty Process on board, put the Vessell and Cargo under an arrest, and threaten to dispose of as much as will pay the demands of the Sailors *really subjects of the United States*, in defiance of the sacred Contract made with the Capt. of the aforesaid Brigantine, Rachel.

On remonstrating to their Lordships please refer to their answer in paper marked S, where they say, if you don't like this determination, bring your Actions at Law, and we will there Judge on them; No one would be weak enough to suppose, that their Lordships, or any depending Court on them, would give relief contrary to the Judgement pronounced by directions of their Lordships and I must therefore decline, doing anything farther in this Business or indeed in any other case similar untill I receive instructions from Congress. I purpose writing you again in a few days in the meantime, I am with great respect & esteem, Sir, Your most Obedient & Most Humble Servant,   JOSHUA JOHNSON

RC (DNA: RG 76, Great Britain, unsorted papers); at foot of text: "Thomas Jefferson Esqr. Secretary for the department of State"; endorsed by Remsen as received 20 Aug. 1791 and so recorded in SJL. FC (DNA: RG 59, CD); at head of text: "Mr. Sterett." There are some differences in phraseology between RC and FC. Enclosures: Texts of all save one of the 17 enclosures identified by Johnson as A

through s (J being omitted) have been found and are presented below in full or in summary. All are transcripts, lettered as indicated. No text of the missing enclosure P has been found. But see note to o below.

MOTHER-BANK: A shoal between the mainland and the Isle of Wight forming the northwest boundary of Spithead.

ENCLOSURES

A

Nicholas Duff to Joshua Johnson

London, 3 Mch. 1791. As Johnson is acquainted with the three months' detention of *Rachel*, he will not restate the particulars. One of the officers of the Customs had brought suit against him and he was obliged to give bail of £500 sterling before *Rachel*, not being given entry in any British port, could proceed to Ostend where her cargo was landed by order of the consignees. There he took on board 40 pipes of brandy and 100 cases of Geneva bound for New York. Since it was "absolutely necessary" for him to touch at the Mother Bank to learn the fate of the prosecution against himself, he did so and on 24 Feb. informed the Commissioners of Customs that he had put in there for this sole purpose. On the 25th they granted his request on condition that he compensate the officer. This he did so that his bailsmen would be relieved and he could proceed on his voyage. *Rachel* had reached Mother Bank on the 21st but because of bad weather he could not report until 24th to Portsmouth collector, who directed him to turn over register and papers. To these he added bills of lading and cargo manifest. The collector said he would have to send all to the Commissioners. The suit had been quashed and he had received orders to proceed to New York, so on 25th he asked for his papers. The collector said he had had no answer from London. He called upon him each day from Saturday through Tuesday and received the same answer. On Wednesday the 2d. he was told that the Commissioners had ordered him to seize both vessel and cargo. This was done about noon the same day when *Rachel* was boarded by the "Collector, and Comptroller of the Customs at Portsmouth, with a Pilot, and eight hands, and putting a Chalk Mark upon the Mainmast and Foremast, declared that they had seized her, and her Cargo, and taking her by force into their possession, conducted her from the Mother Bank, where she was then lying at Anchor, into the Harbour of Portsmouth." He left *Rachel* there that night in order to come to London to appeal to Johnson as the American consul "to take such immediate Measures as may be necessary and effectual" to save him and the parties at interest – all of them citizens of the United States – "from the Distress, Delay, and Embarrassment which such an arbitrary stretch of Power may occasion."

Tr (DNA: RG 76, Great Britain, unsorted papers).

B

Joshua Johnson to the Commissioners of the Customs

London, 4 Mch. 1791. Yesterday, Nicholas Duff, commander of the brigantine *Rachel*, New York, the property of subjects of the United States, informed him that the vessel was seized on the 2d at the Mother Bank by the collector and comptroller by the Commissioners' direction. "Annext your Honours will find a statement of all Captain Duff's Proceedings, and as his Case is peculiarly hard, and he has done nothing with intent of fraud, but his putting into an English Port was to pay respect to the Laws of this Country, and to liberate his Bail in a Prosecution . . . which your Honours has ordered to be quasht, I humbly beg that your Honours will be pleased to take this matter into your immediate Consideration, and give Orders for the liberation of the Brig Rachel, and her Cargo, that Captain Duff may proceed for New York, and that you direct the Comptroller, and Collector at Portsmouth to make Compensation for the detention. – Should your Honours desire any farther Explanation to the facts stated, I will with pleasure attend you."

Tr (DNA: RG 76, Great Britain, unsorted papers); docketed by Remsen. Tr (PRO: FO 4/10, f. 42). The annexed papers were: (1) Memorial of Jacob Wilkinson, London, to the Commissioners of the Treasury, 22 Oct. 1790, stating that *Rachel*'s cargo from New York consisted of pearl and potash, staves, and pig iron consigned to him; that, since the vessel was French built but American property, she could not be given entry; and that, inasmuch as this arose from ignorance of the owner and as such merchandize does not pay duty, he asks that it be allowed entry as if imported in an American bottom. (2) Affidavit of William Green, 4 Mch. 1791, sworn before Robert Smith, stating that he was a New York merchant residing at present in Great Portland street; that the brandies and Geneva on *Rachel* were shipped by Theodore van Moorsel & Co. of Ostend by order of Jacob Wilkinson for the account of William Green; and that neither the whole nor any part was intended for any port in the British dominions. (3) Affidavit of Nicholas Duff, sworn before Robert Smith, 4 Mch. 1791, stating that *Rachel*, commanded by him, arrived in London on 22 Oct. 1790; that he presented her register and papers to the collector of customs but was refused entry because she had been built in France, though she had long been owned by American citizens, registered under laws of the United States, and admitted several times to ports in England and Ireland; that she remained in London from that date until 17 Jan. 1791 while the Commissioners of the Treasury were deciding whether she could enter; that, when she was finally denied entry, the consignee directed him to proceed to Ostend and deliver the cargo to Theodore van Moorsel & Co., who, on the consignee's order, laded her with brandies and Geneva for shipment to New York on the account of William Green; that, having been prosecuted by the Commissioners of Customs on complaint of one of their tidewaiters and obliged to give bail in the amount of £500 "because he had landed without sufferance an English gun made by Mortimer in Fleet street, in order to have it repaired, and because he had turned the said Officer out of his Cabin, who attempted to make it a Cooking place for his provision, he was . . . permitted by the Consignee to put into

Portsmouth" in order to take up his bail; that, on arrival, he informed the Commissioners of Customs and asked that "he might be permitted to compromise the matter with the Officer who had preferred the Complaint against him and proceed on his way to New York"; that the Commissioners, on or about the 24th of February granted his request "and the matter was accordingly compromised . . . at a very heavy and ruinous expence" to himself; that when this was done he immediately demanded the liberation of *Rachel* and his register and papers which the collector had taken away from him but was refused, that official saying he had sent them to London and was awaiting the Commissioners' instructions; that he was put off with this answer from day to day until the 2d of March when *Rachel* was seized and taken into Portsmouth harbor; and that no part of the cargo had been intended for English ports but was destined for New York and he had been ordered to proceed there "with all possible dispatch," stopping only at Teneriffe to take in wines. (Trs of all in DNA: RG 76, Great Britain, unsorted papers; other Trs in PRO: FO 4/10, f. 43-9, as enclosed with the above letter in Johnson's letter to Stephens of 25 May 1791, the whole being docketed: "Copy sent to the Treasury March 25th"; see Enclosure o below.)

C

Memorial of Joshua Johnson to the Duke of Leeds

London, 25 Mch. 1791. Rachel, an American vessel, is owned, registered, and navigated agreeably to the laws of the United States, and her cargo is the property of an American citizen. She arrived in London 22 Oct. 1790 with a cargo consigned to an English merchant, but since her register did not state that she was built in America and her construction appeared French, the Commissioners of Customs refused her entry, alleging that for this reason she was not entitled to the privileges of an American vessel. In consequence, the Lords of the Treasury were asked a day or two after her arrival to allow her to discharge her cargo as she had been permitted to do in ports of England and Ireland many times. No answer was received until the end of December, when the appeal was denied and *Rachel* was obliged to proceed to Ostend. "It may be necessary here most respectfully to remark to your Grace that this American Vessel after being detained in a British Port upwards of twelve weeks, was compelled to leave it and make a Deposit of her Cargo in a Foreign Port. . . . Captain Duff the Commander of the said Vessel having been prosecuted . . . for landing whilst in the Port of London an English fowling-piece made by the celebrated Mortimer of this City in order to have it repaired by the Maker . . . he was obliged to put in with his Vessel at Spithead on her way to North America in order to redeem his recognizances or to surrender his Person and take his trial agreeably to the Laws of England, and upon his arrival at Spithead on the twenty second Ultimo the said Hon'ble Commissioners of the Customs were acquainted therewith, and petitioned on account of the notorious hardship of the Case to order the prosecution to be stopt which they were pleased to consent to upon condition of his paying the Bills of their Solicitors, satisfying the Informer who represented to the Board that he had landed an English made fowling-piece, and paying the said Informer's expences which Captain Duff was obliged to do and which cost him upwards of Seventy Pounds Sterling, or he would have been committed to an English Jail under the prosecution of the Crown Lawyers. – This Sum is upwards of a year's pay to the Captain of so small a Vessel. . . . The Collector at Portsmouth to whom Captain Duff had made a report of his arrival and of every item of his Cargo demanded his Papers which Captain Duff gave up, and when the Commissioners were pleased to stay this prosecution on account of the fowling-piece . . . he called on the Collector for a return of his Papers which he refused to relinquish alledging that he could not until he had received orders from the Hon'ble Commissioners of the Customs. And pretending to have received these orders on the second of this Month the said Collector came off with a number of other Persons and forcibly taking possession of the said American Vessel and Cargo, conducted her . . . to the Harbour of Portsmouth.

"A conduct like this so likely to sow the seeds of Discord between Great Britain and the United States of America being represented to your Grace's Memorialist He found himself immediately under the necessity of representing the same to the Hon'ble Commissioners of His Majesty's Customs (a Copy of which representation, with the Owners and Captain's Affidavit No. 2, 3, and 4, is inclosed herewith) requiring that the Collector who had committed this act of violence should be immediately ordered to give up the said Vessel and Cargo and to make satisfaction to the parties injured for the losses and damages his conduct had occasioned.

"It is now three Weeks since this Memorial was presented, and yesterday your Grace's Memorialist was given to understand that the . . . Commissioners had ordered the Collector at Portsmouth to give up the said Vessel and a considerable part of her Cargo, nearly in the following words 'The Spirits in small quantities to be prosecuted, the Ship and Cargo to be liberated on satisfaction being made to the Seizing Officer.'

"In order to obviate the consequences of a System so destructive to the harmony with which the Subjects of the two Countries should ever regard each other, and which it is your Grace's Memorialist's earnest desire to cultivate, this Memorial is therefore submitted, and this Appeal made to your Grace's justice, with a repetition of the requisition, that the Hon'ble Commissioners of the Customs be instructed to give orders to their Collector at Portsmouth immediately to deliver up the said Vessel and all her Cargo, to the Captain thereof, and be likewise ordered to make full and ample compensation for the loss and damage which has been occasioned by his conduct."

Tr (DNA: RG 76, Great Britain, unsorted papers). Another Tr (DNA: RG 59, CD). RC (PRO: FO 4/10, f. 42). Enclosure: Johnson to the Commissioners of Customs, 4 Mch. 1791 (Enclosure B preceding), and its three enclosures.

D

Joshua Johnson to the Duke of Leeds

May it please your Grace   [London] 19 April 1791

It is with extreme concern that I am under the necessity of applying again to your Grace upon the situation of the American Brigantine Rachel, Nicholas Duff, Master, concerning which I had the honor of presenting a Memorial to your Grace on the 25th. Ultimo, to which no answer has been given. Altho' it has been mentioned to me, that the matter has been referred to the Right Honorable the Lords of His Majesty's Treasury, and again by their Lordships, to the Commissioners of the Customs; upon this occasion, I beg leave respectfully to remark to your Grace, that the matter appears thus to have been immediately referred to the very Men, under whose authority, an Injury to one of the Subjects of the United States has been committed. That Vessel is yet laying perishing at Portsmouth, and this is now the fifth Month that she has been detained here, at an heavy Loss, and Expence to the Owners of both the Vessel, and Cargo. I think it my Duty respectfully to submit to your Grace the novelty of a Circumstance so extraordinary as that of taking possession by force of a Vessel, and Cargo, belonging to a Subject of a Friendly Power, where no breach of your Laws had been committed, or intended, and the suffering a Collector of the Customs with impunity to dismantle the Vessel, strip her of a part of her Cargo, and exact a Fine at his own pleasure, appears to me contrary to Justice, as it allows his making his own will, in that respect, a supreme Law. Respectfully referring your Grace to my Memorial upon this Subject, I beg leave to solicit an early Answer, I have the Honor to be My Lord Duke Your Grace's very Obedt. and most Humble Servant, [JOSHUA JOHNSON]

Tr (DNA: RG 76, Great Britain, unsorted papers); docketed by Remsen. Another Tr (DNA: RG 59, CD). RC (PRO: FO 4/9, f. 236).

E

Commissioners of Customs to the Lords of the Treasury

[*London*], *29 April 1791.* [Charles] Long in his of the 6th indicating that he had placed before the Lords of the Treasury a letter from [J. B.] Burgess of 25 Mch. transmitting Johnson's memorial together with the documents referred to therein and that he had been commanded to lay these documents before the Commissioners of the Customs, they report: that *Rachel* "was discovered on Monday the 21 of February last at Anchor amongst the Ships at Spithead. – That although the Law requires immediate notice be given, by the Master of the unavoidable necessity of coming into Port, (if any such necessity exists) yet the Master of this Vessel did not go to the Custom House to make any Report, until the Thursday following, when he produced his Manifest, and informed the Collector and Controller that his reason for coming into Port was *to wait for Orders* – That it appeared by the Manifest the Cargo consisted of the undermentioned Goods 40 Pipes and a Quarter Cask of Brandy 124 Cases and a Quarter Cask of Geneva 14 ℔. Weight of Coffee and 1 Gross of Playing Cards. That the 2 Quarter Casks, and the whole of the Cases are prohibited Packages and it being represented to us that the Wind was fair for this Vessel to have proceeded on her Voyage at the time she came into Port, that the Crew were not in want of any Provisions, and that the Vessel was not driven in by necessity or distress of Weather – Our Officers conceived that the Plea of coming into Port, merely to wait for Orders, was not a sufficient or legal excuse for so doing, and therefore stoped the said Vessel's Cargo, and it appearing that both were subject to forfeiture We directed them to be prosecuted accordingly. But on Application lately made to us by Mr. Johnson . . . We again considered all the circumstances of the Case, and directed the delivery of the Vessel and Cargo (except the small Casks and Cases of Spirits) upon a Satisfaction to the Seizing Officers. — We are of opinion that the Parties have already received all the indulgence, that they are reasonably entitled to, and therefore cannot recommend to your Lordships the granting them any further relief."

Tr (DNA: RG 76, Great Britain, unsorted papers); docketed by Remsen. The documents transmitted by Long were Johnson's memorial (Enclosure B above) and its enclosures.

F

Charles Long to George Aust

[*London*], *Treasury Chambers*, *13 May 1791*. Having placed before the Lords of the Treasury Aust's letter of 20 Apr. transmitting by direction of the Secretary of State Johnson's memorial renewing his application in behalf of *Rachel*, he is commanded by them to submit to him a copy of the report of the Commissioners of the Customs and, for the information of Lord Grenville, to say that they agree with the opinion "that the Parties are not entitled to any further Indulgence."

Tr (DNA: RG 76, Great Britain, unsorted papers); docketed by Remsen.

G

George Aust to Joshua Johnson

Whitehall May 16th. 1791

Mr. Aust presents his Compliments to Mr. Johnson and takes the earliest opportunity of transmitting him Copies of the Answers received from the Treasury, in answer to his application respecting the American Ship Rachel.

Tr (DNA: RG 76, Great Britain, unsorted papers); docketed by Remsen. Enclosures: See E and F preceding.

H

Joshua Johnson to Commissioners of the Customs

Gentlemen   London May 18th. 1791

A Report said to have been made from your Board on the 29th. ulto. respecting the Brigantine Rachel, Nichs. Duff, Commander, and which the Right Honorable the Lords of His Majesty's Treasury quote as the ground and basis of their refusal to give any Compensation for the loss and damages which the Owners of the said Vessel have sustained by her detention, having been transmitted me from the Office of His Majesty's Secretary of State for Foreign Affairs, I cannot avoid expressing my surprize and concern at its perusal, since what is there called a Statement of facts, deviates so essentially from the truth, that I should betray the trust reposed in me by my Country for the protection of its Commerce, were I to pass it over in silence. The Remarks I have to offer follow:

1st. The said Captain Duff was held to bail in recognizances to the amount of five hundred Pounds Sterling for landing in this Port last December an English made fowling-piece to have it repaired. He could not proceed to North America without settling this matter, and on the very day Thursday the 24th February when the said Report states that he delivered a Manifest of his Cargo to your Officers at Portsmouth, to my knowledge a Memorial on his part was presented to your own Board in London, praying the said Prosecution to be remitted, and stating fully, that to be the sole cause of his putting into that Port. On Friday the next day you were pleased to grant his Prayer, on satisfaction being made to the Complaining Officer, which with the Expences to your Solicitors and others, cost the poor Man upwards of Ninety Pounds Sterling or more than a year's pay.

2dly. This Affair having been thus settled the Captain presumed he might proceed on his Voyage and demanded his Papers from your said Officers, for they had at his first arrival illegally demanded and taken them away from him which they refused to give up, until they heard as they said from your Board. The Captain of the said Vessel in the mean time had committed no new offence against Law or Justice, and on Wednesday or Thursday the 3d or 4th. day of March, under real or pretended orders from your Board, the said Officers went on board at the Mother Bank and seized both Vessel and Cargo, and forcibly carried the said Vessel from her Anchorage at the said place into the Harbour of Portsmouth, so that she was not seized until ten days after her arrival there, and seven, after its purpose had been formally notified to your own Board, and that Board had formally acted upon it, as may be known by your reference to your own Records. The Vessel would not have remained there a day after February 26th. when the news of your decision reached Portsmouth but for the said detention of her Papers.

3dly. Reports from Men so extremely interested as these Officers are, since your deliberations generally conclude, with Satisfaction to the Seizing Officer, should be received with precaution at all times, and upon this occasion I believe it would be found that their date of the Captain's delivery of his Manifest is erroneous, and that they had written Thursday for Tuesday, the Captain says the bad Weather prevented his getting on Shore at all the first day for it blew a Gale of Wind. Upon a reference to your Records it also will be found, that altho' as you admit the Vessel arrived on Monday (not at Spithead) at the Mother Bank, that on the Thursday following yourselves were in a regular Memorial presented with all the facts, so that allowing the first day's delay in Writing to its true cause, bad Weather, the earliest advices of her arrival could not have reached London till Wednesday noon, and on the next day Thursday the 24th. day of February you were presented with the Captain's Memorial containing a fair, candid and just statement of facts.

I trust it will enter naturally into your minds that the Commerce of the Subjects and Citizens of the United States of America, are no longer subject to your Revenue Regulations, and I ought to add that the freightage of British Shipping employed in the transport of American produce last year, amounted to upwards of Four hundred thousand pounds Sterling, which is a greater National profit than any that arises to Great Britain from any other part, or perhaps from the whole of her remaining Carrying Trade with other Foreign Nations.

As Consul of the United States I cannot understand that part of your Report which enjoins *a Satisfaction to the Seizing Officers*, is it in the nature of a verbal or written apology from Captain Duff to these Men, or are they to have a Sum of Money and what Sum is there to be paid to them, after detaining an American Vessel three Months, to induce them to release her, and is the amount of that Sum to depend upon their will, or is there any regular tarif for Impositions of this kind, by which the American Merchant may regulate himself in future.

I am sorry to find myself under the necessity of transmitting an account of these matters to the Congress of the United States of America, and I shall also transmit Copies of this Address to you, to The Right Honorable the Lords of His Majesty's Treasury and to His Majesty's Secretary of State for Foreign Affairs.

In future when I have occasion to write you either Letters or Memorials on Public matters, May I beg that Instructions be given to your Secretary to answer them in some Official way, since no Answer has ever yet been regularly given to the Memorial which I addrest to you upon the Rachel in March last. I have the Honor to be, Gentlemen, Your most Obedient Humble Servant,

[JOSHUA JOHNSON]

Tr (DNA: RG 76, Great Britain, unsorted papers).

I

Joshua Johnson to Nicholas Duff

London, 18 May 1791. He encloses a letter to the officers of the customs. "You will wait on those Gentlemen and deliver the same, requesting that they will be pleased to give you their Answer, and which you will forward to me without loss of time. I would have you refer to your Log Book, and see what Day you arrived at the Mother Bank, what Day you went on Shore, and what Day you made your Report at the Custom House; you will be very particular in this, and transmit the Account."

Tr (DNA: RG 76, Great Britain, unsorted papers); docketed by Remsen. Enclosure: Johnson to the Principal Officers of the Customs at Portsmouth, 18 May 1791, stating that since the Commissioners of the Customs have ordered *Rachel* and brandies in pipe to be given up "on *a sat-* *isfaction being made to the seizing officers,* which term I have adopted as it is their own," he desires them to inform him in writing "what that means, and if it means the payment of a Sum of Money to you, what that sum is" (Tr in DNA: RG 59, CD).

K

Nicholas Duff to Joshua Johnson

Portsmouth, 19 May 1791. He delivered the letter enclosed in Johnson's of the 18th. The collector answered that it did not solely rest with him and that he would consult the comptroller and give their answer. – "I arrived at Spithead on the night of the 21st of Feby. had the Revenue Cutter on board on the morning of the 22d. and rec'd two Officers from her. I reported on the 23d. and had my papers taken on the 24th. I am" &c.

Tr (DNA: RG 76, Great Britain, unsorted papers); docketed by Remsen. Another Tr (DNA: RG 59, CD).

Joshua Johnson to the Commissioners of Customs

Gentlemen   London 24 May 1791

Since writing my Letter of the 21 Instant, I have received a Letter from your Officers John Whitway, and James Peers at Portsmouth, whereby they demand Sixty Pounds Sterling for releasing the Brig Rachel, and the remaining part of her Cargo. I desire to have the honor of receiving from you a Notification whether that is what you term Satisfaction to the seizing Officer, and whether the Sum of Sixty Pounds is to be paid to the said Officer before the Vessel is to be permitted to proceed on her Voyage to America, over and above the Loss which has fallen on her Cargo. I beg a speedy, and explicit Answer, that Men, who have already lost so much, may suffer as little addition to the Misfortune as possible. I have the Honor to be Gentlemen Your most Obedient Humble Servant,   [JOSHUA JOHNSON]

Tr (DNA: RG 76, Great Britain, unsorted papers); docketed by Remsen. Another Tr (DNA: RG 59, CD). No letter from Johnson to the Commissioners of the Customs of 21 May 1791 has been found. This letter may have been Enclosure P, which is also missing.

Officers of the Customs to Joshua Johnson

Portsmouth, 20 May 1791. Acknowledging and summarizing Johnson's letter of the 18th by Captain Duff. In answer, they inform him that the Commissioners of the Customs had directed them to deliver the vessel and brandies upon satisfaction being made to the seizing officers. "In consequence whereof we immediately sent for Captn. Duff to whom we communicated this Order, and at the same time . . . proposed £60, as a Satisfaction to us the Seizing Officers; his answer was, he looked upon it to be a very reasonable sum, and that he would write you thereon by that days post."

Tr (DNA: RG 76, Great Britain, unsorted papers); at foot of text: "Jno. Whiteway Con: Ja. Peers D. Compr."; docketed by Remsen.

Affidavit of Nicholas Duff and Adam Masterman

Gosport, 26 May 1791. Duff as master and Masterman as chief mate of *Rachel* swear that Thomas Ure swore in their presence and before John Wilkes, notary, in New York on 8 Sep. 1790 that he was a bona fide American of New York and agreed to ship as boatswain on *Rachel* to London and elsewhere and return at the rate of $9 per month, part of which was to be paid to his wife, monthly, during the voyage; that, on the morning of 27 Apr. 1791, Ure refused to do duty and, contrary to Duff's orders, absented himself "and hath not since returned"; that John Cutler, Charles Chamberland, and Joseph Robinson shipped, respectively, on 21 and 28 Dec. 1790 and 10 Jan. 1791 on *Rachel* at London, declared themselves Americans, and "did sign with their own hands the Articles of the United States of North America to proceed . . . to Ostend, and elsewhere, to New York and there to be paid their wages and discharged"; that George Collins on 28 Dec. did the same, declaring himself born in Sweden but of Boston; and that Collins, Cutler, Chamberland, and Robinson on the morning of 27 Apr. absented themselves from *Rachel*, "denying their Duty to both Master and Mate."

Tr (DNA: RG 76, Great Britain, unsorted papers); docketed by Remsen as sworn before J. M. Bingham at Gosport.

O

Joshua Johnson to Philip Stephens

Sir   London 25 [i.e. 26] May 1791

A Person stiling himself the King's Solicitor, having on the 19 Instant, in company with a Tide Surveyor, and two of his Officers, gone on board the American Brigantine Rachel, Nicholas Duff, Master, now in Portsmouth Harbour, tho' outward bound to New York, and having affixed what he called an Admiralty Paper on the Main Mast, signed by Thomas Ure, and sundry other of her Crew who had ran away from her, and entered into the King's Service in the Navy, and having delivered her the said Brigantine, and Cargo, into the charge of the said Officers, with a threat, in six Days to return, and sell as much of her Cargo as will pay the said Deserters their Wages, which they have forfeited by their Articles with the Captain, in consequence of their said Desertion, which Deserters had all entered on board of her as Americans. I am to request as Consul of the United States of America, that the Lords Commissioners of the Admiralty, will give instant, and effectual Orders to put an immediate stop to the perpetration of so insolent an Outrage, and I doubt not, their Lordships will see the propriety of putting a check to Practices that have a tendency so alarming to the present amicable Sentiments of the United States of America towards Great Britain.

I beg to have the honor of an Answer as soon as possible, and remain with due Consideration Sir Your most Obedient Humble Servant,

[JOSHUA JOHNSON]

Tr (DNA: RG 76, Great Britain, unsorted papers); docketed by Remsen as addressed to Stephens as secretary to the Admiralty; at foot of text: "Inclosed you have Captain Nicholas Duff's, and his Mate Adam Masterton's Affidavit proving the within mentioned Crew belonging to the Brig Rachel, to have shipt as Americans." Another Tr (DNA: RG 59, CD).

Joshua Johnson to Charles Long

Sir   London May 27th. 1791.

His Grace the Duke of Leeds late His Majesty's Secretary of State for Foreign Affairs having transmitted to the Lords of the Treasury a Memorial which I presented to His Grace, as Consul of the United States of America representing the Case of the American Brigantine Rachel, Nichs. Duff, Master and claiming a compensation for the loss and damage arising to the Owners from the unprecedented treatment she had met with from Persons acting under the authority of His Majesty's Commissioners of the Customs and their Lordships having referred my Memorial to the said Commissioners for a Report, which was by them again referred to their Officers at Portsmouth, the very Men whose conduct had occasioned the Memorial, and the said Commissioners having in consequence after a long delay made a Report to their Lordships differing essentially from a Statement of the truth in consequence of which their Lordships were pleased to answer the Duke of Leeds and to deny the prayer of my said Memorial. I have now the honor to transmit you a Copy of my Remarks on the conduct of the said Commissioners which I beg you will lay before their Lordships as an accurate detail of the circumstances respecting that Vessel and her Cargo, Copies of which it is my duty to transmit by the June Packet to the Congress of the United States. I believe it to be a novel practice either in Politics or Justice to refer the Complaint of a Public Grievance to the Men who had committed the wrong and against whom that Complaint had been made and who were to benefit by its perpetration. This observation points directly at the Custom House Officers at Portsmouth.

Upon a National Subject I have found it my duty to Memorialize one of His Majesty's Ministers, that Memorial has been referred to His Majesty's Treasury, then again by their Lordships to the Commissioners of the Customs, these Commissioners refer it a third time to two Custom House Officers at Portsmouth and these persons are permitted to decide upon a State paper, their decision passes upwards until it reaches again His Majesty's Ministers and becomes sanctioned by the highest authority of Office.

The direct tendency of this kind of conduct is too obvious to render any remarks of mine necessary and I hope their Lordships will see the absolute necessity of giving it a period.

The Rachel is still at Portsmouth and I cannot give my consent to the Conditions of her release imposed by the Commissioners of the Customs, which is that of subjecting an American Vessel to an arbitrary fine imposed at the will and discretion of Men (the said Custom House Officers at Portsmouth) who had before under frivolous pretences pillaged her of a considerable part of her Cargo. I beg you will lay my address inclosed herewith before their Lordships and that I may be favored with their resolution hereupon, so that it may be transmitted if possible also by the June Packet to be laid before Congress.

It is painful to me to be under the necessity of making this representation, but a sense of duty to the United States irresistibly supercedes every other consideration. I have the honor to be with great respect, Sir Your most Obedient Humble Servant,   [JOSHUA JOHNSON]

Tr (DNA: RG 76, Great Britain, unsorted papers); docketed as addressed to Long as joint secretary to the Treasury. Another Tr (DNA: RG 59, CD).

R
Joshua Johnson to Lord Grenville

My Lord   London 27 May 1791

Having had occasion to present a Memorial to his Grace the Duke of Leeds, your Lordships Predecessor, in the Month of March last, complaining of the treatment which the American Brigantine Rachel, Nicholas Duff, Master had met with at Portsmouth, from Persons acting under the Authority of his Majesty's Commissioners of the Customs, and soliciting a Compensation in redress for the same: His Grace referred my Memorial to the Right Honorable the Lords of His Majesty's Treasury, their Lordships were again pleased to refer it to the Commissioners of the Customs, and the Commissioners of the Customs again to two Custom House Officers at Portsmouth. In the course of my frequent Applications at your Lordship's Office, for an Answer to my Memorial, I had the mortification to learn what sort of a progress it was making, upon which I addressed a Letter to his Grace, to which I humbly beg your Lordship will now please to advert, representing the extreme uncertainty, and irregularity of that mode of proceeding, seeing that the decision of a State Paper, complaining of a gross Outrage, committed upon a Vessel, and Cargo, the property of a Citizen of the United States of America, and bearing its Flag, had been ultimately referred for it's decision, to two Custom House Officers at Portsmouth, the perpetrators of that very outrage. The report made by these Men, having been adopted by His Majesty's Commissioners of the Customs, and transmitted under their sanction to the Lords of the Treasury, and their Lordships having also adopted it, and past it to your Lordships Office, from that Office it came to me with a Negative upon the Prayer of my Memorial, and I confess to your Lordship, I was more concerned than surprised to find that report so essentially deviate from a true statement of Facts, for what other event could be expected from Men who found their Interest in misrepresentation. I could not pass over in silence the very extraordinary Conduct of His Majesty's Commissioners of the Customs upon this occasion, and I do myself the Honor to inclose herewith for your Lordship's perusal the Copy of my Letter to them, dated the 21 Instant, it is painful to me to be under the necessity of adding, that after having for three Months ineffectually endeavoured to procure redress from his Majesty's Ministers, and from a subordinate Board, I feel it my indispensible Duty to take the earliest opportunity of transmitting Copies of my Memorials, and of my Correspondence upon this Subject to be laid before the Congress of the United States of America. The Rachel is still at Portsmouth, in the fourth Month of her detention, nor can I consent to suffer an American Vessel which has offended against no Law, to be subject to an arbitrary fine imposed for the benefit, and by the will of two Custom House Officers at Portsmouth, who have already under frivolous Pretences, stript her of a considerable part of her Cargo. I wish much to deprecate the consequences of this line of Political Conduct, and I hope your Lordship will readily see the propriety of preventing it's repetition. I have the honor to be with great respect Your Lordship's most obedient humble Servant,   [JOSHUA JOHNSON]

Tr (DNA: RG 76, Great Britain, unsorted papers); docketed by Remsen. Another Tr (DNA: RG 59, CD).

s
Philip Stephens to Joshua Johnson

Admiralty Office, 30 May 1791. He acknowledges [and summarizes the contents of] Johnson's letter of the 25th, which he has laid before the Lords of the Admiralty. He is commanded by them "to acquaint you, that the several Men at whose instance the Brigantine has been seized by Process from the High Court of Admiralty, for the recovery of their Wages, and Cloaths, having declared themselves severally to be British Subjects, their Lordships are advised that if the Master, or Owner of the Vessel intend to dispute that fact, it is only necessary, in order to liberate the Vessel, that Bail be given to the several Suits, after which, the Causes will be regularly proceeded on to issue, and determination."

Tr (DNA: RG 76, Great Britain, unsorted papers); docketed by Remsen.

III. William Green to the Secretary of State

SIR   New York Decembr. 6th. 1791

Mr. Johnson, the Consul for the United States at the Port of London, having Communicated to you, the Causes, and, some of the Consequences of the detention there, and, at Portsmouth, of the Brigantine Rachel, Nicholas Duff Master, and belonging to me; I think it my duty to lay before you, the sequel of that detail in as few words as possible.

The Rachel was detained in the Port of London, on her arrival with a Cargo from this Port, on the 22nd day of October 1790, to the 18th of the following January, whilst His Britannic Majesty's Ministers were deliberating, whether, Vessels naturalized by the United States, should be admitted to the same privileges in British Ports, as they are allowed, in all other Ports of Europe: and, having decided in the Negative, on the 18th. of January the Rachel sailed with the same Cargo on board, to the Port of Ostend.

But, whilst the Vessel lay in the Port of London, the Captain delivered from on board an English-made fowling piece the property of Mr. Henry Cruger of this City, and which was returned to the Maker, for repair or alteration and had been carried on board the Vessel, as part of the Baggage of Mr. Knox the Consul for Dublin.

For this act, Captain Duff was taken ignominiously out of the Vessel, in virtue of a Judges warrant, and Conveyed to the Common Goal, until he found Sureties for his penal responsibility to the Amount of Five Hundred pounds Sterling: Having given the bail in question, he was permitted to proceed, as is already Stated, with the Vessel to Ostend, and there having discharged the said Cargo and taken in a Cargo of Brandies and Geneva for this Port, he proceeded on his Voyage, but put in to the Mother Bank and Come to Anchor off Spithead untill the event of a Memorial to the Commissioners of the Customs, for putting an end to this Malicious prosecution against him, could be known. If the Commissioners consented to his request, he had only to get instantly under way and proceed on his first Voyage, but if they had persisted to bring the matter into any of their Courts of Justice, then, Captain Duff must have quitted his employ, and remained behind in England, where also the greater part of the Crew of the Vessel must have been kept to testify his Innocence. In any event, the poor Man must have been ruined by the expence, for the Crown of England is not liable for Cost and Damages. But the Commissioners were pleased to suffer him to compromise the matter, which he did at a heavy expence and he would have sailed on his Voyage on the 25th. day of February, agreeably to the permission of the Said Commissioners, if their Officers at that Port, had not on that day, taken possession both of Vessel and Cargo, under pretence, that no Vessel with Brandies and Geneva in Cases on board, could legally put into any British Port.

The case being referred to the Commissioners of the Customs, they most unjustly Sanctioned their said Officers, to pillage the Vessel of all the Geneva she had on board, but added a permission to the Rachel, afterwards to proceed on her Voyage, provided a farther and indefinite Satisfaction in Money was made to their Officers at Portsmouth. – As Mr. Johnson has acquainted you with the absolute refusal of the British Ministry, to redress such an accumulation of gross Injury and damage, I shall only add, that after a Contest for Justice, which lasted five Months, I was obliged to give up the point, and to pay the fee, they, the said Officers demanded, over and above the Amount of the property of which they had before robbed the Vessel: for, I had no other alternative but that of abandoning both Vessel, and Cargo, to the possession of those Harpies, or, of acquiescing after so long a resistance in a Public Wrong and Indignity to the Independance of the United States. I confess after a positive annihilation of a Capital of upwards of Two hundred Thousand Dollars, employ'd in the Commerce of the United States to the East Indies, and which had been destroyed by British Policy, the recollection of my family (four of my Children are Natural born Subjects of the United States) decided me to yeild, and I took back my Vessel and Cargo upon their own terms. She is since safely arrived here after an absence of thirteen Months, on this Voyage to Europe.

One other circumstance I ought not to Omit, is, that during the time of her detention by the Customs, five of her People, after attempting to rob the Cargo, run away from the Rachel, and thereby according to their American Articles forfeited their Wages. The case was so notorious, that no private Law-Practitioner could be found, hardy enough to Sue for the defaulters: It remain'd therefore for the British Government to take up the Cause, which it did, by engeniously converting the said Deserters (who had by this time entered on board a Ship of War) into American Loyalists, the Vessel was accordingly taken possession of, by a Gaurd, but on a Spirited Memorial being presented to the Admiralty, by Mr. Johnson, that Gaurd was withdawn, and I really thought the affair ended, until I went down with that part of my family which had Accompanied me to Europe, to embark on board, for my return to this City, and after the pillage of the Custom House had been finally accomplished and Settled: and then, another Gaurd was put on board by the Admiralty, with orders not to Suffer her to move, untill the said Demand was discharged, and Mr. Johnson at the same time was officially informed, that unless it was fully done with Costs and Charges, both Vessel and Cargo would be appraised, and Sold. This was a Second pillage, and there was no resisting an Admiralty Mandate thus enforced.

During the time of the Vessels detention at Portsmouth, she was Compleatly dismantled by the Custom House, and her sails Carried on shore, nay such was the uncommon rigor of Conduct to her, that altho the Captain repeatedly required permission to sight his Anchor, for the purpose of releiving his Cable he was constantly refused. The consequence was that the Cable which had just before cost him in London Eighty Pounds Sterling, was ruined, and almost unfit for any farther Service. I should not have Subjoined the Mention of this singular Circumstance, had it not been to have the extraordinary asperity, and hostility with which the Commerce of the Citizens and Subjects of the United States are treated by the British Government and its unprincipled and profligate Subalterns.

I have the honor to enclose you an Account of the Damage this

Vessels detention has Occasioned to me her Owner and which Amount to the sum of seven thousand Dollars and upwards, I humbly hope the humanity Wisdom and Spirit of the Federal Government will be interposed for the Indemnification of the Citizens of the United States under such Circumstances. I have the honor to be with the greatest respect Sir Your most Obedient & Most humble Servant,

WILLIAM GREEN

RC (DNA: RG 76, Great Britain, unsorted papers); in clerk's hand, signed by Green; endorsed by TJ as received 16 Dec. 1791 and so recorded in SJL. Enclosure: Estimate of damages sustained by Green, owner of *Rachel*, "by her detention for the Space of Nine Months . . . in the Ports of London and Portsmouth": (1) loss and expense by detention of *Rachel*, fully manned and victualled, for 89 days from 22 Oct. 1790 to 18 Jan. 1791 while government deliberated whether she, as "a Naturalized American bottom, should be allowed an Entry in a British Port . . . moderately and humbly estimated per diem at 20 Dollars," $1,780; (2) extra insurance of vessel and cargo at $12,500 and super freight on 175 ton vessel from London to Ostend, $475; (3) damage to potash which could not be recovered from underwriters, $400; (4) demurrage for 166 days at $20 per diem from 22 Feb. to 6 Aug. 1791 while *Rachel* lay at Portsmouth, where she had put in to enable Captain Duff to redeem his bail in a prosecution because he had landed a fowling piece – "Actually . . . landed, with the Verbal permission of the Surveyors general, Officers of the Customs," totalling $3,320; (5) under date "Feby. 22," 125 cases of Holland Geneva at $4 per case, "pillaged from the Cargo . . . by the Custom House Officers . . . and which pillage was sanctioned by the Ministers of His Britannic Majesty who refused redress to all the representations of Mr. Johnson, the Consul for the United States," $500; (6) fee extorted from Captain Duff by customs officers despite protests of Johnson, an extortion sanctioned by government by not permitting *Rachel* to sail until it was paid, $88. 8/9, recorded as paid 29 July 1791; (7) sundry expenses resulting from the prosecution of *Rachel* to recover wages of five American seamen who, "after having attempted to rob the cargo, had run away from her, to avoid punishment, and had

therefore, conformable to their American Articles, forfeited their Wages," but whom the captain was compelled to pay in full despite their desertion and the fact that sundry payments "had been made to their order in New York, during their absence" – all because, through the "ingenuity" of the Admiralty, "they had entered Volunteers on board a British ship of War, having Converted the said Seamen, into American Loyalists," $301. 1/9; and finally (8), under 4 Aug. 1791, sundry expenses incurred by Captain Duff in the prosecution against him for landing an English fowling piece, $427. 4/9 – the whole aggregating $7,292. 4/9 (DNA: RG 76, Great Britain, unsorted papers; signed by Green and dated at New York, 6 Dec. 1791).

When Green returned to the United States in August, deluding himself with the hope that Congress would indemnify him for losses produced by "a Public Wrong and Indignity to the Independance of the United States," he could not have helped himself by the letter of introduction he bore from Thomas Paine to the President. Paine, who had been advanced £50 by Green, described him as his friend. "He has a troublesome affair on his hands here," Paine wrote, "and is in danger of losing thirty or forty thousand pounds, embarked under the flag of the United States in East India property. . . . He wishes to state the case to Congress, not only on his own account, but as a matter that may be nationally interesting" (Paine to Washington, 21 July 1791, DLC: Washington Papers). In bearing this letter, which arrived in the midst of the acrimonious "contest of Burke and Paine . . . in America," Green also conveyed the fifty copies of *Rights of Man* which Paine sent to the President and other friends, including TJ (see Editorial Note and group of documents at 26 Apr. 1791).

From Benjamin Harrison, Jr.

Richmond, 1 June 1791. "The Abuses that are practicing here every day, and the cheat that is thereby put on the public, particularly the Ignorant and poor, by the mutilation of our money, is become of a serious nature. Supposing the remedy within your department . . . and knowing your wish for information on all subjects, I have a few days ago picked up the enclosed pieces of money from a Silver Smith in this Town, who tells me that he gets some hundred of Ounces of them yearly from a variety of people here, and I know myself that after these p[iece]s are taken off, the remainder is passed on the ignorant for the full original value. The Broad p[iece]s are taken from the Pistereen when whole, the narrower from the Bit after it has gone fairly cut into the Hands of the offender."

This letter is sent by his friend John Gregory, originally of Dunkirk but of late years of Petersburg, whom TJ will find worthy. "As Americans we have to regret his return to France with his Lady, retiring into private life in that Land of Liberty on an ample fortune left him by his Father lately dead."

RC (DNA: RG 59, MLR); addressed: "The Honble. Thos. Jefferson Philadelphia J: Gregory Esqr."; signature clipped; endorsed by TJ as received 29 Aug. 1791 and so recorded in SJL.

From James Swan

Paris, "Rue de Montmorency No. 63," 2 June 1791. The proposals described in his of 8 [i.e., 3] Oct. to exchange provisions for the American debt were defeated by the opposition of Fleurieu and by the propositions of Schweizer, Jeanneret & Co. of Paris "for some Genoese Capitalists, who proposed to pay the debt in money at once." On that day the Assembly decreed that after 1 Jan. 1791 provisions for the marine should be made by public adjudication to the lowest bidder, in which case Swan and his partners would have been the furnishers. Afterward, they would have proposed to the Assembly to give them the debt in payment, "which would have been very agreeable." But Fleurieu, minister of marine, in contempt of the decree never asked for bids "but continued even for the whole of this Year, the old Regie. I have very certain knowledge why he did so." He was twice called on by the Assembly to account for this, but he did not even deign to reply. He is out, and the present one has asked a repeal of the decree to allow him to "make the furniture by a private Copropriété. To meet this a french and American company is made up." Robert Morris, himself, and some other Americans are to do the principal part; the French are to give 3.2 million livres as security to government. Gouverneur Morris will have nothing to do with it. "The interest we have got near the Minister, the support we have of the Intendants, promises every success. I hope in a few weeks to have the pleasure to inform you that it is closed: it will be a fortunate thing for the United States, and beneficial to the individuals concern'd."

As for his timber contract, threat of war last summer suspended deliveries. This spring he has applied several times to get assurance of payment in specie or allowed depreciation in accordance with "the spirit and intention" of both parties in making the contract. Fleurieu said he could not do it. Present minister wishes to put it, as a foreign supply, on specie list, but fears censure. Decision will be made in a few days. If he does not, it must be suspended, since depreciation makes a difference of 80,000 livres annually.

RC (DNA: RG 59, MLR); endorsed by TJ as received 9 Aug. 1791 and so recorded in SJL.

From La Rochefoucauld d'Enville

Paris, 3 June 1791. TJ's letter of 3 Apr. 1790 arrived a little late, but he reproaches himself with the long silence and will frankly explain the cause. Being charged by the National Assembly to take part in the framing of levies, he had hoped that certain parts would offer occasions to bind France more closely with America. "C'est un voeu qui est dans l[e coeur de tous] bons patriotes." But the principles guiding the proceedings did not allow the opportunity to be seized as he had desired. Perhaps M. de Ternant will bring TJ a decree of yesterday expressing the desire of the Assembly to negotiate a commercial treaty beneficial to the interest of both powers and to unite them in commerce as they are in political principles. The letter from the President to the Pennsylvania legislature will develop these sentiments. – De Ternant will inform TJ that they have just convened their successors; he will leave it to him to put him *au courant* of their affairs. "Je me bornerai, faute de tems, à ne vous parler que des regrets de tous vos amis et surtout de notre famille, et à vous renouveller l'homage du sincere et tendre attachement avec [lequel j'ai l'honneur] d'être, Monseiur, Votre très humble et très [obeissant Serviteur." . . . [P.S.] "Ma mere et ma femme me char[gent de leurs] complimens pour vous."

RC (DLC); mutilated, so that some words have been lost and are supplied in part conjecturally; endorsed by TJ as received 9 Aug. 1791 and so recorded in SJL.

For comment on President Bureaux-Pusy's letter to the Pennsylvania legislature, see Editorial Note and group of documents on the death of Franklin, at 26 Jan. 1791. See also Bureaux-Pusy's letter to TJ, 6 June 1791, and its enclosure.

From the President of the National Assembly

Paris le six Juin 1791.

L'Assemblée Nationale de France, Monsieur, qui avait reçu avec la plus vive sensibilité la réponse du Président du Congrès des Etats unis d'Amérique, à la communication qui lui avoit été fait des dernieres marques d'honneurs décernés par les représentans d'un peuple libre à votre illustre compatriote Benjamin Franklin, n'a pas été moins touchée des nouveaux témoignages d'amitié fraternelle que vous lui adressés au nom du Congrès.

Elle m'a chargé de vous faire part du Décret qu'elle a rendu sur le rapport de son Comité Diplomatique. Il sera pour les Etats unis d'Amérique la preuve du vif desir de l'Assemblée nationale de voir se resserrer par tous les moyens de bienveillance, d'affection et d'utilité reciproque les liens qui doivent à jamais unir deux peuples qui, nés à la liberté l'un par l'autre, semblent destinés à vivre en communauté d'interrêts comme de principes.

Je m'applaudis, Monsieur, d'être dans cette occasion l'organe de l'Assemblée, nationale et de pouvoir transmettre l'expression de ses sentimens à un homme qui a concouru si essentiellement à la révolution et à la législation de son pays, et qui, après avoir contemplé dans le nôtre le berceau de notre liberté naissante, nous a quittés en emportant l'amitié des Français dont il avoit depuis longtems la considération et l'estime.

Par ordre de l'Assemblée nationale de France

J.X. Bureaux-Pusy
Président

RC (DNA: RG 59, NL); at foot of text: "M. Jefferson Ministre du Congrès des Etats unis d'Amérique"; endorsed by Remsen: "Letters &c. from the National Assembly of France"; endorsed by TJ as received 9 Aug. 1791 and so recorded in SJL. Enclosure printed below.

On 2 June 1791, Fréteau-Saint-Just, reporting to the National Assembly for the Diplomatic Committee, read to that body TJ's letter of 8 Mch. 1791 to the accompaniment of "Applaudissements à gauche." Referring to Washington's letter of 27 Jan. 1791, also addressed to the President of the Assembly, he explained that this second letter had been written by the Secretary of State at the direction of Congress in order to give "une nouvelle preuve des sentiments de fraternité qui l'unissent à ce royaume" and to express their desire to continue in peace and unity with France – scarcely an exact statement either for the authority for TJ's letter or for the sentiments of Congress. Fréteau-Saint-Just then read the address of the Pennsylvania legislature of 8 Apr. 1791 (for comment on the political context of these and related documents, see Editorial Note and texts of documents relating to the death of Franklin

under 26 Jan. 1791). After the reading of the Pennsylvania address, several members of the National Assembly called for it to be printed. Another suggested that a copy be sent to Abbé Raynal, who two days earlier had outraged the Assembly with a letter very critical of its proceedings (see Short to TJ, 6 June 1791). Several members then exclaimed that Fréteau-Saint-Just's report had not been completed, whereupon, having read the two documents, the reporter stretched their meaning still further by declaring them to be the sentiments of the American people. Bureaux-Pusy did not include the text of the Pennsylvania address in the communication, though that, like TJ's own letter, formed a part of the report of the Diplomatic Committee which preceded its comment upon their meaning and its recommendation that a new treaty of commerce be negotiated. In his communication of the same date to the Pennsylvania legislature, Bureaux-Pusy included TJ's letter as a part of the report but naturally omitted the text of the Pennsylvania address. This letter and its enclosure, along with the text of the address itself, were published in Bache's *General Advertiser*, 29 Aug. 1791, as well as in other newspapers. When the communication was read in the House of Representatives two days earlier, it was first laid on the table and then, in an action which indicated that the divisions which had been manifested on the same subject during the debates of the previous session were still present, it was moved "and by special order . . . taken up for a second reading, and the original letter with the translation was ordered to be entered on the journals of the house" (same). A few days later Bache declared that the communication from the National Assembly "breathes a spirit of liberty which would do honor to the freest republican government. The reference . . . to our revolution, as being indirectly the cause of their regeneration, exhibits a degree of candor not very common with other European Courts. The wishes expressed, to be united to us by the closest commercial ties, is a favorable omen of benefits to be derived by an intercourse with that country, to the advantage of our commerce and agriculture" (*General Advertiser*, 1 Sep. 1791). The allusion to the want of candor in other courts was obviously directed toward that of England. Whether in publishing and commenting upon these documents Bache was influenced by TJ, who had tried to make his a balanced national newspaper, is not known.

But there can be no doubt that it was the Secretary of State who released to the press the copy of Fréteau-Saint-Just's report which came with the above letter. TJ's choice of newspaper as well as his timing was clearly calculated. He had received Bureaux-Pusy's letter and its enclosure early in August and of course could have trans-

lated these himself and made them available to Bache even before the text was made public by the Pennsylvania legislature. Instead he held the report until November, after Congress had convened and after Ternant had arrived as the new French minister. It was at this session, too, that TJ expected to submit his report on commerce calling for a navigation act aimed at Great Britain, a proposal to which the friendly expressions of the National Assembly and the decree calling for a new treaty of commerce with the United States could only have given added strength. TJ perhaps would have waited for this favorable conjunction of events in any case. But just a few days before he received Bureaux-Pusy's letter and its gratifying enclosure, Philip Freneau had announced to him his intention to establish a newspaper at the seat of government, as Madison and TJ had urged him to do (Freneau to TJ, 4 Aug. 1791). Within a few days Freneau also accepted appointment as translator to the Department of State. Thus what was perhaps the first translating assignment given the new departmental member became simultaneously one of the most gratifying and timely communications that the Secretary of State could make available to the newly established and favored *National Gazette*. Fréteau-Saint-Just's report, including TJ's letter of 8 Mch. 1791 to the President of the National Assembly, but not the address of the Pennsylvania legislature, appeared in the issue of 17 Nov. 1791. Bache's *General Advertiser* carried an incomplete text of the report two days later.

ENCLOSURE

Report of the Diplomatic Committee of the National Assembly of France

Gentlemen

You have been made acquainted with the sentiments of the Americans, and their expressions of grateful respect and particular good will towards you.[1]

The honesty and upright moral character of that people are to us the best pledges of their sincerity and affection.

Our interests and theirs must in future be considered the same; and we are reciprocally attached to each other by every tie of duty and regard.

We have assisted them in repulsing their enemies and vindicating themselves into freedom. In return they have taught us a just and humane spirit of toleration, to respect the obligation of oaths, to pay obedience to the Laws, to honour in man the dignity of his species, and even to undervalue the brilliancy of genius, whether displayed in Legislation or successful warfare, when set in competition with the horrors of sanguinary contests and brutal violence. They have also taught us how to pay a proper regard to the lives and honours of our fellow creatures, as well as their fortunes, and lastly they have set us the example in a quiet submission to lawful authority.

A Nation actuated by such ideas can boast of being more than the conquerors of a world. They are at once our great example and support. Into their ports and marts of trade then, to the peaceable and happy country they inhabit, should it be our great endeavour, in preference to all others, to introduce our Merchants to inform themselves in the Nature of their Commerce and imbibe the virtues which alone can cause it to flourish, that is to say, œconomy, simplicity, purity of morals, integrity, and honesty.

From the foregoing considerations it is the opinion of the Committee; that the National Assembly should use every possible Means to cherish and encourage a reciprocal commercial intercourse between France and America.

Lewis the Sixteenth having gained the title of Restorer of the Liberties of France may with no less justice lay claim to that of Benefactor of the New World. So far then are you from infringing his Royal Prerogative in being the first to notify him of your intentions on this head, that, on the contrary your views and his perfectly co-incide and co-operate in the glorious plan which he has so much at heart, to draw closer than ever those ties of connexion which unite the French Nation to the brave citizens of the United States of America, whose uniform and generous spirit of equity, next to the justice of their cause, the energy of their exertion, and their invincible courage, was heretofore, as it is at this day, the only firm support and the surest pledge of their Independence.

Decree of the National Assembly, June 2d. 1791

The National Assembly having heard a Letter read from the Minister of the United States of America, that was addressed to their President signed "Jefferson"; and also another letter from the Representatives of the State of Pennsylvania, dated the 8th of April last, and by them addressed to the President of the Assembly, together with the report of their official Committee,

Ordered, that the two Letters abovementioned be printed and inserted in the Journals of the session.

The President is requested to answer the Letter from the Representatives of the State of Pennsylvania, and to inform the Minister of the United States of America, that it is the earnest desire of the National Assembly to strengthen more and more the ties of friendship and brotherly affection which at this day constitute a bond of union between the two Nations.

Decreed, finally, that the King be prayed to cause to be negociated with the United States, a New Treaty of Commerce that may tend to strengthen those mutual relations of friendship and good understanding, so highly beneficial to them both.

Signed
Besse, Curate of St. Aubin
Secretary
[Huot-Goncourt][2]
Ricard Dep[uté] de Toulon

Tr (DNA: RG 59, DD); in the hand of Freneau, who translated it from the French. RC (same); in French, in clerk's hand except for the signatures, one of which was not included in Freneau's translation, perhaps because of its difficult handwriting (see note 2 below); endorsed by TJ as received 9 Aug. 1791 and so recorded in SJL. Dupl (same); in French, in another hand except for the three signatures.

Surprisingly for so gifted a writer as Freneau, his translation of Fréteau-Saint-Just's report does not do justice either to its style or to its sentiments. It is understandable that he should have omitted Huot-Goncourt's all but illegible signature, but his rendition of the text was at times loose, awkward, and even imprecise. It is a fair presumption, based on a number of examples that might be cited, that a translation by TJ himself would have been more faithful to the original both in its substance and in its elevated style. (See, for example, TJ's translation of Condorcet's letter and its enclosure at 3 May 1791.) It is difficult to imagine TJ rendering the brief and forceful "Nos intérêts vont désormais se confondre, et des devoirs plus étroits vont nous unir" as "Our interests and theirs must in future be considered the same; and we are reciprocally attached to each other by every tie of duty and regard." Nor is it likely that he would have translated "ils nous instruisent à leur tour à être tolerans, justes et humaines" as "In return they have taught us a just and humane spirit of toleration." Certainly he could not have put into English "à préférer à toutes les qualités brillantes, même aux dons du Génie dans la politique, et aux faveurs du sort dans les Combats, l'horreur du Sang et de la violence, le respect pour la vie et l'honneur de nos Semblables, et pour les propriétés, enfin la Soumission aux autorités légitimes" such a long and confused version as Freneau rendered in the corresponding passage above. In view of the importance TJ attached to this timely document as indicated by his authorizing Freneau to make it public, it is surprising that he did not add to its force by providing a more adequate version of the original. Perhaps he felt that the essential part of the message was not its official expression of friendship for the American people, which would have been discounted in any case by those preferring stronger ties with England, but its announcement of the decree of the National Assembly calling for a new treaty of commerce. That, strengthened by the arrival of Ternant, would not likely be dismissed as mere rhetoric. TJ knew that the decree had been adopted at Lafayette's suggestion to palliate the effect of the tobacco and other decrees because various French interests were too powerful to permit a modification of them (Short to TJ, 6 June 1791). But he made the most of the report by releasing it to the press.

[1] Fréteau-Saint-Just's report to the National Assembly included TJ's letter to the President, 8 Mch. 1791, and the address of the Pennsylvania legislature, 8 Apr. 1791, to which this passage alludes, but Bureaux-Pusy naturally omitted these in the text sent TJ.

[2] Huot-Goncourt's signature appears in RC but is here supplied because Freneau omitted it in his Tr.

From William Short

DEAR SIR   Paris June 6. 1791.

I received a few days ago by Mons. Terrasson your letter of March. 8. together with the papers it inclosed. – The report on the fisheries has been lent to a member of the committee of finance, who not understanding English himself told me he purposed having it translated for the use of the committee. I was pleased with this as a pamphlet which I had published on the affair of tobacco whilst I was in Holland cost so dear as to make me averse to such things in future. – Your letter to the President of national assembly was well received. It was brought forward as well as an address from the legislature of Pennsylvania which had arrived by the way of London, by the diplomatic committee, on whose report, as you will see by the journals and will learn by M. de Ternant, the King is requested to form a new treaty of commerce with the U.S. The moment was exceedingly favorable for your letter and the address of Pennsylvania as the assembly was still sore under the scourges received the day before from a letter of the Abbe Raynal read to them by their permission because they were not acquainted with its contents.

I cannot know what will be the disposition of the U.S. with respect to this treaty, and I see a considerable difficulty in the business on account of their islands. The assembly having desired the King however to negotiate it is an advantage as it will render the ministry more bold in meeting that question on proper ground. M. de Montmorin has certainly much more liberal ideas respecting it and would be disposed to treat it with more freedom than the assembly, where the influence of the merchants, is manifest in all matters of commerce. I think you will find Ternant well disposed also, at least as far as I can judge from his conversation and assurances. – It will be proper to examine perhaps whether the U.S. would find it for their interest to render all rights common between American and French citizens (the islands included) in both countries; if so this is certainly the proper time to propose it and thus reduce the treaty to one simple article, and give a great example which if followed by other nations would abolish at once three fourths of the causes of war. – Such a proposition would be more likely to be adopted under present circumstances than any which present themselves to me as probable for some time to come. I should think it impolitic for the U.S. to clog themselves with a number of articles in a treaty of commerce and particularly with this country at this time. At any rate it seems to me that an admission into the islands on a tolerably free footing should be a *sine qua non*, and I cannot help believing they will refuse this unless it is ushered in by some new and leading system, such as mentioned above, which would find strong supporters here among all the economists.

Mr. McHenry's papers were received and attention shall be paid to them in the manner you desire. They were sent to his agent with this information and M. de la fayette says he will lend his aid also.

I received also by M. Terrasson your letters of March 12. 15. and 19. You will be as much mortified no doubt as I have been, at the copy of your letter to Mr. Carmichael and the papers alluded to therein, as stated in your letter of March 12. having not come to my hands. Those alone which relate to the case of Ste. Marie came inclosed. I immediately however communicated the matter agreeably to your desire to M. de la fayette, whom I found perfectly in the dispositions which might have been expected. His zeal in favor of the liberty and independence of the Floridas would have carried him beyond what I consider as our interest, since his wish was that the U.S. without stopping for negotiation should proceed at once to wrest them from Spain and incorporate them in the union. I stated to him the embarassing position in which that would place France and brought him easily to adopt a more moderate plan. – He persisted however in treating as chimerical any idea that this or any future National assembly would ever consent to undertake a war to reduce the Floridas to Spanish dominion or against us for endeavouring to withdraw them from it. He thinks that he alone whether in or out of such assembly would unquestionably be able to prevent them from it. It would not have been well to have shewn apprehensions of the contrary, and I am persuaded in such an extremity the first impulsion of the assembly would be in favor of the liberty and independence of the Floridas. Yet it is impossible to say how far this might be changed by maturer reflexion, when they would find themselves under the necessity of acting in a contrary direction or risking the loss of their alliance with Spain, and therefore the U.S. should not lose sight of such an embarassment, although I still think it more than probable they would not take an active part. I speak of them in a future and more settled condition than the present, for at this moment it may be considered I think as certain that either the novelty of the enthusiasm for liberty, or the situation of their affairs at home, or their apprehensions from abroad would prevent their acting in a case of this kind.

After having ascertained the dispositions of M. de la fayette I asked a rendezvous with M. de Montmorin and laid open to him with the confidence he deserves the present position of this affair. He entered fully of himself into the situation of the U.S. and the impossibility of their restraining the western inhabitants or abandoning them. He told me he had long foreseen that this would happen, that when at Madrid he had pressed that court to remove the difficulty by an amicable arrangement taken then, as the moment was more favorable for their interests than any which could be contemplated in future, that they rejected all idea of an arrangement in such a manner at that time as to leave him no hopes that they would listen to it at present, that he was confirmed in this opinion by his knowledge of the mode of thinking of that court, that the influence of France would at all times have been ineffectual against their prejudices in matters of this kind, but at present would be entirely vain, he feared, as the Spanish cabinet would necessarily consider any terms proposed by them, as dictated by their partiality in favor of the U.S. on account of the new system which has taken place in France. – Still he assured me, and in this I am persuaded of his sincerity, of his disposition to use every effort for having this difficulty removed agreeably to the desire of the U.S. He added that the navigation of the Mississipi was a matter of *necessity* to the U.S. and that it was always useless to struggle against *necessity*. – He seemed concerned when I shewed him the danger there was that the western inhabitants might descend the Mississipi without waiting for the event of negotiation, not because he considered there was anything to be hoped from negotiation, but as he said, because in that case we should be considered as the agressors. I observed to him that the seizure of Ste. Marie's goods within the limits of the U.S. and carrying off forcibly those in whose charge they were, was such a violation of the territory of the U.S. and of their rights as would naturally be considered as the first aggression. To this he did not reply directly but he shewed no disposition to deny it. – He considered also the invitation held out by the Spanish government, to strangers, even *protestants*, to come and settle on their side of the Mississipi as plainly indicative of designs that the U.S. could not wait the execution of.

Finally he desired I would write to him on the subject, that he might send my letter to Madrid, and instruct the French Resident thereon. He told me he would direct him particularly to support Mr. Carmichael in the representations he should make to that court. In consequence of this I wrote him the letter, of which I inclose you a copy, and delivered it to him myself with a desire that he would read it, and if he should find anything that he wished to be changed, that he would say so in order to such alterations being made as should be found proper. For this purpose I wrote it in French, we read over the letter together and spoke on the several articles as we went along. He told me he saw nothing that he wished to be altered, that he would forward it and give instructions for supporting the claims therein stated. – I think on reading the letter, Sir, you will find that the Minister promises to go as far as my No. 46. gave hopes of, and that I have no reason to repent having communicated the ideas therein contained.

M. de Montmorin told me also he would speak of this matter to the Spanish Ambassador here, whom he considered as more likely to be disposed to listen to reason on this subject than M. de Florida Blanca. He said however he was sure they would not agree to have the subject treated here, as you seem to desire. He added also that even if the Spanish Ambassador should be convinced, he did not think it would be anything gained, as it did not appear to him, that he had influence at court. I had supposed the contrary, but I rely more on M. de Montmorin's opinion than that which I had taken up.

There was one circumstance in the course of our conversation, after he had read my letter which I cannot pass unnoticed, although he said he mentioned it to me in confidence and not at all in his ministerial capacity. It was that he thought the best thing to be done was, for Congress to let the western inhabitants act for themselves, in going down the Mississipi and taking New Orleans, without undertaking to support them or legitimate the act.

On the whole it seems to me: 1. That at present this country is in a disposition of mind which would certainly prevent their interfering actively against the U.S. on this question. 2. That in future when their own affairs shall be settled and their government in force, although they would in the first moment be in our favor also, and although it is probable they would continue to refuse acting offensively in such a cause, yet it will be less certain than at present, as they will then also be more cool in listening to the dictates of their political and commercial interests dependent on the alliance with Spain. 3. That the present ministry is better disposed towards the U.S. with respect to this question, than any future one will probably be. 4. That there is no doubt they will use their influence by negotiation to obtain for the U.S. the navigation of the Mississipi on the footing they desire, or if that cannot be done, by a free port established at N. Orleans or in its neighborhood.

It may not be amiss to mention at present that the Marquis de la fayette can no longer be considered as having the same influence as when I wrote you my No. 46. This decline has come from that progression in human affairs which allows nothing to be long at a stand, and from his having too much virtue and patriotism to allow himself to make use of improper means for extending and rivetting his power and influence. The sentiments of M. de Montmorin on this subject may therefore be considered as spontaneous, and consequently more conformable to the wishes of the U.S. – I hope I shall continue to receive your instructions regularly on this important business, and particularly that the copy of your letter to Mr.

Carmichael and papers it refers to, as mentioned in your letter of March 12. will be sent. If I could have shewn them to M. de Montmorin as was your intention, it would certainly have been a mark of confidence that would have been agreeable.

The medal which you desire to be made for M. de Moutier shall be executed as soon as I can have the *coins* finished. You will no doubt be much astonished at this delay, but the Engraver has been so devoted to the affair of their money which is contending for by all the artists that it has been impossible to get him to finish the work he had undertaken for the U.S. and which was nearly completed last fall. This delay cannot last much longer and he assures me he will shorten it as much as possible. He is to write me a letter that I may send it to M. de la Luzerne and shew him that the delay does not proceed from me. I don't know by what opportunity to send you the *dies*. There is no other than that by the public carriages to Havre, and at present they would be stopped and examined by several of the municipalities who would take them, from their weight to be specie, to be exported, which they do not allow notwithstanding the decrees of the assembly.

I received with your letter of March 15. the report of the committee inclosed. It has been inserted in a gazette here. I do not think it would be proper to have it printed apart and circulated, as it would be at once known from whence it came. The gazette which inserted it and which you will receive committed some errors, but their correction is not essential at this moment as it is certain the national assembly will not again resume the subject.

You will learn from M. de Ternant the efforts that have been made to induce the assembly to change their decrees 1. As to the difference made between French and American vessels importing tobacco. 2. As to the augmented duty of 6 ₶ per quintal on American oils. 3. As to the abolition of the sales of American vessels in the French ports. M. de Ternant has been active and used his utmost efforts. There were various interests opposed to the changes desired, and finally several of the committees assembled to take into consideration my letter to M. de Montmorin and the alterations proposed by M. de Ternant, after discussing the subject fully with him and with M. de la fayette, determined it would be unsafe to propose the alterations to the assembly at present as they feared they would be rejected. It was agreed among them, at the instigation particularly of M. de la fayette to palliate this by something agreeable for the U.S. in protestations of a desire to become more united &c. In this disposition your letter arrived, and on it the report mentioned above was adopted.

You say that the President was authorized to employ workmen for the mint, but you add nothing respecting *Drost*. I sent you from Mr. Grand his proposals last year. Among the papers which I forward to the Secretary of the Treasury you will find observations by *Dupré*, in which *Drost's* mode is objected to, and Dupré tells me he is convinced it cannot answer for striking money although proper for medals when few only are wanted. – *Drost* has been here and on the list of the artists in competition for the new coinage projected. *Dupré's* devices have received the preference; and they are now delivered to the artists to be engraved in competition. It is probable also I think that Dupré will be preferred for this part of the business.

You will receive by M. de Ternant the journals of the assembly and gazettes to the present day. I have added to those you generally receive, the *Patriote François* and *Gazette universelle*, the first as the best respecting colonial matters, and the second for European politics. – The *moniteur* will be sent by the way of Havre. It is the best for domestic affairs and is also considered with the *journal logographique*, as much the most accurate with respect to the debates of the assembly.

The most important decrees passed since my last are those for ordering the elections of the new legislature and concerning the colonies. You will see them in the journals. The deputies of the colonies have withdrawn themselves from the assembly and express much discontentment at the decree which gives the rights of citizenship in future to free mulattoes who have a sufficient property. – It is thought this assembly will fix the term of the meeting for the next at the end of August. If an alarming crisis takes place either from the non perception of taxes, or disorder of any kind, they may do it. Otherwise I do not think they will separate so soon. Notwithstanding appearances there is certainly a large majority who desire to remain as long as their places are tenable.

I think I may venture to assure you that the letters are no longer opened in the post-office of this country which you desire to know. The assembly have expressed themselves in such a manner on this subject as would certainly break ancient habits. Besides the administration is changed and no funds are allowed for that purpose. I beg you to continue to be persuaded of the sentiments of sincere attachment & perfect respect with which I have the honor to be Dear Sir Your most obedient & most humble servant,

W. SHORT

P.S. The length of this letter induces me to refer you to the newspapers for the general politics of Europe. Still I suppose it proper to mention to you that it is probable peace will not be interrupted between England and Russia. The opposition which Mr. Pitt saw in the nation, induced him to make modifications which will as it is thought present the means of successful negotiation. In the mean time the truce between the Emperor and the Porte is near its expiration, and it is not known that steps are taken for prolonging it. If not this may change the scene. The Turks have had some success lately against the Russians which have revived their hopes and pretensions as to the *status quo*.

PrC (DLC: Short Papers); at head of text: "*No.67*"; at foot of text: "Thomas Jefferson Secretary of State Philadelphia." Tr (DNA: RG 59, DD). Recorded in SJL as received 9 Aug. 1791. Enclosure: (1) Copy of a paper given him by the Russian chargé concerning one Luc Rauss, a native of Cronstadt, who had studied theology at the University of Jena beginning in 1742 and seven years later had emigrated to America, where he served as pastor in the Lutheran church of Germantown and then, according to a letter he wrote his parents in 1781, had been transferred to Yorktown in Virginia. The statement indicated that his sister Justine, who had married one Raab of Cronstadt, had died without issue on 12 Feb. 1789 and that her brother, if still living, was entitled to his share of her estate (Tr in DNA: RG 59, DD). (2) Short to Montmorin, 1 June 1791, printed below.

Short's bold suggestion that it would be timely to propose "some new and leading system," in which a treaty of a single article making all rights reciprocal between American and French citizens would constitute its essence, was scarcely new. TJ had actually incorporated such a proposal in a draft treaty six years earlier. In sending the draft to John Adams, he acknowledged that such a treaty would be beyond the powers of the American commissioners "and beyond the powers of Congress too," but stated that he was prepared to assume the risk of proposing it to England and France if Adams was (TJ to Adams, 28 July 1785, with enclosure). Such a proposal, coming from the young republic at a time when the powers of Congress were limited and being offered to the two most powerful monarchies of Europe, was no doubt unrealistic. John Adams did not respond. But

now, as Short pointed out, circumstances in France seemed propitious. Also, adoption of a new system of government in the United States had removed the constitutional impediment TJ had recognized in 1785, and responsibility for the conduct of foreign policy was now in the hands of the President and himself. TJ still entertained a cordial disposition to meld "the two nations . . . into one as nearly as possible" at least in respect to commercial matters. But he no longer entertained the idea of a reciprocal guarantee of all rights of citizenship as he had proposed earlier. Also, as he had already warned Montmorin through Otto, and would soon do so through Ternant, this disposition to "grant naturalization to French citizens in matters respecting commerce" would be jeopardized if the recent decrees respecting tobacco, whale oil, and American-built vessels were not modified (TJ to Short, 29 Aug. 1791; Otto to Montmorin, 4 Apr. 1791, quoted above in Editorial Note on the French protest on the tonnage acts, 18 Jan. 1791; Ternant to Montmorin, 24 and 27 Oct. 1791, noted Vol. 18: 278). In actuality, even this narrowed objective was doomed by the divisions in the American government and by the situation in France. As for the latter, Short's description of it as propitious for the proposal of a "new and leading system" was contradicted by his simultaneous assessment of the decree calling for a new commercial treaty as only a palliative designed to soften the blow of the tobacco and other decrees.

TJ's letter to the President of the National Assembly was that of 8 Mch. 1791. Its context, with that of the address of the Pennsylvania legislature, is discussed above in the Editorial Note on the political repercussions which followed the death of Franklin (Vol. 19: 78-115). The report of

the Diplomatic Committee and the resultant decree were enclosed in the response
of the President (see Bureaux-Pusy to TJ,
6 June 1791). Short's "No. 46" was his
dispatch of 6 Nov. 1790 and the passage
to which he alludes is identified there in
note 1. TJ was so impressed by the hopes

thus held out that he made an extract of
the passage and sent it to Washington, urging that the Mississippi question be pressed
"on a broader bottom" than that of the St.
Marie claim. (See Editorial Note on the
threat of disunion in the West, 10 Mch. 1791,
and TJ to Washington, 18 Mch. 1791.)

ENCLOSURE

Short to Montmorin

Monsieur   Paris le 1er. Juin 1791.

Je suis chargé par le President des Etats Unis d'avoir l'honneur de porter
à votre connoissance, Monsieur, la position dans la quelle ils se trouvent vis a
vis de l'Espagne dans ce moment ci relativement à la navigation du Mississipi.

Jusqu'a présent ils ont respecté l'indecision de l'Espagne sur ce sujet, per-
suadés que le tems, la vue des circonstances et l'interet même de cette Puissance l'engageroient à se desister de ses pretensions avant qu'il ne devint
indispensable de l'exiger. Mais le moment est actuellement arrivé ou il n'est
pas permis aux Etats Unis d'attendre plus long tems la decision de cette question, comme vous vous convaincrez facilement, Monsieur, pas les considerations
qui suivent.

D'abord plainte a été regulièrement portée au President des Etats Unis
que le Gouvernement Espagnol a fait saisir sur le territoire reconnu des Etats
Unis des marchandises appartenantes à leurs citoyens, qui ont été transportées
au fort Espagnol et confisquées par l'officier qu'y commandoit. Il a ajouté en
même tems que les ordres qu'il avoit reçu du Gouverneur de la Louisiane
portoient qu'il avoit à saisir tout ce qu'il trouvoit appartenant aux Etats Unis
sur les deux bords du Mississipi au dessous de l'embouchure de l'Ohio et
d'envoyer les proprietaires prisonniers à la nouvelle Orleans.

Ensuite le Gouvernement de l'Espagne a fait inviter tous les etrangers catho-
liques et protestants, par la promesse de la livre navigation de ce fleuve de
venir s'etablir dans ses possessions. Ainsi en defendant cette navigation à ceux
qui resteroient attachés aux Etats Unis et en l'accordant à ceux qui s'en
detacheroient pour passer le Mississipi et devenir sujets espagnols il a montré
clairement que la navigation exclusive etoit un systême du quel il ne contoit
pas se departir, mais au contraire s'en assurer en se servant même des citoyens
des Etats Unis expatriés pour cet objet.

Encore, les habitants de cette partie des Etats Unis ont été retenus dans
des bornes jusqu'a present par notre Gouvernement parce qu'il leur persuadoit,
comme il etoit persuadé lui même, qu'ils obtiendroient par le tems sans autre
effort, la reconnoissance parfaite et paisible de leurs droits. Ces habitants con-
vaincus actuellement du contraire par des raisons que je viens d'avoir l'honneur
Monsieur, de vous citer, indiquent clairement qu'ils ne veulent plus attendre.

Je vous ai fait ces observations seulement, Monsieur, pour vous montrer
l'alternative à la quelle les Etats Unis se trouvent reduits dan ce moment ci,
et qui n'est autre chose que de se separer de ces citoyens et ainsi reduire de
moitié l'etendue des Etats Unis, ou de les soutenir dans leurs justes reclamations. Quand à la premiere partie vous ne la trouverez certainement pas,

Monsieur, digne d'une remarque; il n'y à donc que la seconde à adopter, et par consequent à chercher la maniere la plus convenable d'y parvenir.

C'est pour cela, Monsieur, que les Etats Unis s'addressent a la France avec toute la confiance et la franchise dont ils ont toujours usé. On ne peut se dissimuler que le droit de naviguer sur le Mississipi deviendroit illusoire se le batiments qui descendent le fleuve et ceux qui viennent de la mer n'avoient pas un port commun ou ils pourroient se rencontrer et se decharger mutuellement. On sent aussi que si ce port etoit sous une jurisdiction etrangere il donneroit lieu journellement à des abus et des plaintes de part et d'autre qui ne pourroient manquer à la longue d'affoiblir les liens de confiance et d'amitié que les Etats Unis desirent conserver avec l'Espagne sans les voir exposés à aucune interruption.

Sur ces considerations, Monsieur, ainsi que sur des preuves d'attachment le plus désinteressé que les Etats Unis ont si souvent reçu de la France, le President se croit fondé à esperer que vous ne refuseriez pas votre ministre à appuyer les demandes qu'il a chargé leur President a Madrid de faire auprès de cette cour, et qui consistent à obtenir de L'Espagne la reconnoissance des droits des Etats Unis de naviguer librement sur le Mississipi – et pour que ces droits ne soient pas illusoires et en même tems n'exposent pas les deux pays aux inconvenieniens dejà mentionnés, de les assurer en leur cedant un port ou leurs vaisseaux peuvent se decharger sujets à leur propre jurisdiction seulement.

Le President des Etats Unis se plait à croire, Monsieur, que l'Espagne eclairee sur ses veritables interets par l'interposition amicale de la France n'hesitera pas d'adopter une mesure dont les avantages pour toutes les parties interesseés sont evidents. Son premier effet seroit d'eloigner tout pretexte de mésintelligence entre deux pays egalement attachés à la France et qui ont tant d'interets en commun avec elle.

Comptant sur l'efficacité que les bons offices de la France ne pourront pas manquer d'avoir, Monsieur, en mettant cette question dans son vrai jour, je ne me permettrai pas d'envisager les inconveniens qui pourroient s'ensuivre si contre toute attente l'Espagne se refusant a être eclaireé persistoit dans des pretensions que la conduite de ses agens sur le Mississipi paroit indiquer. Ils doivent necessairement se presenter en foule à vous, Monsieur, qui etes plus que personne à même de les apprecier. J'ai l'honneur d'etre avec des sentimens du plus profond respect & du plus parfait attachment, Monsieur, Votre très obeissant serviteur,
                                                        W. SHORT

Tr (DNA: RG 59, DD).

The above letter accurately reflects TJ's policy concerning the navigation of the Mississippi as set forth in his letters to Short of 12 and 19 Mch. 1791 and more fully in that of 10 Aug. 1790 and its enclosures. But it is important to note that, as Short indicates, he was ignorant of what TJ had said to Carmichael in his letter of 12 Mch.

1791 enclosing the memorial of St. Marie, which Short did receive (Short to TJ, 20 July 1791). For a discussion of the effect Short's letter had when Montmorin transmitted it to Spain, see Editorial Note on the threat of disunion in the West, 10 Mch. 1791.

From David Humphreys

Mafra, 7 June 1791. Acknowledging TJ's of 11 Apr. with dispatches for Carmichael. After trying in vain for some weeks to get a private conveyance, he "made interest" to have TJ's former letter to Carmichael carried by the Portuguese from the office for foreign affairs. He expects to use same means to dispatch those now received, which will be sent as soon as possible. He will be pleased to be channel of communication until a better one established. He has not heard from Carmichael since 15 Apr. though he said he would write soon and two or three letters are unacknowledged, perhaps due to ill health. He imagines he will not live long unless removed: "His health is ruined, his spirits depressed and he seems unhappy. Certain I am, no consideration would induce me to remain so long in that Country as he has done."

In his first conversation with De Pinto he mentioned first item in ciphered part of TJ's letter. He had written asking when he would receive business visits to talk further on this. De Pinto replied that he was always ready to do business, but "it was the Style for Diplomatic Characters to make previous arrangements with him" lest illness or avocations disappoint, and as soon as his health permitted he would not delay an instant to talk on the subject. — Humphreys will take care to comply with the second item ciphered.

Chevalier de Caâmans, Spanish brigadier and *chargé*, paid him repeated visits after he left his ceremonial card. As he was never in, he called on him thinking he had something particular in mind. He is ambitious to be Spanish minister to U.S., said he had written Florida Blanca about Humphreys, expressed a desire to be acquainted, and fell into conversation on America. Humphreys believes this would be a "good channel for communicating obliquely and apparently unintentionally information to . . . Florida Blanca." He gave him true account of western country, growing population, and general resources. He received this with avidity, repeated his question about population on western waters, &c., and convinced Humphreys he planned an official letter. He offered him his newspapers and public documents about U.S. as soon as he could get them from the Duke de Alfoñes to whom he had lent them. De Caâmans reads English "and discovered an uncommon eagerness that I would not forget my proposal."

In conversation with Corrêa on American enterprise, he said Mears' account showed Americans had extended navigation from Boston much farther than English. He lamented that they did not also publish accounts of voyages and discoveries, as this " 'would undoubtedly reflect great credit on their national character and perseverance.' — He then added, 'let me engage you to write to some of your friends to have this done.' " Since then Humphreys was informed "that a very intelligent and accurate journal was kept by one of the officers on board of the Washington." He mentions these things to show importance of getting newspapers and other publications. The English there, from the minister down, "have scarcely any true ideas of . . . the U.S." as they get their information mainly through English papers, as do the nations of Europe. The census returns, facts, and observations in the *Museum* and other publications "are calculated to do us vast service in Europe. Even the dissemination of the knowledge of the minuter improvements in Agriculture, Mills, Fabrics, Card-Manufactures &c. is not without its use. And particularly the Remarks on

Lord Sheffield's illusive Work are admirably adapted to dispel the mists of prejudice. – Formerly we were ignorant ourselves of the capacities and resources of the different parts of the Union." Not having but one set of these periodicals, he has not been able to present them to the minister for foreign affairs, the minister of marine, and several other distinguished characters who read English. The more that is known of Americans and the more they know of the world the better. It is unfortunate for American farmers and merchants that last wheat crop not sent sooner. "A vast quantity might have been disposed of at a ready and good market." Timely arrival would have prevented sale of forty cargoes, not long since arrived from the north, since quality of American wheat gives it a decided preference. If Dutch merchants had known arrangements for sending American grain here, they probably would not have sent a single cargo. To increase quantity of our produce, farmers must have high probability of selling it at good prices: it is thus especially important to take measures to increase demand in old markets and to find new ones.

Has British papers by the last packet, but cannot send them as they belong to a gentleman in Lisbon. They contain accounts of military operations in India favorable to English. Other than this, few remarkable occurrences: Russian victories, English fleet preparations, discontents in Constantinople, adoption of modified order of civil policy by Polish Diet, and ill-will between France and the Pope, with "the burning of the latter in effigy in the Capitol of the former."

RC (DNA: RG 59, DD); at head of text: "(No. 21?"; endorsed by TJ as received 22 Aug. 1791 and so recorded in SJL. Tr (same).

From David Humphreys

Mafra, 7 June 1791. Knowing extreme jealousy of Spanish government and rigid regulations of this respecting all kinds of books, he almost despairs of being able to get those named in TJ's private letter. Even if he had received it at Madrid, he could not have brought the books with him. But he will "revolve the matter in different views; and consult . . . my acquaintances" on means to effect it. In this and all other commands, nothing would give him more pleasure than to demonstrate by prompt compliance his "great esteem and sincere friendship."

RC (DLC); at head of text: "Private"; endorsed by TJ as received 22 Aug. 1791 and so recorded in SJL.

From Lafayette

MY DEAR FRIEND   Paris june the 7th 1791

Altho Every Motive of Regard and Affection Conspire to Make me Lament our separation, I Lament it still more on Account of our Revolution wherein Your Advices would Have Greatly Helped us, and Could Not fail to Have Had a Great Weight Among our Constitution Makers. You left us on the Point of that dissolution of the Patriotic Party which I then did, and I Have ever in Vain Endeavoured to Unite into Mutual Concessions of self interest, and self importance. You left me on the Eve to Add Greatly to My Responsability with the Nation, as the Assembly and the King Had Not Yet fixed their Abode Within these Quarters. So Many Courts Have passed Since, So Many Accounts Have from time to time Been sent to You that I will only say the Assembly is Shortly to Make Room for all Constituted Powers. How far we May induce them to Mend the Constitution Before they Go, I do not know. This I Can say that it will not Be a Voluminous Work, and that leaving Much to Be Corrected By Common legislation, We May Hope this Constitution, such as it will Be Presented, will Have a fair trial, and Give time to prepare a More proper one for the Next Convention, to Be Convocated in a short period. At least our principles are Sound – *Liberté, Egalité,* are the Motto, and if the people Can Be Brought to a proper scale of obedience to the Law, which much depends on some Alterations to Be Made in the Administrative and judiciary parts of the Constitution, We May do Very well, and Apologize for the work in Considering By whom, and for whom it Has Been Made. May Education Better fit for liberty the Ensuing Generations! Enough it will Be for this, to Have Broke the fetters, destroied Prejudices, and laid a Good Ground to Be Sowed By our successors, and Cultivated By posterity.

M. de Ternant will Acquaint You with the state of our internal and External Politics. To Him I Refer Myself. You Have thought with me He is the Best Man to Be sent to America. I Had in the Course of the Revolution Many opportunities to Experience His Abilities, Honesty, and friendship. He will deliver to You a letter of our National Assembly, Expressing sentiments Most sincerely felt. He will Explain How it Happened the Assembly Blunderd in the duties on oil and tobacco, and I Hope You will Be satisfied with His Accounts on these Matters.

Our friend Short who Continues to Conciliate to Himself Universal Esteem and Affection will write to You Respecting New orleans. France will do what she Can with Spain, and that is Not a great Guarantee for the Negociation. I Had My Private sentiments long Ago fixed on the subject, and Never thought it was possible, Much less desireable to prevent Louisiana from declaring Herself independant – That You Could Not stop an Adress from Kentucky to Congratulate them on the Occasion – and that it should Be Hard

Not to Have Provided a Bundle of Proofs that Spain Has Been in twenty Circumstances the Agressing power. Adieu, My dear friend, Remember me Most Affectionately and Respectfully to the two ladies. Most Friendly I am for ever Yours,

LAFAYETTE

RC (DLC); endorsed by TJ as received 9 Aug. 1791 and so recorded in SJL.

From William Short

DEAR SIR   Paris June 7. 1791.

My last private to you was sent by Petit who sailed in the French May packet. It was lengthy as are most of the letters I write to you in hopes of their inducing you to follow the example. Yours by M. Terrasson of Mar. 16. is the last I have recieved from you (private). Next before that was that of Jan. 24. which is the only one received since yours of Sep. 30. 90. – The private letters which I have written to you and of which the reciept is not yet acknowleged are Sep. 9. Oct. 30. Nov. 7. (as you have acknowleged my No. 46. I take it for granted you recieved that which accompanied it, but had not time to acknowlege it) Dec. 29. Jan. 17. Feb. 18. March. 30. April 26. May 2. – You have acknowleged the reciept of others written in the months of Sep. Oct. Nov. and Dec. – I cannot help here asking the favor of you to be particular in marking the letters received as well public as private. I have already mentioned to you one or two instances in which I supposed there must be some mistake, similar to that which I am about to mention. In your private of March. 16 you say mine of Oct. 25. was received Jan. 27, and yet you state my No. 44. in your letters of march as missing. These both went by the same hand (M. de St. Triest), and probably under the same cover. I cannot concieve how they could be separated. – You acknowlege the reciept of my letters but say nothing in answer to them. That of Oct. 25. particularly asked you for information concerning several matters.

If I were not afraid of being importunate and if you had not resided here yourself and experienced yourself the disadvantage of recieving so few letters from Congress, I should state to you the various inconveniences resulting from it and the real prejudice it is of to the public service. I leave out of the account the personal desagrément it occasions to him who is employed here. – As your own experience must enable you to appreciate this as fully as I can, I will not allow myself to say any thing further respecting it so far as it concerns official correspondence. I cannot help adding however that as far as it relates to our private correspondence, it has been impossible for me not to feel myself much mortified by your long silence and particularly on subjects which regard you or your family. Besides the mortification of being sometimes months without hearing from you, and of learning generally through other channels alone what regards you, I have that of reflecting that this silence can proceed only from a supposition that such intelligence must be indifferent to me. – I should have hoped also that you would have given me more information in detail concerning a subject which concerns me. I mean the nomination of diplomatic characters here—such as the cause of the delay after the bill passed last July, and which was hurried in order that the appointments might be immediately made. Your previous letter mentioned this and afterwards without knowing any reason for it I learned that no appointment would take place till the winter and of course that my 'successor would not come out until the spring.' From that time therefore that is to say during the whole winter I have been waiting in daily and anxious expectation of learning something definitive. I now suppose that no appointment will take place before october and still it is impossible to be sure of it. So that without knowing why it happens or when it will cease I see the uncertainty of my position prolonged at least during the summer. In one respect I ought to be pleased with this uncertainty as it cannot but be useful to my wishes still it has become so disagreeable as well on account of the present situation of this country, as the time it has lasted that I cannot help wishing it to cease. I may say so boldly now because I suppose after the arrival of Ternant the delay cannot be continued. If I am definitively appointed here I shall think myself well rewarded for the uncertainty I have remained in. But if I am superseded, the longer I shall have remained here the more disagreeable, as the greater must be and will be considered my demerit, since experience could not enable me to counterbalance the qualities of my successor who of course will be without experience. – I will say no more because I feel I am not to be the judge of these considerations, and because I fear of forgetting myself as formerly and saying too much. Still as I take it for granted that the appointments will not be made before this letter arrives and that they will be at the next session I cannot help adding here that although my desire to remain at Paris has much diminished since the last year, for the reasons mentioned in my last letter, still I should like better remaining minister here than going to any other court. That next to this I should prefer London if a minister is named there, and after that the Hague. I hope the grade there will be the same with that of Lisbon, because in these little places diplomatick characters are much in evidence, and because the title of chargé des affaires is always and in all places considered as a character par interim, and often as a makeshift. Besides after remaining here so long to be sent to an inferior place with the same title would be considered as a means of providing for me in order to remove me from hence and would put me in the awkward posture of being superseded for want of merit. The title of *minister-resident* as that of Lisbon would be much more agreeable and in my case particularly of being removed from hence, much more honorable. Still I must confess, although I should be mortified, I would accept the grade of chargé des affaires rather than nothing, and that merely because I do not wish at present on account of the circumstances of my affairs and family to return in this moment to fix in the U.S. But whatever appointment I may recieve I should not wish to continue in it more than two or three years at most – and after all I should prefer being settled in Virginia and a member of the federal senate from that State to any appointment that could be given me in Europe, and in such a case it would be agreeable and honorable to have been minister in Europe. – Should it be decided to send another person here and to place me at the Hague there is one thing which would give me the greatest pleasure if it could be effected and I should hope it might if you desired it. It would be to allow me a congé to return to America in the next spring. No inconvenience could result from it as the principal business for the U.S. in Holland is that at Amsterdam and it might be very well attended to by the minister sent here. This congé might be obtained on that consideration and my long absence from the U.S. I own to you however that my reason for desiring it would be in order to return to Virginia and if I could be elected into the senate the fall after to remain there. This I mention of course to you alone, but it is what I should desire above all things. Such a consideration would induce me to encounter the sea with the risk of recrossing it notwithstanding my hitherto unconquerable aversion to it. My mind has come to this by regular gradation in which my fear of the ocean has diminished in proportion as my desire to go and make an attempt to settle myself in America has increased. – Should you find such a congé not to be obtained (and yet I cannot think it when the length of my absence from the U.S. and the little inconvenience of delay in settling at the Hague is considered) then I should prefer returning to the U.S. under the following circumstances to being a meer *chargé des affaires* at the

Hague. Supposing that it should be found necessary that you should have an assistant in your department for the foreign correspondence with the title of *under Secretary of State* or some such name or that the foreign department should be given to some one under your direction, which is nearly the same thing, with a decent salary say 1800 or 2000 dollars, if I was thought proper for it I should like it better than being removed from hence to the Hague with the same grade I have here. – But I should prefer being *minister Resident* at the Hague with the alternative of the congé as mentioned above as it would give me the chance of the senate. – In the case of being appointed under you I hope it would be so contrived as to allow me to go out in the spring only on account of the season, and the opportunity it would give me of passing a short time in England which I should desire much in order to become better acquainted with the politics of that country which I should hope would not be time lost. – I beg you a thousand pardons my dear Sir for all these minute and personal details. I hope and believe you will excuse them when you consider the distance I am from you and the necessity I am [under] of expressing my sentiments to you respecting them. It is to you alone that I could do it and it is the best proof of my constant attachment and friendship, and unbounded reliance on yours.

You will recieve by M. Kellerman who goes to join M. Ternant at Rochefort the tin proofs of P. Jones's medal which you desired. – Piranesi's drawings shall be sent to you by Havre, as well as Desgodetz. I will settle also your correspondence with Froullé. Several new books have come out here which I should suppose you would like. They are mostly on political subjects and you will see them spoken of in the gazettes. I have not thought myself authorized to send them to you. You did well to purchase the little encyclopedias when you did. I have been obliged lately to pay 190. ₶ for an edition. They cannot now be bought for less. I am making my collection of books in order to prepare myself for a retreat. I shall purchase as few as possible on account of the uncertainty of the life I am to lead in future.

Tolozan has recieved his box and desires to be remembered to you with his thanks, and I have been solliciting Mr. Grand to have your account made out for some time though in vain. The articles purchased for you, and the wine for the President &c. will be charged to you. You will have credit for the bill sent me last fall and the article mentioned in my letter by Petit. The balance will be remitted to Messrs. V. Staphorst. This will be done in a few days. Mr. Grand gave me his word it should be done long ago. The balance will be a trifle.

You said in your letters of March you would write in future by the French and English packets. I shall be happy if you do it. Put your letters sent by the English packet under cover to Messr. Donald & Burton, London. I have an account open with them for postage. Of course they will not be burthened with the expence and will forward my letters with pleasure. You may write to me with as much certainty by that means as if I was in Baltimore.

I am sorry you do not give me some accounts of our improvements in manufactures and new productions. It is a most interesting subject. I hear a good deal of the refineries of sugar at Philadelphia and New York, but as you say nothing about them and as I see nothing of them in the late newspapers I do not know what to think of them. I tasted of the sugar in Amsterdam and it appeared to me equal fully to the single refined of the islands. It was not doubted in Amsterdam that it would succeed fully. The subject is much talked of here and particularly since Warville's travels have appeared. Mde. D'Enville asks me to beg you to send her a sample of the sugar. I will thank you to do it by the first opportunity to Havre or to some one of the consuls who may send it on by the diligence. Let me know if it can be sold as cheap as that of the islands. The Duke de la Rochefoucauld tells me has just received a book printed in the U.S. with types and on paper made there and that the impression is superb. He has promised to send it to me, but I have not yet seen it.

I know not what to do with respect to my funds in America. I have thought much on the subject since your letter of Mar. 16. I know no agent on whom I could rely after the exception you make. Colo. Skipwith has treated me I fear very ill, at least with unpardonable and cruel neglect. Besides my funds being Virga. State certificates if the State undertakes to provide for them as I have heard they will do and as Maryland has done, it is better than funding them as proposed by the late law which is abominably unjust as to State certificates. They could not therefore be placed in the bank without considerable loss as they must be sold, or funded agreeable to the late law, in order to do it. I shall write to Mr. Donald however to authorize Mr. Brown of Richmond to vest one half of them in the bank by sale or funding if he finds it proper on the then view of circumstances. Mr. Donald tells me that full discretion in all cases may be left to Mr. Brown and yet it is certain that Mr. Brown is concerned himself and owner of similar funds. – I have not given and shall not give any reason to Mr. Donald for wishing to vest my funds or a part of them in the bank. Should any remarkable circumstance take place I hope my dr. Sir, you will get over your scruples and from your friendship for me and direct Mr. Brown of Richmond [con]fidentially what to do. He will of course follow your instructions. – Adieu. Let me hear from you and believe me your friend & servant,   W Short

RC (DLC); at head of text: "*Private*"; endorsed by TJ as received 9 Aug. 1791 and so recorded in SJL. PrC (PHi).

From William Short

Paris, 7 June 1791. Introducing M. Kellerman, nephew to De Marbois, who goes to America with De Ternant and who carries two letters to the Secretary of the Treasury to be given to De Ternant at Rochefort, also a packet of newspapers for TJ. Other papers and journals were sent by De Ternant and Dupont, who left Paris successively. They are to meet at Rochefort. His public letter begun yesterday not yet finished and cannot go by Kellerman, but will be sent to De Ternant at Rochefort. He asks TJ's civilities and attentions to Kellerman.

RC (DLC); endorsed by TJ as received 10 Aug. 1791 and so recorded in SJL. PrC (DLC: Short Papers).

From Alexander Hamilton

[Philadelphia], "*Treasury Department*," *8 June 1791.* He thinks it would be useful if an officer of the U.S. in each foreign country where there is one were directed to transmit occasional state of the coins of the country, specifying standards, weights, and values, also periodical listing of market prices of gold and silver in coin and bullion, the rates of foreign exchange, and the wages of labor both in manufactures and in tillage. – He requests that, if no inconvenience in the idea appears to TJ, an instruction for this purpose be sent and copies of statements received be furnished the Treasury.

RC (DLC: Madison Papers); in clerk's hand except for signature; endorsed by TJ as received 21 June 1791 and so recorded in SJL. Full text appears in Syrett, *Hamilton*, VIII, 450.

The presence of the above letter in Madison's Papers suggests that TJ consulted his close collaborator on this as on almost all other matters of public interest. So also does the inclusion there of another docu-

ment in which TJ recorded the available sources of information concerning questions raised by Hamilton. This shows that for France, Spain, Portugal, England, and Holland, data on the "State of the coin" were readily accessible in the *Encyclopédie*. For stocks and foreign exchange, the *Gazette de France* was given as the source for France and Lloyd's List for England, with none for the other three nations. For the market price of bullion and coin, Lloyd's

List for England was the only recorded source. Understandably, there was none for any of the five countries on the price of labor in tillage and manufactures (undated MS in tabular form, in TJ's hand; DLC: Madison Papers). The result of Hamilton's suggestion was a cautionary response reflecting TJ's characteristic disinclination to trouble American officials abroad with requests for needless or duplicative information, coupled with an invitation to discuss the matter and ascertain what was already available before proceeding further (TJ to Hamilton, 25 June 1791). The ac-count of the episode in Leonard D. White's *The Federalists*, p. 227n., contains a number of errors and omissions, among them the following: TJ did not neglect the request, Hamilton did not in precise terms renew it in his letter of 26 Dec. 1792, and Washington's instruction to the Secretary of State of 20 Mch. 1793 was required by the Act for regulating foreign coins, not, as implied, because of Hamilton's urging. In consequence the intended conclusion – that this was an instance of TJ's failure to cooperate with his colleague – cannot be accepted.

From Stephen Cathalan, Jr.

Marseilles, 10 June 1791. Encloses another letter from O'Bryen and Stephens. Parret thinks that to obtain an advantageous treaty with Algiers the first step is to redeem the prisoners. Spain lost millions by not doing so. Parret thinks, and he agrees, that about £40,000 sterling in money, vessels, or presents would be adequate, after which peace could be obtained. Will give Parret and de Kersey, recent French consul at Algiers, introduction to Short. – Has had no news from Short for a long time about his "Petition to M. de Montmorrin" about his consular rank. In the meantime he is not given rights and duties of consul because he is named *vice*-consul. Annexes one print of the consular seal just received from Paris and hopes it will be approved. Lists commodity prices. "Whale oil is in the greatest demand, and none in Town. . . . Assignats have very much hurted the Publick credit. Foreigners have not Confidence in Transacting Bussiness with France, in this Time." Raynal's petition to the National Assembly will show the real sentiments of the nation. The people suffer and do not know when their sufferings will end. Self-interest and intrigues guide the machine and will "conduct France to it's entire Destruction and Ruin; your Constitution has been made with Calm, wisdom and Prudence, and you Enjoy now the Benefit." – The National Assembly has just directed that a new treaty of alliance and trade should be made with the United States. Fears this comes too late because the tobacco decree is against American interests and that forbidding purchase of foreign vessels is harmful to French merchants. Also England appears desirous of making such a treaty.

RC (DNA: RG 59, CD); endorsed by TJ as received 22 Sep. 1791 and so recorded in SJL. The letter from O'Bryen and Stephens of 1 Apr. 1791 (not found) was not enclosed with the above letter but was forwarded in a brief covering note from Cathalan of 12 June 1791 (DNA: RG 59, CD; endorsed by TJ as received 22 Sep. 1791 and so recorded in SJL).

From William Short

This is sent after M. de Ternant in hopes of its overtaking him at Rochefort and as merely to inclose you a copy of the report of the diplomatic committee and the decree of the national assembly thereon. You will recieve the same together with their President's letter to yours, by the same opportunity, the Marquis de la fayette having taken them in order to send them after M. de Ternant by this day's post.

This decree is considered here as rendering any changes in those they have lately made respecting our commerce, as unnecessary. Of course I despair now of their diminishing or abolishing the difference of duty imposed on tobacco imported in French and American vessels. I hoped for some time they would do it in consequence of my letter to M. de Montmorin on that subject. He himself desired it much and pressed it on the diplomatic committee. The committees also were disposed to do it, but they feared it would not pass in the assembly and therefore substituted the decree inclosed to the changes asked on this subject and that with respect to oils, and the sale of American built vessels.

I learn from the ports that a number of French vessels are freighted there to be sent to the U.S. for tobacco and indeed the difference of duty being more than the whole price of the freight it is impossible that American vessels can be employed in that business at all unless Congress should make some counter-regulation as to tobacco. This of course must comprehend other foreign vessels. Still I should suppose better to do this than to submit to have our vessels excluded from sharing in the transportation of that part of our own productions so far as it regards the importation into France. – This is so just that it cannot affect the treaty of commerce they express a desire to see negotiated. On the contrary if we submit to such regulations they may consider stipulations as useless and even disadvantageous.

With respect to the augmented duty on oils M. de Ternant was persuaded that it was a mistake in the assembly and that their intention was to have placed them on the same footing that they would have been under the *arrêt du conseil*. This was the case with some of the members, but with the greater number it was certainly design, and the error voluntary. One of the leading members of the committee of commerce still persists in asserting that the intention of the *Arret du conseil* was to subject the American oils to the fabrication duties, notwithstanding all the proofs adduced to the contrary as well from the minister's letter as the registers of the farm.

Ignorance and a sacrifice of general interests to those of particular classes have been the causes of the faults committed by this assembly with respect to their commerce with the U.S. The same causes will necessarily continue though in a less degree for some time. I am persuaded they will cease with time, still I cannot undertake to assure you, as many people here think that it will be with the next legislature. Should a treaty be negotiated that will of course correct the errors, but if that is postponed it will be prudent and proper for Congress to adopt measures on the supposition that the present regulations will continue here for some time to come unless counteracted by them.

The assembly deputed one of their members to day to enquire of the Minister of marine what had been done with respect to the decrees of May 13. and 14. concerning the colonies. The answer of the minister was that vessels were now ready to carry thither the last decrees sanctioned. – The assembly resolved at the same time that the colonial committee should present on monday next their code to be proposed to the colonies for their constitution, in order that the same vessels may be charged with it.

The alarm in the assembly with respect to the efforts of the Prince de Condé and the designs of foreign powers, increases every day although it does not appear that it is warranted by authentic information. The gazettes will have informed you of all that is known or believed in the public. The assembly resolved also to-day that the diplomatic committee should make a report to-morrow on the present state of the frontiers.

The present dispositions of a great number of the officers of the army, who are manifestly opposed to the revolution have long given uneasiness to the assembly. They are so much alarmed by them at present, a report was made to day in the name of six committees on this subject. They propose that the officers shall sign a new submission and give their word of honor to adhere to it, that such as will not do it shall retire with a pension &c. The report was debated on but is adjourned to-morrow. Some members for licensing the army and re-establishing it immediately employing only such officers and were judged proper for service under the present constitution. – The plan of the committee will probably pass. I have the honor to be as you know me, Dear Sir, your most obedt. servant,

W. SHORT

PrC (DLC: Short Papers); at head of text: "*No. 68.*" Tr (DNA: RG 59, DD). Recorded in SJL as received 9 Aug. 1791.

From John Rutledge, Jr.

Charleston, 14 June 1791. Acknowledging receipt of TJ's of 20 Feb. His friendly information about President's tour was their first intelligence of it. He immediately "communicated this very pleasing information to my fellow Citzens," who at once began to prepare for his reception. This was "splendid and handsome, and in this great and good man's tour through this State, people of all denominations shewed the highest veneration possible for his character, and the greatest affection for his person."

Yesterday Mr. Dease of Charleston, who knew TJ in Paris, was tried "for having murdered, in a duel, his cousin a Mr. Inglis." Despite evidence unfavorable to him and the court's recommending no verdict short of manslaughter, "yet custom has so sanctioned this sort of murder, that the jury found *not guilty.*" It is to be regretted that, "notwithstanding the progress of philosophy and reason, and our appearing to live in a blaze of light and knowledge, . . . duelling is the only mode of settling disputes." It is much to be lamented that frequency of settling the most trivial disputes in this way seems peculiar to this country. "I hope the time will soon arrive when this crime shall attract the notice of the Legislature, and that it may establish some manner of settling disputes less gothic than the present. It has hitherto been imagined that no other can be devised, but a revolution in the minds of people on this subject, will be much less surprizing than the revolutions which have lately happened." He encloses a letter for Short to be forwarded. His father desires to be "remembered affectionately" to TJ.

RC (DLC); addressed: "The Honorable Mr. Jefferson Philadelphia"; endorsed by TJ as received 25 June 1791 and so recorded in SJL.

From George Washington

SIR   Mount-Vernon, June 15. 1791.

I acknowledged the receipt of your letter of the 2nd. of April from Richmond, since which I have only received two letters from you of the 10th. of April and 15th. of May.

Concluding that some of your dispatches may have been forwarded to Taylor's ferry (by which route I did not return) I have to request, if that should have been the case, and the communications were of a particular or pressing nature, that duplicates may be addressed to me at Mount-Vernon, where I shall remain until the 27th. of the present month, when, by an appointment before I went to the southward, I am to meet the Commisioners at Georgetown. – I cannot now determine how long I may be there, but it is probable

I shall not make any particular communications to you before my return to Philadelphia.

If the suggestion contained in your letter of the 10th. of April, respecting the engravings, can be carried into effect at a moderate expence, I think it may answer a good purpose. – I am Sir, Your most obedient Servant, Go: WASHINGTON

A letter from Major Shaw, Consul at Canton, of the 7th. of December last, with it's enclosures, and a very unexpected address from some Persons styling themselves, "free people of colour of the Island of Grenada," are herewith transmitted for your consideration, and your opinions thereon when I see you in Philadelphia.

Go. WASHINGTON

RC (DLC); in William Jackson's hand except for signatures; endorsed by TJ as received 19 June 1791 and so recorded in SJL. Dft (DNA: RG 59, MLR); also in Jackson's hand. FC (DNA: RG 59, SDC). Enclosures: (1) Samuel Shaw to Washing-ton, 7 Dec. 1790 (printed as enclosure in TJ to Van Berckel, 14 July 1791); (2) Memorial of "Tous Les Citoyens libres de Couleur de . . . Grenade aux antilles," 24 Jan. 1791 (printed below).

ENCLOSURE

Louis Lagrenade and Others to the President

May it please your Excellency [24 Jan. 1791]

We The free coloured people of the Island of Grenada, having taken into Consideration a Writing, the purpose of which (they are informed) is your Excellency's generous disposition of giving that unfortunate Class of People, an Asylum in the southern parts of the States of your Excellency's Government; have inclosed herewith, a Copy of the same humbly requesting your Excellency to Confirm its authenticity; in order that they may have that faith in it which a subject of such magnitude requires. Such an Act of your Excellency's Generosity, will excite their deepest gratitude and they will deem themselves peculiarly blest, if their unhappy Situation in these Islands can have touched your Breast so as to move your Benevolence to furnish them with the means of coming out of their Captivity, and to introduce them into a new Canaan, where they will enjoy all the Happiness of that precious Liberty, which, you gloriously and generously defended, and maintained in favor of Your illustrious Countrymen. Your Excellency's rendering this a Certainty, will determine Sixty thousand free Coloured Individuals, to Settle in Your Country for the Honor and prosperity of their Family's, and there to enjoy a tolerable existence; them and their Slaves be fully sufficient to form their Establishments.

It will be then that the plains of America (from that time become the Happy residence of People capable of the Highest Gratitude, for the Clemency bestowed upon them, by Your Excellency and the Honourable Congress) will be with greater Certainty, the Asylum of Peace free from the disturbance, of all those who might endeavour to interrupt the Continuance of the Happiness of our Benefactors; which we would always support with the same resolution, and ardour, as they themselves have shewed; an example to all the Nations of World, in procuring for themselves that independency which they now enjoy. It is with those sentiments that we are in Hopes to attain to those days, so Happy and so desirable, which will enable us to prove to You, all the veneration, and respect, with which we Have the Honor to be. May it please Your Excellency Your most Humble and Most Obedient Servants The Committee,

Los. Lagrenade
J. N. Pre. Saulger
F. Julien
Joseph Green

RC (DLC: Washington Papers); in clerk's hand except for signatures. RC (same); in French, signed; addressed: "His Excellency Georges-Washington, Esquire. Président of the United States of America &c &c. &cra. Philadelphia"; endorsed as received 12 July (i.e., June) 1791.

The enclosure accompanying this "very unexpected address" was an unsigned and undated communication addressed "To the Free Men of Colour in the West India Islands." This extraordinary document opened with the assurance that it was being transmitted by a person deeply interested in "the future ease and happyness of a people . . . who seems to be almost without Existance in their present situation." The undisclosed author, inspired by the spectacle of a free, prosperous, and independent America, declared that while mankind for many centuries had suffered oppression and calamities in utter darkness, "the Great Arbiter of the Universe" had so illumined the minds of men that kingdoms and states could now establish themselves in righteousness forever. He pointed to the Americans as having founded their independence on principles of liberty and justice, thereby setting a glorious example for Europe and all the universe. But, while the free colored people of the West Indies were numerous enough to obtain such blessings, their circumstances were in stark contrast to those enjoyed by Americans.

The unknown author therefore urged this oppressed people to establish themselves as a free and independent society. Far from being a mere exhortation, the document — referred to by its author as a "Narrative" — conveyed the specific suggestion that the free persons of color in the islands establish themselves as a "Colony in the Southern parts of North America . . . from which Noble and Wise Institution they will be able to extricate themselves and their offspring from a Land of torment and misery wherein they are despisd, and Ill treated by Laws which is unreasonable for any Freeman to endure neither can they bear up against it so as to merit a reform to their advantage. . . . O! ye free Coloured People of the West Indies and your offspring instead of flourishing round ye like the young olive plants are daily dwindling into thorns and Briars for want of proper Cultivation and rural amusements. Your sons for want of Education under a free Government are rais'd up in Idleness and your Daughters are all Sacraficed as Victims to the Brutish lust of those whom have no other Generosity or respect towards them than to your eternal disgrace and to their shame and Confusion." Such was the unhappy state of the free persons in the islands, but it was one from which they could escape.

This was made possible, the author asserted, by the free and generous sons of America. Having enlightened all Europe and made manifest their determination always to support with their lives and fortunes the great birthright of mankind, liberty and independence, they now offered as a lasting testimony of their concern for the good of mankind "a full and free Asylum to all the World to partake of the Blessings of Peace free liberty and ample protection in her extensive and Fertile plains and City's." The golden choice lay with the islanders: "It is to you Free Coloured people that is wandering in the West India Islands and have no place of abode, That I now do myself the Honour to address. Now is the time for ye to be rais'd from your Slumbers and enlighten yourselves and look forward to a land Now offer'd to you

[552]

a Land of Freedom and ease flowing with milk and honey. A Land of great comforts where you may form a Colony of your own appoint your own Laws and Government under your own People for your Mutual prosperity and the encouragement of arts Sciences and agriculture. Your young men will then be taught to tread the paths of Virtue and Wisdom and your Daughters will be esteem'd the Virtuous and amiable and which must in a short time make you a Nation of great Respectability by freely embracing the present Moment of Establishing your selves to be a Free people, For who cannot but tremble at your former as well as present Situation which is little short of the Most abject Slavery a Character greatly to be dispised by all [Men] of genus and generosity."

The "Narrative" closed with a glowing account of this New Canaan waiting for settlement: "The Clime is mild and Healthy. The Soil rich and Fertile Capable of producing all manner of Necessaries for the subsistance of Mankind. Cotton. Indigo. Tobacco. Wheat. Rye. Oats. Barley. Corn. peas. potatoes. and all manner of Vegetables . . . and also white oak Staves. Pitch pine. Cyprys shingles For Turpintine and Pitch. The Forrest is well stored with Game. The Rivers affords a great variety of Fish and the extensive Meadows is Capable of raising immense Herds of Cattle. Indeed it can be said with much propriety that no part of the Continent of North America can boast of superior advantages and none equal in Salubrity of Climate and Fertility of Soil" (Unsigned and undated Tr, in clerk's hand, in DLC: Washington Papers).

It is not surprising that Lagrenade and the other members of the committee who transmitted this astonishing communication to the President should have sought to have its authenticity confirmed. The document was wholly devoid of the kind of specific details that even so dubious a venture as the Scioto Company felt obliged to give to prospective emigrants. It pointed to no particular part of southern America for the location of the proposed independent "Colony." It did not define the terms upon which the free persons of color could claim title and stipulated nothing as to the extent of territory they might expect to inhabit. It did not, as Lagrenade and the others indicated, suggest that the invitation

was extended by the President of the United States but only presumed to speak on behalf of the free and generous sons of America. Possibly the person who conveyed the document to the islanders sought to provide such particulars, including – if the original lacked a signature – the identity of the author.

That unknown person, writing with evangelical fervor, may have been prompted by a concern for the good of mankind in general and for the oppressed islanders in particular. But that this was his sole object is very doubtful. The suggestion that the independent "Colony" be established in the South, the timing of the proposal (which must have been written in the late autumn of 1790), and the glowing description of the climate, soil, and productivity of the region all indicate the presence of another and less altruistic motive. They also point to a particular source. On 20 October 1790 a gentleman in Lexington, Kentucky, writing to his friend in Philadelphia, gave a description of upwards of a million acres lying on and about the Yazoo River to which the South Carolina Yazoo Company claimed title under a 1789 grant from Georgia. This description appeared in Bache's *General Advertiser*, 24 Nov. 1790, and reads in part as follows: "The soil is superior to the very best in Kentucky . . . and the whole face of extensive country is well watered, abounding in sweet springs – the woods replenished with game, and the rivers, creeks and brooks with fish of all kinds. The whole territory is well timbered . . . the finest country on earth for horned cattle, horses, sheep and hogs, and deemed the very best for corn, tobacco, indigo, cotton, hemp and flax. . . . The lands abound with pitch pine trees, although no pine barren. The staples will therefore be staves, heading, lumber, tobacco, cotton, corn, indigo, silk, naval stores, provisions of salted flesh, fish, coarse linens, cordage, sail duck, Indian meal and flour."

The lengthy communication from the gentleman in Lexington also stated that 100 families had already taken possession of the Company's territory; that its Agent General would soon depart for the land with a battalion of cavalry, artillery, and riflemen; that General Scott would follow with 500 families; that General Wilkinson would bring 1,000 fighting men and their families by Christmas; that General Sevier would take a similar number; and that both Indians and Spaniards had been reconciled to the settlement. Internal evidence in this communication proves beyond question that its author, whose assertions of fact existed chiefly in his own imagination, was James O'Fallon, physician, soldier, adventurer, land speculator, and dabbler in foreign intrigue who in the autumn of 1790 was in Lexington as Agent General of the South Carolina Yazoo Company and who had been indiscreet enough not only to describe the lands and the military preparations for their settlement in the letter published in the newspaper, but also to do the same in a communication to Washington asking authority to proceed – all in direct violation of the laws governing intercourse with the Indians as announced in the President's proclamation issued only a month earlier (O'Fallon to the President, 25 Sep. 1790, ASP, *Indian Affairs*, I, 115-17; see O'Fallon's comparable descriptions of his plans in letters to Governor Esteban Miró and others in "Spain in the Mississippi Valley, 1765-1794," ed. Lawrence Kinnaird, AHA, *Ann. Rpt. 1945*, III, pt. II, 338, 338-41, 341-2, 357-64, 379, 395, 395-8).

The obvious parallel between the description of the territory given in the communication to the free persons of color and that in O'Fallon's letter to his friend in Philadelphia does not prove that the adventurer was the author of both. But the former was written by an American who, for some reason, hoped to see an independent black settlement in the southern parts of America, a region whose occupation by westerners was being more conspicuously advocated by O'Fallon at that moment than by anyone else. O'Fallon's overweening ambition to establish on the Yazoo "the most flourishing . . . settlement ever formed"; his assurances to Governor Miró that this would be a barrier between the Spanish territories and those of the United States, from which the Yazoo colony would secede; his similar assurances that the settlement would protect his own country from Indians and Spaniards, made at the very time that he informed an accomplice, secretly and wholly without foundation, that Washington had promised his protection to the venture; his prolix, flamboyant, repetitious style with its gram-matical awkwardnesses and peculiar phrasing (*e.g.*, "reiteratedly repeated") – these and other factors seem to point to O'Fallon as the most likely author of the proposal for a black state in the South. Among other circumstances lending support to the conjecture, perhaps none could have been more compelling to O'Fallon than the need for his proposed settlement to have a barrier to protect itself against Indians and Spaniards. Perhaps the unknown emissary who conveyed the letter to the islanders may have indicated, as O'Fallon did in the letter published in Bache's *General Advertiser*, that adjacent to the Yazoo settlement lay 500,000 acres suitable for rice, the cultivation of which would have been more congenial to the island blacks than to emigrants from Kentucky. Settlement at that location, too, would have provided a barrier to protect the Yazoo colonists. It should be noted in this connection that Lagrenade and his associates pledged to Washington their support "against all . . . who might endeavour to interrupt the Continuance of the Happiness of our Benefactors." This was the same kind of assurance O'Fallon had given both to the Spanish and to the Americans. It is plausible to suppose that the emissary conveying the letter to the free blacks may have prompted them to make such a pledge.

It is also pertinent to note that O'Fallon was a friend of Thomas Paine, having arrived in America the same year the author of *Common Sense* did; that his writings in support of the patriot cause were considered so inflammatory for the time as to land him in prison in North Carolina; and that, two decades later, Paine in Paris complimented him with this appeal: "If [you are] as yet in the habits of writing; this My Dear Doctor, is your precious time. Never was there a cause so deserving of your pen" (Paine to O'Fallon, 17 Feb. 1793, "Letter of Thomas Paine, 1793," Louise P. Kellogg, ed., AHR, XXIX [Apr. 1924], 501-5). The letter "To the Free Men of Colour in the West India Islands" rings with the same kind of ardor for the principles of the Revolution that O'Fallon had exhibited when he first came to America. In the absence of the original of that letter, its authorship cannot with certainty be attributed to him. But both in its grandiloquent style and in its quixotic proposal it seems to accord with all that is known of his overblown schemes and intrigues, every one of which – like this one – was doomed to failure.

The free blacks of Grenada and their slaves were denied even a reply to the appeal to Washington. TJ advised Washington to ignore the matter since any action by the United States would amount to an intervention in the internal affairs of another government. But the prospect of an independent settlement of 60,000 free blacks on the southern borders, even if justifiable in terms of international law, he also regarded as undesirable (TJ to Washington, 20 June 1791; see also note to the opinion of the Attorney General on legal action to be taken against O'Fallon, which TJ helped prepare, 14 Feb. 1791, and Murray to TJ, 12 May 1791).

From Henry Remsen, Jr.

Philadelphia, 16 June 1791. He did not receive TJ's of 28th until 7th, hence did not send letters and packets to Bennington or Hartford as they could not have reached even latter place in time. All of the letters and Fenno's papers he has put up in 7 packets and sent to New York, keeping back a book and a roll of some size. Among letters is one from Brown of Richmond opened at request of captain. The two hogsheads of bacon mentioned in it are lodged in cellar and freight paid out of money left by TJ. There is also a letter from Maxwell of Norfolk about crab cider.

Four baskets and four boxes covered in oil cloth have come from France for TJ. He presumes they are wine and has placed in cellar. Also the chariot and sulky came by same vessel, the carriage of the first damaged by sea water. Carr, the coachmaker who was employed by Francis to unpack and house them, says this was due to improper packing and should be attended to at once. If TJ stays a day or so in New York and thinks it necessary for him to do what is proper, he asks for directions. The duty on these items has not been paid, but he has given bond to the collector for the amount and oath that a due entry will be made. Lear took charge of the President's wine. Also, 14 cases of wine for TJ have come via Charleston and placed in cellar, with freight paid. He has inquired at Baltimore stage office about wine from there, but has not heard of it.

Brown's paper of this evening mentions President's return to Mt. Vernon. The letters for him, Thomas M. Randolph, and Currie are forwarded. No letter from President has come with the expected commission for Eveleigh's successor. Lear has applied for and received several commissions for inspectors of revenue in southern states, all duly minuted. Remsen observes in Fenno's last the arrival of "Dr. Josef Jaudens Commissioner from his Catholic Majesty to the United States."

The business between Currie and Griffin remains as TJ left it. On directions from former, he had an attachment levied on any effects belonging to Griffin in possession of "the Messrs. Potters, W. Hazlehurst, W. McConnell and W. Shannon, and judging that Mr. Robt. Morris might have property of Mr. Griffin, I have desired Mr. Barton to extend the attachment to that." Griffin is now in New York, and he recommends that TJ apply to him again, since it is uncertain whether he has any property in Philadelphia and since Currie says there is none in Virginia "and begs a resort to any measures that may reimburse him." The 6% stock has risen to 17/ and he again urges TJ to see

Griffin and insist on a settlement "as the only chance left to Dr. Currie to obtain it."

No business has occurred at the office to demand TJ's return earlier than proposed. "The workmen are going on *gradually* with your book-room and stable, but Mr. Leiper has had the house painted. Mr. Eppes has been and continues well. I hope that you have been so, and that your journey has been perfectly agreeable."

RC (DLC); endorsed by TJ as received 21 June 1791 and so recorded in SJL.

From David Humphreys

Mafra, 17 June 1791. Nothing final received by packet from England about war between Russians and Turks. Fox' speech gives "a just representation of the interfering, restless and bullying conduct of the British Ministry for some years past; with the probable disgrace, disadvantage and humiliation to be expected from it." – A real novelty appears in "true accounts of the prosperous condition of the United States" in English papers widely circulated in Europe. They assert America's credit reestablished, its new Government supported by the people, and its affairs "happily conducted by an able Administration." – Change in government of Poland "certainly one of the wonderful events of this age." It is said the King stated the new constitution to be modelled after English and American constitutions. – Nothing new in Portugal. The people violently irritated against French because of burning of Pope in effigy in Paris.

RC (DNA: RG 59, DD); at head of text: "(No.22)"; endorsed by TJ as received 22 Aug. 1791 and so recorded in SJL. Tr (same).

From James Monroe

DEAR SIR   Richmond June 17. 1791.

I have been favor'd with 2 letters from you since my arrival with Paine's pamphlet in one, and should have answer'd them sooner, but knew of your departure Eastward and of course that it would not have been sooner received. By the 25th. we shall be settled in Albemarle upon my plantation, the unfinish'd state of the buildings having prevented the removal there sooner. The appeals and general court are sitting. Their respective terms will not expire so as to enable me to get home by that time, but my own business will be finish'd and I shall not stay longer.

Upon political subjects we perfectly agree, and particularly in the reprobation of all measures that may be calculated to elevate the government above the people, or place it in any respect without its natural boundary. To keep it there nothing is necessary, but virtue in a part only (for in the whole it cannot be expected) of the high publick servants, and a true development of the principles of those acts which have a contrary tendency. The bulk of the people are for democracy, and if they are well inform'd the ruin of such enterprizes will infallibly follow. I shall however see you in Sepr. at which time we will confer more fully on these subjects.

I have been associated in the room of Mr. Pendleton with the Commissioners for revising the laws of this State. The appointment was communicated to me yesterday by the Executive and as it was neither wish'd nor expected, I can give no information of the extent of the duty or the time it will take to execute it. Upon the hope of completing what is expected from us before the meeting of the next Congress I have accepted the appointment.

I am extremely anxious to procure rooms near you for the next session. If such should be known to you which may be preingag'd, to be occupied on the commencement of the session, shall thank you to contract for them in my behalf. I shall certainly be there at that time, for having accepted this appointment I am resolv'd to pursue and not be diverted from it by any consideration whatever. Remember me to Mr. Madison. Mrs. M. was well when I left her. With great respect & esteem I am affectionately yr. friend & servant,

JAS. MONROE

RC (DLC); endorsed by TJ as received 23 June 1791 and so recorded in SJL.

From George Washington

SIR   Mount-Vernon, June 17th. 1791.

By the last post from the southward I received your letters of the 17th. and 24th. of April, with their enclosures.

In a letter of the 7th. of May, which I wrote to the Secretary of the Treasury from Charleston, I expressed my approbation of what he informed me had been determined by the Vice-President and the Heads of Departments, relative to Mr. Short's negociation at Amsterdam, and the further progress of the loans in Holland. I am, Sir, Your most obedient Servant,   Go: WASHINGTON

RC (DLC); in clerk's hand, except for signature; at foot of text: "The Secretary of State"; endorsed by TJ as received 21 June and so recorded in SJL. Dft (DNA: RG 59, MLR). FC (DNA: RG 59, SDC).

To George Washington

SIR   Philadelphia June 20. 1791.

I am honoured with yours of the 15th. instant, and not a little mortified with the miscarriage of so many of my letters. They have been of the following dates

Mar. 27.	Apr. 24.
Apr. 2.	May 1.
Apr. 10.	May 8.
Apr. 17.	May.15.

June. 5. from Bennington. Of these it appears that only the three first and that of May 15. had come to hand, and probably that of June 5. has been recieved ere this. Those of Apr. 17. and 24. and May 1. and 8. were sent, the two first to Charleston, and the two last to Taylor's ferry. I now send copies of them, tho their contents are not at this time very interesting.

The papers from the free people of colour in Grenada, which you did me the honour to inclose, I apprehend it will be best to take no notice of. They are parties in a domestic quarrel, which I think we should leave to be settled among themselves. Nor should I think it desireable, were it justifiable, to draw a body of sixty thousand free blacks and mulattoes into our country. – The instructions from the government of the United Netherlands, by which Mr. Shaw has suffered, merit serious notice. The channel thro which application shall be made is the only difficulty; Dumas being personally disagreeable to that government. However, either thro' him or some other it should certainly be conveyed.

Mr. Remsen had unluckily sent off to New York all my letters on the very day of my arrival here, which puts it out of my power to give you the state of things brought by the last packet. I expect they will be returned tomorrow, and that my next may communicate to you whatever they contain interesting.

I recieved yesterday a letter from Colo. Ternan informing me of his appointment and that he should sail about the latter end of May. – The court of Madrid has sent over a Don Joseph Jaudenes as a joint commissioner with de Viar, till a Chargé shall be named. He presented me the letter of Credence from the Count de Florida Blanca when I was at New York. He is a young man who was under Secretary to Mr. Gardoqui when here.

Our tour was performed in somewhat less time than I had calculated. I have great hopes it has rid me of my head-ach, having scarcely had any thing of it during my journey. Mr. Madison's health is very visibly mended. I left him at New York, meditating a journey as far Eastward as Portsmouth. – I have the honor to be with the most respectful attachment, Sir, Your most obedient & most humble servt, Th: Jefferson

RC (DNA: RG 59, MLR); endorsed by Washington. PrC (DLC). FC (DNA: RG 59, SDC). The letter from Ternant was that of 8 Mch. 1791.

To Seth Jenkins

SIR   Philadelphia June 21. 1791.

According to my promise when I had the pleasure of seeing you at Hudson, I have examined my notes made when I was at Bordeaux and find that the lowest priced white wines of that canton cost 75 livres the ton, which contains 1000 French pints, their pint almost exactly our quart: that they yeild from a fifth to a sixth of spirit on distillation, and that the smallest wines make the best brandy. According to this a ton will yeild 200 quarts or 50 gallons of spirit, which will be 30 sous or 2/3 New York money the gallon. I think you told me this was the price of a gallon of molasses now in the West Indies. It is then to be considered whether a saving may not be made in the freight, and a gain by the superior quality of the spirit distilled from wine. You have probably a correspondent at Bordeaux: if not, and you cannot readily get one well recommended, you may safely address yourself to Mr. Fenwick a native of Maryland, consul at Bordeaux for the United states, who is an honest man, and pretty well acquainted with the subject of wines.

I inclose you one of my reports on the whale and cod fisheries, and will be obliged to you if, in reading it, you will have a pen in your hand, and make notes, ever so roughly, of any errors you may discover in it, and any new facts you can furnish me with, and be so obliging as to send me the notes. I am with great esteem Sir Your most obedient humble servt,   Th: Jefferson

RC (William I. Davis, Newark, Ohio, 1944); at foot of text: "Capt. Seth Jenkins." PrC (DLC); mutilated, so that about a third of the text is lost.

Captain Seth Jenkins was a Nantucket whaler who, with his brother Thomas Jenkins, Alexander Coffin, and others, founded the whaling port of Hudson in 1783. The town prospered so that within three years it had four fine wharves, several ware-houses, a ropewalk, a sail loft, a spermaceti factory, a distillery, and about 150 dwellings (Edouard A. Stackpole, *The Sea-Hunters*, p. 100-1). TJ saw Jenkins at Hudson when he and Madison passed through on May 25, 1791. They breakfasted at the thriving port after spending the night at Claverack. TJ clearly had two objects in view for Jenkins' distillery: in arguing that better and cheaper spirits could be produced from wine than from molasses, he hoped to lessen American dependence upon the British West Indies and to increase trade relations with France. With the distillery exporting a thousand hogsheads of rum annually, TJ must have been disappointed that his argument was not convincing to Jenkins (Jenkins to TJ, 5 July 1791).

To James Madison

DEAR SIR   Philadelphia June 21. 1791.

I arrived here on Sunday evening. Yesterday I sent your note to Lieper who immediately called and paid the 200 Dollars, which I have exchanged for a post note and now inclose. I mentioned to the Atty Gen. that I had a note on him, and afterwards sent it to him, saying nothing as to time. I inclose you also a post note for 35. Dollars to make up my deficit of expences (25.94 D.) to pay Mr. Elsworth and the smith, and also to get me from Rivington's Hamilton More's practical navigator, if his be the 6th. edition, as I believe it is. This is the last edition revised and printed under the author's eye. The later editions are so incorrect as to be worth nothing.

The President will leave Mt. Vernon on the 27th. He will be stayed a little at Georgetown. – Colo. H. Lee is here. He gives a very different account from Carrington's of the disposition of the upper country of Virginia towards the Excise law. He thinks resistance possible. – I am sorry we did not bring with us some leaves of the different plants which struck our attention, as it is the leaf which principally decides *specific* differences. You may still have it in your power to repair the omission in some degree. The Balsam tree at Govr. Robinson's is the Balsam poplar, Populus balsamifera of Linnaeus. The Azalea I can only suspect to be the Viscosa, because I find but two kinds the nudiflora and viscosa acknoleged to grow with us, and I am sure it is not the nudiflora. The White pine is the Pinus Strobus. I will thank you if in your journey Northward you will continue the enquiries relative to the Hessian fly, and note them. The post is almost on it's departure so Adieu. – Your's affectionately,   TH: JEFFERSON

RC (DLC: Madison Papers); addressed: "James Madison esquire at Mr. Elsworth's Maiden lane New York"; franked; postmarked: "21 IU" and "FREE." PrC (DLC).

From C. W. F. Dumas

The Hague, 22 June 1791. He sends this by the *Harmony*, Captain Folger, for Baltimore, with duplicate by Amsterdam. Parliament adjourned without being able to learn the designs of the British court, their fleet ready to depart, the press of sailors continuing, the armistice between the Turks and Hungary expired – all indicate continuation and extension of war.

[P.S.] *26 June*. His dispatch by Amsterdam had gone before arrival of the troubling news of the escape of the King, Queen, and Monsieur [the Comte de Provence]. The last is at Mons, but no one knows today where the King is. After tomorrow we fear news of assassination.

FC (Dumas Letter Book, Rijksarchief, The Hague; photostats in DLC); at head of text: "No. 78." RC (missing) recorded in SJL as received 22 Oct. 1791.

From William Short

DEAR SIR   Paris June 22. 1791.

I have to communicate to you a very unexpected event which has taken place here and occupies the National assembly at present. The King with the Queen and Royal family retired from Paris without being observed the night before last. It is not yet known how they got out of the *Chateau*, in what manner they set off, nor whither they are gone. What renders this extraordinary circumstance the more remarkable is that the *comité des recherches*; the Municipality, and M. de la fayette were all warned of the intended flight, and had increased the guard and doubled their vigilance that night.

The event has so astonished every body and is so unaccountable in itself that no probable conjecture is formed of the manner in which it was effected. It became known between eight and nine o'clock in the morning of yesterday and expresses were sent off immediately to spread this information and stop the King or any part of the Royal family. As yet no intelligence of any kind whatever has been recieved of them.

It seems probable that the King counts on foreign aid and in that case he will endeavour to get out of the Kingdom for the present by the safest route. It is thought he will go through bye ways into the low countries or perhaps to Worms where he will find the Count D'Artois and Prince de Condé.

Previous to his departure he drew up an address *à tous les Francois à sa sortie de Paris*. He protests against the decrees he has sanctioned since Octob. 89. He forbids the ministers to sign any act in his name without further orders from him and commands the *Garde du sceau* to send him the seal of the State when he shall require it.

The National Assembly have taken provisionary measures for the exercise of the government during the King's absence as you will see by their proceedings of yesterday which are inclosed in this letter and its copies which I shall send by several conveyances.

In consequence of their decrees M. de Montmorin has written a circular letter to the foreign ministers here. I inclose you a copy of that addressed to me. I subjoin also a copy of one I recieved yesterday from the Spanish Ambassador, since when I have heard nothing further from him.

It is surprizing that the King's departure should have produced so little effect here. – There reigns the most perfect tranquillity and business goes on in almost the ordinary style. It is impossible to say how long this will continue. A few days however will probably shew more clearly the dispositions of all parties. The people murmured much against M. de la fayette, but his irreproachable character and known virtue saved him from their violence and he seems now to have fully their confidence, as he has certainly that of the National assembly. – I am with sentiments of sincere attachment & affection Dear Sir, your friend & servant, W. SHORT

P.S. 10 o'clock p.m. An express has just arrived with intelligence that the King has been stopped at Varrennes near the frontier of Luxemburg. He was recognized by the postmaster of the village. He is now surrounded by thousands of *gardes nationales* who flocked in from all quarters and are escorting him here. The assembly will conduct themselves with moderation, but it is impossible to answer for the excesses of the people and particularly with respect to the Queen. The crisis is really tremendous and may have a disastrous issue.

PrC (DLC: Short Papers); at head of text: "No. 69." Tr (DNA: RG 59, DD). Entries in SJL show, without identification, that RC, Dupl, and Tripl were received on 23 Aug., 20 Sep., and 22 Oct. 1791. Enclosures: (1) Montmorin to Short, 22 June 1791, informing him that the uncertainty caused by the King's departure for an unknown refuge the night before last had caused the National Assembly to assure him of the will of the French nation to continue the friendly relationship existing between France and the United States (Tr in DNA: RG 59, DD). (2) Communication from the Spanish Ambassador to Short expressing his conviction that, in the existing critical and uncertain circumstances, it was advisable and even necessary for the honor and safety of the diplomatic corps to follow a uniform course in its conduct; that he had written to Montmorin to inquire what his intentions were in this respect; and that Montmorin had just answered his inquiry, saying he was then on his way to the National Assembly to receive orders he was confident would be appropriate in the cruel circumstances in which they found themselves (undated but written on 21 June 1791; Tr in DNA: RG 59, DD).

The Declaration of Louis XVI to the people of France, issued at Paris on 20 June 1791, explaining the reasons for his departure, forbidding his ministers to sign any order in his name without further instructions, and commanding the Keeper of the Seal to transmit it to him when directed to do so, was read the next day to the stunned members of the National Assembly (*Ar-*

chives Parlementaires, XXVII, 378-83). Under the compelling necessity of providing for the exercise of the powers of government in future and in order to validate all of the decrees it had adopted since 1789, the National Assembly could do no more than make provisional arrangements. Its action, followed by Montmorin's communication to the diplomatic corps, was of course essential for the continuity of formal relations with other nations because each of its members was accredited to Louis XVI as sovereign. The ambassador from Spain was particularly sensitive to the implications of "les cruelles circonstances" because of the alliance of the Spanish and French Bourbons under the Family Compact.

To William Carmichael

SIR   Philadelphia June 23. 1791.

My letters to you of the present year have been of the 12th. and 17th. of Mar. the 11th. of Apr. and 16th. of May. Yours of Jan. 24. is still the only one I have from you. We have not yet been able to fix on a satisfactory subject for the Consulship of Cadiz which would furnish a convenient channel of conveyance for letters between this place and Madrid. The present goes by the way of Lisbon. – A regulation of the government of Spain relative to foreign wheat imported has appeared in our papers and excites much uneasiness. Such impediments thrown in the way of our agriculture must lead us to confine that to our own consumption and turn our superfluous labour to manufactures, so as to be independant as much as possible on the fluctuating councils of other countries. – An extraordinary drought which has prevailed very generally thro our states will occasion the crop of wheat of this year to be very short. – Our domestic paper continues high, and we have unequivocal proofs of the preeminence of our credit in Europe. – The Indians North of the Ohio have hitherto continued their little depredations, but we are tolerably confident that the measures now in a course of execution will lead them to peace. With the present I send a continuation of the newspapers, and am with great esteem, Sir, your most obedt. & most humble servt,   TH: JEFFERSON

PrC (DLC). FC (DNA: RG 59, DCI).

From Tench Coxe

[Philadelphia], *23 June 1791*. Enclosing account of Cuba and statement of Newfoundland fishery for three years. Also sends the Virginia imports which TJ will see are "near a half a million greater in value" than register's return, owing to later quarterly returns from some customhouses which were then deficient.

RC (DLC); endorsed by TJ as received 22 June 1791 and so recorded in SJL – an error in date made either by Coxe or by TJ. Enclosures: (1) An account by Oliver Pollock of the military and naval forces in Cuba and of the exports from Havana. As to the former, Pollock stated that some 200,000 men were on the island, about half of whom were in or near Havana, being "one third nearly white, and one third of colour, and the remaining third Black"; that the Havana militia were well disciplined but not likely to sustain any test of prowess, while the country militia were scattered, inefficient, and could not be depended on in any emergency whatever; that the fortifications were very strong, particularly near Havana, though the strongest fort was not finished; that the marine consisted of only one 74-gun ship, two badly manned frigates, and a 100-gun ship under construction, though the workmen on it and on the fortifications were idle because of the financial difficulties of the government; and that "The Inhabitants of the whole Island of Cuba may without any exception be pronounced universally dissatisfied, with the heavy Yoke, imposed by their despotic System of Government, and they doubtless will at some future period, eagerly embrace the earliest favourable opportunity, to shake off the Galling Chain, nay even the military part are far from being pleased with their situation." Pollock estimated that imports totalled 40,000 barrels of flour and an equal amount of beef, pork, rice, gammon, lard, butter, cheese, spermaceti candles, beeswax, apples, potatoes, codfish, beer, cider, masts, iron, and steel, the whole of which he thought could be valued at $800.000. As to the latter, he gave a detailed account based on customs records of the exports from Havana for 1783 and 1784, consisting principally of sugar, molasses, spirits, tobacco, lumber, tar, pitch, raw hides, beeswax, and gold and silver, both in coins and in ingots – the figures for these being unreliable because of smuggling. "The slightest view of the soil and attention to the happy Climate of this Fertile Island," Pollock concluded, "must force conviction, that were the Inhabitants permitted to purchase slaves proportioned to their abilities to pay for them, their exports . . . would be increased many fold, for no industry is to be expected from the exertions of the white Inhabitants of that region of Sloth" (MS in DLC: TJ Papers, 65: 11200-2, signed by Pollock; undated, with the following note added by Coxe: "date unknown, but subsequent to 1784"; endorsed by TJ: "Military Force &c. at Havana"). (2) A table of shipping and imports for the various ports of Newfoundland from 10 Oct. 1786 to 10 Oct. 1789, showing that 335 vessels with tonnage of 37,913 arrived from Great Britain while only 11 with tonnage of 1,395 were from Canada, Nova Scotia, and the United States; that the principal imports were bread, flour, beef, pork, butter, cheese, salt, tea, sugar, molasses, rum, wine, gin, cider, tobacco, coffee, soap, candles, coal, pitch, tar, lumber, oxen, sheep, and poultry. A note to the table indicated that articles not specified – linens, woollens, sailcloth, cordage, leather, and iron – were all imported from Great Britain and Ireland. It also stated that the table covered those parts of the coast of Newfoundland where the fishery of Great Britain was carried on and provided a summary of its results for the years covered (MS in tabular form in DLC: TJ Papers, 65: 11203; in clerk's hand, undated).

The enclosures provided further information for the report on commerce which TJ expected to submit at the ensuing session of Congress (see Report on Commerce, 16 Dec. 1793).

To Christopher Gore

SIR   Philadelphia June 23. 1791.

I am favoured with yours of May 20. and have now the honour to inclose you a post note for 5 D. 84 C. which will be taken up by any custom house officer of the U.S. This should not have been so long delayed, but that I have been absent on a journey from which I am but just returned. The continuance of your attention to procure the laws between 1772. and 1780. which you are so kind as to promise is very obliging. I have it much at heart to have one complete set of the laws of all the states in a deposit where they will be tolerably sure of being preserved. – I have the honour to be with great respect Sir Your most obedt humble servt, TH: JEFFERSON

PrC (DLC). FC (DNA: RG 360, PCC No. 120).

Gore's letter of 20 May, responding to TJ's of 29 Mch., informed TJ that he had not yet procured copies of the laws of Massachusetts passed between 1772 and 1780, but that he would cheerfully do everything in his power to "fill up the chasm." He enclosed a receipt for the cost of those already furnished (RC in DNA: RG 59, MLR; endorsed by both TJ and Remsen as received 21 June 1791 and so recorded in SJL).

To David Humphreys

DEAR SIR   Philadelphia June 23. 1791.

My last letters to you have been of Apr. 11. and May 13 and I am now to acknowlege the receipt of yours of Mar. 6. No. 13. for 14. Mar. 31. No. 15. Apr. 8. No. 16. Apr. 30. No. 17. May 3. No. 18.

As yet no native candidate, such altogether as we would wish, has offered for the Consulate of Lisbon, and as it is a distinguished place in our commerce, we are somewhat more difficult in that than other appointments. – Very considerable discouragements are recently established by France, Spain and England with respect to our commerce: the first as to whale oil, tobacco, and ships, the second as to corn, and the third as to corn and ships. Should these regulations not be permanent, still they add to the proofs that too little reliance is to be had on a steady and certain course of commerce with the countries of Europe to permit us to depend more on that than we cannot avoid. Our best interest would be to employ our principal labour in agriculture, because to the profits of labour which is dear this adds the profits of our lands which are cheap. But the risk of hanging our prosperity on the fluctuating councils and caprices of others renders it wise in us to turn seriously to manufactures; and if Europe will not let us carry our provisions to their manufacturers we must endeavor to bring their manufacturers to our provisions. A very uncommon drought has prevailed thro most of the states, so that our crop of wheat will be considerably shorter than common. Our public paper continues high, and the proofs that

[565]

our credit is now the first in Europe are unequivocal. The Indians North of the Ohio have hitherto continued their little depredations, but we are in daily expectation of hearing the success of a first excursion to their towns by a party of 7. or 800 mounted infantry under Genl. Scott. Two or three similar expeditions will follow successively under other officers, while a principal one is preparing to take place at a later season.

I thank you for your communication from Mr. Carmichael. His letter of Jan. 24. is still the only one we have from him. Until some surer means of hearing from Madrid can be devised, I must beg of you to give us from time to time all the intelligence you can from that capital. The conveyance by the British packets is tolerably sure, when direct conveyances fail.

You will recieve herewith a continuation of the newspapers, for yourself, as also a letter and newspapers for Mr. Carmichael which I must beg the favour of you to convey as safely as you can. – The President is expected here the beginning of the ensuing month, being arrived at Mt. Vernon on his return from his Southern tour. – I am with great & sincere esteem Dear Sir your most obedt. & most humble servt,   TH: JEFFERSON

RC (W. B. Jefferson, San Francisco, 1946); addressed. PrC (DLC). FC (DNA: RG 59, DCI).

TJ's allusion to the possibility that the United States might be driven by the fluctuating councils and caprices of other nations to entice European manufacturers to establish themselves in America near the raw materials must be read in the context of the times. At this moment Hamilton's Society for Establishing Useful Manufactures was being organized, as TJ well knew. Tench Coxe had sent him a copy of its plan and had long since been engaged in efforts to attract English artisans to the United States (Coxe to TJ, 15 Apr. 1791; see also note to Digges to TJ, 28 Apr. 1791). TJ had opposed these efforts, but he knew how strongly the President felt otherwise (Washington to TJ, 13 Feb. 1789). George Beckwith and Phineas Bond both reported the developments to their government, and British manufacturers also made their concern known. It is not surprising, therefore, that TJ should have expressed the view that he did to both Humphreys and Carmichael (see TJ to Carmichael, 13 June 1791). His use of the current interest in manufactures was as an instrument of diplomacy, and the object in view was the promotion of commercial relations, not American manufactures.

From James Madison

DEAR SIR   New York June 23d. 1791.

I recieved your favor of the 21st. yesterday, inclosing post notes for 235 dollars. I shall obtain the bills of Mrs. Elsworth and the Smith this afternoon and will let you know the amount of them.

There is a bill also from the Taylor amounting to £6.7. which I shall pay. The articles for which it is due are in my hands and will be forwarded by the first opportunity. If a good one should fall within your notice, it may be well for you to double the chance of a conveyance by giving a commission for the purpose. I have applied to Rivington for the Book but the only copies in Town seem to be of the *8th. Edition*. This however is advertised as "enlarged &c. by the author," who I am told by Berry & Rogers is now living and a correspondent of theirs. It is not improbable therefore that your reason for preferring the 6th. Ed: may be stronger in favor of this. Let me know your pleasure on the subject and it shall be obeyed.

I am at a loss what to decide as to my trip to the Eastward. My inclination has not changed but a journey without a companion, and in the stage which besides other inconveniences travels too rapidly for my purpose, makes me consider whether the next fall may not present a better prospect. My horse is more likely to recover than at the time of your departure. By purchasing another, in case he should get well, I might avoid the stage, but at an expence not altogether convenient.

You have no doubt seen the French Regulations on the subject of Tobo. which commence hostilities against the British Navigation Act. Mr. King tells me an attack on Payne has appeared in a Boston paper under the name of Publicola, and has an affinity in the stile as well as sentiments to the discourses on Davila. I observed in a late paper here an extract from a Philada. pamphlet on the Bank. If the publication has attracted or deserves notice I should be glad of a copy from you. I will write again in a few days; in the mean time remaining Yrs. mo: affecly,   Js. MADISON JR.

RC (DLC: Madison Papers); endorsed by TJ as received 25 June 1791 and so recorded in SJL.

From James Maury

Liverpool, 23 June 1791. He has received none of TJ's letters since his of 2 Mch. Sends the corn law, just "finished." Many expect it will be amended more favorably to foreign countries before it goes into operation. In accordance with TJ's of 26 Aug. he has required particulars of masters. "Some conform, but many will not." He will continue to make requisitions, but has not applied to civil authority to assist him in compelling compliance. American vessels continue to engross carrying from England to U.S., and their arrivals have increased this year. Ports of this kingdom are open to foreign corn and entirely under direction of Privy Council until 15 Nov. next.

RC (DNA: RG 59, CD); endorsed by TJ as received 20 Aug. 1791 and so recorded in SJL. Enclosure: Copy of Hawkesbury's Corn Law of 1791. This was the first copy that TJ received from abroad (see TJ to Maury, 30 Aug. 1791).

To Martha Jefferson Randolph

MY DEAR DAUGHTER   Philadelphia June 23. 1791.

I wrote to each of you once during my journey, from which I returned four days ago, having enjoyed thro' the whole of it very perfect health. I am in hopes the relaxation it gave me from business has freed me from the almost constant headach with which I had been persecuted thro the whole winter and spring. Having been entirely clear of it while travelling proves it to have been occasioned by the drudgery of business. I found here on my return your letter of May 23. with the pleasing information that you were all in good health. I wish I could say when I shall be able to join you: but that will depend on the movements of the President who is not yet returned to this place. – In a letter written me by young Mr. Franklin, who is in London, is the following paragraph. 'I meet here with many who ask kindly after you, among these the D. of Dorset, who is very particular in his enquiries. He has mentioned to me that his niece had wrote once or twice to your daughter since her return to America; but not receiving an answer had supposed she meant to drop her acquaintance, which his neice much regretted. I ventured to assure him[1] that that was not likely, and that possibly the letters might have miscarried. – You will take what notice of this you may think proper.' – Fulwar Skipwith is on his return to the United States. – Mrs. Trist and Mrs. Waters often ask after you. – Mr. Lewis being very averse to writing, I must trouble Mr. Randolph to enquire of him relative to my tobacco, and to inform me about it. I sold the whole of what was good here. 17. hogsheads only are yet come, and by a letter of May 29. from Mr. Hylton there were then but 2. hogsheads more arrived at the warehouse. I am uneasy at the delay, because it not only embarrasses me with guessing at excuses to the purchaser, but is likely to make me fail in my payment to Hanson, which ought to be made in Richmond on the 19th. of next month. I wish much to know when the rest may be expected. – In your last you observe you had not received a letter from me in five weeks. My letters to you have been of Jan. 20. Feb. 9. Mar. 2. 24. Apr. 17. May 8. which you will observe to be pretty regularly once in three weeks. – Matters in France are still going on safely. Mirabeau is dead; also the Duke de Richlieu; so that the Duke de Fronsac has now succeeded to the head of the family, tho' not to the title, these being all abolished. Present me affectionately to Mr. Randolph and Polly, and kiss the little one for me: Adieu my dear Your's affectionately,   TH: JEFFERSON

RC (NNP). PrC (MHi). Not recorded in SJL.

is that of 6 Apr. 1791. With one exception, TJ copied the passage exactly.

William Temple Franklin's letter to TJ

[1] Franklin wrote "his Grace."

To Tobias Lear

June 24th. 1791.

Th: Jefferson presents his compliments to Mr. Lear. He has been endeavoring this morning, while the thing is in his mind to make a statement of the cost and expences of the President's wines, but not having a full account of the whole from Fenwick he is unable to do it but on sight of the account rendered by him to the President. If Mr. Lear, the first time any circumstance shall give him occasion of doing Th: J. the honour of calling on him, will put that account in his pocket, the matter can be completed in two or three minutes. – The cloudiness of the present day renders it favourable to remove the 4. hampers of Champagne from Th: J's cellar, if Mr. Lear thinks proper to send for them. It would be well to open a case of every kind and place the bottles on their shelves that they may be settled before the President's return.

RC (Estate of Col. Charles William Whipple, New York, 1945); addressed: "Mr. Lear." Not recorded in SJL.

To William Short

DEAR SIR   Philadelphia June 24. 1791.

Mr. Custis, a citizen of Virginia, proposing to make application to the government of France for redress of a wrong which he thinks he has sustained from them, I am to ask your patronage of his claims so far as they shall be just and so far also as a denial or delay of justice in the ordinary modes of application may render an extraordinary interference necessary. – I am with great & sincere esteem, Dear Sir Your friend & servant,   TH: JEFFERSON

PrC (DLC); at foot of text: "William Short esq. Chargé des affaires of the U. S. at Paris." FC (DNA: RG 59, DCI).

To Fulwar Skipwith

Sir   Philadelphia June 24th. 1791

This letter will be handed you by the person who goes to Martinique as agent for those interested in the Sloop Jane of Baltimore lately commanded by Captain Woodrough. This vessel, according to the evidence handed me, appears to have been taken at Sea off the island of Martinique, carried into the port of Cazenaviere of that island, the cargo disposed of under authority of the Government, and the vessel itself retained and converted into a cruizer. How far these appearances may be qualified by further evidence cannot be estimated here. If the troubles then existing in the island rendered the vessel and cargo necessary for the purposes of Government, justice will certainly induce them to make ample indemnification to the individuals interested, and our dispositions towards that Nation are too friendly to press anything further. I am to desire you will patronize the applications for redress as far as shall be necessary and just.

My letter of the 13th. of May last will have informed you that the circumstances of the moment induce us not to press for the literal execution of the Consular Convention so far as regards your exequatur. At the same time we are assured that your applications on behalf of our commerce informally made, shall be substantially attended to and respected. It is in this way we desire you to interfere in the present case if necessary. — I am with great esteem Dear Sir Your most obedient & most humble Servt.

PrC (DLC); in Remsen's hand, unsigned. FC (DNA: RG 59, DCI).

To Alexander Hamilton

Sir   Philadelphia June 25. 1791.

Your favour of the 8th. inst. could only be recieved on my return here, and I have this morning been considering of it's contents. I think with you that it will be interesting to recieve from different countries the details it enumerates. Some of these I am already in a regular course of recieving. Others when once well executed, will scarcely need to be repeated. As to these I already possess what may answer your views in part. I must therefore give you the trouble to call on me in some of your walks, in order that after seeing what I possess, we may decide on the proper supplement. I think it adviseable not to trouble gentlemen abroad with sending what we have already, because the less we give them to do the more secure we shall be of having it done. I am with the most respectful esteem Dr. Sir Your most obedt & most humble servt,

TH: JEFFERSON

PrC (DLC); at foot of text: "The Secretary of the Treasury." FC (DNA: RG 360, PCC No. 120).

To Mary Jefferson

MY DEAR MARIA   Philadelphia June 26. 1791.

I hope you have recieved the letter I wrote you from lake George, and that you have well fixed in your own mind the geography of that lake, and of the whole of my tour, so as to be able to give me a good account of it when I shall see you. On my return here, I found your letter of May 29. giving me the information it is always so pleasing to me to recieve that you are all well. Would to god I could be with you to partake of your felicities, and to tell you in person how much I love you all, and how necessary it is to my happiness to be with you. – In my letter to your sister written to her two or three days ago, I expressed my uneasiness at hearing nothing more of my tobacco and asked some enquiries to be made of Mr. Lewis on the subject, but I received yesterday a letter from Mr. Lewis with full explanations, and another from Mr. Hylton informing me the tobo. was on it's way to this place. Therefore desire your sister to suppress that part of my letter and say nothing about it. Tell her from me how much I love her, kiss her and the little one for me and present my best affections to Mr. Randolph, assured of them also yourself from your's,   TH: J.

RC (ViU); addressed: "Miss Maria Jefferson Monticello." PrC (ViU).

To Nicholas Lewis

DEAR SIR   Philadelphia June 26. 1791.

On my return here from a journey of a month I found a letter of Mr. Hylton's dated May 29. informing me there were yet but 2 more hhds. of my tobo. arrived at Richmond (after the 17 which he had sent.) Uneasy at this, from the engagement I had entered into here, in my letter of two or three days ago to my daughter, I desired her to have this mentioned to you lest there should be a stoppage of the Bedford tobo. somewhere, of which you might not be apprised. However the receipt of your letter which came to hand yesterday, and one from Mr. Hylton informing me that 22. hhds. more were shipped for Philadelphia, have relieved all my anxiety on that subject. These when arrived will make 39. and those you speak of as yet to come will fill up the expectations I had given the purchaser. – I observe Wilson only states the money he has paid to Dobson. What I was desirous of knowing was how much we might count upon from the bonds which had been put into his hands and not yet accounted for. You know in our estimate, we supposed that, with interest, it would amount to £525. From this however there will be a deduction of Mr. Randolph's account and interest. I had not supposed I had recieved so much flour from him, but I have always reason to distrust my memory, and none to doubt his account, which therefore is to be credited. Whenever you can inform me exactly or nearly how much the bonds still due (and counted by us at £525) will really be I shall be obliged to you. The two hogsheads of hams are arrived, but we have not yet opened them. – The time of my return home is not yet fixed. I suppose it will be towards the latter part of August, and to remain to the middle of October. As there are generally things to be done by the carpenters which can only be done when I am present to direct them, I should be glad if it could be so contrived as that they shall be disengaged and in Albemarle while I am at home. – The last part of your letter shall be last answered. It is with infinite regret, my dear Sir, that I learn your purpose of withdrawing from the direction of my affairs. My confidence in you has been so entire, that since they have been in your hands I have never had an anxiety about them. I saw indeed that you took a great deal more trouble about them than I could expect or wish, and I feared it would lead you to an entire relinquishment of them. Instead of having a right to urge a continuance of such a drudgery on you, it is my duty to be thankful that you have submitted to it so long, and I am so, sincerely and thoroughly. What I am next to do with them, I am utterly at a loss to devise. Stewards of the common description are a most unhopeful dependance. I must ask you to turn this matter in your mind, and to advise with me when I come home on what I can best do. With respect to Clarke, I shall be for doing exactly what you think best, and will be glad to confirm any arrangement you may be so good as to make with him for me, in his present concern. Present me very affectionately to Mrs. Lewis, & be assured of the esteem & attachment of Dear Sir Your sincere friend & servt,   TH: JEFFERSON

RC (NHi); addressed: "Colo. Nicholas Lewis near Charlottesville." PrC (MHi).

TJ's expression of relief from anxiety about the experiment of selling his tobacco in Philadelphia was premature, as his later correspondence with Hylton soon revealed. Robert Coventry had reported for James Brown that "two Hhds. of Bacon had been received from Lewis on 18 May and forwarded the next day" (Coventry to TJ, 19 May 1791, enclosing bill of lading showing shipment by the sloop *Phoenix*, Capt. John Sheppard, with freight charges of $6; RC and enclosure in MHi; endorsed by TJ as received 21 June 1791 and so recorded in SJL). The shipment, as TJ indicates, contained hams. The term *bacon* was occasionally applied to hams (DAE).

Hylton's letter of 17 June and that of Lewis of 20 June 1791, both dated at Richmond, are recorded in SJL as received on the 25th. Lewis evidently replied to the above letter on 16 Aug. 1791 since one of that date, written from Albemarle, is recorded in SJL as received on the 26th. None of these letters has been found.

From Richard Peters

DEAR SIR   [Belmont], 26 June 1791.

Almost as soon as I saw you advertized in a New York News Paper your Return was announced in one of ours. I have been in Town twice since I left the Assembly and once I called to enquire after you but you had eloped. My Strawberries are gone and I have no Temptations to offer you. Come then from disinterested Motives when you wish for a little Country Air and you will get it here. Should it create an Apetite I will give you something to eat. I do not esteem you as Men do many things for your Scarcity. If this could make you more valuable than you are there would be no End to the Calculation. Possibly if you resided at the Potowmack you would make a Northern Excursion from Curiosity. Madison I saw not thro' the Winter except now and then *en passant*. In this I suppose we were both to blame. I hear not whether he is in Philada. or gone Southward. As he is said to be the *Fox* of America, I suppose he was too cunning to let our Paragraphists get hold of him. I wish the News Factors had made a better Comparison. For our Fox has every thing I love and the other, except his Talents, everything I hate. – Yours very Sincerely,   R. PETERS

MS not found; text printed from *Jefferson Correspondence*, Bixby, p. 47-8. Recorded in SJL as received 27 June 1791.

From William Short

DEAR SIR   Paris June 26. 1791.

My last of the 22d. inst. of which copies were sent by several conveyances, will inform you of the King's departure from Paris and his arrestation at Varennes near the frontier of Luxemburg. He was accompanied by the Queen, their two children, Madame Elisabeth, the Gouvernante du Dauphin, two femmes de chambre, and three gardes du corps dressed in the habit of couriers and acting in that capacity. Monsieur and Madame left Paris the same night and taking a different route have arrived safe in the low countries. From the depositions which have been taken it appears that the King, Queen and their company got out of the chateau, by a secret door which was always kept shut as useless, and for which false keys were made.

The King's carriage was stopped at Varennes without their knowing who he was. It was thought the suspicions against them arising from the circumstances of their taking a different route to get to Varennes, from that which they had at first directed for Verdun, their being escorted by several hussards, their apparent confusion when questioned &c. were sufficient to authorize their being stopped under present circumstances. In a short time the King was recognized by an inhabitant of Varennes. The alarm was spread through the country. The gardes nationales from all quarters rushed in. The order of the Marquis de la fayette and that added to it by the National assembly for stopping the King and Royal family arrived there by one of the Aides du camp sent off in pursuit of them, and immediately the return towards Paris commenced.

The Hussards who escorted the King had been posted on the route by M. de Bouillé under pretence of conducting the supplies of money intended for the army. As soon as they found it was the King they declared their attachment to the *nation* and the horror of what they had been deceived to do. I mention this as a sample of the present spirit of the army.

My former letter will have informed you of the National assembly having immediately on the King's departure taken the whole government on themselves. Addresses from all quarters are coming in daily declaring their confidence in the assembly and their adhesion to their measures. They continued the several ministers in their functions, decreed that the sanction of the King should for the present be dispensed with, and prescribed a new form of an oath to be taken to the national assembly. All the military of the assembly immediately took it, and what is remarkable all the members of what is called the *cote droit*, without excepting the most hostile to the revolution, took it with a seeming pleasure; all parties seemed to make a point of honor of uniting and acting in concert. The oath was also sollicited by M. D'affry an old courtier at the head, and in the name of the officers of the Swiss guards. The garde nationale of Paris have followed this example and citizens of all classes and parties do the same.

The assembly dispatched three of their members to go and meet the King with absolute powers to take all the measures necessary for conducting him safely to Paris and protecting him and the Royal family from injury or insult. – They sent other members also to the frontiers with unlimited powers for their defense, and among others that of suspending such of the officers of the army as they should consider subject to suspicion. They decreed at the same time the suspension and arrestation of M. de Bouillé the commandant of Metz, suspected of having been concerned in what is now called the King's *evasion*, after having at first been called his *enlevement*. It is reported that M. de Bouillé has found means to escape out of the Kingdom.

When the King was first stopped he produced a passeport in the usual form signed Montmorin &c. It was for a Baronne de Corme and her suite. Immediately on this passeport being sent to the assembly, M. de Montmorin was denounced as having contributed to the King's evasion. – The assembly ordered him to be escorted immediately to their bar to answer to it, and this exciting the suspicions of the people, they run in crowds to his house and would probably have proceeded to violence if the *garde nationale* had not prevented them. M. de Montmorin found no difficulty in satisfying the assembly that this passeport had been given in the usual manner at the request of M. de Simolin. No further enquiry has been yet made respecting it so as to shew whether Simolin obtained it with improper views. The assembly being satisfied with M. de Montmorin's explanation appeased the people, who remained several hours in a menacing posture at his house.

The assembly you know had ordered the elections for the next Legislature. The electors are forming throughout the Kingdom. They have now thought proper in consequence of present circumstances to suspend these elections until ordered by a future decree. How long this will be delayed depends absolutely on circumstances. There is no doubt that a majority of the assembly will be disposed to delay it as long as possible, notwithstanding their assertions individually to the contrary.

Yesterday morning previous to the King's arrival the assembly decreed on the report of the committee of constitution the following articles.

Art. 1er. Aussitôt que le Roi sera arrivé au chateau des Thuilleries, il lui sera donné provisoirement une garde, qui sous les ordres du commandant de la garde nationale Parisienne veillera à sa sûreté et repondra de sa personne.

2. Il sera provisoirement donné à l'heritier presomptif de la couronne une garde particuliere, de même sous les ordres du commandant general, et il sera nommé un gouverneur par l'assemblée nationale.

3. Tous ceux qui ont accompagné la Famille Royale seront mis en etat d'arrestation et interrogés. Le Roi et la Reine seront entendus dans leur déclaration le tout sans delai, pour être pris ensuite par l'assemblée nationale les resolutions qui seront jugées necessaires.

4. Il sera provisoirement donné une garde particuliere à la Reine.

5. Jusqu'à ce qu'il en ait été autrement ordonné le decret rendu le 21. de ce mois qui enjoint au ministre de la justice d'apposer le sceau de l'état aux decréts de l'assemblée nationale sans qu'il soit besoin de la sanction ou de l'acceptation du Roi continuera d'etre executé dans toutes ses dispositions.

6. Les ministres et les commissaires du Roi pour la trésorerie nationale, la caisse de l'extraordinaire et la direction de la Liquidation, sont de même autorisés provisoirement de faire chacun dans leur département et sous leur responsabilité les fonctions du pouvoir executif.

7. Le present decret sera publié à l'instant même au son de trompe dans tous les quartiers de la capitale, d'après les ordres du ministre de l'interieur transmis au directoire du Departement de Paris.

This decree will give you some idea of the present situation of the government and the measures intended to be taken. You will easily conceive that the post of M. de la fayette becomes the most disagreeable and dangerous that can be imagined. He will probably insist on the assembly's tracing with more particularity the conduct he is to pursue in this new kind of safekeeping. The Duke de la Rochefoucauld will I think be appointed Governor of the Dauphin. This place will be less dangerous but cannot fail to be exceedingly disagreeable under present circumstances.

The assembly will not determine probably until after the declaration of the King and Queen, in what character they will consider him in future. It does not seem that a doubt enters into the head of any body about their right to declare him King or no King according as they may judge proper. The assembly themselves or a majority of them would prefer I think keeping him as a shadow of monarchy and exercising all the functions of government without him. The people of Paris headed by some popular ambitious persons declare loudly in favor a republican government. They have much influence on the deliberations of the assembly; still I do not know how far they will succeed. – The question will be kept undecided by the assembly as long as possible. Great numbers now wish that the King had escaped, as well those who are zealous republicans as those who are attached to the King's person. The former think that his absence would have shewn that he was an useless part of the government. As it is, all parties are embarassed and doubt what will be done. We have no idea of what the King will say himself or of what foreign powers will say. It would seem certain that he had been well assured of their support before undertaking the risk of a flight, although he affirmed to the commissaries of the assembly that he never had an intention of quitting the Kingdom but should have stopped at Mont Médi on the frontier: which seems probable enough, as he would in all likelihood have called there an Austrian garrison.

I was yesterday evening in the assembly when the three commissaries who had been sent to meet the King, returned there after seeing him and the Royal family safe in their appartments. They gave a particular detail of all the circumstances that took place after their joining him. In addition to the King's affirmation mentioned above, they said he expressed his sensibility, on their reading him the decree of the assembly, at the sollicitude of the assembly for the safety of his person and the precautions taken for insuring it. They say that the most perfect order and obedience to the decrees of the assembly was observed by all the citizens on the route and that they were surrounded every where with demonstrations of their zeal and implicit confidence and reliance on the national assembly.

An alarm took place at the moment of the King's carriage stopping before the door of the palace. To avoid the crowd of the streets the convoy had followed the boulevard without the new walls and came in by the champs elysées entering the Thuilleries on the pont tournant. The people forced the guard and entered the Thuilleries so as to be present when the carriages stopped. The three gardes du corps dressed as couriers were said among the people to be the Duke de Guiche and two other persons of the court disguised in order to assist the King's flight. They were placed on the coachman's seat of the King's carriage and in alighting a movement was made among the people and the garde nationale which seemed to threaten them. The three commissaries and M. de la fayette exerted themselves to calm their fury. It is doubtful whether they would have succeeded if the assembly, warned of the danger, had not sent several of their members to assist in relieving them. Their presence restored order and induced the people to desist – except this the arrival in Paris passed with much tranquillity. Dispositions sometimes appeared among the people to hiss and insult the King but were immediately suppressed by the garde nationale. In general much silence was observed and a determined resolution to shew none of the accustomed marks of respect, insomuch that the people allowed no body to keep their hats off as the Royal family passed.

The King expressed his surprize after his arrival that the ministers were not present, as he was not then informed of the decree of yesterday morning. M. de Montmorin went to wait on him this morning, though not to take his orders and I know not in what manner the decree was communicated to him. The corps diplomatique remain inactive as a body. Individually they will treat with M. de Montmorin though I suppose the most of them will suspend as much as possible their correspondence for the present, and particularly the family ambassadors.

I forgot to mention to you that when the Aide du camp of M. de la fayette arrived at Varennes and informed the King of his being sent after him, he and the Queen both forgot for a moment their position and went into the most unbounded abuse as well of the aide de camp as of M. de la fayette. He has for some time been the person on whom the Queen's hatred has concentered and the King has lately followed her example, notwithstanding it is certain that they both owe their lives to him and that he has lost the favor of numbers of the garde nationale and people on account of what they considered as his complaisance for them.

These are the principal details that have passed respecting this most unfortunate event. The influence it will have on the future situation of this country must be great, but it is impossible to say at present in what manner it will operate. I will take care to keep you informed of it in proportion as it is developed.

I have to acknowlege the reciept of your letter of April 25. together with the newspapers and the box containing the proceedings of the former Congress. I have seen M. Drost. He is now engaged in contending with other artists for the engraving of the new money to be struck here. Of course he could not engage immediately to go to America. The question however will be decided in fifteen days. I doubt whether he will succeed as his rivals and judges are both academicians. Should he not succeed he will undertake the business on the terms sent to you, and of which you returned me a copy. He says it will be indispensable to have the presses made here, and that it will be best to have the other instruments also as it will be more economical and as they may be made at the same time as the presses. He says they cannot be finished before the winter, and that he could not go until the spring, but that in the mean time he could send directions for erecting the necessary buildings so that no delay would ensue. He would recommend the having four presses made here, but says two may suffice for the present. They will cost about 22,000₶ each. I hope you will instruct me with respect to the number you would chuse. He hopes that if he should succeed in the struggle he is engaged in here that he might still find time to go to America for the purpose you wish, or if not he thinks that he could have a mint erected and established there by having the proper instruments made here and giving the proper directions to a person he could send from hence. He is to give me his answer with respect to his going in fifteen days. I hope he will agree to undertake the voyage as I do not see from your letter that I am to engage another in the case of his refusal. – He tells me he does not understand the business of assaying but that it is so simple an art that he will undertake to make himself master of it if he should go, and will instruct in it any person you may designate, not chusing to meddle with the operation practically himself on account of the delicacy of the subject. I am particularly happy that he undertakes this part of the business, as your letter and the copy of that of the Sec. of the Treasury to you left me in doubt whether I was to send another person for this purpose and on what terms. On the whole, I think you may count on M. Drost for the next spring, but you shall hear further from me on the subject very soon.

This letter and its duplicate will be sent to London to go by the two first conveyances. I beg you to be assured of the sentiments of affection & attachment with which I am my dear Sir, your friend & servant,   W. SHORT

PrC (DLC: Short Papers); at head of text: "*No. 70*"; at foot of text: "Thomas Jefferson Secretary of State, Philadelphia." Tr (DNA: RG 59, DD).

From George Washington

SIR   Mount Vernon, June 26. 1791.

The last post brought me your letter of the 20th. instant, and the duplicates of your letters, which were missing when I last wrote to you, the originals of which have since been received. This acknowledgement is all the notice I shall take of them until I have the pleasure of seeing you.

I have selected the letters written by you to me while you were in the administration of the government of this State, and I will take them with me to Philada.

The enclosed letters have been received since my return to Mount Vernon. — I am Sir, Your most obedient Servant,

GO: WASHINGTON

RC (DLC); in Jackson's hand, except for signature; endorsed by TJ as received 30 June 1791 and so recorded in SJL. Dft (DNA: RG 59, MLR); also in Jackson's hand, unsigned. Tr (DNA: RG 59, SDC).

From Samuel Hopkins

RESPECTED FRIEND   Newyork 27th. 6 mo 1791

Thomas Jefferson. I take the liberty of offering for thy acceptance an address to the Manufacturers of Pot and Pearl-ash, containing an account of the process and according to the Principles of my Patent. Thou wilt observe my having succeeded in Canada, and by accounts from those who have commenced opperating I am flatterd to believe that the business is in a fair way of fully answering what I have held out.

After making some further arangements here propose returning to Philadelphia when intind personally to wait on thee, and hope I shall have it in my power to give farther satisfaction. In mean time believe me, Thy Assured Friend,   SAM HOPKINS

RC (MHi); endorsed as received 30 June 1791 and so recorded in SJL. Enclosure: *An address to the manufacturers of pot and pearl ash, with an explanation of Samuel Hopkins's patent method of making the same . . . Also, copy of the patent granted to Samuel Hopkins* (New York, Childs and Swaine, 1791; Roger P. Bristol, comp., *Supplement to Charles Evans' American Bibliography*, Charlottesville, 1970, B7629). TJ bound the enclosed address with Charles Williamos' translation of Lavoisier's *The art of manufacturing alkaline salts and potashes* (Sowerby, No. 1222). Hopkins' patent was granted 31 July 1790 for his "new Apparatus and Process . . . in the making of Pearl ash 1st. by burning the raw Ashes in a Furnace, 2d. by dissolving and boiling them when so burnt in Water, 3rd. by drawing off and settling the Ley, and 4th. by boiling the Ley into Salts which then are the true Pearl-ash; and also in the making of Pot-ash by fluxing the Pearl-ash . . . which Operation of burning the raw Ashes in a Furnace, preparatory to their Dissolution and boiling in Water, is new, leaves little Residuum, and produces a much greater Quantity of Salt" (MS Letters Patent in Remsen's hand, signed by Washington, certified by Edmund Randolph to be in accord with the Act to promote the useful arts; with Great Seal impressed on paper; 31 July 1790; ICHi).

From James Madison

DEAR SIR   New York June 27. 1791.

By a Capt: Simms who setts off this afternoon in the Stage for Philadelphia I forward the Bundle of Cloaths from the Taylor. His bill is inclosed with that of Mrs. Elsworth including the payment to the Smith.

I have seen Col: Smith more than once. He would have opened his budget fully to me, but I declined giving him the trouble. He has written to the President a state of all his conversations with the British Ministry, which will get into your hands of course. He mentioned to me his wish to have put them there in the first instance and your situation on his arrival as an apology for not doing it. From the complexion of the little anecdotes and observations which dropped from him in our interviews I suspect that report has as usual far overrated the importance of what has been confided to him. General professions which mean nothing, and the sending a Minister which can be suspended at pleasure or which if executed may produce nothing, are the amount of my present guesses.

Mr. Adams seems to be getting faster and faster into difficulties. His attack on Payne which I have not seen, will draw the public attention to his obnoxious principles, more than every thing he has published. Besides this, I observe in McLean's paper here, a long extract from a sensible letter republished from Poughkeepsie, which gives a very unpopular form to his antirepublican doctrines, and presents a strong contrast of them with a quotation from his letter to Mr. Wythe in 1776.

I am still resting on my oars with respect to Boston. My Horse has had a relapse which made his recovery very improbable. Another favorable turn has taken place, and his present appearance promises tolerably well. But it will be some time before he can be [reco]verd if he should suffer no other check. Adieu Yrs.

Js. MADISON JR.

RC (DLC: Madison Papers); date added to endorsement by Madison when letter was later returned to him; endorsed by TJ as received 29 June 1791 and so recorded in SJL.

P. N. Godin to Robert Morris

St. Eustatius, 28 June 1791. Recommending as consul on St. Eustatius David M. Clarkson "whose amiable Character makes [him] more fit for it than an other Gentleman named Stevenson, who . . . would by no means be agreeable to me."

RC (DLC: Washington Papers); endorsed by TJ: "Clarkson for St. Eustatius, lre. handed in by Mr. R. Morris. recd. July 16. 1791." Clarkson was confirmed as consul for St. Eustatius on 20 Feb. 1793 (JEP, I, 130-1).

To James Madison

DEAR SIR   Philadelphia June 28. 1791.

Yours of the 23d. has been duly recieved. The parcel from the taylor will probably come safely by the stage. With respect to the edition of Hamilton More's book I took pains to satisfy myself of the best edition when I was in a better situation than I now am to do it with success. The result was that the 6th. edn. was the last published under the examination of the author, and that the subsequent editions, in order to cheapen them, had been so carelessly supervised as to be full of typographical errors in the tables. I therefore prefer waiting till I can get the 6th. I learned further that after the 6th. edn. the author abandoned all attention to the work himself. I inclose you the pamphlet on the bank, and must trouble you to procure a pamphlet for me which is only in a private hand in N. York. This is a Description of the Genisee country, but more particularly of Mr. Morris's purchase of Goreham and Phelps, in 4to. with a map. It was printed in London under the agency of W. T. Franklin to captivate purchasers. There is no name to it. Colo. Smith brought in 6. copies. If one of them can be drawn from him I should be very glad of it. – Will you also be so good as to ask of him whether he can give me any information of the progress of the map of S. America, which he, at my request, put into the hands of an engraver. The French proceedings against our tobo. and ships are very eccentric and unwise. With respect to the former however, which you consider as a *commencement* of hostilities against the British navigation act, it is only a continuation of the decision of the council of Berni, since which the importation of tobo. into France in any but American or French bottoms has been prohibited. The Spanish as well as English proceedings against our commerce are also serious. – Nobody doubts here who is the author of Publicola, any more than of Davila. He is very indecently attacked in Brown's and Bache's papers. – From my European letters I am inclined to think peace will take place between the Porte and Russia. The article which separates them is so minute that it will probably be got over, and the war is so unpopular in England that the ministers will probably make that an excuse to the K. of Prussia for not going all lengths with him. His only object is Thorn and Dantzic, and he has secretly intimated at Petersbg. that if he could be accomodated with this he would not be tenacious against their keeping Oczakoff. This has leaked out, and is working duly in Poland. – I think the President will contrive to be on the road out of the reach of ceremony till after the 4th. of July. Adieu my dear Sir, Yours' affectionately,

TH: JEFFERSON

RC (DLC: Madison Papers). PrC (DLC).

From George Rogers Clark

DEAR SIR   Jefferson Co[un]ty June 29th. 1791

Judge Innis has admitt'd me to a perusal of part of a Letter of yours to that Gentleman which strongly evidenced your friendly recollection of me. I have in consequence signified to the Judge by letter the high sense I had entertained of your partiality in my favour and beged him to have imparted to you the heartfelt respect and gratitude which I have ever felt and still entertain for Mr. Jefferson, as well for his personal qualifications, as for his uniform favourable propensities towards me.

At the time of having perused that part of your Letter above alluded to, I deemed it obligatory on my feelings, to have expressed by Letter to the Judge the gratitude I entertained for the friendly remembrance of an old servant to your government, with which you was pleased to honour me. Since then, Sir, I have considered that the terms of the Letter was such and so friendly as to have demanded at my hands that this acknowledgement however inadequate should be personally addressed to yourself. Be pleased then to accept it from a heart teeming with the warmest regard for your person, but untainted with the sordid desire of cultivating your patronage from selfish views. I am above that design but (when duly called on) I shall never be above the service of my Country at the risque of Life and reputation, Blood and Treasure. I might have been and yet may be saved.

The little Factions of those Western Cuntries, so incident to all infant settlements, have induc'd me to spurn at competition and Rivalry. My pride soared above them, and although long since re-tired into the vale of private Life in which the eye of observation is generally more acute disinterested and clear sighted, yet I felt myself constrained from the pressure of distress with which Kentucky was overwhelm'd at the time by Indian hostilitys to come forward as a private citizen and to exert all the Influance I had possessed with the people to forward the late expedition. On no public occasion shall my exertion be wanting. My country and yourself may at all times, command me. I remain Dr. Sir yr Most respectfull & obliged Humble Servt,   G R CLARK

RC (DLC); endorsed by TJ as received 3 Oct. 1791 and so recorded in SJL.

From William Short

DEAR SIR   Paris June 29. 1791.

I informed you in my last of the 26th. inst. of the arrival of the King and Royal family at Paris, and the decree of the national assembly relative thereto and the present exercise of government. The part of the decree for recieving the declaration of the King and Queen has since been carried into execution and you will recieve inclosed the one and the other. With respect to that part which relates to the appointing a governor for the Dauphin, some dispositions were made yesterday and among others it was determined that the members of the assembly should be ineligible. This proceeds from the jealousy which has always reigned among the members of the several parties and from a desire to please those out of doors. – The Duke de la Rochefoucauld would have been certainly appointed though he had with much propriety determined to refuse it. It is highly probable at present that it will be M. de Condorcet. The Marquis de la fayette begun his new function of the King's keeper immediately on his return to Paris. He postpones asking the assembly to particularize their decree so as that he may have only to follow precise instructions with respect to this custody; for which he is blamed by some of his friends. On the whole his post becomes every day more untenable. He is too generous to act with respect to the King and Queen as the people of Paris exact. This confirms the popular opinion of his connivance with them for which he is publicly denounced in a number of clubs and journals. In the mean time the necessity of a vigilant guard forces him to do many things which present him in the most insupportable and tyrannical posture both to the King and Queen and even to a great number of the patriotic part of the assembly. It seems impossible under these circumstances that he should be long without losing the attachment of both parties and the confidence of the people.

The assembly are daily recieving addresses from all quarters of the Kingdom and from all orders civil and military. Most of these were written before the King's arrestation was known and are in a style alarmingly republican. It is this circumstance which contributed to induce the assembly, of which a majority are decidedly for supporting the shadow of monarchy, to suspend the election of their successors. The electors, in a neighbouring department had been chosen. They immediately sent a deputation to the assembly to inform them of this circumstance and to express their obedience to the assembly particularly with respect to the suspension of the elections. This example will probably be followed by most of the departments in the first instance, as in such cases men naturally follow one another; but I doubt whether it will last long. It seems clear to me that a great opposition is forming in the spirit of the people without, to that of the members within, the assembly. The latter as I have said wish to support the form of a monarchy. The former are becoming every day under the influence of their clubs, leaders and journals, more and more averse both to the substance and form. You may judge of the spirit of the people of Paris who have much influence on those of the provinces, from the popular journals which you will recieve by the way of Havre together with the usual papers. – These journals are hawked about the streets, cried in every quarter of Paris and sold cheap or given to the people who devour them with astonishing avidity. Should this spirit propagate itself as seems certain, the present assembly will be obliged to abandon the helm. They are already denounced by these journals as being sold to the court, as forging the addresses from the provinces (this you know is a reproach which has been long made to them by the aristocrats and often with reason) approbatory of their present proceedings. The most popular members are accused of wishing to reestablish despotic government in the person of the monarch, whose usual epithet is now *Louis le faux* or *Louis le parjure*. Depositions are printed as having been taken from people who have a perfect knowlege of the Marquis de la fayette and M. Bouillé having favored the King's escape, and having endeavoured to escape themselves. A thousand such extravagances repeated every day cannot fail in the end to produce an effect on the minds of the people. The Queen's declaration seems to inculpate the Marquis as she says they passed through a door which he had informed the assembly had been particularly guarded that night, as information had been given that they were to pass there. Some think still that they went through another passage for which false keys were made. If so it is probably with a design to injure the Marquis that the contrary is asserted. In addition to this his insisting on the King's being allowed to go to St. Cloud, and resigning because the guard refused to obey him in it, and his connexion with and responsibility having always taken on him to answer for M. de Bouillé, are constantly quoted in proof.

It is now known that he was the chief of the plan for the King's leaving Paris and had given orders for arranging the troops under his command so as to secure his journey to, and stay at, Montmedi. The troops were not in the secret, but it was thought that the presence of their sovereign would insure their fidelity. Many suppose also that an Austrian garrison for greater security would have been marched to Montmedi which is in the neighbourhood of Luxemburg.

As yet nothing is known of the effect which the King's arrestation has produced abroad. The present uncertain state of politics among the principal European States leaves it impossible to conjecture whether any or what measures will be adopted in consequence of it. If they act separately their interference will produce no effect, and it would seem little probable that powers who have all the appearance of being at the eve of hostilities among themselves could act in concert.

The negotiations at Sistovic still continue but give little hopes of a speedy reconciliation. The Emperor gives symptoms by the disposition of his troops, of expecting to renew the war with the Turk. The Empress redoubles her preparations in the Baltic and speaks in a tone correspondent to the respectable state of defense she has prepared. G. Britain continues her naval equipments and it is said is only now waiting for the return of an express from Petersburg in order to take decisive measures. All the symptoms indicate that the fleet is to go into the Baltic. Still I am told that there has been a much greater rise on the Mediterranean than the Baltic insurance. This circumstance astonishes a good deal here and is considered as inexplicable from any of M. de la Luzerne's letters.

The person sent by the King to the Prince de Condé with the decree of the assembly injoining his return, writes that he was at Worms the 22d., that he had been well recieved, and was to follow the Prince to Coblentz where he is to have his answer. Numbers of French refugees and all the Princes are assembled in that quarter. Their inveteracy against the present order of things is as great as it can be, but it does not appear that they have any well grounded hopes of being supported from abroad and it is certain they have no means of doing any thing of themselves.

Simolin has exempted himself from all suspicion in the affair of the passeport by a letter written to M. de Montmorin and published in the journals. It appears that the person for whom he asked it was really a Russian, and by strategem induced him to obtain a duplicate which was given to the King.

The assembly have passed a decree prohibiting any person's leaving the Kingdom without a passeport. Foreigners are to recieve it from their respective ministers; citizens, from the municipalities. In both cases the *signalement* of the several persons is to be expressed in the passeport.

I omitted in my last inclosing you a copy of my answer to M. de Montmorin. Several of the corps diplomatique, and particularly the Spanish Ambassador told me they intended answering it somewhat in that style. I have not heard any thing for a long time from Carmichael. I will inform you in a letter I shall write by the way of Havre of a conversation I had with Reyneval on the subject of your letter of March 19. Things relative thereto remain as when I last wrote to you.

You will recieve also inclosed a letter for the Secretary of the treasury and a copy of my No. 69. This letter will go by the English Packet.

I mentioned in my No. 70. that I had seen Drost, that he hopes he shall be able to comply with your wishes in going to America, but that he is certain it cannot be before next spring, that in the mean time he would have the proper instruments made here and could give directions for the buildings to be erected before his arrival so as to lose no time, that he thinks it would be best to have four presses made, but that two would do for the present, that they will cost about 22,000 ₶ each, that he will undertake to teach the art of assaying to any person you may designate, and finally that he was to determine in a fortnight whether he would engage to go. I am with the sentiments of attachment & affection, of which I hope you are well persuaded, my dear Sir, your friend and servant,

W. SHORT

P.S. In your letter of March 15. you observe that the papers had not been recieved from my secretary as I expected during my absence. They were certainly regularly sent, and I hope will have been recieved with time. You add that nothing had been addressed to him, his name being unknown to you. I did not suppose it necessary to give you his name for the purpose of your addressing any thing to him, as my absence being for three months only it was certain that I should be back before any letter from you addressed to him could arrive. I have always forgotten to give this explanation in my letters written since the reciept of.yours of March 15.

PrC (DLC: Short Papers); at head of text: "No.71."; at foot of text: "Thomas Jefferson Secretary of State Philadelphia." Tr (DNA: RG 59, DD). Recorded in SJL as received 23 Aug. 1791.

From Sylvanus Bourne

Cape François, 30 June 1791. He has not been favored by any communication from TJ since his of 27 Apr. After more than three months he has not been officially received, despite his "arguments . . . drawn from the tenor of explicit compact, and conveyed in firm but cool language." They reply that they have never been officially notified of the Consular Convention, it cannot be registered, and of course they are not bound by it. But this is specious: the real motives are "less honourable and such as never ought to have influence in public Councils." The fact is that admiralty and customs officers say they would lose many fees under the Convention that they now enjoy, while those who execute the *droit d'aubaine* would lose "their future chances of pillaging our Countrymen under the sanction of an *infamous* Statute . . . a disgrace to any civilized Country and more especially one which boasts of strides to freedom and clear perception in the simple relative rights of Men."

This law applied in case of a Mr. Myers of Aux Cayes, mentioned in his last. He has since received a letter from George Saunderson, a reputable American merchant there, dated 21 Apr. 1791, in response to his of the 14th asking information of the case. Saunderson says that Myers died intestate on the 5th, with none of his friends or relatives present; that, though he supposed the *droits d'aubaine* annihilated by the change in government, the officers "in *my* absence and that of many other Americans" affixed their seals, inventoried the effects, and disposed of them by auction on the 20th. On receiving this news Bourne discussed the question with the Governor General, who has written to his government about promulgation of the Convention. Bourne pointed out to him that treaties were the supreme law of the land and that their promulgation by royal proclamation gave them immediate effect throughout the kingdom which all officers were bound to obey, otherwise certain branches of government, acting on their particular interests, might nullify their effect, as had been done in some provinces of France that had refused to register royal edicts. To this he received "no satisfactory reply."

Though he is thus placed in "so painful a situation, yet in no one instance have they shewn me that attention which might evidence the truth of their assertion [of regret at not receiving the Convention] or tend to meliorate the effects of that neglect." Divesting himself "of every degree of personal chagrin of resentment," he nevertheless points out that "the flagrant breaches of Treaty" in respect to the *droit d'aubaine*, of such importance to American commercial interests, and to the treatment of American consuls in the West Indies would "not fail to meet the pointed notice of the Government of the U.S." All else proving ineffectual to obtain official recognition, he awaits the arrival of the *commissaires* from the National Assembly, who are said to have power to decide. He doubts this, for those lately arrived at Martinique have recognized Skipwith, but he embarks for America. Even if he is received, he doubts whether he can remain, "as the Government of the U.S. neglect . . . support of their Consular Establishment" and do not guarantee by law funds necessary.

Even if received the day he arrived, he doubts whether he could have obtained clearance data desired by TJ. Several captains have told him they were not bound to report clearances to him, there being no law requiring it. American sailors in distress have appealed to him for relief here or conveyance home. As to former, motives of humanity led him to aid them, "tho without any promise of reimbursement from my Government." As to latter, his appeals to captains "have been treated with contempt and some times insult." His commission, then, brings him "pain and chagrin in lieu of honour or Reward." Contrary to arguments of "those Gentlemen in Congress who are opposed to granting any compensation to our Consuls," the captains trading there think it incompatible with his official duty to engage in trade and have expressed surprise, on learning the fact, that consuls get neither fees nor salary. They acknowledge that consuls "placed . . . on proper principles" in foreign ports would save more than the cost of their support "by checks on the impositions of the lower officers in the customs." But lest he be thought biased, he will say no more.

He has reports of several Chambers of Commerce requested by National Assembly. If adopted, these will circumscribe American trade "as they seem to take very critically the principles of the British navigation acts and support the idea of an exclusive monopoly to the Mother country of the trade with the Colonies." He will try his private establishment for two or three months longer, seeing "no grounds to prop my reliance on any specific support from my Government." If he does not succeed, he must quit the country as the expenses are enormous and "the climate such as to require a valuable object . . . to justify one in a constant risque of health," returning to America to deliver to the President a commission he sees no prospect of "retaining with personal reputation or public advantage." [P.S.] He apologizes for "a few interlines in this espistle": being ill it pains him to copy it. He hopes he will have "soon the honour of an answer."

RC (DNA: RG 59, CD); endorsed by TJ as received 16 July 1791 and so recorded in SJL.

From Tench Coxe

[Philadelphia], *30 June 1791*. Enclosing "some notes on the Portuguese regulations" based on reliable sources and according with his own previous knowledge and the "known spirit of the Portuguese commercial System." He will furnish a similar paper on the other cases, meanwhile adding summary data on the Swedish subject.

Their West India trade (at St. Bartholomew's) as free as possible, all sorts of goods importable and exportable in all sorts of vessels at trifling duty, thought to be $\frac{1}{4}$%. Tobacco duties $\frac{1}{3}$ higher into Sweden in foreign than Swedish vessels. Cod and pickled fish, not wanted from abroad, could not be admitted, nor biscuit. Grain, rice, flour admitted on moderate duties, so also beef and pork in casks, of which a good deal is imported from Ireland. Oak timber the only article of lumber admitted, except masts. Potash and pearlash made there in great quantities, no demand for foreign and none admitted. Duty on indigo moderate, on tobacco considerable. "Oil of *whales* admitted. The East India Trade a monopoly . . . no foreign ships can introduce India articles." All foreign manufactures prohibited even in Swedish ships, but large quantities are introduced in their freeport Mastrandt and the Danish freeport Elsinore. Only about 12 or 1500 tierces of rice of 5 Cwt. each required, consumption being confined to affluent families. Naval stores and flaxseed neither wanted nor admitted. Demand for tobacco said to be 12,000 hhds.

"Foreign built ships prohibited to be made free bottoms, but for the recovery of debts, after sale for insufficiency, and repair &c. by which means some collusive naturalizations of them are effected. All foreigners Vessels are on the same footing. – Lord Sheffield on the proposed corn law will be found in this enclosure, as also the return of exports at large, and in the rough state a fair copy not being in the office. It will be perceived from this document that large contraband importations from the U. S. into foreign Countries take place."

RC (DLC); endorsed by TJ. Not recorded in SJL. Enclosure: "Notes of the commercial and navigating regulations of the Kingdom of Portugal and its dominions, which affect the exports, imports, and vessels of the United States" (undated MS in DLC: Jefferson Papers, 65: f.11309-12, with erroneous attribution of date [19? July 1791]).

To Richard Peters

June 30. 1791.

I should sooner have answered your kind note, my dear Sir, but that I had hoped to meet you the day before yesterday, and to tell you vivâ voce that, even without that, I meant to be troublesome to you in my afternoon excursions: that being the part of the day which business and long habit have allotted to exercise with me. I shall certainly feel often enough the inducements to Belmont, among the chief of which will be your society and the desire of becoming acquainted with Mrs. Peters. Call on me, in your turn, whenever you come to town: and if it should be about the hour of three, I shall rejoice the more. You will find a bad dinner, a good glass of wine, and a host thankful for your favor, and desirous of encouraging repetitions of it without number, form or ceremony. When Madison returns you will often find him here without notice and always with it: and if you complain again of not seeing him, it will be that the place of rendezvous does not enjoy your favour. He is at present in New York, undecided as to his next movement. Adieu. Your affectionate friend & servt,   TH: JEFFERSON

RC (PHi); addressed: "Honble Richard Peters, at Belmont"; endorsed by Peters, probably much later: "Friendly Note from Mr. Jefferson, with whom and Mr. Madison I had long been in Habits of Friendship." Not recorded in SJL.

From Tench Coxe

[ca. June 1791]

Mr. Coxe has the honor to enclose to Mr. Jefferson a state of the exports of Sugar, coffee, cocoa and Cotton from Surinam for 1787, and some smaller articles for other years. None of these articles can be shipt elsewhere than to Europe, nor in any other than Dutch bottoms.

A Dutch Merchant having informed Mr. Coxe that he has furnished Mr. Fitzsimmons with the Dutch account of Duties for Mr. Jefferson they are omitted to be noticed here.

East India goods (except Spices) can yet be shipt to Holland from the United States but this it is expected will very soon be altered.

American built Ships can be bought and employed as Dutch Ships, except in the *Fisheries*, *East India Trade*, and *West India Trade*, about which there is some uncertainty.[1]

All foreigners are prohibited at the Dutch East India settlements, beyond *Good Hope*, into which port all are admitted.

All kinds of meal are prohibited to be imported into Holland, all other goods are admitted on low duties, spices (and I suspect fish) excepted.

All kinds of goods may be shipt from Holland.

No distinction is made between foreign ships. Nor any between native and foreign except in the East India Trade, fisheries and West India Trade.

RC (DLC); in clerk's hand; endorsed by TJ: "Mr. Coxe, Dutch" and "Holland, Surinam." Not recorded in SJL. Dft (PHi: Coxe Papers), with some slight variations (see note 1). Enclosure: Tabular "State of the Exports from the Colony of Surinam" showing some few items (such as indigo, tobacco, wax, and "Bois de Lettre") for various years from 1722 to 1763, but principally the following for the year 1787:

15,744 hhds. of sugar; 12,129,756 pounds of coffee; 802,724 pounds of cacao; and 925,967 pounds of cotton (MS in clerk's hand in DLC). The 1787 figures were interlined by Coxe in Dft underneath the appropriate articles.

[1] The last clause was added after the letter was first written.

From David Humphreys

Lisbon, 1 July 1791. Enclosing his account, as requested in TJ's of 15 Mch. He wrote Willink, Van Staphorst & Hubbard to ask if they had received orders to pay him the sums stated in that letter, but has had no reply and has not drawn the whole due him, not needing remainder until furniture ordered from England arrives. He has not been able to state amount of postage with precision, but it is not considerable and he has not charged it as contingent expenses nor claimed it in his public account. He wishes to know if *etrennes* fall "in that predicament" to any specific amount. He understands Franklin charged them, and Carmichael says Adams wrote that he should do the same. "A liberality in that Article, beyond what the Salary . . . will conveniently allow, may, perhaps, not be without its use. – But of this you are a much more competent judge than I can pretend to be."

He has ordered newspapers sent from different countries to him, to be forwarded to "the Office of foreign Affairs" and charged to the public. None as yet has arrived. P.S. Three days ago he received TJ's of 2 May introducing Wilcock and will pay attention to its subject.

RC (DNA: RG 59, DD); at head of text: "(No. 23)"; endorsed by TJ as received 22 Sep. 1791 and so recorded in SJL. Tr (same).

From George Skene Keith

"Keith hall," Scotland, 1 July 1791. He is sending "a small publication" which he hopes TJ will accept, concerning "an universal Equalization of Weights Measures and Coins. And if I thought any man in America had bestowed more Labour on this than I have done I should not have given you this trouble."

As for TJ's proposed rod pendulum vibrating seconds as the standard, he surely knows that "the *Length of pendulum*," always measured from the point of suspension to the center of oscillation and supposed to have neither breadth nor weight, is about 39.13 inches and "the same either in the ball pendulum or Rod pendulum which I prefer."

"The System which I propose was founded upon a discovery, which astonished myself when I first made it. A cubic vessel whose side is equal to the seconds pendulum, holds *almost exacly a Tun* of distilled water of 60° heat, Amsterdam weight. This I proposed to divide decimally. Other advantages you will see in the pamphlet. – If you, or any Gentleman from N. America, choose to correspond with me, my address is – The Reverend Geo: Skene Keith Minr. of Keith hall by Aberdeen N. Britain."

RC (MWA); endorsed by TJ as received 4 Apr. 1792 and so recorded in SJL.

From James Madison

New York, 1 July 1791. He received TJ's of the 28th yesterday and this morning obtained from Col. Smith the pamphlet and map, here enclosed, the former to be kept and the latter returned as it is the last copy. As to the map of South America, he says it was obtained "from the engraver by Pitt and Grenville during the squabble with Spain, and remained in their hands for that period as the best geographical information to be had; that it has since been returned to him according to promise, is about ⅔ engraved, and will probably be out this fall."

He encloses letter from Le Havre with account of the price of tobacco which TJ may not have seen "and which it may not be amiss for Leiper to see."

He has been somewhat indisposed for several days, with a fever and pretty "decided symptoms of bile," confining him to the house but not to his room. He is now better, especially at being relieved "from a nausea and irritation in the stomach . . . the more disagreeable as they threatened a more serious attack." Though he still has a slight fever and loss of appetite, he hopes the cause is fugitive and the effects going off. His horse seems out of danger, but has much flesh to regain. He sends "a little of the true guinea corn from Jamaica where it forms a great proportion of the food of the Slaves. It grows on the top of the Stalk like broom Corn, and in a figure not unlike a bunch of Sumac berries. This the first time I have seen the grain, tho' it may be familiar to you. The small-eared corn which I have seen in Virginia under the same name is a very different thing. Yrs. mo: affecly."

RC (DLC: Madison Papers); date added to endorsement by Madison later when letter was returned to him; endorsed by TJ as received 6 July 1791 and so recorded in SJL.

From Daniel Carroll

Georgetown, 2 July 1791. Mr. Wederstrandt, whose enclosed letter solicits consulship in Isle of France for his son, is a native of France who came to Maryland before the Revolution, married into a very respectable Eastern Shore family, was employed by the state or Congress during the war, and has "a very fair Character." The young gentleman is not yet of age but will be soon after Congress meets. He served apprenticeship with Messrs. Zacharie Coopman & Co., merchants of character in Baltimore. He may be the bearer of this letter, and TJ will make use of it with the President as he "may see occasion."

RC (DLC: Washington Papers); endorsed by TJ as received 13 July 1791 and so recorded in SJL. Enclosures: (1) Wederstrandt to Carroll, 27 June 1791, asking him to recommend his son to the Secretary of State and permit him to deliver the letter himself; (2) Zacharie Coopman & Co. to Wederstrandt, 20 June 1791 (enclosed in the foregoing), stating the apprentice served with irreproachable fidelity for five years and displayed assiduity in business, docility of temper, and good character (same).

The father, Conrad T. Wederstrandt, was not employed by Congress but served as commissary of purchases for Maryland during the war (JCC, XIX, 179). The French consul in Baltimore, Charles François D'Anmours, also gave young Wederstrandt a letter of introduction and recommendation to TJ, saying that he had known him since infancy and that he had deserved the applause and esteem of all acquainted with him (D'Anmours to TJ, 8 July 1791, RC in DLC: Washington Papers; endorsed by TJ as received 13 July 1791 and so recorded in SJL). Young Wederstrandt did not get the appointment.

From Joshua Johnson

London, 2 July 1791. His last, 31 May, went by Sterett on New York packet. On 29th ult. he received TJ's two letters of 13 May; those enclosed have been delivered. To his other he will reply in a few days, "tho' . . . I must confess that I began to consider your silence, neglect; or that my communications were not worth attention." But, doubts removed, he informs TJ that Thomas Walpole, minister to the Palatine Elector, was offered appointment of minister to U.S. but, on advice of friends, declined it. George Hammond, late secretary to Lord St. Helens, ambassador to Spain, "was appointed two or three days ago, and I understand, is to go out very soon." TJ may know something of him: "he is the son of Mr. Hammond of Hull, and was with David Hartley. Esq., when he was sent to negotiate with the American Commissioners at Paris; I know nothing of his Character, or abilities, more than that I hear he is a heavy man."

Preparations for war are still going on, "and the trouble, and Vexation I have had with our Seamen &ca. is infinite beyond any conception. Notwithstanding all this, many think it will end in nothing." He would write fuller, but is pressed by the captain.

Dupl (DNA: RG 59, CD); at head of text: "The original ⅌ the London Packet, Capt Fohey, via Baltimore." Recorded in SJL as received 2 Oct. 1791. FC (same).

Johnson refers to TJ's two letters of 13 May 1791, but only one of that date is recorded in SJL, and only one has been found. Since Johnson mentions enclosures in one of the two letters, the second must have been a covering note asking him to forward the consular instructions to others, such as Knox, Maury, Church, and Auldjo.

To Alexander Martin

Sir   Philadelphia July 2. 1791.

I recieved yesterday the letters of May 10. and 20. with which your Excellency was pleased to honour me, and have to return you my thanks for your attention to my request relative to the lands of the U. S. and to express the gratification it will be to me to recieve at an early day the information you have been pleased to direct from the Secretary of your state and from Colo. Armstrong.

On the 26th. of January last I had the honor of writing to your Excellency a letter of which the inclosed is a copy and at the same time two copies of the laws of the first session of Congress were forwarded on to you, as you will see by the inclosed note from the Chief clerk of my office, who made up the dispatch. I now inclose another copy, and deliver it to the gentleman who was the bearer of your letter, and who undertakes to find a safe conveyance. I hope it will be more fortunate in it's passage than the former copies have been. I have the honour to be with great respect Your Excellency's most obedt. & most humble servt., TH: JEFFERSON

PrC (DLC). FC (DNA: RG 360, PCC No. 120). Listed in SJL as written 1 July 1791, no doubt erroneously, for on the same date the letters of Martin received YESTERDAY are recorded. Martin's letters have not been found.

From Henry Lee

DEAR SIR   Philada. July 3d. 91

The preservation of the relative importance of Virginia among her sister states must be held highly consequential to her future interests, whether fate shall allot to America undisturbed felicity, or difficultys dangers and vicissitudes.

The idea you suggested relative to a purchase of a tract of land contiguous to Lake Erie and Beaver creek is certainly worthy of every consideration, and if executable ought to be done for public purposes without loss of time. — I have since I saw you continued my enquirys on the subject and find that my memory was right as to the reservation of soil by the State of connecticut of a large tract of country south of the Pensylvania line, lying on lake Erie and passing down the lake below the mouth of Cayohoga. I have seen a sale by deed from the State of Connecticut of 4000 acres of this land adjoining and comprehending the Salt Springs on Beaver creek.

By referring to the Journals of Congress for the year 86 I think the act of cession made by the State of Connecticut will be found, which will give every requisite information on this point. Since the assumption of the State debts, the object for which this reservation was made, ceases, and the State will probably sell their lands with facility for a lower price than was originally contemplated.

Mr. Wadsworth who is one of the partners with Mr. Morris in the purchase from Massachusetts has turned his views to this object and waits [only] for the meeting of the Legislature to enter into treaty for a part or all of the reserved lands. I understand only the first mentioned tract of 4000 acres has yet been sold. From the statement it seems obvious, that measures ought to be taken expeditiously with or without the concurrence of Mr. Wadsworth to secure the object necessary to our country, or it may be irrevocably lost.

If I determine to accompany Mr. Madison to Boston, I will pass thro Connecticut and avail myself of every information within my reach and do any thing else which may be advised to accomplish this business.

In the mean time you will have it in your power to consider the intelligence now given, to compare it with the act of cession, and to furnish me with such remarks as may result from your farther investigation of the matter when your leisure will permit. – I have the honor to be sir with great respect your h: ser, HENRY LEE

RC (DLC); addressed: "The Honl. Mr. Jefferson Secretary of State"; endorsed by TJ as received 3 July 1791 and so recorded in SJL.

From John Carey

[Philadelphia], *"Monday, July 4 [1791], No..96, South Street."* Apologizes for trouble given him about Irenæus and is mortified to discover his mistake. Mr. Crawford, who purchased the book, has positively assured him he mentioned Justin Martyr, not Irenæus, though, as TJ had already bought one of the two copies of Justin Martyr, he "cannot possibly account for the error."

Having yesterday taken up *Notes on Virginia* and had his "imagination so hurried away by the united streams of Shenandoah and Patowmac, bursting forth at your command, as at the touch of Moses' rod, and forcing their way through opposing mountains," he lost sight of every consideration pointing out impropriety of asking TJ's attention to a trifling plan which some would think useless and others impracticable. But he hopes "the philosophic writer of the Notes on Virginia will excuse me for hazarding an idea, even though it should, upon investigation, prove erroneous – and for venturing to address it to *Him*, in preference to men less capable of deciding on its merit."

To keep the legislative body comfortably warm in winter presents no great difficulty. But in summer it would perhaps be desirable to keep them comfortably cool, especially if not expensive or troublesome. "Now Saltpetre is universally known to be a very powerful refrigerant: and Saltpetre will, no doubt, be among the military stores, of which government must constantly have an adequate provision. Suppose, then, that under the Rooms, which are to be erected, for . . . Congress, on the banks of Patowmac, space sufficient were allowed (without descending to the damp) for Magazines of Saltpetre. Communications, between these and the Rooms of Congress, might be easily contrived in a variety of modes, so as not to hurt the eye, by disfiguring the appearance of the latter. Tubes or Trunks might be fastened to the apertures underneath, and the lower end of each either lodged in a heap of the Saltpetre, or as near to it, as would be consistent with the free circulation of the air. In this case, if the windows of the rooms above were kept close shut, to exclude the warm air of the surrounding atmosphere, any accession of air, to that already contained in the rooms, must come directly through the Saltpetre, cool and fresh, and purified (I would suppose) from many of those noxious particles, of which the frost happily rids us every winter.

"In the ceiling, an opening will, no doubt, be left, for the purpose of ventilating the Rooms of Congress. Suppose, however, it were thought advisable to aid the ordinary ascensive motion of the warm air, and consequently the influx of cool air from the Saltpetre-rooms, Quære, whether — (ridiculous as the idea may, at first sight, appear to some people) — the force of fire might not be made subservient to this end? The effects of fire upon air, and (if I may be allowed to coin a new expression) the *ignipetal* force of the latter, are too well known, to need a demonstration. Suppose, then, that, over the aperture for ventilating the Room, there were contrived, in the roof or dome of the house, a funnel of proper dimensions, in which a stove should be placed, at such distance from the ventilator, as to attract the air through *it*, rather than from any other part: this stove might be kept constantly heated during the sitting of Congress in warm weather; and would thus accelerate the circulation of the whole volume of air, between the Saltpetre-rooms and the roof."

He does not know how far it would be necessary to establish the height at which outside air should be introduced to the saltpeter area, but this could be determined by experiment, with "trunks run up (in a Northern aspect) along the walls, or funnels left open in the masonry)." Not being versed in natural philosophy, he cannot vouch for the practicability of the plan or say how far it will admit useful improvements. "With doubt and hesitation, therefore, I beg leave to present it to a philosopher, as I would present a rough stone to a skillful statuary, who can at once decide whether it is susceptible of a polish — and, if it be, can call forth, from the rude mass, a twin sister to the Medicean Venus, or a younger brother to the Apollo of Belvedere."

RC (MHi); endorsed by TJ as received 4 July 1791 and so recorded in SJL.

A copy of Justin Martyr's *Opera* (Paris, 1636) is in the Library of Congress and bears the signature of John Carey. It was probably the copy under discussion here (see Sowerby, No. 1581). If TJ responded to Carey's interesting suggestion about air-conditioning the halls of Congress, the fact is not of record.

To John Dobson

SIR   Philada. July 4. 1791.

A bond of mine for £500. sterl. part of Mr. Wayles's debt to Farrell & Jones being payable the 19th. inst. and being come to your hands, it is necessary for me to give you the following information. These bonds were subject to written conditions expressed in articles of the same date with the bonds. One of these provided that Mr. Hanson should receive and collect the bonds for which we should sell property, and not demand the money from us unless the obligors should prove insolvent. In the mean time we were to apply the profits of our estates as they should arise towards the discharge of the earliest bonds. In November last I informed Mr. Hanson that according to the best judgment which could then be formed of my crop of that year, I should have 55,000 ℔. of good tobo. and 14,000 ℔. of indifferent to apply to the payment of my bond of this year to him, and of another to another person of which he knew. In another letter of April I informed him that the low price of tobo. in Virginia had induced me to order my good tobo. here and to sell it here: but that as they made a difference of 5/ between new and old tobo. and would consider none as old till the month of September, I had been obliged to give credit to the end of that month, and consequently to delay his payment between 2. and 3 months in order to enlarge it. This was to the interest of his principal as well as myself. He informed me in answer that he had assigned my bond to you, which is the cause of my troubling you with the communication of what had passed between him and me. I have reason to expect as much tobo. will come here as I had notified him of: but I fear, from a letter received from Colo. Lewis, mentioning some expences which had occurred and on which he had not calculated, that perhaps he may have been obliged to apply a part, if not all, of the 14,000 ℔. to other purposes. As I shall be with him in September I shall then be able to concert with him the quickest means we can find of making up the deficiency which the payment from hence will leave, either from the 14,000 ℔. of tobo. beforementioned or from the resources furnished by the present year. I shall be glad, between this and October, to know from you whether I can make payment to any person here for you, and whether you will recieve money at the current exchange, or must have a bill. The former would be most agreeable to me. I am Sir Your very humble servt,

Th: Jefferson

PrC (CSmH).

From Jonathan Edwards

New Haven, 4 July 1791. In April or May last he sent two books of his father, the copyright to which he claims as proprietor, and requested a certificate. Receiving none, he concludes either that he had omitted some step or that this had escaped notice among more important objects. "If the former be the fact, will you kindly inform me in a line, what the omission is? If the latter, you will pardon me, that I have refreshed your memory. That may be very important to me, which is of no consequence to others." He desires the certificate to show that the books were deposited at the time received, "as that if I understand the law, is an important circumstance."

RC (DNA: RG 59, MLR); endorsed by TJ as received 9 July 1791 and so recorded in SJL.

In the summer of 1790 Jonathan Edwards (1745-1801), son of the famous theologian and metaphysician, had sent TJ a copy of his *The salvation of all men strictly examined* (New Haven, 1790) to be registered for copyright and had asked for certification of the fact if this were necessary (Edwards to TJ, 9 Aug. 1790; RC in DNA: RG 59, MLR, not recorded in SJL). In April 1791 he sent two books "the copyright of which I claim as *proprietor*, having published them from the manuscripts of the authour: and I request a certificate, that I have . . . deposited them in your office" (Edwards to TJ, 26 Apr. 1791; RC in same, not recorded in SJL). These works, as indicated in the above letter, were those of his father. Their titles were *True grace distinguished* (Elizabethtown, 1791) and *Two dissertations* (Philadelphia, 1791). Edwards could scarcely have avoided knowing that TJ had passed through Connecticut a short while before this letter was written, a fact which may give added mean-ing to his allusion to those "more important objects" which might have caused his request to escape notice. TJ closed the correspondence with his response of 14 July 1791. He could never have found Edwards philosophically congenial, but he was much interested in and acquired a copy of Edwards' *Observations on the language of the Muhhekaneew Indians* (New Haven, 1788). On the basis of his own youthful experience among the Mohican Indians, Edwards compiled a comparative vocabulary of the Mohican, Shawanee, and Chippewa languages, much as TJ had caused to be done with many other tribes. Edwards' *Observations* attempted to show the extent of the Mohican language in North America, to trace its grammatical nature, and to point out "some of its peculiarities, and some instances of Analogy between that and the Hebrew" (Sowerby, No. 4050).

From Eliphalet Pearson

SIR   Cambridge, 4th July, 1791.

The American Academy of Arts and Sciences has directed me to present each corresponding society, and each of its own members, not resident in this State, a copy of Judge Lowell's Eulogy on its late worthy President, which I have now the honor to transmit. With sentiments of due respect, I am, Sir, Your most obedient, humble servant,   ELIPHALET PEARSON

RC (DLC); printed, signed by Pearson as Corresponding Secretary; endorsed by TJ as received 22 Oct. 1791 and so recorded in SJL. Enclosure: *An eulogy, on the honourable James Bowdoin, Esq. L.L.D. late President of the American Academy of Arts and Sciences. Who died at Boston, November 6, A.D. 1790. Delivered before the Society, January 26, 1791, by John Lowell* . . . (Boston, 1791; see Sowerby, No. 521, for a description of the copy enclosed).

TJ received the *Eulogy* as a member of the Academy, having been elected in 1787 when Bowdoin was President (see Willard to TJ, 16 Jan. 1790).

From Elias Porter

Baltimore, 4 July 1791. As a stranger, he apologizes for delay in sending a letter from London by brig *Minerva*, being mislaid "or it certainly would bin sent . . . before." – He saw Humphreys in Lisbon in Dec. on his way to Madrid. He received a small packet of letters from him to TJ, which he gave to Capt.

Steavens at Cadiz, "bound to Philadelphia, being bound My self to London in the Schooner Federalist which I have sense had the Misfortune to lose on the Coast of England."

RC (DNA: RG 59, MLR); endorsed by TJ as received 6 July 1791 and so recorded in SJL. The letter sent by *Minerva* has not been identified. Those sent from Cadiz were Humphreys' dispatches of 14 and 28 Oct. and 19 and 30 Nov. 1790, all received on 11 Feb. 1791.

To Burrill Carnes

SIR   Philadelphia July 5. 1791.

The bearer hereof Thomas Newell, a citizen of the United States of America, having occasion to sollicit justice before the tribunals of France within your Consulate, I take the liberty of recommending him to your patronage and attention so far as the justice of his case shall authorize. I have the honour to be Sir your very humble servt.,

TH: JEFFERSON

PrC (DLC); at foot of text: "Mr. Burrell Carnes. Consul at Nantes." Recorded in SJL as "for Capt. Newell." FC (DNA: RG 59, DCI).

From Stephen Cathalan, Jr.

Marseilles, 5 July 1791. He wrote on 10th of June by a vessel for New York. This goes by one direct for Philadelphia and is only to convey a letter from Captain Richard O'Bryen which will inform TJ of the situation of the captives in Algiers better than he could. He awaits TJ's orders on that business and will not go further until he answers his letter of [22] Jan.

He hopes that the olive trees will succeed in Carolina. The parcel of 197 hhds. of tobacco mentioned in his of 20 [*i.e.,* 23] May sold at about £45.₶ per quintal. Little remains unsold. The first arrivals will find ready sales and good prices. No American wheat or flour has arrived. Wheat would bring £35₶ to 36.₶ and flour 38. ₶ France has been in a crisis on account of the flight of the King and his family. There were no fatal accidents on his return because of the good measures taken by Lafayette. What turn events will take God knows! Foreign powers may interpose if a total change in the form of government should be adopted. Meanwhile, foreign envoys have declared to Montmorin that they could no longer correspond with him until they receive orders from their courts.

He is yet without news from William Short. He has performed sundry legal acts for merchants of Marseilles who have business in the United States, doing this "*Gratis,* till the Law will be established for Perquisites of the Consular offices." [P.S.] He hopes all parties will save the kingdom from total ruin by "a Sincere reunion of hearths to a Single Sprit."

RC (DNA: RG 59, CD). Recorded in SJL as received 22 Sep. 1791. Enclosure: "Abstract of a Letter from Capn. Richd. Obrien to Stephen Cathalan, Junr. at Marseilles," dated "City of Bondage" 11 June 1791, acknowledging his of the 5th and assuring him that the Regency would never abate the price asked for their release, since it required slaves to build and fit out its cruisers; that the efforts of Lamb and others were known to be under the authority of Congress, hence the plain question to be faced is for that body or its envoys to declare that the price of 17,225 sequins is too great and the captives will not be redeemed on such terms, since this is the manner of the Algerines' dealings with all nations; that he hoped "to the Almighty God that an answer will be given, either Liberty or Bondage, not to keep us in this state of suspence," this being the sixth year of their captivity, during which time Congress has been kept fully informed of their situation; that he fears the favorable opportunity Congress had to make peace with the Regency has been almost irrevocably lost; that the sum asked for their release is not high considering the current price of slaves; and that no business could be done with the Regency without bribing the ministry. O'Bryen thanked Cathalan for his offers to help, but assured him that even the most miserable of the slaves would view this as a confirmation of a longer captivity and might "perhaps be the means through an abyss of Dispair and Grief of making some of us try to get clear of a Life which seems to be a Burthen of Torment." He concluded by assuring Cathalan that anything he wrote would be kept as a profound secret and that any light he could shed on the subject of their ransom would be gratefully received, "Particularly what may be the answer of Congress to the enquiries of Monsr. Paret," since all depended on that important response (Tr in DNA: RG 59, CD; attested by Cathalan with the seal of the consulate attached on 4 July 1791, from "the original . . . in the Chancelary of the Consulate").

From Seth Jenkins

Hudson, 5 July 1791. Acknowledging TJ's of 21 June about cost of "low Wines" in southern France. If "that heavy Duty was out of the way," they might serve a good purpose. But at present they "cannot answer for Distilling in this Country."

He has carefully read TJ's report and "I find your information to be so good that I can bear no light on the . . . Whale and Cod fisheries." His best information from Nantucket is that they will carry their whale fisheries to France as they have [added] five new ships to their fleet this year from 200 to 240 tons. "I think . . . this cannot support them in the now situation of the business."

RC (MHi); endorsed by TJ as received 12 July 1791 and so recorded in SJL.

From Alexander Donald

London, 6 July 1791. Acknowledging TJ's of 13 May. The next day he delivered that to Lackington with his own hand. As TJ is much engaged in public business, he sets a higher value on his letters, if possible, than formerly. Nothing can give him more pleasure than to be of service to TJ: "I have ever been proud of your Friendship."

The idea of a regie in France for tobacco seems at present given up, and he hopes the same may soon be said of the difference in duty on it in French and

American bottoms. If not, "you will no doubt adopt such measures as will force it, for . . . it operates as a prohibition against your ships carrying Tobo. to France." Short was in Amsterdam when this decree was passed. He immediately notified him and pointed out its disadvantage for American shipping. – Tobacco is very low at every market in Europe, the quantity far exceeding the consumption. He hopes Virginians "will bend their labour in some other way for two or three years" and thus perhaps get a better price. He is glad TJ sold his last crop so well and is "vastly pleased with the high prices for wheat in America last winter and Spring. Those who shipped it for Europe, must suffer much by it." He thanks TJ for Virginia news. Tucker had informed him of his intended marriage. The fleet is still at Spithead and the press for seamen very hot, but he does not think there will be war between England and Russia. – He says nothing of the extraordinary event in France of the 21st, supposing Short will have written fully by the letter he sent TJ via New York a few days ago and by the two now forwarded by the New York packet. – He is greatly indebted to TJ for his directions about wine.

RC (DLC); endorsed by TJ as received 23 Aug. 1791 and so recorded in SJL.

To James Madison

Dear Sir   Philadelphia July 6. 1791.

I have duly recieved your favours of June 27. and July 1. The last came only this morning. I now return Colo. Smith's map with my acknolegements for the pamphlet and sight of the map. – I inclose you a 60. Dollar bill, and beg the favor of you to remit 30. Dollars with the inclosed letter to Prince, also, as I see Maple sugar, *grained*, advertised for sale at New York in boxes of 400 ℔. each, if they can be induced to sell 100 ℔. only and to pack and send it to Richmond, I will thank you to get it done for me. The box to be directed to me 'to the care of James Brown, merchant Richmd. to be forwarded to Monticello.' You see I presume on your having got over your indisposition; if not, I beg you to let all this matter rest till you are. Colo. Harry Lee thinks of going on tomorrow, to accompany you to Portsmouth, but he was not quite decided when I saw him last. The President arrived about 10. minutes ago, but I have not yet seem him. – I recieved safely the packet by Capt. Sims. The Guinea corn is new to me, and shall be taken care of. My African upland rice is flourishing. I inclose you a paper estimating the shares of the bank as far as was known three days before it opened. When it opened 24,600 subscriptions were offered, being 4,600 more than could be recieved, and many persons left in the lurch, among these Robt. Morris and Fitzsimmons. They accuse the Directors of a misdeal, and the former proposes to sue them, the latter to haul them up before Congress. Every 25 dollars actually deposited, sold yesterday for from 40. to 50. dollars with the future rights and burthens annexed to the deposit. We have no authentic news from Europe since the last packet. Adieu my dear Sir, take care of yourself and let me hear soon that you are quite re-established. Your's affectionately,   TH: JEFFERSON

P.S. If you leave N. York, will you leave directions with Mr. Elsworth to forward to me the two parcels of Maple seed, and that of the Birch bark respectively as they arrive. The last I think had better come by water.

RC (DLC: Madison Papers); addressed: "James Madison esquire at Mr. Elsworth's Maiden lane New-York"; postmarked "7 IV" and "FREE"; franked. PrC (DLC). Enclosures: (1) TJ to Prince, July 6, 1791. (2) Memorandum showing distribution of subscriptions to "The capital stock of the bank, ten millions of dollars, divided into *25,000 shares*," as follows: "to be subscribed by the President [on behalf of the United States], 5,000 shares; already subscribed, Boston, 4,000; already subscribed, New York, 6,400; will be subscribed by Philada. 5,000; already subscribed, Baltimore, 2,400; already subscribed, Charleston, 700," totalling 23,500 shares, with 1,500 remaining to be subscribed (undated memorandum in Remsen's hand, with TJ's recapitulation on verso balancing the 10,400 subscriptions in Boston and New York against the 8,100 in Philadelphia, Baltimore, and Charleston, with the government's subscription and the unsubscribed remainder in the middle of the geographical equation; MS in DLC: Madison Papers). The act of 22 Feb. 1791 incorporating the Bank of the United States provided that the capital stock should amount to $10 million divided into 25,000 shares at $400 each and that subscriptions should be opened in Philadelphia on 1 Apr. 1791. The President was authorized to subscribe within eighteen months for not more than $2 million, or one-fifth of the total number of shares. The supplementary act of 2 Mch. 1791 provided that subscriptions should not be opened until 1 July 1791; that no one, except on behalf of the government, could subscribe for more than thirty shares – a drastic reduction from the limit of one thousand shares originally stipulated; and that, while the payment of three-fourths in public securities was deferred until Jan. 1792, the one-fourth in specie had to be paid at the time of subscribing.

To William Prince

SIR   Philadelphia July 6. 1791.

When I was at your house in June I left with you a note to furnish me with the following trees, to wit

Sugar maples. All you have.

bush cranberries. All you have.

3. balsam poplars

6. Venetian sumachs.

12. Burée pears.

To these I must now desire you to add the following; the names of which I take from your catalogue, to wit

6. Brignola plumbs.
12. apricots. I leave to you to fix on three or four of the best kinds, making in the whole 12 trees.
6. red Roman nectarines.
6. yellow Roman nectarines
6. green nutmeg peaches.
6. large yellow clingstone peaches ripening Oct. 15.
12. Spitzenberg apples. I leave to you to decide on the best kind, as I would chuse to have only one kind.
6. of the very earliest apples you have.
Roses. Moss Provence. Yellow. Rosa mundi. Large Provence. The monthly. The white damask. The primrose. Musk rose. Cinnamon rose. Thornless rose. 3 of each, making in all 30.
3. Hemlock spruce firs.
3. large silver firs
3. balm of Gilead firs.
6 monthly honey suckles.
3 Carolina kidney bean trees with purple flowers.
3. balsam of Peru.
6. yellow willows.
6. Rhododendrons.
12. Madeira nuts.
[...] fill-buds.

According to your estimate and the prices in your catalogue these will be covered by 30. dollars which sum you will recieve herewith. I must trouble you to send them yourself to Richmond, addressed to the care of Mr. James Brown merchant of that place, who will recieve them and pay freight &c. Send them to no other port of that country for I shall never get them, and there are vessels going from New York to Richmond very frequently. Be so good as to forward them as soon as the season will admit. I am Sir your very humble servt,   TH: JEFFERSON

PrC (MHi); at foot of text: "Mr. Wm. Prince, at Flushing landing Long isld."

From David Humphreys

SIR   Lisbon July 7th. (6 o'Clock A.M.) 1791.

The day before yesterday, when the Nuncio and the Diplomatic Corps were at my house, the former with some of the latter mentioned the existence of a private report, that the King of France had attempted to make his escape and that he had been arrested near

Strasbourg. Yesterday, I dined with the Duke of Alafoñes, where the same rumour was repeated. Last night, at the Royal Academy, I met with M. de Pinto, who told me, "that Madame Lebzeltern (wife to the Imperial Minister at this Court) had received a letter which contained the News of the escape of the French King from Paris, with the report of his being stopped near the frontiers: but that the latter part of the information seemed more doubtful than the former." I enquired of him respecting the circumstances of, and agents in this extraordinary affair. He answered, "that the Royal Family were said to have left the Capital on the evening of the 20th Ulto. and that their departure was not known until 9 O'Clock the next morning": he farther added, "that the Compte Fersen (sent for the purpose by the Compte d'Artois) was reported to have been the Instrument of effecting this business."

As I am to pass this day at the Quinta of the Nuncio possibly I may hear more on the subject. But, in order not to lose an opportunity, which is offered at this moment, of forwarding this letter to America; I hasten to conclude in repeating the assurances of perfect consideration & esteem, with which, I have the honor to be Sir Your Most obedient & Most humble Servant,

D: HUMPHREYS

RC (DNA: RG 59, DD); at head of text: "(No. 24)"; endorsed by TJ as received 22 Sep. 1791 and so recorded in SJL. Tr (same).

From Thomas Mann Randolph, Jr.

DEAR SIR   Monticello July 7. 1791.

Your letter of June 23. arrived at Monticello on the 4. of July and made us happy by mentioning the beneficial effects of your journey. We take the first opportunity to inform you that we are in good health ourselves.

In a late letter you desire us to let you know our success with the seeds you sent from Philadelphia. The Sugar maple has failed entirely, a few plants only having appeared which perished allmost immediately. The yellow rice failed allso from the badness of the seed, but the dark colored came up tolerably well and the plants are thriving. The first kind was transmitted to Colo. Lewis on your account by a Gentleman in Jamaica, the 2d. you left in one of the Niches in the parlour here. For both of these and the maple we preferred the flat ground below the park on the little stream which passes thro' it, being the natural situation of the latter, and more suitable to the former than the garden.

The Pacans have not appeared as yet. Thinking that they would not bear transplantation I took the liberty to place them partly on each side of the new way leading from the Gate to the house and partly in the Garden. Several of those in the garden were destroyed unluckily by the Hogs before it was inclosed. I am ashamed to say that we will scarcely have a double quantity of the White Wheat. Colo. Lewis desired that a part of it might be intrusted to him and as there was then no prospect of the garden being inclosed in time to sow it, I reserved a few grains only, which were put into the ground in February. From the difficulty the hogs met with in taking up such small seeds a few escaped, which produced a good crop, the greater part of that again in spite of all our attention has been destroyed by the fowls. Colo. Lewis laid his part by, during the frost and unluckily forgot it. There is sufficient however to establish it in two years with proper care. You have not been more fortunate in your attempt to render the Shepherds dog common in America. We have had seven of pure blood, five of which perished by a distemper which has allmost rendered any regulation of the Virginia Assembly with respect to Dogs unnecessary; one by accident and one, fortunately a male, has arrived at considerable size. A Spurious brood of Six has been more fortunate and is not disregarded, as perhaps the animals may have some value with you.

I am informed by Colo. Lewis that all the Tobacco except 5 or 6 Hhds. which have not yet gone down the river from Lynchburg, has been shiped by Mr. Hylton for Philadelphia. The crop at Poplar Forest a fortnight ago was promising and the Wheat which before this is all secured, is uncommonly fine. The Wheat throughout the country is of a superior quality this year and the whole quantity produced is supposed to be at least ½ greater than the most favorable year has ever given. ⅞ Dollar is the price at present of the Wheat of the last crop in Richmond. ⅚ has been offered for the new. – Colo. Lewis supposes that there are at least 3000 bushels here and at Shadwell.

Mr. Henderson has been offered 1400£. Virginia money for his Mill and it is generally supposed that he may get 2000 for it. He refused peremptorily the first offer. I am informed that Mr. George Dyvers is one of a company which wishes to purchase it and carry on the manufacture of flour on an extensive scale by a joint Stock. The situation has shewn its advantages this Summer when allmost all the mills in the country have stoped.

This is the first summer day we have had this month. The weather has been cold enough to render fires comfortable. The following is an extract from my Diary.

July	Sun rise.		2 o clock.	Sun set.
	B.	T.		
1.	29.1.	63. f. — 29.1.	67. f. — 29.1.	63. f. a. r.
2.	29.2.	59. c. — 29.2½.	61. f. — 29.3.	62. f.
3.	29.3⅔.	55. f. — 29.4	61. f. — 29.4.	61. f.
4.	29.4.	55. f. — 29.4.	60. f. — 29.4.	60. c.
5.	29.3½.	56. c. — 29.3.	59. c. — 29.3.	55. r.
6.	29.2⅓.	52. c. — 29.2½.	60. c. — 29.2½.	60. f.
7.	29.2½	60. f. — 29.2½.	65. f. —	

I am Dear Sir Your most obedt. & affectionate Servt.,

T. M. RANDOLPH

RC (MHi); endorsed by TJ as received 16 July 1791 and so recorded in SJL.

From Thomas Auldjo

Cowes, 8 July 1791. Despite repeated applications, his commission not yet recognized and the under secretaries have given only "flimsy and foolish pretext" for the failure. He will continue to officiate to the limit of his power. Little political or commercial information to report. "American shipping meet no interruption in this port." The only thing causing him trouble "is . . . your American Seamen calling themselves English" to get wages due or advances, which occurs every day. "Even seamen with passes as American's from the Consul in London, have left their Ships here and gone on board men of war . . . to get their wages paid them. . . . I wish you could find a remedy for it, but I confess I think it will be a difficult point." Encloses list of American ships in port there for preceding six months, with their cargoes, arranged in a manner he hopes will be approved.

RC (DNA: RG 59, CD); endorsed by TJ as received 23 Aug. 1791 and so recorded in SJL. Enclosure: "An Account of American Ships and vessels with their Cargoes at the Port of Cowes between 1st. January and 30th June 1791" (actually between 25 Apr. and 3 July). The matter was arranged in tabular form showing dates of arrival and departure, names of masters and owners, place of registry, tonnage, number of men, and cargoes. There were eight vessels in all, the smallest of 99 tons and the largest of 272, employing 69 men. All save one were freighting rice from South Carolina (3,180 barrels) and tobacco from Virginia (934 hogsheads). The exception was *Abigail* of Boston, bound from London for Georgia with "Bale Goods," but windbound at Cowes (MS in DNA: RG 59, CD; dated at Cowes 30 June 1791 and signed by Auldjo). The form indicated that all of the cargoes save hers were destined for Cowes, but *Minerva* of Philadelphia, owned by Robert Morris and carrying 450 hogsheads of tobacco, entered Cowes 3 July and departed the same day for Havre de Grace, to which port her cargo was obviously destined.

From William Irvine and John Kean

SIR   Philadelphia July 8th: 1791

The great loss of papers in the several States, but more especially in those to the Southward, renders it necessary for us to seek information from every source, in order to form the best possible judgement on their respective claims.

We have reason to believe that many papers filed in the office of the late Secretary of Congress and which have fallen under your care, will throw material light on the expenditure of the States alluded to – such as letters &ca from the Governors of the States – Generals commanding in seperate departments – Committees of Congress and Heads of departments.

The secret Journals of Congress may also be serviceable – because claims are made said to be authorised by them and others are also made which are said to be authorised by discretionary powers vested in General officers of the United States.

To enable us to gain proper information we have to sollicit your permission, that we may be allowed from time to time to make such extracts from any books or papers in your office as will assist us in the business before us, which may be done either by one of our own body or by a confidential person to be appointed for that purpose. – With sentiments of high esteem We are Sir Your most obedient & very humble servants,

WM. IRVINE } Commissioners
JOHN KEAN } of Accounts

RC (DNA: RG 59, MLR); endorsed by TJ as received 9 July 1791 and so recorded in SJL.

From William Short

DEAR SIR   Paris July 8. 1791.

This letter will be sent by the French Packet and will acknowlege the reciept of yours of the 10th. of May. – I recieved also a few days ago, from the American consul at London, four letters for the American consuls in France. They were addressed in the handwriting of your office and came under a blank cover to me. They have been forwarded except that for Mr. Barrett who declines I believe entering on the functions of his office. He has informed you of the reasons and is about returning to America. He is expected soon in Paris when I shall deliver him your letter.

No change has taken place in the government of this country since my last. The decree of the assembly for the temporary suspension and imprisonment of the King, which I sent to you by several routes, still continues in force. The several ministers under it exercise such parts of the executive functions in their respective departments as the committees of the assembly please to leave them.

It is impossible to say when this order of things will cease or whether the assembly will have sufficient force to restore the King to the throne as a majority of them desires. The plan which they are preparing in two of the committees is to form the whole of the constitution and then present it to the King for his free acceptation as they term it. All persons seem sensible of the inconveniencies and objections which may and will be made to this plan. Still they say no other less objectionable can be devised. I cannot conjecture what will be the issue. In the mean time the King, the Queen and Dauphin are closely guarded. It is with much difficulty that access is had to them and that always under the inspection of officers named by the Marquis de la fayette for the purpose of guarding them.

The corps diplomatique are not admitted. The Spanish Ambassador made an indirect application and as that did not succeed nothing further has been done. Things will probably remain as they are until answers are recieved from the several courts to M. de Montmorin's communication, already inclosed to you. – The Spanish and English Ambassadors have corresponded with M. de Montmorin, the first to contradict the information sent by a municipality that the Spanish troops had invaded the Kingdom – the second to complain of the garde nationale of Nantes having forcibly entered and detained two merchant vessels of that nation in their port.

A list of the persons to be voted for as Governor of the Dauphin was published eight days ago. The number is about ninety and many of them obscure and improper. It was moved and carried to put off this nomination for fifteen days under pretence of obtaining information with respect to them. Some think the nomination will be still delayed until the affairs of government are settled.

Nothing is yet known with respect to the time that the new elections will be allowed to go on. It is certain however that so far as it depends on the assembly it will not be until after the constitution shall have been presented to the King in the mass. This cannot be in less than a month supposing no incidental interruption to take place. But as such interruptions must happen often it is impossible to form any guess with respect to the progress of this business.

You will recieve by the way of Havre some of the popular journals.

I have thought it proper to send them to you at present on account of the peculiar circumstances of this country and to shew you the spirit of those who unfortunately have too much influence on them. At any other period such publications would be disgusting and unworthy of being read.

I inclose you a paper which contains sentiments so strongly expressed for the abolition of monarchy that a motion was made in the assembly for arresting the author. It was what he desired and for that purpose had signed the placart and pasted it up in large characters in all the frequented quarters of Paris. The assembly prudently rejected the motion. The author is the M. Duchatelet that you have frequently seen at the Hotel de la Rochefoucauld. It was supposed that the Abbé Sieyes was the chief of this republican party, but he has written a letter declaring himself explicitly in favor of monarchical government.

The assembly have thought that their present situation authorized them to violate one of the articles of their declaration of rights. Of course they have forbidden every citizen to leave the Kingdom under any pretence whatsoever, unless he is a merchant and in that case he is to have a passeport from his municipality. Foreigners cannot go out of the Kingdom either but with a passeport from the office of foreign affairs granted on one to be given by the resident of the country to which he belongs, and the passeports in all cases are to have the description of the person marked in it. – The natural effect of this decree is operating sensibly, viz. to inspire a desire to leave the country and an aversion to return to it. This circumstance may induce the assembly soon to repeal it, but it will be a long time before the municipalities will be induced to discontinue an inquisition so much to their taste and of course such passeports will be necessary long after the repeal of the decree.

The pensions and salaries of all those who are out of the kingdom are suspended without excepting those of *Monsieur* and the *Count D'Artois*. The assembly are about to take other measures also against the absentees. Additional taxes, sequestration of estates during absence, or some such plan will probably be adopted.

The King's brothers met at Brussels and had many conferences with the principal refugees of whom great numbers had assembled there. The King's arrestation has averted all their projects; still however many officers of the frontier garrisons continue to go over to them.

Some of these officers have lately written to the soldiers of their regiments to join them, adding that the Count D'Artois had full powers from the King for continuing their pay &c. The King wrote yesterday to the assembly to deny these assertions. They did not know at first how to recieve his letter but at length determined that it should be inserted in the *proces verbal*.

I inclose you also a paper containing a letter from M. de Bouillé to the assembly, or rather the substance of the letter. You will find it more full and correct in the *Journal logographe.* – It gives some idea of the measures intended to be pursued by the King and the motives which induced him to make such an effort for leaving Paris. The manner in which M. de Bouillé announced foreign interference gave uneasiness in the first moment, but it seems now to have passed. Yet I cannot help thinking that he must be persuaded of what he advances; and foreign interference will probably be determined by this internal situation of France. It is unfortunately too true that this will rather invite than repel it.

Several causes will however probably prevent their interference for the present, such as the unsettled state of foreign politics, and the danger to which it would expose the King and Queen. – The longer this is delayed also the less France will be in a state of defense I should fear from the natural progress of things. The military ardor of the *gardes nationales* is such at present that on every trifling ungrounded alarm they are under arms. This ardor cannot last. Dissensions from want of subordination must necessarily take place, discontentment if they are not paid, and ruin to the public resources if they are. As a proof of this I need only mention what has lately taken place in some of the maritime provinces. – Two or three sail of vessels were leaving the coast of France to carry refugees from Brittany to Jersey or Guernsey. A municipality took the alarm and spread it, of its being an English fleet of twenty Sail of the line arriving on the coast. The *gardes nationales* in the neighbouring departments immediately assembled under this idea, and it is supposed that they were on the whole three hundred thousand in number. Such things also have taken place though in a smaller degree on the other frontiers.

Supposing peace to be concluded among the other European powers, as seems probable during the summer (notwithstanding the Congress of Sistovie have separated without being able to agree on any thing) and that they should be disposed to interfere in the affairs of France next year, they would certainly have more influence than at present. Many difficulties however would naturally occur among the foreign powers themselves.

I shall continue to send by the way of Havre the accustomed

journals and gazettes to which I refer you for other particulars as to the proceedings of the assembly, and the politics of Europe. You will recieve with them Mr. Necker's book on the affairs of this country, which though not the most flattering, is certainly the truest that has been given of them. In the journals you will see also the decrees of the assembly respecting the colonies.

I have mentioned to M. de Montmorin what you say respecting consuls there. He seemed well satisfied and promised that proper attention should be paid to the persons named, on the footing you mention.

You desire to know whether letters are opened in the French post office. The decrees of the asembly are formal and severe against it and no funds being allowed I take it for granted it is not done, and I think you may safely consider it so. You said you intended writing also by the English packets. As they are regular it would be exceedingly agreeable to recieve letters by them. I suppose however that letters are read in that office. If addressed to the Consul or Mr. Donald in London they would arrive with the greatest safety. I am with perfect sincerity my dear Sir, your friend & servant,

W: Short

PrC (DLC: Short Papers); at head of text: "*No. 72.*"; at foot of text: "Thomas Jefferson Secretary of State, Philadelphia." Tr (DNA: RG 59, DD). Recorded in SJL as received 22 Oct. 1791.

The book by Jacques Necker that Short admired was a defense of his administration of French finances, *Sur l'administration de M. Necker* (Paris, 1791; see Sowerby, No. 2546). For TJ's own estimate of Necker and for a similar characterization drawn by a friend of his which TJ copied and sent to the Secretary for Foreign Affairs, see TJ to Jay, 17 June 1789, and its enclosure.

From Tobias Lear

"*United States,*" *9 July 1791.* By President's command he transmits letter from Francisco Chiappe, forwarded by James Simpson, "which the President requests the Secretary to take into consideration."

PrC (DNA: RG 59, MLR). Tr (DNA: RG 59, SDC). Recorded in SJL as received the same day. Enclosures: (1) James Simpson to the President, Gibraltar, 13 Apr. 1791, sending "another packet . . . from Mr. Chiappe" by the English *Roman Eagle*, Samuel Glover master, for New York (RC in DNA: RG 59, CD). (2) Francisco Chiappe to the President, 22 Mch. 1791 (RC in DNA: RG 360, PCC No. 98, M-247/125; endorsed by TJ as "delivered to Th: J. July 9"). See note, TJ to Francisco Chiappe, 13 May 1791.

To Charles Carter

DEAR SIR   Philadelphia July 10. 1791.

Your letter of May 21. arrived here soon after my departure on a journey to the lakes. I found it here on my return, which is but lately, and immediately set about the enquiries necessary for your satisfaction. I am well acquainted with Dr. Barton, and can assure you he merits the high character you have heard of him. I have no doubt that a student will be perfectly well placed under him. Should your son board in the town, I find that the lowest terms of boarding are 3. dollars a week, and the boarder finds his own firewood, candles and washing, which may be estimated at 40. dollars a year, to which must be added clothing and pocket-money. I believe it is essential also that he attend a course of anatomical lectures and dissections, which will cost 4. guineas.[1] I am possessed of an accurate estimate of the expences of an economical student at Edinburgh, which are about 400. Dollars a year. This is probably something less than the whole expences will be here annually. It cannot be denied that both the reputation and the reality of the means of information are in favor of Edinburgh: against which however a parent will feel some advantages in favor of this place. After weighing all circumstances should you decide in favor of this place, I shall with great pleasure be of any service I can to your son, while I may be here. Be so good as to present me in the most affectionate terms to Mrs. Carter, and to be assured yourself of the regard with which I am Dear Sir your most obedt humble servt,

TH: JEFFERSON

RC (Miss Eleanor Peck, Brooklyn, N.Y., 1950); addressed: "Charles Carter esquire of Ludlow at Fredericksburg"; franked; postmarked: "11 IV" and "FREE." PrC (MHi). Tr (CtY); in an unidentified hand, but written in an obvious – and unsuc- cessful – attempt to imitate TJ's hand, sig- nature, and address.

[1] At this point in PrC there is a blank: "4. guineas" was added to RC after PrC was executed.

To James Currie

DEAR SIR   Philadelphia July 10. 1791.

My letter written on the day of my departure informed you of the promises which had been made by your debtor, and which, though I could not confide in very firmly, yet neither could I consider them altogether as nothing. They turned out so however; and Mr. Remsen engaged Mr. Barton an attorney to levy an attachment on his property in the hands of the Potters, Hazlehurst, Shannon, and Mc-Connel, all of which I had informed you would be random shot, as it was only guessed there might be property in the hands of the three last; and tho' it was known there was property in the hands of the Potters, yet it was also known it would little more than cover their debt. I found this to be the state of things on my return, and that no attachment had been levied in the hands of Mr. Morris. Yet it is most highly probable that the mass of his property is in Mr. Morris's hands, at least so he says, and so says common opinion. I had the attachment therefore immediately extended to him, and I will take some good opportunity of bespeaking his favour to your claim. The return will be made into court this month, but I have not learned when a judgment may be expected. Probably soon. I shall press the attorney from time to time, and when any thing new, either in fact or prospect turns up, I will do myself the pleasure of apprising you of it and of repeating, as I do now, assurances of the sincere esteem of dear Sir your friend & servt, TH: JEFFERSON

PrC (DLC).

To Daniel L. Hylton

DEAR SIR   Philadelphia July 10. 1791.

Your favour of May 29. came here after my departure on a journey to the lakes. That of June 17. is since recieved, and in consequence I send you a post-bank note for 21 D.-25. c. being the addition of 24/ to £5-3-6 as noted in your letter to be the probable amount of your disbursements for the 22. hhds. of tobo. forwarded by Capt. Stratton. He is not yet arrived. But the season admits of no anxiety on that account. A late letter from Havre in France informs me that the *best* tobacco had risen there to 45. ₶ the French hundred, say 8 D.-33. c. for 109 ℔. American. The demand there must increase and be of considerable duration, as there can be at present very few hhds. of tobo. in a country which has always kept 60,000 hhds. of unwrought stock in hand. As both the public managers, and private merchants are free to buy and sell, it is to be hoped the price will become considerable. We have no news from the Westward yet, and are anxious to hear the event of Scott's expedition. Present my affectionate compliments to Mrs. Hylton, & be assured of the sincere esteem of Dear Sir Your friend & servt,   TH: JEFFERSON

PrC (MHi).

From Joshua Johnson

London, 10 July 1791. Encloses a copy of his of 2d. Has heard nothing of Hammond's preparations for departing, nor is his appointment yet publicly known. He has taken infinite pains to obtain a report of the Committee of the Lords of Trade. One hundred copies printed for the Privy Council "but so very careful are they of them, that it is impossible to get one for you; I procured a Sight of one for a few hours, and even in the hurried manner in which I scanned it over, I see, if they make that the Basis of Mr. Hammonds negotiation, that nothing will be done." – The report is based on questions put and answers received from a committee of merchants of London, Bristol, Liverpool and Glasgow. The two former were very moderate and rather friendly. That of Liverpool recommended immediate retaliation. The Glasgow committee advised negotiation on limited principles and, if that failed, retaliation. "Lord Hawkesbury, who it is said was the principal in drawing up the Report, has laboured very hard, to shew that the trade of this Country is increasing, and that of the United States is declining; he however has Modesty enough to admit, that the remaining trade to America is beneficial to this, and advises a commercial regulation, provided Congress, do not demand admission for their Vessells to the West India Islands, but, should they do that . . . an immediate end be put to any farther negotiation, and that this Country adopt retaliation. I lament very much that I cannot procure this curious production for you; that Congress might be in possession of the sentiments of this Government, towards the United States, which I think are not friendly."

All astonished at continued arming and cannot tell the motive. American shipping much distressed from impressment, warmer than ever. In many instances they have taken whole crews, and, because of difficulty of proving American birth, many valuable men are lost. – He will soon send copies of correspondence with the Secretary of State [for Foreign Affairs], the Lords of the Treasury, and the Lords of the Admiralty in order to put him in full possession of all his proceedings.

RC (DNA: RG 59, CD). FC (same). Recorded in SJL as received 22 Oct. 1791.

The next day Johnson sent by the same conveyance his quarterly account of inward and outward entries of American vessels in the port of London, also a statement of his account with the United States showing a balance in his favor of £33-4-0 (Johnson to TJ, 11 July 1791; FC in same). Two months before TJ received the above letter, he obtained through the agency of William Temple Franklin an abstract of Hawkesbury's Report to the Privy Council of 28 Jan. 1791 (see Editorial Note on commercial and diplomatic relations with Great Britain, at 15 Dec. 1790).

To James Madison

My dear Sir   Philadelphia July 10. 1791.

Your indisposition at the date of your last, and hearing nothing from you since, make me fear it has continued. The object of the present is merely to know how you do, and from another hand, if you are not well enough. – We have little new but what you will see in the public papers. You see there the swarm of anti-publicolas. The disavowal by a Printer only does not not appear to satisfy. We have no news yet of the event of Scott's expedition. The Marquis Fayette has certainly resumed his command and on a ground which must strengthen him and also the public cause. – The subscriptions to the bank from Virginia were almost none. Pickett, Mc.lurg and Dr. Lee are the only names I have heard mentioned. This gives so much uneasiness to Colo. H. that he thinks to propose to the President to sell some of the public shares to subscribers from Virga. and N. Carolina, if any more should offer. This partiality would offend the other states without pleasing those two: for I presume they would rather the capitals of their citizens should be employed in commerce than be locked up in a strong box here: nor can sober thinkers prefer a paper medium at 13 per cent interest to gold and silver for nothing. Adieu my dear friend. Yours affectionately,

TH: JEFFERSON

P.S. Osgood is resigning the Postmaster's place. I shall press Paine for it.

RC (DLC: Madison Papers). PrC (DLC).

From James Madison

DEAR SIR   N. York July 10. 1791

Your favor of the 6th. came to hand on friday. I went yesterday to the person who advertised the Maple Sugar for the purpose of executing your commission on that subject. He tells me that the cargo is not yet arrived from Albany, but is every hour expected; that it will not be sold in parcels of less than 15 or 16 hundred lb. and only at auction, but that the purchasers will of course deal it out in smaller quantities; that a part is grained and part not; and that the price of the former will probably be regulated by that of good Muscavado which sells at about £5. N.Y. Currency, a Ct. I shall probably be at Flushing in two or three days and have an opportunity of executing your other Commission on the spot. In case of disappointment, I shall send the Letter and money to Prince by the best conveyance to be had. The Maple Seed is not arrived. The Birch-Bark has been in my hands some days and will be forwarded as you suggest.

The Bank-Shares have risen as much in the Market here as at

Philadelphia. It seems admitted on all hands now that the plan of the institution gives a moral certainty of gain to the Subscribers with scarce a physical possibility of loss. The subscriptions are consequently a mere scramble for so much public plunder which will be engrossed by those already loaded with the spoils of individuals. The event shews what would have been the operation of the plan, if, as originally proposed, subscriptions had been limited to the 1st. of april and to the favorite species of Stock which the Bank-Jobbers had monopolized. It pretty clearly appears also in what proportions the public debt lies in the Country, what sort of hands hold it, and by whom the people of the U.S. are to be governed. Of all the shameful circumstances of this business, it is among the greatest to see the members of the Legislature who were most active in pushing this Jobb, openly grasping its emoluments. Schuyler is to be put at the Head of the Directors, if the weight of the N.Y. subscribers can effect it. – Nothing new is talked of here. In fact Stockjobbing drowns every other subject. The Coffee House is in an eternal buzz with the gamblers.

I have just understood that Freneau is now here and has abandoned his Philada. project. From what cause I am wholly unable to divine: unless those who know his talents and hate his political principles should have practised some artifice for the purpose.

I have given up for this season my trip Eastward. My bilious situation absolutely forbade it. Several lesser considerations also conspired with that objection. I am at present free from a fever, but have sufficient evidence, in other shapes, that I must adhere to my defensive precautions.

The pamphlet on Weights &c. was put into my hands by Doctr. Kemp with a view to be forwarded after perusal to you. As I understand it is a duplicate and to be kept by you. Always, & mo: affecly. Yrs.,   Js. MADISON JR.

RC (DLC: Madison Papers); date added to endorsement by Madison after letter was returned to him; endorsed by TJ as received 12 July 1791 and so recorded in SJL.

To Louis Osmont

July 10. 1791.

Th: Jefferson presents his compliments to Mr. Osmont, and informs him that having found that Colo. Pickering would probably leave the Oneida country before a letter could reach him, he has inclosed Mr. Osmont's paper to Mr. Renslaer member of Congress from Albany, with a request to make enquiry into the case at Albany and in the Oneida country, between which two places there is considerable intercourse.

PrC (DLC).

Louis Osmont was a young Frenchman whom Madame D'Houdetot had asked William Short to recommend to TJ for counsel about his plans to settle in America and to engage in commerce. Short was embarrassed, but could not refuse such a request from TJ's good friend (Short to TJ, 7 Nov. 1790, where Osmont is incorrectly named in the text as Ormont). The young man was in straitened circumstances, and TJ took some pains to assist him, especially because he had been so "particularly recommended." Timothy Pickering was at the moment negotiating a treaty with the Six Nations, and TJ knew that a letter to him concerning Osmont's claim to Oneida lands would not arrive in time. He therefore appealed to Jeremiah Van Rensselaer to transmit a statement of the claim to appropriate persons in Albany (TJ to Van Rensselaer, 10 July 1791). TJ was favorably impressed by young Osmont (TJ to Short, 28 July 1791).

To Martha Jefferson Randolph

MY DEAR DAUGHTER   Philadelphia July 10. 1791.

I have no letter from Monticello later than Maria's of May 29. which is now six weeks old. This is long, when but one week is necessary for the conveyance. I cannot ascribe all the delay to the Charlottesville post. However to put that out of the way I am negotiating with the postmaster the establishment of a public post from Richmond to Staunton. In this case all the private riders will be prohibited from continuance, let their contracts be what they will, and the whole being brought into one hand, the public will be better served. I propose that the post shall pass by Tuckahoe, Goochld. courthouse, Columbia and Charlottesville in order that as many may be served by it as possible. The price on each newspaper will be to be settled between the printers and their customers. – I have no information whether the things sent by Stratton have got safe to hand: tho' hope they have. I expect him here daily, and shall send by him some stores against my arrival at Monticello, the time of which however is not yet fixable. I rather expect it will be earlier than the last year, because my return here must be earlier. Tell Maria I shall expect to find her improved in all good things and particularly in her music, of which I hope you also are mindful. Kiss her for me and the little one, and present my best esteem to Mr. Randolph. – Your's, my dear, affectionately,   TH: JEFFERSON

RC (NNP). PrC (MHi).

To Jeremiah Van Rensselaer

SIR   Philadelphia July 10. 1791.

Inclosed is a statement of a claim to some lands in the Oneida country given by the Indians to one Le Tonnelier, and by him sold to a Mr. Osmont. This latter gentleman is arrived from France and has fixed himself here. Being a stranger, without the means of informing himself what chance there is, and what should be his proceedings to recover the lands, and having been very particularly recommended to me from France, I am anxious to aid his enquiries. The circumstance of Le Tonnelier's having married in Albany, and the relations between that place and the Oneida country have induced me to suppose it a good place to make the necessary enquiries. Not having the advantage of any particular acquaintance at Albany, I have presumed on behalf of Mr. Osmont to address myself to you, relying for my excuse on the motives which lead to this liberty, and on your own goodness which will find in an injured and friendless stranger a proper object for it's exercise. If therefore you can either at Albany, or by the means of any acquaintance you may have within reach of the lands, obtain information of the reality of Le Tonnelier's rights and the means of availing Osmont of them, the communication of it will be esteemed a very singular favor by Sir your most obedt. & most humble servt.,   TH: JEFFERSON

RC (Frank Glenn, Kansas City, Mo., 1955); addressed: "The honble Jeremiah Van Renslaer Member of Congress at Albany"; franked; postmarked: "11 IY" and "FREE." PrC (MHi). Enclosure not found (see TJ to Osmont, 10 July 1791).

From C. W. F. Dumas

The Hague, 12 July 1791. He acknowledges TJ's of 13 May and has made good use of his account of the prosperity of the United States. If the volume of European quarrels allows space for this felicitous example set by the New World, it will be seen in the newspapers.

He has written Luzac to continue sending the gazette by the English packet boats. As for the question of American packets, this must wait for another day. But since the government does not wish to bear the cost, this could be an object of speculation by merchants under a concession from which the government would profit.

He knows from reliable sources that American securities of the first two loans of Messrs. Stadnitsky and Staphorst sell today at ƒ1430 the 1000 — that is, at least 43% above par; those of subsequent loans correspondingly; and those of the loans authorized by Congress at 5% through Messrs. Willink and Staphorst are sought for, the last like the first at 1% above par.

He says nothing of European affairs. The most clairvoyant are baffled and know no more than what appears in the gazettes. He thinks the National Assembly has taken the wisest course and does not believe any power will attack France in its present state of ferment.

P.S. *13 July*. TJ will see in the *Gazette de Leide* of the 12th the account of American prosperity outlined by him. All prudent readers will be struck by the agreeable contrast between this and the European news. He is also sending this article to the brave man who edits the *Gazette de Harlem*, a paper which he will begin sending the first of the month. This gazette and that of Leyden are regarded by the Dutch as the most informed and best edited of all the Holland journals. The others are partisan and strident. The worst of all and the most contemptible for its impudence is that published at The Hague, called the *Gazette de la Cour*.

P.S. *17 July*. Certain people here profess that a Congress of certain powers will soon assemble at Aix-la-Chapelle to intervene in French affairs. He does not believe it. If this were to happen, it would be so much the worse for those powers, not for France.

FC (Dumas Letter Book, Rijksarchief, The Hague; photostats in DLC); at head of text: "No. 79." RC (missing) is recorded in SJL as received 22 Oct. 1791.

From David Humphreys

Lisbon, 12 July 1791. The news in his of the 7th about secret flight of French King has been confirmed. Assumption by National Assembly of executive powers notified in circular to diplomatic representatives. Yesterday, dining with diplomatic corps at Walpole's, he was shown by him a letter from Lord Gower in Paris dated 25 June containing news of arrest of the King and his entourage, of ministers of state being required to take orders from the National Assembly, and of tranquillity prevailing, due to care in posting national guard. The Duke of Luxembourg is said to have received news of King's return to Paris. – Many rumors about "the evasion and arrest of the Royal Family." Fersen a principal agent. De Bouillé, commandant at Metz, was in the plot and sent two bodies to bring the King there. "The Soldiers grounded their Arms. This Event frustrates the high expectations of the Aristocrats and their favorers in this and other Countries. The news of the King's being captured, which is said to have caused many tears in this Court, induced the Masters of French vessels in this harbour to testify their joy by hoisting their Colours, as on Gala days. – Every thing had been matured for a Crisis on the expected arrival of the King of France at Metz. It is even now imagined external Hostilities will immediately commence against that Country, but all is conjecture. The Duke de Luxembourg and others of the same party here are in the most profound Distress."

RC (DNA: RG 59, DD); at head of text: "(No. 25)"; endorsed by TJ as received 22 Oct. 1791 and so recorded in SJL.

To William Irvine and John Kean

GENTLEMEN   Philadelphia July 12. 1791.

I am honoured with your letter of the 5th.[1] instant and shall be happy to give every facility to the settlement of the public accounts, which the papers in my office may afford, and their nature admit. You will readily concieve that there may be some (as the secret journals for instance) which could not be suffered to go out of the office, nor to be examined there but by persons of the highest confidence. The few papers which are in this predicament, I am in hopes you would not think it too much trouble for one of yourselves to examine in the office where they are. But as to the residue which probably constitute the great mass of those which may be of any service to you they shall be delivered to your clerk on his leaving a reciept for them at the office. – I have the honour to be with great respect Gentlemen Your most obedient & most humble servt,

TH: JEFFERSON

PrC (DLC). FC (DNA: RG 59, PCC No. 120).

[1] Thus in MS; their letter was dated the 8th.

From James Maury

Liverpool, 12 July 1791. Since his of the 23rd he has received TJ's of 1 and 13 May. He will attend particularly to the matter Mr. Coxe desired. Far from thinking himself neglected, he was aware TJ's time was "much engrossed by more important concerns" than writing. – Two American vessels, chartered in Virginia for Guernsey, delivered their tobacco there and came here to take freights home, "under no aprehension of . . . having done any Thing illegal." They have been seized by the customs, but as it is "notoriously an Error of Ignorance" he hopes the owners will not suffer. He is highly delighted by TJ's account of the prosperity of the United States.

"The 4th Instant being observed by most of our Countrymen in this port as an Holiday, the Crewes of many of their Vessells collected together and getting too much Drink behaved in most disorderly and disrespectful Manner to the people of the Country, which had well nigh been attended with very serious Consequences. Happily it terminated otherwise. It will however be a Caution on future Occasions."

RC (DNA: RG 59, CD); endorsed by TJ as received 3 Oct. 1791 and so recorded in SJL.

From George Washington

GW. TO MR. J.   Tuesday 12th. June[1] 1791

The enclosed I send this afternoon, for your perusal. Tomorrow, 8'oclock, I shall send the person who was the bearer of it, to you. – It being the hour, he left word, when he left the letter, that he should call upon me. – If Mr. Pearce merits the character given him by T: D. he will unquestionably merit encouragement, and you can put him in the way to obtain it. – Yrs. ever,   GW.

RC (DLC); addressed: "Mr. Jefferson"; endorsed by TJ as received 13 July 1791 and so recorded in SJL.

The enclosed letter has not been found, but its author and its object cannot be doubted: it was a letter from Thomas Digges, probably dated late in April, introducing the British artisan William Pearce whom Digges had encouraged to emigrate to the United States with models of his looms (two similar letters from Digges to the President, dated 1 July and 12 Nov. 1791, urged that Pearce be given assistance; these are in DNA: RG 59, MLR). The collaboration between Digges and Pearce was contrary to the laws of both Britain and Ireland, and it was for this reason that, only a few months earlier, TJ had persuaded Washington not to give official countenance to such activity. Yet, in this unusual and unequivocal directive, the Secretary of State was commanded to do something not only contrary to his earlier counsel to the President but also at variance with the principles he believed should govern relations with other countries. For a comment on the means by which TJ avoided this embarrassment, see note to Digges to TJ, 28 Apr. 1791.

[1] At this point TJ interlined the correct date: "July."

To John Bulkeley & Son

GENTLEMEN   Philadelphia July 13. 1791.

I am now to acknolege the reciept of your favor of Jan. 18. together with the samples of wine forwarded. That marked No. 2. and called Termo was exactly the quality desired. Next to this was No. 4. Torres. The other qualities not liked. I am now therefore to pray you to send me a pipe of the kind called Termo, the oldest and best you can procure. You will recieve from Mr. Barclay, the bearer of this, 75. dollars on my account, which if I calculate rightly your millreas, will cover the cost of the pipe and the samples. Should any miscalculation, or any advance of price for an older or better quality render it insufficient, Colo. Humphreys will perhaps be so good as to make it up, or I will pay it to your correspondent here at your choice. – I am with great regard Gentlemen Your most obedt. humble servt,   TH: JEFFERSON

PrC (MHi).

Early in 1791, in an undated memorandum, David Humphreys informed TJ that "Messrs. John Bulkeley & Son have engaged to send by the first vessel to Philadelphia different specimens of the dry Lisbon Wines, with the prices, for the inspection of Mr. Jefferson. They are well acquainted with the subject and may be expected to deal with the strictest honor" (RC in Humphreys' hand, endorsed by TJ; MHi). The letter from Bulkeley & Son of 18 Jan. 1791, which must have been written in compliance with Humphreys' instructions, is recorded in SJL as received on 28 Feb. 1791 but has not been found. Another letter from the firm, dated 7 Feb., is recorded as received 30 Mch. 1791 but is also missing.

From Tench Coxe

[Philadelphia], 13 July 1791. He received TJ's note by Pearce and will give his attention "to fix a man who appears of so much importance to the United States. He communicated . . . very freely, and finding on my cautioning him about foreign seduction that he had been attacked in that way already at New York, I have prevailed on him to deposit his articles at once in the patent office. This will frustrate all attempts and cut off the hopes of getting him away." He encloses Pearce's signed order to Mr. Seton to deliver the apparatus to such persons as TJ will direct. He will wait on TJ that evening or next day to "submit the proceeding, which appears proper in the Case," and will then return the letter to the President, wishing to revise it more carefully than the hours of office afford. Pearce intends to proceed at once to make the frames for his machinery, which he says he can "exhibit at work in a weeks time." – He encloses the British act consolidating their duties, which TJ desired.

RC (DLC); endorsed by TJ as received 13 July 1791 and so recorded in SJL. Enclosure: William Pearce to William Seton, 13 July 1791, requesting him to deliver the two boxes or cases containing his machinery to the order of "the Honorable Thomas Jefferson Esqr. Secretary of the United States who is one of the Members of the Board for granting Patents. The two cases which I mean are those directed to 'His Excellency General Washington, and marked with the letters G. W.'" (Tr in clerk's hand, PHi: Coxe Papers, with notes by TJ and Coxe as given below).

TJ's note of this date introducing William Pearce has not been found and is not recorded in SJL. For comment on the circumstances which caused TJ to introduce Pearce to Coxe, see notes to Washington to TJ, 12 July 1791, and Digges to TJ, 28 Apr. 1791. Coxe, in advising Pearce, took the liberty of having him authorize Seton to deliver the apparatus to anyone the Secretary of State would designate. Even this degree of involvement was more than TJ could accept. On the original of Pearce's letter to Seton he therefore placed responsibility back upon Coxe with the following note: "Mr. Jefferson is desired to deliver the above cases to the order of Mr. Tench Coxe, by his humble servant. Signed (Thomas Jefferson)" (RC missing; TJ's undated note appended to enclosure as described above). TJ then returned Pearce's letter to Coxe, who found himself obliged to add his own directive to Seton authorizing him "to dispose of the within agreeably to a Letter of this 15th July 1791" (same). The rebuff to Coxe is conclusive proof that TJ did not, as has been claimed, write directly to Seton authorizing him to reimburse Pearce for his travel and other expenses (see note to Digges to TJ, 28 Apr. 1791).

To David Humphreys

Mr. Barclay having been detained longer than was expected, you will receive this, as well as my Letter of May 13th. from him. Since the date of that I have received your No. 15 March 31, No. 16 April 8, No. 17 April 30, No. 18 May 3, and No. 20. May 21.

You are not unacquainted with the situation of our Captives at Algiers. Measures were taken, and were long depending, for their redemption. During the time of their dependance we thought it would forward our success to take no notice of the captives. They were maintained by the Spanish Consul, from whom applications for reimbursement through Mr. Carmichael often came: no answer of any kind was ever given. A certainty now that our measures for their redemption will not succeed, renders it unnecessary for us to be so reserved on the subject, and to continue to wear the appearance of neglecting them. Though the Government might have agreed to ransom at the lowest price admitted with any Nation (as, for instance, that of the French order of Merci) they will not give anything like the price which has been lately declared to be the lowest by the Captors. It remains then for us to see what other means are practicable for their recovery. In the mean time it is our desire, that the disbursements hitherto made for their subsistence by the Spanish Consul or others be paid off, and that their future comfortable subsistence be provided for. As to past disbursements, I must beg the favor of you to write to Mr. Carmichael that you are authorised to pay them off, and pray him to let you know their amount, and to whom payments are due. With respect to future provision for the captives, I must put it into your hands. The impossibility of getting letters to or from Mr. Carmichael renders it improper for us to use that channel. As to the footing on which they are to be subsisted, the ration and cloathing of a soldier would have been a good measure were it possible to apply it to articles of food and cloathing so extremely different as those used at Algiers. The allowance heretofore made them by the Spanish Consul, might perhaps furnish a better rule, as we have it from themselves that they were then comfortably subsisted. Should you be led to correspond with them at all, it had better be with Capt. Obrian, who is a sensible man, and whose conduct since he has been there has been particularly meritorious. It will be better for you to avoid saying anything which may either encrease or lessen their hopes of ransom. I write to our Bankers to answer your draughts for these purposes, and enclose you a duplicate to be forwarded with your first draught. The prisoners are fourteen in number – their names and qualities as follows – Richard Obrian and Isaac Stephens Captains, Andrew Montgomery and Alexander Forsyth Mates, Jacob Tessanier a french passenger, William Paterson, Philip Sloan, Peleg Lorin, John Robertson, James Hall, James Cathcart, George Smith, John Gregory, James Hermet Seamen. They have been twenty one or twenty two.

We are in hourly expectation of hearing the event of Genl. Scott's irruption into the Indian country at the head of between 7 and 800 mounted infantry. Perhaps it may yet be known in time to communicate to you by this opportunity. Our Bank was filled with subscriptions the moment it was opened. Eight millions of dollars were the whole permitted to be subscribed, of which two millions were deposited in cash, the residue to be public paper. Every other symptom is equally favorable to our credit.

The President is returned from his southern tour in good health. You will receive herewith the newspapers up to the present date. – I have the honor to be with great esteem Dear Sir Your most obedient & most humble Servt.   TH: JEFFERSON

RC (NjP); in Remsen's hand, except for signature; endorsed. PrC (DLC); lacks signature; at foot of text in TJ's hand (not in RC): "Colo. Humphries" – a notation evidently added at a much later date. FC (DNA: RG 59, DCI). Enclosure: Duplicate of TJ to Willink, Van Staphorst & Hubbard, 13 July 1791.

From Edmund Pendleton

Caroline, 13 July 1791. He has just received a letter from his nephew, Nathaniel Pendleton, Jr., of Georgia, informing him of the resignation of Mr. Rutledge as "one of the Judges of the Supreme Fœdral Court" and asking his influence in being appointed.

He hands TJ his pretentions founded on supposition that the vacancy will be filled by a citizen of the Southern District; that, as North and South Carolina have already been gratified thus, it will fall to a Georgian; and that his being District Judge will place him foremost there. "How far this is well founded, the President will judge, and you, Sir, if, as is probable, you are consulted on such Occasions." He hears that his reputation is high in Georgia, and Pendleton will be obliged if, consistent with the public good, TJ can serve him there.

RC (DLC); endorsed by TJ as received 19 July 1791 and so recorded in SJL.

George Washington to William Stephens Smith

SIR   Philadelphia July 13[1] 1791.

I have recieved, since my return to this place, the letter which you were so kind as to write on the 6th. of June, and am now to make you my acknowledgements for the information it contained. Very soon after I came to the government, I took measures for enquiring into the dispositions of the British cabinet on the matters in question between us: and what you now communicate corresponds very exactly with the result of those enquiries. Their intention indeed to send a Minister is more strongly indicated on this occasion, as one of the Secretaries of state has come forward voluntarily to say so. How far they may be disposed to settle the other points which are really interesting to us, is still a subject of conjecture. In all events we are to thank you for the trouble you have taken, and the lights you have contributed to throw on this subject.[2] – I am &c.   G W

PrC (DLC); entirely in TJ's hand. FC (DLC: Washington Papers); with variations as indicated below.

For comment on Smith's private mission to England, his interview with Grenville, his report to Washington in his letter of 6 June 1791, and the effect of the above response to that letter which the President asked TJ to draft, see Editorial Note to the group of documents on commercial and diplomatic relations with Great Britain, at 15 Dec. 1790. For a different interpretation of the result of Smith's mission and of TJ's response to his report, see Charles R.

Ritcheson, *Aftermath of Revolution*, p. 119-22.

[1] Date blank in TJ's draft, supplied from FC.

[2] FC has the following sentence not in TJ's draft: "Having taken copies of the documents which accompanied your letter, I herewith return the originals." Washington's copies of the enclosures, which are identified in notes 91, 92, 96, 98, and 100 in Editorial Note to relations with Great Britain at 15 Dec. 1790, are in DNA: RG 59, MLR.

To Willink, Van Staphorst & Hubbard

GENTLEMEN   Philadelphia July 13th. 1791

Col: Humphreys is charged with the payment of some arrearages due for the maintenance of our captives at Algiers from the time of their captivity down to the present. The amount is unknown to me, and I can therefore only desire you to answer his draughts for this purpose whatever they be, and charge them in your general account with the Secretary of State. He is also to see to their future subsistence. They are fourteen in number, and he will draw on you from time to time for this purpose, which draughts be pleased to answer also and charge in the same account. I have the Honor to be Gentlemen Your most obedient humble Servant,

TH: JEFFERSON

RC (NjP); in Remsen's hand except for signature and address by TJ: "Messrs. Willinks, Van Staphorsts & Hubard. Bankers Amsterdam"; at head of text TJ wrote "Duplicate." PrC (DLC); lacks signature. FC (DNA: RG 59, DCI). Enclosed in TJ to Humphreys, this date.

Sylvanus Bourne to Henry Remsen, Jr.

Cape François, 14 July 1791. Having noticed in late American newspapers that TJ is on tour and "may not probably return very soon," he asks that his last letters [29 Apr. and 30 June 1791] be communicated to the President. If the Commissaries, daily expected from France, refuse to recognize him, he will feel justified in returning to America without further notice. If recognized, he will need advice whether to remain. — News has just arrived that the National Assembly passed a decree "giving the privileges of freemen to the Mulattoes in their Island." The Commissaries are expected to be attended by troops to enforce the decree. If so, he fears the horrors of a civil war, as the whites are "pursuing every step towards a severe opposition." He will send full information on "how this affair operates." He hopes for replies to his several letters.

RC (DNA: RG 59, CD); addressed: "Mr. Henry Remsen in the office of the Secy. of State Philadelphia"; endorsed by TJ as received 11 Aug. 1791 and so recorded in SJL.

To Nathaniel Chipman

SIR   Philadelphia July 14. 1791.

Your favour of May 10. came to hand on the 21st. of June. The Commission to you as judge of the district of Vermont was made out at the same time with those for the Attorney and Marshal, and, as the chief-clerk of my office assures me, it was put under the same cover with them to one of your deputies then at New York. I inclose you a copy of the letter which accompanied it. Having learned however that it had never reached your hands I had another commission prepared, which was signed by the President on his return, and is now inclosed. I hope this will come safely to hand, and with sincere expressions of satisfaction that your country will have the benefit of your talents employed in it's service, I have the honour to assure you of the esteem & respect with which I am Sir Your most obedt. & most humble servt,   TH: JEFFERSON

RC (ViU); at foot of text: "Honble. Mr. Chipman." PrC (DLC). FC (DNA: RG 59, PCC No. 120).

To the complications which attended the admission of Vermont were added the difficulties which Nathaniel Chipman experienced in obtaining his commission as federal judge for the district. When the state was admitted as of 4 Mch. 1791, Washington, on TJ's advice, called a special meeting of the Senate on that day to act upon nominations to the following offices in addition to that of Chipman: Stephen Jacobs, district attorney; Lewis R. Morris, marshal; and Stephen Keyes, collector for the port of Alburg. All were confirmed, and, on the same day, TJ dispatched their commissions (see Editorial Note and group of documents on admission of Vermont and Kentucky, at 4 Mch. 1791). Two months later Chipman reported to TJ that he had never received his (Chipman to TJ, 10 May 1791; recorded in SJL as received 21 June but not found). The duplicate commission which TJ enclosed with the above letter met with the same fate, according to a communication from Chipman to TJ of 28 Aug. 1791 (recorded in SJL as received 22 Sep. 1791 but also missing). Remsen received that letter during TJ's absence in Virginia and, by direction of the President, immediately issued a triplicate commission which went forward directly to Chipman without being attested by TJ (Remsen to TJ, 9 Sep. 1791). Apparently the other federal officers in Vermont received their commissions without experiencing such difficulty.

To Jonathan Edwards

Sir   Philadelphia July 14. 1791.

I have duly recieved your favor of the 4th. inst. The books you mention had come to hand and been regularly entered. I have assured myself by an examination of my own notes of letters recieved, made in the moment of recieving them, and also of the letters filed in the office, that no letter came with those books. In such cases, where there is no indication whither or how the certificate is to be sent, we do not venture to send it out at random. The right however is secured by the entry; the certificate is nothing more than an evidence of it. I have now the honor to inclose yours and to assure you of the regard with which I am Sir Your most obedt. humble servt,   Th: Jefferson

PrC (DLC). FC (DNA: RG 59, PCC No. 120).

The works mentioned by Edwards are identified in the note to his letter to TJ of 4 July 1791. TJ did not record in SJL receipt of Edwards' letter of 26 Apr. 1791, but, whether that letter accompanied the books or not, it did come to rest in the departmental files (RC in DNA: RG 59, MLR).

Peter de Franchi to Robert Morris

Tenerife, Port Orotava, 14 July 1791. Recommends his friend and neighbor, John Culnan, for the consulship of these islands as he knows "no person better qualifyed in every respect to serve his Country, as he did during the war in capacity of Deputy Clothier Genl." He will be further indebted to Morris for his exertions, joined to his "powerful influence to carry my friends point."

RC (DLC: Washington Papers); endorsed by TJ: "Culnan for Teneriffe. given in by Mr. R. Morris." Enclosures: (1) Pasley Barry & Little to Morris, 14 July 1791; (2) John Cologan & Sons to Robert Morris, 16 Aug. 1791, both recommending Culnan; (3) statement dated 12 Aug. 1791, signed by John Cologan & Sons, John Pasley & A. Little, and Peter de Franchi, testifying to the genuineness of an enclosed copy of an affidavit sworn to in Philadelphia on 4 Dec. 1782 by Plunket Fleeson stating that John Culnan, "a Gentleman from Ireland, hath voluntarily taken and subscribed the Oath of Allegiance, and Fidelity as directed by an Act of General Assembly of Pennsylvania" (same; all in the same clerk's hand except for signatures).

On a later list of candidates for appointment as U.S. consuls, TJ wrote and then struck out the following note after Teneriffe: "John Culnan. of   to be Consul. recommended by John and   Moylan and others. see the papers. there is rather more reason for than against the appointment, tho it is not very important" (List of U.S. Consuls, 15 Feb. 1793, PrC: DLC). On 30 Dec. 1793 Stephen Moylan wrote to TJ urging Culnan's appointment. On verso TJ wrote: "John Culnan to be Consul for Oratava in Teneriffe" (RC in DLC: Washington Papers). Culnan was appointed consul there 29 May 1794 and served until 1 Jan. 1800 (JEP, I, 158).

To F. P. Van Berckel

SIR   Philadelphia July 14. 1791.

I take the liberty of troubling you with the perusal of the inclosed papers from Mr. Shaw, consul for the U.S. in the East Indies, wherein you will observe he complains of a prohibition from the government of Batavia to *American* ships *by name* to have any trade in that port, while such trade was permitted to other nations. I do not hesitate to presume that something has been misunderstood in this case. My presumption is founded on those sentiments of general amity which subsist between our government and that of the United Netherlands, and also on the whole tenor of our treaty which secures to us always the treatment of the most favored nation. Nevertheless the refusal by the government of Batavia has been so formal, so deliberate and pointed as to render it necessary to ask for some explanation. If you will allow me the honour of a moment's conference on this subject the first time you come to town, I shall be obliged to you: and in the mean time have that of assuring you of those sentiments of esteem and respect with which I am Sir Your most obedt. & most humble servt,   TH: JEFFERSON

PrC (DLC). FC (DNA: RG 59, PCC No. 120, IV).

Washington transmitted Shaw's letter and its enclosures to TJ in his of 15 June, requesting him to consider them and, on his return to Philadelphia, to be prepared to render an opinion. TJ responded immediately, concluding that the matter was serious enough to warrant a formal representation but that it should not be made through Dumas, the American agent at The Hague, because he was out of favor with the government (TJ to Washington, 20 June 1791). The disturbing implications of Shaw's letter also prompted TJ to solicit Tench Coxe's information about American trade with Holland and her possessions for use in preparing the report on commerce which he expected to present at the opening of Congress (see Coxe to TJ, ca. June and 19 July 1791).

There is no record in SJPL to indicate that TJ gave his opinion in writing concerning the nature of his proposed representation. But, as was his custom in matters of importance, he must have submitted the above letter for Washington's approval before dispatching it. Van Berckel, resident minister of the Netherlands whom TJ chose as the channel of communication, gave his disappointing response almost a year later (Van Berckel to TJ, 31 May 1792). There was no further exchange of letters on the subject, but TJ did submit to the minister "*privately and informally*" an extract of that part of his report on commerce concerning Dutch-American trade and asked him to verify its accuracy (TJ to Van Berckel, 13 Feb. 1793; Van Berckel to TJ, 22 Feb. 1793; see TJ's Report on Commerce, 16 Dec. 1793).

ENCLOSURE

Samuel Shaw to George Washington

SIR   Canton in China December 7th. 1790.

The commerce of a nation being one of the principal objects of the attentions of it's rulers, I hope it will not be deemed inconsistent with the duties of the office with which you have been pleased to honor me, that I submit to your consideration some particulars relative to the trade of the Citizens of the United States with those of the United Netherlands at Batavia, the capital of their establishments in India.

Having sailed from Boston the latter end of March last, in an entire new Ship, built, navigated, and owned by Citizens of America, I arrived at Batavia, the first Port of my destination, on the 30th. of August following; when to my no small astonishment I was informed by the head officer of the customs, that all commerce with the Americans was prohibited by orders from Holland, and that we should be allowed to take only the necessary refreshments for our passage to Canton, my second port of destination. Notwithstanding this information from the Shabander, I thought it my duty to exercise the right of petitioning to the Governor General and the Council for permission to trade, as had been heretofore the custom; and accordingly I was the next morning presented to his Excellency at his Levee, and in two hours after delivered to him my petition, at the Council board, where I received for answer, that the prayer of it could not be granted.

After informing myself, from the Shabander, of the reasons on which the prohibition of the Americans to trade at Batavia was grounded, I thought it incumbent on me as Consul for the United States, to make a representation to the Governor and Council on a matter which I conceived so nearly to concern the welfare of our Country. On communicating to the Shabander this my determination, he assented to the propriety of it, and observed that though the prohibition was in the highest degree injurious both to the Americans and to

[630]

the inhabitants of Batavia, yet if the former did not complain to the supreme authority, when they had an opportunity, it would ill become that respectable body to take any notice of the matter to the Administration in Holland. Accordingly on Saturday the 4th. of September, I drew up a memorial to the Governor and Council and enclosed it in a letter to the Shabander, requesting him to take the earliest opportunity of having it presented. On seeing that Gentleman afterwards, he assured me that the memorial should be presented on the ensuing Tuesday, and that it would be favorably received, it being the wish not only of the inhabitants, but of the Government also, that the commerce at Batavia should be as free for the Americans as it was for any other nation.

To the aforegoing particulars I take the liberty of adding copies of the letter and declaration above mentioned, and of begging that you will believe me to be, with the most respectful attachment, Sir Your most obedient humble Servant,
SAMUEL SHAW

PrC (DLC); in hand of William Blackwell; at head of text: "To the President of the United States of America." FC (DNA: RG 59, PCC No. 120, IV). Enclosures: (1) "Letter from Samuel Shaw, Consul for the United States of America, to the honble. Nicholas Englehard, Shabander of Batavia, 4th Septemr. 1790," stating that on his arrival there on 30 Aug. in the American ship *Massachusetts* of Boston, bound for Canton, he had requested privileges hitherto accorded American citizens trading there; that he was grateful for the Shabander's politeness in presenting him to the governor general and the council in order to request such permission to dispose of articles for this market as had been given him on his voyage in 1786; but that to his surprise he had been told that all commerce with Americans was absolutely prohibited. Shaw then concluded: "My acquaintance with and respect for the Law of Nations teach me that, in such circumstances, implicit obedience is a virtue and I shall accordingly, on the morrow, proceed in my voyage, declaring as owner of . . . ship and cargo, that no article of the same has been or will be sold during our stay; and that nothing has been purchased here, except water, vegetables, and other refreshments for our passage to Canton. – At the same time that I make this declaration, permit me, sir, to observe to you, that I have reason to believe this prohibition is laid upon my Countrymen on account of evil reports, which have been propagated to their prejudice by persons unfriendly to both Countries; and I have therefore, as Consul for my Nation, taken the liberty of making a

Representation to the Government here upon the subject, which I herewith enclose, and request you will [take] the earliest opportunity of having it presented. As a public officer and a good citizen, I feel for the honor of my Country. As a merchant, the prohibition is extremely detrimental to my interest. These motives I hope will plead my excuse for troubling you on the present occasion" (PrC in Blackwell's hand in DLC; word in brackets missing from text and supplied from FC in DNA: RG 59, PCC No. 120, IV). (2) Declaration of Samuel Shaw to the Governor General and Council of Batavia, 4 Sep. 1790, stating that, as supercargo and part owner of the ship *Hope* from New York, he stopped at Batavia in July 1786 for twenty days, during which time neither he nor anyone acting for him violated trade laws by clandestine exportation of pepper, coffee, or spices; that he then left for Canton and remained there as U.S. consul until January 1789 when he took passage for America; that he believed other American shipowners and captains stopping at Batavia since 1786 had likewise observed its laws and customs; that "Coffee from the Isles of France and Bourbon, pepper from the coast of Malabar and other places in India, and spices from Batavia" could be purchased by Americans from English ships at Canton as well as from the Chinese on terms affording them a reasonable profit; that, in consequence of reports to the prejudice of his countrymen, "they have not only been prohibited all commerce here, but have been . . . classed with smugglers"; that, because of this prohibition, the large amount of non-contraband articles he had brought from America expressly for the market of Batavia would have to be carried to Canton, where they were not wanted, thereby greatly injuring him as owner; that in a particular manner it thus became his duty as consul for his nation "to use every means in his power to vindicate it from the unjust aspersions under which it suffers"; and that, believing this could be done in a little time, he "confides in the justice of the administration in Holland, and in that of Batavia, that his Countrymen will then be admitted to the full enjoyment of all privileges allowed to any other nation, more especially as the connection at present happily subsisting between their Republic and the United States of America has . . . the equitable principle of reciprocal good for its immediate object" (PrC in Blackwell's hand in DLC; FC in DNA: RG 59, PCC No. 120, IV).

From Joseph Fenwick

Bordeaux, 15 July 1791. Enclosing entry and clearance of American vessels there for period 1 Jan. to 30 June. Return for cargoes laden there as particular as the nature of customhouse clearances and "the general disposition of the Shippers to conceal their expeditions" permit. — The Consular Convention has never been promulgated, hence consuls dependent on captains and consignees for information desired, which makes exercise of their functions "rather an act of courtesy than right." Short informs him that ministers promise to publish it without delay, having theretofore been prevented by "the multitude of business." This has prevented his establishing agents in neighboring ports and giving account of American produce received at Bayonne, Charente, Rochefort, the islands of Oleron, and Ré.

In April he sent TJ the act levying general import duties. American whalebone, after the arrêt of 29 Dec. 1787, pays 6₶-13s-4d. per cwt., other foreign bone 15₶ per cwt. on the gross weight. All articles pay on gross weight save tobacco, which is accorded tare of 12% as are a few fine articles. Marseilles has lately become a free port. Bayonne and Dunkirk retain their freedom, but it is probably to be desired they be put on same footing as others, since tobacco trade shows their disadvantage to national revenue and to commerce in general. "Tobacco is pored in there from all quarters, and sold not higher than in other ports where it is manufactured and introduced illicitly . . . without paying duty, to the injury of the fair trader and manufacturer." — If some measure not speedily taken to put carrying of tobacco on more equal footing, American navigation will soon lose "all proportion of the freights" for French consumption. The lesser duty on that in French vessels, though they may navigate at greater expense, gives such a decided advantage that Americans cannot compete. Also, the law denying French papers to any foreign built ships "will totally preclude any masque of their colours." Several ships sent from different ports for tobacco have already had a great influence on price and sale, none buying save for immediate use in anticipation of a price nearly equal to the difference in duty favoring French bottoms. Sale is now very dull and slow throughout France at 25 to 40 per cwt.

The new Constitution is nearly finished, with internal peace and no danger of foreign attack apprehended, though there are some fears from the English armament and threats from French refugees and parts of German empire.

Assignats lose from 8 to 20%, varying with the sum in different parts: at Bordeaux they lose 4 to 15%. Exchange is 20 to 23% under par. Yet labor, living, and merchandise not affected by exchange have not increased in cost.

He has received TJ's of 13 May and notes "with infinate pleasure . . . the unparalled prosperity of our Country." He hopes it may long enjoy the happiness and prosperity that "Nature, the wisdom of its Rulers, and the prudence of its Citizens have lay'd the foundation for."

RC (DNA: RG 59, CD); endorsed by TJ as received 22 Oct. 1791 and so recorded in SJL.

From Mary Jefferson

MY DEAR PAPA   Monticello, July 16th. 1791

I have received both your letters, that from Lake George and of June 26th. I am very much obliged to you for them, and think that the bark you wrote on prettier than paper. Mrs. Monroe and Aunt Bolling are here. My aunt would have written to you, but she was unwell. She intends to go to the North Garden. Mr. Monroe is gone to Williamsburg to stay two or three weeks, and has left his lady here. She is a charming woman. My sweet Anne grows prettier every day. I thank you for the pictures and nankeen that you sent me, which I think very pretty. Adieu, dear papa. I am your affectionate daughter,   MARIA JEFFERSON

MS not found; text taken from Randolph, *Domestic Life*, p. 170, where the date is given as 10 July 1791. Recorded in SJL as written 16 July and as received 9 Aug. 1791. The date was evidently blurred or unclear, for in his letter to Martha of 14 Aug. 1791 TJ referred to "Maria's . . . of July 16." and a week later in his response to Mary he referred to it as "Your letter of July 10." The Editors have accepted the date given above as the more probable one since it gained TJ's approval two out of three times.

From John Pemberton

ESTEEMED FRIEND   7th month. 16th. 1791.

I send the Books thou paid for 2 months past. They are not in such good order as I could have wished. They suffered while in the Bookseller's hands — that if thou does not approve of them, I cannot insist on thy taking them.

6 vol; Plutarch's lives Greek.⎱
7 vol; do. . . . . . . Latin. ⎰ 2. 10. –

Thy friend,   JOHN PEMBERTON

I have not as yet received any reply to the Letter I wrote my Brother Isaac Zane respecting the Other books thou pointed out from the Catalogue.

RC (MHi); addressed: "For Thomas Jefferson"; endorsed by TJ as received 16 July 1791 and so recorded in SJL.

On the day before TJ departed on his northern tour, he paid Pemberton $6.66 for the two sets of Plutarch's *Lives* in Greek and Latin editions (Account Book, 16 May 1791). These were but two titles out of a total of fifty-two, aggregating 223 volumes, in which he had indicated an interest. These were offered at £243-4-3, which was not much less than TJ's quarterly salary. Pemberton, a Quaker missionary, was a member of one of Philadelphia's wealthiest and most philanthropic families, long experienced in the Indian and shipping trade. But in this transaction he was dealing with one of the most astute and knowledgeable bookmen of the day, just returned from Europe where he had dealt with the leading booksellers of Paris, London, and Amsterdam. We know what titles TJ had asked Pemberton to set aside for his consideration and what TJ offered because of the letter that Pemberton wrote to his brother-in-law, Isaac Zane – the latter a friend and legislative colleague of TJ's of long standing. Pemberton's letter to Zane reads in part: "Loving Brother . . . I annex a list of some books which T. Jefferson has some mind to take, but his terms are such I thot, it right to Consult thee first. I offered to take £110 for them, but he says he would not give £60. Thou may see they are many of them in Latin and Greek, and so not like to suit every man. They have lain long and probably may remain yet Long unless sold Low. But his Offer is so far below the valuation in 1782. I Could not Consent to it, until I had informed thee, and desire thy Spedy Answer as he will want to know the re[sult]" (John Pemberton to Isaac Zane, 14 May 1791, PHi: Zane Papers). The enclosed list is as follows:

			Vols.	Price in the Catalogue		
Folio	No. 8	Montfaucon	10	£35		
	237	Rycauts Peru	1	1		
	293.	Ligons history of Barbados	1		7.	6.
Quarto.		Dauphin Editions, in Latin				
			vols.	Price.		
	No. 12	Plautus Comedies	2	£4		
	14.	the same, (elegant)	2.	4.4		
	15	Statius	2.	4.4		
	16	Apuleius works	2.	4.4		
	17	Cicero on Oratory	2.	4.4		
	18	Horace	2.	4.4		
	19	Plinys Natural histy	5.	10 10		
	20	Quintus Curtius	1.	2.2		
	22	Panegyrici Umberes	1	2.2		
	23	Aurelius' Compendium	1.	2.2		
	24	Boethius	1.	2.2		
	25	Livy's history	6.	12.12		
	26	Cornelius Nepos	1.	2.2		
	27	Tacitus	4.	8.8		
	28	Ovid	4.	8.8		
	29	Petronius	2.	4.4		
	30	Justin	1.	2		
	31.	Salust	1.	2		
	32	Phedrus	1.	1.1		
	33	Paterculus	1.	1.1		

		Price in the Catalogue			
		vols.	Price.		
34	Eutropius	1.	1.1		
35	Ciceros Orations	3.	6.6.		
36	Valerius Maximus	1.	2.2		
37.	Claudian	1.	2.2		
38	Prudentius	1.	2.2		
39	Aulius Gellius	1.	2.2		
40	Juvenal & Persius	1.	2.2		
42	Manilius' Astronomy	1.	2.2		
43	Martials Epigrams	1.	2.2		
44	Pompius Sextus	1.	2.2		
45	Ciceros Epistles	1.	2.2		
46	Terence	1.	2.2		
48	Quintilian &ca.	2.	3		
49	Catullus &ca.	2.	3.5		
50	Quintilian	2.	3.10		
51.	Florus	1.	2		
52	Dictys Cretensis	1.	2	127	16
54.	History of the french Academy of Sciences	26	30		
60	Acta erudita	43	25		
87.	Philosophical Transactions	29	15		
142	Marcellinus	1		5	
74.	Sales 2d. Voyage to America	1		5	
104	Plutarchs' Lives, Greek	6	1.	10	
132	Glauber	1		3.	9
133	ditto	1		5	
202	Boyle's works	4	1		
3	Journal de Scavans	24	3		
38	Plutarch's Lives—Latin	7	2		
345	Boyle's Philosophical works	4		12	
		223. vols	£243.	4.	3

Octavo (applies to rows 142, 74, 104, 132, 133)

Duodo. (applies to rows 202, 3, 38, 345)

At the foot of the text Pemberton added a note showing that the prices were "from the Catalogue delivered Wm. Pritchard" and that "Thomas Jefferson offers £57. for the whole in this List or he will leave out Monfaucon £35 – the Dauphin Editions £127.16," totalling £162-16-0. For the remainder, valued at £80-8-3, TJ offered £25 (enclosure, undated, PHi: Zane Papers). In brief, TJ offered about a fourth of the list price for the whole and about a third for the remnant. Apparently the offer was not accepted.

TJ owned several editions of Plutarch's works, including the first printed edition of the *Lives* (Florence, Giunta, 1517) and the first complete edition of his *Opera* (Geneva, Stephanus, 1572), the latter hav-ing been acquired from the library of Colonel William Byrd of Westover (Sowerby, Nos. 68, 69, 1312, and 1313). Indeed, one of his last library acquisitions was *Plutarchi politica*, published in Paris in 1824 (*President Jefferson's Library*, Poor sale, Washington, 1829, No. 641). Why, then, on the eve of his departure on his northern tour did he single out and pay for Plutarch's *Lives* from the lot offered by Pemberton and leave the acquisition of the remainder to be decided after his return? Surely, on a journey of observation of a month's duration, under rather strenuous conditions and through a section of the nation he had never before travelled, he would not have added to his luggage thirteen volumes, even in duodecimo. It beggars credulity to suppose that, on such a tour of topographical, political, economic, and botanical exploration, he would have wished to read about Greeks and Romans whose lives had long since become familiar to him. Only one explanation for his selection of Plutarch at this particular moment seems to accord with plausibility. Young John Wayles Eppes had just arrived in Philadelphia and was being guided by TJ in his studies. He was eighteen and perhaps had not been given the kind of instruction in the classics that TJ had received under the Rev. James Maury, thereby acquiring the lifelong habit and the inestimable "Luxury of reading the Greek and Roman authors in all the beauties of their originals" – an acquisition for which he felt more indebted to his father "than for all the other luxuries his cares and affections have placed within my reach" (TJ to John Brazer, 24 Aug. 1819; on TJ's classical education, see Malone, *Jefferson*, I, 40-6, and L. B. Wright, "Thomas Jefferson and the Classics," Am. Phil. Soc., *Procs.*, LXXXVII [July, 1943], 223-33). Whether or not TJ thought Eppes deficient in the classics, he was at this time

much concerned about the need for keeping the youth on the straight path of his studies at an age when he might be "more susceptible of delights from other sources" (TJ to John Brazer, 24 Aug. 1819). It is easy to imagine TJ, as he was about to leave his nephew alone in the capital for a month, advising him to read and profit from the moralistic parallels set forth in Plutarch's biographies of eminent Greeks and Romans (on his concern about Eppes' course of studies and temptations that might interfere, see his letters to Eppes' parents, 15 May 1791). Didactic and disciplinary with his own children, he would have been quite in character if, in presenting the volumes to Eppes, he had gently admonished him that he would expect a report of progress on his return. It is also plausible to assume that TJ may have had Eppes' training in the classics in mind when he offered to purchase the Dauphin editions of classical works, many of which he already possessed in other editions at Monticello and some of which had come in the shipment of books he received from Paris a few months earlier (see note, Short to TJ, 7 Nov. 1790).

To William Smith

SIR   Philadelphia July 16. 1791.

The President of the United States desiring to avail the public of your services as Auditor of the Treasury of the U. S. I have now the honor of enclosing you the Commission. You will readily concieve from the nature of this office that every day's suspension of its functions adds new instances of inconvenience to the public, and to individuals. While I indulge myself therefore in expressing my hopes and felicitations for the public, that you will undertake a trust so important for them, I am charged to add the desire that you may find it convenient to come on with all practicable dispatch. I have the honour to be with sentiments of the most perfect esteem & respect, Sir Your most obedient & most humble servt.

TH: JEFFERSON

PrC (DLC); mutilated, so that about a fourth of the line endings are lost, these being supplied from FC (DNA: RG 59, PCC No. 120).

Soon after reaching Mount Vernon on returning from his southern tour, Washington informed Hamilton of his intention to appoint Wolcott to succeed Eveleigh as

Comptroller of the Treasury. At the same time he said that he would not name an Auditor until he reached Philadelphia (Washington to Hamilton, 13 June 1791, Syrett, *Hamilton*, VIII, 470-1; see also Editorial Note and group of documents on Coxe's candidacy for the Comptrollership, at 16 Apr. 1791). But several weeks before this communication was written, Hamilton, acting on the understandable assumption that his choice of Wolcott would be supported, sought to interest his own candidates in the office of Auditor. His agency in the matter was James McHenry, and, while his letter on the subject is missing, it is clear that his first choice was Otho H. Williams and his second William Smith, both of Maryland. Early in May McHenry approached Williams, mentioned Hamilton's "power and disposition," and held out the promise of further advancement. Williams gave the impression that he would have accepted the office of Comptroller but declined the lesser post on the ground of health. McHenry then tried to persuade William Smith, who, he reported to Hamilton, "with less shew of talents will make a much better auditor. He will have as little to learn as the General; is as systematic, a more perfect and correct accountant, of great respectability and of longer standing in society. I found also here that the comptrollership was a more darling object." McHenry finally persuaded Smith to permit him to use his discretion in the matter, thus giving the same latitude to Hamilton.

"I was obliged to intimate," McHenry reported, "that from the opinion you had of him, I would entertain no doubt but his appointment would be certain unless the President got entangled to the Southward" (McHenry to Hamilton, 3 May 1791, Syrett, *Hamilton*, VIII, 321-2). Hamilton understood as clearly as McHenry and others that one of Washington's leading principles in the distribution of patronage was to see that the various sections were fairly represented, a factor which no doubt induced him to look southward with the Comptrollership being clearly destined for a New Englander.

Thus, within ten days after Washington returned to Philadelphia, Hamilton had put forward the candidacy of William Smith, and this recommendation, like that of Wolcott, was unhesitatingly accepted. TJ's letter transmitting Smith's commission on behalf of the President reveals both the urgency with which the matter was being pressed and the uncertainty as to whether the appointment would be accepted. The doubt was well-founded. Smith acknowledged the above letter on 22 July 1791, and, while his letter has not been found, it is clear that he declined the office. Late in November Washington nominated Richard Harrison, a merchant of Alexandria, as Auditor. The Senate, after inquiring which of the several Richard Harrisons in the United States was meant, promptly confirmed him (JEP, I, 90).

From Philip Wilson

London, 16 July 1791. On 4 Feb. he sent TJ a schedule and affidavit of the truth of papers furnished through Judge McKean and now encloses a further petition concerning those "most oppressive evasions and wrongs." – Relying on TJ's humane character, he hopes for his official attention to a matter of such striking injustice done to "a once prosperous Merchant, now Empoverished; not by his own Errours; but from National, or Governmental, breach of Duty, Honour, and Justice, by a breach of an agreement come under between the British and American Governments, on both of which I have a claim of Justice."

Tr (DNA: RG 76, British Spoliations); at head of text: "Duplicate"; at foot of text: "then from No. 57 Marsham-street West-minster London." Records in SJL show that one version of text was received 27 Oct. 1791 and another 10 Feb. 1792.

An account of Philip Wilson's long and unsuccessful effort to obtain redress for the loss of his ship *Mentor* is given in the note to TJ to McKean, 23 Dec. 1790. The documents which TJ returned with that letter are to be found in Wilson's transcripts of his various appeals in DNA: RG 76, British Spoliations. The schedule mentioned as having been transmitted in Wilson's letter of 4 Feb. 1791 may be found in the same series, but that letter, recorded in SJL as received 2 Apr. 1791, is missing. With the above, Wilson enclosed his petition, dated at Westminster 16 July 1791, "To his Excellency the most Honourable President, Vice-President, Senators; and the Right Honourable Congress of the United States of North America." In this Wilson referred to his three former petitions of 11 Mch. and 4 and 31 July 1790 and stated that, on "the 3d of February last," he had sent to "the Honourable Thomas Jefferson . . . Secretary of Foreign and Domestick affairs" a schedule of fifteen papers with documents from the High Court of Admiralty concerning his case; that he hoped for a remonstrance from the United States against the injury done him by the British government in "this complicated Act of Wrong and breach of Treaty and Law"; and that he had left at the Treasury Office accounts proving the cost of *Mentor* and a manifest of her cargo showing his total damages to be £11,797-6-3½ sterling. In the course of this petition Wilson quoted the full text of his appeal to the Lords Commissioners of Appeals for Prize Causes, in which he stated that, in response to a petition to the Senate of the United States, he had been assured a claim for the destruction of *Mentor* would be made "by the American Ambassador that may in time be sent to the English Court," but that in the meantime he might perish in prison and his family be destitute for food. He therefore prayed for a recommendation to the Privy Council urging immediate relief. This petition, as recorded in the one enclosed with the above letter, was dated at Westminster 19 May 1791. Two days later, as Wilson set forth in his petition to the American government, he attended the Privy Council and "went up to the head of the Board where the Lord President Earl of Camden, and Mr. Pitt the Minister sat; and begged of their Lordships, *Justice and immediate relief*; and told Mr. Pitt that he had delivered his papers at the Treasury Office twelve months ago agreeable to his instructions: The Earl of Camden got up and, rather warmly, said 'We can do nothing more for you here, we have recommended your Case,' and . . . (lowering his eyes and voice towards Mr. Pitt and the petitioner) said 'It is a compassionate Case,' and, as Mr. Pitt was going away without answering, His Lordship the Earl of Camden, stoped him and, it is supposed, told him of the petitioner's application to the American Government, or Senate of the United States."

Camden's compassion drove Wilson to frame another petition to the Lords Commissioners of Appeals and the Privy Council, dated 25 May 1791, which he also quoted at length in the appeal enclosed in the above letter. In the former he declared that his was " 'a compassionate Case' not from want of Right by Law, but from the scanty and wrong dispensations thereof, in the High Court of Admiralty; and from the breach of the Statutes of this Country, and of hospitality to the pauper in Doctors Commons; as well as from the Delay of Duty in his Majesty's Government." In consequence, after reciting at length the proceedings which he regarded as a miscarriage of justice, Wilson asked a review of his case on appeal that he might not "sink in the distinction between *Legal Right* and *Compassion*; but receive some immediate relief" (quoted in Wilson's petition to the President and Congress, 16 July 1791; DNA: RG 76, British Spoliations; endorsed by TJ).

TJ did not respond to the above appeal, nor did he submit the petition to Congress. He probably saw no need even to consult the President on the matter. While SJL shows that TJ received letters from Wilson dated 28 Nov. 1791, 28 Mch. and 3 Dec. 1792, 27 July 1797, 28 July 1798, 25 Mch. 1801, 13 and 15 Apr. 1802, 17 June 1804, and 28 Jan. and 15 July 1805 – most of which are missing – there is no evidence that he ever responded to any official or private communication from the unfortunate man. He did, however, recommend his case to the attention of the new minister to Great Britain (TJ to Pinckney, 11 June 1792). Possibly Wilson's imprudence in making statements to the British government to the effect that the Senate had assured him it would espouse his claim, together with other assertions set forth in the two petitions quoted in that to the American government, influenced TJ's attitude of aloofness. Wilson had a far more defensible claim at law than that of William Green and his brig *Rachel* which Joshua Johnson prosecuted with such vigor and which TJ also handled with silence (see Editorial Note and group of documents at 31 May 1791). But the owner of *Mentor*, while earning the compassion of Camden and others, was not his own best advocate. In his petition to the Lords Commissioners of Appeals and the Privy Council of 25 May 1791 Wilson added this postscript: "The petitioner not having Legal Counsel nor a Proctor assigned to him, wishes to express himself as inoffensively and well as he can, so as to be Clear and Intelligible." This he did, but without success even in a good cause and before sympathetic officials.

From William Blount

"Territory of the United States of America south of the River Ohio, W. Cobbs," *17 July 1791.* He received TJ's letter of 12 March on 19 May and had already recommended that census be taken in every county of Territory on the last Saturday of July by the militia captains and had given the form as required by act of Congress except in that recommended by himself. In order to know whether there are 5,000 free white males of full age in the Territory, the second column lists free white males of 21 and upwards instead of 16 and upwards, while third column lists free white males under 21 instead of under 16. With the Indian claim by the treaty of 2 July with the Cherokees being extinguished, he has ordered a census to be taken in August in the land south of French Broad. – He received TJ's of 26 March on 22 May. "Besides the three exceptions of private claims which have been stated to you against the General right of Congress to the whole land Ceded by North Carolina there are two others, that is the lands entered in the entry Offices of the Counties of Washington and Sullivan in this Territory." Immediately on receiving TJ's letter he ordered a return to be made of the lands entered in these offices and expects a report in a few days. – He has been unable to take the bearings of the mountains marking the eastern Territorial boundary because of his attendance at the Cherokee treaty, but this will be done during the present week and the information forwarded by the next conveyance.

RC (DNA: RG 59, SWT; M-471/1). Recorded in SJL as received 5 Aug. 1791.

From Charles Carter

Ludlow Farm, 17 July 1791. He is obliged for the information in TJ's of the 10th. He will leave it to his son to decide, but his own choice would be for an American education. "The prejudices formerly imbibed, by the Americans . . . sent to Brittain for an education, I always thought, were too strong, ever to be overcome. But since our Independance, I hope that no such consequences will derive. Indeed if I were to Judge of what has come within my own observation, in the political line, I woud clearly decide in favor of an American Education. But in Physick, their experience must be greater then ours can possably be, and the opportunities a student will there have, especially in the Anato'mal line far superior."

He now encroaches a little further on TJ's goodness and asks whether a loan can be obtained from the Bank with land as security. "The very great scarcity of money in this State distresses many men, me at this time greatly so. . . . coud I obtain 1500 It woud enable me . . . to pay my just Debts, compleat the Education of my four Sons, and to live in a comfortable manner, and I hope untill my Children are setled in the world." The 5,000 acres he recovered from Robert Carter in Loudoun would be the security, the rents of which, even at the present low rate, exceed the interest. But as many of the most valuable lots "are for the life of Old Robert Carter only, the rise will be great, so much so, as in a few Years to discharge the debt. Unless I can accomplish this desirable object, I shal be torn to pieces by my Creditors and indeed nothing, but a Jail, can I expect. Another good purpose will be answered, Mrs. Carter, and my Sons will have an opportunity of working between 40 and 50 valuable Slaves to great advantage. The lands are within 30 to 40 miles of George Town, the intended seat of Government. I am happy to hear, our worthy President is returned well, I had the pleasure of seing him as he went, and returnd, he had a very fortunate journey. I shall be glad to hear, yours very much to your satisfaction, and my very much respected Friend Mr. Maddison, was restored to a perfect state of Health. Be so good as to present my respects to him, and be assured Dr. Sr that I am with esteem Yr Affe. Friend."

RC (MHi); endorsed by TJ as received 21 July 1791 and so recorded in SJL.

From Robert Montgomery

Alicante, 17 July 1791. He has been deprived of TJ's favors since his of 13 Mch. – He encloses two letters "from one of our slaves at Algiers." The pirates continue to cruise. A 20-gun "Xebeque" touched at Carthagena for water and provisions last Sunday after having been, he reported, 40 days in the Atlantic. Also, a 2-gun rowboat off Malaga spoke of several vessels now in quarantine here. But despite the friendly reception their vessels meet with on the coast of Spain, the Bey of Mascara continues the seige of Oran with all his power, being no doubt supported by his master, the Dey of Algiers. The Spanish force makes a brilliant resistance, but the garrison is by no means out of danger.

RC (DNA: RG 59, CD); endorsed by TJ as received 22 Oct. 1791 and so recorded in SJL. On this day TJ recorded receipt of only one letter (missing) from Richard O'Bryen, dated 28 Apr. 1791.

To Thomas Mann Randolph, Jr.

Dear Sir   Philadelphia July 17. 1791.

Your favor of the 7th. came to hand yesterday and brought me the news, always welcome, of your being all well. I have taken effectual means of repairing the loss of the sugar maple seed, by bespeaking a new supply of seed, and purchasing a considerable number of young trees from Prince in Long-island who will forward them to Richmond in the fall. The species of rice which has succeeded, is that I believe which was the best for our climate, as requiring less sun than the other. I am happy to hear the crop of wheat is likely to turn out well. 3000 bushels of wheat will be of double the value of the tobo. made by the same hands at the same places the last year, which was a favorable year too: and when we consider that the first year of transition from one species of culture to another is subject to disadvantages, it gives favorable hopes of the change in future. It is an additional proof that 100 bushels of wheat are as easily made as 1000 ℔. of tobo. – The last 22. hhds. shipt by Mr. Hylton are arrived here. – Tobacco of the first quality in France has got to 45/9 Virginia money the hundred. – Stratton, who brought my tobo. will take on board some stores for me. I suppose they will be at Richmond before the last of the month, after which I shall beg the favor of you to have them brought up as occasion shall offer. My visit to Albemarle is at present under a more unfavorable aspect than when I wrote last. It is now rather believed that the President will not go to Mount Vernon this year. If so, tho' it will not prevent my visit altogether, it will very much shorten it. From the 7th. to the 14th. of July we have had the most intolerable heats. I hardly remember to have ever suffered so much. The greatest height of the thermometer was 94. or 95.° – I mentioned in my last week's letter that I was endeavoring to get a regular post established from Richmond thro' Columbia and Charlottesville to Staunton, so as to cost nothing to the public. This will render all private riders illegal, a circumstance to be attended to in contracts with them. Remember me affectionately to my daughters, and be assured of the sincere attachment of Dear Sir Yours affectionately,

TH: JEFFERSON

RC (DLC). TJ erroneously recorded this letter in SJL as being addressed to Martha Jefferson Randolph.

From William Short

DEAR SIR   Paris July 17. 1791.

I inclose you a note of your account as given to me by Mr. Grand and by which you will see that there remains a balance in your favor of 2709 ᵗᵗ. 18. which has been remitted agreeably to your desire to Messrs. V. Staphorst & Hubbard. The clock which I am now promised daily and the mending your reveille watch will be to be paid out of this balance and I shall accordingly draw on it for that purpose when Chanterot shall be ready. – Mr. Gautier desired me also to inclose you the letters of the Jeweller to him concerning the price of the diamonds. – I hope you will recieve safely by Petit the picture from which they were detached.

My late private letters to you were May 2. by Petit and two dated June 7. one by M. de Ternant and the other by M. de Kellerman. They were as usual very full of myself, the latter particularly as I had at the time of writing it a kind of certainty that it would get to your hands before any thing would be done with respect to the nomination for this place. I am tempted to renew the subject at present only from the consideration of the possibility of that letters miscarrying, and from this being a private conveyance. The present therefore is merely a duplicate of that and I hope you will excuse it when you consider the circumstances under which it is written. It seems now certain that no nomination will take place before October next, and it would seem probable that the person appointed will not come out before the spring. In this position of affairs it is impossible for me not to carry my reflexions forward. Although it may appear singular that without knowing whether I shall be thought proper for any place, I should be saying what place I should chuse, yet I cannot help allowing myself to express my sentiments on a subject which interests me so nearly to a person to whom I have been so long accustomed to say every thing.

Should my last letter have been recieved this will become useless as it is a repetition of it. I take it for granted that Ministers plenipotentiary will be appointed here and to London. The expression of the wish of the national assembly for negotiating a treaty of commerce carried out by Ternant will probably hasten the first, as M. de Montmorin has told me that Ternant is directed to inform the American government of the desire of this that their representative here should recieve instructions for that purpose. – The late events and the present situation of affairs here (of which you are informed) may however shew the improbability of any negotiation being effected until something permanent takes place, perhaps the impropriety of setting the negotiation on foot. Of this you alone can judge. I must however add that it is impossible for the present to say when this crisis is to end, or what is to be the issue – of course what kind of government will be established or by whom exercised. This can only effect the time of commencing the negotiation for or rather the conclusion of, a treaty of commerce and not at all the nomination of a minister which has been long intended and is independent of the situation of affairs here. – To return to that subject; should this appointment take place it is of course what I should prefer for the reasons I have so often given and repeated, next to it London, and thirdly the Hague. I take it for granted and hope that the grade will be the same with that at Lisbon. I mentioned to you in my last how disagreeable and how little honorable it would be for me to be superseded here after having been remained so long, and that by a person who would of course be supposed to know much less of the ground. It could not possibly be attributed to any thing but an absolute want of merit on my part. It would be the same thing if I were sent to an inferior place with the same grade. Besides in those little places the diplomatick characters being much more in view than in Paris or London, inferior grades are much more disagreeable. After all I should imagine the Hague would be considered equal to Lisbon, and from the flattering manner in which the Secretary of the treasury has expressed himself to me on my late mission in Holland, and also from the time I have been employed in Europe I should hope it could not be on my account particularly that the grade would be kept inferior. – I mentioned in my last letter what I repeat here that if destined to that place I should be glad to recieve a congé at the same time which would allow me to return in the spring to the U.S. I mentioned also by what degrees I had come to this, and for what reasons I desired it. Even if I were appointed minister here I should like such a conditional congé as would allow me to return if I thought proper, as it is possible that the affairs of this country may be in such a state that a residence here would be useless. In that case it would be highly agreeable to have the possibility of making use of that time for visiting the U.S. and endeavouring to fix myself there. But this however I submit entirely to you. – My desire to have this congé will of course be proportioned to the place I am to have, and as I suppose the lowest would be that of chargé des affaires at the Hague it is under it that I should wish for it the most. If however I am definitively to go there with that grade, the sooner the more agreeable to me, because the longer I remain here in that character the more it will appear against me to give place here to another, and to accept of an inferior grade, viz. an equal grade at an inferior place.

I should prefer much to this what I mentioned in my last. I suppose Congress will soon find it necessary to give you an assistant say for the foreign department in the character of under Secretary of State, with a decent salary of 1800, or 2000. dollars. In such a case if I were thought proper for it I should like better that mode of retiring from Paris than going to the Hague as chargé des affaires. I need not repeat here that should I be allowed to return to America on congé, it would be with a desire to be employed in the manner you mentioned in a former letter and which I should ultimately prefer to any thing else whatever. – In all events I beg you my dear Sir to be so good as to write to me on these subjects. During such a state of uncertainty and anxiety your conjectures would be of much resource and consolation.

The present situation of affairs here and the state of anxiety in which all classes are render this place far from agreeable at this moment. Of course the worst position in Europe is remaining here as at present with the uncertainty of the time I am to continue and even the probability that as soon as the storm passes I shall be sent away. The apprehension therefore that I shall be kept in this posture during the whole of the next winter is exceedingly disagreeable under a variety of considerations. I hope and beg that something definitive may be done in the fall, and that if another person is to come here that he will arrive before the winter, unless it should be contrived so that I could be sure of having the congé in the spring, and in that case I should have no objection to remaining here, if thought necessary, during the winter, instead of going to the Hague or wherever I may be sent. What would be highly disagreeable would be to be obliged to remain here for some time after my successor should be named, if I had not some other appointment which would shew that I was not entirely deprived of the confidence of my country such as that mentioned under you, or something superior to what I have here in some other place.

I have lately recieved from Mr. Brown of Richmond an account of my funds put into his hands by Colo. Skipwith. I hear nothing from the latter and I cannot be much surprized at it, as I cannot concieve how he can reconcile this with the letters he formerly wrote to me. Mr. Brown seems to have the intention of funding these State securities agreeable to the plan of the Secretary. Of course I suppose it was unavoidable as the plan is intolerably unjust as to State securities. I imagine he will do for the best and is certainly much more capable of judging being on the spot than I can be here. I hope if indispensable you will be so kind as to give him your advice, as he may consult you confidentially. But I should have hoped the State of Virginia would have put these securities on a better footing than the funding bill does.

I have heard that you were with Mr. Madison at Boston the 12th.

of June. I don't doubt that you would have found every thing prosperous in this tour. As you were to have been in Philadelphia about
the middle of that month I hope I may now soon hear from you. – You
will recieve with the newspapers which go by Havre an odd volume
which I think must belong to your library; I found it among my
books. –

I have seen here lately a loaf of the maple sugar refined at Philadelphia. I am promised a piece of it for the old Dutchess D'Enville
who had desired me to write to ask you to send her a sample. I
have heard nothing yet of the seeds you promised should be sent to
her. The Duke de la Rochefoucauld begged I would ask you to send
him a few grafts of your best peaches. Don't they come from the
stone simply? He cannot think any peach in the world equal to the
Parisian. Paine has lately left this place. The success of his answer
to Burke seems to have had much weight on him. He was here the
avowed apostle of republicanism and begun to alarm all moderate
people by his counsel for the abolition of monarchy. You will see
in the Moniteur his letter to the Abbe Sieyes and the answer. The
litigation will probably end there, as I hope he will not return here
for some time. He is gone to London and intends going from thence
to Ireland. I think he would have done harm here if he had remained.
I know not what he will do in England or Ireland. He is sure that
the English government is afraid of him but in this he may be
decieved. Adieu my dear Sir. Be so good as to let me hear from you
and believe me sincerely your friend & servant,   W: SHORT

RC (DLC); at foot of text: "Thomas
Jefferson Secretary of State Philadelphia";
at head of text: "*Private*"; endorsed by TJ
as received 22 Oct. 1791 and so recorded
in SJL. PrC (PHi). Enclosure: "Notte du
Compte de Monsieur Jefferson" with Grand
& Cie. showing on the credit side a total
of 9,994₶-6, of which 9,405₶ were received "pour un portrait de brillants." Deb-
its amounting to 7,284₶-8 included 1,680₶
for the President's champagne; 222₶ to
Cathalan for olive trees; 1200₶ to Tolozan
and 800₶ to Sequeville; 2,500₶ to Fenwick
for wines; 282₶-8 to Delamotte for expenses on TJ's carriages, transportation,
and duty on the champagne; and 120₶ "to
Houdon for the dress" (MS dated at Paris,
4 July 1791, with note by Grand & Cie.
showing that ƒ959-14 had been remitted
to Van Staphorst & Hubbard for the bal-

ance of 2,709₶-18, to which Short added
notes to explain the charges in favor of
Fenwick, Delamotte, and Houdon; DLC:
TJ Papers, 65:11232). See Short's addi-
tion to this account in note to his letter to
TJ of 6 Oct. 1791.

The diamonds were taken from the portrait of Louis XVI given to TJ by the King.
For TJ's instructions to Short about this
secret transaction involving the sale of the
diamonds, out of the proceeds of which
the customary gratuities to Tolozan and
Sequeville of the foreign office were to be
taken, see TJ to Short, 24 Jan. 1791, and
Editorial Note on TJ's policy concerning
gifts to foreign diplomats, at 20 Apr. 1790.
For TJ's order of "the costume . . . for the
President's statue," see TJ to Short, 25
Aug. 1790.

From William Linn

SIR,   New-York, July 18th. 1791.

Allow me to present you a sermon on the blessings of that country, the character and privileges of which you have ably and successfully vindicated, and of which you are among its greatest ornaments. – I am, with very great respect, Sir, Your most obedient and most humble servant,   WM. LINN

RC (ViW); endorsed by TJ as received 20 July 1791 and so recorded in SJL. For note on the enclosed sermon and on the subsequent relations between TJ and Linn, see TJ to Linn, 31 July 1791.

From Tench Coxe

July 19th. 1791

Mr. Coxe has the honor to make his acknowledgements to Mr. Jefferson for Sir John St. Clair's pamphlet – the last nine lines of which are as free from reason and as full of passion as anything in Lord Sheffield. The little publication relative to Scotland is curious, and in parts interesting even to the United States. Mr. Coxe begs leave to add a few facts relative to the dutch commercial regulations, the first page of which is from an eminent Dutch Merchant, *here*, the remainder from the same work that contained the account of the Dutch fisheries included in Mr. C's notes of Novemr. last.

MS (DLC). Not recorded in SJL. Enclosures: (1) Information on Dutch trade restrictions indicating that an American-built ship owned by a Dutch citizen may sail between Holland and all other ports except Surinam or any Mediterranean port. Also, American fish and whale and fish oil could be imported into Holland. (2) List of duties on Dutch imports and prohibited articles (in clerk's hand; docketed by Coxe: "Some commercial regulations and duties of Ud. Netherlands"; endorsed by TJ: "Holland"; not recorded in SJL; MS in DLC).

The items from Sinclair that TJ sent to Coxe are described in Vol. 18:367n.

To Henry Knox

DEAR GENERAL   July 19. 1791.

When the hour of dinner is approaching, sometimes it rains, sometimes it is too hot for a long walk, sometimes your business would make you wish to remain longer at your office or return there after dinner, and make it more eligible to take any sort of a dinner in town. Any day and every day that this would be the case you would make me supremely happy by messing with me, without ceremony or other question than whether I dine at home. The hour is from one quarter to three quarters after three, and, taking your chance as to fare, you will be sure to meet a sincere welcome from Yours affectly. & respectfully, Th: Jefferson

PrC (DLC).

From Henry Knox

My dear Sir   July 19. 1791

I have received your friendly note of this morning for which I sincerely thank you. I shall frequently avail myself of your kindness, and I should have done so this day, in order to evince my impressions on the occasion, had I not previously engaged to Mrs. Knox, that I would dine with her being the first time since her late confinement. – I am my dear Sir respectfully and affectionately Yours,

H Knox

RC (MHi); endorsed by TJ as received 19 July 1791 and so recorded in SJL. Dft (MHi: Knox Papers).

From Tench Coxe

Treasury Department, 20 July 1791. In the unavoidable absence of the Secretary of the Treasury, Coxe requests the Secretary of State to have prepared and sent to the Treasury a correct list of U.S. consuls and their places of residence, being necessary for the collectors of the impost.

RC (DNA: RG 59, MLR); in a clerk's hand; endorsed by Remsen as received 20 July 1791, but not recorded in SJL.

From Jean François Froullé

Paris, 20 July 1791. By direction of Mr. Short, he has sent TJ, by way of Delamotte of Le Havre, a little box packed with straw and wrapped in oilcloth containing Desgodets' "L'architecture" in folio at 72℔; plus several journals sent by Short, with the first volume of Millot's *Eléments de l'histoire de France*; to these he has added Le Clerc's *Geométrie* at 6℔; "L'ordre d'architecture" in octavo at 5℔; and he sends 12 numbers of *L'Argus Patriotique*, a new journal which he presumes TJ will like, the subscription to which is 30℔ per year and which he will send if TJ wishes. For the box and packing, 2℔; total, 85℔. – He will always be honored to fill any of TJ's orders: "vous connoissé mon devoument. Soyez assuré quil ne deminura point, non plus que le respect avec lequel jai l'honneur d'être pour vous Monsieur Votre tres humble et tres obéissant Serviteur." [P.S.] He has looked for Piranesi's "Les Monuments de Rome" but only found the complete work in 26 vols., offered to him at 750^{tt}.

RC (MHi); at foot of text: "Mr. cheferson Philadelphia   r: s v P"; endorsed by TJ as received 24 Oct. 1791 and so recorded in SJL.

From William Short

DEAR SIR   Paris July 20. 1791.

You will recieve by the way of Havre the journals of the assembly which will inform you fully of their late proceedings, and particularly those with respect to the King's retreat from Paris, and the organisation of Government[1] in consequence thereof. The report of the seven committees was for prosecutions being carried on against the several persons suspected of being instrumental in the King's retreat. The King was not comprehended in the proposed decree. This brought on a long debated question on his inviolability. The most popular members, viz. four or five of them who are the friends and companions of Brissot de Warville insisted on his being tried also. They composed however a very small minority on the decision of the question, and the plan of the committee passed. In order to render it more palatable to the club des Jacobins and the people of Paris who had loudly manifested contrary sentiments, some articles were previously decreed determining certain cases which should be considered as an abdication on the part of the King. It has been decreed that the present suspension of Regal functions should continue until the completion of the constitution, that is to say as long as it pleases the assembly.

You will see in the journals the various arguments on these questions. I inclose you a paper containing Warville's speech at the Jacobins from which the members of the assembly took every thing they said on that side. This speech is considered as the most able and eloquent that has been made here since Mirabeau.

I mentioned to you in a former letter the Republican party that was forming here. The late question has shewn that their number was small in the assembly, but strong out of it. They were proceeding to petition and even protest against the decree that exempted the King from prosecution. You will see by a paper inclosed that M. de Condorcet, supports the Republican side by his pen. There is no member of the assembly of your acquaintance on that side.

The decree became the pretext for disorders which were so alarming as they were in immediate opposition to the authority of the assembly that it has been thought necessary to try rigorous measures. Crowds assembled during two or three days successively in the champ de Mars under pretence of signing petitions to the assembly against the decree. They were joined always by persons who have been long distinguished here for preaching doctrines of resistance under pretence of liberty, and who are generally supposed the emissaries of foreign powers. You will see by the papers the excesses to which they proceeded and which induced the municipality to proclame the law martial. On the garde nationale approaching the champ de Mars to dissipate them, they were insulted and fired on. The guard fired in their defense. Ten or twelve of the rioters were killed and as many wounded. The rest were immediately dispersed and Paris has been since that event which happened three days ago perfectly quiet. – The assembly have approved the conduct of the municipality and made a decree for punishing mutinous people and incendiary writers.

Two persons have been arrested among numberless other disorderly people, suspected of being employed here by foreign powers. One of them is the Jew Ephraim long famous in the intrigues of Europe. Among his papers they have found the commencement of a letter in cypher to the King of Prussia. It is said to have been decyphered and shews an intention in the King of Prussia to meddle at a proper time in the affairs of this country.

It becomes every day more probable that other powers have the same intention as it seems now certain that England and Prussia will abandon the Porte to its own fate rather than go to war with the two Empires. It begins to be believed that the aversion of Prussia to break with the Emperor, and the conferences of the ministers of England and Prussia sent into Italy to join the Emperor indicate strongly that there is some common object between them. If so it must be France either directly or indirectly. – The Diet of Ratisbon has hitherto been in favor of pacific measures for securing the rights of the Empire attacked by the decrees of the National assembly. They shew now less temperance. On the whole foreign interference which of course will ever depend on the internal situation of France becomes more and more probable. The way of negotiation will probably be first tried, the injuries suffered by the members of the Empire be made the pretext, and after that the personal situation of the Royal family here be made to enter into the account. – As yet these things are on the scale of probabilities only, much as it appears to me mounting every day. I must add however that the diplomatic committee are or affect to be of a different opinion.

The King remains as when I last wrote to you still under guard. M. de la fayette is equally reproached by the courtiers for the harsh manner in which he exercises the post of what they call a jailer, and by the people for the little precaution he takes against future escape. The corps diplomatique are not admitted to pay their court to the Royal family. That matter remains as formerly mentioned. It is whispered that several of them will soon be recalled if no change takes place. Spain will probably give the first example. I inclose you an official communication lately made by the Spanish Ambassador which he has had printed and distributed here. Nothing later has taken place, and in general the several powers of Europe have shewn no marks of their future intentions with respect to the personal situation[2] of the King.

The assignats and the exchange with foreign countries seem to have been not at all affected by the Kings absence and the events subsequent thereto. The sales of ecclesiastical property go on in the same manner and sell as well as before. This circumstance and the indifference shewn in several parts of the Kingdom is what the Republicans plead as proof that the people are sufficiently enlightened to change the government and thus economise thirty millions a year. Several addresses having however been sent to the assembly from the different departments approbatory of the late decree concerning the exemption of the King from criminal prosecution this is considered as testimony in favor of monarchical government, and the republicans at Paris where their force and numbers are greatest seem to be yielding for the present. It is much to be apprehended however that they will be revived some time hence. As soon as the constitution is finished it is to be offered to the King who is then to remount the throne or not at his election. No doubt he will prefer the first. He must then of course be restored to his liberty. It is highly probable he will make use of the first opportunity to go to the frontiers or out of the kingdom, and in that case the friends of monarchy and republicanism must come to issue and even supposing no foreign interferences determine the question by the sword.

The emigrants who are now in considerable numbers and have the force which rage and despair give, will take part. They are not strong enough to be formidable so long as the internal dissensions are kept within bounds, but will have weight enough then to induce an attempt for a much higher handed system than the monarchists here have at present any idea of.

These emigrants are at present much divided among themselves. The Baron de Breteuel is now at Aix la chapelle and is the soul of one party which may be called the Queen's. M. de Calonne and M. de Bouillé are the chiefs of the other which is the Count D'Artois'—he is now with Monsieur and Madame at Coblentz. M. de Calonne has just arrived in London, and M. de Bouillé remains at Luxemburg from whence he is using every exertion to induce the officers and soldiers of the French army to join him. He has succeeded with many of the former but none of the latter.—Besides these two great divisions there are various shades in their designs and pretensions. The more moderate desire the re-establishment of order in France, and a fixed government capable of securing their persons and property agreeable to the seance Royale of June 29. These are the richer class. Others insist on a rigorous statu quo as at the beginning of the revolution. These are the parliamentary people &c. Others again, the poor nobility of the gardes du corps, gendarmarie &c. like the janissaries of all countries desire nothing more than struggle and confusion.

I have mentioned to you already that I had no hopes of inducing the assembly to change any of their decrees relative to our commerce since their authorisation of the King to negotiate a treaty with us. It will be necessary therefore perhaps that Congress should correct that which virtually excludes our vessels from participating in the carrying of tobacco by some counter-regulation. This can do no harm if the treaty is made and if not will be indispensable. I learn that many French vessels are chartered to be sent to the U.S. for that article.

When I spoke to you formerly of the idea of rendering by treaty the rights of American and French citizens common in the two countries, I did not attend to the difficulty arising from several nations enjoying here as well as in America the *rights of the most favored*. This clause which is justly considered as the child of diplomatic indolence will of course prevent such an arrangement, or at least I do not at present see any mode of getting the better of it: but it should be a lesson for future negotiations.

You will see by the journals of the assembly that they do not lose sight of the Nantucket colony—that is to say that merchants connected with these people induce the assembly from the hope of recovering the whale fishery to foster the establishment. By a late decree they are exempted from that which prohibits the sale of American vessels in France. Of course they may as formerly bring their vessels from the U.S. and such as may come to settle in France in future are to enjoy the same privileges. It is said that the number of whale men has increased considerably in this country, that is to say the vessels fitted out by the Nantucket men. I hope soon to have a true state of them which I will send to you.

Drost has not succeeded in his competition for the place of Engraver general of the mint here; it is given to Dupré. I saw Drost two days ago and he seemed now determined to go to America. He observes that it is indispensable to have two *Balanciers* at least made here. He even desired to have four made, but as I apprehend that you did not count on such an operation, from the length of time it will take to make them, I shall insist on the smallest number possible. He found it impossible to have these machines executed in England without the assistance of workmen whom he was obliged to send for from Paris. Of course I suppose them within the meaning of the Secretary's expression, *difficult of execution*. Drost says they will cost about 22,000.ᵗᵗ each and that they cannot be finished before the next winter. He offers to have them executed by employing workmen in detail and charging their salaries to the U.S., or to contract to furnish them at a stipulated price. This latter mode will be preferred as being the best in all cases for a government. The other instruments he tells me will be inconsiderable. He is to decide finally in two or three days whether he will go or not, and I have little doubt of his going. In that case he will not embark before the next spring because the instruments cannot be finished sooner. – The money which was deposited in Mr. Grand's hands for the Algerine business and which has been long lying idle and depreciating there shall be applied to these expences unless I recieve contrary orders. It amounted in the beginning to 60,000.ᵗᵗ and only your house rent has been paid out of it as formerly mentioned.

Drost wishes that you would send him the intended devices of the money to be struck. He says he would ingrave one of the dyes here which he seems to speak of as a means of shewing his talents in that way, perhaps with a view to being employed by the U.S. as the engraver of their money.

I have had a long conversation with Rayneval relative to the navigation of the Mississipi. He gave me a full detail of this business as it formerly passed here between Count D'Aranda and Mr. Jay; and the ideas he communicated on the subject, being chosen by them as a kind of arbitrator – all which he says were made known to Congress by Count Vergennes who sent them a copy of his (Raynevals) memoire made on this question, in order to shew that he did not merit the inculpations, which had been laid to his charge of a want of good faith towards the U.S. in wishing to sacrifice their interests to those of Spain. The memoire he tells me was perfectly satisfactory to Congress, and that it appears to him that there is no other way of terminating the business than by adopting the result which his researches then brought him to. This memoire must of course be known to you. The principal feature as he tells me is that the Spaniards should make a free port of New-Orleans, where the Americans might stop load and unload their goods without being subject to any of the molestations of entering a foreign country.

This does not come up to your idea perfectly, as you seem to think a place extraterritorial and of course extrajudicial, essential to the preservation of peace. Mr. Carmichael I suppose is fully informed of your ideas as to the free port. The copy of your letter to him intended to have been sent me with yours of March 12. having not been recieved leaves me ignorant of whatever was not mentioned to me. I do not see that inconvenience will result from it at present, as well on account of the impossibility of bringing the negotiation to this place, as the turn which it seems to be taking at Madrid.

M. de Montmorin has informed me that it has a much more promising aspect there than he could have hoped for. He is informed by the French chargé des affaires that the Spanish ministry are disposed to renew the negotiation and will probably consent to yield to the U.S. a slip on the river where the river and sea craft may meet and exchange their loads without being subject to the Spanish laws and regulations. He observed also that the idea of making New-Orleans a free port was rejected entirely by the Spanish ministry, so that it seems that the cession of territory is more agreeable to them. This was the state of things previous to its being known at Madrid that the King of France had protested against the constitution and left Paris. M. de Montmorin does not seem to apprehend that it will produce any change in the sentiments of that cabinet relative to the Mississipi business. It has been a long time since I have heard from Mr. Carmichael, but I don't doubt that he keeps you fully informed of the progress of this affair.

I thought there was some reason to believe some time ago that the English and Spanish courts were disposed to get over all misunderstandings by forming closer connexions. It was whispered here that the Secretary of the English Embassy who passed through this place on his way to London was intrusted with confidential communications on this subject. M. de Montmorin says this was not the case, and that at the time of his leaving Madrid, which was previous to the King's departure from Paris, the coolness between these two courts was rather increasing. He knows not how that event may effect the Spanish cabinet as to this country and of course as to England. The official communication inclosed and mentioned above is all that is yet public.

It seems certain that the affairs of that country are getting into difficulties. The abuses of administration and the enormous expences of the court at the same time that they discontent the people weaken the arm of government. The example of this country shews what such causes are capable of producing, and although it will serve perhaps also to teach that government how to avoid a similar fate, yet I should suppose from the present view of circumstances that Spain will be a less powerful enemy some time hence than at present. I mention this in the case of the negotiation not terminating to the wishes of the United States. Besides, a short time also will raise the curtain which at present conceals the secret and active negotiations which are carrying on among almost all the cabinets of Europe. When it shall have appeared what scenes are to be acted and what part Spain assigns to herself in the drama it will be more easy to appreciate her future means in relation to the United States.

I inclose in this letter the gazette of Leyden and beg leave to refer you to the other papers sent by the diligence to Havre for an account of the ceremony of translating Voltaire to Paris, in which the national assembly took part. It is an attempt towards training the French to that enthusiastic love of great actions and great men for which the inhabitants of Greece and Rome have been so celebrated.

July 21. The Jew Ephraim mentioned in my letter of yesterday has been interrogated and discharged. It was said that the report as to the beginning of his letter to the King of Prussia is not true. It is certain that several letters were found on him in the hand writing of the King of Prussia. The committee before whom he was examined say that nothing appeared relative to France which was not friendly. Opinions vary as to this matter. Some think that the fear of the King of Prussia made them set him at liberty and that they conceal such things as were found and would have authorized his being confined. Others think that the Jew has had address enough to persuade them that the King of Prussia wishes to negotiate an alliance with the nation and that he is the confidential agent employed to pave the way to it. It is certain that he is treated very differently from any of the numberless persons arrested here within these few days past. They are all in close confinement and will probably most of them remain there a long time, as in the present system no true act of habeas corpus existing or any substitute for it, there is always difficulty in extricating even an innocent person from prison. – Among those arrested are some of the authors of the popular journals of which I have sent you some numbers as a specimen of the present liberty of the press here.

M. Du Veyrier whom the King had sent with a letter and the decree of the assembly, to the Prince de Condé has just arrived here. I mentioned to you that his long silence had appeared unaccountable and given uneasiness. The express sent by M. de Montmorin in search of him had returned without being able to find him. It seems that on passing through Luxemburg he had taken alarm on hearing that M. de Bouillé was there, and had changed his name. This circumstance rendering him suspect he was arrested and not allowed to write.

Mr. Barrett who goes immediately to America will take charge of this letter: the newspapers, journals, and the book of ancient architecture sent according to your desire he will find at Havre. – I remain with the attachment & respect which I hope are well known to you, Dear Sir, your affectionate friend & servant, W: SHORT

PrC (DLC: Short Papers); at head of text: "*No. 73*"; at foot of text: "Thomas Jefferson Secretary of State Philadelphia." Tr (DNA: RG 59, DD). Recorded in SJL as received 22 Oct. 1791.

[1] The words "of Government" are taken from the Tr.
[2] The Tr reads "personal safety."

From Fulwar Skipwith

Richmond, 20 July 1791. He will not repeat reasons for leaving Martinique given in two letters written from there, being assured TJ will understand that his return as consul cannot take place with propriety or justice to himself until France shall communicate the Convention and until Congress provides for the support and authority of consuls. He has left in Martinique a capable representative in Mr. Nathaniel Barrett, nephew of Senator Langdon. His departure is not viewed as a relinquishment of his consulate. – It is painful to report that a longer continuance there would more probably fix him "in the limits of a jail than in the functions of . . . office," for in the distressed situation of the island it was impossible to succeed in trade. – If, as many imagine, consuls will remain inadmissible in the French islands and Congress continue to regard them "as Servants entitled to no support," he is persuaded that justice will cause them to reimburse him for late expenditures and that the President and TJ will not deem him an object unworthy of consideration.

RC (ViW); endorsed by TJ as received 26 July 1791 and so recorded in SJL.

From David Humphreys

Sir   Mafra July 21st. 1791

I came to this place a few days ago, in order to avoid the heat of Lisbon. But before I left Lisbon, I had a conference with M. de Pinto, on the subject suggested for his consideration in your letter of March 15th, and enforced on me in the beginning of the cyphered part of your letter dated April 11th. He seemed to accord fully with you in his ideas of the propriety and utility of the measure. But observed that it rested with the Board of Commerce to arrange all regulations of that nature, and requested a copy of the Report of the Committee of Congress to lay before that Board. I gave him a copy accordingly. I conjecture the proceedings of these Boards are slow, and that no decision must be soon expected. On proper occasions, I shall not omit to resume the conversation on such topics as I may judge most likely to conduce to the accomplishment of your wishes.

By the first private intelligence from France, after the return of the Royal Family to Paris, we learned, that the King, Queen, and other Branches of it were kept seperately, with five Centinels at their doors. By the last advices, the opinion is more prevalent than it has lately been, that every thing will settle into quiet, and that the Nation will not be exposed to the immediate horrors of a foreign or civil war.

The neighbouring Powers appear to be too much occupied with their own affairs, to interfere in those of France, in the manner which their inclinations might prompt them to do. The Government of Spain is not without apprehension, that the same spirit may insinuate itself into that Kingdom, which has wrought such changes in the neighbour-State. This apprehension, which has for some time past excited great precautions, has lately produced some Regulations favorable to the Subjects of that Government.

The Congress of Sistove not having been able to effect a pacification in the North, there is a probability hostilities will recommence between the Emperor and the Port, which will not leave the former at liberty to interpose his force in attempts to thwart the Revolution of France.

In this Country perfect tranquility exists. – The recent publication of a small Theological work, written by an Ecclesiastic, who is a Member of the Tribunal for the examination and licensing of Books, has surprised me more than any other circumstance which has happened since my residence here. It is an Analysis of the Profession of Faith of Pope Pius IV, and inculcates very different opinions from those entertained by bigotted Roman Catholics. The Writer does not believe in the Infallibility of the Successors of St. Peter: on the contrary he shews that they have published many Bulls replete with errors, particularly with respect to interference in affairs of civil Government. It is said the farther impression and sale of this Work is prohibited, in consequence of a private Order obtained by the Nuncio from the Court. But I have had the perusal of one of the Copies. – With Sentiments of the highest esteem I have the honor to be, Sir, Your Most obedt & most humble servant,

D. HUMPHREYS

RC (DNA: RG 59, DD); at head of text: "(No. 26)"; endorsed by TJ as received 22 Oct. 1791 and so recorded in SJL. Tr (same).

The small theological work which surprised Humphreys was *Analyse da professão da fé do Santo Padre Pio IV, por A. Pereira de Figueiredo* (Lisbon, 1791).

To James Madison

MY DEAR SIR   Philadelphia July 21. 1791.

Your favors of July 10. and 13. have been duly recieved and I now return the pamphlet inclosed in the latter, with thanks for the perusal. The author has the appearance of knowing better what has past in England than in America. As to the latter to be sure he has been ignorant enough. I am sincerely sorry that Freneau has declined coming here. Tho' the printing business be sufficiently full here, yet I think he would have set out on such advantageous ground as to have been sure of success. His own genius in the first place is so superior to that of his competitors. I should have given him the perusal of all my letters of foreign intelligence and all foreign newspapers; the publication of all proclamations and other public notices within my department, and the printing of the laws, which added to his salary would have been a considerable aid. Besides this, Fenno's being the only weekly or half weekly paper, and under general condemnation for it's toryism and it's incessant efforts to overturn the government, Freneau would have found that ground as good as unoccupied. – P——e [Paine] will not be appointed to the place I had recommended him for. – I have a letter from Mazzei asking information of his affairs. I must therefore ask from you the letter you were to write me as to Dohrman. He desires to be affectionately remembered to you. He is declared, with the consent of the Diet, Chargé des affaires of the king and nation. – No news yet from Genl. Scott. – Mr. Randolph writes me that our harvest is safely in in general, that the quantity will be half as much again as the acre usually yeilds, and the quality of first rate. – The price offered is 5/6 at Richmd. Tobo. there is still 18/ to 20/. – I have European letters and papers to the 8th. of May. The Empress has notified the English factory in Russia, that the peace between her and Gr. Britain is likely to be broken, but knowing their good conduct they shall be welcome to remain in her dominions, she pays a compliment to the British nation, and says she considers it only as a war with their ministers. Denmark has made a warm offer of mediating alone. Prussia has notified the Porte that they are free to conclude a peace with Russia without any mediation, and that it will not be disagreeable to him. But the Porte has refused to relinquish the mediation of Prussia and England, and has also declined accepting that offered by Spain. France is going on steadily with it's work. On the 7th. of May a report of a committee was given in to the assembly, confirming their former plan as to the mode of settling the constitution of their colonies, adding further that the Colonies should have the initiative (exclusively) as to the condition of the people of colour, and that each colony should send deputies to the French part of St. Martin's to a Congress which should propose a general form of constitution. This was ordered to be printed and taken up at a future day, and there was some symptom of a disposition in the Assembly to over-rule the report so far as it related[1] to the *condition* of the people of colour. Comparing the date[1] of this with the news said by the gazettes to have arrived at St. Domingo July 1. I cannot help suspending my belief of the latter.

I hope your health is better established. Your friends here anxiously enquire after it. Your letters now therefore are doubly interesting, and very feelingly so to Dear Sir your affectionate friend & servt.,   TH: JEFFERSON

RC (DLC: Madison Papers); slightly mutilated when seal was broken; see note 1. PrC (DLC).

[1] Word supplied from PrC.

To Henry Knox

DEAR SIR   Philadelphia July 22. 1791.

It having been agreed among us at a former session of the board of arts that the descriptions to be inserted in patents should be handed to us separately at our lodgings to be examined at leisure and approved with or without amendments, I now hand on to you the inclosed which came to me from the Attorney General who had proposed some amendments to them; I have also proposed some of a trifling nature, merely to render the construction clearer, which are pencilled only, in my hand writing. We have endorsed on each our separate examination. When you shall have been so good as to have examined also, and proposed any amendments you may wish, if there be no material difference among us, Mr. Remsen will prepare a description accomodated to what shall appear to be agreed, and present it to us on Saturday next at our meeting. If there be a material diversity, it will await our meeting. I trouble you with this explanation, because the inclosed are the first which have been offered since we agreed on this plan. Hereafter they shall be sent you with a simple sketch of the amendments only. – Your's respectfully & affectionately,   TH: JEFFERSON

PrC (DLC). Not recorded in SJL. Enclosure not found, but it was presumably the description of Jonathan Dickerson's improvement in tide mills to be inserted in the patent. At the meeting on "Saturday next" – 30 July 1791 – Dickerson was granted his patent, the only one issued on that date.

From Louis Guillaume Otto

Philadelphia, 22 July 1791. He hastens to send the enclosed letter from Montmorin which he has been directed to communicate officially to the government. – He cannot observe without surprise that even in the United States some ill-disposed persons have given credit to wholly untrue rumors concerning the intentions of the King and the probability of a counter-revolution in France. Faithful to the principles he has consistently professed, Otto has done all within his power to deny these calumnies and false insinuations of the pretended friends of the King who, under the cloak of an assumed interest in the peace and glory of His Majesty, hide their chagrin at the success of the revolution and their regret at the triumph of principles diametrically opposed to their own. Some, led into error by the insidious reports of gazettes and foreign pamphlets whose real aim they should have easily discerned, have become victims of their illusion to the point of taking up the pen and deducing from these false facts consequences even more absurd. But he has a deep-seated conviction that the government of the United States, being as enlightened as it is impartial and equally the friend of truth and liberty, has never shared such opinions. He is also persuaded that the declarations contained in the enclosed letter will put in their true light the sincerity and magnanimity of His Majesty and will leave no doubt about the stability of a revolution which will always be a source of prosperity for France, of confidence for her allies, and of regret for her enemies.

Tr (Arch. Aff. Etr., Paris, Corr. Pol., E.-U., xxxv; photocopy in DLC); in French; at head of text in clerk's hand: "Philadelphie avec le No 63 du juillet 1791" (i.e., enclosed in Otto's dispatch to Montmorin of that date). Enclosure printed below.

ENCLOSURE
Montmorin to Otto

S<small>IR</small>   [Paris, 23 April 1791]

The King has charged me to inform you that it is his will that you make known his sentiments respecting the Revolution and the French Constitution to the Court at which you reside. The same orders are transmitted to the Ambassadors and Ministers of France, at all the Courts of Europe, to the end that no doubt may remain with regard to his Majesty's intentions, his free acceptation of the new form of government, or his irrevocable oath to maintain it.

His Majesty had convoked the States General of his kingdom, and resolved in his Council, that the Commons should, in that Assembly, have a number of Deputies equal to those of the two other orders then existing. This act of provisional legislation which the circumstances of the moment did not allow to be more favourable, sufficiently announced his Majesty's wish to restore to the nation all its rights.

The States General met, and took the title of the National Assembly; and, in a short time, a constitution, fitted to secure the happiness of France and of the Monarch, took place of the ancient order of things, under which the apparent power of the king only served to conceal the real power of certain aristocratic bodies.

The National Assembly adopted the representative form of government, conjoined with hereditary monarchy. The legislative body was declared permanent; the choice of the ministers of public worship, of magistrates, and judges, was given to the people; the executive power was conferred on the King, the formation of laws on the legislative body, and the power of sanction on the Monarch. The public force, both internal and external, was organized on the same principles, and in conformity with the fundamental basis of a distribution of powers. Such is the new constitution of the kingdom.

That which is called a revolution, is no more than the abrogation of numerous abuses, that have been accumulating for ages, through the errors of the people, or the power of the Ministers which was never the power of the King. Those abuses were no less prejudicial to the nation than to the Monarch. Authority, under happy reigns, had never ceased to attack these abuses, but without being able to destroy them. They exist no longer; the nation, now the sovereign, has no citizens but such as are equal in rights; no despot but the law; no organs but public officers, and of those officers the King is the first. Such is the French revolution.

This must naturally have for its enemies all those who, in the first moment of error, regret, on account of personal advantages, the abuses of the ancient government. Hence the apparent division which shewed itself in the kingdom, and which is daily becoming less; hence perhaps some severe laws and circumstances which time will correct; but the King, whose true power can never be distinct from that of the nation, who has no aim but the happiness of the people, and no authority but that which is delegated to him, the King has adopted, without hesitation, a happy constitution, which will at once regenerate the nation, the monarchy, and his authority. All his powers are preserved to him, except the dreadful power of making laws. He remains charged with the power of negociating with foreign nations, with the care of defending the kingdom, and repelling its enemies, but the French nation will in future have no external enemies, but its aggressors; no internal enemies but those who, still flattering themselves with vain hopes, believe that the will of twenty-four millions of men, restored to their natural rights, after having organized the kingdom in such a manner as to leave only the memory of ancient form and abuses, is not an immovable and irrecoverable constitution.

The most dangerous of those enemies are they who affect to disseminate doubts of the intentions of the Monarch. These men are much to blame, or much deceived. They suppose themselves the friends of the King, and they are the only enemies of royalty. They would have deprived the King of the love and the confidence of a great nation, if his principles and his probity had been less known. What has the King not done to shew that he considered both the Revolution and the French Constitution as his titles to glory! – After having accepted and sanctioned all the laws, he has neglected no means of causing them to be executed. Since the month of February, of the last year, he has promised in the bosom of the National Assembly, to maintain them. He has taken an oath to do so, in the midst of the general federation of the kingdom. Dignified by the title of the Restorer of French Liberty, he will transmit to his son more than a Crown – he will transmit a Constitutional Royalty.

The enemies of the constitution are constantly repeating that the King is not happy; as if it were possible for a King to enjoy any happiness but the happiness of his people. They say that his authority is lessened, as if authority, founded on force were not less powerful, and more precarious, than authority founded on law. Finally that the King is not free: a calumny atrocious, if they suppose that his will could be constrained; absurd, if they take for a want of freedom the consent repeatedly expressed by his Majesty to remain among the citizens of Paris, a consent that was due to their patriotism, even to their fears, but above all to their love.

Those calumnies, however, have reached foreign Courts; they have been repeated there by Frenchmen, who are voluntary exiles from their country, instead of sharing its glory, and who, if they are not enemies, have at least deserted their stations as citizens. The King, Sir, charges you to defeat their intrigues and their projects. The same calumnies, while they spread the falsest ideas respecting the French revolution, have rendered the intentions of French travellers suspected by several neighbouring nations; and the King expressly orders you to protect and defend them. Represent the French constitution in the same light as that in which the King views it; and leave no doubt of his intention to maintain it, to the utmost of his power. By securing the liberty and the equality of the citizens, that constitution founds the national prosperity on the most immovable basis; it confirms the royal authority by the laws; it prevents, by a glorious revolution, a revolution which the abuses of the old government would probably soon have effected by a dissolution of the empire; and, finally, it will constitute the happiness of the King. To justify it, to defend it, and to consider it as the rule of your conduct ought to be your first duty.

I have frequently before communicated to you his Majesty's sentiments on this head; but after the information he has received of the opinion endeavored to be established at foreign Courts, respecting what is passing in France, he has ordered me to charge you to make known the contents of this letter to the government with which you reside; and that it may be still more public, his Majesty has ordered it to be printed.   MONTMORIN

Philadelphia, July 25, 1791.

The above is a faithful translation of a letter communicated to me officially by Mr. Otto, chargé des affaires of France, and rendered public at his desire.

THOMAS JEFFERSON
Secretary of State

Brown's *Federal Gazette*, 26 July 1791; at head of text, in engraved script: "*By Authority*"; to which is added: "Copy of a letter from the Minister of foreign affairs, and addressed, by order of the King, to all the ambassadors and ministers of his Majesty in Foreign Courts." The text of Montmorin's letter, followed by TJ's note of 25 July 1791, was printed in Fenno's *Gazette of the United States*, 3 Aug. 1791, exactly as it appeared in the *Federal Gazette*. A slightly different version appeared in Bache's *General Advertiser* on 21 July 1791. That copy carried the date of the letter as well as the reaction of the National Assembly to a reading of it, a brief address from that body to the king, and the king's response (Tr in French in Arch. Aff. Etr., Corr. Pol., E.-U., xxxv).

From Pio

MONSIEUR   à Paris ce 22. Juillet 1792 [i.e., 1791]

Les sentimens que vous m'avez inspiré ne s'effaceront jamais de mon coeur, et vous me permettrez que je cherche toutes les occasions pour vous le dire me procurant par là la satisfaction, bien douce pour moi, de me rappeler à votre souvenir. Je vous ai écrit une autre fois, il y a bientôt deux ans par Mr. *Rutlidge*, mais je crains que ma lettre ne vous ait pas été rendue. Plût au ciel que celle-ci n'ait pas le même sort. Je ne vous demande qu'une seule ligne de votre écriture; dites moi, si vous vous portez bien, si vous êtes content et si vous ne regrettez pas quelquefois la *Grille de Chaillot*. Moi, je ne puis pas y penser sans eprouver une tendre commotion; des hommes comme vous, Monsieur, ne se remplacent pas. Que votre conversation me seroit necessaire dans cette crise politique! Les hommes ne sont plus les mêmes; j'ai perdu tous les amis, la Patrie seule me reste, et vous savez sans doute que c'est la *France libre*. Voilà mon Idole. Je ne vous donne pas de nouvelles; vous les recevez sans doute par des autres canaux. Pour Mr. *Short*, jadis mon ami, je serois presque tenté de vous en demander des nouvelles; nous pensions toujours de même dans le tems du Despotisme; dans le regne de la Liberté nos idées ne se rencontrent plus, et par consequent nos personnes non plus. L'auriez vous jamais cru? Je n'ai actuellement que Locke sous les yeux, Sidney, Milton, J.J.Rousseau, et Th. Payne; voilà toute ma bibliothèque; j'ai brulé le reste, excepté *Machiavel*, que tous les Diplomates ont, mais qu'ils n'osent pas avouer, et que les hommes libres doivent placer à coté de la *Declaration des Droits.* Mais notre Revolution n'est pas achevée, et je crains que le choc soit plus fort d'or en avant qu'il ne l'a eté jusqu'à present. Nous desirons ardemment une nouvelle Legislature, comme nous avons desiré ces jours ci une Monarchie sans monarque; celle ci a manqué; serons nous aussi malheureux pour l'autre? – Je suis corde et animo tout à vous, et bien fraternellment,

Pio

RC (MoSHi); misdated by Pio; endorsed by TJ as received 22 Oct. 1791 and so recorded in SJL.

From Chantrot

Monsieur   A paris Ce 24 juillet 1791

La personne Chargé de vous acheter une Pendule a demie Seconde au prix fixe n'ayant pas trouvé Ce que vous désiriez, Ce monsieur m'en à fait part. Je lai engage de mencharge, Sachant que Setoit pour vous, je me suis Empresse de vous faire une pendule dont vous n'ayez rien à desirer pour ce qui regarde lorlogerie. Je me flatte après avoir porter tous les soins qu'il convient pour vous livrer une excellente pendule que vous vous adresseréz à moi quand vous aurez besoin de quel que piece d'orlogerie. En place d'une soit pour tenire le balancier c'est un morceaux d'acier fait en forme de lame de couteau à la quelle il y à une petite tête au bout pour empecher le balencier de S'echapper. Vous trouverez un petit chassis de cuivre au bout de latige du balancier dans le quel il y à une gouttier en àcier. Il faut la passer dans ce petit morceau d'acier fait en forme de couteau qui tient au coq en place de Soit Ce qui vaux beaucoup mieux et qui est bien moins suget. Vous trouverez apres lechassi qui tient la fourchette dans le quel le balancier doit entrer une vis sur le côté que lon peux tournés avec les doigts pour la pouvoir mettre parfaitement dans Son Echappement. Pour voir Si cette pendule est bien dans son Echappement il faut quand vous l'aurez placée dans l'endroit que vous voulez quelle occupe laisser le Balancier arrêter d'apres cela vous verez si en le faissent échapper de droite à gauche de gauche à droite en le tenent avec les doights. Si la distance est egale la pendule doit se trouvé dans son Echappement. Si elle fait plus de chemaint d'un côté que de l'autre alors la pendule n'est point dans son echappement. Il faut tournet cette petite vis qui fait mouvoir la fourchette dans le quel le peti morceau

de cuivre qui est au milieu de latige de votre balancier entre ce qui est cache par le timbre. Vous trouverez le balencier envelopper den du papier dans un coin de la Caisse de meme que la clef et leguille a segond. Pour mettre cette Eguille apres le mouvement il faut l'entrer dessus une petit bout de tige qui se trouve au centre des Eguilles. Si, comme je l'espere vous êtes Satisfait, je vous prie de m'en acuser la reception quand vous an trouverez l'occasion. Ce qui me fera le plus grand plaisir étant jalous de vous satisfaire. — Je suis avec un Profon respec Monsieur Votre tres humble et tre obeisent serviteur,
CHANTROT
Successeur de Mr. Meyer

RC (MHi); endorsed by TJ as received 24 Oct. 1791 and so recorded in SJL.

To Augustine Davis

SIR   Philadelphia July 24. 1791.

The necessity of establishing a communication from Richmond into the upper parts of Virginia induced me to ask from the late postmaster-general a plan for establishing cross posts consistently with law. He has furnished me with the inclosed deed, by which you will percieve that certain covenants are to be entered into between the future postmaster general and an undertaker, in such a way as that the latter shall have the whole postage and nothing more; so that the cross post is to support itself, and not to bring any expence to the public. After the contract executed, no rider can take pay for the carriage of letters; consequently that profit will go exclusively to the post, to which will be added whatever yourself, your brother printers or the subscribers will give him for newspapers. Satisfied that a rider plying weekly through Columbia, and Charlottesville to Staunton and back, may be supported by the postage of letters and premium on newspapers, I have had the inclosed deed prepared for that route, and wish you to engage some trusty person to undertake it immediately, and to execute the deed. You will shortly know the name of the Postmaster general to be inserted.

But a more material cross post will be that from Richmond along the Buckingham road, by New-London and the peaks of Otter into Montgomery, Wythe, and Washington, and along the Holston &ca. on the route, as far as may be done, towards the seat of the South Western government. How far the profits of this cross post will enable you to extend it along that route, I know not: but after deciding on the best roads, having regard to the populousness of the country through or near which they pass, so as to accomodate as many people as possible, and consequently get into the way of as many contributions towards it's support as possible, my idea would be that you should set it up to the *farthest* bidder, that is to say, engage it to him who will go *farthest* on the route for the profits it may afford. I shall be glad if, after considering this proposition, and making due enquiries, you will be so good as to let me know what you think of it's practicability, and to what extent along the route you think it may be pushed, stating also the particular roads which, in order to increase custom, it may be best for the undertaker to pursue. — I am Sir your very humble servt, TH: JEFFERSON

PrC (DLC). Enclosure: Form of contract to be executed between Samuel Osgood, Postmaster General, and the person engaging to carry the mail on the cross-post in Virginia. This was the customary form for such contracts, transcribed by a clerk in Osgood's office, which TJ altered in various ways by pencilled notations. Knowing that Osgood would soon resign, he bracketed his name wherever it appeared. Where the form obligated the contractor to "carry the Mail or ensure it to be carried," TJ altered this to read: "carry Mails or ensure them to be carried." He filled in all of the blanks specifying the route and frequency of the cross-post, as indicated in the italicized words of the passage requiring the contractor to carry mail "from the Post Office in Richmond to *Columbia, Charlottesville and Staunton* in the state of Virginia and from *Columbia, Charlottesville and Staunton* so as to form *one* compleat Tour *once* at least in each Week." TJ of course left untouched the blanks to be filled with the name of the contractor. The person assuming responsibility for conducting the cross-post was required to supply all equipment necessary for the purpose; to forfeit an unspecified sum in case he failed to make any trip, unless this was due to unavoidable accident; to be accountable for all postage due to the United States and to settle in gold or silver coin after deducting postage for any letters or packets not delivered; to take an oath "not to open detain or delay, Embezzle or destroy" any letters or packets in his care; to be liable for damages sustained by any losses occurring through carelessness or neglect; and

to give bond for the faithful performance of his duties. In return the contractor was given exclusive right to carry the mail along the specified route; to enjoy all the emoluments and profits arising therefrom; to have authority to establish post offices between Richmond and Staunton; and to appoint suitable persons to manage such offices, they being accountable to him (undated form in clerk's hand except for TJ's interpolations, in DLC: TJ Papers, 69: 11996-7; endorsed by TJ).

TJ's concern for the establishment of a cross-post reaching into the western parts of Virginia was no doubt augmented by the uncertainty and the slowness of the posts. But his desire to serve the public interest by promoting better transportation of letters and newspapers was also stimulated by the anxiety he had experienced in recent months in hearing so seldom from his family at Monticello. While he was keenly aware of the need for better communication with officials in the Southwest Territory, he submitted the proposal for a post along that route only for Davis' consideration. Davis advertised it, however, as if he had been authorized to negotiate a contract in the same manner as for the route to Staunton (see Davis to TJ, 1 Aug. 1791; TJ to Washington, 7 Aug. 1791; Tatham to TJ, 15 Aug. 1791).

It was perhaps at this time that TJ obtained from the Postmaster General's office the following tabulation of existing mail contracts on the post road from Boston to Richmond (undated MS in clerk's hand, DLC: TJ Papers, 69: 11995):

Contracts for carrying the Mail

	Names of the Contractors	From what places	No. Miles	How carried	how often.	Total cost.	Cost of. one trip.	Rate pr. mile by the year one trip weekly
1	Levi Pease	Boston to New York	253	Stage	twice in winter & 3 times in Sumr.	2,500.	19.23	3.95
2	John Inskeep	New York to Phila.	95	4 monthly on Horses & eight pr Stages	5 times Weekly	1,860.67	7.16	3.90
3	Inskeep & Vanhorne	Phila. to Baltimore	102	Ditto	3 Do.	1,466.67	9.40	4.79
4	Van Horne	Baltimore to Alexandria	54	Stages	3 Do.	597.33	3.83	3.69
5	John Hoomes	Alexa. to Richmond	122	Stages	3 Do.	1,475.68	9.46	4. 3
			626				49. 8	20.36

To John Dobson

SIR   Philadelphia July 24. 1791.

Your favor of July 6. came to hand on the 12th. In the mean time you must have recieved mine of the 4th. informing you of the circumstances which had obliged me to give credit for my tobacco till the last of September, and consequently that no payment could be made till my return hither from Virginia in October. This being the situation of things, I can only repeat it by way of answer to your's of the 6th. I shall hope that what the tobacco may be deficient, can be made up by the sale of the wheat of the present crop which I hear is a good one. — I am with great esteem Sir Your most obedt. humble servt,   TH: JEFFERSON

PrC (MHi).

Dobson's letter of the 6th, recorded in SJL as received 12 July 1791, has not been found.

To James Madison

MY DEAR SIR   Philadelphia July 24. 1791.

Yours of the 21st. came to hand yesterday. I will keep my eye on the advertisements for Halifax. The time of my journey to Virginia is rendered doubtful by the incertainty whether the President goes there or not. It is rather thought he will not. If so, I shall go later and stay a shorter time. I presume I may set out about the beginning of September, and shall hope your company going and coming. – The President is indisposed with the same blind tumour, and in the same place, which he had the year before last in New York. As yet it does not promise either to suppurate or be discussed. He is obliged to lye constantly on his side, and has at times a little fever. The young grandson has had a long and dangerous fever. He is thought better to-day. No news yet from Genl. Scott: nor any thing from Europe worth repeating. Several merchants from Richmond (Scotch, English &c.) were here lately. I suspect it was to dabble in federal filth. Let me hear of your health. Adieu my dear Sir yours affectionately,   TH: JEFFERSON

P.S. The inclosed are for yourself, being duplicates.

RC (DLC: Madison Papers). PrC (DLC).

From James Madison

DEAR SIR   N. York July 24. 1791.

Your favor of the 21st. came to hand last evening. It was meant that you should keep the pamphlet inclosed in it. I have seen Freneau, and, as well as Col: H. Lee, have pressed the establishment of himself in Philada. where alone his talents can do the good or reap the profit of which they are capable. Though leaning strongly against the measure, under the influence of little objections which his modesty magnified into important ones, he was less decided on the subject than I had understood. We are to have a further conversation, in which I shall renew my efforts, and do not despair, though I am not sanguine, of success. If he yeilds to the reasoning of his friends, it is probable that he will at least commence his plan in alliance with Childs as to the emoluments. In the conduct and title of the paper, it will be altogether his own. – I am not much disappointed tho' I much regret the rejection of P——e [Paine] in the late appointment. Another opportunity of doing him some justice may not occur and at the present moment it was to be wished for a thousand reasons that he might have received from this Country such a token of its affection and respect. I must see Dorhman again before I can enable you to answer Mazzei. I will endeavor to do it tomorrow and will write you without delay.

You will recollect that the Pretensions of T. C. [Tench Coxe] to the place now filled by Wolcot went thro' your hands and with my knowledge. Would you believe that this circumstance has got into

[667]

circulation in the shape of an attempt in you and myself to intermeddle with the Treasury department, to frustrate the known wishes of the head of it, and to keep back the lineal successor, from a Southern antipathy to his Eastern descent! Col: Lee got hold of the Report and finding that it had made some impression on Hamilton, asked of me an explanation of the matter. As far as I could call to mind, what had left so faint an impression, I enabled him to contradict the misrepresentation. Last evening a favorable opportunity offering, I touched on the subject to Col: Hamilton, who had certainly viewed it thro' a very wrong medium, but seemed disposed to admit the right one. I believe he is now satisfied that misrepresentations had been made to him, that our agency, if to be so called was the effect of complaisance rather than of solicitude for or against the candidates – and particularly that it was impossible from the very nature of the case, it would have involved the idea of thwarting his purposes in his own department. – This is not the only instance I find in which the most uncandid and unfounded things of a like tendency have been thrown into circulation.

I promised a gentleman who lately sailed for Halifax on his way to England, to send him a copy of the Remarks on Sheffields Book. May I trouble you to send to Cary's or wherever may be proper for a Copy, and let me have it in the course of the week, the earlier the better. I shall endeavor to convey it by the hands of some passenger in the Packet which sails early next week. Will you be so good also as first to let the inclosed letter on the subject of Mr. N. Pendleton be handed to Mr. Lear as from me. He will of course let the President see the pretensions of that gentleman, and I shall then have sufficiently discharged the trust consigned to me by his Unkle. This is the mode in which I have generally conveyed applications to the President.

My health is much improved by the precautions I have observed. From the state of my appetite I hope I have got pretty much rid of my bile. My horse is also nearly well. He has had a third relapse, and there are still remains of the tumor as well as of his leanness. I have already asked when you think of setting out for Virginia. I mean to join you whenever you are ready, and shall be in Philada. in due time for the purpose. – Always & mo: affecty. Yours,

Js. Madison Jr

RC (DLC: Madison Papers); date added to endorsement by Madison after letter was returned to him; endorsed by TJ as received 26 July 1791 and so recorded in SJL. On verso of final page TJ jotted down in pencil a list of items for his reply: "pamphlets, E. P.'s lre, My journal, Mazzei."

To Peter Marks

DEAR SIR   Philadelphia July 24. 1791.

I have never been inattentive to the application made on behalf of your son: but there has been no vacancy, till now, to which he could be appointed. I have no doubt he will so conduct himself as to justify the recommendations which were handed to me, and on which I founded his claim.

I hope to have the pleasure of seeing my neighbors in Albemarle in the course of the fall, tho I am unable yet to foresee the particular moment. They have all my wishes for their happiness and prosperity, adding for yourself particular assurances of the sincere esteem of Dear Sir Your most obedt. humble servt,   TH: JEFFERSON

PrC (DLC).

From Robert Montgomery

Alicante, 24 July 1791. He has this moment received news from Algiers that at 6 a.m. on the 12th the Dey died and was immediately succeeded by Ali Hassan, who has been "in many instances our perticular friend," about which he will write more fully by the next post to Lisbon and Cadiz.

RC (DNA: RG 59, CD); endorsed by TJ as received 27 Oct. 1791 and so recorded in SJL.

John Montgomery, by special request of his brother, also informed TJ that the Dey of Algiers had died; that his successor "was always Mr. Montgomery's friend"; and that "Sior. Seliman an Algerian Noble Man who paid him a Diet at Alicante" had been promoted. He added that "Mr. Montgomery has no doubt that Something might be done towards a peace at this Critical period, if proper measures was now adopted by Congress" (John Montgomery to TJ, Boston, 14 Oct. 1791; RC in DNA: RG 59, MLR; endorsed by TJ as received 22 Oct. 1791 and so recorded in SJL).

To Edmund Pendleton

DEAR SIR   Philadelphia July 24. 1791.

I recieved duly your favour of the 13th. and communicated it to the President. The titles of your relation were unquestionably strong of themselves and still strengthened by your recommendation. But the place was before proposed to another whose acceptance will probably fix it.

The President is indisposed with a tumour like that he had in New York the year before last. It does not as yet seem as if it would come to a head.

We are wonderfully slow in recieving news from Genl. Scott. The common accounts give reason to hope his expedition has succeeded well. – You will have seen the rapidity with which the subscriptions to the bank were filled. As yet the delirium of speculation is too strong to admit sober reflection. It remains to be seen whether in a country whose capital is too small to carry on it's own commerce, to establish manufactures, erect buildings &c. such sums should have been withdrawn from these useful pursuits to be employed in gambling? Whether it was well judged to force on the public a paper circulation of so many millions for which they will be paying about 7. per cent per annum and thereby banish as many millions of gold and silver for which they would have paid no interest? I am afraid it is the intention to nourish this spirit of gambling by throwing in from time to time new aliment.

The question of war and peace in Europe is still doubtful. The French revolution proceeds steadily, and is I think beyond the danger of accident of every kind. The success of that will ensure the progress of liberty in Europe, and it's preservation here. The failure of that would have been a powerful argument with those who wish to introduce a king, lords and commons here, a sect which is all head and no body. Mr. Madison has had a little bilious touch at New York, from which he is recovered however. Adieu my dear Sir Your affectionate friend & servt.,   TH: JEFFERSON

RC (MHi: Washburn Collection); addressed: "The honorable Edmund Pendleton Caroline county by the Port-royal mail"; franked; postmarked: "25 IY" and "FREE"; endorsed. PrC (DLC).

To Martha Jefferson Randolph

MY DEAR DAUGHTER   Philadelphia July 24. 1791.

Your last letter come to hand was of May 23. Consequently it is now two months old.

Petit arrived here three or four days ago, and accosted me with an assurance that he was come pour rester toujours avec moi. The principal small news he brings is that Panthemont is one of the convents to be kept up for education, that the old Abbess is living, but Madame de Taubenheim dead, that some of the nuns have chosen to rejoin the world, others to stay, that there are no English pensioners there now, Botidour remains there, &c. &c. &c. Mr. Short lives in the Hotel d'Orleans where I lived when you first went to Panthemont.

The President is indisposed with a complaint similar to that he had in New York the year before last. It is commonly called a blind bile, and is in fact a tumour which will not come to a head. – I do not yet know when I shall go to Virginia, and fear the visit will be short. It will probably be the beginning of September. I sent off yesterday by Capt. Stratton 4. boxes and 14. kegs with stores to be delivered to Mr. Brown to be forwarded to Monticello. But I beg you not to await my coming for the opening and using of them, as they are for the common use. Kiss Maria and the little Anne for me and accept cordial love from your's affectionately,   TH: J.

RC (NNP). PrC (MHi).

To Thomas Mann Randolph, Jr.

DEAR SIR   Philadelphia July 24. 1791.

I had always intended to endeavor to engage with some miller of capital here to erect my mill on such plan as he should chuse and then rent it to him for a term of years. Your letter informing me that Mr. Divers and others were proposing to take Mr. Henderson's mill, but that they had not been able to agree, induces me to suppose it possible they might be willing to take mine. I should propose to make the necessary stoppages in the river and to build the millhouse on such plan as the tenant should chuse, and for this I should ask 10. per cent per annum on account of the risk and decay to which they would be exposed. I should finish the canal and ask 5. per cent on the cost of that, to which I should add a reasonable interest on the value of the position, water fall &c. they to erect their own running gear and of course to pay no rent on them. I should be willing to rent for such term as their running gear might be supposed to last, or for double that term if they should prefer it. If you should have an opportunity of sounding Mr. Divers on this subject I will be obliged to you: and if he is disposed to the contract it shall be concluded when I come to Virginia. Tho' I believe it would be better for the neighborhood that there should be two rival mills, yet I suppose the Miller would rather be without rivality.

I inclose letters for Mr. P. Marks and Mr. de Rieux, which be so good as to have safely delivered, and be assured of the sincere attachment of Dr. Sir Your's affectionately,   TH: JEFFERSON

RC (DLC); in both this and the preceding letter TJ changed the date by overwriting from 23 to 24 July and entered both in SJL under the latter date. PrC (CSmH). Enclosures: (1) TJ to Marks, 24 July 1791. (2) Letter from Mme. Plumard de Bellanger, 14 Apr. 1791 (not found, but see Derieux to TJ, 12 Aug. 1791).

From William Short

Paris July 24. 1791.

I had the honor of writing to you four days ago by Mr. Barrett. This will be sent also by the way of Havre and will contain a letter for the Secretary of the Treasury.

A very lengthy report has been made to the assembly in the name of the two committees, diplomatick and of war, on the situation of France with respect to her neighbours, and her military force. From it it appeared that the politics of Europe are not settled as yet – that if a league of the leading powers should be formed against the French constitution, they could not possibly concert their measures and begin to act before the next spring – of course nothing to be apprehended for the present from thence – that there were about 4, or 5,000 emigrants at Worms and other places on the frontiers – that the Emperor had about 40, or 45,000 men in the low countries, of which the circumstances of those countries would not allow him to employ against France (even if he were disposed and nothing indicated such a disposition) more than 15, or 20,000 – that the German princes who had regular troops would probably aid the emigrants so as to raise their numbers to 15, or 20,000 men. Supposing therefore every thing at the worst, the greatest number of troops that could be brought against France at present would be 40,000 men. The reporter shewed that the emigrants being led by men who had given so many proofs of designs without calculation, of projects without the possibility of execution, might adopt that of entering the country by force, with the succours mentioned above or a part of them, in the ill grounded hopes of being joined by the discontented within and rendering their force formidable.

France had to oppose to such an invasion 64,000 regular troops which when the regiments were completed would amount to 91,000 posted from Dunkirk to Belfort. The whole army in France is now 143,000 men and when completed will be 213,000.

After such a picture it might have been expected that they would have been satisfied with their present means of resistance. Instead of which the committees proposed and the assembly decreed that there should be immediately raised in addition an army of garde nationale volunteers of 97,000 men, who are to have 15. sous a day. Such measures must be always expected from numerous assemblies which exercise all the functions of government. Many inconveniences are to be apprehended without counting the additional expence, from the present. Such a body of turbulent indisciplined men if they find no employment from the enemy will either return disgusted and thus have used in vain the first and fiery zeal from which volunteers derive their greatest force – or remaining embodied will endeavour to find employment even at the risk of violating public tranquillity. Their want of discipline will tend to destroy the little which remains among the regular troops with whom they will serve, and their superior pay will probably create discontentment and jealousy among those troops.

Count Rochambeau commands on the Northern frontier and by the open and decided part he has taken in the revolution enjoys the full confidence of the assembly and of his troops. – Should France be attacked M. de la fayette will take command in the active army.

It is certain that England and Prussia will abandon the Porte. A forced peace will therefore take place. M. de Montmorin has informed the diplomatic committee that this circumstance and the present posture of negotiation among the several European powers rendered it every day more probable that they meant to take the questions relative to France into consideration. I mentioned to you in my last how I thought this business would be begun.

They will perhaps use as much delay as possible in hopes that the French government not being organised, the taxes not being collected, the credit falling, the expected internal tranquility not arriving, may disgust many against the present order of things. The parties which are forming in the country among those who wish for the revolution, but differ in their opinions about the constitution, resemble so much those which took place in Brabant, and the advantage which the Emperor derived from delay will weigh much in the adoption of such a system.

Acts of rigour are now used against that class of people who have been long employed as the arms of the revolution and who had become too strong for the government. Their disgust will necessarily increase and it will not be surprizing if in time they act against their former leaders in favor of any party who should be strong enough to offer them a change. It is the misfortune of this country to have too many of those who will always desire disorder and changes because having nothing to lose they have nothing to fear.

It must be agreed also that the conduct of the assembly gives fair play to their enemies whether Royalists or Republicans. The acts of irregularity and despotism which they tolerate or authorize are overlooked by a great many as they consider them the only remedy to the greater evil of anarchy. But they are reproached by many also as the indirect cause of this anarchy in taking the government into their own hands instead of organizing and separating its parts. It is evident that the true principles of liberty are either not known or not attended to. They are avowedly violated every day under the long known pretext of public good. Where such things will lead to or when they will end it is impossible to say, but it is evident that they obscure the horizon and give alarm to such as have time to reflect on their future progress.

M. Duveyrier whom I mentioned in my last has been called before the assembly to give an account of his mission. He had not changed his name as was said at Luxemburg. He was arrested there because his passeport was for one person only and he had a companion, and because he was suspected of wishing to debauch the garrison. He was confined three weeks without being allowed to write. He was set at liberty and escorted to the French territory before M. de Montmorin's reclamation arrived at Brussels.

In addition to what I mentioned of Spain in my last, I think it well to send you the following account which has been printed here and which I have reason to believe is nearly exact. – the population about ten millions – the mean amount of its revenues taken on ten years £4,172,648 sterling, annual expences £4,888,514. The revenue now amounts to £5,000,000 sterling owing to a better system of collections. – It is said also that the expences have not increased in the same proportion, which I take to be erroneous, as it is generally supposed there is an annual deficit. – Land forces 70, or 80,000 men of which a large body is cavalry. – 73 ships of the line.

It is published in the English newspapers that war is inevitable between the U. S. and Spain and that preparations are making for it on both sides. M. de Montmorin asked me how the business stood at present and seemed somewhat surprized at my telling him that I knew nothing later than what I had formerly mentioned to him. I have in more than one instance experienced the inconvenience of being without information. In this it is disagreeable as it may have the appearance with M. de Montmorin of my having something to conceal from him which not being the case it would be wrong that he should be allowed to take up such an idea. I observed that I did not suppose there was any new circumstance as you had not informed me of it.

I have just recieved a letter from the Consul at Bordeaux who informs me that hitherto the decrees of the assembly have had a good effect both on our oils and tobacco as to price. He adds that several French vessels sent to America for the latter article are soon expected which will lower the price 5.₶ or 6.₶. They will of course exclude our vessels altogether unless counteracted by some means or other.

I have not seen Drost since my last. He then told me he would come in two or three days and take final arrangements if he determined to go which I have little doubt will be the case. I hope to be able to assure you of it in my next. In the mean time I beg you to be persuaded of the sincerity with which I am, Dear Sir, your affectionate friend & servant, W: SHORT

PrC (DLC: Short Papers); at head of text: "*No. 74*"; at foot of text: "Thomas Jefferson Secretary of State Philadelphia." Tr (DNA: RG 59, DD). Recorded in SJL as received 22 Oct. 1791. Enclosure: William Short to Alexander Hamilton, 24 July 1791 (text printed in Syrett, *Hamilton*, VIII, 573-6).

From James Currie

Richmond, 25 July 1791. Acknowledging TJ's favor written the day he departed on his trip "to the N. and Eastward," which he hopes was pleasant and salutary. He corresponded with Remsen as TJ advised and is astonished at the conduct of his debtor. "Humanity in the reverses of fortune frequently exhibits Phænomena that astonishes even those who before thought themselves very intimately acquainted with it. My debtor I think is entitled to rank among the first of that Class." He will always keep in grateful remembrance the very uncommon, indeed unparalleled pains TJ took on his behalf. The issue he must still commit to his friendly care. "All your friends at Monticello were very well a few days ago. Mr. R[andolph] . . . dind with me on his way home from . . . Varina. Mrs. Currie who will go in a few days to the Green Springs intends herself the pleasure of visiting at Mr. Walkers, and the family at Monticello. She joins me in warmest wishes for your health and happiness."

RC (DLC); endorsed by TJ as received 15 Aug. 1791 and so recorded in SJL.

From Delamotte

Le Havre, 25 July 1791. Acknowledging TJ's of 13 May and informing him that his recent silence was caused by a six weeks' absence in Paris; that he saw Mr. Short there and was reimbursed by him for advances to the American sailor Benjamin Huls; and that he had forwarded dispatches from Short and would consult him about the propriety of publishing an extract from TJ's letter concerning the prosperity of the United States. He had already conveyed this to the American captains there and believed that such publication at that moment might help establish reciprocal confidence.

Evidence of this, he thought, was the establishment there of two French and Dutch houses to engage in American trade. Also, a considerable amount of merchandise had been sent to Boston by those hoping to import salt provisions, candles, timber, and other articles. – The difference in duty on tobacco in

American ships had injured trade with America, but he thought that this would not last; that the United States would soon retaliate; and that the decree calling for a new treaty would make possible a change in the one on tobacco.

On the 14th an English house there, speaking for the English captains, asked permission of the municipality to dress their ships in tribute to the French revolution. This was granted, and it responded by inviting them to attend the ceremony; it gave them cockades; and the public was eager to show them its gratitude. Without being a servile copyist, he could not let the Americans be silent. The ships of the two foreign nations displayed their own flags at the stern, the French flag at the mainmast, and the Province flag at the foremast. After several fêtes, the Society of Friends of the Constitution at Le Havre bestowed on the President of the United States a little flag uniting the flags of the three nations. It was displayed at a dinner of 200 persons, given to the Americans and the English as a symbol of the reunion of the three nations. He will send this flag to the President. He hopes TJ will not find his conduct blamable; if so, he should consider that he was led into this by the English and by the love of the French for their revolution.

Mr. Barrett, departing for Boston, will give TJ his reasons for not accepting the consulate at Rouen. Delamotte has appointed the following agents: *Rouen*, Pierre Barthelmy Le Couteulx; *Honfleur*, Jean Frederic Lallemand; *Fécamp*, Laurent Berigny; *Dieppe*, Jacques Eugénes Le Baron; *St. Vallery sur Somme*, François Marie Masset; *Caen*, Pierre Le Cavelier. – In his next he will give the names of those at Dunkirk, Boulogne, and Cherbourg. He encloses list of American ships entered there to the end of June, and in January he will report on all entries from Dunkirk to Cherbourg. He also encloses Capt. Raser's receipt.

RC (DNA: RG 59, CD); in clerk's hand except for signature, with receipt from Captain Bernard Raser of the ship *Molly* for "one Box address'd to Mr. Th: Jefferson Philadelphia, which I'll deliver faithfully, paying me for my freight, One Dollar. Signed Double Havre July the 30th 1791." Dupl (same). Recorded in SJL as received 22 Oct. 1791.

On the same day, Delamotte wrote Short enclosing a copy of that part of the above concerning the Fourth of July celebration and expressing the hope that his conduct would be approved. He also announced that two ships would leave on the 30th for Philadelphia (RC in DLC: Short Papers). Short replied that he considered as proper "any conduct which may be agreeable to yourself and at the same time present the Americans in their true and friendly dispositions with respect to the inhabitants of your port and the citizens of France in general." He added that he had addressed to Delamotte "a clock for Mr. Jefferson well packed to be sent by the diligence in hopes of its arriving in time for one of the vessels going to Philadelphia" (Short to Delamotte, 29 July 1791; PrC in same). The clock, made to TJ's design by Chanterot (see Vol. 16: xxxiii, and illustration opposite p. 52), did not arrive in time. Delamotte at first reported that the clock would come by the *Minerva*, Captain Wood, then that it had gone by *Le Jeune Eole*, and later that it had after all been given to Wood (Delamotte to TJ, 12 and 24 Aug. 1791; Delamotte to Short, 17 Aug. 1791, DLC: Short Papers). The box referred to in Captain Raser's receipt attached to the above letter probably contained the works of Desgodets and others that TJ had bought of Froullé (see Froullé to TJ, 20, July 1791).

From David Humphreys

Mafra, 25 July 1791. A packet from Falmouth brings no news of sailing of British fleet or peace in the north. Fawkener, British envoy at Petersburg, momentarily expected at London with conclusive news, which public judgment thinks will be peace. Yet bounty for seamen extended to end of July. All accounts indicate the Empress stands by her original demands, and the fresh rupture between Austrians and Turks is favorable to her object.

"Mr. Hammond, who was formerly (as you may recollect) with Mr. David Hartley at Paris, now Secretary of Embassy at Madrid, had just arrived at London Express from Lord St. Helens. The occasion of his coming was not certainly known, but it was believed to be on account of some impediments which the Court of Spain had thrown in the way of the final adjustment of the Articles of the Convention respecting the Nootka Sound affair."

He encloses newspapers from Paris, showing the tranquillity of the nation, its unanimity, the firmness of the governing power, and the preparations for opposing domestic or foreign foes having the temerity to attempt force. Also the Portuguese gazettes showing operations between Spaniards and Moors at Oran.

RC (DNA: RG 59, DD); at head of text: "(No. 27)"; endorsed by TJ as received 22 Oct. 1791 and so recorded in SJL. Tr (same).

To David Humphreys

DEAR SIR   Philadelphia July 26. 1791.

Mr. Robert Morris this moment informs me that a person of the name of William Duncan, formerly of this state, sailed from hence about the year 1785,[1] and has never been since heard of till lately that his mother has been informed by some one, who says he has been at Algiers, that this Wm. Duncan is there in captivity. I am therefore to ask the favour of you to take the first opportunity of having enquiry made at Algiers into this fact, and if you find it true, Mr. Morris wishes you to ransome the person and obliges himself to answer the ransom-money. I presume Capt. Obrian can inform you if there be such a person, and it might be well to ask of him further if there be any Americans in the dominion of Algiers other than those I have named to you. – I am with sincere esteem Dear Sir Your friend & servt,   TH: JEFFERSON

RC (NjP); addressed: "A Monsieur Monsieur Humphreys Resident des E. U. d'Amerique à Lisbonne"; endorsed. PrC (DLC). FC (DNA: RG 59, DCI).

William Duncan, presumably lost at sea, was never one of the captives of the Al-

gerines (Humphreys to TJ, 30 Mch. 1792). The "some one" who informed his mother that he was held prisoner there was one James Reynolds. On the circumstances which suggest that this was another instance of imposition practised upon the families of Algerine captives and that the person making the report was none other than James Reynolds, a known reprobate who was involved in the notorious episode concerning Alexander Hamilton's affair with Maria Reynolds, see Vol. 18: Appendix, note 89. The fact that Robert Morris interested himself in the case lends support to the supposition there advanced. It is also possible that Morris was the one who prompted the similar appeal to the British government in May 1791 which is referred to in that note.

William Duncan was probably the person of that name who was part owner of the ship *Rebecca*. She was registered in Philadelphia in 1775 and was built there the preceding year (PMHB, XXXIX, 195).

[1] Thus in MS, probably an error for 1775 (see Vol. 18: Appendix, note 89).

From James Madison

DEAR SIR   N.Y. July 26. 1791

I am just in possession of your favor of the 24 inst: and thank you for the pamphlet which I shall look over without delay. Mr. Dorhman has this moment handed me a letter to Mazzei which will give him the change of prospect as to the balance of the debt. I really believe D's misfortunes to have been great and real. Mazzei must rest contented with his ultimate security in the land which I consider as satisfactory. It probably could not at this moment be converted into money at all; and certainly not without an absolute sacrifice of D's interest. – The maple sugar was principally bought by the manufacturers to be refined. After some research I have found a parcel from which you can be supplied. But the quality is so far below the standard formed by my imagination, that I inclose a sample in order to have your own decision on the case. The price is £3. 8. N.-Y. Currency. Nothing new. Yrs. mo: affy.,

Js. MADISON JR

RC (DLC: Madison Papers); date added to endorsement by Madison when letter was returned to him; endorsed by TJ as received 28 July 1791 and so recorded in SJL.

From Robert Montgomery

Alicante, 26 July 1791. As reported in his of the 24th, Ali Hassan, "after having ordered the Aga to be strangled for an attempt to oppose him," succeeded the late Dey of Algiers. – Ali had shown great wisdom and talents while minister of marine, an office he filled for many years until made prime minister. "He is considered as a man of uncommon Abilities and a Wise politician" who showed partiality for the United States. Montgomery has known him for twenty years, and since being established at Alicante he has had a friendly intimacy with his confidant, "Hagge Suliman Benchellon a Moore of some Learning and Knowledge of European Languages and manners," who has been sent by

Ali on frequent missions to Spain. During these trips, "I made him make my House his home With every other mark of civility which Could tend to Secure his friendship and confidance. . . . my views you may suppose were Pointed at this crisis when my friend and his master Should both be at the Summit of Power." If TJ will get him permission to try, peace with Algiers may be obtained on honorable terms and at an expense fully compensated "by a very few years trade with this Country."

He would not ask or recommend being sent there at first by Congress. He could go over as a merchant and easily get permission from the Dey and be well received by Suliman, both of whom "already know my hearty desire to bring about a Concilliation." He would point out that the few American slaves were picked up by accident; that they could expect no more, Americans now being on guard; that profits from war would never equal advantages of peace on such terms as Americans could afford; and that Suliman, wishing to serve him, could never have so good an opportunity as to enable him to have the honor of bringing about a peace. Such language, and what TJ might think proper, could be used without an interpreter since he understands Spanish.

No nation has been able to make peace without paying for it, but some armed vessels and naval stores, the produce of America, could serve. Of course a visit there would first be necessary. If TJ would approve and honor him with his confidence, he would immediately go there, purchase wheat for this market, gain information, and then report advices to be laid before Congress. If TJ desired to write in cypher, someone should be sent with the communications to the resident in London, whence they could be forwarded "pretty safely by post." Or, if TJ preferred, he could leave his business in the hand of a partner and come to America to wait on him in person for instructions. He encloses a letter from "one of our Slaves," which contains "pretty good information," and so he transmits "it original" to TJ. He speaks of Cathalan of Marseilles as "a very respectable character" in trade and of Burchara as "a Jew settled in Algiers; Captn. O Bryan seems to have discover'd at last that both one and the other would wish to make the best of his business." He apprehends that "some improper Jobbing in the business has done us more injury with the late Dey than we ever have been aware of." There have been several cruisers on the coast. Should they go westward of Cadiz and Lisbon they must certainly pick up some of our vessels. The Portuguese squadron is by no means vigilant. Should Portugal make peace, we can expect their cruisers on the coast "and in the Bays of America the summer following." The seige of Oran continues. [P.S.] The Algerians have raised four new batteries commanding greater part of the works. The Moors have again renewed the war with Spain and recommenced the siege of Ceuta.

RC (DNA: RG 59, CD); lacks final page, text of which is provided by Dupl (same). Another Dupl (same); mutilated and slightly variant in phraseology; endorsed by TJ as received 22 Oct. 1791 and so recorded in SJL. Enclosure: Richard O'Bryen to TJ, dated at Alicante, 22 Apr. 1791, recorded in SJL as received 22 Oct. 1791 but not found.

To Gouverneur Morris

Dear Sir   Philadelphia July 26. 1791.

Your favors of Feb. 26. and Mar. 16. have been duly recieved. The conferences which you held last with the British minister needed no apology. At the time of writing my letter desiring that communications with them might cease, it was supposed possible that some might take place before it would be recieved. They proved to be such as not to vary the opinion formed, and indeed the result of the whole is what was to have been expected from known circumstances. Yet the essay was perhaps necessary to justify as well as induce the measures proper for the protection of our commerce. – The first remittance of a thousand dollars to you was made without the aid of any facts which could enable the government to judge what sum might be an indemnification for the interference of the business referred to you with your private pursuits. Your letter of Feb. 26. furnishing grounds for correcting the first judgment, I now inclose you a bill on our bankers in Holland for another sum of a thousand dollars. In the original remittance, as in this supplement to it, there has been no view but to do what is right between the public and those who serve them.

Tho' no authentic account is yet recieved, we learn through private channels that Genl. Scott is returned from a successful expedition against the Indians; having killed about 30. warriors, taken fifty odd women and children prisoners, and destroyed two or three villages, without the loss of a man, except three drowned by accident. A similar expedition was to follow immediately after the first, while preparations are making for measures of more permanent effect: so that we hope this summer to bring the Indians to accept of a just and general peace, on which nothing will be asked of them but their peace.

The crops of wheat in the U.S. are rather abundant and the quality good. Those of tobacco are not promising as yet. I have heard nothing of the Rice crops. – I am with very great esteem Dear Sir Your most obedient & most humble servt.,   Th: Jefferson

PrC (DLC). FC (DNA: RG 59, DCI). Enclosure: Bill of exchange, dated 26 July 1791, drawn on Willink, Van Staphorst & Hubbard for $1,000 in favor of Morris (missing). TJ's letter of advice gave the facts as stated (TJ to Willink, Van Staphorst & Hubbard, 26 July 1791; PrC in DLC; FC in DNA: RG 59, DCI).

TJ submitted the above letter to the President for his approval before dispatching it (see TJ to Washington, 27 July 1791).

From William Blount

["*Territory of the United States of America South of the River Ohio*"], *27 July 1791*. Enclosing all information he has on Territorial boundaries and private claims to be excepted from right of Congress to dispose of lands ceded by North Carolina. The bearer, Major Mountflorence, a Nashville lawyer, is well informed, conversant with laws of his state, and would be happy to serve TJ. [P.S.] Reports of entries in Washington and Sullivan counties, being too bulky to be enclosed, are "committed to the Bearer."

RC (DNA: RG 59, SWT M-471/1); endorsed by TJ as received 15 Aug. 1791 and so recorded in SJL. The enclosures, which have not been found, were acknowledged in TJ to Blount, 17 Aug. 1791, and were used in preparing TJ's Report on Public Lands, 8 Nov. 1791.

James Cole Montflorence, born in France of Irish parents, emigrated to North Carolina in 1778. An officer during the Revolution, he later practiced law in Nashville. At this time he was returning to France, where he remained (see Carter, *Terr. Papers*, IV, 71-2).

From William Channing

Newport, 27 July 1791. Transmits copies of laws of his state written before receipt of TJ's letter of "29th. of May [i.e., March] last" and all printed copies of other laws he has been able to procure. He regrets this collection is not more complete and will furnish additional copies when obtained in future. He encloses bill of his "disbursements in this business."

RC (DNA: RG 59, MLR); endorsed by TJ and by Remsen as received 8 Aug. 1791 and so recorded in SJL.

From Edward Church

Bordeaux, 27 July 1791. After a long and tedious passage he arrived on the 1st and would have proceeded to Bilbao but for extreme illness of one of his daughters. He has been told he might not be allowed to function there as consul, and so has written to "the American Minister at . . . Madrid" for advice. As it is impracticable and expensive to move a large family from place to place, he will await Carmichael's answer to avoid an unnecessary and fruitless voyage.

It is argued that the recent decree respecting tobacco operates against American interest, but viewed on the whole, "abstracted from the pernicious prejudice of Americans in favor of the british interest – from the interest of british Factors, and british subjects in America – and from the too credulous confidence of Americans in general in the immaculate faith of british Merchants," he sees cogent arguments for a contrary opinion. In any case, "France has done no more than followed the example of Britain, who is generally supposed to be commercially wise, but no unprejudiced American can presume to question the right of other nations to consult their own interest." He offers this in support of the American consul who has given umbrage by what is thought to be "a too scrupulous regard to the laws of the Country," which may lead to complaint against him based on this as the real "or *pretended*" cause. – He thinks Fenwick is censured because he would not connive in the effort of masters of two American vessels to deceive the customs officers. They are said to have claimed entry direct from America, but their papers show clearly an entry and clearance from Falmouth. The deception could not be supported by Fenwick on any pretence. The customs officers might have been duped at first to permit an entry and sale, but the indirect route was a matter of general notoriety and could not long be concealed. Hence Fenwick adopted the wisest plan, especially since duplicity would not have produced any "essential advantage" and might in the end have injured the owners of the tobacco and his character as a public servant, which he was "doubly bound to preserve inviolate." He hopes TJ will approve Fenwick's conduct and acquit himself "of any culpability" for joining in his opinion.

RC (DNA: RG 59, CD); endorsed by TJ as received 22 Oct. 1791 and so recorded in SJL.

To James Madison

MY DEAR SIR   Philadelphia July 27. 1791.

I inclose you the pamphlet desired in your's of July 24. also the one on Weights and measures recieved through you, of which having another copy, be pleased to keep it. In turning over some papers I came across my journal through France, and Italy, and fancied you might be willing to acquire of that country a knowlege at second hand which you refuse to acquire at the first. It is written in the way you seemed to approve on our journey. – I gave E.P.'s letter to Mr. Lear. I write to Mazzei by a vessel which sails on Monday; so shall hope to hear from you by that time. – Nobody could know of T.C.'s application but himself, H. you and myself. Which of the four was most likely to give it out at all, and especially in such a form? Which of the four would feel an inclination to excite an opinion that you and myself were hostile to every thing not Southern? – The President is much better. An incision has been made, and a kind suppuration is brought on. If Colo. Lee be with you present my respects to him. Adieu. Yours affectionately,   TH: JEFFERSON

P.S. Dispatches from Genl. Scott confirm the newspaper accounts of his success, except that he was not wounded.

RC (DLC: Madison Papers). PrC (DLC).

The pamphlet which Madison had requested was Tench Coxe's *A brief exami-* nation of Lord Sheffield's observations on the commerce of the United States (Philadelphia, 1791). TJ failed to inclose it in the above letter, which Madison received two days later and replied: "I have this instant received yours of the 27th in which you refer to as enclosed the pamphlet desired by me. . . . as it is not enclosed I snatch this sudden opportunity to request you to forward it by Monday's mail. I thank you for the other enclosures and have only time to add that I am &c. Js. Ma[dison] Jr. N.Y.

Friday" (Madison to TJ, 29 July 1791; RC in DLC: Madison Papers; addressed: "Mr. Jefferson Secretary of State Philadelphia"; endorsed by TJ as received 31 July 1791 and so recorded in SJL). See Madison to TJ, 31 July 1791.

From William Short

DEAR SIR   Paris July 27. 1791

Having had an opportunity of writing to you by private hands on the 20th. and 24th. inst., this by the English packet is sent merely to shew you that I do not omit that regular conveyance.

The circumstances of this country remain as mentioned in those letters. There is so much zeal shewn among the Parisians for marching to the frontiers that they have been obliged to allow the capital a larger quota than was at first determined of the 97.000 thousand volunteer *gardes nationales*. They are now encamped near the *champ de Mars* and are only waiting for marching orders. There is every reason to believe that the other departments also will furnish their quotas with the same facility. It is a misfortune that this first enthusiasm should be thus lost, as it will certainly be the next year before they can have any enemy in face sufficient to render their services necessary.

The probability of their having such an one then increases every day, in proportion as peace to the North becomes more certain. There is no doubt it will be effected in the course of this summer. It is possible it may be already signed as the conferences of Sistovie have been renewed on one hand and the English minister sent extraordinarily to Petersburg for negotiating the peace has presented his powers in form on the other.

As yet the only cabinet which has expressed its sentiments on the present situation of the King, is Spain, whose official communication I have already sent to you. – The Emperor has just arrived at Vienna and it is expected he will soon say something either as head of the empire, with respect to the reclamations of the German princes – or as brother to the Queen and connected with the Royal family, with respect to their present treatment. Royal affections generally are subservient to political considerations so that if there was no other motive there would be little to fear from foreign influence, but the present posture of the King of France will necessarily bring the subject nearer home to the several crowned heads of Europe and render them the personal, as they have ever been the political, enemies of the present order of things in France. It is expected that several of them will soon break the silence they have hitherto scrupulously observed. How far they will go will depend of course on the internal situation of this country. There seems among the leading members a fixed determination to enter into no kind of transaction with any foreign power relative to the constitution – even those who disapprove many parts of that which has been decreed by peacemeals are determined to submit to its defects and support them to the last; rather than allow any change to be made by foreign interference; even if more conformable to their principles.

All parties seem impatient to see the whole of the constitution completed. The two committees of constitution and revision have been for some time employed in extracting it from the indigested mass of decrees. It will be proposed to the assembly in a few days. The committees have laid aside numberless of those articles which have been hitherto ridiculously called constitutional. As soon as the assembly shall have ratified the whole of the constitution as thus proposed, it will be offered to the King, who will no doubt accept it, and in that case he is to resume the reins of government. This is the present plan of the assembly. It may be thwarted from abroad or perhaps from within. Should that not be the case they will as they say immediately order the new elections.

D[roz] has been with me this morning. He determines to go, but says it will be impossible to leave this place in less than six months for the reasons mentioned in my No. 73. He is to have articles of agreement drawn up by Mr. Grand on the basis proposed, and then submit them to me.

The kind of warfare which has for some time subsisted between the Spaniards and Moors still continues. It is nothing more than an intermittent siege of the Spanish forts on the coast of Africa. – I am with sentiments of the most perfect respect & attachment Dear Sir your affectionate friend & servant,   W: SHORT

PrC (DLC: Short Papers); at head of text: "*No. 75*"; at foot of text: "Thomas Jefferson Secretary of State Philadelphia." Tr (DNA: RG 59, DD). Recorded in SJL as received 22 Oct. 1791.

To George Washington

July 27. 1791.

Th: Jefferson has the honour to inclose to the President his letter to G. Morris, to which he will add any thing the President pleases by way of Postscript or by incorporating it into the letter. – A ship sailing from hence for Havre on Monday Th: J. proposes to send his letters for France by that rather than by the French packet.

RC (DNA: RG 59, MLR); addressed: "The President of the U. S." Not recorded in SJL or SJPL.

It is possible that Washington replied to the above on the 28th. His private note of that date concerned a different subject but was clearly related to Morris. Another of the same date, presumably public and recorded in SJPL, has not been found. Whether in the missing communication or in consultation, Washington obviously gave his approval to TJ's letter to Morris, 26 July 1791, as written. In his own letter commenting on Morris' letters on European affairs, Washington wrote: "This letter goes with one from Mr. Jefferson, to which I must refer you for what respects your public transactions, and I shall only add to it the repeated assurances of regard and affection" (Washington to Morris, 28 July 1791, *Writings*, ed. Fitzpatrick, XXXI, 330).

From Pierre Guide

Baltimore, 28 July 1791. Acknowledging TJ's of the 21st stating that he had found the first case of wine and the raisins. He is very sorry that this gave TJ trouble and delay, but in consigning them he gave emphatic directions. He has received TJ's note on the Baltimore collector of customs for "Douze gourdes." – He has sent two shipments of tobacco to his brother at Nice under the American flag, which he hopes will succeed in strengthening relations between Sardinia and the United States. – He proposes to go next week to Philadelphia and will take the liberty of waiting on TJ.

RC (MHi); endorsed by TJ as received 30 July 1791 and so recorded in SJL. TJ's letter to Guide of 21 July 1791 is recorded in SJL but has not been found.

From John Macpherson

[*Philadelphia*], *Almond Street, No. 50, 28 July 1791.* He asks TJ to read the enclosed papers; he will call the next day to get them back. For seven years he has struggled between the first law of nature and parental affection; none but a tender parent can know what he has suffered; and now self preservation and duty to other children have prevailed: "I must now prove to the public, that I have been Cursed with a Son, more deceitfull, Ungrateful, Unjust, Unnatural and Inhuman than any Character I have read of in history." The charges made in the letters are but part of what he will prove in a court of justice. He has two objects: to do justice to himself and to "make his Fall a

Warning to Sons Yet Unborn." [P.S.] He troubles TJ with these papers to keep the defamations of his son and others from influencing him. He encloses some verses he published after his son refused a reconciliation.

RC (MHi); in clerk's hand, except for signature; endorsed by TJ as received 28 July 1791 and so recorded in SJL. Enclosures not found.

To John Macpherson

SIR   Philadelphia July 28. 1791.

I have duly received your letter of this day with the papers it contained, and gave the hasty perusal which my occupations would permit to so much of them as served to shew me it was the case of a variance between father and son, which I sincerely lament, but wish to be left ignorant of the facts or faults which may have produced it. If my recommendation of mutual forgiveness and union, or at least of mutual silence, could have weight, it should be pressed: but no circumstance gives me a right to expect it. Wishing therefore to be permitted to have no opinion on the subject I am Sir Your very humble servt,   TH: JEFFERSON

PrC (MHi); at foot of text: "Capt. John Macpherson."

To James Madison

MY DEAR SIR   Philadelphia July 28. 1791.

I this moment recieve yours of the 26th. The sugar of which you inclose a sample would by no means answer my purpose, which was to send it to Monticello, in order, by a proof of it's quality, to recommend attention to the tree to my neighbors. — In my letter of yesterday I forgot to tell you there is a brig here to sail for Halifx in 10. days. She is under repair, and therefore may possibly protract her departure. Adieu. Your's affectionately,

TH: JEFFERSON

PrC (MHi).

To William Short

DEAR SIR   Philadelphia July 28th. 1791

Since my last I have received Letters from you as follows.

No. 59	March 4.	received	June 21.	No. 63	April 8	received	July 8.
60	" 11	"	" 21.	64	" 25	"	" 23.
61	" 12	"	" 22.	65	May 3	"	" 19.
62	" 30	"	" 21	66	" 8	"	" 19.

Mine to you unacknowledged were of March 8. 12. 15. 19, April 25 and May 10. Your two last letters mention the length of time you have been without intelligence, having then received mine of January 23d. only. You will perceive by the above that six letters of a later date were on their way to you. The receipt of these with the newspapers, journals, laws and other printed papers accompanying them will have relieved your anxiety, by answering several articles of your former letters, and opening to you some new and important matters. I scarcely ever miss the opportunity of a private vessel going from hence or New York to any port of France, without writing to you and sending you the newspapers &ca. In the winter, occasions are very rare, this port particularly being blocked up with ice. The reason of so long an interval between the last and present letter, has been the journey of a month which that informed you I was about to take. This is the first vessel which has offered since my return: she is bound to Havre, and will carry the newspapers as usual.

The difference of 62. ₶ 10 the hogshead established by the National Assembly on tobacco brought in their and our ships, is such an act of hostility against our navigation as was not to have been expected from the friendship of that Nation. It is as new in it's nature as extravagant in it's degree, since it is unexampled that any Nation has endeavoured to wrest from another the carriage of it's own produce, except in the case of their Colonies. The British navigation act, so much and so justly complained of, leaves to all nations the carriage of their own commodities free. This measure too is calculated expressly to take our own carriage from us, and give the equivalent to other nations: for it is well known that the shipping of France is not equal to the carriage of their whole commerce; but the freight in other branches of navigation being on an equal footing with only 40. ₶ the hogshead in ours, and this new arrangement giving them 62. ₶ 10 the hogshead in addition to their freight, that is to say 102. ₶ 10 instead of 40. ₶, their vessels will leave every other branch of business to fill up this. They will consequently leave a void in those other branches, which will be occupied by English, Dutch and Swedes, on the spot. They complain of our Tonnage duty; but it is because it is not understood. In the ports of France we pay fees for anchorage, buoys and beacons, fees to measurers, weighers and guagers, and in some countries for light-houses. We have thought it better that the Public here should pay all these, and reimburse itself by a consolidation of them into one fee, proportioned to the tonnage of the vessel, and therefore called by that name. They complain that the *foreign* tonnage is higher than the domestic. If this complaint had come from the English it would not have been wonderful, because the foreign tonnage operates really as a tax on their commerce, which, under this name, is found to pay 16½ dollars for every dollar paid by France. It was not conceived that the latter would have complained of a measure calculated to operate so une- qually on her rival, and I still suppose she would not complain if the thing were well understood. The refusing to our vessels the faculty of becoming national bottoms on sale to their citizens was never before done by any nation but England. I cannot help hoping that these were wanderings of a moment, founded in misinforma- tion — which reflection will have corrected before you receive this.

Whenever jealousies are expressed as to any supposed views of ours on the dominion of the West Indies, you cannot go farther than the truth in asserting we have none. If there be one principle more deeply rooted than any other in the mind of every American, it is that we should have nothing to do with conquest. As to commerce indeed we have strong sensations. In casting our eyes over the earth, we see no instance of a nation forbidden, as we are, by foreign powers to deal with neighbours, and obliged with them to carry into another hemisphere the mutual supplies necessary to relieve mutual wants. This is not merely a question between the foreign power and our neighbour. We are interested in it equally with the latter, and noth- ing but moderation, at least with respect to us, can render us in- different to it's continuance. An exchange of surplusses and wants between neighbour nations, is both a right and a duty under the moral law, and measures against right should be mollified in their exercise, if it be wished to lengthen them to the greatest term pos- sible. Circumstances sometimes require that rights the most un- questionable should be advanced with delicacy. It would seem that the one now spoken of would need only a mention to be assented to by an unprejudiced mind: But with respect to America, Euro- peans in general have been too long in the habit of confounding force with right. The Marquis de la Fayette stands in such a relation between the two countries, that I think him perfectly capable of seizing what is just as to both. Perhaps on some occasion of free conversation you might find an opportunity of impressing these truths on his mind, and that from him they might be let out at a proper moment, as meriting consideration and weight, when they shall be engaged in the work of forming a Constitution for our neighbours. In policy, if not in justice, they should be disposed to avoid oppression, which falling on us, as well as on their Colonies, might tempt us to act together.[1]

The element of measure adopted by the National Assembly excludes, ipso facto, every nation on earth from a communion of measure with them; for they acknowledge themselves, that a due portion for admeasurement of a meridian crossing the 45th. degree of latitude and terminating at both ends in the same level, can be found in no country on earth but theirs. It would follow then, that other nations must trust to their admeasurement, or send persons into their country to make it themselves, not only in the first instance, but whenever afterwards they should wish to verify their measures. Instead of concurring then in a measure which, like the pendulum, may be found in every point of the 45th. degree and through both hemispheres, and consequently in all the countries of the earth lying under that parallel, either Northern or Southern, they adopt one which can be found but in a single point of the Northern parallel, and consequently only in one country, and that country is theirs.

I left with you a statement of the case of Schweighauser & Dobree, with the original vouchers on which it depends. From these you will have known, that being authorized by Congress to settle this matter I began by offering to them an arbitration before honest and judicious men of a neutral nation. They declined this, and had the modesty to propose an arbitration before *merchants* of *their own town*. I gave them warning then, that as the offer on the part of a sovereign nation to submit to a private arbitration was an unusual condescendence, if they did not accept it then it would not be repeated, and that the United States would judge the case for themselves hereafter. They continued to decline it, and the case now stands thus. The territorial judge of France has undertaken to call the United States to it's jurisdiction, and have arrested their property, in order to enforce appearance, and possess themselves of matter whereon to found a decree: But no Court can have jurisdiction over a sovereign nation. This position was agreed to; but it was urged that some act of Mr. Barclay's had admitted the jurisdiction. It was denied that there had been any such act by Mr. Barclay, and disavowed if there was one, as without authority from the United States, the property on which the arrest was made having been purchased by Dr. Franklin and in his possession till taken out of it by the arrest. On this disavowal it was agreed there could be no further contest, and I received assurance that the property should be withdrawn from the possession of the Court by an evocation of the cause before the King's council, on which, without other proceedings, it should be delivered to the United States. Applications were repeated as often as dignity or even decency would permit, but it was never done. Thus the matter rests, and thus it is meant it should rest. No answer of any kind is to be given to Schweighauser & Dobree. If they think proper to apply to their Sovereign, I presume there will be a communication either through you or their representative here, and we shall have no difficulty to shew the character of the treatment we have experienced.

I will observe for your information that the sustenance of our captives at Algiers is committed to Col: Humphreys.

You will be so kind as to remember that your public account, from the 1st. day of July 1790 to the last of June 1791 inclusive, is desired before the meeting of Congress, that I may be able to lay before them the general account of the foreign fund for that year.

General Scott has returned from a successful expedition against the Northern Indians, having killed 32 warriors, taken 58 women and children prisoners, and destroyed three towns and villages with a great deal of corn in grain and growth. A similar expedition was to follow immediately, while preparation is making for measures of more permanent effect; so that we may reasonably hope the Indians will be induced to accept of Peace, which is all we desire.

Our funds have risen nearly to par. The eight millions for the bank was subscribed as fast as it could be written, and that stock is now above par. Our crops of Wheat have been rather abundant, and of excellent quality. Those of Tobacco are not very promising as yet. The Census is not yet completed, but from what we hear, we may expect our whole numbers will be nearer four than three millions. I enclose a sketch of the numbers as far as we yet know them. – I am with great and sincere esteem Dear Sir Your sincere friend & Servt.,   TH: JEFFERSON

RC (Lloyd W. Smith, Madison, N.J., 1946); in Remsen's hand except for signature; partly in code, with interlinear decoding in Short's hand; endorsed by Short as received 26 Sep. 1791. PrC (DLC); unsigned, accompanied by PrC of text *en clair*, also in Remsen's hand, with following caption: "Explication of that part of Mr. Jefferson's letter to Mr. Short of July 28th. 1791, which is *in cyphers*" (text for the encoded part of the above letter is taken from this "Explication"; see note 1 below). FC (DNA: RG 59, DCI); with the encoded portion of the text *en clair*.

Since this carefully wrought and firm statement of the government's position on the decrees of the National Assembly concerning tobacco and shipping, on trade with the West Indies, on the standard of measure adopted by France, and on the French judicial decision in the claim of Schweighauser & Dobree represented an unusual declaration of policy on specific issues, TJ submitted it to the President. The degree of discretion permitted to Short in the encoded passage gave TJ the opportunity to express a "perfect knowlege of his judgment" and to imply full confidence in him. Coming immediately after Washington had made available to TJ the letters of Gouverneur Morris, which sought to correct accounts of French affairs reaching the President "thro other Channels" – a clear disparagement of Short's well-informed and penetrating dispatches – this letter may well have been contrived to advance the pretensions of Short for appointment as minister to France (Washington to TJ, 28 July 1791; TJ to Washington, 30 July 1791; Washington to TJ, 30 July 1791). It is equally plausible to assume, in the context of the Paine episode and Washington's silence on the controversy, that TJ supposed

Morris' thrust was aimed at him and therefore, employing unusually forceful language, he sought to rebut the insinuation. Morris' surprising derogation of Lafayette and TJ's full expression of confidence in him in the encoded passage of the letter lends support to this interpretation. If TJ had this dual object in view, timing his statement with the arrival of Ternant as minister and knowing of the French proposal for a new commercial treaty, he succeeded only in making clear that his policies could defend American rights and interests as firmly against France as against England. Ironically, Short's view of affairs in France was one that shared Morris' skepticism, but he was more objective in his reports, enjoyed the confidence of Montmorin to a greater extent, and understood the role of a diplomat far better than the man whom Washington appointed to succeed him.

[1] This paragraph is in code.

To William Short

DEAR SIR   Philadelphia July 28. 1791.

My last private letter to you was of Mar. 16. Yours to me recieved since that date have been of Nov. 7. Dec. 29. Jan. 17. Feb. 18. Mar. 30. Apr. 26. May 2.

Young Osmont arrived here safely, and is living with Colo. Biddle in a mercantile line. He appears to me a young man of extraordinary prudence. I am endeavoring to help him in the case of his purchase of le Tonnelier, if the latter had any right to the lands he pretended to sell. – Mazzei's debt may rest between him and me, and I shall endeavor to arrange it here. He was certainly a good hand to employ with the abbé Morellet, from whom I understand there is no hope, and but little from Barrois who is the real debtor. Perhaps Barrois would pay me in books. If he has a complete set of the Greek Byzantine historians this would balance the account. – The wines from Champagne and Bordeaux, dress from Houdon, press from Charpentier, reveille and carriages are arrived. So is Petit. You have not informed me of the cost of the Champagne, and of it's transportation to Paris, so that my account with the President remains still open. I inclose you a bill of exchange for £131-5 sterl. drawn by John Warder of this place on John Warder & co. merchants of

London which I have indorsed to you. Be pleased to let me know what it yeilds in livres, specie, at Paris that I may credit the President accordingly. You will be so good as to place it to my credit either with yourself, or Mr. Grand or the V. Staphorsts as you think best. I have received my private account with you to Dec. 30. 1790. but as there has been subsequent transactions, I refer looking into it till I receive them. Your public account to July 1. 1790. is also recieved. As soon as that to July 1. 1791. comes to hand, I will take up the whole so as to make one job of it. In yours of May 2. you speak of your house rent, and expences to Amsterdam. As to the former you had better not charge it, because I think it will not be allowed, and because you charge it on the ground of abandoning any claim to an Outfit. If you continue in Europe an Outfit will certainly be allowed you: if you do not, still a partial allowance may be justly claimed. In whatever form I recieve your account, I will take the liberty of modelling it so as to preserve to you every interest which justice and usage will admit. With respect to the expences of your journey to and from Amsterdam and your stay there, it has been the usage for those residing at a court when sent on any extraordinary mission out of the country of their residence to charge their expences. In my journies to London and Amsterdam I charged carriage hire, horse hire, and subsistence. The latter included my tavern expences, lodging do. servants &c. the whole time, but nothing for clothes, pocket money, vales &c. I think you may do the same. If your account is come off before you recieve this, send me immediately the necessary amendment and I will insert it. – No diplomatic appointment will be made till the next session of Congress. Nothing more is known on that subject now than when I wrote you last. Your brother is expected here daily. He is well, and is making a fortune in Kentuckey. – They say R.H. Lee will resign his Senatorial appointment on account of his health. – The following is the translation of the cyphered passage of my letter of Jan. 24. which the mistake of 1287. for 128. and 460. for 466 had confounded. 'Humphries is gone to Lisbon, the grade not settled.' It was since however settled to be Resident. – Paine's pamphlet has been published and read with general applause here. It was attacked by a writer under the name of Publicola, and defended by a host of republican volunteers. None of the defenders are known. I have desired Mr. Remsen to make up a complete collection of these pieces from Bache's papers, the tory-paper of Fenno rarely admitting any thing which defends the present form of government in opposition to his desire of subverting it to make way for a king, lords and commons. There are high names here in favour of this doctrine, but these publications have drawn forth pretty generally expressions of the public sentiment on this subject, and I thank god to find they are, to a man, firm as a rock in their republicanism. I much fear that the honestest man of the party will fall a victim to his imprudence on this occasion, while another of them, from the mere caution of holding his tongue and buttoning himself up, will gain what the other loses.

I trouble you with the care of the inclosed letters. That to Mr. G. Morris is important, as containing a bill of exchange. Accept warm & sincere assurances of the unalterable esteem & attachment of Dear Sir Your affectionate friend & servt,

Th: Jefferson

P.S. Always be so good as to remember me to enquiring friends as if I had named them. – Since writing the above, Petit informs me he has been all over the town in quest of Vanilla, and it is unknown here. I must pray you to send me a packet of 50. pods (batons) which may come very well in the middle of a packet of newspapers. It costs about 24s. a baton when sold by the single baton. Petit says there is great imposition in selling those which are bad; that Piebot generally sells good, but that still it will be safe to have them bought by some one used to them.

RC (ViW); accompanied by a separate sheet in Short's hand containing code symbols and Short's interlinear decoding – the marginal encoded text being so tightly written that it did not permit the decoding to be done on the original, as Short customarily did; endorsed by Short as received 26 Sep. 1791. PrC (DLC); accompanied by a separate sheet in TJ's hand containing the text *en clair* of the encoded marginal passage (varying slightly from Short's decoding): "Adams, Jay, Hamilton, Knox, many of the Cincinnati. The 2d says nothing. The 3d is open. Both are dangerous. They pant after union with England as the power which is to support their projects, and are most determined Antigallicans. It is prognosticated that our republic is to end with the President's life. But I believe they will find themselves all head and no body" (MS in DLC: TJ Papers, 65: 11344). Recorded in SJL as "Private." Enclosed: TJ to Morris, 26 July 1791.

The HONESTEST MAN OF THE PARTY was unmistakenly John Adams, while AN-OTHER OF THEM was John Jay. On Short's use of the anti-*Publicola* pieces sent him from Bache's *General Advertiser*, see note to TJ to Paine, 29 July 1791 (Document XI at 26 Apr. 1791).

From George Washington

Dear Sir   Thursday Afternoon 28th July

I have just given the enclosed Letters an acknowledgment, and was about to file them; but not recollecting whether I had ever shewn them to you, or not – I now, as they contain information, and opinions on Men and things, hand them to you for your perusal. – By comparing them with others, and the predictions at the times they were written with the events which have happened, you will be able to judge of the usefulness of such communications from the person communicating them. – I am Yrs. sincerely,

GO: WASHINGTON

ENCLOSURES

I

Gouverneur Morris to George Washington

DEAR SIR   Paris 22d Novr. 1790

I wrote to you a Note on the 19th. to accompany your Plateaux. My last Letter was of the twenty fourth of September. Since that Period I have past thro Flanders and a Part of Germany, and having coasted the Rhine to Strasbourgh came thence to this City.

As I conjectured, so it has happened, that my longer Continuance in London would have been useless. Spain finding from the Revolt of the marine and other Circumstances, that whatever might be the Intention or rather wish of France no real aid could be hoped for from a Country where even the Semblance of Authority is gone, has submitted to the imperious Demands of Britain. This is a great Point in the general System. From henceforth the Benefit derived by Spain from her Colonies must wither away, and if she should hereafter wage War to cancel an onerous Compact, it is highly probable that one or more independent Monarchies may be established in that large Portion of the new World which she now occupies. Nothing of this Sort can be indifferent to us. In the great Course of Events which divine Providence may have marked, human Wisdom can do but little: and to effect that little we must approach as nearly as possible to our Comprehension the View of Futurity, and bestow on the present that cool Consideration with which every one can examine the Deeds that were done in the old Time before us. The Independence of all America will place us forward as the Bulwark of our Neighbours, and at the same Time it must loosen our Hold upon Europe. I consider the several Colonies to the South of us as a Pledge in our Hands for the good Conduct of those Powers to which they belong. We now derive an Influence from their reciprocal Jealousies which we shall soon I trust secure by our own internal Force. This Subject opens a Field too vast for present Discussion but it leads to another of narrower Compass which we now tread.

England will not I am persuaded enter into Treaty with us unless we give for it more than it is worth now, and infinitely more than it can be worth hereafter. Had they got engaged in a War, and could they in such War have obtained our Aid, they would have paid high; but no Price could in my poor opinion have compensated to us the ill Consequences which must have followed. In Proportion as her Commerce with our Neighbours becomes more extensive and her naval Force more evident, in that same Proportion shall we find the Advantage of being freed from any Stipulations with her. A present Bargain would be that of a young Heir with an old Usurer. Beleiving in our Wants, she will impose Terms which we ought not, cannot consent to. This at least is my serious Beleif. A different Idea may be entertained by others who have better Information more Experience or clearer Judgement: and the Propriety of each Opinion must be decided by the Arbitrament of Time. At present we may consider the Western Posts which belong to us, as a Part of what Britain means to give for Privileges of Trade which in her Hands turn always to Gold. This which is very like buying us with our own Money, would enable the Minister to go down to the House of Commons with perfect Ease and Self Complacency.

The Country I now inhabit on which so many other Countries depend, having sunk to absolute Nothingness, has deranged the general State of Things in every Quarter. And what complicates the Scene in no small Degree is the Incertitude which prevails as to her future Fate because a new System calculated on the palsied State of France would be as effectually deranged by her Recovery, as that which leant upon her Greatness heretofore, and fall with her Fall.

The Northern Courts, removed at a greater Distance from her Influence, have provided for themselves by an Alliance which took Place immediately after the Peace between Sweden and Russia. I think I hinted in a former Letter my Expectation that a new System would arise there. The Effect a Treaty under and between what may be called the Baltic Powers, will have considerable Influence hereafter upon the general System. When you recollect that they are exclusively the Magazine of naval Stores in this Hemisphere, your comprehensive Mind will seize at once the Consequences which may follow to America from Combinations where such Articles are indispensible. This same Baltic is also a Granary for southern Europe. Hence a new Source of important Reflection. I think that occasions will ere long present themselves in which America may be essentially concerned. But to come nearer to my present Position, the Emperor disengaged from the Turk and likely to be soon repossessed of Flanders, will be there in the Command of 50,000 Men besides the Resource which every Sovereign derives from successless Revolt. The King of Prussia is no longer at the Head of an effective germanic League. The fear of Austria and her Connections has for evident Reasons subsided, and the Baron Hertzberg rather a Pedant than Politician, but illy fills that great Void which was left by the Death of Frederick. In Fact Prussia seems to be that Country in Shape Extent Fertility Population Connection and Relation which one would have chosen to shew what great Genius can do with incompetent Materials, and what a Dream is human Greatness. The Emperor is in Possession of Proofs that the Spirit of Revolt thro all his Dominions was fostered by that Court and would have broken out in every Quarter at the Instant of a War. Hence the sudden Pacification at Reichenbach of which the Prussian was the Dupe tho he dictated the Terms. You will readily suppose that Leopold neither as a Man nor a Statesman can look on such Conduct 'in the calm Lights of mild Philosophy.' Hereditary Claims to Dominion which his Rival is possessed of, a long opposition of jarring Interests, and the Bitterness of that Cup he has just been forced to drink, must lead him to seek and to seize the Moment of Vengeance. Forgiveness is not a Family Feature in the House of Lorraine, neither is Italy the School of Christian Meekness. On the other Hand the Alliance between him and the late Sovereign of this Country is rent to Tatters. Not formally cancelled it is effectually annulled. The french Nation hate the Emperor and detest a Connection which seems nevertheless to be the wisest that could have been formed. The great Power of this Monarchy has been for

Centuries an insurmountable Barrier to imperial Ambition. Leopold must therefore wish to see it injured and even dismembered. Many of the german Princes who have rights within the Boundaries of France secured to them by numerous Treaties, and guaranteed by the germanic Corps but lately violated by the national Assembly wish the whole Empire to insist on Restitution; and in Case of Refusal to engage in a War whose Object would be the Recovery of Alsace and Lorraine. Many of the discontented Nobles and Clergy of France are urgent with the Chief of the Empire to avenge the Insults offered to his unfortuante Sister. So fair a Pretext, such plausible Reasons both public and private, joined to a great political Interest and personal territorial Claims might determine an enterprizing Prince. But he is cautious, trusting more in Art than in Force. He sits on a Throne which lately tottered and is hardly yet confirmed. He has before him the Example of a Predecessor whose incessant Toils brought only an Encrease of laborious Care, whose Anxieties wore away the Web of his Existence, and whose mighty Projects were but 'the baseless Fabric of a Vision.' The Germanic Body itself is distracted between the Duty of supporting it's Members and a Dread of destroying the Check upon it's Chief.

This unhappy Country, bewildered in the Pursuit of metaphysical Whimsies, presents to our moral View a mighty Scene. Like the Remnants of antient Magnificence we admire the Architecture of the Temple, while we detest the false God to whom it was dedicated. Daws and Ravens, and the Birds of Night now build their Nests in its Niches. The Sovereign humbled to the Level of a Beggar's Pity, without Resources, without Authority, without a Friend. The Assembly at once a Master and a Slave. New in Power wild in Theory raw in Practice, it engrosses all Functions tho incapable of exercising any, and has taken from this fierce ferocious People every Restraint of Religion and of Respect. Sole Executors of the Law and therefore supreme Judges of it's Propriety, each District measures out its Obedience by its Wishes: and the great Interests of the whole split up into factional Morsels depend on momentary Impulse and ignorant Caprice. Such a State of Things cannot last.

But how will it end? Here Conjecture may wander thro unbounded Space. What Sum of Misery may be requisite to change the popular Will, Calculation cannot determine. What Circumstances may arise in the order of divine Providence to give Direction to that Will, our Sharpest Vision cannot discover. What Talents may be found to seize those Circumstances, to influence that Will, and above all to moderate the Power which it must confer, we are equally ignorant. One Thing only seems to be tolerably ascertained: that the glorious Opportunity is lost, and (for this Time at least) the Revolution has failed. In the Consequences of it we may however find some Foundations of future Prosperity. Such are 1st. the Abolition of those different Rights and Privileges which kept the Provinces asunder, occasioning thereby a Variety of Taxation, increasing the Expences of Collection, impeding the useful Communications of Commerce, and destroying that Unity in the System of distributive Justice which is one Requisite to social Happiness. 2ly. The Abolition of feudal Tyranny by which the Tenure of real Property is simplified the Value reduced to Money Rent is more clearly ascertained and the Estimation which depended upon idle Vanity or capricious Taste or sullen Pride is destroyed. 3ly. The Extension of the Circle of Community to those vast Possessions held by the Clergy in Mortmain which conformed great Wealth to the Wages of Idleness, damped the Ardor of Enterprize and impaired that steady Industry which increase the Stock of national riches. 4ly. The Distruction of a System of venal Jurisprudence which arrogating a Kind of legislative Veto, had established the Pride and Privileges of the few on the Misery and Degradation of the general Mass. 5ly. Above all the Promulgation and Extension of those Principles of Liberty which will I hope remain to chear the Heart, and cherish a Nobleness of Soul, when the metaphisic Froth and Vapor shall have been blown away. The Awe of that Spirit which has been thus raised will I trust excite in those who may hereafter possess Authority, a proper Moderation in the Exercise, and induce them to give to this People a real Constitution of Government, fitted to the natural, moral, social, and political State of their Country.

How and when these Events may be brought about I know not. But I think from the Chaos of Opinion, and the Conflict of its jarring Elements a new Order will at length arise which tho in some Degree the Child of Chance, may not be less productive of human Happiness, than the forethought Provisions of human Speculation.

In the Beginning of this Year I mentioned the Conviction that during the Course of it, the then Ministry would *wear out*. This has been literally verified and Mr. de Montmorin is the only remaining Shred of the old Garment. As to the present temporary Set, I shall say Nothing just now, reserving to a better Opportunity some Sentiments on particular Men. The Object of this Letter is as you will observe to communicate as nearly as I can that State of Things which may in a greater or smaller Degree be forced upon your Attention. I must add the Conviction that my Letters present very different Prospects from those which may reach you thro other Channels. You who know Mankind thoroughly will be able to form a solid Opinion, and however that may vary from mine I shall still rejoice if even by the Display of false Ideas I shall have cast any additional Light upon those which are true. – I am always my dear Sir very truly yours,   GOUV. MORRIS

RC (DLC); endorsed by Washington.

II
Gouverneur Morris to George Washington

DEAR SIR   Paris 1 December 1790

I had the Honor to address to you a Letter on the 22d of last Month in the Close of which I mentioned the Intention of saying at a future Period some few Words of the People who are now on the Stage. To begin then with our friend La fayette, who has hitherto acted a splendid Part. Unfortunately both for himself and his Country he has not the Talents which his Situation requires. This important Truth known to the few from the very Beginning is now but too well understood by the People in general. His Authority depends on Incidents and sinks to Nothing in a Moment of Calm, so that if his Enemies would let him alone his twinkling Light would expire. He would then perhaps raise Commotions in order to quell them. This his Enemies have long charged him with unjustly I believe but I would not answer for the future. The King obeys but detests him. He obeys because he fears. Whoever possesses the royal Person may do what he pleases with the royal Character and Authority. Hence it happens that the Ministers are of la fayette's Appointment. A short Description of their Use was given the other Day by Mirabeau. 'We make Ministers (says he) as we used formerly to send Servants to keep our Boxes at the Play House.' I gave you the Explanation of this Jest while I was in London. La fayette thinks that these his Creatures will worship their Creator but he is mightily mistaken. You know du portail the Minister of War. He is said to be violent in favor of the Revolution. It is more than a year since I have seen him, excepting a short Visit of Congratulation the other Day: My Judgment therefore should have little Weight but I beleive he is too much the Friend of Liberty to approve of the Constitution. For the Rest, he has as you know that Command of himself and that Simplicity of exterior deportment which carry a Man as far as his Abilities will reach. He may perhaps remember his Creator in his ministerial Youth in order that his Days may be long in the Land of Office, but I venture to predict that his duteous observance will not endure one half Second beyond the Moment of Necessity. I believe I did not mention to you about a Year ago the Intention to appoint him, but at that Time I endeavored to take his Measure. The Minister of the Marine I know Nothing about. They say he is a good Kind of Man which is saying very little. The Keeper of the Seals Monsieur du port de tertre was a Lawyer of no Eminence. Thrown up into Notice by the Circumstances of the Moment he is said to possess both Abilities and Firmness. Monsieur de Lessart the Minister of the Finances is rather above than below Mediocrity and possesses that Kind of civil Assent which never compromises the Possessor tho it seldom travels in Company with Greatness.

There is not a Man among them fitted for the great Tasks in which they are engaged, and greater Tasks are perhaps impending. I have no Proofs but I have a well founded Opinion that the Leaders of one Party wish what those of the other fear and both expect viz the Interference of foreign Powers. One previous Step would be to carry off if possible the King and Queen. The latter at least, for there is every Reason to apprehend for their Safety should violent Measures be adopted while they are here.

For my own Part I do not beleive in any such Interference. Neither do I think that the Opposers of the Assembly have sufficient Energy of Character to make a civil War. Their Attempt if any will I imagine be feeble and consequently ruinous to themselves. If indeed they had a considerable Part of the Army commanded by the Prince of Condé and the Person of the King in his Possession, and if they came forward to establish a proper Constitution adopting such good Things as the Assembly have done and rejecting the Evil, then indeed there would be different Ground of Expectation. But I consider this rather as the visionary Hope of a few than as the fixed Plan of Persons who can carry it into Execution. I am always Yours,   GOUV. MORRIS

RC (DLC: Washington Papers); endorsed by Washington.

III
Gouverneur Morris to George Washington

DEAR SIR   London 24 Decr. 1790

A Duplicate of your favor of the fourteenth of August was handed to me Yesterday. The Delay has probably arisen from the Circumstance of my Absence when Colo. Humphreys arrived in this City. I have already informed you of what passed in Relation to the Ballance due to you by Mr. Welch and also of the Mode proposed for Reimbursement of Monies applied according to your

Orders in this City, which I hope may have proved agreable to your Wishes. I hope also that the Articles sent may have arrived safely at their Destination, and answer the Ends for which they were intended. Any further Orders which you may incline to give, while I am on this Side of the Atlantic, I shall be happy to execute.

Mr. Jefferson having written to me on Subjects of a public Nature, I am hence led to presume that it is your wish my future Communications should go thro that Channel, and I shall of Course conform thereto.

Accept I pray you my best Wishes that you may for many Years enjoy all earthly Blessings, and dispense the inestimable Benefits of good Government to a grateful Country. With sincere and respectful Affection I am my dear Sir very truly yours,   GOUV. MORRIS

RC (DLC: Washington Papers); addressed: "George Washington Esqr. President of the United States Philadelphia."

IV
Gouverneur Morris to George Washington

DEAR SIR   Paris 9 March 1791

I am to acknowlege the Receipt of yours of the seventeenth of December which reached me several Days ago, but no good Opportunity then presented itself to convey a Reply. The Idea you formed of the british Cabinet was I am persuaded perfectly just. This Government has lately taken some Steps which cannot but be advantageous to their Rivals for I am persuaded that the late Decrees laying a heavy Duty on Oil, giving a great Preference of Duty on Tobacco imported in french Ships, and declaring that none but those built in France shall be reputed french Bottoms will excite much ill Humor in America. Those who rule the Roost here seem to think that because the old Government was sometimes wrong, Every Thing contrary to what they did must be right; like Jack in the Tale of the Tub who tore his Cloaths to Pieces in pulling off the Fringe Points and Trimmings that Peter had put on, or like the old Congress in its young Days who rejected the Offer of valuable Contracts and employed a Host of Commissaries and Quarter Masters because Great Britain dealt with Contractors. In the Debate on the Subject one of the Lameth's gave it as his Opinion that America was not in a Situation to be either sought or feared for some time to come. This, which is not however the Sentiment of the Party occasioned some Hints in the Close of Observations I sent to Monsieur de Montmorin and of which a Copy has been transmitted to Mr. Jefferson. I hope that the Congress will not act precipitately in Consequence of these Decrees, for I beleive that proper Representations at a proper Moment will produce a Change, and really in the present Effervescence very few Acts of the Assembly can be considered as deliberate Movements of national Will. There still continue to be three Parties here. The *Enragées*, long since known by the Name of *Jacobins*, have lost much in the public Opinion, so that they are less powerful in the Assembly than they were, but their Committees of Correspondence, called *Societes patriotiques*, spread all over the Kingdom, have given them a deep strong Hold of the People. On the other Hand the numerous Reforms, some of them unnecessary, and all either harsh precipitate or extreme, have thrown into the aristocratic Party a great Number of discontented. The Military, who *as such* look up to the Sovereign, are somewhat less factious than they were. But yet they are rather a Mob than an Army, and must I think fall either to the aristocratic or Jacobine Side of the Question. The middle Men are in a Whimsical Situation. In the Senate they follow the Jacobine Counsels rather than appear Connected with the other Party. The same Principle of Shamefacedness operates on great Occasions out of Doors but as the Aristocrats have been forced down by a Torrent of Opinion from the Heighth of their absurd Pretensions, and as the middle Men begin to be alarmed at the Extremities to which they have been hurried, these two Parties might come together if it were not for personal Animosities among the Leaders. This middle Party could be the strongest if the Nation were virtuous, but alas! This is not the Case, and therefore I think it will only serve as a stepping Stone for those who may find it convenient to change Sides. In the Midst however of all their Confusions, what with confiscating the Church Property selling the Domains curtailing Pensions, and destroying Offices, but especially by that great Liquidator of public Debts a paper Currency, the Nation is working it's Way to a new State of active Energy which will I think be displayed as soon as a vigorous Government shall establish itself. The intervening Confusions will probably call forth Men of Virtue to form such Government and to exert it's Powers.

In a Letter I had the Honor to write on the twenty second of November I mentioned a Treaty made between the Baltic Powers. I do not know whether I drew this Idea from Information or Conjecture, but it was in my Mind and still continues there. While in England waiting at Whitehall for the Duke of Leeds who was accidently prevented from keeping his Appointment, I had a long Conversation with Mr. Burgess who seemed desirous of convincing me that he was an efficient Man in the Office of foreign Affairs. I asked him whether such Treaty existed, insinuating that he must certainly be informed of every Movement in that as in every other Quarter. He assured me possitively that it did not, but that Assurance did not alter my Opinion. Indeed the Object of my Question was to discover whether they were at all upon Terms with Sweden, and from what afterwards passed I am persuaded that they are not. I must add that my Enquiries here have been answered in the same Way, but yet I beleive that such a Treaty exists. We spoke a good deal of the Convention with Spain and I declared freely my Opinion which being favorable to Administration drew from him in Support of it a History of the Negotiation. It ended (as he said) in this remarkable Manner. The Count de florida blanca upon hearing the Revolt of the french Marine told the british Embassador 'you insist on the Terms to which I am now about to agree not because they are just but because I am compelled to it. If France could assist us I would never submit, but we are not able singly to cope with you and therefore you must do as you please.' You will judge, my dear Sir, how long such a Treaty is likely to last.

I am delighted with the Account you give me of our public Affairs. There can be no Doubt that a Publication of the Census and a clear State of our Finances will impress a Sense of our Importance on the Statesmen of Europe. We are now getting forward in the right Way, not by little skirmishing Advantages of political Manœuvers but in a solid Column of well form'd national Strength. Like Father Mason's aristocratic Screw, which you doubtless remember, at every Turn we shall now gain and hold what we get. — It is no Evil that you should have a little of the old Leaven. I have always considered an Opposition in free Governments as a Kind of outward Consciences which prevent Administration from doing many Things thro Inadvertence which they might have Reason to repent. By their Means both Men and Measures are sifted, and the Necessity of appearing as well as of being right confirms and consolidates the good Opinion of Society. I expect and am indeed certain that this good Opinion will live with you during Life and follow weeping to your Grave. I know you will continue to deserve it, and I hope you may long live to vex your Enemies by serving your Country. Adieu my dear Sir Beleive me always I pray you, very sincerely yours,   Gouv. Morris

RC (DLC: Washington Papers); endorsed by Washington.

From Nathaniel Barrett

Le Havre, 29 July 1791. He has received TJ's of 13 May. The deranged state of trade there, the disinclination of the National Assembly to grant any special favors to American commerce, the burdens on oil business, and unfortunate situation of his family rendered uncertain his permanent fixture there. He consulted Short on propriety of handing in his commission when he would probably return to America for a year or two to begin a commercial exchange with France which, if it succeeded, would "be on a very great scale." – He has done all in his power to assist Short in getting reduced duty on oils. "A very contrary System has taken place" – that of inducing American fishermen to settle in France and making their vessels French, entitling them to the bounty. The English fishery hitherto not successful. He has a minute of it in his trunk on shipboard and will send it on arrival. He leaves Sunday for Boston and has asked Delamotte, for the present, to regard his place as in his district. He has made Le Couteulx agent, who speaks English well. He hopes TJ will approve. He will wait on him on arrival. Letters given him by Short will be sent by Delamotte with others on vessel bound for Philadelphia, as Short wished. "All was quiet 2 days since in paris. Monsieur de la fayette begs his Compliments to you."

RC (DNA: RG 59, CD); endorsed by TJ as received 22 Oct. 1791 and so recorded in SJL.

From Daniel Carroll

Georgetown, 29 July 1791. Introducing Mr. Cabot of Massachusetts who wishes to be acquainted with TJ. His character, respectable connections, and qualities as "a sensible, intelligent Gentleman" readily induce him to obtain that pleasure for Cabot. He has been mentioned in some letters to the President from the East. He has settled there and is anxious to embrace anything advantageous respecting the public buildings and the Federal City. He has been in treaty with directors of the Potomac Co. about supplying "a number of his Countrymen" to make canal at Little Falls: "they did not agree." He goes to Philadelphia with L'Enfant, and Carroll supposes "many matters will be talk'd over respecting the business on hand." He asks TJ to "assist Mr. Cabot in his views, on their appearing to coincide with the public interest." [P.S.] He asks TJ to take charge of enclosed letter to Madison, having lately written him at Philadelphia and presuming he may be in New York. He refers TJ to what he has written him. – If TJ passes Georgetown on his way to Virginia, he asks him "if not inconvenient to bring a few of the plans of Chatau's you show'd," which will be taken care of and given him on his return.

RC (DLC); endorsed by TJ as received 29 Aug. 1791 and so recorded in SJL.

From Giuseppe Ceracchi

STIMATISSIMO SIGNORE   [Philadelphia] dal allogio 29 luglio 1791

Ricevo dalla stampa la discrizione della mia idea di cui le ne includo due copie.

Il solo onore mi ha fatto impegnare in questo glorioso soggetto, qualunque siasi la riuscita mi sarà sempre lodevole l'averlo progettato, tanto più che non posso aver alcun motivo di rimproverarmi ne il tempo, ne le somme che impiego a quest' effetto perchè le mie commode circostanze possono facilmente supplire, e al uno, e al altro.

Altro non mi resta a desiderare che la sodisfazione di vedere Vosignoria compiacersi delle mie bene intenzionate produzioni, mentre pieno di respetto sono di Vostra Signoria Umilissimo Servo

G. CERACCHI

RC (DLC); endorsed by TJ as received 29 July 1791. Entry in SJL reads: "1791. July 29. Ciracchi. Phila. July 29." In what was obviously a later endorsement, TJ misread "allogio" (lodging) and docketed the letter as dated "May 29," an error which led to its being catalogued under that date in the original DLC microfilm of the Jefferson Papers.

From Nathaniel Cutting

Le Havre, 29 July 1791. Enclosing letter from Short, to which he will not add since he presumes it contains every public occurrence worthy of TJ's notice. – Believing from many circumstances a more extensive and advantageous trade "will speedily take place between France and North America," he has decided to establish himself there and has become interested in Le Mesurier & Cie. Hence, if the consulate for that port remains vacant, he would cheerfully render his country all possible service in that office. – Business at once calls him to St. Domingue, and he will probably leave next month, from there going to America, and he hopes to be in Philadelphia in Feb. next. If there is any way he can serve TJ there, TJ's commands should be sent to James Perkins at Cape François or Messrs. J. G. Roux at St. Marc. – He asks TJ to present "my kind Compliments to both your Daughters."

RC (DNA: RG 59, CD); endorsed by TJ as received 22 Oct. 1791 and so recorded in SJL. FC (MHi: Cutting Papers). Enclosure: Short to TJ, 24 July 1791.

To Lewis Littlepage

DEAR SIR   Philadelphia July 29. 1791.

I am to acknowledge the reciept of your favor of March 5. and to thank you for the view of European politics it conveyed. With respect to the letter of Feb. 25. 1790. which you mention to have written to the President, he authorises me to assure you he never recieved that or any other from you. It is most probable it was intercepted either in it's passage from you to M. de la Fayette, or from him to it's port of embarcation.

There is no better sign than when a nation can say we have no news. This is exactly our case. An unusual tide of prosperity produces it. This proceeds from 4. years successive of plentiful crops and high prices, from a general diffusion of domestic manufactures, from a return to economy, and a great deal of faith in our new government. Some hostilities by the Indians indeed have obliged us to arm against them. Genl. Scott is returned from a very successful expedition against them, and a second and third are preparing, so that we have little doubt they will be induced to accept of peace which is all we ask as the price of victory.

Mr. Paine's Rights of man have been received and read here with great avidity and pleasure. A writer under the signature of Publicola having attacked him, has served only to call forth proofs of the firmness of our citizens in their republicanism. Some great names here have been preaching and patronising the doctrine of king, lords and commons, and as men generally do, they believed what they hoped, that the people might be led to crown or coronet them at least. Tho' checked, they are not yet desperate. But I am happy in a general evidence that they will be found to be all head, without a body. If the revolution in France had failed, it might have intimidated some weak nerves here, but, for the happiness of mankind, that has succeeded.

Kentucke and Vermont have been declared independant members of the Union. Maine and Frankland will soon come forward. Our Census, according to the progress made in it promises our numbers to be about three millions and a half, of which Virginia will be about 700,000 exclusive of Kentucké which is about 74,000.

I shall be happy to hear from you when Europe offers anything interesting. Be so good as to proffer my respects to the Princesses Czaterisky, Count Potoskis, and my friend the Abbé Piattoli: with assurances of great & sincere esteem I am Sir Your most obedient & most humble servt.,   TH: JEFFERSON

PrC (DLC).

From James Maury

Liverpool, 29 July 1791. His last was of the 12th. He had expected to complete his six months' report, but "the Irregularity of the Masters" prevents. He cannot furnish properly until he has "authority to compel," and he asks TJ's express instructions. – The two American vessels remain under seizure and arrivals still increase, having decided preference for freights in trade to U.S. though price is from 50 to 100% more than in British ships. General opinion is that ports will remain open to foreign corn until 15 Nov. and that peace is about to be fixed between Russia and Turkey.

RC (DNA: RG 59, CD); endorsed by TJ as received 22 Oct. 1791 and so recorded in SJL.

To George Washington

SIR   Philadelphia July 30. 1791.

I have the honour to inclose for your perusal a letter which I have prepared for Mr. Short.

The ill humour into which the French colonies are getting, and the little dependance on the troops sent thither, may produce a hesitation in the National assembly as to the conditions they will impose in their constitution. In a moment of hesitation small matters may influence their decision. They may see the impolicy of insisting on particular conditions which operating as grievances on us, as well as on their colonists, might produce a concert of action. I have thought it would not be amiss to trust to Mr. Short the sentiments in the cyphered part of the letter, leaving him to govern himself by circumstances whether to let them leak out at all or not, and whether so as that it may be known, or remain unknown, that they come from us. A perfect knowlege of his judgment and discretion leave me entirely satisfied that they will be not used, or so used, as events shall render proper. But if you think that the possibility that harm may be done, overweighs the chance of good, I would expunge them, as in cases of doubt it is better to say too little than too much. I have the honour to be with the most perfect respect & attachment Sir Your most obedient & most humble servant,

TH: JEFFERSON

RC (DNA: RG 59, MLR); endorsed by Lear. PrC (DLC). FC (DNA: RG 360, PCC No. 120). Tr (DNA: RG 59, SDC). Enclosure: TJ to Short, 28 July 1791.

From George Washington

SIR   Philadelphia July 30th 1791
  I have given your letter to Mr. Short, dated the 28th. instant an attentive perusal. – As you place confidence in his judgment and discretion, I think it is very proper that the sentiments which are expressed in the cyphered part of it, should be handed to him; and approve the communicating of them to him accordingly.

GO: WASHINGTON

RC (DLC); at foot of text: "The Secretary of State"; endorsed by TJ as received 31 July 1791 and so recorded in SJL. FC (DNA: RG 59, SDC).

To Charles Carter

DEAR SIR   Philadelphia July 31. 1791.
  On the reciept of your favour of the 17th. I applied to Mr. Willing, President of the bank, to answer your enquiry as to loans of money on a deposit of lands. He assured me it was inadmissible by the laws of their institution. – From subsequent enquiries and information here I am the more confirmed in my opinion of the superior advantages of Edinburgh for the study of physic, and also in point of economy. Still perhaps you will find it more comfortable to have your son where you can oftener hear from him. – There being nothing new worth communicating, I have only to add my respectful compliments to Mrs. Carter & assurances of the regard with which I am Dear Sir Your most obedt. humble servt.,

TH: JEFFERSON

PrC (DLC).

To Mary Jefferson

Philadelphia July 31. 1791.

The last letter I have from you, my dear Maria, was of the 29th. of May. which is 9 weeks ago. Those which you ought to have written the 19th. of June and 10th. of July would have reached me before this if they had been written. – I mentioned in my letter of the last week to your sister that I had sent off some stores to Richmond which I should be glad to have carried to Monticello in the course of the ensuing month of August. They are addressed to the care of Mr. Brown. – You mentioned formerly that the two Commodes were arrived at Monticello. Were my two sets of ivory chessmen in the drawers? They have not been found in any of the packages which came here, and Petit seems quite sure they were packed up. How goes on the music, both with your sister and yourself? Adieu, my dear Maria; kiss and bless all the family for me. – Your's affectionately,   TH: JEFFERSON

RC (ViU); addressed: "Miss Maria Jefferson." PrC (CSmH).

To William Linn

SIR   Philadelphia July 31. 1791.

I am to return you my thanks for the copy of the sermon you were so good as to send me, which I have perused with very great pleasure. It breathes that spirit of pure fraternity which exists in nature among all religions, and would make the ornament of all: and with the blessings we derive from religious liberty, makes us also sensible how highly we ought to value those of a temporal nature with which we are surrounded. I sincerely wish you in abundance those of every kind, being with sentiments of perfect respect, Sir Your most obedt & most humble servt,

TH: JEFFERSON

PrC (DLC).

William Linn (1752-1808), whose great-grandfather had emigrated from Ireland and settled in Pennsylvania, entered Columbia College before he was fourteen, was graduated in 1795, and began the study of law under Alexander Hamilton but soon gave it up and prepared himself for the ministry (W. B. Sprague, *Annals of the American Pulpit*, IV [New York, 1858], 210-11). The sermon which he transmitted to TJ in a letter describing him as one of the nation's greatest ornaments was his *The Blessings of America . . . preached in the Middle Dutch Church on the Fourth of July, 1791 . . . At the request of the Tammany Society, or Columbian Order* (New York, Thomas Greenleaf, 1791); see Linn to TJ, 18 July 1791; Greenleaf to TJ, 14 Aug. 1791; and

Sowerby, No. 1647. In his enumeration of America's blessings, Linn praised the Constitution, which gave "no undue preference . . . to one denomination of religion above another," a sentiment which naturally evoked TJ's warm sympathy. Linn and TJ later corresponded about their common interest in the American Indian tribes and their languages (Linn to TJ, 25 May 1797; 8 Feb. and 4 Apr. 1798; TJ to Linn, 3 June 1797; 5 Feb. and 2 Apr. 1798).

But the political animosities of the times brought their correspondence to an end. In 1800 Linn published anonymously *Serious considerations on the election of a President* (Trenton, 1800), in which he professed gratitude for the services TJ had rendered his country but argued against his election solely on the basis of "his disbelief of the Holy Scriptures . . . his rejection of the Christian Religion and open profession of Deism." He suspected TJ of being an atheist and said that one of the effects of his election would be to "destroy religion, introduce immorality, and loosen all the bonds of society" (see Sowerby, No. 3226). DeWitt Clinton, as *Grotius*, replied to the "furious priest" with *A vindication of Thomas Jefferson* (New York, 1800); Sowerby, No. 3197. Years later, when TJ received a copy of the defense from Clinton, he said that he had read *Serious considerations* when it came out, had guessed Linn to be its author, and had left him with other "slanderers . . . to the scourge of public opinion" (TJ to Clinton, 24 May 1807).

To James McHenry

[*Philadelphia, 31 July 1791.* "Will Dr. McHenry do Thomas Jefferson the favour to make one of a small committee of friends to dine tomorrow at half after three? Sunday July 31, 1791." MS sold at City Book Auction Sale No. 420, 18 Sep. 1948, lot 84. Not found and not recorded in SJL.]

From James Madison

MY DEAR SIR   N. York July 31. 1791

I received yours of the 28th. last evening. Your preceding one covering among other things your memorandums through France was acknowledged by a few lines put into the hands of a young gentleman bound to Philada. in the Stage of yesterday. The purpose of them was to apprize you that you had omitted Coxe's answer to Sheffeild and to request the favor of you to send it by Monday's mail. Should the bearer have failed in his trust I take the liberty of repeating the request. I should be glad to have the pamphlet on Tuesday, but if forwarded after the receipt of this it may possibly be in time, especially if one of your young men should light on a passenger for Wednesday's Stage that runs thro' in one day. I do not wish however any trouble to be taken in enquiring for such a conveyance, and am really sorry that so much in so trifling a matter should have been given to yourself.

Col: H. Lee left this a day or two ago. He will probably mention to you the comments circulated as to the affair of the Comptroller. It is a little singular no doubt that so serious a face should have been put on it by —— who ought to have known the circumstances which explained the nature of the interference complained of. He referred in his conversation with me, to another candidate whom he could not properly name, as the channel thro' which he had received his wrong impressions.

I am running over yo[ur] memorandums; but I find that to enjoy the pleasure fully I must repeat them with a Map of France before me, which I cannot at present command. – Yrs. mo: affecly.,

Js. MADISON JR.

RC (DLC: Madison Papers); date added to endorsement by Madison after letter was returned to him; endorsed by TJ as received 2 Aug. 1791 and so recorded in SJL.

The person indicated by a dash was of course the Secretary of the Treasury. On the charge that TJ and Madison had sought to interfere in the Treasury Department by promoting Tench Coxe for the office of Comptroller – a charge which TJ had good reason to believe originated with Hamilton himself – see note to Coxe to TJ, 16 Apr. 1791. The other candidate to whom Hamilton referred in his conversation with Madison may have been Timothy Pickering, who of course could have learned of TJ's role in the affair only at second hand, most likely from Hamilton or Knox.

To Fulwar Skipwith

DEAR SIR   Philadelphia July 31. 1791.

Your favor of the 20th. has come duly to hand, and with my congratulations on your safe arrival in your own country, am sorry to mix expressions of concern that your position in the West Indies has turned out the contrary of your expectations. The events indeed which have happened in France and it's dependances are such as could not have been calculated on. But whilst I participate sincerely in the disappointment of your expectations, my duty to you as well as the public obliges me to notice those expressed in your letter that the public will reimburse you your expenditures in the undertaking. The footing on which the consulships stood when you were appointed, was that of serving without emolument from the public. A proposition indeed was afterwards made to allow some small fees, but I informed you before your departure, that it was doubtful whether it would pass with Congress. In fact it failed, and there exists no power at present to make any allowances for Consular services. Nothing less than a law of Congress will do it, and hitherto they have shewn no disposition to make any. Should they however do it hereafter, it will only be some little fee on the vessels arriving in port. Were the precedent once set of reimbursing expences, no one could tell to what it would lead. I have therefore thought it would be wrong in me to leave you a moment under such an expectation because it would be a delusive one, the laws not permitting it to be made good. – I sincerely wish, my dear Sir, I could have given you a different answer: but this does not depend on me, and your candour will distinguish between my will and that of the laws of the land. With every wish for your felicity I am with great esteem Dear Sir Your most obedt. & most humble servt,

TH: JEFFERSON

RC (CtY); addressed: "Mr. Fulwar Skipwith Richmond"; franked; postmarked: "FREE" and "1 AU"; endorsed as received 6 Aug. PrC (DLC).

To James Sullivan

Philadelphia July 31. 1791.

Th: Jefferson presents his compliments to Mr. Sullivan and thanks him for the perusal of the pamphlet he was so kind as to send him. He sees with great pleasure every testimony to the principles of pure republicanism; and every effort to preserve untouched that partition of the sovereignty which our excellent constitution has made, between the general and particular governments. He is firmly persuaded that it is by giving due tone to the latter, that the former will be preserved in vigour also, the constitution having foreseen it's incompetency to all the objects of government and therefore confined it to those *specially described*. When it shall become incompetent to these also, instead of flying to monarchy for that semblance of tranquillity which it is the nature of slavery to hold forth, the true remedy would be a subdivision as Mr. Sullivan observes. But it is hoped that by a due poise and partition of powers between the general and particular governments we have found the secret of extending the benign blessings of republicanism over still greater tracts of country than we possess, and that a subdivision may be avoided for ages, if not for ever.

PrC (DLC).

The PAMPHLET acknowledged by TJ was undoubtedly Sullivan's *Observations upon the Government of the United States of America*, Boston, [1791] (Sowerby, No. 3155).

Robert Morris' Notes on Commerce

[ca. July 1791]

The exportation of Rice from America to Spain, has I think been in a progressive State for some years.

Bread Grains and Meals are Received in Spain from the U S without any obligation to be exported. Consequently may be Consumed in Spain or exported to their Colonies and in Times of Scarcity are actually Consumed in Spain to large extent.

The prohibition to the importation of American flour into Portugal, took its rise from misrepresentations made by *Interested* Persons and ought to be removed.

The difference of Duties paid on Tobo. imported into France in American Ships more than in French – *Must* – be Removed or We must Counter Act it in America which will be unpleasant. The Sale of our Ships must be permitted in France if possible to obtain the permission.

MS (DLC: TJ Papers, 65: 11308); undated, in Morris' hand; endorsed by TJ: "R. Morris's notes." Not recorded in SJL.

Morris' notes were no doubt solicited by TJ for the report on commerce which he expected to submit at the ensuing Congress, just as he had sought information from other merchants, such as Thomas FitzSimons and John Ross (see Report on Commerce, 16 Dec. 1793).

To Nathaniel Burwell

DEAR SIR   Philadelphia Aug. 1. 1791.

Being to write shortly to Mr. Paradise I should be very happy to be able to hand him any information with respect to the prospect of raising money to pay his debts. You know there was some hope from the cutting and selling of timber. Is this likely to be realised? I recollect he had a considerable sum of public paper. As I am on the spot where the science in that line is mathematically exact, I would be obliged to you to inform me of what amount and description Mr. Paradise's paper is? On knowing exactly what kind of certificates &c. he has, I can enquire here what it will sell for in it's present form, or whether it can be converted into any other form, and sell more advantageously, and communicate the information to you to do thereon what you think best. If it can be sold at near par, it will lop off a sensible part of his debt. If you will have the goodness to favour me with an answer, put into the post office by the 16th. inst. I shall receive it in time to communicate it to him by the sure opportunity in contemplation. I am with very great esteem Dear Sir Your most obedt. & most humble servt.,   Th: Jefferson

PrC (DLC); mutilated, so that about a third of the lines on the right margin are lost; this portion of the text is supplied from Tr (ViU), in the hand of Nicholas P. Trist.

From Augustine Davis

Richmond, 1 Aug. 1791. Acknowledging TJ's of the 24th authorizing him to establish two cross-posts. Without knowing anyone who would undertake the business, he inserted the enclosed advertisement in the newspaper. His enquiries promise success, especially as to that at Staunton. It has been recommended that he try to get it "extended to the Shoula Springs, about 120 miles further," placing Staunton in the middle and requiring the route to be run weekly, so also from New London on the other route. — Supposing considerable aid will be given by David Ross in both instances, he will try to get his opinion and patronage before proceeding. "On Main Holston, about 300 miles hence, Mr. Ross has a considerable Iron-Works; from thence to Kentucky, and to the Cumberland Country, (I am informed) travellers generally go in Companies, so that a pointed Contract could not be expected further." — He will be glad to have TJ's commands and instructions regularly.

RC (DLC); endorsed by TJ as received 6 Aug. 1791 and so recorded in SJL.

ENCLOSURE

Proposal for the Establishment of Cross-posts in Virginia

Notice!

I am authorised to contract for the Establishment of two Cross Posts, for one year, from this place; One through Columbia and Charlottesville, to Staunton; the other towards the Holston Settlements, along the Buckingham road, and the Peaks of Otter, into Montgomery, Wythe, and Washington, and on the Route as far as may be towards the Seat of the South-Western Government. The design is, that the Undertaker is to derive all the benefit from the Establishment, whether from private subscriptions for the benefit of Newspapers, or from the customary postage of letters; so that the Cross Post is to support itself, and not to bring any expence to the public. A regular discharge of the duties will be required, which the Undertakers it is presumed may well afford, and to which their own interests will be a further inducement. As it is the object of the Government to open as much as possible communications to the most interior parts of the country, the person who will undertake to go *farthest* will be preferred.

It is presumed that if the Undertaker should extend as far as Main Holston, that letters from the Western Government on Cumberland, and from Kentucky, would be greatly profitable. Applications to be made at this office.

AUGUSTINE DAVIS

Post Office Richmond, Aug. 1. 1791.

N.B. The routes to and from Staunton, and to and from New London, to be performed weekly; for which certain Covenants are to be entered into between the postmaster General and the Undertaker.   A. D.

MS (DLC); in Davis's hand.

From C. W. F. Dumas

The Hague, 1 Aug. 1791. A letter from Paris reports that the Constitution, reduced to essentials, will be presented this week to the King, not to be sanctioned but accepted. After that the King will no longer be uneasy. They will lose no time in finishing the elections already begun for a new Assembly, to which the present one will gloriously give way. If the news of this solemn event takes place after his next dispatch, he will immediately send another. The enclosures, of which he can guarantee the authenticity, concern the peace between the Emperor and the Turks.

He will say nothing of the atrocities at Birmingham, except that it appears they were committed by some ecclesiastics in collusion with someone in the ministry (apparently Grenville). It was a crime of the feudal ecclesiastical hierarchy, perpetrated in hatred on the 14th of July, a day celebrated anywhere else in an irreproachable manner. P.S. *2 Aug.* The Dutch ambassador at Paris is said to have reported on 29 July that the Constitution would be presented to the King on 4 Aug. and he would be given the remainder of the month to decide whether to accept or refuse it.

FC (Dumas Letter Book, Rijksarchief, The Hague; photostats in DLC); at head of text: "No. 80." RC (missing) recorded in SJL as received 22 Oct. 1791. Enclosures not found.

The riots at Birmingham began with the mob's attack on the hotel at which a dinner was held on the 14th of July to commemorate the fall of the Bastille. Mistakenly assuming that Joseph Priestley was the organizer—he had been dissuaded from attending—the mob attacked his home and destroyed most of his papers, books, and apparatus. The rioting continued for two days, with seven homes and two meeting-houses being burned and much property destroyed. Dumas, having contempt for Grenville and believing him to be the dominant person in the ministry, found it easy to hold him responsible.

From Thomas Leiper

Philadelphia, 2 Aug. 1791. He called on TJ about an hour ago and found him not at home. He wished to speak about the addition Carstairs is making to the library room; his labor, he says, will cost £20. "If he says Twenty, a few more Pound may be added." His bill for the room itself will be £100, "and by the Same ru[le] Something more." This, with the other bills, will make it "a very expensive building"; his friends and he think the value added to the house will not equal the cost. Before proceeding he wishes to "be Certain of one thing. If I understood you when we was Speaking . . . of rent you was of the opinion that Six per Cent was too much for Houses. I am of opinion it is a reasonable rent and what I have fixed upon after your time Expires . . . the 7th Jany. 1792." When he let the house to Mr. Franklin at £150 per annum he was very clear he would have 6% for his lot and advances, but is mistaken. If his terms are agreeable, he will go on with Carstairs' addition. If not, he wishes TJ would mention it. He would not have gone this far if he had not believed TJ would give 6% "and a prospect of remaining in the House for Some Time. In that Case Extra Buildings would not have been so much against me."

MS missing, and text taken from a typed transcript provided by Mrs. A. Waldo Jones, Atlanta, Ga., and made by her from a MS copy by Thomas L. Kane in 1854-5 (communication from Mrs. Jones to the Editors, 3 Feb. 1954). Recorded in SJL as received 2 Aug. 1791.

To Philip Mazzei

DEAR SIR   Philadelphia Aug. 2. 1791.

Your favor of Sep. 3. 1790. came to hand Dec. 15. and that of Apr. 12. is just recieved.

I inclose you a letter from Dohrman forwarded me by Mr. Madison from New York. He thinks that Dohrman's expectations of making payment, within any short time, are not to be counted on, but that the land mortgaged is a solid security for the debt ultimately. – I inclose you a copy of Mr. Blair's account. He paid me the balance of £8-14-6-¾ Virginia currency = 157℔-2 for which you are to debit me. – As I have little chance of ever seeing Bowdoin again, or the note of mine to you which he possessed, tho' unindorsed, I credit you it's amount as I formerly mentioned. – I inclose you copies of the papers you gave me on my departure from Paris, according to the desire expressed in your letter of Sep. 3. – I wrote yesterday morning to E. Randolph to inform him of this opportunity of answering your letter, and that I would take care of it. If his letter comes in time, I will inclose it. If he does not write, it will be because the Supreme court met yesterday and engages him. I must leave to him to inform you as to the prospect in Forster Webb's affair. – You will see in Mr. Blair's account that he received from George Nicholas the £6-2 paid by Garth. Nicholas indeed seems to have charged it to you twice, which was an error. However neither that nor any other matter of account is worth enquiring into as to him, as he has settled that and all his immense debts by an insolvency and retirement to Kentuckey. – Mr. Blair consulted with me this day on the subject of your Virginia certificates, which, settled by the depreciation table, are between two and three thousand dollars. The question was whether he should transfer them to the funds of the general government, as is allowed if desired. Virginia, like the other states, has abandoned the idea of providing for these debts since they have been assumed by the general government. If transmuted into the paper of the U.S. four ninths will be at 6. per cent interest, payable as it arises, and may now be sold for 20/ the pound cash. Two ninths will be at 3. per cent, payable as it arises, and may now be sold for 12/ the pound cash. The remaining three ninths is to be at 6. per cent. after 10 years, and may now be sold for 12/ the pound. You will ask why all this gibberish and nonsense? Were the two ninths and the three ninths a less sacred debt than the four ninths? I know no reason but that they might be a puzzle like the funds of England. Mr. Blair and myself both concur in opinion to turn your paper into Continental. You may then if you please turn the four ninths into cash at above par, and by letting the rest lie they will rise to a higher price. But we will consult with E. R. and also have J. M's opinion if it can be got from N. York before Mr. Blair leaves this place. – I shall go to Monticello in September, and then certainly sell Colle. A twelvemonth's credit must be given, or the sale would suffer much. I will take care to have the money in sure hands. I presume you may count on about £150. – There is at present a symptom of the trade at Richmond ceasing to climb up Shockoe-hill. It is at present fixed at the foot of that hill. This gives a hope it may take it's natural course down the river, and raise the value of your lots from the annihilation into which they had fallen. As to these then, I think it prudent to wait awhile. – I will continue to press Mr. Eppes to secure Hylton's debt if possible. – I have thus, I think, gone through every article of your affairs, as far as I am conusant of them. – A word now of my own. Barrois is the real debtor for the money due to me for the map. Tho' he cannot pay money, perhaps he can give me books to that amount. If he has the Byzantine historians, Gr. and Lat. printed at Paris, it would pay the debt. If he has not, then any other saleable books, reasonably valued. If you can save me this, it will be so much got out of the fire. – I am sincerely glad that you have got under the wings of the Diet as well as of the king, and equally so that you take the prudent resolution of not spending your whole allowance. I am in an office of infinite labour, and as disagreeable to me as it is laborious. I came into it utterly against my will, and under the cogency of arguments derived from the novelty of the government, the necessity of it's setting out well &c.; but I pant after Monticello and my family, and cannot let it be long before I join them. My elder daughter is well, happy in her marriage and living at Monticello. She has made me a grandfather. The younger one is with her, but will come here with me. Your friends all well, as far as I recollect. Present me affectionately to the Dutchess Danville, the D. and Dss. de la Rochefoucault. I have left so much of my affection there, that I but half exist here. Adieu, my dear Sir. Your affectionate friend & servt,   TH: JEFFERSON

RC (Mrs. Charles W. Engelhard, Far Hills, N.J., 1978). PrC (DLC); mutilated, so that most of the line endings are lost. Tr (ViU); in the hand of Nicholas P. Trist. Enclosures not found.

Mazzei's letter of 3 Sep. 1790 has not been found, but TJ included an extract from it in his letter to Madison of 15 Dec. 1790. The letter of 12 Apr. 1791 is recorded in SJL as received 19 June 1791, but it also is missing. TJ's letter to Edmund Randolph is not recorded in SJL and has not been found.

To James Madison

DEAR SIR   Philada. Aug. 3. 1791.

Your favours of July 31. and Aug. 1. are recieved, but not that of the 30th. which was trusted to a private hand. Having discovered on Friday evening only that I had not inclosed Coxe's pamphlet, I sent it off immediately to the post office. However I suppose it did not leave this place till the post of Monday nor get to your hands till Tuesday evening.

Colo. Lee is here still, and gives me hopes of your coming on soon. The President is got well. If he goes to Mount Vernon at all it will be about the beginning of October. However I must go a month sooner. One of my carriage horses is dangerously ill, and become in a few days death-poor and broke out full of sores. I fear his situation portends a difficulty. — I inclose you the map belonging to my journal, being the one I had in my pocket during the journey. Adieu, my dear Sir. Your's affectly.,   TH: JEFFERSON

RC (DLC: Madison Papers); addressed: "Mr. Madison at Mr. Elsworth's Maiden Lane New York"; franked; postmarked: "FREE" and "4 AV"; endorsed. PrC (MHi).

To George Washington

[Philadelphia, 3 Aug. 1791]
Th: Jefferson has the honor to inclose to the President a note of such articles as he supposes will be interesting to Mr. Young, so far as he is enabled to do it with some degree of certainty.

RC (DLC: Washington Papers); undated, but date is established from that on enclosure and from entry in SJL reading: "[Aug.] 3. Washington Presidt. for Young."

E N C L O S U R E

Notes on Virginia Lands

Aug. 3. 1791.

The writer hereof is best acquainted with that tract of land which crosses Virginia from North East to South-West by the names of the Bull-run mountains, South-West mountains and Green mountains, and is generally 6 or 8 miles wide, one half of which is the mountain itself and therefore steep; the residue lies at the foot on each side, in large waving hills, perfectly accessible to the plough. It is of a dark red colour. The richest of it is a pure mould or loam, without the least mixture of sand or grit, though often a good deal of broken stone. When first cleared of it's timber, it lies loose for about a foot depth. That is to say as far down as the frosts have penetrated. But below that, for many feet, the earth is still the same, but hard, as having never yet been opened by the frost. When it is turned up by the plough and has been exposed to the frost a winter or two, it is nearly as rich as the original first soil. This land is excellent for wheat and rye, but yields poorly in oats. For Indian corn it is midling. The fruits which abound are apples, peaches, and cherries. The country perfectly healthy, and the climate more moderate in summer than that below, and in winter than that above. Most of the parcels of land held by individuals have been so laid out as to contain about one third of the first quality as above described, one third of a midling quality, and one third of barrens well timbered. The husbandry is in general very slovenly. Under such as it is, the lands of the first quality will produce 30. bushels of wheat to the acre when fresh, and being tended alternately in wheat and Indian corn (the latter of which is a great exhauster) without ever being rested or manured, they fall at length down to 8. or 10. bushels the acre. The soil of midling quality will yield 12 or 15 bushels of wheat the acre when fresh, and fall down to about 8. The grasses which have been found to succeed best are red clover and orchard grass. Greenswerd does well also. Only one good cutting of these can be counted on unless the ground can be watered.

A tract consisting of the three qualities before mentioned in equal quantities, in that part which lies near the Rivanna river, say about Charlottesville, will sell for about 22/6 to 27/6 sterl. the acre on an average. It will be more or less in proportion as there is more or less of the best or worst qualities. Produce is water-borne from hence to the tide-waters 70 miles distant. Advancing North-Eastwardly along the same mountains these lands are dearer, tho' their produce cannot be water-borne till they reach the Patowmac. Going South Westwardly

along the same mountains, lands become cheaper. Where they cross the Flu-
vanna or James river they are about ⅔ of the price before-mentioned, and from
that part their produce may be also waterborne to tide waters, 130 miles distant.

Ordinary prices about Charlottesville are as follows. A labouring negro man
is hired by the year for 9.£ sterl. his clothes & food. A good plough horse costs
£10 to 12£ sterl. A cow 30/ – a sheep 6/ – a sow 10/ a goose or turkey 2/ – a
dunghill fowl 6d. – a bushel of wheat 3/ – of rye 22d.½ – of Indian corn 1/
6 – beef in autumn and pork in the winter 16/ the 100 ℔. – bacon 6d to 8d
the ℔. – hay 45/ the ton.

MS (DLC: Washington Papers); entirely in TJ's hand. PrC (DLC).

From James Madison

My Dear Sir   N. York Aug: 4. 1791
It being probable that I shall leave this place early in the ensuing
week I drop you an intimation of it, that you may keep back any
letters that may fall into your hands for me, or that you might intend
to favor me with.

The outward bound packet for Halifax and London sailed to day.
The one expected for some time past is not yet arrived, and I do
not learn that any foreign news is received thro' any other channel.
Stock and script continue to be the sole domestic subjects of conversation. The former has mounted in the late sales above par, from
which a superficial inference would be drawn that the rate of interest
had fallen below 6 per Ct. It is a fact however which explains the
nature of these speculations, that they are carried on with money
borrowed at from 2½ pr. Ct. a month to 1 pr. Ct. a week. Adieu.
Yrs. mo. affecly.   Js. Madison Jr.

RC (DLC: Madison Papers); date added to endorsement by Madison after letter was
returned to him; endorsed by TJ as received 6 Aug. 1791 and so recorded in SJL.

From John Nicholson

[*Philadelphia*], "*Compt Genls Office*," *4. Aug. 1791*. Gen. William Thompson, some time before he died at end of 1781, sent his resignation to Congress.
Some claims on the public make it desirable to see that letter. He thus requests
permission to take a copy of it or that one be sent him, whichever is more
agreeable to TJ.

RC (DNA: RG 59, MLR); endorsed by Remsen as received 4. Aug. 1791. FC
(PHMC: Nicholson Letter Book). Not recorded in SJL.

From Fulwar Skipwith

Richmond, 4 Aug. 1791. He encloses a packet lately received from the governor of Martinique, the purpose of which is to solicit from "the . . . Cincinnatus their honorary badge." If granted, he will be happy to convey it to the governor.

RC (DNA: RG 59, CD, T/431); endorsed by TJ as received 11 Aug. 1791 and so recorded in SJL.

Jefferson, Freneau, and the Founding of the *National Gazette*

I. PHILIP FRENEAU TO THOMAS JEFFERSON, 4 AUGUST 1791

II. PROSPECTUS FOR THE *NATIONAL GAZETTE*, [BEFORE 9 AUGUST 1791]

III. APPOINTMENT OF PHILIP FRENEAU AS CLERK, 16 AUGUST 1791

IV. GABRIEL HENNO TO THOMAS JEFFERSON, [BEFORE 2 AUGUST 1791]

V. THOMAS JEFFERSON TO GABRIEL HENNO, 4 DECEMBER 1791

VI. PHILIP FRENEAU TO THOMAS JEFFERSON, 27 JANUARY 1792

VII. THOMAS JEFFERSON TO PHILIP FRENEAU, 13 MARCH 1792

VIII. THOMAS JEFFERSON TO THOMAS BELL, 16 MARCH 1792

IX. RESIGNATION OF PHILIP FRENEAU AS CLERK, 11 OCTOBER 1793

EDITORIAL NOTE

The Editor of the "National Gazette" receives a salary from government.

Quere – whether this salary is paid him for *translations*: or for *publications*, the design of which is to vilify those to whom the voice of the people has committed the administration of our public affairs – to oppose the measures of government, and by false insinuations, to disturb the public peace?

In common life it is thought ungrateful for a man to bite the hand that puts bread into his mouth; but if the man is hired to do it, the case is altered.

—*T.L.* in *Gazette of the United States*, 25 July 1792.

The author of this blunt question about the dual role of Philip Freneau, editor of the *National Gazette* and clerk for foreign languages in the Department of State, was the Secretary of the Treasury. With this thrust at the editor as a tool of the Secretary of State, Hamilton brought into the open convictions he and his friends had shared for some time. Two months earlier he had unburdened himself to Edward Carrington in a long letter expressing his serious alarm at the political situation in a critical election year. He believed Madison and Jefferson were at the head of a hostile faction, being *"actuated by views . . . subversive of the principles of good government and dangerous to the union, peace and happiness of the Country."* He was convinced that Jefferson was a man of profound ambition and violent passions who aimed "with ardent desire at the Presidential Chair." To accomplish this ambition, he felt certain, the Secretary of State had patronized Freneau in order to establish a newspaper at the seat of government for the purpose of subverting the measures of the Secretary of the Treasury and pursuing a course "generally unfriendly to the Government." Hamilton was certain that Madison had conducted the negotiations with Freneau, thus being equally responsible for the establishment of the paper and the ill consequences that might be imputed to it.[1] The query put by *T.L.* in the *Gazette of the United States* was phrased more cautiously than the charges in this private and confidential letter, but the insinuation was clear enough to precipitate an acrimonious exchange which intensified partisan feelings, brought embarrassment to the Secretary of State, and infuriated the editor of the *National Gazette*.

Three days after *T.L.* posed his question Freneau declared it to be "beneath reply" – and then proceeded to compare his free and impartial newspaper with that of "a vile sycophant, who obtaining the emoluments from government, far more lucrative than the salary alluded to . . . finds his interest in attempting to poison the minds of the people by propagating and disseminating principles and sentiments utterly subversive of the true republican interests of this country, and flattering and recommending *every* and *any* measure of government, however pernicious its tendency might be, to the great body of the people." Freneau acknowledged that he received "a small stipend for services rendered as French translator to the department of state" but declared that, as editor of a free newspaper, he admitted "into his publication impartial strictures on the proceedings of government."[2] This gave Hamilton an opening which he promptly seized. In a second *T.L.* squib he quoted Freneau as saying he was paid "for service rendered as French Translator to the Department of State, and, *as Editor of a free newspaper*." With this distortion of the meaning, Hamilton, aiming at his real target, asked to be informed "what inducement our rulers can have to hire a man to abuse them." He hinted that the mystery might be solved when the Treasury reports were published.[3] Within the week, writing as *An American*, he accused Jefferson of having introduced something new in the history of American politics by creating, as a public official, a newpaper whose editor was in effect pensioned by the government. Freneau, he declared, "is the faithful and devoted servant of the head of a party, from whose hand he receives the boon. The whole complexion of his paper is an exact copy of the politics of his employer foreign and domestic, and exhibits a decisive internal

[1] Hamilton to Carrington, 26 May 1792 (Syrett, *Hamilton*, XI, 426-45). On the same day that Hamilton made his views public in Fenno's paper, he wrote to Rufus King about Francis Childs, who, with John Swaine, was publisher of the *American Daily Advertiser*: "Francis Childs is a very cunning fellow. In Philadelphia in the person of his proxy Freneau, he is a good Antifœderalist and Clintonian; in New York he is a good Fœderalist and Jayite – Beckley and Jefferson pay him for the first and the Fœderal Citizens of New York for the last" (same, XII, 100).

[2] *National Gazette*, 28 July 1792.

[3] *T.L.* to Fenno, dated 28 July 1792 and printed in the *Gazette of the United States*, 1 Aug. 1792 (Syrett, *Hamilton*, XII, 123-4).

evidence of the influence of that patronage under which he acts." Then followed the most penetrating thrust of all, carefully framed as questions:[4]

> Is it possible that Mr. Jefferson, the head of a principal department of the Government can be the Patron of a Paper, the evident object of which is to decry the Government and its measures? If he disapproves of the Government itself and thinks it deserving of opposition, could he reconcile to his own personal dignity and the principles of probity to hold an office under it and employ the means of official influence in that opposition? If he disapproves of the leading measures . . . could he reconcile it with the principles of delicacy and propriety to continue to hold a place in that administration, and at the same time to be instrumental in vilifying measures which have been adopted by majorities of both branches of the Legislature and *sanctionned by the Chief Magistrate of the Union*?

With this essay, Hamilton laid before the public the sense of alarm he had expressed to Carrington two months earlier, even at times employing the same phraseology. The ethical question thus raised would remain.

The first response to the probing question came two days later when Freneau issued an affidavit, swearing under oath that he had never opened any negotiation with the Secretary of State for the establishment of the *National Gazette*; that his coming to Philadelphia as its publisher "was at no time urged, advised, or influenced" by that officer; that this was his own voluntary act and neither he nor his paper "was ever . . . directed, controuled, or attempted to be influenced in any manner, either by the Secretary of State, or any of his friends"; that there was never "a line . . . directly or indirectly, written, dictated, or composed for it by that officer"; and that he as editor had "consulted his own judgement alone in the conducting of it – free – unfettered – and uninfluenced." The affidavit was published in Fenno's *Gazette of the United States*, together with a comment by Freneau on the charges made against him in which he left it to the public to decide whether "the whole is not a *lie*."[5]

This was such a vulnerable defense as to give Hamilton, again thinly disguised as *An American*, the opportunity to extend his indictment to Madison. Examining the sworn testimony with a skillful lawyer's reasoning, he readily conceded that, in a literal sense, it might be true Freneau had not himself opened negotiations with the Secretary of State. This, however, was immaterial. Incontestable proof, he warned, might be brought forward to show that the negotiation for an appointment and for the creation of an opposition newspaper was "carried on by a very *powerful, influential* and *confidential* friend and associate of that Gentleman." He thought it shocking that Freneau should have made a sworn statement he could not possibly have verified – that Jefferson had never directly or indirectly written, dictated, or composed a single line for the *National Gazette* – and declared that such testimony would have been invalidated in a court of justice even if it had come from a disinterested witness. Again he raised the moral problem: "It is impossible for a correct mind not to

---

[4] *An American* to Fenno, 4 Aug. 1792, published in *Gazette of the United States* of that date. A sentence in Hamilton's draft referring to Freneau's "talents for invective and abuse" as exemplified in his writings for Bailey's *Freeman's Journal* was omitted in the published version (Syrett, *Hamilton*, xii, 158, note 7).

[5] *Gazette of the United States*, 8 Aug. 1792. Both Freneau's sworn statement, 6 Aug. 1792, and his subjoined comment are printed in full in Syrett, *Hamilton*, xii, 188-9.

pronounce, that, in the abstract, a connection like that which is acknowledged to subsist between . . . the *Editor of a News Paper* and the *head* of a department of the Government, is *indelicate* and *unfit*. . . . A connection of that sort in a free country, is a pernicious precedent, inconsistent with those pretensions to extraordinary republican purity, of which so suspicious a parade is upon every occasion exhibited." Then, dismissing Freneau, Hamilton conceded that his strictures were directed toward a character of greater importance:[6]

> They aim at explaining a public Officer, who has too little scrupled to embarras and disparage the government, of which he is a member, and who has been the prompter open or secret of unwarrantable aspersions on men, who as long as actions not merely professions shall be the true test of patriotism and integrity need never decline a comparison with him of their titles to public esteem.

In accusing Jefferson of unscrupulous official conduct as the hidden sponsor of the *National Gazette*, Hamilton described a relationship which was applicable in substance if not in form to his own patronage of Fenno's *Gazette of the United States*. This was what Freneau had had in mind when he publicly denounced Fenno as a vile sycophant. Jefferson made the same point in a private letter to the President, though he stopped short of naming Hamilton as Fenno's patron:[7]

> [Freneau] and Fenno are rivals for the public favor. The one courts them by flattery, the other by censure: and I believe it will be admitted that the one has been as servile, as the other severe. But is not the dignity, and even decency of government committed, when one of it's principal ministers enlists himself as an anonymous writer or paragraphist for either the one or the other of them?

In the same letter Jefferson professed to be not at all concerned with the merits of the *National Gazette*. This scarcely accorded either with his active role in patronizing Freneau or with his repeated expressions to others of the need for "a whig vehicle of intelligence" that would be national in scope. But his overriding concern was to make it clear to the President that his known opposition to Hamiltonian measures had been seized upon by his colleague to accuse him, in terms of scurrility and personal abuse, of harboring views subversive of principles of good government and dangerous to the Union. This was the first time that the head of one department had made a direct public attack on another. The profound cleavage in the Cabinet was now suddenly and sensationally made public knowledge.

Washington, Jefferson, and Madison were all in Virginia when Hamilton thus brought on the confrontation. Like other informed readers of Fenno's paper, none of them needed to be told the identity of *T.L.* and *An American*. Madison called the writings an extraordinary calumny founded upon a gross perversion of facts, and declared that "the quarter, the object, and the motives

---

[6] *An American*, in the *Gazette of the United States*, 11 Aug. 1792. In the same issue Hamilton, as *T.L.*, drawing upon Aesop, declared that if Freneau were in the pay of government, his conduct "forcibly reminds us of the Fable of the Viper which stung to death the Countryman, the genial warmth of whose bosom had reanimated its frozen carcase." The pieces by both *An American* and *T.L.* are given in full in Syrett, *Hamilton*, XII, 188-94.

[7] TJ to Washington, 9 Sep. 1792.

. . . speak for themselves."[8] Washington, deeply disturbed over the dissensions within the Cabinet and the depths to which the newspaper controversy had sunk, called upon all of the principal officers of government to supplant wounding suspicious and irritable charges with "liberal allowances, mutual forbearances, and temporising yieldings *on all sides*."[9] In response to this appeal Hamilton admitted that he had "had some instrumentality . . . in the retaliations . . . upon certain public characters," but candidly declared himself to be in such a situation as not to be able "to recede *for the present*."[10] Jefferson in his reply placed responsibility for the attack on himself squarely upon Hamilton: "neither the style, matter, nor venom of the pieces alluded to," he wrote, "can leave a doubt of their author." He readily admitted that he had furnished Freneau with copies of the *Gazette de Leide* in order to provide the President and the public "juster views of the affairs of Europe than could be obtained from any other public source." Then, in terms comparable to Freneau's sworn disclaimer, he declared:[11]

[8] Madison to Edmund Randolph, 13 Sep. 1792 (Extract in DLC: Madison Papers). Madison at first thought of publishing a rebuttal over his own name, but, among other reasons, he did not know whether TJ would approve. He explained to Randolph that his decision not to do so was later sanctioned by "two or three judicious and neutral friends" whom he consulted.

[9] Washington to TJ, 23 Aug. 1792; Washington to Hamilton, 26 Aug. 1792; Washington to Randolph, 26 Aug. 1792 (*Writings*, ed. Fitzpatrick, XXXII, 128-32, 132-4, 135-6). The letters to TJ and Hamilton were substantially the same and in some instances — as in that quoted above — were identical in phraseology. But there were subtle differences in tone. The letter to Hamilton closed with expressions of "sincere and affectionate regard" — that to TJ with "sincere esteem and friendship."

[10] Hamilton to Washington, 18 Aug. and 9 Sep. 1792 (Syrett, *Hamilton*, XII, 229, 348).

[11] TJ to Washington, 9 Sep. 1792. Shortly after writing this letter, TJ stopped at Mount Vernon where he had a "full, free, and confidential conversation with the President," the particulars of which he promised to communicate to Madison (TJ to Madison, 1 Oct. 1792). These details have been lost to history, but it is to be doubted that TJ's position as expressed in his letter to Washington was altered in any significant way.

The Editors have found no evidence that TJ every employed a newspaper pseudonym to impugn the character of a political opponent (see Vol. 16: 247). Rufus Griswold, *The Republican Court* (1854), asserted Freneau had "confessed" that TJ wrote some of the most offensive pieces in the *National Gazette* attacking Washington. The alleged confession cannot be accepted on Griswold's authority alone, and Philip M. Marsh has properly dismissed it in "The Griswold Story of Freneau and Jefferson," AHR, LI (Oct. 1945), 68-73.

Nevertheless, TJ went too far in saying that he had never written anything "*in . . . any other gazette*" to which his name was not affixed — an assertion which was made even stronger a few days later when he said that, early in life, he had resolved never to write in a public paper without subscribing his name and had always adhered to this resolution (TJ to Randolph, 17 Sep. 1792). Yet, both before and after making these statements, he did write anonymously to newspapers, as in 1784, when he posed as an officer who had served in the Revolution, and again in 1817, when he wrote "A letter from a correspondent of the Editor of the [Richmond] Enquirer" (see TJ to Dumas, 20 Nov. 1784 and its enclosure; TJ to Ritchie, 28 Aug. 1817 and its enclosure). In these and other instances, however, he employed concealment not to vilify an individual but to correct misrepresentations, to advance a cause, or, as he expressed it to Ritchie, to avoid being drawn by "cavillers . . . personally into contest before the public."

But as to any other direction or indication of my wish how his press should be conducted, what sort of intelligence he should give, what essays encourage, I can protest in the presence of heaven, that I never did by myself, or any other, directly or indirectly, say a syllable, nor attempt any kind of influence. I can further protest, in the same awful presence, that I never did by myself or any other, directly or indirectly, write, dictate or procure any one sentence or sentiment to be inserted *in his, or any other gazette*, to which my name was not affixed, or that of my office.

Hamilton's comment on Freneau's sworn testimony implied that the editor had perjured himself, and contemporary polemicists thought Jefferson's role in the founding of the *National Gazette* "a perfect example of his lies and intrigue."[12] Timothy Dwight in 1793 described Freneau as "a mere incendiary, or rather as a despicable tool of bigger incendiaries, and his paper as a public nuisance."[13] But in the extensive body of literature on the subject such assessments have generally been rejected as born of political prejudice. Subsequent commentators, accepting with varying degrees of qualification the not unbiased judgment of Madison that "in the whole catalogue of American printers, not one could rival Freneau in character, talent, and principles," have ranked him as the most gifted journalist of the day, his journal as the best and most influential republican newspaper, and his character, independence, and patriotism as impeccable.[14]

Such generally favorable estimates of Freneau and his relation with Jefferson may have been influenced in part by Hamilton's tactics. In the spring of 1792, alarmed by Freneau's bold and continuing assault on every aspect of his fiscal program, Hamilton had responded by concealing his identity, by charging his Cabinet colleague with improper conduct as a public official, and by distorting the record concerning Jefferson's stand on the Constitution and the debt to France. Had he confined himself to the ethical question, he would have been

[12] George L. Roth, "Verse Satire on 'Faction,' 1790-1815," WMQ, XVII (Oct. 1960), 480. V. F. Calverton, "Philip Freneau, Apostle of Liberty," *Modern Monthly*, VII (Oct. 1933), 543, declared flatly that Freneau had perjured himself and thought it unlikely that TJ would have refrained from writing for the *National Gazette* – an opinion, as indicated below, not shared by other writers on the subject.

[13] George Gibbs, *Memoirs of the Administrations of George Washington and John Adams*, I (New York, 1846), 107.

[14] Such is the conclusion of so careful a scholar as Malone, *Jefferson*, II, 423-7, 460-3. Another thorough investigator of the subject who shares this view is Philip M. Marsh, whose extensive investigations include the following works: "Freneau and Jefferson," *Am. Lit.*, VIII (May 1936), 180-9; "Freneau and his Circle," PMHB, LXIII (Jan. 1939), 37-59; "Madison's Defense of Freneau," WMQ, XXX (Apr. 1946), 269-80; "Jefferson and Journalism," *Huntington Lib. Qu.*, IX (Feb. 1946), 209-12; "The Jefferson-Madison Vacation and Monroe's Draft of the Defense of Freneau," PMHB, LXXI (Jan. 1947), 70-6; "Jefferson and Freneau," *Am. Scholar*, XVI (1947), 201-10; *The works of Philip Freneau, A critical study* (Metuchen, 1968). See also Lewis Leary, *That rascal Freneau, A study in literary failure* (Rutgers, 1941); Jacob Axelrad, *Philip Freneau Champion of democracy* (Austin, 1967); Mary Weatherspoon Bowden, *Philip Freneau* (Boston, 1976); Merrill Peterson, *Thomas Jefferson and the new nation* (New York, 1970), 444-6, 468-70; Irving Brant, *Madison*, III, 334-6; Ralph Ketcham, *James Madison* (New York, 1971), 326-7, 332-3; John C. Miller, *Alexander Hamilton* (New York, 1959), 343-52; Broadus Mitchell, *Alexander Hamilton*, II (New York, 1962), 207-21.

less vulnerable. But to a greater extent than Hamilton could have known, Freneau's sworn testimony concealed much and, on the central point, could not be reconciled with verifiable facts. In his own detailed explanation to the President, Jefferson acknowledged that he welcomed the establishment of the *National Gazette*, that he had made the *Gazette de Leide* accessible to Freneau just as he had done with Fenno and Bache, and that he had supported the paper by soliciting subscriptions for it. All of this was true enough, but it was by no means the whole story.

I

Political leaders of every persuasion, well aware of the critical role of the press in preparing the public mind for independence and for the transformation in government that followed, had long since perceived the advantage of supporting newspaper editors who shared or could be induced to share their views. By 1791 the political and sectional cleavages had become so obvious as to intensify the desire for such understandings between politicians and printers. The founding of the *National Gazette* was only the most famous example of these mutual arrangements which, however hidden and informal, helped to crystallize the formation of parties and ultimately to bring about the triumph of the opposition in 1800.[15] Partisan aims in the narrow sense cannot be justly attributed to Madison and Jefferson in their sponsorship of Freneau. But, among all of the hundreds of gazettes in existence during the divisive years of Federalist administration, urban or rural, daily or weekly, none received such powerful political patronage as the *National Gazette*, the very name of which reflected Jefferson's persistent effort to create at the seat of government a newspaper which would inform the public on all essential measures of government and would circulate throughout the Union. As its editor, Freneau was promised and was accorded advantages enjoyed by no other journalist of the time. Given this unique opportunity to espouse his own deep-rooted republican principles before the nation, his hesitancy and even vacillation in arriving at a decision suggests much about the man and his fitness for such a role at the center of political power.

In his letter to the President, Jefferson did not indicate that Madison was the one who had recommended Freneau for office. Nor did he need to do so. The President and other informed readers of the *Gazette of the United States* knew as well as Jefferson and Madison did whom Hamilton was referring to when he said that the negotiations for Freneau's appointment and for the creation of an opposition journal were "carried on by a very *powerful, influential, and confidential* friend and associate" of the Secretary of State.[16] This was the thrust that went to the heart of the matter. Jefferson's sensitivity on the point is indicated in the pains he took to persuade the President that he could not recall whether he had learned of Freneau's intention to set up a newspaper at

---

[15] The best treatments are Donald H. Stewart, *The opposition press of the Federalist period* (Albany, 1969); Noble E. Cunningham, Jr., *The Jeffersonian Republicans The formation of party organizations, 1789-1801* (Chapel Hill, 1957); and Culver H. Smith, *The press, politics, and patronage The American government's use of newspapers, 1789-1875* (Athens, Ga., 1977).

[16] *An American No. II*, in *Gazette of the United States*, 11 Aug. 1792; Syrett, *Hamilton*, XII, 192.

Philadelphia before or after the appointment was made. Madison naturally shared his concern over the charge of official impropriety and joined with Monroe in preparing a vindication of Jefferson — an effort of which the latter was well aware. Indeed, on his return to Philadelphia, Jefferson stopped at Madison's home, received from him the third of his and Monroe's essays defending the appointment and personally conveyed it to the printer — not to the *National Gazette*, where its source might have been more easily guessed, but to *Dunlap's American Daily Advertiser*.[17] The essence of the argument in defense was that Freneau's appointment was based on merit alone and had no connection with the establishment or the conduct of the *National Gazette*. The authors, knowing it to be the President's own rule, rested their case on the solitary principle governing every appointment to public office — "That the man appointed . . . be irreproachable in point of morality and in other respects well qualified to discharge its duties with credit to himself and advantage to his country." In terms which only Madison could have provided, they portrayed Freneau as a man of liberal eduation, unblemished morals, and sound republicanism who had a record of service and suffering in the Revolution. What difference did it make, Jefferson's defenders asked, whether one deserving of even higher office had already set up a press or was about to do so when given the appointment? "The conduct of the press itself," they flatly declared, "is, in every respect, a distinct thing, and for which Mr. Jefferson can be no way accountable."[18] Put in other terms, this was the impression Jefferson had sought to give to the President. But the distinction is one which cannot be reconciled either with the plausibilities or with the known facts.

It was in the closing days of the First Congress that Madison recommended Freneau for an official appointment. Jefferson extended the invitation a few days later. In doing so, he told Freneau he had just been informed that it might be convenient for him to accept because the duties of translating clerk were so light as not to interfere with "any other calling." Freneau declined the "unsollicited proposal" because, as he expressed it, he felt committed to the patrons of his proposed rural gazette in New Jersey.[19] Madison, being well aware that the translating clerk was required to be available at the capital, would scarcely have recommended the appointment without informing Jefferson of his hope that Freneau would give up his plan and instead establish in Philadelphia "a

[17] In conveying the document, TJ gave considerable alarm to Madison, who feared it might have been among some papers he had lost on the road from Mount Vernon to Alexandria. Madison hoped that a *"safe* train had been laid" to recover particularly the one put under seal because of the possibility of its falling into base hands (TJ to Madison, 1 Oct. 1792; Madison to TJ, 9 Oct. 1792). The papers, which did not include the essay, were found by one of Washington's neighbors, and the President himself forwarded them to TJ (Washington to TJ, 7 Oct. 1792; TJ to Madison, 17 Oct. 1792).

[18] The third part of the vindication appeared in *Dunlap's American Daily Advertiser*, 20 Oct. 1792, and in Fenno's *Gazette of the United States* four days later; the text is reprinted in Marsh, "Madison's Defense of Freneau," wmq, iii (Apr. 1946), 275-80.

[19] TJ to Freneau, 28 Feb. 1791; Freneau to TJ, 5 Mch. 1791. Freneau's reference to TJ's offer as "unsollicited" may lend support to the account William Bradford gave Elisha Boudinot that Freneau had received the offer "in dudgeon, as striking at his independence, &c., and wrote a very insulting answer, which he showed to Mr. Childs, who prevented him from sending it" (Boudinot to Hamilton, 16 Aug. 1792, Syrett, *Hamilton*, xii, 210-11). The information given Hamilton that Madison had handled the negotiations was also attributed to Childs.

free paper meant for general circulation and edited by a man of genius and republican principles."[20] A few weeks later, on learning that Freneau might be induced to change his mind, he gave him a letter of introduction to Jefferson. He hoped Freneau would give his friends in Philadelphia "an opportunity of aiding his decision by their information and counsel." In informing Jefferson of this he said that Freneau had been in the habit of translating the *Gazette de Leide* and thus was fitted for the task allotted him. Jefferson of course had no official need for a translator of the Leyden paper. His purpose, as he frankly told Washington, was to make it available to the American public, as he had tried to do through Fenno and Bache. But Freneau — proud and independent but indecisive, ambitious for literary distinction but unsure of his talent — remained uncommunicative in New Jersey for more than two months. Jefferson assumed he had changed his mind again and expressed his regret.[21] In July Madison informed him that Freneau had abandoned his "Philada. project." Jefferson, revealing both his awareness of the plan and the extent of the patronage he was prepared to offer in addition to the clerkship, said that he would have given Freneau the printing of the laws, the publication of proclamations and public notices of the department, and "the perusal of all . . . letters of foreign intelligence and all foreign newspapers." He considerably understated the case when he said that these privileges, when "added to his salary would have been a considerable aid."[22]

The extensive patronage Jefferson was prepared to offer provided Madison with further arguments. With Henry Lee, he interviewed Freneau twice in New York. Late in July the reluctant editor promised to meet their wishes if financial arrangements could be worked out. This was done when Francis Childs and John Swaine agreed to finance the printing of the paper, admitting Freneau to an equal share of the profits, exempting him from any liability for losses, and permitting him full control as editor.[23] In informing Jefferson of this development, Freneau alluded to the hint about establishing the paper that Jefferson and Madison had given him when they met in New York.[24] Years

---

[20] Madison to Edmund Randolph, 13 Sep. 1792 (Extract in Madison's hand in DLC: Madison Papers). Madison told Randolph his first concern had been Freneau's own interests and that the suggestion of an official appointment had come from "another Gentleman," whom he later identified in a note on the letter as Henry Lee.

[21] Madison to TJ, 1 May 1791. The letter of introduction given to Freneau has not been found and was probably never presented. TJ to Madison, 9 May 1791.

[22] Madison to TJ, 10 July 1791; TJ to Madison, 21 July 1791.

[23] Madison to TJ, 24 July 1791; Freneau to Madison, 25 July 1791 (DLC: Madison Papers). The printing of the paper was done in the shop of Childs and Swaine in Philadelphia, which John Swaine had been managing since the government moved there (Leary, *Freneau*, p. 191). Thus, according to Freneau's account of the partnership, the editor of the *National Gazette* would not even have to bear the costs of printing his paper. It is very unlikely, however, that Childs and Swaine did not charge printing costs when calculating profits or loss of the paper. The terms of the agreement are known only through Freneau's statement made in 1800 (Charleston *City Gazette*, 31 Dec. 1800; reprinted in Marsh, "Freneau and Jefferson," *Am. Lit.*, VIII [May 1936], 185; Freneau errs in dating the agreement June 1791).

[24] Freneau to TJ (Document I). TJ had told the President he thought he could not have discussed the plan for a newspaper with Freneau prior to the latter's appointment because he had met him only once, "at a public table, at breakfast" (TJ to Washington, 9 Sep. 1792). See Editorial Note to group of documents at 20 May 1791.

later, in an attempt to defend Jefferson against Hamilton's charges, he said that when he called on the Secretary of State in Philadelphia he was told the clerkship was still vacant. He then added that in this conversation[25]

> . . . not a single word passed on either side on the subject of the National Gazette, in the establishment of which I was influenced by no one, but undertook it from the powerful necessity of such a paper at the seat of government, to expose in some degree . . . the approaches of royalty, and to hold up to America the baseness and duplicity of certain influential characters, in their desertion of almost every principle of the revolution of 1776.

In fact, Freneau not only discussed his plans for the paper with Jefferson but sought – and unquestionably received – his advice about its prospectus.[26] Ten days after that conversation, Freneau was appointed clerk for foreign languages in the Department of State. His salary began immediately, but by his own admission, he left for New Jersey at once and did not return until late October. Jefferson's gratification at the outcome – to say nothing of his attitude toward the more important object in view – was made clear in the promise he gave to David Humphreys shortly after Freneau's visit and two months before the paper came into existence. He assured the minister to Portugal that he would soon send him another newspaper "written in a contrary spirit to that of Fenno." These two, he added, would reveal "both sides of our politics."[27]

In his effort to prove that Jefferson was "the *Institutor* and *Patron* of the National Gazette . . . an incendiary and pernicious publication," Hamilton did not fail to point out that others possessing linguistic competence could have been found and thus all suspicion of official impropriety avoided.[28] This was a

[25] "To the Citizens of South Carolina," in the *Aurora*, 14 Aug. 1802, as reprinted in Marsh, "Freneau and Jefferson," *Am. Lit.*, VIII (May 1936), 185.

[26] Freneau to TJ, 4 Aug. 1791 (Document I). See notes to prospectus (Document II).

[27] TJ to Humphreys, 23 Aug. 1791.

[28] *An American*, 4 Aug. 1791, *Gazette of the United States* of the same date (Syrett, *Hamilton*, XII, 158, notes 7 and 8). On Hamilton's efforts to obtain documentary proof of Madison's key role in the negotiations, see Hamilton to Jonathan Dayton, 13 Aug. 1792; Elisha Boudinot to Hamilton, 16 Aug. 1792; Dayton to Hamilton, 26 Aug. 1792; *Catullus No. I*, 15 Sept. 1792 (same, XII, 196, 210-11, 275, 385). A few days before *Catullus* appeared, Hamilton told Washington that, on the basis of evidence he possessed, he could not doubt that "the National Gazette was instituted by [Jefferson] for political purposes" (Hamilton to Washington, 9 Sep. 1792, same, XII, 348).

Oliver Wolcott was one of those who assisted Hamilton in his effort to obtain information about Freneau's appointment. In *An American No. II* (published in *Gazette of the United States*, 11 Aug. 1792; Syrett, *Hamilton*, XII, 190) there is the following: "Daily Advertiser of Oct. 26, 1791. – We hear from Phil. that the hon T. J. Esq Secy of State for the U. S. has appointed Capt. P. Fr. Interpreter of the F. L. for the deptmt. of State." *An American* copied this exactly from an unsigned paper which contained only this announcement, addressed "Hon. Oliver Wolcot Comptroller of the Treasury U. S." On its verso Hamilton caused his clerk John Meyer to calculate the number of days from the presumed time of Freneau's employment as of 26 Oct. 1791 to the date of *An American No. II*, 8 Aug. 1792. The MS which Hamilton used is not in the hand of Jonathan Dayton or Elisha Boudinot (MS in DLC: Hamilton Papers, undated but before 8 Aug. 1792). Lacking other information, Hamilton assumed erroneously that Freneau had been appointed on the date of the announcement in the *Daily Advertiser*, which appeared in the issue of 24 Oct. 1791, not that of two days later as the unsigned MS indicates. To this announcement in *American No. II* Hamilton appended the following note: "It is

telling point. Hamilton undoubtedly knew that John Meyer, a clerk in his own department, had offered his services to the Secretary of State as "translator of the French, German, and Low dutch Languages."[29] This was exactly a year before the post was given to Freneau, who was not too facile in the one language he was able to translate. Meyer had not been appointed. During all of this time, with many others available in the capital who were skilled in languages, the clerkship had remained vacant. This was due less to any desire to await the outcome of Freneau's unpredictable changes of mind than it was to the lack of urgent need for a translator. Jefferson himself was largely responsible for this because of his insistence upon close control of all diplomatic correspondence, which he permitted his clerks to see only after it had passed under his own scrutiny. Almost all of the communications in foreign languages were in French and Spanish, both of which he handled with competence. In general, only those letters and documents were translated which he deemed important enough to bring to the attention of the President or which had to be submitted to Congress. Such translations were usually done by himself or, occasionally, by his chief clerk.[30] During Freneau's incumbency as translating clerk, the most important, the most sensitive, and the most numerous diplomatic exchanges in languages other than English involved American relations with France and Spain. Yet no evidence has been found to indicate that Freneau was ever required — or permitted — to translate any of the communications received by the Secretary of State from the French ministers, Ternant and Genet, or from the Spanish representatives, Viar and Jaudenes. Occasionally Jefferson even went so far as to have his chief clerk translate extracts of communications intended for publication, thus placing upon that overburdened officer a task for which Freneau was simultaneously compensated as clerk and benefited as editor.[31]

---

believed that Mr. Freneau could throw light upon this question, by naming the date when his salary commenced." He then stated as a fact that Freneau dared not deny that his clerkship "was *cotemporary* with or rather *antecedent* to the *commencement* of the National Gazette."

[29] John Meyer to TJ, 12 Aug. 1790. Meyer's application may have been ignored because TJ suspected an attempt by Hamilton to infiltrate his department (see note to Meyer's letter, Vol. 17: 351-3). Shortly after the government moved to Philadelphia, TJ made at least one inquiry about the possibility of employing a person skilled in foreign languages. A native of Sweden, one Kullen, who claimed to be "Master of the French, Spanish, English, and Swedish Tongues," was highly recommended to him, but nothing came of it (Swanwick to TJ, [14] Dec. 1790). George Taylor himself, on learning that Pintard would not remove to Philadelphia, applied for appointment as translating clerk in addition to his other duties. TJ, however, declined making the appointment — but not (as Leary, *Freneau*, p. 391, suggests) because TJ reserved the place for Freneau. Taylor's application, which testifies to the lightness of the translating clerk's duties, was made before the government left New York (Taylor to Timothy Pickering, 23 Jan. 1809, MHi: Pickering Papers).

[30] At times TJ translated documents because he deemed them of such confidentiality as to make them improper to be given to clerks. See note 61 below. On TJ's method of handling diplomatic correspondence, see note to Remsen's memoranda on office procedures (Vol. 17: 387).

[31] Usually, but not always, this was done when the extract was released both to the *National Gazette* and to the *Gazette of the United States*.

In applying for office in 1789, George Taylor, Jr., who succeeded Remsen as chief

Even though the duties of the translating clerk were thus reduced to a minimum, Freneau in his reply to Hamilton referred to his annual compensation of $250 as a "small stipend." His later description of his duties and his being required to pay for translating other languages is more fanciful than factual. He claimed that

> . . . there were sent from the several departments of government so many foreign papers and letters, directed to official characters in this country, from Russia, Holland, Prussia, Germany, and elsewhere; the translations of which I was obliged to procure at an exorbitant rate of charge; the place was beginning to be rather a loss than a matter of emolument.

Freneau even gave as one of his reasons for resigning the clerkship his fear that he might be required to translate Chinese, Turkish, or Arabic.[32] The fact is that, considering the extremely light duties placed upon him because Jefferson himself assumed most of them, his compensation was anything but trivial. At the time of his appointment it was half that of the other clerks, who by contrast presented "one continued scene of drudgery in copying papers and close attendance from morning till night."[33] If Freneau was required to have any documents other than French translated, which is doubtful, the cost to himself could only have been an extremely small fraction of his salary. Yet his own grossly exaggerated and inaccurate statements about his duties, his compensation, and the costs which he had to bear have never been challenged.[34]

The unavoidable conclusion is that the offer of official patronage and the founding of the *National Gazette*, despite disclaimers by Jefferson, Madison, and Freneau, were unquestionably interconnected. It is not likely that the appointment to the clerkship tipped the scales with so independent a person

---

clerk on 1 Apr. 1791, said that he had "a tolerable Proficiency in the Study of the french Language" (Taylor to the President, 1 May 1789, DLC: Washington Papers). In 1793 Taylor was given extra compensation in the amount of $40 for translating the whole of Genet's correspondence. This was probably in preparation for the meeting of the Cabinet on 2 Aug. 1793, where TJ presented and read all of it (TJ's memorandum of the meeting, 1 Aug. 1793; Contingent Expenses of the Department of State, Vol. 17: 375). This of course was a duty Freneau was paid to perform.

When, after years of service in the Department of State, Taylor was summarily dismissed by Timothy Pickering, he stated that he had in some cases assisted a Dutch gentleman "to translate french documents put into his hands by Mr. Freneau" (Taylor to Pickering, 23 Jan. 1809, MHi: Pickering Papers). Taylor was a man of veracity "and the most perfect integrity" for whom TJ had high regard (see TJ's certificates of 31 Dec. 1793 and 22 Feb. 1798). Freneau, as TJ's occasional corrections show, was not skilled in the French language. On Taylor's dismissal by Pickering, see Vol. 17: 358.

[32] The *Aurora*, 14 Aug. 1802, as from the Charleston *City Gazette*, 31 Dec. 1800; reprinted in Marsh, "Freneau and Jefferson," *Am. Lit.*, VIII (May 1936), 185-6. Freneau, of course, was required to translate only for the Department of State, not for the whole executive branch as he asserts.

[33] TJ to Barton, 1 Apr. 1792. For an account of personnel, compensation, and TJ's relations with his staff, see note to the salary account of the Department of State, Vol. 17: 356-9. The chief clerk received $800, the others $500.

[34] See, for example, Malone, *Jefferson*, II, 426. Axelrad, *Freneau*, p. 215, goes so far as to assert that Freneau "often paid out more for foreign translations than he received in salary." Not even Freneau made so extravagant a claim. No evidence has been found as to what amounts, if any, he was obliged to pay for translations.

as Freneau, sensitive as he always was to the suspicion of being influenced in his actions by another. The arrangement with Childs and Swaine which freed him of financial responsibility was probably the most decisive factor. But this is irrelevant to the question of improper conduct raised by Hamilton. In seeking – and unquestionably receiving – Jefferson's prior counsel on the planning of the newspaper, Freneau contradicted his sworn testimony that the Secretary of State had at no time "urged, advised, or influenced" his coming to Philadelphia as editor. By the same token, the impression Jefferson sought to give the President – and his defenders to convince the public – that the appointment and the founding of the paper were unrelated is not persuasive. Considering the nominal duties given to the translating clerk and the highly disproportionate compensation he received, it can scarcely be denied that Jefferson had in fact offered and Freneau had accepted what can only be described as a political sinecure.[35]

II

Soon after Freneau made known his plans and accepted the clerkship, Childs and Swaine announced that *"The National Gazette*, a periodical Miscellany of News, Politics, History, and Polite Literature" under Freneau's editorship would soon begin publication, provided a sufficient number of subscriptions could be procured.[36] Even before the announcement was made the paper's

[35] On 11 Feb. 1785 Congress directed that all documents submitted by the Secretary for Foreign Affairs be accompanied by English translations and that he be allowed to pay for that the sum he deemed sufficient but never to exceed the salary of a clerk (JCC, XXVIII, 29, 30, 56). Some indication of the amount paid for translating languages other than French may be gained from the following: Isaac Pinto received only £8-12-4 as Spanish interpreter for three years (Pinto to Jay, 13 Nov. 1789, DNA: RG 59, MLR). From 1786 to 1790 the Rev. John Daniel Gros received £5 for translating "a number of German papers at different periods." Henry Remsen, Jr., while serving as chief clerk, was paid £3-4-10 for translating Dutch papers in 1789-1790. In 1790 Pinto was paid £20-15-9 for translating various Spanish papers over an indeterminate period. During the entire year preceding Freneau's assumption of duties there were no expenditures at all for translating, obviously because TJ himself took care of such French and Spanish documents as required it (Contingent Expenses of the Department of State, 1790-1793; Vol. 17: 359-75). TJ had made no changes in the arrangements that prevailed when his predecessor left office (TJ to Speaker of the House, 2 Jan. 1793).

[36] *Daily Advertiser*, 25 Aug. 1791. This announcement was repeated in the issue of 28 Oct. 1791 with little change, the only one of significance being the omission of the condition stated – "if a sufficient number of subscribers are procured." The omission testifies to the success of the concerted effort by Madison, Jefferson, and others to procure subscriptions. See also TJ to Freneau, 13 Mch. 1792; TJ to Bell, 16 Mch. 1792 (Documents VI and VIII). An excellent summary of the efforts of TJ, Madison, and others to obtain subscribers is presented in Cunningham, *The Jeffersonian Republicans*, p. 17-18. TJ subscribed to only five sets of Fenno's paper for departmental use while ordering seven of Freneau's (Contingent Expenses of the Department of State, Vol. 17: 367, 370). See also Madison to Mann Page, 1 Aug. 1791; Carroll to Madison, 22 Nov. 1791; William Madison to Madison, 3 Dec. 1791; Lee to Madison, 8 Dec. 1791; Madison to Lee, 18 Dec. 1791; Madison to his father, 13 Nov. 1791 (all in DLC: Madison Papers). In a letter to Joseph Jones introducing Childs, Madison described Freneau as "a man of genius, of literature, of experience in the business he is to conduct, and of great integrity" (quoted in Parke-Bernet Catalogue No. 2988, 17 Feb. 1970). See TJ to

political patrons had begun a vigorous and sustained effort to procure subscriptions. Madison appears to have been the first to act. Besides soliciting subscribers himself, he wrote letters to prominent Virginians introducing Francis Childs, who made a journey southward for the purpose. Jefferson frankly admitted to Washington that this was one form of assistance he had rendered. During the month he spent at Monticello before the first issue of the *National Gazette* came from the press, he urged his Albemarle friends to subscribe. He also entered seven subscriptions for use by the Department of State to counterbalance Fenno's *Gazette of the United States*, which he had been sending to American representatives abroad. Daniel Carroll made solicitations in Maryland and Henry Lee in Virginia. Aaron Burr lent his patronage in New York. With such leading political figures bringing powerful influence to bear, it is not surprising that Freneau could announce after six months that subscriptions had "succeeded beyond the Editor's most sanguine expectations."[37] The distribution of the paper, however, was less national in scope than its sponsors had hoped. Most of the subscribers were in the South and West. It was more than a year after the *National Gazette* began publication that Jefferson could say that it was "getting into Massachusets under the patronage of Hancock and Sam Adams."[38]

Subscriptions were essential, but everything depended upon the contents of the paper. Here, too, Freneau enjoyed an advantage over all other editors. The official documents, essays, and correspondence that his sponsors contributed or procured for the *National Gazette* held out the promise that its character would be such as to sustain their high hopes for its important mission. "I need not write you news," Jefferson remarked to a friend in the spring of 1792, "as you recieve Freneau's paper." Then, in one of many instances showing how well informed he was about the operation of the paper, he added: "In his next after this date will be an interesting report of a committee of Congress on the causes of the failure of the last campaign."[39] To another, speaking as an informed reader of many journals, he said that Freneau's was the best he "ever saw published in America."[40]

Official documents alone, domestic and foreign, made the *National Gazette* an important and in some respects an unrivalled vehicle of intelligence in its initial stage. Most of the space in five issues was given over to Hamilton's report on manufactures. His reports on the public debt and on the execution

---

Randolph, 20 Nov. 1791. An entry in SJL shows that TJ received on 9 Feb. 1792 a letter from William Hunter pertaining to "subscriptions for Freneau," but it has not been found.

[37] *National Gazette*, 7 May 1792. Later he asserted that the paper was supported "by upwards of thirteen hundred subscriptions from honest and independent citizens . . . through every part of the Union" (same, 20 Oct. 1792).

[38] TJ to Randolph, 16 Nov. 1792.

[39] TJ to Gilmer, 11 May 1792.

[40] TJ to Bell, 16 Mch. 1792 (Document VIII). Among the many papers TJ subscribed to were Brown's *Federal Gazette*, 1789-1797; Fenno's *Gazette of the United States*, 1789-1796; Bache's *General Advertiser*, 1791-1797; and Dunlap's *American Daily Advertiser*, 1791-1795 (Sowerby, Nos. 540, 542, 543, 544, 545, 546-602). TJ also had the Department of State subscribe to various newspapers in the United States and in Europe. In a later comment which revealed his knowledge of the political attitudes of various newspapers, he said that to judge a country from them, one should have to know their character (TJ's Notes on Ebeling's letter of 30 July 1795).

of the excise law were also published. Jefferson's reports on public lands, on the census, and on the ratification of the first ten amendments to the Constitution were given in full. Such documents were of course available to all newspapers as public records. But others could only have been furnished from the files of the Department of State. Freneau himself often gave hints of this, as when he printed the laws passed in the Northwest Territory and proudly announced: "*Authentic. (Never before printed). . . . Made out from the Original Records in the Office of the Secretary for the said Territory.*"[41] Freneau similarly informed his readers of the authenticity of the full text of the Constitution of Kentucky, which had been made available to him by Madison and Jefferson.[42] In foreign affairs, especially those of France, Freneau also enjoyed particular advantages. Jefferson, perhaps because of his negotiations with Hammond and Ternant, made available copies of his letter to the National Assembly and its decree calling for the negotiation of a treaty of commerce with the United States.[43] From the proceedings of the National Assembly and other official documents transmitted by William Short or published in French newspapers, Freneau was able to publish other materials in which Jefferson had a particular interest, such as the French law on patents, to which the *National Gazette* devoted much space. Documents pertaining to the slave insurrections in Santo Domingo also were given extensive coverage, including the petition of its legislature for arms and supplies and the similar appeals to the National Assembly.[44]

In the early stage of the paper, Freneau was privileged to fill its pages with essays from his influential backers. Madison's alone lifted the discussion of important public topics to the level of his contributions to the *Federalist* papers. Jefferson thought his essay on population and emigration so important that, immediately on its appearance, he urged William Short to have it translated and published in the Paris newspapers.[45] In other essays Madison argued that

[41] *National Gazette*, 19 and 22 Dec. 1791. The laws had indeed been copied from the originals in the office of the Secretary for the Northwest Territory, but the text used by Freneau was the copy in the Department of State.

[42] *National Gazette*, 25 and 28 June 1792. The copy of the Constitution was forwarded to TJ by Madison in his letter of 12 June 1792. Madison had enclosed other documents which he urged TJ to read and then handle as he might judge best. These documents have not been identified but, like the Constitution of Kentucky, Madison may have intended them for use by Freneau. In the same letter he advised TJ to pass on to the editor a hint about the "tax" on newspapers—that is, postage—because this, like the excise, had become a subject of grievance and unless something were done about it, subscriptions to the *National Gazette* might be lost. Freneau had already published an announcement of a meeting to be held in Richmond to protest the "tax" as an alarming interference with the free circulation of newspapers (*National Gazette*, 28 May 1792, quoting the *Virginia Gazette* of the 19th).

[43] *National Gazette*, 17 Nov. 1791; the decree is that of 8 June 1791, enclosed in Short to TJ, 10 June 1791. See TJ to the President of the National Assembly, 8 Mch. 1791.

[44] The appeals of the Santo Domingo legislature to the King and to the National Assembly, both dated 13 Sep. 1791, were printed in the *National Gazette*, 21 Nov. 1791, with this editorial note: "The two following State Papers are translated from the original French, and may be relied on as authentic." The authorization of the legislature to send a delegation to the United States, dated 11 Oct. 1791, is recorded in an extract from its journal (DNA: RG 59, MLR). The legislature's appeal to the United States, dated 13 Oct. 1791, was published by Freneau on 24 Nov. 1791 as read to Congress on the 21st.

[45] TJ to Short, 24 Nov. 1791; *National Gazette*, 21 Nov. 1791.

public opinion, setting limits to all governments and being the real sovereign in every free one, required among other things "a free press, and particularly a *circulation of newspapers throughout the entire body of the people*"; that America had initiated the most triumphant epoch in history; that the experiment, involving as it did a complicated form of federalism, required more than an ordinary reverence for authority, throwing upon the citizens responsibility for defending liberty against power and power against licentiousness; that, while political parties were unavoidable, the great objects should be to achieve political equality and to keep one interest from being favored at the expense of another; and that the political system of the United States was that for which philosophy had been searching and humanity fighting since the most remote ages and which it was "the glory of America to have invented, and her unrivalled happiness to possess."

These eloquent tributes to the American experiment and warnings against those tendencies which might cause it to fail breathed the spirit of republicanism which Madison and other sponsors of the *National Gazette* wished it to convey to the public. It is not likely that all of Madison's contributions to the paper have been identified, but it is worth noting that of the fifteen pieces that can with certainty be attributed to him, all save one fell in the first six months of its existence. Just as Madison may be regarded as the initiator and most persuasive proponent of the undertaking, so may his cogent and eloquent defense of the American proposition be considered as having set the example of what he and Jefferson hoped the character of the paper would be — one of rational discussion, inspiring the citizenry to go beyond mere opposition to federal encroachments and, by working with those of differing opinions, to "erect over the whole one paramount empire of reason, benevolence, and brotherly affection."[46]

The contributions made by Jefferson to the *National Gazette*, despite the solemn assurance given to the President that he had never written or procured a single sentence for it, were more varied and more extensive than those of Madison. They were also of a different character. No evidence has been found to indicate that Jefferson himself wrote anything for the paper, except of course official documents, which he signed as Secretary of State and also caused to be published in Fenno's *Gazette of the United States* and other newspapers. He unquestionably induced others to contribute to it, though only a few of these can be identified with any degree of certainty. He persuaded David Rittenhouse to supply weekly meteorological observations, which he did faithfully for most of the paper's existence.[47] It is plausible to assume that Jefferson's views of the inadequacy of the patent system prompted him to give a hint to his friend Joseph Barnes on that subject. Barnes, who thought the protection provided by the 1790 law worse than none, urged adoption of the French system and

---

[46] The one exception is Madison's "Candid State of Parties," which appeared in the *National Gazette*, 26 Sep. 1792, after Hamilton as *An American* and *Catullus* had attacked TJ and implicated himself in the founding of Freneau's paper. The other essays — the longest of which was on money, written in 1780 — appeared in the paper on 5, 19 (two in this issue), and 22 Dec. 1791; 2, 19, 23, and 30 Jan. 1792; 2, 6, and 20 Feb. 1792; 5, 22, and 29 Mch. 1792; and 2 Apr. 1792. All are printed in Madison, *Writings*, ed. Hunt, VI, 43-105.

[47] TJ to Randolph, 27 Nov. 1791. Without naming TJ as the one who had made this arrangement, Freneau announced Rittenhouse's contribution in the paper of the next day.

supplied Freneau with copies of the pertinent statute and regulations, which he published in full.[48]

It is also virtually certain that Jefferson encouraged his friend George Logan, a prolific essayist on agricultural and political subjects, to lend his facile pen to the *National Gazette*. He regarded Logan as the best experimental farmer in Pennsylvania, both in theory and practice, and sought his advice on the rotation of crops and other matters.[49] He was a frequent visitor at Stenton, enjoyed conversing with Logan's charming wife, Deborah – as did she with him – and undoubtedly found Logan's reports of his experiments a welcome relief from official chores. As a reader of Oswald's *Independent Gazeteer*, Jefferson knew that Logan was the author of several essays under the pseudonym *A Farmer*. In 1791 these were gathered and published as *Letters addressed to the yeomanry of the United States* and he obtained a copy, perhaps as a gift from Logan himself.[50] He did not fully share Logan's somewhat doctrinaire and at times dogmatic opinions in political economy, derived in large part from the Physiocrats. But he was wholly in accord with the master of Stenton in thinking that the foundation of the republic was the independent yeoman, cultivating his own land and trying to improve both it and himself through honest toil, improved methods of farming, and a vigilant attention to the measures of government. He also recognized in Logan one of the earliest opponents of the Hamiltonian system.[51]

Freneau himself seems to have provided the opening for this vigorous spokesman for the opposition to be added to the influential contributors to his paper. Late in January, three months after the *National Gazette* was established, he published an inquiry from a gentleman in Virginia about the plan of organization of the Philadelphia Society for Promoting Agriculture and about any agricultural discoveries that had resulted. The next day he sent the same query to Jefferson.[52] Up to that time Logan had apparently contributed nothing to Freneau's paper, since Eleazer Oswald had made his stoutly republican *Independent Gazetteer* freely available to him. Whether, on receiving Freneau's inquiry, Jefferson prompted Logan to make the response cannot be determined, but it is scarcely conceivable that he would have failed to encourage his friend to do so. In any event Logan seized the opportunity with his usual vigor and enthusiasm. He did not submit the plan of the Philadelphia Society for Pro-

---

[48] Barnes to Freneau, 4 July 1792 (*National Gazette*, 7 July 1792). The texts of the French law and regulations appeared in the issues of 11 and 14 July 1792. See TJ's draft of a bill for promoting useful arts, 1 Dec. 1791.

[49] TJ to Logan, 1 July 1793; TJ to Randolph, 28 July 1793.

[50] The full title discloses the theme: *Letters addressed to the yeomanry of the United States: shewing the necessity of confining the public revenue to a fixed proportion of the net produce of the land; and the bad policy and injustice of every species of indirect taxation and commercial regulations* (Philadephia, Eleazer Oswald, 1791); Sowerby, No. 3156. These essays appeared in Oswald's *Independent Gazetteer* for 13 Mch., 24 Apr., 8 May, and 14 Aug. 1790, and 8 Jan. 1791. Logan's pieces by *A Farmer* appeared in the *National Gazette*, 20, 23, and 27 Feb.; 1, 12, and 26 Mch.; 5 and 23 Apr.; 25 July, 1 Aug., and 8 Sep. 1792. Other pieces by Logan appeared in the issues of 3 May, 24 Oct. 1792, and 1 June 1793.

[51] This is the carefully considered opinion of Frederick B. Tolles, whose "George Logan, Agrarian Democrat," PMHB, LXXV (July 1951), 260-78, is the best account of all of Logan's writings.

[52] *National Gazette*, 26 Jan. 1792; Freneau to TJ, 27 Jan. 1792 (Document VI).

moting Agriculture, since that organization – of which he was a charter member – was made up largely of merchants and professional men. Instead, writing as *A Farmer*, he sent to Freneau a copy of the constitution of the Pennsylvania Society for the Promotion of Agriculture and Domestic Manufactures, an organization restricted to actual farmers.[53] With this initial step, *A Farmer* enthusiastically embarked upon a new series of "Letters to the Yeomanry" in which he envisioned a national network of societies for promoting improvements in agriculture, communicating the results of their investigations, and opposing measures so highly injurious to the farmer as the funding system, the bank, the excise, and manufactories aided by government such as Hamilton had proposed. He thought these societies should operate much as the committees of safety did at the time of the Revolution. Their members, he pointed out in the first letter, should be few in number, active, and endeavor "to stimulate each other to support their rights *as men*." The letters of *A Farmer*, some of them reprinted by request from Oswald's *Independent Gazetteer*, were directed in part to such agricultural topics as rotation of crops, beekeeping, the cultivation of flax, and reports of farming experiments, but most of them voiced the political opposition of the agricultural interest. Within a few weeks *A Farmer* boldly attacked Hamilton and his friends for inducing the New Jersey legislature to enact the law creating the Society for Establishing Useful Manufactures, which he described as "one of the most unjust and arbitrary laws . . . that ever disgraced the government of a free people" because of monopolistic and unconstitutional grants of special privileges to a few wealthy men.[54] Freneau thought so highly of these letters that he later reprinted some parts of them when they appeared in pamphlet form.[55] Jefferson could scarcely have agreed with some of Logan's arguments – his opposition to canals, for example – but he and *A Farmer* stood together in opposing the general tendency of the Hamiltonian system.

This final series of "Letters to the Yeomanry" appeared in the *National Gazette* in the winter and spring of 1793, resulting in another pamphlet which Logan's most perceptive biographer has appraised as his "most eloquent and cogently argued tract."[56] In lending his pen to Freneau's paper, Logan had written more for it than any other, with the possible exception of the editor himself. But while Freneau's writings were largely colored with satire and personal invective, *A Farmer* based his arguments on fundamental principles, thereby proving

[53] *National Gazette*, 20 Feb. 1792.

[54] *National Gazette*, 1 Mch. 1792.

[55] *National Gazette*, 29 Aug. 1792; 19 and 22 Sep. 1792. The full title of the pamphlet made explicit its chief purpose: *Five letters, addressed to the yeomanry of the United States, containing some observations on the dangerous scheme of Governor Duer and Mr. Secretary Hamilton, to establish national manufactories* (Philadelphia, 1792); Sowerby, No. 3157.

[56] Tolles, "George Logan, Agrarian Democrat," PMHB, LXXV (July 1951), 271. The final series began in the *National Gazette* on 31 Jan. 1793. The pamphlet was published by Childs and Swaine early in May under the title *Letters addressed to the yeomanry of the United States, containing some observations on funding and bank systems* (Philadelphia, 1793).

TJ's influence on this series is evident in Logan's use of the doctrine that the earth belongs in usufruct to the living, the dead having neither power nor right over it. Some of Logan's expressions are remarkably similar to those in TJ to Madison, 6 Sep. 1789, in which he expounded the doctrine (Tolles, "George Logan, Agrarian Democrat," PMHB, LXXV [July 1951], 271-2).

himself a far more formidable propagandist for the opposition. By the same measure, Logan's attack on the Society for Establishing Useful Manufactures, which created a vigorous newspaper controversy in the summer of 1792, must have been one of the chief reasons for Hamilton's retaliatory charges against Jefferson as the patron of the *National Gazette*.

III

The extent to which Jefferson made available to Freneau domestic and foreign intelligence in the form of newspapers, official documents, consular dispatches, private letters, pamphlets, and other records cannot be completely or accurately measured. But precisely identifiable examples of Freneau's use of materials from departmental records and from Jefferson's own personal files exist in sufficient number to demonstrate beyond question that the editor of the *National Gazette* enjoyed special privileges not accorded any other journalist. The sheer mass of material from which selections were made available for publication undoubtedly exceeded in quantity alone the total contributions by Madison, Logan, and the writings of such prolific spokesmen for the opposition as *Brutus*, *Sidney*, *Timon*, and *Franklin*. With a few exceptions, these materials also differed from theirs in consisting chiefly of political intelligence and reports of events at home and abroad rather than being discussions of principles and policies of government. Even so, the selections made from the mass reflected Jefferson's view of political issues, as he had made clear to Washington in informing him of his long effort to have the *Gazette de Leide* give a more balanced representation of the momentous happenings in Europe than the American press received by way of the British newspapers.

The Leyden paper was only one of many received by the Department of State that Freneau had the privilege of using. Like other journalists, he of course could and did exchange the *National Gazette* with other newspapers free of postage. This was an extremely important means by which editors could obtain news and gauge public opinion in all sections of the country. But for Freneau the need to bear the expense of exchanging his paper for others was greatly diminished by the large number of journals accessible to him in the department of which he was a clerk. American papers alone amounted in Jefferson's estimate to about twenty.[57] But exchanges free of postage did not extend to foreign journals, and the number of these received by the Department of State was even greater, putting Freneau in an enviable position with respect to his competitors. Newspapers of all sorts from Paris, London, Amsterdam, Leyden, Rotterdam, Brussels, Lisbon, and Madrid, as well as from Canada and the West Indies, were transmitted to the Department of State by Short, Humphreys, Pinckney, Morris, members of the consular establishment, and private individuals. It is not possible, and indeed not necessary, to make a comparative analysis of this rich resource and the use Freneau made of it. But

[57] Estimate of Expenses of the Department of State beginning 1 Jan. 1793 (DNA: RG 59, DL; Vol. 78, f. 13458). This was in addition to the papers selected for printing the laws, which in 1791 numbered five. TJ hoped to extend this category to all states, a goal he was not able to achieve until he became President. This opened up an important potential for political patronage, as the character of the papers chosen and the grateful letters of editors illustrate (see DNA: RG 59, Letters, Printing, and Distribution of the Laws, 1790-1809).

it is clear that he was able to present in compact form a variety and extent of European news and opinion that his rivals could not match. It is equally clear that his selections reflected his own deep antipathy to the British people and their government, his uncritical acceptance of all propaganda favorable to the progresss of the revolution in France, his hatred of monarchy and all its manifestations, and his devotion to the principles of the American Revolution as he understood them. One example is illustrative. A few days before the first issue of the *National Gazette* appeared, Jefferson received from William Short a number of French journals to show to what extremes their editors went in appealing to popular prejudices. "At any other period," Short declared, "such publications would be disgusting and unworthy of being read."[58] In the second issue of his paper Freneau quoted one of these journals, *L'Argus Patriote*, and referred to it as "a French paper of estimation." A few days later he printed an extract from it asserting that liberty of the press was dead in England, its carcass gnawed upon by worms, but it had been revived in France, the freest nation in all the universe, whose constitution had been brought to perfection.[59]

Edmund Randolph, writing as *Aristides* in vindication of Jefferson, declared categorically that the Secretary of State had refused in any instance to mark a single paragraph in the foreign journals for publication in the *National Gazette*. Hamilton, as *Catullus*, regarded the assertion as an act of deception. Even if such refusals had occurred, he asked, what other printer would make such applications to the head of any other department of government? In any case, *Aristides'* declaration he took as proof of the connection between Freneau's paper and the Secretary of State.[60] In a literal sense, Jefferson may not have marked the *Gazette de Leide* and other European journals to call Freneau's attention to particular items. In the absence of the files of these papers, the question cannot be answered one way or the other. But in respect to other departmental and private documents that were made available to the *National Gazette*, there can be no doubt that Jefferson selected letters and documents he thought worthy of publication, made extracts from them when necessary, wrote captions for them, and on occasion indicated when the names of the authors should be given or withheld.

When Jefferson told Madison that he had been prepared to give Freneau "the perusal of all . . . letters of foreign intelligence," he wrote under the impression that the plan to establish the *National Gazette* had been given up. He could not have intended then or ever to give the editor free access to the whole range of departmental files. Even Henry Remsen, Jr., the highly trusted chief clerk, was permitted to handle diplomatic correspondence only after Jefferson himself had screened it for such confidential documents as he thought should be kept in his own locked chest or shown perhaps only to the President.[61] The selections he made for publication included much important information for the public, especially that relating to political affairs in Europe and the West Indies and to American commerce. Not all concerned politics, for he also

[58] Short to TJ, 8 July 1791; received 22 Oct. 1791.

[59] *National Gazette*, 3 and 17 Nov. 1791.

[60] *Aristides*, in the *National Gazette*, 26 Sep. 1792; *Catullus No. IV*, in the *Gazette of the United States*, 17 Oct. 1792, reprinted in Syrett, *Hamilton*, XII, 586-7.

[61] See, for example, TJ to Washington, 13 Jan. 1793, concerning documents which he took most of the day to translate himself — and of course did not require Freneau to do it — because he thought them improper to be shown to clerks.

contributed such items as a reported discovery about the Nantucket shoals and an announcement of the investigation of the Hessian fly by the committee of the American Philosophical Society of which he was chairman.[62] Some communications, such as those from consuls urging that manifests of American vessels and proof of citizenship of seamen be properly authenticated and that merchants be warned of the prohibition against shipping tobacco to Guernsey and Jersey, were published at the suggestion of the authors and over their names. These, of course, were made available to all newspapers when copies were sent by Jefferson both to Fenno's *Gazette of the United States* and Freneau's *National Gazette*. There were also essays discussing subjects having direct bearing on matters under discussion in Congress.

One of the first of such essays that Jefferson sent to Freneau was Paine's "Thoughts on the Establishment of a Mint." He had decided to have the essay published even before he knew that the *National Gazette* would be established. But when the fact became known, he delayed publishing it until he could let Freneau have it, after deleting passages containing facts relative to particular persons. Jefferson's views on the creation of a mint were in general in agreement with those of Hamilton, but they differed on the controversial issue of copper coinage and even more so on the question of making the standard of the money unit the same as that for weights and measures. The timing of publication of Paine's essay — when Congress was about to take up the President's recommendations for establishing a mint and creating a system of weights and measures and when Jefferson himself was seeking through Monroe and Madison to have Congress link the weight of the dollar to the universal standard he had proposed — was deliberate because Jefferson thought Paine's influence might defeat the contrary plan then under consideration.[63]

Another well-timed contribution Jefferson made to the *National Gazette* at the beginning may have been calculated to show, among other things, that the paper would be receptive to writings on measures of which he was known to

[62] *National Gazette*, 14 June 1792. Perhaps through TJ's suggestion the paper also carried announcements of election of members of the Society and of the establishment of its Magellanic Fund created in 1786 by John Hyacinth de Magellan of London (*National Gazette*, 28 Nov. 1791 and 2 Feb. 1792).

[63] TJ to Paine, 29 July 1791. See also TJ to Hamilton, 24 Jan. 1791, in group of documents on coinage at 31 Dec. 1790; Paine to TJ, 28 Sep. 1790, with enclosed essay on a mint for the United States; Washington's Address to Congress, 25 Oct. 1791 (*Writings*, ed. Fitzpatrick, xxxi, 402).

In a memorandum to Monroe before the Senate acted on Washington's recommendation, TJ suggested that the excessive alloy provided in the bill be allowed to stand, thus making alteration in the House more probable. He knew that opposition in the Senate would be unsuccessful, thus "drawing disreputation without doing any good" (MS in TJ's hand, undated but before 12 Jan. 1792, in NjP). About the same time TJ sent Monroe another memorandum suggesting that the question be grounded on the final decision of Congress of 1786 (MS in TJ's hand, undated, in NN: Monroe Papers; see JCC, xxxi, 876-8; Monroe to TJ, 12 Oct. 1786). After the Senate passed the bill, TJ urged Madison to propose an amount of alloy which would link the money unit to the general system of weights and measures he had proposed — and would "try the dispositions of the Representatives towards that system." (TJ's "Notes on the alloy of the Dollar," undated but after 12 Jan. and before 2 Apr. 1792; MS in DLC: Madison Papers). TJ's effort failed: the House allowed the amount of alloy fixed by the Senate bill to stand unaltered.

disapprove. Early in August, two days before learning of Freneau's decision, he received a brief communication covering a long essay by one Gabriel Henno, a native of Flanders then residing in Connecticut. At first glance the 63-page manuscript would have seemed more appropriate for Fenno's *Gazette of the United States* because of its ardent advocacy of governmental encouragement of infant manufactures. But it also argued for measures which Hamilton would never have approved and which, at this juncture, Jefferson wished to have enacted into law. Perhaps it was because Henno's essay seemed to be politically impartial that Jefferson decided to hold it for use by the *National Gazette*. He later explained to the author that his "observations on manufactures" were thought entirely suited for publication but that he had not been able for some months to have this done.[64] This was obviously a circumlocution. The opening of Congress, Hamilton's expected report on manufactures, that of Jefferson on commerce, the arrival of the new minister from Great Britain, and the nature of the policies advocated by Henno must have influenced his choice of means and timing of publication.

Henno's essay was entitled "Memoire *to the administrators*. . . . Recherche politique des moiens D'ameliorer le commerce Des etats" and was published in four early issues of the *National Gazette*. The translation was presumably that of Freneau, who eliminated a few passages which Jefferson described as insubstantial "embellishments," gave added emphasis to some points, and in other ways took liberties with the text. One example of this, important only as changing the emphasis from the general to the particular, occurs in the title, which the translator rendered as "*A political enquiry into the best means of improving the Commerce of the American States.*" Freneau also described the essay as a "Letter addressed to the Government of the United States," translated for the *National Gazette* "from the original French manuscript of the Author, dated *New-London*, May 17, 1791." As in other instances, the omission of the author's name was very likely done at Jefferson's request. It is also improbable that Freneau would have described the essay as addressed "to the Government of the United States" if Jefferson had not desired it, since this was almost the equivalent of announcing that it had been received by the Secretary of State and transmitted by him for publication. Hamilton would certainly have known that it could not have been released by himself or the Secretary of War, least of all by the President. No written evidence of its being communicated to the press or of any instructions regarding the manner of publication has been found. None is recorded in Jefferson's register of correspondence. But that there was direct communication on the subject between Jefferson and Freneau is proved by the letter of the former to the author transmitting the four issues of the newspaper in which the essay appeared.

Henno's major theme, stripped of its Gallic style and its many classical allusions, might have been written by Tench Coxe or Alexander Hamilton himself. He argued that the government should lend every encouragement to infant industries; that one means of doing this would be to encourage foreign artisans, mechanics, and ingenious persons to emigrate to America; and that

---

[64] TJ to Henno, 4 Dec. 1791 (Document v). Henno had asked for an immediate reply. The essay appeared in the *National Gazette* for 21, 24, and 28 Nov. and 1 Dec. 1791. Madison's essays and TJ's contribution of Henno's piece and other communications virtually dominated the paper in these early weeks of its existence.

by producing manufactures to meet its essential needs, the true national interest would be served by making the new republic less dependent upon the monarchical powers of Europe. Nothing could have been further from Jefferson's concept of national policy than this, which is essentially what Hamilton advocated in his report on manufactures — soon to be taken under consideration by Congress — and what he was trying to accomplish as the leading proponent of the Society for Establishing Useful Manufactures.[65]

There was much in the essay, however, which Jefferson would have approved. As the home of liberty, Henno argued, America should seek its preservation by attending to the great objects of agriculture and commerce. All nations of Europe, more than at any period of history, had now fixed their attention upon trade. The most flourishing of these powers were those which encouraged the reciprocally beneficial arts and sciences and which — the very phrase was Jeffersonian — promoted the general diffusion of knowledge. Commerce, founded upon produce of the land, had back of it the inexhaustible resources of America. Again voicing an opinion Jefferson had long entertained, Henno thought the high cost of labor and the cheapness of land would make manufacturing establishments impracticable so long as these conditions obtained. So also was his contention that a constant repetition of the same function by an artisan and the use of children at low wages made it possible for England to sell the best goods at a cheaper rate than other nations.

But Alexander Hamilton surely would not have accepted the conclusion derived from this premise. Reinforced by Freneau's emphasis as translator, Henno, seeking in ancient history the secret motives and springs of action of the British ministry, argued that Great Britain would contrive "to dishearten and ruin those who first attempt manufactures in America."[66] They would do this by persuading Americans of the hopelessness of establishing manufactures in competition with theirs, by driving artisans out of the United States or into other occupations, and by inundating the nation with British fabrics, thereby compelling its citizens to pay a sort of tribute to foreign merchants. Thus, with a single dash of his pen, a British minister could determine the commercial fate of the nation and render tributary and dependent a people in the bosom of liberty itself. But, Henno pointed out, America had the means to defend herself against these baneful consequences by which Great Britain founded her commercial supremacy on the ruins of her neighbors. The very language employed echoed that of Jefferson in his Report on Fisheries, with its sensational charge that the British government had "begun . . . mounting their navigation on the ruins of ours."[67] Jefferson's use of such blunt language had aroused fears both in England and among supporters of the British interest in the United States that the result would be a retaliatory navigation act. Freneau's added emphasis in the translation could not have been intended to lessen those fears.[68]

[65] Hamilton's report on manufactures was submitted two weeks after the first installment of Henno's essay appeared; the entire report was published in the *National Gazette* for 26 and 29 Dec. 1791, and 2, 5, and 9 Jan. 1792. For TJ's opposition to the government's encouraging artisans and mechanics to emigrate, see, for example, note to Digges to TJ, 28 Apr. 1791.

[66] Freneau added the word "first" in his translation, thus seeming to point to Hamilton's plan for the SUM. Henno's remarks about British policy were also made more emphatic by the translator.

[67] TJ's Report on Fisheries, 1 Feb. 1791.

[68] In those passages in which Henno traced through ancient and modern history the

Lest the point be lost, Freneau summarized Henno's intent in a prefatory note to the second installment of the essay: "In this part of his address, the author proves from the experience of history, that government ought, by every proper means, to exert its endeavors to procure from Europe and elsewhere, persons skilled in the useful arts, in order to manufacture the raw materials produced, or capable of being produced, in this country."[69] This was by way of preface to Henno's argument on the need for a united commercial policy, which he regarded as a fundamental principle for all states seeking to become prosperous and economically independent. Freneau emphasized the passage by arguing the absolute necessity – the comparable phrase was not employed by Henno – "for the United States to preserve a unity of interests among themselves; the first object of which . . . should be the putting it out of the power of any body of men, an individual, or a foreigner, to thwart" the national interest.

The appeal for unity, the strong criticism of British policy, the manipulated translation, and the timing of publication all suggest that Jefferson saw the advantage of publishing Henno's essay as a prelude to his negotiations with George Hammond, the British minister to the United States who had just arrived.[70] The possibility of a commercial treaty with Great Britain and the nature of its terms were of great concern both to Hamilton and Jefferson. Henno's essay seemed on its face to support Hamilton's ambitious plans for stimulating American manufactures, but it must also have appeared to Jefferson a convenient means of suggesting to Hammond that on the question of encouraging both industry and commerce, the national counsels were united. But no newspaper essay could have concealed from the British envoy the irreparable breach over policy existing within the administration. Hammond in fact had been instructed to address himself to the leader of the British interest in America and his very appointment as minister, as he well understood, resulted from the mounting influence of the Secretary of State and from the fear that the navigation bill he and Madison advocated would be adopted. If Jefferson, a political realist, did in fact make use of Henno's essay as a last desperate effort to unify the government's counsels, it was a strategy doomed to failure. A short while later, after Hamilton had privately given guidance to Hammond just as he had done earlier in his discussions with Beckwith, Jefferson no doubt would have realized the hopelessness of such an attempt.

On being informed that the Secretary of State had seen fit to publish his first

---

policies of wise rulers in encouraging manufactures and the cultivation of wool, flax, and silk, Freneau followed the original with some fidelity. But whenever Henno sought to reveal the springs of British policy or to suggest countervailing measures, the translator made the arguments more pointed for American readers and the need for retaliatory policy more explicit.

[69] *National Gazette*, 24 Nov. 1791.

[70] In the first issue of the *National Gazette* Freneau announced Hammond's arrival in terms which may have been an intentional misrepresentation: "Mr. Hammond . . . has it in commission to conclude a treaty of commerce between England and this country. The outlines of this treaty have been already discussed, and we learn that some very considerable commercial advantages are held out to America as the basis of it, which will in time supplant the greater part of the trade of Russia with England." There was no foundation in fact for the assertion. TJ at the time was trying to discover just what powers Hammond possessed, being under no illusion about the outcome after having read Hawkesbury's secret Report to the Privy Council of 28 Jan. 1791 (see group of documents and Editorial Note at 15 Dec. 1790).

essay, Henno was so greatly pleased that he immediately composed another which he thought a necessary analogue. He explained that in the meantime he had begun a work entitled "Observations sur les interêts de la france dans L'archipel Américain," but on finding that it would lead to conclusions diametrically opposed to American interests, he had abandoned that task and resumed the topic of his earlier essay. The result he immediately dispatched to Jefferson, who handed it over to the *National Gazette*, where it appeared in four installments.[71] Freneau introduced the first of these as "the work of an intelligent French Gentleman residing at New-London, who has recently transmitted to us some further ideas on the same subject; a translation of which the Editor flatters himself will be equally acceptable to the generality of our readers." The second essay was largely repetitious, lacking the pronounced thrust of the first against British commercial policy, but it reinforced both Jefferson's interest in advocating diffusion of scientific knowledge and Hamilton's efforts in sponsoring immigrant artisans. It also anticipated George Logan's essay in the *National Gazette* in urging the formation of voluntary societies for the promotion of agriculture and home manufactures and in suggesting rules and regulations by which they might effectively advance the general good. In a comment which sounds much like one of Freneau's interpolations and which was certainly applicable to Hamilton's projected Society for the Establishment of Useful Manufactures, the essay pronounced it to be truth that "the success of all such establishments does not depend merely upon *political association*, or simple incorporation of bodies with exclusive privileges." Henno's plan, like Logan's, called for the creation of voluntary societies of individuals whose primary obligation would be to engage in research and experimentation in everything pertaining to the improvement of agriculture and home industries – "scientific bodies who study the theory of things, and consider it as a part of their duty to publish to the nation and to the world, whatever can be of public service."

Jefferson did not acknowledge this second essay, but Henno nevertheless contributed a third. Freneau, contradicting the impression he had previously given his readers, told Jefferson he found it "like the others, generally superficial, tedious, and too little of argumentative discussion." He promised to include such items as he found interesting when nothing better offered. A fourth and final essay came from the zealous French émigré, but it, too, was dismissed.[72] Henno's essays had aroused no comment and had had no discernible effect that Jefferson might have hoped for at the opening of Congress. But at least their appearance in the *National Gazette* through Jefferson's direct inter-

[71] Henno to TJ, 25 Dec. 1791 (RC in DNA: RG 59, MLR; endorsed by TJ as received 30 Dec. 1791 and so recorded in SJL). This essay appeared in the *National Gazette* for 12, 16, 19, and 30 Jan. 1792. The original MS of Henno's second essay has not been found.

[72] No letter of transmittal of this third part has been found and none is recorded in SJL, but clearly it had been received by TJ and sent by him to Freneau (Freneau to TJ, 27 Jan. 1792; Document VI). Three months later Henno informed TJ that he felt honor bound to conclude the work he had begun and enclosed a final essay (Henno to TJ, 12 Mch. 1792; RC in DNA: RG 59, MLR; endorsed by TJ as received 20 Mch. 1792 and so recorded in SJL). An entry in SJL shows that Henno wrote again on 20 Mch. 1792 and that TJ received the letter on the 30th, but it has not been found. To neither of these communications did TJ respond. The concluding essay has been lost to history, and if TJ thought it worth sending to Freneau, which is doubtful, it did not appear in the *National Gazette*.

vention placed in its proper context his solemn assurance to Washington that he never did "directly or indirectly, write, dictate, or procure any one sentence or sentiment" for Freneau's paper.

As Jefferson went through his official and personal files to sort out those to be made available to Freneau, he revealed at least in part the criteria determining his choices. For obvious reasons and with few exceptions, he omitted documents and letters whose substance repeated information to be found in the *Gazette de Leide* and other newspapers. But no printed sources could convey such reliable and detailed information about the slave uprisings in Santo Domingo as the eye-witness accounts Jefferson received from his friend Nathaniel Cutting. These, without exception but with some unimportant changes in phraseology, were passed on to Freneau and were published almost in full. Jefferson did instruct the editor to withhold Cutting's name, and the letters appeared under such rubrics as "*Authentic copy of a letter from a gentleman of character and information in Cape-François to his friend in this city.*"[73] A second category of materials Jefferson almost entirely withheld included the official dispatches of American ministers abroad – William Short, David Humphreys, Gouverneur Morris, and Thomas Pinckney. The only exceptions to this were three letters from Humphreys and one from Pinckney, the former being carefully extracted and confined to such subjects as the prohibition by Holland against foreigners' importation of tea, the failure of crops, the desire of artisans to emigrate to America, and the health of the Queen of Portugal.[74] The one extract from Pinckney's dispatches – a postscript giving the substance of a bill in parliament providing the death penalty for all treasonable correspondence and commerce with the enemy – naturally omitted the minister's name and his reference to a conversation with Grenville on the subject.[75]

The primary reason for excluding almost all of the correspondence with American ministers abroad was, of course, the need to respect the confidentiality of their conversations with officials of the courts to which they were accredited. But even the ministers' reports could have been used selectively, and Jefferson could have disguised their source as he did for most of those items he did release to Freneau. Had his purpose been to achieve narrow partisan aims or even to support particular policies, he might have made use of Joshua Johnson's strictures on the harsh treatment of American seamen by British naval officers, his frustrating collisions with admiralty, customs, and treasury officials, and

[73] See Cutting to TJ, 4 and 28 Dec. 1791; 21 and 24 Jan. and 13 Apr. 1792. These appeared with some slight alterations in the *National Gazette*, 2 Jan., 9 Feb., 5 Mch., and 7 May 1792. The "*Translation of an original State Paper recently received from Cape-François,*" which appeared in the issue of 23 Feb. 1792, was probably an enclosure in Cutting's letter of 28 Dec. 1792. On that letter, beneath Cutting's signature, TJ wrote in pencil: "The names of the persons to whom the letter refers are not to be mentioned."

[74] Humphreys to TJ, 18 Aug. 1791; 18 and 25 Mch. 1792, published in *National Gazette*, 3 Nov. 1791 and 21 May 1792. In each case TJ directed that Humphreys' name be withheld, bracketed the portions to be printed, and provided such captions as "*Extract of a letter from a gentleman of the first information at Lisbon, to his correspondent in this city.*"

[75] Pinckney to TJ, 5 Apr. 1793, published in *National Gazette*, 22 May 1793, as an "*Extract from a well informed correspondent*" in London. In his letter Pinckney urged that American merchants be put on guard to the possibility that the bill would be passed. TJ omitted this and other parts of the letter, but passed the extract of the postscript on to both Freneau and Fenno.

especially his strong recommendation that the United States adopt a navigation act in retaliation against Great Britain.[76] Jefferson did not inform anyone save the President, much less Freneau and the press, that he had received two months before the establishment of the *National Gazette* the substance of Lord Hawkesbury's highly secret report to the Privy Council on trade with the United States. This important document he retained as an advantage in his negotiations with Hammond. So also, on the question of the debt to France, could he have used William Short's private and official communications under careful concealment had his intent been to confront his Cabinet colleague on the manner in which the proceeds of the Holland loans were being employed — or not employed. Protection of the confidentiality of diplomatic communications led understandably to the exclusion of all correspondence between the Secretary of State and the French and British ministers to the United States, except of course that part made public to all newspapers by submission to Congress.

It would be a mistake, however, to assume that the need for confidentiality alone caused Jefferson to withhold from Freneau every part of the long, perceptive, and highly important dispatches of William Short. In his intimate knowledge of affairs in France, in his appraisals of leading public figures, and in his ability to anticipate the course of events, Short provided Jefferson with the most important budgets of information of any of the American representatives abroad. Gouverneur Morris, who preferred to communicate with the President because he thought information channeled through the Secretary of State would be biased, also provided much useful intelligence about the drift of affairs in France.[77] But both Short in his modest, studious accounts and Morris in his self-confident but generally accurate appraisal of men and measures, were in substantial agreement about the extreme revolutionists and the likelihood that they would destroy the bright hopes for the French republic. The nature of their skeptical reports, added to the need for confidentiality, helps to explain why Jefferson declined to allow Freneau in any instance to make use of any part of the dispatches of these two astute observers of the European scene. But if he avoided publishing anything from their estimates of the course of events, so also did he withhold from Freneau the accounts of such idealistic and overly optimistic sympathizers with the revolutionary cause as his friends the abbés Arnoux and Chalut.[78] Freneau, as Jefferson could not have failed to observe, had shown himself too uncritical in accepting everything favorable about the changes taking place in France and in rejecting or condemning anything to the contrary.

On the other hand, those excerpts from official and private files which Jefferson made available to Freneau concerning affairs in England scarcely gave the British government the benefit of any doubt. Late in November Jefferson wrote the following note on the address cover of a letter he had just received

[76] In the absence of diplomatic relations, Johnson acted as a sort of *de facto* minister as well as the consul at London. See Editorial Note and group of documents at 31 May 1791.

[77] Gouverneur Morris to Washington, 22 Nov. 1790, Enclosure II in Washington to TJ, 28 July 1791.

[78] Arnoux and Chalut to TJ, 20 May 1791. On Short's dispatches, see for example 30 June and 7 July 1791, received just prior to the establishment of the *National Gazette*. See also Pio to TJ, 22 July 1791.

from the nephew of Richard Price: "Perhaps Mr. Freneau may think the paragraph marked within to be worth a place in his paper. The names of the persons from and to whom the letter was written not to be mentioned."[79] The paragraph in question spoke glowingly of the spirit of reformation in England, depicted Paine as one who had contributed to it, and reported that, while Burke raved in the House of Commons, his friends had deserted him and Paine's *Rights of Man* was in all hands making converts. So also did Jefferson make extensive use of two long letters from William Knox reporting that, while three-fourths of the population of Ireland consisted of Catholics, they were denied the rights of citizenship, could not serve as magistrates or on grand juries, or even to vote for Protestant members of Parliament; that, in consequence, petitions had been presented to that body seeking an end to discriminatory legislation; and that if these requests were denied – as they were – there would be such a general ferment in Ireland as had not been seen for a century. The matter selected from these letters for publication is accented by the fact that Jefferson excluded that part about the flourishing American trade, the immense amount of smuggling of tobacco, and the difficulties of impressment, inadequate registration of American vessels, and so on.[80]

By far the major portion of letters and extracts that Jefferson permitted Freneau to publish came from American consuls and vice-consuls, chiefly those in France. These selections were concerned largely but not exclusively with commercial matters. Of these the chief contributor was Joseph Fenwick, consul at Bordeaux, whose dispatches selected for publication urged that Americans should become better acquainted with manufactures and other products obtainable in France cheaper than in England; that Congress should establish arsenals in which French clothing and other supplies could be used; and that increase in this infant trade would make it easier for the United States to end its troubles with the Algerines. In general, Fenwick took an optimistic view of French politics, as when he reported that rumors of a league forming on the continent against France were nothing more than a chimera.[81] The dispatches of Stephen Cathalan, Jr., vice-consul at Marseilles, were not so numerous as those of Fenwick, but Jefferson's interest in fostering trade with the Mediterranean doubtless prompted him to make some of them available to Freneau.

---

[79] George Morgan to TJ, 17 May 1791, received by TJ on 19 Nov. 1791 and published in the *National Gazette* on the 21st as "*Extract of a letter from Hackney, England, September 2.*" In the passage discussing Burke, Freneau inserted a sentence not in the original: "It is remarkable that in his debates he frequently refers to Paine's book, and thereby shows how much it galls him." This is a good example of a number of instances in which Freneau altered dates and made changes in the texts.

[80] William Knox to TJ, 17 Jan. and 15 Feb. 1792; both published in *National Gazette*, 12 Apr. 1792, as "*Extract of a letter from a gentleman in Dublin*" and "*Extract of another letter from the same gentleman.*" See also Johnson to TJ, 10 Aug. 1791 (his second of that date), published as "*Extract of a letter from London, Sept. 6,*" in *National Gazette*, 3 Nov. 1791.

[81] Fenwick's letters made available to Freneau, with some enclosures, were those of 25 Sep., 28 Oct., and 24 Dec. 1791; 11 and 28 Sep. 1792; 20 Jan. and 12 May 1793; printed in the *National Gazette*, 16 Jan., 2 Apr., and 22 Dec. 1792; 5 Jan., 1 May, 27 and 31 July 1793. Usually these were printed with such captions as "*Authentic extract of a letter, dated Bordeaux . . . to a gentleman in this city.*" But in those of 11 and 28 Sep. 1792 – just after TJ had explained his connection with the *National Gazette* to Washington – the extracts were bracketed by TJ and Fenwick's name as consul given.

Cathalan's report of a ship laden with a fine cargo of brandies, soap, olive oil, anchovies, umbrellas, fans, and silks was marked by Jefferson for publication, but the name of the Baltimore consignee, Robert Gilmor & Company, was omitted. His transmission of a petition from the municipality of Marseilles to the President pointing out the scarcity of wheat and flour in that vicinity and urging that American trade be encouraged was also published. In another letter given to Freneau after the outbreak of the war, Cathalan gave assurance that the French fleet would protect American vessels coming to the Mediterranean. Jefferson always excluded Cathalan's generally gloomy and sometimes desperate account of the state of affairs in France.[82] The letters from Delamotte at Le Havre also urged increased trade with the United States, predicted that the national spirit stirring France could only result in improvements, and expressed the belief that the two nations understood and sympathized with each other more and more. "Your loan in Holland," he added, "your policies, and your public securities create a sensation in Europe."[83] The flattering hopes for the revolutionists' cause fell far short of the reliable reports being given by William Short, but the published extract must have seemed grateful both to Hamiltonians and to the opposition. In general, the consular dispatches from Europe gave little if any information about commerce not more readily and perhaps more accurately known to the mercantile community. Thus even before Cathalan's urgent appeals for wheat and flour had reached Jefferson, the markets of Marseilles and other ports of southern France and Spain were already glutted because of the earlier intelligence received by American shippers. The political views expressed by Fenwick and other consuls were also frequently belied by the onrush of events. Such news events as the death of the Emperor of Morocco reported by Thomas Barclay – with both his identity and the nature of his mission concealed – did, however, provide useful facts.[84]

In the number of items selected and in the manner of presentation, with Jefferson and his clerks at times doing the translations from French and Spanish documents which it was the duty of the clerk for foreign languages to perform, the contributions of the Secretary of State to the *National Gazette* stand unique among all others. Like the essays of Madison, Logan, *Brutus*, and *Sidney*, most of the pieces that Jefferson made available fell in the first year of the paper's existence. Unlike theirs, his were not discussions of public issues from his own pen but were selected by him from private and official communications, being intended to inform and to present a more balanced and reliable account of

[82] Cathalan to TJ, 11 Mch. and 24 Aug. 1792 (the latter enclosing the petition to the President), and 17 Feb. 1793; published in the *National Gazette*, 10 May, 10 and 14 Nov. 1792, and 4 May 1793. Cathalan's letter, with its author identified as vice-consul, and the petition to the President, which of course would not have been published without his consent, were also sent to Fenno and appeared in *Gazette of the United States*, 14 Nov. 1792.

[83] Delamotte to TJ, 15 and 27 Oct. 1791; and 5 Oct. 1792; published in *National Gazette*, 13 Feb. 1792 and 16 Jan. 1793, under such captions as "*Authentic Extract of a letter from a gentleman of the best information, at Havre.*" In the first of these letters TJ bracketed the paragraph to be published and then wrote in the margin: "This passage to be translated and sent to Mr. Freneau," thus placing upon another clerk (probably Taylor) the task for which Freneau was paid.

[84] Barclay to TJ, 1 and 16 Mch. 1792, published in the *National Gazette* of 24 May 1792, with important deletions, as "*Extract of a letter from a gentleman at Gibraltar, to his correspondent in this city.*"

events. As selections, they naturally reflected his own judgment as to what was significant, and, in general, represented his own views of foreign policy. But the important fact lies not in their number or even in their carefully selected subjects but in the relationship between a member of the Cabinet and the editor of a newspaper which they exemplified. The essential fact is that Jefferson's making available such a variety of materials through his own personal selection and under his own directions to the printer was a particular act of favoritism which the Secretary of State did not extend to any other editor and which he bestowed upon one of his clerks to assist him in his private enterprise. It was the number and the kind of special privileges accorded Freneau which set the *National Gazette* apart from earlier and later manifestations of Jefferson's interest in such newspapers as those of John Fenno, Andrew Brown, Benjamin F. Bache, William Duane, and Samuel H. Smith. Undeniably, Jefferson made this extraordinary effort in collaboration with Madison because both were so deeply concerned about the tendency of Hamiltonian measures, a concern so profound as to create fears of what Jefferson regarded as the worst of all evils – disunion. But, however exalted the motive, such official bestowal of special privilege did not and could not dispose of the ethical question Hamilton had raised. The fact that Hamilton himself was far more vulnerable on questions of official propriety does not affect the validity of the point he made.

IV

Despite the most concerted and the most powerful political influence enjoyed by any journal of the time, the *National Gazette* failed to achieve the high goal its sponsors set for it. In its first few months, because of their varied and important contributions, if was in fact an impressive and useful journal of information and reasoned discussion. Gratifying expressions of appreciation of its character provided testimony to this, especially from the South.[85] But the *National Gazette* never realized the hopes of its patrons that it would become a truly national paper of the sort they had planned. In the South and West, where most of its subscribers were located, it preached to the already converted about the evils of the funding system, the bank, the excise, and every manifestation of monarchical tendencies in the government. The Middle States were well served by a number of ably edited competitive journals which supported both the administration and the opposition points of view. In Federalist New England the *National Gazette* never gained a foothold, being regarded at best as a nuisance and at worst as an instrument wielded by Jefferson and his supporters to subvert the established order. It was, however, occasionally quoted by such republican papers as Thomas Adams' *The Independent Chronicle* of Boston and Anthony Haswell's *Vermont Gazette* in Bennington.

The largely sectional nature of Freneau's paper was not, however, the real cause of its failure. Financial difficulties have generally been regarded as the chief reason for the termination of its brief career. These were undoubtedly real. Delivery was slow and uncertain, especially in the South, and collection of arrearages from subscribers – to whom Freneau appealed frequently and

---

[85] Randolph to TJ, 23 June 1792; Henry Lee to Madison, 6 Feb. 1792 (DLC: Madison Papers). Occasional commendatory pieces were also published in the *National Gazette*, especially in the beginning.

threateningly in the last few months—was even worse.[86] "Mark this plain observation from experience," William Duane wrote in 1798 about the financial situation of Bache's paper, *"Newspaper debts are the worst of all others."*[87] The crowning blow came in September 1793, when, according to Freneau, Francis Childs told him to stop publication immediately if continuance depended upon his advances, since the paper theretofore had been to him a perpetual loss.[88] The only evidence of Childs' withdrawal of support is Freneau's later statement in defense of Jefferson, which was also self-serving and in some essential respects inaccurate. In his final issue Freneau announced that he was only suspending the paper, that he had recently acquired new and elegant types from Europe, and that he hoped to resume publication by the time Congress convened.[89] If this contemporary announcement actually represented Freneau's intention at the time, it can scarcely be reconciled with his later statement that it was Childs' withdrawal of support which caused cessation of publication.

While financial problems undoubtedly existed even for a paper with a sub-scription list far beyond what Freneau claimed for the *National Gazette*, it is difficult to believe that this alone explains why it failed. It is significant that Childs and Swaine continued to operate the shop where it had been printed. Also, there were other Philadelphia papers which survived the financial diffi-culties afflicting all, among them Bache's *General Advertiser*, Brown's *Federal Gazette*, Dunlap's *American Daily Advertiser*, and Fenno's *Gazette of the United States*. These journals—even the last, which was provided with financial as-sistance through Hamilton and his friends—lacked the special advantages of political patronage that had been bestowed upon the *National Gazette*. Why, then, did it cease to exist after only two years? By then partisan lines had become more sharply drawn, political contentions were more bitter, and the need for such a national journal as Jefferson and Madison had envisaged was far greater than when Freneau was persuaded to embark upon the venture. In the summer of 1793 that need was expressed by Jefferson in an almost desperate appeal to Madison to answer efforts made by Hamilton as *Pacificus* to destroy the alliance with France. "For god's sake, my dear Sir," Jefferson wrote, "take up your pen, select the most striking heresies, and cut him to pieces in the face

[86] On subscribers' complaints of non-delivery in the first few weeks of the paper's existence, see Daniel Carroll to Madison, 22 Nov. 1791 (DLC: Madison Papers); Henry Lee to Madison, 8 Jan. and 6 Feb. 1792 (same).

[87] William Duane to Tench Coxe, 15 Oct. 1798 (PMHB, XCVI [Oct. 1972], 524).

[88] Freneau "To the Citizens of South Carolina," 31 Dec. 1800 (Philadelphia *Aurora* of 14 Aug. 1802; reprinted in Marsh, "Freneau and Jefferson," *Am. Lit.*, VIII [May 1936], 186).

[89] *National Gazette*, 26 Oct. 1793. Freneau's statement in 1800 asserted that Childs' notification for immediate cessation came in September. This was at least a month before the paper ceased to exist. The new types were acquired by the Philadelphia printing shop of Childs and Swaine. The last three issues were printed on half-sheets, which Freneau explained as being due to a shortage of paper. The yellow fever epidemic may have been responsible for this and may also have contributed to the announced suspension of the paper, as it did in the case of Fenno's *Gazette of the United States*. Some subscribers at a distance from Philadelphia feared to handle the paper because of the epidemic, and Freneau had to explain that is was not printed in that part of the city where the disease was most prevalent and that none of the printers had contracted it.

of the public. There is nobody else who can and will enter the lists with him."[90] This earnest appeal was written only a few months before the *National Gazette* ceased publication. But when Madison complied with his notable *Letters of Helvetius*, these were published not in Freneau's paper but in that of Fenno.

Long before this it must have become clear to Freneau's original sponsors that a perceptible and to them distressing change had taken place in the character of the *National Gazette*. Hints of this had appeared at the outset, but by late summer of 1792 the alteration was clearly discernible, especially after Hamilton had accused the editor of being a hireling of the Secretary of State. Up to then the publication of important official documents, the reporting of Congressional debates, the cogent essays of Madison, the reasoned analyses of government measures by Logan, *Brutus*, *Sidney*, and others, and the carefully selected items of foreign intelligence contributed by Jefferson had made it a new and impressive vehicle for the opposition. Thereafter, with occasional important exceptions, it became more and more a narrowly polemical journal marked by satire, invective, scurrility, personal abuse, and repetitive harping upon all evidences of monarchy and aristocracy which its editor discovered in every aspect of government and society. John Adams' argument for the necessity of titles and distinctions among men was an easy target for Freneau's incessant barbs, but all honorifics – even the time-honored and innocuous use of "Esquire" – now became absurd in a republic. The climax came with the arrival of Genet as French minister to the United States. The enthusiastic reception given him by the people in his calculated progress from Charleston to Philadelphia was echoed and magnified to an inordinate degree in the pages of the *National Gazette*, with Freneau himself taking a prominent part in the hero's welcome accorded Genet in Philadelphia. Not surprisingly, such adulation had its impact upon the new minister, upon Freneau, upon the *National Gazette*, and – in a harmful manner quite unintended – upon the Franco-American Alliance itself. Jefferson, who had to contend in the Cabinet with Hamilton over the issue, was dismayed by Genet's conduct. "Never, in my opinion," he confided to Madison, "was so calamitous an appointment made as that of the present minister. . . . Hotheaded, all imagination, no judgment, passionate, disrespectful and even indecent towards the P[resident] in his written as well as verbal communications, talking of appeals from him to Congress, from them to the people, urging the most unreasonable and groundless propositions, and in the most dictatorial style &c. &c. &c." He predicted, accurately, that if it ever became necessary to make Genet's communications public, they would excite universal indignation. Then, revealing his knowledge of the altered character

---

[90] TJ to Madison, 7 July 1793. Hamilton's *Pacificus* pieces appeared in *Gazette of the United States*, 19 June, 3 and 6 July 1793; printed in Syrett, *Hamilton*, xv, 33-43, 55-63, 65-9. Madison's *Letters of Helvetius* appeared in *Gazette of the United States*, 24 and 28 Aug.; 7, 11, 14, and 18 Sep. 1793; printed in Madison, *Writings*, ed. Hunt, vi, 138-88. In transmitting these to TJ, Madison said that he could not get them to Fenno without TJ's aid. He also asked TJ to go over the paper, especially those parts marked, for such alterations as he thought should be made. In addition, he enclosed "a little thing" of Lord Chatham's for publication. TJ changed only part of one sentence in Madison's pieces but did not send the Chatham item to Fenno because he thought it would be attributed to himself and, in any case, would have more effect after the meeting of Congress (Madison to TJ, 11 Aug. 1793; TJ to Madison, 18 Aug. and 1 Sep. 1793).

of the *National Gazette*, he added: "To complete our misfortune we have no channel of our own through which we can correct the irritating representations he has made."[91] A few days later Jefferson declared to Monroe that Genet's conduct was "indefensible by the most furious Jacobin."[92]

But Freneau, ardent in his Jacobinism, was one of two or three journalists who supported Genet to the end. He denounced the President's proclamation and thought the impartial position of the government amounted to desertion of a friend and ally. "The cause of France is the cause of mankind," one typical editorial pronounced, "and neutrality is desertion."[93] When meetings of citizens and merchants all over the country began to adopt resolutions supporting the President's policy, expressing friendship and gratitude to France, and calling for support of the alliance while condemning the conduct of Genet, Freneau never deviated from the course he had taken in the beginning. The changed character of the *National Gazette* reflected the unchanged character of its editor, who repeated endlessly the old accusations against those who differed with him on the Genet mission, who revealed his inability to analyze the issue in terms of constitutional and international law, and who became more and more isolated from the growing numbers of his countrymen who rallied in support of the administration's policy of neutrality.

This intransigent stand is only the most conspicuous of many proofs that Freneau was never the hireling of the Secretary of State as Hamilton had charged. Endowed with an unbending pride and an invincible conviction of personal rectitude, he was extraordinarily sensitive to any intimation that he could be manipulated as a political instrument. Though he was capable of sympathetic feelings for man in general, he was closer in spirit to Rousseau and Condorcet than to such political pragmatists of the American Enlightenment as Jefferson and Madison. He was primarily a man of passion, not of reason. His capacity for hatred — exemplified in his savage indictment of the British people as the most cruel people on earth, so much so that even the birds and beasts of that island shared their depravity — carried him beyond the limit of rationality. For those who held his convictions about government and society, no praise could be sufficient. For those who believed or reasoned otherwise, no expression of contempt was too severe. So also for those who seemed to him to betray a public trust. Thus Louis XVI, who in the early days of the *National Gazette* was hailed as "the Patriot 'King of the French'" later became the "perjured monarch," his decapitation not to be regretted but hailed as the triumph of a just and sovereign people. All monarchs in his view were enemies of the human race. George III was a tyrant who ruled over a people not only servile but also stupid. When the Queen of Portugal was treated by an English doctor, Freneau denounced him as a quack and expressed the hope that he would be no more successful in treating *rabies monarchica* than in dealing with the disease in other animals. In the beginning, too, he declared that the President's birthday had been observed with suitable ceremony, but the following year he denounced this occasion along with presidential soirees and levees as absurd evidences of monarchical pomp and parade.

Thus the failure of the *National Gazette*, as indicated also by the brief association of Freneau with Bailey's *Freeman's Journal*, Childs and Swaine's *Daily*

[91] TJ to Madison, 7 July 1793.
[92] TJ to Monroe, 14 July 1793.
[93] *National Gazette*, 15 May 1793.

Advertiser, and, later, his own short-lived *Jersey Chronicle* and *The Time-Piece*, lay primarily within himself.[94] The chief weapons with which he consistently and ardently championed republican principles throughout life, both in prose and verse, were instinctual and emotional, expressed in satire, ridicule, scurrility, vituperation, and even on occasion scatological abuse.[95] He was possessed of natural talents for light verse and, in his way, was an undaunted defender of republican principles. But always, in the end, his efforts in journalism failed because his vituperative personal assaults on those who differed with him alienated those of his audience who preferred reasoned discussion of public issues. To his corrosive style Freneau also brought an innate aversion to the demanding tasks of journalism. In a revealing statement in one of the last issues of the *National Gazette*, he expressed the opinion that newspapers, the most useful of all publications, were also the most difficult to conduct. Lawyers, divines, physicians, and other professionals, having only one subject to approach, could easily win fame and recognition from posterity. By contrast, he pointed out, the editor had to treat of the entire range of knowledge and be censured for not pleasing everyone. Moreover, he was obliged to do this "on stated days, whether . . . ready or not."[96] It is thus not suprising that all of Freneau's journalistic endeavors were brief and unsuccessful. The scurrilous, vituperative, and abusive style that he brought to the discussion of men and measures was only one cause of his failure as an editor. Another factor was more fundamental. He has been called the ablest editor of his day, but his natural endowments did not include the stamina, the discipline, and the temperament demanded of the professional editor. The truth is that he failed in all of his spasmodic and short-lived journalistic efforts because he lacked these essential qualities, so much so that he did not succeed even when aided by the most concerted and influential patronage bestowed upon any practitioner of the craft in his time.

The silence of Freneau's sponsors at the demise of the *National Gazette* and the manner in which he severed his relations with the Department of State are

---

[94] The *Jersey Chronicle*, of which Freneau was both editor and printer at his home in Monmouth, lasted only from 2 May 1795 to 30 Apr. 1796. A facsimile of the only known copy of the broadside announcing Freneau's plans for the paper (which naturally differed substantially from the Proposals for the *National Gazette*) is reproduced in Victor Hugo Paltsits, *A bibliography of the separate and collected works of Philip Freneau* (New York, 1903), p. 10. A few months after that paper expired, Freneau wrote Madison that he had almost completed plans to go into partnership with Greenleaf in his two papers, the *Argus* and the *New-York Journal*, and that he hoped to revive something in the spirit of the *National Gazette* and to succeed "with proper assistance." He acknowledged his inability to become known to the principal characters of New York and asked Madison for an introduction to Chancellor Livingston (Freneau to Madison, 1 Dec. 1796). That venture never came to fruition: the kind of assistance that had brought the *National Gazette* into existence was no longer available. Freneau launched *The Time-Piece* in New York on 13 Mch. 1797 in partnership with A. Menut, but the partnership was dissolved six months later. Another partnership was then formed, and, just a year after the paper had begun, Freneau left the enterprise.

[95] See, for example, *National Gazette*, 26 Apr. 1792 and 27 Feb. 1793. When Freneau was associated with Bailey's *Freeman's Journal*, his resort to coarseness of this sort caused that paper to be referred to as "Bailey's Chamber Pot" (Axelrad, *Freneau*, p. 136). Vituperation, scurrility, and coarseness also characterized the short-lived *Jersey Chronicle* and the *Time-Piece*.

[96] *National Gazette*, 9 Oct. 1793.

illuminating. His curt note of resignation was written before he announced his hope of resuming publication of the paper. If this was accompanied by any expression of friendship, of gratitude for many favors bestowed, or of regret at the failure of the *National Gazette*, no evidence of the fact has been found. To Freneau's brief note of resignation Jefferson made no response.[97] The contrast between the end of this official relationship and that, for example, between Jefferson and his chief clerk, Henry Remsen, Jr., who remained a lifelong friend, is striking. It was under these circumstances, just a short while before he left office as Secretary of State, that Jefferson said he had been told the *National Gazette* would be resumed under the editorship of John Swaine. If it is, he added, "I think it will be well executed."[98] Swaine's death soon thereafter, Jefferson's retirement from office, and other factors may have prevented resumption of the paper under a different editor. But his avowal of confidence in Swaine, unaccompanied by any expression of disappointment at the departure of Freneau, is eloquent in its omission.

The *National Gazette* had been worse than a failure caused by the miscasting of its editor. Like Genet, Freneau had become a liability to the cause he so

---

[97] See Document IX. Entries in SJL show that Freneau wrote TJ on 7 and 21 Nov. 1793, no doubt from Philadelphia, since both were received on their respective dates. Neither has been found. The contents can only be conjectured, though the first must have enclosed Freneau's resignation, since both that and the letter were received on the same day.

It is significant that, except for appeals by Freneau for TJ's subscription to his published poems, this closed their correspondence. An entry in SJL shows that TJ wrote to Freneau on 22 Oct. 1795, but the letter has not been found. This almost certainly was in response to an unrecorded appeal from Freneau for a subscription to his *Poems written between the years 1768 and 1794 . . . printed at the Press of the Author, at Mount-Pleasant* (1795), a copy of which TJ procured (Sowerby, No. 4437). The next communication was a brief note from Freneau of 8 Apr. 1809 enclosing proposals for publishing his poems in two volumes and suggesting that some of TJ's friends in Virginia might be influenced to subscribe. TJ subscribed for one set but politely declined to solicit subscriptions from others (TJ to Freneau, 22 May 1809). Freneau, claiming that TJ had misunderstood and that he had not wished to put him at the pains of collecting subscriptions, then proved that this had been his object by saying he had intended no more than that TJ give such of his neighbors as might choose to do so a chance to put down their names (Freneau to TJ, 27 May 1809). TJ did not respond, but when he received the volumes he must have been astonished to find his name as a subscriber for ten sets, with an eleventh especially bound for him. Characteristically, he asked the publisher to check the subscription list and promised to pay if he had actually ordered so many copies (Lydia Bailey to TJ, 22 Mch. 1810; TJ to Mrs. Bailey, 18 Apr. 1810). On verifying the list, Mrs. Bailey found that TJ's name was indeed down for ten sets but that the handwriting was certainly not his. "Some person wanting principle," she added, "must have taken the unwarrantable liberty" (Lydia Bailey to TJ, 8 May 1810). At her suggestion, TJ returned all save the set he had ordered (TJ to Lydia Bailey, 6 Dec. 1810). The implication is that the person wanting principle who had thus padded the order was the author, certainly not the publisher. See Sowerby, No. 4438.

Freneau also made an appeal to Madison, asking him to solicit subscriptions for the 1809 edition. Madison's name headed the list for ten sets. Freneau heard nothing from the President about their receipt and learned later that they had perished when the White House was burned in 1814 (Freneau to Madison, 8 Apr., 12 May, and 7 Aug. 1809; 12 Jan., 3 Mch., and 10 May 1815; all in DLC: Madison Papers).

[98] TJ to Randolph, 8 Dec. 1793.

ardently championed. His venture into national journalism, coming so close on the heels of Jefferson's public embarrassment over Paine's *Rights of Man* and being so conspicuously sponsored by the chief leaders of the opposition, had dealt a severely damaging blow to the republican cause. The *National Gazette* won few if any converts in the South and West, where criticism of its virulent attacks on the President and its emotional defense of Genet steadily increased. Among the Federalists of New England it had the effect of consolidating and reinforcing the supporters of those measures and policies against which it had directed its fire. But advantages sometimes emerge even from failure. If the *National Gazette* helped bring defeat to the republican opposition in this initial battle, the Federalists, encouraged by victory, moved on step by step in their exercise of national power until at last the people emphatically reversed the progression by the Revolution of 1800. The extreme polemics of Freneau and the failure of the *National Gazette* may have led those exercising power into the error of overconfidence. But it was the leadership of Jefferson, embodying in precept and practice the principles of government he had drafted a quarter of a century earlier, which expressed the mood of the nation and ultimately triumphed in that most crucial of elections.

For Jefferson himself the failure of the *National Gazette* was not the only legacy of the ill-starred venture. There remained the accusation that he had betrayed a public trust by an improper use of patronage. This for him was the permanent consequence, rankling all the more because of the large element of truth in it and because, in his lifelong devotion to the public interest, his concept of official propriety and his grasp of the implications of self-government caused him more than any of his contemporaries to draw a sharp line of distinction between private and public interest. The *National Gazette* did not touch his personal concerns, but it did cause him to suspend for this moment and for a greater cause his profound convictions about the probity and disinterestedness required of a public officer in a free society. This may have been in his consciousness when, on resigning office and thanking Washington for all of his indulgences, he said his need for them was all the greater because he could claim nothing on his part other than a firm pursuit of what appeared to be right — "and a thorough disdain of all means which were not as open and honorable, as their object was pure."[99]

The disappointing effort to establish the *National Gazette*, begun with such high hopes, was only one of Jefferson's continuing attempts to demonstrate the absolute necessity of a free press in a free society. But it was not until he became President that, largely through his persuasive influence, his dream became a reality with the founding of the first truly national newspaper. Its editor, Samuel Harrison Smith, had unintentionally brought acute embarrassment to Jefferson over the Paine incident of 1791 at a time when they were strangers to each other. But they became firm friends, and Smith proved to be the kind of responsible journalist for whom Jefferson had been seeking so long. *The National Intelligencer* — its title also reflecting Jefferson's deeply cherished hopes and perhaps his influence as well — came as near to matching his elevated standards for the press as any newspaper ever did.

[99] TJ to Washington, 31 Dec. 1793.

I. Philip Freneau to Thomas Jefferson

Sir   New-York August 4th. 1791

So many difficulties occurred in regard to my removing from this city to Philadelphia and personally establishing the paper, the hint of which you, Sir, in conjunction with Mr. Madison were pleased to mention to me in May last, that I had determined in my own mind not to attempt it.

However, upon recently talking over the matter with Mr. Madison and Col. Lee I have proposed a concern (which they have accepted) with Messieurs Childs and Swaine in a press at the seat of Government for the purpose abovementioned.

I am now so far advanced on our plan as to have finished a *copy of Proposals* for the National Paper I have in view, and which upon my arrival at Philadelphia on Tuesday next I shall request the favour of you to glance your eye over, previous to its being printed. – I have the honour to be, Sir, with the highest respect Your most obedient humble servant,   Philip Freneau

RC (DLC); endorsed by TJ as received 6 Aug. 1791 and so recorded in SJL.

II. Prospectus for the *National Gazette*

To the Public

The Editor of the *National Gazette* having found his proposals for establishing a paper of that kind attended with all the success he could reasonably expect, considering the short time that has elapsed since his first acquainting the public with his design, takes this opportunity in his *first* number, briefly to remind his subscribers, and others, of the plan upon which he originally intended, and still proposes to proceed.

The National Gazette shall be published on the *Monday* and *Thursday* mornings of every week, in the city of Philadelphia, and sent to the more distant subscribers by the most ready and regular modes of conveyance. Such persons, resident in the city of Philadelphia, as incline to become subscribers, shall be supplied early on the mornings of publication, at their own houses. The price will be Three Dollars a year; the first half yearly payment to be made in three months from the time of subscribing, and future payments every six months.

The paper shall contain, among other interesting particulars, the most important foreign intelligence, collected not only from the British, French, and Dutch newspapers (a constant and punctual supply of which has been engaged) but also from original communications, letters, and other papers to which the Editor may have an opportunity of recurring for the most authentic information relative to the affairs of Europe.

The department for domestic news will be rendered as complete and satisfactory as possible, by inserting a judicious detail of such occurrences as shall appear worthy the notice of the public.

The most respectful attention shall be paid to all decent productions of entertainment in prose or verse that may be sent for insertion, as well as to such political essays as have a tendency to promote the general interests of the Union. There will also be inserted during the sessions of Congress, a brief History of the Debates and Proceedings of the Supreme Legislature of the United States, executed, it is hoped, in such a manner as to answer the expectations and gratify the curiosity of every reader.

Persons at a distance who may subscribe for fifteen papers, and will become responsible for the subscription money, shall receive with the packet a sixteenth, gratis.

Subscriptions are received at the Office, No. 239 High-street; also at the respective Bookstores of Mr. Francis Bailey, and Mr. Thomas Dobson.

From the *National Gazette*, Vol. 1, No. 1, 31 Oct. 1791. Freneau restated the plan and policy of his paper in the issues of 1 and 17 Nov. 1791. In variant form his statement of editorial policy appeared in the issue of 7 May 1792.

No manuscript text of the Proposals which Freneau refers to in the opening paragraph has been found. But Childs and Swaine's *Daily Advertiser*, 25 Aug. 1791, announced that the paper would be established provided a sufficient number of subscribers could be procured. The text of the Proposals, however, was drawn up before 9 Aug. 1791, since Freneau promised to show it to TJ on that date (Freneau to TJ, 4 Aug. 1791; Document I). On 25 Aug. and again on 28 Oct. 1791, with slight variation, the *Daily Advertiser* announced "Proposals for publishing, in Philadelphia, On the Second Day of November next, *The National Gazette*, A Periodical Miscellany of News, Politics, History, and Polite Literature: BY PHILIP FRENEAU." This, pre-

sumably, was essentially the form in which the original text appeared when Freneau showed it to TJ early in August. The shift in the time of publication as announced in the *Daily Advertiser* from Wednesdays and Saturdays to Mondays and Thursdays as stated above may have been suggested by TJ so that the paper could more easily meet the southbound post from Philadelphia and the cross-post from Richmond. The second section of the Proposals, as printed in the *Daily Advertiser*, stated in substance if not in direct terms TJ's original concept: "The proposed paper being . . . intended (as intimated in the title) to circulate throughout the United States, particular pains will be taken to convey the most authentic foreign and domestic information from the Seat of Government to every part of the Union." The third section of the Proposals, including the direct quotation of a maxim which may possibly have been provided by TJ when the text of the Proposals was shown to him and which certainly expressed his views, also suggests his influence: "In all political essays, or such writings as relate to the governmental concerns of our country, the utmost freedom and latitude of discussion will be encouraged and invited: time and experience having rendered the maxim indubitable that 'a patient and candid attention to a multiplicity of opinions, is the surest method of arriving at the truth of any question.' "

This text of the Proposals in broadside form was probably employed by Madison, TJ, and others in their efforts to solicit subscriptions for the *National Gazette* – an effort begun even before TJ received Freneau's letter announcing his arrangement with Childs and Swaine to establish the paper.

The announcement to the public as printed above summarized the essential nature of the Proposals as printed in the *Daily Advertiser*. But there was one very important and revealing difference. The assurance that a constant and punctual supply of British, French, and Dutch newspapers had been engaged and also that original communications, letters, and other papers accessible to the editor for the most authentic information of affairs in Europe did not appear in the Proposals as announced by Childs and Swaine. This assurance described precisely what resulted from Freneau's relationship to the Department of State. It was one that only TJ could have authorized.

III. Appointment of Philip Freneau as Clerk

Department of state of the United States.

Philip Freneau is hereby appointed Clerk for foreign languages in the office of Secretary of State with a salary of two hundred and fifty dollars a year, to commence from the time he shall take the requisite oaths of qualification. Given under my hand this 16th day of August. 1791. TH: JEFFERSON

MS (DLC); entirely in TJ's hand, containing on verso certificate of William Lewis, federal district judge for Pennsylvania, dated 17 Aug. 1791, stating that Freneau had appeared before him that day "and did solemnly swear that he will support the Constitution of the United States and also that he will well and faithfully execute the Trust committed to him as Clerk for foreign Languages in the office of Secretary of State" (in clerk's hand, signed by Lewis).

IV. Gabriel Henno to Thomas Jefferson

[New London, before 2 Aug. 1791]

L'auteur de ce mémoire désire en recevoir un reçu dans peu de tems dans lequel il sera bien aise d'apprendre s'il doit continuer ses recherches. Son adresse est chez monsieur louis maniere new london.

GABRIEL HENNO
ne dans la flandre autrichienne

RC (DNA: RG 59, MLR); the following appears on a separate leaf: "tho' the author understand english, he has thought proper to writ the following observations in french language with which he is more acquainted"; endorsed by TJ as received 2 Aug. 1791 and so recorded in SJL. The above is almost certainly the conclusion of Henno's letter, being without salutation or date as in the case of his other letters to TJ. Nor can there be any doubt that it was addressed to the Secretary of State, since TJ retained it and its enclosure in the departmental files. The most plausible explanation for the missing initial portion, if there was such, would seem to be that TJ separated that part of the letter as an accompaniment to the enclosure when he released it to the press. Enclosure: A 63-page manuscript entitled "Mémoire *to the administrators. Singula quaque notando. hor*. Recherche politique des moiens D'améliorer le commerce Des etats," bearing at head of text: "new london 17 May 1791." See Editorial Note for summary of contents.

V. Thomas Jefferson to Gabriel Henno

SIR   Philadelphia Dec. 4. 1791.

Tho Your observations on manufactures came to my hands long ago, and were considered as entirely worthy of communication to the public, yet it is not till lately that I have been able to have them so communicated. I inclose you the gazettes containing them, wherein you will see that the printer has taken the liberty of omitting some passages which he considered as matter of embellishment rather than of substance. His object was to save space in his paper, he thinks also that it is thereby more accomodated to the taste of his readers. – I am with great consideration Sir Your most obedt. humble servt,   TH: JEFFERSON

PrC (MHi); at foot of text: "Mr. Gabriel Henno, chez Monsr. Louis Maniere New London."

Although Henno had requested an immediate reply so that he might know whether to proceed with his research, TJ waited four months before responding. It seems clear that he did so in order to place the essay in the *National Gazette* rather than in some other paper.

VI. Philip Freneau to Thomas Jefferson

SIR   Morning Jan. 27. [1792]

Two or three days ago I received a Letter from Mr. Nelson, of Augusta County, Virginia, in which he wishes me to inform him of the Nature or plan of the organization of the Pennsylvania Society for the improvement of agriculture. He mentions that possibly Mr. Jefferson can give me some information, that will enable me to write him on the subject. Mr. Jefferson will be pleased to recollect if he has any documents relative to this Society, and I will call tomorrow morning, to be informed.

I have just glanced over Mr. Henno's last essay, you were so kind as to send. It is much like the others, generally superficial, tedious, and too little of argumentative discussion for the subject, to please the generality of readers. However, there are here and there some good things interspersed, which we will give the public when nothing more interesting offers. – I am Sir with great respect Your very humble Servt.,   PH. FRENEAU

RC (MHi); endorsed by TJ as received 27 Jan. 1792 but recorded in SJL as received on the day preceding. The error in date may have been that of Freneau, who made frequent errors in dates of letters published in the *National Gazette*. At times he did this deliberately, as examples cited in the Editorial Note indicate.

For the response to this inquiry as made by George Logan and published in the *National Gazette*, see Editorial Note.

VII. Thomas Jefferson to Philip Freneau

[Philadelphia] March 13. 92

Thomas Jefferson sends to Mr. Frenau a list of persons in Charlottesville who have desired to receive his paper. This mail should go by the Friday morning's post always, which will meet the Charlottesville post at Richmond on the Thursday evening following, and on Saturday the mail will be at Charlottesville.

Thos. J. will pay Mr. Frenau the necessary advances as soon as he will be so good as to furnish him a note of them.

Tr (DLC); in an unidentified hand; the names of subscribers are bracketed in the margin and are the same eleven, given in the same order, which TJ listed in his letter to Thomas Bell on the 16th.

Entries in Account Book show that on 23 May 1792 TJ paid John Fenno for half a year's subscription to *Gazette of the United* States; that on 8 Jan. 1793 he paid Freneau for a year's subscription (two copies); and that on 22 Nov. 1793 he "gave Philip Frenau order on bank for 18.75 to wit for myself to Oct. 26.93. 6 [dollars]." The last payment perhaps covered subscriptions for some of the individuals named in TJ's letter to Bell of 16 Mch. 1792 as well as that of two copies for himself.

VIII. Thomas Jefferson to Thomas Bell

DEAR SIR   Philadelphia Mar. 16. 1792.

Having learned by Mr. Randolph's last letter th[at the] post to Charlottesville is now regularly established, I ha[ve given] in to Freneau the list of subscribers you sent me to wit –

John Nicholas

Thomas Bell

Nicholas Lewis junr.

Robert Jouett

George Divers

George Bruce

William Woods

Divers & Lindsay

Isaac Miller

Peter Derieux

George Gilmer

and have desired him to send off the [papers] by every Friday's post, so that you will receive them eight days afterwards. He is to give me a note of the advances necessary to be made, which I am to pay him for the subscribers, and must get you to settle with them for me. I am in hopes indeed that you will send forward five names more, and so be entitled to your paper gratis, for collecting the rest. In this manner the business can be done between them and Freneau by you and myself. I am in hopes his paper will give satisfaction: it is certainly the best I ever saw published in America. I am with great and sincere esteem to yourself and my friends of your place and vicinity Dear Sir your friend & servt.   TH: JEFFERSON

PrC (DLC); slightly mutilated, with the missing words being given in brackets (supplied) from a Tr in unidentified hand (DLC). TJ listed the names in a box inset in the text.

IX. Resignation of Philip Freneau as Clerk

Philadelphia, October 11th. 1793

The Within contains the appointment of Philip Freneau to the office of clerkship of foreign Languages in the department of State by Mr. Jefferson.

I hereby resign the same appointment, from October 1st. 1793.

PHILIP FRENEAU

RC (DLC); endorsed by TJ as received 7 Nov. 1793 and recorded in SJL with date of letter omitted. Enclosure: TJ's appointment of Freneau, 16 Aug. 1791 (Document III).

Indexes covering Vols. 1-6, 7-12, and 13-18 have been published. A comprehensive index of persons, places, subjects, etc., arranged in a single consolidated sequence for Vols. 1-20, will be issued as Vol. 21. Beginning with Vol. 22, each volume will contain its own index, although cumulative indexes may be published periodically.